CODE OF FEDERAL REGULATIONS

Title 14
Aeronautics and Space

Parts 200 to 1199

Revised as of January 1, 2019

Containing a codification of documents of general applicability and future effect

As of January 1, 2019

Published by the Office of the Federal Register
National Archives and Records Administration
as a Special Edition of the Federal Register

Table of Contents

Cite this Code: CFR

To cite the regulations in this volume use title, part and section number. Thus, 14 CFR 200.1 *refers to title 14, part 200, section 1.*

Explanation

The Code of Federal Regulations is a codification of the general and permanent rules published in the Federal Register by the Executive departments and agencies of the Federal Government. The Code is divided into 50 titles which represent broad areas subject to Federal regulation. Each title is divided into chapters which usually bear the name of the issuing agency. Each chapter is further subdivided into parts covering specific regulatory areas.

Each volume of the Code is revised at least once each calendar year and issued on a quarterly basis approximately as follows:

Title 1 through Title 16..............as of January 1
Title 17 through Title 27..............as of April 1
Title 28 through Title 41..............as of July 1
Title 42 through Title 50..............as of October 1

The appropriate revision date is printed on the cover of each volume.

LEGAL STATUS

The contents of the Federal Register are required to be judicially noticed (44 U.S.C. 1507). The Code of Federal Regulations is prima facie evidence of the text of the original documents (44 U.S.C. 1510).

HOW TO USE THE CODE OF FEDERAL REGULATIONS

The Code of Federal Regulations is kept up to date by the individual issues of the Federal Register. These two publications must be used together to determine the latest version of any given rule.

To determine whether a Code volume has been amended since its revision date (in this case, January 1, 2019), consult the "List of CFR Sections Affected (LSA)," which is issued monthly, and the "Cumulative List of Parts Affected," which appears in the Reader Aids section of the daily Federal Register. These two lists will identify the Federal Register page number of the latest amendment of any given rule.

EFFECTIVE AND EXPIRATION DATES

Each volume of the Code contains amendments published in the Federal Register since the last revision of that volume of the Code. Source citations for the regulations are referred to by volume number and page number of the Federal Register and date of publication. Publication dates and effective dates are usually not the same and care must be exercised by the user in determining the actual effective date. In instances where the effective date is beyond the cut-off date for the Code a note has been inserted to reflect the future effective date. In those instances where a regulation published in the Federal Register states a date certain for expiration, an appropriate note will be inserted following the text.

OMB CONTROL NUMBERS

The Paperwork Reduction Act of 1980 (Pub. L. 96–511) requires Federal agencies to display an OMB control number with their information collection request.

Many agencies have begun publishing numerous OMB control numbers as amendments to existing regulations in the CFR. These OMB numbers are placed as close as possible to the applicable recordkeeping or reporting requirements.

PAST PROVISIONS OF THE CODE

Provisions of the Code that are no longer in force and effect as of the revision date stated on the cover of each volume are not carried. Code users may find the text of provisions in effect on any given date in the past by using the appropriate List of CFR Sections Affected (LSA). For the convenience of the reader, a "List of CFR Sections Affected" is published at the end of each CFR volume. For changes to the Code prior to the LSA listings at the end of the volume, consult previous annual editions of the LSA. For changes to the Code prior to 2001, consult the List of CFR Sections Affected compilations, published for 1949-1963, 1964-1972, 1973-1985, and 1986-2000.

"[RESERVED]" TERMINOLOGY

The term "[Reserved]" is used as a place holder within the Code of Federal Regulations. An agency may add regulatory information at a "[Reserved]" location at any time. Occasionally "[Reserved]" is used editorially to indicate that a portion of the CFR was left vacant and not accidentally dropped due to a printing or computer error.

INCORPORATION BY REFERENCE

What is incorporation by reference? Incorporation by reference was established by statute and allows Federal agencies to meet the requirement to publish regulations in the Federal Register by referring to materials already published elsewhere. For an incorporation to be valid, the Director of the Federal Register must approve it. The legal effect of incorporation by reference is that the material is treated as if it were published in full in the Federal Register (5 U.S.C. 552(a)). This material, like any other properly issued regulation, has the force of law.

What is a proper incorporation by reference? The Director of the Federal Register will approve an incorporation by reference only when the requirements of 1 CFR part 51 are met. Some of the elements on which approval is based are:

(a) The incorporation will substantially reduce the volume of material published in the Federal Register.

(b) The matter incorporated is in fact available to the extent necessary to afford fairness and uniformity in the administrative process.

(c) The incorporating document is drafted and submitted for publication in accordance with 1 CFR part 51.

What if the material incorporated by reference cannot be found? If you have any problem locating or obtaining a copy of material listed as an approved incorporation by reference, please contact the agency that issued the regulation containing that incorporation. If, after contacting the agency, you find the material is not available, please notify the Director of the Federal Register, National Archives and Records Administration, 8601 Adelphi Road, College Park, MD 20740-6001, or call 202-741-6010.

CFR INDEXES AND TABULAR GUIDES

A subject index to the Code of Federal Regulations is contained in a separate volume, revised annually as of January 1, entitled CFR INDEX AND FINDING AIDS. This volume contains the Parallel Table of Authorities and Rules. A list of CFR titles, chapters, subchapters, and parts and an alphabetical list of agencies publishing in the CFR are also included in this volume.

An index to the text of "Title 3—The President" is carried within that volume.

The Federal Register Index is issued monthly in cumulative form. This index is based on a consolidation of the "Contents" entries in the daily Federal Register.

A List of CFR Sections Affected (LSA) is published monthly, keyed to the revision dates of the 50 CFR titles.

REPUBLICATION OF MATERIAL

There are no restrictions on the republication of material appearing in the Code of Federal Regulations.

INQUIRIES

For a legal interpretation or explanation of any regulation in this volume, contact the issuing agency. The issuing agency's name appears at the top of odd-numbered pages.

For inquiries concerning CFR reference assistance, call 202–741–6000 or write to the Director, Office of the Federal Register, National Archives and Records Administration, 8601 Adelphi Road, College Park, MD 20740-6001 or e-mail *fedreg.info@nara.gov.*

SALES

The Government Publishing Office (GPO) processes all sales and distribution of the CFR. For payment by credit card, call toll-free, 866-512-1800, or DC area, 202-512-1800, M-F 8 a.m. to 4 p.m. e.s.t. or fax your order to 202-512-2104, 24 hours a day. For payment by check, write to: US Government Publishing Office – New Orders, P.O. Box 979050, St. Louis, MO 63197-9000.

ELECTRONIC SERVICES

The full text of the Code of Federal Regulations, the LSA (List of CFR Sections Affected), The United States Government Manual, the Federal Register, Public Laws, Public Papers of the Presidents of the United States, Compilation of Presidential Documents and the Privacy Act Compilation are available in electronic format via *www.govinfo.gov.* For more information, contact the GPO Customer Contact Center, U.S. Government Publishing Office. Phone 202-512-1800, or 866-512-1800 (toll-free). E-mail, *ContactCenter@gpo.gov.*

The Office of the Federal Register also offers a free service on the National Archives and Records Administration's (NARA) World Wide Web site for public law numbers, Federal Register finding aids, and related information. Connect to NARA's web site at *www.archives.gov/federal-register.*

The e-CFR is a regularly updated, unofficial editorial compilation of CFR material and Federal Register amendments, produced by the Office of the Federal Register and the Government Publishing Office. It is available at *www.ecfr.gov.*

OLIVER A. POTTS,
Director,
Office of the Federal Register
January 1, 2019.

THIS TITLE

Title 14—Aeronautics and Space is composed of five volumes. The parts in these volumes are arranged in the following order: Parts 1–59, 60–109, 110–199, 200–1199, and part 1200–End. The first three volumes containing parts 1–199 are comprised of chapter I—Federal Aviation Administration, Department of Transportation (DOT). The fourth volume containing parts 200–1199 is comprised of chapter II—Office of the Secretary, DOT (Aviation Proceedings) and chapter III—Commercial Space Transportation, Federal Aviation Administration, DOT. The fifth volume containing part 1200–End is comprised of chapter V—National Aeronautics and Space Administration and chapter VI—Air Transportation System Stabilization. The contents of these volumes represent all current regulations codified under this title of the CFR as of January 1, 2019.

For this volume, Susannah C. Hurley was Chief Editor. The Code of Federal Regulations publication program is under the direction of John Hyrum Martinez, assisted by Stephen J. Frattini.

Title 14—Aeronautics and Space

(This book contains parts 200 to 1199)

CHAPTER II—OFFICE OF THE SECRETARY, DEPARTMENT OF TRANSPORTATION (AVIATION PROCEEDINGS)

EDITORIAL NOTE: Chapter II was transferred from the Civil Aeronautics Board to the Department of Transportation on January 1, 1985. For a document giving the disposition of CAB regulations once the Agency ceased to exist, see 50 FR 452, Jan. 4, 1985.

EDITORIAL NOTE: Nomenclature changes to chapter II appear by Doc. No. DOT–OST–2008–0173, 73 FR 33327, June 12, 2008.

SUBCHAPTER A—ECONOMIC REGULATIONS

SUBCHAPTER B—PROCEDURAL REGULATIONS

SUBCHAPTER A—ECONOMIC REGULATIONS

PART 200—DEFINITIONS AND INSTRUCTIONS

AUTHORITY: 49 U.S.C. Chapters 401, 411, 413, 415, 417, 461.

§ 200.1 Terms and definitions.

Unless otherwise specifically stated, words and phrases other than those listed in this section have the meaning defined in the Statute.

(a) *Board* or *CAB* means the Civil Aeronautics Board.

(b) *Department* or *DOT* means the Department of Transportation.

(c) *Act* means the Federal Aviation Act of 1958, as amended.

(d) *Section* refers to a section of the Statute or a section of the regulations in this chapter, as indicated by the context. The terms *this section*, *pursuant to this section*, *in accordance with the provisions of this section*, and words of similar import when used in this chapter refer to the section of this subchapter in which such terms appear.

(e) *Rule*, *regulation*, and *order* refer to the rules, regulations, and orders prescribed by the Board or the Department pursuant to the Statute.

(f) *Statute* when used in this chapter means Subtitle VII of Title 49 of the United States Code (Transportation).

(g) *FAA* means the Federal Aviation Administration, U.S. Department of Transportation.

(h) *BTS* means the Bureau of Transportation Statistics, U.S. Department of Transportation.

[Doc. No. 47939, 57 FR 40100, Sept. 2, 1992, as amended by Doc. No. OST–95–397, 60 FR 43523, Aug. 22, 1995; 60 FR 66722, Dec. 26, 1995]

§ 200.2 Instructions.

The regulations of the Department may be cited by section numbers. For example, this regulation may be cited as "§ 200.2 of the Aviation Economic Regulations." The sections contained in the Rules of Practice may also be cited by appropriate rule numbers. (See § 302.1(c) of this chapter.) For example, 14 CFR 302.10 may be cited as "rule 10 of the Rules of Practice."

[Doc. No. 47939, 57 FR 40100, Sept. 2, 1992, as amended at 65 FR 6456, Feb. 9, 2000]

PART 201—AIR CARRIER AUTHORITY UNDER SUBTITLE VII OF TITLE 49 OF THE UNITED STATES CODE—[AMENDED]

AUTHORITY: 5 U.S.C. 1008; 49 U.S.C. Chapters 401, 411, 413, 415, 417.

SOURCE: Docket No. 47582, 57 FR 38765, Aug. 27, 1992, unless otherwise noted.

Subpart A—Application Procedures

§ 201.1 Formal requirements.

(a) Applications for certificates of public convenience and necessity under section 41102 of the Statute and for interstate all-cargo air transportation certificates under section 41103 of the Statute shall meet the requirements set forth in part 302 of this chapter as to general requirements, execution, number of copies, service, and formal specifications of papers.

(b) Any person desiring to provide air transportation as a commuter air carrier must comply with the provisions of part 298 of this chapter and submit data to support a fitness determination in accordance with part 204 of this chapter. An executed original plus two (2) true copies of the fitness data shall be filed with DOT Dockets, 1200 New Jersey Avenue, SE., Washington, DC 20590–0002. Requests for confidential treatment of documents should be filed in accordance with the requirements of part 302 of this chapter.

(Approved by the Office of Management and Budget under control number 2106–0023)

[Doc. No. 47582, 57 FR 38765, Aug. 27, 1992, as amended at 60 FR 43523, Aug. 22, 1995; 64 FR 3212, Jan. 21, 1999; 70 FR 25767, May 16, 2005]

§ 201.2 Amendments.

If, after receipt of any application, the Department asks the applicant to supply additional information, such information shall be furnished in the form of a supplement to the original application.

§ 201.3 Incorporation by reference.

Incorporation by reference shall be avoided. However, where two or more applications are filed by a single carrier, lengthy exhibits or other documents attached to one may be incorporated in the others by reference if that procedure will substantially reduce the cost to the applicant.

§ 201.4 General provisions concerning contents.

(a) All pages of an application shall be consecutively numbered, and the application shall clearly describe and identify each exhibit by a separate number or symbol. All exhibits shall be deemed to constitute a part of the application to which they are attached.

(b) All amendments to applications shall be consecutively numbered and shall comply with the requirements of this part.

(c) Requests for authority to engage in interstate air transportation shall not be included in the same application with requests for authority to engage in foreign air transportation. Similarly, requests for authority to engage in scheduled air transportation under section 41102 of the Statute shall not be included in the same application with requests for authority to engage in charter air transportation under section 41102 of the Statute or with requests for authority to engage in interstate all-cargo air transportation under section 41103 of the Statute.

(d) Each application shall specify the type or types of service (passengers, property or mail) to be rendered and whether such services are to be rendered on scheduled or charter operations.

(e) Each application for foreign scheduled air transportation shall include an adequate identification of each route for which a certificate is desired, including the terminal and intermediate points to be included in the certificate for which application is made.

(f) Each application shall give full and adequate information with respect to each of the relevant filing requirements set forth in part 204 of this chapter. In addition, the application may contain such other information and data as the applicant shall deem necessary or appropriate in order to acquaint the Department fully with the particular circumstances of its case; however, the statements contained in an application shall be restricted to significant and relevant facts.

(Approved by the Office of Management and Budget under control number 2106–0023)

[Doc. No. 47582, 57 FR 38765, Aug. 27, 1992, as amended at 60 FR 43523, Aug. 22, 1995]

§ 201.5 Advertising and sales by applicants.

(a) An applicant for new or amended certificate or commuter air carrier authority shall not:

(1) Advertise, list schedules, or accept reservations for the air transportation covered by its application until the application has been approved by the Department; or

(2) Accept payment or issue tickets for the air transportation covered by its application until the authority or amended authority has become effective or the Department issues a notice authorizing sales.

(b) An applicant for new or amended certificate or commuter air carrier authority may not advertise or publish schedule listings for the air transportation covered by its application after the application has been approved by the Department (but before all authority issued by DOT, including the FAA, becomes effective) unless such advertising or schedule listings prominently state: "This service is subject to receipt of government operating authority."

Subpart B—Certificate Terms, Conditions, and Limitations

§ 201.6 Applicability.

Unless the certificate or the order authorizing its issuance shall otherwise provide, such terms, conditions and limitations as are set forth in this part, and as may from time to time be prescribed by the Department, shall apply to the exercise of the privileges granted by each certificate issued under section 41102 or section 41103 of the Statute.

[Doc. No. 47582, 57 FR 38765, Aug. 27, 1992, as amended at 60 FR 43523, Aug. 22, 1995]

§ 201.7 General certificate conditions.

(a) It shall be a condition upon the holding of a certificate that any intentional failure by the holder to comply with any provision of Statute or any order, rule, or regulation issued thereunder or any term, condition, or limitation of such certificate shall be a failure to comply with the terms, conditions, and limitations of the certificate within the meaning of section 41110 of the Statute even though the failure to comply occurred outside the territorial limits of the United States, except to the extent that such failure shall be necessitated by an obligation, duty, or liability imposed by a foreign country.

(b) Failure to file the reports required by part 241, 291, or 298 of this chapter shall be sufficient grounds to revoke a certificate.

(c) The authority to transport U.S. mail under a certificate is permissive, unless the Department, by order or rule, directs a carrier or class of carriers to transport mail on demand of the U.S. Postal Service; such certificate confers no right to receive subsidy, for the carriage of mail or otherwise.

(d) An all-cargo air transportation certificate shall confer no right to carry passengers, other than cargo attendants accompanying a shipment, or to engage in any air transportation outside the geographical scope of interstate cargo transportation. Such certificate shall not, however, restrict the right of the holder to provide scheduled, charter, contract, or other transportation of cargo, by air, within that geographical scope.

(e) It shall be a condition upon the holding of a certificate that the holder have and maintain in effect and on file with the Department a signed counterpart of Agreement 18900 (OST Form 4523), and a tariff (for those carriers otherwise generally required to file tariffs) that includes its terms, and that the holder comply with all other requirements of part 203. OST Form 4523 may be obtained from the Office of Aviation Analysis, Special Authorities Division.

[Doc. No. 47582, 57 FR 38765, Aug. 27, 1992, as amended at 60 FR 43523, Aug. 22, 1995]

PART 203—WAIVER OF WARSAW CONVENTION LIABILITY LIMITS AND DEFENSES

AUTHORITY: 49 U.S.C. Chapters 401, 411, 413, 415, 417.

SOURCE: ER–1324, 48 FR 8044, Feb. 25, 1983, unless otherwise noted.

§ 203.1 Scope.

This part requires that certain U.S. and foreign direct air carriers waive the passenger liability limits and certain carrier defenses in the Warsaw Convention in accordance with the provisions of Agreement 18900, dated May 13, 1966, and provides that acceptance of authority for, or operations by the carrier in, air transportation shall be considered to act as such a waiver by that carrier.

[ER–1324, 48 FR 8044, Feb. 25, 1983, as amended by Doc. No. 47939, 57 FR 40100, Sept. 2, 1992]

§ 203.2 Applicability.

This part applies to all direct U.S. and foreign direct air carriers, except for air taxi operators as defined in part

298 of this chapter that (a) are not commuter air carriers, (b) do not participate in interline agreements, and (c) do not engage in foreign air transportation.

§ 203.3 Filing requirements for adherence to Montreal Agreement.

All direct U.S. and foreign air carriers shall have and maintain in effect and on file in the Department's Documentary Services Division (Docket 17325) on OST Form 4523 a signed counterpart to Agreement 18900, an agreement relating to liability limitations of the Warsaw Convention and Hague Protocol approved by CAB Order E–23680, dated May 13, 1966 (the Montreal Agreement), and a signed counterpart of any amendment or amendments to such Agreement that may be approved by the Department and to which the air carrier or foreign air carrier becomes a party. U.S. air taxi operators registering under part 298 of this chapter and Canadian charter air taxi operators registering under part 294 of this chapter may comply with this requirement by filing completed OST Forms 4507 and 4523, respectively, in accordance with the provisions of those parts.

[Doc. No. 47939, 57 FR 40100, Sept. 2, 1992, as amended at 60 FR 43523, Aug. 22, 1995; 70 FR 25767, May 16, 2005]

§ 203.4 Montreal Agreement as part of airline-passenger contract and conditions of carriage.

(a) As required by the Montreal Agreement, carriers that are otherwise generally required to file tariffs shall file with the Department's Tariffs Division a tariff that includes the provisions of the counterpart to Agreement 18900.

(b) As further required by that Agreement, each participating carrier shall include the Agreement's terms as part of its conditions of carriage. The participating carrier shall give each of its passengers the notice required by the Montreal Agreement as provided in § 221.175 of this chapter.

(c) Participation in the Montreal Agreement, whether by signing the Agreement, filing a signed counterpart to it under § 203.3, or by operation of law under § 203.5, shall constitute a special agreement between the carrier and its passengers as a condition of carriage that a liability limit of not less than $75,000 (U.S.) shall apply under Article 22(1) of the Warsaw Convention for passenger injury and death. Such participation also constitutes a waiver of the defense under Article 20(1) of the Convention that the carrier was not negligent.

(The reporting provisions contained in paragraph (a) were approved by the Office of Management and Budget under control number 3024–0064.)

[ER–1324, 48 FR 8044, Feb. 25, 1983, as amended by ER–1338, 48 FR 31013, July 6, 1983; Doc. No. 47939, 57 FR 40100, Sept. 2, 1992]

§ 203.5 Compliance as condition on operations in air transportation.

It shall be a condition on the authority of all direct U.S. and foreign carriers to operate in air transportation that they have and maintain in effect and on file with the Department a signed counterpart of Agreement 18900, and a tariff (for those carriers otherwise generally required to file tariffs) that includes its provisions, as required by this subpart. Notwithstanding any failure to file that counterpart and such tariff, any such air carrier or foreign air carrier issued license authority (including exemptions) by the Department or operating in air transportation shall be deemed to have agreed to the provisions of Agreement 18900 as fully as if that air carrier or foreign air carrier had in fact filed a properly executed counterpart to that Agreement and tariff.

[ER–1324, 48 FR 8044, Feb. 25, 1983, as amended by Doc. No. 47939, 57 FR 40100, Sept. 2, 1992]

PART 204—DATA TO SUPPORT FITNESS DETERMINATIONS

Subpart A—General Provisions

Subpart B—Filing Requirements

AUTHORITY: 49 U.S.C. Chapters 401, 411, 417.

SOURCE: Docket No. 47582, 57 FR 38766, Aug. 27, 1992, unless otherwise noted.

Subpart A—General Provisions

§204.1 Purpose.

This part sets forth the fitness data that must be submitted by applicants for certificate authority, by applicants for authority to provide service as a commuter air carrier to an eligible place, by carriers proposing to provide essential air transportation, and by certificated air carriers and commuter air carriers proposing a substantial change in operations, ownership, or management. This part also contains the procedures and filing requirements applicable to carriers that hold dormant authority.

[72 FR 20036, Apr. 23, 2007]

§204.2 Definitions.

As used in this part:

(a) *All-cargo air carrier or section 41103 carrier* means an air carrier holding an all-cargo air transportation certificate issued under section 41103 of the Statute authorizing the transportation by aircraft in interstate air transportation of only property or only mail, or both.

(b) *Certificate authority* means authority to provide air transportation granted by the Department of Transportation or Civil Aeronautics Board in the form of a certificate of public convenience and necessity under section 41102 of the Statute or an all-cargo air transportation certificate to perform all-cargo air transportation under section 41103 of the Statute. *Certificated carriers* are those that hold certificate authority.

(c) *Citizen of the United States* means:

(1) An individual who is a citizen of the United States;

(2) A partnership each of whose partners is an individual who is a citizen of the United States; or

(3) A corporation or association organized under the laws of the United States or a State, the District of Columbia, or a territory or possession of the United States, of which the president and at least two-thirds of the board of directors and other managing officers are citizens of the United States, which is under the actual control of citizens of the United States, and in which at least 75 percent of the voting interest is owned or controlled by persons that are citizens of the United States.

(d) *Commuter air carrier* means an air carrier holding or seeking authority under part 298 of this Chapter that carries passengers on at least five round trips per week on at least one route between two or more points according to its published flight schedules that specify the times, days of the week, and places between which those flights are performed.

(e) *Eligible place* means a place in the United States that—

(1) Was an eligible point under section 419 of the Federal Aviation Act of 1958 as in effect before October 1, 1988;

(2) Received scheduled air transportation at any time between January 1, 1990, and November 4, 1990; and

(3) Is not listed in Department of Transportation Orders 89–9–37 and 89–12–52 as a place ineligible for compensation under Subchapter II of Chapter 417 of the Statute.

(f) *Essential air service* is that air transportation which the Department has found to be essential under Subchapter II of Chapter 417 of the Statute.

(g) *Fit* means fit, willing, and able to perform the air transportation in question properly and to conform to the provisions of the Statute and the rules, regulations and requirements issued under the Statute.

(h) *Interstate air transportation* means the transportation of passengers or property by aircraft as a common carrier for compensation, or the transportation of mail by aircraft—

(1) Between a place in—

(i) A State, territory, or possession of the United States and a place in the

District of Columbia or another State, territory, or possession of the United States;

(ii) Hawaii and another place in Hawaii through the airspace over a place outside Hawaii;

(iii) The District of Columbia and another place in the District of Columbia; or

(iv) A territory or possession of the United States and another place in the same territory or possession; and

(2) When any part of the transportation is by aircraft.

(i) *Key personnel* include the directors, president, chief executive officer, chief operating officer, all vice presidents, the directors or supervisors of operations, maintenance, and finance, and the chief pilot of the applicant or air carrier, as well as any part-time or full-time advisors or consultants to the management of the applicant or air carrier.

(j) *Normalized operations* are those which are relatively free of start-up costs and temporary barriers to full-scale operations posed by the carrier's limited experience.

(k) *Relevant corporations* are the applicant or air carrier, any subsidiary thereof, any predecessor thereof (*i.e.*, any air carrier in which any directors, principal officers or persons having a substantial interest have or once had a substantial interest), and any company (including a sole proprietorship or partnership) which has a significant financial or managerial influence on the applicant or air carrier. The latter includes:

(1) Any company (including a sole proprietorship or partnership) holding more than 50 percent of the outstanding voting stock of the applicant or air carrier, and

(2) Any company (including a sole proprietorship or partnership) holding between 20 percent and 50 percent of the outstanding voting stock of the applicant or air carrier and which has significant influence over the applicant or air carrier as indicated, for example, by 25 percent representation on the board of directors, participation in policy-making processes, substantial inter-company transactions, or managerial personnel with common responsibilities in both companies.

(l) *Substantial change in operations, ownership, or management* includes, but is not limited to, the following events:

(1) Changes in operations from charter to scheduled service, cargo to passenger service, short-haul to long-haul service, or (for a certificated air carrier) small-aircraft to large-aircraft operations;

(2) The filing of a petition for reorganization or a plan of reorganization under Chapter 11 of the federal bankruptcy laws;

(3) The acquisition by a new shareholder or the accumulation by an existing shareholder of beneficial control of 10 percent or more of the outstanding voting stock in the corporation; and

(4) A change in the president, chief executive officer or chief operating officer, and/or a change in at least half of the other key personnel within any 12-month period or since its latest fitness review, whichever is the more recent period.

(m) *Substantial interest* means beneficial control of 10 percent or more of the outstanding voting stock.

[Doc. No. 47582, 57 FR 38766, Aug. 27, 1992, as amended at 60 FR 43523, Aug. 22, 1995; 64 FR 12085, Mar. 11, 1999; 72 FR 20036, Apr. 23, 2007]

Subpart B—Filing Requirements

§ 204.3 Applicants for new certificate or commuter air carrier authority.

An applicant for a type of certificate authority it does not currently hold or for commuter air carrier authority shall file the data set forth in paragraphs (a) through (v) of this section. In addition, the Department may require an applicant to provide additional data if necessary to reach an informed judgment about its fitness. If the applicant has previously formally filed any of the required data with the Department or with another Federal agency and they are available to the Department, and those data continue to reflect the current state of the carrier's fitness, the applicant may instead identify the data and provide a citation for the date(s) and place(s) of filing. Prior to filing any data, the applicant may contact the Air Carrier Fitness Division to ascertain what data required by this section are already available to the Department and need not be included in the filing.

NOTE: If the applicant intends to use as evidence data it has previously filed pursuant to part 241 reporting requirements and those data contain errors, the applicant must first file corrected reports in accordance with § 241.22(g).

(a) The name, address, and telephone number of the applicant.

(b) The form of the applicant's organization.

(c) The State law(s) under which the applicant is organized.

(d) If the applicant is a corporation, a statement provided by the Office of the Secretary of State, or other agent of the State in which the applicant is incorporated, certifying that the applicant corporation is in good standing.

(e) A sworn affidavit stating that the applicant is a citizen of the United States.

(f) The identity of the key personnel who would be employed by the applicant, including:

(1) Their names and addresses;

(2) The experience, expertise, and responsibilities of each;

(3) The number of shares of the applicant's voting stock held by each and the percentage of the total number of such shares issued and outstanding, and the citizenship and principal business of any person for whose account, if other than the holder, such interest is held;

(4) The citizenship of each; and

(5) A description of the officerships, directorships, shares of stock (if 10 percent or more of total voting stock outstanding), and other interests each holds or has held in any air carrier, foreign air carrier, common carrier, person substantially engaged in the business of aeronautics or persons whose principal business (in purpose or fact) is the holding of stock in or control of any air carrier, common carrier or person substantially engaged in the business of aeronautics.

(g) A list of all persons having a substantial interest in the applicant. Such list shall include:

(1) Each person's name, address and citizenship;

(2) The number of shares of the applicant's voting stock held by each such person and the corresponding percentage of the total number of such shares issued and outstanding, and the citizenship and principal business of any person for whose account, if other than the holder, such interest is held;

(3) If any two or more persons holding a substantial interest in the applicant are related by blood or marriage, such relationship(s) shall be included in the list; and

(4) If any person or subsidiary of a person having a substantial interest in the applicant is or has ever been

(i) An air carrier, a foreign air carrier, a common carrier, or

(ii) Substantially engaged in the business of aeronautics, or

(iii) An officer or director of any such entity, or

(iv) A holder of 10 percent or more of total outstanding voting stock of any such entity, the list shall describe such relationship(s).

(h) A list of the applicant's subsidiaries, if any, including a description of each subsidiary's principal business and relationship to the applicant.

(i) A list of the applicant's shares of stock in, or control of, any air carrier, foreign air carrier, common carrier, or person substantially engaged in the business of aeronautics.

(j) To the extent any relevant corporation has been engaged in any business prior to the filing of the application, each applicant shall provide:

(1) Copies of the 10K Annual Reports filed in the past 3 years by any relevant corporation required to file such reports with the Securities and Exchange Commission, and

(2) Copies of recently filed 10Q Quarterly Reports, as necessary, in order to show the financial condition and results of operations of the enterprise current to within 3 months of the date of the filing of the application.

(k) If 10K Reports are not filed with the Securities and Exchange Commission, the following, for the 3 most recent calendar or fiscal years, reflecting the financial condition and results of operations of the enterprise current to within 3 months of the date of the filing of the application:

(1) The Balance Sheet of each relevant corporation;

(2) The Income Statement of each relevant corporation;

(3) All footnotes applicable to the financial statements, including:

(i) A statement as to whether the documents were prepared in accordance with Generally Accepted Accounting Principles, and

(ii) A description of the significant accounting policies of each relevant corporation, such as for depreciation, amortization of intangibles, overhauls, unearned revenues, and cost capitalization;

(4) A statement of significant events occurring subsequent to the most recent Balance Sheet date for each relevant corporation; and

(5) A statement identifying the person who has prepared the financial statements, his or her accounting qualifications, and any affiliation he or she has with the applicant.

(l) A list of all actions and outstanding judgments for more than $5,000 against any relevant corporation, key personnel employed (or to be employed) by any relevant corporation, or person having a substantial interest in any relevant corporation, including the amount of each judgment, the party to whom it is payable, and how long it has been outstanding.

(m) The number of actions and outstanding judgments of less than $5,000 against each relevant corporation, key personnel employed (or to be employed) by any relevant corporation, or person having a substantial interest in any relevant corporation, and the total amount owed by each on such judgments.

(n) A description of the applicant's fleet of aircraft, including:

(1) The number of each type of aircraft owned, leased and to be purchased or leased;

(2) Applicant's plans, including financing plans, for the purchase or lease of additional aircraft; and

(3) A sworn affidavit stating that each aircraft owned or leased has been certified by the FAA and currently complies with all FAA safety standards.

(o) A description of the current status of all pending investigations, enforcement actions, and formal complaints filed by the Department, including the FAA, involving the applicant or any relevant corporation, any personnel employed (or to be employed) by any relevant corporation or person having a substantial interest in any relevant corporation, regarding compliance with the Statute or orders, rules, regulations, or requirements issued pursuant to the Statute, and any corrective actions taken. (If an applicant has a compliance history that warrants it, additional information may be required.)

(p) A description of all charges of unfair or deceptive or anticompetitive business practices, or of fraud, felony or antitrust violation, brought against any relevant corporation or person having a substantial interest in any relevant corporation, or member of the key personnel employed (or to be employed) by any relevant corporation in the past 10 years. Such descriptions shall include the disposition or current status of each such proceeding.

(q) A description of any aircraft accidents or incidents (as defined in the National Transportation Safety Board Regulations, 49 CFR 830.2) experienced by the applicant, its personnel, or any relevant corporation, which occurred either during the year preceding the date of application or at any time in the past and which remain under investigation by the FAA, the NTSB, or by the company itself, including:

(1) The date of the occurrence;

(2) The type of flight;

(3) The number of passengers and crew on board and an enumeration of any injuries or fatalities;

(4) A description of any damage to the aircraft;

(5) The FAA and NTSB file numbers and the status of the investigations, including any enforcement actions initiated against the carrier or any of its personnel; and

(6) Positive actions taken to prevent recurrence. (If an applicant's history of accidents or incidents warrants it, additional information may be required.)

(r) A brief narrative history of the applicant.

(s) A description of all Federal, State and foreign authority under which the applicant has conducted or is conducting transportation operations, and the identify of the local FAA office and personnel responsible for processing an application for any additional FAA authority needed to conduct the proposed operations.

(t) A description of the service to be operated if the application is granted, including:

(1) A forecast Balance Sheet for the first normal year ending after the initially proposed operations have been incorporated, along with the assumptions underlying the accounts and amounts shown; and

(2) A forecast Income Statement, broken down by quarters, for the first year ending after the initially proposed operations are normalized, and an itemization of all pre-operating and start-up costs associated with the initiation of the proposed service. Such Income Statement shall include estimated revenue block hours (or airborne hours, for charter operators) and revenue miles by type of aircraft, number of passengers and number of tons of mail and cargo to be carried, transport revenues and an estimate of the traffic which would be generated in each market receiving the proposed service. Such statements shall also include a statement as to whether the statements were prepared on the accrual or cash basis, an explanation of how the estimated costs and revenues were developed, a description of the manner in which costs and revenues are allocated, how the underlying traffic forecasts were made, and what load factor has been assumed for the average and peak month. Pre-operating and start-up costs should include, but are not limited to, the following: Obtaining necessary government approval; establishing stations; introductory advertising; aircraft, equipment and space facility deposits and rent; training; and salaries earned prior to start-up.

(u) A signed counterpart of Agreement 18900 (OST Form 4523) as required by part 203 of this chapter.

(v) The following certification, which shall accompany the application and all subsequent written submissions filed by the applicant in connection with its application:

Pursuant to title 18 United States Code section 1001, I [the individual signing the application, who shall be a principal owner, senior officer, or internal counsel of the applicant], in my individual capacity and as the authorized representative of the applicant, have not in any manner knowingly and willfully falsified, concealed or covered up any material fact or made any false, fictitious, or fraudulent statement or knowingly used any documents which contain such statements in connection with the preparation, filing or prosecution of the application. I understand that an individual who is found to have violated the provisions of 18 U.S.C. section 1001 shall be fined nor more than $10,000 or imprisoned not more than five years, or both.

(The reporting requirements contained in this section were approved by the Office of Management and Budget under control number 2106–0023)

[Doc. No. 47582, 57 FR 38766, Aug. 27, 1992, as amended at 60 FR 43524, Aug. 22, 1995]

§ 204.4 Carriers proposing to provide essential air service.

Applicants proposing to provide essential air service have been divided into two categories, and are subject to differing data submission requirements as set forth in paragraphs (a) and (b) of this section. However, if a carrier has previously filed any of the required data with the Department or other Federal agency and they are available to the Department, and these data continue to reflect the current state of the carrier's fitness, the carrier may instead identify the data and provide a citation for the date and place of filing. All carriers may contact the Air Carrier Fitness Division to ascertain what information is already available to the Department and thus may not need to be resubmitted.

(a) Carriers who propose to begin or expand non-subsidized essential air service when the incumbent leaves the market must file the following information:

(1) All of the information required under § 204.3 of this part.

(2) A description of the back-up aircraft available to the applicant, including:

(i) The number of each type of such aircraft;

(ii) The conditions under which such aircraft will be available to the carrier;

(iii) The carrier's plans for financing the acquisition or lease of such additional aircraft; and

(iv) A sworn affidavit stating that all such aircraft have been certified by the

FAA and currently comply with all FAA safety standards.

(3) A description of the fuel available to perform the proposed essential air services and the carrier's contracts with fuel suppliers.

(4) The carrier's systemwide on-time and completion record for the preceding year and, if applicable, in the subject market(s).

(5) A list of the markets the carrier serves and the number of weekly round trips it provides in each.

(6) A description of the average number of block hours each type of aircraft is currently flown per day.

(7) An estimate of the impact the proposed essential air service would have on the carrier's utilization of its aircraft fleet.

(8) A detailed schedule of the service to be provided, including times of arrivals and departures, the aircraft to be used for each flight, and the fares to be charged.

(9) A pro-forma income statement for the proposed operation for the first annual period.

(b) Carriers filing proposals to provide subsidized service in response to an order inviting proposals shall file:

(1) All of the information required under § 204.3 of this part.

(2) All of the information required under paragraph (a) of this section.

(3) A forecast Income Statement covering the operations conducted in essential air service for the first year following the initiation of the proposed essential services. Such statement shall include:

(i) Subsidy needed;

(ii) Estimated block hours and revenue miles by type of aircraft;

(iii) Total projected revenue including volumes of passengers and freight by essential air service market and the associated fares and rates;

(iv) An explanation of the derivation of estimates of operating expenses; and

(v) A description of the manner in which costs and revenues are allocated.

(4) A traffic forecast including a load factor analysis on all segments between the small community and the hub; and an estimate of the number of seats available to and from the eligible point each day.

(Approved by the Office of Management and Budget under control number 2106–0023)

[Doc. No. 47582, 57 FR 38766, Aug. 27, 1992, as amended at 60 FR 43524, Aug. 22, 1995]

§ 204.5 Certificated and commuter air carriers undergoing or proposing to undergo substantial change in operations, ownership, or management.

(a) A certificated or commuter air carrier proposing a substantial change in operations, ownership or management shall file the data set forth in § 204.3. These data must be submitted in cases where:

(1) The proposed change requires new or amended authority, or

(2) The change substantially alters the factors upon which its latest fitness finding is based, even if no new authority is required.

(b) Information which a carrier has previously formally filed with the Department, or with another Federal agency where they are available to the Department, which continues to reflect the current state of the carrier's fitness may be omitted. The carrier instead should identify the data and provide a citation for the date(s) and place(s) of filing. Prior to filing any data, the carrier may contact the Department (Air Carrier Fitness Division) to ascertain what data required by this section, if any, are already available to the Department or are not applicable to the substantial change in question and need not be included in the filing.

(c) Information filings pursuant to this section made to support an application for new or amended certificate authority shall be filed with the application and addressed to Docket Operations, M–30, U.S. Department of Transportation, Washington, DC 20590, or by electronic submission at *http://dms.dot.gov*.

(d) Information filed in support of a certificated or commuter air carrier's continuing fitness to operate under its existing authority in light of substantial changes in its operations, management, or ownership, including changes that may affect the air carrier's citizenship, shall be addressed to the Chief, Air Carrier Fitness Division, Office of the Secretary, U.S. Department of Transportation, Washington, DC 20590.

(Approved by the Office of Management and Budget under control number 2106–0023)

[Doc. No. 47582, 57 FR 38766, Aug. 27, 1992, as amended at 72 FR 20036, Apr. 23, 2007]

§ 204.6 Certificated and commuter air carriers proposing a change in operations, ownership, or management which is not substantial.

Carriers proposing to make a change which would not substantially affect their operations, management, or ownership, such as certificated carriers applying for additional authority which would not substantially change their operations, will be presumed to be fit and need not file any information relating to their fitness at time of the change. However, if the Department concludes, from its own analysis or based on information submitted by third parties, that such change may bring the carrier's fitness into question, the Department may require the applicant carrier to file additional information.

§ 204.7 Revocation for dormancy.

(a) An air carrier that has not commenced any type of air transportation operations for which it was found fit, willing, and able within one year of the date of that finding, or an air carrier that, for any period of one year after the date of such a finding, has not provided any type of air transportation for which that kind of finding is required, is deemed no longer to continue to be fit to provide the air transportation for which it was found fit and, accordingly, its authority to provide such air transportation shall be revoked.

(b) An air carrier found fit which commences operations within one year after being found fit but then ceases operations, shall not resume operations without first filing all of the data required by § 204.3 at least 45 days before it intends to provide any such air transportation. Such filings shall be addressed to the Documentary Services Division, Department of Transportation, 1200 New Jersey Avenue, SE., Washington, DC 20590. The Department will entertain requests for exemption from this 45-day advance filing requirement for good cause shown. If there has been no change in fitness data previously formally filed with the Department, the carrier shall file a sworn statement to that effect signed by one of its officers. The carrier may contact the Department (Air Carrier Fitness Division) to ascertain which data are already available to the Department and need not be refiled. A carrier to which this paragraph applies shall not provide any air transportation for which it is required to be found fit, willing, and able until the Department decides that the carrier continues to be fit, willing, and able to perform such air transportation. During the pendency of the Department's consideration of a data submission under this paragraph, the expiration period set out in paragraph (a) of this section shall be stayed. If the decision or finding by the Department on the issue of the carrier's fitness is favorable, the date or that decision or finding shall be the date considered in applying paragraph (a) of this section.

(c) For purposes of this section, the date of a Department decision or finding shall be the service date of the Department's order containing such decision or finding, or, in cases where the Department's decision or finding is made by letter, the date of such letter.

(d) For purposes of this section, references to operations and to the providing of air transportation shall refer only to the actual performance of flight operations under an operating certificate issued to the carrier by the FAA.

(Approved by the Office of Management and Budget under control number 2106–0023)

PART 205—AIRCRAFT ACCIDENT LIABILITY INSURANCE

Sec.

AUTHORITY: 49 U.S.C. Chapters 401, 411, 413, 417.

SOURCE: ER–1253, 46 FR 52577, Oct. 27, 1981, unless otherwise noted.

§ 205.1 Purpose.

This part contains the rules for aircraft accident liability insurance coverage needed by U.S. direct air carriers to obtain or to exercise authority from the Department to operate in interstate or foreign air transportation, and by foreign direct air carriers to operate under permit or other authority in foreign air transportation. It further requires a disclosure statement to shippers about cargo liability limits and insurance coverage for U.S. and foreign direct air carriers.

[ER–1253, 46 FR 52577, Oct. 27, 1981, as amended by Doc. No. 47939, 57 FR 40100, Sept. 2, 1992; Doc. No. OST–96–1269, 61 FR 19165, May 1, 1996]

§ 205.2 Applicability.

These rules apply to all U.S. direct air carriers, including commuter air carriers and air taxi operators as defined in § 298.2 of this chapter, and foreign direct air carriers, including Canadian charter air taxi operators as defined in § 294.2(c) of this chapter.

[Doc. No. 47939, 57 FR 40100, Sept. 2, 1992]

§ 205.3 Basic requirements.

(a) A U.S. or foreign direct air carrier shall not engage in air transportation unless it has in effect aircraft accident liability insurance coverage that meets the requirements of this part for its air carrier or foreign air carrier operations. The minimum amounts of coverage required by this part may be provided either by insurance policies or by self-insurance plans. The currently effective policy of insurance or complete plan for self-insurance shall be available for inspection by the Department at the carrier's principal place of business. The current certificate of insurance or a summary of the complete self-insurance plan on file with the Department, as required by § 205.4, shall be available for public inspection at the carrier's principal place of business.

(b) For purposes of this part, a certificate of insurance is one or more certificates showing insurance by one or more insurers (excluding reinsurers) of currently effective and properly endorsed policies of aircraft accident liability insurance in compliance with this part. When more than one such insurer is providing coverage, the limits and types of liability assumed by each insurer (excluding reinsurers) shall be clearly stated in the certificate of insurance. Insurance policies and self-insurance plans named in a certificate of insurance that accompanies an application for initial registration or for operating authority shall become effective not later than the proposed starting date for air carrier operations as shown in the application.

(c) The certificate of insurance shall list the types or classes of aircraft, or the specific aircraft by FAA or foreign government registration number, with respect to which the policy of insurance applies, or shall state that the policy applies to all aircraft owned or operated by the carrier in its air transportation operations. With respect to certificates of insurance that list aircraft by government registration number, the policy or self-insurance plan shall state that, while an aircraft owned or leased by the carrier and declared in the policy is withdrawn from normal use because of its breakdown, repair, or servicing, such insurance as is provided by the policy or plan for that aircraft shall apply also to another aircraft of similar type, horsepower, and seating capacity, whether or not owned by the insured, while temporarily used as a substitute aircraft.

(d) Each certificate of insurance shall be signed by an authorized officer, agent, or other representative of the insurer or the insurance broker.

(e) Insurance coverage to meet the requirements of this part shall be obtained from one or more of the following:

(1) An insurer licensed to issue aircraft accident liability policies in any State, Commonwealth, or Territory of the United States, or in the District of Columbia;

(2) Surplus line insurers named on a current list of such insurers issued and approved by the insurance regulatory authority of any State, Commonwealth, or Territory of the United States or of the District of Columbia; or

(3) Insurers licensed or approved by a foreign government.

This requirement may be waived by the Department in the public interest.

[ER-1253, 46 FR 52577, Oct. 27, 1981, as amended by Doc. No. 47939, 57 FR 40100, Sept. 2, 1992]

§ 205.4 Filing of evidence of insurance.

(a) A U.S. or foreign air carrier shall file a certificate of insurance or a complete plan for self-insurance with the Department. Each carrier shall ensure that the evidence of aircraft accident liability coverage filed with the Department is correct at all times. The Department will normally notify the carrier within 20 days of receipt if the certificate or plan does not meet the requirements of this part. Certificates of Insurance shall be filed on OST Form 6410 for U.S. air carriers, including commuter air carriers and air taxi operators, and OST Form 6411 for foreign air carriers, including Canadian air taxi operators. The Department may return the certificate or self-insurance plan to the carrier if it finds for good cause that such certificate or plan does not show adequate evidence of insurance coverage under this part. Forms may be obtained from and should be filed with the Department at the addresses specified in paragraph (c) of this section. Forms may also be obtained on the Internet at *http://ostpxweb.dot.gov.*

(b) If the coverage is by type or class of aircraft or by specific aircraft, endorsements that add previously unlisted aircraft or aircraft types or classes to coverage, or that delete listed aircraft, types, or classes from coverage, shall be filed with the Department at the addresses specified in paragraph (c) of this section not more than 30 days after the effective date of the endorsements. Aircraft shall not be listed in the carrier's operations specifications with the FAA and shall not be operated unless liability insurance coverage is in force.

(c) Certificates of insurance and endorsements required in paragraphs (a) and (b) of this section shall be submitted to the Department of Transportation, Federal Aviation Administration, Program Management Branch, AFS-260, 800 Independence Avenue, SW., Washington, DC 20591. For those air carriers that have a mailing address in the State of Alaska, the forms shall be submitted to the Department of Transportation, Federal Aviation Administration, Alaskan Region Headquarters, AAL-230, 222 West 7th Avenue, Box 14, Anchorage, Alaska 99513. For Canadian air taxis, the forms shall be submitted to the Department of Transportation, Special Authorities Division, X-46, 1200 New Jersey Avenue, SE., Washington, DC 20590.

(Approved by the Office of Management and Budget under control number 2106-0030)

[Doc. No. 47939, 57 FR 40100, Sept. 2, 1992, as amended by Doc. No. OST-96-1269, 61 FR 19165, May 1, 1996; 70 FR 25767, May 16, 2005]

§ 205.5 Minimum coverage.

(a) Insurance contracts and self-insurance plans shall provide for payment on behalf of the carrier, within the specific limits of liability in this section, of all sums that the carrier shall become legally obligated to pay as damages, excluding any deductible in the policy, for bodily injury to or death of a person, or for damage to the property of others, resulting from the carrier's operation or maintenance of aircraft in air transportation provided under its authority from the Department.

(b) U.S. and foreign direct air carriers, including commuter air carriers but excluding U.S. air taxi operators and Canadian charter air taxi operators, shall maintain the following coverage:

(1) Third-party aircraft accident liability coverage for bodily injury to or death of persons, including non-employee cargo attendants, other than passengers, and for damage to property, with minimum limits of $300,000 for any one person in any one occurrence, and a total of $20,000,000 per involved aircraft for each occurrence, except that for aircraft of not more than 60 seats or 18,000 pounds maximum payload capacity, carriers need only maintain coverage of $2,000,000 per involved aircraft for each occurrence.

(2) Any such carrier providing air transportation for passengers shall, in addition to the coverage required in

paragraph (b)(1) of this section, maintain aircraft accident liability insurance coverage for bodily injury to or death of aircraft passengers, with minimum limits of $300,000 for any one passenger, and a total per involved aircraft for each occurrence of $300,000 times 75 percent of the number of passenger seats installed in the aircraft.

(c) U.S. air taxi operators registered under part 298 shall maintain the following coverage:

(1) Third-party aircraft accident liability coverage for bodily injury to or death of persons, including nonemployee cargo attendants, other than passengers, with minimum limits of:

(i) $75,000 for any one person in any one occurrence, and a total of $300,000 per involved aircraft for each occurrence, and

(ii) A limit of a least $100,000 for each occurrence for loss of or damage to property.

(2) U.S. air taxi operators carrying passengers in air transportation shall, in addition to the coverage required in paragraph (c)(1) of this section, maintain aircraft accident liability insurance coverage for bodily injury to or death of aircraft passengers, with minimum limits of $75,000 for any one passenger, and a total per involved aircraft for each occurrence of $75,000 times 75 percent of the number of passenger seats installed in the aircraft.

(d) Canadian charter air taxi operators registered under part 294 of this chapter shall maintain the following coverage:

(1) Third-party aircraft accident liability coverage for bodily injury to or death of persons, including nonemployee cargo attendants, other than passengers, and for damage to property, with a minimum coverage of $75,000 for any one person in any one occurrence, and a total of $2,000,000 per involved aircraft for each occurrence, except that Canadian charter air taxi operators operating aircraft of more than 30 seats or 7,500 pounds maximum cargo payload capacity, and a maximum authorized takeoff weight on wheels not greater than 35,000 pounds shall maintain coverage for those aircraft of $20,000,000 per involved aircraft for each occurrence.

(2) Canadian charter air taxi operators engaging in passenger charter air service under part 294 of this chapter shall, in addition to the coverage required in paragraph (d)(1) of this section, maintain aircraft accident liability coverage for bodily injury to or death of aircraft passengers, with a minimum coverage of $75,000 for any one passenger and a total per involved aircraft for each occurrence of $75,000 times 75 percent of the total number of passenger seats installed in the aircraft.

(e) Notwithstanding paragraphs (b), (c) and (d) of this section, the carrier may be insured for a combined single limit of liability for each occurrence. The combined single-limit coverage must be not less than the combined required minimums for bodily injury and property damage coverage plus, if the aircraft is used in passenger service, the required total passenger coverages stipulated in paragraph (b) of this section for U.S. and foreign direct air carriers and commuter carriers, paragraph (c) of this section for U.S. air taxi operators, or paragraph (d) of this section for Canadian charter air taxi operators.[1] The single-limit liability policy for the required aircraft accident liability coverage may be provided by a single policy or by a combination of primary and excess policies.

(f) The liability coverage shall not be contingent upon the financial condition, solvency, or freedom from bankruptcy of the carrier. The limits of the liability for the amounts required by this part shall apply separately to each occurrence. Any payment made under the policy or plan because of any one occurrence shall not reduce the coverage for payment of other damages resulting from any other occurrence.

[Doc. No. 47939, 57 FR 40101, Sept. 2, 1992; 57 FR 52590, Nov. 4, 1992]

[1] For example: the minimum single limit of liability acceptable for any aircraft in air taxi passenger service with 16 passenger seats would be computed on the basis of limits set forth in paragraph (c) as follows: 16 × .75 equals 12; 12 × $75,000 equals $900,000; $900,000 plus $300,000 (nonpassenger liability per occurrence) plus $100,000 (property damage per occurrence) equals $1,300,000. The latter amount is the minimum in which a single-limit liability policy may be written.

§ 205.6 Prohibited exclusions of coverage.

(a) No warranty or exclusion in the policy or plan or in any endorsement or amendment to the policy or plan, nor any violation of the policy or plan by the carrier, shall remove the liability coverage required by this part, except as specifically approved by the Department. This requirement shall not limit the right of insurers to recover from the carrier for amounts paid.

(b) A policy of insurance or a self-insurance plan required by this part shall not contain the following exclusions:

(1) Violation of any safety-related requirement imposed by statute or by rule of a government agency.

(2) Liability assumed by the carrier under an agreement to raise the liability limitations of the Warsaw Convention by signing a counterpart to the agreement of carriers (such as the Montreal Agreement, 18900, as approved by Board Order E-23680, May 13, 1966, agreeing to a limit on the carrier's liability for injury or death of passengers of $75,000 per passenger), or any amendment to such agreement that may be approved by the Department and to which the carrier becomes a party.

[ER-1253, 46 FR 52577, Oct. 27, 1981, as amended by Doc. No. 47939, 57 FR 40100, 40101, Sept. 2, 1992]

§ 205.7 Cancellation, withdrawal, modification, expiration, or replacement of insurance coverage.

(a) Each policy of aircraft accident liability insurance and plan for self insurance shall specify that it shall remain in force, and may not be replaced, canceled, withdrawn, or in any way modified to reduce the minimum standards set forth in this part, or to change the extent of coverage, by the insurer or the carrier, nor expire by its own terms, in regard to coverage for the carrier in its common carrier operations in air transportation, until 10 days after written notice by the insurer (in the event of replacement, by the retiring insurer), or by the insurer's representative, or by the carrier, describing the change, to the Department at the addresses specified in § 205.4(c), which 10-day notice period shall start to run from the date such notice is actually received at the Department. For purposes of this part, a policy will not be considered to have expired if the same insurer renews its coverage without reduction in the extent of coverage or amounts of coverage, and without a break in coverage, whether or not a new policy is issued, and notice to the Department is not required in that event. If the coverage being changed is by type or class of aircraft or by specific aircraft, endorsements adding or deleting specific aircraft or types or classes of aircraft, for which prior notice would be required by this paragraph, shall be filed in accordance with § 205.4(b), and prior notice of the change need not be given under this paragraph.

(b) The requirements of this section shall not apply if the policy contains a lesser time period for cancellation in a war risk exclusion. If the war risk exclusion is activated by the insurer, the insurer or its representative shall immediately notify the Department.

[Doc. No. 47939, 57 FR 40100, 40101, Sept. 2, 1992, as amended at 70 FR 25768, May 16, 2005]

§ 205.8 Cargo liability disclosure statement.

Every direct U.S. or foreign air carrier providing air cargo service in air transportation shall give notice in writing to the shipper, when a shipment is accepted, of the existence or absence of cargo liability insurance, and the limits on the extent of its liability, if any. The notice shall be clearly and conspicuously included on or attached to all of its rate sheets and airwaybills.

[ER-1282, 47 FR 16173, Apr. 15, 1982]

PART 206—CERTIFICATES OF PUBLIC CONVENIENCE AND NECESSITY: SPECIAL AUTHORIZATIONS AND EXEMPTIONS

Sec.

AUTHORITY: 49 U.S.C. Chapters 401, 415, 417, 419.

§ 206.1 Emergency transportation.

Notwithstanding the provisions of section 41101 of the Statute, and any term, condition or limitation attached to the exercise of the privileges of an air carrier certificate of public convenience and necessity which prohibits an air carrier from engaging in air transportation between any points on its route, the air carrier may carry between such points (a) any person or persons certified by a physician to be in need of immediate air transportation in order to secure emergency medical or surgical treatment together with any necessary attendant or attendants and (b) any medical supplies certified by a physician as requiring immediate air transportation for the protection of life. Air carriers offering to provide this emergency transportation shall file appropriate tariffs pursuant to Chapter 415 of the Statute.

(Secs. 204, 416, 72 Stat. 743, 771; 49 U.S.C. 1324, 1386)

[ER–261, 24 FR 1860, Mar. 14, 1959, as amended at 60 FR 43524, Aug. 22, 1995]

§ 206.2 Exemption from schedule filing.

All air carriers are hereby exempted from the requirements of section 41902(b) of the Statute, which provides that each air carrier must periodically provide the Department and the U.S. Postal Service a listing of all of its regularly operated aircraft schedules and schedule changes, showing for each schedule the points served and the departure and arrival times.

[Doc. No. 47939, 57 FR 40101, Sept. 2, 1992, as amended at 60 FR 43524, Aug. 22, 1995]

§ 206.3 Transportation of newspersons by all-cargo carriers.

Notwithstanding the provisions of section 41101 and Chapter 415 of the Statute and part 221 of this chapter, an air carrier holding a certificate of public convenience and necessity for the transportation of only property and mail may provide transportation to persons on regularly scheduled cargo flights for the purpose of collecting data for preparation of feature news, pictorial or like articles provided that the transportation is limited to the writer, journalist, or photographer engaged in the preparation of data for use in feature news, pictorial, or like articles which are to appear in newspapers or magazines, or on radio or television programs and which will publicize the regularly scheduled cargo operations of the carrier.

[Doc. No. 47939, 57 FR 40102, Sept. 2, 1992, as amended at 60 FR 43524, Aug. 22, 1995]

§ 206.4 Exemption of air carriers for military transportation.

Air carriers providing air transportation pursuant to a contract with the Department of Defense are hereby exempted from Chapter 415 of the Statute, and from part 221, §§ 207.4 and 208.32, of this chapter, with respect to those services.

[Doc. No. 47939, 57 FR 40102, Sept. 2, 1992, as amended at 60 FR 43524, Aug. 22, 1995]

§ 206.5 Small aircraft operations by certificated carriers.

(a) A carrier holding an effective certificate issued under section 41102 of the Statute, when conducting operations with small aircraft, is exempt from the requirements of the Statute as set forth in subpart B of part 298 of this chapter, except section 41708 of the Statute, and is subject to the requirements set forth in the following provisions of this chapter:

(1) Part 205, with the minimum coverage requirements of § 205.5(b),

(2) Part 215,

(3) Part 298, subpart D, §§ 298.30, and 298.38, and subpart H, and

(4) Part 298, subpart F, if the certificated carrier conducts operations with small aircraft only (a certificated carrier conducting operations with both small and large aircraft is subject only to the reporting requirements contained in part 241 of this chapter).

(b) If a certificated carrier, when conducting operations with small aircraft, provides foreign air transportation that includes a segment for which tariff filing is required and another segment for which tariff filing is not required, then for through service over that routing the carrier has the option of filing a tariff or charging the sum of the applicable local rates, fares, or charges. If the carrier files a tariff for through service, it is not exempt from Chapter 415 or section 41310 of the Statute for that air transportation.

[Doc. No. 47939, 57 FR 40102, Sept. 2, 1992, as amended at 60 FR 43524, Aug. 22, 1995]

PART 207—CHARTER TRIPS BY U.S. SCHEDULED AIR CARRIERS

AUTHORITY: 49 U.S.C. 40101, 40102, 40109, 40113, 41101, 41102, 41103, 41301, 41504, 41702, 41708, 41712, 46101.

SOURCE: Docket No. OST–97–2356, 63 FR 28236, May 22, 1998, unless otherwise noted.

§ 207.1 Applicability.

This part establishes the terms, conditions, and limitations applicable to charter air transportation conducted by air carriers holding certificates under 49 U.S.C. 41102 authorizing the operation of scheduled air transportation services.

§ 207.2 Terms of service.

Charter air transportation under this part shall be performed in accordance with the provisions of part 212 of this chapter.

PART 208—CHARTER TRIPS BY U.S. CHARTER AIR CARRIERS

AUTHORITY: 49 U.S.C. 40101, 40102, 40109, 40113, 41101, 41102, 41103, 41301, 41504, 41702, 41708, 41712, 46101.

SOURCE: Docket No. OST–97–2356, 63 FR 28236, May 22, 1998, unless otherwise noted.

§ 208.1 Applicability.

This part establishes the terms, conditions, and limitations applicable to charter air transportation conducted by air carriers holding certificates under 49 U.S.C. 41102 authorizing the operation of charter air transportation services.

§ 208.2 Terms of service.

Charter air transportation under this part shall be performed in accordance with the provisions of Part 212 of this chapter.

PART 211—APPLICATIONS FOR PERMITS TO FOREIGN AIR CARRIERS

Subpart A—General

Subpart B—General Requirements

Subpart C—Information Requirements

Subpart D—Freely Associated State Air Carriers

AUTHORITY: 49 U.S.C. Chapters 401, 411, 413, 415, 417.

SOURCE: ER–1386, 49 FR 33439, Aug. 23, 1984, unless otherwise noted.

EDITORIAL NOTE: Nomenclature changes to part 211 appear at 61 FR 34725, July 3, 1996.

Subpart A—General

§ 211.1 Purpose.

This part sets forth the filing and evidence requirements for foreign air carriers applying for authority to engage in foreign air transportation under section 41301 of Title 49 of the United States Code (Transportation).

(Approved by the Office of Management and Budget under control number 3024–0068)

[ER–1386, 49 FR 33439, Aug. 23, 1984, as amended by ER–1397, 49 FR 50027, Dec. 26, 1984]

§211.2 Applicability.

(a) Except as provided in paragraph (b) of this section, this part applies to all foreign air carriers seeking initial foreign air carrier permits or the transfer, renewal, or amendment of an existing foreign air carrier permit.

(b) Canadian charter air taxi operators, foreign indirect air carriers of property, and foreign charter operators are not required to submit applications under this part. Instead, Canadian charter air taxi operators shall register under part 294 of this chapter, foreign indirect air carriers of property shall register under part 297 of this chapter, and foreign charter operators shall register under subpart F of part 380 of this chapter.

(Approved by the Office of Management and Budget under control number 3024–0068)

[ER–1386, 49 FR 33439, Aug. 23, 1984, as amended by ER–1397, 49 FR 50027, Dec. 26, 1984]

Subpart B—General Requirements

§211.10 Filing specifications.

(a) Except as provided in paragraph (b) of this section, applicants shall follow the requirements in §302.3 of this chapter as to execution, number of copies, and formal specifications of papers.

(b) Mexican air taxi operators filing applications for foreign air carrier permits authorizing charter flights across the Mexico-United States border with small aircraft (a maximum passenger capacity of 60 seats or less, or a maximum payload capacity of 18,000 pounds or less) shall file an original and two copies of the application. The application shall conform to the instruction document available from the Foreign Air Carrier Licensing Division, Office of International Aviation, Department of Transportation, 1200 New Jersey Avenue, SE., Washington, DC 20590.

(c) An application shall have consecutively numbered pages, and shall clearly describe and identify each exhibit by a separate number or symbol. All exhibits are part of the application to which they are attached.

(d) Applications shall state all weights, measures and monetary units in U.S. terms, and all text in English.

(Approved by the Office of Management and Budget under control number 3024–0068)

[ER–1386, 49 FR 33439, Aug. 23, 1984, as amended by ER–1397, 49 FR 50027, Dec. 26, 1984; 61 FR 34725, July 3, 1996]

§211.11 Verification.

Applications shall be verified and subscribed and sworn to before a Notary Public or other officer authorized to administer oaths in the jurisdiction in which the application is executed. An application verified before a United States consular officer meets the requirements of this section.

(Approved by the Office of Management and Budget under control number 3024–0068)

[ER–1386, 49 FR 33439, Aug. 23, 1984, as amended by ER–1397, 49 FR 50027, Dec. 26, 1984]

§211.12 Filing and service.

All types of applications for foreign air carrier permits (initial, renewal, amendment, or transfer) are filed as of the date the applications are received at the Department's Docket Facility. Each applicant shall serve those persons as required in part 302, subpart B, of this chapter.

(Approved by the Office of Management and Budget under control number 3024–0068)

[ER–1386, 49 FR 33439, Aug. 23, 1984, as amended by ER–1397, 49 FR 50027, Dec. 26, 1984; 65 FR 6456, Feb. 9, 2000]

§211.13 Amendments to applications.

An applicant shall submit any information required by this part that is omitted from the original application, or any additional information, as an amendment to the original application. Applicants shall consecutively number amendments to applications and shall comply with the requirements of this subpart.

(Approved by the Office of Management and Budget under control number 3024–0068)

[ER–1386, 49 FR 33439, Aug. 23, 1984, as amended by ER–1397, 49 FR 50027, Dec. 26, 1984]

§211.14 Incorporation by reference.

Where two or more applications are filed by a single carrier, the applicant may incorporate lengthy exhibits, or other documents, attached to one application into others by reference. The applicant may not incorporate by reference and update any information from a previous docket unless submitted within the past 2 years. The applicant must identify the docket, and the page number or exhibit number being incorporated, and state that there has been no change in that information since submitting the original information.

(Approved by the Office of Management and Budget under control number 3024–0068)

[ER–1386, 49 FR 33439, Aug. 23, 1984, as amended by ER–1397, 49 FR 50027, Dec. 26, 1984]

§211.15 Statements of fact.

The applicant shall include only significant and relevant facts in an application. Each application shall contain adequate information with respect to the evidence required in subpart C of this part. The application may contain other information and data the applicant considers necessary to explain particular circumstances.

(Approved by the Office of Management and Budget under control number 3024–0068)

[ER–1386, 49 FR 33439, Aug. 23, 1984, as amended by ER–1397, 49 FR 50027, Dec. 26, 1984]

§211.16 Oral hearing.

If an oral evidentiary hearing is convened, the applicant must make available witnesses who are competent and able to testify to the accuracy of the statements and documents submitted.

(Approved by the Office of Management and Budget under control number 3024–0068)

[ER–1386, 49 FR 33439, Aug. 23, 1984, as amended by ER–1397, 49 FR 50027, Dec. 26, 1984]

Subpart C—Information Requirements

§211.20 Initial foreign air carrier permit or transfer of a permit.

A person applying for an initial foreign air carrier permit or the transfer of a permit shall submit the information listed below. The applicant must fully comply with this requirement. If the applicant is unable to respond to an item, the application shall contain an explanation, and include substitute information most closely approximating the information requested. The Department may require an applicant to provide additional information as necessary.

(a) State the name and address of the applicant, the nature of its organization (individual, partnership, corporation, etc.), and, if other than an individual, the name of the country under the laws of which it is organized and the statutory citation of such laws, if any.

(b) State the name and official address of the government air transport authority of applicant's country of citizenship having regulatory jurisdiction over applicant.

(c) Supply the following information regarding the services proposed:

(1) A complete statement of the authority sought; and

(2) A description of the services proposed, specifying:

(i) The point or points in the United States proposed to be served:

(ii) The frequency of service planned at the start of operations, indicating any seasonal variations; whether the service proposed is to be scheduled, nonscheduled or charter; whether the service would be passenger, or property and mail, or a combination; and the type of equipment (and configuration) to be used; and

(iii) A service schedule stating the manner in which the service will be operated (e.g., nonstop or multi-stop, and the identity of proposed intermediate traffic and nontraffic points).

(d) Provide the names, addresses (both residence and business), and citizenship of all Directors, Officers and key management personnel, including the President, Vice Presidents, the Directors or Supervisors of Operations, Maintenance, and Finance, and the chief pilot and chief inspector. Indicate whether any of these persons are related by blood or marriage.

(e) Provide the names and citizenship of all persons holding five percent (5%) or more of the capital stock or capital of the applicant. Also indicate the number and percentage of shares of stock or percentage of capital held by each. If five percent or more of the applicant's stock is held by a corporation or partnership, set forth the name and citizenship of each person holding five percent or more of the entire capital stock or capital of that corporation or partnership and the respective interest of each. If any shares are held for the benefit of another person, give the name and citizenship of that person.

(f) If the applicant is not wholly owned by its homeland government, state whether the applicant (each officer, director, manager, or holder of five percent or more of the capital stock) holds any interest directly or indirectly (through brokers or holding companies) in any of the entities listed below. If no interest is held, so state.

(1) Any U.S. carrier;

(2) Any other foreign air carrier;

(3) Any persons engaged in the business of aeronautics; and

(4) Any common carrier, or any person whose principal business is the holding of stock in, or control of, any air carrier.

(g) Indicate the relationship between the applicant and its homeland government. If the applicant is wholly owned or substantially owned by the government, indicate which governmental department has responsibility for managerial decisions.

(h) State whether the applicant's insurance coverage meets or exceeds the liability limits of 14 CFR part 205. State the name(s) of its insurance carrier(s).

(i) Supply certified evidence, in English, of the applicant's operating authority issued by its government that relates to the operations proposed. This evidence must include a description of the applicant's present authority, the expiration date of this authority, and the manner in which it is expected to be renewed.

(j) Summarize the operating history of the applicant. Include the types of transportation services rendered, points served, etc., from the beginning of operations to the present. Also, if the applicant is a new airline (*i.e.*, an airline that began direct air services within the past 12 months), briefly summarize the business experience of each officer, director and key management personnel, emphasizing any air transportation experience.

(k) Provide a list of the aircraft owned, leased and operated by the applicant. State each aircraft registration number and the country of registration. If leased, state the address and citizenship of each lessor. Describe any plans for the acquisition or lease of additional aircraft if the present permit application is granted as proposed. If any of the listed aircraft will not be used exclusively by the applicant, explain its proposed use. State whether any aircraft are or will be wet-leased.

(l) State where and by whom the maintenance of the aircraft is or will be performed. State whether the applicant's maintenance program complies with the provisions of ICAO Pilots and Airmen Annexes 1, 6 (Part 1) and 7. Also state whether the applicant's home country is a contracting State to the Convention on International Civil Aviation.

(m) Briefly describe any agreements or cooperative working arrangements (e.g., block-space, wet-lease), both oral and written, entered with and between the applicant, or on behalf of the applicant, and any U.S. or foreign air carrier, affecting the proposed services to the United States that are not on file with the Department. If there are no such agreements, so state.

(n) Supply financial data summaries, setting forth in U.S. dollars the applicant's profit and loss statements and balance sheets for the 2 most recent available years (calendar or fiscal). These summaries must be accompanied by a statement from the applicant's official responsible for preparation of the summaries that the submissions are complete and accurate. These summaries must include the following data, but need not be more detailed than the financial data summaries published by ICAO:

(1) The profit and loss summary shall identify:

(i) Total air transport operating revenues (separated into three categories: passenger, cargo, and other transport revenues);

(ii) Total air transport operating expenses;

(iii) Operating result (difference between (i) and (ii));

(iv) Non-operating items; and

(v) Profit or loss after income taxes.

(2) The balance sheet summary shall state and identify:

(i) Current assets;

(ii) Flight equipment (after depreciation);

(iii) Other assets;

(iv) Total assets (sum of (i) through (iii));

(v) Current liabilities;

(vi) Other liabilities;

(vii) Long-term debt;

(viii) Capital stock;

(ix) Retained earnings (balance including capital surplus); and

(x) Total liabilities and equity (sum of (v) through (ix)).

(o) Describe the amount, type and reason for financial assistance received or expected from the applicant's home government, if any.

(p) Submit an estimate showing the total traffic and the financial results of the proposed services for the first full year of normal operations and the supporting data employed to calculate the financial forecast.

(q) If the air transportation proposed is not covered by an air transport agreement, state in narrative form each of the elements of reciprocity or comity relied upon for the requested authority. If the authority requested is governed by an agreement, state whether the applicant has been formally designated by its homeland government, and, if so, cite the diplomatic note.

(r) To the extent not described in paragraph (q), state the policy of the applicant's homeland government with respect to U.S. carriers' applications for scheduled and charter authority. Specifically state whether the homeland government grants Fifth Freedom traffic rights to U.S. carriers.

(s) For the preceding 5 years, state whether the applicant has been involved in any safety or tariff violations or any fatal accidents. If so, furnish details.

(t) Submit 3 completed copies of OST Form 4523 (Waiver of liability limits under the Warsaw Convention).

(Approved by the Office of Management and Budget under control number 3024–0068)

[ER–1386, 49 FR 33439, Aug. 23, 1984, as amended by ER–1397, 49 FR 50027, Dec. 26, 1984; 61 FR 34725, July 3, 1996]

§211.21 Amendments or renewal of foreign air carrier permits.

A person applying for an amendment or renewal of a foreign air carrier permit shall submit the information listed below. The applicant must comply fully with this requirement. If the applicant is unable to respond to an item, the application shall contain an explanation and include substitute information most closely approximating the information requested. The Department may require an applicant to provide any additional information necessary.

(a) The information required in paragraphs (a), (b), (i), (o), (q), (r), and (s), of §211.20.

(b) Except if seeking renewal of existing authority, the information specified in paragraphs (c) and (p) of §211.20 regarding the new or altered services proposed to be operated.

(c) If the financial material for the applicant on file with the Department is more than 2 years old, financial summaries setting forth, in U.S. dollars, the applicant's profit and loss statements and balance sheets for the 2 most recent available years (calendar or fiscal) as required in paragraph (n) of §211.20, together with the statement of completeness and accuracy required by that paragraph. If the financial material on file with the Department is 2 years old or less, the applicant may incorporate that information by reference as described in §211.14 of this part.

(d) If the ownership and control of the applicant are substantially unchanged, so state. If a change has occurred, the applicant shall respond to the paragraph in §211.20 that most closely relates to the change that has taken place.

(e) A statement that applicant's maintenance program continues to comply with the provisions of ICAO Pilots and Airmen Annexes 1, 6 (Part 1) and 7.

[ER–1386, 49 FR 33439, Aug. 23, 1984]

Subpart D—Freely Associated State Air Carriers

SOURCE: Amdt. 211–18, 52 FR 5442, Feb. 22, 1987, unless otherwise noted.

EDITORIAL NOTE: Nomenclature changes to subpart D of part 211 appear at 61 FR 34725, July 3, 1996.

§ 211.30 Eligibility.

Foreign carriers owned and controlled by citizens of the Federated States of Micronesia, the Marshall Islands, Palau and/or the United States may, in accordance with the provisions of paragraph 5(b) of Article IX of the Federal Programs and Services Agreement, implementing section 221(a)(5) of the Compact of Free Association between the United States and those governments, apply for authority as "Freely Associated State Air Carriers." The permit application for such authority shall be labeled on the front page, "Application for Freely Associated State Foreign Air Carrier Permit."

§ 211.31 Application.

The application shall include, in addition to other requirements of this part, documentation clearly establishing:

(a) That the carrier is organized under the laws of the Federated States of Micronesia, the Marshall Islands, Palau or the United States;

(b) That substantial ownership and effective control of the carrier are held by citizens of the Federated States of Micronesia, the Marshall Islands, Palau and/or the United States;

(c) That citizens of other countries do not have interests in the carrier sufficient to permit them substantially to influence its actions, or that substantial justification exists for a temporary waiver of this requirement;

(d) That the Administrator of the Federal Aviation Administration has determined that the carrier complies with such safety standards as the Administrator considers to be required.

(e) That the government or governments of the Freely Associated States concerned have consented to the carrier's operation as a "Freely Associated State Air Carrier."

§ 211.32 Issuance of permit.

If the Department is satisfied that the applicant meets the requirements of § 211.31 (a) through (e), and that grant of all or part of the requested authority would otherwise be in the public interest, the Department may, subject to Presidential review under section 801(a) of the Federal Aviation Act, issue a "Freely Associated State Foreign Air Carrier Permit" to the applicant, including such terms, conditions or limitations as the Department may find to be in the public interest.

§ 211.33 Interstate and interstate authority.

(a) An application under this subpart may include a request, in addition to other foreign air transportation, for authority to engage in interstate air transportation between Guam, the Commonwealth of the Northern Mariana Islands and Honolulu, Hawaii, and interstate air transportation within the Commonwealth of the Northern Mariana Islands. A request for all or part of such limited interstate air transportation authority shall be supported by documentation establishing:

(1) The impact of such interstate air transportation services on the economic projections of the carrier's proposed operations;

(2) The need for such proposed interstate air transportation by the affected U.S. points;

(3) The economic impact of such interstate air transportation on services provided by other carriers providing essential air transportation services to eligible Freely Associated State points within the scope of part 272 of this chapter.

(b) The Department may grant a Freely Associated State Air Carrier authority to engage in all or part of the interstate air transportation requested in paragraph (a) of this section provided that the Department finds:

(1) That grant of such interstate air transportation authority would be in furtherance of the objectives of the Compact of Free Association and related agreements between the United States and the Freely Associated States, and would otherwise be in the public interest; and

(2) That grant of such interstate air transportation authority would not

significantly impair the economic viability of existing services providing essential air transportation to any eligible Freely Associated State point within the scope of part 272 of this chapter, or significantly increase compensation that may be required to maintain any such essential air transportation.

(c) The Department may, at any time, subject to Presidential review under section 41307, suspend, modify, or revoke such interstate authority if it concludes that the requirements specified in paragraph (b) of this section are not then being met.

[Amdt. 211–18, 52 FR 5442, Feb. 22, 1987]

§211.34 Other permits.

Nothing in this section shall be construed as limiting the authority of the Department to issue a foreign air carrier permit, other than a Freely Associated State Foreign Air Carrier Permit, to a carrier owned or controlled, in whole or in part, by citizens of the Federated States of Micronesia, the Marshall Islands or Palau, that does not meet the requirements of this section.

§211.35 Termination of eligibility.

The eligibility of a carrier owned or controlled, in whole or in part, by citizens of the Federated States of Micronesia, the Marshall Islands or Palau, respectively, for issuance of a Freely Associated State Foreign Air Carrier Permit under this subpart shall exist only for such period as subparagraphs (a), (d), and (e) (eligibility for Freely Associated State essential air transportation subsidy compensation), or subparagraph (c) (limited interstate air transportation authority), of paragraph (5) of the Agreement on Civil Aviation Economic Services and Related Programs (Article IX of the Federal Programs and Services Agreement) remain in effect between the Government of those States and the Government of the United States, insofar as authority is conferred by such permits for purposes specified in those subparagraphs.

[Amdt. 211–18, 52 FR 5442, Feb. 22, 1987]

PART 212—CHARTER RULES FOR U.S. AND FOREIGN DIRECT AIR CARRIERS

AUTHORITY: 49 U.S.C. 40101, 40102, 40109, 40113, 41101, 41103, 41504, 41702, 41708, 41712, 46101.

SOURCE: Docket No. OST–97–2356, 63 FR 28236, May 22, 1998, unless otherwise noted.

§212.1 Scope.

This part applies to all charter flights, and all other flights carrying charter passengers or cargo, in interstate and/or foreign air transportation by U.S. certificated air carriers or in foreign air transportation by foreign air carriers. It does not apply to any flights performed by a commuter air carrier, air taxi operator, or certificated air carrier operating "small aircraft" under part 298 of this chapter. Nothing in this part gives authority to operate a type or level of service not authorized by certificate, foreign air carrier permit, or exemption, except that a certificated air carrier authorized to conduct scheduled operations may conduct charter flights, in interstate and/or foreign air transportation, without limitation as to the points served.

§212.2 Definitions.

For the purposes of this part:

Affinity (pro rata) charter means a charter arranged by an organization on behalf of its membership, and which meets the requirements of §212.5.

Certificated air carrier means a U.S. direct air carrier holding a certificate issued under 49 U.S.C. 41102.

Charter flight means a flight operated under the terms of a charter contract between a direct air carrier and its charterer or lessee. It does not include scheduled interstate air transportation, scheduled foreign air transportation, or nonscheduled cargo foreign air transportation, sold on an individually ticketed or individually waybilled basis.

Charter operator means:

(1) A "Public Charter operator" as defined in §380.2 of this chapter, or

(2) An "Overseas Military Personnel Charter operator" as defined in §372.2 of this chapter.

Direct air carrier means a certificated or foreign air carrier that directly engages in the operation of aircraft under a certificate, permit, or exemption issued by the Department.

Fifth freedom charter means a charter flight carrying traffic that originates and terminates in countries other than the carrier's home country, regardless of whether the flight operates via the home country.

Foreign air carrier means a direct air carrier which is not a citizen of the United States as defined in 49 U.S.C. 40102(a) that holds a foreign air carrier permit issued under 49 U.S.C. 41302 or an exemption issued under 49 U.S.C. 40109 authorizing direct foreign air transportation.

Fourth freedom charter means a charter flight carrying traffic that terminates in the carrier's home country having originated in another country.

Gambling junket charter means a charter arranged by a casino, hotel, cruise line, or its agents, the purpose of which is to transport passengers to the casino, hotel, or cruise ship where gambling facilities are available, and which meets the requirements of §212.6.

Long-term wet lease means a wet lease which either—

(1) Lasts more than 60 days, or

(2) Is part of a series of such leases that amounts to a continuing arrangement lasting more than 60 days.

Mixed charter means a charter, the cost of which is borne partly by the charter participants and partly by the charterer, where all the passengers meet the eligibility requirements for "affinity (pro rata)" charters of §212.5.

Part charter means flight carrying both charter and scheduled passenger traffic.

Seventh-freedom charter means a charter flight carrying traffic that originates and terminates in a country other than the foreign air carrier's home country, where the flight does not have a prior, intermediate, or subsequent stop in the foreign air carrier's home country.

Single entity charter means a charter the cost of which is borne by the charterer and not by individual passengers, directly or indirectly.

Sixth-freedom charter means a charter flight carrying traffic that originates and terminates in a country other than the country of the foreign air carrier's home country, provided the flight operates via the home country of the foreign air carrier.

Third freedom charter means a charter flight carrying traffic that originates in the carrier's home country and terminates in another country.

Wet lease means a lease between direct air carriers by which the lessor provides all or part of the capacity of an aircraft, and its crew, including operations where the lessor is conducting services under a blocked space or codesharing arrangement.

[Doc. No. OST–97–2356, 63 FR 28236, May 22, 1998, as amended at 71 FR 5784, Feb. 3, 2006]

§212.3 General provisions.

(a) Certificated and foreign air carriers may conduct charter flights as described in this part, and may carry charter passengers on scheduled flights, or charter cargo on scheduled or nonscheduled flights (or on the main deck or in the belly of passenger charter flights), subject to the requirements of this chapter and any orders of, or specific conditions imposed by, the Department.

(b) Charter flights may be operated on a round-trip or one-way basis, with no minimum group, shipment, or contract size.

(c) Contracts to perform charter flights must be in writing and signed by an authorized representative of the certificated or foreign air carrier and the charterer prior to the operation of the flights involved. The written agreement shall include:

(i) The name and address of either the surety whose bond secures advance charter payments received by the carrier, or of the carrier's depository bank to which checks or money orders for the advance charter payments are to be made payable as escrow holder pending completion of the charter trip; and

(2) A statement that unless the charterer files a claim with the carrier, or, if the carrier is unavailable, with the surety, within 60 days after the cancellation of a charter trip with respect to which the charterer's advance payments are secured by the bond, the surety shall be released from all liability under the bond to such charterer for such trips.

(d) A certificated or foreign air carrier must make a reasonable effort to verify that any charterer with which it contracts, and any charter it conducts, meets the applicable requirements of this chapter.

(e) The certificated or foreign air carriers shall require full payment of the total charter price, including payment for the return portion of a round trip, or the posting of a satisfactory bond for full payment, prior to the commencement of any portion of the air transportation, *provided*, however, that in the case of a passenger charter for less than the entire of an aircraft, the carrier shall require full payment of the total charter price, including payment for the return portion of a round trip, from the charterers not less than 10 days prior to the commencement of any portion of the transportation, and such payment shall not be refundable unless the charter is canceled by the carrier or unless the carrier accepts a substitute charterer for one which has canceled a charter, in which case the amount paid by the latter shall be refunded. For the purpose of this section, payment to the carrier's depository bank, as designated in the charter contract, shall be deemed payment to the carrier.

(f) A certificated or foreign air carrier operating a U.S.-originating passenger charter shall be responsible to return to his or her point of origin any passenger who purchased round trip transportation on that charter and who was transported by that carrier on his or her outbound flight; except that this provision shall not apply in cases where the return transportation is to be provided by another certificated or foreign air carrier.

(g) A certificated or foreign air carrier may not perform any charter flight for which a statement of authorization is required under §212.9 until one has been granted by the Department. In addition, if a foreign air carrier is required to obtain a statement of authorization under paragraph (e) of that section, neither it, not any charter operator, or any other person shall advertise or sell any passenger charter services except those that have been specifically authorized by the Department.

(h) A certificated air carrier may not operate charters where such operations would result in a substantial change in the scope of its operations within the meaning of part 204 of this chapter.

(i) A certificated air carrier may not limit its baggage liability for interstate charter flights except as set forth in part 254 of this chapter.

(j) A certificated air carrier may not, except as set forth in part 121 of the Federal Aviation Regulations (14 CFR part 121), limit the availability, upon reasonable request, of air transportation and related services to a person who may require help from another person in expeditiously moving to an emergency exit for evacuation of an aircraft.

(k) A certificated air carrier holding a certificate to conduct only cargo operations may not conduct passenger charters.

(l) A certificated air carrier may not perform any charter in interstate commerce within the State of Alaska.

(m) A foreign air carrier may operate charters in foreign air transportation only to the extent authorized by its foreign air carrier permit under 49 U.S.C. 41302 or exemption authority under 49 U.S.C. 40109, and only to the extent to which such operations are consistent with the provisions of any applicable bilateral aviation undertaking.

§ 212.4 Authorized charter types.

Certificated and foreign air carriers may conduct the following charter types, subject to the provisions of this part:

(a) Affinity (pro rata) charters.

(b) Single entity charters, including:

(1) Wet leases involving the carriage of passengers and/or cargo, provided, that the wet lessee holds appropriate economic authority from the Department to conduct the proposed operations; and

(2) Charters pursuant to contracts with the Department of Defense, provided, that foreign air carriers may conduct charters for the Department of Defense only to the extent that such operations are consistent with the provisions of 49 U.S.C. 40118.

(c) Mixed charters.

(d) Gambling junket charters.

(e) Public Charters in accordance with part 380 of this chapter (including operations by educational institutions as defined in that part).

(f) Overseas military personnel charters in accordance with part 372 of this chapter.

(g) Cargo charters.

§ 212.5 Operation of affinity (pro rata) charters.

An affinity (pro rata) charter operated by a certificated or foreign air carrier must meet the following criteria:

(a) The aircraft must be chartered by an organization, no part of whose business is the formation of groups for transportation or solicitation or sale of transportation services, for the purpose of providing air transportation to its members and their immediate families.

(b) The charter must be organized by the organization itself, or by a person or company who acts not as a principal, but as an agent for the chartering organization or the certificated or foreign air carrier.

(c) No solicitation, sales, or participation may take place beyond the bona fide members of an eligible chartering organization, and their immediate families (spouse, children, and parents). All printed solicitation materials shall contain the following notice in boldface, 10-point or larger type—

Some of the Federal rules that protect against tour changes and loss of passengers' money in publicly sold charters do not apply to this charter flight.

(d) "Bona fide members" are members of an organization who: Have not joined the organization merely to travel on a charter flight; and who have been members of the chartering organization for a minimum of six months prior to the date of commencement of the affected flight; *provided*, that the "six month" rule does not apply to:

(1) Employees of a single commercial establishment, industrial plant, or government agency, or

(2) Students and employees of a single school.

(e) The charter price due the direct air carrier shall be prorated equally among all the charter passengers, except that children under 12 may be offered discounted or free transportation.

(f) The certificated or foreign air carrier shall make reasonable efforts to assure that passengers transported meet the eligibility requirements of this section. The certificated or foreign air carrier shall also obtain (no later than the date of departure), and maintain for two years, a certification by an authorized representative of the chartering organization that all passengers are eligible for transportation under this section.

§ 212.6 Operation of gambling junket charters.

A gambling junket charter operated by a certificated or foreign air carrier must meet the following criteria:

(a) The aircraft must be chartered by

(1) A casino, hotel, or cruise line duly licensed by the government of any state, territory or possession of the United States, or by a foreign government, or

(2) An agent of such a casino, or cruise line on behalf of that casino, hotel, or cruise line.

(b) The casino, hotel, or cruise line or its agents, may not require a passenger to incur any expense in taking the trip, *provided*, that this provision shall not preclude the casino, hotel, or cruise line or its agents, from requiring prospective passengers to pay nominal reservation fees that are duly refundable by the casino, hotel, or cruise line before the flight, establish a minimum line-of-credit at the casino, hotel, or cruise line, bring (but not necessarily spend) a specified minimum amount of money, or meet other requirements that do not place them in financial jeopardy; nor does it preclude the casino, hotel, or cruise line, or its agents, from offering operational land packages for a fee.

§212.7 Direct sales.

(a) Certificated and foreign air carriers may sell or offer for sale, and operate, as principal, Public Charter flights under part 380 of this chapter directly to the public.

(b) Each certificated or foreign air carrier operating a charter trip under this section shall comply with all the requirements of part 380 of this chapter, except that:

(1) Those provisions of part 380 relating to the existence of a contract between a charter operator and a direct air carrier do not apply;

(2) A depository agreement shall comply with §380.34a (d) and (f);

(3) A security agreement shall comply with §380.34 (c) and (d); and

(i) If no depository agreement is used, protect charter participant payments (including those for ground accommodations and services) and assure the certificated or foreign air carrier's contractual and regulatory responsibilities to charter participants in an unlimited amount (except that the liability of the securer with respect to any charter participant may be limited to the charter price paid by or on behalf of such participant);

(ii) If used in combination with a depository agreement, protect charter participant payments (including those for ground accommodations and services) and assure the certificated or foreign air carrier's contractual and regulatory responsibilities to charter participants in the amount of at least $10,000 times the number of flights, except that the amount need not be more than $200,000. The liability of the securer with respect to any charter participant may be limited to the charter price paid by or on behalf of such participant.

(c) The Department reserves the right to limit or prohibit the operation of direct sales Public Charters by a foreign air carrier upon a finding that such action is necessary in the public interest.

§212.8 Protection of customers' payments.

(a) Except as provided in paragraph (c) of this section, no certificated air carrier or foreign air carrier shall perform any charter trip (other than a cargo charter trip) originating in the United States or any Overseas Military Personnel Charter trip, as defined in part 372 of this chapter, nor shall such carrier accept any advance payment in connection with any such charter trip, unless there is on file with the Department a copy of a currently effective agreement made between said carrier and a designated bank, by the terms of which all sums payable in advance to the carrier by charterers, in connection with any such trip to be performed by said carrier, shall be deposited with and maintained by the bank, as escrow holder, the agreement to be subject to the following conditions:

(1) The charterer (or its agent) shall pay the carrier either by check or money order made payable to the depository bank. Such check or money order and any cash received by the carrier from a charterer (or its agent) shall be deposited in, or mailed to, the bank no later than the close of the business day following the receipt of the check or money order or the cash, along with a statement showing the name and address of the charterer (or its agent); provided, however, that where the charter transportation to be performed by a carrier is sold through a travel agent, the agent may be authorized by the carrier to deduct its commission and remit the balance of the advance payment to the carrier either by check or money order made payable to the designated bank.

(2) The bank shall pay over to the carrier escrowed funds with respect to a specific charter only after the carrier has certified in writing to the bank that such charter has been completed; provided, however, that the bank may

be required by the terms of the agreement to pay over to the carrier a specified portion of such escrowed funds, as payment for the performance of the outbound segment of a round-trip charter upon the carrier's written certification that such segment has been so completed.

(3) Refunds to a charterer from sums in the escrow account shall be paid directly to such charterer its assigns. Upon written certification from the carrier that a charter has been canceled, the bank shall turn over directly to the charterer or its assigns all escrowed sums (less any cancellation penalties as provided in the charter contract) which the bank holds with respect to such canceled charter, provided however, that in the case of a split charter escrowed funds shall be turned over to a charterer or its assigns only if the carrier's written certification of cancellation of such charter includes a specific representation that either the charter has been canceled by the carrier or, if the charter has been canceled by the charterer, that the carrier has accepted a substitute charterer.

(4) The bank shall maintain a separate accounting for each charter flight.

(5) As used in this section the term "bank" means a bank insured by the Federal Deposit Insurance Corporation.

(b) The escrow agreement required under paragraph (a) of this section shall not be effective until approved by the Department. Claims against the escrow may be made only with respect to the non-performance of air transportation.

(c) The carrier may elect, in lieu of furnishing an escrow agreement pursuant to paragraph (a) of this section, to furnish and file with the Department a surety bond with guarantees to the United States Government the performance of all charter trips (other than cargo charter trips) originating in the United States and of all overseas military personnel charter trips, as defined in part 372 of this chapter, to be performed, in whole or in part, by such carrier pursuant to any contracts entered into by such carrier. The amount of such bond shall be unlimited.[1] Claims under the bond may be made only with respect to the non-performance of air transportation.

(d) The bond permitted by this section shall be in the form set forth as the appendix to this part. Such bond shall be issued by a bonding or surety company—

(1) Which is listed in Best's Insurance Reports (Fire and Casualty) with a general policyholders' rating of "A" or better or

(2) Which is listed in the U.S. Department of Treasury's notice listing companies holding Certificates of Authority as acceptable sureties on Federal bonds and as acceptable reinsuring companies, published in the FEDERAL REGISTER on or about July 1. The bonding or surety company shall be one legally authorized to issue bonds of that type in the State in which there is located the office or usual residence of the agency designated by the carrier under 49 U.S.C. 46103 to receive service of notices, process and other documents issued by or filed with the Department of Transportation. For the purposes of this section the term "State" includes any territory or possession of the United States, or the District of Columbia. If the bond does not comply with the requirements of this section, or for any reason fails to provide satisfactory or adequate protection for the public, the Department will notify the certificated or foreign air carrier by registered or certified mail, stating the deficiencies of the bond. Unless such deficiencies are corrected within the time limit set forth in the notification, no amounts payable in advance by customers for the subject charter trips shall be accepted by the carrier.

(e) The bond required by this section shall provide that unless the charterer files a claim with the carrier, or, if the carrier is unavailable, with the surety, within 60 days after cancellation of a charter trip with respect to which the charterer's advance payments are secured by the bond, the surety shall be

[1] While the face amount of the bond is unlimited, claims are limited to amounts that are paid to carrier for U.S.-originating passenger charter flights that carrier fails to perform or to refund.

released from all liability under the bond to such charterer for such charter trip. The contract between the carrier and the charterer shall contain notice of this provision.

§212.9 Prior authorization requirements.

(a) Certificated air carriers shall obtain a statement of authorization for each long-term wet lease to a foreign air carrier.

(b) Foreign air carriers shall obtain a statement of authorization for each:

(1) Fifth-, sixth- and/or seventh-freedom charter flights to or from the United States;

(2) Long-term wet lease;

(3) Charter flight for which the Department specifically requires prior authorization under paragraph (e) or (f) of this section; or

(4) Part charter.

(c) The Department may issue blanket statements of authorization to foreign air carriers to conduct fifth freedom charters. The standards for issuing such blanket authorizations shall be those stated in §212.11. The Department may revoke any authority granted under this paragraph at any time without hearing.

(d) The Department may at any time, with or without hearing, but with at least 30 days' notice, require a foreign air carrier to obtain a statement of authorization before operating any charter flight. In deciding whether to impose such a requirement, the Department will consider (but not be limited to considering) whether the country of the carrier's nationality:

(1) Requires prior approval for third or fourth freedom charter flights by U.S. air carriers;

(2) Has, over the objection of the U.S. Government, denied rights of a U.S. air carrier guaranteed by a bilateral agreement; or

(3) Has otherwise impaired, limited, or denied the operating rights of U.S. air carriers, or engaged in unfair, discriminatory, or restrictive practices with respect to air transportation services to, from, through, or over its territory.

(e) The Department, in the interest of national security, may require a foreign air carrier to provide prior notification or to obtain a statement of authorization before operating any charter flight over U.S. territory.

[Doc. No. OST–97–2356, 63 FR 28236, May 22, 1998, as amended at 71 FR 5785, Feb. 3, 2006]

§212.10 Application for statement of authorization.

(a) Application for a statement of authorization shall be submitted on OST Form 4540 except that for part charters or long-term wet leases the application may be in letter form. An application for a long-term wet lease shall describe the purpose and terms of the wet lease agreement. Except for an application for a long-term wet lease involving a codeshare agreement, an original and two copies of an application shall be submitted to the Department of Transportation, Office of International Aviation, U.S. Air Carrier Licensing Division, X–44 (for an application by a certificated air carrier), or Foreign Air Carrier Licensing Division, X–45 (for an application by a foreign air carrier), 1200 New Jersey Avenue, SE., Washington, DC 20590; an original and two copies of an application for a long-term wet lease involving a codeshare agreement shall be submitted to DOT Dockets, PL–401, 1200 New Jersey Avenue, SE., Washington, DC 20590, or by electronic submission to DOT Dockets according to procedures at the DOT Dockets website. Upon a showing of good cause, the application may be transmitted by facsimile (fax) or telegram, or may be made by telephone, provided, that in the case of a fax or telephone application, the applicant must confirm its request (by filing an original and two copies of its application as described above) within three business days.

(b) A copy of each application for a long-term wet lease shall also be served on the Director of Flight Standards Service (AFS–1), Federal Aviation Administration, 800 Independence Avenue, SW., Washington, DC 20591, and on each certificated air carrier that is authorized to serve the general area in which the proposed transportation is to be performed.

(c)(1) Applicants for statements of authorization filed by foreign air carriers shall include documentation to establish the extent to which the country of the applicant's nationality deals with U.S. air carriers on the basis of reciprocity for similar flights, if such flights are not subject to a bilateral agreement, and

(i) The Department has not established that the country accords reciprocity;

(ii) The Department has found reciprocity defective in the most recent prior approval application involving the country; or

(iii) Changes in reciprocity have occurred since the most recent Department finding for the country in question.

(2) Applications filed by certificated or foreign air carriers to conduct long-term wet leases shall include, for the country of the lessee's nationality, the documentation specified in paragraph (c)(1) of this section.

(d)(1) Applications shall be filed at least 5 business days before commencement of the proposed flight or flights, except as specified in paragraphs (d)(2), (d)(3), and (d)(4) of this section. Late applications may be considered upon a showing of good cause for the lateness.

(2) Applications for a part charter or for a long-term wet lease shall be filed at least 45 calendar days before the date of the first proposed flight.

(3) Applications specifically required under §212.9(d) shall be filed at least 30 calendar days before the proposed flight or flights (10 calendar days for cargo charters), unless otherwise specified by the Department.

(4) Applications required by a Department order under §212.9(e) shall be filed at least 14 calendar days before the proposed flight or flights, unless otherwise specified by the Department.

(5) Where an application is required by more than one provision of this part and/or order of the Department, only one application need be filed, but it must conform to the earliest applicable filing deadline.

(6) The Department may require service of applications as it deems necessary.

(e)(1) Any part in interest may file a memorandum supporting or opposing an application. Three copies of each memorandum shall be filed within 7 business days after service of the application or before the date of the proposed flight or flights, whichever is earlier. Memorandums will be considered to the extent practicable; the Department may act on an application without waiting for supporting or opposing memorandums to be filed.

(2) Each memorandum shall set forth the reasons why the application should be granted or denied, accompanied by whatever data, including affidavits, the Department is requested to consider.

(3) A copy of each memorandum shall be served on the certified or foreign air carrier applying for approval.

(f)(1) Unless otherwise ordered by the Department, each application and memorandum filed in response will be available for public inspection at the Office of International Aviation immediately upon filing. Such information with respect to codeshare applications and responsive pleadings will be available for public inspection at DOT Dockets or at the DOT Dockets website. Notice of the filing of all applications shall be published in the Department's Weekly List of Applications Filed.

(2) Any person objecting to public disclosure of any information in an application or memorandum must state the grounds for the objection in writing. If the Department finds that disclosure of all or part of the information would adversely affect the objecting person, and that the public interest does not require disclosure, it will order that the injurious information be withheld.

[Doc. No. OST-97-2356, 63 FR 28236, May 22, 1998, as amended at 64 FR 3213, Jan. 21, 1999]

§212.11 Issuance of statement of authorization.

(a) The Department will issue a statement of authorization if it finds that the proposed charter flight, part charter, or wet lease meets the requirements of this part and that it is in the public interest. Statements of authorization may be conditioned or limited.

(b) In determining the public interest the Department will consider (but not be limited to) the following factors:

(1) The extent to which the authority sought to covered by and consistent with bilateral agreements to which the United States is a party.

(2) The extent to which an applicant foreign air carrier's home country (and, in the case of a long-term wet lease, the lessee's home country) deals with U.S. air carriers on the basis of substantial reciprocity.

(3) Whether the applicant or its agent has previously violated the provisions of this part.

(4) Where the application concerns a long-term wet lease:

(i) Whether the lessor (applicant) or its agent or the lessee (charterer) or its agent has previously violated the provisions of the Department's charter regulations.

(ii) Whether, because of the nature of the arrangement and the benefits involved, the authority sought should be the subject of a bilateral agreement.

(iii) To what extent the lessor owns and/or controls the lessee, or is owned and/or controlled by the lessee.

(c) The Department will submit any denial of an authorization specifically required of a foreign air carrier under § 212.9(d) to the President of the United States at least 10 days before the proposed departure. The denial will be subject to stay or disapproval by the President within 10 days after it is submitted. A shorter period for Presidential review may be specified by the Department where the application for authorization is not timely or properly filed. Denial of a late-filed application need not be submitted to the President. For the purposes of this paragraph, an application filed by a foreign air carrier under § 212.9(d) to conduct a cargo charter will be considered as timely filed only if it is filed at least 30 calendar days before the proposed flight, notwithstanding the 10-day filing requirement for cargo charters in § 212.10(d)(3).

(d) The Department will publish notice of its actions on applications for statements of authorization in its Weekly List of Applications Filed. Interested persons may upon request obtain copies of letters of endorsed forms advising applicants of action taken on their applications.

§ 212.12 Waiver.

The Department may grant a waiver of any of the provisions of this part upon a finding that such waiver is in the public interest. A certificated or foreign air carrier may request a waiver by filing a written application with the Department, citing the specific provision to be waived and providing justification for such waiver.

APPENDIX A TO PART 212—CERTIFICATED OR FOREIGN AIR CARRIER'S SURETY BOND UNDER PART 212 OF THE REGULATIONS OF THE DEPARTMENT OF TRANSPORTATION (14 CFR PART 212)

Know all persons by these presents, that we ________ (Name of certificated or foreign air carrier) of ________, (City) ________ (State or Country) as Principal (hereinafter called Principal), and ________ (name of Surety) a corporation created and existing under the laws of the State of ________ (State) as Surety (hereinafter called Surety) are held and firmly bound unto the United States of America in an unlimited amount, as required by 14 CFR 212.8, for which payment, well and truly to be made, we bind ourselves and our heirs, executors, administrators, successors, and assigns, jointly and severally, firmly by these presents.

Whereas the principal, a certificated air carrier holding a certificate of public convenience and necessity issued under 49 U.S.C. 41102, or a foreign air carrier holding a foreign air carrier permit issued under 49 U.S.C. 41302 or an exemption issued under 49 U.S.C. 40109 authorizing that foreign air carrier to engage in charter trips in foreign air transportation, is subject to rules and regulations of the Department of Transportation relating to security for the protection of charterers of civil aircraft and has elected to file with the Department of Transportation such a bond as will guarantee to the United States Government the performance of all charter trips (other than cargo charter trips) originating in the United States and of all Overseas Military Personnel Charters, as defined in 14 CFR part 372, to be performed, in whole or in part, by such certificated or foreign air carrier pursuant to contracts entered into by such carrier after the execution date of this bond, and

Whereas this bond is written to assure compliance by the Principal with rules and regulations of the Department of Transportation relating to security for the protection of charterer of civil aircraft for charter trips (other than cargo charters) originating in the United States or of Overseas Military Personnel Charter trips and shall inure to the benefit of any and all such charterers to whom the Principal may be held legally liable for any of the damages herein described.

Now, therefore, the condition of this obligation is such that if the Principal shall pay or cause to be paid to such charterer any sum or sums for which the Principal may be held legally liable by reason of the Principal's failure faithfully to perform, fulfill, and carry out all contracts made by the Principal while this bond is in effect for the performance of charter trips (other than cargo charter trips) originating in the United States and of Overseas Military Personnel Charter trips, then this obligation shall be void, otherwise to remain in full force and effect.

The liability of the Surety shall not be discharged by any payment or succession of payments hereunder in any specified amount. The surety agrees to furnish written notice to the Department of Transportation forthwith of all suits filed, judgments rendered, and payments made by said Surety under this bond.

This bond is effective the _____ day of _______________, _______, 12:01 a.m., standard time at the address of the Principal as stated herein and shall continue in force until terminated as hereinafter provided. The Principal or the Surety may at any time terminate this bond by written notice to the Department of Transportation at its office in Washington, D.C., such termination to become effective thirty (30) days after actual receipt of said notice by the Department. The Surety shall not be liable hereunder for the payment of the damages hereinbefore described which arise as the result of any contracts for the performance of air transportation services made by the Principal after the termination of this bond becomes effective, as herein provided, but such termination shall not affect the liability of the Surety hereunder for the payment of any such damages arising as the result of contracts for the performance of air transportation services made by the Principal after the termination of this bond becomes effective. Liability of the Surety under this bond shall in all events be limited only to a charterer who shall within sixty (60) days after the cancellation of a charter trip with respect to which the charterer's advance payments are secured by this bond give written notice of claim to the certificated or foreign air carrier, or, if it is unavailable, to the Surety, and all liability on this bond for such charter trip shall automatically terminate sixty (60) days after the termination date thereof except for claims filed within the time provided herein.

In witness whereof, the said Principal and Surety have executed this instrument on the _____ day of _______________, _______.

Principal

Name ____________________

By: Signature and title ____________________

Witness ____________________

Surety

Name ____________________

By: Signature and title ____________________

Witness ____________________

Bonding or surety company must be listed in Best's Insurance Reports (Fire and Casualty) with a general policyholders' rating of "A" or better or in the Department of the Treasury listing of companies holding certificates of authority as acceptable sureties on Federal bonds. In addition, the bonding or surety company shall be one legally authorized to issue bonds of that type in the State(s) in which the charter flight(s) originate. Agents must provide satisfactory proof that they have the requisite authority to issue this bond.

APPENDIX B TO PART 212—CERTIFICATION OF COMPLIANCE

Organization Charterworthiness for Affinity Charter Air Transportation and Eligibility of All Prospective Passengers for Such Flights Under Part 212 of the Regulations of the Department of Transportation (14 CFR Part 212)

I declare under penalty of perjury under the laws of the United States of America that the foregoing is true and correct.

PART 213—TERMS, CONDITIONS AND LIMITATIONS OF FOREIGN AIR CARRIER PERMITS

AUTHORITY: 49 U.S.C. Chapters 401, 411, 413, 415, 417.

SOURCE: ER–624, 35 FR 8881, June 9, 1970, unless otherwise noted.

EDITORIAL NOTE: Nomenclature changes to part 213 appear at 61 FR 34725, July 3, 1996.

§ 213.1 Applicability.

This regulation sets forth terms, conditions, and limitations applicable to foreign air carrier permits issued under section 41302 of Title 49 of the United

States Code (Transportation) authorizing scheduled foreign air transportation. Unless such permits or the orders issuing such permits otherwise provide, the exercises of the privileges to engage in scheduled foreign air transportation granted by any such permit shall be subject to the terms, conditions, and limitations as are set forth in this part, and as may from time to time be prescribed by the Department.

[ER-680, 36 FR 7306, Apr. 17, 1971, as amended at 61 FR 34725, July 3, 1996]

§213.2 Reports of traffic data.

The Department may at any time require any foreign air carrier to file with the Department traffic data disclosing the nature and extent of such carrier's engagement in transportation between points in the United States and points outside thereof. The Department will specify the traffic data required in each such instance. Interested persons seeking reconsideration of a Department determination under this section may file a petition pursuant to Rule 14 of part 302 within 10 days after Department action.

[ER-624, 35 FR 8881, June 9, 1970, as amended at 65 FR 6456, Feb. 9, 2000]

§213.3 Filing and approval of schedules.

(a) In the absence of provisions to the contrary in the permit and of Department action pursuant to this section, a foreign air carrier may determine the schedules (including type of equipment used) pursuant to which it engages in transportation between points in the United States and points outside thereof.

(b) In the case of a foreign air carrier permit for scheduled air transportation which is not the subject of an air transport agreement between the United States and the government of the holder, the Department, if it finds that the public interest so requires, may with or without hearing order the foreign air carrier to file with it within 7 days after service of such order, an original and three copies of any or all of its existing schedules of service between any point in the United States and any point outside thereof, and may require such carrier thereafter to file an original and three copies of any proposed schedules of service between such points at least 30 days prior to the date of inauguration of such service. Such schedules shall contain all schedules of aircraft which are or will be operated by such carrier between each pair of points set forth in the order, the type of equipment used or to be used, the time of arrival and departure at each point, the frequency of each schedule, and the effective date of any proposed schedule.

(c) In the case of any foreign air carrier permit for scheduled air transportation which is the subject of an air transport agreement between the United States and the government of the holder, the Department may with or without hearing issue an order, similar to that provided for in paragraph (b) of this section, if it makes the findings provided for in that subsection and, in addition, finds that the government or aeronautical authorities of the government of the holder, over the objections of the U.S. Government, have: (1) Taken action which impairs, limits, terminates, or denies operating rights, or (2) otherwise denied or failed to prevent the denial of, in whole or in part, the fair and equal opportunity to exercise the operating rights, provided for in such air transport agreement, of any U.S. air carrier designated thereunder with respect to flight operations to, from, through, or over the territory of such foreign government.

(d) The carrier may continue to operate existing schedules, and may inaugurate operations under proposed schedules 30 days after the filing of such schedules with the Department, unless the Department with or without hearing issues an order, subject to stay or disapproval by the President of the United States within 10 days after adoption, notifying the carrier that such operations, or any part of them, may be contrary to applicable law or may adversely affect the public interest. If the notification pertains to a proposed schedule, service under such schedule shall not be inaugurated; if the notification pertains to existing schedules, service under such schedules shall be discontinued on the date specified in the Department's order. Such date shall be not less than ten days after adoption of the Department's order unless affirmative Presidential approval is obtained at an earlier date.

(e) No petitions for reconsideration may be filed with respect to Department orders issued pursuant to paragraph (b), (c), or (d) of this section. Nevertheless, if the Department serves a notification under paragraph (d) of this section, the carrier may make application to the Department for approval of any or all existing or proposed schedules, pursuant to the provisions of § 213.5. The Department may with or without hearing withdraw, in whole or in part, its notification at any time and may permit existing or proposed schedules to be operated for such period or periods as the Department may determine.

(f) The date of service on a foreign air carrier of orders and notifications pursuant to this section shall be the date of mailing thereof, by certified or registered mail, to the agent designated by the foreign air carrier pursuant to 49 U.S.C. 46103 or, if the foreign air carrier has failed to designate an agent, the date of mailing by registered air mail to the foreign air carrier's home office.

[ER–624, 35 FR 8881, June 9, 1970, as amended by ER–870, 39 FR 30843, Aug. 26, 1974; ER–1107, 47 FR 46495, Oct. 19, 1982; 61 FR 34725, July 3, 1996]

§ 213.4 [Reserved]

§ 213.5 Filing and service of schedules and applications for approval of schedules; procedure thereon.

(a) *Number of copies and certificate of service.* An original and three copies of each schedule, and an original and seven (7) copies of application for approval of schedules (§ 213.3(e)) shall be filed with the Department, each setting forth the names and addresses of the persons, if any, required to be served, and stating that service has been made on all such persons by personal service or by registered or certified mail (if the addressee is located within the United States, its territories and possessions) or by registered air mail (if the addressee is located outside the United States, its territories and possessions) and the date of such service. In the case of service by mail, the date of mailing shall be considered the date of service.

(b) *Pleadings by interested persons.* Any interested person may file and serve upon the foreign air carrier a memorandum in opposition to, or in support of, schedules or an application for approval of schedules within 10 days of the filing opposed or supported. All memoranda shall set forth in detail the reasons for the position taken together with a statement of economic data and other matters which it is desired that the Department officially notice, and affidavits stating other facts relied upon. Memoranda shall contain a certificate of service as prescribed in paragraph (a) of this section. An executed original and seven (7) true copies shall be filed with the Department's Docket Facility. Unless otherwise provided by the Department, further pleadings will not be entertained.

(c) *Determination and petitions for reconsideration.* The Department may make its determination upon the application and other pleadings or, in its discretion, after hearing. Interested persons seeking reconsideration of the Department's determination on an application approval of schedules may file a petition pursuant to Rule 14 of part 302 of this chapter within 10 days of Department action. Any interested person may file an answer in opposition to, or in support of, the petition within 10 days after it is filed. An executed original and 19 copies of such petition for reconsideration or memorandum shall be filed with the Docket Facility. All petitions for reconsideration shall contain a certificate of service in the form prescribed by paragraph (a) of this section. Unless ordered by the Department upon application or upon its own motion, further pleadings will not be entertained.

[ER–624, 35 FR 8881, June 9, 1970, as amended by ER–644, 35 FR 14382, Sept. 12, 1970; 61 FR 34725, July 3, 1996; 65 FR 6456, Feb. 9, 2000]

§ 213.6 Compliance.

Any violation by the foreign air carrier of applicable provisions of Subtitle

VII of Title 49 of the U.S. Code or of orders, rules or regulations issued thereunder, or of the terms, conditions or limitations applicable to the exercise of the privileges granted by the permit shall constitute a failure to comply with the terms, conditions and limitations of such permit: *Provided*, That upon a showing that a violation of a provision not mandatorily prescribed by law resulted from the observance by the holder of an obligation, duty or liability imposed by a foreign country, the Department may excuse the violation.

[ER-624, 35 FR 8881, June 9, 1970, as amended at 61 FR 34725, July 3, 1996]

§213.7 Filing requirements for adherence to Montreal Agreement.

It shall be a condition upon the holding of a foreign air carrier permit or other authority authorizing direct foreign scheduled air transportation that the holder have and maintain in effect and on file with the Department a signed counterpart of Agreement 18900 (OST Form 4523), and a tariff (for those carriers otherwise generally required to file tariffs) that includes its provisions, and comply with all other requirements of part 203 of this chapter. That form can be obtained from the Foreign Air Carrier Licensing Division (X-45), Office of International Aviation, Department of Transportation, 1200 New Jersey Avenue, SE., Washington, DC 20590.

(Approved by the Office of Management and Budget under control number 3024-0064)

[ER-1330, 48 FR 8050, Feb. 25, 1983, as amended by ER-1346, 48 FR 31014, July 6, 1983; 61 FR 34725, July 3, 1996]

PART 214—TERMS, CONDITIONS, AND LIMITATIONS OF FOREIGN AIR CARRIER PERMITS AUTHORIZING CHARTER TRANSPORTATION ONLY

§214.1 Applicability.

This part establishes the terms, conditions, and limitations applicable to charter foreign air transportation pursuant to foreign air carrier permits authorizing the holder to engage in charter transportation only.

(Secs. 204, 402, Pub. L. 85-726, as amended, 72 Stat. 743, 757; 49 U.S.C. 1324, 1371)

[ER-1223, 46 FR 28379, May 26, 1981]

§214.2 Terms of service.

Charter air transportation under this part shall be performed in accordance with the provisions of part 212 of this chapter.

(Secs. 204, 402, Pub. L. 85-726, as amended, 72 Stat. 743, 757; 49 U.S.C. 1324, 1371)

[ER-1223, 46 FR 28379, May 26, 1981]

PART 215—USE AND CHANGE OF NAMES OF AIR CARRIERS, FOREIGN AIR CARRIERS AND COMMUTER AIR CARRIERS

AUTHORITY: 49 U.S.C. Chapters 401, 411, 413, 417.

SOURCE: 53 FR 17923, May 19, 1988, unless otherwise noted.

§215.1 Applicability.

This part applies to all certified air carriers, commuter air carriers, and foreign direct air carriers and to initial or amended applications for authority, applications for certificate or permit transfers or reissuances, and registration of business names.

§215.2 Purpose.

This part sets rules under which direct air carriers may use the names in their operating authorizations and change those names. It further provides for notification to air carriers that may be affected by the use by other air carriers of the same or similar names. Its purpose is to place the responsibility for resolving private disputes about the use of similar names with the air carriers involved, through recourse to the trade names statutes and the courts. These rules do not preclude Department intervention or enforcement action should there be evidence of a significant potential for, or of actual, public confusion.

§ 215.3 Use of name.

In holding out to the public and in performing air transportation services, a direct air carrier or foreign direct air carrier subject to this part shall use only the name in which its operating authorization is issued or trade name is registered, and shall not operate or hold out to the public in a name not acknowledged by the Department to be so registered. Minor variations in the use of this name, including abbreviations, contractions, initial letters, or other variations of the name that are identifiable with the authorized name, are permitted. Slogans and service marks shall not be considered names for the purpose of this part, and their use is not restricted.

[53 FR 17923, May 19, 1988, as amended at 70 FR 25768, May 16, 2005]

§ 215.4 Change of name or use of trade name.

(a) *Registrations.* Any air carrier subject to this part that desires to change the name in which its operating authorization has been issued, or to use a trade name, or to obtain initial operating authority must register the name with the Department. The Department will construe any application for initial, reissued, or transferred authority as containing a "registration" of the intended name. A separate name registration document need not be filed. A carrier registering use of a trade name, without seeking reissuance of its underlying certificate commuter or foreign air carrier permit or exemption authority, must file a statement that complies with §§ 302.3 and 302.4 of this chapter registering its intended name with the Air Carrier Fitness Division if it is a U.S. certificated or commuter carrier, or within the Licensing Division if it is a foreign air carrier.

(b) *Montreal Agreement.* Each registration under this section shall be accompanied by three copies of a counterpart to the Montreal Agreement (Agreement 18900) (OST Form 4523) signed by the carrier using the proposed name. Upon arrival of the application, the Department will place a copy of the signed OST form 4523 in Docket 17325.

(Reporting and recordkeeping requirements in paragraph (b) were approved by the Office of Management and Budget under control number 3024–0064.)

[53 FR 17923, May 19, 1988, as amended at 70 FR 25768, May 16, 2005]

§ 215.5 Procedure in case of similarity of names.

The Department will compare the proposed name in any registration filed under this part or in an application for new, reissued, or transferred authority with a list of names used by existing certificated, commuter and foreign direct air carriers. The Department will notify the applicant of any other certificated, foreign or commuter carriers that may have an identical or similar name. The registrant must then notify those carriers of its registration. The notification will identify the applicant and state its proposed name or the name requested, area of operation or proposed area of operation, type of business, and other pertinent matters. The registrant must then file a certificate of service of the notification with the Department.

§ 215.6 Acknowledgment of registration.

After completion of the filing and notification requirements of this part, the Department may acknowledge the registration by notice in the action granting the application for initial operating authority, transfer, or reissuance or by separate notice in the case of use of a trade name. Non-action under this provision shall not be construed as an adjudication of any rights or liabilities.

[53 FR 17923, May 19, 1988, as amended at 70 FR 25768, May 16, 2005]

PART 216—COMMINGLING OF BLIND SECTOR TRAFFIC BY FOREIGN AIR CARRIERS

216.6 Existing unauthorized operations.

AUTHORITY: 49 U.S.C. Chapters 401, 413, 417.

SOURCE: ER–525, 33 FR 692, Jan. 19, 1968, unless otherwise noted.

§216.1 Definitions.

(a) As used in this part, unless the context otherwise requires:

Act means the Federal Aviation Act of 1958, as amended.

Blind sector traffic means revenue traffic, carried by a foreign air carrier on a flight operating in air transportation, which is enplaned at one foreign point and deplaned at another foreign point, where at least one of such points is not named as a terminal or intermediate point in the carrier's applicable foreign air carrier permit.

NOTE: This definition shall not be deemed to include the carriage of authorized *beyond homeland* traffic (*i.e.*, traffic carried between a point named in a carrier's foreign air carrier permit and a point beyond a homeland terminal point authorized under such permit).

Revenue traffic means persons, property or mail carried for compensation or hire.

(b) Terms defined in section 101 of the Act have the meaning expressed in such definitions.

§216.2 Applicability.

This part sets forth the requirements applicable to foreign air carriers for obtaining a Special Authorization from the Board with respect to any deviation from an authorized foreign air transportation route for the purpose of commingling blind sector traffic with air transportation traffic carried pursuant to a foreign air carrier permit issued by the Board. The deviation by a foreign air carrier from its authorized route for the purpose of combined carriage to or from the United States of nonrevenue or other traffic, the carriage of which does not constitute engaging in foreign air transportation, is governed by the provisions of part 375 of this chapter.

§216.3 Prohibition.

No foreign air carrier shall carry any blind sector traffic, as defined in this part, on any flight operating in air transportation pursuant to the authority of a foreign air carrier permit issued under section 402 of the Act, unless the combined carriage of such traffic has been specifically authorized by such permit, or by a Special Authorization issued under §216.4.

§216.4 Special authorizations.

(a) *Applications*. Any foreign air carrier may apply to the Board for a Special Authorization, as required by this part, for the carriage of blind sector traffic on a particular flight, series of flights, or for a specified or indefinite period of time between specified points. Applications shall be submitted directly to the Board, addressed to the attention of the Director, Bureau of International Aviation. One original and two copies in conformity with the requirements of §§302.3(b) and 302.4 (a) and (b) of this chapter shall be filed. The applications shall contain a proper identification of the applicant; the flight or flights upon which it is proposed to carry such blind sector traffic, including routing, nontraffic stops, and dates or duration of the authority sought; a full description of such traffic, and points between which such traffic will be carried; information or documentation as to whether the country of which the applicant is a national grants reciprocal privileges to U.S. carriers; and the reasons for requesting such authorization together with such additional information as will establish that the grant of such authority will otherwise be in the public interest. Such additional information as may be specifically requested by the Board shall also be furnished.

(b) *Service*. Applications shall be served upon each direct U.S. air carrier certificated to engage in individually ticketed or waybilled foreign air transportation over any portion of the route to which the application pertains, and on such other persons as the Board may require, and proof of such service shall accompany the application as provided in §302.7 of this chapter. Notice of such applications shall also be published in the Board's Weekly List of Applications Filed.

(c) *Memoranda in support or opposition*. Any interested person may file a memorandum in support of or in opposition to the grant of an application.

Such memorandum shall set forth in detail the reasons why it is believed that the application should be granted or denied and shall be accompanied by such data, including affidavits, which it is desired that the Board consider. Copies of the memorandum shall be served upon the applicant. Nothing in this subparagraph shall be deemed to preclude the Board from granting or denying an application when the circumstances so warrant without awaiting the filing of memoranda in support of or in opposition to the application.

(d) *Time for filing.* (1) Applications seeking authority to engage in blind sector operations for a period of 3 months or longer, shall be submitted at least 60 days in advance of the proposed commencement of such operations. Memoranda in response to such an application shall be submitted within 15 days after the date of filing thereof.

(2) Applications seeking authority to engage in blind sector operations for a period less than three months shall be filed at least 20 days in advance of the proposed commencement of such operations, and memoranda in response thereto within 7 days after the date of filing thereof: *Provided,* That the Board may consider late filed applications upon a showing of good cause for failure to adhere to this requirement.

(e) *General procedural requirements.* Except as otherwise provided herein, the provisions of part 302, subpart A, of this chapter shall apply to the extent applicable.

(f) *Issuance of Special Authorization.* A Special Authorization authorizing the carriage of blind sector traffic will be issued only if the Board finds that the proposed carriage is fully consistent with applicable law and this part, and that grant of such authority would be in the public interest. The application may be granted or denied in whole or in part without hearing, and a Special Authorization made subject to any conditions or limitations, to the extent that such action is deemed by the Board to be in the public interest. Special Authorizations are not transferable.

(g) *Nature of the privilege conferred.* A Special Authorization issued pursuant to this section shall constitute a privilege conferred upon a carrier, which may be enjoyed only to the extent that its continued exercise remains in the interest of the public. Accordingly, any Special Authorization issued pursuant to this section may be revoked, suspended, amended or restricted without hearing.

(Sec. 204(a) of the Federal Aviation Act of 1958, as amended, 72 Stat. 743 (49 U.S.C. 1324); Reorganization Plan No. 3 of 1961, 75 Stat. 837, 26 FR 5989 (49 U.S.C. 1324 (note)))

[ER–525, 33 FR 692, Jan. 19, 1968, as amended by ER–910, 40 FR 23844, June 3, 1975; ER–1060, 43 FR 34117, Aug. 3, 1978; 65 FR 6456, Feb. 9, 2000]

§ 216.5 Existing permits.

"Foreign aircraft permits" issued by the Board under the provisions of part 375 of the Board's Special Regulations, authorizing the combined carriage of blind sector traffic as defined in this part, shall continue in effect in accordance with their terms until their expiration date unless sooner terminated, revoked or modified by the Board. Such permits shall, upon the effective date of this part, be deemed to constitute a Special Authorization issued pursuant to § 216.4.

§ 216.6 Existing unauthorized operations.

Notwithstanding the provisions of § 216.3, if within 30 days after the effective date of this part a carrier files an application for a Special Authorization to continue to perform existing blind sector operations which have been regularly performed by such carrier commencing on a date prior to August 9, 1967, such carrier may continue to engage in such blind sector operations until final decision by the Board on such application: *Provided,* That any such application shall, in addition to the requirements of § 216.4(a), contain a statement that the carrier is relying upon this section for continuance of preexisting blind sector operations, and shall fully describe such operations including the date inaugurated, and the frequency and continuity of performance.

PART 217—REPORTING TRAFFIC STATISTICS BY FOREIGN AIR CARRIERS IN CIVILIAN SCHEDULED, CHARTER, AND NON-SCHEDULED SERVICES

Sec.

AUTHORITY: 49 U.S.C. 329 and chapters 41102, 41301, 41708, and 41709.

SOURCE: 53 FR 46294, Nov. 16, 1988, unless otherwise noted.

§217.1 Definitions.

As used in this part:

Foreign Air Carrier means a non-U.S. air carrier holding a foreign air carrier permit or exemption authority from the Department of Transportation.

Nonrevenue passenger means: a person traveling free or under token charges, except those expressly named in the definition of *revenue passenger;* a person traveling at a fare or discount available only to employees or authorized persons of air carriers or their agents or only for travel on the business of the carriers; and an infant who does not occupy a seat. (This definition is for 14 CFR part 217 traffic reporting purposes and may differ from the definitions used in other parts by the Federal Aviation Administration and the Transportation Security Administration for the collection of Passenger Facility Charges and Security Fees.)

The definition includes, but is not limited to the following examples of passengers when traveling free or pursuant to token charges:

(1) Directors, officers, employees, and others authorized by the air carrier operating the aircraft;

(2) Directors, officers, employees, and others authorized by the air carrier or another carrier traveling pursuant to a pass interchange agreement;

(3) Travel agents being transported for the purpose of familiarizing themselves with the carrier's services;

(4) Witnesses and attorneys attending any legal investigation in which such carrier is involved;

(5) Persons injured in aircraft accidents, and physicians, nurses, and others attending such persons;

(6) Any persons transported with the object of providing relief in cases of general epidemic, natural disaster, or other catastrophe;

(7) Any law enforcement official, including any person who has the duty of guarding government officials who are traveling on official business or traveling to or from such duty;

(8) Guests of an air carrier on an inaugural flight or delivery flights of newly-acquired or renovated aircraft;

(9) Security guards who have been assigned the duty to guard such aircraft against unlawful seizure, sabotage, or other unlawful interference;

(10) Safety inspectors of the National Transportation Safety Board or the FAA in their official duties or traveling to or from such duty;

(11) Postal employees on duty in charge of the mails or traveling to or from such duty;

(12) Technical representatives of companies that have been engaged in the manufacture, development or testing of a particular type of aircraft or aircraft equipment, when the transportation is provided for the purpose of in-flight observation and subject to applicable FAA regulations;

(13) Persons engaged in promoting air transportation;

(14) Air marshals and other Transportation Security officials acting in their official capacities and while traveling to and from their official duties; and

(15) Other authorized persons, when such transportation is undertaken for promotional purpose.

Reporting carrier for T–100(f) purposes means the air carrier in operational control of the flight, i.e., the carrier that uses its flight crews under its own operating authority.

Revenue passenger means: a passenger for whose transportation an air carrier receives commercial remuneration. (This definition is for 14 CFR part 217 traffic reporting purposes and may differ from the definitions used in other parts by the Federal Aviation Administration and the Transportation Security Administration for the collection of Passenger Facility Charges and Security Fees.) This includes, but is not limited to, the following examples:

(1) Passengers traveling under publicly available tickets including promotional offers (for example two-for-one) or loyalty programs (for example, redemption of frequent flyer points);

(2) Passengers traveling on vouchers or tickets issued as compensation for denied boarding or in response to consumer complaints or claims;

(3) Passengers traveling at corporate discounts;

(4) Passengers traveling on preferential fares (Government, seamen, military, youth, student, etc.);

(5) Passengers traveling on barter tickets; and

(6) Infants traveling on confirmed-space tickets.

Statement of Authorization under this part means a statement of authorization from the Department, pursuant to 14 CFR part 207, 208, or 212, as appropriate, that permits joint service transportation, such as blocked space agreements, part-charters, code-sharing or wet-leases, between two direct air carriers holding underlying economic authority from the Department.

Wet-Lease Agreement means an agreement under which one carrier leases an aircraft with flight crew to another air carrier.

[53 FR 46294, Nov. 16, 1988, as amended at 67 FR 49223, July 30, 2002; 67 FR 58689, Sept. 18, 2002]

§ 217.2 Applicability.

This part applies to foreign air carriers that are authorized by the Department to provide civilian passenger and/or cargo service to or from the United States, whether performed pursuant to a permit or exemption authority.

[Doc. No. OST–98–4043, 67 FR 49223, July 30, 2002]

§ 217.3 Reporting requirements.

(a) Each foreign air carrier shall file BTS Form 41 Schedule T–100(f) "Foreign Air Carrier Traffic Data by Nonstop Segment and On-flight Market." All traffic statistics shall be compiled in terms of each flight stage as actually performed.

(b) The traffic statistics reported on Schedule T–100(f) shall be accumulated in accordance with the data elements prescribed in § 217.5 of this part, and these data elements are patterned after those in section 19–5 of part 241 of this chapter.

(c) One set of Form 41 Schedule T–100(f) data shall be filed.

(d) Schedule T–100(f) shall be submitted to the Department within thirty (30) days following the end of each reporting month.

(e) Reports required by this section shall be submitted to the Bureau of Transportation Statistics in a format specified in accounting and reporting directives issued by the Bureau of Transportation Statistics' Director of Airline Information.

[53 FR 46294, Nov. 16, 1988, as amended at 60 FR 66722, Dec. 26, 1995; 75 FR 41583, July 16, 2010]

§ 217.4 Data collected (service classes).

(a) The statistical classifications are designed to reflect the operating elements attributable to each distinctive class of service offered for scheduled, nonscheduled and charter service.

(b) The service classes that foreign air carriers shall report on Schedule T–100(f) are:

(1) F Scheduled Passenger/Cargo

(2) G Scheduled All-Cargo

(3) L Nonscheduled Civilian Passenger/Cargo Charter

(4) P Nonscheduled Civilian All-Cargo Charter

(5) Q Nonscheduled Services (Other than Charter). This service class is reserved for special nonscheduled cargo flights provided by a few foreign air carriers under special authority granted by the Department.

§ 217.5 Data collected (data elements).

(a) Within each of the service classifications prescribed in § 217.4, data shall be reported in applicable traffic elements.

(b) The statistical data to be reported on Schedule T–100(f) are:

(1) *Air carrier.* The name and code of the air carrier reporting the data. The

carrier code is assigned by DOT. The Office of Airline Information (OAI'S) will confirm the assigned code upon request; OAI's address is in the appendix to §217.10 of this part.

(2) *Reporting period date.* The year and month to which the reported data are applicable.

(3) *Origin airport code.* This code represents the industry designator as described in the appendix to §217.10 of this part. A common private industry source of these industry designator codes is the *Official Airline Guides* (OAG). Where none exists, OAI will furnish a code upon request. OAI's address is in the appendix to §217.10 of this part.

(4) *Destination airport code.* This represents the industry designator, from the source described in §217.5(b)(3).

(5) *Service class code.* For scheduled and other services, the applicable service class prescribed in §217.4 of this part shall be reported.

(6) *Aircraft type code.* This code represents the aircraft type, as specified in the appendix to §217.10 of this part. Where none exists, OAI will furnish a code upon request.

(7) *Revenue aircraft departures performed (Code 510).* The number of revenue aircraft departures performed.

(8) *Revenue passengers transported (Code 130).* The total number of revenue passengers on board over a flight stage, including those already on the aircraft from previous flight stages. Includes both local and through passengers on board the aircraft.

(9) *Revenue freight transported (kilograms) (Code 237).* The volume, expressed in kilograms, of revenue freight that is transported. As used in this part, "Freight" means revenue cargo other than passengers or mail.

(10) *Total revenue passengers in market (Code 110).* The total number of revenue passengers enplaned in a market, boarding the aircraft for the first time. While passengers may be transported over several flight stages in a multisegment market, this data element (code 110) is an unduplicated count of passengers originating within the market.

(11) *Total revenue freight in market (kilograms) (Code 217).* The amount of revenue freight cargo (kilograms) that is enplaned in a market, loaded on the aircraft for the first time.

(12) *Available capacity-payload (Code 270).* The available capacity is collected in kilograms. This figure shall reflect the available load (see load, available in 14 CFR part 241 Section 03) or total available capacity for passengers, mail and freight applicable to the aircraft with which each flight stage is performed.

(13) *Available seats (Code 310).* The number of seats available for sale. This figure reflects the actual number of seats available, excluding those blocked for safety or operational reasons. Report the total available seats in item 310.

[53 FR 46294, Nov. 16, 1988 and 53 FR 52404, Dec. 28, 1988, as amended at 54 FR 7183, Feb. 17, 1989; 60 FR 66722, Dec. 26, 1995; 62 FR 6718, Feb. 13, 1997]

§217.6 Extension of filing time.

(a) If circumstances prevent the filing of a Schedule T–100(f) report on or before the due date prescribed in section 22 of part 241 of this chapter and the appendix to §217.10 of this part, a request for an extension must be filed with the Director, Office of Airline Information.

(b) The extension request must be received at the address provided in §217.10 at least 3 days in advance of the due date, and must set forth reasons to justify granting an extension, and the date when the report can be filed. If a request is denied, the air carrier must submit the required report within 5 days of its receipt of the denial of extension.

[53 FR 46294, Nov. 16, 1988, as amended at 60 FR 66722, Dec. 26, 1995]

§217.7 Certification.

The certification for BTS Form 41 Schedule T–100(f) shall be signed by an officer of the air carrier with the requisite authority over the collection of data and preparation of reports to ensure the validity and accuracy of the reported data.

[53 FR 46294, Nov. 16, 1988, as amended at 60 FR 66722, Dec. 26, 1995]

§217.8 Reporting procedures.

Reporting guidelines and procedures for Schedule T–100(f) are prescribed in the Appendix to §217.10 of this part.

§217.9 Waivers from reporting requirements.

(a) A waiver from any reporting requirement contained in Schedule T–100(f) may be granted by the Department upon its own initiative, or upon the submission of a written request of the air carrier to the Director, Office of Airline Information, when such a waiver is in the public interest.

(b) Each request for waiver must demonstrate that: Existing peculiarities or unusual circumstances warrant a departure from the prescribed procedure or technique; a specifically defined alternative procedure or technique will result in substantially equivalent or more accurate portrayal of the operations reported; and the application of such alternative procedure will not adversely affect the uniformity in reporting applicable to all air carriers.

[53 FR 46294, Nov. 16, 1988, as amended at 60 FR 66722, Dec. 26, 1995]

§217.10 Instructions.

(a) Reports required by this section shall be submitted to the Bureau of Transportation Statistics in a format specified in accounting and reporting directives issued by the Bureau of Transportation Statistics' Director of Airline Information.

(b) The detailed instructions for preparing Schedule T–100(f) are contained in the appendix to this section.

APPENDIX TO SECTION 217.10 OF 14 CFR PART 217—INSTRUCTIONS TO FOREIGN AIR CARRIERS FOR REPORTING TRAFFIC DATA ON FORM 41 SCHEDULE T–100(f)

(a) General instructions.

(1) Description. Form 41 Schedule T–100(f) provides flight stage data covering both passenger/cargo and all cargo operations in scheduled and nonscheduled services. The schedule is used to report all flights which serve points in the United States or its territories as defined in this part.

(2) Applicability. Each foreign air carrier holding a §41302 permit or exemption authority shall file Schedule T–100(f).

(3) Reports required by this section shall be submitted to the Bureau of Transportation Statistics in a format specified in accounting and reporting directives issued by the Bureau of Transportation Statistics' Director of Airline Information.

(4) Filing period. Form 41 Schedule T–100(f) shall be filed monthly and is due at the Department thirty (30) days following the end of the reporting month to which the data are applicable.

(5) Number of copies. A single set of legible Form 41 Schedule T–100(f) data and certification shall be submitted.

(6) Foreign air carrier certification. Each foreign air carrier shall submit a certification statement (illustrated at the end of this Appendix) as an integral part of each monthly Schedule T–100(f), as prescribed in §217.5 of this part.

(7) [Reserved]

(b) Preparation of Form 41 Schedule T–100(f):

(1) Explanation of nonstop segments and on-flight markets. There are two basic categories of data, one pertaining to nonstop segments and the other pertaining to on-flight markets. For example, the routing (A-B-C-D) consists of three nonstop segment records A-B, B-C, and C-D, and six on-flight market records A-B, A-C, A-D, B-C, B-D, and C-D.

(2) Guidelines for reporting a nonstop segment. A nonstop segment is reported when one or both points are in the United States or its territories. These data shall be merged with that for all of the other reportable nonstop operations over the same segment. Nonstop segment data must be summarized by aircraft type, under paragraph (h)(1), and class of service, paragraph (g)(1)(v).

(3) Rules for determining a reportable on-flight market. On-flight markets are reportable when one or both points are within the U.S., with the following exceptions: (i) Do not report third country to U.S. markets resulting from flight itineraries which serve a third country prior to a homeland point in flights passing through the homeland bound for the U.S.; and (ii) do not report U.S. to third country markets resulting from itineraries serving third country points subsequent to a homeland point in flights outbound from the U.S. and passing through the homeland. In reporting data pertaining to these two exceptions, the traffic moving to or from the U.S. relating to the applicable prior or subsequent third countries (referred to as "behind" or "beyond" traffic) is to be combined with the applicable foreign homeland gateway point, just as though the traffic were actually enplaned or deplaned at the homeland gateway, without disclosure of the actual prior or subsequent points. Applicable flights are illustrated in examples (6) and (7) under paragraph (c).

(c) *Examples of flights.* Following are some typical flight itineraries that show the reportable nonstop segment and on-flight market entries. The carrier's homeland is the key factor in determining which on-flight markets are reportable.

(1) SQ flight # 11 LAX—NRT—SIN. This is an example of a flight with an intermediate foreign country. It is not necessary to report anything on the NRT—SIN leg.

SQ—Singapore Airlines
LAX—Los Angeles, USA
NRT—Tokyo-Narita, Japan
SIN—Singapore, Singapore

A-3—Airport code	A-4—Airport code	A-5—Service class (mark an X)					By aircraft type—				Sum of all aircraft types—	
Origin	Destination	F	G	L	P	Q	B-1—Aircraft type code	B-2—Revenue aircraft departures	B-3—Revenue passengers transported	B-4—Revenue freight transported (kg)	C-1—Total revenue passengers in market	C-2—Total revenue freight in market (kg)
LAX	NRT	X	....	....	....	....	8161	12	2400	4800	400	500
LAX	SIN	X	....	....	....	....	....	....	....	....	2000	4300

(2) SQ flight #15 LAX—HNL—TPE—SIN. This is an example of two U.S. points, an intermediate third country, and a homeland point. Information is reportable on only the on-flight markets and nonstop segments that consist of one or both U.S. points.

SQ—Singapore Airlines
LAX—Los Angeles, USA
HNL—Honolulu, USA
TPE—Taipei, Taiwan
SIN—Singapore, Singapore

A-3—Airport code	A-4—Airport code	A-5—Service class (Mark an x)					By aircraft type—				Sum of all aircraft types—	
Origin	Destination	F	G	L	P	Q	B-1—Acft. type code	B-2—Revenue aircraft departures	B-3—Revenue passengers transported	B-4—Revenue freight transported (kg)	C-1—Total revenue passengers in market	C-2—Total revenue freight in market (kg)
LAX	HNL	X	....	....	....	....	8161	12	2700	5300	0	0
LAX	TPE	X	....	....	....	....	....	....	....	....	700	1300
LAX	SIN	X	....	....	....	....	....	....	....	....	2000	4000
HNL	TPE	X	....	....	....	....	8161	12	2200	6800	1200	800
HNL	SIN	X	....	....	....	....	....	....	....	....	1000	6000

(3) LB flight # 902 LPB-VVI-MAO-CCS-MIA. This flight serves two homeland points and two different foreign countries before terminating in the U.S. Nonstop segment information is required only for the nonstop segment involving a U.S. point. On-flight market information is required in 4 of the 10 markets, LPB-MIA and VVI-MIA, since these involve homeland and U.S. points; MAO-MIA is necessary to show traffic carried into the U.S., and CCS-MIA for the same reason, and also because in all cases where a nonstop segment entry is required, a corresponding on-flight market entry must also be reported.

LB—Lloyd Aero Boliviano
LPB—La Paz, Bolivia
VVI—Santa Cruz-Viru Viru, Bolivia
MAO—Manaus, Brazil
CCS—Caracas, Venezuela
MIA—Miami, USA

A-3—Airport code	A-4—Airport code	A-5—Service class (mark an x)					By aircraft type—				Sum of all aircraft types—	
Origin	Destination	F	G	L	P	Q	B-1—Acft. type code	B-2—Revenue aircraft departures	B-3—Revenue passengers transported	B-4—Revenue freight transported (kg)	C-1—Total revenue passengers in market	C-2—Total revenue freight in market (kg)
CCS	MIA	X	....	....	....	....	8161	31	6900	71000	0	0
LPB	MIA	X	....	....	....	....	....	....	....	....	1100	20000

A-3—Airport code	A-4—Airport code	A-5—Service class (mark an x)					By aircraft type—				Sum of all aircraft types—	
Origin	Destination	F	G	L	P	Q	B-1—Acft. type code	B-2—Revenue aircraft departures	B-3—Revenue passengers transported	B-4—Revenue freight transported (kg)	C-1—Total revenue passengers in market	C-2—Total revenue freight in market (kg)
VVI	MIA	X									4000	30000
MAO	MIA	X									1000	12000

(4) LY flight #005 TLV-AMS-ORD-LAX. This flight serves a single foreign intermediate point and two U.S. points after its homeland origination. The information on the TLV-AMS leg is not reportable.

LY—El Al Israel Airlines
TLV—Tel Aviv, Israel
AMS—Amsterdam, Netherlands
ORD—Chicago, USA
LAX—Los Angeles, USA

A-3—Airport code	A-4—Airport code	A-5—Service class (mark an x)					By aircraft type—				Sum of all aircraft types—	
Origin	Destination	F	G	L	P	Q	B-1—Acft. type code	B-2—Revenue aircraft departures	B-3—Revenue passengers transported	B-4—Revenue freight transported (kg)	C-1—Total revenue passengers in market	C-2—Total revenue freight in market (kg)
AMS	ORD	X					8161	1	350	10000	50	1500
TLV	ORD	X									150	4000
TLV	LAX	X									125	3000
ORD	LAX	X					8161	1	150	4500	0	0
AMS	LAX	X									25	1500

(5) QF flight #25 SYD—BNE—CNS—HNL—YVR. This flight serves three homeland points, a U.S. point, and a subsequent third country. Nonstop segment information is required on the respective legs into and out of the United States. All on-flight market entries involving the U.S. point HNL are also required. Data are not required on the homeland to homeland markets, or the homeland—third country markets.

QF—Qantas Airways (Australia)
SYD—Sydney, Australia
BNE—Brisbane, Australia
CNS—Cairns, Australia
HNL—Honolulu, USA
YVR—Vancouver, Canada

A-3—Airport code	A-4—Airport code	A-5—Service class (mark an x)					By aircraft type				Sum of all aircraft types	
Origin	Destination	F	G	L	P	Q	B-1—Acft. type code	B-2—Revenue aircraft departures	B-3—Revenue freight transported	B-4—Revenue freight transported (kg)	C-1—Total revenue passengers in market	C-2—Total revenue freight in market (kg)
CNS	HNL	X					8161	5	2200	41000	400	8000
SYD	HNL	X									600	10000
BNE	HNL	X									600	9000
HNL	YVR	X					8161	5	750	15700	150	1700

(6) JL flight #002 HKG—NRT—SFO. This flight originates in a third country prior to the homeland. No data is required on the HKG-NRT leg, but the HKG-SFO passengers and cargo shall be shown as enplanements in the NRT-SFO on-flight market entry. These volumes are included by definition in the passenger and cargo transported volumes of the NRT-SFO nonstop segment entry.

JL—Japan Air Lines
HKG—Hong Kong, Hong Kong
NRT—Tokyo-Narita, Japan
SFO—San Francisco, USA

A–3—Airport code	A–4—Airport code	A–5—Service class (mark an x)					By aircraft type				Sum of all aircraft types	
Origin	Destination	F	G	L	P	Q	B–1—Acft. type code	B–2—Revenue aircraft departures	B–3—Revenue passengers transported	B–4—Revenue freight transported (kg)	C–1—Total revenue passengers in market	C–2—Total revenue freight in market (kg)
NRT	SFO	X					8161	3	1200	18000	1200	18000

(7) JL flight #001 SFO-NRT-HKG. This flight is the reverse sequence of flight #002 above; it requires a nonstop segment entry covering SFO-NRT, and a single on-flight market entry also for SFO-NRT. In this case, the on flight traffic enplaned at SFO and destined for HKG, a beyond homeland point, shall be included in the SFO-NRT entry; a separate SFO-HKG entry is not required.

JL—Japan Air Lines
SFO—San Francisco, USA
NRT—Tokyo-Narita, Japan
HKG—Hong Kong, Hong Kong

A–3—Airport code	A–4—Airport code	A–5—Service class (mark an x)					By aircraft type				Sum of all aircraft types	
Origin	Destination	F	G	L	P	Q	B–1—Acft. type code	B–2—Revenue aircraft departures	B–3—Revenue passengers transported	B–4—Revenue freight transported (kg)	C–1—Total revenue passengers in market	C–2—Total revenue freight in market (kg)
SFO	NRT	X					8161	1	400	20000	400	20000

(8) BA flight #5 LHR-ANC-NRT-OSA. This example contains a single homeland point and a single U.S. point followed by two third country points. It is necessary to report the nonstop segments into and out of the U.S., and all three of the on-flight markets which have the U.S. point ANC as either an origin or destination.

BA—British Airways
LHR—London, England
ANC—Anchorage, USA
NRT—Tokyo-Narita, Japan
OSA—Osaka, Japan

A–3—Airport code	A–4—Airport code	A–5—Service class (mark an x)					By aircraft type				Sum of all aircraft types	
Origin	Destination	F	G	L	P	Q	B–1—Acft. type code	B–2—Revenue aircraft departures	B–3—Revenue passengers transported	B–4—Revenue freight transported (kg)	C–1—Total revenue passengers in market	C–2—Total revenue freight in market (kg)
LHR	ANC	X					8161	10	3000	50000	100	1000
ANC	NRT	X					8161	10	3150	55000	100	2500
ANC	OSA	X					....	....	....	....	150	1500

(d) Provisions to reduce paperwork:

(1) Nonstop Segment Entries. The flight stage data applicable to nonstop segment entries must be summarized to create totals by aircraft equipment type, within service class, within pairs-of-points.

(2) On-flight Market Entries. The applicable on-flight market entries shall be summarized to create totals by service class within pair-of-points.

(e) Preparation of Schedule T–100 (f):

(1) Section A—Indicative and flight pattern information. A copy of Schedule T–100(f) is shown at the end of this Appendix. Section A defines the origin and destination points and the service class code to which the nonstop segment data in Section B and the on-flight market data in Section C are applicable. Section A information, along with the carrier code and report date, must be included on each schedule.

(2) Section B—Nonstop segment information. Section B of the schedule is used for reporting nonstop segment information by aircraft type. To reduce the number of schedules reported, space is provided for including

data on multiple different aircraft types. Similarly, the on-flight market section has been included on a single Schedule T–100(f), along with the nonstop segment data, rather than on a separate schedule.

(3) Section C—On-flight market information. Section C of the schedule is used for reporting on-flight market data. There will always be an on-flight market that corresponds to the nonstop segment. Because the on-flight market data are reported at the service class level rather than by aircraft type, a specific flight may produce more on-flight markets than nonstop segments, (see examples in paragraph (c) of this Appendix), resulting in data reported in sections A and C only.

(f) [Reserved]

(g) Data element definitions:

(1) Service pattern information.

(i) Line A–1 Carrier code. Use the carrier code established by the Department. This code is provided to each carrier in the initial reporting letter from the Office of Airline Information (OAI). If there are any questions about these codes, contact the OAI Data Administration Division at the address in paragraph (a)(3) of this Appendix.

(ii) Line A–2 Report date. This is the year and month to which the data are applicable. For example, 200009 indicates the year 2000, and the month of September.

(iii) Line A–3 Origin airport code. This is the departure airport, where an aircraft begins a flight segment, and where the passengers originate in an on-flight market. Use the 3-letter code from the City/Airport Codes section of the *Official Airline Guide Worldwide Edition*. If no 3-letter code is available, OAI will assign one; the address is in paragraph (a)(3) of this Appendix.

(iv) Line A–4 Destination airport code. This is the arrival airport, where an aircraft stops on a flight segment, and where passengers deplane (get off the flight) after reaching their destination in a market. Use the 3-letter code from the source described in paragraph (g)(1)(iii) of this Appendix.

(v) Line A–5 Service class code. Select one of the following single letter codes which describes the type of service being reported on a given flight operation.

F = Scheduled Passenger/cargo Service
G = Scheduled All-cargo Service
L = Nonscheduled Civilian Passenger/Cargo Charter
P = Nonscheduled Civilian All-Cargo Charter
Q = Nonscheduled Services (Other than Charter)

(2) Nonstop segment information:

(i) Line B–1 Aircraft type code. Use the four digit numeric code prescribed in paragraph (h)(1) of this Appendix. If no aircraft type code is available, OAI will assign one. The address is in paragraph (a)(3) of this Appendix.

(ii) Line B–2 Aircraft departures performed. This is the total number of physical departures performed with a given aircraft type, within service class and pair-of-points.

(iii) Line B–3 Revenue passengers transported. This is the total number of revenue passengers transported on a given nonstop segment. It represents the total number of revenue passengers on board over the segment without regard to their actual point of enplanement.

(iv) Line B–4 Revenue freight transported. This item is the total weight in kilograms (kg) of the revenue freight transported on a given nonstop segment without regard to its actual point of enplanement.

(3) On-flight market information:

(i) Line C–1 Total revenue passengers in market. This item represents the total number of revenue passengers, within service class, that were enplaned at the origin airport and deplaned at the destination airport.

(ii) Line C–2 Total revenue freight in market. This item represents the total weight in kilograms (kg) of revenue freight enplaned at the origin and deplaned at the destination airport.

(h) [Reserved]

(i) Joint Service.

(1) The Department may authorize joint service operations between two direct air carriers. Examples of these joint service operations are:

Blocked-space agreements;
Part-charter agreements;
Code-sharing agreements;
Wet-lease agreements, and similar arrangements.

(2) Joint-service operations shall be reported on BTS Form 41 Schedules T–100 and T–100(f) by the air carrier in operational control of the flight, i.e., the air carrier that uses its flight crew to perform the operation. If there are questions about reporting a joint-service operation, contact the BTS Assistant Director—Airline Information at the address in paragraph (a)(3) of this appendix.

(j) [Reserved]

[53 FR 46294, Nov. 16, 1988, as amended at 54 FR 7183, Feb. 17, 1989; 60 FR 66722, Dec. 26, 1995; 67 FR 49223, July 30, 2002; 75 FR 41583, July 10, 2010]

§ 217.11 Reporting compliance.

(a) Failure to file reports required by this part will subject an air carrier to civil penalties prescribed in Title 49 United States Code section 46301.

(b) Title 18 U.S.C. 1001, Crimes and Criminal Procedure, makes it a criminal offense subject to a maximum fine of $10,000 or imprisonment for not more than 5 years, or both, to knowingly and willfully make, or cause to be made, any false or fraudulent statements or representations in any matter within the jurisdiction of any agency of the United States.

[53 FR 46294, Nov. 16, 1988, as amended at 67 FR 49223, July 30, 2002]

PART 218—LEASE BY FOREIGN AIR CARRIER OR OTHER FOREIGN PERSON OF AIRCRAFT WITH CREW

Sec.

AUTHORITY: Secs. 204(a), 402, Pub. L. 85–726, as amended, 72 Stat. 743, 757 (49 U.S.C. 1324, 1372).

SOURCE: ER–716, 36 FR 23148, Dec. 4, 1971, unless otherwise noted.

§ 218.1 Definitions.

For the purpose of this part the term *lease* shall mean an agreement under which an aircraft is furnished by one party to the agreement to the other party, irrespective of whether the agreement constitutes a true lease, charter arrangement, or some other arrangement.

§ 218.2 Applicability.

This part applies to foreign air carriers and other persons not citizens of the United States which, as lessors or lessees, enter into agreements providing for the lease of aircraft with crew to a foreign air carrier for use in foreign air transportation. For purposes of section 402 of the Act, the person who has operational control and safety responsibility is deemed to be the carrier, and is required to have appropriate operating authority.

[ER–716, 36 FR 23148, Dec. 4, 1971, as amended by ER–1250, 46 FR 47770, Sept. 30, 1981]

§ 218.3 Prohibition against unauthorized operations employing aircraft leased with crew.

(a) No foreign air carrier, or other person not a citizen of the United States, shall lease an aircraft with crew to a foreign air carrier for use by the latter in performing foreign air transportation unless either:

(1) The lessor holds a foreign air carrier permit issued under section 402 of the Act or an approved registration issued under part 294 of this chapter, and any statement of authorization required by part 212 of this chapter; or

(2) The Board has issued an exemption under section 416 of the Act specifically authorizing the lessor to engage in the foreign air transportation to be performed under the lease; or

(3) The Board has issued an order under §218.6 disclaiming jurisdiction over the matter.

(b) For purposes of this part, an aircraft shall be considered to be leased with crew if:

(1) The pilot in command or a majority of the crew of the aircraft, other than cabin attendants:

(i) Is to be furnished by the lessor;

(ii) Is employed by the lessor;

(iii) Continues in the employ of the lessor in the operation of services other than those provided for in the agreement between the parties; or

(iv) Has been employed by the lessor prior to the lease, and the employment of whom by the lessee is coextensive with the period or periods for which the aircraft is available to the lessee under the lease; or

(2) The aircraft is operated under operations specifications issued to the lessor by the Federal Aviation Administration.

[ER–716, 36 FR 23148, Dec. 4, 1971, as amended by ER–1250, 46 FR 47770, Sept. 30, 1981; ER–1260, 46 FR 52598, Oct. 27, 1981]

§ 218.4 Condition upon authority of lessee.

In any case where a foreign air carrier leases from another foreign air carrier or other person not a citizen of the United States an aircraft with crew for use in performing foreign air transportation, it shall be a condition upon the authority of the lessee to perform such foreign air transportation that compliance be achieved with the requirements of this part.

§ 218.5 Application for disclaimer of jurisdiction.

The parties to a lease with crew as described in § 218.3(b) may apply to the Board for an order disclaiming jurisdiction over the matter. The application shall be filed jointly by both parties to the lease, and shall generally conform to the procedural requirements of part 302, subpart A, of this chapter. It shall be served upon any air carrier providing services over all or any part of the route upon which air transportation services will be provided pursuant to the agreement. The application should set forth in detail all evidence and other factors relied upon to demonstrate that true operational control and safety responsibility for the air transportation services to be provided are in the hands of the lessee rather than the lessor. A copy of the agreement and all amendments thereof, as well as a summary interpretation of its pertinent provisions, shall be included with the applications. Any interested person may file an answer to the application within 7 days after service hereof. Until the Board has acted upon the application, no operations in foreign transportation shall be performed pursuant to the agreement.

§ 218.6 Issuance of order disclaiming jurisdiction.

If the Board finds that true operational control and safety responsibility will be vested in the lessee and not in the lessor (*i.e.*, that the lease transaction is in substance a true lease of aircraft rather than a charter or series of charters), and that the performance of the operations provided for in such lease will not result in the lessor's being engaged in foreign air transportation, it will issue an order disclaiming jurisdiction over the matter. Otherwise the application for disclaimer of jurisdiction will be denied.

§ 218.7 Presumption.

Whether under a particular lease agreement the lessor of the aircraft is engaged in foreign air transportation is a question of fact to be determined in the light of all the facts and circumstances. However, in circumstances where the lessor furnishes both the aircraft and the crew, there is a presumption that true operational control and safety responsibility are exercised by the lessor, and that the agreement constitutes a charter arrangement under which the lessor is engaged in foreign air transportation. The burden shall rest upon the applicants for disclaimer of jurisdiction in each instance to demonstrate by an appropriate factual showing that the operation contemplated will not constitute foreign air transportation by the lessor.

PART 221—TARIFFS

Subpart A—General

Subpart B—Who Is Authorized To Issue and File Tariffs

Subpart C—Specifications of Tariff Publications

Subpart D—Manner of Filing Tariffs

Subpart E—Contents of Tariff

Subpart F—Requirements Applicable to all Statements of Fares and Charges

AUTHORITY: 49 U.S.C. 40101, 40109, 40113, 46101, 46102, chapter 411, chapter 413, chapter 415 and chapter 417, subchapter I.

SOURCE: 64 FR 40657, July 27, 1999, unless otherwise noted.

Subpart A—General

§ 221.1 Applicability of this part.

All tariffs and amendments to tariffs of air carriers and foreign air carriers filed with the Department pursuant to chapter 415 of the statute shall be constructed, published, filed, posted and kept open for public inspection in accordance with the regulations in this part and orders of the Department.

§ 221.2 Carrier's duty.

(a) *Must file tariffs.* (1) Except as provided in paragraph (d) of this section, every air carrier and every foreign air carrier shall file with the Department, and provide and keep open to public inspection, tariffs showing all fares, and charges for foreign air transportation between points served by it, and between points served by it and points served by any other air carrier or foreign air carrier, when through service and through rates shall have been established, and showing to the extent required by regulations and orders of the Department, all classifications, rules, regulations, practices, and services in connection with such foreign air transportation.

(2) Tariffs shall be filed, and provided in such form and manner, and shall contain such information as the Department shall by regulation or order prescribe. Any tariff so filed which is not consistent with chapter 415 of the statute and such regulations and orders may be rejected. Any tariff so rejected shall be void, and may not be used.

(b) *Must observe tariffs.* No air carrier or foreign air carrier shall charge or demand or collect or receive a greater or less or different compensation for foreign air transportation or for any service in connection therewith, than the fares and charges specified in its currently effective tariffs; and no air carrier or foreign air carrier shall, in any manner or by any device, directly or indirectly, or through any agent or broker, or otherwise, refund or remit any portion of the fares, or charges so specified, or extend to any person any privileges or facilities, with respect to matters required by the Department to be specified in such tariffs, except those specified in such tariffs.

(c) *No relief from violations.* Nothing contained in this part shall be construed as relieving any air carrier or foreign air carrier from liability for violations of the statute, nor shall the filing of a tariff, or amendment thereto, relieve any air carrier or foreign air carrier from such violations or from violations of regulations issued under the statute.

(d) *Exemption authority.* Air carriers and foreign air carriers, both direct and indirect, are exempted from the requirement of section 41504 of the statute and any requirement of this chapter to file, and shall not file with the Department, tariffs for operations under the following provisions:

(1) Part 291, Domestic Cargo Transportation;

(2) Part 296, Indirect Air Transportation of Property;

(3) Part 297, Foreign Air Freight Forwarders and Foreign Cooperative Shippers Association;

(4) Part 298, Exemption for Air Taxi Operations, except to the extent noted in § 298.11(b);

(5) Part 380, Public Charters;

(6) Part 207, Charter Trips and Special Services;

(7) Part 208, Terms, Conditions, and Limitations of Certificates to Engage in Charter Air Transportation;

(8) Part 212, Charter Trips by Foreign Air Carriers;

(9) Part 292, International Cargo Transportation, except as provided in part 292.

(10) Part 293 International Passenger Transportation, except as provided in part 293.

§221.3 Definitions.

As used in this part, terms shall be defined as follows:

Add-on means an amount published for use only in combination with other fares for the construction of through fares. It is also referred to as "proportional fare" and "arbitrary fare".

Add-on tariff means a tariff which contains add-on fares.

Area No. 1 means all of the North and South American Continents and the islands adjacent thereto; Greenland; Bermuda; the West Indies and the islands of the Caribbean Sea; and the Hawaiian Islands (including Midway and Palmyra).

Area No. 2 means all of Europe (including that part of the former Union of the Soviet Socialist Republics in Europe) and the islands adjacent thereto; Iceland; the Azores; all of Africa and the islands adjacent thereto; Ascension Island; and that part of Asia lying west of and including Iran.

Area No. 3 means all of Asia and the islands adjacent thereto except that portion included in Area No. 2; all of the East Indies, Australia, New Zealand, and the islands adjacent thereto; and the islands of the Pacific Ocean except those included in Area No. 1.

Bundled normal economy fare means the lowest one-way fare available for unrestricted, on-demand service in any city-pair market.

CRT means a video display terminal that uses a cathode ray tube as the image medium.

Capacity controlled fare means a fare for which a carrier limits the number of seats available for sale.

Carrier means an air carrier or foreign air carrier subject to section 41504 of 49 U.S.C. subtitle VII.

Charge means the amount charged for baggage, in excess of the free allowance, accompanying or checked by a passenger or for any other service ancillary to the passenger's carriage.

Conditions of carriage means those rules of general applicability that define the rights and obligations of the carrier(s) and any other party to the contract of carriage with respect to the transportation services provided.

Contract of carriage means those fares, rules, and other provisions applicable to the foreign air transportation of passengers or their baggage, as defined in the statute.

Department means the Department of Transportation.

Direct-service market means an international market where the carrier provides service either on a nonstop or single-flight-number basis, including change-of-gauge.

Electronic tariff means an international passenger fares or rules tariff or a special tariff permission application transmitted to the Department by means of an electronic medium, and containing fares for the transportation of persons and their baggage, and including such associated data as arbitraries, footnotes, routings, and fare class explanations.

Fare means the amount per passenger or group of persons stated in the applicable tariff for the air transportation thereof and includes baggage unless the context otherwise requires.

Field means a specific area of a record used for a particular category of data.

Filer means an air carrier, foreign air carrier, or tariff publishing agent of such a carrier filing tariffs on its behalf in conformity with this subpart.

Item means a small subdivision of a tariff and identified by a number, a letter, or other definite method for the purpose of facilitating reference and amendment.

Joint fare means a fare that applies to transportation over the joint lines or routes of two or more carriers and which is made and published by arrangement or agreement between such carriers evidenced by concurrence or power of attorney.

Joint tariff means a tariff that contains joint fares.

Local fare means a fare that applies to transportation over the lines or routes of one carrier only.

Local tariff means a tariff that contains local fares.

Machine-readable data means encoded computer data, normally in a binary format, which can be read electronically by another computer with the requisite software without any human interpretation.

On-line tariff database means the remotely accessible, on-line version, maintained by the filer, of:

(1) The electronically filed tariff data submitted to the Department pursuant to this part and Department orders, and

(2) The Departmental approvals, disapprovals, and other actions, as well as any Departmental notation concerning such approvals, disapprovals, or other actions, that subpart R of this part requires the filer to maintain in its database.

Original tariff refers to the tariff as it was originally filed exclusive of any supplements, revised records or additional records.

Passenger means any person who purchases, or who contacts a ticket office or travel agent for the purpose of purchasing, or considering the purchase of, foreign air transportation.

Passenger tariff means a tariff containing fares, charges, or governing provisions applicable to the foreign air transportation of persons and their baggage.

Publish means to display tariff material in either electronic or paper media.

Record means an electronic tariff data set that contains information describing one (1) tariff price or charge, or information describing one (1) related element associated with that tariff price or charge.

SFFL means the Standard Foreign Fare Level as established by the Department of Transportation under 49 U.S.C. 41509.

Statute means subtitle VII of Title 49, United States Code.

Statutory notice means the number of days required for tariff filings in § 221.160(a).

Tariff publication means a tariff, a supplement to a tariff, or an original or revised record of a tariff, including an index of tariffs and an adoption notice (§ 221.161).

Through fare means the total fare from point of origin to destination. It may be a local fare, a joint fare, or combination of separately established fares.

Ticket office means a station, office or other location where tickets are sold or similar documents are issued, that is under the charge of a person employed exclusively by the carrier, or by it jointly with another person.

Unbundled normal economy fare means the lowest one-way fare available for on-demand service in any city-pair market which is restricted in some way, e.g., by limits set and/or charges imposed for enroute stopovers or transfers, exclusive of capacity control.

United States means the several States, the District of Columbia, and the several Territories and possessions of the United States, including the Territorial waters and the overlying air space thereof.

Warsaw Convention means the Convention for the Unification of Certain Rules Relating to International Transportation by Air, 49 Stat. 3000.

§ 221.4 English language.

All tariffs and other documents and material filed with the Department pursuant to this part shall be in the English language.

§ 221.5 Unauthorized air transportation.

Tariff publications shall not contain fares or charges, or their governing provisions, applicable to foreign air transportation which the issuing or participating carriers are not authorized by the Department to perform, except where the Department expressly requests or authorizes tariff publications to be filed prior to the Department's granting authority to perform the foreign air transportation covered by such tariff publications. Any tariff publication filed pursuant to such express request or authorization which is not consistent with chapter 415 and this part may be rejected; any tariff publication so rejected shall be void.

Subpart B—Who is Authorized To Issue and File Tariffs

§221.10 Carrier.

(a) *Local or joint tariffs.* A carrier may issue and file, in its own name, tariff publications which contain:

(1) Local fares of such carrier only, and provisions governing such local fares, and/or

(2) Joint fares which apply jointly via such issuing carrier in connection with other carriers (participating in the tariff publications under authority of their concurrences given to the issuing carrier as provided in §221.140) and provisions governing such joint fares. Provisions for account of an individual participating carrier may be published to govern such joint fares provided §221.40(a)(9) is complied with. A carrier shall not issue and file tariff publications containing local fares of other carriers, joint rates or fares in which the issuing carrier does not participate, or provisions governing such local or joint fares.

(3) Rules and regulations governing foreign air transportation to the extent provided by this part and/or Department order. Rules and regulations may be published in separate governing tariffs, as provided in subpart G.

(b) *Issuing officer.* An officer or designated employee of the issuing carrier shall be shown as the issuing officer of a tariff publication issued by a carrier, and such issuing officer shall file the tariff publication with the Department on behalf of the issuing carrier and all carriers participating in the tariff publication.

§221.11 Agent.

An agent may issue and file, in his or its own name, tariff publications naming local fares and/or joint fares, and provisions governing such fares, and rules and regulations governing foreign air transportation to the extent provided by this part and/or Department order, for account of carriers participating in such tariff publications, under authority of their powers of attorney given to such issuing agent as provided in §221.150. The issuing agent shall file such tariff publications with the Department on behalf of all carriers participating therein. Only one issuing agent may act in issuing and filing each such tariff publication.

Subpart C—Specifications of Tariff Publications

§221.20 Specifications applicable to tariff publications.

(a) *Numerical order.* All items in a tariff shall be arranged in numerical or alphabetical order. Each item shall bear a separate item designation and the same designation shall not be assigned to more than one item.

(b) *Carrier's name.* Wherever the name of a carrier appears in a tariff publication, such name shall be shown in full exactly as it appears in the carrier's certificate of public convenience and necessity, foreign air carrier permit, letter of registration, or whatever other form of operating authority of the Department to engage in air transportation is held by the carrier, or such other name which has specifically been authorized by order of the Department. A carrier's name may be abbreviated, provided the abbreviation is explained in the tariff.

(c) *Agent's name and title.* Wherever the name of an agent appears in tariff publications, such name shall be shown in full exactly as it appears in the powers of attorney given to such agent by the participating carriers and the title "Agent" or "Alternate Agent" (as the case may be) shall be shown immediately in connection with the name.

(d) *Statement of prices.* All fares and charges shall be clearly and explicitly stated and shall be arranged in a simple and systematic manner. Complicated plans and ambiguous or indefinite terms shall not be used. So far as practicable, the fares and charges shall be subdivided into items or similar units, and an identifying number shall be assigned to each item or unit to facilitate reference thereto.

(e) *Statement of rules.* The rules and regulations of each tariff shall be clear, explicit and definite, and except as otherwise provided in this part, shall contain:

(1) Such explanatory statements regarding the fares, charges, rules or other provisions contained in the tariff as may be necessary to remove all doubt as to their application.

(2) All of the terms, conditions, or other provisions which affect the fares or charges for air transportation named in the tariff.

(3) All provisions and charges which in any way increase or decrease the amount to be paid by any passenger, or which in any way increase or decrease the value of the services rendered to the passenger.

(f) *Separate rules tariff.* If desired, rules and regulations may be published in separate governing tariffs to the extent authorized and in the manner required by subpart G.

(g) *Rules of limited application.* A rule affecting only a particular fare or other provision in the tariff shall be specifically referred to in connection with such fare or other provision, and such rule shall indicate that it is applicable only in connection with such fare or other provision. Such rule shall not be published in a separate governing rules tariff.

(h) *Conflicting or duplicating rules prohibited.* The publication of rules or regulations which duplicate or conflict with other rules or regulations published in the same or any other tariff for account of the same carrier or carriers and applicable to or in connection with the same transportation is prohibited.

(i) Each tariff shall include:

(1) A prominent D.O.T. or other number identifying the tariff in the sequence of tariffs published by the carrier or issuing agent;

(2) The name of the issuing carrier or agent;

(3) The cancellation of any tariffs superseded by the tariff;

(4) A description of the tariff contents, including geographic coverage;

(5) Identification by number of any governing tariffs;

(6) The date on which the tariff is issued;

(7) The date on which the tariff provisions will become effective; and

(8) the expiration date, if applicable to the entire tariff.

Subpart D—Manner of Filing Tariffs

§ 221.30 Passenger fares and charges.

(a) Fares tariffs, including associated data, shall be filed electronically in conformity with subpart R. Associated data includes arbitraries, footnotes, routing numbers and fare class explanations. See § 221.202(b)(8).

(b) Upon application by a carrier, the Department's Office of International Aviation shall have the authority to waive the electronic filing requirement in this paragraph and in Subpart R in whole or in part, for a period up to one year, and to permit, under such terms and conditions as may be necessary to carry out the purposes of this part, the applicant carrier to file fare tariffs in a paper format. Such waivers shall only be considered where electronic filing, compared to paper filing, is impractical and will produce a significant economic hardship for the carrier due to the limited nature of the carrier's operations subject to the requirements of this part, or other unusual circumstances. Paper filings pursuant to this paragraph shall normally conform to the requirements of § 221.195 and other applicable requirements of this part.

§ 221.31 Rules and regulations governing passenger fares and services.

(a) Tariff rules and regulations governing passenger fares and services other than those subject to § 221.30 may be filed electronically in conformity with subpart R. Such filings shall conform to criteria approved by the Department's Office of International Aviation as provided in § 221.180 and shall contain at a minimum the information required by § 221.202(b)(9).

(b) Applications for special tariff permission may be filed electronically, as provided in § 221.212.

(c) Tariff publications and applications for special tariff permission covered by paragraphs (a) and (b) of this section may be filed in a paper format, subject to the requirements of this part and Department orders.

Subpart E—Contents of Tariff

§ 221.40 Specific requirements.

(a) In addition to the general requirements in § 221.20, the rules and regulations of each tariff shall contain:

(1) *Aircraft and seating.* For individually ticketed passenger service, the

name of each type of aircraft used in rendering such service by manufacturer model designation and a description of the seating configuration (or configurations if there are variations) of each type of aircraft. Where fares are provided for different classes or types of passenger service (that is, first class, coach, day coach, night coach, tourist, economy or whatever other class or type of service is provided under the tariff), the tariff shall specify the type of aircraft and the seating configuration used on such aircraft for each class or type of passenger service. When two or more classes or types of passenger service are performed in a single aircraft, the seating configuration for each type or class shall be stated and described.

(2) *Rule numbers.* Each rule or regulation shall have a separate designation. The same designation shall not be assigned to more than one rule in the tariff.

(3) *Penalties.* Where a rule provides a charge in the nature of a penalty, the rule shall state the exact conditions under which such charge will be imposed.

(4) *Vague or indefinite provisions.* Rules and regulations shall not contain indefinite statements to the effect that traffic of any nature will be "taken only by special arrangements", or that services will be performed or penalties imposed "at carrier's option", or that the carrier "reserves the right" to act or to refrain from acting in a specified manner, or other provisions of like import; instead, the rules shall state definitely what the carrier will or will not do under the exact conditions stated in the rules.

(5) *Personal liability rules.* Except as provided in this part, no provision of the Department's regulations issued under this part or elsewhere shall be construed to require the filing of any tariff rules stating any limitation on, or condition relating to, the carrier's liability for personal injury or death. No subsequent regulation issued by the Department shall be construed to supersede or modify this rule of construction except to the extent that such regulation shall do so in express terms.

(6) *Notice of limitation of liability for death or injury under the Warsaw Convention.* Notwithstanding the provisions of paragraph (a)(5) of this section, each air carrier and foreign air carrier shall publish in its tariffs a provision stating whether it avails itself of the limitation on liability to passengers as provided in Article 22(1) of the Warsaw Convention or whether it has elected to agree to a higher limit of liability by a tariff provision. Unless the carrier elects to assume unlimited liability, its tariffs shall contain a statement as to the applicability and effect of the Warsaw Convention, including the amount of the liability limit in dollars. Where applicable, a statement advising passengers of the amount of any higher limit of liability assumed by the carrier shall be added.

(7) *Extension of credit.* Air carriers and foreign air carriers shall not file tariffs that set forth charges, rules, regulations, or practices relating to the extension of credit for payment of charges applicable to air transportation.

(8) *Individual carrier provisions governing joint fares.* Provisions governing joint fares may be published for account of an individual carrier participating in such joint fares provided that the tariff clearly indicates how such individual carrier's provisions apply to the through transportation over the applicable joint routes comprised of such carrier and other carriers who either do not maintain such provisions or who maintain different provisions on the same subject matter.

(9) *Passenger property which cannot lawfully be carried in the aircraft cabin.* Each air carrier shall set forth in its tariffs governing the transportation of persons, including passengers' baggage, charges, rules, and regulations providing that such air carrier receiving as baggage any property of a person traveling in air transportation, which property cannot lawfully be carried by such person in the aircraft cabin by reason of any Federal law or regulation, shall assume liability to such person, at a reasonable charge and subject to reasonable terms and conditions, within the amount declared to the air carrier by such person, for the full actual loss or damage to such property caused by such air carrier.

(b) [Reserved]

§ 221.41 Routing.

(a) *Required routing.* The route or routes over which each fare applies shall be stated in the tariff in such manner that the following information can be definitely ascertained from the tariff:

(1) The carrier or carriers performing the transportation,

(2) The point or points of interchange between carriers if the route is a joint route (via two or more carriers),

(3) The intermediate points served on the carrier's or carriers' routes applicable between the origin and destination of the fare and the order in which such intermediate points are served.

(b) *Individually stated routings—Method of publication.* The routing required by paragraph (a) of this section shall be shown directly in connection with each fare or charge for transportation, or in a routing portion of the tariff (following the fare portion of the tariff), or in a governing routing tariff. When shown in the routing portion of the tariff or in a governing routing tariff, the fare from each point of origin to each point of destination shall bear a routing number and the corresponding routing numbers with their respective explanations of the applicable routings shall be arranged in numerical order in the routing portion of the tariff or in the governing routing tariff.

Subpart F—Requirements Applicable to All Statements of Fares and Charges

§ 221.50 Currency.

(a) *Statement in United States currency required.* All fares and charges shall be stated in cents or dollars of the United States except as provided in paragraph (b) of this section.

(b) *Statements in both United States and foreign currencies permitted.* Fares and charges applying between points in the United States, on the one hand, and points in foreign countries, on the other hand, or applying between points in foreign countries, may also be stated in the currencies of foreign countries in addition to being stated in United States currency as required by paragraph (a) of this section: Provided, that:

(1) The fares and charges stated in currencies of countries other than the United States are substantially equivalent in value to the respective fares and charges stated in cents or dollars of the United States.

(2) Each record containing fares and charges shall clearly indicate the respective currencies in which the fares and charges thereon are stated, and

(3) The fares and charges stated in cents or dollars of the United States are published separately from those stated in currencies of other countries. This shall be done in a systematic manner and the fares and charges in the respective currencies shall be published in separate records.

§ 221.51 Territorial application.

(a) *Specific points of origin and destination.* Except as otherwise provided in this part, the specific points of origin and destination from and to which the fares apply shall be specifically named directly in connection with the respective fares.

(b) *Directional application.* A tariff shall specifically indicate directly in connection with the fares therein whether they apply "from" and "to" or "between" the points named. Where the fares apply in one direction, the terms "From" and "To" shall be shown in connection with the point of origin and point of destination, respectively, and, where the fares apply in both directions between the points, the terms "Between" and "And" shall be shown in connection with the respective points.

§ 221.52 Airport to airport application, accessorial services.

Tariffs shall specify whether or not the fares therein include services in addition to airport-to-airport transportation.

§ 221.53 Proportional fares.

(a) *Definite application.* Add-on fares shall be specifically designated as "add-on" fares on each page where they appear.

(b) A tariff may provide that fares from (or to) particular points shall be determined by the addition of add-ons to, or the deduction of add-ons from, fares therein which apply from (or to) a base point. Provisions for the addition or deduction of such add-ons shall be shown either directly in connection with the fare applying to or from the base point or in a separate provision which shall specifically name the base point. The tariff shall clearly and definitely state the manner in which such add-ons shall be applied.

(c) *Restrictions upon beyond points or connecting carriers.* If an add-on fare is intended for use only on traffic originating at and/or destined to particular beyond points or is to apply only in connection with particular connecting carriers, such application shall be clearly and explicitly stated directly in connection with such add-on fare.

§221.54 Fares stated in percentages of other fares; other relationships prohibited.

(a) Fares for foreign air transportation of persons or property shall not be stated in the form of percentages, multiples, fractions, or other relationships to other fares except to the extent authorized in paragraphs (b), (c), and (d) of this section with respect to passenger fares and baggage charges.

(b) A basis of fares for refund purposes may be stated, by rule, in the form of percentages of other fares.

(c) Transportation rates for the portion of passengers' baggage in excess of the baggage allowance under the applicable fares may be stated, by rule, as percentages of fares.

(d) Children's, infants' and senior citizen's fares, may be stated, by rule, as percentages of other fares published specifically in dollars and cents (hereinafter referred to as base fares): Provided, that:

(1) Fares stated as percentages of base fares shall apply from and to the same points, via the same routes, and for the same class of service and same type of aircraft to which the applicable base fares apply, and shall apply to all such base fares in a fares tariff.

(2) Fares shall not be stated as percentages of base fares for the purpose of establishing fares applying from and to points, or via routes, or on types of aircraft, or for classes of service different from the points, routes, types of aircraft, or classes of service to which the base fares are applicable.

§221.55 Conflicting or duplicating fares prohibited.

The publication of fares or charges of a carrier which duplicate or conflict with the fares of the same carrier published in the same or any other tariff for application over the same route or routes is hereby prohibited.

§221.56 Applicable fare when no through local or joint fares.

Where no applicable local or joint fare is provided from point of origin to point of destination over the route of movement, whichever combination of applicable fares provided over the route of movement produces the lowest charge shall be applicable, except that a carrier may provide explicitly that a fare cannot be used in any combination or in a combination on particular traffic or under specified conditions, provided another combination is available.

Subpart G—Governing Tariffs

§221.60 When reference to governing tariffs permitted.

(a) *Reference to other tariffs prohibited except as authorized.* A tariff shall not refer to nor provide that it is governed by any other tariff, document, or publication, or any part thereof, except as specifically authorized by this part.

(b) *Reference by fare tariff to governing tariffs.* A fare tariff may be made subject to a governing tariff or governing tariffs authorized by this subpart: Provided, that reference to such governing tariffs is published in the fare tariff in the manner required by §221.20(h).

(c) *Participation in governing tariffs.* A fare tariff may refer to a separate governing tariff authorized by this subpart only when all carriers participating in such fare tariff are also shown as participating carriers in the governing tariff: Provided, that:

(1) If such reference to a separate governing tariff does not apply for account of all participating carriers and is restricted to apply only in connection with local or joint fares applying over routes consisting of only particular carriers, only the carriers for whom such reference is published are required to be shown as participating carriers in the governing tariff to which such qualified reference is made.

(2) [Reserved]

(d) *Maximum number of governing tariffs.* A single fare tariff shall not make reference to conflicting governing tariffs.

§ 221.61 Rules and regulations governing foreign air transportation.

Instead of being included in the fares tariffs, the rules and regulations governing foreign air transportation required to be filed by §§ 221.20 and 221.30 and/or Department order which do not govern the applicability of particular fares may be filed in separate governing tariffs, conforming to this subpart. Governing rules tariffs shall contain an index of rules.

§ 221.62 Explosives and other dangerous or restricted articles.

Carriers may publish rules and regulations governing the transportation of explosives and other dangerous or restricted articles in separate governing tariffs, conforming to this subpart, instead of being included in the fares tariffs or in the governing rules tariff authorized by § 221.61. This separate governing tariff shall contain no other rules or governing provisions.

§ 221.63 Other types of governing tariffs.

Subject to approval of the Department, carriers may publish other types of governing tariffs not specified in this subpart, such as routing guides.

Subpart H—Amendment of Tariffs

§ 221.70 Who may amend tariffs.

A tariff shall be amended only by the carrier or agent who issued the tariff (except as otherwise authorized in subparts P and Q).

§ 221.71 Requirement of clarity and specificity.

Amendments to tariffs shall identify with specificity and clarity the material being amended and the changes being made. Amendments to paper tariffs shall be accomplished by reissuing each page upon which a change occurs with the change made and identified by uniform amendment symbols. Each revised page shall identify and cancel the previously effective page, show the effective date of the previous page, and show the intended effective date of the revised page. Amendments in electronic format shall conform to the requirements of § 221.202 and other applicable provisions of subpart R.

§ 221.72 Reinstating canceled or expired tariff provisions.

Any fares, rules, or other tariff provisions which have been canceled or which have expired may be reinstated only by republishing such provisions and posting and filing the tariff publications (containing such republished provisions) on lawful notice in the form and manner required by this part.

Subpart I—Suspension of Tariff Provisions by Department

§ 221.80 Effect of suspension by Department.

(a) *Suspended matter not to be used.* A fare, charge, or other tariff provision which is suspended by the Department, under authority of chapter 415 of the statute, shall not be used during the period of suspension specified by the Department's order.

(b) *Suspended matter not to be changed.* A fare, charge, or other tariff provision which is suspended by the Department shall not be changed in any respect or withdrawn or the effective date thereof further deferred except by authority of an order or special tariff permission of the Department.

(c) *Suspension continues former matter in effect.* If a tariff publication containing matter suspended by the Department directs the cancellation of a tariff or any portion thereof, which contains fares, charges, or other tariff provisions sought to be amended by the suspended matter, such cancellation is automatically suspended for the same period insofar as it purports to cancel any tariff provisions sought to be amended by the suspended matter.

(d) *Matter continued in effect not to be changed.* A fare, charge, or other tariff provision which is continued in effect as a result of a suspension by the Department shall not be changed during the period of suspension unless the change is authorized by order or special tariff permission of the Department, except that such matter may be reissued without change during the period of suspension.

§221.81 Suspension supplement.

(a) *Suspension supplement.* Upon receipt of an order of the Department suspending any tariff publication in part or in its entirety, the carrier or agent who issued such tariff publication shall immediately issue and file with the Department a consecutively numbered supplement for the purpose of announcing such suspension.

(b) The suspension supplement shall not contain an effective date and it shall contain the suspension notice required by paragraph (c) of this section.

(c) *Suspension notice.* The suspension supplement shall contain a prominent notice of suspension which shall:

(1) Indicate what particular fares, charges, or other tariff provisions are under suspension,

(2) State the date to which such tariff matter is suspended,

(3) State the Department's docket number and order number which suspended such tariff matter, and

(4) Give specific reference to the tariffs (specifying their D.O.T. or other identifying numbers), original or revised records and paragraphs or provisions which contain the fares, charges, or other tariff provisions continued in effect.

§221.82 Reissue of matter continued in effect by suspension to be canceled upon termination of suspension.

When tariff provisions continued in effect by a suspension are reissued during the period of such suspension, the termination of the suspension and the coming into effect of the suspended matter will not accomplish the cancellation of such reissued matter. In such circumstances, prompt action shall be taken by the issuing agent or carrier to cancel such reissued provisions upon the termination of the suspension in order that they will not conflict with the provisions formerly under suspension.

§221.83 Tariff must be amended to make suspended matter effective.

(a) When the Department vacates an order which suspended certain tariff matter in full or in part, such matter will not become effective until the termination of the suspension period unless the issuing agent or carrier amends the pertinent tariffs in the manner prescribed in this subpart (except as provided in paragraph (b) of this section).

(b) If the Department vacates its suspension order prior to the original published effective date of the tariff provisions whose suspension is vacated, such provisions will become effective on their published effective date.

§221.84 Cancellation of suspended matter subsequent to date to which suspended.

(a) *Endeavor to cancel prior to expiration of suspension period.* When an order of the Department requires the cancellation of tariff provisions which were suspended by the Department and such cancellation is required to be made effective on or before a date which is after the date to which such tariff provisions were suspended, the issuing carrier or agent shall, if possible, make the cancellation effective prior to the date to which such tariff provisions were suspended.

(b) *When necessary to republish matter continued in effect by suspension.* If suspended tariff provisions become effective upon expiration of their suspension period and thereby accomplish the cancellation of the tariff provisions continued in effect by the suspension, the issuing agent or carrier shall republish and reestablish such canceled tariff provisions effective simultaneously with the cancellation of the suspended provisions in compliance with the Department's order. The tariff amendments which reestablish such canceled tariff provisions shall bear reference to this subpart and the Department's order.

Subpart J—Filing Tariff Publications With Department

§221.90 Required notice.

(a) *Statutory notice required.* Unless otherwise authorized by the Department or specified in a bilateral agreement between the United States and a foreign country, all tariff filings shall be made on the following schedule, whether or not they effect any changes:

(1) At least 30 days before they are to become effective, for tariffs stating a passenger fare within the zone created by section 41509(e) of the statute or stating a rule that affects only such a fare;

(2) At least 25 days before they are to become effective, for matching tariffs that are to become effective on the same date as the tariff to be matched and that meet competition as described in § 221.94(c)(1)(v); and

(3) At least 60 days before they are to become effective, for all other tariffs.

(b) *Computing number of days' notice.* A tariff publication shall be deemed to be filed only upon its actual receipt by the Department, and the first day of any required period of notice shall be the day of actual receipt by the Department.

(c) *Issued date.* All tariff publications must be received by the Department on or before the designated issued date.

§ 221.91 Delivering tariff publications to Department.

Tariff publications will be received for filing only by delivery thereof to the Department electronically, through normal mail channels, or by delivery thereof during established business hours directly to that office of the Department charged with the responsibility of processing tariffs. No tariff publication will be accepted by the Department unless it is delivered free from all charges, including claims for postage.

§ 221.92 Number of copies required.

Two copies of each paper tariff, tariff revision and adoption notice to be filed shall be sent to the Office of International Aviation, Department of Transportation, Washington, DC 20428. All such copies shall be included in one package and shall be accompanied by a letter of tariff transmittal.

§ 221.93 Concurrences or powers of attorney not previously filed to accompany tariff transmittal.

When a tariff is filed on behalf of a carrier participating therein under authority of its concurrence or power of attorney, such concurrence or power of attorney shall, if not previously filed with the Department, be transmitted at the same time such tariff is submitted for filing.

§ 221.94 Explanation and data supporting tariff changes and new matter in tariffs.

When a tariff is filed with the Department which contains new or changed local or joint fares or charges for foreign air transportation, or new or changed classifications, rules, regulations, or practices affecting such fares or charges, or the value of the service thereunder, the issuing air carrier, foreign air carrier, or agent shall submit with the filing of such tariff:

(a) An explanation of the new or changed matter and the reasons for the filing, including (if applicable) the basis of rate making employed. Where a tariff is filed pursuant to an intercarrier agreement approved by the Department, the explanation shall identify such agreement by DOT Docket number, DOT order of approval number, IATA resolution number, or if none is designated, then by other definite identification. Where a tariff is filed on behalf of a foreign air carrier pursuant to a Government order, a copy of such order shall be submitted with the tariff.

(b) Appropriate Economic data and/or information in support of the new or changed matter.

(c) *Exceptions.* (1) The requirement for data and/or information in paragraph (b) of this section will not apply to tariff publications containing new or changed matter which are filed:

(i) In response to Department orders or specific policy pronouncements of the Department directly related to such new or changed matter;

(ii) Pursuant to an intercarrier agreement approved by the Department setting forth the fares, charges (or specific formulas therefor) or other matter: Provided that the changes are submitted with the number of the DOT order of approval and fully comply with any conditions set forth in that order;

(iii) To the extent fares for scheduled passenger service are within a statutory or Department-established zone of fare flexibility; and

(iv) To meet competition: Provided, that

(A) Changed matter will be deemed to have been filed to meet competition only when it effects decreases in fares or charges and/or increases the value of service so that the level of the fares or charges and the services provided will be substantially similar to the level of fares or charges and the services of a competing carrier or carriers.

(B) New matter will be deemed to have been filed to meet competition only when it establishes or affects a fare or charge and a service which will be substantially similar to the fares or charges and the services of a competing carrier or carriers.

(C) When new or changed matter is filed to meet competition over a portion of the filing air carrier's system and is simultaneously made applicable to the balance of the system, such matter, insofar as it applies over the balance of the system, will be deemed to be within the exception in this paragraph (c)(1)(iv) of this section only if such carrier submits an explanation as to the necessity of maintaining uniformity over its entire system with respect to such new or changed matter.

(D) In any case where new or changed matter is filed to meet competition, the filing carrier or agent must supply, as part of the filing justification, the complete tariff references which will serve to identify the competing tariff matter which the tariff purports to meet. In such case the justification or attachment shall state whether the new or changed matter is identical to the competing tariff matter which it purports to meet or whether it approximates the competing tariff matter. If the new or changed matter is not identical, the transmittal letter or attachment shall contain a statement explaining, in reasonable detail, the basis for concluding that the tariff publication being filed is substantially similar to the competing tariff matter.

(2) [Reserved]

Subpart K—Availability of Tariff Publications for Public Inspection

§ 221.100 Public notice of tariff information.

Carriers must make tariff information available to the general public, and in so doing must comply with either:

(a) Sections 221.101, 221.102, 221.103, 221.104, 221.105, and 221.106, or

(b) Sections 221.105, 221.106 and 221.107 of this subpart.

§ 221.101 Inspection at stations, offices, or locations other than principal or general office.

(a) Each carrier shall make available for public inspection at each of its stations, offices, or other locations at which tickets for passenger transportation are sold and which is in charge of a person employed exclusively by the carrier, or by it jointly with another person, all tariffs applicable to passenger traffic from or to the point where such station, office, or location is situated, including tariffs covering any terminal services, charges, or practices whatsoever, which apply to passenger traffic from or to such point.

(b) A carrier will be deemed to have complied with the requirement that it "post" tariffs, if it maintains at each station, office, or location a file in complete form of all tariffs required to be posted; and in the case of tariffs involving passenger fares, rules, charges or practices, notice to the passenger as required in § 221.105.

(c) Tariffs shall be posted by each carrier party thereto no later than the filed date designated thereon except that in the case of carrier stations, offices or locations situated outside the United States, its territories and possessions, the time shall be not later than five days after the filed date, and except that a tariff which the Department has authorized to be filed on shorter notice shall be posted by the carrier on like notice as authorized for filing.

§ 221.102 Accessibility of tariffs to the public.

Each file of tariffs shall be kept in complete and accessible form. Employees of the carrier shall be required to give any desired information contained in such tariffs, to lend assistance to seekers of information therefrom, and to afford inquirers opportunity to examine any of such tariffs without requiring the inquirer to assign any reason for such desire.

§ 221.103 Notice of tariff terms.

Each carrier shall cause to be displayed continuously in a conspicuous public place at each station, office, or location at which tariffs are required to be posted, a notice printed in large type reading as follows:

Public Inspection of Tariffs

All the currently effective passenger tariffs to which this company is a party and all passenger tariff publications which have been issued but are not yet effective are on file in this office, so far as they apply to traffic from or to. (Here name the point.) These tariffs may be inspected by any person upon request and without the assignment of any reason for such inspection. The employees of this company on duty in this office will lend assistance in securing information from the tariffs.

In addition, a complete file of all tariffs of this company, with indexes thereof, is maintained and kept available for public inspection at. (Here indicate the place or places where complete tariff files are maintained, including the street address, and where appropriate, the room number.)

§ 221.105 Special notice of limited liability for death or injury under the Warsaw Convention.

(a)(1) In addition to the other requirements of this subpart, each air carrier and foreign air carrier which, to any extent, avails itself of the limitation on liability to passengers provided by the Warsaw Convention, shall, at the time of delivery of the ticket, furnish to each passenger whose transportation is governed by the Convention and whose place of departure or place of destination is in the United States, the following statement in writing:

Advice to International Passengers on Limitations of Liability

Passengers embarking upon a journey involving an ultimate destination or a stop in a country other than the country of departure are advised that the provisions of a treaty known as the Warsaw Convention may be applicable to their entire journey including the portion entirely within the countries of departure and destination. The Convention governs and in most cases limits the liability of carriers to passengers for death or personal injury to approximately $10,000.

Additional protection can usually be obtained by purchasing insurance from a private company. Such insurance is not affected by any limitation of the carrier's liability under the Warsaw Convention. For further information please consult your airline or insurance company representative.

(2) Provided, however, That when the carrier elects to agree to a higher limit of liability to passengers than that provided in Article 22(1) of the Warsaw Convention, such statement shall be modified to reflect the higher limit. The statement prescribed herein shall be printed in type at least as large as 10-point modern type and in ink contrasting with the stock on:

(i) Each ticket;

(ii) A piece of paper either placed in the ticket envelope with the ticket or attached to the ticket; or

(iii) The ticket envelope.

(b) Each air carrier and foreign air carrier which, to any extent, avails itself of the limitation on liability to passengers provided by the Warsaw Convention, shall also cause to be displayed continuously in a conspicuous public place at each desk, station, and position in the United States which is in the charge of a person employed exclusively by it or by it jointly with another person, or by any agent employed by such air carrier or foreign air carrier to sell tickets to passengers whose transportation may be governed by the Warsaw Convention and whose place of departure or destination may be in the United States, a sign which shall have printed thereon the statement prescribed in paragraph (a) of this section: Provided, however, That an air carrier, except an air taxi operator subject to part 298 of this subchapter, or foreign air carrier which provides a higher limitation of liability than that set forth in the Warsaw Convention and has signed a counterpart of the agreement among carriers providing for such higher limit, which agreement was approved by the Civil Aeronautics Board by Order E–23680, dated May 13, 1966 (31 FR 7302, May 19, 1966), may use the alternate form of notice set forth in the proviso to § 221.106(a) of this chapter in full compliance with the posting requirements of this paragraph. And provided further, That an air taxi operator subject to part 298 of this subchapter, which provides a higher limitation of liability than that set forth in the Warsaw Convention and has signed a counterpart of the agreement among carriers providing for such higher limit, which agreement was approved by the Civil Aeronautics Board by Order E-23680, dated May 13, 1966 (31 FR 7302, May 19, 1966), may use the following notice in the manner prescribed by this paragraph in full compliance with the posting requirements of this paragraph. Such statements shall be printed in bold faced type at least one-fourth of an inch high.

Advice to International Passengers on Limitation of Liability

Passengers traveling to or from a foreign country are advised that airline liability for death or personal injury and loss or damage to baggage may be limited by the Warsaw Convention and tariff provisions. See the notice with your ticket or contact your airline ticket office or travel agent for further information.

§221.106 Notice of limited liability for baggage; alternative consolidated notice of liability limitations.

(a)(1) Each air carrier and foreign air carrier which, to any extent, avails itself of limitations on liability for loss of, damage to, or delay in delivery of baggage shall cause to be displayed continuously in a conspicuous public place at each desk, station, and position in the United States which is in the charge of a person employed exclusively by it or by it jointly with another person, or by any agent employed by such air carrier or foreign air carrier to sell tickets to persons or accept baggage for checking, a sign which shall have printed thereon the following statement:

Notice of Limited Liability for Baggage

For most international travel (including domestic portions of international journeys) liability for loss, delay, or damage to baggage is limited to approximately $9.07 per pound for checked baggage and $400 per passenger for unchecked baggage unless a higher value is declared and an extra charge is paid. Special rules may apply for valuables. Consult your carrier for details.

(2) Provided, however, That an air carrier or foreign air carrier which provides a higher limitation of liability for death or personal injury than that set forth in the Warsaw Convention and has signed a counterpart of the agreement approved by the Civil Aeronautics Board by Order E-23680, dated May 13, 1966 (31 FR 7302, May 19, 1966), may use the following notice in full compliance with the posting requirements of this paragraph and of §221.105(b):

Advice to Passengers on Limitations of Liability

Airline liability for death or personal injury may be limited by the Warsaw Convention and tariff provisions in the case of travel to or from a foreign country.

For most international travel (including domestic portions of international journeys) liability for loss, delay or damage to baggage is limited to approximately $9.07 per pound for checked baggage and $400 per passenger for unchecked baggage unless a higher value is declared and an extra charge is paid. Special rules may apply to valuable articles.

See the notice with your tickets or consult your airline or travel agent for further information.

(3) Provided, however, That carriers may include in the notice the parenthetical phrase "($20.00 per kilo)" after the phrase "$9.07 per pound" in referring to the baggage liability limitation for most international travel. Such statements shall be printed in bold-face type at least one-fourth of an inch high and shall be so located as to be clearly visible and clearly readable to the traveling public.

(b)(1) Each air carrier and foreign air carrier which, to any extent, avails itself of limitations of liability for loss of, damage to, or delay in delivery of, baggage shall include on or with each ticket issued in the United States or in a foreign country by it or its authorized agent, the following notice printed in at least 10 point type:

Notice of Baggage Liability Limitations

For most international travel (including domestic portions of international journeys) liability for loss, delay, or damage to baggage is limited to approximately $9.07 per pound for checked baggage and $400 per passenger for unchecked baggage unless a higher value is declared in advance and additional charges are paid. Excess valuation may not be declared on certain types of valuable articles. Carriers assume no liability for fragile or perishable articles. Further information may be obtained from the carrier.

(2) Provided, however, That carriers may include in their ticket notice the parenthetical phrase "($20.00 per kilo)" after the phrase "$9.07 per pound" in referring to the baggage liability limitation for most international travel.

(c) It shall be the responsibility of each carrier to insure that travel agents authorized to sell air transportation for such carrier comply with the notice provisions of paragraphs (a) and (b) of this section.

(d) Any air carrier or foreign air carrier subject to the provisions of this section which wishes to use a notice of limited liability for baggage of its own wording, but containing the substance of the language prescribed in paragraphs (a) and (b) of this section may substitute a notice of its own wording upon approval by the Department.

(e) The requirements as to time and method of delivery of the notice (including the size of type) specified in paragraphs (a) and (b) of this section and the requirement with respect to travel agents specified in paragraph (c) of this section may be waived by the Department upon application and showing by the carrier that special and unusual circumstances render the enforcement of the regulations impractical and unduly burdensome and that adequate alternative means of giving notice are employed.

(f) Applications for relief under paragraphs (d) and (e) of this section shall be filed with the Department's Office of International Aviation not later than 15 days before the date on which such relief is requested to become effective.

(g) Notwithstanding any other provisions of this section, no air taxi operator subject to part 298 of this subchapter shall be required to give the notices prescribed in this section, either in its capacity as an air carrier or in its capacity as an agent for an air carrier or foreign air carrier.

§ 221.107 Notice of contract terms.

(a) *Terms incorporated in the contract of carriage.* (1) A ticket, or other written instrument that embodies the contract of carriage for foreign air transportation shall contain or be accompanied by notice to the passenger as required in paragraphs (b) and (d) of this section.

(2) Each carrier shall make the full text of all terms that are incorporated in a contract of carriage readily available for public inspection at each airport or other ticket sales office of the carrier: Provided, That the medium, *i.e.*, printed or electronic, in which the incorporated terms and conditions are made available to the consumer shall be at the discretion of the carrier.

(3) Each carrier shall display continuously in a conspicuous public place at each airport or other ticket sales office of the carrier a notice printed in large type reading as follows:

Explanation of Contract Terms

All passenger (and/or cargo as applicable) contract terms incorporated into the contract of carriage to which this company is a party are available in this office. These provisions may be inspected by any person upon request and for any reason. The employees of this office will lend assistance in securing information, and explaining any terms.

In addition, a file of all tariffs of this company, with indexes thereof, from which incorporated contract terms may be obtained is maintained and kept available for public inspection at. (Here indicate the place or places where tariff files are maintained, including the street address and, where appropriate, the room number.)

(4) Each carrier shall provide to the passenger a complete copy of the text of any/all terms and conditions applicable to the contract of carriage, free of charge, immediately, if feasible, or otherwise promptly by mail or other delivery service, upon request at any airport or other ticket sales office of the carrier. In addition, all other locations where the carrier's tickets may be issued shall have available at all times, free of charge, information sufficient to enable the passenger to request a copy of such term(s).

(b) *Notice of incorporated terms.* Each carrier and ticket agent shall include on or with a ticket or other written instrument given to the passenger, that embodies the contract of carriage, a conspicuous notice that:

(1) The contract of carriage may incorporate terms and conditions by reference; passengers may inspect the full text of each applicable incorporated term at any of the carrier's airport locations or other ticket sales offices of the carrier; and passengers, shippers and consignees have the right to receive, upon request at any airport or other ticket sales office of the carrier, a free copy of the full text of any/all such terms by mail or other delivery service;

(2) The incorporated terms may include, among others, the terms shown in paragraphs (b)(2) (i) through (iv) of this section. Passengers may obtain a concise and immediate explanation of the terms shown in paragraphs (b)(2) (i) through (iv) of this section from any location where the carrier's tickets are sold.

(i) Limits on the carrier's liability for personal injury or death of passengers (subject to §221.105), and for loss, damage, or delay of goods and baggage, including fragile or perishable goods.

(ii) Claim restrictions, including time periods within which passengers must file a claim or bring an action against the carrier for its acts or omissions or those of its agents.

(iii) Rules about re-confirmations or reservations, check-in times, and refusal to carry.

(iv) Rights of the carrier and limitations concerning delay or failure to perform service, including schedule changes, substitution of alternate carrier or aircraft, and rerouting.

(c) *Explanation of incorporated terms.* Each carrier shall ensure that any passenger can obtain from any location where its tickets are sold or any similar documents are issued, a concise and immediate explanation of any term incorporated concerning the subjects listed in paragraph (b)(2) or identified in paragraph (d) of this section.

(d) *Direct notice of certain terms.* A passenger must receive conspicuous written notice, on or with the ticket, or other similar document, of the salient features of any terms that restrict refunds of the price of the transportation, impose monetary penalties on customers, or permit a carrier to raise the price or impose more restrictive conditions of contract after issuance of the ticket.

§221.108 Transmission of tariff filings to subscribers.

(a) Each carrier required to file tariffs in accordance with this part shall make available to any person so requesting a subscription service as described in paragraph (b) of this section for its passenger tariffs issued by it or by a publishing agent on its behalf.

(b) Under the required subscription service one copy of each new tariff publication, including the justification required by §221.94, must be transmitted to each subscriber thereto by first-class mail (or other equivalent means agreed upon by the subscriber) not later than one day following the time the copies for official filing are transmitted to the Department. The subscription service described in this section shall not preclude the offering of additional types of subscription services by carriers or their agents.

(c) The carriers or their publishing agents at their option may establish a charge for providing the required subscription service to subscribers: *Provided,* That the charge may not exceed a reasonable estimate of the added cost of providing the service.

Subpart L—Rejection of Tariff Publications

§221.110 Department's authority to reject.

The Department may reject any tariff which is not consistent with section 41504 of the statute, with the regulations in this part, or with Department orders.

§221.111 Notification of rejection.

When a tariff is rejected, the issuing carrier or agent thereof will be notified electronically or in writing that the tariff is rejected and of the reason for such rejection.

§ 221.112 Rejected tariff is void and must not be used.

A tariff rejected by the Department is void and is without any force or effect whatsoever. Such rejected tariff must not be used.

Subpart M—Special Tariff Permission To File on Less Than Statutory Notice

§ 221.120 Grounds for approving or denying Special Tariff Permission applications.

(a) *General authority.* The Department may permit changes in fares, charges or other tariff provisions on less than the statutory notice required by section 41505 of the statute.

(b) *Grounds for approval.* The following facts and circumstances constitute some of the grounds for approving applications for Special Tariff Permission in the absence of other facts and circumstances warranting denial:

(1) *Clerical or typographical errors.* Clerical or typographical errors in tariffs constitute grounds for approving applications for Special Tariff Permission to file on less than statutory notice the tariff changes necessary to correct such errors. Each application for Special Tariff Permission based on such grounds shall plainly specify the errors and contain a complete statement of all the attending facts and circumstances, and such application shall be presented to the Department with reasonable promptness after issuance of the defective tariff.

(2) *Rejection caused by clerical or typographical errors or unintelligibility.* Rejection of a tariff caused by clerical or typographical errors constitute grounds for approving applications for Special Tariff Permission to file on less than statutory notice, effective not earlier than the original effective dates in the rejected tariff, all changes contained in the rejected tariff but with the errors corrected. Each application for the grant of Special Tariff Permission based on such grounds shall plainly specify the errors and contain a complete statement of all the attending facts and circumstances, and such application shall be filed with the Department within five days after receipt of the Department's notice of rejection.

(3) *Newly authorized transportation.* The fact that the Department has newly authorized a carrier to perform foreign air transportation constitutes grounds for approving applications for Special Tariff Permission to file on less than statutory notice the fares, rates, and other tariff provisions covering such newly authorized transportation.

(4) The fact that a passenger fare is within a statutory or Department-established zone of fare flexibility constitutes grounds for approving an application for Special Tariff Permission to file a tariff stating that fare and any rules affecting them exclusively, on less than statutory notice. The Department's policy on approving such applications is set forth in § 399.35 of this chapter.

(5) *Lowered fares and charges.* The prospective lowering of fares or charges to the traveling public constitutes grounds for approving an application for Special Tariff Permission to file on less than statutory notice a tariff stating the lowered fares or charges and any rules affecting them exclusively. However, the Department will not approve the application if the proposed tariff raises significant questions of lawfulness, as set forth in § 399.35 of this chapter.

(c) *Filing notice required by formal order.* When a formal order of the Department requires the filing of tariff matter on a stated number of days' notice, an application for Special Tariff Permission to file on less notice will not be approved. In any such instance a petition for modification of the order should be filed in the formal docket.

§ 221.121 How to prepare and file applications for Special Tariff Permission.

(a) *Form.* Each application for Special Tariff Permission to file a tariff on less than statutory notice shall conform to the requirements of § 221.212 if filed electronically.

(b) *Number of paper copies and place of filing.* For paper format applications, the original and one copy of each such application for Special Tariff Permission, including all exhibits thereto and amendments thereof, shall be sent to the Office of International Aviation,

Department of Transportation, Washington, DC 20590.

(c) *Who may make application.* Applications for Special Tariff Permission to file fares, or other tariff provisions on less than statutory notice shall be made only by the issuing carrier or agent authorized to issue and file the proposed tariff. Such application by the issuing carrier or agent will constitute application on behalf of all carriers participating in the proposed fares, or other tariff provisions.

(d) *When notice is required.* Notice in the manner set forth in paragraph (e) of this section is required when a carrier files an application for Special Tariff Permission:

(1) To offer passenger fares that would be outside a Department-established zone of price flexibility or, in markets for which the Department has not established such a zone, outside the statutory zone of price flexibility; or

(2) To file any price increase or rule change that the carrier believes is likely to be controversial.

(e) *Form of notice.* When notice of filing of a Special Tariff Permission application affecting passenger fares is required by paragraph (d) of this section, the carrier shall, when it files the application, give immediate telegraphic notice or other notice approved by the Office of International Aviation, to all certificated and foreign route carriers authorized to provide nonstop or one-stop service in the markets involved, and to civic parties that would be substantially affected. The application shall include a list of the parties notified.

§221.122 Special Tariff Permission to be used in its entirety as granted.

Each Special Tariff Permission to file fares, or other tariff provisions on less than statutory notice shall be used in its entirety as granted. If it is not desired to use the permission as granted, and lesser or more extensive or different permission is desired, a new application for Special Tariff Permission conforming with §221.121 in all respects and referring to the previous permission shall be filed.

§221.123 Re-use of Special Tariff Permission when tariff is rejected.

If a tariff containing matter issued under Special Tariff Permission is rejected, the same Special Tariff Permission may be used in a tariff issued in lieu of such rejected tariff provided that such re-use is not precluded by the terms of the Special Tariff Permission, and is made within the time limit thereof or within seven days after the date of the Department's notice of rejection, whichever is later, but in no event later than fifteen days after the expiration of the time limit specified in the Special Tariff Permission.

Subpart N—Waiver of Tariff Regulations

§221.130 Applications for waiver of tariff regulations.

Applications for waiver or modification of any of the requirements of this part 221 or for modification of chapter 415 of the statute with respect to the filing and posting of tariffs shall be made by the issuing carrier or issuing agent.

§221.131 Form of application for waivers.

Applications for waivers shall be in the form of a letter addressed to the Office of International Aviation, Department of Transportation Washington, DC 20590, and shall:

(a) Specify (by section and paragraph) the particular regulation which the applicant desires the Department to waive.

(b) Show in detail how the proposed provisions will be shown in the tariff under authority of such waiver if granted (submitting exhibits of the proposed provision where necessary to clearly show this information).

(c) Set forth all facts and circumstances on which the applicant relies as warranting the Department's granting the authority requested. No tariff or other documents shall be filed pursuant to such application prior to the Department's granting the authority requested.

Subpart O—Giving and Revoking Concurrences to Carriers

§ 221.140 Method of giving concurrence.

(a) A concurrence prepared in a manner acceptable to the Office of International Aviation shall be used by a carrier to give authority to another carrier to issue and file with the Department tariffs which contain joint fares or charges, including provisions governing such fares or charges, applying to, from, or via points served by the carrier giving the concurrence. A concurrence shall not be used as authority to file joint fares or charges in which the carrier to whom the concurrence is given does not participate, and it shall not be used as authority to file local fares or charges.

(b) *Number of copies.* Each concurrence shall be prepared in triplicate. The original of each concurrence shall be filed with the Department, the duplicate thereof shall be given to the carrier in whose favor the concurrence is issued, and the third copy shall be retained by the carrier who issued the concurrence.

(c) *Conflicting authority to be avoided.* Care should be taken to avoid giving authority to two or more carriers which, if used, would result in conflicting or duplicate tariff provisions.

§ 221.141 Method of revoking concurrence.

(a) A concurrence may be revoked by filing with the Department a Notice of Revocation of Concurrence prepared in a form acceptable to the Office of International Aviation.

(b) *Sixty days' notice required.* Such Notice of Revocation of Concurrence shall be filed on not less than sixty days' notice to the Department. A Notice of Revocation of Concurrence will be deemed to be filed only upon its actual receipt by the Department, and the period of notice shall commence to run only from such actual receipt.

(c) *Number of copies.* Each Notice of Revocation of Concurrence shall be prepared in triplicate. The original thereof shall be filed with the Department and, at the same time that the original is transmitted to the Department, the duplicate thereof shall be sent to the carrier to whom the concurrence was given. The third copy shall be retained by the carrier issuing such notice.

(d) Amendment of tariffs when concurrence revoked. When a concurrence is revoked, a corresponding amendment of the tariff or tariffs affected shall be made by the issuing carrier of such tariffs, on not less than statutory notice, to become effective not later than the effective date stated in the Notice of Revocation of Concurrence. In the event of failure to so amend the tariff or tariffs, the provisions therein shall remain applicable until lawfully canceled.

§ 221.142 Method of withdrawing portion of authority conferred by concurrence.

If a carrier desires to issue a concurrence conferring less authority than a previous concurrence given to the same carrier, the new concurrence shall not direct the cancellation of such previous concurrence. In such circumstances, such previous concurrence shall be revoked by issuing and filing a Notice of Revocation of Concurrence in a form acceptable to the Office of International Aviation. Such revocation notice shall include reference to the new concurrence.

Subpart P—Giving and Revoking Powers of Attorney to Agents

§ 221.150 Method of giving power of attorney.

(a) *Prescribed form of power of attorney.* A power of attorney prepared in accordance with a form acceptable to the Office of International Aviation shall be used by a carrier to give authority to an agent and (in the case of the agent being an individual) such agent's alternate to issue and file with the Department tariffs which contain local or joint fares or charges, including provisions governing such fares or charges, applicable via and for account of such carrier. Agents may be only natural persons or corporations (other than incorporated associations of air carriers). The authority conferred in a power of attorney may not be delegated to any other person.

(b) *Designation of tariff issuing person by corporate agent.* When a corporation has been appointed as agent it shall forward to the Department a certified excerpt of the minutes of the meeting of its Board of Directors designating by name and title the person responsible for issuing tariffs and filing them with the Department. Only one such person may be designated by a corporate agent, and the title of such designee shall not contain the word "Agent". When such a designee is replaced the Department shall be immediately notified in like manner of his successor. An officer or employee of an incorporated tariff-publishing agent may not be authorized to act as tariff agent in his/her individual capacity. Every tariff issued by a corporate agent shall be issued in its name as agent.

(c) *Number of copies.* Each power of attorney shall be prepared in triplicate. The original of each power of attorney shall be filed with the Department, the duplicate thereof shall be given to the agent in whose favor the power of attorney is issued, and the third copy shall be retained by the carrier who issued the power of attorney.

(d) *Conflicting authority prohibited.* In giving powers of attorney, carriers shall not give authority to two or more agents which, if used, would result in conflicting or duplicate tariff provisions.

§221.151 Method of revoking power of attorney.

(a) A power of attorney may be revoked only by filing with the Department in the manner specified in this section a Notice of Revocation of Power of Attorney in a form acceptable to the Office of International Aviation.

(b) *Sixty days' notice required.* Such Notice of Revocation of Power of Attorney shall be filed on not less than sixty days' notice to the Department. A Notice of Revocation of Power of Attorney will be deemed to be filed only upon its actual receipt by the Department, and the period of notice shall commence to run only from such actual receipt.

(c) *Number of copies.* Each Notice of Revocation of Power of Attorney shall be prepared in triplicate. The original thereof shall be filed with the Department and, at the same time that the original is transmitted to the Department, the duplicate thereof shall be sent to the agent in whose favor the power of attorney was issued (except, if the alternate agent has taken over the tariffs, the duplicate of the Notice of Revocation of Power of Attorney shall be sent to the alternate agent). The third copy of the notice shall be retained by the carrier.

(d) *Amendment of tariffs when power of attorney is revoked.* When a power of attorney is revoked, a corresponding amendment of the tariff or tariffs affected shall be made by the issuing agent of such tariffs, on not less than statutory notice, to become effective not later than the effective date stated in the Notice of Revocation of Power of Attorney. In the event of failure to so amend the tariff or tariffs, the provisions therein shall remain applicable until lawfully canceled.

§221.152 Method of withdrawing portion of authority conferred by power of attorney.

If a carrier desires to issue a power of attorney conferring less authority than a previous power of attorney issued in favor of the same agent, the new power of attorney shall not direct the cancellation of such previous power of attorney. In such circumstances, such previous power of attorney shall be revoked by issuing and filing a Notice of Revocation of Power of Attorney in a form acceptable to the Office of International Aviation. Such revocation notice shall include reference to the new power of attorney.

Subpart Q—Adoption Publications Required To Show Change in Carrier's Name or Transfer of Operating Control

§221.160 Adoption notice.

(a) When the name of a carrier is changed or when its operating control is transferred to another carrier (including another company which has not previously been a carrier), the carrier which will thereafter operate the properties shall immediately issue, file with the Department, and post for public inspection, an adoption notice in a form and containing such information as is approved by the Office of International Aviation. (The carrier under its former name or the carrier from whom the operating control is transferred shall be referred to in this subpart as the "former carrier", and the carrier under its new name or the carrier, company, or fiduciary to whom the operating control is transferred shall be referred to in this subpart as the "adopting carrier".)

(b) The adoption notice shall be prepared, filed, and posted as a tariff. The adoption notice shall be issued and filed by the adopting carrier and not by an agent.

(c) *Copies to be sent to agents and other carriers.* At the same time that the adoption notice is transmitted to the Department for filing, the adopting carrier shall send copies of such adoption notice to each agent and carrier to whom the former carrier has given a power of attorney or concurrence. (See § 221.163.)

§ 221.161 Notice of adoption to be filed in former carrier's tariffs.

At the same time that the adoption notice is issued, posted, and filed pursuant to § 221.160, the adopting carrier shall issue, post and file with the Department a notice in each effective tariff issued by the former carrier providing specific notice of the adoption in a manner authorized by the Office of International Aviation and which shall contain no matter other than that authorized.

§ 221.162 Receiver shall file adoption notices.

A receiver shall, immediately upon assuming control of a carrier, issue and file with the Department an adoption notices as prescribed by §§ 221.160 and 221.161 and shall comply with the requirements of this subpart.

§ 221.163 Agents' and other carriers' tariffs shall reflect adoption.

If the former carrier is shown as a participating carrier under concurrence in tariffs issued by other carriers or is shown as a participating carrier under power of attorney in tariffs issued by agents, the issuing carriers and agents of such tariffs shall, upon receipt of the adoption notice, promptly file on statutory notice the following amendments to their respective tariffs:

(a) Cancel the name of the former carrier from the list of participating carriers.

(b) Add the adopting carrier (in alphabetical order) to the list of participating carriers. If the adopting carrier already participates in such tariff, reference to the substitution notice shall be added in connection with such carrier's name in the list of participating carriers.

§ 221.164 Concurrences or powers of attorney to be reissued.

(a) Adopting carrier shall reissue adopted concurrences and powers of attorney. Within a period of 120 days after the date on which the change in name or transfer of operating control occurs, the adopting carrier shall reissue all effective powers of attorney and concurrences of the former carrier by issuing and filing new powers of attorney and concurrences, in the adopting carrier's name, which shall direct the cancellation of the respective powers of attorney and concurrences of the former carrier. The adopting carrier shall consecutively number its powers of attorney and concurrences in its own series of power of attorney numbers and concurrence numbers (commencing with No. 1 in each series if it had not previously filed any such instruments with the Department), except that a receiver or other fiduciary shall consecutively number its powers of attorney or concurrences in the series of the former carrier. The cancellation reference shall show that the canceled power of attorney or concurrence was issued by the former carrier.

(b) If such new powers of attorney or concurrences confer less authority than the powers of attorney or concurrences which they are to supersede, the new issues shall not direct the cancellation of the former issues; in such instances, the provisions of §§ 221.142 and 221.152 shall be observed. Concurrences and powers of attorney which will not be replaced by new issues shall be revoked in the form and manner and upon the notice required by §§ 221.141 and 221.151.

(c) *Reissue of other carriers' concurrences issued in favor of former carrier.* Each carrier which has given a concurrence to a carrier whose tariffs are subsequently adopted shall reissue the concurrence in favor of the adopting carrier. If the carrier which issued the concurrence to the former carrier desires to revoke it or desires to replace it with a concurrence conferring less authority, the provisions of §§221.141 and 221.142 shall be observed.

§221.165 Cessation of operations without successor.

If a carrier ceases operations without having a successor, it shall:

(a) File a notice in each tariff of its own issue and cancel such tariff in its entirety.

(b) Revoke all powers of attorney and concurrences which it has issued.

Subpart R—Electronically Filed Tariffs

§221.170 Applicability of the subpart.

(a) Every air carrier and foreign air carrier shall file its international passenger fares tariffs consistent with the provisions of this subpart, and part 221 generally. Additionally, any air carrier and any foreign air carrier may file its international passenger rules tariffs electronically in machine-readable form as an alternative to the filing of printed paper tariffs as provided for elsewhere in part 221. This subpart applies to all carriers and tariff publishing agents and may be used by either if the carrier or agent complies with the provisions of subpart R. Any carrier or agent that files electronically under this subpart must transmit to the Department the remainder of the tariff in a form consistent with part 221, Subparts A through Q, on the same day that the electronic tariff would be deemed received under §221.190(b).

(b) To the extent that subpart R is inconsistent with the remainder of part 221, subpart R shall govern the filing of electronic tariffs. In all other respects, part 221 remains in full force and effect.

§221.180 Requirements for electronic filing of tariffs.

(a) No carrier or filing agent shall file an electronic tariff unless, prior to filing, it has signed a maintenance agreement or agreements, furnished by the Department of Transportation, for the maintenance and security of the on-line tariff database.

(b) No carrier or agent shall file an electronic tariff unless, prior to filing, it has submitted to the Department's Office of International Aviation, Pricing and Multilateral Affairs Division, and received approval of, an application containing the following commitments:

(1) The filer shall file tariffs electronically only in such format as shall be agreed to by the filer and the Department. (The filer shall include with its application a proposed format of tariff. The filer shall also submit to the Department all information necessary for the Department to determine that the proposed format will accommodate the data elements set forth in §221.202.)

(2) The filer shall provide, maintain and install in the Public Reference Room at the Department (as may be required from time to time) one or more CRT devices and printers connected to its on-line tariff database. The filer shall be responsible for the transportation, installation, and maintenance of this equipment and shall agree to indemnify and hold harmless the Department and the U.S. Government from any claims or liabilities resulting from defects in the equipment, its installation or maintenance.

(3) The filer shall provide public access to its on-line tariff database, at Departmental headquarters, during normal business hours.

(4) The access required at Departmental headquarters by this subpart shall be provided at no cost to the public or the Department.

(5) The filer shall provide the Department access to its on-line tariff database 24 hours a day, 7 days a week, except, that the filer may bring its computer down between 6:00 a.m. and 6:00 p.m. Eastern Standard Time or Eastern Daylight Saving Time, as the case may be, on Sundays, when necessary, for maintenance or for operational reasons.

(6) The filer shall ensure that the Department shall have the sole ability to approve or disapprove electronically any tariff filed with the Department and the ability to note, record and retain electronically the reasons for approval or disapproval. The carrier or agent shall not make any changes in data or delete data after it has been transmitted electronically, regardless of whether it is approved, disapproved, or withdrawn. The filer shall be required to make data fields available to the Department in any record which is part of the on-line tariff database.

(7) The filer shall maintain all fares and rules filed with the Department and all Departmental approvals, disapprovals and other actions, as well as all Departmental notations concerning such approvals, disapprovals or other actions, in the on-line tariff database for a period of two (2) years after the fare or rule becomes inactive. After this period of time, the carrier or agent shall provide the Department, free of charge, with a copy of the inactive data on a machine-readable tape or other mutually acceptable electronic medium.

(8) The filer shall ensure that its on-line tariff database is secure against destruction or alteration (except as authorized by the Department), and against tampering.

(9) Should the filer terminate its business or cease filing tariffs, it shall provide to the Department on a machine-readable tape or any other mutually acceptable electronic medium, contemporaneously with the cessation of such business, a complete copy of its on-line tariff database.

(10) The filer shall furnish to the Department, on a daily basis, on a machine-readable tape or any other mutually acceptable electronic medium, all transactions made to its on-line tariff database.

(11) The filer shall afford any authorized Departmental official full, free, and uninhibited access to its facilities, databases, documentation, records, and application programs, including support functions, environmental security, and accounting data, for the purpose of ensuring continued effectiveness of safeguards against threats and hazards to the security or integrity of its electronic tariffs, as defined in this subpart.

(12) The filer must provide a field in the Government Filing File for the signature of the approving U.S. Government Official through the use of a Personal Identification Number (PIN).

(13) The filer shall provide a leased dedicated data conditioned circuit with sufficient capacity (not less than 28.8K baud rate) to handle electronic data transmissions to the Department. Further, the filer must provide for a secondary or a redundancy circuit in the event of the failure of the dedicated circuit. The secondary or redundancy circuit must be equal to or greater than 14.4K baud rate. In the event of a failure of the primary circuit the filer must notify the Chief of the Pricing and Multilateral Affairs Division of the Department's Office of International Aviation, as soon as possible, after the failure of the primary circuit, but not later than two hours after failure, and must provide the name of the contact person at the telephone company who has the responsibility for dealing with the problem.

(c) Each time a filer's on-line tariff database is accessed by any user during the sign-on function the following statement shall appear:

The information contained in this system is for informational purposes only, and is a representation of tariff data that has been formally submitted to the Department of Transportation in accordance with applicable law or a bilateral treaty to which the U.S. Government is a party.

§221.190 Time for filing and computation of time periods.

(a) A tariff, or revision thereto, or a special tariff permission application may be electronically filed with the Department immediately upon compliance with §221.180, and anytime thereafter, subject to §221.400. The actual date and time of filing shall be noted with each filing.

(b) For the purpose of determining the date that a tariff, or revision thereto, filed pursuant to this subpart, shall be deemed received by the Department:

(1) For all electronic tariffs, or revisions thereto, filed before 5:30 p.m.

local time in Washington, DC, on Federal business days, such date shall be the actual date of filing.

(2) For all electronic tariffs, or revisions thereto, filed after 5:30 p.m. local time in Washington, DC, on Federal business days, and for all electronic tariffs, or revisions thereto, filed on days that are not Federal business days, such date shall be the next Federal business day.

§ 221.195 Requirement for filing printed material.

(a) Any tariff, or revision thereto, filed in paper format which accompanies, governs, or otherwise affects, a tariff filed electronically, must be received by the Department on the same date that a tariff or revision thereto, is filed electronically with the Department under § 221.190(b). Further, such paper tariff, or revision thereto, shall be filed in accordance with the requirements of subparts A through Q of part 221. No tariff or revision thereto, filed electronically under this subpart, shall contain an effective date which is at variance with the effective date of the supporting paper tariff, except as authorized by the Department.

(b) Any printed justifications, or other information accompanying a tariff, or revision thereto, filed electronically under this subpart, must be received by the Department on the same date as any tariff, or revision thereto, filed electronically.

(c) If a filer submits a filing which fails to comply with paragraph (a) of this section, or if the filer fails to submit the information in conformity with paragraph (b) of this section, the filing will be subject to rejection, denial, or disapproval, as applicable.

§ 221.200 Content and explanation of abbreviations, reference marks and symbols.

(a) *Content.* The format to be used for any electronic tariff must be that agreed to in advance as provided for in § 221.180, and must include those data elements set forth in § 221.202. Those portions that are filed in paper form shall comply in all respects with part 221, subparts A through Q.

(b) *Explanation of abbreviations, reference marks and symbols.* Abbreviations, reference marks and symbols which are used in the tariff shall be explained in each tariff.

(1) The following symbols shall be used:

R—Reduction
I—Increase
N—New Matter
X—Canceled Matter
C—Change in Footnotes, Routings, Rules or Zones
E—Denotes change in Effective Date only.

(2) Other symbols may be used only when an explanation is provided in each tariff and such symbols are consistent throughout all the electronically filed tariffs from that time forward.

§ 221.201 Statement of filing with foreign governments to be shown in air carrier's tariff filings.

(a) Every electronic tariff filed by or on behalf of an air carrier that contains fares which, by international convention or agreement entered into between any other country and the United States, are required to be filed with that country, shall include the following statement:

> The rates, fares, charges, classifications, rules, regulations, practices, and services provided herein have been filed in each country in which filing is required by treaty, convention, or agreement entered into between that country and the United States, in accordance with the provisions of the applicable treaty, convention, or agreement.

(b) The statement referenced in § 221.201(a) may be included with each filing advice by the inclusion of a symbol which is properly explained.

(c) The required symbol may be omitted from an electronic tariff or portion thereof if the tariff publication that has been filed with any other country pursuant to its tariff regulations bears a tariff filing designation of that country in addition to the D.O.T. number appearing on the tariff.

§ 221.202 The filing of tariffs and amendments to tariffs.

All electronic tariffs and amendments filed under this subpart, including those for which authority is sought to effect changes on less than bilateral/statutory notice under § 221.212, shall contain the following data elements:

(a) A Filing Advice Status File—which shall include:

(1) Filing date and time;

(2) Filing advice number;

(3) Reference to carrier;

(4) Reference to geographic area;

(5) Effective date of amendment or tariff;

(6) A place for government action to be recorded; and

(7) Reference to the Special Tariff Permission when applicable.

(b) A Government Filing File—which shall include:

(1) Filing advice number;

(2) Carrier reference;

(3) Filing date and time;

(4) Proposed effective date;

(5) Justification text; reference to geographic area and affected tariff number;

(6) Reference to the Special Tariff Permission when applicable;

(7) Government control data, including places for:

(i) Name of the government analyst, except that this data shall not be made public, notwithstanding any other provision in this or any other subpart;

(ii) Action taken and reasons therefor.

(iii) Remarks, except that internal Departmental data shall not be made public, notwithstanding any other provision in this or any other subpart;

(iv) Date action is taken; and

(v) Personal Identification Number; and

(8) Fares tariff, or proposed changes to the fares tariffs, including:

(i) Market;

(ii) Fare code;

(iii) One-way/roundtrip (O/R);

(iv) Fare Amount;

(v) Currency;

(vi) Footnote (FN);

(vii) Rule Number, provided that, if the rule number is in a tariff, reference shall be made to that tariff containing the rule;

(viii) Routing (RG) Number(s), provided that the abbreviation MPM (Maximum Permissible Routing) shall be considered a number for the purpose of this file;

(ix) Effective date and discontinue date if the record has been superseded;

(x) Percent of change from previous fares; and

(xi) Expiration date.

(9) Rules tariff, or proposed changes to the rules tariffs.

(i) Rules tariffs shall include:

(A) Title: General description of fare rule type and geographic area under the rule;

(B) Application: Specific description of fare class, geographic area, type of transportation (one way, round-trip, etc.);

(C) Period of Validity: Specific description of permissible travel dates and any restrictions on when travel is not permitted;

(D) Reservations/ticketing: Specific description of reservation and ticketing provisions, including any advance reservation/ticketing requirements, provisions for payment (including prepaid tickets), and charges for any changes;

(E) Capacity Control: Specific description of any limitation on the number of passengers, available seats, or tickets;

(F) Combinations: Specific description of permitted/restricted fare combinations;

(G) Length of Stay: Specific description of minimum/maximum number of days before the passenger may/must begin return travel;

(H) Stopovers: Specific description of permissible conditions, restrictions, or charges on stopovers;

(I) Routing: Specific description of routing provisions, including transfer provisions, whether on-line or interline;

(J) Discounts: Specific description of any limitations, special conditions, and discounts on status fares, e.g. children or infants, senior citizens, tour conductors, or travel agents, and any other discounts;

(K) Cancellation and Refunds: Specific description of any special conditions, charges, or credits due for cancellation or changes to reservations, or for request for refund of purchased tickets;

(L) Group Requirements: Specific description of group size, travel conditions, group eligibility, and documentation;

(M) Tour Requirements: Specific description of tour requirements, including minimum price, and any stay or accommodation provisions;

(N) Sales Restrictions: Specific description of any restrictions on the sale of tickets;

(O) Rerouting: Specific description of rerouting provisions, whether on-line or inter-line, including any applicable charges; and

(P) Miscellaneous provisions: Any other applicable conditions.

(ii) Rules tariffs shall not contain the phrase "intentionally left blank".

(10) Any material accepted by the Department for informational purposes only shall be clearly identified as "for informational purposes only, not part of official tariff", in a manner acceptable to the Department.

(c) A Historical File—which shall include:

(1) Market;

(2) Fare code;

(3) One-way/roundtrip (O/R);

(4) Fare amount;

(5) Currency;

(6) Footnote (FN);

(7) Rule Number, provided that, if the rule number is in a tariff other than the fare tariff, reference shall be made to that tariff containing the rule;

(8) Rule text applicable to each fare at the time that the fare was in effect.

(9) Routing (RG) Number(s), provided that the abbreviation MPM (Maximum Permissible Routing) shall be considered a number for the purpose of this file;

(10) Effective Date;

(11) Discontinue Date;

(12) Government Action;

(13) Carrier;

(14) All inactive fares (two years);

(15) Any other fare data which is essential; and

(16) Any necessary cross reference to the Government Filing File for research or other purposes.

§221.203 Unique rule numbers required.

(a) Each "bundled" and "unbundled" normal economy fare applicable to foreign air transportation shall bear a unique rule number.

(b) The unique rule numbers for the fares specified in this section shall be set by mutual agreement between the filer and the Department prior to the implementation of any electronic filing system.

§221.204 Adoption of provisions of one carrier by another carrier.

When one carrier adopts the tariffs of another carrier, the effective and prospective fares of the adopted carrier shall be changed to reflect the name of the adopting carrier and the effective date of the adoption. Further, each adopted fare shall bear a notation which shall reflect the name of the adopted carrier and the effective date of the adoption, provided that any subsequent revision of an adopted fare may omit the notation.

§221.205 Justification and explanation for certain fares.

Any carrier or its agent must provide, as to any new or increased bundled or unbundled (whichever is lower) on-demand economy fare in a direct-service market, a comparison between, on the one hand, that proposed fare and, on the other hand, the ceiling fare allowed in that market based on the SFFL.

§221.206 Statement of fares.

All fares filed electronically in direct-service markets shall be filed as single factor fares.

§221.210 Suspension of tariffs.

(a) A fare, charge, rule or other tariff provision that is suspended by the Department pursuant to section 41509 of the statute shall be noted by the Department in the Government Filing File and the Historical File.

(b) When the Department vacates a tariff suspension, in full or in part, and after notification of the carrier by the Department, such event shall be noted by the carrier in the Government Filing File and the Historical File.

(c) When a tariff suspension is vacated or when the tariff becomes effective upon termination of the suspension period, the carrier or its agent shall refile the tariff showing the effective date.

§221.211 Cancellation of suspended matter.

When, pursuant to an order of the Department, the cancellation of rules, fares, charges, or other tariff provision is required, such action shall be made by the carrier by appropriate revisions to the tariff.

§221.212 Special tariff permission.

(a) When a filer submits an electronic tariff or an amendment to an electronic tariff for which authority is sought to effect changes on less than bilateral/statutory notice, and no related tariff material is involved, the submission shall bear a sequential filing advice number. The submission shall appear in the Government Filing File and the Filing Advice Status File, and shall be referenced in such a manner to clearly indicate that such changes are sought to be made on less than bilateral/statutory notice.

(b) When a filer submits an electronic tariff or an amendment to the electronic tariff for which authority is sought to effect changes on less than bilateral/statutory notice, and it contains related paper under §221.195, the paper submission must bear the same filing advice number as that used for the electronic submission. Such paper submission shall be in the form of a revised tariff page rather than as a separate request for Special Tariff Permission. All material being submitted on a paper tariff page as part of an electronic submission will clearly indicate the portion(s) of such tariff page that is being filed pursuant to, and in conjunction with, the electronic submission on less than bilateral/statutory notice.

(c) Departmental action on the Special Tariff Permission request shall be noted by the Department in the Government Filing File and the Filing Advice Status File.

(d) When the paper portion of a Special Tariff Permission that has been filed with the Department pursuant to paragraph (b) of this section is disapproved or other action is taken by the Department, such disapproval or other action will be reflected on the next consecutive revision of the affected tariff page(s) in the following manner:

(1) Example of disapproval statement:

The portion(s) of ___ Revised Page ___ filed under EFA No. ___ was/were disapproved by DOT.

(2) Example of other action:

The portion(s) ___ Revised Page ___ filed under EFA No. ___ was/were required to be amended by DOT.

(e) When the Department disapproves in whole or in part or otherwise takes an action against any submission filed under this part, the filer must take corrective action within two business days following the disapproval or notice of other action.

(f) All submissions under this section shall comply with the requirements of §221.202.

§221.300 Discontinuation of electronic tariff system.

In the event that the electronic tariff system is discontinued, or the source of the data is changed, or a filer discontinues its business, all electronic data records prior to such date shall be provided immediately to the Department, free of charge, on a machine-readable tape or other mutually acceptable electronic medium.

§221.400 Filing of paper tariffs required.

(a) After approval of any application filed under §221.180 of this subpart to allow a filer to file tariffs electronically, the filer in addition to filing electronically must continue to file printed tariffs as required by subparts A through Q of part 221 for a period of 90 days, or until such time as the Department shall deem such filing no longer to be necessary. *Provided* that during the period specified by this section the filed printed tariff shall continue to be the official tariff.

(b) Upon notification to the filer that it may commence to file its tariffs solely in an electronic mode, concurrently with the implementation of filing electronically the filer shall:

(1) Furnish the Department with a copy of all the existing effective and prospective records on a machine-readable tape or other mutually acceptable electronic medium accompanied by an

affidavit attesting to the accuracy of such records; and

(2) Simultaneously cancel such records from the paper tariff in the manner prescribed by subparts A through Q of part 221.

§221.500 Transmission of electronic tariffs to subscribers.

(a) Each filer that files an electronic tariff under this subpart shall make available to any person so requesting, a subscription service meeting the terms of paragraph (b) of this section.

(b) Under the required subscription service, remote access shall be allowed to any subscriber to the on-line tariff database, including access to the justification required by §221.205. The subscription service shall not preclude the offering of additional services by the filer or its agent.

(c) The filer at its option may establish a charge for providing the required subscription service to subscribers: Provided that the charge may not exceed a reasonable estimate of the added cost of providing the service.

(d) Each filer shall provide to any person upon request, a copy of the machine-readable data (raw tariff data) of all daily transactions made to its on-line tariff database. The terms and prices for such value-added service may be set by the filer: Provided that such terms and prices shall be non-discriminatory, *i.e.*, that they shall be substantially equivalent for all similarly-situated persons.

§221.550 Copies of tariffs made from filer's printer(s) located in Department's public reference room.

Copies of information contained in a filer's on-line tariff database may be obtained by any user at Departmental Headquarters from the printer or printers placed in Tariff Public Reference Room by the filer. The filer may assess a fee for copying, provided it is reasonable and that no administrative burden is placed on the Department to require the collection of the fee or to provide any service in connection therewith.

§221.600 Actions under assigned authority and petitions for review of staff action.

(a) When an electronically filed record which has been submitted to the Department under this subpart, is disapproved (rejected), or a special tariff permission is approved or denied, under authority assigned by the Department of Transportation's Regulations, 14 CFR 385.13, such actions shall be understood to include the following provisions:

(1) *Applicable to a record or records which is/are disapproved (rejected).* The record(s) disapproved (rejected) is/are void, without force or effect, and must not be used.

(2) *Applicable to a record or records which is/are disapproved (rejected), and to special tariff permissions which are approved or denied.* This action is taken under authority assigned by the Department of Transportation in its Organization Regulations, 14 CFR 385.13. Persons entitled to petition for review of this action pursuant to the Department's Regulations, 14 CFR 385.50, may file such petitions within seven days after the date of this action. This action shall become effective immediately, and the filing of a petition for review shall not preclude its effectiveness.

(b) [Reserved]

PART 222—INTERMODAL CARGO SERVICES BY FOREIGN AIR CARRIERS

Sec.

AUTHORITY: Secs. 204, 402, Pub. L. 85–726, as amended, 72 Stat. 743, 757; 49 U.S.C. 1324, 1372.

SOURCE: ER–1228, 46 FR 32556, June 24, 1981, unless otherwise noted.

§222.1 Applicability.

This part applies to all air transportation of property that includes both air movement by a direct foreign air carrier and surface transportation to or from any point within the United States (hereafter referred to as "intermodal cargo services").

§ 222.2 Scope of permissible intermodal cargo services.

(a) Under its foreign air carrier permit, a direct foreign air carrier may provide or control the surface portion of intermodal cargo services within a zone extending 35 miles from the boundary of the airport or city it is authorized to serve. A direct foreign air carrier shall not provide or control the surface portion of intermodal cargo services outside of this 35-mile zone unless authorized to do so by the Board in accordance with §§ 222.3, 222.4 and 222.5.

(b) A direct foreign air carrier shall be considered to control the surface portion of intermodal cargo services if it has or publicly represents that it has any responsibility for or control over the movement of, or has any ownership, controlling or exclusive dealing relationship with, the carrier actually providing the surface transportation.

(c) Except as provided in paragraphs (a) and (b) of this section with respect to control by a direct foreign air carrier, any U.S. or foreign indirect air carrier, surface carrier or surface freight forwarder may provide the surface portion of intermodal cargo services without limitation as to geographic area within the United States.

(d) The Board may withdraw the authority of an indirect foreign air carrier to provide the surface portion of intermodal cargo services, or the authority of a direct foreign air carrier to offer intermodal cargo services pursuant to joint fares with other carriers providing the surface transportation, at any time, with or without hearing, if the Board finds it in the public interest.

§ 222.3 Application for Statement of Authorization.

(a) Application for a Statement of Authorization shall be filed with the Board's Regulatory Affairs Division, Bureau of International Aviation, in duplicate, on CAB Form 222 (obtainable from the Civil Aeronautics Board, Publications Services Division, Washington, D.C. 20428), attached as Appendix A. In most cases the Board will act upon applications for Statements of Authorization within 60 days.

(b) Persons objecting to an application for a Statement of Authorization shall file their objections with the Regulatory Affairs Division, Bureau of International Aviation, within 28 days of the filing date of the application. The Board will list the names and nationalities of all persons applying for Statements of Authorization in its Weekly Summary of Filings.

(c) An application shall include a copy of any bilateral agreement, memorandum of consultations, or diplomatic note or letter, in support of the authority requested. Documents that appear in official U.S. publications may be incorporated by reference.

(Approved by the Office of Management and Budget under control number 3024–0045)

[ER–1228, 46 FR 32556, June 24, 1981, as amended by ER–1348, 48 FR 31635, July 11, 1983]

§ 222.4 Procedure on receipt of application for Statement of Authorization.

(a) After review of an application form filed under § 222.3, the Board will take one or more of the following actions:

(1) Indicate by stamp on CAB Form 222 the effective date of the Statement of Authorization, and return to the carrier the duplicate copy of Form 222 as evidence of approval under this part;

(2) Request additional information from the applicant;

(3) Set the application for notice and hearing procedures;

(4) Disapprove the application or approve it subject to such terms, conditions, or limitations as may be required by the public interest; or

(5) Reject the application on the grounds that there is no agreement by the United States authorizing the proposed services.

(b) An order disapproving an application or subjecting it to conditions or limitations shall be transmitted to the President for stay or disapproval. If the President does not stay or disapprove the Board's order, it shall become effective on the 31st day after transmittal to the President, or within any longer time period established in the order.

§222.5 Cancellation or conditioning of a Statement of Authorization.

A Statement of Authorization may be canceled or made subject to additional terms, conditions, or limitations, at any time, with or without hearing, if the Board finds that it is in the public interest to do so. An order canceling or conditioning a Statement of Authorization shall be submitted to the President for stay or disapproval and shall become effective on the 31st day after transmittal or within any longer time period established by the Board.

Appendix A to Part 222—CAB Form 222

Appendix A

CAB Form 222

UNITED STATES OF AMERICA
CIVIL AERONAUTICS BOARD

FOREIGN AIR CARRIER APPLICATION FOR
STATEMENT OF AUTHORIZATION FOR
INTERMODAL CARGO SERVICES

DO NOT WRITE - FOR
OFFICIAL USE ONLY

TO: CIVIL AERONAUTICS BOARD
ATTENTION: Regulatory Affairs Division
Bureau of International Aviation
Washington, D.C. 20428

Application is made for a Statement of Authorization to conduct intermodal cargo services under provisions of the applicants' foreign air carrier permit and Economic Regulation Part 222.

☐ Initial Application ☐ Change of Name/Address/Nationality

☐ Application for Removal of conditions

1. Name of Applicant:

Nationality:

2. Send Authorization to:
(Name and Address)

3. (a) estimated annual tonnage of cargo to be shipped by surface transportation: ______________

(b) percentage of total air cargo to be shiped by surface transportation beyond 35-mile pick-up and delivery zone.

4. Area in the United States to be served by surface transportation

CERTIFICATION

I certify that the information contained in this application, and in the attachments hereto, is complete and accurate to the best of my knowledge.

Signature: ______________________

Date: ________________ Name: ______________________
(please type)

Place: ________________ Title: ______________________
(see note)

NOTE: Application must be signed by a responsible officer, such as the President, Vice President, Secretary, or Treasurer of a corporation, or a partner or owner of other non-corporate applicants.

FOR CAB USE ONLY

Special conditions or limitations/reasons for disapproval/rejection/findings.

PART 223—FREE AND REDUCED-RATE TRANSPORTATION

Subpart A—General Provisions

Subpart B—Domestic Travel

Subpart C—International Travel

AUTHORITY: Secs. 204, 403, 404, 405(j), 407, 416, Pub. L. 85–726, as amended, 72 Stat. 743, 758, 760, 766, 771, 49 U.S.C. 1325, 1373, 1374, 1375, 1377, 1386, sec. 2 of the Postal Reorganization Act, 84 Stat. 767, 39 U.S.C. 5007.

SOURCE: ER–1371, 48 FR 57118, Dec. 28, 1983, unless otherwise noted.

Subpart A—General Provisions

§ 223.1 Definitions.

As used in this part, unless the context otherwise requires:

An *affiliate* of a carrier means a person:

(a) Who controls that carrier, or is controlled by that carrier or by another person who controls or is controlled by that carrier; and

(b) Whose principal business in purpose or in fact is:

(1) The holding of stock in one or more carriers;

(2) Transportation by air or the sale of tickets therefor;

(3) The operation of one or more airports, one or more of which are used by that carrier or by another carrier who controls or is controlled by that carrier or that is under common control with that carrier by another person; or

(4) Activities related to the transportation by air conducted by that carrier or by another carrier that controls or is controlled by that carrier or which is under common control with that carrier by another person.

Air carrier means the holder of a certificate of public convenience and necessity issued by the Board under section 401 of the Act authorizing the carriage of persons.

Attendant means any person required by a handicapped person in order to travel, whether or not that person's services are required while the handicapped passenger is in an aircraft.

Carrier means:

(a) An air carrier;

(b) An all-cargo air carrier operating under section 401 or section 418 of the Act;

(c) A foreign air carrier;

(d) An intrastate carrier;

(e) An air taxi (including a commuter air carrier) operating under parts 294 or 298 of this chapter; and

(f) Any person operating as a common carrier by air, or in the carriage of mail by air, or conducting transportation by air, in a foreign country.

Control, as used in this section, means the beneficial ownership of more than 40 percent of outstanding capital stock unless, ownership of more than 40 percent of outstanding capital stock unless, in a specific case, the Board determines under section 408 of the Act that control does not exist. Control may be direct or by or through one or more intermediate subsidiaries likewise controlled or controlling through beneficial ownership of more than 40 percent of outstanding voting capital stock.

Delivery flight means a flight from a point in the United States where a carrier has taken delivery of a newly manufactured aircraft to any point or points on its route system.

Foreign air carrier means the holder of a permit issued by the Board under section 402 of the Act authorizing the carriage of persons.

Free transportation means the carriage by an air carrier or foreign air carrier of any person or property (other than property owned by that carrier) in air transportation without compensation therefor.

Handicapped passenger means any person who has a physical or mental impairment (other than drug addiction or alcoholism), that substantially limits one or more major life activities.

Inaugural flight means a flight on an aircraft type being introduced by a carrier for the first time on a route, even if that aircraft type has been used by that carrier on other routes or on that route by other carriers.

Pass means a written authorization, other than actual ticket stock, issued by a carrier for free or reduced-rate transportation of persons or property.

Reduced-rate transportation means the carriage by an air carrier or foreign air carrier of any person or property (other than property owned by such carrier) in air transportation for a compensation less than that specified in the tariffs of that carrier on file with the Board and otherwise applicable to such carriage.

Retired means:

(a) With respect to carrier directors, officers, and employees, persons receiving retirement benefits from any carrier;

(b) With respect to the general public, persons not regularly working at a full-time paying job, and not intending to do so in the future.

§223.2 Exemption from section 401 of the Act.

(a) Any all-cargo carrier is exempted from section 401 of the Act to the extent necessary to carry, for purposes of in-flight observation, technical representatives of companies that have been engaged in the manufacture, development, or testing of aircraft or aircraft equipment.

(b) Every carrier providing transportation under this section shall also comply with the applicable regulations of the Federal Aviation Administration such as regulations pertaining to admission of persons to the aircraft flight deck.

§223.3 Mandatory free transportation.

Every air carrier shall carry, without charge, on any aircraft that it operates, the following persons:

(a) Security guards who have been assigned to the duty of guarding such aircraft against unlawful seizure, sabotage or other unlawful interference, upon the exhibition of such credentials as may be prescribed by the Administrator of the Federal Aviation Administration;

(b) Safety inspectors of the National Transportation Safety Board or of the Federal Aviation Administration who have been assigned to the duty of inspecting during flight such aircraft or its equipment, route facilities, operational procedures, or airman competency upon the exhibition of credentials or a certificate from the agency involved in authorizing such transportation; and

(c) Postal employees on duty in charge of the mails or traveling to or from such duty, upon the exhibition of the credentials issued by the Postmaster General.

§223.4 Transferability of passes.

Any pass authorizing free or reduced-rate transportation issued by a carrier may be made transferable to the extent specified by the granting carrier.

§223.5 Responsibility of agencies.

The Federal Aviation Administration, National Transportation Safety Board, National Weather Service, and the Postal Service shall be responsible for the following:

(a) The issuance of any credentials or certificates to their personnel eligible for free or reduced-rate transportation under this part; and

(b) The promulgation of any internal rules that are necessary to obtain compliance by such personnel with this part.

§223.6 Carrier's rules.

(a) Each air carrier and foreign air carrier shall maintain at its principal office either a copy or all instructions to its employees and of all company rules governing its practice in connection with the issuance and interchange of free and reduced-rate transportation passes or a statement describing those practices.

(b) The rules or statement required by this section shall, at a minimum, include the following:

(1) The titles of its officials upon whose authorizations passes may be issued;

(2) The titles of other officials who are authorized by these officials to

countersign passes on their behalf, and the extent of the authority granted to them; and

(3) The titles of persons who are authorized to request passes from other carriers.

(c) The rules, instructions, or statement required by this section shall be furnished to the Board upon request or to a member of the public upon payment of a reasonable charge for this service.

(Approved by the Office of Management and Budget under control number 3024–0002)

Subpart B—Domestic Travel

§ 223.11 Free and reduced-rate transportation permitted.

Air carriers may charge any rate or fare for interstate and overseas air transportation.

Subpart C—International Travel

§ 223.21 Free and reduced-rate transportation authorized by statute or regulation.

(a) Any air carrier or foreign air carrier may provide free or reduced-rate foreign air transportation to any classes of persons specifically named in section 403(b) of the Act or free transportation to those named in § 375.35 of this chapter.

(b) Air carriers and foreign air carriers may offer reduced fares for foreign air transportation to ministers of religion, the elderly, retired, and handicapped passengers, and to attendants required by handicapped passengers, but shall file tariffs for such fares. Carriers may establish reasonable tariff rules to assist in identifying those who qualify for reduced fares.

§ 223.22 Other persons to whom free and reduced-rate transportation may be furnished.

Air carriers and foreign air carriers are exempted from sections 403 and 404(b) of the Act and part 221 of this chapter to the extent necessary to provide free or reduced-rate foreign air transportation, including passes, to the following:

(a) Directors, officers, employees, and retirees and members of their immediate families, of any carrier or of any affiliate of such carrier, subject to the requirements of § 223.25.

(b) Persons to whom the carrier is required to furnish such transportation by law or government directive or by a contract or agreement between the carrier and the government of any country served by the carrier. The Board may, without prior notice, direct the carrier to file a tariff covering such transportation if it finds that the law or government directive in question requires the provision of such transportation. This transportation may be provided only if:

(1) The contract or agreement is filed with the Board, and it is not disapproved by the Board; and

(2) The law or government directive does not require the furnishing of such transportation to the general public or any segment thereof.

(c) Technical representatives of companies that have been engaged in the manufacture, development or testing of a particular type of aircraft or aircraft equipment, when the transportation is provided for the purposes of in-flight observation, and subject to applicable regulations of the Federal Aviation Administration such as regulations pertaining to admission of persons to the aircraft flight deck.

(d) Any person in return for goods or services provided by such person whether the transportation is used by that person or any designee of such person;

(e) Persons engaged in promoting transportation and their immediate families, when such transportation is undertaken for a promotional purpose;

(f) Persons being transported on an inaugural flight or delivery flight of the carrier except that, in the case of delivery flights, this exemption extends only to free, and not reduced-rate, transportation;

(g) Any law-enforcement official, including any person who has the duty of guarding government officials traveling on official business against unlawful interference;

(h) As compensation to persons that file a complaint or claim against the carrier;

(i) Charitable organizations; and

(j) Any person in an aviation-related occupation when the transportation is provided for the purpose of technical in-flight observation.

§223.23 Applications for authority to carry other persons.

(a) Any air carrier or foreign air carrier desiring special authorization to provide free or reduced-rate foreign air transportation to persons to whom the carrier would not otherwise be authorized to furnish such transportation under the previous provisions of this part may apply to the Board, by letter or other writing, for such authorization.

(b) The application shall include the following information:

(1) The identity of the persons to whom the transportation is to be furnished;

(2) The points between which the transportation is to be furnished;

(3) The approximate time of departure; and

(4) The carrier's reasons for desiring to furnish such transportation.

(c) No transportation for which approval is required shall be furnished by the carrier until that approval is received by the carrier.

(Approved by the Office of Management and Budget under control number 3024–0002)

§223.24 Transportation of empty mail bags.

Any carrier authorized to engage in foreign air transportation may transport in foreign air transportation empty air mail bags from any country to the country of origin of such bags, free of charge, on a voluntary space-available basis.

§223.25 List of affiliates.

(a) Each carrier shall maintain at its principal office a list containing all of that carrier's affiliates, showing the exact relationship of each affiliate to the carrier.

(b) No pass may be issued under §223.22(a) to a director, officer, employee, or members of their immediate family, of any affiliate, unless that affiliate is on the list required by paragraph (a) of this section.

(c) The list required by paragraph (a) of this section shall be furnished to the Board upon request.

(Approved by the Office of Management and Budget under control number 3024–0002)

PART 232—TRANSPORTATION OF MAIL, REVIEW OF ORDERS OF POSTMASTER GENERAL

Sec.

AUTHORITY: 49 U.S.C. Chapters 401, 419.

SOURCE: 41 FR 49479, Nov. 9, 1976, unless otherwise noted.

§232.1 Applications for review.

(a) Any person who would be aggrieved by an order of the Postmaster General issued under and within the meaning of section 41902 of the Statute may, within not more than 10 days after the issuance of such order, apply to the Department for a review thereof.

(b) An application for review filed under this part shall be made in writing and shall be conspicuously entitled Application for Review of Order of the Postmaster General under section 41902 of the Statute. Except as otherwise provided in paragraph (c) of this section, such application for review shall specify:

(1) The schedule affected and identity of the order complained of;

(2) The manner in which the applicant is or would be aggrieved by the order;

(3) The relief sought;

(4) The facts relied upon to establish that the public convenience and necessity require that such order be amended, revised, suspended, or canceled by the Department;

(5) An estimate of the total economic impact (including nonmail revenues) on the carrier of complying with the Postmaster General's order;

(6) A history of the flight or flights in question and any predecessor flights cooperated in the market at or about

the same hours, including when they were first operated and whether they have been operated continuously since that time: *Provided*, That this history need not extend beyond the last three years;

(7) A detailed statement of the reasons for the schedule change, including copies of any economic data considered by carrier management in reaching that determination;

(8) Any other schedule changes in the affected market which accompany the schedule change in question, or a statement to the effect that there are no such changes;

(9) Monthly load-factor data on the flight or flights in question for the most recent twelve-month period;

(10) Profit and loss data for the flight or flights in question for the most recent twelve-month period, provided that the data be submitted on a fully allocated cost by functional account number or by some other method in which costs are determined on a fully allocated basis and which is explained in complete detail; and

(11) A statement indicating whether the carrier is willing to seatload sack mail on the flight or flights in question.

(c) Where the application is for review of an order which does not involve disapproval, alteration, or amendment of a change or changes which a carrier sought to make in its own schedule(s), the application need not include items 6 through 11, inclusive, specified in paragraph (b) of this section.

[41 FR 49479, Nov. 9, 1976, as amended by Doc. No. 47939, 57 FR 40102, Sept. 2, 1992; 60 FR 43524, Aug. 22, 1995]

§ 232.2 Answers to applications for review.

(a) Any interested person may, within not more than ten days after the filing of an application for review, serve and file with the Department an answer in opposition to, or in support of, such applications. Such answer shall set forth the economic data and other facts upon which it is based.

(b) An answer of the Postmaster General or U.S. Postal Service shall contain the following particular information, where applicable:

(1) The Postal Service's critical time frame for the movement of the mail in question together with a detailed explanation of the operational factors which support that estimate;

(2) The alternate air and surface services (including air taxi service) available in the market in question together with a statement of the costs of using such alternate services and, where appropriate, an explanation of why such services are unacceptable;

(3) An estimate of the average amount and expected actual density of mail which will be tendered to the carrier if the order in question is upheld;

(4) An estimate of the amount and type of containers which will be tendered to the carrier if the order in question is upheld;

(5) The volume (including density of mail, amount and types of containers) of mail historically carried on the flight or flights in question;

(6) An estimate of the volume (including density of mail, amount and types of containers) of mail historically carried on the flight or flights in question which could be accommodated on other flights serving the market without significant impairment of service under the mail delivery time standards of the Postal Service, together with an explanation of how that estimate was computed; and

(7) An estimate of the impact of the flight or flights in question on mail delivery time standards of the Postal Service, together with an explanation of how that estimate was computed.

[41 FR 49479, Nov. 9, 1976, as amended by Doc. No. 47939, 57 FR 40102, Sept. 2, 1992]

§ 232.3 Replies to answers to applications for review.

Any interested person may, within not more than seven days after the filing of an answer to an application for review, serve and file with the Department a reply in opposition to, or in support of, such answer.

[41 FR 49479, Nov. 9, 1976, as amended by Doc. No. 47939, 57 FR 40102, Sept. 2, 1992]

§ 232.4 Applications to postpone the effective date of an order of the Postmaster General; answers thereto.

(a) Any person who would be aggrieved by an order of the Postmaster

General within the meaning of section 41902 of the Statute may, within not more than four calendar days after the issuance of such order, apply to the Department for a postponement of the effective date of that order pending review: *Provided*, That if the final day of the four day period is a Saturday, Sunday, or holiday for the Department, the application may be filed with the Department no later than the end of the next day which is neither a Saturday, Sunday, or holiday.

(b) An application for postponement of the effective date filed under this part may be made in writing or by telegram, and shall be conspicuously entitled Application for Postponement of the Effective Date of Order of the Postmaster General Pending Review Under section 41902 of the Statute. Such application for postponement shall specify:

(1) The schedule affected and identity of the order complained of;

(2) The manner in which the applicant is or would be aggrieved by the order;

(3) The relief which will be sought;

(4) That the applicant intends to file a timely application for review of the order under § 232.1; and

(5) A summary of the justification and facts relied upon to establish that the stay should be granted.

(c) Any interested person may, within not more than four calendar days after the service of an application for postponement of the effective date, serve and file with the Department an answer in opposition to, or in support of, the application: *Provided*, That if the final day of the four day period is a Saturday, Sunday, or holiday for the Department, the application may be filed with the Department no later than the end of the next day which is neither a Saturday, Sunday, or holiday: *Provided further, however*, That the Department need not consider any answer filed later than eight calendar days after issuance of the Postmaster General's order.

[41 FR 49479, Nov. 9, 1976, as amended by Doc. No. 47939, 57 FR 40102, Sept. 2, 1992; 60 FR 43524, Aug. 22, 1995]

§ 232.5 Filing and service of applications, answers, and replies.

(a) An application, answer or reply filed hereunder shall be deemed to have been filed on the date on which it is actually received by the Department at its offices in Washington, D.C.

(b) At the time a written or telegraphic application, answer, or reply is filed under this part, a copy thereof shall be served by personal service, registered mail, or telegraph upon the Postmaster General and upon the air carrier operating or ordered to operate the mail service in question. Except in the case of telegraphic delivery each copy so served shall be accompanied by a letter of transmittal stating that such service is being made pursuant to this section. In the case of telegraphic delivery the copy shall be accompanied by a telegraphic statement that service is being made pursuant to this section.

(c) The execution, number of copies, and verification of a written application, answer, or reply filed under this part, and the formal specifications of papers included in such application, answer, or reply shall be in accordance with the requirements of the Rules of Practice relating to applications generally (see part 302 of this chapter).

[41 FR 49479, Nov. 9, 1976, as amended by Doc. No. 47939, 57 FR 40102, Sept. 2, 1992]

PART 234—AIRLINE SERVICE QUALITY PERFORMANCE REPORTS

Sec.

AUTHORITY: 49 U.S.C. 329, 41101, and 41701.

SOURCE: Amdt. 234-1, 52 FR 34071, Sept. 9, 1987, unless otherwise noted.

NOTE: The reporting requirements contained in this part have been approved by the

Office of Management and Budget under control number 2138–0041.

§ 234.1 Purpose.

The purpose of this part is to set forth required data that certain air carriers must submit to the Department and to computer reservations system vendors in computerized form, except as otherwise provided, so that information on air carriers' quality of service can be made available to consumers of air transportation. This part also requires that service quality data be disclosed directly to consumers.

§ 234.2 Definitions.

For the purpose of this part:

Cancelled flight means a flight operation that was not operated, but was listed in a carrier's computer reservation system within seven calendar days of the scheduled departure.

Discontinued flight means a flight dropped from a carrier's computer reservation system more than seven calendar days before its scheduled departure.

Diverted flight means a flight which is operated from the scheduled origin point to a point other than the scheduled destination point in the carrier's published schedule. For example, a carrier has a published schedule for a flight from A to B to C. If the carrier were to actually fly an A to C operation, the A to B segment is a diverted flight, and the B to C segment is a cancelled flight.

Extra-section flight means a flight conducted as an integral part of scheduled passenger service, that has not been provided for in published schedules and is required for transportation of traffic that cannot be accommodated on the regularly scheduled flight.

Flight means any nonstop scheduled passenger flight segment with a specific flight number scheduled to be operated pursuant to a published schedule within a specific origin-destination city pair, other than transborder or foreign air transportation. In the case of reporting to computer reservations system vendors, *flight* also means one-stop or multi-stop single plane scheduled operations that include any flight segments for which performance is reported pursuant to this part.

Late or *late flight* means a flight that arrives at the gate 15 minutes or more after its published arrival time.

Mishandled-baggage report means a report filed with a carrier by or on behalf of a passenger that claims loss, delay, damage or pilferage of baggage.

Mishandled checked bag means a checked bag that is lost, delayed, damaged or pilfered, as reported to a carrier by or on behalf of a passenger.

New flight means a flight added to a carrier's schedule to operate in a specific origin-destination city pair and not scheduled to depart within 30 minutes of any discontinued flight that was contained in the carrier's published schedules for the same city pair during the previous month.

On-time means a flight that arrives less than 15 mintues after its published arrival time.

On-time performance means the percentage of scheduled operations of a specific flight that an air carrier operates on-time during a month.

On-time performance code means a single character determined in accordance with the provisions of this part that reflects the monthly on-time performance of certain nonstop flights and single plane one-stop or multi-stop flights, the schedule and availability of which are listed in a computer reservation system (*CRS*) regulated by 14 CFR part 255.

Reportable flight. (1) Reportable flight for air transportation taking place before January 1, 2018 means any nonstop flight, including a mechanically delayed flight, to or from any airport within the contiguous 48 states that accounts for at least 1 percent of domestic scheduled-passenger enplanements in the previous calendar year, as reported to the Department pursuant to part 241 of this title. Qualifying airports will be specified periodically in accounting and reporting directives issued by the Office of Airline Information.

(2) Reportable flight for air transportation taking place on or after January 1, 2018 means any domestic nonstop scheduled passenger flight, including a mechanically delayed flight, held out to the public under the reporting carrier's code, to or from any U.S. large, medium, small, or non-hub airport as

defined in 49 U.S.C. 47102. Qualifying airports will be specified periodically in accounting and reporting directives issued by the Office of Airline Information.

Reporting carrier. (1) Reporting carrier for air transportation taking place before January 1, 2018 means an air carrier certificated under 49 U.S.C. 41102 that accounted for at least 1 percent of domestic scheduled-passenger revenues in the most recently reported 12-month period as defined by the Department's Office of Airline Information, and as reported to the Department pursuant to part 241 of this title. Reporting carriers will be identified periodically in accounting and reporting directives issued by the Office of Airline Information.

(2) Reporting carrier for air transportation taking place on or after January 1, 2018 means an air carrier certificated under 49 U.S.C. 41102 that accounted for at least 0.5 percent of domestic scheduled-passenger revenus in the most recently reported 12-month period as defined by the Department's Office of Airline Information, and as reported to the Department pursuant to part 241 of this chapter. Reporting carriers will be identified periodically in accounting and reporting directives issued by the Office of Airline Information.

[Amdt. 234-1, 52 FR 34071, Sept. 9, 1987, as amended by Doc. No. 48524, 59 FR 49797, Sept. 30, 1994; 60 FR 66722, Dec. 26, 1995; Dockt. No. DOT-RITA-2011-0001, 81 FR 76306, Nov. 2, 2016; Dockt. No. DOT-OST-2014-056; 81 FR 76826, Nov. 3, 2016]

§234.3 Applicability.

For air transportation taking place before January 1, 2018, this part applies to reportable flights as defined in §234.2 that are held out to the public by certificated air carriers that account for at least 1 percent of domestic scheduled passenger revenues. As stated in §234.7, certain provisions also apply to voluntary reporting of on-time performance by carriers. For air transportation taking place on or after January 1, 2018, this part applies to reportable flights as defined in §234.2 that are held out to the public by certificated air carriers that account for at least 0.5 percent of domestic scheduled passenger revenues. As stated in §234.7, certain provisions also apply to voluntary reporting of on-time performance by carriers.

[Dockt. No. DOT-OST-2014-0056, 81 FR 76826, Nov. 3, 2016]

§234.4 Reporting of on-time performance.

(a) Each reporting carrier shall file BTS Form 234 "On-Time Flight Performance Report" with the Office of Airline Information of the Department's Bureau of Transportation Statistics on a monthly basis, setting forth the information for each of its reportable flights operated by the reporting carrier and held out to the public on the reporting carrier's Web site and the Web sites of major online travel agencies, or in other generally recognized sources of schedule information. (See also paragraph (k) of this section.) The reportable flights include, but are not limited to, cancelled flights, mechanically cancelled flights, diverted flights, new flights and wet-leased flights. The report shall be made in the form and manner set forth in accounting and reporting directives issued by the Director, Office of Airline Statistics, and shall contain the following information:

(1) Carrier and flight number.

(2) Aircraft tail number.

(3) Origin and Destination airport codes.

(4) Published OAG departure and arrival times for each scheduled operation of the flight.

(5) CRS scheduled arrival and departure time for each scheduled operation of the flight.

(6) Actual departure and arrival time for each operation of the flight.

(7) Difference in minutes between OAG and CRS scheduled arrival times.

(8) Difference in minutes between OAG and CRS scheduled departure times.

(9) Actual wheels-off and wheels-on times for each operation of the flight.

(10) Date and day of week of scheduled flight operation.

(11) Scheduled elapsed time, according to CRS schedule.

(12) Actual elapsed time.

(13) Amount of departure delay, if any.

(14) Amount of arrival delay, if any.

(15) Amount of elapsed time difference, if any.

(16) Causal code for cancellation, if any.

(17) Minutes of delay attributed to the air carrier, if any.

(18) Minutes of delay attributed to extreme weather, if any.

(19) Minutes of delay attributed to the national aviation system, if any.

(20) Minutes of delay attributed to security, if any.

(21) Minutes of delay attributed to a previous late arriving aircraft, if any.

(22) For gate returns, first gate-departure time at origin airport.

(23) Total ground time away from gate for all gate/air returns at origin airport, including cancelled flights—actual minutes.

(24) Longest time away from gate for gate return or cancelled flight.

(25) Three-letter code of airport where diverted flight landed.

(26) Wheels-on time at diverted airport.

(27) Total time away from gate at diverted airport.

(28) Longest period of time away from gate at diverted airport.

(29) Wheels-off time at diverted airport.

(b) Repeat fields (25) through (29) for each subsequent diverted airport landing.

(c) When reporting the information specified in paragraph (a) of this section for diverted flights, a reporting carrier shall use the original scheduled flight number and the origin and destination airport codes except for item (25).

(d) A reporting carrier shall report the information specified in paragraph (a) of this section for a new flight beginning with the first day of the new scheduled operation.

(e) A reporting carrier shall not report the information specified in paragraph (a) of this section for any discontinued or extra-section flight.

(f) Actual arrival, departure and elapsed times shall be measured by the times at which the aircraft arrived at and departed from the gate or passenger loading area.

(g) The published arrival time and departure time of a flight shall be, respectively, the scheduled arrival and departure times in effect on the date of the scheduled operation of the flight, as shown in the most recent *Official Airline Guide*, and in computer reservations systems. Each carrier shall designate a single computer reservations system in addition to the *Official Airline Guide* as the sources of scheduled arrival time and departure time data in its reports to the Department and shall report the scheduled arrival times and departure times listed in those sources for each flight. Scheduled elapsed times, amount of departure and/or arrival delay, and elapsed time difference shall be calculated using the scheduled times shown in the designated CRS source.

(h) Reporting carriers should use the following codes to identify causes for cancelled flights:

Code
A—Air Carrier
B—Extreme Weather
C—National Aviation System (NAS).
D-Security

(1) Air Carrier cancellations are due to circumstances that were within the control of the air carrier (e.g., lack of flight crew, maintenance, etc.).

(2) Extreme weather cancellations are caused by weather conditions (e.g., significant meteorological conditions), actual or forecasted at the point of departure, en route, or point of arrival that, in accordance with applicable regulatory standards and/or in the judgment of the air carrier, prevents operation of that flight and/or prevents operations of subsequent flights due to the intended aircraft being out of position as a result of a prior cancellation or delay attributable to weather.

(3) NAS cancellations are caused by circumstances within the National Aviation System. This term is used to refer to a broad set of conditions: weather-non-extreme, airport operations, heavy traffic volume, air traffic control, etc.

(4) Security cancellations may be the result of malfunctioning screening or other security equipment or a breech of security that causes the evacuation of the airport or individual concourses, or the need to re-screen passengers.

(i) Reporting carriers should use the following causes to identify the reasons for delayed flights:

CAUSE
Air Carrier
Extreme weather
NAS
Security
Late arriving aircraft

(1) Air carrier delays are due to circumstances within the control of the air carrier.

(2) Extreme weather delays are caused by weather conditions (e.g., significant meteorological conditions, actual or forecasted at the point of departure, en route, or point of arrival that, in accordance with applicable regulatory standards and/or in the judgment of the air carrier, prevents operation of that flight and/or prevents operations of subsequent flights due to the intended aircraft being out of position as a result of a prior cancellation or delay attributable to weather.

(3) NAS delays are caused by circumstances within the National Aviation System. This term is used to refer to a broad set of conditions: weather-non-extreme, airport operations, heavy traffic volume, air traffic control, etc.

(4) Security delays may be the result of malfunctioning screening or other security equipment or a breech of security that causes the evacuation of the airport or individual concourses or the need to re-screen passengers.

(5) Late arriving aircraft delays are the result of a late incoming aircraft from the previous flight.

(j) When reporting causal codes in paragraph (a) of this section, reporting carriers are required to code delays only when the arrival delay is 15 minutes or greater; and reporting carriers must report each causal component of the reportable delay when the causal component is 5 minutes or greater.

(k) For air transportation taking place on or after January 1, 2018, each reporting carrier shall also file a separate BTS Form 234 "On-Time Flight Performance Report" with the Office of Airline Information on a monthly basis, setting forth the information for each of its reportable flights held out with only the reporting carrier's airline designator code on the reporting carrier's Web site, on the Web sites of major online travel agencies, or in other generally recognized sources of schedule information, and operated by any code-share partner that is a certificated air carrier or commuter air carrier. If the operating carrier of the flight is not a reporting carrier, the non-operating reporting carrier must file a BTS Form 234 "On-time Flight Performance Report" with the Office of Airline Information on a monthly basis, setting forth the information regarding those flights in a form and manner consistent with the requirements set forth in paragraph (a) through (j) of this section. If the operating carrier of the flight is a reporting carrier, the non-operating reporting carrier must file a simplified BTS Form 234 "On-Time Flight Performance Report" with the Office of Airline Information on a monthly basis, setting forth the information regarding those flights in a form and manner consistent with the requirements set forth in paragraph (a)(1) through (a)(4) and paragraph (a)(10) of this section, and in accordance with the requirements set forth in accounting and reporting directives issued by the Office of Airline Information.

[Amdt. 234-1, 52 FR 34071, Sept. 9, 1987, as amended by Doc. No. 48524, 59 FR 49797, Sept. 30, 1994; 60 FR 66722, Dec. 26, 1995; 67 FR 70544, Nov. 25, 2002; Doc. No. RITA 2007-28522, 73 FR 29431, May 21, 2008; Dockt. No. DOT-OST-2014-0056; 81 FR 76826, Nov. 3, 2016]

§ 234.5 Form of reports.

Except where otherwise noted, all reports required by this part shall be filed within 15 days of the end of the month for which data are reported. The reports must be submitted to the Office of Airline Information in a format specified in accounting and reporting directives issued by the Bureau of Transportation Statistics' Assistant Director for Airline Information.

[Doc. No. DOT-OST-2000-8164, 67 FR 70545, Nov. 25, 2002]

§ 234.6 Baggage-handling statistics.

(a) For air transportation taking place before January 1, 2019, an air carrier certificated under 49 U.S.C. 41102 that accounts for at least 1 percent of domestic scheduled-passenger revenues in the most recently reported 12-month period as defined by the Department's Office of Airline Information, and as reported to the Department pursuant to part 241 of this title shall, for the flights it operates, report monthly to the Department on a domestic system basis, excluding charter flights, the total number of passengers enplaned system-wide and the total number of mishandled-baggage reports filed with the carrier for any nonstop flight, including a mechanically delayed flight, to or from any airport within the contiguous 48 states that accounts for at least 1 percent of domestic scheduled-passenger enplanements in the previous calendar year, as reported to the Department pursuant to part 241 of this title.

(b) For air transportation taking place on or after January 1, 2019, an air carrier certificated under 49 U.S.C. 41102 that accounts for at least 0.5 percent of domestic scheduled-passenger revenues in the most recently reported 12-month period as defined by the Department's Office of Airline Information, and as reported to the Department pursuant to part 241 of this title shall report monthly to the Department on a domestic system basis, excluding charter flights:

(1) The total number of checked bags enplaned, including gate checked baggage, "valet bags," interlined bags, and wheelchairs and scooters enplaned in the aircraft cargo compartment for any domestic nonstop scheduled passenger flight, including a mechanically delayed flight, operated by the carrier to or from any U.S. large, medium, small or non-hub airport as defined in 49 U.S.C. 41702 and separately for any domestic nonstop scheduled passenger flight, including a mechanically delayed flight, held out with only the carrier's designator code to or from any U.S. large, medium, small, or non-hub airport as defined in 49 U.S.C. 47102 and operated by any code-share partner that is a certificated air carrier or commuter air carrier;

(2) The total number of wheelchairs and scooters that were enplaned in the aircraft cargo compartment for any domestic nonstop scheduled passenger flight, including a mechanically delayed flight, operated by the carrier to or from any U.S. large, medium, small or non-hub airport as defined in 49 U.S.C. 41702 and separately for any domestic nonstop scheduled passenger flight, including a mechanically delayed flight, held out with only the carrier's designator code to or from any U.S. large, medium, small, or non-hub airport as defined in 49 U.S.C. 47102 and operated by any code-share partner that is a certificated air carrier or commuter air carrier;

(3) The number of mishandled checked bags, including gate-checked baggage, "valet bags," interlined bags and wheelchairs and scooters that were enplaned in the aircraft cargo compartment for any domestic nonstop scheduled passenger flight, including a mechanically delayed flight, operated by the carrier to or from any U.S. large, medium, small or non-hub airport as defined in 49 U.S.C. 41702 and separately for any domestic nonstop scheduled passenger flight, including a mechanically delayed flight, held out with only the carrier's designator code to or from any U.S. large, medium, small, or non-hub airport as defined in 49 U.S.C. 47102 and operated by any code-share partner that is a certificated air carrier or commuter air carrier; and

(4) The number of mishandled wheelchairs and scooters that were enplaned in the aircraft cargo compartment for any domestic nonstop scheduled passenger flight, including a mechanically delayed flight, operated by the carrier to or from any U.S. large, medium, small or non-hub airport as defined in 49 U.S.C. 41702 and separately for any domestic nonstop scheduled passenger flight, including a mechanically delayed flight, held out with only the carrier's designator code to or from any U.S. large, medium, small, or non-hub airport as defined in 49 U.S.C. 47102 and operated by any code-share partner that is a certificated air carrier or commuter air carrier.

(c) The information in paragraphs (a) and (b) of this section shall be submitted to the Department within 15 days after the end of the month to which the information applies and must be submitted with the transmittal accompanying the data for on-time performance in the form and manner set forth in accounting and reporting directives issued by the Director, Office of Airline Information.

[Dockt. No. DOT–OST–2014–0056, 82 FR 14604, Mar. 22, 2017]

§234.7 Voluntary reporting.

(a) In addition to the data for each reportable flight required to be reported by this part, a reporting carrier may report to DOT for every other nonstop domestic flight that it schedules, the reportable flight data specified in this part.

(b) Any air carrier that is not a reporting carrier may file the data specified in this part for every reportable flight that it schedules, or for every nonstop domestic flight that it schedules.

(c) Voluntary reports containing information not required to be filed (1) must be submitted in the same form and manner, and at the same time, as reports containing data required to be filed, and (2) must be accompanied by a written statement describing in detail the information that is being voluntarily submitted. A carrier that files a voluntary report must continue to do so for a period of not less than 12 consecutive months.

§234.8 Calculation of on-time performance codes.

(a) Each reporting carrier shall calculate an on-time performance code in accordance with this section and as provided in more detail in accounting and reporting directives issued by the Director, Office of Airline Information. The calculations shall be performed for each reportable flight, except those scheduled to operate three times or less during a month. In addition, each reporting carrier shall assign an on-time performance code to each of its single plane one-stop or multi-stop flights, or portion thereof, that the carrier holds out to the public through a CRS, the last segment of which is a reportable flight.

(b) The on-time performance code shall be calculated as follows:

(1) Based on reportable flight data provided to the Department, calculate the percentage of on-time arrivals of each nonstop flight. Calculations shall not include discontinued or extra-section flights for which data are not reported to the Department.

(2) Based upon the on-time performance percentage calculated in paragraph (b)(1) of this section, assign a single digit code to each flight that reflects the percentile of on-time performance achieved by the flight, as set forth in the following table:

ON TIME PERFORMANCE

Code:	Percentage
9	90–100
8	80–89.9
7	70–79.9
6	60–69.9
5	50–59.9
4	40–49.9
3	30–39.9
2	20–29.9
1	10–19.9
0	0–9.9

(3) For a one-stop or multi-stop flight, or portion thereof, listed in a CRS, the performance code for the nonstop flight segment arriving at the destination listed in the CRS shall be used.

(4) In the case of a new flight, carriers shall assign a performance code consisting of the letter "N." A flight that is not a new flight shall be assigned the performance code calculated for the flight that it replaces, even if the two flights do not have the same flight number. In the case of a flight scheduled to operate three times or less during a month, carriers shall assign a performance code consisting of the letter "U."

(c) Carriers shall calculate on-time performance percentages and assign on-time performance codes on a monthly basis. This process shall be completed no later than the 15th day of each month, when the reports required by this part are due to the Department, and the codes shall reflect the previous month's operations.

[Amdt. 234-1, 52 FR 34071, Sept. 9, 1987, as amended by Amdt. 234-3, 52 FR 48397, Dec. 22, 1987; 53 FR 27677, July 22, 1988; Doc. No. 48524, 59 FR 49798, Sept. 30, 1994; 60 FR 66722, Dec. 26, 1995]

§234.9 Reporting of on-time performance codes.

No later than the 15th day of each month, each reporting carrier shall deliver, or arrange to have delivered, to each system vendor, as defined in 14 CFR part 255, the on-time performance codes required to be determined above. Carriers may report the codes by insuring that they are included in basic schedule tapes provided to CRS vendors or by providing a separate tape that will permit the CRS vendors to match the performance codes with basic schedule tapes.

§ 234.10 Voluntary disclosure of on-time performance codes.

(a) Any air carrier may determine, in accordance with the provisions of § 234.8 of this part, the on-time performance codes for the flights for which it voluntarily provides flight information to the Department pursuant to § 234.7 of this part.

(b) A carrier may supply these additional on-time performance codes to system vendors at the same time and in the same manner as the required disclosures are made to system vendors, provided that voluntary disclosures must continue for a period of not less than 12 consecutive months, and must be supplied either

(1) For each of the carrier's reportable flights and each of its single plane one-stop or multi-stop flights, or portions thereof, that it holds out to the public through a CRS, the last segment of which is a reportable flight or

(2) For each of the carrier's domestic flights.

§ 234.11 Disclosure to consumers.

(a) During the course of reservations or ticketing discussions or transactions, or inquiries about flights, between a carrier's employees or contractors and the public, the carrier shall disclose upon reasonable request the on-time performance code for any flight that has been assigned a code pursuant to this part.

(b) For each domestic flight for which schedule information is available on its Web site, including domestic code-share flights, a reporting carrier shall display the following information regarding the flight's performance during the most recent calendar month for which the carrier has reported on-time performance data to the Department: the percentage of arrivals that were on time—*i.e.*, within 15 minutes of scheduled arrival time, the percentage of arrivals that were more than 30 minutes late (including special highlighting if the flight was late more than 30 minutes of scheduled arrival time more than 50 percent of the time), and the percentage of flight cancellations if 5 percent or more of the flight's operations were canceled in the month covered. The information must be provided by showing all of the required information on the initial listing of flights or by showing all of the required information via a prominent hyperlink in close proximity to each flight on the page with the initial listing of flights.

(c) The first time each carrier must load the information whose disclosure is required under paragraphs (a) and (b) of this section onto its Web site is on Saturday, July 24, 2010, for June data. Carriers must load all subsequent flight performance information on the fourth Saturday of the month following the month that is being reported.

(d) A reporting carrier must meet the requirements of paragraphs (b) and (c) of this section by June 29, 2010.

[Doc. No. DOT–OST–2007–0022, 74 FR 69002, Dec. 30, 2009, as amended by Doc. No. DOT–OST–2010–0039, 75 FR 17052, Apr. 5, 2010; Doc. No. DOT–OST–2007–0022, 75 FR 34927, June 21, 2010]

§ 234.12 Waivers.

Any carrier may request a waiver from the reporting requirements of this part. Such a request, at the discretion of the Director, Bureau of Transportation Statistics may be granted for good cause shown. The requesting party shall state the basis for such a waiver.

[Doc. No. 48524, 59 FR 49798, Sept. 30, 1994, as amended at 60 FR 66722, Dec. 26, 1995]

PART 235—REPORTS BY AIR CARRIERS ON INCIDENTS INVOLVING ANIMALS DURING AIR TRANSPORT

Sec.

AUTHORITY: 49 U.S.C. 41721.

SOURCE: 79 FR 37945, July 3, 2014, unless otherwise noted.

§ 235.1 Definitions.

For the purposes of this part:

Air transport includes the entire period during which an animal is in the custody of an air carrier, from the time that the animal is tendered to the air carrier prior to departure until the air carrier tenders the animal to the owner, guardian or representative of the shipper of the animal at the animal's final destination. It does not include animals that accompany a passenger at his or her seat in the cabin and of which the air carrier does not take custody.

Animal means any warm- or cold-blooded animal which, at the time of transportation, is being kept as a pet in a family household in the United States and any dog or cat which, at the time of transportation, is shipped as part of a commercial shipment on a scheduled passenger flight, including shipments by trainers and breeders.

§235.2 Applicability.

This part applies to the scheduled domestic and international passenger service of any U.S. air carrier that operates such service with at least one aircraft having a designed seating capacity of more than 60 passenger seats. The reporting requirements of this part apply to all scheduled-service passenger flights of such carriers, including flights that are operated with aircraft having 60 or fewer seats.

§235.3 Reports by air carriers on incidents involving animals during air transport.

(a) Each covered carrier shall, within 15 days after the end of the month to which the information applies, submit to the United States Department of Transportation's Aviation Consumer Protection Division a report on any incidents involving the loss, injury, or death of an animal during air transport provided by the air carrier, including incidents on flights by that carrier that are operated with aircraft having 60 or fewer seats. The report shall be made in the form and manner set forth in reporting directives issued by the Deputy General Counsel for the U.S. Department of Transportation and shall contain the following information:

(1) Carrier and flight number;

(2) Date and time of the incident;

(3) Description of the animal, including name, if known;

(4) Name and contact information of the owner(s), guardian, and/or shipper of the animal;

(5) Narrative description of the incident;

(6) Narrative description of the cause of the incident;

(7) Narrative description of any corrective action taken in response to the incident; and

(8) Name, title, address, and telephone number of the individual filing the report on behalf of the air carrier.

(b) Within 15 days after the end of December of each year, each covered carrier shall submit the following information (this information may be included in any report that the carrier may file for the loss, injury, or death of animals during the month of December):

(1) The total number of incidents involving an animal during air transport provided by the air carrier for the entire calendar year, including incidents on flights by that carrier that are operated with aircraft having 60 or fewer seats. The report shall include subtotals for loss, injury, and death of animals. Report "0" for any category for which there were no such incidents. If the carrier had no reportable incidents for that calendar year, it shall report "0" in each category. Covered carriers shall use the following data table when reporting the total number of animal incidents during air transport provided by the air carrier for the entire calendar year:

	Total number in the calendar year
Deaths Injuries Loss	

(2) The total number of animals transported in the calendar year. If the carrier did not transport any animals for that calendar year, it shall report "0."

(3) The December report must contain the following certification signed by the carrier's authorized representative: "I, the undersigned, do certify that this report has been prepared under my direction in accordance with the regulations in 14 CFR part 235. I affirm that, to the best of my knowledge

and belief, this is a true, correct and complete report.''

PART 240—INSPECTION OF ACCOUNTS AND PROPERTY

§ 240.1 Interpretation.

(a) In the exercise of the authority granted by section 407(e) of the Act, the authority of any special agent or auditor to inspect and examine lands, buildings, equipment, accounts, records, memorandums, papers or correspondence shall include the authority to make such notes and copies thereof as he deems appropriate.

(b) The term ''special agent'' and ''auditor'' are construed to mean any employee of the Bureau of Enforcement and any other employee of the Board specifically designated by it or by the Director, Office of Facilities and Operations.

(c) The issuance in the form set forth below of an identification card and credentials to any such employee shall be construed to be an order and direction of the Board to such individual to inspect and examine lands, buildings, equipment, accounts, records, and memorandums in accordance with the authority conferred on the Board by the Act.

UNITED STATES OF AMERICA, CIVIL AERONAUTICS BOARD, WASHINGTON, D.C.

Number __________
Expires __________

[photo]

Signature

This is to certify that__________, whose signature and photograph appear hereon is a duly designated __________

of the Civil Aeronautics Board and is authorized and directed to perform the duties of said office in accordance with the laws of the United States and regulations thereunder, and his authority will be respected accordingly.

By authority of the Civil Aeronautics Board.

Secretary

CIVIL AERONAUTICS BOARD

Name __________
Date Issued __________
Number __________
Height __________
Weight __________
Hair __________
Eyes __________
Date of Birth __________

The holder hereof is authorized to investigate violations of the Federal Aviation Act, as amended, collect evidence in cases in which the regulatory authority of the Civil Aeronautics Board is or may be involved and perform other duties imposed upon him by law.

Under the Federal Aviation Act and part 240 of the Economic Regulations of the Civil Aeronautics Board (14 CFR part 240), the duly accredited special agents and auditors of the Board are empowered at all times to obtain access to all lands, buildings and equipment of any air carrier or foreign air carrier and to inspect, examine, and make notes and copies of all accounts, records, memorandums, documents, papers and correspondence kept or required to be kept by any air carrier, foreign air carrier or ticket agent.

The issuance of these credentials to the holder hereof constitutes an order and direction on the part of the Civil Aeronautics Board to such individual to carry out these duties as aforesaid and as more fully described in part 240 of the Board's Economic Regulations.

Failure to honor these credentials will result in penalties as provided by law.

UNITED STATES OF AMERICA,
CIVIL AERONAUTICS BOARD,
WASHINGTON, D.C.

(Secs. 204, 407, 701, 72 Stat. 743; 49 U.S.C. 1324, 1377, 1441)

[ER–822, 38 FR 26601, Sept. 24, 1973, as amended by ER–914, 40 FR 27017, June 26, 1975; ER–941, 40 FR 58850, Dec. 19, 1975]

§ 240.2 Obligation of air carriers, foreign air carriers, and ticket agents.

Upon the demand of a special agent or auditor of the Board, and upon the presentation of the identification card and credentials issued to him in accordance with this part: (a) Any air carrier or foreign air carrier shall forthwith permit such special agent or auditor to inspect and examine all lands, buildings and equipment; (b) any air carrier, foreign air carrier or ticket agent shall forthwith permit such special agent or auditor to inspect and examine all accounts, records, memorandums, documents, papers and correspondence now or hereafter existing, and kept or required to be kept by the air carrier, foreign air carrier, or ticket agent, and shall permit such special agent or auditor to make such notes and copies thereof as he deems appropriate.

(Sec. 204(a), Federal Aviation Act of 1958, as amended, 72 Stat. 743; (49 U.S.C. 1324))

[ER–914, 40 FR 27017, June 26, 1975]

PART 241—UNIFORM SYSTEM OF ACCOUNTS AND REPORTS FOR LARGE CERTIFICATED AIR CARRIERS

AUTHORITY: 49 U.S.C. 329 and chapters 41101, 41708, and 41709.

SOURCE: ER–755, 37 FR 19726, Sept. 21, 1972, unless otherwise noted.

Section 01 Authority Under Which Accounting and Reporting Rules and Regulations are Prescribed and Administered

This Uniform System of Accounts and Reports for Large Certificated Air Carriers is issued, prescribed and administered under the following provisions of the Federal Aviation Act of 1958, as amended (72 Stat. 731, 49 U.S.C. 1301):

GENERAL POWERS

SEC. 204. (a) The Board is empowered to perform such acts, to conduct such investigations, to issue and amend such orders, and to make and amend such general or special rules, regulations, and procedure, pursuant to and consistent with the provisions of this Act, as it shall deem necessary to carry out the provisions of, and to exercise and perform its powers and duties under, this Act.

FILING OF REPORTS

SEC. 407. (a) The Board is empowered to require annual, monthly, periodical, and special reports from any air carrier; to prescribe the manner and form in which such reports shall be made; and to require from any air carrier specific answers to all questions upon which the Board may deem information to be necessary. Such reports shall be under oath whenever the Board so requires. The Board may also require any air carrier to file with it a true copy of each or any contract, agreement, understanding, or arrangement, between such air carrier and any other carrier or person, in relation to any traffic affected by the provisions of this Act.

DISCLOSURE OF STOCK OWNERSHIP

SEC. 407. (b) Each air carrier shall submit annually, and at such other times as the Board shall require, a list showing the names of each of its stockholders or members holding more than 5 per centum of the entire capital stock or capital, as the case may be, of such air carrier, together with the name of any person for whose account, if other than the holder, such stock is held; and a report setting forth a description of the shares of stock, or other interest, held by such air carrier, or for its account, in persons other than itself.

FORM OF ACCOUNTS

SEC. 407. (d) The Board shall prescribe the forms of any and all accounts, records, and memoranda to be kept by air carriers, including the accounts, records, and memoranda of the movement of traffic, as well as of the receipts and expenditures of money, and the length of time such accounts, records, and memoranda shall be preserved; and it shall be unlawful for air carriers to keep any accounts, records, or memoranda other than those prescribed or approved by the Board: *Provided*, That any air carrier may keep additional accounts, records, or memoranda if they do not impair the integrity of the accounts, records, or memoranda prescribed or approved by the Board and do not constitute an undue financial burden on such air carrier.

INSPECTION OF ACCOUNTS AND PROPERTY

SEC. 407. (e) The Board shall at all times have access to all lands, buildings, and equipment of any carrier and to all accounts, records, and memoranda, including all documents, papers, and correspondence, now or hereafter existing, and kept or required to be kept by air carriers; and it may employ special agents or auditors, who shall have authority under the orders of the Board to inspect and examine any and all such lands, buildings, equipment, accounts, records, and memoranda. The provisions of this section shall apply, to the extent found by the Board to be reasonably necessary for the administration of this Act, to persons having control over any air carrier, or affiliated with any air carrier within the meaning of section 5(8) of the Interstate Commerce Act, as amended.

CLASSIFICATION

SEC. 416. (a) The Board may from time to time establish such just and reasonable classifications or groups of air carriers for the purposes of this title as the nature of the services performed by such air carriers shall require; and such just and reasonable rules and regulations, pursuant to and consistent with the provisions of this title, to be observed by each such class or group, as the Board finds necessary in the public interest.

SAFETY, ECONOMIC AND POSTAL OFFENSES

SEC. 901. (a)(1) Any person who violates (A) any provision of Title III, IV, V, VI, VII, or XII of this Act, or any rule, regulation, or order issued thereunder, or under section 1002(i), or any term, condition or limitation of any permit or certificate issued under Title IV, or (B) any rule or regulation issued by the Postmaster General under this Act, shall be subject to a civil penalty of not to exceed $1,000 for each such violation. If such violation is a continuing one, each day of such violation shall constitute a separate offense: *Provided*, That this subsection shall not apply to members of the Armed Forces of the United States, or those civilian employees of the Department of Defense who are subject to the provisions of the Uniform Code of Military Justice, while engaged in the performance of their official duties; and the appropriate military authorities shall be responsible for taking any necessary disciplinary action with respect thereto and for making to the Administrator or Board, as appropriate, a timely report of any such action taken.

(2) Any such civil penalty may be compromised by the Administrator in the case of violations of Titles III, V, VI, or XII, or any rule, regulation, or order issued thereunder, or by the Board in the case of violations of Titles IV or VII, or any rule, regulation or order issued thereunder, or under section 1002(i), or any term, condition, or limitation

of any permit or certificate issued under Title IV, or by the Postmaster General in the case of regulations issued by him. The amount of such penalty, when finally determined, or the amount agreed upon in compromise, may be deducted from any sums owing by the United States to the person charged.

FAILURE TO FILE REPORTS; FALSIFICATION OF RECORDS

SEC. 902. (e) Any air carrier, or any officer, agent, employee, or representative thereof, who shall, knowingly and willfully, fail or refuse to make a report to the Board or Administrator as required by this Act, or to keep or preserve accounts, records, and memoranda in the form and manner prescribed or approved by the Board or Administrator, or shall, knowingly and willfully, falsify, mutilate, or alter any such report, account, record, or memorandum, or shall knowingly and willfully file any false report, account, record, or memorandum, shall be deemed guilty of a misdemeanor and, upon conviction thereof, be subject for each offense to a fine of not less than $100 and not more than $5,000.

REFUSAL TO TESTIFY

SEC. 902. (g) Any person who shall neglect or refuse to attend and testify, or to answer any lawful inquiry, or to produce books, papers, or documents, if in his power to do so, in obedience to the subpena or lawful requirement of the Board or Administrator, shall be guilty of a misdemeanor and, upon conviction thereof, shall be subject to a fine of not less than $100 nor more than $5,000, or imprisonment for not more than one year, or both.

FILING OF COMPLAINTS AUTHORIZED

SEC. 1002. (a) Any person may file with the Administrator or the Board, as to matters within their respective jurisdictions, a complaint in writing with respect to anything done or omitted to be done by any person in contravention of any provisions of this Act, or of any requirement established pursuant thereto. If the person complained against shall not satisfy the complaint and there shall appear to be any reasonable ground for investigating the complaint, it shall be the duty of the Administrator or the Board to investigate the matters complained of. Whenever the Administrator or the Board is of the opinion that any complaint does not state facts which warrant an investigation or action, such complaint may be dismissed without hearing. In the case of complaints against a member of the Armed Forces of the United States acting in the performance of his official duties, the Administrator or the Board, as the case may be, shall refer the complaint to the Secretary of the department concerned for action. The Secretary shall, within ninety days after receiving such a complaint, inform the Administrator or the Board of his disposition of the complaint, including a report as to any corrective or disciplinary actions taken.

INVESTIGATIONS ON INITIATIVE OF ADMINISTRATOR OR BOARD

SEC. 1002. (b) The Administrator or Board, with respect to matters within their respective jurisdictions, is empowered at any time to institute an investigation, on their own initiative, in any case and as to any matter or thing within their respective jurisdictions, concerning which complaint is authorized to be made to or before the Administrator or Board by any provision of this Act, or concerning which any question may arise under any of the provisions of this Act, or relating to the enforcement of any of the provisions of this Act. The Administrator or the Board shall have the same power to proceed with any investigation instituted on their own motion as though it had been appealed to by complaint.

ENTRY OR ORDERS FOR COMPLIANCE WITH ACT

SEC. 1002. (c) If the Administrator or the Board finds, after notice and hearing, in any investigation instituted upon complaint or upon their own initiative, with respect to matters within their jurisdiction, that any person has failed to comply with any provision of this Act or any requirement established pursuant thereto, the Administrator or the Board shall issue an appropriate order to compel such person to comply therewith.

[ER–755, 37 FR 19726, Sept. 21, 1972, as amended by ER–1400, 50 FR 11, Jan. 2, 1985]

Section 02 [Reserved]

Section 03 Definitions for Purposes of This System of Accounts and Reports

Account, clearing. An account used as a medium for the temporary accumulation of costs that are redistributed to appropriate applicable accounts.

Acquisition, date of. The date on which the title to owned property or equipment (or the right to use or control the reassignment of leased property or equipment) passes to the air carrier.

Act. The Federal Aviation Act of 1958, as amended.

Addition, property. Additional equipment, land, structures, and other tangible property; extensions of fuel, water, and oil distribution equipment; additions to buildings and other structures; and additional safety devices applied to equipment not previously thus equipped. (See also *Modification.*)

Affiliated group. A combination of companies comprised of the air carrier, any person controlling the air carrier or under common control with the air carrier, and organizational divisions (as defined in sections 1–6) of and persons controlled by the air carrier.

Agency, cargo. Any person (other than the air carrier preforming the direct air transportation or one of its bona fide regular employees or an indirect air carrier lawfully engaged in air transportation under authority conferred by any applicable part of the Economic Regulations of the Department) who for compensation or profit: (1) Solicits, obtains, receives or furnishes directly or indirectly property or consolidated shipments of property for transportation upon the aircraft of an air carrier subject to this part, or (2) procures or arranges for air transportation of property upon aircraft of an air carrier subject to this part by charter, lease, or any other arrangement.

Agent, ticket. Any person (other than the air carrier performing the direct air transportation or one of its bona fide regular employees, or an air carrier which subcontracts the performance of charter air transportation which it has contracted to perform) who for compensation or profit: (1) Solicits, obtains, receives, or furnishes directly or indirectly passengers or groups of passengers for transportation upon the aircraft of an air carrier subject to this part, or (2) procures or arranges for air transportation of passengers or groups of passengers upon aircraft of an air carrier subject to this part by charter, lease, or any other arrangement.

Agreement. Any oral or written agreement, contract, understanding, or arrangement, and any amendment, revision, modification, renewal, extension, cancellation or termination thereof.

Air carrier. Any citizen of the United States who undertakes, whether directly or indirectly or by a lease or any other arrangement, to engage in air transportation.

Air carrier, charter. An air carrier holding a certificate issued under 49 U.S.C. 41102(a)(3).

Air carrier, large certificated. An air carrier holding a certificate issued under 49 U.S.C. 41102, as amended, that: (1) Operates aircraft designed to have a maximum passenger capacity of more than 60 seats or a maximum payload capacity of more than 18,000 pounds; or (2) conducts operations where one or both terminals of a flight stage are outside the 50 states of the United States, the District of Columbia, the Commonwealth of Puerto Rico and the U.S. Virgin Islands.

Air carrier, surviving. An entity (air carrier) which, as the result of a business combination, has acquired the net assets, and carries on the operations of, one or more predecessor air carriers, and which may be newly organized at the time of the combination or may be one of the predecessor air carriers.

Aircraft. Any contrivance now known or hereafter invented, used or designed for navigation of or flight in the air.

Aircraft days assigned to service-carrier's equipment means the number of days that aircraft owned or acquired through rental or lease are in the possession of the reporting air carrier and are available for service on the reporting carrier's routes plus the number of days such aircraft are in service on routes of others under wet-lease agreements. Includes days in overhaul, or temporarily out of service due to schedule cancellations. Excludes days that newly acquired aircraft are on hand but not available for productive use, days dry-leased or rented to others, and days in possession but formally withdrawn from air transportation service.

Aircraft day assigned to service-carrier routes—same as *aircraft days assigned to service carrier's equipment* but excluding the number of days owned or rented equipment are in the possession of others under interchange agreements and including the number of days aircraft of others are in the possession of the air carrier under interchange agreements.

Aircraft, leased (rented). Aircraft obtained from (or furnished to) others under lease or rental arrangements. Leased and rented aircraft do not include those used under interchange agreements designed to provide oneplane service over the routes of the air carriers involved.

Aircraft type. A distinctive model as designated by the manufacturer.

Airport. A landing area regularly used by aircraft for receiving or discharging passengers or cargo.

Airport, alternate. An approved airport to which a flight may proceed if a landing at the airport to which the flight was dispatched becomes inadvisable.

Airport-to-airport distance. The great circle distance between airports, measured in statute miles in accordance with part 247 of this chapter.

Air transportation. The carriage by aircraft of persons, property, or mail.

Air transportation, charter. Air transportation authorized pursuant to section 401(d)(3).

Airworthiness (or Airworthy). When applied to a particular aircraft or component part, it denotes the ability of such aircraft or component part to perform its function satisfactorily through a range of operations determined by the Federal Aviation Administration.

Allocate. To assign an item or group of items of investment, revenue, or cost to an object, activity, process, or operation, in accordance with cost responsibilities, benefits received, or other measure of apportionment.

Allocation, bases of. Bases of distribution whereby revenues, expenses, and/or costs are equitably apportioned among revenue, expense, property and equipment, and other accounts.

Amortization. The gradual extinguishment of an amount in an account by distributing such amount over a fixed period, over the life of the asset or liability to which it applies or over the period during which it is anticipated the benefit will be realized.

Asset, contingent. An asset the existence, value, or ownership of which depend upon the occurrence or nonoccurrence of a specific event or upon the performance or nonperformance of a specified act.

Associated company. A company in which the accounting air carrier holds 5 percent or more of the outstanding proprietary interest; or a company which holds 5 percent or more of the outstanding proprietary interest of the accounting air carrier; or a company that, directly or through one or more intermediaries, controls or is controlled by, or is under common control with the accounting air carrier. Companies owned or controlled jointly with other air carriers shall be regarded as associated companies for purposes of this system of accounts. (See also *Control.*)

Betterment. Any improvement to property or equipment through the substitution of superior parts for inferior parts retired, the object of which is to make such property more useful or of greater capacity than at the time of acquisition or installation. (See also *Modification.*)

BTS. The Bureau of Transportation Statistics.

Cargo. All traffic other than passengers.

Cargo transported. Cargo on board each flight stage.

Certificated point. A city, place or population center authorized to receive scheduled air service under a *Certificate of Public Convenience and Necessity* or under an exemption issued to an air carrier.

Certificate of Public Convenience and Necessity. A certificate issued to an air carrier under 49 U.S.C. 41102, by the Department of Transportation authorizing the carrier to engage in air transportation.

Company, predecessor. An air carrier whose net assets and operations have been taken over by one or more other air carriers.

Compensation (of personnel). Remuneration to air carrier employees for personal services. Includes salaries, wages, overtime pay, cost-of-living differentials, bonuses, etc., as distinguished from per diem allowances or reimbursement for expenses incurred by personnel for the benefit of the air carrier.

Continental United States. The 48 contiguous States and the District of Columbia.

Control (including the terms *Controlling, Controlled by,* and *Under common control*). The possession, directly or indirectly, of the power positively to direct, or cause the direction of or negate the direction of, the management and policies of a company, whether such power is through one or more intermediary companies or alone or in conjunction with or pursuant to an agreement, and whether such power is established through a majority or minority ownership or voting of securities, common directors, officers, or stockholders, voting trusts, holding trusts, associated companies, contract, or any other direct or indirect means.

Controlling person. (See *Person Controlling an air carrier*)

Cost. The amount of cash (or its equivalent) actually paid for property, materials and supplies, and services, including that amount paid to put the property or materials and supplies in readiness for use. It includes such items as transportation charges, installation charges, and customs duties, less any cash or other discounts.

Cost, book. The amount at which an asset is recorded in an account without the deduction of amounts in related allowances or other accounts.

Cost, depreciated. The cost of property and equipment less the related allowances for depreciation.

Cost, removal. The cost of demolishing, dismantling, tearing down, or otherwise removing property and equipment, including the cost of related transportation and handling.

Debt, expense on. Expenses incurred by or for the air carrier in connection with the issuance and sale of evidences of debt (exclusive of the sale of reacquired securities), such as fees for drafting mortgages and trust deeds; fees and taxes for issuing or recording evidences of debt; cost of engraving and printing bonds, certificates of indebtedness, and other commercial paper; specific costs of obtaining governmental authority for issuance and filing notices thereunder; fees for legal services; fees and commissions paid underwriters, brokers, and salesmen for marketing such evidences of debt; fees and expenses of listing on exchanges; and other like costs.

Deferred taxes. Tax effects which are deferred for allocation to income tax expense of future periods.

Department. Department of Transportation.

Departures completed, percent scheduled. The percent of scheduled departures that were performed.

Departures completed, scheduled. The number of takeoffs performed at each airport pursuant to published schedules, exclusive of extra sections to scheduled departures.

Departure performed. A takeoff made at an airport.

Departure, scheduled. A takeoff scheduled at an airport, as set forth in published schedules.

Depreciation (of depreciable property and equipment). The loss in service value, not restored by current maintenance, incurred in the course of service from causes known to be in current operation, against which the carrier is not protected by insurance, and the effect of which can be forecast with reasonable accuracy. The causes of depreciation include wear and tear, decay, action of the elements, inadequacy, obsolescence, changes in the art, changes in demand, and requirements of public authorities.

Discount (of securities issued or assumed by the air carrier). The excess of (1) the par or stated value of securities over (2) the then current money value of the consideration received from their sale less the amount included for dividends or for interest accrued.

DOT. Department of Transportation.

Equipment. Tangible property other than land, structures, and improvements.

Equity security. Any instrument representing ownership shares (for example, common, preferred, and other capital stock), or the right to acquire (for example, warrants, rights, and call options) or dispose of (for example, put options) ownership shares in an enterprise at fixed or determinable prices. The term does not encompass preferred stock that by its terms either must be redeemed by the issuing enterprise or is redeemable at the option of the investor, nor does it include treasury stock or convertible bonds.

Equivalent unit. A new unit substituted for an existing unit that is worn out, is damaged beyond repair, or has become inadequate in service, the substituted unit having substantially no greater capacity than the unit for which substituted.

Estimated economic life of leased property. The estimated remaining period during which the property is expected to be economically usable by one or more users, with normal repairs and maintenance, for the purpose for which it was intended at the inception of the lease, without limitation by the lease term.

Expense, capital stock. Expenses incurred by or for the air carrier in connection with the initial issuance and sale of capital stock (exclusive of the sale of reacquired capital stock), such as fees and commissions paid to promoters, underwriters, brokers, and salesmen; fees for legal services; cost of soliciting subscriptions for capital stock; including fees, commissions, and advertising, specific costs of obtaining governmental authority for issuance and filing notices thereunder; fees and taxes for issuance of capital stock and listing on exchanges; and the cost of preparing, engraving, printing, issuing, and distributing prospectuses and stock certificates.

Flight, developmental. A flight for (1) the development of a new route either prior or subsequent to certification by the Department of Transportation; (2) the extension of an existing route; or (3) the integration of a new type of aircraft or service.

Flight, extra section. A flight, conducted as an integral part of scheduled service, that has not been provided for in published schedules and is required for transportation of traffic that cannot be accommodated on a regularly scheduled flight. Flights made in ferrying aircraft to meet schedules, or for similar operational reasons, are not extra sections and are classified as nonrevenue flights even if an occasional shipment, as a matter of special accommodation, is on board.

Flight, ferry. A flight for the purpose of returning an aircraft to base, equipment equalization, or moving an aircraft to and from a maintenance base.

Flight, paid positioning. A flight for the purpose of positioning an empty aircraft in connection with a charter flight for which a specific charge is set forth in a tariff or contract for application directly to the positioning miles operated. Such flights are considered revenue flights for Form 41 reporting purposes.

Flight, personnel training. A flight for the purpose of obtaining flying time for flight personnel or a flight in connection with a personnel training program.

Flight stage. The operation of an aircraft from takeoff to landing. For purposes of classifying flight stages as between "domestic", "territorial", and "international", technical stops are disregarded. (See Stops, technical.)

Freight. Property, other than mail, transported by air.

Generally accepted accounting principles (GAAP). The body of authoritative accounting knowledge governing the recording, presenting and disclosing of financial transactions, as incorporated in the pronouncements of the Financial Accounting Standards Board.

Group basis (in depreciation accounting). A plan under which (1) depreciation is based upon the application of a single depreciation rate to the total book cost of all property included in a given depreciable property and equipment account or class, despite differences in service life of individual items of property and equipment, (2) the full original cost, less any salvage realized, of an item of depreciable property or equipment retired is charged to the allowance for depreciation regardless of the age of the item, and (3) no gain or loss is recognized on the retirement of individual items of property or equipment.

Horsepower, maximum continuous for reciprocating engines. The brake horsepower developed in standard atmosphere at a specified altitude and under the maximum conditions of crankshaft rotational speed and engine manifold pressure, and approved for use during periods of unrestricted duration.

Horsepower, maximum continuous for turbine engines. The brake horsepower developed at specified altitudes, atmospheric temperatures, and flight speeds and under the maximum conditions of rotor shaft rotational speed and gas temperature, and approved for use during periods of unrestricted duration.

Thrust, maximum continuous for turbine engines. The jet thrust developed at specified altitudes, atmospheric temperatures, and flight speeds and under the maximum conditions of rotor shaft rotational speed and gas temperature, and approved for use during periods of unrestricted duration.

Hours, aircraft. The airborne hours of aircraft computed from the moment an aircraft leaves the ground until it touches the ground at the end of a flight.

Hours flown, revenue aircraft. The aircraft hours of flights performed in revenue service.

Hours in capitalized projects, aircraft. Aircraft hours applicable to ferrying newly acquired aircraft from the factory, to capitalized extension and development preoperating projects and to other costs which have been capitalized.

Hours per aircraft per day—carrier's equipment, revenue. Average hours of productive use per day in revenue service of reporting carrier's equipment determined by dividing (1) Aircraft days assigned to service—carrier's equipment into (2) Revenue aircraft hours minus Revenue hours on other carrier's interchange equipment plus Total hours by others on the carrier's interchange equipment.

Hours per aircraft per day—carrier's routes, revenue. Average hours of productive use per day in revenue service on reporting carrier's routes determined by dividing (1) Aircraft days assigned to service-carrier's routes into (2) Revenue aircraft hours.

Hours, ramp-to-ramp. The aircraft hours computed from the moment the aircraft first moves under it own power for purposes of flight, until it comes to rest at the next point of landing.

Improvement. An addition or alteration to land, a building, or a unit of equipment that results in a better piece of property, in the sense of greater durability, or in increased productivity or efficiency. (See also *Modification.*)

Income tax expense. The amount of income taxes (whether or not currently payable or refundable) allocable to a period in the determination of net income.

Income taxes. Taxes based on income determined under provisions of the United States Internal Revenue Code and foreign, State, and other taxes (including franchise taxes) based on income.

Insurance, self. The assumption by an air carrier of a risk of loss or liability arising from an accident or other contingent event.

Interchange agreement. An agreement under which aircraft of one air carrier are utilized to provide one-plane service over its own routes and the routes of other air carriers.

Interperiod tax allocation. The process of apportioning income taxes among periods.

Inventory, perpetual. A book inventory kept in continuous agreement with stock on hand by means of a detailed record.

Investor controlled company (for purposes of applying the equity method of accounting). Any business entity in which the accounting air carrier is able to exercise significant influence over operating and financial policies of the issuing company. Significant influence will be presumed, unless established to the contrary by waiver request, with ownership of 20 percent or more of the outstanding voting capital stock. Ability to exercise influence may be indicated in several ways, such as representation on the Board of Directors, participation in policy-making processes, material intercompany transactions, interchange of managerial personnel, or technological dependency. Investor controlled companies shall also be regarded as associated companies for purposes of this system of accounts (see also Associated company).

Item, delayed. An item relating to transactions that occurred during a prior accounting period and that requires further accounting treatment for a true statement of financial condition or operating results. It includes adjustments of errors in the operating revenue, operating expense, and other income accounts for prior periods.

Liability, contingent. A possible source of obligation of an air carrier dependent upon the fulfillment of conditions regarded as uncertain.

Load, available. Represents the maximum salable load. It is the allowable gross weight less the empty weight, less all justifiable aircraft equipment, and less the operating load (consisting of minimum fuel load, oil, flight crew, steward's supplies, etc.). For passenger aircraft, the available load must not exceed the weight of the maximum number of passengers who can be accommodated in the seats installed in the aircraft plus the weight of the traffic that can be accommodated in the cargo space.

Load, average revenue. The average total revenue tons carried in revenue services, determined by dividing total revenue ton-miles by aircraft miles flown in revenue services.

Load, average revenue passenger. Average number of revenue passengers carried in passenger services, determined by dividing revenue passenger-miles by aircraft miles flown in revenue passenger services.

Load factor, over-all revenue. The percent that total revenue ton-miles (passenger plus nonpassenger) are of available ton-miles in revenue services.

Load factor, revenue passenger. The percent that revenue passenger-miles are of available seat-miles in revenue passenger services.

Load, minimum fuel. The minimum quantity of fuel with which an aircraft may be dispatched in accordance with the safety operating needs of the air carrier.

Load, salable. (See *Load, available.*)

Mail, nonpriority. All mail for which transportation by air is provided on a space available basis.

Mail, priority. All mail for which transportation by air is provided on a priority basis.

Mile. A statute mile (5,280 feet).

Miles completed, percent scheduled aircraft. The percent of scheduled aircraft miles which were performed.

Miles completed, scheduled aircraft. The aircraft miles performed on scheduled flights computed between only those scheduled points actually served.

Miles flown, aircraft. The miles (computed in airport-to-airport distances) for each flight stage actually completed, whether or not performed in accordance with the scheduled pattern. For this purpose, operation to a flag stop is a stage completed even though a landing is not actually made. In cases where the interairport distances are inapplicable, aircraft miles flown are determined by multiplying the normal crusing speed for the aircraft type by the airborne hours.

Miles flown, nonrevenue aircraft. The aircraft miles flown on nonrevenue flights, such as ferry (including empty backhauls to MAC one-way charters), personnel training, extension and development, and abortive revenue flights.

Miles, revenue aircraft. The aircraft miles flown in revenue service.

Miles, scheduled aircraft. The sum of the airport-to-airport distances of all flights scheduled to be performed over the air carrier's certificated routes pursuant to published flight schedules. Flights listed in the published schedules for operation only as extra sections, when traffic warrants, are excluded.

Modification. An alteration in a structure or unit of equipment that changes its design and is made to correct an error, increase production, improve efficiency of operation, or for some other reason.

Obsolescence. The process of becoming out of date due to progress of the arts and sciences, changed economic conditions, legislation, etc., which ultimately results in the retirement or other disposition of property.

Off-Line. Installations maintained or facilities used for other than scheduled certificated air services.

On-Line. Installations maintained or facilities used in conducting scheduled certificated air services.

Domestic. Flight stages with both terminals within the 50 States of the United States and the District of Columbia.

Territorial. Flight stages with both terminals within territory under U.S. jurisdiction where at least one of the terminals is not within a State or the District of Columbia.

International. Flight stages with one or both terminals outside of territory under U.S. jurisdiction.

Operations, systems. The over-all operations of an air carrier including all of the operating entities of an air carrier having multiple operations.

Passenger-mile. One passenger transported 1 mile. Passenger-miles are computed by multiplying the aircraft miles flown on each flight stage by the number of passengers transported on that stage.

Passenger-mile, nonrevenue. One nonrevenue passenger transported one mile.

Passenger-mile, revenue. One revenue passenger transported one mile.

Passenger, nonrevenue. A person traveling free or under token charges, except those expressly named in the definition of revenue passenger; a person traveling at a fare or discount available only to employees or authorized persons of air carriers or their agents or only for travel on the business of the carriers; and an infant who does not occupy a seat. (This definition is for 14 CFR part 241 traffic reporting purposes and may differ from the definitions used in other parts by the Federal Aviation Administration and the Transportation Security Administration for the collection of Passenger Facility Charges and Security Fees.)

The definition includes, but is not limited to following examples of passengers when traveling free or pursuant to token charges:

(1) Directors, officers, employees, and others authorized by the air carrier operating the aircraft;

(2) Directors, officers, employees, and others authorized by the air carrier or another carrier traveling pursuant to a pass interchange agreement;

(3) Travel agents being transported for the purpose of familiarizing themselves with the carrier's services;

(4) Witnesses and attorneys attending any legal investigation in which such carrier is involved;

(5) Persons injured in aircraft accidents, and physicians, nurses, and others attending such persons;

(6) Any persons transported with the object of providing relief in cases of general epidemic, natural disaster, or other catastrophe;

(7) Any law enforcement official, including any person who has the duty of guarding government officials who are traveling on official business or traveling to or from such duty;

(8) Guests of an air carrier on an inaugural flight or delivery flights of newly-acquired or renovated aircraft;

(9) Security guards who have been assigned the duty to guard such aircraft against unlawful seizure, sabotage, or other unlawful interference;

(10) Safety inspectors of the National Transportation Safety Board or the FAA in their official duties or traveling to or from such duty;

(11) Postal employees on duty in charge of the mails or traveling to or from such duty;

(12) Technical representatives of companies that have been engaged in the manufacture, development or testing of a particular type of aircraft or aircraft equipment, when the transportation is provided for the purpose of in-flight observation and subject to applicable FAA regulations;

(13) Persons engaged in promoting air transportation;

(14) Air marshals and other Transportation Security officials acting in their official capacities and while traveling to and from their official duties; and

(15) Other authorized persons, when such transportation is undertaken for promotional purpose.

Passenger, revenue. A passenger for whose transportation an air carrier receives commercial remuneration. (This definition is for 14 CFR part 241 traffic reporting purposes and may differ from the definitions used in other parts by the Federal Aviation Administration and the Transportation Security Administration for the collection of Passenger Facility Charges and Security Fees.) This includes, but is not limited to, the following examples:

(1) Passengers traveling under publicly available tickets including promotional offers (for example two-for-one) or loyalty programs (for example, redemption of frequent flyer points);

(2) Passengers traveling on vouchers or tickets issued as compensation for denied boarding or in response to consumer complaints or claims;

(3) Passengers traveling at corporate discounts;

(4) Passengers traveling on preferential fares (Government, seamen, military, youth, student, etc.);

(5) Passengers traveling on barter tickets; and

(6) Infants traveling on confirmed-space tickets.

Passengers transported. Passengers on board each flight stage.

Person controlling an air carrier. Any person, as defined in 49 U.S.C. 40102, whom the Department has found, in any proceeding, to control an air carrier, or who holds, directly or indirectly, the legal or beneficial ownership of more than 50 percent of the outstanding voting capital stock or capital of an air carrier, and who does not make a proper showing to the Department that he or she does not control the carrier despite such stock ownership, shall be deemed to be a person controlling the carrier for the purpose of this part. A brokerage firm which holds record ownership of securities merely for the convenience of the customer beneficially owning the stock shall not be deemed a person controlling an air carrier.

Premium (as applied to securities issued or assumed by the air carrier). The excess of (1) the then current money value of the consideration received from their sale, less the amount included therein for dividends or interest accrued, over (2) their par or stated value.

Pretax accounting income. Income or loss for a period exclusive of related income tax expense.

Property (as applied to traffic). (See *Cargo.*)

Replacement. Substitution of new for existing facilities that are worn out, damaged beyond repair, or have become inadequate in service.

Reporting carrier for T–100 purposes means the air carrier in operational control of the flight, i.e., the carrier that uses its flight crew under its own FAA operating authority.

Residual value. The predetermined portion of the cost of a unit of property or equipment excluded from depreciation. It shall represent a fair and reasonable estimate of recoverable value as at the end of the service life over which the property or equipment is depreciated and shall give due consideration to the proceeds anticipated from disposition of the property or equipment and the extent to which costs attaching to property or equipment are otherwise recoverable through charges against income.

Retirement. The permanent withdrawal of assets from services of the corporate entity through sale, abandonment, demolition, or other disposal.

Retirement, date of. The date on which property or equipment is permanently withdrawn from services of the corporate entity.

Route, certificated. The route(s) over which an air carrier is authorized to provide air transportation by a Certificate of Public Convenience and Necessity issued by the Department of Transportation pursuant to section 401(d) (1) or (2) of the Act.

Salvage value. The amount received for property retired, less the expenses incurred in connection with the sale or in the preparation of the property for sale; or, if retained, the amount at which the material recovered is charged to materials and supplies or other appropriate account.

Seats available. Installed seats in an aircraft (including seats in lounges) exclusive of any seats not offered for sale to the public by the carrier; provided that in no instance shall any seat sold be excluded from the count of available seats.

Seats, average available. The average number of seats available for passengers, determined by dividing available seat-miles by revenue aircraft miles flown in passenger service.

Seat-miles available, revenue. The aircraft miles flown on each flight stage multiplied by the number of seats available for revenue use on that stage.

Section 41103 cargo operations. The carriage, pursuant to 49 U.S.C. 41103, by aircraft of property and/or mail as a common carrier for compensation or hire in commerce between a place in any State of the United States, or the District of Columbia, or Puerto Rico, or the U.S. Virgin Islands, and a place in any other of those entities, or between places in the same State or other entity through the air-space over any place outside thereof, or between places within the District of Columbia, Puerto Rico, or the U.S. Virgin Islands. This includes commerce moving partly by aircraft and partly by other forms of transportation, as well as commerce moving wholly by aircraft.

Segment, service. A pair of points served or scheduled to be served by a single stage of at least one flight within any given time period.

Service, charter. Nonscheduled air transport service in which the party receiving transportation obtains exclusive use of an agreed upon portion of the total capacity of an aircraft with the remuneration paid by the party receiving transportation accruing directly to, and the responsibility for providing transportation is that of, the accounting air carrier.

Service, coach (tourist). Transport service specifically established for the carriage of passengers at special reduced passenger fares that are predicated on both the operation of specifically designated aircraft space and a reduction in the quality of service regularly and ordinarily provided.

Service, first class. Transport service established for the carriage of passengers moving at either standard fares or premium fares, or at reduced fares not predicated upon the operation of specifically allocated aircraft space, and for whom standard or premium quality services are provided.

Service life. The period between the date of installation of property or equipment and its date of retirement.

Service, mixed. Transport service for the carriage of both first-class and coach passengers on the same aircraft.

Service, nonpassenger. Transport service established for the carriage of traffic other than passengers.

Service, nonscheduled. Includes transport service between points not covered by Certificates of Public Convenience and Necessity issued by the Department of Transportation to the air carrier; services pursuant to the charter or hiring of aircraft; other revenue services not constituting an integral part of the services performed pursuant to published schedules; and related nonrevenue flights.

Service, passenger-cargo. Transport service established for the carriage of passengers which may also be used jointly for the transportation of cargo.

Service, scheduled. Transport service operated pursuant to published flight schedules, including extra sections and related nonrevenue flights.

Service, transport. The operation of facilities for the carriage of traffic by air.

Services, all. The total of scheduled and nonscheduled transport services.

Stop, flag. A point on an air carrier's operating system that is scheduled to be served only when traffic is to be picked up or discharged.

Stops, technical. Aircraft landing made for purposes other than enplaning or deplaning traffic. For purposes of identifying reporting entities, landings made for stopover passengers are regarded as technical stops.

Tariff, published. A publication containing fares and rates applicable to the transportation of persons or cargo and rules relating to or affecting such fares or rates of transportation, filed with the Department of Transportation.

Taxable income. The excess of revenues over deductions or the excess of deductions over revenues to be reported for income tax purposes for a period.

Tax effects. Differentials in income taxes of a period attributable to (1) revenue or expense transactions which enter into the determination of pretax accounting income in one period and into the determination of taxable income in another period, (2) deductions or credits that may be carried backward or forward for income tax purposes, and (3) adjustments of prior periods (or of the opening balance of retained earnings) and direct entries to other stockholders' equity accounts which enter into the determination of taxable income in a period but which do not enter into the determination of pretax accounting income of that period. A permanent difference does not result in a "tax effect" as the term is used in this System of Accounts and Reports.

Ton. A short ton (2,000 pounds).

Ton-mile. One ton transported 1 mile. Ton-miles are computed by multiplying the aircraft miles flown on each flight stage by the number of tons transported on that stage.

Ton-mile, nonrevenue. One ton of nonrevenue traffic transported 1 mile.

Ton-mile, passenger. One ton of passenger weight (including all baggage) transported 1 mile. (See also *Weight, passenger.*)

Ton-mile, revenue. One ton of revenue traffic transported 1 mile.

Ton-miles available, revenue. The aircraft miles flown on each flight stage multiplied by the ton capacity available for use on that stage.

Traffic, deplaned. A count of the number of passengers getting off and tons of cargo unloaded from an aircraft. For this purpose, passengers and cargo on aircraft leaving a carrier's system on interchange flights are considered as deplaning and the interchange point; and passengers and cargo moving from one operation to another operation of the same carrier, for which separate reports are required by the Department of Transportation, are considered as deplaning at the junction point.

Traffic, enplaned. A count of the number of passengers boarding and tons of cargo loaded on an aircraft. For this purpose, passengers and cargo on aircraft entering a carrier's system on interchange flights are considered as enplaning at the interchange point; and passengers and cargo moving from one operation to another operation of the same carrier, for which separate reports are required by the Department of Transportation, are considered as enplaning at the junction point.

Traffic, nonrevenue. Passengers and cargo transported by air for which no remuneration or token service charges are received by the air carrier. Airline employees, officers and directors, or other persons, except for ministers of religion, who are traveling under reduced-rate transportation authorized by 49 U.S.C. 41511(a) and 14 CFR part 223, as well as travel agents, cargo agents, and tour conductors traveling at reduced fares are also considered nonrevenue traffic.

Traffic office. A facility where air transportation is sold, and related processes of documentation and reservation confirmation are performed.

Traffic, revenue. Passengers and cargo transported by air for which remuneration is received by the air carrier. Airline employees, officers and directors, or other persons, except for ministers of religion, who are traveling under reduced-rate transportation authorized by 49 U.S.C. 41511(a) and 14 CFR part 223, travel agents, cargo agents, and tour conductors traveling at reduced fares, and other passengers and cargo carried for token service charges, are not considered as revenue traffic.

Transportation, free. The carriage of any person or cargo (other than cargo owned by the air carrier) without compensation.

Unit basis (in depreciation accounting). A plan under which depreciation expenses is accrued upon the basis of the book cost of the individual item of property in relation to the service life and salvage value of the particular item.

Value, service. The difference between the book cost and the residual value of property and equipment.

Weight, allowable gross. The maximum gross weight (of the aircraft and its contents) which an aircraft is licensed to carry into the air on each flight stage.

Weight, average available. The average capacity available for revenue traffic, determined by dividing available ton-miles by aircraft miles in revenue service.

Weight, empty. The weight of the airframe, engines, propellers, and fixed equipment of an aircraft. Empty weight excludes the weight of the crew and payload, but includes the weight of all fixed ballast, unusable fuel supply, undrainable oil, total quantity of engine coolant, and total quantity of hydraulic fluid.

Weight, passenger. For the purposes of this part, a standard weight of 200 pounds per passenger (including all baggage) is used for all civil operations and classes of service. Other weights may be prescribed in specific instances upon the initiative of the Department of Transportation or upon a factually supported request by an air carrier.

Wet-Lease Agreement means an agreement under which one carrier leases an aircraft with flight crew to another air carrier.

[ER-755, 37 FR 19726, Sept. 21, 1972, as amended by Amdt. 241-58, 54 FR 5590, Feb. 89, 1989]

EDITORIAL NOTE: For FEDERAL REGISTER citations affecting Section 03, see the List of CFR Sections Affected, which appears in the Finding Aids section of the printed volume and at *www.govinfo.gov*.

Section 04 Air Carrier Groupings

(a) All large certificated air carriers are placed into three basic air carrier groupings based upon their level of operations and the nature of these operations. In order to determine the level of operations, total operating revenues for a twelve-month period are used. The following operating revenue ranges are used to establish air carrier groupings:

Carrier Group	Total Annual Operating Revenues
I	0–$100,000,000
II	$100,000,001–$1,000,000,000
III	$1,000,000,001 +

For reporting purposes, Group I air carriers are further divided into two subgroups: (1) Air carriers with total annual operating revenues from $20,000,000 to $100,000,000 and (2) Air carriers with total annual operating revenues below $20,000,000.

(b) Both the criteria for establishing air carrier groupings and the assignment of each air carrier to a specific group of carriers will be reviewed periodically by the Director, Office of Airline Information, to assure the maintenance of appropriate standards for the grouping of carriers. When an air carrier's level of operations passes the upper or lower limit of its currently assigned carrier grouping, the carrier is not automatically transferred to a different group and a new level of reporting. The Office of Airline Statistics will issue an updated listing of the carrier groups on an annual basis. A carrier may petition for reconsideration of its assigned carrier grouping or request a waiver from the accounting and reporting requirements that are applicable to a particular group under the provisions of section 1–2 of this Uniform System of Accounts and Reports.

[Amdt. 241–60, 56 FR 12658, Mar. 27, 1991, as amended at 60 FR 66723, Dec. 26, 1995]

GENERAL ACCOUNTING PROVISIONS

Section 1 Introduction to System of Accounts and Reports

Sec. 1–1 Applicability of system of accounts and reports.

Each large certificated air carrier shall keep its books of account, records and memoranda and make reports to the BTS in accordance with this system of accounts and reports. The BTS reserves the right, however, under the provisions of sections 49 U.S.C. 41701 and 41708, to expand or otherwise modify the classes of carriers subject to this system of accounts and reports.

[ER–1400, 50 FR 11, Jan. 2, 1985, as amended at 60 FR 66723, Dec. 26, 1995]

Sec. 1–2 Waivers from this system of accounts and reports.

A waiver from any provision of this system of accounts or reports may be made by the BTS upon its own initiative or upon the submission of written request therefor from any air carrier, or group of air carriers, provided that such a waiver is in the public interest and each request for waiver expressly demonstrates that: existing peculiarities or unusual circumstances warrant a departure from a prescribed procedure or technique; a specifically defined alternative procedure or technique will result in a substantially equivalent or more accurate portrayal of operating results or financial condition, consistent with the principles embodied in the provisions of this system of accounts and reports, and the application of such alternative procedure will maintain or improve uniformity in substantive results as between air carriers.

[ER–755, 37 FR 19726, Sept. 21, 1972, as amended at 60 FR 66723, Dec. 26, 1995]

Sec. 1–3 General description of system of accounts and reports.

(a) This system of accounts and reports is designed to permit limited contraction or expansion to reflect the varying needs and capacities of different air carriers without impairing basic accounting comparability as between air carriers. In its administration three air carrier groups, designated Group I, Group II, and Group III, respectively (see section 04), are established by the BTS. This grouping will be reviewed from time to time upon petition of individual air carriers or by initiative of the BTS with the view of a possible regrouping of the air carriers.

(b) Under the system of accounts prescribed, balance sheet elements are accounted for by all air carrier groups within a fixed uniform pattern of specific accounts. All profit and loss elements are accounted for within specific objective accounts established for each air carrier group resulting from dual classifications, designated for each air carrier group, which are descriptive of both basic areas of financial activity, or functional operation, and objective served. The profit and loss elements of the three air carrier groups can be reduced to broad objectives and general or functional classifications which are comparable for all air carrier groups. Both balance sheet and profit and loss accounts and account groupings are designed, in general, to embrace all activities, both air transport and other than air transport, in which the air carrier engages and provide for the separation of elements identifiable exclusively with other than air transport activities. Profit and loss elements which are recorded during the current accounting year are subclassified as between (1) those which relate to the current accounting year and adjustments of a recurrent nature applicable to prior accounting years, and (2) extraordinary items of material magnitude.

(c) In order to afford air carriers as much flexibility and freedom as possible in establishing ledger and subsidiary accounts to meet their individual needs, a minimum number of account subdivisions have been prescribed in this Uniform System of Accounts. It is intended, however, that each air carrier, in maintaining its accounting records, will provide subaccount and subsidiary account segregations of accounting elements which differ in nature of accounting characteristics, in a manner which will render individual elements readily discernible and traceable throughout the accounting system, and will provide for relating profit and loss elements to applicable balance sheet counterparts.

[ER–755, 37 FR 19726, Sept. 21, 1972, as amended at 60 FR 66723, Dec. 26, 1995]

Sec. 1–4 System of accounts coding.

(a) A four digit control number is assigned for each balance sheet and profit and loss account. Each balance sheet account is numbered sequentially, within blocks, designating basic balance sheet classifications. The first two digits of the four digit code assigned to each profit and loss account denote a detailed area of financial activity or functional operation. The first two digits, thus assigned to each profit and loss account, are numbered sequentially within blocks, designating more general classifications of financial activity and functional operation. The second two digits assigned to profit and loss accounts denote objective classifications.

(b) A fifth digit, appended as a decimal, has been assigned for internal control by the BTS of prescribed subdivisions of the primary objective balance sheet and profit and loss classifications. A different fifth digit code number from that assigned by the BTS may be adopted for internal recordkeeping by the air carrier provided the prescribed subclassification of objective accounts is not impaired and the code number assigned by the BTS is employed in reporting to the BTS on Form 41 Reports.

[ER–755, 37 FR 19726, Sept. 21, 1972, as amended at 60 FR 66723, Dec. 26, 1995]

Sec. 1–5 Records.

(a) The general books of account and all books, records, and memoranda which support in any way the entries therein shall be kept in such manner as to provide at any time full information relating to any account. The entries in each account shall be supported by such detailed information as will render certain the identification of all facts essential to a verification of the nature and character of each entry and its proper classification under the prescribed Uniform System of Accounts. Registers, or other appropriate records, shall be maintained of the history and nature of each note receivable and each note payable.

(b) The books and records referred to herein include not only accounting records in a limited technical sense, but all other records such as organization tables and charts, internal accounting manuals and revisions thereto, minute books, stock books, reports, cost distributions and other accounting work sheets, correspondence, memoranda, etc., which may constitute necessary links in developing the history of, or facts regarding, any accounting or financial transaction.

(c) All books, records and memoranda shall be preserved and filed in such manner as to readily permit the audit and examination thereof by representatives of the DOT. All books, records, and memoranda shall be housed or stored in such manner as to afford protection from loss, theft, or damage by fire, flood or otherwise and no such books and records shall be destroyed or otherwise disposed of, except in conformance with 14 CFR part 249 for the preservation of records.

[ER–755, 37 FR 19726, Sept. 21, 1972, as amended at 60 FR 66723, Dec. 26, 1995]

Sec. 1–6 Accounting entities.

(a) Separate accounting records shall be maintained for each air transport entity for which separate reports to the BTS are required to be made by sections 21(g) and for each separate corporate or organizational division of the air carrier. For purposes of this Uniform System of Accounts and Reports, each nontransport entity conducting an activity which is not related to the air carrier's transport activities and each transport-related activity or group of activities qualifying as a nontransport venture pursuant to paragraph (b) of this section, whether or not formally organized within a distinct organizational unit, shall be treated as a separately operated organizational division; except that provisions of this paragraph and paragraph (b) shall not apply to leasing activities.

(b) As a general rule, any activity or group of activities comprising a transport-related service provided for in transport-related revenue and expense accounts 09 through 18 shall be considered a separate nontransport venture under circumstances in which either: (1) A separate corporate or legal entity has been established to perform such services, (2) the aggregate annual revenue rate, as determined in section 2–1(d), during either of the prior two years exceeds the greater of $1 million per annum or one percent of the air carrier's total annual transport revenues, or (3) the aggregate annual expense rate, as determined in section 2–1(d), during either of the prior two years exceeds the greater of $1 million or one percent of the carrier's total annual operating expenses: *Provided*, That revenues and expenses from in-flight sales, and interchange sales shall be considered related to air transportation and accounted for accordingly, regardless of the revenue or expense standard set forth above.

(c) The records for each required accounting entity shall be maintained with sufficient particularity to permit a determination that the requirements of section 2–1 have been complied with.

[ER–755, 37 FR 19726, Sept. 21, 1972, as amended by ER–841, 39 FR 11994, Apr. 2, 1974; ER–1022, 42 FR 46495, Sept. 15, 1977; ER–1027, 42 FR 60127, Nov. 25, 1977; 60 FR 66723, Dec. 26, 1995]

Sec. 1–7 Interpretation of accounts.

To the end that uniform accounting may be maintained, questions involving matters of accounting significance which are not clearly provided for should be submitted to the Director, Office of Airline Information, K–25, Bureau of Transportation Statistics, for explanation, interpretation, or resolution.

[Amdt. 241–58, 54 FR 5591, Feb. 6, 1989, as amended at 60 FR 66723, Dec. 26, 1995]

Sec. 1–8 Address for reports and correspondence.

Reports required by this section shall be submitted to the Bureau of Transportation Statistics in a format specified in accounting and reporting directives issued by the Bureau of Transportation Statistics' Director of Airline Information.

[Doc. No. OST–2006–26053, 75 FR 41583, July 16, 2010]

Section 2 General Accounting Policies

Sec. 2–1 Generally accepted accounting principles.

(a) The accounting provisions contained in this part are based on generally accepted accounting principles (GAAP). Persons subject to this part are authorized to implement, as prescribed by the Financial Accounting Standards Board, newly issued GAAP pronouncements until and unless the Director, Office of Airline Information (OAI), issues an Accounting Directive making an initial determination that implementation of a new pronouncement would adversely affect the Department's programs.

(b) The Director, OAI, shall review each newly issued GAAP pronouncement to determine its affect on the Department's regulatory programs. If adopting a specific change in GAAP would adversely affect the Department's programs, the Director will issue the results of the review in the form of an Accounting Directive. The directive will state the reasons why the particular change should not be incorporated in the uniform system of accounts and contain accounting guidance for maintaining the integrity of the Department's air carrier accounting provisions.

(c) Objections and comments relating to the Department's decision not to implement a change in generally accepted principles may be addressed to Director, Office of Airline Information, K–25, U.S. Department of Transportation, 1200 New Jersey Avenue, SE., Washington, DC 20590. If significant objections are raised urging adoption of a particular GAAP pronouncement, the Department will institute a rulemaking.

[[Amdt. 241–58, 54 FR 5592, Feb. 6, 1989, as amended at 60 FR 66723, Dec. 26, 1995]

Sec. 2–2 Basis of allocation between entities.

(a) The provisions of this section shall apply to each person controlling an air carrier, each person controlled by the air carrier, as well as each transport entity and organizational division of the air carrier for which separate records must be maintained pursuant to section 1–6.

(b) Each transaction shall be recorded and placed initially under accounting controls of the particular air transport entity or organizational division of the air carrier or member of an affiliated group to which directly traceable. If applicable to two or more accounting entities, a proration shall be made from the entity of original recording to other participating entities on such basis that the statements of financial condition and operating results of each entity are comparable to those of distinct legal entities. The allocations involved shall include all debits and credits associated with each entity.

(c) For purposes of this section, investments by the air carrier in resources or facilities used in common by the regulated air carrier and those transport-related revenue services defined as separate nontransport ventures under section 1–6(b) shall not be allocated between such entities but shall be reflected in total in the appropriate accounts of the entity which predominately uses those investments. Where the entity of predominate use is a nontransport venture, the air carrier shall reflect the investment in account 1510.3, Advances to Associated Companies.

(d) For purposes of this Uniform System of Accounts and Reports, all revenues shall be assigned to or apportioned between accounting entities on bases which will fully recognize the services provided by each entity, and expenses, or costs, shall be apportioned between accounting entities on such bases as will result: (1) With respect to transport-related services, in the assignment thereto of proportionate direct overheads, as well as direct labor and materials, of the applicable expense functions prescribed by this system of accounts and reports, and (2) with respect to separate ventures, in the assignment thereto of proportional general and administrative overheads as well as the direct overheads, labor, and materials.

[ER–755, 37 FR 19726, Sept. 21, 1972, as amended by ER–841, 39 FR 11994, Apr. 2, 1974; ER–1401, 50 FR 238, Jan. 3, 1985. Redesignated and further amended by Amdt. 241–58, 54 FR 5592, Feb. 6, 1989]

Sec. 2–3 Distribution of revenues and expenses within entities.

(a) Revenues and expenses attributable to a single natural objective account or functional classification shall be assigned accordingly.

(b) Revenue and expense items which are common to two or more natural objective accounts shall be recorded in the objective accounts to which they predominantly relate.

(c) Expense items contributing to more than one function shall be charged to the general overhead functions to which applicable except that where only incidental contribution is made to more than a single function an item may be included in the function to which primarily related, provided such function is not distorted by including an aggregation of amounts applicable to other functions. When assignment of expense items on the basis of the primary activity to which related does not in the aggregate result in a fair presentation of the expenses applicable to each function, apportionment shall be made between functions based upon a study of the contribution to each function during a representative period.

[ER–755, 37 FR 19726, Sept. 21, 1972. Redesignated by Amdt. 241–58, 54 FR 5592, Feb. 6, 1989]

Sec. 2–4 Accounting period.

(a) The accounting year of each air carrier subject to this Uniform System of Accounts shall be the calendar year unless otherwise approved by the BTS.

(b) Each air carrier shall keep its financial accounts and records on a full accrual basis for each quarter so that all transactions, as nearly as may reasonably be ascertained, shall be fully reflected in the air carrier's books for the quarter in which revenues have been earned and the costs attaching to the revenues so earned in each quarter have been incurred independently of the incidence of sales or purchases and settlement with debtors or creditors.

(c) Expenditures incurred during the current accounting year which demonstrably benefit operations to be performed during subsequent accounting years to a significant extent shall be deferred and amortized to the period in which the related operations are performed when of sufficient magnitude to distort the accounting results of the year in which incurred.

(d) Expenditures charged directly or amortized to operations within one accounting year shall not be reversed in a subsequent accounting year and reamortized or charged directly against operations of subsequent years except that retroactive adjustments are permitted where necessary to conform with adjustments required by the DOT for ratemaking purposes.

[ER–755, 37 FR 19726, Sept. 21, 1972, as amended by ER–1027, 42 FR 60127, Nov. 25, 1977; ER–1188, 45 FR 48870, July 22, 1980; 60 FR 66723, 66725, Dec. 26, 1995]

Sec. 2–5 Revenue and accounting practices.

(a) Revenue accounting practices shall conform to the provisions of account 2160, Air Traffic Liability.

(b) Each route air carrier shall physically verify the reliability of its passenger revenue accounting practice at least once each accounting year.

(c) For those carriers who use the yield or average-fare method to determine earned revenue, the analysis supporting the verification shall include:

(1) The cutoff date for the liability to be verified; such cutoff date shall be at the end of a calendar month.

(2) The number of months after the cutoff date during which documents were examined to verify the liability; the number of months after the cutoff date during which documents are examined shall not exceed the maximums set forth below:

Class of carrier	Maximum months [1]
TWA	18
Trunks (except TWA)	12
All other route air carriers	6

[1] Applies only to carriers on a yield or average-fare basis.

(3) The nature of the documents which were examined for purposes of the verification.

(4) The totals for each of the various types of documents examined, on actual or sampling basis.

(5) A description of the sampling technique and conversion to totals, if sampling was employed.

(6) The amount and basis for all estimates employed in the verification.

(7) The amount of resulting adjustments and the quarter in which such adjustments were, or are to be, made in the accounts.

(d) For those carriers who use the sales-lift match method to determine earned revenue, the analysis supporting the physical inventory verification shall include:

(1) The cutoff date for the liability to be verified; such cutoff date shall be at the end of a calendar month.

(2) A trial balance as of the cutoff date of all subaccounts supporting the Air Traffic Liability control account; the subsidiary trial balance must agree with the Air Traffic Liability control account or a reconciliation statement furnished.

(3) A statement to the effect that a sales listing of the value of all unmatched auditor coupons has been compiled and compared to the general ledger control figure; the statement required by this subparagraph shall indicate whether or not the value of the unmatched coupons is in agreement with the general ledger. If the sales listing is not in agreement with the Air Traffic Liability control account, the amount of such difference shall be shown on such statement.

[ER–948, 41 FR 12290, Mar. 25, 1976, as amended by ER–1401, 50 FR 238, Jan. 3, 1985. Redesignated at Amdt. 241–58, 54 FR 5592, Feb. 6, 1989; 60 FR 66725, Dec. 26, 1995]

BALANCE SHEET CLASSIFICATIONS

Section 3 Chart of Balance Sheet Accounts

[See footnotes at end of table]

Name of account	General classification	
Current assets:		
Cash		1010
Short-term investments		1100
Notes receivable		1200
Accounts receivable		1270
Allowance for uncollectible accounts		1290
Spare parts and supplies		1300
Allowance for obsolescence—Spare parts and supplies		1311
Prepaid items		1410
Other current assets		1420

[See footnotes at end of table]

Name of account	General classification	
Investments and special funds:		
Investments in associated companies	....	1510
Investments in investor controlled companies	....	1510.1
Investments in other associated companies	....	1510.2
Advances to associated companies	....	1510.3
Other investments and receivables	....	1530
Special funds	....	1550
Property and equipment	....	1600–1700
	Operating	Nonoperating
Airframes	1601	1701
Airframes	1601.1	1701.1
Unamortized airframe overhauls	1601.2	1701.2
Aircraft engines	1602	1702
Aircraft engines	1602.1	1702.1
Unamortized aircraft engine overhauls	1602.2	1702.2
Improvements to leased flight equipment	1607	1707
Flight equipment rotable parts and assemblies	1608	1708
Airframe parts and assemblies	[1] 1608.1	[1] 1708.1
Aircraft engine parts and assemblies	[1] 1608.5	[1] 1708.5
Other parts and assemblies	[1] 1608.9	[1] 1708.9
Flight equipment	1609	1709
Allowance for depreciation:		
Airframes	1611	1711
Aircraft engines	1612	1712
Improvements to leased flight equipment	1617	1717
Flight equipment rotable parts and assemblies	1618	1718
Flight equipment airworthiness allowance	[2] 1629	[2] 1729
Equipment	1630	1730
Furniture, fixtures and office equipment	1636	1736
Improvements to leased buildings and equipment	1639	1739
	General classification	
Buildings	1640	1740
Maintenance buildings and improvements	1640.1	1740.1
Other buildings and improvements	1640.9	1740.9
Ground property and equipment	1649	1749
Allowance for depreciation:		
Equipment	1650	1750
Improvements to leased buildings and equipment	1654	1754
Furniture, fixtures, and office equipment	1656	1756
Buildings	1660	1760
Maintenance buildings and improvements	1660.1	1760.1
Other buildings and improvements	1660.9	1760.9

[See footnotes at end of table]

Name of account	General classification	
Allowance for depreciation of flight equipment and ground property and equipment, and amortization of overhaul and airworthiness costs	1668	1768
Land	1679	1779
Equipment purchase deposits and advance payments	1685	1785
Construction work in progress	1689	1789
Leased property under capital leases	1695	1795
Capital leases—flight equipment	1695.1	1795.1
Capital leases—other property and equipment	1695.2	1795.2
Leased property under capital leases, accumulated amortization	1696	1796
Accumulated amortization—capitalized flight equipment	1696.1	1796.1
Accumulated amortization—capitalized other property and equipment	1696.2	1796.2
Property on operating-type lease to others and property held for lease	....	1797
Property on operating-type lease to others and property held for lease, accumulated depreciation	....	1798
Other assets:		
Long-term prepayments	....	1820
Unamortized developmental and preoperating costs	....	1830
Other assets and deferred charges	....	1890
Current liabilities:		
Current maturities of long-term debt	....	2000
Notes payable:		
Banks	....	2005
Other	....	2015
Trade accounts payable	....	2021
Accounts payable—other	....	2025
Current obligations under capital leases	....	2080
Accrued salaries, wages	....	2110
Accrued vacation liability	....	2120
Accrued interest	....	2125
Accrued taxes	....	2130
Dividends declared	....	2140
Air traffic liability	....	2160
Other current liabilities	....	2190
Noncurrent liabilities:		
Long-term debt	....	2210
Advances from associated companies	....	2240
Pension liability	....	2250
Noncurrent obligations under capital leases	....	2280
Other noncurrent liabilities	....	2290
Deferred credits:		
Deferred income taxes	....	2340
Deferred investment tax credits	....	2345
Other deferred credits	....	2390
Stockholders' equity:		
Preferred stock	....	2820
Common stock	....	2840

[See footnotes at end of table]

Name of account	General classification	
Additional capital invested	....	2890
Premium on capital stock ...	....	2890.*1*
Discount on capital stock ...	....	2890.*2*
Other capital stock transactions	....	2890.*3*
Retained earnings	....	2900
Subscribed and unissued stock	2860	
Treasury stock	....	2990

[1] Prescribed for group II and group III air carriers only.

[2] At the option of the air carrier, these accounts may be assigned Nos. 2629 and 2729, respectively, for accounting purposes.

Note: Digits to right of decimals and italicized codes established for BTS control purposes only.

[ER–1401, 50 FR 239, Jan. 3, 1985, as amended by Amdt. 248–58, 54 FR 5592, Feb. 6, 1989; 60 FR 66723, Dec. 26, 1995]

Section 4 General

(a) The balance sheet accounts are designed to show the financial condition of the air carrier as at a given date, reflecting the asset and liability balances carried forward subsequent to the closing or constructive closing of the air carrier's books of account.

(b) The balance sheet accounts prescribed in this system of accounts for each air carrier group are set forth in Section 3, Chart of Balance Sheet Accounts. The balance sheet elements to be included in each account are presented in section 6.

[ER–755, 37 FR 19726, Sept. 21, 1972, as amended by Amdt. 241–58, 54 FR 5592, Feb. 6, 1989]

Section 5 [Reserved]

Section 6 Objective Classification of Balance Sheet Elements

SOURCE: ER–980, 42 FR 29, Jan. 3, 1977, unless otherwise noted.

CURRENT ASSETS

1010 Cash.

(a) Record here all general and working funds available on demand as of the date of the balance sheet which are not formally restricted or earmarked for specific objectives. Funds deposited for special purposes which are to be satisfied within one year shall be included in account 1100 Short-term Investments and funds restricted as to general availability, which are not offset by current liabilities, shall be included in account 1550 Special Funds.

(b) Each air carrier shall subdivide this account in such manner that the balance can be readily segregated as between balances in United States currency and the balances in each foreign currency.

1100 Short-term Investments.

(a) Record here the cost of short-term investments such as special deposits and United States Government securities, any other temporary cash investments, and the allowance for unrealized gain or loss on current marketable equity securities.

(b) Special deposits for more than one year, not offset by current liabilities, shall not be included in this account but in account 1550 Special Funds.

(c) This account should be charged or credited for discount or premium on United States Government securities or other securities which should be amortized to profit and loss account 80 Interest Income.

1200 Notes Receivable.

(a) Record here current notes receivable including those from associated companies, company personnel, and all other sources.

(b) Balances of notes payable to associated companies shall not be offset against amounts carried in this account. Balances with associated companies which are not normally settled currently shall not be included in this account but in balance sheet account 1510.3 Advances to Associated Companies.

[ER–980, 42 FR 29, Jan. 3, 1977, as amended by ER–1401, 50 FR 241, Jan. 3, 1985]

1270 Accounts Receivable.

(a) Record here current accounts receivable including those due from the United States Government, foreign governments, associated companies, company personnel, and other amounts due for the performance of air transportation.

(b) Amounts due from the United States Government shall be maintained in such fashion as will clearly and separately identify service mail pay receivables, subsidy receivables and other than mail transportation receivables.

(c) Amounts due for the performance of air transportation shall include gross amounts due whether settled through airline clearing houses or with individual carriers. Amounts payable collected as agent shall not be credited to this account, but should be included in account 2190 Other Current Liabilities.

(d) Balances payable to associated companies shall not be offset against amounts carried in this account. Balances with associated companies which are not normally settled currently shall not be included in this account but in balance sheet account 1510.3 Advances to Associated Companies.

[ER-980, 42 FR 29, Jan. 3, 1977, as amended by ER-1401, 50 FR 241, Jan. 3, 1985]

1290 Allowance for Uncollectible Accounts.

(a) Record here accruals for estimated losses from uncollectible accounts.

(b) All accounts against which allowances have been established shall be examined quarterly for the purpose of redetermining the basis of accruals to be applied to subsequent accounting periods and the reasonableness of allowances already provided.

1300 Spare parts and supplies.

(a) Record here the cost of:

(1) Flight equipment replacement parts of a type which ordinarily would be recurrently expended and replaced rather than repaired and reused;

(2) Unissued fuel inventories for use in the overall or system operations of the carrier. Adjustments of inventories for aircraft fuel due to retroactive price increases and decreases shall not be entered in this account but in profit and loss account 45, Aircraft Fuels and Oils; and

(3) Unissued and unapplied materials and supplies held in stock such as unissued shop materials, expendable tools, stationery and office supplies, passenger service supplies, and restaurant and food service supplies.

(b) Costs paid by the air carrier such as transportation charges and customs duties; excise, sales, use and other taxes; special insurance; and other charges applicable to the cost of spare parts and supplies shall be charged to this account when they can be definitely allocated to specific items or units of property. If such costs cannot be so allocated, or if of minor significance in relation to the cost of such property, such amounts may be charged to balance sheet account 1890 Other Assets and Deferred Charges and cleared either by a suitable "loading charge" as the parts are used or by current charges to appropriate expense or property accounts; so long as the method of application does not cause material distortion in operating expenses from one accounting period to another.

(c) Reusable spare parts and supplies recovered in connection with construction, maintenance, or retirement of property and equipment shall be included in this account at fair and reasonable values but in no case shall such values exceed original cost. Recoveries of normally reparable and reusable parts of a type for which losses in value may be covered on a practical basis through valuation allowance provisions shall be included in this account on an original cost basis. Scrap and nonusable parts, expensed from this account and recovered, shall be included at net amounts realizable therefrom with contra credit to the expense accounts initially charged.

(d) The cost of rotable parts and assemblies of material value included in this account which ordinarily are repaired and reused and possess a service life approximating that of the primary property types to which related shall not be recorded in this account but in balance sheet account 1608 Flight Equipment Rotable Parts and Assemblies. For purposes of identifying rotable parts and assemblies of insignificant unit value which may be included in this account, a reasonable maximum unit value limitation may be established.

(e) Any losses sustained or gains realized upon the abandonment or other disposition of flight equipment expendable parts shall be taken up as capital gains or losses in the periods in which sustained or realized. (See balance sheet account 1311.)

(f) Items in this account shall be charged to appropriate expense accounts as issued for use. Profit and loss on sales of inventory items as a routine service to others shall be included in profit and loss accounts 14 General Service Sales—Associated Companies, or 16 General Service Sales—Outside, and the parts sold shall be removed from this accounts at full cost.

(g) Materials and supplies held in small supply and purchased currently may be charged to appropriate expense accounts when purchased.

(h) An allowance for inventory adjustment applicable to materials and supplies is prohibited. Items in this account shall be charged to appropriate expense accounts as issued for use.

(i) Subaccounts shall be established within this account for the separate recording of each class or type of spare parts and supplies.

[ER–980, 42 FR 29, Jan. 3, 1977, as amended by ER–1401, 50 FR 241, Jan. 3, 1985]

1311 Allowance for Obsolescence—Spare Parts and Supplies.

(a) Accruals shall be made to this account when allowances are established for losses in the value of expendable parts. The accruals to this account shall be made by charges to profit and loss account 73 Provisions for Obsolescence and Deterioration—Expendable Parts. Records shall be maintained with sufficient detail to permit association of the allowances with each class or type of expendable parts.

(b) The accruals to this account shall be based upon a predetermination by the air carrier of that portion of the total inventory of each class and type of expendable parts against which an allowance for loss is to be accrued. Expendable parts issued for use in operations shall be charged to operating expenses as issued and shall not be charged to this account. If at the end of any calendar year the amount of the allowance exceeds the product of the applicable inventory for the year determined consistently on a year-end or average basis, and the sum of the standard percentage accrual rates for all prior years including the current, the allowance shall be adjusted downward by the amount of the excess. Such adjustments shall be charged to this account and credited to profit and loss account 73 Provisions for Obsolescence and Deterioration—Expendable Parts.

(c) Where changing conditions necessitate a revision or adjustment in rates of accrual, such revision or adjustment shall be made applicable to current and subsequent accounting periods and shall not be applied retroactively to prior accounting periods. Following retirement of airframe or aircraft engine types to which related, any balance remaining in this account shall be offset against related balances carried in balance sheet account 1300 Spare Parts and Supplies and the net cleared to profit and loss accounts 88.5 Capital Gains and Losses—Operating Property or 88.6 Capital Gains and Losses—Other.

[ER–980, 42 FR 29, Jan. 3, 1977, as amended by ER–1401, 50 FR 241, Jan. 3, 1985]

1410 Prepaid Items.

Record here prepayments of obligations which if not paid in advance would require the expenditure of working capital within one year, such as prepaid rent, insurance, taxes, interest, etc. Unexpired insurance and miscellaneous prepayments applicable to periods extending beyond one year where significant in amount shall be charged to balance sheet account 1820 Long-Term Prepayments.

1420 Other Current Assets.

Record here current assets not provided for in balance sheet accounts 1010 to 1410, inclusive.

INVESTMENTS AND SPECIAL FUNDS

1510 Investments in Associated Companies.

(a) Record here net investments in associated companies.

(b) [Reserved]

(c) This account shall be subdivided by all air carrier groups as follows:

[ER–980, 42 FR 29, Jan. 3, 1977, as amended by ER–1027, 42 FR 60128, Nov. 25, 1977; ER–1188, 45 FR 48870, July 22, 1980]

1510.1 *Investments in Investor Controlled Companies.*

Record here the cost of investments in investor controlled companies except that permanent impairment in the value of securities may be reflected through charges to profit and loss classification 8100, Nonoperating Income or Expense—Net. This account shall also include the equity in undistributed earnings or losses since acquisition. In the event dividends are declared by such companies, the air carrier shall credit this account for its share in dividends declared and debit balance sheet account 1270 Accounts Receivable. This account shall separately state: (a) The cost of such investments at date of acquisition and (b) the equity in undistributed earnings or losses since acquisition.

[Amdt. 241–58, 54 FR 5592, Feb. 6, 1989]

1510.2 *Investments in Other Associated Companies.*

Record here the cost of investments in associated companies other than investor controlled companies. Cost shall represent the amount paid at the date of acquisition without regard to subsequent changes in the net assets through earnings or losses of such associated companies. However, permanent impairment in the value of securities may be reflected through charges to profit and loss classification 8100, Nonoperating Income or Expense—Net.

[Amdt. 241–58, 54 FR 5592, Feb. 6, 1989]

1510.3 *Advances to Associated Companies.*

(a) Record here advances, loans, and other amounts not settled currently with investor controlled and other associated companies and nontransport divisions. Balances receivable from and payable to different associated companies and different nontransport divisions shall not be offset.

(b) In the case of nontransport divisions three subaccounts shall be maintained:

(1) Net investment;

(2) current net profit or loss; and

(3) current accounts receivable or payable between the air carrier and the nontransport division.

(c) Each nontransport division shall be accounted for separately in net amounts receivable which shall be included in this account or net amounts payable which shall be included in balance sheet account 2240 Advances from Associated Companies.

[ER–980, 42 FR 29, Jan. 3, 1977. Redesignated by ER–1401, 50 FR 241, Jan. 3, 1985]

1530 Other Investments and Receivables.

Record here notes and accounts receivable not due within one year, investments in securities issued by others, investments in leveraged leases, the noncurrent net investment in direct financing and sales-type leases, and the allowance for unrealized gain or loss on noncurrent marketable equity securities. Securities held as temporary cash investments shall not be included in this account but in balance sheet account 1100 Short-Term Investments. Investments in and receivables from associated companies which are not settled currently shall be included in balance sheet account 1510 Investments in Associated Companies.

[Amdt. 241–58, 54 FR 5592, Feb. 6, 1989]

1550 Special Funds.

Record here special funds not of a current nature and restricted as to general availability. Include items such as sinking funds, cash and securities posted with courts of law, employee's funds for purchase of capital stock, pension funds under the control of the air carrier and equipment purchase funds.

Operating Property and Equipment

"Operating Property and Equipment" shall encompass items used in air transportation services and services related thereto.

1601 Airframes.

(a) Record here the total cost to the air carrier of airframes of all types and classes together with the full complement of instruments, appurtenances and fixtures comprising complete airframes including accessories necessary to the installation of engines and flight control and transmission systems, except as specifically provided otherwise in accounts 1602 and 1607. Also record here in separate subaccounts the costs of airframes overhauls accounted for on a deferral and amortization basis.

(b) Airframes designed to permit multiple payload configurations shall be recorded in this account at the total cost of the maximum complement of instruments, appurtenances, and fixtures used in the air carrier's operations.

(c) This account shall be subdivided as follows by all air carriers:

1601.1 *Airframes.*

1601.2 *Unamortized Airframe Overhauls.*

[ER–980, 42 FR 29, Jan. 3, 1977, as amended by Amdt. 241–58, 54 FR 5593, Feb. 6, 1989]

1602 Aircraft Engines.

(a) Record here the total cost to the air carrier of complete units of aircraft engines of all types and classes together with a full complement of accessories, appurtenances, parts and fixtures comprising fully assembled engines as delivered by the engine manufacturer ready for operation in test but without the accessories necessary to its installation in airframes. Also record here in separate subaccounts the costs of aircraft engine overhauls accounted for on a deferral and amortization basis.

(b) This account shall be subdivided as follows by all air carriers:

1602.1 *Aircraft Engines.*

1602.2 *Unamortized Aircraft Engine Overhauls.*

[ER–980, 42 FR 29, Jan. 3, 1977, as amended by Amdt. 241–58, 54 FR 5593, Feb. 6, 1989]

1607 Improvements to Leased Flight Equipment.

Record here the total cost incurred by the air carrier for modification, conversion or other improvements to leased flight equipment. Also record here, in separate subaccounts, the costs of airframe and aircraft engine overhauls of leased aircraft accounted for on a deferral and amortization basis.

[Amdt. 241–58, 54 FR 5593, Feb. 6, 1989]

1608 Flight Equipment Rotable Parts and Assemblies.

(a) Record here the total cost to the air carrier of all spare instruments, parts, appurtenances and subassemblies related to the primary components of flight equipment units provided for in balance sheet accounts 1601 through 1607, inclusive. This account shall include all parts and assemblies of material value which are rotable in nature, are generally reserviced or repaired, are used repeatedly and possess a service life approximating that of the property type to which they relate. Items of an expendable nature which generally may not be repaired and reused, shall not be recorded in this account but in account 1300 Spare Parts and Supplies. Except for recurrent service sales, flight equipment parts recorded in this account shall not be charged to operating expenses as retired. Profit or loss on sales of parts as a routine service to others shall be included in profit and loss account 14 General Service Sales, and parts sold shall be removed from this account at full cost irrespective of any allowance for depreciation which has been provided.

(b) This account shall be subdivided as follows by Group II and Group III air carriers:

1608.1 *Airframe Parts and Assemblies.*

1608.5 *Aircraft Engine Parts and Assemblies.*

1608.9 *Other Parts and Assemblies.*

[ER–980, 42 FR 29, Jan. 3, 1977, as amended by Amdt. 241–58, 54 FR 5593, Feb. 6, 1989]

1609 Flight Equipment.

This classification is established only for purposes of control by the BTS and shall reflect the total cost of property and equipment of all types and classes used in the in-flight operations of aircraft.

[ER–980, 42 FR 29, Jan. 3, 1977, as amended at 60 FR 66723, Dec. 26, 1995]

1629 Flight Equipment Airworthiness Allowances.

(a) Record here accumulated provisions for overhauls of flight equipment.

(b) Separate subaccounts shall be established for recording accumulated provisions related to each type of airframe and aircraft engine, respectively.

NOTE: At the option of the air carrier, the number "2629" may be assigned to this account for accounting purposes. However, for purposes of reporting on BTS Form 41, the balance in this account shall be reported under account "1629."

[ER–980, 42 FR 29, Jan. 3, 1977, as amended by Amdt. 241–58, 54 FR 5593, Feb. 6, 1989; 60 FR 66723, Dec. 26, 1995]

1630 Equipment.

Record here the total cost to the air carrier of ground equipment to include the following:

(a) Equipment assigned to aircraft or active line operations as opposed to items held in stock for servicing passengers such as broilers, bottleware, dishes, food boxes, thermos jugs, blankets, first aid kits, etc. Spare items shall be carried in balance sheet account 1300 Spare Parts and Supplies and shall be charged directly to expense upon withdrawal from stock for replacing original complements.

(b) Equipment used in restaurants and kitchens.

(c) Equipment of all types and classes used in enplaning and handling traffic and in handling aircraft while on ramps, including motorized vehicles used in ramp service. Classes of equipment used interchangeably between handling aircraft on ramps and in maintaining aircraft may be classified in accordance with normal predominant use.

(d) Nonairborne equipment of all types and classes used in meteorological and communication services which is not a part of buildings.

(e) Equipment of all types and classes including motorized vehicles used in engineering and drafting services and in maintaining, overhauling, repairing and testing other classes of property and equipment.

(f) Property and equipment of all types and classes used in ground and marine transportation services.

(g) Property and equipment of all types and classes used in storing and distributing fuel, oil and water, such as fueling trucks, tanks, pipelines, etc.

(h) All other ground equipment of all types and classes such as medical, photographic, employees' training equipment, and airport and airway lighting equipment.

[ER–980, 42 FR 29, Jan. 3, 1977, as amended by Amdt. 241–58, 54 FR 5593, Feb. 6, 1989]

1636 Furniture, Fixtures, and Office Equipment.

Record here the total cost to the air carrier of furniture, fixtures and office equipment of all types and classes wherever used or located.

[Amdt. 241–58, 54 FR 5593, Feb. 6, 1989]

1639 Improvements to Leased Buildings and Equipment.

Record here the total cost to the air carrier incurred in connection with modification, conversion, or other improvements to leased buildings and equipment.

1640 Buildings.

Record here the total cost to the air carrier of owned buildings, structures and equipment and related improvements. Each air carrier shall maintain the following subaccounts in which the values fairly assignable to maintenance and other operations shall be separately recorded:

1640.9 *Other Buildings and Improvements.*

1640.1 *Maintenance Buildings and Improvements.*

[Amdt. 241–58, 54 FR 5593, Feb. 6, 1989]

1649 Ground Property and Equipment.

This classification is established only for purposes of control by the BTS and shall reflect the total cost of property and equipment of all types and classes other than flight equipment, equipment purchase deposits and advance payments, land, and work in progress.

[ER–980, 42 FR 29, Jan. 3, 1977, as amended at 60 FR 66723, Dec. 26, 1995]

1668 Allowance for Depreciation of Flight Equipment and Ground Property and Equipment and Amortization of Overhaul and Airworthiness Costs.

(a) Record in accounts 1611 and 1618, inclusive, and 1650 through 1660, inclusive, accruals for depreciation of flight equipment and ground property and equipment.

(b) As set forth in section 3, Chart of Balance Sheet Accounts, separate accounts shall be established for depreciation allowances to parallel balance sheet accounts 1601 through 1608 established for recording the cost of flight equipment and accounts 1630 through 1640 established for recording the cost of ground property and equipment.

(c) This account shall be used as a control account and shall reflect the total amounts recorded in balance sheet accounts 1611 through 1618 and

1650 through 1660 in addition to account 1629 Flight Equipment Airworthiness Allowance.

1679 Land.

Record here the initial cost and the cost of improving land.

[Amdt. 241–58, 54 FR 5593, Feb. 6, 1989]

1685 Equipment Purchase Deposits and Advance Payments.

Record here the amount of purchase deposits and advance payments made to acquire operating property and equipment under outstanding purchase commitments. Funds set aside but not deposited or used as advance payments should not be included in this account but in Account 1550 Special Funds.

1689 Construction Work in Progress.

(a) Record here all direct and indirect costs of the air carrier that are expended for constructing and readying property and equipment of all types and classes for installation in operations. The amount reported shall reflect all such expenses that are accumulated to the balance sheet date. Where properly includable in the property and equipment classification, record here also the accumulated costs for uncompleted overhauls of airframes, aircraft engines, or other material units of property.

(b) At the option of the air carrier this account may be used as a clearing account for recording the cost of property and equipment acquisitions prior to a distribution thereof to the appropriate property accounts, whether or not conditioning or modification is necessary before placing in service.

[ER–980, 42 FR 29, Jan. 3, 1977, as amended by Amdt. 241–58, 54 FR 5594, Feb. 6, 1989]

1695 Leased Property Under Capital Leases.

(a) Record here the total costs to the air carrier for all property obtained under capital leases.

(b) This account shall be subdivided by all air carrier groups as follows:

1695.1 *Capital Leases—Flight Equipment.*

1696.2 *Capital Leases—Other Property and Equipment.*

[ER–1401, 50 FR 241, Jan. 3, 1985, as amended by Amdt. 241–58, 54 FR 5594, Feb. 6, 1989]

1696 Leased Property Under Capital Leases—Accumulated Amortization.

(a) Record here accruals for amortization of leased property obtained under capital leases.

(b) This account shall be subdivided by all air carrier groups as follows:

1696.1 *Accumulated Amortization—Capitalized Flight Equipment.*

1696.2 *Accumulated Amortization—Capitalized Other Property and Equipment.*

[ER–1401, 50 FR 241, Jan. 3, 1985, as amended by Amdt. 241–58, 54 FR 5594, Feb. 6, 1989]

NON-OPERATING PROPERTY AND EQUIPMENT

"Nonoperating Property and Equipment" includes investments in property and equipment not separately accounted for within a nontransport division but assigned to other than air transportation and transport-related services, and property and equipment held for future use.

1700 Non-operating Property and Equipment.

The total cost to the air carrier of nonoperating property and equipment and related allowances for depreciation shall be recorded in balance sheet accounts 1701 through 1796 which, as set forth in section 3, Chart of Balance Sheet Accounts, parallel balance sheet accounts 1601 through 1689, for recording the cost of operating property and equipment. In addition to these accounts, Account 1797 has been established for recording the cost of property on operating-type leases to others and property held for lease; any accumulated depreciation applicable to the assets contained in Account 1797 shall be recorded in Account 1798.

[ER–1013, 42 FR 37515, July 21, 1977]

1797 Property on Operating-type Lease to Others and Property Held for Lease.

Record here the total cost to the air carrier of property on operating-type lease to others and property held for lease.

[Amdt. 241-58, 54 FR 5594, Feb. 6, 1989]

1798 Property on Operating-type Lease to Others and Property Held for Lease—Accumulated Depreciation.

Record here accruals for depreciation of property on operating-type leases to others and property held for lease.

[Amdt. 241-58, 54 FR 5594, Feb. 6, 1989]

OTHER ASSETS

1820 Long-Term Prepayments.

Record here prepayments of obligations applicable to periods extending beyond one year such as payments on leased property and equipment and other payments and advances for rents, rights, or other privileges.

1830 Unamortized Developmental and Preoperating Costs.

(a) Record here costs accumulated and deferred by the air carrier pertaining to the development of new routes or extension of existing routes, preparation for operation of new routes subsequent to certification by the DOT, the integration of new types of aircraft or services, and other preparations for substantial alterations in operational characteristics.

(b) Costs chargeable to this account shall include items directly related to each specific developmental or preoperating project, such as travel and incidental expenses, legal expenses, flight crew training expenses, and regulatory proceedings expenses. Expenses which would be otherwise incurred in the normal air transport operations conducted by the air carrier during the current accounting period shall not be allocated to developmental or preoperating projects and charged to this account. Nor shall this account be credited for revenues from aircraft flights of a developmental or preoperating character the operating costs of which are charged to this account. Any such revenues shall be included in the profit and loss account for the respective type of revenue. This account shall include charges for only those costs associated with projects directed at obtaining new operating authority or expanding the physical capacity of the air carrier and shall not include costs incurred for the purpose of generating revenues through rate adjustment. Accordingly, costs associated with regulatory proceedings involving route awards or amendments, whether successful or unsuccessful to the carrier, shall be included in this account whereas costs associated with regulatory proceedings involving rate or other revenue generation matters shall be charged to appropriate expense accounts.

(c) Records shall be established for new routes or extensions of existing routes to record separately: (1) Costs incurred in acquiring or applying for the routes, including all costs incurred prior to certification by the DOT and inauguration of service by the air carrier, and (2) costs incurred after revenue operations begin over the new routes or extensions.

(d) Subclassifications shall be established to record for each developmental project the period covered and the purpose of each item of expense. Each air carrier shall classify the costs of all projects included in this account between: (1) Those related and contributing to the normal air transportation services currently conducted by the air carrier; (2) those related to services conducted by the air carrier which are extraneous to or are not otherwise related to the air transportation services currently conducted; and (3) those held in suspense pending status determination in terms of possible contribution to the air transportation services and inauguration of the service or operation to which related.

(e) Amounts included in this account which contribute to or protect the position of the normal air transportation services currently conducted by the carrier shall be amortized to profit and loss account 74 Amortization, unless otherwise approved or directed by the DOT. Other amounts included in this account shall be amortized or charged to profit and loss account 89.9 Other Miscellaneous Nonoperating Debits.

[ER-980, 42 FR 29, Jan. 3, 1977, as amended at 60 FR 66723, Dec. 26, 1995]

1890 Other Assets and Deferred Charges.

(a) Record here other assets and deferred charges not provided for elsewhere.

(b) Record here debits, the proper final disposition of which cannot be determined until additional information has been received. This account shall include the accumulated cost of labor, materials and outside services used in the process of manufacturing flight equipment expendable parts and materials and supplies for stock, the accumulated cost of jobs in process for others, projects to be charged to expense upon completion. This account shall also include unamortized debt expense, property acquisition adjustments and intangible assets.

(c) This account shall be charged with property loss and other costs related to casualties and credited with recoveries from purchased insurance and salvage. A debit or credit balance in this account related to property retired as a result of a casualty shall be recorded in profit and loss account 88.5 Capital Gains and Losses—Operating Property or 88.6 Capital Gains and Losses—Other; however, any balances related to property not retired or to other casualties shall be recorded in profit and loss account 58 Injuries, Loss and Damage. Proceeds from purchased insurance for property damage, received prior to repair of such damage, shall not be credited to this account but to balance sheet account 2390 Other Deferred Credits pending repair. The records for each major casualty shall be kept in such manner as to clearly disclose insurance recoveries and the total costs, which shall include charges for the depreciated cost of property damaged or destroyed, costs for clearing wrecks and damaged property and equipment, including salaries and wages for the repair thereof, and payments for damages to property of others. The cost of casualties shall not be charged directly against retained earnings or appropriations thereof, but shall be cleared through the applicable profit and loss accounts in accordance with the foregoing.

(d) Record here the unamortized debt expense related to the assumption by the air carrier of debt of all types and classes. Amounts recorded shall be amortized to profit and loss account 84 Amortization of Debt Discount, Premium and Expense.

(e) Unamortized debt expense shall not include the excess of the par value of debt securities over the cash value of consideration received. Instead, discounts shall be recorded in a subaccount of the related liability.

(f) Record here the cost of patents, copyrights and other intangible properties, rights and privileges acquired as a part of a business from other air carriers and other intangibles not provided for elsewhere. This account shall be subdivided to reflect the nature of each intangible asset included in this account.

(g) Record here the difference between the purchase price to the air carrier of property and equipment acquired as a part of a business from another air carrier through consolidation, merger, or reorganization, pursuant to a plan approved by the DOT, and the depreciated cost to the predecessor company at date of acquisition. Record here also such differences relating to purchases of property and equipment from associated companies unless other treatment is approved by the BTS. Separate subaccounts shall be established to record the amounts applicable to each such acquisition.

(h) Balances in this account relating to property acquisition adjustments shall be amortized by charges to profit and loss account 89.9 Other Miscellaneous Nonoperating Debits unless otherwise directed or approved by the BTS.

[ER–1401, 50 FR 242, Jan. 3, 1985, as amended at 60 FR 66723, Dec. 26, 1995]

CURRENT LIABILITIES

2000 Current Maturities of Long-term Debt.

Record here the face value or principal amount of debt securities issued or assumed by the air carrier which is payable within 12 months of the balance sheet date unless such debt is to refinance, or where payment is to be made from assets of a type not properly classifiable as current.

2005 Notes Payable—Banks.

Record here the face value of all notes, drafts, acceptances, or other similar evidences of indebtedness payable on demand or within one year to a bank or another financial institution with the exception of current maturities of long-term debt which should be included in account 2000.

2015 Notes Payable—Other.

Record here the face value of all notes, drafts, acceptances, or other similar evidences of indebtedness payable on demand or within one year to an associated company or party other than a financial institution.

2021 Trade Accounts Payable.

Record here all accounts payable within one year which accrued from generally recognized trade practices.

2025 Accounts Payable—Other.

Record here all accounts payable within one year which are not provided for in accounts 2000 to 2021, inclusive.

2080 Current Obligations Under Capital Leases.

Record here the total current liability applicable to property obtained under capital leases.

[ER–1013, 42 FR 37515, July 21, 1977; 42 FR 38555, July 29, 1977; Amdt. 241–58, 54 FR 5594, Feb. 6, 1989]

2110 Accrued Salaries, Wages.

Record here amounts accrued for unpaid compensation to personnel, which have been charged to profit and loss or capitalized, as compensation for the period in which accrued.

2120 Accrued Vacation Liability.

(a) Record here accruals of liabilities for personnel vacations. All vacation policies, plans, or agreements whether oral or written shall be accounted for on an accrual basis whenever a lag exists between vacations earned and vacations taken, thereby resulting in a liability against the carrier under the applicable policy, plan or agreement.

(b) This account shall be credited and the applicable personnel compensation expense account concurrently charged with the cost of any lag between vacations accrued and vacations taken. Accruals may be based upon standard rates of lag, if such standard rates are verified by physical inventory and adjusted accordingly at least once each calendar year. Adjustments of balances in this account shall be cleared to applicable compensation expense accounts.

[ER–980, 42 FR 29, Jan. 3, 1977, as amended by ER–1027, 42 FR 60128, Nov. 25, 1977; ER–1188, 45 FR 48870, July 22, 1980; Amdt. 241–58, 54 FR 5594, Feb. 6, 1989]

2125 Accrued Interest.

Record here interest payable within one year for all outstanding obligations.

2130 Accrued Taxes.

(a) Record here accruals for currently payable income and other forms of taxes which constitute a charge borne by the air carrier as opposed to those collected as an agent for others.

(b) Each air carrier shall disclose in the footnotes of its BTS Form 41 for each calendar quarter whether utilized credits are accounted for by the flow-through method or the deferred method. The method selected shall be consistently followed by the carrier.

[Amdt. 241–58, 54 FR 5594, Feb. 6, 1989, as amended at 60 FR 66723, Dec. 26, 1995]

2140 Dividends Declared.

Record here in separate subdivisions for each class and series of capital stock, all dividends declared but unpaid on capital stock.

2160 Air Traffic Liability.

(a) Record here balances representing the value of unused transportation sold. Transportation sold includes both sales for transportation to be provided by the air carrier and transportation to be provided by another air carrier.

(b) Earned revenue, determined by the yield or average fare method or by the sales-lift-match method, shall be consistently and periodically cleared by debit to this account, and by credit to the appropriate profit and loss revenue account. Amounts receivable for transportation to be provided by the air carrier shall be debited to balance sheet account 1270 Accounts Receivable.

(c) Carriers who determine earned revenue on a yield or average fare method may not accrue income during the accounting year in anticipation of a favorable annual physical inventory determination, nor for unused or unpresented tickets.

(d) Subaccounts to this account shall be established to record balances pertaining to passenger and cargo transportation sold, respectively, and separately to sales in scheduled and nonscheduled services.

[ER–980, 42 FR 29, Jan. 3, 1977, as amended by ER–1401, 50 FR 242, Jan. 3, 1985]

2190 Other Current Liabilities.

Record here current and accrued liabilities, including amounts payable collected as an agent, not provided for in accounts 2110 to 2160, inclusive.

NON-CURRENT LIABILITIES

2210 Long-Term Debt.

(a) Record here the face value of principal amount of debt securities issued or assumed by the air carrier and held by other than associated companies, which has not been retired or cancelled and is not payable within 12 months of the balance sheet date.

(b) In cases where debt coming due within 12 months is to be refunded, or where payment is to be made from assets of a type not properly classifiable as current, the amount payable shall not be removed from this account. In addition, this account shall include short-term debt obligations when both the intent to refinance the short-term obligations on a long-term basis is established and the ability to consummate this refinancing can be demonstrated.

[Amdt. 241–58, 54 FR 5594, Feb. 6, 1989]

2240 Advances from Associated Companies.

Record here net amounts due associated companies and nontransport divisions for notes, loans and advances which are not settled currently. Balances payable to and receivable from different associated companies shall not be offset.

2250 Pension Liability.

Record here the liability of the air carrier under employee pension plans, to which either or both employees and the air carrier contribute, if the plan is administered by the air carrier.

2280 Noncurrent Obligations under Capital Leases.

Record here the total noncurrent liability applicable to property obtained under capital leases.

[ER–1013, 42 FR 37515, July 21, 1977, as amended by Amdt. 241–58, 54 FR 5594, Feb. 6, 1989]

2290 Other Noncurrent Liabilities.

Record here noncurrent liabilities not provided for in balance sheet accounts 2210 to 2280, inclusive, such as the liability for installments received on capital stock from company personnel who are not bound by legally enforceable subscription contracts, accruals for personnel dismissal liability, and accruals of other demonstrable miscellaneous noncurrent liabilities.

[ER–1401, 50 FR 242, Jan. 3, 1985]

DEFERRED CREDITS

2340 Deferred Income Taxes.

Record here credits and debits representing the net tax effect of material timing differences originating and reversing in the current accounting period, giving appropriate recognition to the portion of investment tax credits which would have been allowed if taxes were based on pretax accounting income by a reduction of the deferred tax provision.

[Amdt. 241–58, 54 FR 5594, Feb. 6, 1989]

2345 Deferred Investment Tax Credits.

Record here investment tax credits utilized as reduction of tax liabilities, when the carrier exercises the option to defer such credits for amortization over the service life of the related equipment.

[Amdt. 241–58, 54 FR 5594, Feb. 6, 1989]

2390 Other Deferred Credits.

Record here credits, not provided for elsewhere, the proper final disposition of which cannot be effected until additional information has been received.

STOCKHOLDERS' EQUITY

2820 Preferred Stock.

Record here in separate subdivisions for each class and series, the par or stated value of preferred capital stock issued or in the case of no-par stock without stated value, the full consideration received.

2840 Common Stock.

Record here in separate subdivisions for each class and series, the par or stated value of common stock issued or in case of no-par stock without stated value, the full consideration received.

2860 Subscribed and Unissued Stock.

Record here in separate subdivisions for each class and series, the par or stated value, or the subscription price in the case of stock without par or stated value, of legally enforceable subscriptions to the capital stock of the air carrier.

2890 Additional Capital Invested.

(a) Record herein separate subdivisions for each class and series, the difference between the price at which capital stock is sold and the par or stated value of the stock; gains or losses arising from the reacquisition and the resale or retirement of each class and series of capital stock; donations; the excess of retained earnings capitalized over par or stated value of capital stock issued; adjustments in capital resulting from reorganization or recapitalization; and proceeds attributable to detachable stock purchase warrants related to debt issues. This account shall also include balances of contributions to the business enterprise of individual proprietors or partners.

(b) Each air carrier shall maintain the following subaccounts:

2890.1 *Premium on capital stock.* Record here in separate subdivisions for each class and series of capital stock issued the excess of the cash value of consideration received over the par or stated value and accrued dividends of stock issued together with assessments against stockholders representing payments required in excess of par or stated value.

2890.2 *Discount on capital stock.* Record here in separate subdivisions for each class and series of capital stock issued, the excess of the par or stated value over the cash value of consideration received, less accrued dividends. Discounts applicable to a particular class and series of capital stock may be offset against premiums from the same class and series of capital stock. Discounts and premiums on different classes and series of capital stock shall not be offset. The air carrier may, at its option, record in this subaccount commissions and expenses incurred in the issuance of capital stock and may charge balance sheet account 2900 Retained Earnings to the extent capital stock expense may exceed any existing balance of paid-in capital over the par or stated value of capital stock.

2890.3 *Other Capital Stock Transactions.* Record here in separate subdivisions for each class and series, the balance of credits arising from the reacquisition and resale or cancellation of capital stock, credits arising from a reduction in the par or stated value of capital stock or the net balance of credits or debits resulting from other paid-in capital transactions such as proceeds attributable to detachable stock purchase warrants related to debt issues, not provided for elsewhere, which is identified with a particular class and series of capital stock.

2900 Retained Earnings.

(a) Record here the net income or loss from operations of the air carrier and dividends declared on capital stock.

(b) This account shall not be charged with dividends on treasury stock. If a dividend is not payable in cash, the values entered in this account shall be completely described.

(c) Delayed credits or charges to income shall not be entered in this account directly but in appropriate profit and loss accounts.

(d) Net income or loss accounted for during the current fiscal year shall not be entered in this account until the close of the fiscal year. Individual proprietorships or partnerships may clear net income or loss accounted for during the year directly to balance sheet account 2890 Additional Capital Invested, or optionally, to this account for subsequent transfer to balance sheet account 2890 Additional Capital Invested.

(e) A separate subaccount to this account shall be maintained to record changes in the valuation of marketable equity securities included in noncurrent assets. Such changes shall be reflected in this subaccount to the extent the balance in this subaccount represents a net unrealized loss as of the current balance sheet date.

[ER–980, 42 FR 29, Jan. 3, 1977, as amended by ER–1401, 50 FR 242, Jan. 3, 1985]

2990 Treasury Stock.

(a) Record here the cost of capital stock issued by the air carrier reacquired by it and not retired or canceled.

(b) Separate records shall be established for each class and series of capital stock held in this account.

[ER–980, 42 FR 29, Jan. 3, 1977, as amended by Amdt. 241–58, 54 FR 5594, Feb. 6, 1989]

PROFIT AND LOSS CLASSIFICATION

Section 7 Chart of Profit and Loss Accounts

Objective classification of profit and loss elements	Functional or financial activity to which applicable (00)		
	Group I carriers	Group II carriers	Group III carriers
OPERATING REVENUES AND EXPENSES			
Transport revenues:			
01 Passenger:			
01.*1* Passenger—first class	31, 32	31, 32	31, 32.
01.*2* Passenger—coach	31, 32	31, 32	31, 32.
05 Mail:			
05.*1* Priority	31, 32	31, 32	31, 32.
05.*2* Nonpriority	31, 32	31, 32	31, 32.
05.*3* Foreign	31, 32	31, 32	31, 32.
06 Property:			
06.*1* Freight	31, 32	31, 32	31, 32.
06.*2* Excess passenger baggage	31, 32	31, 32	31, 32.
07 Charter:			
07.*1* Passenger	32	32	32.
07.*2* Property	32	32	32.
19 Air transport—other:			
19.*1* Reservation cancellation fees	31, 32	31, 32	31, 32.
19.*2* Miscellaneous operating revenues	31, 32	31, 32	31, 32.
08 Public service revenues (subsidy)	48	48	48.
Transport-related revenues and expenses:			
09 In-flight sales:			
09.*1* Liquor and food—gross revenues	48	48	48.
09.*2* Movies and stereo—gross revenues	48	48	48.
09.*3* Other—gross revenues	48	48	48.
09.*4* Liquor and food—depreciation expense	71	71	71.
09.*5* Liquor and food—other expense	71	71	71.
09.*6* Movies and stereo—depreciation expense	71	71	71.
09.*7* Movies and stereo—other expense	71	71	71.
09.*8* Other—depreciation expense	71	71	71.
09.*9* Other—expense	71	71	71.
10 Restaurant and food service (ground):			
10.*1* Gross revenues	48	48	48.
10.*2* Depreciation expense	71	71	71.
10.*3* Other expenses	71	71	71.
11 Rents:			
11.*1* Gross revenues	48	48	48.
11.*2* Depreciation expense	71	71	71
11.*3* Other expenses	71	71	71.
12 Limousine service:			
12.*1* Gross revenues	48	48	48.
12.*2* Depreciation expense	71	71	71.
12.*3* Other expenses	71	71	71.
13 Interchange sales:			
13.*1* Associated companies—gross revenues	48	48	48.
13.*2* Outside—gross revenues	48	48	48.
13.*3* Associated companies—depreciation expense	71	71	71.
13.*4* Associated companies—other expense	71	71	71.
13.*5* Outside—depreciation expense	71	71	71.
13.*6* Outside—other expense	71	71	71.
14 General service sales:			
14.*1* Associated companies—gross revenues	48	48	48.
14.*2* Outside—gross revenues	48	48	48.
14.*3* Associated companies—depreciation expense	71	71	71.
14.*4* Associated companies—other expense	71	71	71.

Objective classification of profit and loss elements	Functional or financial activity to which applicable (00)		
	Group I carriers	Group II carriers	Group III carriers
14.*5* Outside—depreciation expense	71	71	71.
14.*6* Outside—other expense	71	71	71.
16 Substitute (replacement) service:			
16.*1* Gross revenues	48	48	48.
16.*2* Expense	71	71	71.
17 Air cargo service:			
17.*1* Gross revenues	48	48	48.
17.*2* Depreciation expense	71	71	71.
17.*3* Other expense	71	71	71.
18 Other transport related items:			
18.*1* Gross revenues	48	48	48.
18.*2* Depreciation expense	71	71	71.
18.*3* Other expense	71	71	71.
19 Other operating revenues:			
19.*1* Reservations cancellation fees	31, 32	31, 32	31, 32.
19.*9* Miscellaneous operating revenues	31, 32, 41	31, 32, 41	31, 32, 41.
Transport expenses:			
21 General management personnel	53, 69	53, 55, 64, 67, 68.	53, 55, 61, 62, 63, 65, 66, 68.
23 Pilots and copilots	51	51	51.
24 Other flight personnel	51, 69	51, 55	51, 55.
25 Maintenance labor:			
25.*1* Labor—airframes and other flight equipment		52	52.
25.*2* Labor—aircraft engines		52	52.
25.*6* Labor—flight equipment	52		
25.*9* Labor—ground property and equipment	52, 53	52, 53	52, 53.
26 Aircraft and traffic handling personnel	69		
26.*1* General aircraft and traffic handling personnel		64, 67	61, 62, 63, 65.
26.*2* Aircraft control personnel		64	61.
26.*3* Passenger handling personnel		64, 67	62, 65.
26.*4* Cargo handling personnel		64, 67	62, 65.
28 Trainees, instructors and unallocated shop labor:			
28.*1* Trainees and instructors	51, 53, 69	51, 53, 55, 64,67, 68.	51, 53, 55, 61, 62, 63, 65, 66, 68.
28.*2* Unallocated shop labor	53	53	53.
30 Communications personnel	53, 69	53, 55, 64, 67, 68.	53, 55, 61, 62, 63, 65, 66, 68.
31 Recordkeeping and statistical personnel	53, 69	53, 55, 64, 67, 68.	53, 55, 61, 62, 63, 65, 66, 68.
32 Lawyers and law clerks	69	68	68.
33 Traffic solicitors	69	67	65.
34 Purchasing personnel	53, 69	53, 68	53, 68.
35 Other personnel	53, 69	53, 55, 64, 67, 68.	53, 55, 61, 62, 63, 65, 66, 68.
36 Personnel expenses	51, 53, 69	51, 53, 55, 64, 67, 68.	51, 53, 55, 61, 62, 63, 65, 66, 68.
37 Communications purchased	53, 69	53, 55, 64, 67, 68.	53, 55, 61, 62, 63, 65, 66, 68.
38 Light, heat, power, and water	53, 69	53, 55, 64, 67, 68.	53, 55, 61, 62, 63, 65, 66, 68.
39 Traffic commissions	69		
39.*1* Commissions—passenger		67	65.
39.*2* Commissions—property		67	65.
40 Legal fees and expenses	69	68	68.
41 Professional and technical fees and expenses	51, 53, 69	51, 53, 55, 64, 67, 68.	51, 53, 55, 61, 62, 63, 65, 66, 68
43 General services purchased:			
43.*1* Airframe and other flight equipment repairs		52	52
43.*2* Aircraft engine repairs	52	52	
43.*6* Flight equipment repairs	52		
43.*7* Aircraft interchange charges	51, 52	51, 52	51, 52
43.*8* General interchange service charges	52, 69	52, 55, 64, 67, 68.	52, 55, 61, 62, 63, 65, 66, 68
43.*9* Other services	52, 53, 69	52, 53, 55, 64, 67, 68.	52, 53, 55, 61, 62, 63, 65, 66, 68
44 Landing fees	69	64	61.
45 Aircraft fuels and oils	51		
45.*1* Aircraft fuels		51	51.
45.*2* Aircraft oils		51	51.
46 Maintenance materials:			
46.*1* Airframes and other flight equipment		52	52

Objective classification of profit and loss elements	Functional or financial activity to which applicable (00)		
	Group I carriers	Group II carriers	Group III carriers
46.*2* Aircraft engines		52	52.
46.*6* Flight equipment	52		
46.*9* Ground property and equipment	52, 53	52, 53	52, 53.
47 Rentals	51, 53, 69	51, 53, 55, 64, 67, 68.	51, 53, 55, 61, 62, 63, 65, 66, 68.
49 Shop and servicing supplies	53, 69	53, 64	53, 61.
50 Stationery, printing, and office supplies	53, 69	53, 55, 64, 67, 68.	53, 55, 61, 62, 63, 65, 66, 68.
51 Passenger food expense	69	55	55.
53 Other supplies	51, 53, 69	51, 53, 55, 64, 67, 68.	51, 53, 55, 61, 62, 63, 65, 66, 68.
54 Inventory adjustments	53, 69	53, 55	53, 55.
55 Insurance—general	51, 53, 69	51, 53, 68	51, 53, 68.
56 Insurance—traffic liability	69	55, 64	55, 62.
57 Employee benefits and pensions	51, 53, 69	51, 53, 55, 64, 67, 68.	51, 53, 55, 61, 62, 63, 65, 66, 68.
58 Injuries, loss and damage	51, 53, 69	51, 53, 55, 64, 67, 68.	51, 53, 55, 61, 62, 63, 65, 66, 68.
59 Schedules and timetables	69	67	65, 66.
60 Advertising	69	67	66.
61 Foreign exchange gains and losses	69	68	68.
62 Other promotional and publicity expenses	69	67	66.
63 Interrupted trips expense	69	55	55.
64 Memberships	53, 69	53, 55, 64, 67, 68.	53, 55, 61, 62, 63, 65, 66, 68.
65 Corporate and fiscal expenses	69	68	68.
66 Uncollectible accounts	69	68	68.
67 Clearance, customs and duties	69	64	61, 62.
68 Taxes—payroll	51, 53, 69	51, 53, 55, 64, 67, 68.	51, 53, 55, 61, 62, 63, 65, 66, 68.
69 Taxes—other than payroll	51, 69	51, 68	51, 68.
71 Other expenses	51, 53, 69	51, 53, 55, 64, 67, 68.	51, 53, 55, 61, 62, 63, 65, 66 68.
72 Aircraft overhauls	52, 53	52, 53	52, 53.
72.*1* Airworthiness allowance provisions—airframes	52, 53	52, 53	52, 53.
72.*3* Airframe overhauls deferred	52, 53	52, 53	52, 53.
72.*6* Airworthiness allowance provisions—aircraft engines	52, 53	52, 53	52, 53.
72.*8* Aircraft engine overhauls deferred	52, 53	52, 53	52, 53.
73 Provisions for obsolescence and deterioration—expendable parts:			
73.*1* Current provisions	70	70	70.
73.*2* Inventory decline credits	70	70	70.
74 Amortizations:			
74.*1* Developmental and preoperating expenses	70	70	70.
74.*2* Other intangibles	70	70	70.
75 Depreciation:			
75.*1* Airframes	70	70	70.
75.*2* Aircraft engines	70	70	70.
75.*3* Airframe parts	70	70	70.
75.*4* Aircraft engine parts	70	70	70.
75.*5* Other flight equipment	70	70	70.
75.*6* Flight equipment	70	70	70.
75.*8* Maintenance equipment and hangars	70	70	70.
75.*9* General ground property	70	70	70.
76 Amortization expense, capital leases:			
76.*1* Amortization—capitalized flight equipment	70	70	70
76.*2* Amortization—capitalized other property and equipment	70	70	70
77 Uncleared expense credits:			
77.*8* Uncleared interchange expense credits	53, 69	53, 55, 64, 67, 68.	53, 55, 61, 62, 63, 65, 66, 68.
77.*9* Other uncleared expense credits	53, 69	53, 55, 64, 67, 68.	53, 55, 61, 62, 63, 65, 66, 68.
78 Direct maintenance—flight equipment	52	52	52.
79 Applied burden Dr/Cr:			
79.*6* Flight equipment	52 Dr, 53 Cr	52 Dr, 53 Cr	52 Dr, 53 Cr.
79.*8* General ground property	52 Dr, 53 Cr	52 Dr, 53 Cr	52 Dr, 53 Cr.
NONOPERATING INCOME AND EXPENSE			
81 Interest on long-term debt and capital leases:			
81.*1* Interest expense, long-term debt	81	81	81
81.*2* Interest expense, capital leases	81	81	81
82 Other interest:			
82.*1* Interest expense, short-term debt	81	81	81

Objective classification of profit and loss elements	Functional or financial activity to which applicable (00)		
	Group I carriers	Group II carriers	Group III carriers
83.*1* Imputed interest capitalized—credit	81	81	81
83.*2* Imputed interest deferred—debit	81	81	81
83.*3* Imputed interest deferred—credit	81	81	81
83.*4* Interest capitalized—credit	81	81	81
84.*1* Amortization of discount and expense on debt	81	81	81
84.*2* Amortization of premium on debt	81	81	81
85 Foreign exchange gains and losse	81	81	81
89 Other nonoperating income and expense-net:			
80.*0* Interest income	81	81	81
86.*0* Income from nontransport ventures	81	81	81
87.*0* Equity in income of investor controlled companies	81	81	81
88.*1* Intercompany transaction adjustment-credit	81	81	81
88.*2* Dividend income	81	81	81
88.*3* Net unrealized gain or loss on marketable equity securities.	81	81	81.
88.*4* Net realized gain or loss on marketable equity securities.	81	81	81.
88.*5* Capital gains and losses—operating property	81	81	81.
88.*6* Capital gains and losses—other	81	81	81.
88.*7* Unapplied cash discounts	81	81	81.
88.*9* Other miscellaneous nonoperating credits	81	81	81.
89.*1* Intercompany transaction adjustment—debit	81	81	81.
89.*9* Other miscellaneous nonoperating debits	81	81	81.
INCOME TAXES			
91 Provision for income taxes:			
91.*1* Income taxes before investment tax credits	91	91	91.
91.*2* Investment tax credits utilized	91	91	91.
92 Provisions for deferred income taxes:			
92.*1* Current provisions for deferred taxes	91	91	91.
92.*2* Application of deferred taxes	91	91	91.
92.*3* Adjustment of deferred taxes	91	91	91.
93 Investment tax credits deferred and amortized:			
93.*1* Investment tax credits deferred	91	91	91.
93.*2* Amortization of deferred investment tax credits	91	91	91.
94 Excess profits taxes	91	91	91.
DISCONTINUED OPERATIONS			
95 Discontinued operations:			
95.*1* Income from discontinued operations	96	96	96.
95.*2* Loss on disposal of discontinued operations	96	96	96.
EXTRAORDINARY ITEMS			
96 Extraordinary items	97	97	97.
97 Income taxes applicable to extraordinary items	97	97	97.
CHANGES IN ACCOUNTING PRINCIPLES			
98 Cumulative effects of change in accounting principles	98	98	98.

[ER–755, 37 FR 19726, Sept. 21, 1972, as amended by ER–781, 37 FR 25223, Nov. 29, 1972; 37 FR 28277, Dec. 22, 1972; ER–797, 38 FR 10926, May 3, 1973; ER–841, 39 FR 11995, Apr. 2, 1974; ER–948, 41 FR 12295, Mar. 25, 1976; ER–980, 42 FR 35, Jan. 3, 1977; ER–1013, 42 FR 37515, July 21, 1977; ER–1401, 50 FR 242, Jan. 3, 1985; Amdt. 241–56, 52 FR 9129, Mar. 23, 1987; Amdt. 241–58, 54 FR 5594, Feb. 6, 1989]

Section 8 General

(a) The profit and loss accounts are designed to reflect, through natural groupings, the elements entering into the derivation of income or loss accruing to the proprietary interests during each accounting period.

(b) The prescribed system of accounts provides for the co-ordinate grouping of all revenues and expenses in terms of both major natural objectives and functional activities and for subdivision of both to provide varying degrees of detail for air carriers of differing accounting capacities and/or requirements.

(c) The detailed objective accounts established for each air carrier group, by the dual subdivision of profit and loss elements in terms of both natural objectives and functional activities, are set forth in section 7, Chart of Profit and Loss Accounts.

(d) The prescribed system of accounts provides generally that profit and loss elements shall be grouped in accordance with their inherent characteristics within the following primary classifications:

(1) *Operating revenues.* (i) This primary classification shall include revenues of a character usually and ordinarily derived from the performance of air transportation and air transportation-related services, which relate to services performed during the current accounting year, and adjustments of a recurrent nature applicable to services performed in prior accounting years.

(ii) Operating revenues shall be subclassified in terms of functional activities as provided in section 9.

(2) *Operating expenses.* (i) This primary classification shall include expenses of a character usually and ordinarily incurred in the performance of air transportation and air transportation-related services, which relate to services performed during the current accounting year, and adjustments of a recurring nature attributable to services performed in prior accounting years.

(ii) Operating expenses shall be subclassified in terms of functional activities as provided in sections 10 and 11.

(3) *Nonoperating income and expense—net.* This primary classification (8100) shall include income and loss incident to commercial ventures not inherently related to the performance of the common carrier air transport services of the accounting entity; other revenues and expenses attributable to financing or other activities which are extraneous to and not an integral part of air transportation or its incidental services; and special recurrent items of a nonperiod nature.

(4) *Income taxes for current period.* This primary classification (9100) shall include provisions for Federal, state, local, and foreign taxes which are based upon the net income of the air carrier for the current period together with refunds for excess profits credits or carryback of losses and increases or reductions of income taxes of prior years of a magnitude which will not distort net income of the current accounting year. Income taxes applicable to special income credits or debits recorded in profit and loss classification 9700 Extraordinary Items, and other material income tax items not allocable to income of the current accounting year, shall not be included in this classification but in profit and loss classification 9700 Extraordinary Items.

(5) *Discontinued operations.* This primary classification (9600) shall include earnings and losses of discontinued nontransport operations and gains or losses from the disposal of nontransport operations the result of which are customarily accounted for through profit and loss objective accounts 86, 87 and 88.2.

(6) *Extraordinary items.* This primary classification (9700) shall include material items characterized by their unusual nature and infrequent occurrence.

(7) *Cumulative effect of changes in accounting principles.* This primary classification (9800) shall include the cumulative effect of material changes in accounting principles.

[ER–755, 37 FR 19726, Sept. 21, 1972, as amended by ER–841, 39 FR 11997, Apr. 2, 1974; ER–980, 42 FR 36, Jan. 3, 1977, Amdt. 241–58, 54 FR 5594, Feb. 6, 1989]

Section 9 Functional Classification—Operating Revenues

3900 Transport Revenues.

This classification is prescribed for all air carrier groups and shall include all revenues from the air transportation of traffic of all classes. It shall consist of the following subclassifications:

3100 *Scheduled Services.*

This subclassification shall include revenues from the transportation by air of individual passengers or cargo shipments (as opposed to charter flights) pursuant to published schedules, including extra sections and other flights performed as an integral part of published flight schedules.

3200 *Nonscheduled Services.*

This subclassification shall include revenues from the transportation by air of traffic applicable to the performance of aircraft charters, and other air transportation services not part of services performed pursuant to published flight schedules (but shall not include data applicable to flights performed as extra sections to published flight schedules, which shall be reported in the subclassification 3100 Scheduled Services).

[ER-755, 37 FR 19726, Sept. 21, 1972, as amended by ER-1401, 50 FR 243, Jan. 3, 1985]

4800 Transport-Related Revenues.

(a) This classification is prescribed for all air carrier groups and shall include all revenues from the United States Government as direct grants or aids for providing air transportation facilities and all revenues from services which grow from and are incidental to the air transportation services performed by the air carrier.

(b) Revenues related to services of a magnitude or scope beyond an incidental adjunct to air transportation services shall not be included in this classification (see section 1-6(b)). Revenues applicable to such services shall be included in profit and loss classification 8100, Nonoperating Income and Expense-Net, and the accounting modified to conform with that of a nontransport division whether or not the service is organized as a nontransport division.

[ER-841, 39 FR 11997, Apr. 2, 1974]

Section 10 Functional Classification—Operating Expenses of Group I Air Carriers

5100 Flying Operations.

(a) This function shall include expenses incurred directly in the in-flight operation of aircraft and expenses attaching to the holding of aircraft and aircraft operational personnel in readiness for assignment to an in-flight status.

(b) This function shall not include expenses incurred in repairing, servicing or storing aircraft, expenses incurred on the ground in protecting and controlling the inflight movement of aircraft, or the compensation of ground personnel and other expenses incurred in scheduling or preparing aircraft or aircraft operational personnel for flight assignment. Such expenses shall be included in function 5400 Maintenance or function 6900 General Services and Administration.

5400 Maintenance.

(a) This function shall include all expenses, both direct and indirect, specifically identifiable with the repair and upkeep of property and equipment as may be required to meet operating and safety standards; in inspecting or checking property and equipment in accordance with prescribed operational standards; and in polishing or cleaning property and equipment when such polishing or cleaning is not an incidental routine in connection with the normal productive use of property and equipment.

(b) This function shall include the cost of direct labor, materials, and outside services and maintenances overhead or other costs specifically associated with maintenance operations regardless of the location at which incurred.

(c) This function shall not include costs incurred in the construction, improvement, or modification of property and equipment even when necessitated to meet new or changed operating or safety standards. Such costs shall be charged to appropriate property and equipment accounts.

(d) Costs incurred by aircraft handling personnel in visual inspection, minor check and servicing of aircraft, while in line service, shall not be included in this function when performed as an incidental routine during the normal productive use of aircraft but shall be included in function 6900 General Services and Administration.

(e) Each Group I air carrier shall maintain the following subfunctions:

5200 *Direct Maintenance.*

a. This subfunction shall include the costs of labor, materials and outside services consumed directly in periodic maintenance operations and the maintenance and repair of property and equipment, of all types and classes, regardless of the location at which incurred, exclusive of costs specifically identified with maintenance property and equipment expenses in balance sheet accounts 1630 Equipment, 1639 Improvements to Leased Buildings and Equipment, and 1640.1 Maintenance Buildings and Improvements which shall be included in subfunction 5300 Maintenance Burden.

b. The cost of direct labor, materials and supplies, as well as outside repairs, used in the maintenance and repair of property and equipment shall be recorded on running job orders or tickets covering repairs and periodic inspections except servicing. Where a number of like items are maintained on a group basis, it will be necessary to maintain only one job order for each group.

c. When supervisory personnel such as crew chiefs, inspectors and foremen are engaged in direct labor in connection with equipment maintenance, a proportionate part of their salaries and wages shall be charged to the appropriate direct labor accounts. The cost of transporting property to and from shops for repair and maintenance shall be included as a part of the cost of the materials and supplies used in the repair or maintenance of such property and equipment. Transportation charges, customs and duties, etc.; shall be included in the cost of repairs and maintenance operations when made by outside parties.

5300 *Maintenance Burden.*

a. This subfunction shall include all overhead or general expenses which are specifically identified with activities involved in periodic maintenance operations and the maintenance and repair of property and equipment of all types and classes, including the cost of direct labor, materials and outside services identified with the maintenance and repair of maintenance property and equipment included in balance sheet accounts 1630 Equipment, 1639 Improvements to Leased Buildings and Equipment, and 1604.1 Maintenance Buildings and Improvements. It shall include expenses specifically related to the administration of maintenance stocks and stores, the keeping of pertinent maintenance operations records, and the scheduling, controlling, planning and supervision of maintenance operations.

b. This subfunction shall not include expenses related to financial accounting, purchasing or other overhead activities which are of general applicability to all operating functions. Such expenses shall be included in function 6900 General Services and Administration.

c. This subfunction shall include only those expenses attributable to the current air transport operations of the air carrier. Maintenance burden associated with capital projects of the air carrier, other than overhauls of airframes and aircraft engines shall be allocated to such projects. Maintenance burden incurred in common with services to other companies and operating entities shall be allocated to such services on a pro rata basis unless the services are so infrequent in performance or small in volume as to result in no appreciable demands upon the air carrier's maintenance facilities. When overhauls of airframes or aircraft engines are as a consistent practice accounted for on an accrual basis instead of being expensed directly, maintenance burden shall be allocated to such overhauls on a pro rata basis. Standard burden rates may be employed for quarterly allocations of maintenance burden provided the rates are reviewed at the close of each calendar year. When the actual burden rate for the year differs materially from the standard burden rate applied, adjustment shall be made to reflect the actual cost incurred for the full accounting year. Allocations of maintenance burden to capital projects, and service sales to others shall be made through the individual maintenance burden objective accounts, except that the air carrier may make such allocations by credits to profit and loss account 77 Uncleared Expense Credits provided that use of that account will not undermine the significance of the individual maintenance burden objective accounts in terms of the expense levels associated with the air carrier's air transport services. Maintenance burden allocated to overhauls shall be credited to profit and loss subaccounts 5372.1 or 5372.6 Airworthiness Allowance Provisions.

[ER–755, 37 FR 19726, Sept. 21, 1972, as amended by ER–980, 42 FR 36, Jan. 3, 1977; ER–1027, 42 FR 60128, Nov. 25, 1977; ER–1188, 45 FR 48870, July 22, 1980; Amdt. 241–58, 54 FR 5595, Feb. 6, 1989]

6900 General Services and Administration.

This function shall include expenses incurred on the ground in controlling and protecting the in-flight movement of aircraft; landing, handling, or servicing aircraft on the ground; selling transportation; servicing and handling traffic of all classes; promoting the development of traffic; administering operations generally; and all other expenses not otherwise provided for in functions 5100 Flying Operations, 5400 Maintenance and 7000 Depreciation and Amortization.

7000 Depreciation and Amortization.

This function shall include all charges to expense to record losses suffered through current exhaustion of the serviceability of property and equipment due to wear and tear from use and the action of time and the elements, which are not replaced by current repairs, as well as losses in serviceability caused by obsolescence, supersession, discoveries, change in demand or actions by public authority. It shall also include charges for the amortization of capitalized developmental and preoperating costs, leased property under capital leases and other intangible assets applicable to the performance of air transportation. (See sections 6–1696, 1830 and 1890.)

[Amdt. 241–58, 54 FR 5595, Feb. 6, 1989]

7100 Transport-Related Expenses.

(a) This function shall include all expense items applicable to the generation of transport-related revenues included in section 9, Function 4800.

(b) Such expense related to services of a magnitude or scope beyond an incidental adjunct to air transportation services shall not be included in this function (see section 1–6(b)). Expenses applicable to the generation of such revenues shall be included in profit and loss classification 8100, Nonoperating Income and Expense-Net, and the accounting modified to conform with that of a nontransport division whether or not the service is organized as a nontransport division.

(c) This function shall also include expenses representing increases in costs incurred in common with the air transport service, to the extent such increases result from the added transport-related services, as well as a pro rata share of the costs incurred by the air carrier in operating facilities which are used jointly with others. As a general rule, this function shall not include those expenses, other than joint facilities costs, which would remain as an essential part of the air transport services if the transport-related services were terminated.

[ER–841, 39 FR 11997, Apr. 2, 1974, as amended by ER–1401, 50 FR 243, Jan. 3, 1985]

Section 11 Functional Classification—Operating Expenses of Group II and Group III Air Carriers

5100 Flying Operations.

(a) This function shall include expenses incurred directly in the in-flight operation of aircraft and expenses attaching to the holding of aircraft and aircraft operational personnel in readiness for assignment to an in-flight status.

(b) This function shall not include expenses incurred in repairing, servicing or storing aircraft, expenses incurred on the ground in protecting and controlling the in-flight movement of aircraft, or compensation of ground personnel and other expenses incurred in scheduling or preparing aircraft or aircraft operational personnel for flight assignment. Such expenses shall be included in function 5400 Maintenance, or function 6400 Aircraft and Traffic Servicing.

5400 Maintenance.

(a) This function shall include all expenses, both direct and indirect, incurred in the repair and upkeep of property and equipment as may be required to meet operating and safety standards; in inspecting or checking property and equipment in accordance with prescribed operational standards; and in polishing or cleaning property and equipment when such polishing or cleaning is not an incidental routine in connection with the normal productive use of property and equipment.

(b) This function shall include the cost of direct labor, materials, and outside services and maintenance overhead or other costs associated with maintenance operations regardless of the location at which incurred.

(c) This function shall not include costs incurred in the construction, improvement, or modification of property and equipment even when necessitated to meet new or changed operating or safety standards. Such costs shall be charged to appropriate property and equipment accounts.

(d) Costs incurred by aircraft handling personnel in visual inspection, minor check and servicing of aircraft, while in line service, shall not be included in this function when performed as an incidental routine during the normal productive use of aircraft but shall be included in function 6400 Aircraft and Tariff Servicing.

(e) Both Group II air carriers and Group III air carriers shall maintain the following subfunctions:

5200 *Direct Maintenance.*

a. This subfunction shall include the costs of labor, materials and outside services consumed directly in periodic maintenance operations and the maintenance and repair of property and equipment of all types and classes, regardless of the location at which incurred, exclusive of maintenance property and equipment included in balance sheet accounts 1630 Equipment, 1639 Improvements to Leased Buildings and Equipment, and 1640.1 Maintenance Buildings and Improvements, which shall be included in subfunction 5300 Maintenance Burden.

b. The cost of direct labor, materials and supplies, as well as outside repairs, used in the maintenance and repair of property and equipment shall be recorded on running job orders or tickets covering repairs and periodic inspections except servicing. Where a number of like items are maintained on a group basis, it will be necessary to maintain only one job order for each group.

c. When supervisory personnel such as crew chiefs, inspectors and foremen are engaged in direct labor in connection with equipment maintenance, a proportionate part of their salaries and wages shall be charged to the appropriate direct labor accounts. The cost of transporting property to and from shops for repair and maintenance shall be included as a part of the cost of the materials and supplies used in the repair or maintenance of such property and equipment. Transportation charges, customs and duties, etc., shall be included in the cost of repairs and maintenance operations when made by outside parties.

5300 *Maintenance Burden.*

a. This subfunction shall include all overhead or general expenses used directly in the activities involved in periodic maintenance operations and the maintenance and repair of property and equipment of all types and classes, including the cost of direct labor, materials and outside services used in the maintenance and repair of maintenance property and equipment included in balance sheet accounts 1630 Equipment, 1639 Improvements to Leased Buildings and Equipment, and 1640.1 Maintenance Buildings and Improvements. It shall include expenses related to the administration of maintenance stocks and stores, the keeping of pertinent maintenance operation records, and the scheduling, controlling, planning and supervision of maintenance operations.

b. This subfunction shall not include expenses related to financial accounting, purchasing or other overhead activities which are of general applicability to all operating functions. Such expenses shall be included in function 6800 General and Administrative.

c. This subfunction shall include only those expenses attributable to the current air transport operations of the air carrier. Maintenance burden associated with capital projects of the air carrier, other than overhauls of airframes and aircraft engines, shall be allocated to such projects. Maintenance burden incurred in common with services to other companies and operating entities shall be allocated to such services on a pro rata basis unless the services are so infrequent in performance or small in volume as to result in no appreciable demands upon the air carrier's maintenance facilities. When overhauls of airframes or aircraft engines are as a consistent practice accounted for on an accrual basis instead of being expensed directly, maintenance burden shall be allocated to such overhauls on a pro rata basis. Standard burden rates may be employed for quarterly allocations of maintenance burden provided the rates are reviewed at the close of each calendar year. When the actual burden rate for the year differs materially from the standard burden rate applied, adjustment shall be made to reflect the actual costs incurred for the full accounting year. Allocations of maintenance burden to capital projects, and service sales to others shall be made through the individual maintenance burden objective accounts, except that the air carrier may make such allocations by credits to profit and loss account 77 Uncleared Expense Credits under such circumstances in which the use of that account will not undermine the significance of the individual maintenance burden objective accounts in terms of the expense levels associated with the air carrier's air transport services. Maintenance burden allocated to overhauls shall be credited to profit and loss subaccounts 5372.1 or 5372.6 Airworthiness Allowance Provisions.

[ER–755, 37 FR 19726, Sept. 21, 1972, as amended by ER–980, 42 FR 36, Jan. 3, 1977; ER–1401, 50 FR 244, Jan. 3, 1985; Amdt. 241–58, 54 FR 5595, Feb. 6, 1989]

5500 Passenger Service.

This function shall include all expenses chargeable directly to activities contributing to the comfort, safety and convenience of passengers while in flight and when flights are interrupted. It shall not include expenses incurred in enplaning or deplaning passengers, or in securing and selling passenger transportation and caring for passengers prior to entering a flight status. Such expenses shall be included in functions 6400 Aircraft and Traffic Servicing and 6700 Promotion and Sales, respectively.

6400 Aircraft and Traffic Servicing.

(a) This function shall include the compensation of ground personnel and other expenses incurred on the ground incident to the protection and control of the in-flight movement of aircraft, scheduling and preparing aircraft operational crews for flight assignment, handling and servicing aircraft while in line operation, servicing and handling traffic on the ground, subsequent to the issuance of documents establishing the air carrier's responsibility to provide air transportation, and in-flight expenses of handling and protecting all nonpassenger traffic including passenger baggage.

(b) This function shall include only those aircraft servicing and cleaning expenses which are incurred as an incidental routine during the normal productive use of aircraft in line operations. It shall not include expenses incurred in the repair and maintenance of property and equipment, or in checking or inspecting property and equipment in accordance with prescribed operational standards when such activities are not an incidental routine during the normal productive use of aircraft. Such expenses shall be included in function 5400 Maintenance.

(c) This function shall not include expenses incurred in securing traffic, arranging aircraft space for traffic sold or in issuing documents confirming traffic sales and establishing the air carrier's responsibilities to provide air transportation. Such expenses shall be included in function 6700 Promotion and Sales. However, for purposes of this system of accounts, expenses attributable to the operation of airport traffic offices, excluding reservation centers, shall be included in this function. Expenses attributable to the operation of reservation or aircraft space control centers shall be included in function 6700 Promotion and Sales regardless of the location at which incurred.

(d) Group III air carriers shall further subdivide this function as follows:

6100 *Aircraft Servicing.*

a. This subfunction shall include the compensation of ground personnel and other expenses incurred on the ground incident to the protection and control of the in-flight movement of aircraft; scheduling or preparing aircraft operational crews for flight assignment; landing and parking aircraft; visual inspection, routine checking, servicing and fueling of aircraft; and other expenses incurred on the ground incident to readying for arrival and takeoff of aircraft.

6200 *Traffic Servicing.*

a. This subfunction shall include the compensation of ground personnel and other expenses incurred on the ground incident to handling traffic of all types and classes on the ground subsequent to the issuance of documents establishing the air carrier's responsibility to provide air transportation. Expenses attributable to the operation of airport traffic offices shall also be included in this subfunction; expenses attributable to reservations centers shall be excluded. It shall include expenses incurred in both enplaning and deplaning traffic as well as expenses incurred in preparation for enplanement and all expenses subsequent to deplanement.

b. This subfunction shall also include costs incurred in handling and protecting all nonpassenger traffic while in flight. It shall not include expenses incurred in contributing to the comfort, safety and convenience of passengers while in flight or when flights are interrupted. Such expenses shall be included in function 5500 Passenger Service.

6300 *Servicing Administration.*

a. This subfunction shall include expenses of a general nature incurred in performing supervisory or administrative activities relating solely and in common to subfunctions 6100 Aircraft Servicing and 6200 Traffic Servicing.

b. This subfunction shall not include supervisory or administrative expenses which can be charged directly to subfunction 6100 Aircraft Servicing or subfunction 6200 Traffic Servicing. Nor shall this subfunction include expenses of a general administrative character and of significant amount regularly contributing to operating functions generally. Such expenses shall be included in function 6800 General and Administrative.

c. The expenses in this subfunction shall be recorded separately for each geographic location at which incurred.

6700 Promotion and Sales.

(a) This function shall include expenses incurred in creating public preference for the air carrier and its services; stimulating the development of the air transport market; and promoting the air carrier or developing air transportation generally.

(b) It shall also include the compensation of personnel and other expenses incident to documenting sales; expenses incident to controlling and arranging or confirming aircraft space for traffic sold; expenses incurred in direct sales solicitation and selling of aircraft space; and expenses incurred in developing tariffs and schedules for publication.

(c) This function shall not include expenses incurred in handling traffic subsequent to the issuance of documents establishing the air carrier's responsibility to provide air transportation which shall be included in functions 5500 Passenger Service and 6400 Aircraft and Traffic Servicing. However, for purposes of this system of accounts, expenses attributable to the operation of airport traffic offices, excluding reservation centers, shall be included in function 6400 Aircraft and Traffic Servicing. Expenses attributable to the operation of reservation or aircraft space control centers shall be included in function 6700 Promotion and Sales regardless of the location at which incurred.

(d) Group III air carriers shall subdivide this function as follows:

6500 *Reservations and Sales.*

This subfunction shall include expenses incident to direct sales solicitation, documenting sales, controlling and arranging or confirming aircraft space sold, and in developing tariffs and schedules for publication. It shall also include expenses attributable to the operation of city traffic offices. Expenses incurred in stimulating traffic and promoting the air carrier or air transportation generally shall not be included in this subfunction but in subfunction 6600 Advertising and Publicity.

6600 *Advertising and Publicity.*

a. This subfunction shall include expenses incurred in creating public preference for the air carrier and its services; stimulating development of the air transport market; and promoting the air carrier or developing air transportation generally.

b. This subfunction shall not include expenses incurred in direct sales solicitation and selling of aircraft space. Such costs shall be included in subfunction 6500 Reservations and Sales.

6800 General and Administrative.

(a) This function shall include expenses of a general corporate nature and expenses incurred in performing activities which contribute to more than a single operating function such as general financial accounting activities, purchasing activities, representation at law, and other general operational administration, which are not directly applicable to a particular function.

(b) This function shall not include expenses incurred directly in promoting traffic or in promoting relations of the air carrier generally with the public which shall be included in function 6700 Promotion and Sales. Nor shall this function include expenses, regularly applicable in large part to a specific function, which contribute only incidentally, or in small amount, to various other functions. Such expenses when of such size as will not distort the function to which predominantly related, shall be included in the specific function to which regularly related. However, expenses of a general administrative character and of significant amount regularly contributing to operating functions generally shall be included in this function.

7000 Depreciation and Amortization.

This function shall include all charges to expense to record losses suffered through current exhaustion of the serviceability of property and equipment due to wear and tear from use and the action of time and the elements, which are not replaced by current repairs, as well as losses in serviceability occasioned by obsolescence, supersession, discoveries, change in popular demand or action by public authority. It shall also include charges for the amortization of capitalized developmental and preoperating costs, leased property under capital leases, and other intangible assets applicable to the performance of air transportation. (See sections 6–1696, 1830 and 1890.)

[Amdt. 241–58, 54 FR 5595, Feb. 6, 1989]

7100 Transport-Related Expenses.

(a) This function shall include all expense items applicable to the generation of transport-related revenues included in section 9, Function 4800.

(b) Such expense related to services of a magnitude or scope beyond an incidental adjunct to air transportation services shall not be included in this function (see section 1–6(b)). Expenses applicable to the generation of such revenues shall be included in profit and loss classification 8100, Nonoperating Income and Expense-Net, and the accounting modified to conform with that of a nontransport division whether or not the service is organized as a nontransport division.

(c) This function shall also include expenses representing increases in costs incurred in common with the air transport service, to the extent such increases result from the added transport-related services, as well as a pro rata share of the costs incurred by the air carrier in operating facilities which are used jointly with others. As a general rule, this function shall not include those expenses, other than joint facilities, costs, which would remain as an essential part of the air transport services if the transport-related services were terminated.

[ER-841, 39 FR 11997, Apr. 2, 1974, as amended by ER-1401, 50 FR 244, Jan. 3, 1985]

Section 12 Objective Classification—Operating Revenues and Expenses

00 General Instructions.

(a) Basic objective accounts, applicable to all air carrier groups, are established for recording all revenue and expense elements. These basic accounts are in certain areas subdivided to provide greater detail for indicated air carrier groups.

(b) Each air carrier shall credit the gross revenues accruing from services ordinarily associated with air transportation and transportation-related services to the appropriate account established for each revenue source. Expenses incident to transport and transport-related services shall be charged to the accounts established in this section in accordance with the objectives served by each expenditure. However, direct costs of forwarding traffic as a result of interrupted trips, and refunds of sales, shall be charged to the applicable revenue account.

(c) To the end that the integrity of the prescribed objective accounts shall not be impaired, each air carrier shall: (1) Charge the appropriate account prescribed for each service purchased or expense element incurred expressly for the benefit of the air carrier regardless of whether incurred directly by the air carrier or through an agent or other intermediary, and (2) except as provided in objective account 77, Uncleared Expense Credits, credit or charge, as appropriate, the account prescribed for each expense element which may be involved in distributions of expenses between (i) separate operating entities of the air carrier, (ii) transport-related services and transport services, or transport functions, (iii) balance sheet and profit and loss elements, and (iv) the air carrier and others, when the expenses are incurred initially by or for the benefit of the air carrier. At the option of the air carrier, standard rates applicable to each objective account comprising a particular pool of expenses subject to assignment between two or more activities, may be established for proration purposes, provided the rates established are predicated upon the experience of the air carrier and are reviewed and modified as appropriate at least once each year.

TRANSPORT REVENUES

01 Passenger.

(a) Record here revenue from the transportation of passengers by air, including infants transported at reduced fares, berth charges, surcharges for premium services and other similar charges. Revenue from airline employees, officers and directors, or other persons, except for ministers of religion, who are traveling under reduced-rate transportation authorized by 49 U.S.C. 41511(a) and 14 CFR part 223, as well as revenue from travel agents, cargo agents and tour conductors traveling at reduced fares, and revenues from service charges for passengers traveling on a nonrevenue basis shall be recorded in objective account 19 Air Transport—Other.

(b) This account shall be subdivided as follows by all air carrier groups:

01.1 *Passenger—First Class.*

Record here revenue from the air transportation of passengers moving at either standard fares or premium fares, or at reduced fares not predicated upon the use of aircraft space specifically separated from first class, and for whom standard or premium quality services are provided.

01.2 *Passenger—Coach.*

Record here revenue from the air transportation of passengers moving at special fares reduced from the first class or premium fares which are predicated upon both the operation of specifically designated aircraft space and a reduction in the quality of service regularly and ordinarily provided.

[ER-755, 37 FR 19726, Sept. 21, 1972, as amended by ER-980, 42 FR 36, Jan. 3, 1977; 60 FR 66723, Dec. 26, 1995]

05 Mail.

(a) Record here revenue from the transportation by air of both United States and foreign mail.

(b) Fines and penalties imposed by the United States Government and foreign governments in connection with the carriage of mail shall not be charged to this account but to profit and loss account 89.9 Other Miscellaneous Nonoperating Debits.

(c) This account shall be subdivided as follows by all air carrier groups:

05.1 *Priority.*

Record here revenue from United States mail for which transportation by air is provided on a priority basis.

05.2 *Nonpriority.*

Record here revenue from United States mail for which transportation by air is provided on a space available basis.

05.3 *Foreign.*

Record here revenue from the transportation by air of mail other than United States mail.

[ER–980, 42 FR 36, Jan. 3, 1977, as amended by Amdt. 241–58, 54 FR 5595, Feb. 6, 1989]

06 Property.

(a) Record here revenue from the transportation by air of property including excess passenger baggage.

(b) Revenues resulting from services incidental to the transportation services such as collection of shipper's interest insurance premiums and charges and fees for service such as pick-up and delivery, assembly and distribution, storage and handling, and C.O.D. collection shall not be credited to this account but to profit and loss account 17 Air Cargo Services

(c) This account shall be subdivided as follows by all air carrier groups:

06.1 *Freight.*

Record here revenue from the transportation by air of property other than passenger baggage.

06.2 *Excess Passenger Baggage.*

Record here revenue from the transportation by air of passener baggage in excess of fixed free allowance.

[ER–755, 37 FR 19726, Sept. 21, 1972, as amended by ER–1401, 50 FR 244, Jan. 3, 1985]

07 Charter.

(a) Record here the revenue from nonscheduled air transport services (except as otherwise required by profit and loss Account 86 Income from Nontransport Ventures) where the party receiving the transportation obtains exclusive use of an aircraft at either published tariff or other contractual rates and the remuneration paid by the party receiving transportation accrues directly to, and the responsibility for providing transportation is that of, the accounting air carrier. This account shall also include revenues from air transport services other than inter-airport services, whether scheduled or nonscheduled, where each passenger or shipment receiving transportation is individually documented and does not obtain exclusive use of an aircraft.

(b) This account shall not include revenues or fees received from other air carriers for flight facilities furnished or operated by the accounting air carrier where the remuneration paid by the party receiving transportation accrues directly to, and the responsibility for providing transportation is that of other air carriers. Such revenues and related expenses shall be included in profit and loss accounts 11, Rents; 13, Interchange Sales; or 18, Other Transport-Related Revenues and Expenses.

(c) This account shall be subdivided as follows by all air carrier groups:

07.1 *Passenger.*

Record here revenue from the transportation of passengers and their personal baggage.

07.2 *Property*

Record here revenue from the transportation of property.

[ER–755, 37 FR 19726, Sept. 21, 1972, as amended by ER–980, 42 FR 37, Jan. 3, 1977; ER–1401, 50 FR 244, Jan. 3, 1985]

TRANSPORT RELATED REVENUES AND EXPENSES

08 Public Service Revenues (Subsidy).

Record here amounts of compensation received pursuant to the provisions of 49 U.S.C. 41733 under rates established by the Department of Transportation for the provision of essential air service to small communities.

[Amdt. 241–58, 54 FR 5595, Feb. 6, 1989, as amended at 60 FR 66723, Dec. 26, 1995]

09 In-Flight Sales.

(a) Record here revenues from and expenses related to transport-related services performed while in flight.

(b) This account shall be subdivided as follows by all air carrier groups:

09.1 *Liquor and food—gross revenues.*

09.2 *Movies and stereo—gross revenues.*

09.3 *Other—gross revenues.*

09.4 *Liquor and food—depreciation expense.*

09.5 *Liquor and food—other expense.*

09.6 *Movies and stereo—depreciation expense.*

09.7 *Movies and stereo—other expense.*

09.8 *Other—depreciation expense.*

09.9 *Other—expense.*

10 Restaurant and Food Service (Ground).

(a) Record here revenues from and expenses related to the operation of restaurants and similar facilities, and from sales of food. (See section 12–51.)

(b) This account shall be subdivided as follows by all air carrier groups.

10.1 *Gross revenues.*

10.2 *Depreciation expense.*

10.3 *Other expense.*

11 Rents.

(a) Record here revenues from and expenses related to property and equipment owned or leased which has been rented or subleased to others exclusive of associated companies. This account shall not include fees from the use by others of air carrier aircraft under aircraft interchange agreements.

(b) This account shall be subdivided as follows by all air carrier groups:

11.1 *Gross Revenues.*

11.2 *Depreciation Expense.*

11.3 *Other Expenses.*

12 Limousine Service.

(a) Record here revenues from and expenses related to the operation of passenger limousine surface transportation services.

(b) This account shall be subdivided as follows by all air carrier groups:

12.1 *Gross Revenues.*

12.2 *Depreciation Expense.*

12.3 *Other Expenses.*

13 Interchange Sales.

(a) Record here the revenues or fees from and the expenses related to services provided associated companies and other than associated companies by the air carrier under aircraft interchange agreements. This account shall be charged and the applicable operating expense objective accounts shall be credited, except as provided in operating expense objective account 77, Uncleared Expense Credits, with the expenses attaching to services provided all companies under aircraft interchange agreements.

(b) This account shall not include revenues or expenses related to air transportation services performed in the name of and for the account of the accounting air carrier. Such revenues shall be included in applicable transport revenue and operating expense objective accounts.

(c) This account shall be subdivided as follows by all air carrier groups:

13.1 *Associated companies—gross revenues.*

13.2 *Outside—gross revenues.*

13.3 *Associated companies—depreciation expense.*

13.4 *Associated companies—other expense.*

13.5 *Outside—depreciation expense.*

13.6 *Outside—other expense.*

14 General Service Sales.

(a) Record here the revenues, commissions or fees from and expenses related to other than air transportation and aircraft interchange services provided to associated and outside companies by the air carrier. This account shall include the contractual fees or other revenues from and expenses related to services provided to associated and other companies in the operation of facilities which are used jointly with associated and other companies as well as revenues from and the costs related to the sale of supplies, parts and repairs sold directly or furnished as a part of services to associated and other companies.

(b) This account shall not include consideration received from sales of property, equipment, materials or supplies when disposed of as a part of a program involving retirement of property and equipment as opposed to routine sales and services to associated and other companies unless such disposition is conducted as a normal part of the incidental sales activity. Such retirement gain or loss shall be included in capital gains and losses accounts. Maintenance parts, materials or supplies sold as a service to others shall be charged to this account at cost without adjustment of related obsolescence or depreciation allowances.

(c) This account shall be subdivided as follows by all air carrier groups:

14.1 *Associated companies—gross revenues.*

14.2 *Outside—gross revenues.*

14.3 *Associated companies—depreciation expense.*

14.4 *Associated companies—other expense.*

14.5 *Outside—depreciation expense.*

14.6 *Outside—other expense.*

[ER–755, 37 FR 19726, Sept. 21, 1972, as amended by ER–980, 42 FR 37, Jan. 3, 1977]

16 Substitute (replacement) Service.

(a) Record here revenues from and expenses related to substitute service. This account shall include as revenues all monies received from substitute carriers and as expense all monies paid to substitute carriers.

(b) This account shall be subdivided as follows by all air carrier groups:

16.1 *Gross revenue.*

16.2 *Expense.*

17 Air Cargo Services.

(a) Record here fees and other revenues from and expenses related to incidental services performed in connection with cargo shipments such as pickup and delivery fees, shipper's interest insurance charges, storage and handling fees, etc.

(b) This account shall be subdivided as follows by all air carrier groups:

17.1 *Gross Revenues.*

17.2 *Depreciation Expense.*

17.3 *Other Expenses.*

18 Other Transport-Related Revenues and Expenses.

(a) Record here revenues from and expenses related to transport-related services not provided for in profit and loss accounts 10 through 17, inclusive, such as revenues and expenses incident to the operation of flight facilities by the accounting air carrier, except those operated under aircraft interchange agreements, where the remuneration paid by the party receiving transportation accrues directly to, and the responsibility for providing transportation is that of, other air carriers; and the revenues and expenses incident to vending machines, parcel rooms, storage facilities, etc.

(b) [Reserved]

(c) Revenues from the renting or leasing of property and equipment to others shall not be included in this account but in profit and loss account 11 Rents.

(d) This account shall be subdivided as follows by all air carrier groups:

18.1 *Gross Revenues.*

18.2 *Depreciation Expense.*

18.3 *Other Expenses.*

19 Air Transport—Other.

(a) Record here revenues associated with air transportation conducted by the air carrier, not provided for in profit and loss accounts 01 through 09, inclusive, such as revenue from (1) airline employees, officers and directors, or other persons, except for ministers of religion, who are traveling under reduced-rate transportation authorized by 49 U.S.C. 41511(a) and 14 CFR part 223, as well as travel agents, cargo agents and tour conductors traveling at reduced fares, (2) service charges for failure to cancel or for late cancellation of air transportation reservations, and (3) nontransportation service charges collected on both revenue and nonrevenue flights.

(b) Revenues derived from sightseeing, aerial photography, advertising, or other special flights shall not be included in this account but in account 07 Charter.

(c) This account shall be subdivided as follows by all air carrier groups:

19.1 *Reservations Cancellation Fees.*

19.9 *Miscellaneous Operating Revenue.*

[ER–755, 37 FR 19726, Sept. 21, 1972, as amended by ER–820, 38 FR 24352, Sept. 7, 1973; ER–841, 39 FR 11997, Apr. 2, 1974; ER–980, 42 FR 37, Jan. 3, 1977; 60 FR 66723, Dec. 26, 1995]

TRANSPORT EXPENSES

20 General Instructions.

(a) Each element of expense ordinarily associated with air transportation services shall be charged to the accounts established in this section in accordance with the objectives served by each expenditure. Basic objective accounts, applicable to all air carrier groups, are established for recording all expense elements. These basic accounts are in certain areas subdivided to provide greater detail for indicated air carrier groups.

(b) To the end that the integrity of the prescribed objective accounts shall not be impaired, each air carrier shall:

(1) Charge the appropriate account prescribed for each service purchased or expense element incurred expressly for the benefit of the air carrier regardless of whether incurred directly by the air carrier or through an agent or other intermediary, and (2) except as provided in objective account 77 Uncleared Expense Credits, credit or charge, as appropriate, the account prescribed for each expense element which may be involved in distributions of expenses between (i) separate operating entities of the air carrier, (ii) incidental and transport services or transport functions, (iii) balance sheet and profit and loss elements and (iv) the air carrier and others, when the expenses are incurred initially by or for the benefit of the air carrier. At the option of the air carrier, standard rates applicable to each objective account comprising a particular pool of expenses subject to assignment between two or more activities, may be established for proration purposes, provided the rates established are predicated upon the experience of the air carrier and are reviewed and modified as appropriate at least once each year.

21 General Management Personnel.

Record here the compensation, including vacation and sick leave pay, of general officers and supervisors, and immediate assistants regardless of locality at which based, responsible for an activity not provided for in profit and loss accounts 25 through 35, inclusive, or an activity involving two or more such accounts.

23 Pilots and Copilots.

Record here the compensation, including vacation and sick leave pay, of pilots and copilots assigned or held inactive awaiting assignment to flight duty.

24 Other Flight Personnel.

Record here the compensation, including vacation and sick leave pay, of other flight personnel assigned or held inactive awaiting assignment to flight status, not responsible for the in-flight management of aircraft, such as engineers, navigation officers and cabin attendants.

25 Maintenance Labor.

(a) Record here the compensation for time of personnel spent directly on specific property and equipment maintenance projects. (See sections 10 and 11–5200.) Vacation and sick leave pay shall be charged to profit and loss account 28 Trainees, Instructors and Unallocated Shop Labor.

(b) This account shall be subdivided as follows:

GROUP II AND GROUP III AIR CARRIERS

25.1 *Labor—Airframes and Other Flight Equipment.*

Record here the direct labor expended upon airframes, spare parts related to airframes, and other flight equipment (Other than aircraft engines and spare parts related to aircraft engines). Other flight equipment shall include instruments, which encompass all gauges, meters, measuring devices, and indicators, together with appurtenances thereto for installation in aircraft and aircraft engines which are maintaned separately from airframes and aircraft engines.

25.2 *Labor—Aircraft Engines.*

Record here the direct labor expended upon aircraft engines and spare parts related to aircraft engines.

GROUP I AIR CARRIERS

25.6 *Labor—Flight Equipment.*

Record here the direct labor expended upon flight equipment of all types and classes.

ALL AIR CARRIER GROUPS

25.9 *Labor—Ground Property and Equipment.*

Record here the direct labor expended upon ground property and equipment of all types and classes. Direct labor expended upon general ground properties shall be charged to subfunction 5200 Direct Maintenance; and direct labor expended upon maintenance buildings and equipment shall be charged to subfunction 5300 Maintenance Burden.

[ER–755, 37 FR 19726, Sept. 21, 1972, as amended by ER–1401, 50 FR 244, Jan. 3, 1985]

26 Aircraft and Traffic Handling Personnel.

(a) Record here the compensation, including vacation and sick leave pay, of personnel of all types and classes, including direct supervisory personnel, assigned to ground activities, engaged directly in protecting and controlling aircraft in flight, scheduling and preparing flight crews for flight assignment, parking and servicing aircraft incidental to line operations, and of personnel of all types and classes engaged in servicing and handling traffic of all types and classes on the ground.

(b) This account shall be subdivided as follows by Group II and Group III air carriers:

26.1 *General Aircraft and Traffic Handling Personnel.*

Record here compensation of personnel handling or controlling aircraft and generally servicing or handling traffic of all types and classes whose activities are not identifiable with the particular activities provided for in subaccounts 26.2, 26.3, or 26.4, inclusive.

26.2 *Aircraft Control Personnel.*

Record here compensation of personnel whose activities are identifiable with the protection and control of aircraft in flight and in scheduling or preparing flight crews for flight assignment.

26.3 *Passenger Handling Personnel.*

Record here compensation of personnel whose activities are identifiable with the handling of passengers.

26.4 *Cargo Handling Personnel.*

Record here compensation of personnel whose activities are identifiable with the handling of passenger baggage, mail, express, or freight.

28 Trainees, Instructors, and Unallocated Shop Labor.

(a) Record here the compensation, including vacation and sick leave pay, of instructors and personnel in an off-the-job training status; direct maintenance personnel compensation not assigned to specific projects; and vacation or sick leave pay of direct maintenance personnel.

(b) This account shall be subdivided as follows by all air carrier groups:

28.1 *Trainees and Instructors.*

Record here the compensation of instructors and personnel in a training status.

28.2 *Unallocated Shop Labor.*

Record here the pay of direct maintenance personnel which has not been assigned to profit and loss account 25 Maintenance Labor for time spent on specific maintenance projects, and vacation or sick leave pay of direct maintenance personnel.

30 Communications Personnel.

Record here the compensation, including vacation and sick leave pay, of personnel of all types and classes, including direct supervisory personnel, engaged in local, interstation, or groundair communication activities.

This account shall include compensation of personnel such as radio operators, telephone operators, switchboard operators, teletype operators, messengers, etc.

31 Recordkeeping and Statistical Personnel.

Record here the compensation, including vacation and sick leave pay, of personnel including supervisory personnel, whose primary duties relate to maintaining records or conducting economic or other analyses required for general management controls, such as accountants, economists, statisticians, maintenance record clerks, stores record clerks, stores receiving and issuing clerks and file clerks. The account shall not include personnel engaged in documentation or other activities constituting an integral part of activities encompassed by other objective accounts.

32 Lawyers and Law Clerks.

Record here the compensation, including vacation and sick leave pay, of air carrier personnel engaged in law research or representing the air carrier in matters of law.

33 Traffic Solicitors.

Record here the compensation, including vacation and sick leave pay, of personnel engaged directly in solicitation of traffic of all types and classes. This account shall not include compensation of traffic office personnel engaged in soliciting activities incidental to the documenting of sales and assigning aircraft space which shall be included in profit and loss account 26 Aircraft and Traffic Handling Personnel.

34 Purchasing Personnel.

(a) Record here the compensation, including vacation and sick leave pay, of personnel, including direct supervisory personnel, engaged in purchasing activities.

(b) This account shall include compensation of personnel engaged in maintaining purchasing records but shall not include compensation of personnel responsible for the control of inventories or stores which shall be included in objective account 31 Record Keeping and Statistical Personnel. In cases where the responsibility for maintaining purchasing and stores records are inseparable, the related compensation may be accounted for in accordance with dominant responsibilities.

35 Other Personnel.

Record here the compensation, including vacation and sick leave pay, of personnel whose activities are not identifiable with activities provided for in profit and loss accounts 21 through 34, inclusive.

36 Personnel Expenses.

(a) Record here expenses incurred by officers, executives, directors and other personnel, whether for the benefit of the air carrier or for the private benefit of such persons, which are directly or indirectly borne by the air carrier.

(b) This account shall include allowances in lieu of expenses as well as expenses incurred for travel, lodgings, meals, entertainment of individuals or groups of individuals, and membership fees and dues in professional or social clubs and associations.

(c) Records shall be maintained in a conveniently accessible form which will separately and clearly document each charge to this account in terms of its natural characteristics and contribution to the performance of the air carrier's transport operations. The records shall be maintained in such manner as will identify specifically the persons incurring the cost. Costs for standby hotel or other facilities maintained for the air carrier's personnel generally need not be allocated among the individuals using such facilities; however, sufficiently detailed records are required to identify the use made of such facilities by each individual.

[ER-755, 37 FR 19726, Sept. 21, 1972, as amended by ER-948, 41 FR 12295, Mar. 25, 1976]

37 Communications Purchased.

Record here expenses, including related taxes, incurred for rental of communication services and for communication services of all types and classes not provided by personnel of the air carrier, such as telegraph, telephone, teletype, private line services, and charges for communication services from organizations operated jointly with associated companies or others.

38 Light, Heat, Power and Water.

Record here charges related to the provision of light, heat, power and water including related taxes.

39 Traffic Commissions.

(a) Record here charges by others, including associated companies, for commissions arising from sales of transportation. Commissions, fees or other charges incurred for general agency services, as opposed to commissions arising from sales of transportation, shall not be included in this account but in profit and loss account 43 General Services Purchased.

(b) This account shall be subdivided as follows by Group II and Group III air carriers.

39.1 *Commissions—Passenger.*

Record here charges for commissions arising from sales of passenger transportation.

39.2 *Commissions—Property.*

Record here charges for commissions arising from sales of nonpassenger transportation.

40 Legal Fees and Expenses.

Record here expenditures incurred for legal services by counsel retained on a fee basis and related expenses reimbursed or borne directly by the air carrier and other expenses incurred directly by the air carrier for legal supplies not obtainable from the air carrier's general stationery stock. This account shall not be charged with legal fees or expenses incurred in connection with claims occasioned by accidents or other casualties. Such charges shall be accumulated in balance sheet account 1890 Other Assets and cleared to profit and loss account 58 Injuries, Loss and Damage upon settlement of insurance claims. Nor should this account include fees or expenses related to developmental projects. Such expenses shall be included, as appropriate, in profit and loss account 89.9 Other Miscellaneous Nonoperating Debits or balance sheet account 1830 Unamortized Developmental and Preoperating Costs.

[ER–980, 42 FR 37, Jan. 3, 1977]

41 Professional and Technical Fees and Expenses.

Record here fees and expenses, other than legal fees and expenses, incurred for outside professional and technical services which are reimbursed or borne directly by the air carrier. This account shall not include fees or expenses related to developmental projects. Such expenses shall be included, as appropriate, in profit and loss account 89.9 Other Miscellaneous Nonoperating Debits or balance sheet account 1830 Unamortized Developmental and Preoperating Costs.

[ER–980, 42 FR 37, Jan. 3, 1977]

43 General Services Purchased.

(a) Record here charges for services performed for the air carrier by outside and associated companies which are not identifiable with services provided for in profit and loss accounts 37 through 41, inclusive, or which are not expressly identified with other objective expense accounts.

(b) Charges from outside and associated companies for services provided the air carrier under aircraft interchange agreements or other agreements embracing a complete activity or service, such as the operating of jointly used ground facilities, shall be included in this account for each operating function to which the services contribute. Charges for providing aircraft capacity, including charges for depreciation and interest on the capital related to the flight equipment provided, shall be included in function 5100 Flying Operations.

(c) This account shall be subdivided by each air carrier group, as follows:

GROUP II AND GROUP III AIR CARRIERS

43.1 *Airframe and Other Flight Equipment Repairs.*

Record here charges for maintenance or repair of airframes and spare parts related to airframes owned or leased by the air carrier. Charges for maintenance or repair of other flight equipment (including instruments) owned or leased by the air carrier, excluding aircraft engines and spare parts related to aircraft engines, shall also be recorded here. Instruments shall include all gauges, meters, measuring devices, and indicators, together with appurtenances thereto for installation in aircraft and aircraft engines, which are maintained separately from airframes and aircraft engines. Charges by outside and associated companies for maintenance of flight equipment provided under aircraft interchange agreements shall not be included in this subaccount but in subaccount 43.7 Aircraft Interchange Charges.

43.2 *Aircraft Engine Repairs.*

Record here charges for maintenance of repair or aircraft engines, including spare parts related to aircraft engines owned or leased by the air carrier. Charges by outside and associated companies for maintenance of aircraft engines provided under aircraft interchange agreements shall not be included in this subaccount but in subaccount 43.7 Aircraft Interchange Charges.

GROUP I AIR CARRIERS

43.6 *Flight Equipment Repairs.*

Record here charges for maintenance or repair of flight equipment of all types and classes owned or leased by the air carrier. Charges by outside and associated companies for maintenance of flight equipment provided under aircraft interchange agreements shall not be included in this subaccount but in subaccount 43.7 Aircraft Interchange Charges.

ALL AIR CARRIER GROUPS

43.7 *Aircraft Interchange Charges.*

Record here charges by outside and associated companies for providing aircraft capacity or services related to the direct operation or maintenance of flight equipment under aircraft interchange agreements.

43.8 *General Interchange Service Charges.*

Record here charges by outside and associated companies for services provided the air carrier under aircraft interchange agreements, other than charges related to the direct operation or maintenance of flight equipment, including all charges for maintenance and repair of group properties, as well as fees or charges for traffic solicitation and sales, or supervision and administration covered by the aircraft interchange agreements. Charges for depreciation or interest on capital related to flight equipment provided under interchange agreements shall not be included in this subaccount but in subaccount 43.7 Aircraft Interchange Charges.

43.9 *Other Services.*

Record here charges for maintenance and repair of ground property and equipment of all types and classes and other charges for services performed by outside and associated companies not provided for elsewhere. This subaccount shall include only those charges for services not provided for elsewhere in profit and loss accounts 37 to 41, inclusive, and subaccounts 43.1 to 43.8, inclusive, embracing a complete activity or service provided by outside and associated companies such as the operation of traffic offices or other facilities used jointly with the air carrier which do not represent reimbursement of specific expense elements incurred expressly for the benefit of the air carrier. Reimbursement of expenses incurred expressly for the benefit of the air carrier shall be entered in appropriate personnel compensation or other objective expense accounts. The cost of services received in the repair of general ground properties shall be charged to subfunction 5200 Direct Maintenance; and services received in the repair of maintenance buildings and equipment shall be charged to subfunction 5300 Maintenance Burden.

[Amdt. 241–56, 52 FR 9129, Mar. 23, 1987]

44 Landing Fees.

Record here the charges and fees incurred for landing of aircraft while in line operation.

45 Aircraft Fuels and Oils.

(a) Record here the cost of fuels and oils issued from stocks of the air carrier, or delivery directly by others, to aircraft for use in flight operations. Adjustments of inventories of aircraft fuel and oil shall also be entered in this account. The cost of fuels and oils used in repairs and maintenance services and nonrefundable fuel and oil taxes shall not be included in this account but in profit and loss accounts 49 Shop and Servicing Supplies and 69 Taxes—Other than Payroll, respectively.

(b) This account shall be subdivided as follows by Group II and Group III air carriers:

45.1 *Aircraft Fuels.*

Record here the cost of fuels used in flight operations.

45.2 *Aircraft Oils.*

Record here the cost of oils used in flight operations.

46 Maintenance Materials.

(a) Record here the cost of materials and supplies consumed directly in specific property and equipment maintenance projects.

(b) This account shall be subdivided as follows:

GROUP II AND GROUP III AIR CARRIERS

46.1 *Materials—Airframes and Other Flight Equipment.*

Record here the cost of materials and supplies consumed directly in maintenance of airframes and spare parts related to airframes. Other flight equipment (including instruments), excluding aircraft engines and spare parts related to aircraft engines, shall also be recorded here. Instruments shall include all gauges, meters, measuring devices, and indicators, together with appurtenances thereto for installation in aircraft and aircraft engines, which are maintained separately from airframes and aircraft engines.

46.2 *Materials—Aircraft Engines.*

Record here the cost of materials and supplies consumed directly in maintenance of aircraft engines and spare parts related to aircraft engines.

GROUP I AIR CARRIERS

46.6 *Materials—Flight Equipment.*

Record here the cost of materials and supplies consumed directly in the maintenance of flight equipment of all types and classes.

ALL AIR CARRIER GROUPS

46.9 *Materials—Ground Property and Equipment.*

Record here the cost of materials and supplies consumed directly in the maintenance of ground property and equipment of all types and classes. The cost of materials and supplies consumed in the repair of general ground properties shall be charged to subfunction 5200 Direct Maintenance and materials and supplies consumed in the repair of maintenance buildings and equipment shall be charged to subfunction 5300 Maintenance Burden.

[ER–755, 37 FR 19726, Sept. 21, 1972, as amended by ER–1401, 50 FR 245, Jan. 3, 1985]

47 Rentals.

Record here rentals, fee, or charges incurred in the use of property and equipment provided by others. When a lease arrangement provides that the amounts paid include charges for maintenance, insurance, or taxes, the amounts related thereto shall not be recorded in this account but in the appropriate expense account to which related.

49 Shop and Servicing Supplies.

Record here the cost of supplies and expendable small tools and equipment used in maintaining, servicing and cleaning property or equipment the cost of which cannot be directly assigned to a specific job or type of work.

50 Stationery, Printing and Office Supplies.

Record here the cost of stationery and forms used by the air carrier including the cost of engineering and shipping supplies.

51 Passenger Food Expense.

(a) Record here the cost of food and refreshments served passengers except food costs arising from interrupted trips.

(b) If the air carrier prepares its own food, the initial cost and expenses incurred in the preparation thereof shall be accumulated in a clearly identified clearing account through which the cost of food shall be cleared to this account, to profit and loss account 36 Personnel Expenses, and to profit and loss account 10 Hotel, Restaurant and Food Service on bases which appropriately allocate the cost of food served passengers, the cost of food provided employees without charge and the cost of food sold.

53 Other Supplies.

Record here the cost of supplies consumed and not provided for otherwise.

54 Inventory Adjustments.

Record here adjustments for overage, shortage or shrinkage of inventories carried in balance sheet account 1300 Spare Parts and Supplies. Adjustment of aircraft fuel and oil inventories due to retroactive price increases and decreases shall not be included in this account but in profit and loss account 45 Aircraft Fuels and Oils. Gains or losses from retirements of materials and supplies shall not be recorded in this account but in profit and loss account 88.5 Capital Gains and Losses—Operating Property.

[ER–980, 42 FR 37, Jan. 3, 1977]

55 Insurance—General.

Record here the cost of public liability and property damage insurance and all other general insurance except insurance covering liability for injuries, loss, and damage to passengers and cargo, and insurance carried for the protection or welfare of employees.

[ER–948, 41 FR 12295, Mar. 25, 1976]

56 Insurance—Traffic Liability.

Record here the cost of purchased insurance covering liability for injuries, loss and damage to passengers and cargo.

[ER–980, 42 FR 37, Jan. 3, 1977]

57 Employee Benefits and Pensions.

(a) Record here all costs for the benefit or protection of employees including all pension expenses whether for payments to or on behalf of retired employees or for accruals or annuity payments to provide for pensions; and all expenses for accident, sickness, hospital, and death benefits to employees or the cost of insurance to provide these benefits. Include, also, expenses incurred in medical, educational, or recreational activities for the benefit of employees. Do not include vacation and sick leave pay, or salaries of doctors, nurses, trainees, or instructors, which shall be recorded in the regular salary accounts.

(b) [Reserved]

[ER–755, 37 FR 19726, Sept. 21, 1972, as amended by ER–980, 42 FR 37, Jan. 3, 1977; ER–1188, 45 FR 48871, July 22, 1980]

58 Injuries, Loss and Damage.

Record here the remainder of gains, losses or costs resulting from accidents, casualties or mishandlings, after offsetting insurance recoveries, as accumulated until finally determined in balance sheet account 1890 Other Assets and Deferred Charges. This account shall not include gains or losses from retirement of property and equipment resulting from casualties. Such gains or losses shall be recorded in appropriate capital gains or losses accounts.

[Amdt. 241–58, 54 FR 5596, Feb. 6, 1989]

59 Schedules and Timetables.

Record here the production and distribution cost, excluding compensation of air carrier personnel, of all operating schedules, timetables, circulars and related quick reference charts.

[ER–1401, 50 FR 245, Jan. 3, 1985]

60 Advertising.

Record here the cost, excluding compensation of air carrier personnel, of all space, direct mail, spot and other advertising for the purpose of increasing air travel, disseminating air travel information and publicizing services offered by the air carrier.

61 Foreign Exchange Gains and Losses.

Record here gains or losses from transactions involving currency translations resulting from normal, routine, current fluctuations in rates of foreign exchange. Gains or losses of a nonroutine abnormal character and gains or losses which arise from long-term debt principal and interest transactions shall not be entered in this account but in profit and loss account 85, Foreign Exchange Gains and Losses.

[Amdt. 241–58, 54 FR 5596, Feb. 6, 1989]

62 Other Promotional and Publicity Expenses.

Record here the costs, excluding compensation of air carrier personnel, of producing and distributing publicity releases and other expenses, not chargeable to profit and loss accounts 59 and 60, incurred for the purpose of publicizing or improving the public relations of the air carrier generally.

63 Interrupted Trips Expense.

Record here expenses allowed or paid for the care and serving of passengers because of unscheduled interruptions in passenger journeys. Transportation refunds and the cost of forwarding traffic by surface common carrier or otherwise as a result of such interruptions shall not be charged to this account but to the appropriate operating revenue account.

64 Memberships.

Record here the cost of membership dues in trade associations, chambers of commerce, or other business associations and organizations together with special assessments related thereto.

65 Corporate and Fiscal Expenses.

Record here corporate and fiscal fees and expenses of the air carrier and all expenses in connection with exchange and transfer of capital stock excluding expenses in connection with original issuance of capital stock.

66 Uncollectible Accounts.

Record here losses from uncollectible accounts and allowance provisions and adjustments thereto, for such losses. When allowances for uncollectible accounts are established, losses as realized shall be charged against such allowances and shall not be charged to this account.

[ER–980, 42 FR 37, Jan. 3, 1977]

67 Clearance, Customs and Duties.

Record here clearance, customs, duties and brokerage fees and charges applicable to clearing aircraft and traffic.

68 Taxes—Payroll.

Record here all taxes levied against the air carrier based upon or directly relating to compensation of personnel.

69 Taxes—Other Than Payroll.

(a) Record here all taxes levied against the air carrier not otherwise provided for including nonrefundable aircraft fuel and oil taxes. Interest and penalties on delinquent taxes shall not be charged to this account but to profit and loss accounts 82 Other Interest and 89.9 Other Miscellaneous Nonoperating Debits, respectively.

(b) Entries to this account shall clearly reveal each kind of tax and the governmental agency to which paid or payable.

[ER–755, 37 FR 19726, Sept. 21, 1972, as amended by ER–980, 42 FR 37, Jan. 3, 1977]

71 Other Expenses.

Record here all expenses ordinarily associated with air transportation and its incidental services not provided for otherwise.

72 Aircraft Overhauls.

(a) Record here airframe and aircraft engine overhauls of the current period which are transferred to balance sheet subaccounts 1601.2 Unamortized Airframe Overhauls or 1602.2 Unamortized Aircraft Engine Overhauls. This account shall also include the amount of deferred overhauls costs being amortized for the current period. For carriers which elect to continue accruing for aircraft overhauls for aircraft types acquired before January 1, 1976, as well as for other aircraft of the same type acquired after January 1, 1976, the related provisions and charges shall be recorded in the appropriate subaccounts of this account.

(b) This account shall be subdivided as follows by all carrier groups:

72.1 *Airworthiness Allowance Provisions—Airframes.*

Record here current provisions for effecting an equitable distribution of airframe overhaul costs between different accounting periods. Record here also credits for airframe overhaul costs incurred in the current period which have been charged against related airworthiness allowances.

72.3 *Airframe Overhauls Deferred.*

Record here airframe overhauls of the current period transferred to subaccount 1601.2, Unamortized Airframe Overhauls, and the amount of deferred airframe overhaul costs amortized for the current period.

72.6 *Airworthiness Allowance Provisions—Aircraft Engines.*

Record here current provisions for effecting an equitable distribution of aircraft engine overhauls costs between different accounting periods. Record here also credits for aircraft engine overhaul costs incurred in the current period which have been charged against related airworthiness allowances.

72.8 *Aircraft Engine Overhauls Deferred.*

Record here airframe overhauls of the current period transferred to subaccount 1602.2, Unamortized Aircraft Engine Overhauls, and the amount of deferred aircraft engine overhaul costs amortized for the current period.

[ER–948, 41 FR 12295, Mar. 25, 1976, as amended by ER–1401, 50 FR 245, Jan. 3, 1985]

73 Provisions for Obsolescence and Deterioration—Expendable Parts.

(a) Where allowances for loss in value of flight equipment expendable parts are established, provisions for accruals to such allowances shall be charged to this account and credited to balance sheet account 1311 Allowance for Obsolescence in accordance with the provisions of that account.

(b) This account shall be subdivided as follows by all air carrier groups:

73.1 *Current provisions.*

Record here provisions during the current period for losses in value of expendable parts.

73.2 *Inventory decline credits.*

Record here credits applicable to the current period for any adjustments for excess inventory allowance levels determined pursuant to section 6–1311.

[ER–980, 42 FR 37, Jan. 3, 1977]

74 Amortization.

(a) Record here amortization of deferred changes attaching to the air transportation services conducted by the air carrier which are not prepayments of recurrent expenses ordinarily requiring expenditures of working capital within one year.

(b) This account shall be subdivided as follows by all air carrier groups:

74.1 *Developmental and Preoperating Expenses*

Record here amortization of the cost of projects carried in balance sheet account 1830 Unamortized Developmental and Preoperating Costs.

74.2 *Other Intangibles.*

Record here mortization of the cost of intangibles not provided for otherwise.

[ER–755, 37 FR 19726, Sept. 21, 1972, as amended by ER–980, 42 FR 38, Jan. 3, 1977; Amdt. 241–58, 54 FR 5596, Feb. 6, 1989]

75 Depreciation.

(a) Record here provisions for depreciation of property and equipment carried in balance sheet accounts 1601 through 1640, inclusive.

(b) This account shall be subdivided as follows:

ALL AIR CARRIER GROUPS

75.1 *Depreciation—Airframes.*

Record here provisions for depreciation of property and equipment carried in balance subaccount 1601.1 Airframes.

75.2 *Depreciation—Aircraft Engines.*

Record here provisions for depreciation of property and equipment carried in balance sheet subaccount 1602.1 Aircraft Engines.

GROUP II AND GROUP III AIR CARRIERS

75.3 *Depreciation—Airframe Parts.*

Record here provisions for depreciation of spare airframe instruments and parts carried in balance sheet subaccount 1608.1 Airframe Parts and Assemblies.

75.4 *Depreciation—Aircraft Engine Parts.*

Record here provisions for depreciation of spare aircraft engine instruments and parts carried in balance sheet subaccount 1608.5 Aircraft Engine Parts and Assemblies.

ALL AIR CARRIER GROUPS

75.5 *Depreciation—Other Flight Equipment.*

Record here provisions for depreciation of property and equipment carried in balance sheet account 1607 Improvements to Leased Flight Equipment (exclusive of capitalized overhauls accounted for on a deferral and amortization basis) and balance sheet subaccount 1608.9 Other Parts and Assemblies. Group I air carriers shall also include in this subaccount provisions for depreciation of property carried in balance sheet account 1608 Flight Equipment Rotable Parts and Assemblies.

75.6 *Depreciation—Flight Equipment.*

This classification is established only for purposes of control by the BTS and shall include all charges to operating expenses for depreciation of flight equipment of all types and classes.

75.8 *Depreciation—Maintenance Equipment and Hangars.*

Record here provisions for depreciation of maintenance property and equipment included in balance sheet accounts 1630 Equipment, 1639 Improvements to Leased Buildings and Equipment, and 1640.1 Maintenance Buildings and Improvements.

75.9 *Depreciation—General Ground Property.*

Record here provisions for depreciation of property and equipment included in balance of property and equipment included in balance sheet accounts 1630 through 1640, exclusive of provision for depreciation of maintenance property and equipment included in account 75.8.

[ER–755, 37 FR 19726, Sept. 21, 1972, as amended by ER–948, 41 FR 12296, Mar. 25, 1976; ER–980, 42 FR 38, Jan. 3, 1977; 60 FR 66723, Dec. 26, 1995]

76 Amortization Expense—Capital Leases.

(a) Record here amortization charges applicable to assets recorded under capital leases in Account 1695—Leased Property under Capital Leases.

(b) This account shall be subdivided as follows by all air carrier groups:

76.1 *Amortization—Capitalized Flight Equipment.*

Record here amortization charges applicable to flight equipment acquired under capital leases.

76.2 *Amortization—Capitalized Other Property and Equipment.*

Record here the amortization charges applicable to property and equipment, other than flight equipment, acquired under capital leases.

[ER–1401, 50 FR 245, Jan. 3, 1985]

77 Uncleared Expense Credits.

(a) Record here credits to operating expenses, which have not been cleared to the objective accounts to which applicable.

(b) Each air carrier shall credit, or charge as appropriate, the objective account prescribed for each expense element which may be involved in distribution of expenses between separate reporting entities or nontransport divisions of the air carrier. At the option of the air carrier, either the individual applicable objective accounts or this account may be credited with amounts capitalized, charged against incidental services, or otherwise assigned to other than separate operating entities of the air carrier provided the aggregate credits to this account in each function do not, for any accounting year, distort the individual objective accounts of the function to which related and all expense credits applicable to complete individual transactions are consistently credited either to this account or the individual objective accounts to which related. Each air carrier using this account shall establish such standard practices as may be prescribed by the BTS or, in the absence of such action by the Civil Aeronautics Board, such standard practices as will prevent credits to this account from significantly distorting the individual objective accounts of each function to which related.

(c) This account shall not be credited with amounts applicable to objective accounts of the Flying Operations, Depreciation, and Direct Maintenance functions. Credits applicable to such functions shall be carried to the individual objective accounts to which applicable.

(d) This account shall be subdivided as follows by all air carrier groups:

77.8 *Uncleared Interchange Expense Credits.*

Record here credits to operating expenses, from operations performed for others under aircraft interchange agreements, which have not been cleared to the objective accounts to which applicable.

77.9 *Other Uncleared Expense Credits.*

Record here credits to operating expenses, from other than operations under aircraft interchange agreements, which have not been cleared to the objective accounts to which applicable.

[ER–755, 37 FR 19726, Sept. 21, 1972, as amended at 60 FR 66723, Dec. 26, 1995]

78 Direct Maintenance—Flight Equipment.

This classification is established for purposes of control by the BTS and shall include all charges to operating expenses for maintenance of flight equipment of all types and classes.

[ER–755, 37 FR 19726, Sept. 21, 1972, as amended at 60 FR 66723, Dec. 26, 1995]

79 Applied Burden Debit/Credit.

(a) This classification is established only for purposes of control by the BTS and reporting on Form 41 by air carriers, and shall reflect all maintenance burden applied in accordance with the provisions of section 24, schedule P–5 of this system of accounts and reports.

(b) This classification shall be subdivided as follows by all air carrier groups:

79.6 *Applied Burden—Flight Equipment.*

79.8 *Applied Burden—General Ground Property.*

[ER–755, 37 FR 19726, Sept. 21, 1972, as amended by ER–979, 38 FR 10926, May 3, 1973; 60 FR 66723, Dec. 26, 1995]

Section 14 Objective Classification—Nonoperating Income and Expense

80 Interest Income.

Included under account 89 Other Nonoperating Income and Expense—Net.

[ER–1401, 50 FR 245, Jan. 3, 1985]

81 Interest on Long-term Debt and Capital Leases.

(a) Record here interest expense applicable to long-term debt and capitalized leases.

(b) This account shall be subdivided as follows by all air carrier groups:

81.1 *Interest expense—long-term debt.*

Record here interest on all classes of long-term debt. This includes interest expense applicable to all portions of long-term debt which are classified as either current (Account 2000) or long-term (Account 2210) for balance sheet classification purposes.

81.2 *Interest expense—capital leases.*

Record here for all capitalized leases, that portion of each lease payment which represents interest expense.

[ER-1013, 42 FR 37516, July 21, 1977]

82 Other Interest.

(a) This account shall be subdivided as follows by all air carrier groups:

82.1 *Interest Expense—Short-Term Debt.*

Record here interest on all classes of short-term debt.

83.1 *Imputed Interest Capitalized—Credit.*

Record here credits related to imputed interest capitalized and recorded in asset accounts.

83.2 *Imputed Interest Deferred—Debit.*

Record here debits related to imputed interest deferred in balance sheet account 2390, Other deferred credits.

83.3 *Imputed Interest Deferred—Credit.*

Record here periodic credits for imputed interest, cleared to this account as the amount of such interest in the asset accounts is amortized.

83.4 *Interest Capitalized—Credit.*

Record here interest which is capitalized and recorded in asset accounts.

84.1 *Amortization of discount and expense on debt.*

Record here for all classes of debt the amortizations of discount and expense on short-term and long-term obligations.

84.2 *Amortization of premium on debt.*

Record here for all classes of debt the amortizations of premium on short-term and long-term obligations.

(b) [Reserved]

[ER-1401, 50 FR 245, Jan. 3, 1985, as amended by Amdt. 241-58, 54 FR 5596, Feb. 6, 1989]

83 Capitalized Interest.

Included under account 82 Other Interest.

[ER-1401, 50 FR 245, Jan. 3, 1985]

84 Amortization of Debt Discount, Premium and Expense.

Included under account 82 Other Interest.

[ER-1401, 50 FR 245, Jan. 3, 1985]

85 Foreign exchange gains and losses.

Record here gains and losses from transactions involving currency translations resulting from nonroutine abnormal changes in rates of foreign exchange and gains or losses which arise from translations of long-term debt principal and interest transactions.

[Amdt. 241-58, 54 FR 5596, Feb. 6, 1989]

86 Income from Nontransport Ventures.

Included under account 89 Other Non-Operating Income and Expense—Net.

[ER-980, 42 FR 38, Jan. 3, 1977]

87 Equity in Income of Investor Controlled Companies.

Included under account 89 Other Non-operating Income and Expense—Net.

[ER-1401, 50 FR 245, Jan. 3, 1985]

89 Other Nonoperating Income and Expense—Net.

(a) Record here all debits and credits of a nonoperating character which are not otherwise provided for in this section.

(b) This account shall be subdivided as follows by all air carrier groups:

80.0 *Interest Income.*

(a) Record here interest income from all sources. This account shall include as an increase or reduction of interest received the proportionate amortization of any discount or premium on the purchase price of securities of others held by the air carrier.

(b) This account shall not include interest on securities issued or assumed by the air carrier and subsequently reacquired.

86.0 *Income from Nontransport Ventures.*

(a) Record here the gross revenues and expenses applicable to operations not reasonably considered as incidental to the commercial air transport services of the accounting entity; rents from nonoperating properties used by others; income or loss from nontransport divisions; and other income or loss from activities of the air carrier which are extraneous to the air transport and incidental services of the accounting entity.

(b) This account shall include revenues and expenses applicable to nonscheduled transport services performed for the defense establishment when separate reports for such services are required in accordance with section 21 "Introduction to System of Reports." Where the foregoing transport services are not required to be separately reported, gross revenues from such services shall be included in profit and loss account 07 Charter, or other appropriate revenue account, and gross expenses shall be included in the appropriate operating expense functions.

87.0 *Equity in Income of Investor Controlled Companies.*

Record here the equity in the current earnings or losses of investor controlled companies. Dividends declared on the stock of such companies shall not be included in this account as income but shall be entered in balance sheet subaccount 1510.1 Investments in Investor Controlled Companies as a return on investment.

88.1 *Intercompany Transaction Adjustment—Credit.*

Record here all intercompany credits for any differences between amounts at which transactions between the air carrier and its nontransport divisions or associated companies are initially recorded and are to be settled.

88.2 *Dividend income.*

Record here income from dividends declared on stocks of other than investor controlled companies. Dividends declared on stock of investor controlled companies shall not be included in this account but shall be entered in balance sheet subaccount 1510.1 Investments in Investor Controlled Companies.

88.3 *Net Unrealized Gain or Loss on Marketable Equity Securities.*

Record here the net unrealized gain or loss on the valuation of marketable equity securities.

88.4 *Net Realized Gain or Loss on Marketable Equity Securities.*

Record here the net realized gain or loss on the valuation of marketable equity securities.

88.5 *Capital gains and losses—operating property.*

Record here gains or losses on retirements of operating property and equipment, flight equipment expendable parts, or miscellaneous materials and supplies sold or otherwise retired in connection with a general retirement program as opposed to incidental sales performed as a service to others.

88.6 *Capital gains and losses—other.*

Record here gains or losses not required to be reported in accounts 88.3, 88.4 and 88.5 such as gains or losses on retirement of nonoperating property and equipment, investments in other than marketable equity securities, and the transfer of assets in a troubled debt restructuring.

88.7 *Unapplied cash discounts.*

Record here cash discounts on routine purchases of materials, repair parts or supplies. Cash discounts on classes of assets included in property and equipment accounts shall not be recorded in this account but shall be applied as a reduction of the cost of such accounts.

88.9 *Other miscellaneous nonoperating credits.*

Record here all credits of a nonoperating character not provided for otherwise, such as royalties from patents, gains from reacquisition and retirement or resale of debt securities issued by the air carrier, and gains resulting from troubled debt restructurings.

89.1 *Intercompany Transaction Adjustment—Debit.*

Record here all intercompany debits for any differences between amounts at which transactions between the air carrier and its nontransport divisions or associated companies are initially recorded and are to be settled.

89.9 *Other Miscellaneous Nonoperating Debits.*

Record here all debits of a nonoperating character not provided for otherwise, such as the following:

(a) Fines or penalties imposes by governmental authorities;

(b) Costs associated with employment discrimination that include the following:

(1) Fines or penalties paid by the carrier as a result of a judicial or administrative decree; or the amount paid to the complainant in settling or securing a consent decree;

(2) Back pay awards as a result of a judicial or administrative decree or a compromise settlement regardless of admission of guilt;

(3) Attorneys' fees or court costs awarded to the complainant by a judicial or administrative decree or as a result of a compromise settlement regardless of admission of guilt;

(4) The fees of outside legal counsel or of experts retained in the unsuccessful defense of a discrimination suit or in securing a compromise settlement or consent decree, unless the amounts attributable to the discrimination are not reasonably identifiable; or

(5) Any other expenses, such as employee salaries, resulting from employment practices that were found to be discriminatory or that were the subject of a compromise settlement or consent decree where the amounts attributable to discrimination are reasonably identifiable.

(c) Amortization expense attributable to capital leases recorded in balance sheet Account 1795, Leased Property under Capital Leases;

(d) Costs related to property held for future use;

(e) Donations for charitable, social or community welfare purposes;

(f) Losses on reacquired and retired or resold debt securities of the air carrier;

(g) Losses resulting from troubled debt restructurings;

(h) Losses on uncollectible nonoperating receivables; or

(i) Accruals to allowance for uncollectible nonoperating receivables.

(Secs. 204, 404, 407, and 1002 of the Federal Aviation Act of 1958, as amended, 72 Stat. 743, 760, 766, 788, (49 U.S.C. 1324, 1374, 1377, 1482))

[ER-980, 42 FR 38, Jan. 3, 1977, as amended by ER-1013, 42 FR 37516, July 21, 1977; ER-1027, 42 FR 60128, Nov. 25, 1977; ER-1076, 43 FR 46296, Oct. 6, 1978; ER-1401, 50 FR 245, Jan. 3, 1985; Amdt. 241-58, 54 FR 5596, Feb. 6, 1989]

Section 15 Objective Classification—Income Taxes for Current Period

91 Provision for Income Taxes.

(a) Record here quarterly provisions for accruals of Federal, State, local, and foreign taxes based upon net income, computed at the normal tax and surtax rates in effect during the current accounting year. In general, this account shall reflect provisions within each period for currently accruing tax liabilities as actually or constructively computed on tax returns, and any subsequent adjustments. This account shall include credits for refund claims arising from the carryback of losses in the year in which the loss occurs, credits for the carry-forward of losses in the year to which the loss is carried, and investment tax credits in the year in which each credit is utilized to reduce the liability for income taxes.

(b) Income taxes shall be allocated among the transport entities of the air carrier, its nontransport divisions, and members of an affiliated group. Under circumstances in which income taxes are determined on a consolidated basis by an air carrier and other members of an affiliated group, the income tax expense to be recorded by the air carrier shall be the same as would result if determined for the air carrier separately for all time periods, except that the tax effect of carryback and carryforward operating losses, investment tax credits, or other tax credits generated by operations of the air carrier shall be recorded by the air carrier during the period in which applied in settlement of the taxes otherwise attributable to any member, or combination of members, of the affiliated group. Any difference between the income tax so recorded and the amount at which settlement is to be made shall be recorded in subaccount 88.1 Intercompany Transaction Adjustment—Credit or in subaccount 89.1 Intercompany Transaction Adjustment—Debit, as is appropriate.

(c) This account shall be subdivided as follows by all carrier groups:

91.1 *Income Taxes Before Investment Tax Credits.*

Record here accruals of income taxes based upon taxable income of the period.

91.2 *Investment Tax Credits Utilized.*

Record here investment tax credits utilized to reduce the accrued liability for income taxes.

[Amdt. 241-58, 54 FR 5596, Feb. 6, 1989]

92 Provisions for Deferred Income Taxes.

(a) Record here income tax debits and credits deferred in accordance with the provisions of balance sheet account 2340 Deferred Income Taxes for all material timing differences.

(b) This account shall be subdivided as follows by all air carrier groups:

92.1 *Current Provisions for Deferred Taxes.*

92.2 *Application of Taxes Deferred.*

92.3 *Adjustments of Deferred Taxes.*

[ER–948, 41 FR 12296, Mar. 25, 1976]

93 Investment Tax Credits Deferred and Amortized.

(a) Record here investment tax credits of the current period which are transferred to balance sheet account 2345 Deferred Investment Tax Credits in accordance with the provisions of balance sheet account 2130 Accrued Taxes. This account shall also include amounts for previously deferred investment tax credits amortized during the current period.

(b) This account shall be subdivided as follows by all carrier groups:

93.1 *Investment Tax Credits Deferred.*

93.2 *Amortization of Deferred Investment Tax Credits.*

[ER–755, 37 FR 19726, Sept. 21, 1972, as amended by ER–980, 42 FR 39, Jan. 3, 1977]

Section 16 Objective Classification—Discontinued Operations

95 Discontinued Operations.

(a) Record here the earnings (losses) of discontinued nontransport operations. For the purposes of this system of accounts and reports discontinued operations shall refer to the disposal of investor controlled companies and nontransport ventures whether sold, abandoned, spun off, or otherwise disposed of. This account shall not include earnings or losses from discontinued transport or transport-related operations.

(b) This account shall be subdivided as follows by all air carrier groups:

95.1 *Income from Discontinued Operations.*

Record here the results of operations of the discontinued operations.

95.2 *Loss of Disposal of Discontinued Operations.*

Record here the gain or loss on the disposal of an operation. If loss is anticipated it should be provided for at the measurement date. If gain is anticipated it should be recognized when realized.

[ER–948, 41 FR 12296, Mar. 25, 1976]

Section 17 Objective Classification—Extraordinary Items

96 Extraordinary Items.

Record here material items characterized by their unusual nature and infrequent occurrence. Events or transactions which are material and either unusual or nonrecurring, but not both, shall be recorded in the profit and loss accounts to which they relate and disclosed on BTS Form 41 Schedule P–2 with identification as to their nature and financial effects.

[Amdt. 241–58, 54 FR 5596, Feb. 6, 1989, as amended at 60 FR 66723, Dec. 26, 1995]

97 Income Taxes Applicable to Extraordinary Items.

Record here income taxes allocable to items of income included in profit and loss account 96 Extraordinary Items and income tax assessments that do not constitute ordinary adjustments of a recurrent nature. Records supporting entries to this account shall be maintained with sufficient particularity to identify the nature and gross amount of each extraordinary credit and each extraordinary debit.

[ER–948, 41 FR 12296, Mar. 25, 1976]

Section 18 Objective Classification—Cumulative Effect of Changes in Accounting Principles

98 Cumulative Effect of Changes in Accounting Principles.

Record here the difference between the amount of retained earnings at the beginning of the period of a change in accounting principle and the amount of retained earnings that would have been reported at that date if the new accounting principle had been applied retroactively for all periods which would have been affected and by recognizing only the direct effects of a change and the related income tax effect.

[ER–948, 41 FR 12296, Mar. 25, 1976]

OPERATING STATISTICS CLASSIFICATIONS

Section 19 Uniform Classification of Operating Statistics

Sec. 19–1 Applicability.

(a) *United States air carrier.* Each large certificated U.S. air carrier shall file with the Department, on a monthly basis, Form 41 Schedule T–100 "U.S. Air Carrier Traffic and Capacity Data By Nonstop Segment and On-flight Market," and summary data as prescribed in this section and in sections 22 and 25 of this part.

(b) *Foreign (non-U.S.) air carrier:* Each foreign air carrier as required by part 217 of this chapter shall file Form 41 Schedule T–100(f) "Foreign Air Carrier Traffic Data by Nonstop Segment and On-flight Market." The "Instructions to Foreign Air Carriers for Reporting Traffic Data on Form 41 Schedule T-100(f)," (Instructions-Foreign Air Carriers) are included in the Appendix to §217.10 of this chapter.

(c) Reports required by this section shall be submitted to the Bureau of Transportation Statistics in a format specified in accounting and reporting directives issued by the Bureau of Transportation Statistics' Director of Airline Information.

(d) On-flight market and nonstop segment detail data by carrier shall be made public only as provided in section 19–6.

[53 FR 46305, Nov. 16, 1988; 53 FR 52404, Dec. 28, 1988, as amended at 60 FR 66723, Dec. 26, 1995; 67 FR 49223, July 30, 2002; 75 FR 41583, July 16, 2010]

Sec. 19–2 Maintenance of data.

(a) Each air carrier required to file Form 41 Schedule T–100 data shall maintain its operating statistics, covering the movement of traffic in accordance with the uniform classifications prescribed. Codes are prescribed for each operating element and service class. All traffic statistics shall be compiled in terms of each flight stage as actually performed.

(b) Each carrier shall maintain data applicable to the specified traffic and capacity elements prescribed in section 19–5 and section 25, and by general service classes prescribed in section 19–4 of this part.

(c) Operating statistics shall be maintained in accordance with the type of record, either nonstop segment or on-flight market.

(d) Schedule T–100 collects summarized flight stage data and on-flight market data. All traffic statistics shall be compiled in terms of each revenue flight stage as actually performed. The detail T–100 data shall be maintained in a manner permitting monthly summarization and organization into two basic groupings: The nonstop segment information that must be summarized by equipment type, within class of service, within pair-of-points, without regard to individual flight numbers. The second grouping requires that the enplanement/deplanement information be broken out into separate units called "on-flight market records." These records must be summarized by class of service, within pair-of-points, without regard for equipment type or flight number.

(e) The Department may authorize joint-service operations between two direct air carriers. Examples of these joint-services are blocked-space agreements, part-charter agreements, code-share agreements, wet-lease agreements, and other similar arrangements. Joint services operations are reported by the air carrier in operational control of the aircraft. The traffic moving under these agreements is reported on Schedule T–100 the same way as any other traffic on the aircraft.

(f) Any questions regarding T–100 should be e-mailed to *T100.Support@dot.gov.*

[53 FR 46305, Nov. 16, 1988, as amended at 75 FR 41583, July 16, 2010]

Sec. 19–3 Accessibility and transmittal of data.

(a) Each reporting air carrier shall maintain its prescribed operating statistics in a manner and at such locations as will permit ready accessability for examination by representatives of the Department. The record retention requirements are prescribed in part 249 of this chapter.

(b) [Reserved]

(c) Form 41 Schedule T–100 reports shall be transmitted in accordance with the standard practices established by the Department, and must be received by the Department within 30 days following the end of each reporting month.

[53 FR 46305, Nov. 16, 1988; 53 FR 52404, Dec. 28, 1988, as amended at 67 FR 49223, July 30, 2002]

Sec. 19–4 Service classes.

The statistical classifications are designed to reflect the operating elements attributable to each distinctive class of service offered. The operating elements shall be grouped in accordance with their inherent characteristics as follows:

(a) *Scheduled services.* Scheduled services shall include traffic and capacity elements applicable to air transportation provided pursuant to published schedules and extra sections to scheduled flights. Scheduled Passenger/ Cargo (Service Class F) is a composite of first class, coach, and mixed passenger/cargo service. The following classifications shall be reported, as applicable:

U.S. Air Carriers:
- K—Scheduled Services (F + G)
- F—Scheduled Passenger/Cargo
- G—Scheduled All-Cargo

Foreign Air Carriers:
- F—Scheduled Passenger/Cargo
- G—Scheduled All-Cargo

(b) *Nonscheduled services.* Nonscheduled services shall include all traffic and capacity elements applicable to the performance of nonscheduled aircraft charters, and other air transportation services not constituting an integral part of services performed pursuant to published flight schedules. The following classifications shall be reported, as applicable:

U.S. Air Carriers:
- V—Nonscheduled Services (L + N + P + R)
- L—Nonscheduled Civilian Passenger/Cargo
- P—Nonscheduled Civilian Cargo
- N—Nonscheduled Military Passenger/Cargo
- R—Nonscheduled Military Cargo

Foreign Air Carriers:
- L—Nonscheduled Civilian Passenger Cargo
- P—Nonscheduled Civilian All-Cargo Charters
- Q—Nonscheduled Services (Other than Charter)

(c) *All Services.* This classification shall reflect, for the applicable elements, the aggregate amounts for all services performed by the operating entity:

U.S. Air Carriers:
- Z—All Services (V + K)

Sec. 19–5 Air transport traffic and capacity elements.

(a) Within each of the service classifications prescribed in section 19–4, data shall be reported as applicable to specified air transport traffic and capacity elements.

(b) These reported items are as follows:

Code	Description	Segment	Market	Computed by DOT
	Carrier, carrier entity code	S	M	
	Reporting period date	S	M	
	Origin airport code	S	M	
	Destination airport code	S	M	
	Service class code	S	M	
	Aircraft type code	S		
110	Revenue passengers enplaned		M	
130	Revenue passengers transported	S		
140	Revenue passenger-miles			CFD*
210	Revenue cargo tons enplaned			CFD*
217	Enplaned freight		M	
219	Enplaned mail		M	
230	Revenue tons transported			CFD*
237	Transported freight	S		
239	Transported mail	S		
240	Revenue ton-miles			CFD*
241	Revenue ton-miles passenger			CFD*
247	Revenue ton-miles freight			CFD*
249	Revenue ton-miles mail			CFD*
270	Available capacity payload	S		
280	Available ton-miles			CFD*
310	Available seats, total	S		
320	Available seat-miles			CFD*
410	Revenue aircraft miles flown			CFD*
430	Revenue aircraft miles scheduled			CFD*

Code	Description	Segment	Market	Computed by DOT
501	Inter-airport distance			CFD*
510	Revenue aircraft departures performed	S		
520	Revenue aircraft departures scheduled	S		
610	Revenue aircraft hours (airborne)	S		
630	Aircraft hours (ramp-to-ramp)	S		
650	Total aircraft hours (airborne)	S		

*CFD = Computed by DOT from detail Schedule T–100 and T–100(f) data.

(c) These reported items are further described as follows:

(1) *Reporting period date.* The year and month or quarter to which the reported data are applicable.

(2) *Carrier, Carrier entity code.* Each foreign air carrier shall report its name and code (assigned by DOT). Each U.S. air carrier shall report its name and entity code (a five digit code assigned by DOT that identifies both the carrier and its entity) for its particular operations. The Office of Airline Information (OAI) will assign or confirm codes upon request; OAI's address is in the Appendix to section 25 of this part and the Appendix to §217.10 of this chapter.

(3) *Service class code.* The service class codes are prescribed in section 19–4 of this part. In general, classes are divided into two broad categories, either K (scheduled) or V (nonscheduled), where K = F + G for all carriers and V = L + N + P + R for U.S. air carriers and comprises L + P and Q for foreign air carriers. Refer to section 19–4 for the more information on service class codes F, G, L, N, P, R and Q.

(4) *Record type code.* This code indicates whether the data pertain to nonstop segment (record type S) or on-flight market (record type M).

(5) *Aircraft type code.* This code represents the aircraft types, as described in the Appendix to section 25 of this part.

(6) *Origin, Destination airport code(s).* These codes represent the industry designators described in the Appendix to section 25 of this part. A common private industry source of these industry designator codes is the *Official Airline Guides* (OAG). OAI will assign codes upon request if not listed in the OAG.

(7) *110 Revenue passengers enplaned.* The total number of revenue passengers enplaned at the origin point of a flight, boarding the flight for the first time; an unduplicated count of passengers in a market. Under the T–100 system of reporting, these enplaned passengers are the sum of the passengers in the individual on-flight markets. Report only the total revenue passengers enplaned in item 110. For all air carriers and all entities, item 110 revenue passengers enplaned is reported on Form 41 Schedule T–100 in column C–1, as follows:

	Col.	All carrier groups and entities
C–1	110	Revenue passengers enplaned.

(8) *130 Revenue passengers transported.* The total number of revenue passengers transported over single flight stage, including those already on board the aircraft from a previous flight stage. Report only the total revenue passengers transported in item 130. For all air carriers and all entities, item 130 revenue passengers transported is reported on Form 41 Schedule T–100 in Column B–7, as follows:

	Col.	All carrier groups and entities
B–7	130	Revenue passengers transported.

(9) *140 Revenue passenger-miles.* Computed by multiplying the interairport distance of each flight stage by the number of passengers transported on that flight stage.

(10) *210 Revenue cargo tons enplaned.* The total number of cargo tons enplaned. This data element is a sum of the individual on-flight market figures for each of the following categories: 217 Freight and 219 mail. This element represents an unduplicated count of the revenue traffic in a market.

(11) *230 Revenue tons transported.* The number of tons of revenue traffic transported. This element is the sum of the following elements: 231 Passengers transported-total, 237 Freight, and 239 Mail.

(12) *240 Revenue ton-miles—total.* Ton-miles are computed by multiplying the revenue aircraft miles flown (410) on each flight stage by the number of tons transported on that stage. This element is the sum of 241 through 249.

(13) *241 Revenue ton-miles—passenger.* Equals the number of passengers times 200, times interairport distance, divided by 2000. A standard weight of 200 pounds per passenger, including baggage, is used for all operations and service classes.

(14) *247 Revenue ton-miles—freight.* Equals the volume of freight in whole tons times the interairport distance.

(15) *249 Revenue ton-miles—mail.* Equals the volume of mail in whole tons times the interairport distance.

(16) *270 Available capacity-payload.* The available capacity is collected in pounds. This figure shall reflect the payload or total available capacity for passengers, mail and freight applicable to the aircraft with which each flight stage is performed.

(17) *280 Available ton-miles.* The aircraft miles flown on each flight stage multiplied by the available capacity on the aircraft in tons.

(18) *310 Available seats.* The number of seats available for sale. This figure reflects the actual number of seats available, excluding those blocked for safety or operational reasons. Report the total available seats in item 310. For all air carriers and all entities, item 310 available seats, total is reported on Form 41 Schedule T-100 in column B-4, as follows.

	Col.	All carrier groups and entities
B-4	310	Available seats, total.

(19) *320 Available seat-miles.* The aircraft miles flown on each flight stage multiplied by the seat capacity available for sale.

(20) *410 Revenue aircraft miles flown.* Revenue aircraft miles flown are computed in accordance with the airport pairs between which service is actually performed; miles are generated from the data for scheduled aircraft departures (Code 520) times the interairport distances (Code 501).

(21) *430 Revenue aircraft miles scheduled.* The number of revenue aircraft miles scheduled. All such data shall be maintained in conformity with the airport pairs between which service is scheduled, whether or not in accordance with actual performance.

(22) *501 Interairport distance.* The great circle distance, in official statute miles as prescribed in part 247 of this chapter, between airports served by each flight stage. Official interairport mileage may be obtained from the Office of Airline Information at the address included in section 25 of this part.

(23) Revenue aircraft departures performed. The number of revenue aircraft departures performed.

(24) *520 Revenue aircraft departures scheduled.* The number of revenue aircraft departures scheduled, whether or not actually performed.

(25) *610 Revenue aircraft hours (airborne).* The elapsed time, computed from the moment the aircraft leaves the ground until its next landing.

(26) *630 Aircraft hours (ramp-to-ramp).* The elapsed time, computed from the moment the aircraft first moves under its own power from the boarding ramp at one airport to the time it comes to rest at the ramp for the next point of landing. This data element is also referred to as "block" and block-to-block aircraft hours.

(27) *650 Total aircraft hours (airborne).* The elapsed time, computed from the moment the aircraft leaves the ground until it touches down at the next landing. This includes flight training, testing, and ferry flights.

(28) *810 Aircraft days assigned to service—carrier's equipment.* The number of days that aircraft owned or acquired through rental or lease (but not interchange) are in the possession of the reporting air carrier and are available for service on the reporting carrier's routes plus the number of days such aircraft are in service on routes of others under interchange agreements. Includes days in overhaul, or temporarily out of service due to schedule cancellations. Excludes days that newly acquired aircraft are on hand, but not available for productive use, days rented or leased to others (for other than interchange) and days in possession but formally withdrawn from air transportation service.

(29) *820 Aircraft days assigned to service—carrier's routes.* The same as "aircraft days assigned to service—carrier's equipment," but excluding the number of days that the reporting carrier's owned or rented equipment are in the possession of others under interchange agreements and including the number of days aircraft of others are in the possession of the reporting air carrier under interchange agreements.

(30) *921 Aircraft fuels issued (gallons).* The amount of aircraft fuels issued, in U.S. gallons, during the reporting period for both revenue and nonrevenue flights.

[53 FR 46305, Nov. 16, 1988, as amended by Amdt. 241–58, 54 FR 7184, Feb. 17, 1989; 60 FR 66723, Dec. 26, 1995; 62 FR 6718, Feb. 13, 1997; 67 FR 49224, July 30, 2002]

Sec. 19–6 Public disclosure of traffic data.

(a) Detailed domestic on-flight market data and nonstop segment data except military data shall be made publicly available after processing. Domestic data are defined as data from air transportation operations from a place in any State of the United States, the District of Columbia, the Commonwealth of Puerto Rico and the Virgin Islands, or a U.S. territory or possession to a place in any State of the United States, the District of Columbia, the Commonwealth of Puerto Rico and the Virgin Islands, or a U.S. territory or possession. Domestic military operations are reported under service codes N or R.

(b) Detailed international on-flight market and nonstop segment data in Schedule T–100 and Schedule T–100(f) reports, except military data, shall be publicly available immediately following the Department's determination that the database is complete, but no earlier than six months after the date of the data. Military operations are reported under service codes N or R. Data for on-flight markets and nonstop segments involving no U.S. point shall not be made publicly available for three years. Industry and carrier summary data may be made public before the end of six months or the end of three years, as applicable, provided there are three or more carriers in the summary data disclosed. The Department may, at any time, publish international summary statistics without carrier detail. Further, the Department may release nonstop segment and on-flight market detail data by carrier before the end of the confidentiality period as follows:

(1) To foreign governments as provided in reciprocal arrangements between the foreign country and U.S. Government for exchange of on-flight market and/or nonstop segment data submitted by air carriers of that foreign country and U.S. carriers serving that foreign country;

(2) To parties to any proceeding before the Department under Title IV of the Federal Aviation Act of 1958, as amended, as required by the Administrative Law Judge or other decisionmaker of the Department. Parties may designate agents or consultants to receive the data in their behalf, provided the agents or consultants agree to abide by the disclosure restrictions. Any data to which access is granted pursuant to this provision may be introduced into evidence, subject to the normal rules of admissibility of evidence.

(3) To agencies and other components of the U.S. Government for their internal use only.

[Amdt. 241–59, 56 FR 2845, Jan. 25, 1991, as amended at 62 FR 6719, Feb. 13, 1997; 67 FR 49224, July 30, 2002]

Sec. 19–7 Passenger origin-destination survey.

(a) All U.S. large certificated air carriers conducting scheduled passenger operations (except helicopter carriers) shall participate in a Passenger Origin-Destination (O & D) Survey covering domestic and international operations, as described in the instructions manual entitled, *Instructions to Air Carriers for Collecting and Reporting Passenger Origin-Destination Survey Statistics* (Appendix A to this section), and in *Passenger Origin-Destination Directives* issued by the Department's Bureau of Transportation Statistics (BTS), Office of Airline Information (OAI). Copies of these *Instructions* and *Directives* are provided to each large carrier participating in the Survey. Copies are also available from the Office of Airline Information,

K–25, U.S. Department of Transportation, 1200 New Jersey Avenue, SE., Washington, DC 20590. Copies of these *Instructions* and *Directives* are available on the BTS Web page at (*http://www.bts.gov/programs/airline_information/*).

(b) Reports required by this section shall be submitted to the Bureau of Transportation Statistics in a format specified in accounting and reporting directives issued by the Bureau of Transportation Statistics' Director of Airline Information.

(c) A statistically valid sample of light coupons shall be selected for reporting purposes. The sample shall consist of at least 1 percent of the total lifted ticket flight coupons for all large domestic markets listed in the Instructions and 10 percent for all others—including domestic and international markets. The sample shall be selected and reported in accordance with the requirements of paragraph (a) of their section, except that the participating O & D carriers with nonstandard ticketing procedures, or other special operating characteristics, may propose alternative procedures. Such departures from standard O & D Survey practices shall not be authorized unless approved in writing by the Director, Office of Airline Information under the procedures in Sec. 1–2 of 14 CFR part 241. The data to be recorded and reported from selected lifted ticket flight coupons, as stipulated in the *Instructions* and *Directives* shall include the following data elements: Point of origin, carrier on each flight-coupon stage, fare-basis code for each flight-coupon stage, points of stopover or connection (interline and intraline), point of destination, number of passengers, and total dollar value of ticket (fare plus tax).

(d) Data covering the operations of foreign air carriers that are similar to the information collected in the Passenger Origin-Destination Survey are generally not available to the Department, the U.S. carriers, or U.S. interests. Therefore, because of the damaging competitive impact on U.S. carriers and the adverse effect upon the public interest that would result from unilateral disclosure of the U.S. survey data, the Department has determined its policy to be that the international data in the Passenger Origin-Destination Survey shall be disclosed only as follows:

(1) To an air carrier directly participating in and contributing input data to the Survey or to a legal or consulting firm designated by an air carrier to use on its behalf O & D data in connection with a specific assignment by such carrier.

(2) To parties to any proceeding before the Department to the extent that such data are relevant and material to the issues in the proceeding upon a determination to this effect by the Administrative Law Judge or by the Department's decision-maker. Any data to which access is granted pursuant to this section may be introduced into evidence subject to the normal rules of admissability of evidence.

(3) To agencies and other components of the U.S. Government.

(4) To other persons upon a showing that the release of the data will serve specifically identified needs of U.S. users which are consistent with U.S. interests.

(5) To foreign governments and foreign users as provided in formal reciprocal arrangements between the foreign and U.S. governments for the exchange of comparable O & D data.

(e) The Department reserves the right to make such other disclosures of the O & D data as is consistent with its regulatory functions and responsibilities.

APPENDIX A TO §19–7—INSTRUCTIONS TO AIR CARRIERS FOR COLLECTING AND REPORTING PASSENGER ORIGIN-DESTINATION SURVEY STATISTICS

All questions, comments, extension and waiver requests should be e-mailed to *ODsurvey.Support@dot.gov*.

I. GENERAL DESCRIPTION OF O&D SURVEY

A. Flow Chart of O&D Reporting From Tickets

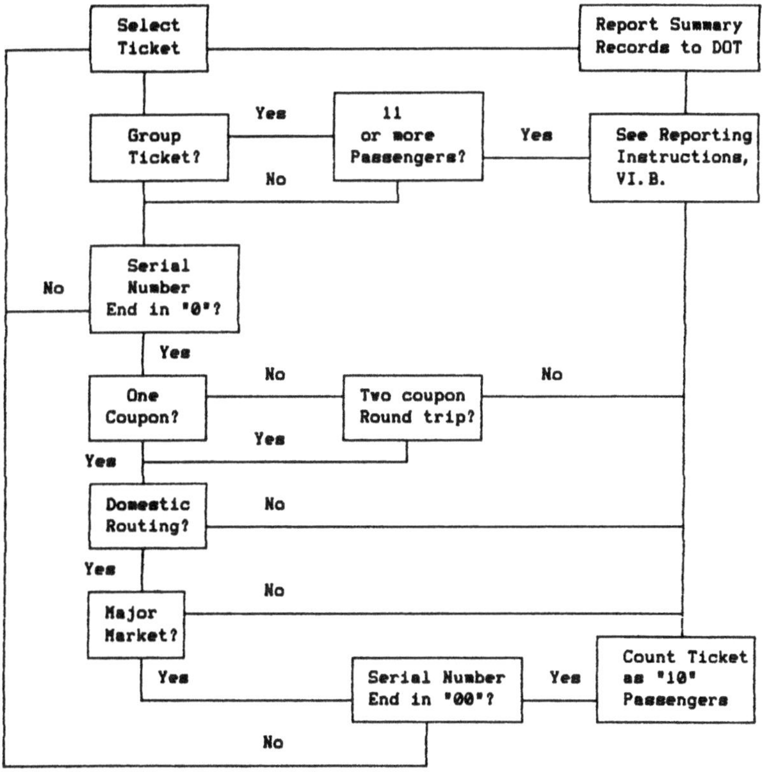

B. Narrative Description

A single O&D Survey is conducted continuously by the large U.S. certificated air carriers. Foreign air carriers do not directly participate in the Survey, although some of their data are captured in the Survey, since passengers who share a ticketed itinerary between a U.S. carrier and a foreign carrier may be sampled by the U.S. carrier. The authority for these instructions is found in 14 CFR part 241, section 19–7, and in the CAB Sunset Act of 1984 (Pub. L. 94–443).

The Survey samples revenue passenger trips moving in whole or in part on domestic and/or international scheduled services of the carriers participating in the Survey. In general, these requirements do not apply to small certificated, all-cargo and all charter carriers.

The source documents for the Survey data are passenger tickets. These data are collected from the "lifted" flight coupons of tickets (a portion of a multi-part ticket booklet of three[1] or more coupons, including one for each stage of the passenger's trip itinerary which is lifted by the carrier as the passenger boards a particular flight segment).

The Survey data are taken from the coupon that is lifted by a participating carrier, unless it is apparent from the lifted coupon that another participating carrier has already recorded and reported the data, in which instance the ticket coupon is non-reportable for the second honoring/participating carrier. The complete passenger itinerary, and related data on type of fare and dollar value of the ticket, is recorded as

[1] Each ticket booklet is comprised of one or more *flight coupons* for passenger travel in a city-pair market, plus a *passenger coupon* (the traveler's receipt) and the *auditor coupon* (for the carrier's internal controls).

one entry from the sampled, reportable flight coupon.

The recording of data from the sampled flight coupon normally consists of transcribing the information exactly as indicated on the ticket. The detail recorded for each trip shows the complete routing from the origin city (airport code) to the destination city (airport code) including, in sequence from the origin, each point of transfer and stopover (intraline and interline), the summarized fare-basis code shown for each flight coupon stage of the itinerary, and the total dollar value of the fare and tax for the entire ticket.

Prior to 1987, the Survey was generally based on a 10-percent sample of passenger tickets. Beginning July 1, 1987, the Survey is collected primarily on the basis of a stratified, scientific sample of at least 1 percent of tickets in domestic major markets and 10 percent of tickets in all other domestic and in all international city-pair markets. The Survey data are taken from the selected flight coupons of the tickets sampled: single-coupon or double-coupon round trips in domestic major markets where the ticket serial number ends in double zero (00) and all other ticket coupons ending in zero (0). This procedure yields a "two-tiered" stratified sample.

Group tickets are included on the basis of a 10-percent sample when the number of passengers on such a group ticket is 10 or less. Group tickets with more than 10 passengers on each ticket are included on the basis of a 100 percent census, *i.e.*, all such tickets are sampled, regardless of serial number, and the total data listed are conformed to a 10 percent sample for inclusion in the O&D Survey.

Following the selection of reportable flight coupons and the recording of data, each participating carrier shall edit and summarize[2] the data into a quarterly report to the Department.

II. EFFECTIVE DATE OF INSTRUCTIONS

These data collection and reporting instructions are effective on and after July 1, 1987 and apply to all flight coupons lifted on or after July 1, 1987.

III. CARRIERS PARTICIPATING IN SURVEY

A. *Participating carriers.* As defined in section 19–7 of the Department's Economic Regulations (14 CFR part 241), the participants in the O&D Survey include all large certificated air carriers conducting scheduled passenger services (except helicopter carriers). These participating carriers collect and report data in accordance with these Instructions, and supplemental *Passenger Origin-Destination Directives* that may be issued periodically. The list of participating carriers will be issued by reporting directive under the authority in 14 CFR 385.27(b).

B. *Amendments to list of participating carriers.* As new carriers begin service, they will be required to file O&D Survey Data. These carriers will not be added to the participating carrier list automatically, but will be added when the next annual review is made.

IV. SUBMISSION OF REPORTS

A. *Period covered by reports.* Reports are to be filed for each calendar quarter of the year as shown below:

Report	Time period covered
1st quarter	Jan. 1 through Mar. 31.
2nd quarter	Apr. 1 through June 30.
3rd quarter	July 1 through Sept. 30.
4th quarter	Oct. 1 through Dec. 31.

B. *Filing date for reports.* Reports are to be filed with the Department on or before the dates listed below. The mailing address is on the inside cover to these instructions.

Report	Due date [1]
1st quarter	May 15
2nd quarter	Aug. 15
3rd quarter	Nov. 15
4th quarter	Feb. 15

[1] Due dates falling on Saturday, Sunday or national holiday will become effective the first following work day.

C. *Format of the Report.* Reports required by this section shall be submitted to the Bureau of Transportation Statistics in a format specified in accounting and reporting directives issued by the Bureau of Transportation Statistics' Director of Airline Information.

D. [Reserved]

E. All reports shall be filed with the Bureau of Transportation Statistics in a format specified in accounting and reporting directives issued by the Bureau of Transportation Statistics' Director of Airline Information.

V. SELECTION OF SAMPLE AND RECORDING OF DATA.[4]

A. *Sampling Basis.* Each participating carrier in this O&D Survey shall search all listed flight coupons, whether the coupons are

[2] These summarization procedures include showing two or more passengers with the same itinerary as one O&D record and compressing extremely lengthy itineraries (such as around-the-world tickets) into a standard trip stage length limit (which may be either seven or twenty-three stages, at the carrier's option), as explained in Section V.D.

[4] Upon approval of the Director, Office of Airline Information, carriers may continue current reporting procedures (up to twenty-three stages of a passenger flight) and may report a uniform 10 percent sample of tickets lifted (each zero ending lifted coupon) without reducing the sample size from 10 percent

its own ticket stock or on the ticket stock of another U.S. or foreign carrier (either standard IATA and ARC ticket stock or non-standard ticket stock), and is to *select for reporting purposes* the following flight coupons:

(1) *Major domestic markets.* All single-passenger flight coupons that are either a single flight coupon ticket or part of a round trip, two coupon ticket where the ticket serial number ends in the digits double-zero (00).

NOTE. The list of major domestic markets will be issued by reporting directive under the authority in 14 CFR 385.27(b).

(2) *International markets and all other domestic markets.* (a) All single-passenger flight coupons with ticket serial numbers ending with the digit zero (0);

(b) Those group-ticket flight coupons with 10 or fewer passengers with ticket serial numbers ending with the digit zero (0);

(c) Those group-ticket flight coupons with 11 or more passengers without regard to serial number; and

(d) Itineraries in major domestic markets that comprise more than two coupons are sampled on a uniform 10 percent basis, by selecting all ticket serial numbers ending with the digit zero (0).

B. *Selection of Reportable Flight Coupons.* The flight coupons identified above are to be examined to isolate the reportable flight coupons, i.e. coupons from which data are to be recorded. Flight coupon data are reported only by the first honoring and participating carrier (operating carrier). Such carriers shall report the required data for the entire ticketed itinerary.

If a participating carrier has preceded an examining carrier on any stage in the trip itinerary, including any stage in a conjunction itinerary and any stage in a reissued ticket (either before or after reissue) that coupon is not reportable.

For conjunction tickets, the ticket number for the first ticket booklet determines if the conjunction tickets should be reported in the Survey. Otherwise, conjunction tickets do not require special treatment and are governed by the rules for regular tickets.

No adjustment is made in the Survey for alterations or changes in the trip itinerary subsequent to the stage covered by the reportable coupon.

C. *Optional Use of Other Sampling Procedures.*

(1) Alternative sampling procedures or alternative O&D data systems may be proposed by participating carriers with non-standard ticketing procedures, or other special operating characteristics. Data reported under proposed alternative procedures must approximate the usefulness and statistical validity of the O&D Survey.

(2) Such departures from the prescribed O&D Survey practices shall not be authorized unless approved in writing by the Director, Office of Airline Information (address inside front cover). The proposed alternative O&D Survey procedures must be described in detail in the letter requesting the waiver.

D. *Recording of Data from Reportable Flight Coupons.* (1) The following items are to be reported from the reportable flight coupons:

(a) Point of origin,

(b) Operating carrier on each flight stage (if unknown, identify ticketed carrier),

(c) Ticketed carrier on each flight stage,

(d) Fare-basis on each flight coupon, C, D, F, G, X or Y,

(e) Points of stopover or connection (interline and intraline),

(f) Point of destination,

(g) Number of passengers, and

(h) Total dollar value of ticket (fare plus tax and other charges, such as Passenger Facility Charges).

(2) The individual items are to be recorded in the sequence of occurrence in the itinerary as follows:

(a) All entries for *points* (airport codes[5]) in an itinerary are to be recorded in three-letter airport code data to fit into the stage-length limitation (seven or twenty-three stages at the carrier's option), all airport codes are to be reported, including data on commuter, foreign, intra-state and other carriers' portions of itineraries. Normally codes are recorded as they appear on the ticket. However, if a code is obviously incorrect, *record the correct code.* For instance, if a ticket is coded DCA-NYC or Washington/National to New York when the flight stage actually operated from Washington, Dulles to Newark (EWR), record the correct airport code. When only name spellings of a city appear on the ticket for multi-airport cities (such as Washington, New York, San Francisco, or Los Angeles), record the specific *three letter airport code.* In cases where two airport codes are shown on the ticket for a point, such as when the passenger arrives at an airport such as San Francisco and departs from another local airport such as Oakland, record the code for the arrival airport, enter

to 1 percent for domestic major markets. Note that the domestic major markets will be reviewed each year at June 30, based on the prior 12 months O&D data, and the list amended as necessary. The list could remain static for more than a year, although it will be reviewed annually. Necessary amendments will be effective on January 1 of the following year.

[5] Codes to be used are those appearing in the *Official Airline Guide* at the time the data are being recorded. If a code is not found in the OAG, contact the Director, Office of Airline Information (address inside front cover).

a surface segment indicator (—) to the departure airport, and record the departure airport code. (When the surface portion is at the beginning or end of an itinerary, the surface indicator is to be omitted). For example:

000001	UCA	YV	UA	Y	JFK	TW	TW	X
Passenger(s)	Utica	Mesa Operating Carrier	United Ticketed Carrier	Fare Code	New York Kennedy Airport	TWA Operating Carrier	TWA Ticketed Carrier	Fare Code

SURFACE TRANSPORTATION

SFO			(Blank space)
San Francisco	Operating Carrier	Ticketed Carrier	Fare Code

OAK	UA	UA	G	LAX	DL	DL	F
Oakland	United Operating Carrier	United Ticketed Carrier	Fare	Los Angeles	Delta Operating Carrier	Delta Operating Carrier	Fare Code

SLC	NW	NW	D	PHX	AA	AA	C	LAX
Salt Lake City	Northwest Operating Carrier	Northwest Ticketed Carrier	Fare Code	Phoenix	American Operating Carrier	American Ticketed Carrier	Fare Code	Los Angeles

JL	JL	C	NRT	04596
Japan Air Lines Operating Carrier	Japan Air Lines Ticketed Carrier	Fare Code	Tokyo Narita	Dollars of Fare + Tax

In the above example, the passenger trip stages or segments are compressed into the maximum of 7 stages so that several intermediate city-pairs (Los Angeles to Seattle to Anchorage, or LAX—SEA—Anc) and the related carriers have not been recorded, as prescribed below in this Section V.D.(3)(e). In addition, after the fourth city-pair (Los Angeles-Salt Lake City), the passenger trip itinerary moves from the initial four-part ticket booklet onto another "conjunction" ticket, and the summary fare code data are not recorded beyond the initial four-part ticket.

(b) All entries for operating and ticketed carriers for a coupon stage of an itinerary are to be recorded using two character IATA assigned or DOT codes, as in the above example. Note that the fare code summary was properly inserted after the ticketed carrier's code, i.e., UA for United Air Lines and Y for unrestricted coach class service. When a two-character carrier code is shown on the ticket, record that code for the ticketed carrier. However, if a code is obviously incorrect, record the correct carrier code. If the reporting carrier does not know the operating carrier on a downline code-share segment, it would use the ticketed carrier's code for both the operating and ticketed carriers. The reporting carrier is not responsible for knowing the operating carrier of a downline code-share where it is not a party to the code-share segment. Except for the infrequent compression of data to fit into the stage-length limitation (7 or 23 stages at the carrier's option), all carrier codes are to be recorded, including data on air taxis, commuters, intra-state, and other carrier portions of itineraries. On tickets involving interchange service or other cooperative carrier arrangements, the juncture point(s) where the passenger moves from one carrier system to another is to be recorded as an intermediate point in the itinerary, even when not shown on the ticket and even though the flight may overfly the juncture point.

(c) Entries for fare-basis codes are to be taken from the "fare basis" and "fare description" portions of the ticket and simplified into the appropriate category, as shown below. No attempt shall be made to determine and record fare-basis codes for that portion of a conjunction ticket appearing in the ticket. Fare-basis codes are to be recorded in one-character alphabetic codes. The fare-basis codes are recorded as follows:

C—Unrestricted Business Class
D—Restricted Business Class
F—Unrestricted First Class
G—Restricted First Class
X—Restricted Coach/Economy Class
Y—Unrestricted Coach/Economy Class

U—Unknown (This fare category is used when none is shown on a ticket coupon, or when a fare category is not discernible, or when two or more carrier fare codes are compressed into a single stage of a passenger trip).

(d) In recording the number of passengers, each single-passenger ticket is to be recorded as one passenger. Tickets for infants under two years of age not occupying a seat are not to be counted. A revenue passenger is defined in Section X.

For group tickets of 10 or fewer passengers per ticket record the actual number of passengers on each ticket, *i.e.*, either 2, 3, 4, 5, 6, 7, 8, 9 or 10. For group tickets with 11 or more passengers (those sampled at a 100-percent rate) record the actual number of passengers traveling on each ticket, but keep these entries separate from the group ticket records with 10 or fewer passengers and from the single-passenger ticket records. Group tickets with 11 or more passengers are to be sorted and summarized to combine all passengers for all itineraries which are identical in every respect, *i.e.*, points, carriers, fare basis codes, and average dollar value (as defined in paragraph (e), below). The total number of passengers on each summarized record is to be divided by 10, rounding to the nearest whole passenger. If the quotient ends in 0.5 or more, raise to the next whole passenger. If the quotient ends in less than 0.5, drop the fraction. These large group-ticket records, after division by 10 for compatibility with the other data, are to be merged with the single-passenger records and with the group-ticket entries from tickets of 10 or fewer passengers for the quarterly O&D Survey report.

(e) The total dollar value shall be taken from the "Total" box on each ticket and shall be the sum of the fare plus tax for the entire ticket. Record this amount in whole U.S. dollars, with the cents dropped. Do not round cents to nearest whole dollar.

Amounts on tickets stated in foreign currency are to be converted to U.S. dollar equivalents. For *all group tickets*, the dollar value to be recorded shall be the average amount per passenger, determined by dividing the total dollar value for the entire group by the number of passengers on the group ticket, dropping cents in the average amount.

(3) The *length of the itineraries to be recorded is limited* to a maximum of seven stages or twenty-three stages, at the carrier's option. This recognizes that the vast majority of tickets sampled have seven stages or fewer and that the rare occurrences of extremely lengthy itineraries do not impact the overall Survey results enough to justify their reporting burden. Therefore, trips longer than these limits are *compressed* to fall within the stated maximums. The ticketed origin and destination are retained, but the *intermediate routing is compressed* by applying the following rules, in sequence:

(a) Combine any contiguous open, unknown carrier, or surface stages eliminating the connecting point, and ignoring the fare-basis codes, if different:

(b) Combine any contiguous stages via the same non-U.S. carrier, eliminating the connecting point, and ignoring the fare-basis codes, if different;

(c) Combine any contiguous stages via different non-U.S. carrier, making the carrier "UK", eliminating the connecting point, and ignoring fare-basis codes, if different:

(d) Combine any contiguous stages via the *same U.S. carrier*, eliminating the connecting point, and ignoring the fare-basis codes, if different, and;

(e) If the trip, after applying the four steps above, is still too long, record the compressed routing through to the stage length limitation city (seventh or twenty-third city), enter UK as the final carrier, and then record the ticketed destination as the next (the 8th or 24th) city.

VI. Summarization of Recorded Data

A. *General.* Prior to the submission of each quarterly report to the Department, each carrier is to summarize the data in accordance with the rules in Section VI.B. In special hardship cases, carriers may submit a waiver request (with justification under Section 1–2 of 14 CFR part 241) requesting permission to report their flight coupon records exactly as represented on their lifted tickets. Waiver requests must provide the documentation described in Section VI.C. so that the Department can develop the necessary procedures and edit routines to ensure the accuracy and reliability of the overall O&D Survey results. The granting of such waivers will depend upon the availability of resources for the Department to assume this additional burden, which can only be determined on a case by case basis, after evaluating each carrier's need.

B. *Rules for Summarization.* Sort the recorded entries into sequence by the entire record (excluding the passenger field) *i.e.*, by origin, complete routing (including fare-basis codes), tickets destination, and dollar value of ticket. *All identical records are then to be combined into one summary record.* The number of passengers on the summary record is to be the sum of the passenger amounts of all the individual records combined. Passengers are only summarized where records are identical in all respects except in the number of passengers including dollar value of ticket. *Note:* Do not summarize dollars over identical records. This summarization is to include the entries from group tickets, but only after the entries for *group tickets with 11 or more passengers have been summarized and divided by 10,* as stated in Section V.D.(2)(d).

C. *Waiver Requests.* Requests for permission to depart from the required O&D Survey procedures should include a *procedural statement* describing the process the carrier proposed to employ in *examining, selecting and editing* the data from reportable flight coupons for the O&D Survey, as well as a flow chart diagramming the proposed procedures.

D. *Quantity and Quality Controls.* Carriers are expected to establish and maintain *continuous quantity and quality* controls on the flow of all lifted flight coupons through their system processes to determine the total *number of coupons handled* and the number of reportable *coupons selected.* Such data controls and tests have not been specified by the Department, and necessarily must be developed by each carrier. Each participating carrier shall develop and use on a continuous basis such control tests as are necessary to ensure that all reportable coupons are being selected, recorded and reported as intended by these O&D Survey Instructions. Such controls should extend over all ADP processing, both in-house and that from external service bureaus.

VII. EDITING OF RECORDED DATA

A. *City and Airport Codes.* Prior to submission of O&D Survey reports, each carrier is to edit the recorded data to validate city and airport codes. This edit is to verify that the codes recorded are valid official codes, and it is independent of whether or not the carriers shown actually operated into or out of the airport shown. Any questions about airport codes should be addressed to the Director, Office of Airline Information (see inside of cover).

B. *Edit Responsibility of Carriers.* Each carrier is responsible for developing edit procedures and internal controls over its data entry and processing procedures so that valid and reliable data are captured in the O&D Survey inputs and are properly summarized in the outputs. Since the carriers have many different statistical systems, it is not practicable for the Department of Transportation to prescribe specific controls in this area, and each carrier is responsible for developing the appropriate internal control procedures to edit the O&D Survey data and ensure the integrity of these data. The Department will control the accuracy of its processing of the sampled data upon receipt from the carriers.

C. *System Documentation of Edits.* Carriers are required to maintain written O&D Survey procedural statements and flow charts. As provided in Section VIII, these must be established, or re-certified as of July 1, 1987, and thereafter when significant procedural revisions occur.

VIII. CONTROL OF SAMPLE SELECTION AND DATA RECORDING

A. *Sample Accuracy and Reliability.* In order to maximize the accuracy and reliability of the sample selection and data recording, each carrier is to:

(1) Develop a written statement describing the procedures it will employ in examining and selecting reportable flight coupons and in recording, summarizing, editing, and testing the Survey data.

(2) Submit any proposed changes in the above procedures to the Department's Office of Airline Information, prior to implementation of such changes.

(3) Establish continuous quantity controls on the flow of all lifted flight coupons through the carrier's accounting processing to determine the total number of coupons handled, and the number of reportable coupons selected. Tests are to be made continuously to assure that all reportable coupons are being selected and the data recorded. Such tests should be completed while the "lifted" flight coupons (representing earned passenger revenues for flight segments operated) remain in the possession of the carrier. Establish such other internal control procedures as are necessary for supervising and monitoring the accuracy of the recording of data from reportable flight coupons.

B. *Staff Review.* The OAI staff will review the carrier procedures and practices and may request modifications or the use of special procedures necessary to improve the sample or to bolster the controls for accuracy and reliability.

[Reserved]

X. GLOSSARY OF TERMS

Selected terms used in the foregoing instructions are here defined and explained in the context of the O&D Survey.

ADP. An abbreviation for automated data processing, which is the term applied to all forms of machine processed data.

Carrier. Any scheduled air carrier, U.S. or foreign, that appears on a coupon stage in a ticketed itinerary, including helicopter, air taxi, commuter, intra-Alaska carriers, and intra state carriers

City or origin. (See origin.)

Conjunction ticket. Two or more tickets concurrently issued to a passenger and which together constitute a single contract of carriage.

Connecting point. An intermediate point in an itinerary at which the passenger deplanes from one flight and boards another flight, either on the same carrier or from the flight of one carrier to a flight of another carrier, for continuation of the journey.

Coupon stage. (See flight-coupon stage.)

Destination. The last point in the itinerary and the last point at which the passenger is to deplane at the completion of the journey.

(In roundtrip itineraries, the destination and the origin are the same.)

Dollar value of ticket. (See total dollar value of ticket.)

Domestic. Itineraries within or between the 50 U.S. States and the District of Columbia are considered domestic for this Survey.

Fare basis code. The alphabetic code(s) or combination of alphabetic and numeric codes appearing in the "Fare basis" box on the flight coupon which describe the applicable service and discount to which the passenger is entitled. All fare basis codes are summarized into basic categories; namely C—Unrestricted Business Class, D—Restricted Business Class, F—Unrestricted First Class, G—Restricted First Class, X—Restricted Coach/Economy Class, Y—Unrestricted Coach/Economy Class, and U—Unknown (This fare category is used when none is shown on a ticket coupon, or when a fare category is not discernible, or when two or more carrier fare codes are compressed into a single stage of a passenger trip).

Fare ladder. The "For-issuing-office-only" box of a ticket.

Flight-coupon stage. The portion of an itinerary which lies between two contiguous points in the itinerary and between which points the passenger is to travel on a single flight.

Group ticket. A single ticket valid for the transportation of two or more passengers over the same itinerary.

Interline transfer. An occurrence at an intermediate point in an itinerary where a passenger changes from one carrier to another carrier, with or without a stopover.

Intermediate point. Any point in an itinerary, other than the origin or destination, at which the passenger makes an interline or intraline connection or stopover.

International. The world area outside the 50 U.S. States and the District of Columbia. Itineraries between points outside the 50 States are considered as international for this Survey, as well as itineraries between the 50 States and U.S. possessions, and between or within U.S. possessions.

Intraline transfer. An occurrence at an intermediate point in an itinerary where a passenger changes from a flight of one carrier to another flight of that same carrier, with or without stopover, or where the passenger changes from one class of service to another class of service on the same flight.

Itinerary. All points in the passenger journey, beginning with the origin, followed by the routing, and ending with the destination, in the sequence shown on the ticket.

Operating air carrier. Under a code-share arrangement, the air carrier whose aircraft and flight crew are used to perform a flight segment.

Origin. The first point in the itinerary and the point where the passenger first boards a carrier at the beginning of the itinerary.

Participating carrier. A carrier which is governed by the Survey data collection and reporting instructions contained herein and which is required to file Survey reports with the Department of Transportation.

Point. A city or airport (always identified by its airport code).

Reissued ticket. A ticket issued in exchange for all or part of the unused portion of a previously issued ticket.

Reportable flight coupon. A flight coupon in an itinerary in which the carrier examining the coupon is the first participating carrier to lift a flight coupon in the itinerary and from which coupon the examining carrier records the Survey data.

Reporting carrier. The carrier in a given itinerary which has lifted the reportable flight coupon in that itinerary and which carrier is required to record the Survey data for that itinerary for the report to the Department.

Routing. The carrier on each flight-coupon stage in an itinerary and the intermediate points of routing stopover or connection (interline or intraline) in the sequence of occurrence in the movement of the passenger from origin to destination. The routing also includes fare-basis summary codes on each flight-coupon stage, to the extent these are available from the ticket.

Scheduled service. Transport service operated on a certificated large air carrier's routes pursuant to published flight schedules, including extra sections of scheduled flights.

Stage. (See flight-coupon stage.)

Ticketed air carrier. Under a code-share arrangement, the air carrier whose two-character air carrier code is used for a flight segment, whether or not it actually operates the flight segment.

Total dollar value of ticket. The sum of the fare plus tax for the entire ticketed itinerary, in whole U.S. dollars with cents dropped. For a group ticket, the amount is the average per passenger. For fares stated in foreign currency, it is the equivalent in U.S. dollars.

Transfer. (See interline transfer and intraline transfer.)

[Reserved]

[Amdt. 241–55, 52 FR 6529, Mar. 5, 1987, as amended at 60 FR 66723, 66724, Dec. 26, 1995; 62 FR 43280, Aug. 13, 1997; 67 FR 58690, Sept. 18, 2002; 75 FR 41584, July 16, 2010]

GENERAL REPORTING PROVISIONS—LARGE CERTIFICATED AIR CARRIERS

Section 21 Introduction to System of Reports

(a) Each large certificated air carrier subject to the Federal Aviation Act of 1958, as amended, shall file with the BTS, monthly, quarterly, semiannually, and annually BTS Form 41 Reports of financial and operating statistics as prescribed herein unless waiver has been made by the Civil Aeronautics Board.

(b) The system prescribed provides for the submission by each air carrier of four classes of financial and operating statistics, on individual schedules of the BTS Form 41 Report, grouped as follows:

A. Certification.
B. Balance Sheet Elements.
P. Profit and Loss Elements.
T. Traffic and Capacity Elements.

(c) The prescribed system of reports provides that the frequency of reporting shall be monthly for some schedules, quarterly for some, semiannually for some and annually for others. It also provides in some areas for the classification of large certificated air carriers into Group I, Group II, and Group III with the form and content differentiated as between groups.

(d) Each schedule of the prescribed BTS Form 41 Report has been assigned a specific code. The prefix alphabetical codes A, B, P and T, respectively, have been employed to denote certification, balance sheet, profit and loss, and traffic and capacity. The digits immediately following the alphabetical prefix designate the particular schedule.

(e) [Reserved]

(f) [Reserved]

(g) Four separate air carrier entities shall be established for large certificated air carriers conducting scheduled service for the purpose of submitting the prescribed reports. They are as follows: (1) Domestic operations; (2) operations via the Atlantic Ocean; (3) operations via the Pacific Ocean; and (4) operations in Latin American areas. With respect to the first classification, the domestic entity shall embrace all operations within and between the 50 States of the United States, the District of Columbia, the Commonwealth of Puerto Rico and the U.S. Virgin Islands, and shall also include Canadian transborder operations. The reports to be submitted by each entity shall be comparable to those required of a distinct legal entity whether the reporting entity constitutes such an entity, a semiautonomous physically separated operating division of the carrier, or an entity established for reporting purposes only.

(h) Two separate entities shall be established for large certificated air carriers predominantly engaged in conducting charter activities for the purpose of submitting the prescribed reports: (1) Domestic operations; and (2) international operations. The domestic entity includes all operations within and between the 50 States of the United States, the District of Columbia, the Commonwealth of Puerto Rico, and the U.S. Virgin Islands. All other operations will be in the international entity.

(i) The entities for which separate reports shall be made by the different route and charter air carriers will be set semiannually by the Office of Airline Information.

(j) As a general rule separate reports shall be filed for the air carrier and for each associated company air carriers as defined in section 03 which is an air carrier. However, transactions of associated companies in which 100 percent equity control resides in the reporting air carrier shall be consolidated with transactions of the reporting air carrier when such associated companies perform services related to the transport operations of the reporting air carrier almost exclusively and are not engaged in air transportation for their own account.

(k) Generally, route air carriers' nonscheduled services shall be treated as an integral part of the reporting entity to which most closely related without regard to the geographic area in which such nonscheduled services may actually be performed. However, supplemental reports shall be made of nonscheduled services (including service for the Department of Defense) in areas not encompassed by the prescribed reporting entity in any month in which the available ton-miles of such nonscheduled services exceed 5 percent of the available ton-miles of the reporting entity. Such supplemental reports shall continue until waived by the BTS upon a showing that such nonscheduled operations will not in the subsequent 12-month period exceed the 5-percent limit. The supplemental reports to be filed each month or calendar quarter, as applicable, shall be comprised of report Schedules P–5, T–1, and T–2. Transport and nontransport revenues pertaining to such separately reported nonscheduled services shall be reported on Schedule P–2 each quarter.

(l) When and as required in the national interest, any air carrier which performs nonscheduled transport services for the Department of Defense shall, when directed by the Department, make separate reports for such services as if they were conducted by a physically separate transport entity, such reports shall consist of Schedules P–1 through P–7, T–1, and T–2. The letter "D" shall be inserted on such reports, following the schedule number of each P and T schedule. When a carrier has more than one reporting entity, nonscheduled transport and nonscheduled Defense services shall be assigned to the reporting entity to which more closely related.

[ER–1027, 42 FR 60128, Nov. 25, 1977, as amended by ER–1073, 43 FR 40453, Sept. 12, 1978; ER–1073, 44 FR 1970, Jan. 9, 1979; ER–1188, 45 FR 48871, July 22, 1980; ER–1297, 47 FR 32919, July 30, 1982; ER–1400, 50 FR 12, Jan. 2, 1985; ER–1401, 50 FR 247, Jan. 3, 1985; Amdt. 241–56, 52 FR 9130, Mar. 23, 1987; Amdt. 241–60, 56 FR 12658, Mar. 27, 1991; 60 FR 66724, Dec. 26, 1995; 75 FR 41584, July 16, 2010]

Section 22 General Reporting Instructions

(a) One copy of each schedule in the BTS Form 41 report shall be filed with the BTS and shall be received on or before the due date indicated for each such schedule in the list titled "Due Dates of Schedules in BTS Form 41 Report."

LIST OF SCHEDULES IN BTS FORM 41 REPORT

[See footnotes at end of table]

Schedule No.	Title	Filing frequency	Applicability by carrier group		
			I	II	III
A	Certification	Q	(1)	X	X
B–1	Balance sheet	Q	(1)	X	X
B–1.1	Balance sheet	SA	(2)	NA	NA
B–7	Airframe and aircraft engine acquisitions and retirements	Q	NA	X	X
B–12	Statement of changes in financial position	Q	(1)	X	X
B–43	Inventory of airframes and aircraft engines	A	X	X	X
P–1.1	Statement of operations	SA	(2)	NA	NA
P–1.2	Statement of operations	Q	(1)	X	X
P–1(a)	Interim operations report	M	X	X	X
P–2	Notes to RSPA Form 41 report	Q	(1)	X	X
P–5.1	Aircraft operating expenses	Q(1), SA(2)	X	NA	NA
P–5.2	Aircraft operating expenses	Q	NA	X	X
P–6	Operating expenses by objective groupings	Q	(1)	X	X
P–7	Operating expenses by functional groupings—Group III air carriers	Q	NA	NA	X
P–10	Employment statistics by labor category	A	(1)	X	X
P–12(a)	Fuel consumption by type of service and entity	M	(1)	X	X
T–100	U.S. air carrier traffic and capacity data by nonstop segment and on-flight market.	M	X	X	X
T–100(f)	Foreign air carrier traffic data by nonstop segment and on-flight market. (see 14 CFR 217)	M			
T–8	Report of all-cargo operations	A	(3)	(3)	(3)

M = Monthly, Q = Quarterly, SA = Semiannually, A = Annually, NA = Not Applicable, X = All Carriers.
(1) Applicable to Group I Air Carriers with annual operating revenues of $20 million or more.
(2) Appilcable to Group I Air Carriers with annual operating revenues below $20 million.
(3) Applicable to Air Carriers conducting 49 U.S.C. 41103 all-cargo operations.

DUE DATES OF SCHEDULES IN BTS FORM 41 REPORT

Due dates [1]	Financial data on schedule No.	Traffic and capacity data on schedule No.
January 20	P–12(a)	
January 30	P–1(a)	T–100, T–100(f)
February 10 [2]	A, B–1, B–1.1, B–7, B–12, P–1.1, P–1.2, P–2, P–5.1, P–5.2, P–6, P–7, P–10.	
February 20	P–12(a)	
March 1	P–1(a)	T–100, T–100(f),
March 20	P–12(a)	
March 30	B–43, P–1(a).	T–100, T–100(f), T–8
April 20	P–12(a)	
April 30	P–1(a)	T–100, T–100(f)
May 10	A, B–1, B–7, B–12, P–1.2, P–2, P–5.1, P–5.2, P–6, P–7.	
May 20	P–12(a)	
May 30	P–1(a)	T–100, T–100(f)
June 20	P–12(a)	
June 30	P–1(a)	T–100, T–100(f)
July 20	P–12(a)	
July 30	P–1(a)	T–100, T–100(f)
August 10	A, B–1, B–1.1, B–7, B–12, P–1.1, P–1.2, P–2, P–5.1, P–5.2, P–6, P–7.	
August 20	P–12(a)	
August 30	P–1(a)	T–100, T–100(f)
September 20	P–12(a)	
September 30	P–1(a)	T–100, T–100(f)
October 20	P–12(a)	
October 30	P–1(a)	T–100, T–100(f)
November 10	A, B–1, B–7, B–12, P–1.2, P–2, P–5.1, P–5.2, P–6, P–7.	
November 20	P–12(a)	
November 30	P–1(a)	T–100, T–100(f)
December 20	P–12(a)	
December 30	P–1(a)	T–100, T–100(f)

[1] Due dates falling on a Saturday, Sunday or national holiday will become effective the first following work day.

[2] Reporting due dates on Form 41 Schedules B and P are extended to March 30 if preliminary schedules are filed at the Department by February 10

(b) Each large certificated air carrier shall file the applicable schedules of the BTS Form 41 Report with the BTS in accordance with the above instructions with the following exceptions:

(1) The time for filing B and P report schedules for the final quarter or semiannual period of each calendar year may be extended to the following March 30 if the preliminary Schedules B–1 or B–1.1 and P–1.1 or P–1.2 are submitted, as applicable, and are received on or before their respective due dates.

(2) For the third month of any calendar quarter, Schedule P–1(a) need not be filed if Schedule P–1.1 or P–1.2 for the quarter or semiannual period, as applicable, is received on the due date prescribed for Schedule P–1(a).

(3) Income and expense data on Schedule P–1(a) for each month will be withheld by the BTS from public disclosure, until such time as (i) the semiannual or quarterly financial reports are due, (ii) the semiannual or quarterly financial reports are filed, or (iii) information covered by monthly reports is publicly released by the carrier concerned, whichever occurs first. Before that time, income and expense data reported on Schedule P–1(a) will be disclosed to parties to any proceeding before the DOT to the extent that such data are relevant and material to the issues in the proceeding upon a determination to this effect by the administrative law judge assigned to the case or by the DOT. Any data to which access is granted may be introduced into evidence, subject to the normal rules of admissibility of evidence. The DOT will make other disclosure of these data upon its own motion or upon application of any interested person, when the DOT finds the public interest so requires. The BTS may, from time to time, publish summary information compiled from Schedule P–1(a) in a form which will not identify the individual carrier. At the request of an air carrier, and upon a showing by such air carriers that public disclosure of its preliminary year-end report would adversely affect its interests and would not be in the public interest, the BTS will withhold such preliminary year-end report from public disclosure until such time as (i) the final report is filed, (ii) the final report is due, or (iii) information covered by the preliminary report is publicly released by the carrier concerned, whichever occurs first.

(c) If circumstances prevent the filing of a report on or before the prescribed due date, consideration will be given to the granting of an extension upon receipt of a written request therefor. To provide ample time for consideration and communication to the air carrier of the action taken, such a request must be delivered to the Board in writing at least three (3) days in advance of the due date, setting forth good and sufficient reason to justify the granting of the extension and the date when the report can be filed. Except in cases of emergency, no such request will be entertained which is not in writing and received by the BTS at least three (3) days before the prescribed due date. If a request is denied, the air carrier remains subject to the filing requirements to the same extent as if no request for extension of time had been made.

(d) [Reserved]

(e) All financial data reported on B, P and G schedules shall reflect the status of the air carrier's books of account for the period for which the report is being made and shall conform to the instructions contained in this Uniform System of Accounts and Reports. At the option of the air carrier, Group III air carriers may round reported financial data to the nearest thousands of dollars by typing "($000)" at the top of each amount column. All Group I and Group II air carriers may, at their option, round reported financial data to the nearest whole dollars by dropping the cents. All rounded amounts must be balanced within and between schedules. This option applies only to the submission of hardcopy reports. Instructions for the submission of data in ADP format are contained in the Accounting and Reporting Directives, which are available from OAI.

(f) Traffic and other operational statistics included in schedules of the BTS Form 41 reports shall reflect data pertaining to the month, quarter or 12-months-to-date period for which the report is being made.

(g) Adjustments correcting errors in previously reported traffic and other operational statistics shall not be included in data reported in schedules for the current period but shall be effected by submission of corrected schedules for the period to which applicable or, if only a few items are involved, by written notice and authorization to the BTS to correct previously filed reports except that any correction which amounts to less than one-half of one percent (0.5%) of the corrected amount for the month to which related may be included in the report for the current month provided the amount of the correction is clearly noted on the Form 41 Report.

(h) All letters and statements of correction or revision of reported data shall be a part of the BTS Form 41 reports.

(i) All changes in accounting methods having a material impact upon the particular financial elements involved, and all changes in methods of computing and reporting traffic and capacity statistics having a material impact upon the particular statistic involved shall be adequately explained and identified in the report first reflecting such changes. Such explanations related to financial position or financial results shall be made on BTS Form 41 Schedule P–2. Changes in methods for computing or reporting traffic and capacity statistics shall be identified and explained on a separate sheet attached to the first report affected. (See sec. 2–16.) The reporting requirements shall not be construed, in any sense, as relieving the air carrier of the responsibility for conforming its procedures to those otherwise prescribed in this system of accounts and reports.

(j) All financial statements released by carriers to the public reflecting a financial position or operating results for dates or reporting periods not covered by reports on file with the Board shall be filed with the Board simultaneously with their public release.

(Approved by the Office of Management and Budget under control number 2138–0013)

[ER–755, 37 FR 19726, Sept. 21, 1972]

EDITORIAL NOTE: For FEDERAL REGISTER citations affecting part 241, section 22, see the List of CFR Sections Affected, which appears in the Finding Aids section of the printed volume and at *www.govinfo.gov*.

FINANCIAL REPORTING REQUIREMENTS

Section 23 Certification and Balance Sheet Elements

Schedule A—Certification

(a) The certification of the BTS Form 41 Report shall be signed by an elective corporate officer, executive, or director. Other persons may be authorized by the carrier to sign the certification provided a written authorization disclosing the individual's name and title is forwarded to the Department of Transportation. Since corrections or revisions of reported data are a part of the BTS Form 41 Report, all correspondence relating to such matters shall be signed only by the person(s) authorized to sign the certification.

(b) The certification of the Form 41 reports, embodied in Schedule A thereof, shall read as follows:

I, the undersigned (Title of officer in charge of accounts) ______ of the (Full name of the reporting company) _____ do certify that this report and all schedules, ADP-media submissions, Passenger Origin-Destination Survey submissions and supporting documents which are submitted herewith or have been submitted heretofore as parts of this report filed for the above indicated period have been prepared under my direction; that I have carefully examined them and declare that they correctly reflect the accounts and records of the company, and to the best of my knowledge and belief are a complete and accurate statement, after adjustments to reflect full accruals, of the operating revenues and expenses, income items, assets, liabilities, capital, retained earnings, and operating statistics for the periods reported in the several schedules, the Schedule T-100 ADP-media submissions, and the Passenger Origin-Destination Survey; that the various items herein reported were determined in accordance with the Uniform System of Accounts and Reports for Large Certificated Air Carriers prescribed by the Department of Transportation; and that the data contained herein are reported on a basis consistent with that of the preceding report except as specifically noted in the financial and statistical statements.

Schedule B–1 Balance Sheet

(a) This schedule shall be filed by all Group II and Group III air carriers and Group I air carriers that have annual operating revenues of $20 million or more.

(b) This schedule shall reflect the balances at the close of business on the last day of each calendar quarter for the overall or system operations of each air carrier in conformance with the provisions of sections 4, 5 and 6.

(c) Individual proprietors or partners shall report the aggregate capital contributed by the proprietor or partners in account 2890 Additional Capital Invested.

Schedule B–1.1—Balance Sheet

(a) This schedule shall be filed semiannually by Group I air carriers with annual operating revenues below $20 million.

(b) Each carrier shall insert in the space provided for "OAG Code" its carrier code as contained in the Official Airlines Guide (OAG). If the OAG does not contain a carrier code for the reporting carrier, a code will be provided by the Office of Airline Information upon request. This code will then be inserted in the space provided for "carrier code."

(c) This schedule shall show the account balances at the close of business on June 30 or December 31, as applicable, of each semiannual reporting period.

(d) "Current Assets" shall include all resources that may reasonably be expected to be realized in cash or sold or consumed within one year. This group of assets is classified into three basic accounts:

(1) "Cash and Equivalents" shall include cash on hand and on deposit, U.S. Government securities, and other temporary cash investments.

(2) "Notes and Accounts Receivable-Net" shall include general traffic accounts receivable, government receivables, notes and receivables from associated companies, officers, employees and others, and a deduction for a reasonable allowance for bad debts.

(3) "Other Current Assets" shall contain all other current assets not provided for in the above classifications. This account shall include, but is not limited to, short-term prepayments, expendable spare parts, supplies and other inventories of flight equipment replacement parts that are usually replaced rather than repaired, and materials and supplies held in stock, such as fuel and oil, expendable tools, office supplies and food service supplies. Spare parts may be reduced by an allowance for obsolescence to provide for losses in value.

(e) "Property and Equipment" shall be segregated into that which is owned and that which is leased under capital leases. All property and equipment, with the deception of land, shall be reported net of accumulated depreciation or amortization.

(f) "Other Assets" shall included all assets not included in the above categories, such as long-term investments, long-term prepayments, long-term receivables, deferred charges, intangible assets, equipment purchase deposits, and construction work in progress.

(g) "Current Liabilities" shall include all obligations, the liquidation of which is reasonably expected to require the use of existing resources within one year. This group of liabilities is classified into three basic accounts:

(1) "Notes and Accounts Payable" shall include any payments on long-term debt, short-term notes and accounts payable, and accrued expenses that are payable within one year.

(2) "Accrued Taxes" shall include tax liabilities, such as those imposed on income,

property and payroll, which are reasonably expected to be liquidated within one year.

(3) "Other Current Liabilities" shall include all current liabilities which are not provided for elsewhere, such as air traffic liabilities for unused transportation sold (includes sales of transportation on both the reporting carrier and other carriers).

(h) "Long-Term Debt" shall include all obligations which are not reasonably expected to be liquidated within one year. Typical examples include bonds payable, long-term notes payable, lease obligations, and pension obligations.

(i) "Other Liabilities" shall include any debts or obligations which are not properly listed in the "Current Liabilities" or "Long-Term Debt" sections.

(j) "Deferred Credits" shall include all credit balances of a general clearing nature, including credits held in suspense pending receipt of further information necessary for final disposition. Included in this account are deferred income taxes and deferred investment tax credits.

(k) "Stockholder's Equity" shall be reported as follows:

(1) "Capital Stock" shall be segregated as between common and preferred. The number of shares outstanding, along with the par or stated value of the stock, shall be reported. In the case of no-par stock without stated value, the full consideration received shall be reported.

(2) "Other Paid-In Capital" shall include the difference between the price at which the capital stock is sold and the par or stated value of the stock.

(3) "Retained Earnings" shall represent the net income or loss from all operations of the corporate entity less dividends.

(4) "Treasury Stock" shall represent the cost of stock issued by the carrier and reacquired by it but not retired or cancelled.

(l) The statement of certification shall be signed by the carrier's chief accounting officer.

(m) All substantive matters that may materially influence interpretations or conclusions in regard to the financial condition or the earnings position of the air carrier which are not clearly identified in the body of the schedule or which represent information that cannot be expressed adequately in monetary terms shall be completely and clearly stated in a note attached to this schedule and cross-referenced to the affected account or accounts.

Schedule B–7 Airframe and Aircraft Engine Acquisitions and Retirements

(a) This schedule shall be filed by all Group II and Group III air carriers.

(b) Data applicable to acquisitions and data applicable to retirements shall be grouped and reported separately. The data reported within each group (acquisitions; retirements) shall be further subgrouped and reported as follows:

(1) Acquisitions: the indicated data shall be reported for each individual airframe, identified by type, model, and design of cabin as to use for passengers exclusively, cargo exclusively, or both passengers and cargo in combination. Data pertaining to aircraft engines shall be reported in aggregate for each type or model; however, leased aircraft engines shall be separately reported under captions entitled: Capital Leases—Aircraft Engines; and Operating Leases—Aircraft Engines. Airframe units leased from others for a period of more than 90 days shall be reported in a separate subsection of this schedule, captioned as follows: Capital Leases—Airframe Units; and Operating Leases—Airframe Units. In addition, a notation shall be made by license number of airframe units of the air carrier returned after lease to others for a period of more than 90 days. Airframe units obtained through interchange lease arrangements shall not be so reported.

(2) Retirements: The indicated data shall be reported for the sale or retirement of each airframe, each type of aircraft engine (stating the number of units retired) and, to the extent retired along with airframes and engines, in aggregates by accounts, operating property and equipment included in accounts 1607 and 1608 and nonoperating property and equipment included in accounts 1707 and 1708. Disposition of properties in accounts 1608 and 1708 not related to airframe and aircraft engine retirements shall be reported in a separate group for each account. Airframe units leased from others for a period of more than 90 days shall be reported, upon return to the lessor, in a separate subsection of this schedule and captioned as follows: Capital Leases—Airframe Units; and Operating Leases—Airframe Units. In addition, a notation shall be made by license number and name of lessee of airframe units leased to others for a period of more than 90 days; moreover, airframe units leased to others under sales-type or direct financing leases shall be separately captioned and reported on this schedule. Airframe units leased under interchange arrangements shall not be so reported. Aircraft engines leased from others for a period of more than 90 days shall be reported, upon return to the lessor, in a separate subsection of this schedule and captioned as follows: Capital Leases—Aircraft Engines; and Operating Leases—Aircraft Engines. In addition, a notation shall be made by model number, number of units, and name of lessee of aircraft engines leased to others for a period of more than 90 days; moreover, aircraft engines leased to others under sales-type or direct financing leases shall be separately captioned and reported on this schedule. Aircraft engines leased under interchange arrangements shall not be so reported.

(c) All dates shall indicate the day, the month and the year; shall be provided on a unit basis for airframes only, and, shall be reported for each aircraft engine group by date of transaction.

(d) Column 1, "Year of First Delivery—Airframe," shall reflect, for each reported airframe, the year that the airframe was first delivered by its manufacturer.

(e) Column 2, "Airframe Manufacturer's Serial Number," shall reflect the serial number assigned to each reported airframe by its manufacturer.

(f) Column 4, "Acquisitions or Retirements," shall be used to indicate, for each item entered, whether it represents an acquisition or retirement. This shall be indicated by inserting in Column 4 an "A" for acquisition or an "R" for retirement.

(g) Column 8, "Maximum Seating Capacity," shall reflect the number of passenger seats installed in each airframe acquired. When airframes are designed for multiple adjustable seating configurations, the maximum number of seats for which designed shall be reported. When the seating configuration of airframes is modified subsequent to original acquisition, the revised passenger capacity of each airfame shall be reported in the quarter in which modified and referenced to identify original capacity reported.

(h) Column 9, "Cost," shall reflect the book cost of reported airframe and aircraft engine acquisitions and retirements.

(i) Column 10, "Amortization/Depreciated Cost," shall reflect the book cost, less amortization or depreciation expense, for airframes and aircraft engines that have been retired.

(j) Column 11, "Realization," shall reflect the proceeds from the disposition of airframes and aircraft engines, including any insurance proceeds.

(k) Column 12, "Acquired From/Disposition," shall reflect: (1) for acquisitions: the name of the person or organization from which airframes and aircraft engines are acquired and (2) for dispositions (retirements): the name of the person or organization to which airframes and aircraft engines are sold or a notation as to the nature of the retirement and the account to which any depreciated cost has been charged, if not sold. Items included in accounts 1607, 1608, 1707, and 1708, sold as a part of an airframe or aircraft sales transaction, shall also be identified by the name of the buyer. Other sales of items included in these accounts shall be reported in a separate group in aggregate for each property account affected.

Schedule B–12—Statement of Cash Flows

(a) This Schedule shall be filed quarterly by all Group II and Group III air carriers and Group I air carriers that have annual operating revenues of $20 million or more.

(b) This schedule shall be filed for the overall or system operations of the air carrier.

(c) The statement of cash flows shall separately disclose the amount of net cash provided or used during the reporting period from the carrier's operating activities, investing activities and financing activities. The effect on cash and cash equivalents of the total amount of net cash provided or used during the quarter from each of the above activities shall be clearly disclosed so as to reconcile beginning and ending cash and cash equivalents.

(d) Carriers may use either the direct or indirect method of reporting cash flows. Under either method, the reporting of cash flows from investing and financing activities will remain the same. However, the reporting of cash flows from operating activities does differ between the two methods.

(e) For carriers electing to use the direct method, cash flows from operating activities are reported as gross amounts of the principal components of cash receipts and cash payments from operating activities, such as cash received from passengers and shippers, cash paid to suppliers, and cash paid to employees. Each carrier using the direct method shall provide as part of its statement of cash flows, a separate schedule that reconciles net income (as reported on Schedule P–1.2 in Account 9899) to cash flow from operating activities.

(f) For carriers electing to use the indirect method, cash flows from operating activities shall reflect net income (as reported on Schedule P–1.2 in Account 9899) along with the adjustments necessary to reconcile net income (Account 9899) to net cash for the period (Net Cash Provided or Used By Operating Activities).

(g) Regardless of the method used, the statement of cash flows shall reflect the amount of net cash flow provided or used by operating activities during the reporting period.

(h) The balance of "Cash and Cash Equivalents," at the beginning and ending of the quarterly period covered by the report, should equal the sum of Accounts 1010, "Cash," and 1100, "Short-term Investments," as reported on the immediately preceding and current quarterly Schedule B–1, "Balance Sheet." If the sum of these two accounts does not equal the total "Cash and Cash Equivalents" reported on the statement of cash flows, then a footnote explaining the difference shall be provided as part of the statement of cash flows.

(i) Carriers shall submit Schedule B–12 in a format specified in accounting and reporting directives issued by the Bureau of Transportation Statistics' Director of Airline Information.

Schedule B-43—Inventory of Airframes and Aircraft Engines

(a) This schedule shall be filed by all Group I, Group II and Group III air carriers.

(b) The indicated data shall be reported for each individual airframe, identified by type, model and design of cabin (main deck) as to use for passengers exclusively, cargo exclusively, or both passengers and cargo in combination. Type and model refers to aircraft models such as B-707-100, B-707-200, DC-10-40, Beech-18, Piper PA-32, etc. Aircraft type designations are prescribed in Accounting and Reporting Directive No. 178, "List of Aircraft Type Numeric Codes." Copies of this directive and subsequent updates to the list of aircraft type codes are available from the Department's Office of Airline Information. Airframes that are authorized for operation over water under FAA regulation FAR 121 shall be so indicated by asterisk.

(c) Data pertaining to aircraft engines shall be reported on a group basis by type of engine and by type of aircraft to which related.

(d) Data in this schedule shall be grouped and subtotaled as data pertaining to airframes and data pertaining to aircraft engines. Data pertaining to nonoperating airframes and aircraft engines shall be reported in a group below the data for operating equipment. Data pertaining to airframes and aircraft engines obtained under operating and capital leases shall be reported, by type of lease, in a separately captioned grouping below nonoperating airframes and aircraft engines and subgrouped within those groups according to operating and nonoperating equipment.

(e) Column 1, "Year of First Delivery—Airframe," shall reflect, for each reported airframe, the year that the airframe was first delivered by its manufacturer.

(f) Column 2, "Airframe Manufacturer's Serial Number," shall reflect the serial number assigned to each reported airframe by its manufacturer.

(g) Data pertaining to airframes and aircraft engines obtained under operating leases shall be listed in Columns 1 through 9; the cost of improvements to equipment under operating leases shall be reported in Columns 10 through 12.

(h) Column 9, "Available Capacity (Weight)," shall reflect, for each reported aircraft type, the available capacity (stated in pounds) that is used in computing the available ton-miles reported on Schedules T-100, T-1, and T-2.

(i) Column 10, "Acquired Cost or Capitalized Value," shall include (1) the acquisition cost of owned airframes and aircraft engines; (2) the total capitalized cost of obtaining airframes and engines under capital leases; and (3) the cost of improvements to airframes and engines obtained under operating leases.

(j) Column 11, "Allowance for Depreciation or Amortization," shall include (1) the accumulations of all provisions for losses due to use and obsolescence that are applicable to owned airframes and aircraft engines, (2) the amount of amortization recorded for amortizing the value of airframes and engines obtained under capital leases, and (3) the amount of amortization recorded for amortizing the value of improvements to airframes and aircraft engines obtained under operating leases.

(k) Column 12, "Depreciated Cost or Amortized Value," shall be calculated as either (1) Acquired Cost (Column 10) less the Allowance for Depreciation (Column 11) or (2) Capitalized Value (Column 10) less Amortization (Column 11).

(l) Column 13, "Estimated Residual Value," shall state, in dollars, the residual value assigned to owned and capital-leased airframes and aircraft engines, including any overhaul value not subject to depreciation.

(m) Column 14, "Estimated Depreciable or Amortizable Life (Months)," shall state the estimated depreciable or amortizable life from the date of acquisition of each airframe and each group of aircraft engines.

[ER-755, 37 FR 19726, Sept. 21, 1972]

EDITORIAL NOTE: For FEDERAL REGISTER citations affecting part 241, section 23, see the List of CFR Sections Affected, which appears in the Finding Aids section of the printed volume and at *www.govinfo.gov*.

Section 24 Profit and Loss Elements

Schedule P-1.1—Statement of Operations

(a) This schedule shall be filed semiannually by Group I air carriers with annual operating revenues below $20 million. Data reported on this schedule shall be for the overall or system operations of the air carrier.

(b) This schedule shall show the results of operations for six-month periods ending June 30 and December 31. Data reported in the "12 Months-to-Date" column shall represent for each individual item the sum of the amount reported in the "Current Period" column and the next previous six-month period.

(c) Each carrier shall insert in the space provided for "OAG Code" its carrier code as contained in the Official Airlines Guide (OAG). If the OAG does not contain a carrier code for the reporting carrier, a code will be provided by the Office of Airline Information upon request. This code will then be placed in the space provided for "carrier code."

(d) "Operating Revenue" shall be put in categories as follows:

(1) "Transport Revenue" shall include the revenue generated by the performance of air transportation services. This category shall be subdivided as follows:

(i) "Scheduled Service" shall include all transport revenue derived from operations between pairs of points which are served on a regularly scheduled basis. Transport revenue received from scheduled service operations shall be subdivided as follows:

(A) *Passengers*. Revenue generated from the transportation of passengers shall be included in this category.

(B) *Other*. Revenue generated by the transportation of property and mail shall be included in this category.

(ii) "Nonscheduled Service" shall include all transport revenue derived from operations between pairs of points which are not served on a regularly scheduled basis.

(2) "Transport-Related Revenue" shall include monies received for providing air transportation facilities associated with the performance of services which flow from and are incidental to air transportation services performed by the air carrier. This category shall be subdivided as follows:

(i) *Public Service Revenue*. This category shall include amounts of compensation paid to the carrier under 49 U.S.C 41733.

(ii) *Other*. This category shall include other transport-related revenue such as in-flight sales, restaurant and food service (ground), rental of property or equipment, limousine service, interchange sales, and cargo pick-up and delivery charges.

(e) "Operating Expense" shall be segregated as follows:

(1) "Flying Operations" shall include expenses incurred directly in the in-flight operation of aircraft and expenses incurred in the holding of aircraft and aircraft operation personnel in readiness for assignment to an in-flight status.

(2) "Maintenance" shall include all expenses which are specifically identifiable with the repair and upkeep of property and equipment used in the performance of air transportation.

(3) "General and Administrative" shall include that portion of all expenses of a general corporate nature and all other expenses not provided for elsewhere which are related to air transport operations either directly or indirectly.

(4) "Depreciation and Amortization" shall include all depreciation and amortization expenses applicable to property and equipment used in providing air transportation services. These expenses shall be segregated between those applicable to owned property and equipment and those applicable to property and equipment which is leased.

(5) "Transport-Related Expense" shall include all expenses associated with the transport-related revenues reported on line 5 of this schedule.

(f) "Operating Profit (Loss)" shall be computed by subtracting the total operating expenses from the total operating revenues.

(g) "Nonoperating Income and Expense" shall include all revenues and expenses resulting from commercial ventures which are not inherently related to the performance of air transport services. For example, the revenues and expenses related to operating a hotel or motel would be reported under this category. This category shall also include the total interest expense incurred from all sources and shall be subdivided as follows:

(1) Interest Expense.

(2) Other Nonoperating (Net).

(h) "Income Tax" shall reflect the provisions for accruals of Federal, State, local, and foreign taxes based upon taxable income, and computed at the normal and surtax rates in effect during the current accounting year.

(i) "Discontinued Operations, Extraordinary Items or Accounting Changes" shall reflect any earnings or losses from discontinued operations, the net of the tax amount of extraordinary items, and the cumulative effect of any changes in accounting principles.

(j) Any air carrier that does not file Schedule P–1(a) in accordance with the filing option described in section 22—General Reporting Instructions shall, for the sixth month of any semi-annual period during which the option is exercised, type in the bottom margin of this statement of operations the total number of full-time and part-time employees to be labeled as such and calculated in accordance with paragraph (d) of the reporting instructions for Schedule P–1(a).

Schedule P–1.2—Statement of Operations

(a) This schedule shall be filed quarterly by all Group II and Group III air carriers and Group I air carriers that have annual operating revenues of $20 million or more.

(b) Route and charter carriers shall file separate statements of operations for each separate operating entity and for the overall, or system operations.

(c) Data reported on this schedule shall conform with the instructions pertaining to profit and loss classifications within this Uniform System of Accounts and Reports.

(d) Data reported in the "12 Months-to-Date" column shall represent for each item the sum of amounts reported in the "Quarter" column for the current and next previous three quarters.

(e) Group III air carriers shall subdivide total Transport Revenues-Passenger (Account 3901) between Accounts 3901.1, Passenger-Flight Class and Account 3901.2 Passenger-Coach, only for operations that are reported in the international entity (Atlantic, Pacific and Latin American). First class and coach passenger revenues associated with transport operations reported in the domestic entity shall be reported as a combined total in Account 3901 Transport Revenues-Passenger.

(f) All Group I and Group II air carriers shall report first class and coach passenger revenues as a combined total in Account 3901

Transport Revenues-Passenger, for both domestic and international entity operations. However, U.S. air carriers in any carrier group that elect to do so may continue to report first class and coach revenue data, if they consider such voluntary reporting to be less burdensome than changing their existing financial reporting system.

(g) Any air carrier that does not file Schedule P–1(a) in accordance with the filing option described in section 22—General Reporting Instructions shall, for the third month of any calendar quarter during which the option is exercised, type in the bottom margin of the system statement of operations the total number of full-time and part-time employees to be labeled as such and calculated in accordance with paragraph (d) of the reporting instructions for Schedule P–1(a).

Schedule P–1(a)—Interim Income Statement

(a) This schedule shall be filed by all air carriers.

(b) This schedule shall be filed for the overall or system operations of the air carrier.

(c) Data reported on this schedule shall reflect the results of operations for the month covered by the report and shall conform to the instructions pertaining to profit and loss classifications within this Uniform System of Accounts and Reports.

(d) Air carriers shall report on this schedule:

(1) Total operating revenues,

(2) Total operating expenses,

(3) Operating profit or loss,

(4) Net income,

(5) Passenger revenues—scheduled service,

(6) Public service revenues (subsidy) and other information on

(7) The total number of full-time and

(8) Part-time employees. Total number of full-time employees and total number of part-time employees shall reflect for the overall or system operations of the air carrier the total number of full-time and part-time employees, respectively, who worked or received pay for any part of the pay period(s) ending nearest the 15th day of the month. For the purposes of this part, "part-time employees" means those employees hired to work less than the number of hours that is customary or standard for their occupational specialty.

(e) In the event of a labor strike, the "number of employees" to be reported on this schedule shall be determined on and actual payroll basis. Actual payroll shall be determined in accordance with paragraph (d) of these reporting instructions. An air carrier that on October 24, 1978, held a certificate issued under 49 U.S.C. 41102 shall also report in a footnote on this schedule the number of full-time employees who were deprived of employment because of a strike (*i.e.*, the number of full-time employees who, but for a strike, would have been included in the number reported in accordance with paragraph (d)(7)).

Schedule P–2—Notes to BTS Form 41 Report

(a) This schedule shall be filed quarterly by all Group II and Group III air carriers and Group I air carriers with annual revenues of $20 million or more. Carriers shall submit Schedule P–2 in a format specified in accounting and reporting directives issued by the Bureau of Transportation Statistics' Director of Airline Information.

(b) Route and charter air carriers shall file this schedule for each separate operating entity and for the overall, or system operations of the carrier.

(c) All substantive matters which may influence materially interpretations or conclusions in regard to the financial condition or the earnings position of the air carrier which are not clearly identified in the body of the Form 41 report or which represent information that cannot be expressed adequately in monetary terms shall be completely and clearly stated in this schedule and cross-referenced to the affected account or accounts. The informative disclosure on this schedule for the system operations of the air carrier shall conform, at the end of each carrier's fiscal or calendar year, with the footnotes prepared for audited financial statements.

(d) The amounts and estimated delivery dates of any purchase commitments of material size and not of a recurrent routine character shall be explained on this schedule. In the case of commitments involving flight equipment, the amount for each equipment type may be given in total, including any engines, airframes and spares; but the number of airframes and the number of engines by type shall be given, as well as the estimated delivery date for each complete aircraft. Reports on commitments other than for flight equipment are required only in the December 31 report of each calendar year.

(e) Each scheduled air carrier shall include on this schedule a description of each interruption in air transport operations, the aggregate effect of which is ten (10) percent or more of the scheduled revenue plane-miles which, except for the interruption, would have been operated during the month or either of 2 consecutive months affected. The information to be reported for each such interruption in operations shall consist of:

(1) For the report period in which partial or complete interruption first occurs, the nature of the interruption and dates of partial and/or complete cessation of operations, as applicable;

(2) For each report period until full resumption of operations, an estimate of the revenue plane-miles canceled in each month of the quarter because of the interruption; and

(3) For the report period in which scheduled operations are resumed, dates of partial and/or complete resumption, as applicable.

Schedule P–5.1—Aircraft Operating Expenses

(a) This schedule shall be filed by all Group I air carriers. Group I air carriers that have annual operating revenues of $20 million or more shall file this schedule quarterly and only report direct operating expense data (lines 1 thru 9). Group I air carriers with annual operating revenues below $20 million shall file this schedule semiannually and report both direct and indirect operating expense data (lines 1 thru 16).

(b) Subject to the provisions of Section 22(a), quarterly reports are due on May 10, August 10, November 10 and February 10 for the first, second, third and fourth calendar quarters, respectively. Semiannual reports are due on August 10 and February 10.

(c) Each carrier shall indicate in the space provided its full corporate name and an "X" shall be inserted in the appropriate box to indicate whether the data being reported are quarterly or six months data. The period-ending data shall be indicated in the space provided.

(d) Route and charter air carriers subject to the quarterly filing requirement shall file this schedule for each operating entity of the air carrier. Air carriers subject to the semi-annual filing requirement shall file this schedule for the overall or system operations of the air carrier.

(e) This schedule shall show the direct and indirect expenses incurred in aircraft operations plus total aircraft hours, gallons of fuel issued, and aircraft days assigned to service. Direct expense data applicable to each aircraft type operated by the carrier shall be reported in separate colums of this schedule. Each aircraft type reported shall be identified at the head of each column in the space provided. "Aircraft Type" refers to aircraft models such as B–707–100, B–707–200, DC–10–40, Beech–18, Piper PA–32, etc, Aircraft Type designations are prescribed in the Accounting and Reporting Directives, which is available from the Board's Information Management Division. In the space provided for "Aircraft Code" carriers shall insert the four digit code which is prescribed in the Accounting and Reporting Directives for the reported aircraft type.

(f) Direct aircraft operating expenses shall be reported in the following categories:

(1) Line 2 "Flying Operations (Less Rental)" shall be subdivided as follows:

(i) Line 3 "Pilot and Copilot" expense shall include pilots' and copilots' salaries, and related employee benefits, pensions, payroll taxes and personnel expenses.

(ii) Line 4 "Aircraft Fuel and Oil" expense shall include the cost of fuel and oil used in flight operations and nonrefundable aircraft fuel and oil taxes.

(iii) Line 5 "Other" expenses shall include general (hull) insurance, and all other expenses incurred in the in-flight operation of aircraft and holding of aircraft and aircraft operational personnel in readiness for assignment to an in-flight status that are not provided for otherwise on this schedule.

(2) Line 6 "Total Flying Operations (Less Rentals)" shall equal the sum of lines 3, 4 and 5.

(3) Line 7 "Maintenance-Flight Equipment" shall include the cost of labor, material and related overhead expended by the carrier to maintain flight equipment, general services purchased for flight equipment maintenance from associated or other outside companies, and provisions for flight equipment overhauls.

(4) Line 8 "Depreciation and Rental-Flight Equipment" expense shall include depreciation of flight equipment, amortization of capitalized leases for flight equipment, provision for obsolescence and deterioration of spare parts, and rental expense of flight equipment.

(5) Line 9 "Total Direct Expense" shall equal the sum of lines 6, 7 and 8.

(g) Line 10 Indirect aircraft operating expenses shall be reported only in total for all aircraft types and shall be segregated according to the following categories:

(1) Line 11 "Flight Attendant Expense" shall include flight attendants' salaries, and related employee benefits, pensions, payroll taxes and personnel expenses.

(2) Line 12 "Traffic Related Expense" shall include traffic solicitor salaries, traffic commissions, passenger food expense, traffic liability insurance, advertising and other promotion and publicity expenses, and the fringe benefit expenses related to all salaries in this classification.

(3) Line 13 "Departure Related (Station) Expense" shall include aircraft and traffic handling salaries, landing fees, clearance, customs and duties, related fringe benefit expenses and maintenance and depreciation on ground property and equipment.

(4) Line 14 "Capacity Related Expense" shall include salaries and fringe benefits for general management personnel, recordkeeping and statistical personnel, lawyers, and law clerks, and purchasing personnel; legal fees and expenses; stationery; printing; uncollectible accounts; insurance purchased-general; memberships; corporate and fiscal expenses; and all other expenses which cannot be identified or allocated to some other specifically identified indirect cost category.

(h) Line 15 "Total Indirect Expense" shall equal the sum of lines 11, 12, 13 and 14.

(i) Line 16 "Total Operating Expense" shall equal the sum of lines 9 and 15.

(j) Line 17 "Total Aircraft Hours" shall equal the sum of revenue and nonrevenue aircraft hours.

(k) Line 18 "Gallons of Fuel Issued" shall equal the aircraft fuels issued (account Z921).

(l) Line 19 "Aircraft Days Assigned to Service" equals the number of days that aircraft owned or acquired through rental or lease are in the possession of the reporting air carrier and are available for service on the reporting carrier's routes plus the number of days such aircraft are in service on routes of others under wet-lease agreements. Includes days in overhaul, or temporarily out of service due to schedule cancellations. Excludes days that newly acquired aircraft are on hand but not available for productive use, days dry-leased or rented to others, and days in possession but formally withdrawn from air transportation service.

Schedule P–5.2—Aircraft Operating Expenses and Related Statistics

(a) This schedule shall be filed by all Group II and Group III air carriers.

(b) Route and charter air carriers shall file this schedule for each operating entity of the air carrier.

(c) Data applicable to each aircraft type operated by the air carrier shall be reported in separate columns of this schedule. "Aircraft Type" refers to aircraft models (such as B–707–100, B–707–300, DC–9–30, etc.) that are prescribed in the *Accounting and Reporting Directives*, which is available from the Office of Airline Information. In the space provided for "Aircraft Code" carriers shall insert the four digit code which is prescribed in the *Accounting and Reporting Directives* for the reported aircraft type. For route air carriers, expenses of operating aircraft provided by other carriers under interchange agreements shall be separately reported in total for all such aircraft as if for a distinct aircraft type. Interchange expenses applicable to aircraft of the same type as those owned or operated by the air carrier shall be distributed in summary memo form as item 98.1 and 98.2 to each aircraft type owned or operated by that air carrier. Aircraft types not generally used in revenue service shall be separately reported. If more than one type of aircraft is involved, a separation of data relating to each type of aircraft shall not be required.

(d) Each aircraft type for which a report is being made shall be identified at the head of each column in the space provided. Data applicable to aircraft designed primarily for cargo services and only incidentally used for passenger services shall be reported in separate columns, and the word "cargo" shall be inserted after the aircraft type at the head of the column. The prescribed reporting by aircraft types may be reviewed from time to time upon request by individual air carriers, or upon the initiative of the BTS, and groupings of aircraft types for reporting purposes may be prescribed or amended in specific instances.

(e) Italicized codes and item titles do not constitute accounts or account numbers prescribed for air carrier accounting, but shall be used for reporting purposes only.

(f) Item 79.6 "Applied Maintenance Burden" shall reflect a memorandum allocation by each air carrier of the total expenses included in subfunction 5300 "Maintenance Burden" between maintenance of flight equipment, by aircraft type, and maintenance of ground property and equipment. The allocation of subfunction 5300 (maintenance burden) shall include the net effect of charges and credits to profit and loss account 5272 Flight Equiment Airworthiness Provisions.

(g) Item 73 "Obsolescence and Deterioration—Expendable Parts" shall reflect (for obsolescence and deterioration of flight equipment expandable parts) the gross provisions for losses in value of expendable parts during the current accounting period offset by any credits applicable to the current period for adjustments for excess inventory levels determined pursuant to section 6–1311.

(h) The total of function 5100 "Flying Operations" reported on this schedule shall agree with corresponding amounts reported on Schedule P–1.2.

Schedule P–6—Operating Expenses by Objective Groupings

(a) This schedule shall be filed quarterly by all Group II and Group III air carriers and Group I air carriers that have annual operating revenues of $20 million or more.

(b) Route and charter air carriers shall file this schedule for each separate operating entity.

(c) Line 36 "Total Operating Expenses" shall agree with the corresponding amount reported on Schedule P–1.

Schedule P–7—Operating Expenses by Functional Groupings—Group III Air Carriers

(a) This schedule shall be filed by all Group III air carriers.

(b) Route and charter air carriers shall file this schedule for each operating entity of the air carrier.

(c) Line 38 "Total Operating Expenses" shall agree with the corresponding amount reported on Schedule P–1.2.

Schedule P–10—Employment Statistics by Labor Category

(a) This schedule shall be filed annually by all Group II and Group III air carriers and Group I air carriers that have annual operating revenues of $20 million or more.

(b) Separate sets of this schedule shall be filed for each operating entity of the air carrier. Employees will be allocated to the reporting entities on a basis consistent with that used in the allocation of salaries for Form 41 financial reporting purposes.

(c) Column 3, "Number of Employees," shall reflect, for each category in column 1, the weighted average number of full-time employees who received pay for any part of the calendar year. In determining the weighted average, all temporary or part-time employees shall be restated, based on their hours paid, as an equivalent number of full-time employees. The calculation shall be based on a standard full-time 2,080/hour year with overtime hours excluded from the computation.

(d) Labor category description—"Other personnel" shall include all employees whose salary is chargeable to accounts 30, 32, 34 and 35 in this Uniform System of Accounts and Reports.

(e) Labor category description—"Transport-related" shall include all employees whose salary is not chargeable to one of the various salary accounts contained in the Uniform System of Accounts and Reports. For example, this category would include those employees who work in transport-related operations and other activities for which a separate payroll account is not prescribed. The number of employees reported as transport-related shall be calculated in accordance with paragraph (c) of these reporting instructions.

Schedule P–12(a)—Fuel Consumption by Type of Service and Entity

(a) This schedule shall be filed monthly by all Group II and Group III air carriers and Group I air carriers that have annual operating revenues of $20 million or more.

(b) A single copy (original only) of this schedule shall be filed to report monthly fuel consumption data by type of service and entity.

(c) For the purposes of this schedule, type of service shall be either scheduled service or nonscheduled service as those terms are defined in section 03 of part 241.

(d) For the purpose of this schedule, scheduled service shall be reported separately for: (1) Intra-Alaskan operations; (2) domestic operations, which shall include all operations within and between the 50 States of the United States (except Intra-Alaska), the District of Columbia, the Commonwealth of Puerto Rico and the United States Virgin Islands and Canadian transborder operations; (3) Atlantic operations (excluding Bermuda); (4) Pacific operations which shall include the North/Central Pacific, South Pacific (including Australia) and the Trust Territories; and (5) Latin American operations which shall include the Caribbean (including Bermuda and the Guianas), Mexico and South/Central America.

(e) For the purpose of this schedule, nonscheduled service shall be reported separately for domestic operations and international operations as defined in paragraph (d) above, except that domestic and international MAC operations shall be reported on separate lines.

(f) The cost data reported on each line shall represent the average cost of fuel, as determined at the station level, consumed in that entity.

(g) The cost of fuel shall include shrinkage but exclude (1) "through-put" and "in to plane" fees, *i.e.*, service charges or gallonage levies assessed by or against the fuel vendor or concessionaire and passed on to the carrier in a separately identifiable form and (2) nonrefundable Federal and State excise taxes. However, "through-put" and "in to plane" charges that cannot be identified or segregated from the cost of fuel shall remain a part of the cost of fuel as reported on this schedule.

(h) Each air carrier shall maintain records for each station showing the computation of fuel inventories and consumption for each fuel type. The periodic average cost method shall be used in computing fuel inventories and consumption. Under this method, an average unit cost for each fuel type shall be computed by dividing the total cost of fuel available (Beginning Inventory plus Purchases) by the total gallons available. The resulting unit cost shall then be used to determine the ending inventory and the total consumption costs to be reported on this schedule.

(i) Where amounts reported for a specific entity include other than Jet A fuel, a footnote shall be added indicating the number of gallons and applicable costs of such other fuel included in amounts reported for that entity.

(j) Where any adjustment(s) recorded on the books of the carrier results in a material distortion of the current month's schedule, carriers shall file a revised schedule P–12(a) for the month(s) affected.

(k) Data reported on this schedule shall be withheld from public release until the quarterly Form 41 P schedules for the calendar quarter to which the monthly schedules relate are due at the BTS. However, aggregate data may be released before that time without identifying individual carriers. Provisions governing the due dates for submitting the quarterly P schedules are contained in paragraphs (a) and (b) of section 22 of this part. Individual carrier fuel data withheld from public disclosure may be disclosed by the BTS to:

(1) Parties to any proceeding before the DOT to the extent such material is relevant and material to the issues in the proceeding upon a determination to this effect by the administrative law judge assigned to the case or by the DOT;

(2) Agencies and other components of the Federal Government for their internal use only; and

(3) Such persons and in such circumstances as the BTS determines to be in the public interest or consistent with its regulatory functions and responsibilities.

(Approved by the Office of Management and Budget under control number 2138–0013)

[ER–755, 37 FR 19726, Sept. 21, 1972, as amended by Amdt. 241–58, 54 FR 5597, Feb. 6, 1989]

EDITORIAL NOTE: For FEDERAL REGISTER citations affecting part 241 section 24, see the List of CFR Sections Affected, which appears in the Finding Aids section of the printed volume and at *www.govinfo.gov*.

TRAFFIC REPORTING REQUIREMENTS

Section 25 Traffic and Capacity Elements

General Instructions. (a) All prescribed reporting for traffic and capacity elements shall conform with the data compilation standards set forth in section 19—Uniform Classification of Operating Statistics.

(b) Carriers submitting Schedule T–100 shall use magnetic computer tape or IBM compatible disk for transmitting the prescribed data to the Department. Upon good cause shown, OAI may approve the request of a U.S. air carrier, under section 1–2 of this part, to use hardcopy data input forms or submit data via e-mail.

Schedule T–8—Report of all-cargo operations.

(a) This schedule shall be filed annually by all air carriers that conduct all-cargo operations under certificates issued under 49 U.S.C. 41103.

(b) [Reserved]

(c) *Statement of operations.* This statement shall include the following elements:

(1) Total operating revenue, categorized as follows:

(i) Transport revenues from the carriage of property in scheduled and nonscheduled service;

(ii) Transport revenues from the carriage of mail in scheduled and nonscheduled service; and

(iii) Transport-related revenues.

(2) Total operating expenses; and

(3) Operating profit or loss, computed by subtracting the total operating expenses from the total operating revenues.

(d) Summary of traffic and capacity statistics. This summary shall include the following elements:

(1) Total revenue ton-miles, which are the aircraft miles flown on each flight stage times the number of tons of revenue traffic carried on that stage. They shall be categorized as follows:

(i) Property; and

(ii) Mail.

(2) Revenue tons enplaned, reflecting the total revenue tons of cargo loaded on aircraft during the annual period;

(3) Available ton-miles, reflecting the total revenue ton-miles available for all-cargo service during the annual period, and computed by multiplying aircraft miles flown on each flight stage by the number of tons of aircraft capacity available for that stage;

(4) Aircraft miles flown, reflecting the total number of aircraft miles flown in cargo service during the annual period;

(5) Aircraft departures performed, reflecting the total number of take-offs performed in cargo service during the annual period; and

(6) Aircraft hours airborne, reflecting the aircraft hours of flight (from take-off to landing) performed in cargo service during the annual period.

Schedule T–100 U.S. Air Carrier Traffic and Capacity Data By Nonstop Segment and On-Flight Market

(a) Schedule T–100 collects detailed on-flight market and nonstop segment data on all revenue flights flown by U.S. certificated air carriers. This schedule is filed monthly. Separate data shall be reported for each operating entity (Latin America, Atlantic, Pacific; International, or Domestic) of the air carrier. Data for each operating entity shall be reported using the five digit entity code prescribed under section 19–5(c) of this part.

(b) Guidelines for reporting the automated monthly Schedule T–100 are included in the Appendix to this section.

(c) Reported data shall be compiled as aggregates of the basic data elements and service classes contained in sections 19–4 and 19–5 of this part.

(d) *Joint-service operations.* The air carrier in operational control of the aircraft (the carrier that uses its flight crews under its own FAA operating authority) must report joint-service operations.

(Approved by the Office of Management and Budget under control number 2138–0013)

[ER–755, 37 FR 19726, Sept. 21, 1972]

EDITORIAL NOTE: For FEDERAL REGISTER citations affecting part 241, section 25, see the List of CFR Sections Affected, which appears in the Finding Aids section of the printed volume and at *www.govinfo.gov*.

PART 243—PASSENGER MANIFEST INFORMATION

Sec.

AUTHORITY: 49 U.S.C. 40101, 40101nt., 40105, 40113, 40114, 41708, 41709, 41711, 41501, 41702, 41712, 44909, 46301, 46310, 46316; section 203 of Pub. L. 101–604, 104 Stat. 3066 (22 U.S.C. 5501–5513), Title VII of Pub. L. 104–264, 110 Stat. 3213 (22 U.S.C. 5501–5513) and Pub. L. 105–148, 111 Stat. 2681 (49 U.S.C. 41313.)

SOURCE: Docket No. OST–95–950, 63 FR 8280, Feb. 18, 1998, unless otherwise noted.

§ 243.1 Purpose.

The purpose of this part is to ensure that the U.S. government has prompt and adequate information in case of an aviation disaster on covered flight segments.

§ 243.3 Definitions.

Air piracy means any seizure of or exercise of control over an aircraft, by force or violence or threat of force or violence, or by any other form of intimidation, and with wrongful intent.

Aviation disaster means:

(1) An occurrence associated with the operation of an aircraft that takes place between the time any passengers have boarded the aircraft with the intention of flight and the time all such persons have disembarked or have been removed from the aircraft, and in which any person suffers death or serious injury, and in which the death or injury was caused by a crash, fire, collision, sabotage or accident;

(2) A missing aircraft; or

(3) An act of air piracy.

Contact means a person not on the covered flight or an entity that should be contacted in case of an aviation disaster. The contact need not have any particular relationship to a passenger.

Covered airline means:

(1) certificated air carriers, and

(2) foreign air carriers, except those that hold Department of Transportation authority to conduct operations in foreign air transportation using only small aircraft (*i.e.*, aircraft designed to have a maximum passenger capacity of not more than 60 seats or a maximum payload capacity of not more than 18,000 pounds).

Covered flight segment means a passenger-carrying flight segment operating to or from the United States (*i.e.*, the flight segment where the last point of departure or the first point of arrival is in the United States). A covered flight segment does not include a flight segment in which both the point of departure and point of arrival are in the United States.

Full name means the given name, middle initial or middle name, if any, and family name or surname as provided by the passenger.

Passenger means every person aboard a covered flight segment regardless of whether he or she paid for the transportation, had a reservation, or occupied a seat, except the crew. For the purposes of this part, passenger includes, but is not limited to, a revenue and non-revenue passenger, a person holding a confirmed reservation, a standby or walkup, a person rerouted from another flight or airline, an infant held upon a person's lap and a person occupying a jump seat. Airline personnel who are on board but not working on that particular flight segment would be considered passengers for the purpose of this part.

United States means the States comprising the United States of America, the District of Columbia, and the territories and possessions of the United States, including the territorial sea and the overlying airspace.

U.S. citizen means United States nationals as defined in 8 U.S.C. 1101(a)(22).

§ 243.5 Applicability.

This part applies to covered flight segments operated by covered airlines. (See § 243.3 of this part)

§ 243.7 Information collection requirements.

(a) For covered flight segments, each covered airline shall:

(1) Collect, or cause to be collected, the full name for each passenger who is a U.S. citizen. U.S.-citizen passengers for whom this information is not obtained shall not be boarded;

(2) Solicit, or cause to be solicited, a name and telephone number of a contact from each passenger who is a U.S. citizen; and

(3) Maintain a record of the information collected pursuant to this section.

(b) The covered airline operating the flight segment shall be responsible for ensuring compliance with paragraph (a) of this section.

§243.9 Procedures for collecting and maintaining the information.

Covered airlines may use any method or procedure to collect, store and transmit the required information, subject to the following conditions:

(a) Information on individual passengers shall be collected before each passenger boards the aircraft on a covered flight segment.

(b) The information shall be kept until all passengers have disembarked from the covered flight segment.

(c) The contact information collected pursuant to section 243.7(a)(2) of this part shall be kept confidential and released only to the U.S. Department of State, the National Transportation Safety Board (upon NTSB's request), and the U.S. Department of Transportation pursuant to oversight of this part. This paragraph does not preempt other governments or governmental agencies that have an independent, legal right to obtain this information.

(d) The contact information collected pursuant to section 243.7(a)(2) of this part shall only be used by covered airlines for notification of family members or listed contacts following an aviation disaster. The information shall not be used for commercial or marketing purposes.

§243.11 Transmission of information after an aviation disaster.

(a) Each covered airline shall inform the Managing Director of Overseas Citizen Services, Bureau of Consular Affairs, U.S. Department of State immediately upon learning of an aviation disaster involving a covered flight segment operated by that carrier. The Managing Director may be reached 24 hours a day through the Department of State Operations Center at (202) 647–1512.

(b) Each covered airline shall transmit a complete and accurate compilation of the information collected pursuant to §243.7 of this part to the U.S. Department of State as quickly as possible, but not later than 3 hours, after the carrier learns of an aviation disaster involving a covered flight segment operated by that carrier.

(c) Upon request, a covered airline shall transmit a complete and accurate compilation of the information collected pursuant to §243.7 of this part to the Director, Family Support Services, National Transportation Safety Board.

§243.13 Filing requirements.

(a) Each covered airline that operates one or more covered flight segments shall file with the U.S. Department of Transportation a brief statement summarizing how it will collect the passenger manifest information required by this part and transmit the information to the Department of State following an aviation disaster. This description shall include a contact at the covered airline, available at any time the covered airline is operating a covered flight segment, who can be consulted concerning information gathered pursuant to this part.

(b) Each covered airline shall file any contact change as well as a description of any significant change in its means of collecting or transmitting manifest information on or before the date the change is made.

(c) All filings under this section should be submitted to OST Docket 98–3305, Dockets Facility (SVC–121.30), U.S. Department of Transportation, 1200 New Jersey Avenue, SE., Washington, DC 20590. The statement shall be filed by July 1, 1998, or, for covered airlines beginning operations after July 1, 1998, prior to the date a covered airline operates a covered flight segment.

§243.15 Conflict with foreign laws.

(a) If a covered airline obtains a waiver in the manner described in this section, it will not be required to solicit, collect or transmit information under this part in countries where such solicitation or collection would violate applicable foreign law, but only to the extent it is established by the carrier that such solicitation or collection would violate applicable foreign law.

(b) Covered airlines that claim that such solicitation, collection or transmission would violate applicable foreign law in certain foreign countries shall file a petition requesting a waiver in the Docket Facility, on or before October 1, 1998, or on or before beginning service between that country and United States. Such petition shall include copies of the pertinent foreign law, as well as a certified translation, and shall include opinions of appropriate legal experts setting forth the basis for the conclusion that collection would violate such foreign law. Statements from foreign governments on the application of their laws will also be accepted.

(c) The U.S. Department of Transportation will notify the covered airline of the extent to which it has been satisfactorily established that compliance with all or part of the data collection requirements of this part would constitute a violation of foreign law.

(d) The U.S. Department of Transportation will maintain an up-to-date listing in OST Docket 98–3305 of countries where adherence to all or a portion of this part is not required because of a conflict with applicable foreign law.

[Doc. No. OST–95–950, 63 FR 8280, Feb. 18, 1998; 63 FR 9413, Feb. 25, 1998]

§ 243.17 Enforcement.

The U.S. Department of Transportation may at any time require a covered airline to produce a passenger manifest including emergency contacts and phone numbers for a specified covered flight segment to ascertain the effectiveness of the carrier's system. In addition, it may require from any covered airline further information about collection, storage and transmission procedures at any time. If the Department finds a covered airline's system to be deficient, it will require appropriate modifications, which must be implemented within the period specified by the Department. In addition, a covered airline not in compliance with this part may be subject to enforcement action by the Department.

PART 244—REPORTING TARMAC DELAY DATA

AUTHORITY: 49 U.S.C. 40101(a)(4), 40101(a)(9), 40113(a), 41702, and 41712.

SOURCE: Docket No. DOT–OST–2010–0140, 76 FR 23160, Apr. 25, 2011, unless otherwise noted.

§ 244.1 Definitions.

Arrival time is the instant when the pilot sets the aircraft parking brake after arriving at the airport gate or passenger unloading area. If the parking brake is not set, record the time for the opening of the passenger door. Also, for purposes of section 244.3 carriers using a Docking Guidance System (DGS) may record the official "gate-arrival time" when the aircraft is stopped at the appropriate parking mark.

Cancelled flight means a flight operation that was not operated, but was listed in an air carrier or a foreign air carrier's computer reservation system within seven calendar days of the scheduled departure.

Certificated air carrier means a U.S. carrier holding a certificate issued under 49 U.S.C. 41102 to conduct passenger service or holding an exemption to conduct passenger operations under 49 U.S.C. 40109.

Commuter air carrier means a U.S. carrier that has been found fit under 49 U.S.C. 41738 and is authorized to carry passengers on at least five round trips per week on at least one route between two or more points according to a published flight schedule using small aircraft as defined in 14 CFR 298.2.

Covered carrier means a certificated carrier, a commuter carrier, or a foreign air carrier operating to, from, or within the United States, conducting scheduled passenger service or public charter service with at least one aircraft having a designed passenger seating capacity of 30 or more seats.

Diverted flight means a flight which is operated from the scheduled origin point to a point other than the scheduled destination point in the carrier's published schedule. For example, a carrier has a published schedule for a flight from A to B to C. If the carrier were to actually fly an A to C operation, the A to B segment is a diverted flight, and the B to C segment is a cancelled flight. The same would apply if the flight were to operate from A to an airport other than B or C.

Foreign air carrier means a carrier that is not a citizen of the United States as defined in 49 U.S.C. 40102(a) that holds a foreign air carrier permit issued under 49 U.S.C. 41302 or an exemption issued under 49 U.S.C. 40109 authorizing direct foreign air transportation.

Gate departure time is the instant when the pilot releases the aircraft parking brake after passengers have boarded and aircraft doors have closed. In cases where the flight returned to the departure gate before wheels-off time and departs a second time, the reportable gate departure time for purposes of this part is the last gate departure time before wheels-off time. In cases of a return to the gate after wheels-off time, the reportable gate departure time is the last gate departure time before the gate return. If passengers were boarded without the parking brake being set, the reportable gate departure time is the time that the last passenger door was closed. Also, the official "gate-departure time" may be based on aircraft movement for carriers using a Docking Guidance System (DGS). For example, one DGS records gate departure time when the aircraft moves more than 1 meter from the appropriate parking mark within 15 seconds. Fifteen seconds is then subtracted from the recorded time to obtain the appropriate "out" time.

Gate Return time means the time that an aircraft that has left the boarding gate returns to a gate or other position at an airport for the purpose of allowing passengers the opportunity to disembark from the aircraft.

Large hub airport means an airport that accounts for at least 1.00 percent of the total enplanements in the United States.

Medium hub airport means an airport accounting for at least 0.25 percent but less than 1.00 percent of the total enplanements in the United States.

Non-hub airport means an airport with 10,000 or more annual enplanements but less than 0.05 percent of the total enplanements in the United States.

Small hub airport means an airport accounting for at least 0.05 percent but less than 0.25 percent of the total enplanements in the United States.

Tarmac delay means the holding of an aircraft on the ground either before taking off or after landing with no opportunity for its passengers to deplane.

§ 244.2 Applicability.

(a) Except as provided in paragraph (b) of this section, this part applies to U.S. certificated air carriers, U.S. commuter air carriers and foreign air carriers that operate passenger service to or from a U.S. airport with at least one aircraft that has an original manufacturer's design capacity of 30 or more seats. Covered carriers must report all passenger operations that experience a tarmac time of more than 3 hours at a U.S. airport.

(b) For foreign air carriers that operate charter flights from foreign airports to U.S. airports, and return to foreign airports, and do not pick up any new passengers in the U.S., the charter flights are not flights subject to the reporting requirements of this part.

(c) U.S. carriers that submit Part 234 Airline Service Quality Performance Reports must submit 3-hour tarmac delay information for public charter flights and international passenger flights to or from any U.S. large hub airport, medium hub airport, small hub airport and non-hub airport. These carriers are already required to submit such information for domestic scheduled flights to or from U.S. large hub airports under art 234 of this chapter. These carriers that are covered by part 234 need only submit information for flights with tarmac delays of more than 3 hours under this part 244 for domestic scheduled passenger flights to or from any U.S. medium hub airport, small hub airport and non-hub airport to the extent they do not report such information under 14 CFR 234.7.

[Docket No. DOT–OST–2010–0140, 76 FR 23160, Apr. 25, 2011, as amended by Dockt. No. DOT–OST–2014–0056, 81 FR 76827, Nov. 3, 2016]

§ 244.3 Reporting of tarmac delay data.

(a) Each covered carrier shall file BTS Form 244 "Tarmac Delay Report" with the Office of Airline Information of the Department's Bureau of Transportation Statistics setting forth the information for each of its covered flights that experienced a tarmac delay of more than 3 hours, including diverted flights and cancelled flights on which the passengers were boarded and then deplaned before the cancellation. The reports are due within 15 days after the end of any month during which the carrier experienced any reportable tarmac delay of more than 3 hours at a U.S. airport. The reports shall be made in the form and manner set forth in accounting and reporting directives issued by the Director, Office of Airline Information, and shall contain the following information:

(1) Carrier code

(2) Flight number

(3) Departure airport (three letter code)

(4) Arrival airport (three letter code)

(5) Date of flight operation (year/month/day)

(6) Gate departure time (actual) in local time

(7) Gate arrival time (actual) in local time

(8) Wheels-off time (actual) in local time

(9) Wheels-on time (actual) in local time

(10) Aircraft tail number

(11) Total ground time away from gate for all gate return/fly return at origin airports including cancelled flights

(12) Longest time away from gate for gate return or canceled flight

(13) Three letter code of airport where flight diverted

(14) Wheels-on time at diverted airport

(15) Total time away from gate at diverted airport

(16) Longest time away from gate at diverted airport

(17) Wheels-off time at diverted airport

(b) The same information required by paragraph (a)(13) through (17) of this section must be provided for each subsequent diverted airport landing.

[Docket No. DOT–OST–2010–0140, 76 FR 23160, Apr. 25, 2011, as amended by Docket No. DOT–OST–2014–0056, 81 FR 76827, Nov. 3, 2016]

PART 247—DIRECT AIRPORT-TO-AIRPORT MILEAGE RECORDS

AUTHORITY: 49 U.S.C. chapter 401.

SOURCE: Amdt. 247–2, 56 FR 67170, Dec. 30, 1991, unless otherwise noted.

§ 247.1 Official mileage record of the Department of Transportation.

The direct airport-to-airport mileage record now maintained, and as hereafter amended or revised from time to time by the Office of Airline Information of the Bureau of Transportation Statistics of the Department of Transportation in the regular performance of its duties, is hereby adopted as the official mileage record of the Department and the mileages set forth therein shall be used in all instances where it shall be necessary to determine direct airport-to-airport mileages pursuant to the provisions of Titles IV and X of the Federal Aviation Act of 1958, as amended, or any rule, regulation, or order of the Department pursuant thereto.

[Amdt. 247–2, 56 FR 67170, Dec. 30, 1991, as amended at 60 FR 66725, Dec. 26, 1995]

PART 248—SUBMISSION OF AUDIT REPORTS

AUTHORITY: 49 U.S.C. 329 and chapters 41102, 41708, and 41709.

SOURCE: ER–420, 29 FR 13799, Oct. 7, 1964, unless otherwise noted.

§ 248.1 Applicability.

The requirements of this part shall be applicable to all air carriers subject to the requirements of part 241 of this subchapter.

§ 248.2 Filing of audit reports.

(a) Whenever any air carrier subject to § 248.1 shall have caused an annual audit of its books, records, and accounts to be made by independent public accountants, such air carrier shall file with the Office of Airline Information, in duplicate, a special report consisting of a true and complete copy of the audit report submitted by such independent public accountants, including all schedules, exhibits, and certificates included in, attached to, or submitted with or separately as a part of, the audit report.

(b) Each air carrier subject to § 248.1 that does not cause an annual audit to be made of its books, records, and accounts for any fiscal year shall, at the close of such fiscal year file with the Board's Office of the Comptroller, as a part of its periodic reports, a statement that no such audit has been performed.

(c) Carriers shall submit their audit reports or their statement that no audit was performed in a format specified in accounting and reporting directives issued by the Bureau of Transportation Statistics' Director of Airline Information.

(Approved by the Office of Management and Budget under control number 2138–0004)

[ER–1351, 48 FR 32756, July 19, 1983, as amended by ER–1362, 48 FR 46265, Oct. 12, 1983; 60 FR 66725, Dec. 26, 1995; 75 FR 41584, July 16, 2010]

§ 248.4 Time for filing reports.

The report required by this part shall be filed with the Office of Airline Information within 15 days after the due date of the appropriate periodic BTS Form 41 Report, filed for the 12-month period covered by the audit report, or the date the accountant submits its audit report to the air carrier, whichever is later.

[ER–1351, 48 FR 32756, July 19, 1983, as amended at 60 FR 66725, Dec. 26, 1995]

§ 248.5 Withholding from public disclosure.

The special reports required to be filed by § 248.2 shall be withheld from public disclosure, until further order of the BTS, if such treatment is requested by the air carrier at the time of filing.

[ER–420, 29 FR 13799, Oct. 7, 1964, as amended at 60 FR 66725, Dec. 26, 1995]

PART 249—PRESERVATION OF AIR CARRIER RECORDS

Subpart A—General Instructions

Subpart B—Preservation of Records by Carrier

Subpart C—Regulations Relating to the Truth-in-Lending Act

AUTHORITY: 49 U.S.C. 329 and chapters 401, 411, 413, 417.

SOURCE: ER–1214, 46 FR 25415, May 6, 1981, unless otherwise noted.

NOTE: The recordkeeping requirements contained in this part have been approved by the Office of Management and Budget under control number 2138–0006.

Subpart A—General Instructions

§ 249.1 Applicability.

Subparts A and B of this part apply to:

(a) Air carriers, as defined in 49 U.S.C. 40102, that hold either certificates of public convenience and necessity or certificates for all-cargo air service.

(b) Public charter operators, as defined in part 380 of this chapter.

(c) Overseas military personnel charter operators, as defined in part 372 of this chapter.

[ER–1214, 46 FR 25415, May 6, 1981, as amended at 60 FR 66725, Dec. 26, 1995]

§ 249.2 Definitions.

For the purposes of this part:

Authorized representatives of the DOT means any persons, including special agents and auditors, designated by the DOT to perform inspections, audits, or examinations within the purview of the DOT's authority.

Certificated air carrier means the holder of a certificate of public convenience and necessity issued by the Department of Transportation under 49 U.S.C. 41102 or a certificate for all-cargo air service issued by the Department of Transportation under 49 U.S.C. 41103.

Final adjudication means the expiration date of the last possible period of review or reconsideration of a given case, by the DOT or by a court, that is provided by applicable statute or regulation.

Open mail rate period means the time interval between the date of institution of a new mail rate proceeding or the start of service over a new route for which no mail rate has previously been fixed, and the date upon which a DOT order setting the final mail rate becomes legally effective.

Pending case means any case that the DOT is empowered to hear before its final adjudication.

Records include all documents that are related to, or constitute integral links in developing the history of, or facts regarding, financial transactions or physical operations of a particular segment, operating division, or entire system of the carrier's operations. The term includes any copy of initially prepared documents which bear approvals, comments, or notations which were added and are of significance to a full explanation of recorded facts or information. The term *records* means not only accounting records in a limited technical sense but all other evidentiary accounts of events such as memoranda, correspondence, working sheets, tabulating equipment listings punched cards, computer-produced listings, microfilm, and magnetic storage media (*i.e.*, magnetic tapes, disks). The term *records* also means microform and/or tape reproductions of documents made as authorized by this subpart. In addition, the term *records* includes any of the above-described materials coming into the possession of the air carrier through merger, consolidation, succession, transfer, or other acquisition.

Supporting papers (records) means any group of documentary papers, such as memoranda, correspondence, working sheets, etc., that assist in upholding the accuracy or clarity of related records.

[ER–1214, 46 FR 25415, May 6, 1981, as amended at 60 FR 66725, Dec. 26, 1995]

§ 249.3 Preservation of records.

(a) All records listed in §§ 249.20 and 249.21 may be preserved on either paper or nonerasable microfilm (see § 249.4). However, a paper or microfilm record need not be created to satisfy the requirements of this part if the record is initially prepared in a machine-readable medium such as punched cards, magnetic tapes, and disks. The records maintained in machine-readable media and the underlying data used in their preparation shall be preserved for the periods prescribed in §§ 249.20 and 249.21. A paper or microfilm record shall not be destroyed after transfer to a machine-readable medium before expiration of the prescribed period: however, a waiver permitting the early destruction of paper or microfilm records transferred to a machine-readable medium may be granted by the Director, Office of Airline Information, when it is demonstrated by the requesting carrier that the substantive purpose of the retention requirement will be met by retention of the information in machine-readable form (see § 249.10).

(b) Each record kept in a machine-readable medium shall be accompanied by a statement clearly indicating the type of data included in the record and certifying that the information contained in it is complete and accurate. This statement shall be executed by a person having personal knowledge of the facts contained in the records. The records shall be indexed and retained in such a manner so that they are easily accessible, and the carrier shall have the facilities available to locate, identify and reproduce the records in readable form without loss of clarity. Authorized representatives of the DOT shall be given immediate access to the carrier's facilities upon request.

(c) If any record which must be retained under the provisions of §§ 249.20

and 249.21 is included as an exhibit to another document which must also be retained, the carrier need only keep in its files one copy of the record to satisfy these record retention requirements. In these cases, the carrier shall establish adequate cross-references to assist in locating the record.

(d) The provisions in this part do not excuse noncompliance with requirements of any other governmental body, Federal or State, prescribing longer retention periods for any records.

[ER–1214, 46 FR 25415, May 6, 1981, as amended at 60 FR 66725, Dec. 26, 1995]

§249.4 Photographic copies.

(a) Any record may be transferred to nonerasable microfilm (including microfiche, computer output microfilm, and aperture cards) at any time. Records so maintained on microfilm shall satisfy the minimum requirements listed in paragraphs (b) through (f) of this section.

(b) The microfilm shall be of a quality that can be easily read and that can be reproduced in paper similar in size to an original without loss of clarity or detail during the periods the records are required to be retained in §§249.20 and 249.21.

(c) Microfilm records shall be indexed and retained in such a manner as will render them readily accessible, and the company shall have facilities available to locate, identify and read the microfilm and reproduce in paper form. Authorized representatives of the DOT shall be given immediate access to these facilities upon request.

(d) Any significant characteristic, feature, or other attribute which microfilm will not preserve shall be clearly indicated at the beginning of each roll of film or series of microfilm records if applicable to all records on the roll or series, or on the individual record, as appropriate.

(e) The printed side of printed forms need not be microfilmed for each record if nothing has been added to the printed matter common to all such forms, but an identified specimen of the form shall be on the film for reference.

(f) Each roll of film or series of microfilm records shall include a microfilm of a certificate stating that the photographs are direct and facsimile reproductions of the original records and they have been made in accordance with prescribed regulations. Such a certificate shall be executed by a person having personal knowledge of these facts. Where the microfilm is computer output, the microfilm certificate shall state that the information is complete and accurate.

[ER–1214, 46 FR 25415, May 6, 1981, as amended at 60 FR 66725, Dec. 26, 1995]

§249.5 Storage of records.

Each carrier shall provide reasonable protection from damage by fire, floods, and other hazards for records subject to the provisions of this part.

§249.6 Destruction of records.

(a) Upon the expiration of the period of preservation prescribed in this regulation, records may be destroyed at the option of the carrier.

(b) Unless otherwise specified, duplicate copies of records may be destroyed at any time if they contain no significant information not shown on the originals.

§249.7 Restrictions on record destruction.

(a) Each carrier that has been named a party to a pending mail rate case shall retain all records remaining in its custody as of the beginning of an "open mail rate period" until the occurrence of one of the following contingencies, whichever is first:

(1) Final adjudication of a DOT order fixing the final mail compensation payable for services rendered during an "open mail rate period."

(2) Receipt of a notice issued by the Director, Office of Airline Information in response to a written application filed by the carrier, authorizing the destruction of specifically identified categories of records. An application should be filed when the carrier believes that certain categories of records are not relevant to the proper processing of a pending mail proceeding. The application should list those categories of records which the carrier wants to destroy and its reasons for believing that the records are not necessary or useful in determining its satutory mail pay.

(b) Each carrier shall preserve records supporting the computation of subsidy mail pay in accordance with the provisions of § 249.20 unless the carrier has been advised that these computations are subject to further review and disposition by the Board. When the DOT is still reviewing the compensation amount after expiration of the normal retention period specified in § 249.20, these records must be retained until the carrier is notified by the Director, Office of Airline Information, that the records may be destroyed.

(c) Each carrier that has been named a party to an enforcement proceeding or against whom a third-party complaint has been filed shall retain all records relating to the case until the receipt of formal notification from the Director, Office of Airline Information, following a written application from the carrier, which authorizes the destruction of these records.

(d) Each carrier that has been named a party to a pending case which is not of a type discussed in paragraphs (a), (b), and (c) of this section, shall preserve all records according to the provisions of § 249.20 unless the Director, Office of Airline Information, notifies the carrier in writing that specific records shall be preserved until final adjudication of the pending case.

(e) Each carrier that is a party to litigation in a Federal court of which the DOT is also a party shall retain all records relating to the case until the receipt of formal notification from the Director, Office of Airline Information, following a written application from the carrier, which authorizes the destruction of these records.

[ER–1214, 46 FR 25415, May 6, 1981, as amended at 60 FR 66725, Dec. 26, 1995]

§ 249.8 Premature loss or destruction of records.

If records are destroyed or lost before the expiration of the prescribed retention period, a statement shall be prepared and submitted to the Director, Office of Airline Information, which lists, as accurately as possible, the unavailable records and describes the circumstances under which they became unavailable.

[ER–1214, 46 FR 25415, May 6, 1981, as amended at 60 FR 66725, Dec. 26, 1995]

§ 249.9 Carriers going out of business.

The records referred to in these regulations may be destroyed after the business is discontinued and the carrier is completely liquidated. The records may not be destroyed until dissolution is final and all transactions and litigations are completed. When a carrier is merged with another company which is regulated by the DOT, the successor company shall preserve records of the merged company in accordance with these regulations.

[ER–1214, 46 FR 25415, May 6, 1981, as amended at 60 FR 66725, Dec. 26, 1995]

§ 249.10 Waiver of requirements.

A waiver from any provision of this regulation may be made by the Director, Office of Airline Information, upon the Director's own initiative or upon submission of a written request by a carrier or group of carriers. Each request for waiver shall demonstrate that unusual circumstances warrant a departure from prescribed retention periods, procedures, or techniques, or that compliance with the prescribed requirements would impose an unreasonable burden on the carrier, and that granting the waiver would be in the public interest.

[ER–1214, 46 FR 25415, May 6, 1981, as amended at 60 FR 66726, Dec. 26, 1995]

Subpart B—Preservation of Records by Carrier

§ 249.20 Preservation of records by certificated air carriers.

Each certificated air carrier shall retain its records according to the provisions of this section. Unless otherwise specified in the "Schedule of Records," each retention period shall begin on the date when the records are created or otherwise come into the possession of the carrier.

SCHEDULE OF RECORDS

[See footnote at end of table]

Category of records	Retention period
1. General and subsidiary ledgers or their equivalents:	
(a) General ledgers; subsidiary or auxiliary ledgers	3 years.
(b) Indexes to general and subsidiary ledgers	Do.
2. Journals and journal vouchers:	
(a) General and subsidiary journals, and journal vouchers	3 years.
(b) Papers forming a part of, or necessary to explain, journal entries; entry numbers	Do.
3. Voucher distribution registers or their equivalent	Do.
4. Accounts receivables and payables:	
(a) Traffic accounts receivable or payable, detailed journals and ledgers or their equivalents, together with supporting papers.	Do.
(b) General accounts receivable or payable, detailed journals and ledgers or their equivalents, together with supporting papers.	Do.
(c) Copies of invoices issued by the carrier which have been settled and all supporting papers.	1 year.
(d) Copies of Postal Service Forms: Weekly Summary of Airmail Dispatch (No. 2729) and POD Airmail Exemption Record (No. 2734) supporting mail pay claims which have been settled.	30 days.
5. Subsidy records:	
(a) For each calendar year, all monthly records of operations, such as tabulations and summaries of miles flown and passenger-miles flown, pertaining to or part of operational records relevant to computation of subsidy mail pay.	3 years.
(b) For each calendar year, all basic original documents, such as pilots' flight logs and passenger lists relevant to a determination of the validity of a carrier's operations described in item (a) above.	Do.
6. The papers, records, or other evidence supporting financial and statistical reports to the BTS. These should include among others the following specific records: Internal administrative or operating reports; system reports of aircraft movements by trip number, showing arrivals, departures, flight delays and related information; bonds and other long-term debt records; stock records; corporate organization records; financial data in support of subsidy claims; minutes of meetings; carrier internal reports on internal controls and other internal audits and procedural studies; operational, management, accounting, financial, and legal service contracts and agreements; records and agreements relating to the lease or purchase and sale of company assets, including title papers, deeds, and similar records; insurance records; property and equipment records; tax records; accountants' and auditors' reports; records of receipts and disbursements including bank statements, check registers and cancelled checks; payroll registers of salaries and wages paid; cost accounting records for work orders; inventories of materials and supplies; and other source documents.	Do.
7. Funds reports and estimates of funds	1 year.
8. Consumer complaints:	
(a) Initial correspondence and record of action taken	3 years.
(b) Initial trip reports:	
(1) Traffic Data: Basic documents showing the number of passengers, and pounds of mail and property carried.	([1]).
(c) Reservations reports and records:	
(1) Cards and charts constituting original source of passengers' names, telephone numbers, etc.	2 months.
(2) Telegrams and radio messages relating to the clearance of space, passenger dispatching, etc.	1 month.
(d) System report of airplane movements by trip number showing arrivals, departures, delays and related information.	3 years.
(e) Sales reports:	
(1) Sales ticket or other similar reports from stations, offices and agents	2 years.
(f) Auditors' coupons	1 year.
(g) Air waybills	Do.
(h) Flight coupons	Do.
(i) Ticket refund claims records and reports	Do.
(j) Records and reports relating to errors, oversales, irregularities and delays in handling passengers.	Do.
9. All documents which relate to the furnishing of transportation to candidates for political office or persons acting on their behalf which are required to be maintained following §374a.7 of the subchapter.	2 years.

SCHEDULE OF RECORDS—Continued

[See footnote at end of table]

Category of records	Retention period
10. Correspondence and working papers relating to rate and route proceedings	3 years.

[1] One year-mail-property; 2 years-passengers.

[ER–1214, 46 FR 25415, May 6, 1981, as amended at 60 FR 66726, Dec. 26, 1995]

§ 249.21 Preservation of records by public charter operators and overseas military personnel charter operators.

Each operator authorized under parts 372 and 380 of this chapter shall retain the following records for 6 months after completion or cancellation of the flight or series of flights. The records shall be made available upon request of an authorized representative of the DOT.

(a) All receipts and statements of travel agents and all other documents which show deposits made by each charter participant or which show refunds to charter participants.

(b) All receipts and statements of travel agents and all other documents which show or reflect commissions received, paid to, or deducted by travel agents in connection with the flight or series of flights.

(c) All statements, invoices, bills, and receipts from suppliers for furnishing of goods or services in connection with the tour or series of tours.

(d) All customer reservations records for each flight.

(e) All contracts with individual tour participants.

(f) All bank statements and reconciliations for escrow bank accounts opened and maintained in accordance with DOT regulations.

[ER–1214, 46 FR 25415, May 6, 1981, as amended at 60 FR 66726, Dec. 26, 1995]

Subpart C—Regulations Relating to the Truth-in-Lending Act

§ 249.30 Applicability.

This subpart is applicable to all air carriers and foreign air carriers as defined in 49 U.S.C. 40102, including, without limitation, direct carriers, air taxi operators registered under part 298 of this chapter, indirect air carriers registered under part 296 of this chapter, charter operators authorized under parts 372 and 380 of this chapter, and foreign air carriers holding permits to engage in indirect foreign air transportation issued under 49 U.S.C. 41302.

[ER–1214, 46 FR 25415, May 6, 1981, as amended at 60 FR 66726, Dec. 26, 1995]

§ 249.31 Preservation and inspection of evidence of compliance.

Air carriers and foreign air carriers shall preserve evidence of compliance with the requirements imposed under Regulation Z of the Board of Governors of the Federal Reserve System (12 CFR part 226), implementing the provisions of Title I (Truth in Lending) and Title V (General Provisions) of the Consumer Credit Protection Act, as amended (15 U.S.C. 1601 *et seq.*) other than the advertising requirements under § 226.10 of regulation Z. This evidence shall be preserved for no less than 2 years after the date each disclosure is required to be made and shall be made available for inspection by authorized representatives of the DOT.

[ER–1214, 46 FR 25415, May 6, 1981, as amended at 60 FR 66726, Dec. 26, 1995]

PART 250—OVERSALES

AUTHORITY: 49 U.S.C. 329 and chapters 41102, 41301, 41708, 41709, and 41712.

SOURCE: ER-1306, 47 FR 52985, Nov. 24, 1982, unless otherwise noted.

§ 250.1 Definitions.

Airport means the airport at which the direct or connecting flight, on which the passenger holds confirmed reserved space, is planned to arrive or some other airport serving the same metropolitan area, provided that transportation to the other airport is accepted (*i.e.*, used) by the passenger.

Alternate transportation means air transportation with a confirmed reservation at no additional charge, operated by a carrier as defined below, or other transportation accepted and used by the passenger in the case of denied boarding.

Carrier means: (1) a direct air carrier, except a helicopter operator, holding a certificate issued by the Department of Transportation pursuant to 49 U.S.C. 41102 or that has been found fit to conduct commuter operations under 49 U.S.C. 41738, or an exemption from 49 U.S.C. 41102, authorizing the scheduled transportation of persons; or (2) a foreign air carrier holding a permit issued by the Department pursuant to 49 U.S.C. 41302, or an exemption from that provision, authorizing the scheduled foreign air transportation of persons.

Class of service means seating in the same cabin class such as First, Business, or Economy class, or in the same seating zone if the carrier has more than one seating product in the same cabin such as Economy and Premium Economy class.

Confirmed reserved space means space on a specific date and on a specific flight and class of service of a carrier which has been requested by a passenger, including a passenger with a "zero fare ticket," and which the carrier or its agent has verified, by appropriate notation on the ticket or in any other manner provided therefore by the carrier, as being reserved for the accommodation of the passenger.

Fare means the price paid for air transportation including all mandatory taxes and fees. It does not include ancillary fees for optional services.

Stopover means a deliberate interruption of a journey by the passenger, scheduled to exceed 4 hours, at a point between the place of departure and the final destination.

Zero fare ticket means a ticket acquired without a substantial monetary payment such as by using frequent flyer miles or vouchers, or a consolidator ticket obtained after a monetary payment that does not show a fare amount on the ticket. A zero fare ticket does not include free or reduced rate air transportation provided to airline employees and guests.

[ER-1306, 47 FR 52985, Nov. 24, 1982, as amended by ER-1337, 48 FR 29680, June 28, 1983; 68 FR 52836, Sept. 8, 2003; Doc. No. OST-01-9325, 73 FR 21033, Apr. 18, 2008; Doc. No. DOT-OST-2010-0140, 76 FR 23161, Apr. 25, 2011]

§ 250.2 Applicability.

This part applies to every carrier, as defined in § 250.1, with respect to scheduled flight segments using an aircraft that has a designed passenger capacity of 30 or more passenger seats, operating in (1) interstate air transportation or (2) foreign air transportation with respect to nonstop flight segments originating at a point within the United States.

[Doc. No. OST-01-9325, 73 FR 21033, Apr. 18, 2008]

§ 250.2a Policy regarding denied boarding.

In the event of an oversold flight, every carrier shall ensure that the smallest practicable number of persons holding confirmed reserved space on that flight are denied boarding involuntarily.

§ 250.2b Carriers to request volunteers for denied boarding.

(a) In the event of an oversold flight, every carrier shall request volunteers for denied boarding before using any other boarding priority. A "volunteer" is a person who responds to the carrier's request for volunteers and who willingly accepts the carriers' offer of compensation, in any amount, in exchange for relinquishing the confirmed reserved space. Any other passenger denied boarding is considered for purposes of this part to have been denied boarding involuntarily, even if that passenger accepts the denied boarding compensation.

(b) Every carrier shall advise each passenger solicited to volunteer for denied boarding, no later than the time the carrier solicits that passenger to volunteer, whether he or she is in danger of being involuntarily denied boarding and, if so, the compensation the carrier is obligated to pay if the passenger is involuntarily denied boarding. If an insufficient number of volunteers come forward, the carrier may deny boarding to other passengers in accordance with its boarding priority rules.

(c) If a carrier offers free or reduced rate air transportation as compensation to volunteers, the carrier must disclose all material restrictions, including but not limited to administrative fees, advance purchase or capacity restrictions, and blackout dates applicable to the offer before the passenger decides whether to give up his or her confirmed reserved space on the flight in exchange for the free or reduced rate transportation. If the free or reduced rate air transportation is offered orally to potential volunteers, the carrier shall also orally provide a brief description of the material restrictions on that transportation at the same time that the offer is made.

[ER–1337, 48 FR 29680, June 28, 1983, as amended at 68 FR 52836, Sept. 8, 2003; Doc. No. OST–01–9325, 73 FR 21034, Apr. 18, 2008; Doc. No. DOT–OST–2010–0140, 76 FR 23161, Apr. 25, 2011; Docket No. DOT–OST–2014–0056, 81 FR 76827, Nov. 3, 2016]

§ 250.3 Boarding priority rules.

(a) Every carrier shall establish priority rules and criteria for determining which passengers holding confirmed reserved space shall be denied boarding on an oversold flight in the event that an insufficient number of volunteers come forward. Such rules and criteria shall reflect the obligations of the carrier set forth in §§ 250.2a and 250.2b to minimize involuntary denied boarding and to request volunteers, and shall be written in such manner as to be understandable and meaningful to the average passenger. Such rules and criteria shall not make, give, or cause any undue or unreasonable preference or advantage to any particular person or subject any particular person to any unjust or unreasonable prejudice or disadvantage in any respect whatsoever.

(b) Boarding priority factors may include, but are not limited to, the following:

(1) A passenger's time of check-in;

(2) Whether a passenger has a seat assignment before reaching the departure gate for carriers that assign seats;

(3) The fare paid by a passenger;

(4) A passenger's frequent-flyer status; and

(5) A passenger's disability or status as an unaccompanied minor.

[ER–1306, 47 FR 52985, Nov. 24, 1982, as amended by ER–1337, 48 FR 29680, June 28, 1983; Doc. No. OST–01–9325, 73 FR 21034, Apr. 18, 2008]

§ 250.5 Amount of denied boarding compensation for passengers denied boarding involuntarily.

(a) Subject to the exceptions provided in § 250.6, a carrier to whom this part applies as described in § 250.2 shall pay compensation in interstate air transportation to passengers who are denied boarding involuntarily from an oversold flight as follows:

(1) No compensation is required if the carrier offers alternate transportation that, at the time the arrangement is made, is planned to arrive at the airport of the passenger's first stopover, or if none, the airport of the passenger's final destination not later than one hour after the planned arrival time of the passenger's original flight;

(2) Compensation shall be 200% of the fare to the passenger's destination or first stopover, with a maximum of $675, if the carrier offers alternate transportation that, at the time the arrangement is made, is planned to arrive at the airport of the passenger's first stopover, or if none, the airport of the passenger's final destination more than one hour but less than two hours after the planned arrival time of the passenger's original flight; and

(3) Compensation shall be 400% of the fare to the passenger's destination or

first stopover, with a maximum of $1,350, if the carrier does not offer alternate transportation that, at the time the arrangement is made, is planned to arrive at the airport of the passenger's first stopover, or if none, the airport of the passenger's final destination less than two hours after the planned arrival time of the passenger's original flight.

(b) Subject to the exceptions provided in §250.6, a carrier to whom this part applies as described in §250.2 shall pay compensation to passengers in foreign air transportation who are denied boarding involuntarily at a U.S. airport from an oversold flight as follows:

(1) No compensation is required if the carrier offers alternate transportation that, at the time the arrangement is made, is planned to arrive at the airport of the passenger's first stopover, or if not, the airport of the passenger's final destination not later than one hour after the planned arrival time of the passenger's original flight;

(2) Compensation shall be 200% of the fare to the passenger's destination or first stopover, with a maximum of $675, if the carrier offers alternate transportation that, at the time the arrangement is made, is planned to arrive at the airport of the passenger's first stopover, or if not, the airport of the passenger's final destination more than one hour but less than four hours after the planned arrival time of the passenger's original flight; and

(3) Compensation shall be 400% of the fare to the passenger's destination or first stopover, with a maximum of $1,350, if the carrier does not offer alternate transportation that, at the time the arrangement is made, is planned to arrive at the airport of the passenger's first stopover, or if not, the airport of the passenger's final destination less than four hours after the planned arrival time of the passenger's original flight.

(c) Carriers may offer free or reduced rate air transportation in lieu of the cash or check due under paragraphs (a) and (b) of this section, if—

(1) The value of the transportation benefit offered, excluding any fees or other mandatory charges applicable for using the free or reduced rate air transportation, is equal to or greater than the cash/check payment otherwise required;

(2) The carrier fully informs the passenger of the amount of cash/check compensation that would otherwise be due and that the passenger may decline the transportation benefit and receive the cash/check payment; and

(3) The carrier fully discloses all material restrictions, including but not limited to, administrative fees, advance purchase or capacity restrictions, and blackout dates applicable to the offer, on the use of such free or reduced rate transportation before the passenger decides to give up the cash/check payment in exchange for such transportation. (See also §250.9(c)).

(d) The requirements of this section apply to passengers with "zero fare tickets." The fare paid by these passengers for purposes of calculating denied boarding compensation shall be the lowest cash, check, or credit card payment charged for a ticket in the same class of service on that flight.

(e) The Department of Transportation will review the maximum denied boarding compensation amounts prescribed in this part every two years except for the first review, which will take place in 2012 in order to put the reviews specified in this section on the same cycle as the reviews of domestic baggage liability limits specified in 14 CFR 254.6. The Department will use any increase in the Consumer Price Index for All Urban Consumers (CPI–U) as of July of each review year to calculate the increased maximum compensation amounts. The Department will use the following formula:

(1) Current Denied Boarding Compensation limit in section 250.5(a)(2) multiplied by (a/b) rounded to the nearest $25 where:

a = July CPI–U of year of current adjustment
b = the CPI–U figure in August, 2011 when the inflation adjustment provision was added to Part 250.

(2) The Denied Boarding Compensation limit in §250.5(a)(3) shall be twice the revised limit for §250.5(a)(2).

(3) The Denied Boarding Compensation limit in paragraph (b)(2) shall be the same as the revised limit for paragraph (a)(2) of this section, and the Denied Boarding Compensation limit in

paragraph (b)(3) shall be twice the revised limit for paragraph (a)(2) of this section.

(f) In addition to the denied boarding compensation specified in this part, a carrier shall refund all unused ancillary fees for optional services paid by a passenger who is voluntarily or involuntarily denied boarding. The carrier is not required to refund the ancillary fees for services that are provided with respect to the passenger's alternate transportation.

[Doc. No. DOT–OST–2010–0140, 76 FR 23162, Apr. 25, 2011, as amended by Doc. No. DOT–OST–2015–0104, 80 FR 30147, May 27, 2015; Doc. No. DOT–OST–2014–0056, 81 FR 76827, Nov. 3, 2016]

§ 250.6 Exceptions to eligibility for denied boarding compensation.

A passenger denied boarding involuntarily from an oversold flight shall not be eligible for denied boarding compensation if:

(a) The passenger does not comply fully with the carrier's contract of carriage or tariff provisions regarding ticketing, reconfirmation, check-in, and acceptability for transportation;

(b) The flight for which the passenger holds confirmed reserved space is unable to accommodate that passenger because of substitution of equipment of lesser capacity when required by operational or safety reasons; or, on an aircraft with a designed passenger capacity of 60 or fewer seats, the flight for which the passenger holds confirmed reserved space is unable to accommodate that passenger due to weight/balance restrictions when required by operational or safety reasons;

(c) The passenger is offered accommodations or is seated in a section of the aircraft other than that specified on the ticket at no extra charge, except that a passenger seated in a section for which a lower fare is charged shall be entitled to an appropriate refund; or

(d) The carrier arranges comparable air transportation, or other transportation used by the passenger at no extra cost to the passenger, that at the time such arrangements are made is planned to arrive at the airport of the passenger's next stopover or, if none, at the airport of the final destination not later than 1 hour after the planned arrival time of the passenger's original flight or flights.

[ER–1337, 48 FR 29680, June 28, 1983, as amended at Doc. No. OST–01–9325, 73 FR 21034, Apr. 18, 2008]

§ 250.7 [Reserved]

§ 250.8 Denied boarding compensation.

(a) Every carrier shall tender to a passenger eligible for denied boarding compensation, on the day and place the denied boarding occurs, except as provided in paragraph (b), cash or an immediately negotiable check for the appropriate amount of compensation provided in § 250.5.

(b) Where a carrier arranges, for the passenger's convenience, alternate means of transportation that departs before the payment can be prepared and given to the passenger, tender shall be made by mail or other means within 24 hours after the time the denied boarding occurs.

[ER–1394, 49 FR 43625, Oct. 31, 1984]

§ 250.9 Written explanation of denied boarding compensation and boarding priorities, and verbal notification of denied boarding compensation.

(a) Every carrier shall furnish passengers who are denied boarding involuntarily from flights on which they hold confirmed reserved space immediately after the denied boarding occurs, a written statement explaining the terms, conditions, and limitations of denied boarding compensation, and describing the carriers' boarding priority rules and criteria. The carrier shall also furnish the statement to any person upon request at all airport ticket selling positions which are in the charge of a person employed exclusively by the carrier, or by it jointly with another person or persons, and at all boarding locations being used by the carrier.

(b) The statement shall read as follows:

COMPENSATION FOR DENIED BOARDING

If you have been denied a reserved seat on (name of air carrier), you are probably entitled to monetary compensation. This notice explains the airline's obligation and the passenger's rights in the case of an oversold flight, in accordance with regulations of the *U.S. Department of Transportation.*

VOLUNTEERS AND BOARDING PRIORITIES

If a flight is oversold (more passengers hold confirmed reservations than there are seats available), no one may be denied boarding against his or her will until airline personnel first ask for volunteers who will give up their reservation willingly, in exchange for compensation of the airline's choosing. If there are not enough volunteers, other passengers may be denied boarding involuntarily in accordance with the following boarding priority of (name of air carrier): (In this space the carrier inserts its boarding priority rules or a summary thereof, in a manner to be understandable to the average passenger.)

COMPENSATION FOR INVOLUNTARY DENIED BOARDING

If you are denied boarding involuntarily, you are entitled to a payment of "denied boarding compensation" from the airline unless:

(1) you have not fully complied with the airline's ticketing, check-in and reconfirmation requirements, or you are not acceptable for transportation under the airline's usual rules and practices; or

(2) you are denied boarding because the flight is canceled; or

(3) you are denied boarding because a smaller capacity aircraft was substituted for safety or operational reasons; or

(4) on a flight operated with an aircraft having 60 or fewer seats, you are denied boarding due to safety-related weight/balance restrictions that limit payload; or

(5) you are offered accommodations in a section of the aircraft other than specified in your ticket, at no extra charge (a passenger seated in a section for which a lower fare is charged must be given an appropriate refund); or

(6) the airline is able to place you on another flight or flights that are planned to reach your next stopover or final destination within one hour of the planned arrival time of your original flight.

AMOUNT OF DENIED BOARDING COMPENSATION

Domestic Transportation

Passengers traveling between points within the United States (including the territories and possessions) who are denied boarding involuntarily from an oversold flight are entitled to: (1) No compensation if the carrier offers alternate transportation that is planned to arrive at the passenger's destination or first stopover not later than one hour after the planned arrival time of the passenger's original flight; (2) 200% of the fare to the passenger's destination or first stopover, with a maximum of $675, if the carrier offers alternate transportation that is planned to arrive at the passenger's destination or first stopover more than one hour but less than two hours after the planned arrival time of the passenger's original flight; and (3) 400% of the fare to the passenger's destination or first stopover, with a maximum of $1,350, if the carrier does not offer alternate transportation that is planned to arrive at the airport of the passenger's destination or first stopover less than two hours after the planned arrival time of the passenger's original flight.

0 to 1 hour arrival delay	No compensation.
1 to 2 hour arrival delay	200% of one-way fare (but no more than $675).
Over 2 hours arrival delay	400% of one-way fare (but no more than $1,350).

International Transportation

Passengers traveling from the United States to a foreign point who are denied boarding involuntarily from an oversold flight originating at a U.S. airport are entitled to: (1) No compensation if the carrier offers alternate transportation that is planned to arrive at the passenger's destination or first stopover not later than one hour after the planned arrival time of the passenger's original flight; (2) 200% of the fare to the passenger's destination or first stopover, with a maximum of $675, if the carrier offers alternate transportation that is planned to arrive at the passenger's destination or first stopover more than one hour but less than four hours after the planned arrival time of the passenger's original flight; and (3) 400% of the fare to the passenger's destination or first stopover, with a maximum of $1,350, if the carrier does not offer alternate transportation that is planned to arrive at the airport of the passenger's destination or first stopover less than four hours after the planned arrival time of the passenger's original flight.

0 to 1 hour arrival delay	No compensation.
1 to 4 hour arrival delay	200% of one-way fare (but no more than $675).
Over 4 hours arrival delay	400% of one-way fare (but no more than $1,350).

Alternate Transportation

"Alternate transportation" is air transportation with a confirmed reservation at no additional charge (by any scheduled airline licensed by DOT), or other transportation accepted and used by the passenger in the case of denied boarding.

METHOD OF PAYMENT

Except as provided below, the airline must give each passenger who qualifies for involuntary denied boarding compensation a payment by cash or check for the amount specified above, on the day and at the place the involuntary denied boarding occurs. If the airline arranges alternate transportation for the passenger's convenience that departs before the payment can be made, the payment shall be sent to the passenger within 24 hours. The air carrier may offer free or discounted transportation in place of the cash payment. In that event, the carrier must disclose all material restrictions on the use of the free or discounted transportation before the passenger decides whether to accept the transportation in lieu of a cash or check payment. The passenger may insist on the cash/check payment or refuse all compensation and bring private legal action.

PASSENGER'S OPTIONS

Acceptance of the compensation may relieve (name of air carrier) from any further liability to the passenger caused by its failure to honor the confirmed reservation. However, the passenger may decline the payment and seek to recover damages in a court of law or in some other manner.

(c) In addition to furnishing passengers with the carrier's written statement as specified in paragraphs (a) and (b) of this section, if the carrier orally advises involuntarily bumped passengers that they are entitled to receive free or discounted transportation as denied boarding compensation, the carrier must also orally advise the passengers of any material restrictions or conditions applicable to the free or discounted transportation and that they are entitled to choose a check instead (or cash if that option is offered by the carrier).

(Approved by the Office of Management and Budget under control number 3024–0003)

[ER–1306, 47 FR 52985, Nov. 24, 1982, as amended by ER–1337, 48 FR 29681, June 28, 1983; ER–1392, 49 FR 40401, Oct. 16, 1984; ER–1394, 49 FR 43625, Oct. 31, 1984; 68 FR 52836, Sept. 8, 2003; Doc. No. OST–01–9325, 73 FR 21034, Apr. 18, 2008; Doc. No. DOT–OST–2010–0140, 76 FR 23162, Apr. 25, 2011; Doc. No. DOT–OST–2015–0104, 80 FR 30147, May 27, 2015]

§ 250.10 Report of passengers denied confirmed space.

(a) Each reporting carrier as defined in § 234.2 of this chapter and any carrier that voluntarily submits data pursuant to § 234.7 of this chapter shall file, on a quarterly basis, the information specified in BTS Form 251. The reporting basis shall be flight segments originating in the United States operated by the reporting carrier. The reports must be submitted within 30 days after the end of the quarter covered by the report. The calendar quarters end March 31, June 30, September 30 and December 31. "Total Boardings" on Line 7 of Form 251 shall include only passengers on flights for which confirmed reservations are offered. Data shall not be included for inbound international flights.

(b) For air transportation taking place on or after January 1, 2018, each reporting carrier and voluntary reporting carrier shall file a separate BTS Form 251 for all flight segments originating in the United States marketed under only the reporting carrier's code, and operated by a code-share partner that is a certificated air carrier or commuter air carrier using aircraft that have a designed passenger capacity of 30 or more seats.

[Docket No. DOT–OST–2014–0056, 81 FR 76827, Nov. 3, 2016]

§ 250.11 Public disclosure of deliberate overbooking and boarding procedures.

(a) Every carrier shall cause to be displayed continuously in a conspicuous public place at each desk, station and position in the United States which is in the charge of a person employed exclusively by it, or by it jointly with another person, or by any agent employed by such air carrier or foreign air carrier to sell tickets to passengers, a sign located so as to be clearly visible and clearly readable to the traveling public, which shall have printed thereon the following statement in boldface type at least one-fourth of an inch high:

NOTICE—OVERBOOKING OF FLIGHTS

Airline flights may be overbooked, and there is a slight chance that a seat will not be available on a flight for which a person has a confirmed reservation. If the flight is overbooked, no one will be denied a seat until airline personnel first ask for volunteers willing to give up their reservation in exchange for compensation of the airline's choosing. If there are not enough volunteers, the airline will deny boarding to other persons in accordance with its particular boarding priority. With few exceptions, including failure to comply with the carrier's check-in deadline (carrier shall insert either "of __ minutes prior to each flight segment" or "(which are available upon request from the air carrier)" here), persons denied boarding involuntarily are entitled to compensation. The complete rules for the payment of compensation and each airline's boarding priorities are available at all airport ticket counters and boarding locations. Some airlines do not apply these consumer protections to travel from some foreign countries, although other consumer protections may be available. Check with your airline or your travel agent.

(b) Every carrier shall include with each ticket sold in the United States the notices set forth in paragraph (a) of this section, printed in at least 12-point type. The notice may be printed on a separate piece of paper, on the ticket stock, or on the ticket envelope. The last two sentences of the notice shall be printed in a type face contrasting with that of the rest of the notice.

(c) It shall be the responsibility of each carrier to ensure that travel agents authorized to sell air transportation for that carrier comply with the notice provisions of paragraphs (a) and (b) of this section.

(d) [Reserved]

(e) Any air carrier or foreign air carrier engaged in foreign air transportation that complies fully with this part for inbound traffic to the United States need not use the last two sentences of the notices required by paragraph (a) of this subsection.

(Approved by the Office of Management and Budget under control number 3024–0018)

[ER–1306, 47 FR 52985, Nov. 24, 1982, as amended by ER–1392, 49 FR 40401, Oct. 16, 1984; Doc. No. OST–01–9325, 73 FR 21035, Apr. 18, 2008]

PART 251—CARRIAGE OF MUSICAL INSTRUMENTS

AUTHORITY: 49 U.S.C. 41724.

SOURCE: 80 FR 166, Jan. 5, 2015, unless otherwise noted.

§ 251.1 Definitions.

As used in this part:

Certificated air carrier means a U.S. carrier holding a certificate issued under 49 U.S.C. 41102 to conduct passenger service or holding an exemption to conduct passenger operations under 49 U.S.C. 40109.

Commuter air carrier means a U.S. carrier that has been found fit under 49 U.S.C. 41738 and is authorized to carry passengers on at least five round trips per week on at least one route between two or more points according to a published flight schedule using small aircraft as defined in 14 CFR 298.2.

Covered carrier means a certificated carrier, a commuter carrier, an air taxi, or a U.S. indirect carrier operating to, from, or within the United States, conducting scheduled passenger service or public charter service.

FAA means the Federal Aviation Administration, an operating administration of the Department of Transportation.

Indirect carrier means a person not directly involved in the operation of an aircraft who sells air transportation services to the general public other than as an authorized agent of a carrier.

§ 251.2 Applicability.

This part applies to U.S. certificated air carriers, U.S. commuter air carriers, air taxis, and U.S. indirect carriers that operate passenger service to, from, or within the United States.

§ 251.3 Small musical instruments as carry-on baggage.

Each covered carrier shall permit a passenger to carry a violin, guitar, or other small musical instrument in the aircraft cabin, without charging the passenger a fee in addition to any standard fee that carrier may require for comparable carry-on baggage, if:

(a) The instrument can be stowed safely in a suitable baggage compartment in the aircraft cabin or under a passenger seat, in accordance with the requirements for carriage of carry-on baggage or cargo established by the FAA; and

(b) There is space for such stowage at the time the passenger boards the aircraft.

§ 251.4 Large musical instruments as carry-on baggage.

Each covered carrier shall permit a passenger to carry a musical instrument that is too large to meet the requirements of § 251.3 in the aircraft cabin, without charging the passenger a fee in addition to the cost of an additional ticket described in paragraph (e) of this section, if:

(a) The instrument is contained in a case or covered so as to avoid injury to other passengers;

(b) The weight of the instrument, including the case or covering, does not exceed 165 pounds or the applicable weight restrictions for the aircraft;

(c) The instrument can be stowed in accordance with the requirements for carriage of carry-on baggage or cargo established by the FAA;

(d) Neither the instrument nor the case contains any object not otherwise permitted to be carried in an aircraft cabin because of a law or regulation of the United States; and

(e) The passenger wishing to carry the instrument in the aircraft cabin has purchased an additional seat to accommodate the instrument.

§ 251.5 Large musical instruments as checked baggage.

Each covered carrier shall transport as baggage a musical instrument that is the property of a passenger traveling in air transportation that may not be carried in the aircraft cabin if

(a) The sum of the length, width, and height measured in inches of the outside linear dimensions of the instrument (including the case) does not exceed 150 inches or the applicable size restrictions for the aircraft;

(b) The weight of the instrument does not exceed 165 pounds or the applicable weight restrictions for the aircraft; and

(c) The instrument can be stowed in accordance with the requirements for carriage of carry-on baggage or cargo established by the FAA.

PART 252—SMOKING ABOARD AIRCRAFT

Sec.

AUTHORITY: Pub. L. 101–164; 49 U.S.C. 40102, 40109, 40113, 41701, 41702, 41706 as amended by section 708 of Pub. L. 106–181 and section 401 of Pub. L. 112–95, 41711, and 46301.

CROSS REFERENCE: For smoking rules of the Federal Aviation Administration, see 14 CFR 121.317(c), 121.571(a)(1)(i), 129.29, 135.117(a)(1), and 135.127(a).

SOURCE: Docket No. DOT–OST–2000–7473, 65 FR 36775, June 9, 2000, unless otherwise noted.

§ 252.1 Purpose.

This part implements a ban on smoking as defined in § 252.3, including the use of electronic cigarettes and certain other devices, on flights by air carriers and foreign air carriers.

[Docket DOT-OST-2011-0044, 81 FR 11427, Mar. 4, 2016]

§ 252.2 Applicability.

This part applies to operations of air carriers engaged in interstate, intrastate and foreign air transportation and to foreign air carriers engaged in foreign air transportation.

[Docket DOT-OST-2011-0044, 81 FR 11427, Mar. 4, 2016]

§ 252.3 Definitions.

As used in this part:

Air carrier means a carrier that is a citizen of the United States undertaking to provide air transportation as defined in 49 U.S.C. 40102.

Foreign air carrier means a carrier that is not a citizen of the United States undertaking to provide foreign air transportation as defined in 49 U.S.C. 40102.

Smoking means the use of a tobacco product, electronic cigarettes whether or not they are a tobacco product, or similar products that produce a smoke, mist, vapor, or aerosol, with the exception of products (other than electronic cigarettes) which meet the definition of a medical device in section 201(h) of the Federal Food, Drug and Cosmetic Act, such as nebulizers.

[Docket DOT-OST-2011-0044, 81 FR 11427, Mar. 4, 2016]

§ 252.4 Smoking ban: air carriers.

Air carriers shall prohibit smoking on the following flights:

(a) Scheduled passenger flights.

(b) Nonscheduled passenger flights, except for the following flights where a flight attendant is not a required crewmember on the aircraft as determined by the Administrator of the Federal Aviation Administration:

(1) Single entity charters.

(2) On-demand services of air taxi operators.

(c) Nothing in this section shall be deemed to require air carriers to permit smoking aboard aircraft.

[Docket DOT-OST-2011-0044, 81 FR 11427, Mar. 4, 2016]

§ 252.5 Smoking ban: foreign air carriers.

(a)(1) Foreign air carriers shall prohibit smoking on flight segments that occur between points in the United States, and between the United States and any foreign point, in the following types of operations:

(i) Scheduled passenger foreign air transportation.

(ii) Nonscheduled passenger foreign air transportation, if a flight attendant is a required crewmember on the aircraft as determined by the Administrator of the Federal Aviation Administration or a foreign carrier's government.

(2) Nothing in this section shall be deemed to require foreign air carriers to permit smoking aboard aircraft.

(b) A foreign government objecting to the application of paragraph (a) of this section on the basis that paragraph (a) provides for extraterritorial application of the laws of the United States may request and obtain a waiver of paragraph (a) from the Assistant Secretary for Aviation and International Affairs, provided that an alternative smoking prohibition resulting from bilateral negotiations is in effect.

[Docket DOT-OST-2011-0044, 81 FR 11427, Mar. 4, 2016]

§ 252.8 Extent of smoking restrictions.

The restrictions on smoking described in §§ 252.4 and 252.5 shall apply to all locations within the aircraft.

[Docket DOT-OST-2011-0044, 81 FR 11428, Mar. 4, 2016]

§ 252.9 Ventilation systems.

Air carriers shall prohibit smoking whenever the ventilation system is not fully functioning. Fully functioning for this purpose means operating so as to provide the level and quality of ventilation specified and designed by the manufacturer for the number of persons currently in the passenger compartment.

§ 252.11 Aircraft on the ground.

(a) Air carriers shall prohibit smoking whenever the aircraft is on the ground.

(b) With respect to the restrictions on smoking described in § 252.5, foreign air carriers shall prohibit smoking from the time an aircraft begins enplaning passengers until the time passengers complete deplaning.

§ 252.17 Enforcement.

Air carriers and foreign air carriers shall take such action as is necessary to ensure that smoking by passengers or crew is not permitted where smoking is prohibited by this part, including but not limited to aircraft lavatories.

[Docket DOT-OST-2011-0044, 81 FR 11428, Mar. 4, 2016]

PART 253—NOTICE OF TERMS OF CONTRACT OF CARRIAGE

Sec.

253.10 Notice of contract of carriage choice-of-forum provisions.

AUTHORITY: 49 U.S.C. 40113; 49 U.S.C. Chapters 401, 415 and 417.

SOURCE: ER–1302, 47 FR 52134, Nov. 19, 1982, unless otherwise noted.

§ 253.1 Purpose.

The purpose of this rule is to set uniform disclosure requirements, which preempt any State requirements on the same subject, for terms incorporated by reference into contracts of carriage for scheduled service in interstate and overseas passenger air transportation.

§ 253.2 Applicability.

This rule applies to all scheduled direct air carrier operations in interstate and overseas air transportation. It applies to all contracts with passengers, for those operations, that incorporate terms by reference.

[ER–1323, 48 FR 6318, Feb. 11, 1983]

§ 253.3 Definitions.

Large aircraft means any aircraft designed to have a maximum passenger capacity of more than 60 seats.

Passenger means any person who purchases, or who contacts a ticket office or travel agent for the purpose of purchasing, or considering the purchase of, air transportation.

Ticket office means station, office, or other location where tickets are sold that is under the charge of a person employed exclusively by the carrier, or by it jointly with another person.

§ 253.4 Incorporation by reference in the contract of carriage.

(a) A ticket or other written instrument that embodies the contract of carriage may incorporate contract terms by reference (*i.e.*, without stating their full text), and if it does so shall contain or be accompanied by notice to the passenger as required by this part. In addition to other remedies at law, an air carrier may not claim the benefit as against the passenger of, and the passenger shall not be bound by, any contract term incorporated by reference if notice of the term has not been provided to that passenger in accordance with this part.

(b) Each air carrier shall make the full text of each term that it incorporates by reference in a contract of carriage available for public inspection at each of its airport and city ticket offices.

(c) Each air carrier shall provide free of charge by mail or other delivery service to passengers, upon their request, a copy of the full text of its terms incorporated by reference in the contract. Each carrier shall keep available at all times, free of charge, at all locations where its tickets are sold within the United States information sufficient to enable passengers to order the full text of such terms.

(The notice requirements contained in paragraphs (b) and (c) were approved by the Office of Management and Budget under control number 3024–0061)

[ER–1302, 47 FR 52134, Nov. 19, 1982, as amended by ER–1309, 47 FR 54764, Dec. 6, 1982]

§ 253.5 Notice of incorporated terms.

Except as provided in § 253.8, each air carrier shall include on or with a ticket, or other written instrument given to a passenger, that embodies the contract of carriage and incorporates terms by reference in that contract, a conspicuous notice that:

(a) Any terms incorporated by reference are part of the contract, passengers may inspect the full text of each term incorporated by reference at the carrier's airport or city ticket offices, and passengers have the right, upon request at any location where the carrier's tickets are sold within the United States, to receive free of charge by mail or other delivery service the full text of each such incorporated term;

(b) The incorporated terms may include and passengers may obtain from any location where the carrier's tickets are sold within the United States further information concerning:

(1) Limits on the air carrier's liability for personal injury or death of passengers, and for loss, damage, or delay of goods and baggage, including fragile or perishable goods;

(2) Claim restrictions, including time periods within which passengers must file a claim or bring an action against the carrier for its acts or omissions or those of its agents;

(3) Rights of the carrier to change terms of the contract. (Rights to change the price, however, are governed by §253.7);

(4) Rules about reconfirmation of reservations, check-in times, and refusal to carry;

(5) Rights of the carrier and limitations concerning delay or failure to perform service, including schedule changes, substitution of alternate air carrier or aircraft, and rerouting.

(Approved by the Office of Management and Budget under control number 3024–0061)

[ER–1302, 47 FR 52134, Nov. 19, 1982, as amended by ER–1309, 47 FR 54764, Dec. 6, 1982; ER–1370, 48 FR 54591, Dec. 6, 1983; ER–1375, 49 FR 5064, Feb. 10, 1984]

§253.6 Explanation of incorporated terms.

Each air carrier shall ensure that any passenger can obtain from any location where its tickets are sold within the United States a concise and immediate explanation of any terms incorporated by reference, concerning the subjects listed in §253.5(b).

(Approved by the Office of Management and Budget under control number 3024–0061)

[ER–1302, 47 FR 52134, Nov. 19, 1982, as amended by ER–1309, 47 FR 54764, Dec. 6, 1982]

§253.7 Direct notice of certain terms.

A carrier may not impose any terms restricting refunds of the ticket price, imposing monetary penalties on passengers, or raising the ticket price consistent with §399.87 of the chapter, unless the passenger receives conspicuous written notice of the salient features of those terms on or with the ticket.

[Doc. No. DOT–OST–2010–0140, 76 FR 23163, Apr. 25, 2011]

§253.8 Qualifications to notice requirements.

(a) If notice is not provided in accordance with §253.5 at a ticket sales location outside of the United States that is not a U.S. air carrier ticket office, the price paid for the portion of such ticket that is for interstate and overseas air transportation shall be refundable without penalty if the passenger refuses transportation by the carrier. Each air carrier shall ensure that passengers who have bought tickets at those locations without the notice required in §253.5 are given that notice not later than check-in for the travel in interstate or overseas air transportation, and that conspicuous notice is included on or with the ticket stating that the price for that travel is refundable without penalty.

(b) An air taxi operator (including a commuter air carrier) not operating under subpart I of part 298 of this chapter shall not be considered to have incorporated terms by reference into its contract of carriage merely because a passenger has purchased a flight segment on that carrier that appears on ticket stock that contains a statement that terms have been incorporated by reference. However, such an air taxi operator may not claim the benefit as against the passenger of, and the passenger shall not be bound by, any contract term incorporated by reference if notice of the term has not been provided to the passenger in accordance with this part.

[ER–1370, 48 FR 54591, Dec. 6, 1983]

§253.9 Retroactive changes to contracts of carriage.

An air carrier may not retroactively apply to persons who have already bought a ticket any material amendment to its contract of carriage that has significant negative implications for consumers.

[Doc. No. DOT–OST–2007–0022, 74 FR 69002, Dec. 30, 2009]

§253.10 Notice of contract of carriage choice-of-forum provisions.

No carrier may impose any contract of carriage provision containing a choice-of-forum clause that attempts to preclude a passenger, or a person who purchases a ticket for air transportation on behalf of a passenger, from bringing a claim against a carrier in any court of competent jurisdiction, including a court within the jurisdiction of that passenger's residence in the United States (provided that the carrier does business within that jurisdiction).

[Doc. No. DOT–OST–2010–0140, 76 FR 23163, Apr. 25, 2011]

PART 254—DOMESTIC BAGGAGE LIABILITY

AUTHORITY: 49 U.S.C. 40113, 41501, 41504, 41510, 41702, and 41707.

SOURCE: ER–1374, 49 FR 5071, Feb. 10, 1984, unless otherwise noted.

§ 254.1 Purpose.

The purpose of this part is to establish rules for the carriage of baggage in interstate and intrastate air transportation. The part sets permissible limitations of air carrier liability for loss, damage, or delay in the carriage of passenger baggage and requires air carriers to provide certain types of notice to passengers.

[ER–1374, 49 FR 5071, Feb. 10, 1984, as amended at 64 FR 70575, Dec. 17, 1999]

§ 254.2 Applicability.

This part applies to any air carrier that provides charter or scheduled passenger service in interstate or intrastate air transportation.

[ER–1374, 49 FR 5071, Feb. 10, 1984, as amended at 64 FR 70575, Dec. 17, 1999]

§ 254.3 Definitions.

Large aircraft means any aircraft designed to have a maximum passenger capacity of more than 60 seats.

§ 254.4 Carrier liability.

On any flight segment using large aircraft, or on any flight segment that is included on the same ticket as another flight segment that uses large aircraft, an air carrier shall not limit its liability for provable direct or consequential damages resulting from the disappearance of, damage to, or delay in delivery of a passenger's personal property, including baggage, in its custody to an amount less than $3,500 for each passenger.

[72 FR 3943, Jan. 29, 2007, as amended at 73 FR 70592, Nov. 21, 2008; 78 FR 14914, Mar. 8, 2013; 80 FR 30147, May 27, 2015]

§ 254.5 Notice requirement.

In any flight segment using large aircraft, or on any flight segment that is included on the same ticket as another flight segment that uses large aircraft, an air carrier shall provide to passengers, by conspicuous written material included on or with its ticket, either:

(a) Notice of any monetary limitation on its baggage liability to passengers; or

(b) The following notice: "Federal rules require any limit on an airline's baggage liability to be at least $3,500 per passenger."

[72 FR 3943, Jan. 29, 2007, as amended by Doc. N. oDOT–OST–2008–0332, 73 FR 70592, Nov. 21, 2008; 78 FR 14914, Mar. 8, 2013; 80 FR 30147, May 27, 2015]

§ 254.6 Periodic adjustments.

The Department of Transportation will review the minimum limit of liability prescribed in this part every two years. The Department will use the Consumer Price Index for All Urban Consumers as of July of each review year to calculate the revised minimum liability amount. The Department will use the following formula:

$2500 × (a/b) rounded to the nearest $100 where:

a = July CPI-U of year of current adjustment
b = the CPI–U figure in December 1999 when the inflation adjustment provision was added to part 254.

[64 FR 70575, Dec. 17, 1999, as amended by Doc. No. DOT–OST–2008–0332, 73 FR 70592, Nov. 21, 2008]

PART 255 [RESERVED]

PART 256—ELECTRONIC AIRLINE INFORMATION SYSTEMS

AUTHORITY: 49 U.S.C. 40101 and 41712.

SOURCE: Docket No. DOT–OST–2014–0056, 81 FR 76828, Nov. 3, 2016, unless otherwise noted.

§ 256.1 Purpose.

(a) The purpose of this part is to set forth requirements for the display of flight options by electronic airline information systems that provide air carrier or foreign air carrier schedule, fare, or availability information, including, but not limited to, global distribution systems (GDSs), corporate booking tools, and internet flight search tools, for use by consumers, carriers, ticket agents, and other business entities so as to prevent unfair or deceptive practices in the distribution and sale of air transportation.

(b) Nothing in this part exempts any person from the operation of the antitrust laws set forth in subsection (a) of the first section of the Clayton Act (15 U.S.C. 12).

§ 256.2 Applicability.

(a) This part applies to any air carrier, foreign air carrier, or ticket agent that operates an electronic airline information system, *e.g.*, GDS, corporate booking tool, or internet flight search tool, that combines the schedules, fares or availability information of more than one air carrier or foreign air carrier for the distribution or sale in the United States of interstate or foreign air transportation.

(b) This part applies only if the electronic airline information system is displayed on a Web site marketed to consumers in the United States or on a proprietary display available to travel agents, business entities, or a limited segment of consumers of air transportation in the United States.

§ 256.3 Definitions.

For purposes of this part:

Availability means information provided in displays with respect to the ability to make a reservation on a particular flight.

Display means the presentation of air carrier or foreign air carrier schedules, fares, or availability to a consumer or agent or other individual involved in arranging air travel for a consumer by means of a computer or mobile electronic device.

Electronic airline information system or EAIS means a system that combines air carrier or foreign air carrier schedule, fare, or availability information for transmission or display to air carriers or foreign air carriers, ticket agents, other business entities, or consumers.

Integrated display means any display that includes the schedules, fares or availability of more than one listed carrier.

§ 256.4 Prohibition on undisclosed display bias.

Each air carrier, foreign air carrier, and ticket agent that operates an EAIS must comply with the requirements of this section.

(a) Each EAIS that uses any factor, not based on user selection or corporate contract travel arrangement, directly or indirectly relating to carrier identity in ordering the information contained in an integrated display must clearly disclose as provided for in § 256.5 that the identity of the carrier is a factor in the order in which information is displayed.

(b) An EAIS's integrated display must not give any carrier's flights a system-imposed preference over any other carrier's flights in that market based on carrier identity unless the preference is prominently disclosed as provided for in § 256.5.

(c) Each EAIS must display information in an objective manner based on search criteria selected by the user (*e.g.*, lowest fare, lowest total cost, date and time of travel, class of service, stopovers, total elapsed time or duration of travel, number of stops, limitations on carriers to be used, particular airport(s), number of passengers, etc.) When providing information in response to a search by a user of the EAIS, the EAIS must order the information provided so that the flight options that best satisfy the parameters of the user-selected search criteria are displayed conspicuously and no less prominently (*e.g.*, in the same or larger font size and the same or more noticeable font color) than any other flight option displayed. Flight options may be presented in sequence, matrix, or other formats, but the flight options that best satisfy the parameters of the user-selected search criteria must be ranked in lists above other flight options, or identified more prominently than other flight options in a matrix or other format. This does not preclude systems from setting default display parameters that are not deceptive or offering users the option to choose a variety of display methods within those parameters.

§ 256.5 Minimum disclosure requirements for biased displays.

To the extent an EAIS engages in display bias based on carrier identity, it must clearly and conspicuously disclose that fact at the top of each search result display presented to the user in response to the user-selected search criteria. The notice must state that the flights are not displayed in neutral order and that certain airlines' fare, schedule or availability information is given preferential treatment in how it is displayed.

§ 256.6 No requirement to provide access to systems.

Nothing in this section requires an air carrier, foreign air carrier, or ticket agent to allow a system to access its internal computer reservation system or to permit "screen scraping" or "content scraping" of its Web site; nor does it require an air carrier or foreign air carrier to permit the marketing or sale of the carrier's services through any ticket agent or other carrier's system. "Screen scraping" as used in this paragraph refers to a process whereby a company uses computer software techniques to extract information from other companies' Web sites without permission from the company operating the targeted Web site.

PART 257—DISCLOSURE OF CODE-SHARING ARRANGEMENTS AND LONG-TERM WET LEASES

Sec.

AUTHORITY: 49 U.S.C. 40113(a) and 41712.

SOURCE: 64 FR 12851, Mar. 15, 1999, unless otherwise noted.

§ 257.1 Purpose.

The purpose of this part is to ensure that ticket agents doing business in the United States, air carriers, and foreign air carriers tell consumers clearly when the air transportation they are buying or considering buying involves a code-sharing arrangement or a long-term wet lease, and that they disclose to consumers the transporting carrier's identity.

§ 257.2 Applicability.

This part applies to the following:

(a) Direct air carriers and foreign air carriers that participate in code-sharing arrangements or long-term wet leases involving scheduled passenger air transportation; and

(b) Ticket agents doing business in the United States that sell scheduled passenger air transportation services involving code-sharing arrangements or long-term wet leases.

§ 257.3 Definitions.

As used in this part:

Air transportation means foreign air transportation or interstate air transportation as defined in 49 U.S.C. 40102 (a)(23) and (25) respectively.

Carrier means any air carrier or foreign air carrier as defined in 49 U.S.C. 40102(2) or 49 U.S.C. 40102(21), respectively, that is engaged directly in scheduled passenger air transportation, including by wet lease.

Code-sharing arrangement means an arrangement whereby a carrier's designator code is used to identify a flight operated by another carrier.

Designator code means the airline designations originally allotted and administered pursuant to Agreements CAB 24606 and 26056.

Long-term wet lease means a lease by which the lessor provides both an aircraft and crew dedicated to a particular route(s), and which either:

(1) Lasts more than 60 days; or

(2) Is part of a series of such leases that amounts to a continuing arrangement lasting more than 60 days.

(g) *Operating carrier* means the carrier that is operating the aircraft in a code-sharing arrangement or long-term wet lease.

Ticket agent has the meaning ascribed to it in 49 U.S.C. 40102(40).

[64 FR 12851, Mar. 15, 1999, as amended by Docket No. DOT–OST–2014–0056, 81 FR 76828, Nov. 3, 2016]

§ 257.4 Unfair and deceptive practice.

The holding out or sale of scheduled passenger air transportation involving a code-sharing arrangement or long-term wet lease is prohibited as unfair and deceptive in violation of 49 U.S.C. 41712 unless, in conjunction with such holding out or sale, carriers and ticket agents follow the requirements of this part.

§ 257.5 Notice requirement.

(a) *Notice in flight itineraries and schedules.* Each air carrier, foreign air carrier, or ticket agent providing flight itineraries and/or schedules for scheduled passenger air transportation to the public in the United States and to the Official Airline Guides and comparable publications, and, where applicable, computer reservation systems, shall ensure that each flight on which the designator code is not that of the operating carrier is clearly and prominently identified and contains the following disclosures. If there is more than one operating carrier for a particular flight (*e.g.*, change of gauge), the required disclosures shall be made for each flight segment where the designator code is not that of the operating carrier.

(1) In flight schedule information provided by an air carrier, foreign air carrier, or ticket agent to U.S. consumers on desktop browser-based Web sites or applications in response to any requested itinerary search, for each flight in scheduled passenger air transportation that is operated by a carrier other than the one listed for that flight, the corporate name of the transporting carrier and any other name under which the service is held out to the public must appear prominently in text format, with font size not smaller than the font size of the flight itinerary itself, on the first display following the input of a search query, immediately adjacent to each code-share flight in that search-results list. Roll-over, pop-up and linked disclosures do not comply with this paragraph.

(2) In flight schedule information provided by an air carrier, foreign air carrier, or ticket agent to U.S. consumers on mobile browser-based Web sites or applications in response to any requested itinerary search, for each flight in scheduled passenger air transportation that is operated by a carrier other than the one listed for that flight, the corporate name of the transporting carrier must appear prominently in text format, with font size not smaller than the font size of the flight itinerary itself, on the first display following the input of a search query, immediately adjacent to each code-share flight in that search-results list. Roll-over, pop-up and linked disclosures do not comply with this paragraph.

(3) For static written schedules, each flight in scheduled passenger air transportation that is operated by a carrier other than the one listed for that flight shall be identified by an asterisk or other easily identifiable mark that leads to disclosure of the corporate name of the operating carrier and any other name under which that service is held out to the public.

(4) Each air carrier and foreign air carrier that provides flight schedule information to any computer reservation system or global distribution system that receives and distributes the U.S. or foreign carrier's fare, schedule, or availability information shall ensure that each flight on which the designator code is not that of the operating carrier is clearly and prominently identified and the corporate name of the transporting carrier and any other name under which the service is held out to the public appears prominently in text format, with font size that is not smaller than the font size of the flight itinerary itself, immediately adjacent to each code-share flight in that search-results list.

(b) *Notice in oral communications with prospective consumers.* In any direct oral communication in the United States with a prospective consumer, and in any telephone call placed from the United States by a prospective consumer, concerning a flight within, to, or from the United States that is part of a code-sharing arrangement or long-term wet lease, a ticket agent doing business in the United States or a carrier shall inform the consumer, the first time that such a flight is offered to the consumer, or, if no such offer was made, the first time a consumer inquires about such a flight, that the operating carrier is not the carrier whose name or designator code will appear on the ticket and shall identify the transporting carrier by its corporate name and any other name under which that service is held out to the public.

(c) *Notice in ticket confirmations.* At the time of purchase, each selling carrier or ticket agent shall provide written disclosure of the actual operator of the flight to each consumer of scheduled passenger air transportation sold in the United States that involves a code-sharing arrangement or long-term wet lease. For any flight on which the designator code is not that of the operating carrier the notice shall state "Operated by" followed by the corporate name of the transporting carrier and any other name in which that service is held out to the public. The following form of statement will satisfy the requirement of this paragraph:

Important Notice: Service between XYZ City and ABC City will be operated by Jane Doe Airlines d/b/a QRS Express. At the purchaser's request, the notice required by this part may be delivered in person, or by fax, electronic mail, or any other reliable method of transmitting written material.

(d) In any written advertisement distributed in or mailed to or from the United States (including those that appear on an internet Web site that is marketed to consumers in the United States) for service in a city-pair market that is provided under a code-sharing arrangement or long-term wet lease, the advertisement shall prominently disclose that the advertised service may involve travel on another carrier and clearly indicate the nature of the service in reasonably sized type and shall identify all potential operating carriers involved in the markets being advertised by corporate name and by any other name under which that service is held out to the public. In any radio or television advertisement broadcast in the United States for service in a city-pair market that is provided under a code-sharing or long-term wet lease, the advertisement shall include at least a generic disclosure statement, such as "Some flights are operated by other airlines."

[Docket No. DOT–OST–2014–0056, 81 FR 76828, Nov. 3, 2016]

§ 257.6 Effective and compliance dates.

(a) This Part is effective as of August 25, 1999.

(b) Compliance with the following sections is mandatory as of August 25, 1999:

(1) § 257.1, § 257.2, § 257.3, § 257.4, § 257.5(d), and § 257.6.

(2) § 257.5(b) to the extent that it requires sellers of air transportation to give consumers oral notice before booking transportation involving a code-share arrangement

(i) Of the fact that the selling carrier is not the transporting carrier and

(ii) Of the transporting carrier's identity (as shown by its two-letter designator code in CRS displays).

(c) Compliance with the following sections is mandatory as of March 15, 2000:

(1) § 257.5(a) and § 257.5(c) in their entirety.

(2) § 257.5(b) insofar as it requires sellers of air transportation to give consumers

(i) Oral notice before booking transportation involving a code-share arrangement of the transporting carrier's corporate name and any other name under which the service is held out to the public and

(ii) The same disclosures for long-term wet leases as for code-sharing arrangements.

[64 FR 46821, Aug. 27, 1999]

PART 258—DISCLOSURE OF CHANGE-OF-GAUGE SERVICES

AUTHORITY: 49 U.S.C. 40113(a) and 41712.

SOURCE: 64 FR 12860, Mar. 15, 1999, unless otherwise noted.

§ 258.1 Purpose.

The purpose of this part is to ensure that consumers are adequately informed before they book air transportation or embark on travel involving change-of-gauge services that these services require a change of aircraft en route.

§ 258.2 Applicability.

This part applies to the following:

(a) Direct air carriers and foreign air carriers that sell or issue tickets in the United States for scheduled passenger air transportation on change-of-gauge services or that operate such transportation; and

(b) Ticket agents doing business in the United States that sell or issue tickets for scheduled passenger air transportation on change-of-gauge services.

§ 258.3 Definitions.

As used in this part:

(a) *Air transportation* has the meaning ascribed to it in 49 U.S.C. 40102(5).

(b) *Carrier* means any air carrier or foreign air carrier as defined in 49 U.S.C. 40102(2) or 49 U.S.C. 40102(21), respectively, that engages directly in scheduled passenger air transportation.

(c) *Change-of-gauge service* means a service that requires a change of aircraft en route but has only a single flight number.

(d) *Ticket agent* has the meaning ascribed to it in 49 U.S.C. 40102(40).

§ 258.4 Unfair and deceptive practice.

The holding out or sale of scheduled passenger air transportation that involves change-of-gauge service is prohibited as an unfair or deceptive practice or an unfair method of competition within the meaning of 49 U.S.C. 41712 unless, in conjunction with such holding out or sale, carriers and ticket agents follow the requirements of this part.

§ 258.5 Notice requirement.

(a) *Notice in schedules.* Carriers holding out or operating change-of-gauge services to, from, or within the United States shall ensure that in the written and electronic schedule information they provide to the public, to the Official Airline Guide and comparable publications, and to computer reservations systems, these services are shown as requiring a change of aircraft.

(b) *Oral notice to prospective consumers.* In any direct oral communication with a consumer in the United States concerning a change-of-gauge service, any carrier or ticket agent doing business in the United States shall tell the consumer before booking scheduled passenger air transportation to, from, or within the United States that the service requires a change of aircraft en route.

(c) *Written notice.* At the time of sale in the United States of transportation that includes a change-of-gauge service to, from, or within the United States, or, if no ticket is issued, no later than the time when the passenger checks in at the airport for the first flight in an itinerary that includes such a service, the selling carrier or ticket agent shall provide the following written notice:

NOTICE: CHANGE OF AIRCRAFT REQUIRED

For at least one of your flights, you must change aircraft en route even though your ticket may show only one flight number and have only one flight coupon for that flight. Further, in the case of some travel, one of your flights may not be identified at the airport by the number on your ticket, or it may be identified by other flight numbers in addition to the one on your ticket. At your request, the seller of this ticket will give you details of your change of aircraft, such as where it will occur and what aircraft types are involved.

§ 258.6 Effective and compliance dates.

(a) This Part is effective as of August 25, 1999.

(b) Compliance with the following sections is mandatory as of August 25, 1999: §§ 258.1, 258.2, 258.3, 258.4, 258.5(a), 258.5(b), and 258.6.

(c) Compliance with § 258.5(c) is mandatory as of March 15, 2000.

[64 FR 46821, Aug. 27, 1999]

PART 259—ENHANCED PROTECTIONS FOR AIRLINE PASSENGERS

AUTHORITY: 49 U.S.C. 40101(a)(4), 40101(a)(9), 40113(a), 41702, and 41712.

SOURCE: 74 FR 69002, Dec. 30, 2009, unless otherwise noted.

§ 259.1 Purpose.

The purpose of this part is to mitigate hardships for airline passengers during lengthy tarmac delays and otherwise to bolster air carriers' accountability to consumers.

§ 259.2 Applicability.

This part applies to all the flights of a certificated or commuter air carrier if the carrier operates scheduled passenger service or public charter service using any aircraft originally designed to have a passenger capacity of 30 or more seats, and to all flights to and from the U.S. of a foreign carrier if the carrier operates scheduled passenger service or public charter service to and from the U.S. using any aircraft originally designed to have a passenger capacity of 30 or more seats, except as otherwise provided in this part. This part does not apply to foreign carrier charters that operate to and from the United States if no new passengers are picked up in the United States.

[Doc. No. DOT–OST–2010–0140, 76 FR 23163, Apr. 25, 2011]

§ 259.3 Definitions.

Certificated air carrier means a U.S. carrier holding a certificate issued under 49 U.S.C. 41102 to conduct passenger service or holding an exemption to conduct passenger operations under 49 U.S.C. 41102.

Commuter air carrier means a U.S. carrier that has been found fit under 49 U.S.C. 41738 and is authorized to carry passengers on at least five round trips per week on at least one route between two or more points according to a published flight schedule using small aircraft as defined in 14 CFR 298.2.

Covered carrier means a certificated carrier, a commuter carrier, or a foreign air carrier operating to, from or within the United States, conducting scheduled passenger service or public charter service with at least one aircraft having a designed seating capacity of 30 or more seats.

Foreign air carrier means a carrier that is not a citizen of the United States as defined in 49 U.S.C. 40102(a) that holds a foreign air carrier permit issued under 49 U.S.C. 41302 or an exemption issued under 49 U.S.C. 40109 authorizing direct foreign air transportation.

Large hub airport means an airport that accounts for at least 1.00 percent of the total enplanements in the United States.

Medium hub airport means an airport accounting for at least 0.25 percent but less than 1.00 percent of the total enplanements in the United States.

Non-hub airport means an airport with 10,000 or more annual enplanements but less than 0.05 percent of the country's annual passenger boardings.

Small hub airport means an airport accounting for at least 0.05 percent but less than 0.25 percent of the total enplanements in the United States.

Tarmac delay means the holding of an aircraft on the ground either before taking off or after landing with no opportunity for its passengers to deplane.

[Doc. No. DOT–OST–2010–0140, 76 FR 23164, Apr. 25, 2011]

§ 259.4 Contingency Plan for Lengthy Tarmac Delays.

(a) *Adoption of Plan.* Each covered carrier shall adopt a Contingency Plan for Lengthy Tarmac Delays for its scheduled and public charter flights at each U.S. large hub airport, medium hub airport, small hub airport and non-hub airport at which it operates or markets such air service and shall adhere to its plan's terms.

(b) *Contents of Plan.* Each Contingency Plan for Lengthy Tarmac Delays shall include, at a minimum, the following:

(1) For domestic flights, assurance that the covered U.S. air carrier will

not permit an aircraft to remain on the tarmac for more than three hours before allowing passengers to deplane unless:

(i) The pilot-in-command determines there is a safety-related or security-related reason (e.g. weather, a directive from an appropriate government agency) why the aircraft cannot leave its position on the tarmac to deplane passengers; or

(ii) Air traffic control advises the pilot-in-command that returning to the gate or another disembarkation point elsewhere in order to deplane passengers would significantly disrupt airport operations.

(2) For international flights operated by covered carriers that depart from or arrive at a U.S. airport, assurance that the carrier will not permit an aircraft to remain on the tarmac at a U.S. airport for more than four hours before allowing passengers to deplane, unless:

(i) The pilot-in-command determines there is a safety-related or security-related reason why the aircraft cannot leave its position on the tarmac to deplane passengers; or

(ii) Air traffic control advises the pilot-in-command that returning to the gate or another disembarkation point elsewhere in order to deplane passengers would significantly disrupt airport operations.

(3) For all flights, assurance that the carrier will provide adequate food and potable water no later than two hours after the aircraft leaves the gate (in the case of a departure) or touches down (in the case of an arrival) if the aircraft remains on the tarmac, unless the pilot-in-command determines that safety or security considerations preclude such service;

(4) For all flights, assurance of operable lavatory facilities, as well as adequate medical attention if needed, while the aircraft remains on the tarmac;

(5) For all flights, assurance that the passengers on the delayed flight will receive notifications regarding the status of the delay every 30 minutes while the aircraft is delayed, including the reasons for the tarmac delay, if known;

(6) For all flights, assurance that the passengers on the delayed flight will be notified beginning 30 minutes after scheduled departure time (including any revised departure time that passengers were notified about before boarding) and every 30 minutes thereafter that they have the opportunity to deplane from an aircraft that is at the gate or another disembarkation area with the door open if the opportunity to deplane actually exists;

(7) Assurance of sufficient resources to implement the plan; and

(8) Assurance that the plan has been coordinated with airport authorities (including terminal facility operators where applicable) at each U.S. large hub airport, medium hub airport, small hub airport and non-hub airport that the carrier serves, as well as its regular U.S. diversion airports;

(9) Assurance that the plan has been coordinated with U.S. Customs and Border Protection (CBP) at each large U.S. hub airport, medium hub airport, small hub airport and non-hub airport that is regularly used for that carrier's international flights, including diversion airports; and

(10) Assurance that the plan has been coordinated with the Transportation Security Administration (TSA) at each U.S. large hub airport, medium hub airport, small hub airport and non-hub airport that the carrier serves, including diversion airports.

(c) *Code-Share Responsibility.* The tarmac delay contingency plan of the carrier under whose code the service is marketed governs, if different from the operating carrier, unless the marketing carrier specifies in its contract of carriage that the operating carrier's plan governs.

(d) *Amendment of plan.* At any time, a carrier may amend its Contingency Plan for Lengthy Tarmac Delays to decrease the time for aircraft to remain on the tarmac for domestic flights covered in paragraph (b)(1) of this section, for aircraft to remain on the tarmac for international flights covered in paragraph (b)(2) of this section, and for the trigger point for food and water covered in paragraph (b)(3) of this section. A carrier may also amend its plan to increase these intervals (up to the limits in this rule), in which case the amended plan shall apply only to departures that are first offered for sale after the plan's amendment.

(e) *Retention of records.* Each carrier that is required to adopt a Contingency Plan for Lengthy Tarmac Delays shall retain for two years the following information about any tarmac delay that lasts more than three hours:

(1) The length of the delay;

(2) The precise cause of the delay;

(3) The actions taken to minimize hardships for passengers, including the provision of food and water, the maintenance and servicing of lavatories, and medical assistance;

(4) Whether the flight ultimately took off (in the case of a departure delay or diversion) or returned to the gate; and

(5) An explanation for any tarmac delay that exceeded 3 hours (*i.e.*, why the aircraft did not return to the gate by the 3-hour mark).

(f) *Unfair and deceptive practice.* A carrier's failure to comply with the assurances required by this rule and contained in its Contingency Plan for Lengthy Tarmac Delays will be considered to be an unfair and deceptive practice within the meaning of 49 U.S.C. 41712 that is subject to enforcement action by the Department.

[Doc. No. DOT–OST–2010–0140, 76 FR 23164, Apr. 25, 2011]

§ 259.5 Customer Service Plan.

(a) *Adoption of Plan.* Each covered carrier shall adopt a Customer Service Plan applicable to its scheduled flights and shall adhere to the plan's terms.

(b) *Contents of Plan.* Each Customer Service Plan shall address the following subjects and comply with the minimum standards set forth:

(1) Disclosing on the carrier's website, at the ticket counter, or when a customer calls the carrier's reservation center to inquire about a fare or to make a reservation, that the lowest fare offered by the carrier may be available elsewhere if that is the case;

(2) Notifying consumers of known delays, cancellations, and diversions as required by 14 CFR 259.8 of this chapter;

(3) Delivering baggage on time, including making every reasonable effort to return mishandled baggage within twenty-four hours, compensating passengers for reasonable expenses that result due to delay in delivery, as required by 14 CFR part 254 for domestic flights and as required by applicable international agreements for international flights, and reimbursing passengers for any fee charged to transport a bag if that bag is lost;

(4) Allowing reservations to be held at the quoted fare without payment, or cancelled without penalty, for at least twenty-four hours after the reservation is made if the reservation is made one week or more prior to a flight's departure;

(5) Where ticket refunds are due, providing prompt refunds, as required by 14 CFR 374.3 and 12 CFR part 226 for credit card purchases, and within 20 days after receiving a complete refund request for cash and check purchases, including refunding fees charged to a passenger for optional services that the passenger was unable to use due to an oversale situation or flight cancellation;

(6) Properly accommodating passengers with disabilities, as required by part 382 of this chapter, and other special-needs passengers as set forth in the carrier's policies and procedures, including during lengthy tarmac delays;

(7) Meeting customers' essential needs during lengthy tarmac delays as required by § 259.4 of this chapter and as provided for in each covered carrier's contingency plan;

(8) Handling "bumped" passengers with fairness and consistency in the case of oversales as required by part 250 of this chapter and as described in each carrier's policies and procedures for determining boarding priority;

(9) Disclosing cancellation policies, frequent flyer rules, aircraft seating configuration, and lavatory availability on the selling carrier's website, and upon request, from the selling carrier's telephone reservations staff;

(10) Notifying consumers in a timely manner of changes in their travel itineraries;

(11) Ensuring responsiveness to consumer problems as required by § 259.7 of this chapter; and

(12) Identifying the services it provides to mitigate passenger inconveniences resulting from flight cancellations and misconnections.

(c) *Self-auditing of plan and retention of records.* Each carrier that is required to adopt a Customer Service Plan shall audit its own adherence to its plan annually. Carriers shall make the results of their audits available for the Department's review upon request for two years following the date any audit is completed.

[Doc. No. DOT–OST–2010–0140, 76 FR 23165, Apr. 25, 2011; 76 FR 45181, July 28, 2011]

§ 259.6 Posting of Contracts of Carriage, Tarmac Delay Contingency Plans and Customer Service Plans on websites.

(a) Each U.S. air carrier that has a website and each foreign air carrier that has a website marketed to U.S. consumers, and that is required to adopt a contingency plan for lengthy tarmac delays, shall post its current contingency plan on its website in easily accessible form.

(b) Each U.S. air carrier that has a website and each foreign air carrier that has a website marketed to U.S. consumers, and that is required to adopt a customer service plan, shall post its current customer service plan on its website in easily accessible form.

(c) Each U.S. air carrier that has a website and each foreign air carrier that has a website marketed to U.S. consumers shall post its current contract of carriage on its website in easily accessible form.

[Doc. No. DOT–OST–2010–0140, 76 FR 23165, Apr. 25, 2011]

§ 259.7 Response to consumer problems.

(a) *Designated advocates for passengers' interests.* Each covered carrier shall designate for its scheduled flights an employee who shall be responsible for monitoring the effects of flight delays, flight cancellations, and lengthy tarmac delays on passengers. This employee shall have input into decisions on which flights to cancel and which will be delayed the longest.

(b) *Informing consumers how to complain.* Each covered carrier shall make available the mailing address and e-mail or web address of the designated department in the airline with which to file a complaint about its scheduled service. This information shall be provided on the U.S. carrier's website (if any) and the foreign carrier's website (if marketed to U.S. consumers), on all e-ticket confirmations and, upon request, at each ticket counter and boarding gate staffed by the carrier or a contractor of the carrier.

(c) *Response to complaints.* Each covered carrier shall acknowledge in writing receipt of each complaint regarding its scheduled service to the complainant within 30 days of receiving it and shall send a substantive written response to each complainant within 60 days of receiving the complaint. A complaint is a specific written expression of dissatisfaction concerning a difficulty or problem which the person experienced when using or attempting to use an airline's services.

(d) *Social networking sites.* Each covered carrier that uses a social networking site (e.g. Facebook, Twitter) and that does not intend for that site to be a vehicle for receipt of written consumer complaints subject to this section shall clearly indicate on the carrier's primary page on that social networking site that it will not reply to consumer complaints on that site and shall direct consumers to the carrier's mailing address and e-mail or website location for filing written complaints.

[Doc. No. DOT–OST–2010–0140, 76 FR 23165, Apr. 25, 2011]

§ 259.8 Notify passengers of known delays, cancellations, and diversions.

(a) Each covered carrier for its scheduled flights to, from or within the U.S. must promptly provide to passengers who are ticketed or hold reservations, and to the public, information about a change in the status of a flight within 30 minutes after the carrier becomes aware of such a change in the status of a flight. A change in the status of a flight means, at a minimum, a cancellation, diversion or delay of 30 minutes or more in the planned operation of a flight that occurs within seven calendar days of the scheduled date of the planned operation. The flight status information must at a minimum be provided in the boarding gate area for the flight at a U.S. airport, on the carrier's website, and via the carrier's telephone reservation system upon inquiry by any person.

(1) With respect to any U.S. air carrier or foreign air carrier that permits passengers and other interested persons to subscribe to flight status notification services, the carrier must deliver such notification to such subscribers, by whatever means the carrier offers that the subscriber chooses.

(2) The U.S. carrier or foreign air carrier shall incorporate such notification service commitment into its Customer Service Plan as specified in section 259.5 of this chapter.

(b) For its scheduled flights to, from or within the U.S, within 30 minutes after the carrier becomes aware of a flight cancellation, a flight delay of 30 minutes or more, or a flight diversion, each covered carrier must update all flight status displays and other sources of flight information that are under the carrier's control at U.S. airports with information on that flight irregularity.

(c) If an airport-controlled display system at a U.S. airport accepts flight status updates from carriers, covered carriers must provide flight irregularity information to that airport for the carrier's scheduled flights to, from or within the U.S. within 30 minutes after the carrier becomes aware of such a change in the status of a flight. Flight irregularity refers to flight cancellations, flight delays of 30 minutes or more, and diversions.

[Doc. No. DOT–OST–2010–0140, 76 FR 23166, Apr. 25, 2011; Docket No. DOT–OST–2014–0056, 81 FR 76829, Nov. 3, 2016]

PART 271—GUIDELINES FOR SUBSIDIZING AIR CARRIERS PROVIDING ESSENTIAL AIR TRANSPORTATION

AUTHORITY: 49 U.S.C. Chapters 401, 417.

SOURCE: ER–1398, 49 FR 49846, Dec. 24, 1984, unless otherwise noted.

§ 271.1 Purpose.

This part establishes the guidelines required by 49 U.S.C. 41736 to be used by the Department in establishing the fair and reasonable amount of compensation needed to ensure the continuation of essential air service to an eligible place under 49 U.S.C. 41731 and 41734. These guidelines are intended to cover normal carrier selection cases and rate renewal cases, and not necessarily emergency carrier selection cases.

[60 FR 43524, Aug. 22, 1995]

§ 271.2 Definitions.

As used in this part:

Eligible place means a place in the United States that—

(1) Was an eligible point under section 419 of the Federal Aviation Act of 1958 as in effect before October 1, 1988;

(2) Received scheduled air transportation at any time between January 1, 1990, and November 4, 1990; and

(3) Is not listed in Department of Transportation Orders 89–9–37 and 89–12–52 as a place ineligible for compensation under Subchapter II of Chapter 417 of the Statute.

Essential air service is that air transportation which the Department has found to be essential under Subchapter II of Chapter 417 of the Statute.

[60 FR 43524, Aug. 22, 1995]

§ 271.3 Carrier subsidy need.

In establishing the subsidy for an air carrier providing essential air service at an eligible place, the Department will consider the following:

(a) The reasonable projected costs of a carrier in serving that place;

(b) The carrier's reasonable projected revenues for serving that place;

(c) The appropriate size of aircraft for providing essential air service at that place; and

(d) A reasonable profit for a carrier serving that place.

[ER–1398, 49 FR 49846, Dec. 24, 1984, as amended at 60 FR 43524, Aug. 22, 1995]

§ 271.4 Carrier costs.

(a) The reasonable costs projected for a carrier providing essential air service at an eligible place will be evaluated:

(1) For costs attributable to the carrier's flying operations (direct expenses), by comparing the projected costs submitted by the carrier with the following:

(i) The carrier's historical direct operating costs with the same or similar aircraft types;

(ii) The direct operating unit costs of similar carriers using the same or similar equipment; and

(iii) Data supplied by the manufacturer of the carrier's aircraft.

(2) For other costs, by one or more of the following methods:

(i) By direct assignment where the indirect costs are attributable to the carrier's operations at the eligible place;

(ii) By comparing the carrier's systemwide indirect operating expenses to those submitted by the carrier for the eligible place; or

(iii) By comparing the indirect operating expenses submitted by the carrier with the ratio of indirect to direct costs that have been experienced by the carrier in other markets or to costs that are representative of the industry.

(3) By considering the unique circumstances of the carrier or the community being served that justify deviations from the costs that would otherwise be established for that carrier under this paragraph.

(4) By determining whether the aircraft to be used by the carrier at the eligible place, and on which its costs are derived, are appropriate for providing essential air service there. The appropriateness of the aircraft to be used is based on the following characteristics of the eligible place:

(i) Traffic levels;

(ii) The level of air service that the Department has decided is essential for the eligible place;

(iii) Distance to the designated hub;

(iv) The altitude at which the carrier must fly to the designated hub; and

(v) Other operational elements involved.

(b) When the essential air service would be made part of the carrier's linear system, the Department might, instead of the factors in paragraph (a) of this section, consider only the incremental costs that the carrier will incur in adding that service to its system.

[ER–1398, 49 FR 49846, Dec. 24, 1984, as amended at 60 FR 43524, 43525, Aug. 22, 1995]

§ 271.5 Carrier revenues.

(a) The projected passenger revenue for a carrier providing essential air service at an eligible place will be calculated by multiplying the following:

(1) A reasonable projected net fare, which is the standard fare expected to be charged for service between the eligible place and the designated hub less any dilution caused by joint fare arrangements, discount fares that it offers, or prorates of fares for through one-line passengers; and

(2) The traffic (including both local and beyond traffic) projected to flow between the eligible place and the designated hub or hubs, which is based on the carrier's own estimates, Department estimates, and on traffic levels in the market at issue when such data are available.

(b) The reasonableness of a carrier's passenger revenue projections will be evaluated by:

(1) Comparing the carrier's proposed fare with the fare charged in other city-pair markets of similar distances and traffic densities; and

(2) Comparing the carrier's proposed pricing structure with historical pricing practices in the market at issue, with the pricing practices of that carrier in other markets, and with any standard industry pricing guidelines that may be available.

(c) An estimate of freight and other transport-related revenue will be included as a component of projected revenues and will be based on recent experience in the market involved and on the experience of the carrier involved in other markets.

[ER–1398, 49 FR 49846, Dec. 24, 1984, as amended at 60 FR 43524, Aug. 22, 1995]

§ 271.6 Profit element.

The reasonable return for a carrier for providing essential air service at an eligible place generally will be set at a flat percentage, typically 5 percent of that carrier's projected operating costs as established under § 271.4, plus any applicable interest expenses on flight equipment.

[ER–1398, 49 FR 49846, Dec. 24, 1984, as amended at 60 FR 43524, 43525, Aug. 22, 1995]

§ 271.7 Subsidy payout formula.

(a) Subsidy will be paid by the Department to the air carrier monthly, based on the subsidy rate established by the Department for the carrier under this part. Payments will not vary except as provided in this section.

(b) While a carrier's subsidy rate will not vary even if actual revenues or costs differ from projections, the actual amount of each payment may vary depending on the following factors:

(1) Seasonal characteristics of the carrier's operations at the eligible place;

(2) The actual number of flights completed, aircraft miles flown, available seat-miles flown, or variations in other operational elements upon which the subsidy rate is based; or

(3) Adjustments to the carrier's subsidy required by § 271.8(b).

(c) Payments will continue for the duration of the rate term established under § 271.8 provided that the carrier continues to provide the required service.

[ER–1398, 49 FR 49846, Dec. 24, 1984, as amended at 60 FR 43524, 43525, Aug. 22, 1995]

§ 271.8 Rate period.

(a) The subsidy rate generally will be set for a 2-year period, or two consecutive 1-year periods. The Department may set the rate for a shorter period in the following situations:

(1) A commuter air carrier is replacing a larger certificated carrier at the eligible place;

(2) Traffic at the eligible place has substantially decreased;

(3) The Department considers the cost or revenue projections of the carrier for the second year to be unrealistic;

(4) It is likely that there will be changes in the eligible place essential air service level; or

(5) The uncertainties of the market or other circumstances warrant a shorter rate period.

(b) The subsidy rate established for a carrier under this part will not be changed during the rate period unless an adjustment is required in the public interest.

(c) At the end of the rate period, the carrier will not have a continuing right to receive subsidy for providing essential air service at the eligible place.

[ER–1398, 49 FR 49846, Dec. 24, 1984, as amended at 60 FR 43524, 43525, Aug. 22, 1995]

§ 271.9 Discrimination prohibited.

(a) All air carriers receiving subsidy under this part shall comply with the following:

(1) The Age Discrimination Act of 1975;

(2) The Civil Rights Act of 1964 and 49 CFR part 21; and

(3) The Rehabilitation Act of 1973, 49 CFR part 27, and part 382 of this chapter.

(b) Within 1 year after it first receives a subsidy under this part, the carrier shall evaluate its practices and procedures for accommodating the handicapped in accordance with § 382.23 of this chapter.

(c) All air carriers seeking a subsidy under this part shall include in their subsidy application the assurances required by 49 CFR parts 20, 21, 27 and 29, and § 382.21 of this chapter.

[ER–1398, 49 FR 49846, Dec. 24, 1984, as amended at 60 FR 43525, Aug. 22, 1995]

PART 272—ESSENTIAL AIR SERVICE TO THE FREELY ASSOCIATED STATES

Sec.

AUTHORITY: 49 U.S.C. Chapters 401, 402, 416, 461, 1102; sec. 221(a)(5) of the Compact of Free Association, and paragraph 5 of Article IX of the Federal Programs and Services Agreement in implementation of that Compact (Pub. L. 99–239; Pub. L. 99–658); Pub. L. 101–219.

SOURCE: Amdt. 272–1, 52 FR 5443, Feb. 23, 1987, unless otherwise noted.

§ 272.1 Purpose.

Paragraph 5 of Article IX of the Federal Programs and Services Agreement implementing section 221(a)(5) of the Compact of Free Association between the United States and the Governments of the Federated States of Micronesia, the Marshall Islands and Palau (the Freely Associated States) provides, among other things, for the Department of Transportation (Department), as successor to the Civil Aeronautics Board (Board), to guarantee essential air service, with compensation if necessary, to certain places in these islands. Subparagraph 5(h) of the Agreement provides that the Department shall adopt rules to implement the provisions of paragraph 5 as it in its discretion deems appropriate. Section 221(a)(5) of the Compact, which was adopted by Congress as public laws (Pub. L. 99–239, Jan. 14, 1986; Pub. L. 99–658, Nov. 14, 1986), provides that the Department (as successor to the Board) has the authority to implement the provisions of paragraph 5 of the Agreement. This part implements these provisions of paragraph 5.

[Amdt. 272–1, 52 FR 5443, Feb. 23, 1987, as amended at 60 FR 43525, Aug. 22, 1995]

§ 272.2 Applicability.

This part establishes the provisions applicable to the Department's guarantee of essential air service to places in the Federated States of Micronesia, the Marshall Islands and Palau, and the payment of compensation for such services. The rule applies to U.S. air carriers and Freely Associated State Air Carriers providing essential air service to these places.

[Amdt. 272–1, 52 FR 5443, Feb. 23, 1987, as amended at 60 FR 43525, Aug. 22, 1995]

§ 272.3 Places eligible for guaranteed essential air service.

(a) Subject to the provisions of this part, and paragraph 5 of Article IX of the Federal Programs and Services Agreement, the Department will make provision for the operation of essential air service, with compensation if necessary, to the following places in the Freely Associated States:

In the *Federated States of Micronesia:* Ponape, Truk and Yap.

In the *Marshall Islands:* Majuro and Kwajalein.

In *Palau:* Koror.

(b) The places specified herein in the Federated States of Micronesia, the Marshall Islands or Palau, respectively, shall cease to be eligible places under this part if any of those Governments withdraw from the subsidy provisions of Article IX of the Federal Programs and Services Agreement in accordance with paragraph 8 of Article IX or Article XII of that Agreement.

[Amdt. 272–1, 52 FR 5443, Feb. 23, 1987, as amended at 60 FR 43525, Aug. 22, 1995]

§ 272.4 Applicability of procedures and policies under 49 U.S.C. 41731–42.

Since the authority of the Department to guarantee essential air service is derived from the Federal Programs and Services Agreement and the Compact of Free Association, the provisions and procedures utilized by the Department in implementation of 49 U.S.C. 41731–42 will be followed only to the extent determined by the Department to be consistent with the obligations assumed by the United States in the Agreement and Compact, and the provisions of this part.

[Amdt. 272–1, 52 FR 5443, Feb. 23, 1987, as amended at 60 FR 43525, Aug. 22, 1995]

§ 272.5 Determination of essential air service.

Procedures for the determination of essential air service under this section, and review of that determination, shall, except to the extent otherwise directed by the Department, be governed by § 325.4 (except the application of 49 U.S.C. 41737 in § 325.4(b)); § 325.6(a); §§ 325.8–325.11; § 325.12 (provided that all documents shall be served on the President and the designated authorities of the Freely Associated State concerned); and §§ 325.13 and 325.14 of this chapter.

[Amdt. 272–1, 52 FR 5443, Feb. 23, 1987, as amended at 60 FR 43525, Aug. 22, 1995]

§ 272.6 Considerations in the determination of essential air service.

(a) In the determination of essential air service to an eligible Freely Associated State place, the Department shall consider, among other factors, the following:

(1) The demonstrated level of traffic demand;

(2) The amount of compensation necessary to maintain a level of service sufficient to meet that demand;

(3) The extent to which the demand may be accommodated by connecting or other services of U.S., Freely Associated State, or foreign carriers by air—through U.S., Freely Associated State, or foreign places—that provide access to the U.S. air transportation system;

(4) Alternative modes of transportation that may be available; and

(5) The peculiar needs of the Freely Associated States for air transportation services.

(b) The Guidelines for Individual Determinations of essential air service set forth in part 398 of this chapter shall be applied only to the extent the Department concludes that they are applicable to the special circumstances affecting transportation to the Freely Associated States and reflective of the provisions of this part.

(c) Nothing in this part shall be construed as providing for a level of essential air service that would exceed the level of service justified by the considerations set forth in paragraph (a) of this section.

[Amdt. 272–1, 52 FR 5443, Feb. 23, 1987, as amended at 60 FR 43525, Aug. 22, 1995]

§ 272.7 Notice of discontinuance of service.

(a) An air carrier or Freely Associated State Air Carrier shall not terminate, suspend, or reduce air service to any eligible Freely Associated State place, unless it has given notice as specified in this section, if as a result of the reduction of such service the aggregate of the remaining air service provided to such place would be below:

(1) If the Department has not made a determination of essential air service for such place, the level of service specified in Order 80–9–63; and

(2) If the Department has made a determination of essential air service for such place, that level of essential air service.

(b) An air carrier or Freely Associated State Air Carrier wishing to terminate, suspend or reduce air service under paragraph (a) shall file a notice of such proposed reduction in service at least 90 days prior to such service reduction, in accordance with the procedures specified in §§ 323.4, 323.6, and 323.7 of this chapter.

(c) The notice shall be served on the President and the designated Authorities of the Freely Associated State concerned, in addition to the persons specified in § 323.7.

(d) The procedures specified in §§ 323.9–323.18, to the extent applicable to 90-day notices filed by certificated air carriers, shall also be applicable to notices of terminations, suspensions or reductions in service filed under this section.

[Amdt. 272–1, 52 FR 5443, Feb. 23, 1987, as amended at 60 FR 43525, Aug. 22, 1995]

§ 272.8 Obligation to continue service.

(a) If the Department finds that a proposed termination, suspension, or reduction in service by an air carrier or Freely Associated State Air Carrier will, or may, reduce service to an eligible Freely Associated State place below the level of essential air service to such place, whether or not the Department has previously determined the level of essential air service to such place, the Department may direct the air carrier or Freely Associated State Air Carrier concerned to maintain service to such place at a level the Department determines will ensure essential air service to such place, pending the commencement of alternative service as required to maintain the level of essential air service previously, or thereafter, determined by the Department.

(b) During any period the Department requires an air carrier or Freely Associated State Air Carrier to maintain a level of service proposed to be terminated, suspended or reduced, following the filing of a 90 day notice in accordance with §272.7, the Department will provide for the payment of compensation to such carrier for any losses incurred by that carrier as a result of such required continuation of service in accordance with the procedures set forth in part 271 of this chapter. If the carrier is already receiving compensation pursuant to §272.9 of this part, the Department will continue to direct payment of such compensation during any period the carrier is required to maintain service. Such payments shall be made by the Department of Interior from funds appropriated for this purpose.

(c) The Department will review its order from time to time and will revise the level of required service as necessary to maintain only the level of essential air service determined by the Department for that place, considering all other service to such place in accordance with §272.6(a)(3).

(d) During the period any such air carrier or Freely Associated State Air Carrier is required to maintain service under this section, the Department will make every effort to obtain alternative service, with compensation if necessary, as required to maintain essential air service to such place.

[Amdt. 272-1, 52 FR 5443, Feb. 23, 1987, as amended at 60 FR 43525, Aug. 22, 1995]

§272.9 Selection of a carrier to provide essential air service and payment of compensation.

(a) If the Department finds that essential air service will not be maintained to an eligible Freely Associated State place, the Department shall invite applications to provide the service required to maintain essential air service to such place.

(b) If the Department determines that essential air service will not be provided to such place in the absence of the payment of subsidy compensation to a carrier or carriers, the Department shall determine the compensation necessary, considering all other service to such place in accordance with §272.6(a)(3), to maintain the level of essential air service determined by the Department under §272.5, and the times and manner of the payment of such compensation.

(c) The compensation determined by the Department to be necessary to maintain essential air service to such place shall be paid by the Department of Interior out of funds appropriated for that purpose, to the carrier or carriers selected by the Department.

(d) The Department shall continue to specify compensation to be paid to a carrier or carriers under this section only as long as the Department determines that essential air service will not be provided to the Freely Associated State in the absence of the payment of such compensation.

(e) Except as permitted in paragraph (f) of this section, the Department shall select a U.S. air carrier or carriers to provide essential air service for compensation.

(f) The Department may select a Freely Associated State Air Carrier, holding a foreign air carrier permit issued in accordance with subpart D of part 211 of this chapter, to provide essential air service for compensation, only if—

(1) No U.S. air carrier is available to provide the required essential air service; or

(2) The compensation necessary for the provision of the required essential air service would be substantially less than the compensation necessary if such essential air service were to be provided by a U.S. air carrier.

(g) Any order of the Department selecting a Freely Associated State Air Carrier to provide such essential air service shall be submitted to the President of the United States not less than 10 days prior to its effective date and shall be subject to stay or disapproval by the President.

(h) Among the criteria that will be considered by the Department in its determination of the carrier or carriers to be selected to perform the required essential air service are:

(1) The desirability of developing an integrated linear system of air transportation whenever such a system most adequately meets the air transportation needs of the Freely Associated States concerned;

(2) The experience of the applicant in providing scheduled air service in the

vicinity of the Freely Associated States for which essential air service is proposed to be provided;

(3) The amount of compensation that will be required to provide the proposed essential air service;

(4) The impact of the proposed service on service provided to other Freely Associated State points; and

(5) The views of the Governments of the Freely Associated States concerned.

(i) The Department may from time to time, on its own motion, or upon application of any carrier or government, review and change its selection of a carrier to provide essential air service, or its determination as to the compensation necessary to provide such essential air service.

(j) All applications or other documents filed or issued in proceedings under this section shall be served upon the President of the Freely Associated State concerned and the Authorities designated by that Government(s) in accordance with Article II, paragraph 10, of the Federal Programs and Services Agreement supplemental to the Compact of Free Association, and such Government shall be a party to any such proceeding. In reaching its determination, the Department will carefully consider any views of such Government that have been submitted.

[Amdt. 272–1, 52 FR 5443, Feb. 23, 1987, as amended at 60 FR 43525, Aug. 22, 1995]

§ 272.10 Conditions applicable to carriers serving a subsidized market.

(a) The Department may, after providing an opportunity for comment by the carrier or carriers affected, impose service, fare or rate conditions on any U.S., Freely Associated State, foreign air carrier, or foreign carrier by air as a precondition to the payment of compensation necessary to maintain essential air service, whether or not the affected carrier is itself receiving subsidy compensation in the market, if it finds that:

(1) Essential air service in a Freely Associated State market or markets will not be provided in the absence of the payment of compensation;

(2) Specified service, rate or fare conditions are or will be necessary or desirable to minimize the required subsidy compensation; and

(3) The imposition of such conditions will not unduly impair the service provided in the market.

(b) To the extent the carrier or carriers upon whom the conditions are imposed pursuant to paragraph (a) of this section do not hold a certificate, permit, or other authority from the Department that may be amended to effectively implement the specified conditions, the Department may notify the Government(s) of the Freely Associated States concerned that the imposition of such conditions on those carriers by those Governments shall be a precondition to the payment of the subsidy compensation required to maintain essential air service in the market in question.

(c) The Department may withhold or suspend its provision for the payment of subsidy compensation required to maintain essential air service unless and until the Freely Associated State(s) concerned take the necessary action to impose the specified conditions on the carriers referred to in paragraph (b) of this section, and those carriers have complied with the specified conditions.

(d) Any order of the Department imposing conditions, or requiring the imposition of conditions, pursuant to this paragraph shall be submitted to the President for review not less than 10 days prior to its effective date, and shall be subject to stay or disapproval by the President.

[Amdt. 272–1, 52 FR 5443, Feb. 23, 1987, as amended at 60 FR 43525, Aug. 22, 1995]

§ 272.11 Effective date of provisions.

The provisions of this part shall not become effective for Palau until the Compact of Free Association and Article IX of the Federal Programs and Services Agreement become effective for Palau.

§ 272.12 Termination.

These provisions shall terminate on October 1, 1998, unless the program of essential air service to the Federated States of Micronesia, the Marshall Islands, and Palau is specifically extended by Congress.

This amendment is issued under the authority of 49 CFR 1.57(l).

[Amdt. 272–2, 56 FR 1732, Jan. 7, 1991, as amended at 60 FR 43525, Aug. 22, 1995]

PART 291—CARGO OPERATIONS IN INTERSTATE AIR TRANSPORTATION

Subpart A—General

Subpart B—All-Cargo Air Transportation Certificates

Subpart C—General Rules for All-Cargo Air Transportation

Subpart D—Exemptions for Cargo Operations in Interstate Air Transportation

Subpart E—Reporting Rules

Subpart F—Enforcement

Subpart G—Public Disclosure of Data

AUTHORITY: 49 U.S.C. 329 and chapters 41103, 41708 and 41709.

SOURCE: ER–1080, 43 FR 53635, Nov. 16, 1978, unless otherwise noted.

Subpart A—General

§ 291.1 Applicability.

This part applies to cargo operations in interstate air transportation by air carriers certificated under section 41102 or 41103 of the Statute. It also applies to applicants for an all-cargo air transportation certificate under section 41103 of the Statute.

[60 FR 43525, Aug. 22, 1995]

§ 291.2 Definitions.

All-cargo air transportation means the transportation by aircraft in interstate air transportation of only property or only mail, or both.

Interstate air transportation means the transportation of passengers or property by aircraft as a common carrier for compensation, or the transportation of mail by aircraft—

(1) Between a place in—

(i) A State, territory, or possession of the United States and a place in the District of Columbia or another State, territory, or possession of the United States;

(ii) Hawaii and another place in Hawaii through the airspace over a place outside Hawaii;

(iii) The District of Columbia and another place in the District of Columbia; or

(iv) A territory or possession of the United States and another place in the same territory or possession; and

(2) When any part of the transportation is by aircraft.

Reporting carrier for Schedule T–100 purposes means the air carrier in operational control of the aircraft, i.e., the carrier that uses its flight crew under its own FAA operating authority.

Section 41102 carrier means an air carrier certificated under section 41102 of the Statute to transport persons, property and mail or property and mail only.

Section 41103 carrier means an air carrier holding a certificate issued under section 41103 of the Statute to provide all-cargo air transportation.

Service, scheduled cargo means transport service operated pursuant to published flight schedules including extra sections. There is no requirement on the number of weekly flights nor is there a requirement that the schedule be published in the Official Airline Guide.

Wet-Lease Agreement means an agreement under which one carrier leases an aircraft with flight crew to another air carrier.

[60 FR 43525, Aug. 22, 1995, as amended at 67 FR 49226, July 30, 2002]

Subpart B—All-Cargo Air Transportation Certificates

§ 291.10 Applications.

Applications for all-cargo air service certificates shall comply with the provisions of part 201 and subpart B of part 302 of this chapter with regard to filing procedures, and with the provisions of part 204 of this chapter with regard to evidentiary requirements.

(Approved by the Office of Management and Budget under control number 2106–0023)

[Doc. No. 47582, 57 FR 38770, Aug. 27, 1992, as amended at 65 FR 6456, Feb. 9, 2000]

Subpart C—General Rules for All-Cargo Air Transportation

§ 291.20 Applicability.

The rules in this subpart apply to cargo operations in interstate air transportation performed by air carriers certificated under sections 41102 or 41103 of the Statute. Section 41103 carriers that operate passenger-only or combination aircraft under section 41102, part 298 of this chapter, or other Department authority, must comply with the rules in this subpart in connection with cargo operations in interstate air transportation, whether provided on all-cargo or combination aircraft, operated pursuant to this authority or otherwise. In case a carrier may operate a particular flight under either a section 41102 certificate or a section 41103 certificate, the flight is presumed to be operated under the carrier's section 41103 authority.

[60 FR 43526, Aug. 22, 1995]

§ 291.22 Aircraft accident liability insurance requirement.

No air carrier shall operate all-cargo aircraft or provide all-cargo air transportation unless such carrier has and maintains in effect aircraft accident liability coverage that meets the requirements of part 205 of this chapter.

[ER–1255, 46 FR 52583, Oct. 27, 1981, as amended at 60 FR 43526, Aug. 22, 1995]

§ 291.23 Record retention.

(a) The provisions of 14 CFR part 249, *Preservation of air carrier accounts, records and memoranda,* shall apply to all carriers, except that records pertaining to transportation provided on aircraft eligible to be operated under part 298 of this title, and records concerning transportation outside the geographic scope of interstate air transportation, need not be maintained unless required by other Department regulations.

(b) Each carrier shall retain for 1 year a copy of each rate sheet, airwaybill contract, and other document reflecting changed, new, or other previously unreported general or special prices or rules governing the carriage of freight in interstate air transportation (except mail), unless the transportation was performed in accordance with an effective tariff on file with the Department. Each carrier shall retain for 1 year a copy of any formula based on standard weight, mileage, or other method used to determine an individual airbill or contract.

(Approved by the Office of Management and Budget under control number 3024–0022)

[ER–1080, 43 FR 53635, Nov. 16, 1978, as amended by ER–1270, 46 FR 63220, Dec. 31, 1981; Doc. No. 47582, 57 FR 38770, Aug. 27, 1992; 60 FR 43526, Aug. 22, 1995]

§ 291.24 Waiver of Department Economic Regulations.

Except for this part and those parts of the Department's Economic Regulations (parts 200 through 299 of this title) specifically referred to in this part, carriers providing cargo operations in interstate air transportation are, with respect to that transportation, relieved from all obligations imposed on air carriers by those economic regulations. Flights operated entirely within interstate air transportation shall be free from those obligations, even though they may also carry shipments to or from points outside that geographic area. This waiver shall not apply to the requirements of part 239 of this title.

[ER-1080, 43 FR 53635, Nov. 16, 1978, as amended by Doc. No. 47582, 57 FR 38770, Aug. 27, 1992; 60 FR 43526, Aug. 22, 1995]

Subpart D—Exemptions for Cargo Operations in Interstate Air Transportation

§ 291.30 General.

The following exemptions, except as otherwise specifically noted, apply only to cargo operations in interstate air transportation. They do not relieve a carrier from obligations derived from other transportation.

[ER-1080, 43 FR 53635, Nov. 16, 1978, as amended at 60 FR 43526, Aug. 22, 1995]

§ 291.31 Exemptions from the Statute.

(a) Each section 41102 or 41103 air carrier providing cargo operations in interstate air transportation is, with respect to such transportation, exempted from the following portions of the Statute only if and so long as it complies with the provisions of this part and the conditions imposed herein, and to the extent necessary to permit it to conduct cargo operations in interstate air transportation:

(1) Sections 41310, 41705,

(2) Chapter 415, and

(3) Chapter 419 for all-cargo operations under section 41103.

(b) Each air carrier providing cargo operations in interstate air transportation under section 41103 of the Statute is exempted from the provisions of section 41106(a) of the Statute to the extent necessary to permit it to compete for and operate cargo charters in interstate air transportation for the Department of Defense under contracts of more than 30 days' duration.

(c) The Department of Defense is exempted from section 41106(a) of the Statute to the extent necessary to permit it to negotiate and enter into contracts of more than 30 days' duration with any section 41103 carrier for operation of cargo charters in interstate air transportation.

[60 FR 43526, Aug. 22, 1995]

Subpart E—Reporting Rules

§ 291.40 [Reserved]

§ 291.41 Financial and statistical reporting—general.

(a) Carriers providing cargo operations in interstate air transportation that also conduct other operations under section 41102 shall comply with the provisions of part 241 of this title.

(b) Carriers providing cargo operations in interstate air transportation under section 41103 certificates shall comply with § 291.42.

(c) Carriers providing cargo operations in interstate air transportation under section 41103, and also providing other services under part 298 of this title, shall report their cargo operations in interstate air transportation operations in accordance with § 291.42, and shall report all other traffic in accordance with the provisions of subpart F of part 298.

[ER-1080, 43 FR 53635, Nov. 16, 1978, as amended at 60 FR 43526, Aug. 22, 1995]

§ 291.42 Section 41103 financial and traffic reporting.

(a) *General instructions.* Carriers operating under section 41103 certificates that are not subject to part 241 of this chapter shall file Form 291-A, "Statement of Operations for Section 41103 Operations", Schedule T-100, "U.S. Air Carrier Traffic and Capacity Data by Nonstop Segment and On-Flight Market", and Schedule P-12(a), "Fuel Consumption by Type of Service and Entity" with the Department's Bureau of Transportation Statistics (BTS).

(1) A single copy of the BTS Form 291-A report shall be filed annually with the Office of Airline Information (OAI) for the year ended December 31, to be received on or before February 10 of the immediately following year. A single copy of the monthly BTS Schedule P-12(a) is due at OAI within 20 days after the end of each month. An electronic filing of the monthly Schedule T-100 is due at OAI within 30 days after the end of each month. Due dates falling on a Saturday, Sunday or Federal holiday will become effective on the next work day.

(2) Reports required by this section shall be submitted to the Bureau of

Transportation Statistics in a format specified in accounting and reporting directives issued by the Bureau of Transportation Statistics' Director of Airline Information.

(b) *Statement of Operations and Statistics Summary for section 41103 operations.* This statement shall include the following elements:

(1) Total operating revenue, categorized as follows:

(i) Transport revenues from the carriage of property in scheduled and nonscheduled service;

(ii) Transport revenue from the carriage of mail in scheduled and nonscheduled service; and

(iii) Transport-related revenues.

(2) Total operating expenses;

(3) Operating profit or loss, computed by subtracting the total operating expenses from the total operating revenues; and

(4) Net income, computed by subtracting the total operating and nonoperating expenses, including interest expenses and income taxes, from the total operating and nonoperating revenues.

(c) *Summary of traffic and capacity statistics.* This summary shall include the following elements:

(1) Total revenue ton-miles, which are the aircraft miles flown on each flight stage times the number of tons of revenue traffic carried on that stage. They shall be categorized as follows:

(i) Property; and

(ii) Mail.

(2) Revenue tons enplaned, reflecting the total revenue tons of cargo loaded on aircraft during the annual period;

(3) Available ton-miles, reflecting the total revenue ton-miles available for all cargo service during the annual period, and computed by multiplying aircraft miles flown on each flight stage by the number of tons of aircraft capacity available for that stage;

(4) Aircraft miles flown, reflecting the total number of aircraft miles flown in cargo service during the annual period;

(5) Aircraft departures performed, reflecting the total number of take-offs performed in cargo service during the annual period; and

(6) Aircraft hours airborne, reflecting the aircraft hours of flight (from take-off to landing) performed in cargo service during the annual period.

[ER–1350, 48 FR 32757, July 19, 1983, as amended by Doc. No. 47582, 57 FR 38770, Aug. 27, 1992; 60 FR 43526, Aug. 22, 1995; 60 FR 66726, Dec. 26, 1995; 67 FR 49226, July 30, 2002; 75 FR 41585, July 16, 2010]

§ 291.43 Statement of operation for section 41103 operations.

Form 291–A contains the following data elements:

(a) Total operating revenue, categorized as follows:

(1) Transport revenues from the carriage of property in scheduled and nonscheduled service;

(2) Transport revenues from the carriage of mail in scheduled and nonscheduled service; and

(3) Transport-related revenues;

(b) Total operating expenses;

(c) Operating profit or loss, computed by subtracting the total operating expenses from the total operating revenues; and

(d) Net income, computed by subtracting the total operating and nonoperating expenses, including interest expenses and income taxes, from the total operating and nonoperating revenues.

[Doc. No. OST–98–4043, 67 FR 49227, July 30, 2002]

§ 291.44 BTS Schedule P–12(a), Fuel Consumption by Type of Service and Entity.

(a) For the purposes of BTS schedule P–12(a), type of service shall be either scheduled service or nonscheduled service as those terms are defined in § 291.45(c)(2) and (3).

(b) For the purpose of this schedule, scheduled service shall be reported separately for:

(1) Intra-Alaskan operations;

(2) Domestic operations, which shall include all operations within and between the 50 States of the United States (except Intra-Alaska), the District of Columbia, the Commonwealth of Puerto Rico and the United States Virgin Islands, or a U.S. territory or possession to a place in any State of the United States the District of Columbia, the Commonwealth of Puerto Rico and the United States Virgin Islands, or a U.S. territory or possession;

(3) International operations are flight stages with one or both terminals outside the 50 States of the United States, the District of Columbia, the Commonwealth of Puerto Rico and the United States Virgin Islands, or a U.S. territory or possession.

(c) For the purpose of this schedule, nonscheduled service shall be reported separately for domestic operations and international operations as defined in paragraphs (b)(2) and (b)(3) of this section, except that domestic and international Military Airlift Command (MAC) operations shall be reported on separate lines.

(d) The cost data reported on each line shall represent the average cost of fuel, as determined at the station level, consumed in that geographic entity.

(e)(1) The cost of fuel shall include shrinkage, but excludes:

(i) "Throughput" and "in to plane" fees, i.e., service charges or gallonage levies assessed by or against the fuel vendor or concessionaire and passed on to the carrier in a separately identifiable form; and

(ii) Nonrefundable Federal and State excise taxes.

(2) However, "through-put" and "in to plane" charges that cannot be identified or segregated from the cost of fuel shall remain a part of the cost of fuel as reported on this schedule.

(f) Each air carrier shall maintain records for each station showing the computation of fuel inventories and consumption for each fuel type. The periodic average cost method shall be used in computing fuel inventories and consumption. Under this method, an average unit cost for each fuel type shall be computed by dividing the total cost of fuel available (Beginning Inventory plus Purchases) by the total gallons available. The resulting unit cost shall then be used to determine the ending inventory and the total consumption costs to be reported on this schedule.

(g) Where amounts reported for a specific entity include other than Jet A fuel, a footnote shall be added indicating the number of gallons and applicable costs of such other fuel included in amounts reported for that entity.

(h) Where any adjustment(s) recorded on the books of the carrier results in a material distortion of the current month's schedule, carriers shall file a revised Schedule P–12(a) for the month(s) affected.

[Doc. No. OST–98–4043, 67 FR 49227, July 30, 2002]

§ 291.45 BTS Schedule T–100, U.S. Air Carrier Traffic and Capacity Data by Nonstop Segment and On-Flight Market.

(a) Each section 41103 all-cargo air carrier shall file Schedule T–100, "U.S. Air Carrier Traffic and Capacity Data by Nonstop Segment and On-Flight Market".

(b) Schedule T–100 shall be filed monthly.

(1) Schedule T–100 collects summarized flight stage data and on-flight market data for revenue flights. All traffic statistics shall be compiled in terms of each flight stage as actually performed. The detail T–100 data shall be maintained in such a manner as to permit monthly summarization and organization into two basic groupings. First, the nonstop segment information which is to be summarized by equipment type, within class of service, within pair-of-points, without regard to individual flight number. The second grouping requires that the enplanement/deplanement information be broken out into separate units called on-flight market records, which shall be summarized by class of service, within pair-of-points, without regard for equipment type or flight number.

(2) *Joint-service operations.* The Department may authorize joint-service operations between two direct air carriers. Examples of these joint-service operations are: blocked-space agreements; part-charter agreements; code-sharing agreements; wet-lease agreements, and similar arrangements.

(i) Joint-service operations are reported by the carrier in operational control of the flight, i.e., the carrier that uses its flight crews under its own FAA operating authority. The traffic moving under these agreements is reported on Schedule T–100 the same way as any other traffic on the aircraft.

(ii) If there are questions about reporting a joint-service operation, contact the BTS Assistant Director—Airline Information (fax no. 202 366–3383, telephone no. 202 366–4373). Joint-service operations are reported in Schedule T–100 in accordance with this paragraph (b).

(iii) *Operational control.* The air carrier in operational control of the aircraft (the carrier that uses its flight crews under its own FAA operating authority) must report joint services.

(c) *Service classes.* (1) The statistical classifications are designed to reflect the operating characteristics attributable to each distinctive type of service offered. The combination of scheduled and nonscheduled operations with passenger, all-cargo, and military services are placed into service classes as follows:

Code	Type of service
F	Scheduled Passenger/Cargo.
G	Scheduled All-Cargo.
L	Nonscheduled Civilian Passenger/Cargo/
P	Nonscheduled Civilian Cargo.
N	Nonscheduled Military Passenger/Cargo.
R	Nonscheduled Military Cargo.

(2) Scheduled services include traffic and capacity elements applicable to air transportation provided pursuant to published schedules and extra sections of scheduled flights. Scheduled Passenger/Cargo (Service Class F) is a composite of first-class, coach, and mixed passenger/cargo service.

(3) Nonscheduled services include all traffic and capacity elements applicable to the performance of nonscheduled aircraft charters, and other air transportation services not constituting an integral part of services performed pursuant to published flight schedules.

(d) *Air transport traffic and capacity elements.* Within each of the service classifications, carriers shall report air transport traffic and capacity elements. The elements are reported on segment and/or market records as follows:

Code	Description	Segment	Market	Computed by DOT
	Carrier, carrier entity code	S	M	
	Reporting period date	S	M	
	Origin airport code	S	M	
	Destination airport code	S	M	
	Service class code	S	M	
	Aircraft type code	S		
110	Revenue passengers enplaned		M	
130	Revenue passengers transported.	S		
140	Revenue passenger-miles			CFD*
210	Revenue cargo tons enplaned			CFD*
217	Enplaned freight		M	
219	Enplaned mail		M	
230	Revenue tons transported			CFD*
237	Transported freight	S		
239	Transported mail	S		
240	Revenue ton-miles			CFD*
241	Revenue ton-miles passenger			CFD*
247	Revenue ton-miles freight			CFD*
249	Revenue ton-miles mail			CFD*
270	Available capacity payload	S		
280	Available ton-miles			CFD*
310	Available seats, total	S		
320	Available seat-miles			CFD*
410	Revenue aircraft miles flown			CFD*
430	Revenue aircraft miles scheduled.			CFD*
501	Inter-airport distance			CFD*
510	Revenue aircraft departures performed.	S		
520	Revenue aircraft departures scheduled.	S		
610	Revenue aircraft hours (airborne).	S		
630	Aircraft hours (ramp-to-ramp)	S		
650	Total aircraft hours (airborne)	S		

*CFD = Computed by DOT from detail Schedule T–100 and T–100(f) data.

(e) These reported items are further described as follows:

(1) *Reporting period date.* The year and month to which the reported data are applicable.

(2) *Carrier, Carrier entity code.* Each air carrier shall report its name and entity code (a five digit code assigned by BTS that identifies both the air carrier and its entity) for its particular operations. The Office of Airline Information (OAI) will assign or confirm codes upon request. Such requests should be transmitted by e-mail to *T100.Support@DOT.gov.*

(3) *Service class code.* The service class codes are prescribed in section 298.45(c). In general, classes are divided into two broad categories, either scheduled or nonscheduled, where scheduled = F + G and nonscheduled = L + N + P + R.

(4) *Record type code.* This code indicates whether the data pertain to nonstop segment (record type S) or on-flight market (record type M).

(5) *Aircraft type code.* This code represents the aircraft types, as described in the BTS' Accounting and Reporting Directives.

(6) *Origin, Destination airport code(s).* These codes represent the industry designators. An industry source of these

industry designator codes is the Official Airline Guide (OAG). OAI assigns codes, upon request, if not listed in the OAG.

(7) *110 Revenue passengers enplaned.* The total number of revenue passengers enplaned at the origin point of a flight, boarding the flight for the first time; an unduplicated count of passengers in a market.

(8) *130 Revenue passengers transported.* The total number of revenue passengers transported over a single flight stage, including those already on the aircraft from a previous flight stage.

(9) *140 Revenue passenger-miles.* Computed by multiplying the inter-airport distance of each flight stage by the number of passengers transported on that flight stage.

(10) *210 Revenue cargo tons enplaned.* The total number of cargo tons enplaned. This data element is a sum of the individual on-flight market figures for each of the following categories: 217 Freight and 219 Mail. This element represents an unduplicated count of the revenue traffic in a market.

(11) *217 Enplaned freight.* The total weight of revenue freight enplaned at the origin point of a flight, loaded onto the flight for the first time; an unduplicated count of freight in a market.

(12) *219 Enplaned mail.* The total weight of mail enplaned at the origin point of a flight, loaded onto the flight for the first time; an unduplicated count of mail in a market.

(13) *230 Revenue tons transported.* The number of tons of revenue traffic transported. This element is the sum of the following elements: 231 Passengers transported-total, 237 Freight, and 239 Mail.

(14) *237 Transported freight.* The total weight of freight transported over a single flight stage, including freight already on the aircraft from a previous flight stage.

(15) *239 Transported mail.* The total weight of mail transported over a single flight stage, including mail already on the aircraft from a previous flight stage.

(16) *240 Revenue ton-miles—total.* Ton-miles are computed by multiplying the revenue aircraft miles flown (410) on each flight stage by the number of tons transported on that stage. This element is the sum of 241 through 249.

(17) *241 Revenue ton-miles—passenger.* Equals the number of passengers times 200, times inter-airport distance, divided by 2000. A standard weight of 200 pounds per passenger, including baggage, is used for all operations and service classes.

(18) *247 Revenue ton-miles—freight.* Equals the volume of freight in whole tons times the inter-airport distance.

(19) *249 Revenue ton-miles—mail.* Equals the volume of mail in whole tons times the inter-airport distance.

(20) *270 Available capacity-payload.* The available capacity is collected in pounds. This figure shall reflect the payload or total available capacity for passengers, mail and freight applicable to the aircraft with which each flight stage is performed.

(21) *280 Available ton-miles.* The aircraft miles flown on each flight stage multiplied by the available capacity on the aircraft in tons.

(22) *310 Available seats.* The number of seats available for sale. This figure reflects the actual number of seats available, excluding those blocked for safety or operational reasons. In the domestic entity, report the total available seats in item 130. Scheduled and nonscheduled available seats are reported in item 130.

(23) *320 Available seat-miles.* The aircraft miles flown on each flight stage multiplied by the seat capacity available for sale.

(24) *410 Revenue aircraft miles flown.* Revenue aircraft miles flown are computed based on the airport pairs between which service is actually performed; miles are generated from the data for scheduled aircraft departures (Code 520) times the inter-airport distances (Code 501).

(25) *430 Revenue aircraft miles scheduled.* The number of revenue aircraft miles scheduled. All such data shall be maintained in conformity with the airport pairs between which service is scheduled, whether or not in accordance with actual performance.

(26) *501 Inter-airport distance.* The great circle distance, in official statute miles as prescribed in part 247 of this chapter, between airports served by each flight stage. Official inter-airport

mileage may be obtained from the Office of Airline Information.

(27) *510 Revenue aircraft departures performed.* The number of revenue aircraft departures performed.

(28) *520 Revenue aircraft departures scheduled.* The number of revenue aircraft departures scheduled, whether or not actually performed.

(29) *610 Revenue aircraft hours (airborne).* The elapsed time, computed from the moment the aircraft leaves the ground until its next landing.

(30) *630 Aircraft hours (ramp-to-ramp).* The elapsed time, computed from the moment the aircraft first moves under its own power from the boarding ramp at one airport to the time it comes to rest at the ramp for the next point of landing. This data element is also referred to as 'block' and 'block-to-block' aircraft hours.

(31) *650 Total aircraft hours (airborne).* The elapsed time, computed from the moment the aircraft leaves the ground until it touches down at the next landing. This includes flight training, testing, and ferry flights.

(f) *Public availability of Schedule T–100 data.* Detailed domestic on-flight market and nonstop segment data in Schedule T–100, except military data, shall be publicly available after processing. Domestic data are defined as data from air transportation operations from a place in any State of the United States, the District of Columbia, the Commonwealth of Puerto Rico and the Virgin Islands, or a U.S. territory or possession to a place in any State of the United States, the District of Columbia, the Commonwealth of Puerto Rico and the Virgin Islands, or a U.S. territory or possession.

APPENDIX TO § 291.45—INSTRUCTIONS TO U.S. AIR CARRIERS FOR REPORTING TRAFFIC AND CAPACITY DATA ON SCHEDULE T–100

(a) *Format of reports*—(1) *Automatic Data Processing (ADP) magnetic tape.* Refer to paragraph (d) of this appendix for instructions pertaining to mainframe and minicomputer reporting. The Department will issue "Accounting and Reporting Directives" to make necessary technical changes to these T–100 instructions. Technical changes which are minor in nature do not require public notice and comment.

(2) *Microcomputer diskette*—(i) *Optional specification.* If an air carrier desires to use its personal computers (PC's), rather than mainframe or minicomputers to prepare its data submissions, the following specifications for filing data on diskette media apply.

(ii) *Reporting medium.* Microcomputer ADP data submission of T–100 information must be on IBM compatible disks. Carriers wishing to use a different ADP procedure must obtain written approval to do so from the BTS Assistant Director—Airline Information. Requests for approval to use alternate methods must disclose and describe the proposed data transmission methodology. Refer to paragraph (i) of this appendix for microcomputer record layouts.

(iii) *Microcomputer file characteristics.* The files will be created in ASCII delimited format, sometimes called Data Interchange Format (DIF). This form of recording data provides for variable length fields (data elements) which, in the case of alphabetic data, are enclosed by quotation marks ('') and separated by a comma (,) or tab. Numeric data elements that are recorded without editing symbols are also separated by a comma (,) or tab. The data are identified by their juxtaposition within a given record. Therefore, each record must contain the exact number of data elements, all of which must be juxtapositionally correct. Personal computer software including most spreadsheets, data base management programs, and BASIC are capable of producing files in this format.

(b) *Filing date for reports.* The reports must be received at BTS within 30 days following the end of each reporting period.

(c) *Address for filing.* Data Administration Division, K–14, Office of Airline Information, Bureau of Transportation Statistics, U.S. Department of Transportation, 1200 New Jersey Avenue, SE., Washington, DC 20590–0001.

(d) *ADP format for magnetic tape*—(1) *Magnetic tape specifications.* IBM compatible 9-track EBCDIC recording. Recording density of 6250 or 1600 bpi. The order of recorded information is:

(i) Volume label.

(ii) Header label.

(iii) Data records.

(iv) Trailer label.

(2) [Reserved]

(e) *External tape label information.* (1) Carrier name.

(2) Report date.

(3) File identification.

(4) Carrier address for return of tape reel.

(f) *Standards.* It is the policy of the Department to be consistent with the American National Standards Institute and the Federal Standards Activity in all data processing and telecommunications matters. It is our intention that all specifications in this application are in compliance with standards promulgated by these organizations.

(g) *Volume, header, and trailer label formats*—(1) *Use standard IBM label formats.* The file identifier field of the header labels should be "T–100.SYSTEM".

(h) *Magnetic tape record layouts for T-100*—(1) *Nonstop segment record layout.*

Field No.	Positions	Mode	Description
1	1	1T ...	Record type code (S = nonstop segment).
2	2–6	5T ...	Carrier entity code.
3	7–12	6T ...	Report date (YYYYMM).
4	13–15	3T ...	Origin airport code.
5	16–18	3T ...	Destination airport code.
6	19	1T ...	Service class code (F, G, L, N, P or R).
7	20–23	4T ...	Aircraft type code.
8	24–28	5N ...	Revenue departures performed (F, G, L, N, P, R510).
9	29–38	10N	Available capacity payload (lbs) (F, G, L, N, P, R270).
10 ..	39–45	7N ...	Available seats (F, L, N310).
11 ..	46–52	7N ...	Passengers transported (F, L, N130).
12 ..	53–62	10N	Rev freight transported (F, G, L, N, P, R237) (in lbs).
13 ..	63–72	10N	Revenue mail transported (F, G, L, N, P, R239) (in lbs).
14 ..	73–77	5N ...	Revenue aircraft departures scheduled (F, G520).
15 ..	78–87	10N	Rev hrs, ramp-to-ramp (F, G, L, N, P, R630) (in minutes).
16 ..	88–97	10N	Rev hrs, airborne (F, G, L, N, P, R610) (in minutes).

T = Text.
N = Numeric.

(2) *On-flight market record layout.*

Field No.	Positions	Mode	Description
1	1	1T ...	Record type: M = on-flight market record.
2	2–6	5T ...	Carrier entity code.
3	7–12	4T ...	Report date (YYYYMM).
4	13–15	3T ...	Origin airport code.
5	16–18	3T ...	Destination airport code.
6	19	1T ...	Service class code (F, G, L, N, P or R).
7	20–26	7N ...	Total passengers in market (F, L, N110).
8	27–36	10N	Rev freight in market (F, G, L, N, P, R217) (in lbs).
9	37–46	10N	Revenue mail in market (F, G, L, N, P, R219) (in lbs).

T = Text.
N = numeric.

(i) *Record layouts for microcomputer diskettes.* The record layouts for diskette are generally identical to those shown for magnetic tape, with the exception that delimiters (quotation marks, tabs and commas) are used to separate fields. It is necessary that the order of fields be maintained in all records.

(1) *File characteristics.* The files will be created in ASCII delimited format, sometimes called Data Interchange Format (DIF). This form of recording data provides for variable length fields (data elements) which, in the case of alphabetic data, are enclosed by quotation marks ('') and separated by a comma (,) or tab. Numeric data elements that are recorded without editing symbols are also separated by a comma (,) or tab. The data are identified by their juxtaposition within a given record. Therefore, it is critical that each record contain the exact number of data elements, all of which must be juxtapositionally correct. PC software including most spreadsheets, data base management programs, and BASIC produce minidisk files in this format.

(2) *File naming conventions for diskettes.* For microcomputer reports, each record type should be contained in a separate DOS file on the same physical diskette. The following DOS naming conventions should be followed:

(i) Record type S = SEGMENT.DAT

(ii) Record type M = MARKET.DAT

[Doc. No. OST-98-4043, 67 FR 49227, July 30, 2002, as amended at 75 FR 41585, July 16, 2010]

Subpart F—Enforcement

§ 291.50 Enforcement.

In case of any violation of any of the provisions of the Statute, or this part, or any other rule, regulation, or order issued under the Statute, the violator may be subject to a proceeding pursuant to section 46101 of the Statute before the Department, or sections 46106 through 46108 of the Statute before a U.S. District Court, as the case may be, to compel compliance therewith; or to civil penalties pursuant to the provisions of section 46301 of the Statute.

[60 FR 43526, Aug. 22, 1995]

Subpart G—Public Disclosure of Data

§ 291.60 Public disclosure of data.

(a) Detailed domestic on-flight market data and nonstop segment data, except military data, shall be made publicly available after processing. Domestic data are defined as data from air transportation operations from a place in any State of the United States, the District of Columbia, the Commonwealth of Puerto Rico and the Virgin Islands, or a U.S. territory or possession to a place in any State of the United States, the District of Columbia, the Commonwealth of Puerto Rico and the Virgin Islands, or a U.S. territory or possession. Domestic military operations are reported under service codes N or R.

(b) Detailed international on-flight market and nonstop segment data in Schedule T-100 and Schedule T-100(f) reports, except military data, shall be publicly available immediately following the Department's determination that the database is complete, but no earlier than six months after the date of the data. Military operations are reported under service codes N or R. Data for on-flight markets and nonstop segments involving no U.S. points shall not be made publicly available for three years. Industry and carrier summary data may be made public before the end of six months or the end of three years, as applicable, provided there are three or more carriers in the summary data disclosed. The Department may, at any time, publish international summary statistics without carrier detail. Further, the Department may release nonstop segment and on-flight market detail data by carrier before the end of the confidentiality period as follows:

(1) To foreign governments as provided in reciprocal arrangements between the foreign country and the U.S. Government for exchange of on-flight market and/or nonstop segment data submitted by air carriers of that foreign country and U.S. carriers serving that foreign country.

(2) To parties to any proceeding before the Department under Title IV of the Federal Aviation Act of 1958, as amended, as required by an Administrative Law Judge or other decision-maker of the Department. Parties may designate agents or consultants to receive the data in their behalf, provided the agents or consultants agree to abide by the disclosure restrictions. Any data to which access is granted pursuant to this provision may be introduced into evidence, subject to the normal rules of admissibility.

(3) To agencies or other components of the U.S. Government for their internal use only.

[Doc. No. OST–98–4043, 67 FR 49230, July 30, 2002]

PART 292—INTERNATIONAL CARGO TRANSPORTATION

AUTHORITY: 49 U.S.C. 40101, 40105, 40109, 40113, 40114, 41504, 41701, 41707, 41708, 41709, 41712, 46101; 14 CFR 1.56(j)(2)(ii).

SOURCE: Docket No. 48827, 60 FR 61478, Nov. 30, 1995, unless otherwise noted.

Subpart A—General

§ 292.1 Applicability.

This part applies to direct air carriers providing scheduled transportation of cargo in foreign air transportation.

§ 292.2 Definitions.

For purposes of this part:

Cargo means property other than baggage accompanied or checked by passengers, or mail.

Cargo tariff means a tariff containing rates, charges or provisions governing the application of such rates or charges, or the conditions of service, applicable to the scheduled transportation of cargo in foreign air transportation.

Direct air carrier means an air carrier or foreign air carrier directly engaged in the operation of aircraft under a certificate, regulation, order, exemption or permit issued by the Department or its predecessor, the Civil Aeronautics Board.

Subpart B—Exemption From Filing Tariffs

§ 292.10 Exemption.

Direct air carriers are exempted from the requirement to file cargo tariffs with the Department of Transportation provided in 49 U.S.C. 41504 and 14 CFR Part 221.

§ 292.11 Revocation of exemption.

(a) The Department, upon complaint or upon its own initiative, may, immediately and without hearing, revoke, in whole or in part, the exemption granted by this part with respect to a carrier or carriers, when such action is in the public interest.

(b) Any such action will be taken in an order issued by the Assistant Secretary for Aviation and International Affairs, and will identify:

(1) The tariff matter to be filed; and

(2) The deadline for carrier compliance.

(c) Revocations under this section will have the effect of reinstating all applicable tariff requirements and procedures specified in the Department's regulations for the tariff material to be filed, unless otherwise specified by Department order.

Subpart C—Effect of Exemption

§ 292.20 Rule of construction.

Carriers holding an effective exemption from the duty to file tariffs under this part shall not, unless otherwise directed by order of the Department, be subject to tariff posting, notification or subscription requirements set forth in 49 U.S.C. 41504 or 14 CFR part 221, *except* as provided in § 292.21 of this part.

§ 292.21 Incorporation of contract terms by reference.

(a) Carriers holding an effective exemption from the duty to file tariffs under this part may incorporate contract terms by reference (*i.e.* without stating their full text) into the waybill or other document embodying the contract of carriage for the scheduled transportation of cargo in foreign air transportation, *provided that:*

(1) The notice, inspection, explanation and other requirements set forth in 14 CFR 221.177(a)(1), (a)(2), (a)(4), (b), (c) and (d) are complied with, to the extent applicable, except that the notice required under 14 CFR 221.177(b)(1) shall refer to the title or general nature of the publication(s) or document(s) containing the full text of the referenced terms rather than to "terms and conditions filed in public tariffs with U.S. authorities";

(b) In addition to other remedies at law, a carrier may not claim the benefit as against a shipper or consignee of, and a shipper or consignee shall not be bound by, any contract term which is incorporated by reference under this part unless the requirements of paragraph (a)(1) of this section are complied with, to the extent applicable; and

(c) The purpose of this section is to set uniform disclosure requirements, which preempt any State requirements on the same subject, for terms incorporated by reference into contracts of carriage for the scheduled transportation of cargo in foreign air transportation.

§ 292.22 Effectiveness of tariffs on file.

(a) Cargo rate tariffs on file with the Department, including related classification and/or applicability rules, cease to be effective as tariffs under 49 U.S.C. 41504 and 41510, as well as under the provisions of 14 CFR Part 221, and they are canceled by operation of law.

(b) As of March 1, 1996, all remaining cargo tariffs on file with the Department cease to be effective as tariffs under 49 U.S.C. 41504 and the provisions of 14 CFR part 221, and are cancelled by operation of law. Any such tariffs may be cancelled voluntarily prior to that date. With respect to terms expressly agreed in the contract of carriage, carriers, agents and other persons are relieved from the requirement of adherence to filed tariffs in 49 U.S.C. 41510 and the related provisions of 14 CFR part 221 as of November 30, 1995.

(c) Applications for filing and/or effectiveness of any cargo tariffs pending on November 30, 1995 are dismissed by operation of law. No new filings or applications will be permitted except as provided under § 292.11.

PART 293—INTERNATIONAL PASSENGER TRANSPORTATION

Subpart A—General

Subpart B—Exemption From Filing of Tariffs

Subpart C—Effect of Exemption

AUTHORITY: 49 U.S.C. 40101, 40105, 40109, 40113, 40114, 41504, 41701, 41707, 41708, 41709, 41712, 46101; 14 CFR 1.56(j)(2)(ii).

SOURCE: 64 FR 40674, July 27, 1999, unless otherwise noted.

Subpart A—General

§ 293.1 Applicability.

This part applies to air carriers and foreign air carriers providing scheduled transportation of passengers and their baggage in foreign air transportation.

§ 293.2 Definitions.

For purposes of this part the definitions in § 221.3 of this chapter apply.

Subpart B—Exemption From Filing Tariffs

§ 293.10 Exemption.

(a) Air carriers and foreign air carriers are exempted from the duty to file passenger tariffs with the Department of Transportation, as required by 49 U.S.C. 41504 and 14 CFR part 221, as follows:

(1) The Assistant Secretary for Aviation and International Affairs will, by notice, issue and periodically update a list establishing the following categories of markets:

(i) In Category A markets, carriers are exempted from the duty to file all passenger tariffs unless they are nationals of countries listed in Category C, or are subject to the provisions of paragraph (c) of this section.

(ii) In Category B markets, carriers are exempted from the duty to file all passenger tariffs except those setting forth one-way economy-class fares and governing provisions thereto, unless they are nationals of countries listed in Category C, or are subject to the provisions of paragraph (c) of this section.

(iii) In Category C markets, carriers shall continue to file all passenger tariffs, except as provided in § 293.10(b);

(2) The Assistant Secretary will list country-pair markets falling in Categories A and C, taking into consideration the factors in paragraphs (a)(2) (i) through (iv) of this section. All country-pair markets not listed in Categories A or C shall be considered to be in Category B and need not be specifically listed.

(i) Whether the U.S. has an aviation agreement in force with that country providing double-disapproval treatment of prices filed by the carriers of the Parties;

(ii) Whether the country's Government has disapproved or deterred U.S. carrier price leadership or matching tariff filings in any market;

(iii) Whether the country's Government has placed significant restrictions on carrier entry or capacity in any market; and

(iv) Whether the country's government is honoring the provisions of the bilateral aviation agreement and there are no significant bilateral problems.

(b) By notice of the Assistant Secretary, new country-pair markets will be listed in the appropriate category, and existing country-pair markets may be transferred between categories.

(c) Notwithstanding a determination that a country is in Category A or B, if the Assistant Secretary finds that effective price leadership opportunities for U.S. carriers are not available between that country and any third country, carriers that are nationals of such country may be required to file tariffs, as provided under part 221 or as otherwise directed in the notice, for some or all of their services between the U.S. and third countries.

(d) Air carriers and foreign air carriers are exempted from the duty to file governing rules tariffs containing general conditions of carriage with the Department of Transportation, as required by 49 U.S.C. 41504 and 14 CFR part 221. A description of the general conditions of carriage will be included in the Assistant Secretary's initial notice.

(e) Notwithstanding paragraph (d) of this section, air carriers and foreign air carriers shall file and maintain a tariff with the Department to the extent required by 14 CFR 203.4 and other implementing regulations.

(f) Authority for determining what rules are covered by paragraph (d) of this section and for determining the filing format for the tariffs required by paragraph (e) of this section is delegated to the Director of the Office of International Aviation.

§ 293.11 Required statement.

Each governing rules tariff shall include the following statements:

(a) "Rules herein containing general conditions of carriage are not part of the official U.S. D.O.T. tariff."

(b) "The rules and provisions contained herein apply only to the passenger fares and charges that the U.S. Department of Transportation requires to be filed as tariffs."

§ 293.12 Revocation of exemption.

(a) The Department, upon complaint or upon its own initiative, may, immediately and without hearing, revoke, in whole or in part, the exemption granted by this part with respect to a carrier or carriers, when such action is in the public interest.

(b) Any such action will be taken in a notice issued by the Assistant Secretary for Aviation and International Affairs, and will identify the tariff matter to be filed, and the deadline for carrier compliance.

(c) Revocations under this section will have the effect of reinstating all applicable tariff requirements and procedures specified in the Department's Regulations for the tariff material to be filed, unless otherwise specified by the Department.

Subpart C—Effect of Exemption

§ 293.20 Rule of construction.

To the extent that a carrier holds an effective exemption from the duty to file tariffs under this part, it shall not, unless otherwise directed by order of the Department, be subject to tariff posting, notification or subscription requirements set forth in 49 U.S.C. 41504 or 14 CFR part 221, except as provided in § 293.21.

§ 293.21 Incorporation of contract terms by reference.

Carriers holding an effective exemption from the duty to file tariffs under this part may incorporate contract terms by reference (*i.e.*, without stating their full text) into the passenger ticket or other document embodying the contract of carriage for the scheduled transportation of passengers in foreign air transportation, provided that:

(a) The notice, inspection, explanation and other requirements set forth in 14 CFR 221.107, paragraphs (a), (b), (c) and (d) are complied with, to the extent applicable;

(b) In addition to other remedies at law, a carrier may not claim the benefit under this section as against a passenger, and a passenger shall not be bound by incorporation of any contract term by reference under this part, unless the requirements of paragraph (a), of this section are complied with, to the extent applicable; and

(c) The purpose of this section is to set uniform disclosure requirements, which preempt any State requirements on the same subject, for incorporation of terms by reference into contracts of carriage for the scheduled transportation of passengers in foreign air transportation.

§ 293.22 Effectiveness of tariffs on file.

(a) One hundred and eighty days after the date of effectiveness of the Assistant Secretary's notice, passenger tariffs on file with the Department covered by the scope of the exemption will cease to be effective as tariffs under 49 U.S.C. 41504 and 41510, and the provisions of 14 CFR part 221, and will be canceled by operation of law.

(b) One hundred and eighty days after the date of effectiveness of the Assistant Secretary's notice, pending applications for filing and/or effectiveness of any passenger tariffs covered by the scope of the exemption, will be dismissed by operation of law. No new filings or applications will be permitted after the date of effectiveness of the Assistant Secretary's notice except as provided under § 293.12.

PART 294—CANADIAN CHARTER AIR TAXI OPERATORS

Subpart A—General

Subpart B—Exemption

Subpart C—Registration for Exemption

Subpart D—General Rules for Registrants

Subpart E—Insurance Requirements

Subpart F—Cancellation of Registration and Presidential Review

Subpart G—Authorizations and Waivers

Subpart H—Violations

Subpart I—Terms, Conditions, and Limitations of This Part

AUTHORITY: 49 U.S.C. Chapters 401, 417.

SOURCE: ER–1257, 46 FR 52591, Oct. 27, 1981, unless otherwise noted.

Subpart A—General

§ 294.1 Applicability and purpose.

This part establishes a classification of foreign air carriers known as "Canadian charter air taxi operators," and establishes registration procedures for these carriers operating or seeking to operate transborder services between Canada and the United States. This part also exempts Canadian charter air taxi operators from certain provisions of the Subtitle VII of Title 49 of the United States Code (Transportation), and establishes rules applicable to their operations in the United States. This part does not provide exemption from the safety regulatory provisions of the Statute that are administered by the U.S. Department of Transportation through the Federal Aviation Administration (FAA), and Canadian charter air taxi operators in the conduct of their operations must observe all applicable safety standards and requirements.

[ER–1257, 46 FR 52591, Oct. 27, 1981, as amended at 60 FR 43526, Aug. 22, 1995]

§ 294.2 Definitions.

As used in this part:

(a) *Agreement* means the *Air Transport Agreement Between the Government of the United States and the Government of Canada*, signed at Ottawa, February 24, 1995, with Annexes and any amendments, supplements, reservations, or supersessions to it.

(b) *Canadian charter air taxi operator* means a foreign air carrier that is substantially owned and effectively controlled by Canadian citizens, the Government of Canada, or both, whose foreign air transportation operations are limited to charter air service between points in Canada and points in the United States, and that does not use large aircraft in those operations.

(c) *Charter air service* means nonscheduled commercial air transportation of persons and their accompanied baggage, and of property, on a time, mileage, or trip basis where the entire planeload capacity of one or more aircraft has been engaged, or the transportation of mail by aircraft.

(d) *Large aircraft* means any aircraft that are not *small aircraft* as defined in this section.

(e) *Maximum authorized takeoff weight* has the meaning assigned to it in regulations of the Canadian Transport Commission.

(f) *Maximum certificated takeoff weight* means the maximum takeoff weight authorized by the terms of the aircraft airworthiness certificate. This weight may be found in the airplane operating record or in the airplane flight manual that is incorporated by regulation into the airworthiness certificate.

(g) *Maximum passenger capacity* means the maximum number of passenger seats for which an aircraft is configured.

(h) *Maximum payload capacity* means the maximum certificated takeoff weight of an aircraft less the empty weight as defined in section 03 of part 241 of this chapter, less all justifiable aircraft equipment, and less the operating load (consisting of minimum fuel load, oil, flight crew, steward's supplies, etc.). For purposes of this part, the allowance for weight of the crew, oil and fuel is as follows:

(1) Crew—200 pounds per crew member required under FAA regulations, (2) oil—350 pounds, (3) fuel—the minimum weight of fuel required under FAA regulations for a flight between domestic points 200 miles apart, assuming VFR weather conditions and flights not involving extended overwater operations. However, in the case of aircraft for which a maximum zero fuel weight is prescribed by the FAA, maximum payload capacity means the maximum zero fuel weight less the empty weight, less all justifiable aircraft equipment, and less the operating load (consisting of minimum flight crew, steward's supplies, etc., but not including disposable fuel or oil).

(2) [Reserved]

(i) *Small aircraft* means any aircraft designed to have:

(1) A maximum passenger capacity of not more than 30 seats and a maximum payload capacity of not more than 7,500 pounds, and/or

(2) maximum authorized takeoff weight on wheels not greater than 35,000 pounds.

[ER-1257, 46 FR 52591, Oct. 27, 1981, as amended by Doc. No. 47939, 57 FR 40102, Sept. 2, 1992; 60 FR 43526, Aug. 22, 1995; 71 FR 49347, Aug. 23, 2006]

§ 294.3 General requirements for Canadian charter air taxi operators.

A Canadian charter air taxi operator shall conduct charter air service between the United States and Canada only if it:

(a) Has been registered by the Department under this part;

(b) Does not directly or indirectly utilize large aircraft in charter air services;

(c) Has and maintains in effect liability insurance coverage that complies with the requirements set forth in subpart E of this part and has and maintains a current certificate of insurance evidencing such coverage on file with the Department;

(d) Has and maintains in effect and on file with the Department a signed counterpart of Agreement 18900 (OST Form 4523) and complies with all other requirements of part 203 of this chapter;

(e) Has effective authority from the Government of Canada to conduct charter air service between the United States and Canada.

(f) Has been granted Federal Aviation Administration operations specifications required under part 129 of the Federal Aviation Regulations;

(g) Is substantially owned and effectively controlled by Canadian citizens, or the Government of Canada, or a combination of both; and

(h) Complies with the terms, conditions, and limitations of this part.

(The reporting requirements contained in paragraph (d) were approved by the Office of Management and Budget under control number 3024–0064)

[ER-1257, 46 FR 52591, Oct. 27, 1981, as amended by ER-1332, 48 FR 8051, Feb. 25, 1983; ER-1342, 48 FR 31015, July 6, 1983; Doc. No. 47939, 57 FR 40102, Sept. 2, 1992; 71 FR 49347, Aug. 23, 2006]

Subpart B—Exemption

§ 294.10 Exemption authority.

Canadian charter air taxi operators registered under this part are exempt from the following provisions of the Statute to the extent necessary to perform charter air service between the United States and Canada, and as long as they comply with the terms, conditions, and limitations of this part:

(a) Section 41302 (permits).

(b) Section 41501 (carrier's duty to observe reasonable rates).

(c) Section 41310 (discrimination).

(d) Section 41313 (aviation disaster family assistance plans for foreign air carriers)

[ER–1257, 46 FR 52591, Oct. 27, 1981, as amended at 60 FR 43526, Aug. 22, 1995; 71 FR 49347, Aug. 23, 2006]

Subpart C—Registration for Exemption

§ 294.20 Applying for registration.

To apply for registration under this part, a Canadian charter air taxi operator shall file with the Department's Office of International Aviation, Special Authorities Division, the following:

(a) A currently effective certificate of insurance (see § 294.40); and

(b) Three copies of OST Forms 4523 and 4505, which may be obtained from the Department's Office of International Aviation, Special Authorities Division. All the information required by OST Form 4505 shall be filled in, and it shall be certified by a responsible officer of the applicant Canadian charter air taxi operator.

(Approved by the Office of Management and Budget under control number 3024–0051)

[ER–1257, 46 FR 52591, Oct. 27, 1981; 46 FR 62054, Dec. 22, 1981, as amended by ER–1363, 48 FR 46265, Oct. 12, 1983; Doc. No. 47939, 57 FR 40102, Sept. 2, 1992; 60 FR 43526, Aug. 22, 1995; 71 FR 49347, Aug. 23, 2006]

§ 294.21 Procedure on receipt of registration form.

(a) The Department will list the names and addresses of all persons applying for registration under this part in its Weekly Summary of Filings.

(b) Any person objecting to the registration of a Canadian charter air taxi operator shall file an objection with the Office of International Aviation, Special Authorities Division, and serve a copy on the applicant within 28 days after the Department receives the properly completed registration application. Objections shall include any facts and arguments upon which they are based.

(c) Any answers to objections shall be filed within 14 days after the date that the objections were due.

(d) After receipt of OST Form 4505, the Department may request additional information.

(e) After the period for objections and answers has expired, the Department will take one of the following actions:

(1) Issue the registration by stamping its effective date on OST Form 4505 and sending a copy of it to the carrier.

(2) Reject the application for failure to comply with this part;

(3) Issue the registration subject to such terms, conditions, or limitations as may be consistent with the public interest; or

(4) Institute evidentiary proceedings to consider whether the registration should be issued.

(f) An action described in paragraph (e) of this section will normally be taken within 60 days after the registration application is received. The Department will consider requests for faster action that include a full explanation of the need for expedited action.

(g) A registration shall not be issued until the Department receives evidence that the applicant has effective authority issued by the Government of Canada. The applicant must provide copies of its Air Carrier Operating certificate and non-scheduled international license issued by the Government of Canada.

(h) Rejection of an application for registration will not preclude the filing of a new application by the same carrier.

[ER–1257, 46 FR 52591, Oct. 27, 1981, as amended by Doc. No. 47939, 57 FR 40102, Sept. 2, 1992; 60 FR 43526, Aug. 22, 1995; 71 FR 49347, Aug. 23, 2006]

§294.22 Notification to the Department of change in operations or identifying information.

Registrants shall refile a copy of OST Form 4505 with the Department's Office of International Aviation, Special Authorities Division, upon any of the following events. The refiling shall be sent by electronic mail, or other means, so as to be received by the Department not later than 30 days after the reported event has occurred.

(a) The carrier changes its name. When a carrier refiles OST Form 4505 to indicate a change of name:

(1) A registration ceases to be in effect unless the Government of Canada amends the registrant's Air Carrier Operating Certificate to reflect the registrant's new name within 60 days of the name change and the registrant submits to the Department a copy of its amended Canadian authority.

(2) The registrant must also refile three copies of Agreement 18900 (OST Form 4523) under its new name;

(3) The registrant must also refile its certificate of insurance under its new name; and

(4) The registrant must also advise the appropriate FAA office referred to in §294.33 of the carrier's new name.

(b) The carrier changes its designated agent.

(c) A change occurs in the carrier's ownership and control resulting in a person acquiring a beneficial or voting interest in the registrant of 10 percent or more. The name(s), address(es), citizenship(s), and percentages of ownership of the new owners shall be indicated on the form. Acquisition of ownership interest by persons who are not citizens of the country of citizenship of the registrant may invalidate the registration.

(d) The carrier temporarily or permanently ceases operations.

(Approved by the Office of Management and Budget under control number 3024–0051)

[ER–1257, 46 FR 52591, Oct. 27, 1981, as amended by ER–1363, 48 FR 46265, Oct. 12, 1983; Doc. No. 47939, 57 FR 40102, Sept. 2, 1992; 60 FR 43526, Aug. 22, 1995; 71 FR 49347, Aug. 23, 2006]

Subpart D—General Rules for Registrants

§294.30 Scope of service and equipment authorized.

(a) Upon fulfillment of the requirements of §294.3 of this part, the registrant will have Department authority to engage in charter air services between any point or points in Canada and any point or points in the United States using small aircraft.

(b) Nothing in this part shall be construed as authorizing the operation of large aircraft in charter air service, and the exemption provided by this part to Canadian charter air taxi operators that register with the Department extends only to the direct operations of charter air service in accordance with the limitations and conditions of this part using aircraft designed to have:

(1) A maximum passenger capacity of no more than 30 seats and a maximum payload capacity of no more than 7,500 pounds, and/or

(2) A maximum authorized takeoff weight on wheels not greater than 35,000 pounds.

(c) A Canadian charter air taxi operator shall not use large aircraft for charter air service until it has been granted a permit by the Department under section 41302 of the Statute or granted an exemption under section 41701 of the Statute. Its application for such a permit or exemption should refer to the registration under this part. Registration under this part will be canceled when a section 41302 permit has been granted by the Department for the use of large aircraft in foreign charter air service.

[ER–1257, 46 FR 52591, Oct. 27, 1981, as amended by Doc. No. 47939, 57 FR 40102, Sept. 2, 1992; 60 FR 43526, Aug. 22, 1995]

§294.31 Use of business name.

(a) A Canadian charter air taxi operator, in holding out charter air service to the public and performing its charter operations, shall do so only in the names in which its registration is issued under this part. The Department may require a Canadian charter air taxi operator to change such names where they appear to be inconsistent with the public interest.

(b) [Reserved]

§ 294.32 Security arrangements for operating Public Charters.

When a Canadian charter air taxi operator performs a Public Charter under part 380 of this chapter, either:

(a) The Canadian charter air taxi operator shall meet the bonding or escrow requirements applicable to foreign air carriers as set forth in § 212.8 of this chapter.

(b) The Canadian charter air taxi operator shall ensure that it does not receive any payments for the charter until after the charter has been completed. In this case, its contracts with the charter operator and the charter operator's depository bank, if any, shall state that the charter operator or bank, as applicable, shall retain control of and responsibility for all participant funds intended for payment for charter air service until after the charter has been completed, notwithstanding any provision of part 380.

[ER–1257, 46 FR 52591, Oct. 27, 1981, as amended by Doc. No. 2006–25691, 71 FR 49347, Aug. 23, 2006]

§ 294.33 Compliance with the regulations of the Federal Aviation Administration.

(a) Registrants under this part shall obtain FAA operations specifications required under part 129 or other applicable rules of the Federal Aviation Regulations prior to beginning operations into the United States. Registrants should write to the FAA office at one of the following addresses to obtain instructions on how to apply for FAA authority.

(b) If the registrant's business address is located on or east of 76 degrees West Longitude (in or east of Ottawa, Ontario) it should write to: Federal Aviation Administration, General Aviation District Office No. 1, Albany County Airport, Albany, New York 12211.

(c) If the registrant's business address is located on or east of 100 degrees West Longitude (in or east of Winnipeg, Manitoba) and west of 76 degrees West Longitude (west of, but not including, Ottawa, Ontario) it should write to: Federal Aviation Administration, Flight Standards District Office, 1 Airport Way, Rochester, New York 14624.

(d) If the registrant's business address is west of Winnipeg, Manitoba, it should write to: Federal Aviation Administration, General Aviation District Office, 1601 Lind Avenue, SW., Renton, Washington 98055.

[ER–1257, 46 FR 52591, Oct. 27, 1981, as amended by Doc. No. 47939, 57 FR 40102, Sept. 2, 1992]

§ 294.34 Advance approval by the Department.

The Department, by order or regulation and without hearing, may require advance approval of individual charter trips conducted by the registrant under the authority granted by this part, if it finds such action to be consistent with the public interest.

Subpart E—Insurance Requirements

§ 294.40 Aircraft accident liability insurance requirements.

No Canadian charter air taxi operator shall engage in charter air service unless such carrier has and maintains in effect aircraft accident liability coverage that meets the requirements of part 205 of this chapter. Evidence of such insurance coverage, in the form of a certificate of insurance, as required in part 205 of this chapter, shall be maintained on file with the Department's Office of International Aviation, Special Authorities Division, at all times.

(Approved by the Office of Management and Budget under control number 3024–0050)

[ER–1257, 46 FR 52591, Oct. 27, 1981, as amended by ER–1342, 48 FR 31015, July 6, 1983; Doc. No. 47939, 57 FR 40102, Sept. 2, 1992; 60 FR 43526, Aug. 22, 1995; 71 FR 49347, Aug. 23, 2006]

Subpart F—Cancellation of Registration and Presidential Review

§ 294.50 Cancellation, revocation, or suspension of registration.

The registration of a carrier subject to this part may be revoked, canceled, suspended, modified, or otherwise subjected to additional terms and conditions by the Department if:

(a) The carrier files with the Department a written notice that it is discontinuing operations;

(b) The carrier is the holder of a section 41302 permit to perform large aircraft charters under the Agreement;

(c) Substantial ownership or effective control is acquired by persons who are not (1) citizens of Canada, (2) the Government of Canada, or (3) a combination of both;

(d) The Government of Canada terminates or suspends authority it granted to the registrant to conduct charter air service between the United States and Canada.

(e) The Agreement between the two countries is terminated;

(f) The registrant fails to have proper insurance coverage, or fails to file or keep a current insurance certificate on file with the Department;

(g) The registrant fails to comply with the terms, conditions, or limitations of this part;

(h) The carrier's operations specifications issued by the FAA are suspended or terminated;

(i) The Department finds that it is in the public interest to do so.

[ER-1257, 46 FR 52591, Oct. 27, 1981, as amended at 60 FR 43526, Aug. 22, 1995; 71 FR 49347, Aug. 23, 2006]

§ 294.51 Presidential review.

A Department order under § 294.50 (e), (g) or (i) shall be subject to stay or disapproval by the President within 60 days.

Subpart G—Authorizations and Waivers

§ 294.60 Applications for authorization to conduct individual operations or programs not otherwise permitted by this part.

(a) Where the terms, conditions, or limitations of this part, particularly § 294.81, require prior approval of individual flights or charter programs, the registrant shall apply for such approval by filing three copies of OST Form 4540 with the Office of International Aviation, Foreign Air Carrier Licensing Division. OST Form 4540 may be obtained from the Foreign Air Carrier Licensing Division.

(b) Action on the application for authorization filed under paragraph (a) of this section will normally be taken within 30 days after the application is filed. The Department will consider requests for faster action that include a full explanation of the need for expedited action.

[ER-1257, 46 FR 52591, Oct. 27, 1981, as amended by Doc. No. 47939, 57 FR 40103, Sept. 2, 1992; 71 FR 49347, Aug. 23, 2006]

§ 294.61 Waivers.

The Department upon application or on its own initiative may waive any of the provisions of this part if it finds such action to be in the public interest.

Subpart H—Violations

§ 294.70 Enforcement.

In case of any violation of any of the provisions of the Statute, or this part, or any other rule, regulation, or order issued under the Statute, the violator may be subject to a proceeding under section 46101 of the Statute before the Department, or sections 46106 through 46108 of the Statute before a U.S. District Court, as the case may be, to compel compliance; or to impose civil penalties under the provisions of section 46301 of the Statute; or in the case of a willful violation, to impose criminal penalties under the provisions of section 46316 of the Statute; or to impose other lawful sanctions, including revocation of registration.

[ER-1257, 46 FR 52591, Oct. 27, 1981, as amended at 60 FR 43527, Aug. 22, 1995]

Subpart I—Terms, Conditions, and Limitations of This Part

§ 294.80 Waiver of sovereign immunity.

By accepting an approved registration under this part, a registrant waives any right it may possess to assert any defense of sovereign immunity in any action or proceeding instituted against it in any court or other tribunal in the United States based upon any claim arising out of its operations under this part.

§ 294.81 Local traffic prohibited.

(a) Except as set forth in paragraph (b) of this section or § 294.60, a registrant shall not carry passengers, cargo, or mail between two or more United States points for compensation or hire.

(b) A registrant may grant stopover privileges at any point or points in the United States to passengers and their accompanied baggage as part of a single continuous operation to or from Canada.

[ER–1257, 46 FR 52591, Oct. 27, 1981, as amended by Doc. No. 2006–25691, 71 FR 49347, Aug. 23, 2006]

§ 294.83 Compliance with certain international agreements.

A registrant shall not operate any aircraft under this part unless it:

(a) Complies with operational safety requirements at least equivalent to Annex 6 of the Chicago Convention;

(b) Complies with all applicable provisions of the Agreement; and

(c) Complies with all applicable provisions of any treaty, convention, or agreement affecting international air transportation to which the United States and Canada are parties.

§ 294.84 Air competency requirements.

Registrants shall conform to the airworthiness and airman competency requirements prescribed by the Government of Canada for Canadian international air service.

§ 294.85 Charterworthiness standards.

(a) Registrants may perform U.S.-originating charters authorized under Annex B (III)(A) of the Agreement as follows: Commercial air transportation of passengers and their accompanied baggage, and of property, on a time, mileage, or trip basis, where the entire planeload capacity of one or more aircraft has been engaged by a person for his own use or by a person for the transportation of a group of persons and/or their property, as agent or representative of such group, or other small aircraft operations as may be authorized under any amendments, supplements, reservations, or supersessions of the Agreement.

(b) Registrants may perform Canadian-originating charters authorized by Annex B (III)(B) of the Agreement and any amendments, supplements, reservations or supersessions of it. Such charters may be performed only to the extent authorized by the Air Carrier Regulations of the Canadian Transport Commission applicable to operations by small aircraft.

§ 294.86 Industrial/agricultural/other nontransport air operations prohibited.

A registrant shall not engage in flights for the purpose of industrial or agricultural operations (e.g., crop dusting, pest control, pipeline patrol, mapping, surveying, banner towing, skywriting, aerial photography) within the United States unless it has obtained a permit from the Department under part 375 of this chapter.

§ 294.87 Compliance with Canadian licenses.

A registrant shall not, in the performance of operations authorized by this part, use any aircraft or conduct any operations except in accordance with the authority and conditions contained in the registrant's applicable Canadian licenses.

PART 295—AIR CHARTER BROKERS

Subpart A—General

Subpart B—Exemption Authority

Subpart C—Consumer Protection

Subpart D—Violations

AUTHORITY: 49 U.S.C. Chapters 401, 411, 413, and 417.

SOURCE: 83 FR 46874, Sept. 17, 2018, unless otherwise noted.

EFFECTIVE DATE NOTE: At 83 FR 46874, Sept. 17, 2018, Part 295 was added, effective Feb. 14, 2019.

Subpart A—General

§ 295.1 Purpose.

Air charter brokers, defined as an indirect air carrier, foreign indirect air carrier or a bona fide agent, provide indirect air transportation of passengers on single entity charters aboard large and small aircraft. This part grants exemptions to such air charter brokers from certain provisions of Subtitle VII of Title 49 of the United States Code (Transportation), and establishes rules, including consumer protection provisions, for the provision of such air transportation by air charter brokers.

§ 295.3 Applicability.

This part applies to any person or entity acting as an air charter broker as defined in this part with respect to single entity charter air transportation that the air charter broker, as an indirect air carrier, foreign indirect air carrier, or a *bona fide agent*, holds out, sells or undertakes to arrange aboard large and small aircraft.

§ 295.5 Definitions.

For the purposes of this part:

(a) *Air transportation* means interstate or foreign air transportation, as defined in 49 U.S.C. 40102(a)(5), 40102(a)(23), and 40102(a)(25).

(b) *Air charter broker* means a person or entity that, as an indirect air carrier, foreign indirect air carrier, or a *bona fide agent*, holds out, sells, or arranges single entity charter air transportation using a direct air carrier.

(c) *Bona fide agent* means a person or entity that acts as an agent on behalf of a single entity charterer seeking air transportation or a direct air carrier seeking to provide single entity charter air transportation, when such charterer or direct air carrier, as principal, has appointed or authorized such agent to act on the principal's behalf.

(d) *Charterer* means the person or entity that contracts with an air charter broker, direct air carrier, or foreign direct air carrier, for the transportation of the passengers flown on a charter flight.

(e) *Charter air transportation* means charter flights in air transportation authorized under Part A of Subtitle VII of Title 49 of the United States Code.

(f) *Direct air carrier and foreign direct air carrier* mean a U.S. or foreign air carrier that provides or offers to provide air transportation and that has control over the operational functions performed in providing that transportation.

(g) *Indirect air carrier and foreign indirect air carrier* mean a person or entity that, as a principal, holds out, sells, or arranges air transportation and separately contracts with direct air carriers and/or foreign direct air carriers.

(h) *Single entity charter* means a charter for the entire capacity of the aircraft, the cost of which is borne by the charterer and not directly or indirectly by individual passengers, except when individual passengers self-aggregate to form a single entity for flights to be operated using small aircraft.

(i) *Statute* means Subtitle VII of Title 49 of the United States Code (Transportation).

(j) *Large aircraft* means any aircraft originally designed to have a maximum passenger capacity of more than 60 seats or a maximum payload capacity of more than 18,000 pounds.

(k) *Small aircraft* means any aircraft originally designed to have a maximum passenger capacity of 60 seats or fewer or a maximum payload capacity of 18,000 pounds or less.

§ 295.7 Agency relationships.

An air charter broker acting as an indirect air carrier or foreign indirect air carrier may choose to act as a bona fide agent in individual cases where a charterer, direct air carrier, or foreign direct air carrier has expressly authorized such agency relationship.

Subpart B—Exemption Authority

§ 295.10 Grant of economic authority; exemption from the statute.

To the extent necessary to permit air charter brokers, acting as indirect air carriers or foreign indirect air carriers, to hold out, sell, and undertake to arrange single entity charter air transportation, such air charter brokers are exempted from the following provisions of Subtitle VII of Title 49 of the United States Code, except for the provisions noted, only if and so long as they comply with the provisions and the conditions imposed by this part: 49 U.S.C. 41101–41113, 49 U.S.C. 41301–41313, and 49 U.S.C. 41501–41511. Air charter brokers are not exempt from the following provision: 49 U.S.C. 41310 (nondiscrimination) with respect to foreign air transportation.

§ 295.12 Suspension or revocation of exemption authority.

The Department reserves the power to alter, suspend, or revoke the exemption authority of any air charter broker acting as an indirect air carrier, without a hearing, if it finds that such action is in the public interest or is otherwise necessary to protect the traveling public.

Subpart C—Consumer Protection

§ 295.20 Use of duly authorized direct air carriers.

Air charter brokers are not authorized under this part to hold out, sell, or otherwise arrange charter air transportation to be operated by a person or entity that does not hold the requisite form of economic authority from the Department and appropriate safety authority from the Federal Aviation Administration and, if applicable, a foreign safety authority. Air charter brokers are not authorized under this part to hold out, sell, or arrange air transportation to be performed by a direct air carrier or direct foreign air carrier that the direct carrier is not authorized in its own right to hold out, sell, or operate. Only direct air carriers that are citizens of the United States as defined in 49 U.S.C. 40102(a)(15) may provide direct air transportation operations in interstate or intrastate air transportation.

§ 295.22 Prohibited unfair or deceptive practices or unfair methods of competition.

An air charter broker shall not engage in any unfair or deceptive practice or unfair method of competition.

§ 295.23 Advertising.

(a) All solicitation materials and advertisements, including internet web pages, published or caused to be published by air charter brokers shall clearly and conspicuously state that the air charter broker is an air charter broker, and that it is not a direct air carrier or a direct foreign air carrier in operational control of aircraft, and that the air service advertised shall be provided by a properly licensed direct air carrier or direct foreign air carrier.

(b) Air charter brokers may display their name and logo on aircraft provided the name of the direct air carrier is displayed prominently and clearly on the aircraft and consumers are not otherwise misled into thinking that the air charter broker is a direct air carrier or direct foreign air carrier.

§ 295.24 Disclosures.

(a) Before entering a contract for a specific flight or series of flights with charterers, air charter brokers must disclose to the charterer the information in paragraphs (a)(1),(2), and (6) of this section. Before entering a contract for a specific flight or series of flights with charterers, air charter brokers must, upon request of the charterer, disclose to the charterer the information in paragraphs (a)(3), (4), and (5) of this section. The six disclosures may be accomplished through electronic transmissions.

(1) The corporate name of the direct air carrier or direct foreign air carrier in operational control of the aircraft on which the air transportation is to be performed and any other names in which that direct carrier holds itself out to the public.

(2) The capacity in which the air charter broker is acting in contracting for the air transportation, *i.e.*, as an indirect air carrier, indirect foreign air carrier, as an agent of the charterer, or

as an agent of the direct air carrier or direct foreign air carrier that will be in operational control of the flight.

(3) If the air charter broker is acting as the agent of the charterer, the air charter broker must disclose the existence of any corporate or business relationship, including a preexisting contract, between the air charter broker and the direct air carrier or direct foreign air carrier that will be in operational control of the flight that may have a bearing on the air charter broker's selection of the direct carrier that will be in operational control of the flight.

(4) The total cost of the air transportation paid by the charterer to or through the air charter broker, including any air charter broker or carrier-imposed fees or government-imposed taxes and fees. Specific individual fees, taxes, or costs may, but are not required to be itemized.

(5) The existence of any fees and their amounts collected by third-parties, if known (or a good faith estimate if not known), including fuel, landing fees, and aircraft parking or hangar fees, for which the charterer will be responsible for paying directly.

(6) The existence or absence of liability insurance held by the air charter broker covering the charterer and passengers and property on the charter flight, and the monetary limits of any such insurance.

(b) If any of the information in paragraph (a) of this section that is required to be disclosed to the charterer or requested by the charterer to be disclosed is not known at the time the contract is entered into or changes thereafter, air charter brokers must provide the information to the charterer within a reasonable time after such information becomes available to the air charter broker, such that the charterer has enough time to make an informed decision as to whether to accept the additional information or accept the change.

(c) If the information in paragraph (a) of this section that is required to be disclosed to the charterer or requested by the charterer to be disclosed is not provided to the charterer within a reasonable time after such information becomes available to the air charter broker, air charter brokers must provide the charterer with the opportunity to cancel the contract for charter air transportation, including any services in connection with such contract, and receive a full refund of any monies paid for the charter air transportation and services.

(d) In all circumstances, air charter brokers must disclose prior to the start of the air transportation the information in paragraph (a) of this section that is required to be disclosed or that the charterer has requested to be disclosed.

(e) If the information in paragraph (a) of this section that is required to be disclosed to the charterer or requested by the charterer to be disclosed changes after the air transportation covered by the contract has begun, air charter brokers must provide information regarding any such changes to the charterer within a reasonable time after such information becomes available to the air charter broker.

(f) If the changes in information described in paragraph (e) of this section are not provided to the charterer within a reasonable time after becoming available to the air charter broker, air charter brokers must provide the charterer with the opportunity to cancel the remaining portion of the contract for charter air transportation, including any services paid in connection with such contract, and receive a full refund of any monies paid for the charter air transportation and services not yet provided.

§295.26 Refunds.

Air charter brokers must make prompt refunds of all monies paid for charter air transportation when such transportation cannot be performed or when such refunds are otherwise due, as required by 14 CFR 374.3 and 12 CFR part 226 for credit card purchases, and within 20 days after receiving a complete refund request for cash and check purchases.

Subpart D—Violations

§ 295.50 Enumerated unfair or deceptive practices or unfair methods of competition.

(a) Violations of this Part shall be considered to constitute unfair or deceptive practices or unfair methods of competition in violation of 49 U.S.C. 41712.

(b) In addition to paragraph (a) of this section, the following enumerated practices, among others, by an air charter broker are unfair or deceptive practices or unfair methods of competition in violation of 49 U.S.C. 41712:

(1) Misrepresentations that may induce members of the public to reasonably believe that the air charter broker is a direct air carrier or direct foreign air carrier when that is not the case.

(2) Misrepresentations as to the quality or kind of service or type of aircraft.

(3) Misrepresentations as to the time of departure or arrival, points served, route to be flown, stops to be made, or total trip-time from point of departure to destination.

(4) Misrepresentations as to the qualifications of pilots or safety record or certification of pilots, aircraft, or air carriers.

(5) Misrepresentations that passengers are directly insured when they are not so insured. For example, where the only insurance in force is that protecting the direct air carrier or air charter broker in event of liability.

(6) Misrepresentations as to fares or charges for air transportation or services in connection therewith.

(7) Misrepresentations as to membership in or involvement with an organization that audits air charter brokers, direct air carriers, or direct foreign air carriers, or that the air charter broker or any direct carriers to be used for a particular flight meets a standard set by an auditing organization.

(8) Representing that a contract for a specified direct air carrier, direct foreign air carrier, aircraft, flight, or time has been arranged without a binding commitment with a direct air carrier or direct foreign air carrier for the furnishing of such transportation as represented.

(9) Selling or contracting for air transportation while knowing or having reason to know or believe that such air transportation cannot be legally performed by the direct air carrier or foreign direct air carrier that is to perform the air transportation.

(10) Misrepresentations as to the requirements that must be met by charterers to qualify for charter flights.

(11) Using or displaying or permitting or suffering to be used or displayed the name, trade name, slogan or any abbreviation thereof, of the air charter broker in advertisements, on or in places of business, or on or in aircraft or any other place in connection with the name of an air carrier or foreign air carrier or with services in connection with air transportation, in such manner that it may mislead or confuse potential consumers with respect to the status of the air charter broker.

§ 295.52 Enforcement.

In case of any violation of any of the provisions of the Statute, or of this part, or any other rule, regulation, or order issued under the Statute, the violator may be subject to a proceeding under 49 U.S.C. 46101 before the Department, or 49 U.S.C. 46106–46108 before a U.S. District Court, as the case may be, to compel compliance. The violator may also be subject to civil penalties under the provisions of 49 U.S.C. 46301, or other lawful sanctions, including revocation of the exemption authority granted in this part. In the case of a willful violation, the violator may be subject to criminal penalties under the provisions of 49 U.S.C. 46316.

PART 296—INDIRECT AIR TRANSPORTATION OF PROPERTY

Subpart A—General

AUTHORITY: 49 U.S.C. Chapters 401, 417.

SOURCE: ER-1261, 46 FR 54727, Nov. 4, 1981, unless otherwise noted.

Subpart A—General

§296.1 Purpose.

This part establishes rules for the indirect air transportation of property. It creates a class of air carriers to provide this air transportation and grants exemptions from certain provisions of the Subtitle VII of Title 49 of the United States Code (Transportation).

[ER-1257, 46 FR 52591, Oct. 27, 1981, as amended at 60 FR 43527, Aug. 22, 1995]

§296.2 Applicability.

This part applies to air transportation of property by indirect cargo air carriers, and to persons entering into control relationships with indirect cargo air carriers.

§296.3 Indirect cargo air carrier.

An indirect cargo air carrier is any U.S. citizen who undertakes to engage indirectly in air transportation of property, and uses for the whole or any part of such transportation the services of an air carrier or a foreign air carrier that directly engages in the operation of aircraft under a certificate, regulation, order, or permit issued by the Department of Transportation or the Civil Aeronautics Board, or the services of its agent, or of another indirect cargo air carrier.

[ER-1261, 46 FR 54727, Nov. 4, 1981, as amended by Doc. No. 47939, 57 FR 40103, Sept. 2, 1992]

§296.4 Joint loading.

Nothing in this part shall preclude joint loading, meaning the pooling of shipments and their delivery to a direct air carrier for transportation as one shipment, under an agreement between two or more indirect air carriers or foreign indirect air carriers.

§296.5 Agency relationships.

An indirect cargo air carrier may act as agent of a shipper, or of a direct air carrier that has authorized such agency, rather than as an air carrier, if it expressly reserves the option to do so when the shipment is accepted.

§296.6 Public disclosure of cargo liability limits and insurance.

Every indirect cargo air carrier shall give notice in writing to the shipper, when any shipment is accepted, of the existence or absence of cargo liability accident insurance, and of the limits on the extent of its liability, if any. The notice shall be clear and conspicuously included on or attached to all of its rate sheets and airwaybills.

Subpart B—Exemption for Indirect Air Transportation of Property

§296.10 Exemption from the Statute.

(a) Indirect cargo air carriers are exempted from the provisions of the Statute only if and so long as they comply with the provisions of this part and its conditions, and to the extent necessary to permit them to organize and arrange their air freight shipments to provide indirect air transportation, except for the following sections:

(1) Section 41510(b) (solicitation of rebates). However, indirect cargo air carriers are exempt from section 41510(b) to the extent necessary to permit them to solicit, accept, or receive fees from direct air carriers.

(2) Section 41702 to the extent required to provide safe service, equipment, and facilities in connection with air transportation.

(3) Section 41310 (nondiscrimination) with respect to foreign air transportation.

(4) Section 41708 (accounts, records, and reports) and section 41709 (inspection of accounts and property);

(5) Section 41712 (unfair or deceptive practices or method of competition);

(6) Section 40102(b) (form of control); and

(7) Section 41711 (inquiry into air carrier management).

(b)–(c) [Reserved]

(d) Direct air carriers are exempted from Chapter 415 of the Statute to the extent necessary to permit them to pay, directly or indirectly, fees to indirect cargo air carriers.

[ER-1261, 46 FR 54727, Nov. 4, 1981, as amended by ER-1335, 48 FR 22705, May 20, 1983; ER-1381, 49 FR 25226, June 20, 1984, 50 FR 31142, July 31, 1985; 60 FR 43527, Aug. 22, 1995]

Subpart C—Violations

§ 296.20 Enforcement.

In case of any violation of any of the provisions of the Statute, or of this part, or any other rule, regulation, or order issued under the Statute, the violator may be subject to a proceeding under section 46101 of the Statute before the Department, or sections 46106 through 46108 of the Statute before a U.S. District Court, as the case may be, to compel compliance. The violator may also be subject to civil penalties under the provisions of section 46301 of the Statute, or other lawful sanctions.

[ER-1261, 46 FR 54727, Nov. 4, 1981, as amended by Doc. No. 47939, 57 FR 40103, Sept. 2, 1992; 60 FR 43527, Aug. 22, 1995]

PART 297—FOREIGN AIR FREIGHT FORWARDERS AND FOREIGN COOPERATIVE SHIPPERS ASSOCIATIONS

Subpart A—General

Sec.

Subpart B—Exemption for Foreign Indirect Air Transportation of Property

Subpart C—Registration for Foreign Air Freight Forwarders and Foreign Cooperative Shippers Associations

Subpart D—General Rules for Foreign Indirect Air Carriers

Subpart E [Reserved]

Subpart F—Violations

AUTHORITY: 49 U.S.C. Chapters 401, 417.

SOURCE: ER-1159, 44 FR 69635, Dec. 4, 1979, unless otherwise noted.

Subpart A—General

§ 297.1 Purpose.

This part establishes registration procedures and operating rules for foreign air carriers that engage indirectly in interstate or foreign air transportation of property. It relieves these carriers from certain provisions of Subtitle VII of Title 49 of the United States Code (Transportation), and establishes simplified reports for them.

[ER-1294, 47 FR 19684, May 7, 1982, as amended at 60 FR 43527, Aug. 22, 1995]

§ 297.2 Applicability.

This part applies to interstate air transportation of property and to foreign air transportation of property outbound from the United States by foreign indirect air carriers. It also applies to applications for registration as a foreign indirect air carrier of property.

[ER-1294, 47 FR 19684, May 7, 1982, as amended at 60 FR 43527, Aug. 22, 1995]

§ 297.3 Definitions.

For purpose of this part:

(a) *Foreign air freight forwarder* means a foreign indirect air carrier that is responsible for the transportation of property from the point of receipt to point of destination, and utilizes for the whole or any part of such transportation the services of a direct air carrier or its agent, of another foreign indirect cargo air carrier as defined in part 296 of this chapter.

(b) *Foreign cooperative shippers association* means a bona fide association of shippers operating as a foreign indirect air carrier on a nonprofit basis that undertakes to ship property by air for the account of such association or its members, and utilizes for the whole or any part of such transportation the services of a direct air carrier or its agent, of a foreign indirect cargo air carrier as defined in part 296 of this chapter.

(c) *Direct air carrier* means an air carrier or foreign air carrier directly engaged in the operation of aircraft under a certificate, regulation, order, or permit issued by the Department of Transportation or the Civil Aeronautics Board.

(d) *Foreign indirect air carrier* means any person, not a citizen of the United States, who undertakes indirectly to engage in the air transportation of property.

[ER-1159, 44 FR 69635, Dec. 4, 1979, as amended by ER-1294, 47 FR 19684, May 7, 1982; Doc. No. 47939, 57 FR 40103, Sept. 2, 1992]

§ 297.4 Joint loading.

Nothing in this part shall preclude joint loading, meaning the pooling of shipments and their delivery to a direct air carrier for transportation as one shipment, under an agreement between two or more indirect air carriers or foreign indirect air carriers.

§ 297.5 Foreign air freight forwarder as agent.

A foreign air freight forwarder may act as agent of a shipper, or of a direct air carrier that has authorized such agency, if it expressly reserves the option to do so when the shipment is accepted. A foreign air freight forwarder shall not act as the agent of any direct air carrier with respect to shipments accepted for forwarding.

§ 297.6 Foreign cooperative shippers association as agent.

A foreign cooperative shippers association may act as agent of a shipper, or of a direct air carrier that has authorized such agency, if it expressly reserves the option to do so when the shipment is accepted. A cooperative shippers association shall not act as an agent of any direct air carrier with respect to shipments accepted in its capacity as an indirect air carrier.

[ER-1235, 46 FR 38496, July 28, 1981]

Subpart B—Exemption for Foreign Indirect Air Transportation of Property

§ 297.10 Exemption from the Statute.

(a) Foreign indirect air carriers with an effective registration under this part are exempted from the following provisions of the Statute only if and so long as they comply with the provisions of this part and the conditions imposed herein, and to the extent necessary to permit them to arrange their air freight shipments:

(1) Section 41302 (Permits);

(2) Sections 41504 and 41510(a) (Tariffs);

(3) Section 41510(b) (Solicitation of rebates) to the extent necessary to permit them to solicit, accept, or receive fees from direct air carriers;

(4) Section 41501 (Carrier's duty to establish just and reasonable rates, etc.); and

(5) If awarded interstate air transportation operating rights, any other provision of the Statute that would otherwise prohibit them from engaging in the interstate indirect air transportation of property.

(6) Section 41310 (nondiscrimination) with respect to interstate and overseas air transportation.

(b) Direct air carriers are exempted from Chapter 415 of the Statute to the extent necessary to permit them to pay, directly or indirectly, fees to foreign air freight forwarders and foreign cooperative shippers associations on consolidated shipments.

[ER-1336, 48 FR 22705, May 20, 1983, as amended by ER-1382, 49 FR 25226, June 20, 1984; Doc. No. 47939, 57 FR 40103, Sept. 2, 1992; 60 FR 43527, Aug. 22, 1995]

§ 297.11 Disclaimer of jurisdiction.

The Department declines to exercise its jurisdiction over foreign indirect air carriers of property with respect to shipments that originate in a foreign country. The Department reserves the right to exercise its jurisdiction over any foreign indirect air carrier of property at any time it finds that such action is in the public interest.

§ 297.12 General requirements.

(a) The direct air transportation provided must be performed by direct air carriers that hold authority under section 41102, 41103, 41302, or 41701 of the Statute or are operating under part 298 of this chapter;

(b) Only U.S. citizen direct air carriers may provide direct air transportation operations in interstate air transportation.

(c) Foreign indirect air carriers that hold authority to engage in foreign air transportation must apply additionally for permission to consolidate freight in interstate air transportation.

[ER–1294, 47 FR 19684, May 7, 1982, as amended at 60 FR 43527, Aug. 22, 1995]

Subpart C—Registration for Foreign Air Freight Forwarders and Foreign Cooperative Shippers Associations

§ 297.20 Filing for registration.

(a) Not later than 60 days before the start of operations as a foreign indirect air carrier, every foreign air freight forwarder and foreign cooperative shippers association shall apply for registration with the Department, unless upon a showing of good cause, the Director, Office of Aviation Analysis, allows application at a later time.

(b) Application shall consist of filing with the Department's Office of Aviation Analysis, Special Authorities Division, two copies of completed OST Form 4506, which may be obtained from the Department of Transportation, Special Authorities Division.

[ER–1159, 44 FR 69635, Dec. 4, 1979, as amended by ER–1265, 46 FR 56602, Nov. 18, 1981; Doc. No. 47939, 57 FR 40103, Sept. 2, 1992; 60 FR 43527, Aug. 22, 1995]

§ 297.21 Objections to registration application.

Persons objecting to registration by a foreign air freight forwarder or foreign cooperative shippers association shall file their objections with the Office of Aviation Analysis, Special Authorities Division, within 28 days of the filing date of the registration forms. The Department will list the names and nationality of all persons applying for registration in its Weekly Summary of Filings.

[ER–1159, 44 FR 69635, Dec. 4, 1979, as amended by Doc. No. 47939, 57 FR 40103, Sept. 2, 1992; 60 FR 43527, Aug. 22, 1995]

§ 297.22 Procedure on receipt of registration application.

After review of a registration form filed under § 297.20, the Department will take one or more of the following actions:

(a) Indicate by stamp on OST Form 4506 the effective date of registration, and return to the carrier the duplicate copy of OST Form 4506 as evidence of registration with the Department under this part;

(b) Reject an application for registration for failure to comply with this part, for reasons relating to the failure of effective reciprocity, or if the Department finds that it is in the public interest to do so.

(c) Request additional information from the applicant;

(d) Issue an order subjecting a carrier's exercise of authority under this part to such terms, conditions, or limitations as may be required by the public interest; or

(e) Institute a proceeding under section 41302 of the Statute.

[ER–1159, 44 FR 69635, Dec. 4, 1979, as amended by ER–1294, 47 FR 19685, May 7, 1982; Doc. No. 47939, 57 FR 40103, Sept. 2, 1992; 60 FR 43527, Aug. 22, 1995]

§ 297.23 Waiver of sovereign immunity.

By accepting an approval registration form under this part, a carrier waives any right it may possess to assert any defense of sovereign immunity from suit in any action or proceeding instituted against the carrier in any court or other tribunal in the United States based upon any claim arising out of operations by the carrier under this part.

§ 297.24 Notification to the Department of change of operations.

(a) Not later than 30 days before any change in its name or address or any temporary or permanent cessation of operations, each foreign indirect air carrier shall notify the Department's Office of Aviation Analysis, Special Authorities Division, of the change by resubmitting OST Form 4506.

(b) The registrant shall apply for an amendment of its registration not later than 30 days after any person listed on its existing registration as owning or holding beneficial ownership of 10 percent or more of the registrant's stock no longer has an interest of 10 percent or more, or after any person not so listed becomes an owner or holder of 10 percent or more. Application for amendment shall be made by resubmitting OST Form 4506, but the existing registration shall remain valid pending Department action on the amendment.

[ER–1159, 44 FR 69635, Dec. 4, 1979, as amended by Doc. No. 47939, 57 FR 40103, Sept. 2, 1992; 60 FR 43527, Aug. 22, 1995]

§ 297.25 Cancellation or conditioning of registration.

The registration of a foreign indirect air carrier may be canceled or subjected to additional terms, conditions or limitations if:

(a) It files with the Department a written notice that it is discontinuing foreign indirect air carrier activities;

(b) It fails to perform air transportation services as authorized;

(c) It fails to file the reports required by this part;

(d) A substantial ownership or control interest is acquired by persons who are not citizens of the country of citizenship of the registrant;

(e) There is a failure of effective reciprocity; or

(f) The Department finds that it is in the public interest to do so.

[ER–1159, 44 FR 69635, Dec. 4, 1979, as amended by ER–1294, 47 FR 19685, May 7, 1982]

Subpart D—General Rules for Foreign Indirect Air Carriers

§ 297.30 Public disclosure of cargo liability insurance.

Every foreign air freight forwarder shall give notice in writing to the shipper, when any shipment is accepted, of the limits of its cargo liability insurance, or of the absence of such insurance, and the limits of its liability, if any. The notice shall be included clearly and conspicuously on all of its rate sheets and airwaybills, and on any other documentation that is given to a shipper at the time of acceptance of the shipment.

§ 297.31 Preparation of airwaybills and manifests.

(a) Each registered foreign indirect air carrier shall prepare an accurate airwaybill describing completely all services rendered to or on behalf of the shipper, including the conditions under which the contract will be completed, in its capacity as a foreign indirect air carrier. A copy of the airwaybill shall be given to the consignor and to the consignee.

(b) Each registered foreign indirect air carrier shall prepare an accurate manifest showing every individual shipment included in each shipment consigned for transportation to a direct air carrier.

(c) A waiver of paragraph (a) of this section may be granted by the Department upon a written application by the foreign indirect air carrier not less than 30 days before the shipment to which it relates is transported, if the waiver is in the public interest, and is warranted by special or unusual circumstances.

Subpart E [Reserved]

Subpart F—Violations

§ 297.50 Enforcement.

In case of any violation of any of the provisions of the Statute, or this part, or any other rule, regulation or order issued under the Statute, the violator may be subject to a proceeding under section 46101 of the Statute before the Department, or sections 46106 through

46108 of the Statute before a U.S. District Court, as the case may be, to compel to compliance; or to civil penalties under the provisions of section 46301 of the Statute; or in the case of willful violation, to criminal penalties under the provisions of section 46316 of the Statute; or other lawful sanctions including cancellation of registration.

[ER–1159, 44 FR 69635, Dec. 4, 1979, as amended at 60 FR 43527, Aug. 22, 1995]

PART 298—EXEMPTIONS FOR AIR TAXI AND COMMUTER AIR CARRIER OPERATIONS

Subpart A—General

Subpart B—Exemptions

Subpart C—Registration for Exemption by Air Taxi Operators

Subpart D—Limitations and Conditions on Exemptions and Operations

Subpart E—Commuter Air Carrier Authorizations

Subpart F—Reporting Requirements

Subpart G—Public Disclosure of Data

Subpart H—Violations

Subpart I—Violations

AUTHORITY: 49 U.S.C. 329 and chapters 41102, 41708, and 41709.

EFFECTIVE DATE NOTE: At 83 FR 46877, Sept. 17, 2018, the authority citation for Part 298 was revised, effective Feb. 14, 2019. For the convenience of the user, the revised text is set forth as follows:

AUTHORITY: 49 U.S.C. 329 and chapters 401, 411, and 417.

SOURCE: ER–929, 40 FR 42855, Sept. 17, 1975, unless otherwise noted.

Subpart A—General

SOURCE: 70 FR 25768, May 16, 2005.

§ 298.1 Applicability of part.

This part establishes classifications of air carriers known as "air taxi operators" and "commuter air carriers," provides certain exemptions to them from some of the economic regulatory provisions of Subtitle VII of Title 49 of the United States Code (Transportation), specifies procedures by which such air carriers may obtain authority to conduct operations, and establishes rules applicable to their operations in interstate and/or foreign air transportation in all States, Territories and possessions of the United States. This part also establishes reporting requirements for commuter air carriers and small certificated air carriers.

§ 298.2 Definitions.

As used in this part:

Air taxi operator means an air carrier as established by § 298.3(a).

Air transportation means interstate air transportation, foreign air transportation, or the transportation of mail by aircraft as defined by the Statute.[1]

Aircraft-hours means the airborne hours of aircraft computed from the moment an aircraft leaves the ground until it touches the ground at the end of a flight stage.

Aircraft miles means the miles (computed in airport-to-airport distances) for each flight stage actually completed, whether or not performed in accordance with the scheduled pattern.

Certificated air carrier means an air carrier holding a certificate issued under section 41102 of the Statute.

Citizen of the United States means:

(1) An individual who is a citizen of the United States;

(2) A partnership each of whose partners is an individual who is a citizen of the United States; or

(3) A corporation or association organized under the laws of the United States or a state, the District of Columbia, or a territory or possession of the United States, of which the president and at least two-thirds of the board of directors and other managing officers are citizens of the United States, which is under the actual control of citizens of the United States, and in which at least 75 percent of the voting interest is owned or controlled by persons that are citizens of the United States.

Commuter air carrier means an air carrier as established by § 298.3(b) that carries passengers on at least five round trips per week on at least one route between two or more points according to its published flight schedules that specify the times, days of the week, and places between which those flights are performed.

Departure means takeoff from an airport.

Eligible place means a place in the United States that—

(1)(i) Was an eligible point under section 419 of the Federal Aviation Act of 1958 as in effect before October 1, 1988;

(ii) Received scheduled air transportation at any time after January 1, 1990; and

(iii) Is not listed in Department of Transportation Orders 89–9–37 and 89–12–52 as a place ineligible for compensation under Subchapter II of Chapter 417 of the Statute; or

(2) Was determined, on or after October 1, 1988, and before the date of the enactment of the Wendell H. Ford Aviation Investment and Reform Act for the 21st Century, by the Department to be eligible to receive subsidized small community air service under section 41736(a) of the Statute.

Flight stage means the operation of an aircraft from takeoff to landing.

Large aircraft means any aircraft originally designed to have a maximum

---

[1] Interstate air transportation is defined in section 40102(a)(25) as the transportation of passengers or property by aircraft as a common carrier for compensation, or the transportation of mail by aircraft (1) between a place in (i) a State, territory, or possession of the United States and a place in the District of Columbia or another State, territory, or possession of the United States; (ii) Hawaii and another place in Hawaii through the airspace over a place outside Hawaii; (iii) the District of Columbia and another place in the District of Columbia; or (iv) a territory or possession of the United States and another place in the same territory or possession; and (2) when any part of the transportation is by aircraft. NOTE: Operations wholly within the geographic limits of a single State are not considered interstate air transportation if in those operations the carrier transports no more than a *de minimis* volume of passengers or property moving as part of a continuous journey to or from a point outside the State.

Foreign air transportation is defined in section 40102(a)(23) of the Statute as the transportation of passengers or property by aircraft as a common carrier for compensation, or the transportation of mail by aircraft, between a place in the United States and a place outside the United States when any part of the transportation is by aircraft.

Air transportation also is defined to include the transportation of mail by aircraft. Section 5402 of the Postal Reorganization Act, 39 U.S.C. 5402, authorizes the carriage of mail by air taxi operators and commuter air carriers in some circumstances under contract with the U.S. Postal Service.

passenger capacity of more than 60 seats or a maximum payload capacity of more than 18,000 pounds.

Maximum certificated takeoff weight means the maximum takeoff weight authorized by the terms of the aircraft airworthiness certificate.[2]

Maximum passenger capacity means the maximum number of passenger seats for which an aircraft is configured.

Maximum payload capacity means: (1) The maximum certificated take-off weight of an aircraft, less the empty weight,[3] less all justifiable aircraft equipment, and less the operating load (consisting of minimum fuel load, oil, flight crew, steward's supplies, etc.). For purposes of this part, the allowance for the weight of the crew, oil, and fuel is as follows:

(i) Crew—200 pounds per crew member required under FAA regulations,

(ii) Oil—350 pounds,

(iii) Fuel—the minimum weight of fuel required under FAA regulations for a flight between domestic points 200 miles apart,[4]

(2) *Provided, however*, That in the case of aircraft for which a maximum zero fuel weight is prescribed by the FAA,[5] maximum payload capacity means the maximum zero fuel weight, less the empty weight, less all justifiable aircraft equipment, and less the operating load (consisting of minimum flight crew, steward's supplies, etc., but not including disposable fuel or oil).

Mile means a statute mile, *i.e.*, 5,280 feet.

Nonrevenue passenger means a person traveling free or under token charges, except those expressly named in the definition of revenue passenger; a person traveling at a fare or discount available only to employees or authorized persons of air carriers or their agents or only for travel on the business of the carriers; and an infant who does not occupy a seat. (This definition is for 14 CFR part 298 traffic-reporting purposes and may differ from the definitions used in other parts by the Federal Aviation Administration and the Transportation Security Administration for the collection of Passenger Facility Charges and Security Fees.) The definition includes, but is not limited to, the following examples of passengers when traveling free or pursuant to token charges:

(1) Directors, officers, employees, and others authorized by the air carrier operating the aircraft;

(2) Directors, officers, employees, and others authorized by the air carrier or another carrier traveling pursuant to a pass interchange agreement;

(3) Travel agents being transported for the purpose of familiarizing themselves with the carrier's services;

(4) Witnesses and attorneys attending any legal investigation in which such carrier is involved;

(5) Persons injured in aircraft accidents, and physicians, nurses, and others attending such persons;

(6) Any persons transported with the object of providing relief in cases of general epidemic, natural disaster, or other catastrophe;

(7) Any law enforcement official, including any person who has the duty of guarding government officials who are traveling on official business or traveling to or from such duty;

(8) Guests of an air carrier on an inaugural flight or delivery flights of newly-acquired or renovated aircraft;

(9) Security guards who have been assigned the duty to guard such aircraft against unlawful seizure, sabotage, or other unlawful interference;

(10) Safety inspectors of the National Transportation Safety Board or the FAA in their official duties or traveling to or from such duty;

---

[2] This weight may be found in the airplane operating record or in the airplane flight manual, which is incorporated by regulation into the airworthiness certificate.

[3] Empty weight is defined in section 03 of part 241 as follows: the weight of the airframe, engines, propellers, and fixed equipment. Empty weight excludes the weight of the crew and payload, but includes the weight of all fixed ballast, unusable fuel supply, undrainable oil, total quantity of engine coolant, and total quantity of hydraulic fluid.

[4] Assumes VFR weather conditions and flights not involving extended overwater operations.

[5] The maximum zero fuel weight is the maximum permissible weight of an airplane with no disposable fuel or oil. The zero fuel weight figure may be found in the FAA's type certificate data sheets, and/or in FAA-approved flight manuals.

(11) Postal employees on duty in charge of the mails or traveling to or from such duty;

(12) Technical representatives of companies that have been engaged in the manufacture, development or testing of a particular type of aircraft or aircraft equipment, when the transportation is provided for the purpose of in-flight observation and subject to applicable FAA regulations;

(13) Persons engaged in promoting air transportation;

(14) Air marshals and other Transportation Security officials acting in their official capacities and while traveling to and from their official duties; and

(15) Other authorized persons, when such transportation is undertaken for promotional purpose.

Passengers carried means passengers on board each flight stage.

Point when used in connection with any territory or possession of the United States, or the States of Alaska and Hawaii, means any airport or place where aircraft may be landed or taken off, including the area within a 25-mile radius of such airport or place; when used in connection with the continental United States, except Alaska, it shall have the same meaning except be limited to the area within a 3-mile radius of such airport or place: Provided, That for the purposes of this part, West 30th Street Heliport and Pan Am Building Heliport, both located in New York City, shall be regarded as separate points.

Reporting carrier for Schedule T–100 purposes means the air carrier in operational control of the flight, *i.e.*, the carrier that uses its flight crews under its own FAA operating authority.

Revenue passenger means a passenger for whose transportation an air carrier receives commercial remuneration. (This definition is for 14 CFR part 298 traffic-reporting purposes and may differ from the definitions used in other parts by the Federal Aviation Administration and the Transportation Security Administration for the collection of Passenger Facility Charges and Security Fees.) This includes, but is not limited to, the following examples:

(1) Passengers traveling under publicly available tickets including promotional offers (for example two-for-one) or loyalty programs (for example, redemption of frequent flyer points);

(2) Passengers traveling on vouchers or tickets issued as compensation for denied boarding or in response to consumer complaints or claims;

(3) Passengers traveling at corporate discounts;

(4) Passengers traveling on preferential fares (Government, seamen, military, youth, student, etc.);

(5) Passengers traveling on barter tickets; and

(6) Infants traveling on confirmed-space tickets.

Revenue passenger-mile means one revenue passenger transported one mile. Revenue passenger-miles are computed by multiplying the aircraft miles flown on each flight stage by the number of revenue passengers carried on that flight stage.

Revenue seat-miles available means the aircraft-miles flown on each flight stage multiplied by the number of seats available for sale on that flight stage.

Revenue ton-mile means one ton of revenue traffic transported one mile. Revenue ton-miles are computed by multiplying the aircraft-miles flown on each flight stage by the number of pounds of revenue traffic carried on that flight stage and converted to ton-miles by dividing total revenue pound-miles by 2,000 pounds.

Revenue ton-miles available means the aircraft-miles flown on each flight stage multiplied by the number of pounds of aircraft capacity available for use on that stage and converted to ton-miles by dividing total pound-miles available by 2,000 pounds.

Scheduled service means transport service operated over routes pursuant to published flight schedules or pursuant to mail contracts with the U.S. Postal Service.

Small aircraft means any aircraft originally designed to have a maximum passenger capacity of 60 seats or less or a maximum payload capacity of 18,000 pounds or less.

Small certificated air carrier means an air carrier holding a certificate issued under section 41102 of the Statute that provides scheduled passenger air service within and between only the 50

States of the United States, the District of Columbia, the Commonwealth of Puerto Rico, and the U.S. Virgin Islands with small aircraft as defined in this section.

Statute means Subtitle VII of Title 49 of the United States Code (Transportation).

Ton means a short ton, *i.e.*, 2,000 pounds.

Wet-Lease Agreement means an agreement under which one carrier leases an aircraft with flight crew to another air carrier.

§ 298.3 Classification.

(a) There is hereby established a classification of air carriers, designated as "air taxi operators," which directly engage in the air transportation of persons or property or mail or in any combination of such transportation and which:

(1) Do not directly or indirectly utilize large aircraft in air transportation;

(2) Do not hold a certificate of public convenience and necessity and do not engage in scheduled passenger operations as specified in paragraph (b) of this section;

(3) Have and maintain in effect liability insurance coverage in compliance with the requirements set forth in part 205 of this chapter and have and maintain a current certificate of insurance evidencing such coverage on file with the Department;

(4) If operating in foreign air transportation or participating in an interline agreement, subscribe to Agreement 18900 (OST Form 4523 or OST Form 4507) and comply with all other requirements of part 203 of this chapter; and

(5) Have registered with the Department in accordance with subpart C of this part.

(b) There is hereby established a classification of air carriers, designated as "commuter air carriers," which directly engage in the air transportation of persons, property or mail, and which:

(1) Do not directly or indirectly utilize large aircraft in air transportation;

(2) Do not hold a certificate of public convenience and necessity;

(3) Carry passengers on at least five round trips per week on at least one route between two or more points according to its published flight schedules that specify the times, days of the week, and places between which those flights are performed;

(4) Have and maintain in effect liability insurance coverage in compliance with the requirements set forth in part 205 of this chapter and have and maintain a current certificate of insurance evidencing such coverage on file with the Department;

(5) Have and maintain in effect and on file with the Department a signed counterpart of Agreement 18900 (OST Form 4523) and comply with all other requirements of part 203 of this chapter; and

(6) Hold a Commuter Air Carrier Authorization issued in accordance with subpart E of this part.

(c) A person who does not observe the conditions set forth in paragraph (a) or (b) of this section shall not be an air taxi operator or commuter air carrier within the meaning of this part with respect to any operations conducted while such conditions are not being observed, and during such periods is not entitled to any of the exemptions set forth in this part.

§ 298.4 Requests for statement of authority.

In any instance where an air taxi operator or commuter air carrier is required by a foreign government to produce evidence of its authority to engage in foreign air transportation under the laws of the United States, the Director, Office of Aviation Analysis (X–50), Office of the Secretary, 1200 New Jersey Avenue, SE., Washington, DC 20590, will, upon request, furnish the carrier with a written statement, outlining its general operating privileges under this part for presentation to the proper authorities of the foreign government.

Subpart B—Exemptions

SOURCE: 70 FR 25768, May 16, 2005.

§ 298.11 Exemption authority.

Air taxi operators and commuter air carriers are hereby relieved from the following provisions of the Statute only if and so long as they comply with the provisions of this part and the conditions imposed herein, and to the extent necessary to permit them to conduct air taxi or commuter air carrier operations:

(a) Section 41101;

(b) Section 41504; except that the requirements of that section shall apply to:

(1) Tariffs for through rates, fares, and charges filed jointly by air taxi operators or commuter air carriers with air carriers or with foreign air carriers subject to the tariff-filing requirements of Chapter 415; and

(2) Tariffs required to be filed by air taxi operators or commuter air carriers which embody the provisions of the counterpart to Agreement 18900 as specified in part 203 of this chapter;

(c) Section 41702, except for the requirements that air taxi operators and commuter air carriers shall:

(1) Provide safe service, equipment, and facilities in connection with air transportation;

(2) Provide adequate service insofar as that requires them to comply with parts 252 and 382 of this chapter;

(3) Observe and enforce just and reasonable joint rates, fares, and charges, and just and reasonable classifications, rules, regulations and practices as provided in tariffs filed jointly by air taxi operators or commuter air carriers with certificated air carriers or with foreign air carriers; and

(4) Establish just, reasonable, and equitable divisions of such joint rates, fares, and charges as between air carriers participating therein which shall not unduly prefer or prejudice any of such participating air carriers;

(d) Section 41310, except that the requirements of that subsection shall apply to through service provided pursuant to tariffs filed jointly by air taxi operators or commuter air carriers with certificated air carriers or with foreign air carriers and to transportation of the handicapped to the extent that that is required by part 382 of this chapter;

(e) Section 41902;

(f) Section 41708.

§ 298.12 Duration of exemption.

The exemption from any provision of the Statute provided by this part shall continue in effect only until such time as the Department shall find that enforcement of that provision would be in the public interest, at which time the exemption shall terminate or be conditioned with respect to the person, class of persons, or service (e.g., limited-entry foreign air transportation market) subject to the finding.

Subpart C—Registration for Exemption by Air Taxi Operators

SOURCE: 70 FR 25768, May 16, 2005.

§ 298.21 Filing for registration by air taxi operators.

(a) Every air taxi operator who plans to commence operations under this part shall register with the Department not later than 30 days prior to the commencement of such operations, unless, upon a showing of good cause satisfactory to the Manager, Program Management Branch (AFS–260), Federal Aviation Administration, registration within a lesser period of time is allowed.

(b) The registration of an air taxi operator shall remain in effect until it is amended by the carrier or canceled by the Department.

(c) Registration by all air taxi operators shall be accomplished by filing with the Department at the address specified in paragraph (d) of this section the following:

(1) Air Taxi Registration (OST Form 4507), executed in duplicate.[6] This form shall be certified by a responsible official and shall include the following information:

(i) The name of the carrier and its mailing address;

(ii) The carrier's principal place of business, if different from its mailing address, and its telephone number and fax number;

(iii) The carrier's FAA certificate number, if any, and the address and telephone number of the carrier's local FAA office;

[6] OST Form 4507 can be obtained from the Manager, Program Management Branch, Federal Aviation Administration, AFS–260, or on the World Wide Web at *http://www.faa.gov/avr/afs/afs200/afs260/Part298.cfm.*

(iv) The type of service the carrier will offer (scheduled passenger,[7] scheduled cargo, mail under a U.S. Postal Service contract, on-demand passenger, on-demand cargo, or other service such as air ambulance operations, firefighting or seasonal operations);

(v) A list of the aircraft that the carrier proposes to operate, or, in the case of an amendment to the registration, the aircraft that it is currently operating in its air taxi operations, and the aircraft type, FAA registration number and passenger capacity of each aircraft;

(vi) For initial registration, the proposed date of commencement of air taxi operations;

(vii) For amendments, whether the carrier has carried passengers in foreign air transportation during the previous 12 months;

(viii) Whether the carrier is a citizen of the United States; and

(ix) A certification that the registration is complete and accurate and that, if the carrier is engaged in foreign air transportation, or participating in an interline agreement, it subscribes to the terms of Agreement 18900 (*see* OST Form 4523).

(2) A certificate of insurance (OST Form 6410) which is currently effective (or in case of initial registration, is to become effective), as defined in part 205 of this chapter;

(3) An 8 dollar ($8) registration filing fee in the form of a check, draft, or postal money order payable to the Department of Transportation.

(d) Registrations required in paragraph (c) of this section shall be submitted to the Department of Transportation, Federal Aviation Administration, Program Management Branch (AFS–260), 800 Independence Avenue, SW., Washington, DC 20591. For those air taxi operators that have a mailing address in the State of Alaska, the registrations shall be filed with the Department of Transportation, Federal Aviation Administration, Alaskan Region Headquarters (AAL–230), 222 West 7th Avenue, Box 14, Anchorage, Alaska 99513.

[7] Companies proposing to provide scheduled passenger service at the level established by this Part for commuter air carriers are not permitted to conduct such operations under their air taxi registration; such companies must first be found fit, willing and able to operate and be issued a Commuter Air Carrier Authorization by the Department.

§ 298.22 Processing by the Department.

After examination of the OST Form 4507 submitted by the carrier, the Department will stamp the effective date of the registration on the form and return the duplicate copy to the carrier to confirm that it has registered with the Department as required by this part. The effective date of the registration shall not be earlier than the effective date of the insurance policy or policies named in the certificate of insurance filed by the carrier under § 298.21(c)(2).

§ 298.23 Notifications to the Department of change in operations.

(a) If any of the information contained on its registration changes, an air taxi operator shall submit an amendment reflecting the updated information. This amendment shall be filed no later than 30 days after the change occurs. There is no filing fee for submitting an amendment.

(b) An amendment shall be made by resubmitting OST Form 4507 to the Department of Transportation, Federal Aviation Administration, Program Management Branch (AFS–260), 800 Independence Avenue, SW., Washington, DC 20591. If the air taxi operator has a mailing address in the State of Alaska, the form shall be mailed to the Department of Transportation, Federal Aviation Administration, Alaskan Region Headquarters (AAL–230), 222 West 7th Avenue, Box 14, Anchorage, Alaska 99513.

§ 298.24 Cancellation of the registration.

The registration of an air taxi operator may be canceled by the Department if any of the following occur:

(a) The operator ceases its operations;

(b) The operator's insurance coverage changes or lapses;

(c) The operator fails to file an amended registration when required by § 298.23;

(d) The operator's Air Carrier Certificate and/or Operations Specifications is revoked by the Federal Aviation Administration;

(e) The operator fails to qualify as a citizen of the United States;

(f) The Department determines that it is otherwise in the public interest to do so.

Subpart D—Limitations and Conditions on Exemptions and Operations

SOURCE: 70 FR 25768, May 16, 2005.

§298.30 Public disclosure of policy on consumer protection.

(a) Every air taxi and commuter air carrier shall cause to be displayed continuously in a conspicuous public place at each desk, station and position in the United States that is in charge of a person employed exclusively by it, or by it jointly with another person, or by any agent employed by it to sell tickets to passengers, a sign located so as to be clearly visible and readable to the traveling public, containing a statement setting forth the air taxi and commuter air carrier's policy on baggage liability and denied boarding compensation.

(b) An air taxi or commuter air carrier shall provide a written notice on or with a passenger's ticket concerning baggage liability as provided in §254.5 of this chapter. These ticket notices are required only for passengers whose ticket includes a flight segment that uses large aircraft (more than 60 seats).

(c) If the substantive terms of the counter sign and ticket notice required by this section differ, the terms contained in the required ticket notice govern.

§298.31 Scope of service and equipment authorized.

Nothing in this part shall be construed as authorizing the operation of large aircraft in air transportation, and the exemption provided by this part to air taxi operators and commuter air carriers that register with the Department extends only to the direct operation in air transportation in accordance with the limitations and conditions of this part of aircraft originally designed to have a maximum passenger capacity of 60 seats or less or a maximum payload capacity of 18,000 pounds or less.

§298.32 Limitations on operations to eligible places.

No person shall provide scheduled passenger service as a commuter air carrier at an eligible place unless it has been found by the Department to be fit, willing, and able to conduct such service and issued a Commuter Air Carrier Authorization as provided in subpart E of this part.

§298.33 Security requirements.

In conducting operations under this part, an air taxi operator or a commuter air carrier is required to adhere to all security requirements established by the Department of Transportation and the Department of Homeland Security applicable to such operations.

§298.34 [Reserved]

§298.35 Limitations on carriage of mail.

An air taxi operator or commuter air carrier is not authorized to carry mail except pursuant to contract with the U.S. Postal Service entered into pursuant to section 5402 of the Postal Reorganization Act (39 U.S.C. 5402).

§298.36 Limitations on use of business name.

(a) An air taxi operator or commuter air carrier in holding out to the public and in performing its services in air transportation shall do so only in the name or names in which its air carrier certificate is issued pursuant to section 44702 of the Statute by the Federal Aviation Administration, and in which it is registered with the Department under this part, or in which its Commuter Air Carrier Authorization is issued or other trade name is registered.

(b) Slogans shall not be considered names for the purposes of this section, and their use is not restricted hereby.

(c) Commuter air carriers are subject to the provisions of part 215 of this chapter with regard to the use and change of air carrier names.

(d) Neither the provisions of this section nor the grant of a permission hereunder shall preclude Department intervention or enforcement action should there be evidence of a significant potential for, or of actual, public confusion.

§ 298.37 Prohibition of services not covered by insurance.

An air taxi operator or commuter air carrier shall not operate in air transportation or provide or offer to provide air transportation unless there is in effect liability insurance which covers such transportation and which is evidenced by a current certificate of insurance on file with the Department as required by part 205 of this chapter.

§ 298.38 Financial security arrangements for operating Public Charters.

When an air taxi operator or commuter air carrier performs a Public Charter under part 380 of this chapter, either:

(a) The air taxi operator or commuter air carrier shall meet the bonding or escrow requirements applicable to certificated air carriers as set forth in § 212.8 of this chapter; or

(b) The air taxi operator or commuter air carrier shall ensure that it does not receive any payments for the charter until after the charter has been completed. In this case, its contracts with the charter operator and the charter operator's depository bank, if any, shall state that the charter operator or bank, as applicable, shall retain control of and responsibility for all participant funds intended for payment for air transportation until after the charter has been completed, notwithstanding any provision of part 380 of this chapter.

Subpart E—Commuter Air Carrier Authorizations

SOURCE: 70 FR 25768, May 16, 2005.

§ 298.50 Application.

(a) Any person desiring to provide air transportation as a commuter air carrier must first obtain a Commuter Air Carrier Authorization. This shall be accomplished by filing with the Department—

(1) An application in accordance with the requirements of parts 201 and 302 of this chapter;

(2) Data in accordance with part 204 of this chapter to support a determination by the Department that the person is "fit, willing, and able" to operate the proposed commuter service; and

(3) A $670 filing fee in the form of a check, draft, or postal money order payable to the Department of Transportation.

(b) An executed original and two true copies of an application for a Commuter Air Carrier Authorization shall be filed with Department of Transportation Dockets, 1200 New Jersey Avenue, SE., Washington, DC 20590.

§ 298.51 Processing by the Department.

In processing applications filed in accordance with § 298.50, the Department will generally follow the procedures set forth in §§ 302.207 through 302.211 of this chapter.

§ 298.52 Air taxi operations by commuter air carriers.

(a) A commuter air carrier that holds an effective Commuter Air Carrier Authorization and otherwise meets the requirements of this part is also authorized to conduct air taxi operations (e.g., scheduled cargo, mail under a U.S. Postal Service contract, on-demand passenger, on-demand cargo, or other service such as air ambulance operations, firefighting or seasonal operations) without having to meet the registration requirements of subpart C of this part, except as provided in paragraph (b) of this section.

(b) Should a commuter air carrier cease conducting all scheduled passenger operations and its Commuter Air Carrier Authorization is suspended pursuant to §§ 298.53 and/or 204.7 of this chapter, it may continue to conduct air taxi operations *provided that* the carrier maintains in effect liability insurance coverage as required for such operations by part 205 of this chapter and, within 10 days of the cessation of scheduled passenger operations, registers as an air taxi operator in accordance with subpart C of this part; and *provided further* that the carrier continues to hold authority from the Federal Aviation Administration to conduct such air taxi operations.

§ 298.53 Suspension or revocation of authority.

A Commuter Air Carrier Authorization may be suspended or revoked if any of the following occur:

(a) The operator fails to maintain insurance coverage as required by part 205 of this chapter for commuter operations;

(b) The scheduled passenger authority under the operator's Air Carrier Certificate is suspended or revoked by the Federal Aviation Administration;

(c) The operator does not commence operations for which it has been found fit, or the operator ceases those operations as provided in § 204.7 of this chapter;

(d) The Department finds that the carrier is not fit, willing, and able to conduct scheduled service or fails to qualify as a citizen of the United States; or

(e) The Department determines that it is otherwise in the public interest to do so.

Subpart F—Reporting Requirements

§ 298.60 General reporting instructions.

(a) Each commuter air carrier and each small certificated air carrier shall file with the Department's Bureau of Transportation Statistics (BTS) the applicable schedules of BTS Form 298-C, A Report of Financial and Operating Statistics for Small Aircraft Operators' and Schedule T–100, AU.S. Air Carrier Traffic and Capacity Data by Nonstop Segment and On-Flight Market'' as required by this section.

(b) A single copy of the BTS Form 298-C report shall be filed quarterly with the Office of Airline Information (OAI) for the periods ended March 31, June 30, September 30 and December 31 of each year to be received on or before May 10, August 10, November 10, and February 10, respectively. An electronic filing of the monthly Schedule T–100 is due at OAI within 30 days after the end of each month. Due dates falling on a Saturday, Sunday or Federal holiday will become effective on the next work day.

(c) Reports required by this section shall be submitted to the Bureau of Transportation Statistics in a format specified in accounting and reporting directives issued by the Bureau of Transportation Statistics' Director of Airline Information.

[ER–1399, 50 FR 19, Jan. 2, 1985, as amended by Doc. No. 47939, 57 FR 40104, Sept. 2, 1992; 60 FR 66726, Dec. 26, 1995; 67 FR 49231, July 30, 2002; 75 FR 41585, July 16, 2010]

§ 298.61 Reporting of traffic statistics.

(a) Each commuter air carrier and small certificated air carrier shall file Schedule T–100, AU.S. Air Carrier Traffic and Capacity Data by Nonstop Segment and On-Flight Market.''

(b) Schedule T–100 shall be filed monthly as set forth in ''298.60.

(1) Schedule T–100 collects summarized flight stage data and on-flight market data from revenue flights. All traffic statistics shall be compiled in terms of each flight stage as actually performed. The detail T–100 data shall be maintained in such a manner as to permit monthly summarization and organization into two basic groupings. The first grouping, the nonstop segment information, is to be summarized by equipment type, within class of service, within pair-of-points, without regard to individual flight number. The second grouping requires that the enplanement/deplanement information be broken out into separate units called on-flight market records, which shall be summarized by class of service, within pair-of-points, without regard for equipment type or flight number.

(2) *Joint-service operations.* The Department may authorize joint service operations between two direct air carriers. Examples of these joint-service operations are: blocked-space agreements; part-charter agreements; code-sharing agreements; wet-lease agreements, and similar arrangements.

(i) Joint-service operations are reported by the carrier in operational control of the flight, i.e., the carrier that uses its flight crews under its own FAA operating authority. The traffic moving under these agreements is reported on Schedule T–100 the same way as any other traffic on the aircraft.

(ii) If there are questions about reporting a joint-service operation, contact the BTS Assistant Director—Airline Information (fax no. 202 366–3383, telephone no. 202 366–4373). Joint-service operations are reported in Schedule T–100 in accordance with this paragraph (b).

(iii) *Operational control.* The air carrier in operational control of the aircraft (the carrier that uses its flight crews under its own FAA operating authority) must report joint-service operations.

(c) *Service classes.* (1) The statistical classifications are designed to reflect the operating characteristics attributable to each distinctive type of service offered. The combination of scheduled and nonscheduled operations with passenger, all-cargo, and military services are placed into service classes as follows:

Code	Type of Service
F	Scheduled Passenger/Cargo
G	Scheduled All-Cargo
L	Nonscheduled Civilian Passenger/Cargo
P	Nonscheduled Civilian Cargo
N	Nonscheduled Military Passenger/Cargo
R	Nonscheduled Military Cargo

(2) Scheduled services include traffic and capacity elements applicable to air transportation provided pursuant to published schedules and extra sections of scheduled flights. Scheduled Passenger/Cargo (Service Class F) is a composite of first class, coach, and mixed passenger/cargo service.

(3) Nonscheduled services include all traffic and capacity elements applicable to the performance of nonscheduled aircraft charters, and other air transportation services not constituting an integral part of services performed pursuant to published flight schedules.

(d) *Air transport traffic and capacity elements.* (1) Within each of the service classifications, carriers shall report air transport traffic and capacity elements. The elements are reported on segment or market records as follows:

Code	Description	Segment	Market	Computed by DOT
	Carrier, carrier entity code	S	M	
	Reporting period date	S	M	
	Origin airport code	S	M	
	Destination airport code	S	M	
	Service class code	S	M	
	Aircraft type code	S		
110	Revenue passengers enplaned		M	
130	Revenue passengers transported.	S		
140	Revenue passenger-miles			CFD*
210	Revenue cargo tons enplaned			CFD*
217	Enplaned freight		M	
219	Enplaned mail		M	
230	Revenue tons transported			CFD*
237	Transported freight	S		
239	Transported mail	S		
240	Revenue ton-miles			CFD*
241	Revenue ton-miles passenger			CFD*
247	Revenue ton-miles freight			CFD*
249	Revenue ton-miles mail			CFD*
270	Available capacity payload	S		
280	Available ton-miles			CFD*
310	Available seats, total	S		
320	Available seat-miles			CFD*
410	Revenue aircraft miles flown			CFD*
430	Revenue aircraft miles scheduled.			CFD*
501	Inter-airport distance			CFD*
510	Revenue aircraft departures performed.	S		
520	Revenue aircraft departures scheduled.	S		
610	Revenue aircraft hours (airborne).	S		
630	Aircraft hours (ramp-to-ramp)	S		
650	Total aircraft hours (airborne)	S		

*CFD = Computed by DOT from detail Schedule T–100 and T–100(f) data.

(2) [Reserved]

(e) These reported items are further described as follows:

(1) *Reporting period date.* The year and month to which the reported data are applicable.

(2) Carrier, Carrier entity code. Each air carrier shall report its name and entity code (a five digit code assigned by BTS that identifies both the carrier and its entity) for its particular operations. The Office of Airline Information (OAI) will assign or confirm codes upon request; OAI's address is Office of Airline Information, BTS, DOT, K–14, 1200 New Jersey Avenue, SE., Washington, DC 20590–0001.

(3) *Service class code.* The service class codes are prescribed in section 298.61(c). In general, classes are divided into two broad categories, either scheduled or nonscheduled, where scheduled = F + G and nonscheduled = L + N + P + R.

(4) *Record type code.* This code indicates whether the data pertain to non-

stop segment (record type S) or on-flight market (record type M).

(5) *Aircraft type code.* This code represents the aircraft types, as described in the BTS' Accounting and Reporting Directives.

(6) *Origin, Destination airport code(s).* These codes represent the industry designators. An industry source of these industry designator codes is the Official Airline Guide (OAG). OAI assigns codes upon request if not listed in the OAG.

(7) *110 Revenue passengers enplaned.* The total number of revenue passengers enplaned at the origin point of a flight, boarding the flight for the first time; an unduplicated count of passengers in a market. Under the T-100 system of reporting, these enplaned passengers are the sum of the passengers in the individual on-flight markets. In the domestic entity, report only the total revenue passengers enplaned in item 110.

(8) *130 Revenue passengers transported.* The total number of revenue passengers transported over a single flight stage, including those already on the aircraft from a previous flight stage. In the domestic entity, report only the total revenue passengers transported in item 130.

(9) *140 Revenue passenger-miles.* Computed by multiplying the inter-airport distance of each flight stage by the number of passengers transported on that flight stage.

(10) *210 Revenue cargo tons enplaned.* The total number of cargo tons enplaned. This data element is a sum of the individual on-flight market figures for each of the following categories: 217 Freight and 219 Mail. This element represents an unduplicated count of the revenue traffic in a market.

(11) *217 Enplaned freight.* The total weight of revenue freight enplaned at the origin point of a flight, loaded onto the flight for the first time; an unduplicated count of freight in a market.

(12) *219 Enplaned mail.* The total weight of mail enplaned at the origin point of a flight, loaded onto the flight for the first time; an unduplicated count of mail in a market.

(13) *230 Revenue tons transported.* The number of tons of revenue traffic transported. This element is the sum of the following elements: 231 Passengers transported-total, 237 Freight, and 239 Mail.

(14) *237 Transported freight.* The total weight of freight transported over a single flight stage, including freight already on the aircraft from a previous flight stage.

(15) *239 Transported mail.* The total weight of mail transported over a single flight stage, including mail already on the aircraft from a previous flight stage.

(16) *240 Revenue ton-miles—total.* Ton-miles are computed by multiplying the revenue aircraft miles flown (410) on each flight stage by the number of tons transported on that stage. This element is the sum of 241 through 249.

(17) *241 Revenue ton-miles—passenger.* Equals the number of passengers times 200, times inter-airport distance, divided by 2000. A standard weight of 200 pounds per passenger, including baggage, is used for all operations and service classes.

(18) *247 Revenue ton-miles—freight.* Equals the volume of freight in whole tons times the inter-airport distance.

(19) *249 Revenue ton-miles—mail.* Equals the volume of mail in whole tons times the inter-airport distance.

(20) *270 Available capacity-payload.* The available capacity is collected in pounds. This figure shall reflect the payload or total available capacity for passengers, mail, and freight applicable to the aircraft with which each flight stage is performed.

(21) *280 Available ton-miles.* The aircraft miles flown on each flight stage multiplied by the available capacity on the aircraft in tons.

(22) *310 Available seats.* The number of seats available for sale. This figure reflects the actual number of seats available, excluding those blocked for safety or operational reasons. In the domestic entity, report the total available seats in item 130. Scheduled and non-scheduled available seats are reported in item 130.

(23) *320 Available seat-miles.* The aircraft miles flown on each flight stage multiplied by the seat capacity available for sale.

(24) *410 Revenue aircraft miles flown.* Revenue aircraft miles flown are computed based on the airport pairs between which service is actually performed; miles are generated from the data for scheduled aircraft departures (Code 520) times the inter-airport distances (Code 501).

(25) *430 Revenue aircraft miles scheduled.* The number of revenue aircraft miles scheduled. All such data shall be maintained in conformity with the airport pairs between which service is scheduled, whether or not in accordance with actual performance.

(26) *501 Inter-airport distance.* The great circle distance, in official statute miles as prescribed in part 247 of this chapter, between airports served by each flight stage. Official inter-airport mileage may be obtained from the Office of Airline Information.

(27) *510 Revenue aircraft departures performed.* The number of revenue aircraft departures performed.

(28) *520 Revenue aircraft departures scheduled.* The number of revenue aircraft departures scheduled, whether or not actually performed.

(29) *610 Revenue aircraft hours (airborne).* The elapsed time, computed from the moment the aircraft leaves the ground until its next landing.

(30) *630 Aircraft hours (ramp-to-ramp).* The elapsed time, computed from the moment the aircraft first moves under its own power from the boarding ramp at one airport to the time it comes to rest at the ramp for the next point of landing. This data element is also referred to as 'block' and 'block-to-block' aircraft hours.

(31) *650 Total aircraft hours (airborne).* The elapsed time, computed from the moment the aircraft leaves the ground until it touches down at the next landing. This includes flight training, testing, and ferry flights.

(f) *Public availability of Schedule T–100 data.* Detailed domestic on-flight market and nonstop segment data in Schedule T–100, except military data, shall be publicly available after processing. Domestic data are defined as data from air transportation operations from a place in any State of the United States, the District of Columbia, the Commonwealth of Puerto Rico and the Virgin Islands, or a U.S. territory or possession to a place in any State of the United States, the District of Columbia, the Commonwealth of Puerto Rico and the Virgin Islands, or a U.S. territory or possession.

[Doc. No. OST–98–4043, 67 FR 49231, July 30, 2002, as amended by Doc. No. OST–2006–26053, 75 FR 41585, July 16, 2010]

§ 298.62 Reporting of financial data.

(a) Each commuter air carrier and each small certificated air carrier shall file BTS Form 298–C, Schedule F–1 "Report of Financial Data." This report shall be filed quarterly as set forth in § 298.60 of this part.

(b) Each carrier shall indicate in the space provided, its full corporate name and the quarter for which the report is filed.

(c) This schedule shall be used to report financial data for the overall or system operations of the carrier. At the option of the carrier, the data may be reported in whole dollars by dropping the cents. Financial data shall be reported in the following categories:

(1) Line 1 "Total Operating Revenues" shall include gross revenues accruing from services ordinarily associated with air transportation and air transportation-related services. This category shall include revenue derived from scheduled service operations, revenue derived from nonscheduled service operations, amounts of compensation paid to the carrier under section 41732 of the Statute and other transport-related revenue such as in-flight sales, restaurant and food service (ground), rental of property or equipment, limousine service, cargo pick-up and delivery charges, and fixed-base operations involving the selling or servicing of aircraft, flying instructions, charter flights, etc.

(2) Line 2 "Total Operating Expenses" shall include expenses of a character usually and ordinarily incurred in the performance of air transporation and air transportation services. This category shall include expenses incurred: directly in the in-flight operation of aircraft; in the holding of aircraft and aircraft personnel in readiness for assignment to an in-flight status; on the ground in controlling and protecting the in-flight movement

of aircraft; landing, handling or servicing aircraft on the ground; selling transportation; servicing and handling traffic; promoting the development of traffic; and administering operations generally. This category shall also include expenses which are specifically identifiable with the repair and upkeep of property and equipment used in the performance of air transportation, all depreciation and amortization expenses applicable to property and equipment used in providing air transportation services, all expenses associated with the transport-related revenues included on line 1 of this schedule, and all other expenses not specifically mentioned which are related to transport operations. Interest expense and other nonoperating expenses attributable to financing or other activities which are extraneous to and not an integral part of air transportation or its incidental services shall not be included in this category.

(3) Line 3 "Net Income or (Loss)" shall reflect all operating and nonoperating items of profit and loss recognized during the period except for prior period adjustments.

(4) Line 4 "Passenger Revenues-Scheduled Service" shall include revenue generated from the transportation of passengers between pairs of points which are served on a regularly scheduled basis.

(d) Data reported on this schedule shall be withheld from public release for a period of 3 years after the close of the calendar quarter to which the report relates.

[ER-1399, 50 FR 20, Jan. 2, 1985, as amended by 53 FR 48528, Dec. 1, 1988; 60 FR 43528, Aug. 22, 1995; 60 FR 66726, Dec. 26, 1995; 67 FR 49234, July 30, 2002]

§ 298.63 Reporting of aircraft operating expenses and related statistics by small certificated air carriers.

(a) Each small certificated air carrier shall file BTS Form 298-C, Schedule F-2 "Report of Aircraft Operating Expenses and Related Statistics." This schedule shall be filed quarterly as prescribed in § 298.60. Data reported on this report shall be for the overall or system operations of the air carrier.

(b) Each carrier shall indicate in the space provided its full corporate name and the quarter for which the report is filed.

(c) This schedule shall show the direct and indirect expenses incurred in aircraft operations. Direct expense data applicable to each aircraft type operated by the carrier shall be reported in separate columns of this schedule. Each aircraft type reported shall be identified at the head of each column in the space provided for "Aircraft Type." "Aircraft Type" refers to aircraft models such as Beech-18, Piper PA-32, etc. Aircraft Type designations are prescribed in the *Accounting and Reporting Directives*, which is available from the BTS' Office of Airline Information. In the space provided for "Aircraft Code" carriers shall insert the three digit code prescribed in the *Accounting and Reporting Directives* for the reported aircraft type. (NOTE: Aircraft of the same type but different cabin configuration may be grouped into a single classification; therefore, carriers are not required to report the fourth digit of an aircraft code indicating cabin configuration.)

(d) Line 1 Direct aircraft operating expenses shall be reported in the following categories:

(1) Line 2 "Flying Operations (Less Rental)" shall be subdivided as follows:

(i) Line 3 "Pilot and Copilot" expense shall include pilots' and copilots' salaries, and related employee benefits, pensions, payroll taxes and personnel expenses.

(ii) Line 4 "Aircraft Fuel and Oil" expense shall include the cost of fuel and oil used in flight operations and nonrefundable aircraft fuel and oil taxes.

(iii) Line 5 "Other" expenses shall include general (hull) insurance, and all other expenses incurred in the in-flight operation of aircraft and holding of aircraft and aircraft operational personnel in readiness for assignment to an in-flight status, which are not provided for otherwise on this schedule.

(2) Line 6 "Total Flying Operations (Less Rentals)" shall equal the sum of lines 3, 4 and 5.

(3) Line 7 "Maintenance-Flight Equipment" shall include the cost of labor, material and related overhead expended by the carrier to maintain

flight equipment, general services purchased for flight equipment maintenance from associated or other outside companies, and provisions for flight equipment overhauls.

(4) Line 8 "Depreciation and Rental-Flight Equipment" expense shall include depreciation of flight equipment, amortization of capitalized leases for flight equipment, provision for obsolescence and deterioration of spare parts, and rental expense of flight equipment.

(5) Line 9 "Total Direct Expense" shall equal the sum of lines 6, 7 and 8.

(e) Line 10 Indirect aircraft operating expenses shall be reported only in total for all aircraft types and shall be segregated according to the following categories:

(1) Line 11 "Flight Attendant Expense" shall include flight attendants' salaries, and related employee benefits, pensions, payroll taxes and personnel expenses.

(2) Line 12 "Traffic Related Expense" shall include traffic solicitor salaries, traffic commissions, passenger food expense, traffic liability insurance, advertising and other promotion and publicity expenses, and the fringe benefit expenses related to all salaries in this classification.

(3) Line 13 "Departure Related (Station) Expense" shall include aircraft and traffic handling salaries, landing fees, clearance, customs and duties, related fringe benefit expenses and maintenance and depreciation on ground property and equipment.

(4) Line 14 "Capacity Related Expense" shall include salaries and fringe benefits for general management personnel, recordkeeping and statistical personnel, lawyers and law clerks, and purchasing personnel; legal fees and expenses; stationery; printing; uncollectible accounts; insurance purchased-general; memberships; corporate and fiscal expenses; and all other expenses which cannot be identified or allocated to some other specifically identified indirect cost category.

(f) Line 15 "Total Indirect Expense" shall equal the sum of lines 11, 12, 13 and 14.

(g) Line 16 "Total Operating Expense" shall equal the sum of lines 9 and 15.

(h) Line 17 "Total Gallons of Fuel Issued" shall include the gallons of fuel used in flight operations related to fuel cost reported in total and by aircraft type on Line 4.

[ER–1399, 50 FR 20, Jan. 2, 1985, as amended by Doc. No. 47939, 57 FR 40104, Sept. 2, 1992; 60 FR 66726, Dec. 26, 1995; 67 FR 49234, July 30, 2002]

§ 298.65 Requests for extensions of time within which to file reports or for waivers from reporting requirements.

(a) If circumstances prevent the filing of BTS Form 298–C on or before the due date, a written request for an extension may be submitted. Except in cases of emergency, the request must be delivered to the BTS's Office of Airline Information in writing at least three days in advance of the due date. The request must state good and sufficient reason to justify the granting of the extension and the date when the reports can be filed. If the request is denied, the air carrier remains subject to the filing requirements to the same extent as if no request for extension of time had been made.

(b) The Office of Airline Information may waive any reporting requirements contained in §§ 298.61, 298.62, 298.63 and 298.64 of this part, upon its own initiative or upon written request from any air carrier if the waiver is in the public interest and the request demonstrates that:

(1) Unusual circumstances warrant such a departure;

(2) A specifically defined alternative procedure or technique will result in a substantially equivalent or more accurate portrayal; and

(3) The application of the alternative procedure will maintain or improve uniformity in reporting between air carriers.

[ER–1399, 50 FR 21, Jan. 2, 1985, as amended by Doc. No. 47939, 57 FR 40104, Sept. 2, 1992; 60 FR 66726, Dec. 26, 1995]

§ 298.66 Reporting exemption for State collection of data.

(a) The Office of Airline Information may exempt a commuter air carrier from the reporting requirements of § 298.61 of this part if a State government collects the information specified in that section and provides it to the Department by the dates specified. The data provided to the Department in this manner must be at least as reliable as if they were collected by the Department directly.

(b) The Office of Airline Information will provide assistance to any State agency interested in participating in this exemption program.

[ER-1399, 50 FR 21, Jan. 2, 1985, as amended by Doc. No. 47939, 57 FR 40104, Sept. 2, 1992; 60 FR 66726, Dec. 26, 1995]

Subpart G—Public Disclosure of Data

§ 298.70 Public disclosure of data.

(a) Detailed domestic on-flight market data and nonstop segment data except military data shall be made publicly available after processing. Domestic data are defined as data from air transportation operations from a place in any State of the United States, the District of Columbia, the Commonwealth of Puerto Rico and the Virgin Islands, or a U.S. territory or possession to a place in any State of the United States, the District of Columbia, the Commonwealth of Puerto Rico and the Virgin Islands, or a U.S. territory or possession. Domestic military operations are reported under service codes N or R.

(b) Detailed international on-flight market and nonstop segment data in Schedule T-100 and Schedule T-100(f) reports, except military data, shall be publicly available immediately following the Department's determination that the database is complete, but no earlier than six months after the date of the data. Military operations are reported under service codes N or R. Data for on-flight markets and nonstop segments involving no U.S. points shall not be made publicly available for three years. Industry and carrier summary data may be made public before the end of six months or the end of three years, as applicable, provided there are three or more carriers in the summary data disclosed. The Department may, at any time, publish international summary statistics without carrier detail.

(c) Schedule F-1 "Report of Financial Data" shall be withheld from public release for a period of 3 years after the close of the calendar quarter to which the report relates.

(d) The Department may release nonstop segment and on-flight market detail data by carrier or individual Schedule F-1 "Report of Financial Data" before the end of the confidentiality period as follows:

(1) To foreign governments as provided in reciprocal arrangements between the foreign country and the U.S. Government for exchange of on-flight market and/or nonstop segment data submitted by air carriers of that foreign country and U.S. carriers serving that foreign country.

(2) To parties to any proceeding before the Department under Title IV of the Federal Aviation Act of 1958, as amended, as required by an Administrative Law Judge or other decisionmaker of the Department. Parties may designate agents or consultants to receive the data in their behalf, provided the agents or consultants agree to abide by the disclosure restrictions. Any data to which access is granted pursuant to this provision may be introduced into evidence, subject to the normal rules of admissibility.

(3) To agencies or other components of the U.S. Government for their internal use only.

[Doc. No. OST-98-4043, 67 FR 49234, July 30, 2002]

Subpart H—Violations

§ 298.80 Enforcement.

In case of any violation of the provisions of the Statute, or this part, or any other rule, regulation, or order issued under the Statute, the violator may be subject to a proceeding pursuant to section 46101 of the Statute before the Department, or sections 46106 through 46108 of the Statute before a U.S. District Court, as the case may be, to compel compliance therewith; or to civil penalties pursuant to the provisions of section 46301 of the Statute; or, in the case of a willful violation, to criminal penalties pursuant to the provisions of section 46316 of the Statute;

or other lawful sanctions including revocation of operating authority.

[ER–929, 40 FR 42855, Sept. 17, 1975, as amended at 60 FR 43528, Aug. 22, 1995]

EFFECTIVE DATE NOTE: At 83 FR 46877, Sept. 17, 2018, § 298.80 was revised, effective Feb. 14, 2019. For the convenience of the user, the revised text is set forth as follows:

§ 298.80 Disclosures.

(a) Before entering a contract for a specific flight or series of flights with charterers, air taxi operators and commuter air carriers must disclose to the charterer the information in paragraphs (a)(1) and (2) of this section. Before entering a contract for a specific flight or series of flights with charterers, air taxi operators and commuter air carriers must, upon request of the charterer, disclose to the charterer the information in paragraphs (a)(3), (4), and (5) of this section. The disclosures may be accomplished through electronic transmissions.

(1) That the flight will be performed by another direct air carrier or direct foreign air carrier if that is the case. The corporate name of the direct air carrier or direct foreign air carrier in operational control of the aircraft on which the air transportation is to be performed and any other names in which that direct carrier holds itself out to the public.

(2) If the flight is to be performed by another direct air carrier or direct foreign air carrier, the capacity in which the air taxi operator or commuter air carrier is acting in contracting for the air transportation, *i.e.*, as a principal, as an agent of the charterer, or as an agent of the direct air carrier that will be in operational control of the flight.

(3) If the flight is to be performed by another direct air carrier or foreign direct air carrier and the air taxi operator or commuter air carrier is acting as the agent of the charterer, the air taxi operator or commuter air carrier must disclose the existence of any corporate or business relationship, including a preexisting contract, between the air taxi operator or commuter air carrier and the direct carrier that will be in operational control of the flight that may have a bearing on the air taxi operator's or commuter air carrier's selection of the direct carrier that will be in operational control of the flight.

(4) The total cost of the air transportation paid by the charterer to or through the air taxi operator or commuter air carrier, including any carrier-imposed fees or government-imposed taxes and fees. Specific individual fees, taxes, or costs may, but are not required to be itemized.

(5) The existence of any fees and their amounts collected by third parties, if known (or a good faith estimate if not known), including fuel, landing fees, and aircraft parking or hangar fees for which the charterer will be responsible for paying directly.

(b) If any of the information in paragraph (a) of this section that is required to be disclosed to the charterer or requested by the charterer to be disclosed is not known at the time the contract is entered into or changes thereafter, air taxi operators and commuter air carriers must provide the information to the charterer within a reasonable time after such information becomes available to the air taxi operator or commuter air carrier, such that the charterer has enough time to make an informed decision as to whether to accept the additional information or accept the change.

(c) If the information in paragraph (a) of this section that is required to be disclosed to the charterer or requested by the charterer to be disclosed is not provided to the charterer within a reasonable time after such information becomes available to the air taxi operator or commuter air carrier, air taxi operators and commuter air carriers must provide the charterer with the opportunity to cancel the contract for air transportation, including any services in connection with such contract, and receive a full refund of any monies paid for the charter air transportation and services.

(d) Except in exigent circumstances particular to a passenger, air taxi operators and commuter air carriers must disclose prior to the start of the air transportation the information in paragraph (a) of this section that is required or requested to be disclosed.

(e) If the information in paragraph (a) of this section that is required to be disclosed to the charterer or requested by the charterer to be disclosed changes after the air transportation covered by the contract has begun, air taxi operators and commuter air carriers must provide information regarding any such changes to the charterer within a reasonable time after such information becomes available to the air taxi operator or commuter air carrier.

(f) If the changes in information described in paragraph (e) of this section are not provided to the charterer within a reasonable time after becoming available to the air taxi operator or commuter air carrier, air taxi operators and commuter air carriers must provide the charterer with the opportunity to cancel the remaining portion of the contract for charter air transportation, including any services paid for in connection with such contract, and receive a full refund of any monies paid for the charter air transportation and services not yet provided.

Subpart I—Violations

SOURCE: 83 FR 46877, Sept. 17, 2018, unless otherwise noted.

EFFECTIVE DATE NOTE: At 83 FR 46877, Sept. 17, 2018, Subpart I was added, effective Feb. 14, 2019.

§ 298.90 Prohibited unfair or deceptive practices or unfair methods of competition.

(a) Violations of this Part shall be considered to constitute unfair or deceptive practices or unfair methods of competition in violation of 49 U.S.C. 41712.

(b) In addition to paragraph (a) of this section, the following enumerated practices, among others, by an air taxi operator or commuter air carrier are unfair or deceptive practices or unfair methods of competition in violation of 49 U.S.C. 41712:

(1) Misrepresentations that may induce members of the public to reasonably believe that the air taxi operator or commuter air carrier will be, or is, in operational control of a flight when that is not the case.

(2) Misrepresentations as to the quality or kind of service or type of aircraft.

(3) Misrepresentations as to the time of departure or arrival, points served, route to be flown, stops to be made, or total trip-time from point of departure to destination.

(4) Misrepresentations as to the qualifications of pilots or safety record or certification of pilots, aircraft, or air carriers.

(5) Misrepresentations that passengers are directly insured when they are not so insured. For example, where the only insurance in force is that protecting the air taxi operator or commuter air carrier in the event of liability.

(6) Misrepresentations as to fares or charges for air transportation or services in connection therewith.

(7) Misrepresentations as to membership in or involvement with an organization that audits direct air carriers or that the direct air carrier to be used for a flight meets a standard set by an auditing organization.

(8) Representing that a contract for a specified direct air carrier, aircraft, flight, or time has been arranged without a binding commitment with a direct air carrier for the furnishing of such transportation as represented.

(9) Selling or contracting for air transportation while knowing or having reason to know or believe that such air transportation cannot be legally performed by the direct air carrier or foreign direct air carrier that is to perform the air transportation.

(10) Misrepresentations as to the requirements that must be met by charterers in order to qualify for charter flights.

(11) Using or displaying or permitting or suffering to be used or displayed the name, tradename, slogan or any abbreviation thereof, of an air charter broker in advertisements, on or in places of business, or on or in aircraft or any other place in connection with the name of the air taxi or commuter air carrier in such manner that it may mislead or confuse potential consumers with respect to the status of the air charter broker.

§ 298.92 Enforcement.

In case of any violation of the provisions of the Statute, or this part, or any other rule, regulation, or order issued under the Statute, the violator may be subject to a proceeding pursuant to section 46101 of the Statute before the Department, or sections 46106 through 46108 of the Statute before a U.S. District Court, as the case may be, to compel compliance therewith; or to civil penalties pursuant to the provisions of section 46301 of the Statute; or, in the case of a willful violation, to criminal penalties pursuant to the provisions of section 46316 of the Statute; or other lawful sanctions including revocation of operating authority.

SUBCHAPTER B—PROCEDURAL REGULATIONS

PART 300—RULES OF CONDUCT IN DOT PROCEEDINGS UNDER THIS CHAPTER

Sec.

AUTHORITY: 49 U.S.C. subtitle I and chapters 401, 411, 413, 415, 417, 419, 421, 449, 461, 463, and 465.

SOURCE: Docket No. 82, 50 FR 2380, Jan. 16, 1985, unless otherwise noted.

§ 300.0 Applicability.

The rules of conduct set forth in this part except as otherwise provided in this or any other DOT regulation shall govern the conduct of the parties and their representatives, and the relationships between the Office of the Secretary of Transportation, the Office of the Assistant Secretary for Aviation and International Affairs, and the Office of the General Counsel, including regular personnel, and officials, special Government employees, consultants, or experts under contract to the Department of Transportation (DOT) and administrative law judges (hereinafter referred to as "DOT employee(s)") and all other persons in all DOT matters involving aviation economic and enforcement proceedings.

[Doc. No. 82, 50 FR 2380, Jan. 16, 1985, as amended by Amdt. 1–261, 59 FR 10061, Mar. 3, 1994; 60 FR 43528, Aug. 22, 1995]

§ 300.0a Applicability of 49 CFR part 99.

(a) Except as provided in paragraph (b) of this section, each DOT employee involved in matters covered by this chapter shall comply with the rules on "Employee Responsibilities and Conduct" in 49 CFR part 99.

(b) The rules in this part shall be construed as being consistent with those in 49 CFR part 99. If a rule in this part is more restrictive than a rule in 49 CFR part 99, the more restrictive rule shall apply.

§ 300.1 Judicial standards of practice.

Certain of DOT's functions involving aviation economic and enforcement proceedings are similar to those of a court, and parties to cases before DOT and those who represent such parties are expected—in fact and in appearance—to conduct themselves with honor and dignity as they would before a court. By the same token, any DOT employee or administrative law judge carrying out DOT's quasi-judicial functions and any DOT employee making recommendations or advising them are expected to conduct themselves with the same fidelity to appropriate standards of propriety that characterize a court and its staff. The standing and effectiveness of DOT in carrying out its quasi-judicial functions are in direct relation to the observance by DOT,

DOT employees, and the parties and attorneys appearing before DOT of the highest standards of judicial and professional ethics. The rules of conduct set forth in this part are to be interpreted in light of those standards.

[Doc. No. 82, 50 FR 2380, Jan. 16, 1985, as amended at 60 FR 43528, Aug. 22, 1995]

§ 300.2 Prohibited communications.

(a) *Basic requirement.* Except as provided in paragraphs (c), (d) and (e) there shall be no substantive communication in either direction between any concerned DOT employee and any interested person outside DOT, concerning a public proceeding, until after final disposition of the proceeding, other than as provided by Federal statute or published DOT rule or order.

(b) *Definitions.* For purposes of this part:

(1) A "substantive communication" is any written or oral communication relevant to the merits of the proceeding.

(2) The "DOT decisionmaker" is defined in 14 CFR 302.2 and 302.18.

(3) A "concerned DOT employee" is a DOT employee who is or may reasonably be expected to be directly involved in a decision which is subject to a public proceeding.

(4) A "public proceeding" is one of the following:

(i) A hearing proceeding (*i.e.*, proceeding conducted on-the record after notice and opportunity for an oral evidentiary hearing as provided in §§ 302.17–302.38)

(ii) A rulemaking proceeding involving a hearing as described in paragraph (b)(4)(i) of this section or an exemption proceeding covered by this chapter. (Other rulemaking proceedings are covered by the ex parte communication policies of DOT Order 2100.2.)

(iii) A tariff filing after DOT has ordered an investigation or a complaint has been filed or docketed.

(iv) A proceeding initiated by DOT show-cause order, after the filing in the docket of an identifiable written opposition to the order's tentative findings.

(v) Any other proceeding initiated by a docket filing, other than a petition for generally applicable rulemaking, after the filing in the docket of an identifiable written opposition to the initiating document.

(c) *General exceptions.* Paragraph (a) of this section shall not apply to the following:

(1) Informal communications between legal counsel, including discussions about stipulations and other communications considered proper in Federal court proceedings.

(2) Information given to a DOT employee who is participating in a hearing case on behalf of an office that is a party, to another DOT employee who is reviewing that work, or to his or her supervisors within that office.

(3) Communications made in the course of an investigation to determine whether formal enforcement action should be begun.

(4) Settlement discussions and mediation efforts.

(5) Information given at the request of a DOT employee acting upon a specific direction of DOT, in a case other than a hearing proceeding as described in paragraphs (b)(4) (i) and (ii) (a "nonhearing case"), where DOT has decided that emergency conditions exist and this rule would otherwise prevent the obtaining of needed information in a timely manner.

(6) Information given at the request of a DOT employee in a tariff matter after a complaint is filed but before an investigation is ordered.

(7) Nonhearing cases that are to be decided within 30 days after the filing of the initiating document.

(8) Nonhearing cases arising under 49 U.S.C. 41731–42.

(9) In nonhearing cases, communications with other Federal agencies not exempted by paragraph (e) of this section, provided the agencies have not participated as parties in the proceeding by making filings on-the-record.

(10) Information given at the request of a DOT career employee in the course of investigating or clarifying information filed, or pursuant to a waiver granted to an applicant or other interested person, in docketed proceedings involving determinations of fitness and/or U.S. citizenship only, for that portion of the proceeding that precedes the issuance of a show-cause order or

an order instituting a formal proceeding. Motions for such waivers and any answers shall be filed in the applicable docket in accordance with § 302.11 of the Department's Procedural Regulations (14 CFR 302.11) and served upon all parties to the proceeding.

(d) *Status and expedition requests.* Paragraph (a) of this section shall not apply to oral or written communications asking about the status, or requesting expeditious treatment, of a public proceeding. However, any request for expeditious treatment should be made in accordance with the Rules of Practice, particularly Rule 11, § 302.11 of this chapter.

(e) *National defense and foreign policy.* In nonhearing cases, paragraph (a) of this section shall not apply to communications concerning national defense or foreign policy matters, including international aviation matters. In hearing cases, any communications on those subjects that would be barred by paragraph (a) of this section are permitted if the communicator's position with respect thereto cannot otherwise be fairly presented, but such communications shall not be included as part of the record on which decisions must be made.

(f) *Communications not considered.* A communication in violation of this section shall not be considered part of a record, or included as available material, for decision in any proceeding.

[Doc. No. 82, 50 FR 2380, Jan. 16, 1985, as amended by Amdt. 300–7, 52 FR 18904, May 20, 1987; 60 FR 10312, Feb. 24, 1995; 60 FR 43528, Aug. 22, 1995; 60 FR 43528, Aug. 22, 1995; 65 FR 6456, Feb. 9, 2000]

§ 300.3 Reporting of communications.

(a) *General.* The following types of substantive communication shall be reported as specified in paragraph (b) of this section:

(1) Any communication in violation of § 300.2(a) of this chapter.

(2) Information given upon determination of an emergency under § 300.2(c)(5) of this chapter.

(3) Information given at the request of a DOT employee in a tariff matter under § 300.2(c)(6) of this chapter.

(4) Communications in nonhearing cases to be decided within 30 days under § 300.2(c)(7) of this chapter.

(5) Communications in nonhearing cases arising under 49 U.S.C. 41731–42, made under § 300.2(c)(8).

(b) *Public filing.* (1) A written communication shall be placed onto the electronic docket management system (DMS) in the file of the docket number corresponding to the proceeding, which shall be available for inspection and copying during business hours in Office of Docket Operations and Media Management.

(2) An oral communication shall be summarized by the DOT employee receiving it. One copy shall be put into a public file as described in paragraph (b)(1) of this section, and another copy shall be mailed to the communicator.

(3) Electronic copies of written communications and oral summaries shall be posted to the DOT's electronic docket. Such docketed materials may be searched, viewed, and downloaded through the Internet at *http://dms.dot.gov.*

(4) Copies of all filings under this part dealing with discontinuances or reductions of air transportation shall be mailed to the directly affected local communities, State agencies, and airport managers.

(c) *Status and expedition requests.* A DOT decisionmaker who receives a communication asking about the status or requesting expeditious treatment of a public proceeding, other than a communication concerning national defense or foreign policy (including international aviation), shall either:

(1) Refer the communicator to Office of Docket Operations and Media Management.

(2) If the DOT decisionmaker responds by advising on the status, put a memorandum describing the exchange in the public file as described in paragraph (b)(1) of this section.

[Doc. No. 82, 50 FR 2380, Jan. 16, 1985, as amended at 60 FR 43528, Aug. 22, 1995; Doc. No. DOT–OST–2002–12200, 67 FR 30325, May 6, 2002]

§ 300.4 Separation of functions in hearing cases.

(a) This section applies after the initiation of a hearing or enforcement case by the Department.

(b) A DOT employee who is participating in a hearing case on behalf of an office that is a party, another DOT employee who is in fact reviewing the position taken, or who has participated in developing the position taken in that case, or, in cases involving accusatory or disciplinary issues (including all enforcement cases) such employees' supervisors within that office, shall have no substantive communication with any DOT decisionmaker, administrative law judge in the case, or other DOT employee advising them, with respect to that or any factually related hearing case, except in accordance with a published DOT rule or order. In addition, each bureau or office supervisor of a DOT employee who is participating in a hearing case on behalf of that office when it is a party shall have no substantive communication with any administrative law judge in the case, or DOT employee advising the judge, in that or any factually related hearing case, except in accordance with a published DOT rule or order. For each hearing case, bureau or office heads shall maintain a publicly available record of those employees who are participating or are in fact reviewing the position taken, or who have participated in developing the position taken in that case.

(c) In hearing cases involving fares or rates, or applications for a certificate or permit under 49 U.S.C. 41102 and 41302, or applications by a holder for a change in a certificate or permit, a supervisor who would not be permitted to advise the DOT decisionmaker under paragraph (a) may advise the DOT decisionmaker in the following manner: The supervisor's advice must either be made orally in an open DOT meeting or by a memorandum placed in the docket or other public file of such matter. Oral advice must be summarized in writing by the supervisor and placed in the docket or file of the matter. A copy of such written memorandum or summary of oral advice must be served on each party to the proceeding within 3 business days after such advice is given to the concerned DOT decisionmaker. Each of the parties may comment in writing on such advice within 5 business days after service or the summary. In no event, however, may a supervisor advise the DOT decisionmaker if he or she acted as the office's counsel or witness in the matter.

(d) In enforcement cases, the Office of the Assistant General Counsel for Aviation Enforcement and Proceedings, under the supervision of the Deputy General Counsel, will conduct all enforcement proceedings and related investigative functions, while the General Counsel will advise the DOT decisionmaker in the course of the decisional process. The Office of the Assistant General Counsel for Aviation Enforcement and Proceedings will report to the Deputy General Counsel. To ensure the independence of these functions, this Office and the Deputy General Counsel, for the purpose of this section, shall be considered an "office" as that term is used in paragraph (a), separate from the General Counsel and the rest of the Office of the General Counsel.

[Doc. No. 82, 50 FR 2380, Jan. 16, 1985, as amended at 60 FR 43528, Aug. 22, 1995]

§ 300.5 Prohibited conduct.

No person shall: (a) Attempt to influence the judgment of a concerned DOT employee by any unlawful means such as deception or the payment of money or other consideration; or

(b) Disrupt or interfere with the fair and orderly disposition of a DOT proceeding.

§ 300.6 Practitioners' standards of conduct.

Every person representing a client in matters before DOT in all contacts with DOT employees, should:

(a) Strictly observe the standards of professional conduct;

(b) Refrain from statements or other actions designed to mislead DOT or to cause unwarranted delay;

(c) Avoid offensive or intemperate behavior;

(d) Advise all clients to avoid improprieties and to obey the law as the attorney believes it to be; and

(e) Terminate the professional relationship with any client who persists in improprieties in proceedings before DOT.

§ 300.7 Conciseness.

Every oral or written statement made in a DOT proceding shall be as concise as possible. Verbose or redundant presentations may be rejected.

§ 300.8 Gifts and hospitality and other conduct affecting DOT employees.

(a) No person, otherwise than as provided by law for the proper discharge of official duty, shall directly or indirectly give, offer, or promise anything of value to any DOT employee for or because of any official act performed or to be performed by such DOT employee (18 U.S.C. 201).

(b) Subject to 49 CFR part 99, it is improper for persons interested in the business of DOT to provide hospitality, gifts, entertainment, or favors to any DOT employee.

(c) Persons interested in the business of DOT should familiarize themselves with (49 CFR part 99), in order that they shall not encourage or cause any violation of the provisions of that part by any DOT employee.

§ 300.9 Permanent disqualification of employees from matters in which they personally participated before joining DOT or the Civil Aeronautics Board.

Any DOT employee shall permanently disqualify himself or herself from participation in every matter before the Department in which he or she previously personally and substantially participated for an interested person or entity, including other agencies of the United States Government, before joining the DOT or the Civil Aeronautics Board. Such disqualification shall be applicable also if a person is closely related to is a DOT employee as partner, associate, employer, or the like, personally and substantially participated in a matter before DOT prior to the employee's employment by the Department or the Civil Aeronautics Board and the circumstances were such that the DOT employee's subsequent participation in the matter as a DOT employee could fairly be said to create the appearance that his or her participation would be affected by his or her prior relationship. Notwithstanding the foregoing, the disqualification of any DOT employee, including any member of a DOT employee's personal staff or a special Government employee, whose prior personal and substantial participation in a DOT or Civil Aeronautics Board proceeding or whose relationship to one who so participated occurred on behalf of another agency of the United States Government shall only be applicable with respect to issues on which the prior governmental employer took a position in the proceeding unless participation could fairly be said to create the appearance that his or her participation would be affected by his or her prior relationship.

§ 300.10 Temporary disqualification of employees from matters in which they had official responsibility before joining DOT.

Any DOT employee shall temporarily disqualify himself or herself from participation in any matter before DOT if he or she represented, was associated with or was employed by an interested person or entity including other agencies of the United States Government before joining DOT, and, although he or she did not personally and substantially participate in the matter, the matter was within his or her "official responsibility," as that term is defined in § 300.14 of this chapter except that the action referred to therein shall be private action as well as "Government" action. Such disqualification shall be applicable also if a person closely related to the DOT employee as partner, associate, employer, or the like, who, while not personally and substantially participating in the matter, had it within his or her "official responsibility" as that term is defined in § 300.14 of this chapter, and modified above, and the circumstances are such that the DOT employee's subsequent participation in the matter as a DOT employee could fairly be said to create the appearance that his or her participation would be affected by his or her prior relationship. Notwithstanding the foregoing, the disqualification of any DOT employee whose prior "official responsibility" or relationship to one with such responsibility occurred on behalf of another agency of the United States Government shall only be applicable with respect to issues on which the prior governmental employer took a position in the proceeding. The temporary disqualification shall run for a period of one year from the date of the termination of the representation, association, or employment with the interested person or entity.

[Doc. No. 82, 50 FR 2380, Jan. 16, 1985, as amended at 60 FR 43528, Aug. 22, 1995]

§300.10a Permanent and temporary disqualification of DOT employees.

The terms of §§300.9 and 300.10 shall not be construed to apply to DOT employees who previously personally and substantially participated in matters before the Board, which have become the subject of DOT proceedings.

[Doc. No. 82, 50 FR 2380, Jan. 16, 1985, as amended at 60 FR 43528, Aug. 22, 1995]

§300.11 Disqualification of Government officers and employees.

No officer or employee of the Federal Government, other than a "special Government employee" as defined in 18 U.S.C. 202, shall represent anyone, otherwise than in the proper discharge of his or her official duties, in any DOT proceeding or matter in which the United States is a party or has a direct and substantial interest.

(18 U.S.C. 205)

§300.12 Practice of special Government employees permitted.

A special Government employee, who qualifies as such under the provisions of 18 U.S.C. 202(a), may participate in DOT proceedings only to the extent and in the manner specified in 18 U.S.C. 205.

§300.13 Permanent disqualification of former Civil Aeronautics Board members and employees and DOT employees from matters in which they personally participated.

No former Board member or employee or DOT employee shall act as agent or attorney before DOT for anyone other than the United States in connection with any proceeding, application, request for a ruling or other determination, contract, claim, controversy, charge, accusation, or other particular matter, involving a specific party or parties, in which the United States is a party or has a direct and substantial interest and in which he or she participated personally and substantially through decision, approval, disapproval, recommendation, rendering of advice, investigation, or otherwise as a Board member or employee or DOT employee.

(18 U.S.C. 207(a))

§300.14 Temporary disqualification of former DOT employees from matters formerly under their official responsibility.

Within one year after termination of employment with DOT, no former DOT employee shall appear personally before DOT on behalf of any person other than the United States in any DOT proceeding or matter in which the United States is a party or has a direct and substantial interest and which was under his or her official responsibility at any time within one year preceding termination of such responsibility. The term "official responsibility" means the direct administrative or operating authority, whether intermediate or final, and either exercisable alone or with others, and either personally or through subordinates, to approve, disapprove, or otherwise direct Government action.

(18 U.S.C. 202(b), 207(b))

[Doc. No. 82, 50 FR 2380, Jan. 16, 1985, as amended at 60 FR 43528, Aug. 22, 1995]

§300.15 Opinions or rulings by the General Counsel.

(a) The General Counsel is authorized to render opinions or rulings to the public on the application of the provisions of this part. When written request is made for such opinions and rulings, they shall be transmitted to DOT and shall be available to the public in the Documentary Services Division after any appeal to or review by the Secretary has been completed or after the time for review has expired. Identifying details shall normally be stricken from copies available to the public unless the public interest requires disclosure of such details.

(b) If any person is disqualified from a particular proceeding under the provisions of §§300.9, 300.10, 300.13, 300.14, and 300.17 of this chapter by a ruling of the General Counsel, or by such person's own action, such disqualification shall be memorialized in a writing filed in the appropriate file of the matter by the General Counsel or such person.

§ 300.16 Waivers.

(a) A former Board member, Board employee or DOT employee with outstanding scientific or technological qualifications who is disqualified from acting in a representative capacity under the provisions of § 300.13 or § 300.14 of this chapter may nevertheless participate in a proceeding in a scientific or technological field pursuant to the terms of a certificate issued in compliance with the proviso following 18 U.S.C. 207 (a) and (b).

(b) An employee who believes his or her prior employment relationships will not affect the integrity of his or her services may request that the prohibition of § 300.9 or § 300.10 of this chapter be waived by the appropriate Ethics Counselor under 49 CFR 99.735–71.

§ 300.17 Disqualification of partners of DOT employees.

No partner of a DOT employee shall act as agent or attorney for anyone other than the United States in any DOT proceeding or matter in which such employee participates or has participated personally and substantially through decision, approval, disapproval, recommendation, rendering advice, investigation, or otherwise, or which is the subject of his or her official responsibility.

§ 300.18 Motions to disqualify DOT employee in review of hearing matters.

In cases to be determined on an evidentiary record, a party desiring that a concerned DOT employee disqualify himself or herself from participating in a DOT decision shall file a motion supported by an affidavit setting forth the grounds for such disqualification in the form and within the periods prescribed in § 302.11 of this chapter. Where review of the administrative law judge's decision can be obtained only upon the filing of a petition for discretionary review, such motions must be filed on or before the date answers are due pursuant to § 302.32. In cases where exceptions are filed to recommended, initial, or tentative decisions or where the DOT decisionmaker orders review of an initial or recommended decision on his or her own initiative, such motions must be filed on or before the date briefs are due pursuant to § 302.35 or § 302.218, as applicable. Failure to file a timely motion will be deemed a waiver of disqualification. Applications for leave to file an untimely motion seeking disqualification of a concerned DOT employee must be accompanied by an affidavit setting forth in detail why the facts relied upon as grounds for disqualification were not known and could not have been discovered with reasonable diligence within the prescribed time.

[Doc. No. OST–97–2090, 65 FR 6456, Feb. 9, 2000]

§ 300.19 Use of confidential information.

No former CAB member or employee or DOT employee, or any person associated with him or her, shall ever use or undertake to use in any DOT proceeding or matter any confidential facts or information which came into the possession of such Member or employee or to his or her attention by reason of his or her employment with the CAB or DOT without first applying for and obtaining the consent of the appropriate ethics counselor for the use of such facts or information.

§ 300.20 Violations.

(a) DOT may disqualify, and deny temporarily or permanently the privilege of appearing or practicing before it in any way to, any person who is found by DOT after written notice of charges and hearing to have engaged in unethical or improper professional conduct. Any violation of this part shall be deemed to be such conduct.

(b) When appropriate in the public interest, DOT may deny any application or other request of a party in a proceeding subject to this part where DOT finds after hearing that such party has, in connection with any DOT proceeding, violated any of the provisions of this part or any of the provisions of Chapter 11 of Title 18 of the United States Code. DOT may also condition its further consideration of such party's application or other request or the effectiveness of any order granting such application or other request upon such party's first taking such action as DOT may deem necessary or appropriate to remedy the violation of this part or Chapter 11 of Title 18 of the United States Code to prevent or deter any repetition of such violation. DOT may in addition issue a cease and desist order against any repetition of such or similar misconduct.

(c) The actions authorized by this section may take place within the framework of the matter during or concerning which the violations occur or in a separate matter, as the DOT decisionmaker or the presiding administrative law judge may direct. A complaint alleging that a violation has occurred in the course of a matter shall be filed in the docket or appropriate public file of such matter unless such complaint is made after DOT's decision of the matter has become final, in which event such complaint may be filed pursuant to part 302, subpart D of the rules of practice. A violation in the course of a matter which may be attributable to or affect the fitness of a party will ordinarily either be disposed of within the framework of such matter or be considered within the context of any subsequent matter involving the interests of such party. Other violations will ordinarily be disposed of in a separate proceeding.

(d) In the case of any violation of the provisions of this part, the violator may be subject to civil penalties under the provisions of 49 U.S.C. 46301. The violator may also be subject to a proceeding brought under 49 U.S.C. 46101 before the Department, or sections 46106 through 46108 of the Statute before a U.S. District Court, as the case may be, to compel compliance with civil penalties which have been imposed.

[Doc. No. 82, 50 FR 2380, Jan. 16, 1985, as amended at 60 FR 43528, Aug. 22, 1995; 65 FR 6456, Feb. 9, 2000]

PART 302—RULES OF PRACTICE IN PROCEEDINGS

DISPOSITION OF APPLICATIONS

302.207 Cases to be decided on written submissions.
302.208 Petitions for oral presentation or judge's decision.
302.209 Procedures for deferral of applications.
302.210 Disposition of applications; orders establishing further procedures.
302.211 Procedures in certificate cases involving initial or continuing fitness.
302.212 Procedures in certificate cases involving international routes.
302.213 Procedures in foreign air carrier permit cases.
302.214 Oral evidentiary hearing.
302.215 Briefs to the administrative law judge.
302.216 Administrative law judge's initial or recommended decision.
302.217 Exceptions to administrative law judge's initial or recommended decision.
302.218 Briefs to the DOT decisionmaker.
302.219 Oral argument before the DOT decisionmaker.
302.220 Final decision of the Department.

Subpart C—Rules Applicable to Exemption and Certain Other Proceedings

302.301 Applicability.
302.302 Filing of applications.
302.303 Contents of applications.
302.304 Service of documents.
302.305 Posting of applications.
302.306 Dismissal or rejection of incomplete applications.
302.307 Answers to applications.
302.308 Replies to answers.
302.309 Requests for hearing.
302.310 Exemptions on the Department's initiative.
302.311 Emergency exemptions.

Subpart D—Rules Applicable to Enforcement Proceedings

302.401 Applicability.
302.402 Definitions.
302.403 Informal complaints.
302.404 Formal complaints.
302.405 Responsive documents.
302.406 Procedure for responding to formal complaints.
302.407 Commencement of enforcement proceeding.
302.408 Answers and replies.
302.409 Default.
302.410 Consolidation of proceedings.
302.411 Motions to dismiss and for summary judgment.
302.412 Admissions as to facts and documents.
302.413 Evidence of previous violations.
302.414 Prehearing conference.
302.415 Hearing.
302.416 Appearances by persons not parties.
302.417 Settlement of proceedings.
302.418 Motions for immediate suspension of operating authority pendente lite.
302.419 Modification or dissolution of enforcement actions.
302.420 Saving clause.

Subpart E—Rules Applicable to Proceedings With Respect to Rates, Fares and Charges for Foreign Air Transportation

302.501 Applicability.
302.502 Institution of proceedings.
302.503 Contents and service of petition or complaint.
302.504 Dismissal of petition or complaint.
302.505 Order of investigation.
302.506 Complaints requesting suspension of tariffs; answers to such complaints.
302.507 Computing time for filing complaints.

Subpart F—Rules Applicable to Proceedings Concerning Airport Fees

302.601 Applicability.
302.602 Complaint by a carrier; request for determination by an airport owner or operator.
302.603 Contents of complaint or request for determination.
302.604 Answers to a complaint or request for determination.
302.605 Replies.
302.606 Review of complaints or requests for determination.
302.607 Decision by administrative law judge.
302.608 Petitions for discretionary review.
302.609 Completion of proceedings.
302.610 Final order.

Subpart G—Rules Applicable to Mail Rate Proceedings and Mail Contracts

302.701 Applicability.

FINAL MAIL RATE PROCEEDINGS

302.702 Institution of proceedings.
302.703 Order to show cause or instituting a hearing.
302.704 Objections and answers to order to show cause.
302.705 Further procedures.
302.706 Hearing.

PROVISION FOR TEMPORARY RATE

302.707 Procedure for fixing temporary mail rates.

INFORMAL MAIL RATE CONFERENCE PROCEDURE

302.708 Invocation of procedure.
302.709 Scope of conferences.
302.710 Participants in conferences.

AUTHORITY: 39 U.S.C. 5402; 42 U.S.C., 4321, 49 U.S.C. Subtitle I and Chapters 401, 411, 413, 415, 417, 419, 461, 463, 471.

SOURCE: Docket No. OST-97-2090, 65 FR 6457, Feb. 9, 2000, unless otherwise noted.

§ 302.1 Applicability and description of part.

(a) *Applicability.* This part governs the conduct of all aviation economic proceedings before the Department whether instituted by order of the Department or by the filing with the Department of an application, complaint, petition, motion, or other authorized or required document. This part also contains delegations to administrative law judges and to the DOT decisionmaker of the Department's function to render the agency decision in certain cases and the procedures for review of those decisions. This part applies unless otherwise specified by order of the Department.

(b) *Description.* Subpart A of this part sets forth general rules applicable to all types of proceedings. Each of the other subparts of this part sets forth special rules applicable to the type of proceedings described in the title of the subpart. Therefore, for information as to applicable rules, reference should be made to subpart A and to the rules in the subpart relating to the particular type of proceeding, if any. In addition, reference should be made to Subtitle VII of Title 49 of the United States Code (Transportation) ("the Statute"), and to the substantive rules, regulations and orders of the Department relating to the proceeding. Wherever there is any conflict between one of the general rules in subpart A and a special rule in another subpart applicable to a particular type of proceeding, the special rule will govern.

(c) *Reference to part and method of citing rules.* This part may be referred to as the "Rules of Practice". Each section, and any paragraph or subparagraph thereof, may be referred to as a "Rule". The number of each rule need include only the numbers and letters at the right of the decimal point. For example, "302.7 *Service of documents*", may be referred to as "Rule 7".

§ 302.2 Definitions.

Administrative law judge as used in this part means an administrative law judge appointed pursuant to 5 U.S.C. 3105.

DOT Decisionmaker as used in this part is the official authorized to issue final decisions of the Department as set forth in § 302.18. This includes the Assistant Secretary for Aviation and International Affairs, the senior career official in the Office of the Assistant Secretary for Aviation and International Affairs, the Deputy Secretary, and the Secretary.

Hearing case or *oral hearing case* means any proceeding that the Department has determined will be conducted on the record using oral evidentiary procedures subject to 5 U.S.C. 556 and 557.

Non-hearing case means any proceeding not involving oral evidentiary procedures.

Party as used in this part includes the person initiating a proceeding, such as an applicant, complainant, or petitioner; any person filing an answer to such filing; and any other persons as set forth in § 302.10.

Statute when used in this chapter means Subtitle VII of Title 49 of the United States Code (Transportation).

Subpart A—Rules of General Applicability

§ 302.3 Filing of documents.

(a) *Filing address, date of filing, hours.* (1) Documents required by any section of this part to be filed with the Department must be filed with Department of Transportation Dockets at the Department's offices in Washington, DC. Documents may be filed either on paper or by electronic means using the process set at the DOT Dockets Management System (DMS) internet website.

(2) Such documents will be deemed to be filed on the date on which they are actually received by the Department. Documents must be filed between the hours of 9:00 a.m. and 5:00 p.m., eastern standard or daylight savings time, whichever is in effect in the District of Columbia at the time, Monday to Friday, inclusive, except on legal holidays. Electronic filings may be made at any time under the process set by the Department. Electronic filings that are received after the specified Dockets Facility hours shall be deemed to be constructively received on the next Dockets Facility business day.

(b) *Formal specifications of documents.* (1) Documents filed under this part must be on white paper not larger than 8½ by 11 inches, including any tables, charts and other documents that may be included. Ink must be black to provide substantial contrast for scanning and photographic reproduction. Text must be double-spaced (except for footnotes and long quotations which may be single-spaced) using type not smaller than 12 point. The left margin must be at least 1½ inches; all other margins must be at least 1 inch. The title page and first page must bear a clear date and all subsequent pages must bear a page number and abbreviated heading. In order to facilitate automated processing in document sheet feeders, documents of more than one page should be held together with removable metal clips or similar retainers. Original documents may not be bound in any form or include tabs, except in cases assigned by order to an Administrative Law Judge for hearing, in which case the filing requirements will be set by order. Section 302.35 contains additional requirements as to the contents and style of briefs.

(2) Papers may be reproduced by any duplicating process, provided all copies are clear and legible. Appropriate notes or other indications must be used, so that the existence of any matters shown in color on the original will be accurately indicated on all copies.

(c) *Number of copies.* Unless otherwise specified, an executed original, along with the number of true copies set forth below for each type of proceeding, must be filed with Department of Transportation Dockets. The copies filed need not be signed, but the name of the person signing the original document, as distinguished from the firm or organization he or she represents, must also be typed or printed on all copies below the space provided for signature. Electronic filers need only submit one copy of the document, which must conform to the submission requirements given in the electronic filing instructions at the specified DOT DMS internet website and in this part, as applicable.

	Number of copies
Airport Fees	9
Agreements:	
International Air Transport Association (IATA)	6
Other (under 49 U.S.C. 41309)	9
Complaints:	
Enforcement	5
Mail Contracts	4
Rates, Fares and Charges in Foreign Air Transportation	6
Unfair Practices in Foreign Air Transportation	7
Employee Protection Program (14 CFR 314)	7
Exemptions:	
Computer Reservations Systems (14 CFR 255)	8
Slot Exemptions (under 49 U.S.C. 41714)	7
Tariffs (under 49 U.S.C. Chapter 415 or 14 CFR 221)	5
Other (under 49 U.S.C. 40109)	7
Foreign Air Carrier Permits/Exemptions	7
International Authority for U.S. Air Carriers (certificates, exemptions, allocation of limited frequencies, designations, or charters)	7
Mail Rate Proceedings	4
Name Change/Trade Name Registrations	4
Suspension of Service (14 CFR 323)	4
Tariff Justifications to exceed Standard International Fare Level	6
U.S. Air Carrier Certificates (involving Initial or Continuing Fitness)	6
Other matters	3

(d) *Prohibition and dismissal of certain documents.* (1) No document that is subject to the general requirements of this subpart concerning form, filing, subscription, service or similar matters will be accepted for filing by the Department, and will not be physically incorporated in the docket of the proceeding, unless:

(i) Such document and its filing by the person submitting it have been expressly authorized or required in the Statute, any other law, this part, other Department regulations, or any order, notice or other document issued by the DOT decisionmaker, the Chief Administrative Law Judge or an administrative law judge assigned to the proceeding, and

(ii) Such document complies with each of the requirements of this paragraph and 302.7, and for those electronically filed, the requirements specified at the DOT DMS internet website, and is submitted as a formal application, complaint, petition, motion, answer, pleading, or similar paper rather than as a letter, telegram, or other informal written communication; *Provided, however*, That for good cause shown, pleadings of any public body or civic organization or comments concerning tariff agreements that have not been docketed, may be submitted in the form of a letter.

(2) If any document initiating, or filed in, a proceeding is not in substantial conformity with the applicable rules or regulations of the Department as to the contents thereof, or is otherwise insufficient, the Department, on its own initiative, or on motion of any party, may reject, strike or dismiss such document, or require its amendment.

(e) *Official docket copy*. With respect to all documents filed under this part, the electronic record produced by the Department shall thereafter be the official docket copy of the document and any subsequent copies generated by the Department's electronic records system will be usable for admission as record copies in any proceeding before the Department.

(f) *Retention of documents by the Department*. All documents filed with or presented to the Department Dockets will be retained in the permanent docket of the Department of Transportation.

§302.4 General requirements as to documents.

(a) *Contents*. (1) In case there is no rule, regulation, or order of the Department that prescribes the contents of a formal application, petition, complaint, motion or other authorized or required document, such document shall contain a proper identification of the parties concerned, a concise but complete statement of the facts relied upon and the relief sought, and, where required, such document shall be accompanied by an Energy Statement, in conformity with the provisions of part 313 of this chapter.

(2)(i) Each document must include with or provide on its first page:

(A) The docket title and subject;

(B) The relevant operating administration before which the application or request is filed;

(C) The identity of the filer and its filing agent, if applicable;

(D) The name and mailing address of the designated agent for service of any documents filed in the proceeding, along with the telephone and facsimile numbers and, if available, electronic mail address of that person; and

(E) The title of the specific action being requested.

(ii) Department of Transportation Dockets has an Expedited Processing Sheet that filers can use to assist in preparing this index for submission of paper documents, and an electronic registration for electronic filing at the DOT DMS internet website.

(3) All documents filed under this part consisting of twenty (20) or more pages must contain a subject index of the matter in such document, with page references.

(b) *Verification:* The following certification shall be included with every pleading filed under this part: "Pursuant to Title 18 United States Code Section 1001, I [*the individual signing the pleading, who shall be a principal owner, senior officer, or internal counsel of the pleader*], in my individual capacity and as the authorized representative of the pleader, have not in any manner knowingly and willfully falsified, concealed or failed to disclose any material fact or made any false, fictitious, or fraudulent statement or knowingly used any documents which contain such statements in connection with the preparation, filing or prosecution of the pleading. I understand that an individual who is found to have violated the provisions of 18 U.S.C. section 1001 shall be fined or imprisoned not more than five years, or both." In addition, electronic subscription requirements shall be those specified at the DOT DMS internet website.

§ 302.5 Amendment of documents.

(a) An application may be amended prior to the filing of answers thereto, or, if no answer is filed, prior to the issuance of an order establishing further procedures, disposing of the application, or setting the case for hearing. Thereafter, applications may be amended only if leave is granted pursuant to the procedures set forth in § 302.11.

(b) Except as otherwise provided, if properly amended, a document and any statutory deadline shall be made effective as of the date of original filing but the time prescribed for the filing of an answer or any further responsive document directed towards the amended document shall be computed from the date of the filing of the amendment.

§ 302.6 Responsive documents.

(a) *Answers.* Answers to applications, complaints, petitions, motions or other documents or orders instituting proceedings may be filed by any person. In hearing cases, answers may be filed by any party to such proceedings or any person who has a petition for intervention pending. Except as otherwise provided, answers are not required.

(b) *Further responsive documents.* Except as otherwise provided, a reply to an answer, reply to a reply, or any further responsive document is not authorized.

(c) *Motions for leave to file otherwise unauthorized documents.* (1) The Department will accept otherwise unauthorized documents for filing only if leave has been obtained from the DOT decisionmaker or, if applicable, the administrative law judge, on written motion and for good cause shown.

(2) Such motions shall contain a concise statement of the matters relied upon as good cause and shall be attached to the pleading or other document for which leave to file is sought, or the written motion may be incorporated into the otherwise unauthorized document for which admission is sought. In such event, the document filed shall be titled to describe both the motion and the underlying documents.

(3) Where unauthorized responsive documents are not permitted, all new matter contained in an answer filed pursuant to paragraph (a) of this section shall be deemed controverted.

(d) *Time for filing.* Except as otherwise provided, an answer, motion, or other further responsive document shall be filed within seven (7) days after service of any document, order, or ruling to which the proposed filing is responsive and must be served on all parties to the proceeding.

§ 302.7 Service of documents.

(a) *Who makes service*—(1) *The Department.* Formal complaints, notices, orders, and similar documents issued by the Department will be served by the Department upon all parties to the proceeding.

(2) *The parties.* Answers, petitions, motions, briefs, exceptions, notices, protests, or memoranda, or any other documents filed by any party or other person with the Department shall be served by such party or other person upon all parties to the proceeding in which it is filed; including, where applicable, all persons who have petitioned for intervention in, or consolidation of applications with, such proceeding. Proof of service shall accompany all documents when they are filed. The Department may require additional service of any document(s).

(b) *How service may be made.* Service may be made by first class mail, express mail, priority mail, registered or certified mail, facsimile transmission, personal delivery, or by electronic mail. The Department may prescribe other means of service by order or notice. The means of service selected must be done in such manner so as to have the same attributes as section 46103 of the Statute, which provides for service of notices and processes in a proceeding by personal service or registered or certified mail.

(c) *Who may be served.* Service upon a party or person may be made upon an individual, or upon a member of a partnership or firm to be served, or upon the president or other officer of the corporation, company, firm, or association to be served, or upon the assignee or legal successor of any of the foregoing, or upon any attorney of record for the party, or upon the agent designated by an air carrier or foreign air carrier under section 46103 of the Statute, but it shall be served upon a person designated by a party to receive service of documents in a particular proceeding in accordance with §302.4(a)(2)(iv) once a proceeding has been commenced.

(d) *Where service may be made.* Service shall be made at the principal place of business of the party to be served, or at his or her usual residence if he or she is an individual, or at the office of the party's attorney of record, or at the office or usual residence of the agent designated by an air carrier or foreign air carrier under section 46103 of the Statute, or at the post office or electronic address or facsimile number stated for a person designated to receive service pursuant to §302.4(a)(2)(iv).

(e) *Proof of service.* Proof of service of any document shall consist of one of the following:

(1) A certificate of mailing executed by the person mailing the document.

(2) A certificate of successful transmission executed by the person transmitting the document by facsimile or electronic mail, listing the facsimile numbers or electronic mail address to which the document was sent, and stating that no indication was received that any transmission had failed. In the event of an electronic transmission failure, any other authorized means of service may be substituted and the appropriate proof of service provided.

(f) *Date of service.* The date of service by post office or electronic mail is the date of mailing. Whenever proof of service by personal delivery or facsimile transmission is made, the date of such delivery or facsimile transmission shall be the date of service.

(g) *Freely Associated State Proceedings.* In any proceeding directly involving air transportation to the Federated States of Micronesia, the Marshall Islands, or Palau, the Department and any party or participant in the proceeding shall serve all documents on the President and the designated authorities of the government(s) involved. This requirement shall apply to all proceedings where service is otherwise required, and shall be in addition to any other service required by this chapter.

§302.8 Computation of time.

In computing any period of time prescribed or allowed by this part, by notice, order or regulation or by any applicable statute, the day of the act, event, or default after which the designated period of time begins to run is not to be included. The last day of the period so computed is to be included, unless it is a Saturday, Sunday, or legal holiday for the Department, in which event the period runs until the end of the next day that is neither a Saturday, Sunday, nor holiday. When the period of time prescribed is seven (7) days or fewer, intermediate Saturdays, Sundays, and holidays shall be excluded in the computation, unless otherwise specified by the DOT decisionmaker or the administrative law judge assigned to the proceeding, as the case may be.

§302.9 Continuances and extensions of time.

(a) Whenever a party has the right or obligation to take action within a period prescribed by this part, by a notice given thereunder, or by an order or regulation, the DOT decisionmaker or the administrative law judge assigned to the proceeding, as appropriate, may:

(1) Before the expiration of the prescribed period, with or without notice, extend such period, or

(2) Upon motion, permit the act to be done after the expiration of the specified period, where good cause for the failure to act on time is clearly shown.

(b) Except where an administrative law judge has been assigned to a proceeding, requests for continuance or extensions of time, as described in paragraph (a) of this section, shall be directed to the DOT decisionmaker. Requests for continuances and extensions of time may be directed to the Chief Administrative Law Judge in the absence of the administrative law judge assigned to the proceeding.

§302.10 Parties.

(a) In addition to the persons set forth in §302.2, in hearing cases, parties shall include Department staff designated to participate in the proceeding and any persons authorized to intervene or granted permission to participate in accordance with §§ 302.19 and 302.20. In any proceeding directly involving air transportation to the Federated States of Micronesia, the Marshall Islands or Palau, these governments or their designated authorities shall be a party.

(b) Upon motion and for good cause shown, the Department may order a substitution of parties, except that in case of the death of a party, substitution may be ordered without the filing of a motion.

(c) An association composed entirely or in part of air carriers may participate in any proceedings of the Department to which the Department's procedural regulations apply if the association represents members that are identified in any documents filed with the Department, and that have specifically authorized the positions taken by the association in that proceeding. The specific authorizations may be informal and evidence of them shall be provided only upon request of the Department. Upon motion of any interested person or upon its own initiative, the Department may issue an order requiring an association to withdraw from a case on the grounds of significant divergence of interest or position within the association.

§ 302.11 Motions.

(a) *Generally.* An application to the DOT decisionmaker or an administrative law judge for an order or ruling not otherwise specifically provided for in this part shall be by motion. If an administrative law judge is assigned to a proceeding and before the issuance of a recommended or initial decision or the certification of the record to the DOT decisionmaker, all motions shall be addressed to the administrative law judge. At all other times, motions shall be addressed to the DOT decisionmaker. All motions shall be made at an appropriate time depending upon the nature thereof and the relief requested therein. This paragraph should not be construed as authorizing motions in the nature of petitions for reconsideration.

(b) *Form and contents.* Unless made during a hearing, motions shall be made in writing in conformity with §§ 302.3 and 302.4, shall state their grounds and the relief or order sought, and shall be accompanied by any affidavits or other evidence desired to be relied upon. Motions made during hearings, answers to them, and rulings on them, may be made orally on the record unless the administrative law judge directs otherwise. Written motions shall be filed as separate documents, and shall not be incorporated in any other documents, except where incorporation of a motion in another document is specifically authorized by the Department, or where a document is filed that requests alternative forms of relief and one of these alternative requests is properly to be made by motion. In these instances the document filed shall be appropriately titled and identified to indicate that it incorporates a motion; otherwise, the motion will be disregarded.

(c) *Answers to motions.* Within seven (7) days after a motion is served, or such other period as the DOT decisionmaker or the administrative law judge may fix, any party to the proceeding may file an answer in support of or in opposition to the motion, accompanied by such affidavits or other evidence as it desires to rely upon. Except as otherwise provided, no reply to an answer, reply to a reply, or any further responsive document shall be filed.

(d) *Oral arguments; briefs.* No oral argument will be heard on motions unless the DOT decisionmaker or the administrative law judge otherwise directs. Written memoranda or briefs may be filed with motions or answers to motions, stating the points and authorities relied upon in support of the position taken.

(e) *Requests for expedition.* Any interested person may by motion request expedition of any proceeding or file an answer in support of or in opposition to such motions.

(f) *Effect of pendency of motions.* The filing or pendency of a motion shall not automatically alter or extend the time to take action fixed by this part or by any order of the Department or of an administrative law judge (or any extension granted thereunder).

(g) *Disposition of motions.* The DOT decisionmaker shall pass upon all motions properly submitted to him or her for decision. The administrative law judge shall pass upon all motions properly addressed to him or her, except that, if the administrative law judge finds that a prompt decision by the DOT decisionmaker on a motion is essential to the proper conduct of the proceeding, the administrative law judge may refer such motion to the DOT decisionmaker for decision.

(h) *Appeals to the DOT decisionmaker from rulings of administrative law judges.* Rulings of administrative law judges on motions may not be appealed to the DOT decisionmaker prior to his or her consideration of the entire proceeding except in extraordinary circumstances and with the consent of the administrative law judge. An appeal shall be disallowed unless the administrative law judge finds, either on the record or in writing, that the allowance of such an appeal is necessary to prevent substantial detriment to the public interest or undue prejudice to any party. If an appeal is allowed, any party may file a brief with the DOT decisionmaker within such period as the administrative law judge directs. No oral argument will be heard unless the DOT decisionmaker directs otherwise. The rulings of the administrative law judge on a motion may be reviewed by the DOT decisionmaker in connection with his or her final action in the proceeding or at any other appropriate time irrespective of the filing of an appeal or any action taken on it.

§302.12 Objections to public disclosure of information.

(a) *Generally.* Part 7 of the Office of the Secretary regulations, Public Availability of Information, governs the availability of records and documents of the Department to the public. (49 CFR 7.1 *et seq.*)

(b) *Information contained in written documents.* Any person who objects to the public disclosure of any information filed in any proceeding, or pursuant to the provisions of the Statute, or any Department rule, regulation, or order, shall segregate, or request the segregation of, such information into a separate submission and shall file it separately in a sealed envelope, bearing the caption of the enclosed submission, and the notation "Confidential Treatment Requested Under §302.12." At the time of filing such submission (or, when the objection is made by a person who is not the filer, within five (5) days after the filing of such submission), the objecting party shall file a motion to withhold the information from public disclosure, in accordance with the procedure outlined in paragraph (d) or (f) of this section, as appropriate. Notwithstanding any other provision of this section, copies of the filed submission and of the motion need not be served upon any other party unless so ordered by the Department.

(c) *Information contained in oral testimony.* Any person who objects to the public disclosure of any information sought to be elicited from a witness or deponent on oral examination shall, before such information is disclosed, make his or her objection known. Upon such objection duly made, the witness or deponent shall be compelled to disclose such information only in the presence of the administrative law judge or the person before whom the deposition is being taken, as the case may be, the official stenographer and such attorneys for and representative of each party as the administrative law judge or the person before whom the deposition is being taken shall designate, and after all present have been sworn to secrecy. The transcript of testimony containing such information shall be segregated and filed in a sealed envelope, bearing the title and docket number of the proceeding, and the notation "Confidential Treatment Requested Under §302.12 Testimony Given by (name of witness or deponent)." Within five (5) days after such testimony is given, the objecting person shall file a motion in accordance with the procedure outlined in paragraph (d) of this section, to withhold the information from public disclosure. Notwithstanding any other provision of this section, copies of the segregated portion of the transcript and of the motion need not be served upon any other party unless so ordered by the Department.

(d) *Form of motion.* Motions to withhold from public disclosure information covered by paragraphs (b) and (c) of this section shall be filed with the Department in accordance with the following procedure:

(1) The motion shall include:

(i) An index listing the information or document sought to be withheld by an identifying number, and including its title, description and number of pages, and, if relevant, the specific location within a document;

(ii) A statement explaining how and why the information falls within one or more of the exemptions from the Freedom of Information Act (5 U.S.C. 552(b)(1)–(9)); and

(iii) A statement explaining how and why public disclosure of the information would adversely affect the interests of the objecting persons and is not required in the interest of the public.

(2) Such motion shall be filed with the person conducting the proceeding, or with the person with whom said application, report, or submission is required to be filed. Such motion will be denied when the complete justification required by this paragraph is not provided.

(3) During the pendency of such motion, the ruling official may, by notice or order, allow limited disclosure to parties' representatives, for purposes of participating in the proceeding, upon submission by them of affidavits swearing to protect the confidentiality of the documents at issue.

(e) *Conditions of disclosure.* The order, notice or other action of the Department containing its ruling upon each such motion will specify the extent to which, and the conditions upon which, the information may be disclosed to the parties and to the public, which ruling shall become effective upon the date stated therein, unless, within five (5) days after the date of the entry of the Department's order with respect thereto, a petition is filed by the objecting person requesting reconsideration by the Department, or a written statement is filed indicating that the objecting person in good faith intends to seek judicial review of the Department's order.

(f) *Objection by Government departments or representative thereof.* In the case of objection to the public disclosure of any information filed by or elicited from any United States Government department or agency, or representative thereof, under paragraph (b) or (c) of this section, the department or agency making such objection shall be exempted from the provisions of paragraphs (b), (c), and (d) of this section insofar as said paragraphs require the filing of a written objection to such disclosure. However, any department, agency, or representative thereof may, if it so desires, file a memorandum setting forth the reasons why it is claimed that a public disclosure of the information should not be made. If such a memorandum is submitted, it shall be filed and handled as is provided by this section in the case of a motion to withhold information from public disclosure.

§ 302.13 Consolidation of proceedings.

(a) *Initiation of consolidations.* The Department, upon its own initiative or upon motion, may consolidate for hearing or for other purposes or may contemporaneously consider two or more proceedings that involve substantially the same parties, or issues that are the same or closely related, if it finds that such consolidation or contemporaneous consideration will be conducive to the proper dispatch of its business and to the ends of justice and will not unduly delay the proceedings. Although the Department may, in any particular case, consolidate or contemporaneously consider two or more proceedings on its own motion, the burden of seeking consolidation or contemporaneous consideration of a particular application shall rest upon the applicant and the Department will not undertake to search its docket for all applications that might be consolidated or contemporaneously considered.

(b) *Time for filing.* Unless the Department has provided otherwise in a particular proceeding, a motion to consolidate or contemporaneously consider an application with any other application shall be filed within 21 days of the original application in the case of international route awards under section 41102 of the Statute (*see* § 302.212), or, where a proceeding has been set for hearing before an administrative law judge, not later than the prehearing conference in the proceeding with which consolidation or contemporaneous consideration is requested. If made at such conference, the motion may be oral. All motions for consolidation or consideration of issues that enlarge, expand, or otherwise change the nature of the proceeding shall be addressed to the DOT decisionmaker, unless made orally at the prehearing conference, in which event the presiding administrative law judge shall present such motion to the DOT decisionmaker for his or her decision. A motion that is not timely filed, or that does not relate to an application pending at such time, shall be dismissed unless the movant shall clearly show good cause for failure to file such motion or application on time.

(c) *Answer.* If a motion to consolidate two or more proceedings is filed with the Department, any party to any of such proceedings, or any person who has a petition for intervention pending, may file an answer to such motion within such period as the DOT decisionmaker may permit. The administrative law judge may require that answers to such motions be stated orally at the prehearing conference in the proceeding with which the consolidation is proposed.

§302.14 Petitions for reconsideration.

(a) *Department orders subject to reconsideration; time for filing.* (1) Unless an order or a rule of the Department specifically provides otherwise:

(i) Any interested person may file a petition for reconsideration of any interlocutory order issued by the Department that institutes a proceeding; and

(ii) Any party to a proceeding may file a petition for reconsideration, rehearing, or reargument of final orders issued by the Department (*See* §302.38), or an interlocutory order that defines the scope and issues of a proceeding or suspends a provision of a tariff on file with the Department.

(2) Unless otherwise provided, petitions for reconsideration shall be filed, in the case of a final order, within twenty (20) days after service thereof, and, in the case of an interlocutory order, within ten (10) days after service. However, neither the filing nor the granting of such a petition shall operate as a stay of such final or interlocutory order unless specifically so ordered by the DOT decisionmaker. Within ten (10) days after a petition for reconsideration, rehearing, or reargument is filed, any party to the proceeding may file an answer in support of or in opposition. Motions for extension of time to file a petition or answer, and for leave to file a petition or answer after the time for the filing has expired, will not be granted except on a showing of unusual and exceptional circumstances, constituting good cause for the movant's inability to meet the established procedural dates.

(b) *Contents of petition.* A petition for reconsideration, rehearing, or reargument shall state, briefly and specifically, the matters of record alleged to have been erroneously decided, the ground relied upon, and the relief sought. If a decision by the Secretary or Deputy Secretary is requested, the petition should describe in detail the reasons for such request and specify any important national transportation policy issues that are presented. If the petition is based, in whole or in part, on allegations as to the consequences that would result from the final order, the basis of such allegations shall be set forth. If the petition is based, in whole or in part, on new matter, such new matter shall be set forth, accompanied by a statement to the effect that petitioner, with due diligence, could not have known or discovered such new matter prior to the date the case was submitted for decision. Unless otherwise directed by the DOT decisionmaker upon a showing of unusual or exceptional circumstances, petitions for reconsideration, rehearing or reargument or answers thereto that exceed twenty-five (25) pages (including appendices) in length shall not be accepted for filing by Department of Transportation Dockets.

(c) *Successive petitions.* A successive petition for rehearing, reargument, reconsideration filed by the same party or person, and upon substantially the same ground as a former petition that has been considered or denied will not be entertained.

NON-HEARING PROCEEDINGS

§ 302.15 Non-hearing procedures.

In cases where oral evidentiary hearing procedures will not be used, § 302.17 through § 302.37, relating to hearing procedures, shall not be applicable except to the extent that the DOT decisionmaker shall determine that the application of some or all of such rules in the particular case will be conducive to the proper dispatch of its business and to the public interest. References in these and other sections of this part to powers or actions by administrative law judges shall not apply.

RULEMAKING PROCEEDINGS

§ 302.16 Petitions for rulemaking.

Any interested person may petition the Department for the issuance, amendment, modification, or repeal of any regulation, subject to the provisions of part 5, Rulemaking Procedures, of the Office of the Secretary regulations (49 CFR 5.1 *et seq.*).

ORAL EVIDENTIARY HEARING PROCEEDINGS

§ 302.17 Administrative law judges.

(a) *Powers and delegation of authority.* (1) An administrative law judge shall have the following powers, in addition to any others specified in this part:

(i) To give notice concerning and to hold hearings;

(ii) To administer oaths and affirmations;

(iii) To examine witnesses;

(iv) To issue subpoenas and to take or cause depositions to be taken;

(v) To rule upon offers of proof and to receive relevant evidence;

(vi) To regulate the course and conduct of the hearing;

(vii) To hold conferences before or during the hearing for the settlement or simplification of issues;

(viii) To rule on motions and to dispose of procedural requests or similar matters;

(ix) To make initial or recommended decisions as provided in § 302.31;

(x) To take any other action authorized by this part or by the Statute.

(2) The administrative law judge shall have the power to take any other action authorized by part 385 of this chapter or by the Administrative Procedure Act.

(3) The administrative law judge assigned to a particular case is delegated the DOT decisionmaker's function of making the agency decision on the substantive and procedural issues remaining for disposition at the close of the hearing in such case, except that this delegation does not apply in cases where the record is certified to the DOT decisionmaker, with or without an initial or recommended decision by the administrative law judge, or in cases requiring Presidential approval under section 41307 of the Statute. This delegation does not apply to the review of rulings by the administrative law judge on interlocutory matters that have been appealed to the DOT decisionmaker in accordance with the requirements of § 302.11.

(4) The administrative law judge's authority in each case will terminate either upon the certification of the record in the proceeding to the DOT decisionmaker, or upon the issuance of an initial or recommended decision, or when he or she shall have withdrawn from the case upon considering himself or herself disqualified.

(b) *Disqualification.* An administrative law judge shall withdraw from the case if at any time he or she deems himself or herself disqualified. If, prior to the initial or recommended decision in the case, there is filed with the administrative law judge, in good faith, an affidavit of personal bias or disqualification with substantiating facts and the administrative law judge does not withdraw, the DOT decisionmaker shall determine the matter, if properly presented by exception or brief, as a part of the record and decision in the case. The DOT decisionmaker shall not otherwise consider any claim of bias or disqualification. The DOT decisionmaker, in his or her discretion, may order a hearing on a charge of bias or disqualification.

§ 302.18 DOT decisionmaker.

(a) *Assistant Secretary for Aviation and International Affairs.* Except as provided in paragraphs (b) and (c) of this section, the Assistant Secretary for Aviation and International Affairs is the

DOT decisionmaker. The Assistant Secretary shall have all of the powers set forth in § 302.17(a)(1) and those additional powers delegated by the Secretary. The Assistant Secretary may delegate this authority in appropriate non-hearing cases to subordinate officials.

(b) *Oral hearing cases assigned to the senior career official.* Carrier selection proceedings for international route authority that are set for oral hearing and such other oral hearing cases as the Secretary deems appropriate will be assigned to the senior career official in the Office of the Assistant Secretary for Aviation and International Affairs, who will serve as the DOT decisionmaker. In all such cases, the administrative law judge shall render a recommended decision to the senior career official, who shall have all of the powers set forth in § 302.17(a)(1) and those additional powers delegated by the Secretary.

(1) Decisions of the senior career official are subject to review by, and at the discretion of, the Assistant Secretary for Aviation and International Affairs. Petitions for discretionary review of decisions of the senior career official will not be entertained. A notice of review by the Assistant Secretary will establish the procedures for review. Unless a notice of review is issued, the decision of the senior career official will be issued as a final decision of the Department and will be served fourteen (14) days after it is adopted by the senior career official.

(2) Final decisions of the senior career official may be reviewed upon a petition for reconsideration filed pursuant to § 302.14. Such a petition shall state clearly the basis for requesting reconsideration and shall specify any questions of national transportation policy that may be involved. The Assistant Secretary will either grant or deny the petition.

(3) Upon review or reconsideration, the Assistant Secretary may either affirm the decision or remand the decision to the senior career official for further action consistent with such order of remand.

(4) Subject to the provisions of paragraphs (b)(1) through (3) of this section, final decisions of the senior career official will be transmitted to the President of the United States when required under 49 U.S.C. 41307.

(c) *Secretary and Deputy Secretary.* The Secretary or Deputy Secretary may exercise any authority of the Assistant Secretary whenever he or she believes a decision involves important questions of national transportation policy.

§ 302.19 Participation by persons not parties.

Any person, including any State, subdivision thereof, State aviation commission, or other public body, may appear at any hearing, other than in an enforcement proceeding, and present any evidence that is relevant to the issues. With the consent of the administrative law judge or the DOT decisionmaker, such person may also cross-examine witnesses directly. Such persons may also present to the administrative law judge a written statement on the issues involved in the proceeding. Such written statements shall be filed and served on all parties prior to the close of the hearing.

§ 302.20 Formal intervention.

(a) *Who may intervene.* Any person who has a statutory right to be made a party to an oral evidentiary hearing proceeding shall be permitted to intervene. Any person whose intervention will be conducive to the public interest and will not unduly delay the conduct of such proceeding may be permitted to intervene.

(b) *Considerations relevant to determination of petition to intervene.* In passing upon a petition to intervene, the following factors, among other things, will be considered and will be liberally interpreted to facilitate the effective participation by members of the public in Department proceedings:

(1) The nature of the petitioner's right under the statute to be made a party to the proceeding;

(2) The nature and extent of the property, financial or other interest of the petitioner;

(3) The effect of the order that may be entered in the proceeding on petitioner's interest;

(4) The availability of other means whereby the petitioner's interest may be protected;

(5) The extent to which petitioner's interest will be represented by existing parties;

(6) The extent to which petitioner's participation may reasonably be expected to assist in the development of a sound record; and

(7) The extent to which participation of the petitioner will broaden the issues or delay the proceeding.

(c) *Petition to intervene*—(1) *Contents.* Any person desiring to intervene in a proceeding shall file a petition in conformity with this part setting forth the facts and reasons why he or she thinks he or she should be permitted to intervene. The petition should make specific reference to the factors set forth in paragraph (b) of this section.

(2) *Time for filing.* Unless otherwise ordered by the Department:

(i) A petition to intervene shall be filed with the Department prior to the first prehearing conference, or, in the event that no such conference is to be held, not later than fifteen (15) days prior to the hearing.

(ii) A petition to intervene filed by a city, other public body, or a chamber of commerce shall be filed with the Department not later than the last day prior to the beginning of the hearing.

(iii) A petition to intervene that is not timely filed shall be dismissed unless the petitioner shall clearly show good cause for his or her failure to file such petition on time.

(3) *Answer.* Any party to a proceeding may file an answer to a petition to intervene, making specific reference to the factors set forth in paragraph (b) of this section, within seven (7) days after the petition is filed.

(4) *Disposition.* The decision granting, denying or otherwise ruling on any petition to intervene may be issued without receiving testimony or oral argument either from the petitioner or other parties to the proceeding.

(d) *Effect of granting intervention.* A person permitted to intervene in a proceeding thereby becomes a party to the proceeding. However, interventions provided for in this section are for administrative purposes only, and no decision granting leave to intervene shall be deemed to constitute an expression by the Department that the intervening party has such a substantial interest in the order that is to be entered in the proceeding as will entitle it to judicial review of such order.

§ 302.21 Appearances.

(a) Any party to a proceeding may appear and be heard in person or by a designated representative.

(b) No register of persons who may practice before the Department is maintained and no application for admission to practice is required.

(c) Any person practicing or desiring to practice before the Department may, upon hearing and good cause shown, be suspended or barred from practicing.

§ 302.22 Prehearing conference.

(a) *Purpose and scope of conference.* At the discretion of the administrative law judge, a prehearing conference may be called prior to any hearing. Written notice of the prehearing conference shall be sent by the administrative law judge to all parties to a proceeding and to other persons who appear to have an interest in such proceeding. The purpose of such a conference is to define the issues and the scope of the proceeding, to secure statements of the positions of the parties and amendments to the pleadings, to schedule the exchange of exhibits before the date set for hearing, and to arrive at such agreements as will aid in the conduct and disposition of the proceeding. For example, consideration will be given to:

(1) Matters that the DOT decisionmaker can consider without the necessity of proof;

(2) Admissions of fact and of the genuineness of documents;

(3) Requests for documents;

(4) Admissibility of evidence;

(5) Limitation of the number of witnesses;

(6) Reducing of oral testimony to exhibit form;

(7) Procedure at the hearing; and

(8) Use of electronic media as a basis for exchange of briefs, hearing transcripts and exhibits, etc., in addition to the official record copy.

(b) *Actions during prehearing conference.* The administrative law judge may require a further conference, or responsive pleadings, or both. If a party refuses to produce documents requested by another party at the conference, the administrative law judge may compel the production of such documents prior to a hearing by subpoena issued in accordance with the provisions of § 302.25 as though at a hearing. Applications for the production prior to hearing of documents in the Department's possession shall be addressed to the administrative law judge, in accordance with the provisions of § 302.25(g), in the same manner as provided therein for production of documents at a hearing. The administrative law judge may also, on his or her own initiative or on motion of any party, direct any party to the proceeding (air carrier or non-air carrier) to prepare and submit exhibits setting forth studies, forecasts, or estimates on matters relevant to the issues in the proceeding.

(c) *Report of prehearing conference.* The administrative law judge shall issue a report of prehearing conference, defining the issues, giving an account of the results of the conference, specifying a schedule for the exchange of exhibits and rebuttal exhibits, the date of hearing, and specifying a time for the filing of objections to such report. The report shall be served upon all parties to the proceeding and any person who appeared at the conference. Objections to the report may be filed by any interested person within the time specified therein. The administrative law judge may revise his or her report in the light of the objections presented. The revised report, if any, shall be served upon the same persons as was the original report. Exceptions may be taken on the basis of any timely written objection that has not been met by a revision of the report if the exceptions are filed within the time specified in the revised report. Such report shall constitute the official account of the conference and shall control the subsequent course of the proceeding, but it may be reconsidered and modified at any time to protect the public interest or to prevent injustice.

§ 302.23 Hearing.

The administrative law judge to whom the case is assigned or the DOT decisionmaker shall give the parties reasonable notice of a hearing or of the change in the date and place of a hearing and the nature of such hearing.

§ 302.24 Evidence.

(a) *Presenting evidence.* Presenting evidence at the hearing shall be limited to material evidence relevant to the issues as drawn by the pleadings or as defined in the report of prehearing conference, subject to such later modifications of the issues as may be necessary to protect the public interest or to prevent injustice, and shall not be unduly repetitious. Evidence shall be presented in such form by all parties as the administrative law judge may direct.

(b) *Objections to evidence.* Objections to the admission or exclusion of evidence shall be in short form, stating the grounds of objections relied upon, and the transcript shall not include argument or debate except as ordered by the administrative law judge. Rulings on such objections shall be a part of the transcript.

(c) *Exhibits.* When exhibits are offered in evidence, one copy must be furnished to each of the parties at the hearing, and two copies to the administrative law judge, unless the parties previously have been furnished with copies or the administrative law judge directs otherwise. If the administrative law judge has not fixed a time for the exchange of exhibits, the parties shall exchange copies of exhibits at the earliest practicable time, preferably before the hearing or, at the latest, at the commencement of the hearing. Copies of exhibits may, at the discretion of the administrative law judge or the DOT decisionmaker, be furnished by use of electronic media in lieu of or in addition to a paper record copy.

(d) *Substitution of copies for original exhibits.* In his or her discretion, the administrative law judge may permit a party to withdraw original documents offered in evidence and substitute true copies in lieu thereof.

(e) *Designation of parts of documents.* When relevant and material matter offered in evidence by any party is embraced in a book, paper, or document containing other matter not material or relevant, the party offering the same shall plainly designate the matter so offered. The immaterial and irrelevant parts shall be excluded and shall be segregated insofar as practicable. If the volume of immaterial or irrelevant matter would unduly encumber the record, such submission will not be received in evidence, but may be marked for identification, and, if properly authenticated, the relevant or material matter may be read into the record, or, if the administrative law judge so directs, a true copy of such matter, in proper form, shall be received as an exhibit, and like copies delivered by the party offering the same to opposing parties or their attorneys appearing at the hearing, who shall be afforded an opportunity to examine the submission, and to offer in evidence in like manner other portions of the exhibit.

(f) *Records in other proceedings.* In case any portion of the record in any other proceeding or civil or criminal action is offered in evidence, a true copy of such portion shall be presented for the record in the form of an exhibit unless:

(1) The portion is specified with particularity in such manner as to be readily identified;

(2) The party offering the same agrees unconditionally to supply such copies later, or when required by the DOT decisionmaker;

(3) The parties represented at the hearing stipulate upon the record that such portion may be incorporated by reference, and that any portion offered by any other party may be incorporated by like reference upon compliance with paragraphs (f)(1) and (2) of this section; and

(4) The administrative law judge directs such incorporation or waives the requirement in paragraph (f)(3) of this section with the consent of the parties.

(g) *Official notice of facts contained in certain documents.* (1) Without limiting, in any manner or to any extent, the discretionary powers of the DOT decisionmaker and the administrative law judge to notice other matters or documents properly the subject of official notice, facts contained in any document within the categories enumerated in this subdivision are officially noticed in all formal economic proceedings except those subject to subpart D of this part. Each such category shall include any document antedating the final Department decision in the proceeding where such notice is taken. The matters officially noticed under the provisions of this paragraph are:

(i) Air carrier certificates or applications therefor, together with any requests for amendment, and pleadings responding to applications when properly filed.

(ii) All Form 41 reports required to be filed by air carriers with the Department.

(iii) Reports of Traffic and Financial Data of all U.S. Air Carriers issued by the Civil Aeronautics Board (CAB) or the Department.

(iv) Airline Traffic Surveys and Passenger Origin-Destination Surveys, Domestic and International, compiled by the CAB or the Department and published and/or made available either to the public or to parties in proceedings.

(v) Compilations of data relating to competition in the airline industry and made available to the public by the CAB or the Department, such as the 1990 Airline Competition Study.

(vi) Passenger, mail, express, and freight data submitted to the CAB or the Department as part of ER–586 Service Segment Data by U.S. carriers, or similar data submitted to the Department by U.S. air carriers (T–100) or by foreign air carriers (T–100F) that is not confidential.

(vii) All tariffs, including the electronic versions, and amendments thereof, of all air carriers, on file with the Department.

(viii) Service Mail Pay and Subsidy for U.S. Certificated Air Carriers published by the CAB and any supplemental data and subsequent issues published by the CAB or the Department.

(ix) Airport Activity Statistics of Certificated Air Carriers compiled and published by the Federal Aviation Administration (FAA) or the Department.

(x) Air Traffic Activity Data issued by the FAA.

(xi) National Plan of Integrated Airport Systems (NPIAS) issued by the FAA.

(xii) Airport Facilities Directory, Form 5010, issued by the FAA.

(xiii) The Airman's Information Manual issued by the FAA.

(xiv) ICAO Statistical Summary, Preliminary Issues and Nos. 1 through 14, and Digest of Statistics, Nos. 15 through 71, prepared by ICAO, Montreal, Canada, with all changes and additions.

(xv) Monthly, quarterly and annual reports of the Immigration and Naturalization Service, U.S. Department of Justice.

(xvi) All forms and reports required by the U.S. Postal Service to be filed by air carriers authorized to transport mail.

(xvii) All orders of the Postmaster General designating schedules for the transportation of mail.

(xviii) Publications of the Bureau of the Census of the U.S. Department of Commerce (DOC) relating, but not necessarily limited, to population, manufacturing, business, statistics, and any yearbooks, abstracts, or similar publications published by DOC.

(xix) ABC World Airways Guide and all Official Airline Guides, including the North American, Worldwide, All-Cargo and quick reference editions, including electronic versions.

(xx) Official Guide of the Railways and Russell's Official National Motor Coach Guide.

(xxi) The Rand McNally Commercial Atlas and Marketing Guide, and the Rand McNally Road Atlas, United States, Canada, and Mexico.

(xxii) Survey of Buying Power published by Sales Management Magazine.

(2) Any fact contained in a document belonging to a category enumerated in paragraph (g)(1) of this section shall be deemed to have been physically incorporated into and made part of the record in such proceedings. However, such taking of official notice shall be subject to the rights granted to any party or intervener to the proceeding under section 7(d) of the Administrative Procedure Act (5 U.S.C. 557(d)).

(3) The decisions of the Department and its administrative law judges may officially notice any appropriate matter without regard to whether or not such items are contained in a document belonging to the categories enumerated in paragraph (g)(1) of this section. However, where the decision rests on official notice of a material fact or facts, it will set forth such items with sufficient particularity to advise interested persons of the matters that have been noticed.

(h) *Receipt of documents after hearing.* No document or other writings shall be accepted for the record after the close of the hearing except in accordance with an agreement of the parties and the consent of the administrative law judge or the DOT decisionmaker.

(i) *Exceptions.* Formal exceptions to the rulings of the administrative law judge made during the course of the hearing are unnecessary. For all purposes for which an exception otherwise would be taken, it is sufficient that a party, at the time the ruling of the administrative law judge is made or sought, makes known the action he or she desires the administrative law judge to take or his or her objection to an action taken, and his or her grounds therefor.

(j) *Offers of proof.* Any offer of proof made in connection with an objection taken to any ruling of the administrative law judge rejecting or excluding proffered oral testimony shall consist of a statement of the substance of the evidence that counsel contends would be adduced by such testimony, and if the excluded evidence consists of evidence in documentary or written form or of reference to documents or records, a copy of such evidence shall be marked for identification and shall constitute the offer of proof.

§ 302.25 Subpoenas.

(a) An application for a subpoena requiring the attendance of a witness at a hearing or the production of documentary evidence may be made without notice by any party to the administrative law judge or, in the event that an administrative law judge has not been assigned to a proceeding or is not available, to the DOT decisionmaker or the Chief Administrative Law Judge, for action.

(b) An application for a subpoena shall be in duplicate except that if it is made during the course of a hearing, it may be made orally on the record with the consent of the administrative law judge.

(c) All such applications, whether written or oral, shall contain a statement or showing of general relevance and reasonable scope of the evidence sought, and shall be accompanied by two copies of a draft of the subpoena sought that, in the case of evidence, shall describe the documentary or tangible evidence to be subpoenaed with as much particularity as is feasible, or, in the case of a witness, the name of the witness and a general description of the matters concerning which the witness will be asked to testify.

(d) The administrative law judge or DOT decisionmaker considering any application for a subpoena shall issue the subpoena requested if the application complies with this section. No attempt shall be made to determine the admissibility of evidence in passing upon an application for a subpoena, and no detailed or burdensome showing shall be required as a condition to the issuance of a subpoena.

(e) Where it appears during the course of a proceeding that the testimony of a witness or documentary evidence is relevant to the issues in a proceeding, the administrative law judge, Chief Administrative Law Judge or DOT decisionmaker may issue on his or her own initiative a subpoena requiring such witness to attend and testify or requiring the production of such documentary evidence.

(f) Subpoenas issued under this section shall be served upon the person to whom directed in accordance with §302.7(b). Any person upon whom a subpoena is served may within seven (7) days after service or at any time prior to the return date thereof, whichever is earlier, file a motion to quash or modify the subpoena with the administrative law judge or, in the event an administrative law judge has not been assigned to a proceeding or is not available, to the DOT decisionmaker or the Chief Administrative Law Judge for action. If the person to whom the motion to modify or quash the subpoena has been addressed or directed, has not acted upon such a motion by the return date, such date shall be stayed pending his or her final action thereon. The DOT decisionmaker may at any time review, upon his or her own initiative, the ruling of an administrative law judge or the Chief Administrative Law Judge denying a motion to quash a subpoena. In such cases, the DOT decisionmaker may order that the return date of a subpoena be stayed pending action thereon.

(g) The provisions of this section are not applicable to the attendance of DOT employees or the production of documentary evidence in the custody thereof at a hearing. The attendance of DOT employees and the production of documentary evidence in their custody are governed by 49 CFR Parts 9 and 7, respectively.

§ 302.26 Depositions.

(a) For good cause shown, the DOT decisionmaker or administrative law judge assigned to a proceeding may order that the testimony of a witness be taken by deposition and that the witness produce documentary evidence in connection with such testimony. Ordinarily an order to take the deposition of a witness will be entered only if:

(1) The person whose deposition is to be taken would be unavailable at the hearing,

(2) The deposition is deemed necessary to perpetuate the testimony of the witness, or

(3) The taking of the deposition is necessary to prevent undue and excessive expense to a party and will not result in an undue burden to other parties or in undue delay.

(b) Any party desiring to take the deposition of a witness shall make application therefor in duplicate to the administrative law judge or, in the event that an administrative law judge has not been assigned to a proceeding or is not available, to the DOT decisionmaker or Chief Administrative Law Judge, setting forth the reasons why such deposition should be taken, the name and residence of the witness, the time and place proposed for the taking of the deposition, and a general description of the matters concerning which the witness will be asked to testify. If good cause be shown, the administrative law judge, the DOT decisionmaker, or the Chief Administrative Law Judge, as the case may be, may, in his or her discretion, issue an order authorizing such deposition and specifying the witness whose deposition is to be taken, the general scope of the testimony to be taken, the time when, the place where, the designated officer (authorized to take oaths) before whom the witness is to testify, and the number of copies of the deposition to be supplied. Such order shall be served upon all parties by the person proposing to take the deposition a reasonable period in advance of the time fixed for taking testimony.

(c) Witnesses whose testimony is taken by deposition shall be sworn or shall affirm before any questions are put to them. Each question shall be recorded and the answers shall be taken down in the words of the witness.

(d) Objections to questions or evidence shall be in short form, stating the grounds of objection relied upon, but no transcript filed by the designated officer shall include argument or debate. Objections to questions or evidence shall be noted by the designated officer upon the deposition, but he or she shall not have power to decide on the competency or materiality or relevance of evidence, and he or she shall record the evidence subject to objection. Objections to questions or evidence not made before the designated officer shall not be deemed waived unless the ground of the objection is one that might have been obviated or removed if presented at that time.

(e) The testimony shall be reduced to writing by the designated officer, or under his or her direction, after which the deposition shall be signed by the witness unless the parties by stipulation waive the signing or the witness is ill or cannot be found or refuses to sign, and certified in usual form by the designated officer. If the deposition is not signed by the witness, the designated officer shall state on the record this fact and the reason therefor. The original deposition and exhibits shall be forwarded to Department of Transportation Dockets and shall be filed in the proceedings.

(f) Depositions may also be taken and submitted on written interrogatories in substantially the same manner as depositions taken by oral examination. Ordinarily such procedure will be authorized only if necessary to achieve the purposes of an oral deposition and to serve the balance of convenience of the parties. The interrogatories shall be filed in quadruplicate with two copies of the application and a copy of each shall be served on each party. Within seven (7) days after service any party may file with the person to whom application was made two copies of his or her objections, if any, to such interrogatories and may file such cross-interrogatories as he or she desires to submit. Cross-interrogatories shall be filed in quadruplicate, and a copy thereof together with a copy of any objections to interrogatories, shall be served on each party, who shall have five (5) days thereafter to file and serve his or her objections, if any, to such cross-interrogatories. Objections to interrogatories or cross-interrogatories, shall be served on the DOT decisionmaker or the administrative law judge considering the application. Objections to interrogatories shall be made before the order for taking the deposition issues and if not so made shall be deemed waived. When a deposition is taken upon written interrogatories, and cross-interrogatories, no party shall be present or represented, and no person other than the witness, a reporter, and the designated officer shall be present at the examination of the witness, which fact shall be certified by the designated officer, who shall ask the interrogatories and cross-interrogatories to the witness in their order and reduce the testimony to writing in the witness's own words. The provisions of paragraph (e) of this section shall be applicable to depositions taken in accordance with this paragraph.

(g) All depositions shall conform to the specifications of §302.3 except that the filing of three copies thereof shall be sufficient. Any fees of a witness, the reporter, or the officer designated to take the deposition shall be paid by the person at whose instance the deposition is taken.

(h) The fact that a deposition is taken and filed in a proceeding as provided in this section does not constitute a determination that it is admissible in evidence or that it may be used in the proceeding. Only such part or the whole of a deposition as is received in evidence shall constitute a part of the record in such proceeding upon which a decision may be based.

§ 302.27 Rights of witnesses; attendance fees and mileage.

(a) Any person appearing as a witness in any proceeding governed by this part, whether in response to a subpoena or by request or permission of the Department, may be accompanied, represented, and advised by counsel and may be examined by that counsel after other questioning.

(b) Any person who submits data or evidence in a proceeding governed by this part, whether in response to a subpoena or by request or permission of the Department, may retain, or, on payment of lawfully prescribed costs, procure, a copy of any document so submitted or a copy of any transcript made of such testimony.

(c) No person whose attendance at a hearing or whose deposition is to be taken shall be obliged to respond to a subpoena unless upon a service of the subpoena he or she is tendered attendance fees and mileage by the party at whose instance he or she is called in accordance with the requirements of paragraphs (c)(1) and (2) of this section; *Provided*, That a witness summoned at the instance of the Department or one of its employees, or a salaried employee of the United States summoned to testify as to matters related to his or her public employment, need not be tendered such fees or mileage at that time.

(1) Witnesses who are not salaried employees of the United States, or such employees summoned to testify on matters not related to their public employment, shall be paid the same per diem, subsistence, and mileage fees paid to witnesses for like service in the courts of the United States that are in effect at the time of travel; *Provided*, That no employee, officer, or attorney of an air carrier who travels under the free or reduced rate provisions of section 41511 of the Statute shall be entitled to any fees or mileage; *And provided further*, That such fees and mileage shall not be applicable for witnesses summoned to testify in Alaska, and that, in Alaska, where permitted by section 41511 of the Statute, the witness may, at his or her option, accept a pass for travel by air. Such witnesses shall be furnished appropriate forms and instructions for the submission of claims for attendance fees, subsistence, and mileage from the Government before the close of the proceedings that they are required to attend. Only persons summoned by subpoena shall be entitled to claim attendance fees, subsistence, or mileage from the Government.

(2) Witnesses who are salaried employees of the United States and who are summoned to testify on matters relating to their public employment, irrespective of at whose instance they are summoned, shall be paid in accordance with applicable Government regulations.

§ 302.28 Transcripts of hearings.

(a) Hearings shall be recorded and transcribed under supervision of the administrative law judge, by a reporting firm under contract with the Department. Copies of the transcript that may, at the discretion of the administrative law judge, be furnished by use of electronic media in addition to the official copy, shall be supplied to the parties to the proceeding by said reporting firm, at the contract price for copies.

(b) The administrative law judge shall determine whether "ordinary transcript" or "daily transcript" (as those terms are defined in the contract) will be necessary and required for the proper conduct of the proceeding and the Department will pay the reporting firm the cost of reporting its proceedings at the contract price for such type of transcript. If the administrative law judge has determined that ordinary transcript is adequate, and has notified the parties of such determination (in the notice of hearings, or otherwise), then any party may request reconsideration of such determination and that daily transcript be required. In determining what is necessary and required for the proper conduct of the proceeding, the administrative law judge shall consider, among other things:

(1) The nature of the proceeding itself;

(2) The DOT decisionmaker's needs as well as the reasonable needs of the parties;

(3) The cost to the Department; and

(4) The requirements of a fair hearing.

(c) If the administrative law judge has determined that ordinary transcript is adequate, or, upon reconsideration, has adhered to such determination, then any party may request the reporting firm to provide daily transcript. In that case, pursuant to its contract with the Department, the reporting firm will be obligated to furnish to the Department daily transcript upon the agreement by the requesting party to pay to the reporting firm an amount equal to the difference between the contract prices for ordinary transcript and daily transcript, provided that the requesting party makes such agreement with the reporting firm at least twenty-four (24) hours in advance of the date for which such transcript is requested.

(d) Any party may obtain from the Office of the Assistant Secretary for Administration, the name and address of the private reporting company with which the Department currently has a contract for transcripts and copies, as well as the contract prices then in effect for such services.

(e) Copies of transcripts ordered by parties other than the Department shall be prepared for delivery to the requesting person at the reporting firm's place of business, within the stated time for the type of transcript ordered. The requesting party and the reporting firm may agree upon some other form or means of delivery (mail, messenger, electronic media, etc.) and the reporting firm may charge for such special service, provided that such charge shall not exceed the reasonable cost of such service.

(f) Changes in the official transcript may be made only when they involve errors affecting substance. A motion to correct a transcript shall be filed with Department of Transportation Dockets, within ten (10) days after receipt of the completed transcript by the Department. If no objections to the motion are filed within ten (10) days thereafter, the transcript may, upon the approval of the administrative law judge, be changed to reflect such corrections. If objections are received, the motion and objections shall be submitted to the official reporter by the administrative law judge together with a request for a comparison of the transcript with the reporter's record of the hearing. After receipt of the report of the official reporter an order shall be entered by the administrative law judge settling the record and ruling on the motion.

§ 302.29 Argument before the administrative law judge.

(a) The administrative law judge shall give the parties to the proceeding adequate opportunity during the course of the hearing for the presentation of arguments in support of or in opposition to motions, and objections and exceptions to rulings of the administrative law judge.

(b) When, in the opinion of the administrative law judge, the volume of the evidence or the importance or complexity of the issues involved warrants, he or she may, either on his or her own motion or at the request of a party, permit the presentation of oral argument, and may impose such time limits on the argument as he or she may determine appropriate. Such argument shall be transcribed and bound with the transcript of testimony and will be available to the Department decisionmaker for consideration in deciding the case.

§ 302.30 Briefs to the administrative law judge.

Within such limited time after the close of the reception of evidence fixed by the administrative law judge, any party may, upon request and under such conditions as the administrative law judge may prescribe, file for his or her consideration briefs which may include proposed findings of fact and conclusions of law that shall contain exact references to the record and authorities relied upon.

§ 302.31 Initial and recommended decisions; certification of the record.

(a) *Action by administrative law judge after hearing.* Except where the DOT decisionmaker directs otherwise, after the taking of evidence and the receipt of briefs which may include proposed findings of fact and conclusions of law, if any, the administrative law judge shall take the following action:

(1) *Initial decision.* If the proceeding does not involve foreign air transportation, the administrative law judge shall render an "initial decision." Such decision shall encompass the administrative law judge's decision on the merits of the proceeding and on all ancillary procedural issues remaining for disposition at the close of the hearing.

(2) *Recommended decision.* In cases where the action of the Department involves foreign air transportation and is subject to review by the President of the United States pursuant to section 41307 of the Statute, the administrative law judge shall render a "recommended decision." Such decision shall encompass the administrative law judge's decision on the merits of the proceeding and on all ancillary procedural issues remaining for disposition at the close of the hearing.

(b) *Certification to the DOT decisionmaker for decision.* At any time prior to the close of the hearing, the DOT decisionmaker may direct the administrative law judge to certify any question or the entire record in the proceeding to the DOT decisionmaker for decision. In cases where the record is thus certified, the administrative law judge shall not render a decision but shall make a recommendation to the DOT decisionmaker as required by section 8(a) of the Administrative Procedure Act (5 U.S.C. 550(a)) unless advised by the DOT decisionmaker that he or she intends to issue a tentative decision.

(c) Every initial or recommended decision issued shall state the names of the persons who are to be served with copies of it, the time within which exceptions to, or petitions for review of, such decision may be filed, and the time within which briefs in support of the exceptions may be filed. In addition, every such decision shall recite that it is made under delegated authority, and contain notice of the provisions of paragraph (d) of this section. In the event the administrative law judge certifies the record to the DOT decisionmaker without an initial or recommended decision, he or she shall notify the parties of the time within which to file with the DOT decisionmaker briefs which may include proposed findings of fact and conclusions of law.

(d) Unless a petition for discretionary review is filed pursuant to § 302.32, exceptions are filed pursuant to § 302.217, or the DOT decisionmaker issues an order to review upon his or her own initiative, the initial decision shall become effective as the final order of the Department thirty (30) days after service thereof; in the case of a recommended decision, that decision shall be transmitted to the President of the United States under 49 U.S.C. 41307. If a petition for discretionary review or exceptions are timely filed or action to review is taken by the DOT decisionmaker upon his or her own initiative, the effectiveness of the initial decision or the transmission of the recommended decision is stayed until the further order of the DOT decisionmaker.

§ 302.32 Petitions for discretionary review of initial or recommended decisions; review proceedings.

(a) *Petitions for discretionary review.* (1) Review by the DOT decisionmaker pursuant to this section is not a matter of right but is at the sole discretion of the DOT decisionmaker. Any party may file and serve a petition for discretionary review by the DOT decisionmaker of an initial decision or recommended decision within twenty-one (21) days after service thereof, unless the DOT decisionmaker sets a different period for filing.

(2) Petitions for discretionary review shall be filed only upon one or more of the following grounds:

(i) A finding of a material fact is erroneous;

(ii) A necessary legal conclusion is without governing precedent or is a departure from or contrary to law, the Department's rules, or precedent;

(iii) A substantial and important question of law, policy or discretion is involved; or

(iv) A prejudicial procedural error has occurred.

(3) Each issue shall be separately numbered and plainly and concisely stated. Petitioners shall not restate the same point in repetitive discussions of an issue. Each issue shall be supported by detailed citations of the record when objections are based on the record, and by statutes, regulations or principal authorities relied upon. Any matters of fact or law not argued before the administrative law judge, but that the petitioner proposes to argue on brief to the DOT decisionmaker, shall be stated.

(4) Petitions for discretionary review shall be self-contained and shall not incorporate by reference any part of another document. Except by permission of the DOT decisionmaker, petitions shall not exceed twenty (20) pages including appendices and other papers physically attached to the petition.

(5) Requests for oral argument on petitions for discretionary review will not be entertained by the DOT decisionmaker.

(b) *Answers.* Within fifteen (15) days after service of a petition for discretionary review, any party may file and serve an answer of not more than fifteen (15) pages in support of or in opposition to the petition. If any party desires to answer more than one petition for discretionary review in the same proceeding, he or she shall do so in a single document of not more than twenty (20) pages.

(c) *Orders declining review.* The DOT decisionmaker's order declining to exercise the discretionary right of review will specify the date upon which the administrative law judge's decision shall become effective as the final decision of the Department. A petition for reconsideration of a Department order declining review will be entertained only when the order exercises, in part, the DOT decisionmaker's discretionary right of review, and such petition shall be limited to the single question of whether any issue designated for review and any issue not so designated are so inseparably interrelated that the former cannot be reviewed independently or that the latter cannot be made effective before the final decision of the Department in the review proceeding.

(d) *Review proceedings.* (1) The DOT decisionmaker may take review of an initial or recommended decision upon petition or on his or her own initiative or both. The DOT decisionmaker will issue a final order upon such review without further proceedings on any or all the issues where he or she finds that matters raised do not warrant further proceedings.

(2) Where the DOT decisionmaker desires further proceedings, he or she will issue an order for review that will:

(i) Specify the issues to which review will be limited. Only those issues specified in the order shall be argued on brief to the DOT decisionmaker, pursuant to § 302.35, and considered by the DOT decisionmaker;

(ii) Specify the portions of the administrative law judge's decision, if any, that are to be stayed as well as the effective date of the remaining portions thereof; and

(iii) Designate the parties to the review proceeding.

§ 302.33 Tentative decision of the DOT decisionmaker.

(a) Except as provided in paragraph (b) of this section, whenever the administrative law judge certifies the record in a proceeding directly to the DOT decisionmaker without issuing an initial or recommended decision in the matter, the DOT decisionmaker shall, after consideration of any briefs submitted by the parties, prepare a tentative decision and serve it upon the parties. Every tentative decision of the DOT decisionmaker shall state the names of the persons who are to receive copies of it, the time within which exceptions to such decision and briefs, if any, in support of or in opposition to the exceptions may be filed, and the date when such decision will become final in the absence of exceptions thereto. If no exceptions are filed to the tentative decision of the DOT decisionmaker within the period fixed, it shall become final at the expiration of such period unless the DOT decisionmaker orders otherwise.

(b) The DOT decisionmaker may, in his or her discretion, omit a tentative decision in proceedings under subpart

B. Final decisions of the DOT decisionmaker are subject to review as provided in § 302.18.

§ 302.34 Exceptions to tentative decisions of the DOT decisionmaker.

(a) *Time for filing.* Within ten (10) days after service of any tentative decision of the DOT decisionmaker, any party to a proceeding may file exceptions to such decision with the DOT decisionmaker.

(b) *Form and contents of exceptions.* Each exception shall be separately numbered and shall be stated as a separate point, and appellants shall not restate the same point in several exceptions. Each exception shall state, sufficiently identify, and be limited to, an ultimate conclusion in the decision to which exception is taken (such as, selection of one carrier rather than another to serve any point or points; points included in or excluded from a new route; imposition or failure to impose a given restriction; determination of a rate at a given amount rather than another). No specific exception shall be taken with respect to underlying findings or statements, but exceptions to an ultimate conclusion shall be deemed to include exceptions to all underlying findings and statements pertaining thereto; *Provided, however,* That exceptions shall specify any matters of law, fact, or policy that were not argued before the administrative law judge but will be set forth for the first time on brief to the DOT decisionmaker.

(c) *Effect of failure to file timely and adequate exceptions.* No objection may be made on brief or at a later time to an ultimate conclusion that is not expressly made the subject of an exception in compliance with the provisions of this section; *Provided, however,* That any party may file a brief in support of the decision and in opposition to the exceptions filed by any other party.

§ 302.35 Briefs to the DOT decisionmaker.

(a) *Time for filing.* Within such period after the date of service of any tentative decision by the DOT decisionmaker as may be fixed therein, any party may file a brief addressed to the DOT decisionmaker in support of his or her exceptions to such decision or in opposition to the exceptions filed by any other party. Briefs to the DOT decisionmaker on initial or recommended decisions of administrative law judges shall be filed only in those cases where the DOT decisionmaker grants discretionary review and orders further proceedings, pursuant to § 302.32(d)(2), and only upon those issues specified in the order. Such briefs shall be filed within thirty (30) days after date of service of the order granting discretionary review unless otherwise specified in the order. In cases where, because of the limited number of parties and the nature of the issues, the filing of opening, answering, and reply briefs will not unduly delay the proceeding and will assist in its proper disposition, the DOT decisionmaker may direct that the parties file briefs at different times rather than at the same time.

(b) *Effect of failure to restate objections in briefs.* In determining the merits of an appeal, the DOT decisionmaker will not consider the exceptions or the petition for discretionary review but will consider only the brief. Each objection contained in the exceptions or each issue specified in the DOT decisionmaker's order exercising discretionary review must be restated and supported by a statement and adequate discussion of all matters relied upon, in a brief filed pursuant to and in compliance with the requirements of this section.

(c) *Formal specifications of briefs*—(1) *Contents.* Each brief shall discuss every point of law, fact, or precedent that the party submitting it is entitled to raise and that it wishes the DOT decisionmaker to consider. Each brief shall include a summary of the argument not to exceed five (5) pages. Support and justification for every point raised shall include itemized references to the pages of the transcript of hearing, exhibit or other matter of record, and citations of the statutes, regulations, or principal authorities relied upon. If a brief or any point discussed in the brief is not in substantial conformity with the requirement for such support and justification, no motion to strike or dismiss such document shall be made but the DOT decisionmaker may disregard the points involved. Copies of briefs may be furnished by use of electronic media in a format acceptable to the Department and the parties.

(2) *Incorporation by reference.* Briefs to the DOT decisionmaker shall be completely self-contained and shall not incorporate by reference any portion of any other brief or pleading; *Provided, however,* That instead of submitting a brief to the DOT decisionmaker a party may adopt by reference specifically identified pages or the whole of his or her prior brief to the administrative law judge if the latter complies with all requirements of this section. In such cases, the party shall file with Department of Transportation Dockets a letter exercising this privilege and serve all parties in the same manner as a brief to the DOT decisionmaker.

(3) *Length.* Except by permission or direction of the DOT decisionmaker, briefs shall not exceed fifty (50) pages including pages contained in any appendix, table, chart, or other document physically attached to the brief, but excluding maps and the summary of the argument. In this case "map" means only those pictorial representations of routes, flight paths, mileage, and similar ancillary data that are superimposed on geographic drawings and contain only such text as is needed to explain the pictorial representation.

§ 302.36 Oral argument before the DOT decisionmaker.

(a) If any party desires to argue a case orally before the DOT decisionmaker, he or she shall request leave to make such argument in his or her exceptions or brief. Such request shall be filed no later than the date when briefs before the DOT decisionmaker are due in the proceeding. The DOT decisionmaker will rule on such request, and, if oral argument is to be allowed, all parties to the proceeding will be advised of the date and hour set for such argument and the amount of time allowed to each party. Requests for oral argument on petitions for discretionary review will not be entertained.

(b) Pamphlets, charts, and other written data may be offered to the DOT decisionmaker at oral argument only in accordance with the following rules: All such material shall be limited to facts in the record of the case being argued and shall be served on all parties to the proceeding with four (4) copies transmitted to Department of Transportation Dockets at least five (5) calendar days in advance of the argument.

§ 302.37 Waiver of procedural steps after hearing.

The parties to any proceeding may agree to waive any one or more of the procedural steps provided in § 302.29 through § 302.36.

§ 302.38 Final decision of the DOT Decisionmaker.

When a case stands submitted to the DOT decisionmaker for final decision on the merits, he or she will dispose of the issues presented by entering an appropriate order that will include a statement of the reasons for his or her findings and conclusions. Such orders shall be deemed "final orders" within the purview of § 302.14(a), in the manner provided by § 302.18.

Subpart B—Rules Applicable to U.S. Air Carrier Certificate and Foreign Air Carrier Permit Licensing Proceedings

§ 302.201 Applicability.

(a) This subpart sets forth the specific rules applicable to proceedings on:

(1) U.S. air carrier certificates of public convenience and necessity and U.S. all-cargo air service certificates under Chapter 411 of the Statute, including renewals, amendments, modifications, suspensions and transfers of such certificates.

(2) Foreign air carrier permits under Chapter 413 of the Statute, including renewals, amendments, modifications, suspensions, and transfers of such permits.

(b) Except as modified by this subpart, the provisions of subpart A of this part apply.

§ 302.202 Contents of applications.

(a) Certificate applications filed under this subpart shall contain the information required by part 201 of this chapter and, where applicable, part 204 of this chapter, and foreign air carrier permit applications shall contain the information required by part 211 of this chapter, along with any other information that the applicant desires the Department to notice officially.

(b) Applications shall include a notice on the cover page stating that any person may support or oppose the application by filing an answer and serving a copy of the answer on all persons served with the application. The notice shall also state the due date for answers. Amendments to applications will be considered new applications for the purpose of calculating the time limitations of this subsection.

(c) Applications shall include a list of the names and addresses of all persons who have been served in accordance with § 302.203.

(d) Where required, each application shall be accompanied by an Energy Statement in conformity with part 313 of this chapter.

§ 302.203 Service of documents.

(a) *General requirements.* (1) Applicants shall serve on the persons listed in paragraph (b) of this section a notice that an application has been filed, and upon request shall promptly provide those persons with copies of the application and supporting documents. The notice must clearly state the authority sought and the due date for other pleadings.

(2) Applicants shall serve a complete copy of the application on the Manager of the FAA Flight Standards District Office responsible for processing the application for any FAA authority needed to conduct the proposed operations.

(3) After an order under § 302.210 has been issued, parties need only serve documents on those persons listed in the service list accompanying the order.

(4) In the case of an application sought to be consolidated, the applicant shall serve the notice required in paragraph (a)(1) of this section on all persons served by the original applicant.

(b) *Persons to be served*—(1) *U.S. air carriers.* (i) In certificate proceedings, except for those proceedings that involve charter-only authority under section 41102(a)(3) of the Statute:

(A) Applicants for certificates to engage in interstate air transportation and other persons who file a pleading in the docket shall serve:

(*1*) The airport authority of each airport that the applicant initially proposes to serve, and

(*2*) Any other person who has filed a pleading in the docket.

(B) Applicants for certificates to engage in foreign air transportation and other persons who file a pleading in the docket shall serve:

(*1*) All U.S. air carriers (including commuter air carriers) that publish schedules in the *Official Airline Guide* or in the *Air Cargo Guide* for the country-pair market(s) specified in the application,

(*2*) The airport authority of each U.S. airport that the applicant initially proposes to serve, and

(*3*) Any other person who has filed a pleading in the docket.

(ii) In certificate proceedings involving charter-only authority under 41102(a)(3) of the Statute, applicants and other persons who file a pleading in the docket shall serve any other person who has filed a pleading in the docket.

(2) *Foreign air carriers.* (i) In permit proceedings, except for those proceedings involving charter-only authority, applicants and other persons who have filed a pleading in the docket shall serve:

(A) All U.S. air carriers (including commuter air carriers) that publish schedules in the *Official Airline Guide* or the *Air Cargo Guide* for the country-pair market(s) specified in the application,

(B) The U.S. Department of State,

(C) The airport authority of each U.S. airport that the applicant initially proposes to serve, and

(D) Any other person who has filed a pleading in the docket.

(ii) In foreign air carrier permit proceedings for charter-only authority, applicants and other persons who file a pleading in the docket shall serve the U.S. Department of State and any other person who has filed a pleading in the docket.

(c) *Additional service.* The Department may, at its discretion, order additional service upon such persons as the facts of the situation warrant. Where only notices are required, parties are encouraged to serve copies of their actual pleadings where feasible. In any proceeding directly involving air transportation to the Federated States of Micronesia, the Marshall Islands or Palau, the Department and any party or participant in the proceeding shall serve all documents on the President and the designated authorities of the government(s) involved.

§ 302.204 Responsive documents.

(a) Any person may file an answer in support of or in opposition to any application. Answers shall set forth the basis for the position taken, including any economic data or other facts relied on. Except as otherwise provided in § 302.212(d), answers shall be filed within twenty one (21) days of the original or amended application and shall be served in accordance with § 302.203.

(b) Replies to answers shall be filed within fourteen (14) days after the filing of the answer.

(c) Persons having common interests shall, to the extent practicable, arrange for the joint preparation of pleadings.

§ 302.205 Economic data and other facts.

Whenever economic data and other facts are provided in any pleading, such information shall include enough detail so that final results can be obtained without further clarification. Sources, bases, and methodology used in constructing exhibits, including any estimates or judgments, shall be provided.

§ 302.206 Verification.

Any pleading filed under this subpart shall include a certification as provided in § 302.4(b).

DISPOSITION OF APPLICATIONS

§ 302.207 Cases to be decided on written submissions.

(a) Applications under this subpart will be decided on the basis of written submissions unless the DOT decisionmaker, on petition as provided in § 302.208 or on his or her own initiative, determines that an oral presentation or an administrative law judge's decision is required because:

(1) Use of written procedures will prejudice a party;

(2) Material issues of decisional fact cannot adequately be resolved without oral evidentiary hearing procedures; or

(3) Assignment of an application for oral evidentiary hearing procedures or an initial or recommended decision by an administrative law judge is otherwise required by the public interest.

(b) The standards employed in deciding cases under § 302.210(a)(1) or (5) shall be the same as the standards applied in cases decided under § 302.210(a)(4). These are the standards set forth in the Statute as interpreted and expanded upon under that Statute.

§ 302.208 Petitions for oral presentation or judge's decision.

(a) Any person may file a petition for oral evidentiary hearing, oral argument, an initial or recommended decision, or any combination of these. Petitions shall demonstrate that one or more of the criteria set forth in § 302.207 are applicable to the issues for which an oral presentation or judge's decision is requested. Such petitions shall be supported by a detailed explanation of the following:

(1) Why the evidence or argument to be presented cannot be submitted in the form of written evidence or briefs;

(2) Which issues should be examined by an administrative law judge and why such issues should not be presented directly to the DOT decisionmaker for decision;

(3) An estimate of the time required for the oral presentation and the number of witnesses whom the petitioner would present; and

(4) If cross-examination of any witness is desired, the name of the witness, if known, the subject matter of the desired cross-examination or the title or number of the exhibit to be cross-examined, what the petitioner expects to establish by the cross-examination, and an estimate of the time needed for it.

(b) Petitions for an oral hearing, oral argument, or an administrative law judge's decision shall be filed no later than the due date for answers in proceedings governed by §§ 302.211, 302.212

and 302.213, and be accompanied with the information specified in paragraphs (a)(1) and (a)(2) of this section. Filing of the information required in paragraphs (a)(3) and (a)(4) of this section may be deferred until the DOT decisionmaker has decided to hold a formal proceeding.

(c) Where a stipulation of disputed facts would eliminate the need for an oral presentation or an administrative law judge's decision, parties shall include in their petitions an offer to withdraw the request should the stipulation be made.

§ 302.209 Procedures for deferral of applications.

Within twenty-eight (28) days after the filing of an application under this subpart, the DOT decisionmaker may defer further processing of the application until all of the information necessary to process that application is submitted. The time periods contained in this subpart with respect to the disposition of the application shall not begin to run until the application is complete. In addition, the DOT decisionmaker may defer action on a foreign air carrier permit application for foreign policy reasons.

§ 302.210 Disposition of applications; orders establishing further procedures.

(a) *General requirements.* The DOT decisionmaker will take one of the following actions with respect to all or any portion of each application:

(1) Issue an Order to Show Cause why the application should not be granted, denied or dismissed, in whole or in part.

(2) Issue a Final Order granting the application if the DOT decisionmaker determines that there are no material issues of fact that warrant further procedures for their resolution.

(3) Issue a Final Order dismissing or rejecting the application for lack of prosecution or if the application does not comply with this subpart or is otherwise materially deficient.

(4) Issue an order setting the application for oral evidentiary hearing. The order will establish the scope of the issues to be considered and the procedures to be employed, and will indicate whether one or more attorneys from the Office of the Assistant General Counsel for Aviation Enforcement and Proceedings will participate as a party. All of the procedures set forth in §§ 302.214 through 302.218 will apply unless the DOT decisionmaker decides otherwise.

(5) Begin to make a determination with respect to the application under simplified procedures without oral evidentiary hearing. In this event, the DOT decisionmaker may indicate which, if any, of the procedural steps set forth in §§ 302.215 through 302.219 will be employed. The DOT decisionmaker may also indicate that other non-oral evidentiary hearing procedures will be employed.

(b) *Additional evidence.* An order establishing further procedures under paragraph (a)(1), (4) or (5) of this section may provide for the filing of additional evidence.

(c) *Petitions for reconsideration.* Petitions for reconsideration of an order issued under this section will not be entertained except to the extent that the order dismissed or rejected all or part of an application. If a petition for reconsideration results in the reinstatement of all or part of an application, the deadline for final Department decision established in § 302.220 will be calculated from the date of the order reinstating the application.

§ 302.211 Procedures in certificate cases involving initial or continuing fitness.

(a) *Applicability.* This section applies to cases involving certificate authority under sections 41102 and 41103 of the Statute, including applications for new authority, renewals, amendments, modifications, suspensions, and transfers of such certificates, where the issues involve a determination of the applicant's fitness to operate. Where such applications propose the operation of scheduled service in limited entry international markets, the provisions of § 302.212 also apply.

(b) *Order establishing further procedures.* Within 90 days after a complete application is filed, the DOT decisionmaker will take action as provided in § 302.210.

§ 302.212 Procedures in certificate cases involving international routes.

(a) *Applicability.* This section applies to cases involving certificates under section 41102 of the Statute that involve international routes, including applications to obtain, renew, amend, transfer, or remove restrictions in such certificates.

(b) *Answers to applications.* Answers shall be filed within twenty one (21) days after the filing of the original application.

(c) *Conforming applications or motions to modify scope.* Any person may file an application for the same authority as sought in an application to obtain, renew, or amend a certificate filed under paragraph (a) of this section. Requests to modify the issues to be decided and to consolidate applications filed in other dockets shall be filed as a "motion to modify scope." Motions and applications under this section shall include economic data, other facts, and any argument in support of the person's position and must be filed within twenty one (21) days after the original application is filed. Later-filed competing applications shall conform to the base and forecast years used by the original applicant and need not contain traffic and financial data for markets for which data have already been submitted by another person.

(d) *Answers to conforming applications or motions to modify scope.* Answers to conforming applications and motions to modify scope filed in accordance with paragraph (b) of this section shall be filed within fourteen (14) days after the filing of the conforming application or motion. Answers may argue that an application should be dismissed. Answers may also seek to consolidate an application filed in another docket if that application conforms to the scope of the proceeding proposed in the motion to modify scope and includes the information prescribed in § 302.202. Answers and applications shall not, however, propose the consideration of additional markets.

(e) *Order establishing further procedures.* Within 90 days after a complete application is filed, the DOT decisionmaker will issue an order as provided in § 302.210.

§ 302.213 Procedures in foreign air carrier permit cases.

(a) *Applicability.* This section applies to cases involving foreign air carrier permits under section 41302 of the Statute, including applications for new authority, renewals, amendments, modifications, suspensions, and transfers of such permits.

(b) *Executive departments.* In addition to the standards set forth in § 302.207(b), the views of other executive agencies, such as the Department of State, and the Federal Aviation Administration's evaluation of the applicant's operational fitness, may be sought in determining the appropriate action on applications filed under this section.

(c) *Order establishing further procedures.* As soon as possible after the date that answers are due and all information needed to reach a decision is filed, the DOT decisionmaker will issue an order as provided in § 302.210.

§ 302.214 Oral evidentiary hearing.

If the DOT decisionmaker determines under § 302.210(a)(4) that an oral evidentiary hearing should be held, the application or applications will be set for oral hearing before an administrative law judge. The issues will be those set forth in the order establishing further procedures. The procedures in §§ 302.17 to 302.38 governing the conduct of oral evidentiary hearings will apply.

§ 302.215 Briefs to the administrative law judge.

Briefs to the administrative law judge shall be filed within the following periods, as applicable:

(a) Fourteen (14) days after the close of the oral evidentiary hearing, unless the administrative law judge determines that, under the circumstances of the case, briefs are not necessary or that the parties will require more time to prepare briefs; or

(b) Fourteen (14) days after the filing of additional evidence called for in the order establishing further procedures if no oral evidentiary hearing is called for, unless the DOT decisionmaker determines that some other period should be allowed.

§ 302.216 Administrative law judge's initial or recommended decision.

(a) In a case that has been set for oral evidentiary hearing under § 302.210(a)(4), the administrative law judge shall adopt and serve an initial or recommended decision within one hundred thirty-six (136) days after the issuance of the order establishing further procedures unless:

(1) The DOT decisionmaker, having found extraordinary circumstances, has by order delayed the initial or recommended decision by a period of not more than thirty (30) days; or

(2) An applicant has failed to meet the procedural schedule adopted by the judge or the DOT decisionmaker. In this case, the administrative law judge may, by notice, extend the due date for the issuance of an initial or recommended decision for a period not to exceed the period of delay caused by the applicant.

(b) In a case in which some of the issues have not been set for oral hearing under § 302.210(a)(4), the administrative law judge shall adopt and serve an initial or recommended decision within the time established by the DOT decisionmaker in the order establishing further procedures, except that that due date may be extended in accordance with paragraph (a)(2) of this section.

(c) The initial or recommended decision shall be issued by the administrative law judge fourteen (14) days after it is served. Unless exceptions are filed under § 302.217 or the DOT decisionmaker issues an order to review on his or her own initiative, an initial decision shall become effective as the final order of the Department the day it is issued. Where exceptions are timely filed or the DOT decisionmaker takes action to review on his or her own initiative, the effectiveness of the initial decision is stayed until further order of the DOT decisionmaker.

(d) In all other respects, the provisions of § 302.31 shall apply.

§ 302.217 Exceptions to administrative law judge's initial or recommended decision.

(a) Within seven (7) days after service of any initial or recommended decision of an administrative law judge, any party may file exceptions to the decision with the DOT decisionmaker.

(b) If timely and adequate exceptions are filed, review of the initial or recommended decision is automatic.

(c) In all other respects, the provisions of § 302.34 shall apply.

§ 302.218 Briefs to the DOT decisionmaker.

(a) In a case in which an initial or recommended decision has been served and exceptions have been filed, any party may file a brief in support of or in opposition to any exceptions. Such briefs shall be filed within fourteen (14) days after service of the initial or recommended decision.

(b) In a case in which no exceptions have been filed, briefs shall not be filed unless the DOT decisionmaker has taken review of the initial or recommended decision on his or her own initiative and has specifically provided for the filing of such briefs.

(c) In all other respect, the provisions of § 302.35 shall apply.

§ 302.219 Oral argument before the DOT decisionmaker.

If the order establishing further procedures provides for an oral argument, or if the DOT decisionmaker otherwise decides to hear oral argument, all parties will be notified of the date and hour set for that argument and the amount of time allowed each party. The provisions of § 302.36(b) shall also apply.

§ 302.220 Final decision of the Department.

In addition to the provisions of § 302.38, the following provisions shall apply.

(a) In the case of a certificate application that has been set for oral evidentiary hearing under § 302.210(a)(4), the Department will issue its final order within ninety (90) days after the initial or recommended decision is issued. If an application has failed to meet the procedural schedule established by the Department, the DOT decisionmaker may, by notice, extend the date for a final decision for a period equal to the period of delay caused by the applicant.

(b) If the DOT decisionmaker does not act in the time period established in paragraph (a) of this section:

(1) in the case of an application for a certificate to engage in foreign air transportation, the recommended decision shall be transmitted to the President of the United States under 49 U.S.C. 41307; or

(2) in the case of an application not subject to review by the President of the United States, the initial decision shall become effective as the final order of the Department.

(c) In the case of a certificate application that has been processed under § 302.210(a)(1) or (5), the Department will issue its final order within one hundred eighty (180) days after the order establishing further procedures. If an applicant has failed to meet the procedural schedule established by the Department, the DOT decisionmaker may, by notice, extend the due date for a final decision for a period equal to the period of delay caused by the applicant.

Subpart C—Rules Applicable to Exemption and Certain Other Proceedings

§ 302.301 Applicability.

(a) This subpart sets forth the specific rules applicable to proceedings for exemptions under sections 40109 and 41714 of the Statute, including the granting of emergency exemptions, as well as applications for frequency allocations and other limited authority under international agreements. Except as modified by this subpart, the provisions of subpart A of this part apply.

(b) Proceedings for the issuance of exemptions by regulation are subject to the provisions governing rulemaking.

§ 302.302 Filing of applications.

(a) Except as provided in paragraphs (b) and (c) of this section, applications for exemption shall conform to the requirements of §§ 302.3 and 302.4.

(b) Applications for exemption from section 41101 or 41301 of the Statute (including those that incorporate an exemption from section 41504) that involve ten (10) or fewer flights may be submitted to the U.S. Air Carrier Licensing Division or the Foreign Air Carrier Licensing Division (as appropriate), Office of International Aviation, on OST Form 4536. However, that form may not be used for:

(1) Applications filed under section 40109(g) of the Statute;

(2) Applications by persons who do not have either:

(i) An effective air carrier certificate or foreign air carrier permit from the Department, or

(ii) A properly completed application for such a certificate or permit, and an effective exemption from the Department for operations similar to those proposed;

(3) Successive applications for the same or similar authority that would total more than ten (10) flights; or

(4) Any other application for which the Department decides the requirements of §§ 302.3 and 302.4 are more appropriate. Upon a showing of good cause, an application may be filed by cablegram, telegram, facsimile, electronic mail (when available), or telephone; all such telephonic requests must be confirmed by written application within three (3) business days of the original request.

(c) Applications for exemption from Chapter 415 of the Statute, from tariffs (except for waivers filed under subpart Q of part 221 of this chapter), or from Department regulations concerning tariffs may be submitted by letter. Three copies of such applications shall be sent to Department of Transportation Dockets. Upon a showing of good cause, the application may also be filed by cablegram, telegram, facsimile, electronic mail (when available), or telephone; all such requests must be confirmed by written application within three (3) business days of the original request.

(d) Applications filed under paragraph (a) of this section shall be docketed and any additional documents filed shall be identified by the assigned docket number.

(e) Applications filed under paragraph (b) or (c) of this section will normally not be docketed. The Department may require such applications to be docketed if appropriate. The Department will publish a notice of such applications in its Weekly List of Applications Filed.

§ 302.303 Contents of applications.

(a) *Title.* An application filed under § 302.302(a) shall be entitled "Application for . . ." (followed by the type of authority request, e.g., exemption, frequency allocation) and, where applicable, shall state if the application involves renewal and/or amendment of existing exemption authority.

(b) *Factual statement.* Each application shall state:

(1) The section(s) of the Statute or the rule, regulation, term, condition, or limitation from which the exemption is requested;

(2) The proposed effective date and duration of the exemption;

(3) A description of how the applicant proposes to exercise the authority (for example, applications for exemption from section 41101 or 41301 of the Statute should include at least: places to be served; equipment types, capacity and source; type and frequency or service; and other operations that the proposed service will connect with or support); and

(4) Any other facts the applicant relies upon to establish that the proposed service will be consistent with the public interest.

(c) *Supporting evidence.* (1) Each application shall be accompanied by:

(i) A statement of economic data, or other matters or information that the applicant desires the Department to officially notice;

(ii) Affidavits, or statements under penalty of 18 U.S.C. 1001, establishing any other facts the applicant wants the Department to rely upon; and

(iii) Information showing the applicant is qualified to perform the proposed services.

(2) In addition to the information required by paragraph (c)(1) of this section, an application for exemption from section 41101 or 41301 of the Statute (except exemptions under section 40109(g)) shall state whether the authority sought is governed by a bilateral agreement or by principles of comity and reciprocity. Applications by foreign carriers shall state whether the applicant's homeland government grants U.S. carriers authority similar to that requested. If so, the application shall state whether the fact of reciprocity has been established by the Department and cite the pertinent finding. If the fact of reciprocity has not been established by the Department, the application shall include documentation to establish such reciprocity.

(d) *Emergency cabotage.* Applications under section 40109(g) of the Statute shall, in addition to the information required in paragraphs (b) and (c) of this section, contain evidence showing that:

(1) Because of an emergency created by unusual circumstances not arising in the normal course of business, traffic in the markets requested cannot be accommodated by air carriers holding certificates under section 41102 of the Statute;

(2) All possible efforts have been made to accommodate the traffic by using the resources of such air carriers (including, for example, the use of foreign aircraft, or sections of foreign aircraft, under lease or charter to such air carriers, and the use of such air carriers' reservation systems to the extent practicable);

(3) The authority requested is necessary to avoid unreasonable hardship for the traffic in the market that cannot be accommodated by air carriers; and

(4) In any case where an inability to accommodate traffic in a market results from a labor dispute, the grant of the requested exemption will not result in an unreasonable advantage to any party in the dispute.

(e) *Renewal applications.* An application requesting renewal of an exemption or other limited authority under this subpart that is intended to invoke the automatic extension provisions of 5 U.S.C. 558(c) shall comply with, and contain the statements and information required by part 377 of this chapter.

(f) *Record of service.* An application shall list the parties served as required by § 302.304.

§ 302.304 Service of documents.

(a) *General requirements.* (1) An application for exemption and responsive pleadings shall be served as provided by § 302.7.

(2) Applicants shall serve on the persons listed in paragraph (b) of this section a complete copy of the application and any supporting documents. Responsive pleadings shall be served on the same persons as applications.

(b) *Persons to be served.* (1) Applicants for scheduled interstate air transportation authority shall serve:

(i) All U.S. air carriers (including commuter air carriers) that publish schedules in the *Official Airline Guide* or the *Air Cargo Guide* for the city-pair market(s) specified in the application,

(ii) The airport authority of each U.S. airport that the applicant proposes to serve, and

(iii) Any other person who has filed a pleading in a related proceeding under section 41102, 41302, or 40109 of the Statute.

(2) Applicants for scheduled foreign air transportation authority shall serve:

(i) All U.S. air carriers (including commuter air carriers) that publish schedules in the *Official Airline Guide* or in the *Air Cargo Guide* for the country-pair market(s) specified in the application,

(ii)The airport authority of each U.S. airport that the applicant proposes to serve, and

(iii) Any other person who has filed a pleading in a related proceeding under section 41102, 41302, or 40109 of the Statute.

(3) Applicants for charter-only or nonscheduled-only authority shall serve any person who has filed a pleading in a related proceeding under section 41102, 41302, or 40109 of the Statute. However, applicants that file fewer than sixteen (16) days prior to the proposed start of service must also serve:

(i) Those U.S. carriers (including commuter carriers) that are known to be operating in the general market(s) at issue and

(ii) Those persons who may be presumed to have an interest in the subject matter of the application.

(4) Applicants for slot exemptions under section 41714 of the Statute shall serve:

(i) All U.S. air carriers (including commuter air carriers) that publish schedules in the *Official Airline Guide* or the *Air Cargo Guide* for the airport(s) specified in the application,

(ii) The manager of each of the affected airports,

(iii) The mayor of the city that each affected airport serves,

(iv) The Governor of the State in which each affected airport is located, and

(v) Any other person who has filed a pleading in a related proceeding under section 41714 of the Statute.

(5) *Additional service.* The Department may, in its discretion, order additional service upon any other person.

[Doc. No. OST-97-2090, 65 FR 6457, Feb. 9, 2000; 65 FR 7418, Feb. 14, 2000]

§ 302.305 Posting of applications.

A copy of every docketed application for exemption shall be posted in Department of Transportation Dockets and listed in the Department's Weekly List of Applications Filed. A copy of every undocketed application shall be posted in the Licensing Division's lobby of the Office of International Aviation.

§ 302.306 Dismissal or rejection of incomplete applications.

(a) *Dismissal or rejection.* The Department may dismiss or reject any application for exemption that does not comply with the requirements of this part.

(b) *Additional data.* The Department may require the filing of additional data with respect to any application for exemption, answer, or reply.

§ 302.307 Answers to applications.

Within fifteen (15) days after the filing of an application for exemption, any person may file an answer in support of or in opposition to the grant of a requested exemption. Such answer shall set forth in detail the reasons why the exemption should be granted or denied. An answer shall include a statement of economic data or other matters the Department is requested to officially notice, and shall be accompanied by affidavits establishing any other facts relied upon.

§ 302.308 Replies to answers.

Within seven (7) days after the last day for filing an answer, any interested party may file a reply to one or more answers.

§ 302.309 Requests for hearing.

The Department will not normally conduct oral evidentiary hearings concerning applications for exemption. However, the Department may, in its discretion, order such a hearing on an application. Any applicant, or any person opposing an application, may request an oral evidentiary hearing. Such a request shall set forth in detail the reasons why the filing of affidavits or other written evidence will not permit the fair and expeditious disposition of the application. A request relying on factual assertions shall be accompanied by affidavits establishing such facts. If the Department orders an oral evidentiary hearing, the procedures in subpart A of this part shall apply.

§ 302.310 Exemptions on the Department's initiative.

The Department may grant exemptions on its own initiative when it finds that such exemptions are required by the circumstances and consistent with the public interest.

§ 302.311 Emergency exemptions.

(a) *Shortened procedures.* When required by the circumstances and consistent with the public interest, the Department may take action, without notice, on exemption applications prior to the expiration of the normal period for filing answers and replies. When required in a particular proceeding, the Department may specify a lesser time for the filing of answers and replies, and notify interested persons of this time period.

(b)(1) *Applications.* Applications for emergency exemption need not conform to the requirements of this subpart or of subpart A of this part (except as provided in this section and in § 302.303(d) concerning emergency cabotage requests). However, an application for emergency exemption must normally be in writing and must state in detail the facts and evidence that support the application, the grounds for the exemption, and the public interest basis for the authority sought. In addition, the application shall state specific reasons that justify departure from the normal exemption application procedures. The application shall also identify those persons notified as required by paragraph (c) of this section. The Department may require additional information from any applicant before acting on an application.

(2) *Oral requests.* The Department will consider oral requests, including telephone requests, for emergency exemption authority under this section in circumstances that do not permit the immediate filing of a written application. All oral requests must, however, provide the information required in paragraph (b)(1) of this section, except that actual evidence in support of the application need not be tendered when the request is made. All oral requests must be confirmed by written application, together with all supporting evidence, within three (3) business days of the original request.

(c) *Notice.* Except when the Department decides that no notice need be given, applicants for emergency exemption shall notify, as appropriate, those persons specified in § 302.304(b) of this subpart. Such notification shall be made in the same manner, contain the same information, and be dispatched at the same time, as the application made to the Department.

Subpart D—Rules Applicable to Enforcement Proceedings

§ 302.401 Applicability.

This subpart contains the specific rules that apply to Department proceedings to enforce the provisions of Subtitle VII of the Statute, and the rules, regulations, orders and other requirements issued by the Department, as well as the filing of informal and formal complaints. Except as modified by this subpart, the provisions of subpart A of this part apply.

§ 302.402 Definitions.

Assistant General Counsel, when used in this subpart, refers to the Assistant

General Counsel for Aviation Enforcement and Proceedings.

Complainant refers to the person filing a complaint.

Parties, when used in this subpart, include the Office of the Assistant General Counsel, the respondent, the complainant, and any other person permitted to intervene under §302.20.

Respondent refers to the person against whom a complaint is filed.

§302.403 Informal complaints.

Any person may submit in writing to the Assistant General Counsel an informal complaint with respect to anything done or omitted to be done by any person in contravention of any provision of the Statute or any requirement established thereunder. Such informal complaints need not otherwise comply with the provisions of this part. Matters so presented may, if their nature warrants, be handled by correspondence or conference with the appropriate persons. Any matter not disposed of informally may be made the subject of an enforcement proceeding pursuant to this subpart. The filing of an informal complaint shall not bar the subsequent filing of a formal complaint.

§302.404 Formal complaints.

(a) *Filing.* Any person may make a formal complaint to the Assistant General Counsel about any violation of the economic regulatory provisions of the Statute or of the Department's rules, regulations, orders, or other requirements. Every formal complaint shall conform to the requirements of §§302.3 and 302.4, concerning the form and filing of documents. The filing of a complaint shall result in the institution of an enforcement proceeding only if the Assistant General Counsel issues a notice instituting such a proceeding as to all or part of the complaint under §302.406(a) or the Deputy General Counsel does so under §302.406(c).

(b) *Amendment.* A formal complaint may be amended at any time before service of an answer to the complaint. After service of an answer but before institution of an enforcement proceeding, the complaint may be amended with the permission of the Assistant General Counsel. After institution of an enforcement proceeding, the complaint may be amended only on grant of a motion filed under §302.11.

(c) *Insufficiency of formal complaint.* In any case where the Assistant General Counsel is of the opinion that a complaint does not sufficiently set forth matters required by any applicable rule, regulation or order of the Department, or is otherwise insufficient, he or she may advise the complainant of the deficiency and require that any additional information be supplied by amendment.

(d) *Joinder of complaints or complainants.* Two or more grounds of complaints involving substantially the same purposes, subject or state of facts may be included in one complaint even though they involve more than one respondent. Two or more complainants may join in one complaint if their respective causes of complaint are against the same party or parties and involve substantially the same purposes, subject or state of facts. The Assistant General Counsel may separate or split complaints if he or she finds that the joinder of complaints, complainants, or respondents will not be conducive to the proper dispatch of the Department's business or the ends of justice.

(e) *Service.* A formal complaint, and any amendments thereto, shall be served by the person filing such documents upon each party complained of, upon the Deputy General Counsel, and upon the Assistant General Counsel.

§302.405 Responsive documents.

(a) *Answers.* Within fifteen (15) days after the date of service of a formal complaint, each respondent shall file an answer in conformance with and subject to the requirements of §302.408(b). Extensions of time for filing an answer may be granted by the Assistant General Counsel for good cause shown.

(b) *Offers to satisfy.* A respondent in a formal complaint may offer to satisfy the complaint through submission of facts, offer of settlement or proposal of adjustment. Such offer shall be in writing and shall be served, within fifteen (15) days after service of the complaint, upon the same persons and in the same manner as an answer. The submittal of an offer to satisfy the complaint shall not excuse the filing of an answer.

(c) *Motions to dismiss.* Motions to dismiss a formal complaint shall not be filed prior to the filing of a notice instituting an enforcement proceeding with respect to such complaint or a portion thereof.

§ 302.406 Procedure for responding to formal complaints.

(a) Within a reasonable time after an answer to a formal complaint is filed, the Assistant General Counsel shall either:

(1) Issue a notice instituting a formal enforcement proceeding in accordance with § 302.407 or

(2) Issue an order dismissing the complaint in whole or in part, stating the reasons for such dismissal.

(b) An order dismissing a complaint issued pursuant to paragraph (a)(2) of this section shall become effective as a final order of the Department thirty (30) days after service thereof.

(c) Whenever the Assistant General Counsel has failed to act on a formal complaint within a reasonable time after an answer is due, the following motions may be addressed to the Deputy General Counsel:

(1) By the complainant to institute an enforcement proceeding by docketing the complaint upon a showing that it is in the public interest to do so; and

(2) By the respondent to dismiss the complaint upon a showing that it is in the public interest to do so.

(d) The Deputy General Counsel may grant, deny, or defer any of the motions, in whole or in part, and take appropriate action to carry out his or her decision.

§ 302.407 Commencement of enforcement proceeding.

(a) Whenever in the opinion of the Assistant General Counsel there are reasonable grounds to believe that any economic regulatory provision of the Statute, or any rule, regulation, order, limitation, condition, or other requirement established pursuant thereto, has been or is being violated, that efforts to satisfy a complaint as provided by § 302.405 have failed, and that the investigation of any or all of the alleged violations is in the public interest, the Assistant General Counsel may issue a notice instituting an enforcement proceeding before an administrative law judge.

(b) The notice shall incorporate by reference the formal complaint submitted pursuant to § 302.404 or shall be accompanied by a complaint by an attorney from the Office of the Assistant General Counsel. The notice and accompanying complaint, if any, shall be formally served upon each respondent and each complainant.

(c) The proceedings thus instituted shall be processed in regular course in accordance with this part. However, nothing in this part shall be construed to limit the authority of the Department to institute or conduct any investigation or inquiry within its jurisdiction in any other manner or according to any other procedures that it may deem necessary or proper.

(d) Whenever the Assistant General Counsel seeks an assessment of civil penalties in an enforcement proceeding, he or she shall serve on all parties to the proceeding a notice of the violations alleged and the amount of penalties for which the respondent may be liable. The notice may be included in the notice instituting a formal enforcement proceeding or in a separate document.

(e) In any proceeding in which civil penalties are sought, any decisions issued by the Department shall state the amount of any civil penalties assessed upon a finding of violation, and the time and manner in which payment shall be made to the United States.

§ 302.408 Answers and replies.

(a) Within fifteen (15) days after the date of service of a notice issued pursuant to § 302.407, the respondent shall file an answer to the complaint attached thereto or incorporated therein unless an answer has already been filed in accordance with § 302.405. Any requests for extension of time for filing of an answer to such complaint shall be filed in accordance with § 302.11.

(b) All answers shall be served in accordance with § 302.7 and shall fully and completely advise the parties and the

Department as to the nature of the defense and shall admit or deny specifically and in detail each allegation of the complaint unless the respondent is without knowledge, in which case, his or her answer shall so state and the statement shall operate as a denial. Allegations of fact not denied or controverted shall be deemed admitted. Matters alleged as affirmative defenses shall be separately stated and numbered and shall, in the absence of a reply, be deemed to be controverted. Any answer to a complaint, or response to a notice, proposing the assessment of civil penalties shall specifically present any matters that the respondent intends to rely upon in opposition to, or in mitigation of, such civil penalties.

(c) The DOT decisionmaker or the administrative law judge may, in his or her discretion, require or permit the filing of a reply in appropriate cases; otherwise, no reply may be filed.

§302.409 Default.

Failure of a respondent to file and serve an answer within the time and in the manner prescribed by §302.408 shall be deemed to authorize the DOT decisionmaker or administrative law judge, as a matter of discretion, to find the facts alleged in the complaint incorporated in or accompanying the notice instituting a formal enforcement proceeding to be true and to enter such orders as may be appropriate without notice or hearing, or, as a matter of discretion, to proceed to take proof, without notice, of the allegations or charges set forth in the complaint or order; *Provided*, that the DOT decisionmaker or administrative law judge may permit late filing of an answer for good cause shown.

§302.410 Consolidation of proceedings.

The DOT decisionmaker or Chief Administrative Law Judge may, upon his or her own initiative, or upon motion of any party, consolidate for hearing or for other purposes, or may contemporaneously consider, two or more enforcement proceedings that involve substantially the same parties or issues that are the same or closely related, if he or she finds that such consolidation or contemporaneous hearing will be conducive to the dispatch of business and to the ends of justice and will not unduly delay the proceedings.

§302.411 Motions to dismiss and for summary judgment.

(a) At any time after an answer has been filed, any party may file with the DOT decisionmaker or the administrative law judge a motion to dismiss or a motion for summary judgment, including supporting affidavits. The procedure on such motions shall be in accordance with the Federal Rules of Civil Procedure (28 U.S.C.), particularly Rules 6(d), 7(b), 12, and 56, except that answers and supporting papers to a motion to dismiss or for summary judgment shall be filed within seven (7) days after service of the motion.

(b) Parties may petition the DOT decisionmaker to review any action by the administrative law judge granting summary judgment or dismissing an enforcement proceeding under the procedure established for review of an initial decision in §302.32.

§302.412 Admissions as to facts and documents.

(a) At any time after an answer has been filed, any party may file with the DOT decisionmaker or administrative law judge and serve upon the opposing side a written request for the admission of the genuineness and authenticity of any relevant documents described in and exhibited with the request or for the admission of the truth of any relevant matters of fact stated in the request with respect to such documents.

(b) Each of the matters of which an admission is requested shall be deemed admitted unless within a period designated in the request, not less than ten (10) days after service thereof, or within such further time as the DOT decisionmaker or the administrative law judge may allow upon motion and notice, the party to whom the request is directed serves upon the requesting party a sworn statement either denying specifically the matters of which an admission is requested or setting forth in detail the reasons why he or she cannot truthfully either admit or deny such matters.

(c) Service of such request and answering statement shall be made as provided in § 302.7. Any admission made by a party pursuant to such request is only for the purposes of the pending proceeding, or any proceeding or action instituted for the enforcement of any order entered therein, and shall not constitute an admission by him or her for any other purpose or be used against him or her in any other proceeding or action.

§ 302.413 Evidence of previous violations.

Evidence of previous violations by any person or of any provision of the Statute or any requirement thereunder found by the Department or a court in any other proceeding or criminal or civil action may, if relevant and material, be admitted in any enforcement proceeding involving such person.

§ 302.414 Prehearing conference.

A prehearing conference may be held in an enforcement proceeding whenever the administrative law judge believes that the fair and expeditious disposition of the proceeding requires one. If a prehearing conference is held, it shall be conducted in accordance with § 302.22.

§ 302.415 Hearing.

After the issues have been formulated, whether by the pleadings or otherwise, the administrative law judge shall give the parties reasonable written notice of the time and place of the hearings. Except as may be modified by the provisions of this subpart, the procedures in §§ 302.17 to 302.38 governing the conduct of oral evidentiary hearings will apply.

§ 302.416 Appearances by persons not parties.

With consent of the administrative law judge, appearances may be entered without request for or grant of permission to intervene by interested persons who are not parties to the proceeding. Such persons may, with the consent of the administrative law judge, cross-examine a particular witness or suggest to any party or counsel therefor questions or interrogations to be asked witnesses called by any party, but may not otherwise examine witnesses and may not introduce evidence or otherwise participate in the proceeding. However, such persons may present to both the administrative law judge and the DOT decisionmaker an oral or written statement of their position on the issues involved in the proceeding.

§ 302.417 Settlement of proceedings.

(a) The Deputy General Counsel and the respondent may agree to settle all or some of the issues in an enforcement proceeding at any time before a final decision is issued by the DOT decisionmaker. The Deputy General Counsel shall serve a copy of any proposed settlement on each party and shall submit the proposed settlement to the administrative law judge for approval. The submission of a proposed settlement shall not automatically delay the proceeding.

(b) Any party to the proceeding may submit written comments supporting or opposing the proposed settlement within ten (10) days from the date of service.

(c) The administrative law judge shall approve the proposed settlement, as submitted, if it appears to be in the public interest, or otherwise shall disapprove it.

(d) Information relating to settlement offers and negotiations will be withheld from public disclosure if the Deputy General Counsel determines that disclosure would interfere with the likelihood of settlement of an enforcement proceeding.

§ 302.418 Motions for immediate suspension of operating authority pendente lite.

All motions for the suspension of the economic operating authority of an air carrier during the pendency of proceedings to revoke such authority shall be filed with, and decided by, the DOT decisionmaker. Proceedings on the motion shall be in accordance with § 302.11. In addition, the DOT decisionmaker shall afford the parties an opportunity for oral argument on such motion.

§302.419 Modification or dissolution of enforcement actions.

Whenever any party to a proceeding, in which an order of the Department has been issued pursuant to section 46101 of the Statute or an injunction or other form of enforcement action has been issued by a court of competent jurisdiction pursuant to section 46106 of the Statute, believes that changed conditions of fact or law or the public interest require that said order or judicial action be modified or set aside, in whole or in part, such party may file with the Department a motion requesting that the Department take such administrative action or join in applying to the appropriate court for such judicial action, as the case may be. The motion shall state the changes desired and the changed circumstances warranting such action, and shall include the materials and argument in support thereof. The motion shall be served on each party to the proceeding in which the enforcement action was taken. Within thirty (30) days after the service of such motion, any party so served may file an answer thereto. The Department shall dispose of the motion by such procedure as it deems appropriate.

§302.420 Saving clause.

Repeal, revision or amendment of any of the economic regulatory provisions of the Statute or of the Department's rules, regulations, orders, or other requirements shall not affect any pending enforcement proceeding or any enforcement proceeding initiated thereafter with respect to causes arising or acts committed prior to said repeal, revision or amendment, unless the act of repeal, revision or amendment specifically so provides.

Subpart E—Rules Applicable to Proceedings With Respect to Rates, Fares and Charges for Foreign Air Transportation

§302.501 Applicability.

This subpart sets forth the special rules applicable to proceedings with respect to rates, fares and charges in foreign air transportation under Chapter 415 of the Statute. Except as modified by this subpart, the provisions of subpart A apply.

§302.502 Institution of proceedings.

A proceeding to determine the lawfulness of rates, fares, or charges for the foreign air transportation of persons or property by aircraft, or the lawfulness of any classification, rule, regulation, or practice affecting such rates, fares or charges, may be instituted by the filing of a petition or complaint by any person, or by the issuance of an order by the Department.

§302.503 Contents and service of petition or complaint.

(a) If a petition or complaint is filed it shall state the reasons why the rates, fares, or charges, or the classification, rule, regulation, or practice complained of are unlawful and shall support such reasons with a full factual analysis.

(b) A petition or complaint shall be served by the petitioner or complainant upon the air carrier against whose tariff provision the petition or complaint is filed.

(c) Answers to complaints, other than those filed under §302.506, shall be filed within seven (7) working days after the complaint is filed.

§302.504 Dismissal of petition or complaint.

If the Department is of the opinion that a petition or complaint does not state facts that warrant an investigation or action on its part, it may dismiss such petition or complaint without hearing.

§302.505 Order of investigation.

The Department, on its own initiative, or if it is of the opinion that the facts stated in a petition or complaint warrant it, may issue an order instituting an investigation of the lawfulness of any present or proposed rates, fares, or charges for the foreign air transportation of persons or property by aircraft or the lawfulness of any classification, rule, regulation, or practice affecting such rates, fares, or charges, and may assign the proceeding for hearing before an administrative law judge. If a hearing is held, except as modified by this subpart, the provisions of § 302.17 through § 302.38 of this part shall apply.

§ 302.506 Complaints requesting suspension of tariffs; answers to such complaints.

(a) Formal complaints seeking suspension of tariffs pursuant to section 41509 of the Statute shall fully identify the tariff and include reference to:

(1) The issued or posting date,

(2) The effective date,

(3) The name of the publishing carrier or agent,

(4) The Department number, and

(5) Specific items or particular provisions protested or complained against. The complaint should indicate in what respect the tariff is considered to be unlawful, and state what complainant suggests by way of substitution.

(b) A complaint requesting suspension of a tariff ordinarily will not be considered unless made in conformity with this section and filed no more than ten (10) days after the issued date contained within such tariff.

(c) A complaint requesting suspension, pursuant to section 41509 of the Statute, of an existing tariff for foreign air transportation may be filed at any time. However, such a complaint must be accompanied by a statement setting forth compelling reasons for not having requested suspension within the time limitations provided in paragraph (b) of this section.

(d) In an emergency satisfactorily shown by the complainant, and within the time limits herein provided, a complaint may be sent by facsimile, telegram, or electronic mail (when available) to the Department and to the carrier against whose tariff provision the complaint is made. Such complaint shall state the grounds relied upon, and must be confirmed in writing within three (3) business days and filed and served in accordance with this part.

(e) Answers to complaints shall be filed within six (6) working days after the complaint is filed.

§ 302.507 Computing time for filing complaints.

In computing the time for filing formal complaints pursuant to § 302.506, with respect to tariffs that do not contain a posting date, the first day preceding the effective date of the tariff shall be the first day counted, and the last day so counted shall be the last day for filing unless such day is a Saturday, Sunday, or legal holiday for the Department, in which event the period for filing shall be extended to the next successive day that is not a Saturday, Sunday, or holiday. The computation of the time for filing complaints as to tariffs containing a posting date shall be governed by § 302.8.

Subpart F—Rules Applicable to Proceedings Concerning Airport Fees

§ 302.601 Applicability.

(a) This subpart contains the specific rules that apply to a complaint filed by one or more air carriers or foreign air carriers ("carriers"), pursuant to 49 U.S.C. 47129(a), for a determination of the reasonableness of a fee increase or a newly established fee for aeronautical uses that is imposed upon the carrier by the owner or operator of an airport. This subpart also applies to requests by the owner or operator of an airport for such a determination. An airport owner or operator is considered to have imposed a fee on a carrier when it has taken all steps necessary under its procedures to establish the fee, whether or not the fee is being collected or carriers are currently required to pay it.

(b) This subpart does not apply to—

(1) A fee imposed pursuant to a written agreement with a carrier using the facilities of an airport;

(2) A fee imposed pursuant to a financing agreement or covenant entered into prior to August 23, 1994, or

(3) Any other existing fee not in dispute as of August 23, 1994.

(c) Except as modified by this subpart, the provisions of subpart A of this part apply.

§ 302.602 Complaint by a carrier; request for determination by an airport owner or operator.

(a) Any carrier may file a complaint with the Secretary for a determination as to the reasonableness of any fee imposed on the carrier by the owner or operator of an airport. Any airport owner or operator may also request such a determination with respect to a fee it has imposed on one or more carriers. The complaint or request for determination shall conform to the requirements of this subpart and §§ 302.3 and 302.4 concerning the form and filing of documents.

(b) If a carrier has previously filed a complaint with respect to the same airport fee or fees, any complaint by another carrier and any airport request for determination shall be filed no later than seven (7) calendar days following the initial complaint. In addition, all complaints or requests for determination must be filed on or before the sixtieth (60th) day after the carrier receives written notice of the imposition of the new fee or the imposition of the increase in the fee.

(c) To ensure an orderly disposition of the matter, all complaints and any request for determination filed with respect to the same airport fee or fees will be considered in a consolidated proceeding, as provided in § 302.606.

§ 302.603 Contents of complaint or request for determination.

(a) The complaint or request for determination shall set forth the entire grounds for requesting a determination of the reasonableness of the airport fee. The complaint or request shall include a copy of the airport owner or operator's written notice to the carrier of the imposition of the fee, a statement of position with a brief, and all supporting testimony and exhibits on which the filing party intends to rely. In lieu of submitting duplicative exhibits or testimony, the filing party may incorporate by reference testimony and exhibits already filed in the same proceeding.

(b) All exhibits and briefs prepared on electronic spreadsheet or word processing programs should be accompanied by standard-format computer diskettes containing those submissions. The disk submission must be in one of the following formats, in the latest two versions, or in such other format as may be specified by notice in the FEDERAL REGISTER: Microsoft Word (or RTF), Word Perfect, Ami Pro, Microsoft Excel, Lotus 123, Quattro Pro, or ASCII tab-delineated files. Parties should submit three copies of each diskette to Department of Transportation Dockets: one copy for the docket, one copy for the Office of Hearings, and one copy for the Office of Aviation Analysis. Filers should ensure that files on the diskettes are unalterably locked.

(c) When a carrier files a complaint, it must also certify:

(1) That it has served on the airport owner or operator and all other carriers serving the airport the complaint, brief, and all supporting testimony and exhibits, and that those parties have received or will receive these documents no later than the date the complaint is filed. Such service shall be by hand, by electronic transmission, or by overnight express delivery. (Unless a carrier has informed the complaining carrier that a different person should be served, service may be made on the person responsible for communicating with the airport on behalf of the carrier about airport fees.);

(2) That the carrier has previously attempted to resolve the dispute directly with the airport owner or operator;

(3) That when there is information on which the carrier intends to rely that is not included with the brief, exhibits, or testimony, the information has been omitted because the airport owner or operator has not made that information available to the carrier. The certification shall specify the date and form of the carrier's request for information from the airport owner or operator; and

(4) That any submission on computer diskette is a true copy of the data file used to prepare the printed versions of the exhibits or briefs.

(d) When an airport owner or operator files a request for determination, it must also certify:

(1) That it has served on all carriers serving the airport the request, brief, and all supporting testimony and exhibits, and that those parties have received or will receive these documents no later than the date the request is filed. Such service shall be in the same manner as provided in § 302.603(c)(1).

(2) That the airport owner or operator has previously attempted to resolve the dispute directly with the carriers; and

(3) That any submission on computer diskette is a true copy of the data file used to prepare the printed versions of the exhibits or briefs.

§ 302.604 Answers to a complaint or request for determination.

(a)(1) When a carrier files a complaint under this subpart, the owner or operator of the airport and any other carrier serving the airport may file an answer to the complaint as provided in paragraphs (b) and (c) of this section.

(2) When the owner or operator of an airport files a request for determination of the reasonableness of a fee it has imposed, any carrier serving the airport may file an answer to the request.

(b) The answer to a complaint or request for determination shall set forth the answering party's entire response. When one or more additional complaints or a request for determination has been filed pursuant to § 302.602(b) with respect to the same airport's fee or fees, the answer shall set forth the answering party's entire response to all complaints and any such request for determination. The answer shall include a statement of position with a brief and any supporting testimony and exhibits on which the answering party intends to rely. In lieu of submitting duplicative exhibits or testimony, the answering party may incorporate by reference testimony and exhibits already filed in the same proceeding.

(c) Answers to a complaint shall be filed no later than fourteen (14) calendar days after the filing date of the first complaint with respect to the fee or fees in dispute at a particular airport. Answers to a request for determination shall be filed no later than fourteen (14) calendar days after the filing date of the request.

(d) All exhibits and briefs prepared on electronic spreadsheet or word processing programs should be accompanied by standard-format computer diskettes containing those submissions as provided in § 302.603(b).

(e) The answering party must also certify that:

(1) it has served the answer, brief, and all supporting testimony and exhibits by hand, by electronic transmission, or by overnight express delivery on the carrier filing the complaint or the airport owner or operator requesting the determination, and that those parties have received or will receive these documents no later than the date the answer is filed; and

(2) that any submission on computer diskette is a true copy of the data file used to prepare the printed versions of the exhibits or briefs.

§ 302.605 Replies.

(a) The carrier submitting a complaint may file a reply to any or all of the answers to the complaint. The airport owner or operator submitting a request for determination may file a reply to any or all of the answers to the request for determination.

(b) The reply shall be limited to new matters raised in the answers. It shall constitute the replying party's entire response to the answers. It shall be in the form of a reply brief and may include supporting testimony and exhibits responsive to new matters raised in the answers. In lieu of submitting duplicative exhibits or testimony, the replying party may incorporate by reference testimony and exhibits already filed in the same proceeding.

(c) The reply shall be filed no later than two (2) calendar days after answers are filed.

(d) All exhibits and briefs prepared on electronic spreadsheet or word processing programs should be accompanied by standard-format computer diskettes containing those submissions as provided in § 302.603(b).

(e) The carrier or airport owner or operator submitting the reply must certify that it has served the reply and all supporting testimony and exhibits on the party or parties submitting the answer to which the reply is directed, and that those parties have received or will receive these documents no later than the date the reply is filed, and that any submission on computer diskette is a true copy of the data file used to prepare the printed versions of the exhibits or briefs.

§302.606 Review of complaints or requests for determination.

(a) Within thirty (30) days after a complaint or request for determination is filed under this subpart, the Secretary will determine whether the complaint or request meets the procedural requirements of this subpart and whether a significant dispute exists, and take appropriate action pursuant to paragraph (b), (c), or (d) of this section. When both a complaint and a request for determination have been filed with respect to the same airport fee or fees, the Secretary will issue a determination as to whether the complaint, the request, or both meet the procedural requirements of this subpart and whether a significant dispute exists within thirty (30) days after the complaint is filed.

(b) If the Secretary determines that a significant dispute exists, he or she will issue an instituting order assigning the complaint or request for hearing before an administrative law judge. The instituting order will—

(1) Establish the scope of the issues to be considered and the procedures to be employed;

(2) Indicate the parties to participate in the hearing;

(3) Consolidate into a single proceeding all complaints and any request for determination with respect to the fee or fees in dispute; and

(4) Include any special provisions for exchange or disclosure of information by the parties.

(c) If the Secretary determines that the complaint or request does not meet the procedural requirements of this subpart, the complaint or request for determination will be dismissed without prejudice to filing a new complaint. The order of the Secretary will set forth the terms and conditions under which a revised complaint or request may be filed.

(d) If the Secretary finds that no significant dispute exists—

(1) If the proceeding was instituted by a complaint, the Secretary will issue an order dismissing the complaint, which will contain a concise explanation of the reasons for the determination that the dispute is not significant.

(2) If the proceeding was instituted by a request for determination, the Secretary will either issue a final order as provided in §302.610 or set forth the schedule for any additional procedures required to complete the proceeding.

§302.607 Decision by administrative law judge.

The administrative law judge shall issue a decision recommending a disposition of a complaint or request for determination within sixty (60) days after the date of the instituting order, unless a shorter period is specified by the Secretary.

§302.608 Petitions for discretionary review.

(a) Within five (5) calendar days after service of a decision by an administrative law judge, any party may file with the Secretary a petition for discretionary review of the administrative law judge's decision.

(b) Petitions for discretionary review shall comply with §302.32(a). The petitioner must also certify that it has served the petition by hand, by electronic transmission, or by overnight express delivery on all parties to the proceeding and that those parties have received or will receive the petition no later than the date it is filed.

(c) Any party may file an answer in support of or in opposition to any petition for discretionary review. The answer shall be filed within four (4) calendar days after service of the petition for discretionary review. The answer shall comply with the page limits specified in §302.32(b).

§302.609 Completion of proceedings.

(a) When a complaint or a request for determination with respect to an airport fee or fees has been filed under this subpart and has not been dismissed, the Secretary will issue a determination as to whether the fee is reasonable within 120 days after the complaint or request is filed.

(b) When both a complaint and a request for determination have been filed with respect to the same airport fee or fees and have not been dismissed, the Secretary will issue a determination as to whether the fee is reasonable within 120 days after the complaint is filed.

§ 302.610 Final order.

(a) When a complaint or request for determination stands submitted to the Secretary for final decision on the merits, he or she may dispose of the issues presented by entering an appropriate order, which will include a statement of the reasons for his or her findings and conclusions. Such an order shall be deemed a final order of the Secretary.

(b) The final order of the Secretary shall include, where necessary, directions regarding an appropriate refund or credit of the fee increase or newly established fee which is the subject of the complaint or request for determination.

(c) If the Secretary has not issued a final order within 120 days after the filing of a complaint by an air carrier or foreign air carrier, the decision of the administrative law judge shall be deemed to be the final order of the Secretary.

Subpart G—Rules Applicable to Mail Rate Proceedings and Mail Contracts

§ 302.701 Applicability.

(a) This subpart sets forth the special rules applicable to proceedings for the establishment of mail rates by the Department for foreign air transportation and air transportation between points in Alaska, and certain contractual arrangements between the U.S. Postal Service and certificated air carriers for the carriage of mail in foreign air transportation entered into pursuant to 39 U.S.C. 5402(a), 84 Stat. 772.

(b) Such contracts must be for the transportation of at least 750 pounds of mail per flight, and no more than five (5) percent, based on weight, of the international mail transported under any such contract may consist of letter mail.

FINAL MAIL RATE PROCEEDINGS

§ 302.702 Institution of proceedings.

(a) Proceedings for the determination of rates of compensation for the transportation of mail may be commenced by the filing of a petition by an air carrier whose rate is to be fixed, or the U.S. Postal Service, or upon the issuance of an order by the DOT decisionmaker.

(b) The petition shall set forth the rate or rates sought to be established, a statement that they are believed to be fair and reasonable, the reasons supporting the request for a change in rates, and a detailed economic justification sufficient to establish the reasonableness of the rate or rates proposed.

(c) In any case where an air carrier is operating under a final mail rate uniformly applicable to an entire ratemaking unit as established by the DOT decisionmaker, a petition must clearly and unequivocally challenge the rate for such entire rate-making unit and not only a part of such unit.

(d) All petitions, amended petitions, and documents relating thereto shall be served upon the U.S. Postal Service by sending a copy to the Assistant General Counsel, Transportation Division, Washington, DC 20260–1124, by registered or certified mail, postpaid, prior to the filing thereof with the Department. Proof of service on the U.S. Postal Service shall consist of a statement in the document that the person filing it has served a copy as required by this section.

(e) Answers to petitions shall be filed within twenty (20) days after service of the petition.

§ 302.703 Order to show cause or instituting a hearing.

Whether the proceeding is commenced by the filing of a petition or upon the Department's own initiative, the DOT decisionmaker may issue an order directing the respondent to show cause why it should not adopt such findings and conclusions and such final rates as may be specified in the order to show cause, or may issue an order setting the matter for hearing before an administrative law judge.

§ 302.704 Objections and answers to order to show cause.

(a) Where an order to show cause is issued, any person having objections to the rates specified in such order shall file with the DOT decisionmaker an answer within forty-five (45) days after the date of service of such order or within such other period as the order may specify.

(b) An answer to an order to show cause shall contain specific objections, and shall set forth the findings and conclusions, the rates, and the supporting exhibits that would be substituted for the corresponding items in the findings and conclusions of the show cause order, if such objections were found valid.

(c) An answer filed by a person who is neither a party nor a person ultimately permitted to intervene in an oral evidentiary hearing if such proceeding is established shall be treated as a memorandum filed under §302.706.

§302.705 Further procedures.

(a) If no answer is filed within the designated time, or if a timely filed answer raises no material issue of fact, the DOT decisionmaker may, upon the basis of the record in the proceeding, enter a final order fixing the rate or rates.

(b) If an answer raising a material issue of fact is filed within the time designated in the Department's order, the DOT decisionmaker may then issue an order authorizing additional pleadings and/or establishing further procedural steps, including setting the matter for oral evidentiary hearing before an administrative law judge.

§302.706 Hearing.

(a) If a hearing is ordered under §302.705, the issues at such hearing shall be formulated in accordance with the instituting order, except that at a prehearing conference, the administrative law judge may permit the parties to raise such additional issues as he or she deems necessary to make a full determination of a fair and reasonable rate.

(b)(1) The parties to the proceeding shall be the air carrier or carriers for whom rates are to be fixed, the U.S. Postal Service, the Office of the Assistant General Counsel for Aviation Enforcement and Proceedings and any other person whom the DOT decisionmaker or administrative law judge permits to intervene in accordance with §302.20.

(2) In addition to participation in hearings in accordance with §302.19, persons other than parties may, within the time fixed for filing an answer to an order to show cause as provided in §302.704, submit a memorandum of opposition to, or in support of, the position taken in the petition or order. Such memorandum shall not be received as evidence in the proceeding.

(c) All direct evidence shall be in writing and shall be filed in exhibit form within the times specified by the DOT decisionmaker or by the administrative law judge.

(d) Except as modified by this subpart, the provisions of §§302.17 through 302.38 of this part shall apply.

Provision for Temporary Rate

§302.707 Procedure for fixing temporary mail rates.

At any time during the pendency of a proceeding for the determination of final mail rates, the DOT decisionmaker, upon his or her own initiative, or on petition by the air carrier whose rates are in issue or by the U.S. Postal Service, may fix temporary rates of compensation for the transportation of mail subject to downward or upward adjustment upon the determination of final mail rates.

Informal Mail Rate Conference Procedure

§302.708 Invocation of procedure.

(a) Conferences between DOT employees, representatives of air carriers, the U.S. Postal Service and other interested persons may be called by DOT employees for the purpose of considering and clarifying issues and factual material in pending proceedings for the establishment of rates for the transportation of mail.

(b) At the commencement of an informal mail rate conference pursuant to this section, the authorized DOT employees conducting such conference shall issue to each person present at such conference a written statement to the effect that such conference is being conducted pursuant to this section and stating the time of commencement of such conference; and at the termination of such conference the DOT employees conducting such conference shall note in writing on such statement the time of termination of such conference.

§ 302.709 Scope of conferences.

The mail rate conferences shall be limited to the discussion of, and possible agreement on, particular issues and related factual material in accordance with sound rate-making principles. The duties and powers of DOT employees in rate conferences essentially will not be different, therefore, from the duties and powers they have in the processing of rate cases not involving a rate conference. The employees' function in both instances is to present clearly to the DOT decisionmaker the issues and the related material facts, together with recommendations. The DOT decisionmaker will make an independent determination of the soundness of the employees's analyses and recommendations.

§ 302.710 Participants in conferences.

The persons entitled to be present in mail rate conferences will be the representatives of the carrier whose rates are in issue, the staff of the U.S. Postal Service, and the authorized DOT employees. No other person will attend unless the DOT employees deem his or her presence necessary in the interest of one or more purposes to be accomplished, and in such case his or her participation will be limited to such specific purposes. No person, however, shall have the duty to attend merely by reason of invitation by the authorized DOT employees.

§ 302.711 Conditions upon participation.

(a) *Nondisclosure of information.* As a condition to participation, every participant, during the period of the conference and for ninety (90) days after its termination, or until the Department takes public action with respect to the facts and issues covered in the conference, whichever is earlier:

(1) Shall, except for necessary disclosures in the course of employment in connection with conference business, hold the information obtained in conference in absolute confidence and trust;

(2) Shall not deal, directly or indirectly, for the account of himself or herself, his or her immediate family, members of his or her firm or company, or as a trustee, in securities of the air carrier involved in the rate conference except that under exceptional circumstances special permission may be obtained in advance from the DOT decisionmaker; and

(3) Shall adopt effective controls for the confidential handling of such information and shall instruct personnel under his or her supervision, who by reason of their employment come into possession of information obtained at the conference, that such information is confidential and must not be disclosed to anyone except to the extent absolutely necessary in the course of employment, and must not be misused. (The term "information", as used in this section, shall refer only to information obtained at the conference regarding the future course of action or position of the Department or its employees with respect to the facts or issues discussed at the conference.)

(b) *Signed statement required.* Every representative of an air carrier actually present at any conference shall sign a statement that he or she has read this entire instruction and promises to abide by it and advise any other participant to whom he or she discloses any confidential information of the restrictions imposed above. Every representative of the U.S. Postal Service actually present at any conference shall, on his or her own behalf, sign a statement to the same effect.

(c) *Presumption of having conference information.* A director of any air carrier that has had a representative at the conference, who deals either directly or indirectly for himself or herself, his or her immediate family, members of his or her firm or company, or as a trustee, in securities of the air carrier involved in the conference, during the restricted period set forth above, shall be presumed to have come into possession of information obtained at the conference knowing that such information was subject to the restrictions imposed above; but such presumption can be rebutted.

(d) *Compliance report required.* Within ten (10) days after the expiration of the time specified for keeping conference matters confidential, every participant, as defined in paragraph (e) of this section, shall file a verified compliance report with Department of Transportation Dockets stating that he or she has complied in every respect with the conditions of this section, or if he or she has not so complied, stating in detail in what respects he or she has failed to comply.

(e) *Persons subject to the provisions of this section.* For the purposes of this section, participants shall include:

(1) Any representative of any air carrier and any representative of the U.S. Postal Service actually present at the conference;

(2) The directors and the officers of any air carrier that had a representative at the conference;

(3) The members of any firm of attorneys or consultants that had a representative at the conference; and

(4) The members of the U.S. Postal Service staff who come into possession of information obtained at the conference, knowing that such information is subject to the restrictions imposed in this section.

§302.712 Information to be requested from an air carrier.

When an air carrier is requested to submit detailed estimates as to traffic, revenues and expenses by appropriate periods and the investment that will be required to perform the operations for a future period, full and adequate support shall be presented for all estimates, particularly where such estimates deviate materially from the air carrier's experience. With respect to the rate for a past period, essentially the same procedure shall be followed. Other information or data likewise may be requested by the DOT employees. All data submitted by the air carrier shall be certified by a responsible officer.

§302.713 DOT analysis of data for submission of answers thereto.

After a careful analysis of these data, the DOT employees will, in most cases, send the air carrier a statement of exceptions showing areas of differences. Where practicable, the air carrier may submit an answer to these exceptions. Conferences will then be scheduled to resolve the issues and facts in accordance with sound ratemaking principles.

§302.714 Availability of data to the U.S. Postal Service.

The representatives of the U.S. Postal Service shall have access to all conference data and, insofar as practicable, shall be furnished copies of all pertinent data prepared by the DOT employees and the air carrier, and a reasonable time shall be allowed to review the facts and issues and to make any presentation deemed necessary; *Provided,* That in cases other than those involving an issue as to the service mail rates payable by the U.S. Postal Service pursuant to section 41901 of the Statute, representatives of the U.S. Postal Service shall be furnished with copies of data under this provision only upon their written request.

§302.715 Post-conference procedure.

No briefs, argument, or any formal steps will be entertained by the DOT decisionmaker after the rate conferences. The form, content and time of the staff's presentation to the DOT decisionmaker are entirely matters of internal procedure. Any party to the mail rate proceeding may, through an authorized DOT employee, request the opportunity to submit a written or oral statement to the DOT decisionmaker on any unresolved issue. The DOT decisionmaker will grant such requests whenever he or she deems such action desirable in the interest of further clarification and understanding of the issues. The granting of an opportunity for such further presentation shall not, however, impair the rights that any party might otherwise have under the Statute and this part.

§302.716 Effect of conference agreements.

No agreements or understandings reached in rate conferences as to facts or issues shall in any respect be binding on the Department or any participant. Any party to mail rate proceedings will have the same rights to file an answer and take other procedural steps as though no rate conference had been held. The fact, however, that a rate conference was held and certain agreements or understandings may have been reached on certain facts and issues renders it proper to provide that, upon the filing of an answer by any party to the rate proceeding, all issues going to the establishment of a rate shall be open, except insofar as limited in prehearing conference in accordance with § 302.22.

§ 302.717 Waiver of participant conditions.

After the termination of a mail rate conference hereunder, the air carrier whose rates were in issue may petition the DOT decisionmaker for a release from the obligations imposed upon it and all other persons by § 302.711. The DOT decisionmaker will grant such petition only after a detailed and convincing showing is made in the petition and supporting exhibits and documents that there is no reasonable possibility that any of the abuses sought to be prevented will occur or that the Department's processes will in any way be prejudiced. There will be no hearing or oral argument on the petition and the DOT decisionmaker will grant or deny the request without being required to assign reasons therefor.

PROCESSING CONTRACTS FOR THE CARRIAGE OF MAIL IN FOREIGN AIR TRANSPORTATION

§ 302.718 Filing.

Any air carrier that is a party to a contract to which this subpart is applicable shall file three (3) copies of the contract in the Office of Aviation Analysis, X–50, Department of Transportation, Washington, DC 20590, not later than ninety (90) days before the effective date of the contract. A copy of such contract shall be served upon the persons specified in § 302.720 and the certificate of service shall specify the persons upon whom service has been made. One copy of each contract filed shall bear the certification of the secretary or other duly authorized officer of the filing air carrier to the effect that such copy is a true and complete copy of the original written instrument executed by the parties.

§ 302.719 Explanation and data supporting the contract.

Each contract filed pursuant to this subpart shall be accompanied by economic data and such other information in support of the contract upon which the filing air carrier intends that the Department rely, including, in cases where pertinent, estimates of the annual volume of contract mail (weight and ton-miles) under the proposed contract, the nature of such mail (letter mail, parcel post, third class, etc.), together with a statement as to the extent to which this traffic is new or diverted from existing classes of air and surface mail services and the priority assigned to this class of mail.

§ 302.720 Service.

A copy of each contract filed pursuant to § 302.718, and a copy of all material and data filed pursuant to § 302.719, shall be served upon each of the following persons:

(a) Each certificated and commuter (as defined in § 298.2 of this chapter) air carrier, other than the contracting carrier, that is actually providing scheduled mail services between any pair of points between which mail is to be transported pursuant to the contract; and

(b) The Assistant General Counsel, Transportation Division, U.S. Postal Service, Washington, DC 20260–1124.

§ 302.721 Complaints.

Within fifteen (15) days of the filing of a contract, any interested person may file with the Office of Aviation Analysis, X–50, Department of Transportation, Washington, DC 20590, a complaint with respect to the contract setting forth the basis for such complaint and all pertinent information in support of same. A copy of the complaint shall be served upon the air carrier filing the contract and upon each of the persons served with such contract pursuant to § 302.720.

§ 302.722 Answers to complaints.

Answers to the complaint may be filed within ten (10) days of the filing of the complaint, with service being made as provided in § 302.720.

§ 302.723 Further procedures.

(a) In any case where a complaint is filed, the DOT decisionmaker shall issue an order dismissing the complaint, disapproving the contract, or taking such other action as may be appropriate. Any such order shall be issued not later than ten (10) days prior to the effective date of the contract.

(b) In cases where no complaint is filed, the DOT decisionmaker may issue a letter of notification to all persons upon whom the contract was served indicating that the Department does not intend to disapprove the contract.

(c) Unless the DOT decisionmaker disapproves the contract not later than ten (10) days prior to its effective date, the contract automatically becomes effective.

§ 302.724 Petitions for reconsideration.

Except in the case of a Department determination to disapprove a contract, no petitions for reconsideration of any Department determination pursuant to this subpart shall be entertained.

APPENDIX A TO PART 302—INDEX TO RULES OF PRACTICE

Appendix A shows the subjects covered by part 302 and the section numbers used before and after the final rule revising part 302, published in the FEDERAL REGISTER on February 9, 2000 and became effective on March 10, 2000.

Subject	Old rule	New rule
ADMINISTRATIVE LAW JUDGES:		
Actions after hearings	§ 302.27(b)	§ 302.31(a)
Actions during prehearing conference	§ 302.23(a)	§ 302.22(b)
Arguments before	§ 302.25	§ 302.29
Briefs	§ 302.26	§ 302.30
Licensing cases	§ 302.1752	§ 302.215
Certification for decision	§ 302.22(d)	§ 302.31(b)
Definition	§ 302.22(a)	§ 302.2
Delegation of authority	§ 302.27(a)	§ 307.17(a)(3)
Exceptions	§ 302.27(a)	§ 307.17(a)(3)
Interlocutory matters	§ 302.27(a)	§ 307.17(a)(3)
Disqualification	§ 302.22(b)	§ 302.17(b)
Exceptions	§ 302.24(e)	§ 302.24(i)
Licensing cases	§ 302.1754	§ 302.217
Hearings before	§ 302.24	§ 302.23
Initial decision (*see* Initial Decision).		
Powers	§ 302.22(c)	§ 302.17(a)
Prehearing conference report	§ 302.23(b)	§ 302.22(c)
Recommended decision (*see* Recommended Decision).		
Termination of authority	§ 302.22(c)	§ 307.17(a)(4)
ADMISSIONS:		
Enforcement proceeding	§ 302.212	§ 302.412
Limitation on use	§ 302.212	§ 302.412(c)
AIRPORT FEES:		
Administrative law judge decision	§ 302.615	§ 302.607
Complaints by U.S. or foreign air carriers	§ 302.603(a)	§ 302.602(a)
Answers	§ 302.607	§ 302.604
Additional complaints	§ 302.603(b)	§ 302.602(b)
Contents	§ 302.605	§ 302.603
Format of exhibits and briefs	§ 302.605(b)	§ 302.603(b)
Service	§ 302.605(c)(1)	§ 302.603(c)(1)
Replies	§ 302.609	§ 302.605
Consolidation of proceedings	§ 302.603(c)	§ 302.602(c)
Dismissal	§§ 302.611(c), (d)	§§ 302.606(c), (d)
Final order	§ 302.621	§ 302.610
Timing	§ 302.619	§ 302.609
Instituting order	§ 302.611(b)	§ 302.606(b)
Petitions for discretionary review	§ 302.617	§ 302.608
Answers	§ 302.617(c)	§ 302.608(c)
Request for determination by airport owner/operator	§ 302.603(a)	§ 302.602(a)
Answers	§ 302.607	§ 302.604
Contents	§ 302.605	§ 302.603
Format of exhibits and briefs	§ 302.605(b)	§ 302.603(b)
Service	§ 302.605(d)(1)	§ 302.603(d)(1)
Replies	§ 302.609	§ 302.605

Subject	Old rule	New rule
Review procedures	§ 302.611	§ 302.606
Significant dispute determination	§ 302.611(b)	§ 302.606(b)
AMENDMENTS OF DOCUMENTS (*see* Documents)		
ANSWERS (*see also* Replies):		
Airport fees	§ 302.607	§ 302.604
Certificate applications:		
Initial fitness	§ 302.1730(c)	§ 302.204
International route awards		
Conforming applications	§ 302.1720(d)	§ 302.212(d)
Motions to modify scope	§ 302.1720(e)	§ 302.212(d)
New authority	§ 302.1720(d)	§ 302.212(b)
Complaints		
Air mail contracts	§ 302.1506	§ 302.722
Airport fees	§ 302.607	§ 302.604
Enforcement matters	§ 302.204(b)	§ 302.405
Suspension of tariffs	§ 302.505	§ 302.506
Consolidation of proceedings	§ 302.12(c)	§ 302.13(c)
Enforcement proceeding, notice instituting	§ 302.207	§ 302.408
Exemption applications	§ 302.406	§ 302.307
Foreign air carrier permit applications	§ 302.1740(c)	§ 302.204
Generally	§ 302.6	§ 302.6
Mail rate proceedings show cause orders	§ 302.305	§ 302.704
Motions, generally	§ 302.18(c)	§ 302.11(c)
Motions to consolidate	§ 302.12(c)	§ 302.13(c)
Motions to dismiss and for summary judgment	§ 302.212	§ 302.411
Motions for modification/dissolution of enforcement proceedings	§ 302.218	§ 302.419
Petitions for discretionary review	§ 302.28(b)	§ 302.32(b)
Petitions for final mail rates	§ 302.303	§ 302.702(e)
Petitions for intervention	§ 302.15(c)(3)	§ 302.20(c)(3)
Petitions for reconsideration	§ 302.37a	§ 302.14
Requests for determination of airport fees	§ 302.607	§ 302.607
APPEALS:		
Administrative Law Judge's ruling	§ 302.18(f)	§ 302.11(h)
Enforcement complaints	§ 302.206(b)	§ 302.406(c)
APPEARANCES:		
Generally	§ 302.11	§ 302.21
Application for admission to practice unnecessary	§ 302.11(a)	§ 302.21(b)
Copy of transcript	§ 302.11(c)	§ 302.27(b)
Retention of counsel	§ 302.11(b)	§ 302.27(a)
Enforcement proceedings	§ 302.214	§ 302.416
APPLICATIONS:		
Admission to practice unnecessary	§ 302.11(a)	§ 302.21(b)
Suspension from practicing before DOT	§ 302.11(a)	§ 302.21(c)
Amendment	§ 302.5	§ 302.5
Certificates for international route awards	§§ 302.1701–1713, 1720	§§ 302.201–206
Conforming applications	§ 302.1720(c)	§ 302.212(c)
Certificates involving initial fitness	§§ 302.1701–1713, 1730	§§ 302.201–206
Consolidation	§ 302.12	§ 302.13
Exemptions	§§ 302.401–405	§§ 302.302–304
Exemptions, emergency	§§ 302.410(b), (c)	§ 302.311
Foreign Air Carrier Permits	§§ 302.1701–1713, 1740	§§ 302.201–206
Licensing cases	§§ 302.1701–1750	§§ 302.201–206
ARGUMENT:		
Before Administrative Law Judge	§ 302.25	§ 302.29
Oral (*see* Oral Arguments)		
ATTENDANCE FEES AND MILEAGE	§ 302.21	§ 302.27(c)
BRIEFS:		
Accompanying motions or answers	§ 302.18(d)	§ 302.11(d)
Failure to restate objections	§ 302.31(b)	§ 302.35(b)
Filing time	§ 302.31(a)	§ 302.35(a)
Formal specifications	§ 302.31(c)	§ 302.35(c)
Incorporation by reference	§ 302.31(b)	§ 302.35(c)(2)
Licensing cases	§§ 302.302.1752, 1755	§§ 302.215, 218
To Administrative Law Judge	§ 302.26	§ 302.30
Licensing cases	§ 302.1752	§ 302.215
To DOT decisionmaker	§ 302.31	§ 302.35
Licensing cases	§ 302.1755	§ 302.218
CERTIFICATE CASES FOR U.S. AIR CARRIERS:		

Subject	Old rule	New rule
Application:		
Answers to	§§ 302.1720(d) 1730(d)	§ 302.204(a)
Contents of	§ 302.1704	§ 302.202
Incomplete	§ 302.1713	§ 302.209
Replies to answers	....	§ 302.204(b)
Service of	§ 302.1705	§ 302.203
Supporting evidence	§ 302.1710	§§ 302.202(a), 205
Verification	§ 302.1707	§ 302.206
Continuing Fitness	§ 302.1730	§ 302.211
Non-hearing procedures	§ 302.1712(a)	§ 302.207
Generally	§§ 302.1701–1790	§§ 302.201–220
Initial Fitness	§ 302.1730	§ 302.211
International Route Awards	§ 302.1720	§ 302.212
Oral evidentiary hearing proceedings	§§ 302.1751–1757	§§ 302.214–220
Petition for	§ 302.1712(b)	§ 302.208
CERTIFICATION:		
Documents	§ 302.4(b)	§ 302.4(b)
Record	§§ 302.22(d), 27, 29	§ 302.31(b)
CHARGES (*see* Rates, Fairs, and Charges; Airport Fees)		
CITATION OF RULES	§ 302.2	§ 302.1(c)
CIVIL PENALTIES	§ 302.206(a)	§§ 302.407(d), (e)
COMPLAINANTS, JOINDER	§ 302.13	§ 302.404(d)
COMPLAINTS:		
Airport fees	§§ 302.603–605	§§ 302.602–603
Contracts for transportation of mail	§§ 302.1505–1507	§ 302.721
Enforcement proceedings	§§ 302.200–204	§§ 302.403–404
Joinder	§ 302.13	§ 302.404(d)
Rates, fares, and charges	§§ 302.501–508	§§ 302.501–507
Suspension of tariffs	§§ 302.505–508	§ 302.506
COMPUTATION OF TIME (*see also* Time)	§ 302.16	§ 302.8
CONSOLIDATION OF PROCEEDINGS	§ 302.12	§ 302.13
Airport fees	§ 302.603(c)	§ 302.602(c)
Answer to motion for	§ 302.12(c)	§ 302.13(c)
Enforcement proceedings	§ 302.210(a)	§ 302.410
Filing time	§ 302:12(b)	§ 302.13(b)
Initiation of	§ 302.12(a)	§ 302.13(a)
CONTINUING FITNESS CERTIFICATE CASES	§ 302.1701–1713	§ 302.212
CONTRACTS (*see* Mail Contracts)		
DECISIONS:		
Final	§ 302.36	§§ 302.38, 220
Initial (*see* Administrative Law Judges)		
Recommended (*see* Administrative Law Judges)		
Tentative	§ 302.29	§ 302.33
Exceptions to	§ 302.30	§ 302.34
DEFINITIONS	NA	§§ 302.2, 402
DELEGATION OF AUTHORITY	§ 302.27	§§ 302.17(a), 18(a)
DEPOSITIONS:		
Application by party for	§ 302.20(b)	§ 302.26(b)
Criteria for order to issue	§ 302.20(a)	§ 302.26(a)
Evidential status	§§ 302.20(h)	§ 302.26(h)
Objections to questions or evidence	§ 302.2(d)	§ 302.26(d)
Specifications	§ 302.20(g)	§ 302.26(g)
Subscription by witness	§ 302.20(e)	§ 302.26(e)
Written interrogatories	§ 302.20(f)	§ 302.26(f)
DISCRETIONARY REVIEW:		
Initial and Recommended decisions	§ 302.28	§ 302.32
Answers in opposition or support	§ 302.28(b)	§ 302.32(b)
Formal requirements	§ 302.28(a)(3)	§§ 302.32(a)(3), (4)
Grounds for	§ 302.28(a)(2)	§ 302.32(a)(2)
Orders declining review	§ 302.28(c)	§ 302.32(c)
Oral arguments	§ 302.28(a)(5)	§ 302.32(a)(5)
Petitions for	§ 302.28(a)(1)	§ 302.32(a)(1)
Review proceedings	§ 302.28(d)	§ 302.32(d)
DISSOLUTION OF ENFORCEMENT ACTION	§ 302.218	§ 302.419
DOCUMENTS:		

Subject	Old rule	New rule
Amendments	§ 302.5	§ 302.5
Leave of Department	§ 302.5	§ 302.5(a)
Timing of	§ 302.5	§ 302.5(b)
Answers (*see* Answers)		
Briefs (*see* Briefs)		
Dismissal	§ 302.5	§ 302.3(d)
Electronic filing	NA	§ 302.3(c)
Exhibits	§§ 302.24(g)	§ 302.24(c)
Filing	§ 302.3	§ 302.3
Address	§ 302.3(a)	§ 302.3(a)
Date	§ 302.3(a)	§ 302.3(a)
Improper filing	§ 302.4e	§ 302.3(d)
Formal specifications	§ 302.3(b)	§ 302.3(b)
General requirements	§ 302.4	§ 302.4
Contents	§ 302.4(a)	§ 302.4(a)(2)
Designation of person to receive service	§ 302.4(c)	§ 302.4(a)
Subscription	§ 302.4(b)	§ 302.4(b)
Memoranda of opposition or support	§ 302.6(c)	§ 302.706(b)(2)
Number of copies	§ 302.3(c)	§ 302.3(c)
Objections to public disclosure	§ 302.39(b)	§ 302.12
Official Notice of facts	§ 302.24(n)	§ 302.24(g)
Partial relevance of	§ 302.24(l)	§ 302.24(e)
Presented at oral argument	§ 302.32(b)	§ 302.36(b)
Receipt after hearing	§ 302.24(k)	§ 302.24(h)
Responsive	§ 302.6	§ 302.6
Retention	§ 302.7	§ 302.3(f)
Service (*see* Service)		
Table of contents/Index	§ 302.3(d)	§ 302.4(a)(3)
Unauthorized	§ 302.4(f)	§ 302.6(c)
DOT DECISIONMAKER:		
Briefs to	§ 302.31	§ 302.35
Licensing cases	§ 302.1755	§ 302.218
Certification of record to	§ 302.22(d)	§ 302.31(b)
Definition	§ 302.22a	§§ 302.2, 18
Final decision	§ 302.36	§ 302.38
Licensing cases	§ 302.1757	§ 302.220
Oral argument	§ 302.32	§ 302.36
Licensing cases	§ 302.1756	§ 302.219
Petitions for reconsideration	§ 302.37	§ 302.14
Review of Administrative Law Judge decision	§ 302.38	§ 302.32
Tentative decision	§ 302.29	§ 302.33
Exceptions	§ 302.30	§ 302.34
ENFORCEMENT PROCEEDINGS:		
Admissions as to facts and documents	§ 302.212	§ 302.412
Complaints:		
Formal	§ 302.201	§ 302.404
Informal	§ 302.200	§ 302.403
Insufficiency of	§ 302.203	§ 302.404(c)
Consolidation of proceedings	§ 302.210a	§ 302.410
Evidence of previous violations	§ 302.216	§ 302.413
Generally	§§ 302.200–217	§§ 302.401–420
Hearings	§ 302.213	§ 302.415
Modification or dissolution of enforcement action	§ 302.218	§ 302.419
Motions to dismiss	§ 302.212	§ 302.411
Motions for summary judgment	§ 302.212	§ 302.402
Settlement proceedings	§ 302.215	§ 302.417
EVIDENCE:		
Exhibits	§§ 302.24(g), (h)	§§ 302.24(c), (d)
Generally	§ 302.24(c)	§ 302.24(a)
Objections to	§ 302.24(d)	§ 302.24(b)
Offers of proof	§ 302.24(f)	§ 302.24(j)
Official notice of facts in certain documents	§ 302.24(n)	§ 302.24(g)
Partial relevance of	§ 302.24(l)	§ 302.24(e)
Previous violations	§ 302.216	§ 302.413
Records in other proceedings	§ 302.24(j)	§ 302.24(f)
EXAMINERS (*see* Administrative Law Judges)		
EXCEPTIONS:		
Administrative Law Judge's rulings	§ 302.24(e)	§ 302.24(i)
Initial decisions	§ 302.30	§ 302.31(c)
Licensing cases	§ 302.1754	§ 302.217
Recommended decisions	§ 302.30	§ 302.31(c)
Request for oral argument	§ 302.32	§ 302.36
Tentative decisions	§ 302.30	§ 302.34
Waiver	§ 302.33	§ 302.37

Subject	Old rule	New rule
EXEMPTION PROCEEDINGS:		
Application:		
Answers to	§ 302.406	§ 302.307
Contents of	§ 302.402	§ 302.303
Filing of	§ 302.401	§ 302.302
Incomplete	§ 302.405	§ 302.306
Posting of	§ 302.404	§ 302.305
Service of	§ 302.403	§ 302.304
Reply to answer	§ 302.407	§ 302.308
Supporting evidence	§ 302.402(c)	§ 302.302(c)
DOT's initiative	§ 302.409	§ 302.310
Emergencies	§ 302.410	§ 302.311
Cabotage	§ 302.402(d)	§ 302.303(d)
Hearing request	§ 302.408	§ 302.309
EXHIBITS (*see also* Evidence):		
Generally	§ 302.24(g)	§§ 302.24(c), (d)
FARES (*see* Rates, Fares, and Charges)		
FEE (*see* Airport Fees)		
FINAL MAIL RATE PROCEEDINGS (*see* Mail Rate Proceedings)		
FINAL ORDERS (*see* Orders)		
FITNESS CASES (*see* Certificate Cases)		
FOREIGN AIR CARRIER PERMIT CASES:		
Application:		
Answers to	§ 302.1740(c)	§ 302.204(a)
Contents of	§ 302.1704	§ 302.202
Incomplete	§ 302.1713	§ 302.209
Replies to answers	....	§ 302.204(b)
Service of	§ 302.1705	§ 302.203
Supporting evidence	§ 302.1710	§§ 302.202(a), 205
Verification	§ 302.1707	§ 302.206
Non-hearing procedures	§ 302.1712(a)	§ 302.207
Generally	§§ 302.1701–1713, 1740–1790	§§ 302.201–220
Oral evidentiary hearing proceedings	§ 302.1751–1757	§§ 302.214–220
Petition for	§ 302.1712(b)	§ 302.208
HEARINGS:		
Airport fee dispute proceedings	§ 302.611(b)	§ 302.606(b)
Argument before Administrative Law Judge	§ 302.25	§ 302.29
Change in rates, fares, or charges	§ 302.506	§ 302.706
Consolidated (*see* Consolidation of Proceedings)		
Documents of partial relevance	§ 302.24(i)	§ 302.24(e)
Enforcement proceedings	§ 302.213	§ 302.415
Evidence (*see* Evidence)		
Expedition of	§ 302.14(a)	§ 302.11(e)
Generally	§ 302.24	§ 302.23
Intervention	§ 302.15	§ 302.20
Licensing cases	§ 302.1751	§ 302.214
Notice	§ 302.24(b)	§ 302.23
Offers of proof	§ 302.24(f)	§ 302.24(j)
Official notice of facts in certain documents	§ 302.24(n)	§ 302.24(g)
Participation by non parties	§ 302.14(b)	§ 302.19
Receipt of documents after hearing	§ 302.24(k)	§ 302.24(h)
Records in other proceedings	§ 302.24(j)	§ 302.24(f)
Request for, on application for exemption	§ 302.408	§ 302.309
Shortened procedure	§ 302.35	§ 302.15
Transcripts	§§ 302.24(l), (m)	§ 302.28
INITIAL DECISION:		
Answer in support or opposition	§ 302.28(b)	§ 302.32(b)
Contents	§ 302.27(b)	§ 302.31(c)
Effect of	§ 302.27(c)	§ 302.31(d)
Licensing cases	§ 302.1753	§ 302.216
Exceptions to	§ 302.1754	§ 302.217
Oral arguments	§ 302.28(a)(5)	§ 302.32(a)(5)
Orders declining review	§ 302.28(c)	§ 302.32(c)
Petitions for discretionary review	§ 302.28	§ 302.32
Service	§ 302.27(b)	§ 302.31(c)
Scope	§ 302.27(a)	§ 302.31(a)(1)
INITIAL FITNESS CERTIFICATE CASES (*see* Certificate Cases)		
INSTITUTING ORDERS (*see* Orders)		
INTERROGATORIES (*see* Depositions)		
INTERVENTION:		
Generally	§ 302.15	§ 302.20
JOINDER OF COMPLAINTS OR COMPLAINANTS	§ 302.13	§ 302.404(d)

Subject	Old rule	New rule
JOINT PLEADINGS:		
Enforcement cases	§ 302.13	§ 302.404(d)
Licensing cases	§ 302.1708	§ 302.204(c)
LAW JUDGE (*see* Administrative Law Judges)		
LICENSING CASES (*see* Certificate Cases; Foreign Air Carrier Permit Cases		
MAIL CONTRACTS:		
Complaint against contract	§§ 302.1505–1507	§§ 302.721–723
Data supporting contract	§ 302.1503	§ 302.719
Explanation of contract	§ 302.1503	§ 302.719
Filing of contract	§ 302.1502	§ 302.718
Petition for reconsideration	§ 302.1508	§ 302.724
Service of contract	§ 302.1504	§ 302.720
MAIL RATE CONFERENCES:		
Availability of data to Postal Service	§ 302.317	§ 302.714
Conditions upon participation	§ 302.314	§ 302.711
Compliance report	§ 302.314(d)	§ 302.711(d)
Non-disclosure of information	§ 302.314(a)	§ 302.711(a)
Signed statement required	§ 302.314(b)	§ 302.711(b)
DOT analysis of data for submission of answers	§ 302.316	§ 302.713
Effect of conference agreements	§ 302.319	§ 302.716
Information to be requested from carrier	§ 302.315	§ 302.712
Participants in conferences	§ 302.313	§ 302.710
Post conference procedure	§ 302.318	§ 302.715
Scope of conferences	§ 302.312	§ 302.709
Time of commencing and terminating conference	§ 302.321	§ 302.708(b)
Waiver of participant conditions	§ 302.320	§ 302.717
MAIL RATE PROCEEDINGS:		
Evidence	§ 302.308	§ 302.706(c)
Further procedures	§ 302.306, 307	§ 302.705
Hearing	§ 302.309	§ 302.706
Institution of proceedings	§ 302.302	§ 302.702
Objections and answers to show cause order	§ 302.305	§ 302.704
Order to show cause	§ 302.303	§ 302.703
Parties and persons other than parties	§ 302.301, 302	§ 302.706(b)
MILEAGE FEES	§ 302.21	§ 302.27(c)
MODIFICATION OF ENFORCEMENT ACTION	§ 302.218	§ 302.419
MOTIONS (*see also* Petitions):		
Answers to	§ 302.18(c)	§ 302.11(c)
Appeals from rulings of Administrative Law Judges	§ 302.18(f)	§ 302.11(h)
Briefs	§ 302.18(d)	§ 302.11(d)
Consolidation of proceedings	§ 302.12	§ 302.13
Enforcement cases	§ 302.210a	§ 302.410
Continuances and extension of time	§ 302.17	§ 302.9
Disposition of	§ 302.18(e)	§ 302.11(g)
Effect of pendency	§ 302.18(g)	§ 302.11(f)
Expedition of case	§ 302.14(a)	§ 302.11(e)
For suspension of operating authority pendente lite	§ 302.217	§ 302.418
For modification or dissolution of orders	§ 302.218	§ 302.419
Form and contents	§ 302.18(b)	§ 302.11(b)
Generally	§ 302.18	§ 302.11(a)
Oral arguments	§ 302.18(d)	§ 302.11(d)
Substitution of parties	§ 302.10	§ 302.10(b)
To correct transcripts	§ 302.24(m)	§ 302.28(f)
To dismiss and for summary judgment	§ 302.212	§ 302.411
To dismiss formal complaint	§ 302.204	§ 302.405(c)
To file unauthorized documents	§ 302.4(f)	§ 302.6(c)
To modify scope in Licensing cases	§ 302.1720(c)	§ 302.212(b)
To quash or modify subpoena	§ 302.19(f)	§ 302.25(f)
To whom motions addressed	§ 302.18(a)	§ 302.11(a)
To withhold information from public disclosure	§§ 302.39(b), (e), (f)	§§ 302.12(d), (e)
NON-HEARING PROCEDURES	§ 302.35	§ 302.15
Licensing cases	§ 302.1712(a)	§ 302.207
OBJECTIONS (*see also* Answers):		
To Public Disclosure of Information	§ 302.39	§ 302.12
OFFERS OF PROOF	§ 302.24(f)	§ 302.24(j)
OFFICIAL NOTICE	§ 302.24(n)	§ 302.24(g)
ORAL ARGUMENTS:		
Before DOT decisionmakers	§ 302.32	§ 302.36
Request for leave	§ 302.32(a)	§ 302.36(a)
Rules on documentary evidence	§ 302.32(b)	§ 302.36(b)
Before Administrative Law Judges	§ 302.25	§ 302.29
Discretionary review	§ 302.28(a)(5)	§ 302.32(a)(5)

Subject	Old rule	New rule
Licensing cases	§ 302.1756	§ 302.219
Waivers	§ 302.33	§ 302.37
ORAL EVIDENTIARY HEARINGS (*see* Hearings)		
ORDERS:		
Declining review of initial decisions	§ 302.28(c)	§ 302.32(c)
Dismissal:		
Airport fee dispute proceedings	§§ 302.611(c), (d)	§§ 302.606(c), (d)
Enforcement complaints	§ 302.205	§ 302.406
Licensing cases	§ 302.1750(a)(2)	§ 302.210(a)(3)
Establishing further procedures (Licensing cases)	§ 302.1750	§ 302.210
Final	§ 302.36	§ 302.38
Airport fee dispute proceedings	§ 302.621	§ 302.610
Licensing cases	§ 302.1750	§ 302.210
Mail contracts	§ 302.1507(a)	§ 302.723(a)
Mail rate proceedings	§ 302.306	§ 302.705
Instituting oral evidentiary hearing:		
Airport fee dispute proceedings	§ 302.611(b)	§ 302.606(b)
Licensing cases	§ 302.1750(a)(1)	§ 302.210(a)(4)
Mail rate proceedings	§§ 302.307, 309	§§ 302.703, 705(b)
Instituting investigation of rates, fares, and charges	§ 302.504	§ 302.505
Show cause:		
Licensing cases	§ 302.1730(d)	§ 302.210(a)(1)
Mail rate proceedings	§ 302.304	§ 302.703
PARTIES:		
Appearances of	§ 302.11	§ 302.21(a)
Defined	§ 302.9	§ 302.2, 10(a)
Enforcement proceedings	§ 302.210	§ 302.402
Licensing cases	§ 302.1709	§ 302.210(a)(4)
Mail rate proceedings	§ 302.301	§ 302.706(b)
Participation by Air Carrier Associations	§ 302.10(a)	§ 302.10(c)
Persons other than parties	§ 302.14	§ 302.19
Substitution of	§ 302.10	§ 302.10(b)
PETITIONS:		
Determination of rates, fares, or charges	§ 302.502(a)	§ 302.502–503
Discretionary review (*see* Discretionary Review)		
Filing Time	§ 302.37(a)	§ 302.14(a)
Institution of mail rate proceedings	§ 302.303	§ 302.302
Intervention	§ 302.15(c)	§ 302.20
Orders subject to reconsideration	§ 302.37(a)	§ 302.14(a)
Repetitive	§ 302.37(c)	§ 302.14(c)
Reconsideration	§ 302.37	§ 302.14
Rulemaking	§ 302.38	§ 302.16
PREHEARING CONFERENCE	§ 302.23	§ 302.22
Actions during	§ 302.23(a)	§ 302.22(b)
Enforcement proceeding	§ 302.211	§ 302.414
Purposed § 302.23(a)	§ 302.23(a)	§ 302.22(a)
Report of	§ 302.23(b)	§ 302.22(c)
Scope	§ 302.23(a)	§ 302.22(a)
PROCEEEDINGS:		
Airport fee dispute proceedings	§§ 302.601–621	§§ 302.601–610
Consolidation of (*see* Consolidation)		
Contemporaneous consideration (*see* Consolidation)		
Enforcement	§§ 302.200–217	§ 302.401–420
Exemption	§§ 302.400–410	§ 302.301–311
Licensing cases	§§ 302.1701–1790	§ 302.201–220
Mail rate	§§ 302.300–321	§ 302.701–717
Rates, fares, and charges	§§ 302.500–508	§ 302.501–507
PUBLIC DISCLOSURE OF INFORMATION:		
Documents	§ 302.39(b)	§ 302.12(b)
Generally	§ 302.39(a)	§ 302.12(a)
Objection to by government	§ 302.39(d)	§ 302.12(f)
Oral testimony	§ 302.39(c)	§ 302.12(c)
RATES, FARES, AND CHARGES—PROCEEDINGS (*see also* Mail Rate Proceedings; Airport Fees):		
Institution of	§ 302.501	§ 302.502
Order of investigation	§ 302.504	§ 302.505
Petition	§ 302.501	§ 302.503
Contents	§ 302.502(a)	§ 302.503(a)
Dismissed	§§ 302.503	§ 302.504
Service	§ 302.502(b)	§ 302.503(b)
Suspension of tariffs	§ 302.505	§ 302.506

Subject	Old rule	New rule
Answers	§ 302.505	§ 302.506(e)
Complaints	§ 302.505	§ 302.506
Time for filing complaint	§ 302.508	§ 302.507
RECOMMENDED DECISIONS (*see* Decisions)		
Answer in support or opposition	§ 302.28(b)	§ 302.32(b)
Contents	§ 302.27(b)	§ 302.31(c)
Effect of	§ 302.27(c)	§ 302.31(d)
Licensing cases	§ 302.1753	§ 302.216
Exceptions to	§ 302.1754	§ 302.217
Oral arguments	§ 302.28(a)(5)	§ 302.32(a)(5)
Orders declining review	§ 302.28(c)	§ 302.32(c)
Petitions for discretionary review	§ 302.28	§ 302.32
Service	§ 302.27(b)	§ 302.31(c)
Scope	§ 302.27(a)	§ 302.31(a)(2)
RECONSIDERATION, REHEARING, REARGUMENT (*see* Petitions for Reconsideration):		
RECORD, CERTIFICATION	§§ 302.22(d), 27(a), 29(a)	§ 302.31(b)
REPLIES:		
Airport fee dispute proceedings	§ 302.609	§ 302.605
Exemption cases	§ 302.407	§ 302.308
Generally	§ 302.6(b)	§ 302.6(b)
Licensing cases	....	§ 302.204(b)
Motions	§ 302.18(c)	§ 302.11(c)
Enforcement proceedings	§ 302.209	§ 302.408
RESPONSIVE DOCUMENTS (*see* Answers; Replies):		
REVIEW (*see* Discretionary Review):		
ROUTE PROCEEDINGS (*see also* Certificate Cases):		
International route awards	§§ 302.1701–1790	§ 302.201–220
RULEMAKING PETITIONS	§ 302.38	§ 302.16
SERVICE:		
Airport fee dispute proceedings	§§ 302.605(c)(1), (d)(1)	§§ 302.603(c)(1), (d)(1)
By the Department	§ 302.8(a)(1)	§ 302.7(a)(1)
Date of	§ 302.8(f)	§ 302.7(f)
Enforcement complaints	§ 302.204(a)	§ 302.404(e)
Exemption cases	§ 302.403	§ 302.304
Generally	§ 302.8	§ 302.7
Licensing cases	§ 302.1705	§ 302.203
Mail rate petitions	§ 302.303(c)	§ 302.702(d)
Persons eligible for service	§ 302.8(c)	§ 302.7(c), (g), (h)
Procedures	§ 302.8(b)	§ 302.7(b)
Proof of	§ 302.8(e)	§ 302.7(e)
Rates, fares, and charges complaints	§ 302.502(b)	§ 302.503(b)
Where to be made	§ 302.8(d)	§ 302.7(d)
SETTLEMENT OFFERS:		
Enforcement proceedings	§ 302.215	§ 302.417
Public disclosure	§ 302.215(d)	§ 302.417(d)
SHORTENED PROCEDURE	§ 302.35	§ 302.15
SHOW CAUSE ORDERS (*see* Orders):		
SUBPOENAS	§ 302.19	§ 302.25
SUSPENSION OF PRACTICE BEFORE DOT	§ 302.11(a)	§ 302.25(f)
TARIFFS:		
Complaints requesting suspension	§ 302.505	§ 302.506
TEMPORARY RATE PROCEEDINGS	§ 302.310	§ 302.707
TENTATIVE DECISIONS (*see* Decisions):		
TESTIMONY (*see* Witnesses):		
TIME:		
Computation of	§ 302.16	§ 302.8
Continuances of	§ 302.17	§ 302.9
Extensions of	§ 302.17	§ 302.9
Licensing cases	§§ 302.1706, 1711	§ 302.209
TRANSCRIPTS OF HEARINGS	§ 302.24(l)	§ 302.28
U.S. AIR CARRIER CERTIFICATION (*see* Certificate Cases):		
VERIFICATION:		
Licensing cases	§ 302.1707	§ 302.206
WAIVERS OF PROCEDURAL STEPS	§ 302.33	§ 302.37
WITNESSES:		
Attendance fees and mileage	§ 302.21	§ 302.27(c)
Cross-examination by nonparties	§ 302.14(b)	§ 302.19
Depositions	§ 302.20	§ 302.26
Objections to public disclosure of testimony	§ 302.39(c)	§ 302.12(c)

Subject	Old rule	New rule
Represented by counsel	§ 302.11(a)	§ 302.27(a)
Subpoenas	§ 302.19	§ 302.25
VIOLATIONS—EVIDENTIAL STATUS IN ENFORCEMENT PROCEEDINGS	§ 302.216	§ 302.413

PART 303—REVIEW OF AIR CARRIER AGREEMENTS

Subpart A—General Provisions

Subpart B [Reserved]

Subpart C [Reserved]

Subpart D—Section 412 Applications

Subpart E—Procedures Upon Application or Review

AUTHORITY: 49 U.S.C. chapters 401, 413, 417.

SOURCE: 50 FR 31142, July 31, 1985, unless otherwise noted.

Subpart A—General Provisions

§ 303.01 Purpose.

These regulations set forth the procedures by which applications may be made to the Department of Transportation under sections 412 and 414 of the Federal Aviation Act, as amended (49 U.S.C. 1382 and 1384) and procedures governing proceedings to enforce these provisions.

[Amdt. 303–2, 54 FR 33499, Aug. 15, 1989]

§ 303.02 Definitions.

(a) The term *Act* refers to the Federal Aviation Act of 1958, as amended. (49 U.S.C. 1301 *et seq.*)

(b) The term *Assistant Secretary* means the Assistant Secretary for Aviation and International Affairs, or as delegated. As provided in 49 CFR 1.43, the Secretary or Deputy Secretary may exercise any authority in lieu of the Assistant Secretary under the provisions of this part.

(c) The term *documents* means (1) all written, recorded, transcribed or graphic matter including letters, telegrams, memoranda, reports, studies, forecasts, lists, directives, tabulations, logs, or minutes and records of meetings, conferences, telephone or other conversations or communications; and (2) all information contained in data processing equipment or materials. The term does not include daily or weekly statistical reports in whose place an annual or monthly summary is submitted.

(d) The term *Documentary Services Division* means the Documentary Services Division of the Office of the Assistant General Counsel for Regulation and Enforcement.

(e) The term *hearing* means either a show cause proceeding as provided in § 303.44 of this part or a full evidentiary hearing as provided in § 303.45 of this part, whichever is determined by the Assistant Secretary to be appropriate.

(f)–(g) [Reserved]

(h) The term *Section 412 transaction* means any contract, agreement or discussion of a cooperative working arrangement within the scope of section 412 of the Act. (49 U.S.C. 1382).

(i) [Reserved]

[50 FR 31142, July 31, 1985, as amended by Amdt. 303–2, 54 FR 33499, Aug. 15, 1989; Amdt. 1–261, 59 FR 10061, Mar. 3, 1994]

§ 303.03 Requirement to file application.

A person who seeks approval of a section 412 transaction must file with the Documentary Services Division an application that conforms to the requirements set forth in §§ 303.04 and 303.05 of this part.

[Amdt. 303–2, 54 FR 33499, Aug. 15, 1989]

§ 303.04 General rules governing application content, procedure and conditions of approval.

(a) Unless specifically exempted by these regulations or by an order of the Assistant Secretary, a person filing an application pursuant to § 303.03 of this part shall prepare and file the application in the manner specified in this section. The application shall also contain the information required by subpart D of this part. An application may be deemed incomplete if it is not in substantial compliance with these requirements.

(b) The parties to the transaction may file either separate applications or one joint application so long as all the information required herein is submitted for each party to the transaction. The Assistant Secretary or Administrative Law Judge, if the matter has been assigned to a judge, upon his or her initiative or upon application, may order the target company or other persons to submit some or all of the information required by this subpart, or other information under 14 CFR 302.25.

(c) Each page of the application and each document submitted with the application shall be marked with the name, initials, or some other identifying symbol of the applicant. The application shall also indicate the date of preparation and the name and corporate position of the preparer.

(d) Where the required information is in data processing equipment, on microfilm, or is otherwise not eye-readable, the applicant shall provide such information in eye-readable form.

(e) The information provided by the applicant shall be updated in a timely fashion throughout the period of consideration of the application.

(f) If any information or documents required by the applicable subpart are not available, the applicants shall file an affidavit executed by the individual responsible for the search explaining why they cannot be produced.

(g) The Assistant Secretary or the Administrative Law Judge may order any applicant to submit information in addition to that required by the applicable subpart.

(h) An applicant may withhold a document required by this part on the grounds that it is privileged, but each document so withheld shall be identified and the applicant shall supply a brief description of the nature of the document, a written statement indicating the basis of the privilege claimed, and the names of the preparers and recipients of the document. If any interested party contests the assertion of privilege, the document shall be promptly submitted to the Assistant Secretary, or the Administrative Law Judge, if the matter has been assigned to a Judge. Where appropriate, an in camera inspection may be ordered.

(i) The person submitting the application to the Department shall send a complete copy of the application to the Chief, Transportation Section, Antitrust Division of the Department of Justice, at the same time as it is filed with the Documentary Services Division.

(j) The applicant shall, if requested, be responsible for expeditiously providing the application to any interested person, whether or not a party.

(k) Unless otherwise specified in this subpart, all applications shall conform generally to the requirements set forth in 14 CFR part 302, subpart A.

(l) In exceptional circumstances, the Assistant Secretary may waive or alter the procedural requirements of this part to permit a transaction to proceed on an expedited basis.

[50 FR 31142, July 31, 1985, as amended by Amdt. 302–2, 54 FR 33499, Aug. 15, 1989; 65 FR 6456, Feb. 9, 2000]

§ 303.05 Applications requesting antitrust immunity.

(a) Each application must state explicitly whether or not the applicant seeks antitrust immunity under the provisions of section 414 of the Act. If antitrust immunity is requested, the application should specify whether the applicant seeks full immunity or immunity only from the provisions of sections 4, 4a and 4c of the Clayton Act, 15 U.S.C. 15, 15a, 15c. Each application seeking antitrust immunity shall contain a statement explaining why the applicant believes immunity is in the public interest and necessary in order for the transaction to proceed.

(b) [Reserved]

(c) Any material misrepresentation of fact in such an application shall be grounds for rescission *nunc pro tunc* of any antitrust immunity granted as a result of the misrepresentation.

(d) A request for renewal of any immunity granted does not operate under section 558 of Administrative Procedure Act, 5 U.S.C. 558(c), to extend the period of immunity conferred.

[50 FR 31142, July 31, 1985, as amended by Amdt. 303-2, 54 FR 33499, Aug. 15, 1989]

§303.06 Review of antitrust immunity.

The Assistant Secretary may initiate a proceeding to review any antitrust immunity previously conferred by the Civil Aeronautics Board or the Department in any section 412 transaction. The Assistant Secretary may terminate or modify such immunity if the Assistant Secretary finds after notice and hearing that the previously conferred immunity is not consistent with the provisions of section 414. In any proceeding to review such immunity, the proponents of the immunity will have the burden of justifying the continuation of previously conferred immunity under the provisions of section 414.

[Amdt. 303-2, 54 FR 33499, Aug. 15, 1989]

§303.07 Transitional rule.

If a section 412 application or a request for antitrust immunity under section 414 is pending on the date this part is amended, such application or request shall be deemed made pursuant to the provisions of this part, as amended.

[Amdt. 303-2, 54 FR 33499, Aug. 15, 1989]

Subpart B [Reserved]

§§303.10–303.19 [Reserved]

Subpart C [Reserved]

§§303.20–303.24 [Reserved]

Subpart D—Section 412 Applications

§303.30 General provisions concerning contents of applications.

A Section 412 application shall contain the following general information:

(a) The name, mailing address and primary line of business of each party to the contract, agreement or request for authority to discuss a possible cooperative working arrangement.

(b) If the contract or agreement for which approval is sought is not evidenced by a resolution of an air carrier association, the application shall contain a copy of the contract or agreement that is certified to be true and complete by each party to the contract of agreement. If the contract or agreement is set forth in an exchange of correspondence, copies of all such correspondence must be submitted and must be certified as true and complete by all parties to the contract or agreement. If the contract or agreement is oral, a memorandum fully describing the agreement must be submitted and must be certified as true and complete by all parties to the contract or agreement. If approval is sought for a request for authority to discuss a possible cooperative working arrangement, the application shall contain a complete description of the possible cooperative working arrangement and all matters to be discussed. The description shall be certified to be true and complete by each party to the proposed discussion.

(c) If the contract, agreement or request for authority to discuss a cooperative working arrangement is evidenced by a resolution or other action of an air carrier association, the application shall contain the resolution or other action and a certification by an authorized employee of the association that the resolution or other action was duly adopted on a certain date. The authorized employee shall also specify in such certification the name of each air carrier that concurred in such resolution or other action and the name of each air carrier member that did not concur. Contracts, agreements and requests for authority to discuss cooperative working arrangements may be filed in this manner only if the Association has complied with 14 CFR part 263.

§ 303.31 Justification for the application.

A section 412 application shall explain the nature and purpose of the contract, agreement or request to discuss a cooperative working arrangement and describe how it changes any price, rule or practice existing under a previously-approved application. The application also, consistent with Department of Transportation and CAB precedent, shall contain factual material, documentation and argument in support of the application. Economic analyses, when required, shall include full explanatory details, including data sources and allocation methods. If the applicants intend to rely on public benefits to justify approval they shall describe these benefits, including foreign policy and comity considerations.

§ 303.32 Service of the application.

(a) Except as provided in paragraph (b) of this section, a section 412 application described in § 303.30(c) of this subpart and any related pleadings shall be served on any person or organization that has previously advised the air carrier association of its desire for service of such agreements. Each application shall contain the names and addresses of all persons served and a notice that any party in interest may within 21 days of the date of the application file comments with the Assistant Secretary in support or opposition to the application.

(b) Service of IATA Traffic Conference agreements and amendments thereto upon any person or organization that previously has advised IATA of its desire for service of agreements may be accomplished by sending a summary notice specifying the filing date; the IATA memorandum number; the particular Conferences involved; the subject matter (e.g., cargo/passenger, tariffs/agency matters/ procedures); the proposed effective date(s); the markets or Conference areas affected; the names of the carriers participating in the agreement; the names of all persons served; and a notice that any party in interest may within 21 days of the date of filing of the application file comments with the Assistant Secretary in support of or opposition to the application. A request for a complete copy of the application can be made under the provisions of § 303.04(j).

§ 303.33 Modifications and cancellations.

This subpart also applies to all modifications or cancellations of contracts or agreements or requests for authority to discuss a possible cooperative working arrangement.

Subpart E—Procedures Upon Application or Review

§ 303.40 Determination of compliance.

(a) Within 10 days after an application is filed pursuant to § 303.03, the Assistant Secretary will determine whether the application complies with the requirements of §§ 303.04 and 303.05.

(b) If the Assistant Secretary determines that the application is incomplete, he or she may issue a notice dismissing the application without prejudice. If the application is dismissed, and statutory time period for completion of proceedings will not begin to run until a completed application is filed.

§ 303.41 Notice.

(a) The Documentary Service Division shall compile a weekly list of all applications filed under §§ 303.04 and 303.05. The list shall include a description of the application, the docket number, date of filing, state that it may be reviewed in the Documentary Services Division, and indicate that interested parties may comment on the application or request a hearing within 21 days of the date of filling or other period as specified. The weekly list will normally be prepared on the following Monday, or as soon as possible, and will be posted on a public bulletin board in the Documentary Services Division. The list also shall be submitted for publication in the FEDERAL REGISTER.

(b) In appropriate case, particularly when an application concerns a matter of broad public significance, the Assistant Secretary may cause a notice of an application and request for public comment to be published separately in the FEDERAL REGISTER.

§ 303.42 Comments on application.

(a) Unless a different comment period is specified in the weekly list, or in a notice of filing published in the FEDERAL REGISTER, any person may file comments, responses to the application, and/or a request for a hearing within 21 days of the filing of an application.

(b) Comments supporting or opposing an application or proposing conditions and responses thereto shall state with particularity the factual basis on which the person commenting relies, and provide affidavits or other material in support of the factual basis, if appropriate.

(c) Requests for a formal oral evidentiary hearing must set out with specificity the material issues of fact in dispute that cannot be resolved without such a hearing. Vague, unsupported allegations will not suffice.

§ 303.43 Action following the comment period.

(a) [Reserved]

(b) *Section 412 applications.* After the period for which comments, requests for a hearing or responses to an order to show cause are due concerning a section 412 application, the Assistant Secretary may proceed by order requesting further information or justification or by order of approval or disapproval or, in appropriate cases, may proceed by order to show cause or by order instituting a full evidentiary hearing.

(c) Notice to the public of any full evidentiary hearing or order to show cause concerning an application shall be made by publication in the FEDERAL REGISTER.

[50 FR 31142, July 31, 1985, as amended by Amdt. 303-2, 54 FR 33500, Aug. 15, 1989]

§ 303.44 Show cause proceedings.

If the Assistant Secretary determines that an application, or review of a previously granted application, will be considered in a show cause proceeding, a tentative decision shall be issued inviting interested persons to show cause why the tentative decision should not be made final. Interested persons may respond to the order within the time specified in the order. Replies to such responses shall be permitted within the time specified in the order. Persons wishing to introduce additional facts into the record should incorporate such information in their responses or replies by affidavit. In the case of applications, show cause orders may be issued after the receipt of initial comments on the application.

§ 303.45 Evidentiary hearings.

(a) If the Assistant Secretary determines that an application, or review of a previous granted application, should be the subject of a full evidentiary hearing, he or she shall issue an order so stating. The term "full evidentiary hearing" includes any hybrid format set out in the instituting order. This order shall set forth the issues that are to be considered in such hearing.

(b) After the issuance of an order for a full evidentiary hearing, the Chief Administrative Law Judge shall promptly appoint an Administrative Law Judge to conduct such hearing in accordance with section 7 of the Administrative Procedure Act, 5 U.S.C. 556, and the Rules of Practice in part 302 of this chapter.

(c) The applicants and the Assistant General Counsel for Aviation Enforcement and Proceedings shall be parties in any full evidentiary hearing held under these regulations. The Assistant Attorney General, Antitrust, shall be a party upon notice filed with the Administrative Law Judge. Other persons may intervene as parties as provided by § 302.20 of this chapter.

(d) Within the time specified in the order instituting the full evidentiary hearing, the Administrative Law Judge shall recommend to the Assistant Secretary that the application be approved or denied or that the previously granted exemption approval or immunity should be terminated or continued in accordance with the standards of the Act. The recommendation shall be in writing, shall be based solely on the hearing record, and shall include a statement of the Administrative Law Judge's findings and conclusions, and the reasons or basis therefore, or all material issues of fact, law or discretion presented on the record. Copies of the recommendation shall be served on each party.

(e) Within 10 days after the date the Administrative Law Judge serves his or her recommendation, any party may file written exceptions to the recommendation for consideration by the Assistant Secretary. Within 21 days after the service date of the judge's recommendation, any party may file a brief in support of or in opposition to any exceptions. This period may be altered by order of the Assistant Secretary, who may also authorize the filing of reply briefs.

[50 FR 31142, July 31, 1985, as amended at 65 FR 6456, Feb. 9, 2000]

§ 303.46 Decision by the Assistant Secretary.

The Assistant Secretary shall decide, on the basis of the record and in accordance with the procedures prescribed in part 302 of this chapter, whether to grant or deny, in whole or in part, the application. A copy of the Assistant Secretary's final decision shall be served on all parties.

PART 305—RULES OF PRACTICE IN INFORMAL NONPUBLIC INVESTIGATIONS

Sec.

AUTHORITY: 49 U.S.C. chapters 401, 417, 461; 5 U.S.C. 555, 556.

SOURCE: Docket No. 82, 50 FR 2421, Jan. 16, 1985, unless otherwise noted.

§ 305.1 Applicability.

The provisions of this part shall govern informal nonpublic investigations, as distinguished from formal investigations and adjudicatory proceedings, undertaken by the Office of the Assistant General Counsel for Aviation Enforcement and Proceedings with a view to obtaining information from any person. While the Department seeks and encourages voluntary cooperation and believes that it is in the best interest of all parties concerned, it will utilize the procedures provided by this part to compel the disclosure of information by any person where DOT wishes to determine whether such person, or any other person, has been or is violating any provisions of Title IV or sections 101(3), 1002, 1003, or 1108(b) of the Act, or any rule, regulation, order, certificate, permit, or letter or registration issued pursuant thereto by DOT and when the information appears to be relevant to the matter under investigation. This part shall not apply to employees or records of other agencies of the U.S. Government, the District of Columbia, or the several States and their political subdivisions.

§ 305.2 Definition.

For the purpose of, and as used in this part, the term *investigation* means a non-adjudicatory, informal nonpublic investigation for the purpose of determining whether formal enforcement action should be instituted with respect to alleged violations of law.

§§ 305.3–305.4 [Reserved]

§ 305.5 Initiation of investigation.

An investigation may be initiated by order of the Department. Attorneys of the Office of the Assistant General Counsel for Aviation Enforcement and Proceedings shall conduct such investigations pursuant to the provisions of this part and they shall be designated Investigation Attorneys. Investigation Attorneys, administrative law judges and the DOT decisionmaker are hereby authorized to exercise and perform their duties and functions under this part in accordance with the provisions of the Act and the rules and regulations of the Department.

§ 305.6 Appearance of witnesses.

Witnesses may be required to appear before any administrative law judge for the purpose of receiving their testimony or receiving from them documents or other data relating to any subject under investigation. Such testimony shall be mechanically or stenographically recorded, and a transcript thereof shall be made and incorporated in the record of the investigation.

§305.7 Issuance of investigation subpenas.

(a) The Deputy General Counsel, the DOT decisionmaker, the chief administrative law judge or the administrative law judge designated to preside at the reception of evidence, may issue a subpena directing the person named therein to appear before a designated administrative law judge at a designated time and place to testify or to produce documentary evidence relating to any matter under investigation, or both. Each such subpena shall briefly advise the person required to testify or submit documentary evidence of the purpose and scope of the investigation, and a copy of the order initiating the investigation shall be attached to the subpena.

(b) Witnesses subpenaed to appear shall be paid the fees and mileage prescribed in §302.7 of the Rules of Practice (14 CFR 302.7). Service of such subpenas shall be made in accordance with the provisions of §302.27(c) of the Rules of Practice (14 CFR 302.27(c)).

[Doc. No. 82, 50 FR 2421, Jan. 16, 1985, as amended at 65 FR 6456, Feb. 9, 2000]

§305.8 [Reserved]

§305.9 Rights of witnesses.

Any person required to testify or to submit documentary evidence shall be entitled to procure, on payment of lawfully prescribed costs, a copy of any document produced by such person and of his or her own testimony as stenographically reported. Any person compelled to testify or to produce documentary evidence may be accompanied, represented, and advised by counsel.

§305.10 Nonpublic character of proceedings.

Investigations shall be attended only by the witnesses and their counsel, the administrative law judge, the Investigation Attorney, other DOT personnel concerned with the conduct of the proceeding and the official stenographer. All orders initiating investigations, motions to quash or modify investigation subpenas, orders disposing of such motions, documents, and transcripts of testimony shall be part of the record in the investigation. Unless DOT determines otherwise, all orders initiating investigations which do not disclose the identity of the particular persons of firms under investigation shall be published in the FEDERAL REGISTER. Except as otherwise required by law, the remainder of the record of such proceedings shall constitute internal DOT documents which shall not be available to the general public. The use of such records in DOT proceedings subject to part 302 of the Rules of Practice shall be governed by §§302.25(g) and 302.12 and by the law of evidence applicable to DOT proceedings.

[Doc. No. 82, 50 FR 2421, Jan. 16, 1985, as amended at 65 FR 6456, Feb. 9, 2000]

§305.11 Procedures after investigation.

Upon completion of the investigation, where the Deputy General Counsel, determines that no corrective action is warranted, the investigation will be closed, and any documentary evidence obtained in the investigation will be returned to the persons who produced it. Where remedial action is indicated by the investigation, the Deputy General Counsel will proceed pursuant to subpart D of part 302 of the Rules of Practice or will take such other action as may be appropriate.

[Doc. No. 82, 50 FR 2421, Jan. 16, 1985, as amended at 65 FR 6456, Feb. 9, 2000]

§305.12 Motions to quash or modify an investigation subpena.

Any person upon whom an investigation subpena is served may, within seven (7) days after such service or at any time prior to the return date thereof, whichever is earlier, file a motion to quash or modify such subpena with the administrative law judge who issued such subpena, or in the event the administrative law judge is not available, with the chief administrative law judge for action by himself or herself or by the DOT decisionmaker. Such motions shall be made in writing in conformity with Rules 3 and 4 of the

Rules of Practice (part 302 of this subchapter); shall state with particularity the grounds therefor and the relief sought; shall be accompanied by the evidence relied upon and all such factual matter shall be verified in accordance with the provisions of Rule 4(b) of the aforesaid Rules of Practice. Written memoranda or briefs may be filed with the motions, stating the points and authorities relied upon. No oral argument will be heard on such motions unless the chief administrative law judge, the administrative law judge or the DOT decisionmaker directs otherwise. A subpena will be quashed or modified if the evidence whose production is required is not reasonably relevant to the matter under investigation, or the demand made does not describe with sufficient particularity the information sought, or the subpena is unlawful or unduly burdensome. The filing of a motion to quash or modify an investigation subpena shall stay the return date of such subpena until such motion is granted or denied. The DOT decisionmaker may at any time review, upon his or her own initiative, the ruling of an administrative law judge or the chief administrative law judge denying a motion to quash a subpena. In such cases, the DOT decisionmaker may order that the return date of a subpena which he or she has elected to review be stayed pending DOT action thereon.

[Doc. No. 82, 50 FR 2421, Jan. 16, 1985, as amended at 65 FR 6457, Feb. 9, 2000]

PART 313—IMPLEMENTATION OF THE ENERGY POLICY AND CONSERVATION ACT

Sec.

AUTHORITY: 42 U.S.C. 6362(b), 49 U.S.C. Chapter 401.

SOURCE: Docket No. 82, 50 FR 2425, Jan. 16, 1985, unless otherwise noted.

§ 313.1 Purpose, scope, and authority.

(a) Chapter 77 (Energy Conservation) of Title 42 (The Public Health and Welfare), authorizes and directs certain actions to conserve energy supplies through energy conservation programs and where necessary, the regulation of certain energy uses, and to provide for improved energy efficiency of motor vehicles, major appliances, and certain other consumer products. In furtherance of these purposes, 42 U.S.C. 6362 requires several transportation regulatory agencies, including DOT, to submit a number of reports to the Congress with respect to energy conservation and efficiency, and where practicable and consistent with the exercise of DOT's authority under other law, to include in any major regulatory action a statement of its probable impact on energy efficiency and energy conservation. 42 U.S.C. 6362(b) directs DOT to define the term "major regulatory action" by rule.

(b) Section 40113 of Subtitle VII of Title 49 of the United States Code (Transportation)("the Statute"), authorizes DOT to establish such rules, regulations, and procedures as are necessary to the exercise of its functions and are consistent with the purposes of the Statute.

(c) The purpose of these regulations is to establish procedures and guidelines for the implementation of DOT's responsibility under 42 U.S.C. 6362 to include in any major regulatory action taken by DOT a statement of the probable impact on energy efficiency and energy conservation.

(d) These regulations apply to all proceedings before DOT, as provided herein.

[Doc. No. 82, 50 FR 2425, Jan. 16, 1985, as amended at 60 FR 43528, 43529, Aug. 22, 1995]

§ 313.2 Policy.

(a) *General.* It is the policy of DOT to view the conservation of energy and the energy efficiency improvement goals of Chapter 77 of Title 42 as part of DOT's overall mandate, to be considered along with the several public interest and public convenience and necessity factors enumerated in section 40101 of the Statute. To the extent practicable and consistent with DOT's authority under the Statute and other law, energy conservation and efficiency are to be weighed in the decision-making process just as are DOT's traditional policies and missions.

(b) *Implementation.* Implementation of this policy is through the integration of energy findings and conclusions into decisions, opinions, or orders in proceedings involving a major regulatory action, as defined in this part.

(c) *Proceedings in progress.* The provisions of this part are intended primarily for prospective application. Proceedings in progress on the effective date of this part, in which an application has been docketed but no final decision made public, shall adhere to § 313.6(a) of this part, provided that the fair, efficient, and timely administration of DOT's regulatory activities is not compromised thereby. Nothing herein shall imply a requirement for new or additional hearings, a reopening of the record, or any other procedures which would tend to delay a timely decision in proceedings in progress.

(d) *Hearings.* Public hearings will not normally be held for the purpose of implementing 42 U.S.C. 6362, particularly in connection with proposed actions which do not require notice and hearing as a prerequisite to decision under the Statute. Hearings may be ordered in exceptional circumstances where the proposed action is of great magnitude or widespread public interest and, in addition, presents complex issues peculiarly subject to resolution through evidentiary hearings and the process of cross-examination.

[Doc. No. 82, 50 FR 2425, Jan. 16, 1985, as amended at 60 FR 43528, 43529, Aug. 22, 1995]

§ 313.3 Definitions.

As used in this part:

(a) *Energy efficiency* means the ratio of the useful output of services in air transportation to the energy consumption of such services.

(b) *Energy statement* is a statement of the probable impact of a major regulatory action on energy efficiency and energy conservation, contained in a decision, opinion, order, or rule.

(c) *Major regulatory action* is any decision by the DOT decisionmaker or administrative law judge requiring an energy statement pursuant to § 313.4 of this part.

(d) *NEPA* means the National Environmental Policy Act of 1969.

(e) *Statute* means Subtitle VII of Title 49 of the United States Code (Transportation).

[Doc. No. 82, 50 FR 2425, Jan. 16, 1985, as amended at 60 FR 43529, Aug. 22, 1995]

§ 313.4 Major regulatory actions.

(a) Any initial, recommended, tentative or final decision, opinion, order, or final rule is a major regulatory action requiring an energy statement, if it:

(1) May cause a near-term net annual change in aircraft fuel consumption of 10 million (10,000,000) gallons or more, compared to the probable consumption of fuel were the action not to be taken; or

(2) Is specifically so designated by DOT because of its precedential value, substantial controversy with respect to energy conservation and efficiency, or other unusual circumstances.

(b) Notwithstanding paragraph (a)(1) of this section, the following types of actions shall not be deemed as major regulatory actions requiring an energy statement:

(1) Tariff suspension orders under section 41509 of the Statute, emergency exemptions or temporary exemptions not exceeding 24 months under section 40109 of the Statute and other proceedings in which timely action is of the essence;

(2) Orders instituting or declining to institute investigations or rulemaking, setting or declining to set applications for hearing, on reconsideration, or on requests for stay;

(3) Other procedural or interlocutory orders;

(4) Actions taken under delegated authority; and

(5) Issuance of a certificate where no determination of public convenience and necessity is required.

(c) Notwithstanding paragraph (a)(1) of this section, DOT may provide that an energy statement shall not be prepared in a proceeding which may result in a major regulatory action, if it finds that:

(1) The inclusion of an energy statement is not consistent with the exercise of DOT's authority under the Statute or other law;

(2) The inclusion of an energy statement is not practicable because of time constraints, lack of information, or other unusual circumstances; or

(3) The action is taken under laws designed to protect the public health or safety.

[Doc. No. 82, 50 FR 2425, Jan. 16, 1985, as amended at 60 FR 43529, Aug. 22, 1995]

§ 313.5 Energy information.

(a) It shall be the responsibility of applicants and other parties or participants to a proceeding which may involve a major regulatory action to submit sufficient information about the energy consumption and energy efficiency consequences of their proposals or positions in the proceeding to enable the administrative law judge or the DOT decisionmaker, as the case may be, to determine whether the proceeding will in fact involve a major regulatory action for purposes of this part, and if so, to consider the relevant energy factors in the decision and prepare the energy statement.

(b) In proceedings involving evidentiary hearings, the energy information shall be submitted at such hearings pursuant to DOT's usual procedural regulations and practices, under control of the administrative law judge or other hearing officer.

(c) In proceedings not involving evidentiary hearings, the energy information shall be submitted at such time as other materials in justification of an application are submitted. Where an application itself is intended as justification for DOT action, the energy information shall be submitted with the application. In rulemakings not involving hearings, the energy information shall normally be submitted along with comments on the notice of proposed rulemaking, or as directed in any such notice or any advance notice.

§ 313.6 Energy statements.

(a) Each major regulatory action shall include, to the extent practicable, consideration of the probable impact of the action taken or to be taken upon energy efficiency and conservation. The administrative law judge or the DOT decisionmaker, as the case may be, shall normally make findings and conclusions about:

(1) The net change in energy consumption;

(2) The net change in energy efficiency; and

(3) The balance struck between energy factors and other public interest and public convenience and necessity factors in the decision.

(b) Energy findings and conclusions contained in any initial or recommended decision are a part of that decision and thus subject to discretionary review by DOT.

(c) In the case of orders to show cause initiated by DOT, energy findings and conclusions may be omitted if adequate information is not available. In such instances, the energy statement shall be integrated into the final decision.

§ 313.7 Integration with environmental procedures.

(a) In proceedings in which an environmental impact statement or a finding of no significant impact is prepared by a responsible official pursuant to DOT's procedures implementing the National Environmental Policy Act of 1969 (NEPA), the energy information called for by this part may be included in that statement or declaration in order to yield a single, comprehensive document. In such instances, the DOT's NEPA procedures shall govern the submission of the energy information. However, it shall remain the responsibility of the administrative law judge or the DOT decisionmaker, as the case may be, to make the findings and conclusions required by § 313.6(a) of this part.

(b) A determination that a major regulatory action within the meaning of 42 U.S.C. 6362 and this part may be involved in a proceeding is independent from any determination that the proceeding is a "major Federal action significantly affecting the quality of the human environment" within the meaning of NEPA, and vice versa.

[Doc. No. 82, 50 FR 2425, Jan. 16, 1985, as amended at 60 FR 43528, 43529, Aug. 22, 1995]

PART 314 [RESERVED]

PART 323—TERMINATIONS, SUSPENSIONS, AND REDUCTIONS OF SERVICE

AUTHORITY: 49 U.S.C. Chapters 401, 411, 417.

SOURCE: Docket No. 82, 50 FR 2430, Jan. 16, 1985, unless otherwise noted.

§323.1 Applicability.

This part applies to certificated air carriers who terminate or suspend service to a point, or in a market, and to all air carriers who terminate, suspend, or reduce service below the level of essential air service under 49 U.S.C. 41731-41742.

[Doc. No. 82, 50 FR 2430, Jan. 16, 1985, as amended by Doc. No. OST-96-1269, 61 FR 19165, May 1, 1996]

§323.2 Definitions.

As used in this part:

Certificated carrier means a direct air carrier holding authority to provide air transportation granted by the Department of Transportation ("DOT") or the former Civil Aeronautics Board ("CAB") in the form of a certificate of public convenience and necessity under section 41102 of the Title 49 of the United States Code (Transportation) ("the Statute") or an all-cargo air transportation certificate to perform all-cargo air transportation under section 41103 of the Statute.

Eligible place means a place in the United States that—

(1) Was an eligible point under section 419 of the Federal Aviation Act of 1958 as in effect before October 1, 1988;

(2) Received scheduled air transportation at any time between January 1, 1990, and November 4, 1990; and

(3) Is not listed in Department of Transportation Orders 89–9–37 and 89–12–52 as a place ineligible for compensation under Subchapter II of Chapter 417 of the Statute. (For availability of Department of Transportation Orders, see 49 CFR part 7, subpart E and appendix A.)

Essential air service is that air transportation which the Department has found to be essential under Subchapter II of Chapter 417 of the Statute.

FAA means the Federal Aviation Administration, U.S. Department of Transportation.

FAA-designated hub means any airport serving a small, medium, or large air traffic hub listed in the Department of Transportation publication, *Airport Activity Statistics of Certificated Route Carriers*.

Statute means Subtitle VII of Title 49 of the United States Code (Transportation).

United States includes the several States, the District of Columbia, and the several territories and possessions of the United States. *State* includes any of the individual entities comprising the United States.

[Doc. No. 82, 50 FR 2430, Jan. 16, 1985, as amended by Doc. No. OST-96-1269, 61 FR 19165, May 1, 1996]

§323.3 Who shall file notices.

(a) *Terminations, suspensions, or reductions by certificated carriers.* The notice described in §323.4(a) shall be filed by any certificated carrier that intends to:

(1) Terminate or suspend all passenger air transportation that it is providing to any eligible place in the United States when that termination or suspension will leave no certificated carriers serving that place. Service shall be considered to be terminated or suspended whenever it is operated less than 5 days per week, with three or more intermediate stops, or in one direction only between the two places;

(2) Reduce passenger air transportation so that any eligible place receives less than the level of essential air service determined by DOT;

(3) Terminate or suspend all passenger air transportation that it is providing to any eligible place in the United States for which DOT has not issued an essential air service determination under either § 325.5 or § 325.7 of this chapter, when that termination or suspension will leave only one certificated carrier serving that place. Service shall be considered to be terminated or suspended whenever it is operated less than 5 days per week, with three or more intermediate stops, or in one direction only between the two places;

(4) Reduce passenger air transportation to any eligible place in Alaska for which DOT has not determined the level of essential air service so that the service between that place and every other place served by a certificated carrier is either:

(i) Less than two round trip flights per week, or

(ii) Less than the average weekly number of round trip flights actually provided during calendar year 1976, or

(iii) Less than the number of flights specified under an agreement between DOT and the State of Alaska; or

(5) Terminate, suspend, or reduce passenger air transportation at an eligible place for which DOT has issued, or is required to issue, an essential air service determination under section 41731 or section 41733 of the Statute so that the total available seats of all the carriers linking that place to FAA-designated hubs will be reduced by 33 percent or more during a 90-day period. Service to a hub shall be considered to be terminated or suspended whenever it is operated less than 5 days per week, with three or more intermediate stops, or in one direction only between two places.

(b) [Reserved]

(c) *Uncertificated carriers.* The notice described in § 323.4(a) shall be filed by any uncertificated carrier that intends to terminate, suspend, or reduce:

(1) Air transportation so that any eligible place receives less than the level of essential air service determined by the DOT;

(2) Passenger air transportation to any eligible place for which DOT has not determined the level of essential air service, other than a place in Alaska, so that there is no FAA-designated hub from which the place receives at least two round trip flights per day, 5 days per week; or

(3) Passenger air transportation to any eligible place in Alaska, for which DOT has not determined the level of essential air service, so that the service between that place and every other place served by a certificated carrier is either:

(i) Less than two round trip flights per week, or

(ii) Less than the average number of weekly round trip flights actually provided during calendar year 1976, or

(iii) Less than the number of flights specified under an agreement between DOT and the State of Alaska.

(d) For the purpose of this section, in ascertaining the level of air transportation being provided to a place or between two places, air transportation that has been the subject of a notice filed under this section shall be considered not in operation for the duration of the notice period.

(e) If a certificated carrier was, before October 24, 1978, granted authority to suspend air transportation, and that authority ends on a stated date, the carrier shall comply with the requirements of this part before continuing the suspension beyond that date.

(f) If a certificated carrier was, before October 24, 1978, granted authority to terminate or suspend air transportation, but has not suspended service, the carrier shall comply with the requirements of this part before terminating or suspending service.

[Doc. No. 82, 50 FR 2430, Jan. 16, 1985, as amended by Doc. No. OST–96–1269, 61 FR 19165, 19166, May 1, 1996]

§ 323.4 Contents of notices.

(a) The notice required under § 323.3 (a) and (c) shall contain:

(1) Identification of the carrier, including address and telephone number.

(2) Statement whether the carrier is a certificated carrier or an uncertificated carrier.

(3) Names of all other air carriers serving the point at the time of filing.

(4) Description of the service to be terminated, suspended, or reduced, including:

(i) Arrival and departure times at the affected points of the flights to be discontinued,

(ii) Aircraft type used,

(iii) Routes of the flights to be discontinued, and a statement of which routes, if any, will be left without nonstop or single-plane service from a certificated carrier by the intended change, and

(iv) Date of intended termination, suspension, or reduction of service.

(5) A statement whether DOT has determined the level of essential air service for the point, and

(i) If such a determination has been made, a statement whether the intended termination, suspension, or reduction will reduce air transportation to the place below the essential level; or

(ii) If such a determination has not been made, and the place is an eligible place, a statement whether the intended termination, suspension, or reduction reasonably appears to deprive the place of essential air service, and an explanation.

(6) If the place is an eligible place, the calendar date when objections are due under § 323.10.

(7) Proof of service upon all persons specified in § 323.7(a). The proof of service shall include the names of all carriers served and the names and addresses of all other persons served.

(b) [Reserved]

(c) DOT may require any carrier filing notice to supply additional information.

(Approved by the Office of Management and Budget under control number 3024–0030)

[Doc. No. 82, 50 FR 2430, Jan. 16, 1985, as amended by Doc. No. OST–96–1269, 61 FR 19165, 19166, May 1, 1996]

§ 323.5 Time for filing notices.

(a) Except as specified by paragraph (b) of this section, a notice required by § 323.3 shall be filed at least:

(1) 90 days before the intended termination, suspension, or reduction, if it is filed by a certificated carrier or by an uncertificated carrier receiving compensation under 49 U.S.C. 41731-41742 for service to the place;

(2) 30 days before the intended termination, suspension, or reduction, if it is filed by an uncertificated carrier not receiving compensation under section 419 of the Act for service to the place.

(b) The notice required by § 323.3(a)(3) shall be filed at least 30 days, and the notice required by § 323.3(a)(1) shall be filed at least 60 days, before the intended termination or suspension.

[Doc. No. 82, 50 FR 2430, Jan. 16, 1985, as amended by Doc. No. OST–96–1269, 61 FR 19165, 19166, May 1, 1996]

§ 323.6 General requirements for notices.

(a) Each notice filed under this part shall, unless otherwise specified, conform to the procedural rules of general applicability in subpart A of part 302 of this chapter.

(b) Each notice filed under this part shall be titled to indicate the place(s) involved, and to indicate whether it is a 30-, 60-, or 90-day notice and whether it involves a termination, a suspension, or a reduction of air transportation.

[Doc. No. 82, 50 FR 2430, Jan. 16, 1985, as amended by Doc. No. OST–96–1269, 61 FR 19166, May 1, 1996]

§ 323.7 Service of notices.

(a) A copy of each notice required by § 323.3 shall be served upon:

(1) The chief executive of the principal city or other unit of local government at the affected place. The principal city is the one named, or previously named, in the section 41102 certificate by virtue of which the place qualifies as an eligible place. For places in Alaska or Hawaii that are designated as eligible places without having been listed on a section 41102 certificate, the principal city is the most populous municipality at the place.

(2) [Reserved]

(3) The State agency with jurisdiction over transportation by air in the State containing any community required to be served under paragraph (a)(1) of this section. If there is no such State agency, the notice shall be sent to the governor of that State.

(4) The manager of, or other individual with direct supervision over and responsibility for, the airport at any

community required to be served under paragraph (a)(1) of this section.

(5) The Postmaster General (marked for the attention of the Assistant General Counsel, Transportation), if the carrier filing the notice is authorized to transport United States mail to or from any community required to be served under paragraph (a)(1) of this section.

(6) Each air carrier providing scheduled service to a non-hub or FAA-designated small hub that is directly affected by the notice.

(7) The DOT Regional Office for the region in which the affected point is located.

(8) Any other person designated by DOT.

(b) [Reserved]

(c) Local communities, State agencies, and airport managers shall be served personally or by registered or certificated mail. All other persons may be served by ordinary mail.

[Doc. No. 82, 50 FR 2430, Jan. 16, 1985, as amended by Doc. No. OST–96–1269, 61 FR 19166, May 1, 1996]

§ 323.8 Exemptions.

Carriers are exempted from paragraphs (a)(1), (a)(3), and (a)(5) of § 323.3 to the extent that those provisions require them to file a notice when terminating or suspending the domestic leg of an international flight (fill-up service).

[Doc. No. OST–96–1269, 61 FR 19166, May 1, 1996]

§ 323.9 Objections to notices.

(a) Any person may file an objection requesting DOT to prohibit any termination, suspension, or reduction of air transportation to an eligible place that is the subject of a notice filed under this part.

(b) Objections shall contain:

(1) Identification of the objector, including address and telephone number.

(2) A statement of DOT action requested.

(3) The schedules, routes, carriers, and aircraft types for all air transportation to the affected place other than that proposed to be terminated, suspended, or reduced.

(4) A suggested reasonable level of essential air service to the affected place.

(5) [Reserved]

(6) A justification of the suggested level of essential air service.

(7) Proof of service on the carrier filing the notice objected to, on all airport managers and State and local governments on whom the notice was filed, and any other person designated by DOT. The proof of service shall include the names of all carriers served and the names and addresses of all other persons served.

(c) Objectors are strongly urged to include in their objections facts to support the suggested level of essential air service (e.g., traffic and enplanement data, other market studies, facts descriptive of the place's isolation or dependence on air transportation).

(Approved by the Office of Management and Budget under control number 3024–0030)

[Doc. No. 82, 50 FR 2430, Jan. 16, 1985, as amended by Doc. No. OST–96–1269, 61 FR 19165, 19166, May 1, 1996]

§ 323.10 Time for filing objections.

(a) Objections shall be filed not later than:

(1) 12 days from the date of filing of a 30-day notice;

(2) 15 days from the date of filing of a 60-day notice; or

(3) 20 days from the date of filing of a 90-day notice.

(b) The Department may accept late-filed objections, upon motion, for good cause shown.

(c) Whenever a notice has been filed earlier than required under § 323.5, the Department may extend the time for filing an objection to that notice.

§ 323.11 Answers to objections.

(a) Any person may file an answer to an objection filed under this part.

(b) An answer must be filed not later than 7 business days after the filing of the objection to which it responds. Late-filed answers may be allowed, and extensions of filing time granted, by the Department for the same reasons as for objections.

(c) An answer may contain the same type of facts and discussion permitted for objections under this part, and must contain:

(1) Proof of service on the objector, on all persons on whom the objection was required to be served, and on any

other person designated by the Department. The proof of service shall include the names and addresses of all persons served.

(2) Identification of the answering party, including address and telephone number.

(Approved by the Office of Management and Budget under control number 3024–0030)

§323.12 General requirements for objections and answers.

(a) Each objection and answer filed under this part shall, unless otherwise specified, conform to the procedural rules of general applicability in subpart A of part 302 of this chapter.

(b) Each objection shall be titled "Objection to Termination, Suspension, or Reduction of Air Service," and shall identify the notice to which it responds. Each answer shall be titled "Answer to Objection to Termination, Suspension, or Reduction of Air Service," and shall identify the objection to which it responds.

§323.13 DOT actions.

(a) If an objection has been filed under this part, DOT will dispose of the objection by order.

(b) If no objection has been filed within the time allowed by §323.10(a), DOT may:

(1) By order prohibit a termination, suspension, or reduction that reasonably appears to deprive any eligible place of essential air transportation;

(2) Issue a notice or a final order that it will take no action on a notice filed under §323.3; or

(3) Take no action.

[Doc. No. 82, 50 FR 2430, Jan. 16, 1985, as amended by Doc. No. OST–96–1269, 61 FR 19166, May 1, 1996]

§323.14 Temporary suspension authority for involuntary interruption of service.

(a) Any air carrier may temporarily suspend service without filing a notice under §323.3 for any interruption of service that the carrier cannot reasonably be expected to foresee or control, such as rules, standards, or other action, or inaction, of the Administrator of the Federal Aviation Administration or of a foreign government, emergency measures, strikes, weather conditions, construction work on airports, or disasters. However, the provisions of this paragraph shall apply to interruptions due to airport inadequacies only if the carrier is unable to serve the place through any airport convenient to the place with the type of equipment last regularly used to serve the place.

(b) In the case of an interruption of service caused by a strike, the carrier shall give immediate notice of the interruption to DOT. Suspension authority under this section due to a strike shall expire 90 days after employees return to work.

(c) If service to a place is interrupted for more than 3 consecutive days for reasons beyond the carrier's control other than a strike, the holder shall give notice to DOT within 3 days following the date of first interruption, setting forth the date of first interruption and a full statement of the reasons for the interruption.

(d) The notice required by paragraph (b) or (c) of this section shall be marked for the attention of the Director, Office of Aviation Analysis.

(Approved by the Office of Management and Budget under control number 3024–0030)

[Doc. No. 82, 50 FR 2430, Jan. 16, 1985, as amended by Doc. No. OST–96–1269, 61 FR 19166, May 1, 1996]

§323.15 Report to be filed after strikes.

(a) Within 15 days following resumption of service after a strike, an air carrier shall file a report with DOT containing a list of all flights that were canceled, the date they were canceled, and the date service was resumed.

(b) The report shall be marked for the attention of the Director, Office of Aviation Analysis.

(Approved by the Office of Management and Budget under control number 3024–0030)

[Doc. No. 82, 50 FR 2430, Jan. 16, 1985, as amended by Doc. No. OST–96–1269, 61 FR 19166, May 1, 1996]

§323.16 Listings in schedule publications.

Each air carrier filing a notice under §323.3 (a)(2), (a)(4), (a)(5), or (c) shall continue to list the affected flights in all generally-distributed schedule publications in which the flight was listed before the notice. The listings shall continue until DOT permits the flights to be discontinued. The listings may include a notice stating that the flights are "to be discontinued as of (date) subject to government approval."

§ 323.17 Delays in discontinuing service.

If transportation that is the subject of a notice under this part is not discontinued within 90 days of the intended date stated in the notice, a new notice must be filed before the service may be discontinued. However, if DOT requires the carrier to provide service beyond the stated date, the carrier need not file a new notice if it discontinues the service within 90 days after DOT permits it to do so.

§ 323.18 Carriers' obligations when terminating, suspending, or reducing air service.

Any air carrier that terminates, suspends, or reduces air service, whether or not subject to the notice requirements of this part, shall make reasonable efforts to contact all passengers holding reservations on the affected flights to inform them of the flights' cancellation.

§ 323.19 Withdrawal notice by exemption carriers in certain limited-entry markets.

As a condition on the exemption, an air carrier operating under exemption authority in an international market which is the subject of a carrier selection proceeding shall file a notice with the Department at least ninety days before it terminates service in that market. Once such a notice has been filed, the carrier may not terminate service in that market during the notice period unless the air carrier chosen in the selection proceeding enters the market and the Department grants the operating carrier permission to do so. The Department may allow earlier termination for good cause when in the public interest.

[Doc. No. 43403, 51 FR 43188, Dec. 1, 1986]

PART 325—ESSENTIAL AIR SERVICE PROCEDURES

AUTHORITY: 49 U.S.C. Chapters 401, 417.

SOURCE: Docket No. 82, 50 FR 2434, Jan. 16, 1985, unless otherwise noted.

§ 325.1 Purpose.

The purpose of this part is to establish procedures to be followed in designating eligible points and in determining essential air transportation levels for eligible points, and in the appeals and periodic reviews of these determinations, under section 419 of the Act.

§ 325.2 Applicability.

This part applies to essential air service determinations for communities designated as eligible under section 419(a) of the Act and to eligible point designations and essential air service determinations for communities that qualify under section 419(b) of the Act. It applies to the gathering of data by the Department, and to the participation of State, local, and other officials and other interested persons in the designation and determination processes.

NOTE: Criteria for designating eligible points under section 419(b) are contained in part 270 of this chapter. Guidelines for deciding essential air service levels are contained in part 398 of this chapter.

§ 325.3 Definitions.

As used in this part, *eligible point* means:

(a) Any point in the United States, the District of Columbia, and the several territories and possessions of the United States to which any direct air carrier was authorized, under a certificate issued by CAB under section 401 of the Act, to provide air service on October 24, 1978, whether or not such service was actually provided;

(b) Any point in the United States and the several territories and possessions of the United States that was deleted from a section 401 certificate between July 1, 1968 and October 24, 1978, inclusive, and that has been designated as an eligible point under the Act; or

(c) Any other point in Alaska or Hawaii that has been designated as an eligible point under the Act.

§ 325.4 State and local participation.

(a) DOT, on a periodic basis, will send a questionnaire to each eligible point that is served by not more than one certificated air carrier, or is designated as an eligible point under section 419(b) of the Act, or for which DOT is reviewing its essential air service needs. The questionnaire will be addressed to:

(1) The chief executive of the principal city, or other unit of local government at the affected point, that is named or has been previously named in a qualifying section 401 certificate. For points in Alaska or Hawaii that are named DOT as eligible points without having been listed on a section 401 certificate, the principal city is the most populous municipality at the point;

(2) The individual or entity with direct supervision over and responsibility for the airport at the eligible point; and

(3) The State agency with jurisdiction over air transportation in the State containing the eligible point. If there is no such State agency, the questionnaire will be sent to the governor of that State.

(b) Within 60 days after receipt of the questionnaire, five copies of the response shall be filed in the Documentary Services Division, unless the Department specifies another date. If no response is received within the period, essential air service for that eligible point may temporarily be set at the minimum level prescribed in section 419(f) of the Act.

(c) Any other interested person may, during the 60-day response period, submit information relevant to the essential air service level of that eligible point by filing in the Documentary Services Division, five copies of a document titled with the name of the point involved.

(d) As necessary, the DOT may request additional information to supplement the questionnaire.

(Approved by the Office of Management and Budget under control number 3024–0037)

§ 325.5 Determinations and designations.

(a) Not later than October 24, 1979, after reviewing all information submitted, CAB issued determinations of the essential level of air service for eligible points that, on October 24, 1978, were served by not more than one direct air carrier holding a certificate under section 401 of the Act for scheduled service to the point.

(b) DOT will issue a determination of the essential level of air service for a point within 6 months after each of the following events:

(1) A notice is received that service to an eligible point will be reduced to only one carrier that holds a section 401 certificate;

(2) A point is designated as an eligible point under section 419(b) of the Act and either paragraph (c) of this section, paragraph (d) of this section, or § 325.7(e); or

(3) A review was conducted of essential air service of that point under § 325.6.

(c) Not later than January 1, 1982, CAB designated the communities described in § 270.2(a) and (b) as eligible points or as ineligible.

(d) After January 1, 1982, DOT may designate communities in Alaska or Hawaii as eligible points if they apply for such designation.

§ 325.6 Periodic reviews.

(a) The Department will start a periodic review of essential air service within 1 year of the date of the previous determination of essential air service for eligible points receiving subsidized service, within 2 years of the date of the previous determination for eligible points in Alaska, and within 3 years of the date of the previous determination for eligible points without subsidized air service.

(b) The review shall be conducted in accordance with the procedures in §§ 325.4, 325.5 and 325.7.

(c) The Department may review the designation under section 419(b) of a community as an eligible point to determine whether that point continues to meet the criteria in part 270 of this chapter.

§§ 325.7–325.9 [Reserved]

§ 325.10 Modification of the designated level of essential air service.

(a) Any person may file with DOT a petition titled "Petition for Modification of Essential Air Service Level," asking to modify the essential air service level at a point.

(b) The petition shall identify the point affected, and specifically state the reasons why the petitioner believes the designated essential level is inadequate. It should contain any facts and arguments that support its requests, and describe the level of essential air service that should be substituted.

(c) Any person may, within 30 days after the filing of a petition for modification, file an answer to that petition titled "Answer to Petition for Modification."

(d) After review, the Department may seek more information and the procedures of §§ 325.5 and 325.7 will be followed.

(Approved by the Office of Management and Budget under control number 3024–0037)

§ 325.11 Form of documents.

All documents filed under this part shall be filed in the Documentary Services Division, U.S. Department of Transportation, 1200 New Jersey Avenue, SE., Washington, D.C. 20590, and on their front page state:

(a) The title of the document;

(b) The name of the affected community;

(c) The name, address, and telephone number of a person who can be contacted for further information concerning the subject of the document; and

(d) In the case of a responsive document, the docket number of the document to which it responds.

§ 325.12 Service of documents.

Any person, except one filing individually as a consumer, who files a document under this part, including responses to the questionnaire, shall serve that document upon those listed in § 325.4(a) of this part and upon the following:

(a) The governor of the State in which the eligible point is located;

(b) Each air carrier providing scheduled service to the affected eligible point;

(c) In the case of a responsive document, the one who filed the document to which it responds; and

(d) The U.S. Postal Service, Assistant General Counsel, Transportation Division, Law Department, Washington, D.C. 20260.

§ 325.13 Environmental evaluations and energy information not required.

Notwithstanding any provision of part 312 or part 313 of this chapter, a person filing a petition or appeal under this part is not required to file an environmental evaluation or energy information with the application.

§ 325.14 Conformity with subpart A of part 302.

Except where they are inconsistent, the provisions of subpart A of part 302 of this chapter shall apply to proceedings under this part.

PART 330—PROCEDURES FOR COMPENSATION OF AIR CARRIERS

Subpart A—General Provisions

Sec.

Subpart B—Application Procedures

Subpart C—Set-Aside for Certain Carriers

AUTHORITY: Pub. L. 107–42, 115 Stat. 230 (49 U.S.C. 40101 note); sec. 124(d), Pub. L. 107–71, 115 Stat. 631 (49 U.S.C. 40101 note).

SOURCE: Docket No. DOT–OST–2001–10885, 67 FR 54066, Aug. 20, 2002, unless otherwise noted.

Subpart A—General Provisions

§330.1 What is the purpose of this part?

The purpose of this part is to establish procedures to implement section 101(a)(2) of the Air Transportation Safety and System Stabilization Act ("the Act"), Public Law 107–42, 115 Stat. 230 (49 U.S.C. 40101 note). This statutory provision is intended to compensate air carriers for direct losses incurred as a result of the Federal ground stop order issued by the Secretary of Transportation, and any subsequent orders, following the terrorist attacks of September 11, 2001, and incremental losses incurred from September 11 through December 31, 2001, as the result of those attacks.

§330.3 What do the terms used in this part mean?

The following terms apply to this part:

Air carrier means any U.S. air carrier, as defined in 49 U.S.C. 40102.

Air taxi operator means an air carrier, other than a commuter air carrier, that holds authority issued under 14 CFR part 298 and 14 CFR part 121 or part 135.

Available seat-miles (ASMs) means the aircraft miles flown on each flight stage by an air carrier multiplied by the number of seats available for revenue use on that stage.

Certificated air carrier means an air carrier holding a certificate issued under 49 U.S.C. 41102 or 41103.

Commuter air carrier means an air carrier as defined in 14 CFR 298.2(e) that holds a commuter air carrier authorization issued under 49 U.S.C. 41738.

Incremental loss means a loss incurred by an air carrier in the period of September 11, 2001–December 31, 2001, as a result of the terrorist attacks on the United States of September 11, 2001. It does not include any loss that would have been incurred if the terrorist attacks on the United States of September 11, 2001, had not occurred.

Regional air carrier means an air carrier that operates at least one large aircraft and has annual operating revenues of less than $100 million.

Revenue ton-miles (RTMs) means the aircraft miles flown on each flight stage by the air carrier multiplied by the number of tons of revenue cargo transported on that stage. For purposes of this part, RTMs include only those resulting from all-cargo flights.

§330.5 What funds will the Department distribute under this part?

Under this part, the Department will distribute up to the full amount of the compensation it determines is payable to air carriers under section 103(b) of the Act, and up to the full amount of the set-aside provided for in subpart C of this part to air carriers eligible for it. The Department may require additional information to support payments to individual carriers in connection with this final payment.

§ 330.7 [Reserved]

§ 330.9 What are the limits on compensation to air carriers?

(a) You are eligible to receive compensation equaling the lesser of your direct and incremental losses or the amount calculated by the formula set forth in section 103(b)(2) of the Act.

(b) If at any time we determine that a carrier has been compensated in an amount that exceeds the amount to which it is entitled under section 103(b) of the Act or the subpart C set-aside program, the Department will notify the carrier of the basis for the determination, the amount that must be repaid, and the procedures to follow for making a repayment. We will follow collection procedures under the Federal Claims Collection Act of 1966 (31 U.S.C. 3701 *et seq.*,) to the extent required by law, in recovering such overpayments. This process will also apply to collection of overpayments by the Department as a result of an audit by representatives of the Department, including the Office of the Inspector General, or the Comptroller General under section 103 of the Act, which may be the subject of a separate collection action.

§ 330.11 Which carriers are eligible to apply for compensation under this part?

(a) If you are a certificated air carrier, a commuter air carrier, an air taxi, or an indirect air carrier, you are eligible to apply for compensation under subpart B of this part.

(b) [Reserved]

(c) If you are a foreign air carrier, commercial operator, flying club, fractional owner, general aviation operator, fixed base operator, flight school, or ticket agent, you are not eligible to apply for compensation under this part.

§ 330.13 If an air carrier received compensation under the Act previously, does it have to submit a third-round application?

Yes, if, as an air carrier, you previously received compensation under section 101(a)(2) of the Act, you must, in all cases, submit a complete Form 330 (Final) and other documents required under this part. You must do so even if you are not seeking additional compensation.

§§ 330.15–330.17 [Reserved]

Subpart B—Application Procedures

§ 330.21 [Reserved]

§ 330.23 To what address must air carriers send their applications?

(a) You must submit your application, and all required supporting information, in hard copy (not by fax or electronic means) to the following address:

U.S. Department of Transportation, Aviation Relief Desk (X–50), 1200 New Jersey Avenue, SE., Washington, DC 20590.

(b) If your complete application is not sent to the address in paragraph (a) of this section as required in this section, the Department will not accept it.

§ 330.25 What are the components of an air carrier's application for compensation?

As an air carrier applying for compensation under this part, you must provide to the Department all materials described in §§ 330.27–330.33. The Department will not accept your application if it does not comply fully with the requirements of this subpart.

§ 330.27 What information must certificated and commuter air carriers submit?

(a) You must submit Form 330 (Final), found in appendix A to this part. Data supplied on Form 330 (Final) in appendix A to this part must be tied only to the airline portion of their businesses and must exclude non-air transportation related expenses.

(b) [Reserved]

(c) Air carriers that operate both passenger/combination aircraft and all-cargo aircraft and routinely report to the Department ASMs and RTMs separately for both types of flights must submit two versions of Form 330 (Final) in appendix A to this part to seek compensation on both an ASM and RTM basis. Financial and operational data (both actual and forecasted) must be disaggregated and correlate exclusively to one or the other type of operation.

(d) You must include the following financial information on Form 330 (Final) for the period September 11, 2001 through December 31, 2001:

(1) Your pre-September 11, 2001, profit/loss forecast for the period beginning September 11, 2001, and ending December 31, 2001. This forecast must reflect seasonal reductions in capacity and the cost savings associated with such reductions. Documentation verifying that the pre-September 11, 2001, forecast was, in fact, completed before that date must also be submitted with your application.

(2) Your actual results for that same period reflecting any losses that were a direct result of the terrorist attacks of September 11, 2001. These actual results must incorporate all cost reductions associated with capacity reductions and furloughs you made due to the reduced demand for air service after the September 11th attacks (e.g., employee pay adjustments and furloughs, changes in aircraft fleet in service, schedule and capacity changes, etc.).

(3) The difference between your forecast profits/losses and actual results for that period (*i.e.*, the difference between the figures in paragraphs (d) (1) and (2) of this section).

(4) The actual losses you report must be net losses, before taxes, taking into account savings from such items as reductions in passenger and cargo handling costs, fuel consumption, landing fees, revenue/traffic-related expenses (e.g., commissions, food and beverage, booking fees, credit card fees), and savings of other costs due to the ground stop and subsequent schedule/capacity/staff reductions (including savings from layoffs of employees, adjusted for severance payments), as well as proceeds from business recovery insurance or other insurance payments. You must not report as losses insurance premium increases that have been or will be compensated by the Government under the Act, or other losses that have been or will be compensated by other subsidies or assistance provided by Federal, state, or local governments.

§330.29 What information must air taxi operators submit on Form 330 (Final) and Form 330–C?

As an air taxi operator, you must complete Form 330 (Final) in accordance with the requirements in §330.27. You must also complete pages 2, 5, and 6 (certifying pages 2 and 5) of Form 330–C as shown in appendix C to this part. Explanatory notes are included on that Form.

§330.31 What data must air carriers submit concerning ASMs or RTMs?

(a) Except as provided in paragraph (d) of this section, if you are applying for compensation as a passenger or combination passenger/cargo carrier, you must have submitted your August 2001 total completed ASM report to the Department for your system-wide air service (e.g., scheduled, non-scheduled, foreign, and domestic).

(b) Except as provided in paragraph (d) of this section, if you are applying for compensation as an all-cargo carrier, you must have submitted your RTM reports to the Department for the second calendar quarter of 2001.

(c) In calculating and submitting ASMs and RTMs under paragraphs (a) and (b) of this section, there are certain things you must not do:

(1) Except at the direction of the Department, or to correct an error that you document to the Department, you must not alter the ASM or RTM reports you earlier submitted to the Department. Your ASMs or RTMs for purposes of this part are as you have reported them to the Department according to existing standards, requirements, and methodologies established by the Office of Airline Information (Bureau of Transportation Statistics).

(2) You must not include ASMs or RTMs resulting from operations by your code-sharing or alliance partners.

(d) If you have not previously reported ASMs or RTMs as provided in paragraphs (a) and (b) of this section for a given operation or operations, you may submit your calculation of ASMs or RTMs to the Department with your application. You must certify the accuracy of this calculation and submit with your application the data and assumptions on which the calculation is based. After reviewing your submission, the Department may modify or reject your calculation.

(1) If you are a direct air carrier that has operated your aircraft for a lessee (*i.e.*, a wet lease, or aircraft, crew, maintenance, and insurance (ACMI) operation), you may submit your calculation of ASMs or RTMs for these flights. Your submission must include the following elements:

(i) Documentation that you otherwise qualify as an air carrier;

(ii) Documentation that you are a wet lessor, and an explanation of why you did not previously report ASMs or RTMs for the operations in question;

(iii) Documentation of the identify of the wet lessees involved in these operations; and

(iv) Accurate and auditable records of ASMs or RTMs actually flown during the relevant time period for these operations.

(2) If you are an indirect air carrier, you may submit your calculation of ASMs or RTMs for flights that direct air carriers have operated for you under contract or other arrangement. Your submission must include the following elements:

(i) Documentation that you otherwise qualify as an air carrier;

(ii) Documentation that you are an indirect air carrier, and an explanation of why you did not previously report ASMs or RTMs for the operations in question;

(iii) Documentation of the identify of the direct air carriers involved in these operations; and

(iv) Accurate and auditable records of ASMs or RTMs actually flown during the relevant time period for these operations.

§ 330.33 Must carriers certify the truth and accuracy of data they submit?

Yes, with respect to all information submitted or retained under §§ 330.27–330.31 and 330.35, your Chief Executive Officer (CEO), Chief Financial Officer (CFO), or Chief Operating Officer (COO) or, if those titles are not used, the equivalent officer, must certify that the submitted information was prepared under his or her supervision and is true and accurate, under penalty of law.

§ 330.35 What records must carriers retain?

As an air carrier that applies for compensation under this part, you must retain records as follows:

(a) You must retain all books, records, and other source and summary documentation supporting your claims for compensation of direct and incremental losses pursuant to Sections 101, 103, and 106 of the Act. This requirement includes, but is not limited to, the following:

(1) You must retain supporting evidence and documentation demonstrating the validity of the data you provide under §§ 330.27–330.31.

(2) You must retain documentation verifying that your pre-September 11, 2001, forecast was the most recent forecast available to that date.

(3) You must also retain documentation outlining the assumptions made for all forecasts and the source of the data and other inputs used in making the forecasts.

(4) You must agree to have your independent public accountant retain all reports, working papers, and supporting documentation pertaining to the agreed upon procedures engagement conducted by your independent public accountant under the requirements of this part for a period of five years. The accountant must make this information available for audit and examination by representatives of the Department of Transportation (including the Office of the Inspector General), the Comptroller General of the United States, or other Federal agencies.

(b) You must preserve and maintain this documentation in a manner that readily permits its audit and examination by representatives of the Department of Transportation (including the Office of the Inspector General), the Comptroller General of the United States, or other Federal agencies.

(c) You must retain this documentation for five years.

(d) You must make all requested data available within one week from a request by the Department of Transportation (including the Office of the Inspector General), the Comptroller General of the United States, or other Federal agencies.

§330.37 Are carriers which participate in this program subject to audit?

(a) All payments you receive from the Department of Transportation under this program are subject to audit. All information you submit with your applications and all records and documentation that you retain are also subject to audit.

(b) Except as provided in paragraph (d) of this section, before you are eligible to receive payment from the final installment of compensation under the Act, there must be an independent public accountant's report based on the performance of procedures agreed upon by the Department of Transportation with respect to the carrier's forecasts and actual results. The independent public accountant's engagement must be performed in accordance with generally accepted professional standards applicable to agreed-upon procedures engagements. You must submit the results of the agreed-upon procedures engagement to the Department with your application for payment of the final installment.

(c) The following are the core requirements for the independent public accountant's review:

(1) Determine that the earnings forecast presented to the Department was inclusive of the entity's full operations as an air carrier and was the most current forecast prepared prior to September 11, 2001;

(2) Determine that, if forecasts presented to the Department for prior periods had material variances from actual results, the carrier provided explanations to account for such variances;

(3) Determine that the methodology for allocating revenue and expenses to the periods September 1–10 and September 11–30, from the forecasted and actual September results, was in accordance with air carrier records and analyses;

(4) Determine that the actual expenses and revenues presented to the Department are in accordance with the official accounting records of the carrier or the financial statements included in the carrier's Securities and Exchange Commission Form 10–Q (for availability, see 17 CFR 249.0–1(b)), and consistent with Generally Accepted Accounting Principles (GAAP), except to the extent that GAAP would require or allow treatment that would be inconsistent with the Act or this part;

(5) Verify that the carrier provided explanations supporting the allocation methodology used if the forecasted and/or actual results for the September 11–30 period was different from allocating 66.7 percent of the total amounts for September;

(6) Determine that the carrier provided full explanations for all material differences between forecast and actual results for the September 11–30, 2001 period and the October 1—December 31, 2001 period;

(7) Determine that the amounts included in management's explanations for such material differences were in accordance with the carrier's analysis of such fluctuations, and the amounts and explanations were traceable to supporting general ledger accounting records or analyses prepared by the carrier;

(8) Determine that the amounts presented to the Department in Form 330 (Final), pages 2–3, in appendix A to this part that the carrier identified as adjustments to the difference between the pre-September 11 forecast and actual results for the period September 11 through December 31, 2001, were in accordance with the official accounting records of the carrier or the financial statements included in the carrier's Securities and Exchange Commission Form 10–Q, and consistent with GAAP, except to the extent that GAAP would require or allow treatment that would be inconsistent with the Act or this part;

(9) Determine that the insurance recoveries and government payments reported by the air carrier and offsetting income were in accordance with the air carrier's general ledger accounting records;

(10) Determine that the information presented in the air carrier's Supplemental Certification were in accordance with the air carrier's general ledger accounting records;

(11) Include in the auditor's report full documentation for each exception taken by the auditor; and

(12) Identify air carrier reports and records utilized in performing the procedures in paragraphs (c)(1) through (11) of this section.

(d) If you are a carrier that reported fewer than 10 million ASMs for the month of August 2001 or fewer than two million RTMs for the quarter ending June 30, 2001, you are not required to report to the Department on the basis of an agreed-upon procedures engagement by an independent public accountant. Instead, you may report on the basis of simplified procedures approved by the Department.

§ 330.39 What are examples of types of losses that the Department does not allow?

(a)(1) The Department generally does not allow air carriers to include in their calculations aircraft impairment charges, charges or expenses attributable to lease buyouts, or other losses that are not actually and fully realized in the period between September 11, 2001 and December 31, 2001.

(2) The Department will consider requests to accept adjustments for extraordinary or non-recurring expenses or revenues on a case-by-case basis. If, as a carrier, you make such a request, you must demonstrate the following to the satisfaction of the Department:

(i) That the expense or revenue was (or was not, as appropriate) the direct result of the terrorist attacks of September 11, 2001;

(ii) That the revenue or expense was reported in accordance with Generally Accepted Accounting Principles (GAAP), except to the extent that the GAAP would require or allow treatment that would be inconsistent with the Act or this part;

(iii) That an expense was fully borne within the September 11—December 31, 2001, period and is permanent; and

(iv) That the resulting additional compensation would not be duplicative of other allowances for compensation.

(b) The Department generally does not accept claims by air carriers that cost savings should be excluded from the calculation of incurred losses. Consequently, the Department will generally not allow such claims to be used in a way that has the effect of increasing the compensation for which an air carrier is eligible.

Subpart C—Set-Aside for Certain Carriers

§ 330.41 What funds is the Department setting aside for eligible classes of air carriers?

The Department is setting aside a sum of up to $35 million to compensate eligible classes of air carriers, for which application of a distribution formula containing ASMs as a factor, as set forth in section 103(b)(2) of the Act, would inadequately reflect their share of direct and incremental losses.

§ 330.43 What classes of air carriers are eligible under the set-aside?

There are two classes of eligible air carriers:

(a) You are a Class I air carrier if you are an air taxi, regional, commuter or indirect air carrier and you reported 75,000 or fewer ASMs to the Department for the month of August, 2001.

(b) You are a Class II air carrier if you are an air taxi, regional, commuter or indirect air carrier and you reported between 75,001 and 10 million ASMs to the Department for the month of August 2001.

[Doc. No. DOT–OST–2001–10885, 67 FR 54066, Aug. 20, 2002, as amended at 68 FR 44458, July 29, 2003]

§ 330.45 What is the basis on which air carriers will be compensated under the set-aside?

(a) Except as provided in paragraph (c) of this section, as an air carrier eligible for compensation through the set-aside, you will be compensated for an amount calculated as provided in paragraph (b) of this section.

(b)(1) As a Class I carrier, your compensation will be calculated using a fixed ASM rate equivalent to the mean losses per ASM for all Class I carriers applying for compensation.

(2) As a Class II carrier, your compensation will be calculated using a graduated ASM rate equivalent to—

(i) The mean loss per ASM for all Class I carriers applying for compensation, for each of the first 75,000 ASMs reported; and

(ii) The mean remaining loss per ASM for all Class II carriers applying for compensation for each ASM in excess of 75,000.

(3) For purposes of this paragraph (b), ASMs are those verified by the Department for August 2001.

(4) Any compensation payments previously made to air carriers eligible for the set-aside will be deducted from the amount calculated as the carrier's total compensation under the set-aside formula.

(c) If you are an air carrier whose compensation is calculated using an ASM rate as provided in paragraph (b) of this section, your compensation will not be less than an amount equivalent to 25 percent of the direct and incremental transportation-related losses you have demonstrated to the satisfaction of the Department were incurred as a direct result of the terrorist attacks of September 11, 2001. Your compensation will not be more than an amount equivalent to the mean percentage of compensation for losses received by passenger and combination air carriers that are not eligible for the set-aside funds, unless you would have been compensated for more than that percentage of losses under the formula set forth in section 103(b)(2) of the Act, in which case you will be compensated under that formula.

[Doc. No. DOT–OST–2001–10885, 67 FR 54066, Aug. 20, 2002, as amended at 68 FR 44458, July 29, 2003]

APPENDIX A TO PART 330—FORMS FOR ALL CARRIERS

FORM 330 (Final)
Page 1 of 6
(for completion by all carriers)

AIR TRANSPORTATION SAFETY AND SYSTEM STABILIZATION ACT APPLICATION FOR COMPENSATION

NAME, ADDRESS, AND TELEPHONE NUMBER OF AIR CARRIER	
TYPE OF DOT ECONOMIC AUTHORITY HELD	
COMPENSATION AMOUNT RECEIVED TO DATE UNDER SECTION 101(A)(2) OF THE ACT	

Forecasted and Actual Losses for the Period September 11, 2001 to December 31, 2001

	Column A	Column B	Column C
Carrier Financial Data	Pre 9/11/01 Forecast for the Period 9/11/01 thru 12/31/01	Actual Results for the Period 9/11/01 thru 12/31/01	Difference Between the Pre 9/11/01 Forecast & Actual Results for 9/11/01 thru 12/31/01 (A-B)
1. Total Operating Revenue			
2. Total Operating Expenses			
3. Total Operating Income (1-2)			
4. Non-Operating Revenue			
5. Non-Operating Expenses			
6. Income Before Taxes (3 + 4 –5)			

Fuel Price Used in Forecast: Average price per gallon of fuel used in the pre-September 11 forecast for the period from September 11, 2001 through December 31, 2001: ____________.

Monthly Profit and Loss Statements: Per section 330.21(h), you must also submit copies of monthly profit and loss statements for the months July 2001 through January 2002, each of which must include the imputed price per gallon average of the fuel used for all aircraft during that month.

FORM 330 (Final)
Page 2 of 6
(for completion by all carriers)

NAME OF AIR CARRIER	

Identification and Explanation of Out-of-Period, Extraordinary or Non-Recurring Revenues and Expenses, and Adjustments to Revenues and Expenses Stemming from Changes Not Directly Related to the Terrorist Events of September 11, 2001

(Note: For definitions and background information in completing this Form, see the sections on "Impairments and Other Extraordinary or Nonrecurring Items" and "Adjustment for Losses Not the Direct Result of the Events of September 11" in the preamble accompanying the original issuance of this form (67 FR 18468; April 16, 2002). See especially the discussion of impairment of assets, lease buyouts, and limitations on treatment of cost reductions below forecast. The three blank lines in each table indicate the format, rather than the expected number of entries.)

In Table 1 below, separately identify and explain any and all out-of-period revenues, extraordinary or non-recurring revenues, and adjustments to actual revenues not directly related to the terrorist events of September 11, 2001 that were **included** in Column B (Boxes B-1 and B-4 on page 1 of this form) but not in Column A, the forecasted revenues. You should use a separate sheet to provide a complete explanation.

Table 1. Adjustments in Included Revenues

Included Revenue Items	Dollar Amount	Explanation (on separate sheet)

In Table 2 below, separately identify and explain any and all out-of-period revenues, extraordinary or non-recurring revenues, and adjustments to actual revenues not directly related to the terrorist events of September 11, 2001 that were **excluded from** Column B (Boxes B-1 and B-4 on page 1 of this form) but not from Column A, the forecasted revenues. You should use a separate sheet if necessary to provide a complete explanation.

Table 2. Adjustments in Excluded Revenues

Excluded Revenue Items	Dollar Amount	Explanation (on separate sheet)

In Table 3 below, separately identify and explain any and all out-of-period expenses, extraordinary or non-recurring expenses, and adjustments to actual expenses not directly related to the terrorist events of September 11, 2001 that were **included** in Column B (Boxes B-2 and B-5 on page 1 of this form) but not in Column A, the forecasted expenses. You should use a separate sheet to provide a complete explanation.

Table 3. Adjustments in Included Expenses

Included Expense Item	Dollar Amount	Explanation (on separate sheet)

In Table 4 below, separately identify and explain any and all out-of-period expenses, extraordinary or non-recurring expenses, and adjustments to actual expenses not directly related to the terrorist events of September 11, 2001 that were **excluded from** Column B (Boxes B-2 and B-5 on page 1 of this form) but not from Column A, the forecasted expenses. You should use a separate sheet to provide a complete explanation.

Table 4. Adjustments in Excluded Expenses

Excluded Expense Item	Dollar Amount	Explanation

FORM 330 (Final)
Page 4 of 6
(to be completed by all-cargo carriers)

NAME OF AIR CARRIER	

ALL-CARGO OPERATIONAL DATA

Cargo Carrier Operating Data	Pre 9-11-01 Forecast for the Period 9-11-01 through 12-31-01	Actual Data for the Period 9-11-01 through 12-31-01	Difference Between the Pre 9-11-01 Forecast and Actual Loss for the Period 9-11-01 thru 12-31-01
Revenue Tons Enplaned			
Revenue Ton Miles (RTMs)			
Available Ton Miles (ATMs)			
Load Factor (%)			
Departures Performed			
Cargo Revenue Yield per RTM			

FORM 330 (Final)
Page 5 of 6
(to be completed by passenger and combination carriers)

NAME OF AIR CARRIER	

PASSENGER AND COMBINATION CARRIER OPERATIONAL DATA

Passenger Carrier Operating Data	Pre 9-11-01 Forecast for the Period 9-11-01 thru 12-31-01	Actual Data for the Period 9-11-01 thru 12-31-01	Difference Between the Pre 9-11-01 Forecast and Actual Loss for the Period 9-11-01 thru 12-31-01
Revenue Passengers Carried			
Revenue Passenger Miles (RPMs)			
Available Seat Miles (ASMs)			
Load Factor (%)			
Breakeven Load Factor (%)			
Average Length of Passenger Haul			
Departures Performed			
Average Passenger Fare ($)			
Passenger Revenue Yield per RPM (cents)			
Operating Revenue per ASM (cents)			
Operating Expense per ASM (cents)			

FORM 330 (Final)
Page 6 of 6

NAME, ADDRESS AND TELEPHONE NUMBER OF AIR CARRIER	

Compensation payments will be made via Electronic Funds Transfer. The Department of Transportation can process this type of payment only if air carrier applicants submit the following banking information with their request:

Air Carrier Bank Routing Number	_ _ _ _ _ _ _ _ _ (9 positions)
Air Carrier Bank Account Number	
Name on Account	
Type of Account (*e.g.*, checking, savings)	
Taxpayer ID Number	

I CERTIFY THAT THE INFORMATION ON FORM 330 (FINAL) AND THE MONTHLY PROFIT AND LOSS STATEMENTS SUBMITED AS PART OF THE APPLICATION ARE TRUE AND ACCURATE UNDER PENALTY OF LAW. FALSIFICATION OF A CLAIM FOR COMPENSATION/PAYMENTS UNDER PUB. L. 107-42 MAY RESULT IN CRIMINAL PROSECUTION RESULTING IN FINE AND/OR IMPRISONMENT.

______________________________ ______________________________
CERTIFYING OFFICER DATE
(CEO, CFO or COO)

Print Name______________________ Telephone Number ______________

Title: ______________________________

APPENDIX B TO PART 330 [RESERVED]

APPENDIX C TO PART 330—FORMS FOR AIR TAXI OPERATORS

FORM 330-C
Page 1 of 7

AIR TRANSPORTATION SAFETY AND SYSTEM STABILIZATION ACT APPLICATION FOR COMPENSATION FOR AIR TAXI OPERATORS

NAME, ADDRESS AND TELEPHONE NUMBER OF AIR TAXI OPERATOR	
DATE OF MOST RECENT PART 298 REGISTRATION OR AMENDMENT	
FAA PART 135 OR 121 CERTIFICATE NUMBER	

PART 1: FORECASTED & ACTUAL LOSSES FOR THE PERIOD SEPTEMBER 11, 2001 TO SEPTEMBER 30, 2001 (in whole dollars)

Air Taxi Financial Data	Contracted/Planned Operations for the Period 9-11-01 through 9-30-01	Actual Results for the Period 9-11-01 through 9-30-01	Difference Between the Pre 09-11-01 Forecast and Actual Results for 9-11-01 through 9-30-01
Total Operating Revenue			
Total Operating Expenses			
Total Operating Income			
Non-Operating Income			
Non-Operating Expenses			
Income Before Taxes			

The operations for hire for which losses are claimed in this chart must have been cancelled entirely, resulting in a complete loss of revenue for those operations. Revenue for these operations must not have been re-captured through subsequent re-accommodation of the same trips. Such non-recovered losses in revenues had associated countervailing reductions in operating expenses that have also been incorporated in the data and calculations in this chart.

FORM 330-C
Page 2 of 7

NAME OF AIR CARRIER	

PART 2: REPORT OF OPERATING STATISTICS FOR AIR TRANSPORTATION FOR HIRE*
(in whole numbers)

FOR AIRCRAFT USED IN PASSENGER, PASSENGER/CARGO & OTHER TRANSPORT SERVICES FOR THE MONTH OF AUGUST 2001						
Aircraft Type	Number of Type in Use for Transport Services**	Number of Seats Available per Aircraft for Use by Paid Passengers	Revenue Aircraft Miles Flown in Transport Services	Available Seat Miles in Transport Services	Revenue Airborne Hours in Transport Services	Revenue Aircraft Departures in Transport Services
1)						
2)						
3)						
4)						
5)						
6)						

FOR AIRCRAFT USED ONLY FOR ALL-CARGO OPERATIONS*** FOR THE QUARTER ENDED JUNE 30, 2001						
Aircraft Type	Number of Type in Use for Transport Services**	Available Payload Capacity (in pounds)	Revenue Aircraft Miles Flown in Transport Services	Cargo Revenue Ton Miles in Transport Services (if known)	Revenue Airborne Hours in Transport Services	Revenue Aircraft Departures in Transport Services
1)						
2)						
3)						
4)						
5)						
6)						

* Air transportation for hire includes only commercial services operated under Part 121 or Part 135 operating certificates. Other services operated under Part 91, as well as dry leases and flights operated for the purpose of flight instructions, maintenance testing and aircraft positioning are excluded.
** This number should be the same number as listed on the operator's current Part 298 registration and current FAA-issued operations specifications.
*** For all-cargo operations, please note aircraft that are operated under contract for another express or all-cargo carrier and identify those carriers and provide details on a separate, attached sheet.

NOTE: If the operator records and reports aircraft miles, the operator should compute and enter available seat miles by multiplying the number of seats times the aircraft miles. If the operator does not report aircraft miles, DOT will compute the available seat miles. If the operator records and reports cargo RTMs, the operator should enter the amounts directly on the form. If not, DOT will estimate the RTMs based on the other data submitted. All carriers, however, must report airborne hours and departures.

FORM 330-C
Page 3 of 7

NAME OF AIR CARRIER	

PART 3: ESTIMATE OF LOSS FOR THE PERIOD
OCTOBER 1, 2001 TO DECEMBER 31, 2001
(in whole dollars)

Air Taxi Financial Data	Pre 09-11-01 Forecast* for the Period 10-01-01 through 12-31-01	Current Forecast for the Period 10-01-01 through 12-31-01	Difference Between the Pre 09-11-01 Forecast and the Current Forecast for the period 10-01-01 through 12-31-01
Total Operating Revenue			
Total Operating Expenses			
Total Operating Income			
Non-Operating Income			
Non-Operating Expenses			
Income Before Taxes			

* For those air taxi operators that do not typically prepare forecasts, use contracted/scheduled services that were scheduled before September 11, 2001 and can be documented.

FORM 330-C
Page 4 of 7

NAME OF AIR CARRIER	

PART 4: OPERATIONAL DATA
(in whole numbers or dollars)

Air Taxi Operational Data		Pre 9-11-01 Forecast for the Period 10-01-01 through 12-31-01	Current Forecast for the Period 10-01-01 through 12-31-01	Difference Between the Pre 9-11-01 Forecast and the Forecast for 10-01-01 through 12-31-01
Total operating revenues				
Total operating expenses				
Total operations for hire (departures)				
Total available seat miles OR				
Total revenue ton miles				
Total aircraft in fleet:				
(Show aircraft types in the next column)	1)			
	2)			
	3)			
	4)			
	5)			
	6)			
Seats available per aircraft:				
(Show aircraft types in the next column)	1)			
	2)			
	3)			
	4)			
	5)			
	6)			
Total aircraft miles flown:				
(Show aircraft types in the next column)	1)			
	2)			
	3)			
	4)			
	5)			
	6)			
Total airborne hours:				
(Show aircraft types in the next column)	1)			
	2)			
	3)			
	4)			
	5)			
	6)			
Available payload capacity (in lbs.) (all-cargo operations only):				
(Show aircraft types in the next column)	1)			
	2)			
	3)			
	4)			
	5)			
	6)			

FORM 330-C
Page 5 of 7

NAME OF AIR CARRIER	

PART 5: HISTORICAL OPERATIONAL DATA
(in whole numbers or dollars)

Air Taxi Operational Data		Month of Sept 2000	Month of Oct 2000	Month of Nov 2000	Month of Dec 2000		Month of July 2001	Month of Aug 2001
Total operating revenues								
Total operating expenses								
Total operations for hire (departures)								
Total available seat miles **OR**								
Total revenue ton miles								
Total aircraft in fleet:								
(Show aircraft types in the next column)	1)							
	2)							
	3)							
	4)							
	5)							
	6)							
Seats available per aircraft:								
(Show aircraft types in the next column)	1)							
	2)							
	3)							
	4)							
	5)							
	6)							
Total aircraft miles flown:								
(Show aircraft types in the next column)	1)							
	2)							
	3)							
	4)							
	5)							
	6)							
Total airborne hours:								
(Show aircraft types in the next column)	1)							
	2)							
	3)							
	4)							
	5)							
	6)							
Available payload capacity (in lbs.) (all-cargo operations only):								
(Show aircraft types in the next column)	1)							
	2)							
	3)							
	4)							
	5)							
	6)							

FORM 330-C
Page 6 of 7

NAME OF AIR CARRIER	

Part 6: ACCOUNT INFORMATION AND CERTIFICATION

Compensation payments will be made via Electronic Funds Transfer. The Department of Transportation can process this type of payment only if air carrier applicants submit the following banking information with their requests:

Air Carrier Bank Routing Number	_ _ _ _ _ _ _ _ _ (9 positions)
Air Carrier Bank Account Number	
Name on Account	
Type of Account (*e.g.*, checking, savings)	
Taxpayer ID Number	

I CERTIFY THAT THE INFORMATION CONTAINED IN PARTS 1 THROUGH 5 OF THIS FORM (FORM 330-C) IS TRUE AND ACCURATE UNDER PENALTY OF LAW. FALSIFICATION OF A CLAIM FOR COMPENSATION/PAYMENTS UNDER PUB. L. 107-42 MAY RESULT IN CRIMINAL PROSECUTION RESULTING IN FINE AND/OR IMPRISONMENT (18 U.S.C. 1001).

Certifying Officer (signature) **Date**

Print Name and Title (CEO, CFO or COO) **Telephone Number**

FORM 330-C
Page 7 of 7

EXPLANATORY NOTES:

1. In order to avoid the possibility of misinterpretation, we are requiring that numbers or notations (for example, "N/A") be entered into all data blocks on all forms even if those numbers are zero. We also note that all amounts are to be reported in whole numbers.

2. The required forecasted amounts should be based on a forecasting and/or budgeting approach or similar accounting system if the air carrier routinely uses that method. For those carriers whose accounting systems or methodologies rely more on actual or short run projections, we ask that they make a "good faith" effort to categorize their revenues and expenses according to the required forms. In this regard, the following may provide additional assistance.

3. As general guidance, we include the following information that has been adapted from 14 CFR Part 298 (Section 298.62) or 14 CFR Part 241. Air transportation for hire includes only commercial services operated under Part 121 or Part 135 operating certificates. Other services operated under Part 91, as well as dry leases and flights operated for the purpose of flight instructions, maintenance testing and aircraft positioning are excluded.

4. Total operating revenues generally include gross revenues accruing from services ordinarily associated with air transportation. It is meant to include revenue derived from scheduled service, on demand and nonscheduled service operations.

5. In general, total operating expenses include expenses of the type usually and ordinarily incurred in the performance of air transportation. It includes expenses incurred: directly in the in-flight operation of aircraft; in the holding of aircraft and aircraft personnel in readiness for assignment to an in-flight status; on the ground, in controlling and protecting the in-flight movement of aircraft; landing and handling aircraft on the ground; selling transportation, servicing and handling passenger and cargo traffic; promoting the development of traffic; and administering operations generally. It shall also include expenses which are specifically identifiable with the repair and upkeep of property and equipment used in the performance of air transportation and all depreciation and amortization expenses applicable to property and equipment used in providing air transportation services.

6. Non-operating income includes such items as interest income and other similar investments. It may also include capital gains (for example, aircraft sales). Non-operating expenses include interest expense and other expenses attributable to financing or other activities that are extraneous to and not an integral part of air transportation or its incidental services. It may also include capital losses (for example, aircraft sales).

7. We note that claims for compensation cannot be based solely on lost revenues, that is, the total revenue that an air taxi operator expected to receive from flights that would have been flown but were cancelled due to the DOT-mandated flight stoppage. While these amounts would provide information on the changes in total operating revenues, it is important to recognize that changes in total operating expenses must also be considered in calculating operating income and net income which is ultimately used to determine compensation. Also, for those carriers with less sophisticated accounting systems, the calculation of forecasted total operating expenses might be based on an analysis of fixed costs (those that stay the same regardless of the number of flights or changes in passenger and cargo traffic) and variable costs (those that change in proportion to the level of operations and traffic volume).

8. All carriers should be able to provide actual financial results for the period of September 11 to September 30, 2001, as required. We will not accept incomplete forms or reports that are submitted in lieu of the required forms and we will not accept the submission of invoices, flight logs, sales records, calendar notations of events or other similar documents in lieu of the required forms. However, supporting documentation must be retained for audit purposes.

PART 331 [RESERVED]

SUBCHAPTER C [RESERVED]

SUBCHAPTER D—SPECIAL REGULATIONS

PART 372—OVERSEAS MILITARY PERSONNEL CHARTERS

Subpart A—General Provisions

Subpart B—Exemption

Subpart C—Conditions and Limitations

Subpart D—Operating Authorization

AUTHORITY: 49 U.S.C. Chapters 401, 411, 413, 417.

SOURCE: SPR–54, 37 FR 11163, June 3, 1972, unless otherwise noted.

Subpart A—General Provisions

§ 372.1 Applicability.

This part establishes the terms and conditions governing the furnishing of overseas military personnel charters in air transportation by direct air carriers or foreign air carriers and by overseas military charter operators. This part also relieves charter operators from the provisions of section 41102 of Title 49 of the United States Code ("the Statute"), for the purpose of enabling them to provide overseas military personnel charters utilizing aircraft chartered from such direct air carriers or foreign air carriers. Nothing contained in this part shall be construed as repealing or amending any provisions of any of the Department's regulations, unless the context so requires.

[SPR–60, 37 FR 19122, Sept. 19, 1972, as amended at 60 FR 43529, Aug. 22, 1995]

§ 372.2 Definitions.

As used in this part, unless the context otherwise requires:

Charter means overseas military personnel charter.

Charter operator means overseas military personnel charter operator.

Charter participant means a member of the overseas military personnel charter group.

Charter price means the total amount of money paid by the charter participant to the charter operator for air transportation.

Immediate family means only the following persons: the spouse, children, parents, parents of the spouse, children of the parents, and children of the parents of the spouse of (1) military personnel on active duty with the United States Armed Forces (including Coast Guard) stationed outside the contiguous states of the United States and the District of Columbia, and (2) civilian employees of the Department of Defense who are citizens of the United States and are stationed in a foreign country, or in a U.S. territory or possession, where U.S. military personnel are stationed.

Overseas military personnel charter means a charter, either one-way or round-trip, limited to military personnel on active duty with the U.S. Armed Forces (including the Coast Guard), stationed outside the 48 contiguous States of the United States and the District of Columbia, and/or civilian employees of the Department of Defense who are citizens of the United States and are stationed in a foreign country, or in a U.S. territory or possession, where such U.S. military personnel are stationed, and/or the immediate families of the foregoing persons, where the following conditions are met: (a) All military personnel and civilian employees of the Department of Defense participating in the charter are on official furlough, leave, pass, or other authorized absence from duty, and (b) the transportation is between a place in the 48 contiguous States of the United States or the District of Columbia and a place in Alaska, Hawaii, or a territory or possession of the United States, or a foreign country in which military personnel of the United States are stationed: *Provided, however*, That nothing contained herein shall preclude an overseas military personnel charter operator from utilizing any unused space on an aircraft chartered by it pursuant to this part for the transportation, on a free or reduced-rate basis, of such charter operator's employees, directors, and officers, and the parents and immediate families of such persons, subject to the provisions of part 223 of this chapter.

Overseas military personnel charter operator means any citizen of the United States, as defined in section 40102(a)(15) of the Statute authorized hereunder to engage in the formation of overseas military personnel charter groups and who complies with the provisions of this part.

Person means any individual, firm, association, partnership, or corporation.

Statute when used in this chapter means Subtitle VII of Title 49 of the United States Code (Transportation).

[SPR–54, 37 FR 11163, June 3, 1972, as amended by SPR–69, 38 FR 14164, May 30, 1973; SPR–109, 41 FR 35158, Aug. 20, 1976; 60 FR 43529, Aug. 22, 1995]

§ 372.3 Waiver.

A waiver of any of the provisions of this regulation may be granted by the Department upon its own initiative, or upon the submission by a charter operator of a written request therefor: *Provided*, That such a waiver is in the public interest and it appears to the Department that special or unusual circumstances warrant a departure from the provisions set forth herein.

§ 372.4 Enforcement.

In case of any violation of the provisions of the Statute, or this part, or any other rule, regulation, or order issued under the Statute, the violator may be subject to a proceeding pursuant to section 46101 of the Statute before the Department, or sections 46106 through 46108 of the Statute before a U.S. district court, as the case may be, to compel compliance therewith, to civil penalties pursuant to the provisions of section 46301 of the Statute, or in the case of willful violation, to criminal penalties pursuant to the provisions of section 46316 of the Statute; or other lawful sanctions.

[SPR–54, 37 FR 11163, June 3, 1972, as amended at 60 FR 43529, Aug. 22, 1995]

§ 372.5 Suspension or revocation of authority.

The Department reserves the power to suspend the authority of any charter operator, without hearing, if it finds that such action is necessary in order to protect the rights of the traveling public, or to revoke such authority for cause.

Subpart B—Exemption

§ 372.10 Exemption.

Charter operators are hereby relieved from the provisions of section 41102 of the Statute only if and so long as they comply with the provisions of this part and the conditions imposed herein, and to the extent necessary to permit them to organize and arrange overseas military personnel charters.

[SPR–176, 46 FR 43960, Sept. 2, 1981, as amended at 60 FR 43529, Aug. 22, 1995]

Subpart C—Conditions and Limitations

§ 372.20 Requirement of operating authorization.

No person shall engage in air transportation as an overseas military personnel charter operator by organizing, providing, selling, or offering to sell, soliciting, or advertising an overseas military personnel charter or charters unless there is in force an operating authorization issued pursuant to

§372.31 authorizing such person to engage in such transportation.

[Doc. No. 47939, 57 FR 40105, Sept. 2, 1992]

§372.21 Solicitation.

Solicitation of charter participants through advertising by charter operators shall be restricted to the following:

(a) Radio and television stations operated by the U.S. Armed Forces;

(b) Newspapers, periodicals, or other printed media disseminated and distributed primarily among military personnel or civilian employees of the Department of Defense: *Provided, however*, That any printed advertisement of a charter operator shall include a statement explaining that eligibility for participation in such charters is limited to military servicemen who are stationed outside of the 48 contiguous States and the District of Columbia, and/or U.S. citizen civilian DOD employees who are stationed in a foreign country, or a U.S. territory or possession, where U.S. military personnel are stationed, and their respective immediate families.

§372.22 Discrimination.

No charter operator shall make, give, or cause any undue or unreasonable preference or advantage to any particular person, port, locality, or description of traffic in air transportation in any respect whatsoever or subject any particular person, port, locality, or description of traffic in air transportation to any unjust discrimination or any undue or unreasonable prejudice or disadvantage in any respect whatsoever.

§372.23 Methods of competition.

No charter operator shall engage in unfair or deceptive practices or unfair methods of competition in air transportation or the sale thereof.

§372.24 Surety bond, depository agreement, escrow agreement.

(a) Before selling or offering to sell, soliciting or advertising any charter flight, a charter operator shall comply with one of the three following requirements:

(1) The charter operator shall furnish a surety bond in an amount not less than the maximum fare held out for charter flights proposed to be operated during each calendar month multiplied by 90 percent of the number of available seats on such flights: *Provided, however*, That the liability of the surety to any charter participant shall not exceed the charter operator's applicable tariff fare. Such bond shall be filed with the Department not less than 45 days prior to the commencement of the calendar month covered by the bond together with a list of flights proposed to be operated during the month showing charter price, departure dates, equipment to be used for each flight and the seating capacity: *Provided, however*, That the amount of the bond shall be increased if additional charter flights are proposed or may be reduced if proposed charter flights are canceled, in which event a substitute bond and amended list of proposed flights shall be filed with the Department within 10 days of the date that the charter operator adds flights or cancels flights previously proposed, but in no event later than 2 days prior to the operation of any such additional charter flights; or

(2) The charter operator shall:

(i) Furnish and file with the Department a surety bond in the amount of $100,000 for the protection of the charter participants: *Provided, however*, That the liability of the surety to any charter participant shall not exceed the charter operator's applicable tariff fare; and

(ii) Enter into an agreement with a bank, the terms of which shall include the following:

(*a*) Each participant shall pay for his deposit and subsequent payments comprising the charter participant's tariff fare only by check or money order payable to such bank which shall maintain a separate accounting for each flight: *Provided, however*, That if the participant makes a cash deposit, the charter operator who receives such cash deposit shall forthwith remit to the designated bank a check for the full amount of the deposit;

(*b*) The bank shall not pay the air carrier or foreign air carrier the charter price for the transportation earlier than 60 days (including day of departure) prior to the scheduled day of departure of the originating or returning flight, upon certification of the departure date and price by the charter operator;

(*c*) The bank shall reimburse the charter operator for refunds made by the latter to the participants upon written notification from the charter operator;

(*d*) If the charter operator notifies the bank that a flight has been canceled, the bank shall make the applicable refunds directly to the participants;

(*e*) Except as provided in paragraph (a)(2)(ii)(*c*) of this section, the bank shall not pay any funds from the account to the charter operator prior to 2 banking days after completion of each flight when the balance in the account shall be paid to the charter operator upon certification of the completion date by the charter operator and direct air carrier;

(*f*) Notwithstanding any provisions above, the amount of total cash deposits required to be maintained in the depository account of the bank may be reduced by one or both of the following: The amount of surety bond in the form prescribed herein in excess of the minimum bond required by paragraph (a)(2)(i) of this section; an escrow with the designated bank of Federal, State, or municipal bonds or other securities, consisting of certificates of deposit issued by banks having a stated policy of redeeming such certificates before maturity at the request of the holder (subject only to such interest penalties or other conditions as may be required by law), or negotiable securities which are publicly traded on a securities exchange, all such securities to be made payable to the escrow account: *Provided,* That such other securities shall be substituted in an amount no greater than 80 percent of the total market value of the escrow account at the time of such substitution: *And provided, further,* That should the market value of such other securities subsequently decrease, from time to time, then additional cash or securities qualified for investment hereunder shall promptly be added to the escrow account, in an amount equal to the amount of such decreased value; or

(3) The charter operator shall:

(i) Furnish and file with the Department a surety bond in the amount of $100,000 for the protection of the charter participants: *Provided, however,* That the liability of the surety to any charter participant shall not exceed the charter operator's applicable tariff fare; and

(ii) Enter into an agreement with a bank, the terms of which shall include the following:

(*a*) Whenever the gross amount of customers' deposits exceeds 25 percent of the charter operator's net worth, as computed under generally accepted accounting principles, the charter operator shall, on or before the 30th day of the succeeding month, place in escrow or in trust with the bank cash in an amount at least equal to the amount by which such deposits exceed 25 percent of its net worth: *Provided,* That negotiable securities may be substituted for cash, but the market value thereof shall at all times be not less than the amount of cash for which they are substituted;

(*b*) The escrow agreement or the trust agreement between the bank and the operator shall not be effective until approved by the Department. Claims against the escrow or trust may be made only with respect to the nonperformance of air transportation.

(b) As used in this section, the term *bank* means a bank insured by the Federal Deposit Insurance Corporation.

(c) Any bond furnished under this section shall insure the financial responsibility of the charter operator and the supplying of the air transportation in accordance with the contract between the charter operator and the charter participants, and shall be in the form set forth as appendix A to this part. Such bond shall be issued by a bonding or surety company (1) whose surety bonds are accepted by the Interstate Commerce Commission under 49 CFR 1084.6; or (2) which is listed in Best's Insurance Reports (fire and casualty) with a general policyholders' rating of "A" or better. The bonding or surety company shall be one legally authorized to issue bonds of that type in the State in which the charter originates or in which the charter operator is incorporated. For purposes of this section, the term "State" includes any territory or possession of the United States, or the District of Columbia. The bond shall be specifically identified by the issuing surety with a company bond numbering system so that the Department may identify the bond with the specific charter or charters to which it relates: *Provided, however,* That these data may be set forth in an addendum attached to the bond which addendum must be signed by the charter operator and the surety company. It shall be effective on or before the date the operating authorization becomes effective. If the bond does not comply with the requirements of this section, or for any reason fails to provide satisfactory or adequate protection for the public, the Department will notify the direct air carrier and the charter operator, by registered or certified mail, stating the deficiencies of the bond. Unless such deficiencies are corrected within the time set forth in such notification, the subject charters shall in no event be operated.

(d) Any bond furnished under this section shall provide that unless the charter participant files a claim with the charter operator, or, if he is unavailable, with the surety, within sixty (60) days after termination of the charter, the surety shall be released from all liability under the bond to such charter participant. The contract between the charter operator and the charter participants shall contain notice of this provision.

(Secs. 101(3), 204(a), 401, and 402 of the Federal Aviation Act of 1958, as amended, 72 Stat. 737, 743, 754, and 757, as amended, 49 U.S.C. 1301, 1324, 1371 and 1372)

[SPR-54, 37 FR 11163, June 3, 1972, as amended by SPR-60, 37 FR 19122, Sept. 19, 1972; SPR-63, 37 FR 22849, Oct. 26, 1972; SPR-95, 40 FR 52355, Nov. 10, 1975; Doc. No. 47939, 57 FR 40105, Sept. 2, 1992]

§ 372.25 Tariffs to be filed for charter trips.

Effective October 1, 1972, a charter operator shall not operate or sell or offer to sell, solicit or advertise, any charter trips unless such operator shall have on file with the Department a currently effective tariff showing all rates, fares, and charges for such charter trips and showing the rules, regulations, practices, and services in connection with such transportation.

§ 372.26 [Reserved]

§ 372.27 Name of operator.

It shall be an express condition upon the exercise of the exemption herein granted and the operating authorizations issued hereunder, that the charter operator concerned, in holding out to the public and performing air transportation services, shall do so only in a name the use of which is authorized under the provisions of part 215 of this chapter.

§ 372.28 Record retention.[1]

(a) Every charter operator conducting a charter pursuant to this part shall retain for 2 years after completion of the charter or series of charters true copies of the following documents at its principal or general office in the United States:

(1) All documents which evidence or reflect deposits made by, and refunds made to, each charter participant;

(2) All statements, invoices, bills, and receipts from suppliers or furnishers of goods and services in connection with the charter or series of charters.

(b) Every charter operator shall make the documents listed in this section available upon request by an authorized representative of the Department and shall permit such representative to make such notes and copies thereof as he deems appropriate.

[SPR-54, 37 FR 11163, June 3, 1972, as amended by Doc. No. 47939, 57 FR 40105, Sept. 2, 1992]

[1] Whoever, in any matter within the jurisdiction of any department or agency of the United States knowingly and willfully falsifies, conceals, or covers up by any trick, scheme, or device, a material fact, or makes any false, fictitious, or fraudulent statements or representations, or makes or uses any false writing of document knowing the same to contain any false, fictitious, or fraudulent statement or entry, shall be fined not more than $10,000 or imprisoned not more than 5 years, or both. Title 18, U.S.C. sec. 1001.

Subpart D—Operating Authorization

§ 372.30 Application.

(a) *Application.* Any person desiring to operate as an overseas military personnel charter operator may apply to the Department for an appropriate operating authorization. Contact the Office of Aviation Analysis, Special Authorities Division, for filing instructions. The application shall be certified by a responsible official of such person and shall contain the following information:

(1) Date;

(2) Name of applicant, trade names, and name in which authorization is to be issued;

(3) Address of principal office and mailing address;

(4) Form of organization (*i.e.*, corporation, partnership, etc.), State under whose laws company is authorized to operate and date company was formed;

(5) A list containing the names of each officer, director, partner, owner, or member of applicant, and holder of more than 5 percent of outstanding stock if a corporation, or owner of more than a 5-percent interest if other than a corporation; an indication as to whether or not 75 percent or more of the voting interest is owned or controlled by citizens of the United States or one of its possessions; if more than 5 percent of applicant's stock is held by a corporation, an indication must be made as to whether or not 75 percent or more of the voting interest in such corporation is owned or controlled by citizens of the United States or one of its possessions;

(6) A description of current business activities and of former business experience in, or related to, the transportation field;

(7) Description of operating authority granted applicant by agencies of the U.S. Government (such as customs broker, surface or air freight forwarder, motor carrier, ocean freight forwarder, etc.), and, if applicable, reasons for revocation or other termination;

(8) List of names of the officers, owners, etc., of applicants who have at any time applied for any type of authority or registration from the Civil Aeronautics Board or the Department of Transportation and, if applicable, reasons for revocation or other termination;

(9) List of officers, owners, etc., of applicant who have at any time been employed by or associated with any air carrier authorized to operate by the Civil Aeronautics Board or the Department of Transportation indicating dates of employment and capacity in which employed;

(10) Any additional information in support of application;

(11) Balance sheet as of a date not more than 3 months prior to application and profit and loss statement for the full year ending as of date of balance sheet;

(12) Brief account of any arrangement by which applicant will have available financial sources and facilities of other companies or individuals;

(13) The charter operator's surety bond and, where applicable, a copy of the depository, escrow or trust agreement with a bank as provided in § 372.24.[2]

(b) *Additional information.* The applicant shall also submit such other additional information pertinent to its proposed activities as may be requested by the Department with respect to any individual application.

[SPR–54, 37 FR 11163, June 3, 1972, as amended by Doc. No. 47939, 57 FR 40105, Sept. 2, 1992; 60 FR 43529, Aug. 22, 1995]

§ 372.31 Issuance.

(a) If, after the filing of an application for an operating authorization, it appears that the applicant is capable of performing the air transportation authorized by this part as an overseas military personnel charter operator and of conforming to the provisions of the Act and all rules and requirements thereunder, and that the conduct of such operations by the applicant will not be inconsistent with the public interest, the applicant will be notified by letter. Such notification will advise

[2] The surety bond and, where applicable, a copy of the depository escrow, or trust agreement with the bank should not be filed with the Department until the applicant is notified by the Department to do so.

the applicant that, upon the filing of a valid tariff pursuant to § 372.25, an operating authorization will be issued to the applicant.

(b) If, after the filing of an application for an operating authorization, it appears that the applicant has not made a due showing of capability or that the conduct of operations by the applicant might otherwise be inconsistent with the public interest, the Department shall by letter notify the applicant of its findings to that effect. The Department may dismiss any such application unless within 30 days of the date of the mailing of such letter, the applicant has in writing requested reconsideration and submitted such additional information as it believes will make the necessary showing, or requested that the application be assigned for hearing, in which case the applicant shall outline the evidence to be presented at such hearing and shall show the need for hearing in order properly to present its case.

(c) In the event that reconsideration or hearing is requested, the Department may, without notice or hearing, enter an order of approval or of disapproval in accordance without notice or hearing, enter an order of approval or of disapproval in accordance with its determination of the public interest upon the showing made, or on its own initiative may assign the application for hearing.

§ 372.32 Effective period.

Each operating authorization shall be effective upon the date specified therein, and shall continue in effect, unless sooner suspended or revoked, during such period as the authority provided by this part shall remain in effect, or if issued for a limited period of time, shall continue in effect until the expiration thereof unless sooner suspended or revoked.

§ 372.33 Nontransferability.

(a) An operating authorization shall be nontransferable and shall be effective only with respect to the person named therein or his successor by operation of law, subject to the provisions of this section. The following persons may temporarily continue operations under an operating authorization issued in the name of another person, for a maximum period of 6 months from the effective date of succession, by giving written notice of such succession to the Department within 60 days after the succession:

(1) Administrators or executors of deceased persons;

(2) Guardians of incapacitated persons;

(3) Surviving partner or partners collectively of dissolved partnerships; and

(4) Trustees, receivers, conservators, assignees, or other such persons who are authorized by law to collect and preserve the property of financially disabled persons.

(b) All operations by successors, as above authorized, shall be performed in the name or names of the prior holder of the operating authorization and the name of the successor, whose capacity shall also be designated. Any successor desiring to continue operations after the expiration of the 6-month period above authorized must file an application for a new operating authorization within 120 days after such succession. If a timely application is filed, such successor may continue operations until final disposition of the application by the Department.

Appendix A to Part 372—Overseas Military Personnel Charter Operator's Surety Bond Under Part 372 of the Special Regulations of the Department of Transportation (14 CFR Part 372)

Know all men by these presents, that we ____________ (name of charter operator) of ____________ (address) as Principal hereinafter called "Principal"), and ____________ (name of surety) a corporation created and existing under the laws of the State of ____________ (State) as Surety (hereinafter called "Surety") are held and firmly bound unto the United States of America in the sum of ____________ (see § 372.24(a), 14 CFR Part 372) for which payment, well and truly to be made, we bind ourselves and our heirs, executors, administrators, successors, and assigns, jointly and severally firmly by these presents.

Whereas Principal is an overseas military personnel charter operator pursuant to the provisions of Part 372 of the Department's

Special Regulations and other rules and regulations of the Department relating to security for the protection of charter participants, and has elected to file with the Department of Transportation such a bond as will insure financial responsibility with respect to all monies received from charter participants for services in connection with overseas military personnel charters to be operated subject to Part 372 of the Department's Special Regulations in accordance with contracts, agreements, or arrangements therefor, and

Whereas this bond is written to assure compliance by Principal as an authorized charter operator with Part 372 of the Department's Special Regulations, and other rules and regulations of the Department relating to security for the protection of charter participants, and shall inure to the benefit of any and all charter participants to whom Principal may be held legally liable for any damages herein described.

Now, therefore, the condition of this obligation is such that if Principal shall pay or cause to be paid to charter participants any sum or sums for which Principal may be held legally liable by reason of Principal's failure faithfully to perform, fulfill and carry out all contracts, agreements, and arrangements made by Principal while this bond is in effect with respect to the receipt of moneys from charter participants, and proper disbursement thereof pursuant to and in accordance with the provisions of Part 372 of the Department's Special Regulations, then this obligation shall be void, otherwise to remain in full force and effect.

The liability of Surety with respect to any charter participant shall not exceed the charter price paid by or on behalf of such participant.

The liability of Surety shall not be discharged by any payment or succession of payments hereunder, unless and until such payment or payments shall amount in the aggregate to the penalty (face amount) of the bond, but in no event shall Surety's obligation hereunder exceed the amount of said penalty.

Surety agrees to furnish written notice to the Office of Aviation Analysis, Department of Transportation, forthwith of all suits or claims made and judgments rendered, and payments made by Surety under this bond.

This bond shall cover the following Charters:[1]

Surety company's bond No. ____________
Date of flight departure ____________
Place of flight departure ____________

This bond is effective on the ____ day of ________, 199_, 12:01 a.m., standard time at the address of Principal as stated herein and as hereinafter provided. Principal or Surety may at any time terminate this bond by written notice to: Special Authorities Division (X–57), Office of Aviation Analysis, U.S. Department of Transportation, Washington, DC 20590, such termination to become effective thirty (30) days after the actual receipt of said notice by the Department. Surety shall not be liable hereunder for the payment of any damages hereinbefore described which arise as a result of any contracts, agreements, undertakings, or arrangements for the supplying of transportation and other services made by Principal after the termination of this bond as herein provided, but such termination shall not affect the liability of the bond hereunder for the payment of any damages arising as a result of contracts, agreements, or arrangements for the supplying of transportation and other services made by Principal prior to the date that such termination becomes effective. Liability of Surety under this bond shall in all events be limited only to a charter participant or charter participants who shall within sixty (60) days after the termination of the particular charter described herein give written notice of claim to the charter operator or, if it is unavailable, to Surety, and all liability on this bond shall automatically terminate sixty (60) days after the termination date of each particular charter covered by this bond except for claims made in the time provided herein.

In witness whereof, the said Principal and Surety have executed this instrument on the ____ day of ________, 199_.

PRINCIPAL

Name ____________
By: Signature and title ____________
Witness ____________

SURETY

Name ____________
By: Signature and title ____________
Witness ____________

Only corporations may qualify to act as surety and they must meet the requirements set forth in § 372.24(c) of Part 372.

[Doc. No. 47939, 57 FR 40105, Sept. 2, 1992, as amended at 60 FR 43529, Aug. 22, 1995]

[1] These data may be supplied in an addendum attached to the bond; however, all pages are to bear the Surety's seal.

PART 374—IMPLEMENTATION OF THE CONSUMER CREDIT PROTECTION ACT WITH RESPECT TO AIR CARRIERS AND FOREIGN AIR CARRIERS

Sec.

AUTHORITY: 15 U.S.C. 1601–1693r; 49 U.S.C. Subtitle VII; and 12 CFR parts 202 and 226.

SOURCE: SPR–175, 46 FR 43960, Sept. 2, 1981, unless otherwise noted.

§374.1 Purpose.

The purpose of this part is to state the Department of Transportation's responsibility to enforce air carrier and foreign air carrier compliance with Subchapters I, III, IV, V and VI of the Consumer Credit Protection Act and Regulations B and Z of the Board of Governors of the Federal Reserve System.

[62 FR 25841, May 12, 1997]

§374.2 Applicability.

This part is applicable to all air carriers and foreign air carriers engaging in consumer credit transactions.

§374.3 Compliance with the Consumer Credit Protection Act and regulations.

(a) Each air carrier and foreign air carrier shall comply with the requirements of the Consumer Credit Protection Act, 15 U.S.C. 1601–1693r. Any violation of the following requirements of that Act will be a violation of 49 U.S.C. Subtitle VII, enforceable by the Department of Transportation:

(1) The Truth in Lending Act, as supplemented by the Fair Credit Billing Act, 15 U.S.C. 1601–1667, requiring disclosure of credit terms to the consumer and prohibiting inaccurate or unfair credit billing and credit card practices.

(2) The Fair Credit Reporting Act, 15 U.S.C. 1681–1681 setting forth requirements to be met by consumer credit reporting agencies and persons who use consumer credit reports.

(b) Each air carrier and foreign air carrier shall comply with the requirements of Regulation B, 12 CFR part 202, and Regulation Z, 12 CFR part 226, of the Board of Governors of the Federal Reserve Board. Any violation of the requirements of those regulations will be a violation of 49 U.S.C. Subtitle VII, enforceable by the Department of Transportation.

[62 FR 25841, May 12, 1997]

§374.4 Enforcement procedure.

The statutes and regulations referred to in §374.3 may be enforced by an enforcement procedure as set forth in part 302 of this chapter or by the assessment of civil penalties under 49 U.S.C. 46301.

[62 FR 25842, May 12, 1997]

PART 374a—EXTENSION OF CREDIT BY AIRLINES TO FEDERAL POLITICAL CANDIDATES

Sec.

AUTHORITY: 49 U.S.C. chapters 401, 411, 415, 417.

SOURCE: SPR–53, 37 FR 9388, May 10, 1972, unless otherwise noted.

§374a.1 Purpose.

Section 401 of the Federal Election Campaign Act of 1971 (Pub. L. 92–225, 86 Stat. 19, 2 U.S.C. 451, enacted February 7, 1972, and hereafter referred to as the "Election Campaign Act") directs the Civil Aeronautics Board to promulgate, within 90 days after enactment, regulations with respect to the extension of unsecured credit by any person regulated by the Board to any candidate for Federal office, or to any person on behalf of such a candidate, for goods furnished or services rendered in connection with the campaign of such candidate for nomination for election, or election, to such office. The purpose of this part is to issue rules pursuant to said section 401 of the Election Campaign Act in accordance with the Civil Aeronautics Board's responsibility thereunder.

§374a.2 Applicability.

This regulation shall be applicable to all air carriers as defined herein.

§ 374a.3 Definitions.

Adequate security means (a) a bond, issued by a surety meeting the standards prescribed for sureties in part 380 of this chapter, in an amount not less than one hundred and fifty percent (150%) of the credit limit established by the air carrier for the candidate, or the person acting on behalf of the candidate, as the case may be, by the terms of which bond the surety undertakes to pay to the air carrier any and all amounts (not exceeding the face amount of the bond) for which the assured candidate or the assured person acting on behalf of a candidate, as the case may be, is or may become legally liable to the air carrier for transportation, as defined in this part; or (b) collateral with a market value equal to one hundred and fifty percent (150%) of the established credit limit for such account, which collateral must be deposited in escrow and must consist of Federal, State, or municipal bonds or other negotiable securities which are publicly traded on a securities exchange.

Air carrier means any air carrier holding a certificate of public convenience and necessity issued under section 401 of the Federal Aviation Act of 1958, as amended.

Candidate means an individual who seeks nomination for election, or election, to Federal office, whether or not such individual is elected. For purposes of this part, an individual shall be deemed to seek nomination for election, or election, if he has (a) taken the action necessary under the law of a State to qualify himself for nomination for election, or election, to Federal office; or (b) received contributions or made expenditures, or given his consent for any other person to receive contributions or make expenditures, with a view to bringing about his nomination for election, or election, to such office.

Election shall have reference to (a) a general, special, primary, or runoff election; (b) a convention or caucus of a political party held to nominate a candidate; (c) a primary election held for the selection of delegates to a national nominating convention of a political party; or (d) a primary election held for the expression of a preference for the nomination of persons for election to Federal office.

Established credit limit means the dollar limit of credit established by the carrier extending credit.

Federal office means the office of President or Vice President of the United States, or of Senator or Representative in, or Delegate or Resident Commissioner to, the Congress of the United States.

Person acting on behalf of a candidate means (a) a political committee acting on behalf of, or a person employed by such candidate or by such political committee to act on behalf of, such candidate in connection with such candidate's campaign for nomination for election, or election, to Federal office; (b) a person acting under a contract with, or as an agent of, such candidate or political committee to engage in activities in connection with such candidate's campaign for nomination for election, or election, to Federal office; or (c) a person for whom such candidate or political committee pays, directly or indirectly, for services purchased by such person. The term includes persons acting on behalf of more than one candidate.

Payment in advance means payment by cash, check, money order, or by credit card (if the issuer of such card is not an air carrier or a subsidiary, parent, or affiliate thereof) prior to performance of such transportation by an air carrier.

Political committee means any committee, association, corporation, or organization which accepts contributions, or makes expenditures, for the purpose of supporting a candidate or candidates for nomination for election, or election, to Federal office.

Transportation means (a) the carriage of persons or property (including services connected therewith) for compensation or hire to or from any place in the United States, or (b) the lease or rental of aircraft, with or without crew.

[SPR–53, 37 FR 9388, May 10, 1972, as amended by SPR–173, 45 FR 80099, Dec. 3, 1980]

§ 374a.4 Conditions governing extension of unsecured credit.

(a) Unless adequate security is posted, or full payment in advance is made, no air carrier shall provide transportation to any person it knows, or has reasons to know, is a candidate or a person acting on behalf of such candidate, in connection with the campaign of such candidate, except in accordance with, and subject to, the following conditions:

(1) At least once a month the air carrier shall submit to each such candidate or person a statement covering all unsecured credit extended to such candidate or person, as the case may be (whether in connection with the campaign of such candidate or otherwise.)

(2) Such statements shall be mailed no later than the second business day following the last day of the billing period, covered by the statement.

(3) The amount of indebtedness shown on each such statement shall be payable in full no later than 25 days after the last day of the billing period, after which time the indebtedness shall be overdue.

(4)(i) Unsecured credit shall not be extended by an air carrier to a candidate, or to any person acting on his behalf in connection with the campaign of such candidate, so long as any overdue indebtedness of such candidate to such air carrier shall remain unpaid, in whole or in part, or so long as such air carrier shall know that any overdue indebtedness of such candidate to any other air carrier remains unpaid, in whole or in part.

(ii) Unsecured credit shall not be extended by an air carrier to a person acting on behalf of a candidate, for transportation in connection with the campaign of such candidate, so long as any overdue indebtedness of such person to such carrier shall remain unpaid, in whole or in part, or so long as such air carrier shall know that any overdue indebtedness of such person to any other air carrier remains unpaid, in whole or in part.

(5)(i) With respect to transportation in connection with the campaign of any candidate to be performed after June 1, 1972, unsecured credit shall not be extended by an air carrier to any person acting on behalf of such candidate unless the carrier is authorized in writing by such candidate to extend such credit. The foregoing sentence shall not be construed as requiring the candidate to assume liability to the carrier for credit so extended.

(ii) Within 7 days after indebtedness becomes overdue for any unsecured credit extended by an air carrier to a person acting on behalf of a candidate in accordance with paragraph (a)(5)(i) of this section, the carrier shall notify the candidate in writing of the amount of the overdue indebtedness, and, unless paid in full within 25 days after the date of such notice, the overdue indebtedness shall be deemed to be the overdue indebtedness of the candidate, for the purposes of paragraph (b)(4)(i) of this section.

(b) It shall be presumed that a candidate or person acting on behalf of a candidate intends to use transportation in connection with the campaign of such candidate for nomination for election, or election, to Federal office.

(Secs. 204, 407 of the Federal Aviation Act of 1958, as amended, 72 Stat. 743, 766; 49 U.S.C. 1324, 1377. Sec. 401 of the Federal Election Campaign Act of 1971, 86 Stat. 19, 2 U.S.C. 451)

[SPR–53, 37 FR 9388, May 10, 1972, as amended by SPR–169, 45 FR 25796, Apr. 16, 1980; SPR–172, 45 FR 53454, Aug. 12, 1980]

§374a.5 Exemption authority.

Air carriers are exempt from the following provisions of Title IV of the Federal Aviation Act of 1958, as amended: (a) Section 403, (b) section 404(b), and any and all other provisions of Title IV of the Federal Aviation Act of 1958, as amended, to the extent necessary to enable air carriers to comply with the provisions of this part.

§374a.6 Reporting requirements.

(a) Air carriers shall make monthly reports to the Bureau of Transportation Statistics with respect to the credit for transportation furnished to candidates, or persons acting on behalf of candidates, during the period from 6 months before nomination, if any, or from 6 months before election, until the date of election. After that 6-month period, air carriers shall file such a report with the Bureau of Transportation Statistics not later than the 20th day following the end of the calendar month in which the election or nomination takes place, and thereafter when any change occurs in that report, until a negative report is filed showing that no debt for such extension of credit is owed to the carrier.

(b)(1) A separate report shall be filed for each candidate with an aggregate indebtedness balance of over $5,000 on the last day of the month to which the report pertains. The report shall cover all debts incurred by the candidate, whether or not incurred in connection with his campaign, and all debts incurred by persons acting on his behalf in connection with such campaign. The indebtedness accounts reported shall be those which the air carrier knows, or has reason to know, have been incurred by or on behalf of a candidate; and it shall be presumed that the transportation for which the indebtedness has been incurred is intended to be used in connection with the campaign of such candidate for nomination for election, or election, to Federal office.

(2) The reports required by this paragraph (b) shall be filed with the Office of Airline Information not later than the 20th day following the end of the calendar month to which the report pertains. They shall include the following data: (i) Name of account; (ii) the credit limit established for such account; (iii) the balance, if any, of the amount payable for transportation not paid for in advance; (iv) any unpaid balance of the charges for such transportation as of the last day of the month covered by the report, and the length of time that such balance has remained unpaid; and (v) a description of the type and value of any bond, collateral, or other security securing such unpaid balance.

(3) The report required by this paragraph (b) shall be in the form attached hereto as appendix A.[1]

(c) A separate report shall be filed for each person acting on behalf of any candidate, if the aggregate indebtedness balance of such person to the reporting air carrier (including all debts incurred by such person, whether or not incurred in connection with the campaign of a candidate, as defined in this part) is over $5,000 on the last day of the month to which the report pertains. The report shall be filed with the Office of Airline Information not later than the 20th day following the end of the calendar month to which the report pertains and shall include (1) the credit limitation established for such person; (2) the balance, if any, of the amount payable for transportation not paid for in advance; (3) any unpaid balance of the charges for such transportation as of the last day of the month covered by the report, and the length of time that such balance has remained unpaid; and (4) a description of the type and value of any bond, collateral, or other security securing such unpaid balance.

[SPR–53, 37 FR 9388, May 10, 1972, as amended by SPR–190, 47 FR 32414, July 27, 1982; 60 FR 66726, Dec. 26, 1995]

§ 374a.7 Record retention requirements.

(a) Every air carrier subject to the part shall retain for 2 years after a Federal election true copies of the following documents at its principal or general office in the United States:

(1) All documents which evidence or reflect the furnishing of transportation to a candidate for political office or a person acting on his behalf;

(2) All statements, invoices, bills, and receipts with respect to the furnishing of such transportation referred to in paragraph (a)(1) of this section.

(b) Every air carrier shall make the documents listed in this section available in the United States upon request by an authorized representative of the DOT and shall permit such representative to make such notes and copies thereof as he deems appropriate.

[SPR–53, 37 FR 9388, May 10, 1972, as amended at 60 FR 66726, Dec. 26, 1995]

§ 374a.8 Prospective application of part.

The provisions of this part shall apply only to the extension of credit by an air carrier to a candidate, or to a person acting on his behalf, which is made subsequent to the effective date of this part, and shall not be applicable to debts incurred prior to such date but which are unpaid as of the effective date of this part. The provisions of this part will be applicable, however, to all credit transactions which occur subsequent to the effective date of the part even though the credit account in

[1] Filed as part of the original document.

which the transaction takes place was opened prior to the effective date of the part.

PART 375—NAVIGATION OF FOREIGN CIVIL AIRCRAFT WITHIN THE UNITED STATES

AUTHORITY: 49 U.S.C. 40102, 40103, and 41703.

SOURCE: OST Doc. No. 42547, 51 FR 7254, Mar. 3, 1986, unless otherwise noted.

Subpart A—General

§375.1 Definitions.

As used in this part:

Act means the Federal Aviation Act of 1958, as amended;

Air transportation means the carriage by aircraft of persons or property as a common carrier for compensation or hire or the carriage of mail by aircraft in interstate, overseas, or foreign commerce (see section 101 (10) and (23) of the Federal Aviation Act, 49 U.S.C. 1301);

Category shall indicate a classification of aircraft such as airplane, helicopter, glider, etc.;

Commercial air operations shall mean operations by foreign civil aircraft engaged in flights for the purpose of crop dusting, pest control, pipeline patrol, mapping, surveying, banner towing, skywriting, or similar agricultural and industrial operations performed in the United States, and any operations for remuneration or hire to, from or within the United States including air carriage involving the discharging or taking on of passengers or cargo at one or more points in the United States, including carriage of cargo for the operator's own account if the cargo is to be resold or otherwise used in the furtherance of a business other than the business of providing carriage by aircraft, but excluding operations pursuant to foreign air carrier permits issued under 49 U.S.C. 41301, exemptions, and all other operations in air transportation.

Exemption means an exemption granted, under section 416(b) of the Act, authorizing air transportation by a foreign air carrier;

Foreign air carrier permit means a permit authorizing foreign air transportation by a foreign air carrier pursuant to section 402 of the Act;

Foreign aircraft permit means a permit authorizing navigation of foreign civil aircraft in the United States pursuant to section 1108(b) of the Act and this part;

Foreign civil aircraft means (a) an aircraft of foreign registry that is not part of the armed forces of a foreign nation, or (b) a U.S.-registered aircraft owned, controlled or operated by persons who are not citizens or permanent residents of the United States;

Stop for non-traffic purposes means a landing for any purpose other than taking on or discharging passengers, cargo or mail, and does not include landings for embarking or disembarking stopover passengers or transshipped cargo or mail, or for other than strictly operational purposes.

Type means all aircraft of the same basic design including all modifications thereto except those modifications that result in a change in handling or flight characteristics.

[OST Doc. No. 42547, 51 FR 7254, Mar. 3, 1986, as amended at 71 FR 15328, Mar. 28, 2006]

§ 375.2 Applicability.

The provisions of this part regulate the admission to, and navigation in, the United States of foreign civil aircraft other than aircraft operated under authority contained in a foreign air carrier permit or exemption. This part also contains provisions that specify the extent to which certain classes of flight operations by foreign civil aircraft may be conducted, and the terms and conditions applicable to such operations. Nothing in this part shall authorize any foreign civil aircraft to engage in air transportation nor be deemed to provide for such authorization by the Department.

§ 375.3 [Reserved]

Subpart B—Authorization

§ 375.10 Certain foreign civil aircraft registered in ICAO member states.

Subject to the observance of the applicable rules, conditions, and limitations set forth in this part:

(a) Foreign civil aircraft manufactured in a State that at the time of manufacture was a member of the International Civil Aviation Organization (ICAO), and registered in a State that at the time of flight is a member of ICAO, may be navigated in the United States;

(b) Foreign civil aircraft manufactured in a State that at the time of manufacture was not a member of ICAO, and registered in a State that at the time of flight is a member of ICAO, may be navigated in the United States,

(1) If the State of registry has notified ICAO that the requirements under which it issues or renders valid certificates of airworthiness are equal to or above the minimum standards established pursuant to the Chicago Convention, or

(2) If such notification has not been made to ICAO at the time of flight, there is on file with the Department a statement by the State of registry that, with regard to aircraft of the type that is proposed to be operated hereunder, the requirements under which certificates of airworthiness are issued or rendered valid are equal to or above the minimum standards established pursuant to the Chicago Convention.

§ 375.11 Other foreign civil aircraft.

A foreign civil aircraft, including unmanned aircraft as defined in § 1.1 of this title, other than those referred to in § 375.10 may be navigated in the United States only when:

(a) The operation is authorized by the Department under the provisions of this part, and

(b) The aircraft complies with any applicable airworthiness standards of the Federal Aviation Administration for its operation.

[80 FR 78648, Dec. 16, 2015]

Subpart C—Rules Generally Applicable

§ 375.19 Nature of privilege conferred.

The provisions of this part, and of any permit issued hereunder, together with section 1108(b) of the Act, are designed, among other purposes, to carry out the international undertakings of the United States in the Chicago Convention, in particular Article 5. That article gives foreign aircraft the privilege of "taking on or discharging passengers, cargo or mail" subject to the right of the State where such embarkation or discharge takes place to impose such regulations, conditions or limitations as it may consider desirable. The U.S. Congress by the 1953 amendment to section 6 of the Air Commerce Act of 1926, now designated as section 1108(b) of the Act, authorizes the Department to permit such operations only where conditions of reciprocity and the interest of the public in the United States are met. Thus, the operator of any foreign registered aircraft is not entitled as a matter of right to the issuance, renewal or freedom from modification or change in a permit issuable pursuant to this authority. Accordingly, any authority conferred by this part may be withheld, revoked, amended, modified, restricted, suspended, withdrawn, or canceled by the Department in the interest of the public of the United States, without notice or hearing.

§ 375.20 Airworthiness and registration certificates.

Foreign civil aircraft shall carry currently effective certificates of registration and airworthiness issued or rendered valid by the country of registry and shall display the nationality and registration markings of that country. However, a foreign civil aircraft may carry, in lieu of such certificate of airworthiness, an effective special flight authorization issued by the Federal Aviation Administration for the operations being performed.

§ 375.21 Airmen.

Members of the flight crew of a foreign civil aircraft shall have in their personal possession valid airman certificates or licenses authorizing them to perform their assigned functions in the aircraft and for the operation involved issued or rendered valid by the country of registry of the aircraft or by the United States. No such flight crew members shall perform any flight duty within the United States that they are not currently authorized to perform in the country issuing or validating the certificate.

§ 375.22 Flight operations.

Flights of foreign civil aircraft in the United States shall be conducted in accordance with the currently applicable rules of the Federal Aviation Administration.

§ 375.23 Maximum allowable weights.

Foreign civil aircraft that are permitted to navigate in the United States on the basis of foreign airworthiness certificates must conform to the limitations on maximum certificated weights prescribed or authorized for the particular variation of the aircraft type, and for the particular category of use, by the country of manufacture of the aircraft type involved.

§ 375.24 Entry and clearance.

All U.S. entry and clearance requirements for aircraft, passengers, crews, baggage and cargo shall be followed.

§ 375.25 Unauthorized operations.

No foreign civil aircraft shall be navigated in the United States unless authorized by this part. Commercial air operations (other than those authorized by § 375.36) shall not be undertaken without a permit issued by the Department.

§ 375.26 Waiver of sovereign immunity.

Owners and operators of aircraft operated under this part that are engaged in proprietary of commercial activities waive any defense of sovereign immunity from suit in any action or proceeding instituted against any of them in any court or other tribunal in the United States for any claim relating to that operation.

Subpart D—Authorized Operations

§ 375.30 Operations other than commercial air operations.

Foreign civil aircraft that are not engaged in commercial air operations into, out of, or within the United States may be operated in the United States and may carry non-revenue traffic to, from or between points in the United States.

§ 375.31 Demonstration flights of foreign aircraft.

Flights of foreign civil aircraft within the United States may be made for the purpose of demonstration of the aircraft or any component thereof (including demonstrations at airshows), provided no persons, cargo or mail are carried for remuneration or hire.

§ 375.32 Flights incidental to agricultural and industrial operations outside the United States.

Foreign civil aircraft that are engaged in agricultural or industrial operations to be performed wholly outside the United States may be navigated into, out of, and within the United States in connection with those operations provided that the aircraft is not at the time engaged in the carriage of passengers, cargo, or mail for remuneration or hire.

§ 375.33 Transit flights, irregular operations.

Foreign civil aircraft carrying passengers, property or mail for remuneration or hire, but not engaged in scheduled international air services, are authorized to navigate nonstop across the territory of the United States and to make stops for non-traffic purposes. The navigation of foreign civil aircraft in the United States is not authorized under this section when the elapsed time between landing and takeoff at a stop in the United States exceeds 24 hours and passengers are permitted to leave the airport or when passengers, property or mail are transferred to another aircraft. Flights involving stops under such circumstances may, however, be performed in the case of emergency relating to the safey of the aircraft, passengers, cargo or crew.

§ 375.34 Indoctrination training.

Foreign civil aircraft may be operated in the United States for the purpose of giving indoctrination training in the operation of the aircraft concerned to a buyer or a buyer's employees or designees. This section does not, however, authorize foreign civil aircraft to be used within the United States for the purpose of flight instruction for remuneration or hire.

§ 375.35 Free transportation.

(a) Foreign civil aircraft may be navigated in the United States by a foreign air carrier for the transportation of persons and property specified in paragraph (b) of this section over the following non-traffic segments provided such transportation is not for compensation or hire:

(1) Between two or more points in the United States;

(2) Between a point in the United States named in the carrier's section 402 permit or exemption, and a point outside the United States not so named, when authorized in accordance with the provisions of part 216 of this chapter to carry blind sector traffic to or from such unnamed foreign point; and

(3) Between a point in the United States and a point outside thereof when the carrier lands at the United States point for non-traffic purposes in exercise of the privilege granted under the International Air Services Transit Agreement.

(b) Free transportation may be provided under this section for the following categories of persons and property:

(1) Directors, officers and employees, and their parents and immediate families, of the foreign air carrier operating the aircraft;

(2) Directors, officers and employees, and their parents and immediate families, of an air carrier or another foreign air carrier traveling pursuant to a pass interchange arrangement;

(3) Travel agents being transported for the purpose of familiarizing themselves with the carrier's services, if the agents are under no obligation to sell the transporting carrier's services;

(4) Witnesses and attorneys attending any legal investigation in which any such foreign air carrier is involved;

(5) Persons injured in aircraft accidents and physicians and nurses attending such persons;

(6) Any persons or property with the object of providing relief in cases of general epidemic, natural disaster or other catastrophe;

(7) Any person who has the duty of guarding foreign government officials travelling on official business; and

(8) Guests of a foreign air carrier (including members of the press) on delivery flights of newly-acquired or newly-renovated aircraft.

(c) A charge reasonably related to the value of meals and beverages furnished enroute shall not be deemed to constitute compensation or hire for purposes of this section.

§375.36 Lease of foreign civil aircraft without crew.

Foreign civil aircraft that are leased without crew to an air carrier or citizen or permanent resident of the United States, and used by the lessee in otherwise authorized air transportation or commercial air operations, may be operated into, out of, and within the United States in accordance with any applicable regulations prescribed by the Federal Aviation Administration.

§375.37 Certain business aviation activities using U.S.-registered foreign civil aircraft.

For purposes of this section, "company" is defined as a person that operates civil aircraft in furtherance of a business other than air transportation. U.S.-registered foreign civil aircraft that are not otherwise engaged in commercial air operations, or foreign air transportation, and which are operated by a company in the furtherance of a business other than transportation by air, when the carriage is within the scope of, and incidental to, the business of the company (other than transportation by air), may be operated to, from, and within the United States as follows:

(a) *Intra-company operations.* A company operating a U.S.-registered foreign civil aircraft may conduct operations for a subsidiary or parent or a subsidiary of its parent on a fully-allocated cost reimbursable basis; provided, that the operator of the U.S.-registered foreign civil aircraft must hold majority ownership in, be majority owned by, or have a common parent with, the company for which it provides operations;

(b) *Interchange operations.* A company may lease a U.S.-registered foreign civil aircraft to another company in exchange for equal time when needed on the other company's U.S. registered aircraft, where no charge, assessment, or fee is made, except that a charge may be made not to exceed the difference between the cost of owning, operating, and maintaining the two aircraft;

(c) *Joint ownership operations.* A company that jointly owns a U.S.-registered foreign civil aircraft and furnishes the flight crew for that aircraft may collect from the other joint owners of that aircraft a share of the actual costs involved in the operation of the aircraft; and

(d) *Time-sharing operations.* A company may lease a U.S.-registered foreign civil aircraft, with crew, to another company; provided, that the operator may collect no charge for the operation of the aircraft except reimbursement for:

(1) Fuel, oil, lubricants, and other additives.

(2) Travel expenses of the crew, including food, lodging, and ground transportation.

(3) Hanger and tie-down costs away from the aircraft's base of operations.

(4) Insurance obtained for the specific flight.

(5) Landing fees, airport taxes, and similar assessments.

(6) Customs, foreign permit, and similar fees directly related to the flight.

(7) In flight food and beverages.

(8) Passenger ground transportation.

(9) Flight planning and weather contract services.

(10) An additional charge equal to 100 percent of the expenses for fuel, oil, lubricants, and other additives.

[Doc. No. DOT–OST–2003–15511, 71 FR 15328, Mar. 28, 2006]

§ 375.38 Other foreign civil aircraft: Small unmanned aircraft operated exclusively as model aircraft.

Foreign civil aircraft that are small unmanned aircraft used exclusively as model aircraft may be operated in the United States only when the individual:

(a) Completes the registration process in accordance with §§ 48.30, 48.100(b) and (c), 48.105, and 48.115 of this title;

(b) Identifies the aircraft in accordance with the aircraft marking requirements in §§ 48.200 and 48.205 of this title; and

(c) Complies with the requirements of Sec. 336 of Pub. L. 112–95 (Feb. 14, 2012).

[80 FR 78648, Dec. 16, 2015]

Subpart E—Operations Requiring Specific Preflight Authorization of Filing

§ 375.40 Permits for commercial air operations.

(a) *Permit required.* Except for aircraft being operated under a foreign air carrier permit, an exemption, or as otherwise provided in subpart D or H of this part, foreign civil aircraft may engage in commercial air operations only if there is carried on board the aircraft a permit issued by the Department in accordance with this subpart authorizing the operations involved.

(b) Aircraft are not authorized to engage in air transportation under this section. Where an operation involves the carriage of persons, property or mail for compensation or hire, the Department will determine whether particular flights for which a permit is sought will be in common carriage, and therefore in air transportation, based on all the facts and circumstances surrounding the applicant's entire operations. The burden rests upon the applicant in each instance to demonstrate by an appropriate factual showing that the contemplated operation will not constitute common carriage from, to or within the United States. In general, an applicant that holds itself out to the public, or to a particular class or segment, as willing to furnish transportation for hire is a common carrier.

§ 375.41 Agricultural and industrial operations within the United States.

Foreign civil aircraft shall not be used for such commercial air operations as crop dusting, pest control, pipeline patrol, mapping, surveying, banner towing, skywriting or similar agricultural or industrial operations within the United States, including its territorial waters and overlying airspace, unless a permit has been issued by the Department and the operation is conducted in accordance with all applicable State and local laws and regulations as well as the applicable provisions of this part.

§ 375.42 Transport operations—occasional planeload charters.

Occasional planeload charters may be authorized where, because of their limited nature and extent, special equipment or facilities utilized, or other circumstances pertaining to them, it appears that they are not within the scope of the applicant's normal holding out of transportation services to the general public. Such charters are normally limited to those in which the entire capacity of the aircraft is engaged by a single charterer, and since they are occasional in nature, should not exceed for any one applicant more than six flights during a calendar year. This part does not authorize operations that involve solicitation of the general public such as is usually involved in the transportation of individually-ticketed passengers or individually-waybilled cargo, or in which the charterer is a travel agent, a charter operator, a broker, an air freight forwarder or any other organization that holds itself out to the general public to provide transportation services. Carriage of cargo for the operator's own account is governed by the provisions of this section if the cargo is to be resold or otherwise used in the furtherance of a business other than the business of providing carriage by aircraft.

§ 375.43 Application for foreign aircraft permit.

(a) Applications for foreign aircraft permits shall be submitted on OST Form 4509, (Appendix A), in duplicate, addressed to the Chief, Discrete Operations Branch, Licensing Division, P-45, Office of Aviation Operations. Upon a showing of good cause, applications may be made by telegram or by telephone.

(b) Applications shall contain a proper identification (including citizenship) of the applicant (the operator of the aircraft concerned) and of the owner thereof (if different from the applicant), a description of the aircraft by make, model, and registration marks; and a full description of the operations for which authority is desired, indicating type and dates of operations and number of flights, and routing. In the case of cargo flights, the names of all contractors, agents, if any, and the beneficial owner of the cargo, and a description of the cargo and of the proposed operations shall be provided. In the case of passenger flights, a full identification and description of the group chartering the aircraft, and identification of the travel agent, if any, shall be provided. Applications shall also contain a statement as to whether the applicant's homeland allows operators of U.S.-registered aircraft to conduct similar operations.

(c) Applications shall be filed at least 15 days in advance of the proposed commencement date of the operations. The Department may direct the applicant to serve copies of its application on additional persons. Late applications may be considered by the Department upon a showing of good cause.

(d)(1) Any party in interest may file a memorandum supporting or opposing an application. Two copies of each memorandum shall be filed within 7 business days after the application is filed but no later than the proposed commencement date of the operations. Memoranda will be considered to the extent practicable; the Department may act on an application without waiting for supporting or opposing memoranda to be filed.

(2) Each memorandum shall set forth the reasons why the applications should be granted or denied, accompanied by whatever data, including affidavits, the Department is asked to consider.

(3) A copy of each memorandum shall be served on the applicant.

(e)(1) Unless otherwise ordered by the Department, each application and memorandum filed in response shall be available for public inspection at the Licensing Division of the Office of Aviation Operations immediately upon filing. Notice of the filing of all applications shall be published in the Department's Weekly List of Applications Filed.

(2) Any person objecting to public disclosure of any information in an application or memorandum must state the grounds for the objection in writing. If the Department finds that disclosure of all or part of the information should be withheld under applicable provisions of law, and the public interest does not require disclosure, it will order that the injurious information be withheld.

(Approved by the Office of Management and Budget under control number 2106-0002)

§375.44 Issuance of permit.

(a) The Department will issue a foreign aircraft permit if it finds that the proposed operations meet the requirements of this part and are in the public interest. Foreign aircraft permits may be conditioned or limited by the Department. Permits must be carried aboard the applicant's aircraft during flight over U.S. territory, and are not transferable.

(b) In determining whether to grant a particular application, the Department will consider, among other factors, the extent to which the country of the applicant's nationality deals with U.S. civil aircraft operators on the basis of substantial reciprocity, and whether the operation is otherwise in the public interest.

§375.45 Records and reports of occasional planeload charters.

(a) *Cargo documents.* The holder of a permit for cargo operations shall issue a manifest or shipping document to its shipper with respect to each shipment.

(b) [Reserved]

(c) *Contents of documents for passenger flights.* The holder of a permit for passenger charters originating or terminating in the United States shall require each charterer to file with it prior to flight a list of names and addresses of all passengers to be transported on each flight.

(d) *Reports of unused authority.* All foreign operators of occasional planeload charters for which authority is granted must notify the Department, in writing, not later than 15 days after the expiration of their permits, or their failure to use this authority. The unused authority shall otherwise be deemed to have been exercised.

Subpart F—Transit Flights

§ 375.50 Transit flights; scheduled international air service operations.

(a) *Requirement of notice.* Scheduled international air services proposed to be operated pursuant to the International Air Services Transit Agreement in transit across the United States may not be undertaken by foreign civil aircraft unless the operator of such aircraft, and (if other than the operator) the carrier offering such service to the public, has, not less than 30 days prior to the date of commencement of such service, filed a Notice of Proposed Transit Flights Pursuant to the International Air Services Transit Agreement in accordance with the provisions of paragraphs (b) and (c) of this section.

(b) *Filing of the notice.* An original and two copies of the Notice shall be filed with the Chief, Discrete Operations Branch, Licensing Division, P–45, Office of Aviation Operations. Copies of the Notice shall be served upon the Department of State and the Administrator of the Federal Aviation Administration. The filing date shall be the date of actual receipt by the Department.

(c) *Content of notice.* A "Notice of Proposed Transit Flights Pursuant to the International Air Services Transit Agreement" shall be clearly labeled as such, and as a minimum shall set forth, with whatever detail may be necessary, the following information:

(1) The name, country or organization, and citizenship of the operator, and, if other than the operator, of the carrier offering the services to the public. If any interest (direct or indirect) in the operator or offeror of services is held by nationals of a country other than the country of organization or citizenship, the nature and extent of such interest must be fully disclosed. If any officer or director of the operator or carrier offering the services is a national of a country other than the country of organization or citizenship, the position of duties of such officer or director, and the officer and director's relevant position in relation to other officers and directors must similarly be fully disclosed. If the information required in this subsection has been previously supplied to the Department, the applicant may incorporate it by reference.

(2) The State of registration of the aircraft proposed to be operated.

(3) A full description of the proposed operations including the type of operations (passenger, property, mail, or combination), date of commencement, duration and frequency of flights, and routing (including each terminal and intermediate point to be served).

(4) A statement as to whether or not any advertisement or publication of the proposed operations has been made in the United States. If there has been any advertisement or publication of the operations in the United States, copies of all such advertisements or publications shall be included.

(5) Any change with respect to these matters (minor changes in schedules or routing excepted) shall also be filed with the Department.

(d) *Authorized operations.* If the operator and the carrier offering services to the public (if different from the operator) have filed a "Notice of Proposed Transit Flights Pursuant to the International Air Services Transit Agreement," at least 30 days before the date of commencement of the proposed operations in accordance with paragraphs (a), (b), and (c) of this section, the described operations may be commenced and performed without further authorization from the Department, unless and until the Department issues an order notifying the operator and/or the carrier offering the services to the public that, considering the matters submitted in the Notice, the Department is of the view that a question may exist as to whether:

(1) The proposed services are authorized pursuant to the terms of the International Air Services Transit Agreement;

(2) Substantial ownership and effective control are vested in nationals of a State party to the International Air Services Transit Agreement;

(3) The proposed operations will be in compliance with the laws of the United States, the Department's rules, or the provisions of this section; or

(4) The operator or its government have performed their obligations under the International Air Services Transit Agreement.

(e) *Prohibited operations.* If the Department issues an order of notification as described in paragraph (d) of this section, neither the operator, nor the carrier offering the services to the public, shall commence the proposed operations, or, except as may be otherwise specified in the order, operate any flights subsequent to receipt of the order, unless and until the Department issues a foreign aircraft permit pursuant to the provisions of section 1108(b) of the Act and this part specifically authorizing such operations.

(f) *Foreign aircraft permit—application and procedures.* If the Department issues an Order of Notification as described in paragraph (d) of this section, the carrier's Notice of Proposed Transit Flights Pursuant to the International Air Services Transit Agreement shall be treated as an application for the required foreign aircraft permit, and further procedures on such application shall be as directed by the Department.

(g) *Short notice filing.* Nothing in this section shall be construed as precluding the filing of an application for a foreign aircraft permit to perform transit operations pursuant to the International Air Services Transit Agreement less than 30 days in advance of the proposed operation. No such flights shall be operated, however, unless or until a specific foreign aircraft permit has been issued by the Department.

(h) *Nature of privilege conferred.* Air transportation is not authorized under this section, and the burden rests upon each operator and carrier to show that the proposed operations will not constitute air transportation within the meaning of the Federal Aviation Act. In addition, each operator and carrier has the burden of demonstrating that the proposed operations are authorized by the International Air Services Transit Agreement, and that the appropriate authorization should not be withheld pursuant to section 5 of Article I thereof. Stopovers for the convenience or pleasure of the passengers are not authorized under this section and stops other than for strictly operational reasons shall not be made. The consolidation on the same aircraft of an operation under this section with a service authorized under section 402 or 416(b) of the Act is not authorized by this section. Any authorization or permit granted under this section is nontransferable, and may be withheld, revoked, suspended, withdrawn, or cancelled by the Department, without notice or hearing, if required by the public interest. Operators of aircraft registered in countries not parties to the International Air Services Transit Agreement shall make special application to the Department under §375.70.

Subpart G—Penalties

§375.60 Penalties.

The operation of a foreign aircraft within the United States or over adjacent territorial waters in violation of the provisions of this part constitutes a violation of the Federal Aviation Act and of this chapter, and may, in addition, constitute a violation of the rules of the Federal Aviation Administration. Such operation makes the person or persons responsible for the violation or violations subject to a civil penalty as provided in section 901 of the Act, and to the alteration, amendment, modification, suspension or revocation of any permit issued under this part and of any U.S. certificate involved as provided in section 609 of the Act. Engaging in air transportation as defined in the Act by a foreign aircraft without a foreign air carrier permit issued pursuant to section 402 of the Act or an exemption, or in violation of the terms of such authority constitutes not only a violation of this part but of title IV of the Act as well, which entails a criminal penalty as set forth in section 902 of the Act.

Subpart H—Special Authorization

§ 375.70 Special authorization.

Any person desiring to navigate a foreign civil aircraft within the United States other than as specifically provided in this part may petition the Department for a special authorization to conduct the particular flight or series of flights. Such authorization may be issued only if the Department finds that the proposed operation is fully consistent with the applicable law, that the applicant's homeland grants a similar privilege with respect to operators of U.S.-registered aircraft, and that the proposed operation is in the interest of the public of the United States.

APPENDIX A TO PART 375—FORM 4509

Approved by OMB
No. 2106-0002
Expires 11/30/87

U.S. Department of Transportation

APPLICATION FOR FOREIGN AIRCRAFT PERMIT OR SPECIAL AUTHORIZATION UNDER PART 375

(See Instructions On Reverse Side)

DO NOT WRITE—FOR OFFICIAL USE ONLY

Disposition of Applications:

☐ Approved

☐ Approved, subject to condition(s) on reverse.

☐ Disapproved/Dismissed for reason(s) cited on reverse.

Under assigned authority ______________

Effective from ________ to ________.

Director, Office of Aviation Operations

TO: Department of Transportation
Licensing Division, P-45
Office of Aviation Operations
Washington, D.C. 20590

1. Name and address of applicant: (operator)

Nationality:

Operations pursuant to this authorization shall conform to Part 375 of the Department's Regulations and Part 91 of the Federal Aviation Regulations. THIS PERMIT MUST BE CARRIED ABOARD AIRCRAFT DURING FLIGHT OVER UNITED STATES TERRITORY.

2. Send authorization to:
   a. Name and address:

   b. Telephone:

3. Aircraft make, model, and registration or identification marks:

4. Country in which aircraft is registered:

5. Name and address of registered owner of aircraft:

6. Name and address of contractor/charterer:

7. Dates of flights:

8. Planned routing of flights (indicate non-traffic stops by asterisks):

9. Description of operations (see instructions) (Check one):
   Passenger ☐ Cargo ☐ Agricultural or Industrial operation ☐

10. Does the nation which is the domicile of the applicant grant to United States carriers a privilege similar to that requested herein?______; if so, has the fact of such reciprocity been established with the Department?______. If the fact has not been established with the Department, provide documentation to establish such reciprocity.

OST Form 4509 (Rev. 2/20/86)

11. If application is being filed late, state reasons for lateness:
12. Other information requested by the Department:

CERTIFICATION

I hereby certify that the flights for which authority is sought herein conform to the requirements of the applicable regulations and orders of the Department of Transportation.

(Date) (Signature and title of authorized officer)

INSTRUCTIONS

1. Prepare an original and one copy of this application according to Section 375.43 of the Department's Regulations. If extra space is required to complete an item, continue on a separate sheet of paper.
2. Under Item 9:
   (a) For passenger flights, provide full identification or description of group contracting for charter, and name and address of travel agent, if any.
   (b) For cargo flights, provide the names of all contractors, description of cargo, beneficial owner of cargo, and provide a full description of the proposed operation including nature of any service to be performed by any exporter, importer, or transportation agent.
   (c) For agricultural or industrial operations, describe area involved and purpose of operations.
3. Send the application to: Department of Transportation, Licensing Division, P–45, Office of Aviation Operations, Washington, D.C. 20590.
4. See Part 91 of Federal Aviation Regulations and 375 of the Department's Regulations (14 CFR 91 and 14 CFR 375) for a full statement of the rules respecting navigation of foreign civil aircraft within the United States.

DO NOT WRITE—FOR OFFICIAL USE ONLY
Exercise of the authorization is subject to the following condition(s): OR Application is disapproved/dismissed for the following reason(s):

PART 377—CONTINUANCE OF EXPIRED AUTHORIZATIONS BY OPERATION OF LAW PENDING FINAL DETERMINATION OF APPLICATIONS FOR RENEWAL THEREOF

Subpart A—General Provisions

Subpart B—Renewal Applications and Procedure Thereon

AUTHORITY: 49 U.S.C. Chapters 401, 461; 5 U.S.C. 558, 559.

Subpart A—General Provisions

§377.1 Definitions.

As used in this part:

Authorization means any agency certificate, approval, statutory exemption or other form of permission granted pursuant to sections 101(3), 401, 402, 408, 409, 412 and 416 of the Federal Aviation Act of 1958, as amended. Where any operating authorization creates more than one separate route, each of these shall be deemed a separate authorization for the purposes of this part.

Renewal application means any application filed in conformity with the requirements of this part which requests either a renewal or a new license and is intended to invoke the provisions of the last sentence of 5 U.S.C. 558(c).

Route means an authorization which permits an air carrier to render unlimited regularly scheduled service between a specifically designated pair of terminal points and intermediate points, if any.

[SPR-84, 40 FR 24998, June 12, 1975, as amended by SPR-184, 47 FR 7212, Feb. 18, 1982]

§377.2 Applicability of part.

(a) This part implements the last sentence of 5 U.S.C. 558(c) with regard to temporary authorizations granted by the Board.

NOTE: The last sentence of 5 U.S.C. 558(c) provides: "When the licensee has made timely and sufficient application for a renewal or a new license in accordance with agency rules, a license with reference to an activity of a continuing nature does not expire until the application has been finally determined by the agency."

(b) Nothing in this part prevents the Board from terminating at any time, in accordance with law, any authorization or any extension of an authorization.

(c) Nothing in this part constitutes a determination that any given authorization is a "license with reference to an activity of a continuing nature" within the meaning of 5 U.S.C. 558(c).

[SPR-184, 47 FR 7212, Feb. 18, 1982]

§377.3 Authorizations not covered by 5 U.S.C. 558(c).

The Board hereby determines that the following authorizations are not licenses "with reference to an activity of a continuing nature" within the meaning of 5 U.S.C. 558(c):

(a) Authorizations granted for a specified period of 180 days or less; and

(b) Authorizations, other than those granted under section 401 of the Act, that by their terms are subject to termination at an uncertain date upon the happening of an event, including fulfillment of a condition subsequent or occurrence of a contingency.

[SPR-184, 47 FR 7212, Feb. 18, 1982]

§377.4 Certain authorizations with alternative termination dates.

Unless granted under section 401 of the Act, an authorization that by its terms is subject to termination alternatively, either at an uncertain date upon the happening of an event or upon the arrival of a specified date:

(a) Will not be considered a "license with reference to an activity of a continuing nature" within the meaning of 5 U.S.C. 558(c), if the event occurs before the specified date; and

(b) Ordinarily (subject to Board interpretation under §377.5) will be considered such a license, if the event does not occur before the specified date and that date is more than 180 days after the effective date of the authorization.

[SPR–184, 47 FR 7212, Feb. 18, 1982]

§ 377.5 Procedure to obtain Board interpretation.

(a) The Board will determine upon written request by the holder of a temporary authorization or by any competitively affected air carrier or foreign air carrier, or upon its own initiative, whether the temporary authorization is a "license with reference to an activity of a continuing nature" within the meaning of 5 U.S.C. 558(c).

(b) A written request for such a Board determination shall be filed at least 60 days before the deadline set forth in § 377.10 for a timely renewal application.

(c) The filing of such a written request shall not affect the timeliness requirements for renewal applications that are set forth in § 377.10 or any other applicable Board rule or order.

[SPR–184, 47 FR 7212, Feb. 18, 1982]

Subpart B—Renewal Applications and Procedure Thereon

§ 377.10 Requirements for, and effect of, renewal applications.

(a) *Identification of authorization covered by renewal application.* Each renewal application shall identify the authorization or authorizations to which it is intended to relate. The application shall indicate the applicant's intention to rely upon 5 U.S.C. 558(c) as implemented by this part. In case of applications for renewal of an authorization for route service, the renewal application shall specifically identify the separate routes which the applicant proposes to continue serving pursuant to the expiring authorization, pending final determination of the renewal application.

(b) *Contents of renewal application.* The application must contain all the information required by law and the Board's regulations, and meet the requirements thereof as to form. The new authorization sought need not be of the same duration as the expiring authorization. If the application relates to renewal of route authority, it must contain, as a minimum, a request for renewed authority to render route service between the terminals named in each separate route for which renewal is requested.

(c) *Timeliness.* The application must be filed and served in compliance with applicable law and the Board's regulations at least 60 days before the expiration date of the outstanding temporary authorization, except that:

(1) For certificates issued under section 401 of the Act with a specified expiration date, the deadline is 180 days before the expiration date;

(2) For certificates issued under section 401 of the Act that terminate by their terms upon the happening of an event that could not be foreseen, the deadline is 30 days after the time that the carrier has notice that the event will occur or has occurred;

(3) For foreign air carrier permits issued under section 402 of the Act and exemptions issued under section 416 to non-U.S. citizens, the deadline is the expiration date itself;

(4) For renewal by substantially equivalent certificate authority of fixed term route authorizations granted by exemption and for interim extension of the exemption, pursuant to § 399.18 of this chapter, the deadline is 90 days before the expiration date; and

(5) Nothing in this part supersedes a requirement for earlier filing contained in any law, Board rule or order, or temporary authorization.

(d) *Effect.* In the case of authorizations which constitute licenses with reference to activities of a continuing nature within the meaning of 5 U.S.C. 558(c), the filing of an application complying in all respects with the requirements of paragraphs (a) through (c) of this section shall extend the authorization to which it relates as then outstanding in its entirety, together with all applicable terms, conditions and limitations, until the application has been finally determined by the Board. In the case of routes granted under section 401 of the Act, the duty to render adequate service continues to attach to every point as provided in the expired authorization which is extended pursuant to this provision. The date of final determination of the application shall be the date when the final order determining the application takes effect, or when the applicable period for filing of petitions for rehearing, reargument or reconsideration expires, or when a timely filed petition therefor is denied, whichever occurs latest.

[SPR–84, 40 FR 24998, June 12, 1975, as amended by SPR–184, 47 FR 7212, Feb. 18, 1982; 65 FR 6457, Feb. 9, 2000]

§377.11 Processing of defective renewal applications.

When the Board determines that a renewal application does not comply with the requirements of this part, or that it does not relate to a license with reference to an activity of a continuing nature, it will so notify the applicant. The applicant may amend his application to cure the deficiency as a matter of right at any time prior to the date when the application was due pursuant to §377.10(c).

[SPR–84, 40 FR 24998, June 12, 1975]

PART 380—PUBLIC CHARTERS

Subpart A—General Provisions

Subpart B—Conditions and Limitations

Subpart C—Requirements Applicable to Charter Operators

Subpart D—Requirements Applicable to Direct Air Carriers

Subpart E—Registration of Foreign Charter Operators

AUTHORITY: 49 U.S.C. 40101, 40102, 40109, 40113, 41101, 41103, 41301, 41504, 41702, 41708, 41712, 46101.

SOURCE: Docket No. OST–97–2356, 63 FR 28241, May 22, 1998, unless otherwise noted.

Subpart A—General Provisions

§380.1 Applicability.

This part applies to Public Charter air transportation of passengers in interstate or foreign air transportation, whether furnished by direct air carriers or Public Charter operators. This part also relieves such charter operators from various provisions of subtitle VII of Title 49 of the United

States Code (statute), formerly Title IV of the Federal Aviation Act of 1958, as amended, for the purpose of enabling them to provide Public Charters utilizing aircraft chartered from such direct air carriers. It also declines jurisdiction over foreign Public Charter operators operating foreign-originating Public Charters.

§ 380.2 Definitions.

For the purposes of this part:

Certificated air carrier means a U.S. direct air carrier holding a certificate issued under the statute.

Charter flight means a flight operated under the terms of a charter contract between a direct air carrier and its customer. It does not include scheduled air transportation, scheduled foreign air transportation, or nonscheduled cargo air transportation, sold on an individually ticketed or individually waybilled basis.

Direct air carrier means a certificated commuter or foreign air carrier, or an air taxi operator registered under part 298 of this chapter, or a Canadian charter air taxi operator registered under part 294 of this chapter, that directly engages in the operation of aircraft under a certificate, authorization, permit or exemption issued by the Department.

Educational institution means a school that is operated as such on a year-round basis and is empowered to grant academic degrees or secondary school diplomas by any government in the United States or by a foreign government.

Foreign air carrier means a direct air carrier that holds a foreign air carrier permit issued under the statute or an exemption issued under the statute authorizing direct foreign air transportation.

Foreign Public Charter opertor means an indirect air carrier which is not a citizen of the United States as defined in the statute, that is authorized to engage in the formation of groups for transportation on Public Charters in accordance with this part.

Indirect air carrier means any person who undertakes to engage indirectly in air transportation operations and who uses for such transportation the services of a direct air carrier.

Public Charter means a one-way or round-trip charter flight to be performed by one or more direct air carriers that is arranged and sponsored by a charter operator.

Public Charter operator means a U.S. or foreign Public Charter operator.

Security agreement means:

(1) A surety bond issued by a company—

(i) That is listed in the Best's Insurance Reports (Fire and Casualty) with a general policyholders' rating of "A" or better, or

(ii) That is listed in the U.S. Department of Treasury's notice listing companies holding Certificates of Authority as acceptable sureties on Federal bonds and as acceptable reinsuring companies, published in the FEDERAL REGISTER in the first week in July; or

(2) A Surety trust agreement or a letter-of-credit, issued by a Federal Deposit Insurance Corporation-insured financial institution, which provides substantially equivalent protection.

Statute means Subtitle VII of Title 49 of the United States Code (Transportation).

Sub-operator means a Public Charter operator that has contracted for its charter seats from a Public Charter operator that has contracted from one or more direct air carriers. A sub-operator is itself an indirect air carrier, not an agent of the Public Charter operator from which it has obtained its seat.

U.S. Public Charter operator means an indirect air carrier that is a citizen of the United States as defined in 49 U.S.C. 40102(a) and that is authorized to engage in the formation of groups for transportation on Public Charters in accordance with this part.

[Doc. No. OST–97–2356, 63 FR 28241, May 22, 1998, as amended at 70 FR 25773, May 16, 2005]

§ 380.3 General provisions.

(a) Public Charters may be operated on a one-way or round-trip basis, with no minimum group or contract size. Public Charters may be sold on an air-only basis, or with mandatory or optional land arrangements.

(b) A U.S. Public Charter operator operating a Public Charter which originates in a foreign country shall not be subject to the requirements of §§ 380.25, 380.28, 380.30 and 380.35.

(c) The Department declines to exercise jurisdiction over a foreign Public Charter operator which operates a Public Charter originating in a foreign country, but reserves the right to exercise its jurisdiction over any foreign Public Charter operator at any time its finds that such action is in the public interest.

(d)(1) An educational institution operating a Public Charter need not comply with the financial security requirements of § 380.34 if each student participant in the charter is enrolled in a formal academic course of study outside the United States, sponsored by or in conjunction with that institution, that is of at least four weeks' duration.

(2) The spouse, children, and parents of a student participant may accompany the participant on a charter operated under this section.

(e) The Department, upon application or on its own initiative, may waive any of the provision of this part if it finds such action to be in the public interest.

§ 380.4 Enforcement.

In the case of any violation of the provision of the Statute or of this part, or any other rule, regulations, or order issued under the Statute, the violator may be subject to a proceeding pursuant to the Statute before the Department or a U.S district court, as the case may be, to compel compliance therewith; to civil penalties pursuant to the provisions of the Statute, or to criminal penalties pursuant to the provisions of the Statute, or other lawful sanctions.

Subpart B—Conditions and Limitations

§ 380.10 Public Charter requirements.

Public Charters under this part shall meet the following requirements:

(a)–(b) [Reserved]

(c) If the charter is on a round-trip basis, the departing flight and returning need not be performed by the same direct air carrier.

(d) The air transportation portion of the charter must be performed by direct air carriers that hold authority under Chapter 411 and 413 of the Statute, or are operating under 14 CFR part 298, except that only U.S. citizen direct air carriers may provide air transportation for operations in interstate air transportation.

§ 380.11 Payment to direct air carrier(s).

Except for air taxi operators and commuter air carriers (which are governed by 14 CFR 298.38) and Canadian charter air taxi operators (which are governed by 14 CFR 294.32), the direct air carrier(s) shall be paid in full for the cost of the charter transportation (for both legs, if a round-trip charter) prior to the scheduled date of flight departure, as provided for in the basic charter regulations applicable to the direct air carrier(s) under part 212 of this chapter.

§ 380.12 Cancellation by charter operator and notice to participants.

(a) The charter operator may not cancel a charter for any reason (including insufficient participation), except for circumstances that make it physically impossible to perform the charter trip, less than 10 days before the scheduled date of departure of the outbound trip.

(b) If the charter operator cancels 10 or more days before the scheduled date of departure, the operator must so notify each participant in writing within 7 days after the cancellation but in any event not less than 10 days before the scheduled departure date of the outbound trip. If a charter is canceled less than 10 days before scheduled departure (*i.e.*, for circumstances that make it physically impossible to perform the charter trip), the operator must get the message to each participant as soon as possible.

§ 380.13 Prohibition on sale of round trips with open returns.

The charter operator shall not accept any participant's payment for return transportation unless the participant has specified a particular return flight.

§ 380.14 Unused space.

Noting contained in this part shall preclude a charter operator from utilizing any unused space on an aircraft by it for a Public Charter for the transportation, on a free or reduced basis, of such charter operator's employees, directors, and officers, and parents and immediate families of such persons.

§ 380.15 Substitution for charter participants.

Subsititues may be arranged for charter participants at any time preceding departure. Participants who provide the charter operator or its sales agent with a substitute participant, or who are substituted for by a participant found by the operator, shall receive a refund of all moneys paid to the operator, except that the operator may reserve the right to retain an administrative fee not to exceed $25 for effecting the substitution.

§ 380.17 Charters conducted by educational institutions.

(a) This section shall apply only to charters conducted by educational institutions for charter groups comprised of bona fide participants in a formal academic course of study abroad which is of at least 4 weeks duration. The charter group may also include a student participant's immediate family (spouse, children, and parents). Except as modified in this section, all terms and conditions of this part applicable to the operation of Public Charters shall apply to charters conducted by educational institutions.

(b) An educational institution conducting such a charter shall submit to the Office of Aviation Analysis, Special Authorities Division, a statement, signed by its president, certifying that it meets the definition of "educational institution" set forth in § 380.2.

(c) An educational institution conducting such a charter need not comply with the requirements of §§ 380.25, 380.28, 380.34, and 380.35.

Subpart C—Requirements Applicable to Charter Operators

§ 380.20 Relief from the Statute.

(a) To the extent necessary to permit them to organize and arrange public charters, charter operators and foreign charter operators are hereby relieved from the following provisions of Subtitle VII of Title 49 of the U.S. Code, only if and so long as they comply with the provisions and the conditions imposed by this part:

(1) Chapter 411.

(2) Chapter 413.

(3) Chapter 415.

(4) Chapter 419.

(5) If foreign charter operators receive interstate air transportation rights, any other provision of the statute that would otherwise prohibit them from organizing and arranging Public Charters in interstate air transportation.

(b) A charter operator who is a citizen of the United States shall not be subject to the following requirements with respect to Public Charters that originate in a foreign country: §§ 380.25, 380.28, and 380.30 through 380.35.

§§ 380.21–380.23 [Reserved]

§ 380.24 Suspension of exemption authority.

The Department reserves the power to deny the exemption authority of any charter operator, without hearing, if it finds that such action is necessary in the public interest or is otherwise necessary in order to protect the rights of the traveling public.

§ 380.25 Prospectus filing and related requirements.

A charter operator may organize and operate a Public Charter only in accordance with this part, and subject to the following conditions:

(a) No charter operator shall operate, sell, receive money from any prospective participant for, or offer to sell or otherwise advertise a charter or series of charters until the Office of Aviation Analysis, Special Authorities Division, has accepted a Public Charter prospectus as described in § 380.28.

(b) If within 10 days after the filing the Department notifies the charter operator that it has rejected the prospectus for noncompliance with this part, the prohibitions set forth in paragraph (a) of this section shall continue until the Department advises that it has accepted the prospectus.

(c) The following amendments to a filed prospectus may be made:

(1) The addition or cancellation of any flight;

(2) A change in any flight, date, origin city or destination city; and

(3) A change in or addition of any direct air carrier, securer, or depository bank.

(d) The charter operator shall amend the prospectus to reflect any change described in paragraph (c) of this section. The amendment shall be filed in the manner and form used for the original prospectus. It shall become effective upon filing unless the operator is otherwise notified.

(e) The charter operator shall notify the depository bank (if any) and the securer of any change described in paragraph (c) of this section not later than when filing a prospectus amendment to reflect the change. If the securer is unable to adjust the security agreement as required by the change, the Office of Aviation Analysis, Special Authorities Division shall be advised of this fact within 2 business days.

(Approved by the Office of Management and Budget under Control Number 2106–0005)

§ 380.26 Discrimination.

No charter operator shall make, give, or cause any undue or unreasonable preference or advantage to any particular person, port, locality, or description of traffic in air transportation in any respect whatsoever, or subject any particular person, port, locality, or description of traffic in air transportation to any unjust discrimination or any undue or unreasonable prejudice or disadvantage in any respect whatsoever.

§ 380.27 Methods of competition.

No charter operator shall engage in unfair or deceptive practices or unfair methods of competition in air transportation or the sale thereof.

§ 380.28 Charter prospectus.

(a) The charter prospectus shall include an original and two copies of the following:

(1) From the charter operator and the direct air carrier:

(i) The proposed flight schedule, listing the origin and destination cities, dates, type of aircraft, number of seats, and charter price for each flight;

(ii) The tour itinerary (if any) including hotels (name and length of stay at each), and other ground accommodations and services; and

(iii) A statement that they have entered into a charter contract that covers the proposed flight schedule, that the contract complies with all applicable Department regulations, and that a copy of the schedule has been sent to the depository bank (if any) and the operator's securer. The schedule shall be identified with a number assigned by the charter operator that does not duplicate any schedule numbers assigned by the operator to other proposed flight schedules. The proposed flight schedule, tour itinerary (if any), and statement shall be filed on OST Form 4532.

(2)(i) From the charter operator and the securer, a statement:

(A) That they have entered into a security agreement covering the proposed flight schedule that complies with § 380.34, including the amount of the coverage, the number assigned to it by the securer, and the amount of any outstanding claims against it, and

(B) That the securer has received a copy of the proposed flight schedule. The statement shall identify the proposed flight schedule by the schedule number assigned by the charter operator in accordance with paragraph (a) of this section. If there are any outstanding claims against the agreement, the charter operator and securer shall also state that they have executed a rider or amendment increasing the coverage by the amount of the claims, or that the securer will separately pay any claims for which it may be liable without impairing the agreement or reducing the amount of its coverage.

(ii) These statements shall be filed an OST Form 4533.

(3) If a depository agreement is used, a statement from the charter operator, the direct air carrier, and the depository bank:

(i) That they have entered into a depository agreement covering the proposed flight schedule that complies with § 380.34, and

(ii) That the bank has received a copy of the proposed flight schedule by the schedule number assigned by the charter operator in accordance with paragraph (a)(1) of this section. This statement shall be filed on OST Form 4534.

(b) Each of the statements described in paragraph (a) of this section shall also include the names and addresses of the parties to it, and the originals shall be signed by those parties.

(c) The prospectus may cover a series of charters performed by one charter operator if the departure of the last charter is not more than one year after the departure of the first.

(d) If the prospectus covers a series of charters and the air transportation will be performed by more than one direct air carrier, the prospectus shall include separate statements in accordance with paragraphs (a)(1) and (a)(3) of this section to cover the flights that will be performed by each direct carrier.

(Approved by the Office of Management and Budget under Control Number 2106–0005)

§ 380.29 Charter contract.

The charter contract between the charter operator or foreign charter operator and the direct air carrier shall evidence a binding commitment on the part of the carrier to furnish the air transportation required for the trip or trips covered by the contract.

§ 380.30 Solicitation materials.

(a) All solicitation materials for a Public Charter shall include the name of the charter operator and the name of the direct air carrier.

(b) Any solicitation material that states a price per passenger shall also include one of the following:

(1) A statement referring to the operator-participant contract for further information about conditions applicable to the charter; or

(2) The full text of the operator-participant contract.

(c) Except as set forth in § 380.33a for operator's option plan contracts, if the charter prospectus names alternative dates or cities, any solicitation material that states a price per passenger shall also state that the actual dates or cities have not yet been selected, if that is the case.

(d) Any solicitation material that names a hotel but does not name every hotel named in the operator-participant contract shall also state that substitutions may be made.

(e) In any solicitation material from a direct air carrier, indirect air carrier, or an agent of either, for a charter, charter tour (*i.e.*, a combination of air transportation and ground accommodations), or a charter tour component (e.g., a hotel stay), any price stated for such charter, tour, or component shall be the entire price to be paid by the participants to the air carrier, or agent, for such charter, tour, or component.

§ 380.31 General requirements for operator-participant contracts.

(a) Except for telephone sales for which payment is made by credit card as described in paragraph (b) of this section, the charter operator shall not accept payment from or on behalf of a prospective participant unless the participant has agreed to the conditions of the charter by signing an operator-participant contract as described in § 380.32. If a member of a group that will travel together pays for the group, that member may sign the contract on behalf of the group.

(b) For telephone sales only, the charter operator may accept payment by credit card without the participant having first signed an operator-participant contract provided that the charter operator first advises the customer:

(1) That he or she has the right to receive the operator-participant contract before making a booking;

(2) That the operator-participant contract will be mailed to the participant within 24 hours of accepting payment by credit card; and

(3) That the operator-participant contract must be signed, and the signed portion returned to the operator, before travel.

(4) A full refund must be made of any amounts charged to a credit card for any participant who cancels before the operator-participant contract is signed.

(c) The contract form may include a space that participants may check to authorize the charter operator to retain their money while attempting to make other arrangements for them if there is no space available on the flight or on specific alternative flights they have requested.

(d) If there is no space available on the flight or specific alternative flights requested by the participant the operator shall return all the participant's money within 7 days after receiving it unless the participant, in accordance with paragraph (c) of this section, has authorized the operator to retain the payments while the operator attempts to make other arrangements for the participant. If the operator retains the payments while attempting to make other arrangements for the participant, it shall notify the participant of the fact within 7 days after receiving the payments, but in no event later than the departure. For the purpose of the time periods in this paragraph, receipt of money by a travel agent on behalf of a charter operator will not be considered as receipt by the operator.

(e) Except as set forth in §380.33a for operator's option plan contracts, the operator-participant contract shall not specify alternative dates for the outbound or return flights, or alternative origin or destination cities for any flight leg.

(f) The contract form shall be printed in 7-point or larger type. The statements required by paragraph (a), (f), (h), (l), (r), (s), and (x) of §380.32 shall be printed so as to contrast with the rest of the contract by the use of boldfaced type, capital letters, or a type size that is at least 50 percent larger than that used for the rest of the contract.

(g) The contract form shall include a space that participants may check to indicate that they wish to be furnished details of trip cancellation, health, and accident insurance.

(h) The contract form shall be designed so as to enable participants to retain a copy of the general terms and conditions after signing it. The specific information supplied by participants (such as choices of dates, cities, or other options) need not be retainable.

§380.32 Specific requirements for operator-participant contracts.

Contracts between charter operators and charter participants shall state:

(a) The name and complete mailing address of the charter operator;

(b) The name of the direct air carrier, the dollar amounts of that carrier's liability limitations for participant's baggage, the type and capacity of the aircraft to be used for the flight, and the conditions governing aircraft-equipment substitutions;

(c) The dates of the outbound and return flights;

(d) The origin and destination cities of each flight leg;

(e) The amount and schedule of payments;

(f) If a depository agreement as provided in §380.34(b) is used: That all checks, money orders, and credit card drafts must be made payable to the escrow account at the depository bank (identifying bank)[1] or, when the charter is sold to the participant by a retail travel agent, checks and money orders may be made payable to the agent, who must in turn make his check payable to the escrow account at the depository bank;

(g) The tour itinerary, if any, including the name and location of the hotels, length of stay at each, and other ground accommodations and services that are part of the tour;

(h) That the charter operator may not cancel the charter less than 10 days before the scheduled departure date, except for circumstances that make it physically impossible to perform the charter tip;

(i) That if a charter is canceled 10 or more days before the scheduled departure date, the operator will notify the participant in writing within 7 days after the cancellation, but in any event at least 10 days before the scheduled departure;

(j) That is a charter is canceled less than 10 days before departure (*i.e.*, for circumstances that make it physically impossible to perform the charter trip), the operator will get the message to the participant as soon as possible;

[1] If the credit card merchant account is separate from the depository account, it must be used solely as a conduit, i.e., all credit card payments toward Public Charter trips must be immediately remitted to the depository account in full, without holdback, or retention of any portion of the participant's payment. If the depository bank is not the credit card merchant bank, the Department must be satisfied that there are adequate procedural safeguards for the protection of participants' payments.

(k) That if the charter is canceled, a refund will be made to the participant within 14 days after the cancellation;

(l) The right to refunds if the participant changes plans is limited;

(m) The right to refunds if the participant changes plans, including

(1) The right to a full refund, for sales made by credit card, until an operator-participant contract is signed; and

(2) That any participant who wishes to cancel will receive a full refund (less any applicable administrative fee, not to exceed $25) upon providing a substitute participant to the charter operator or its sales agent, or upon being substituted for by a participant found by the charter operator;

(n) The procedure for obtaining the refunds described in paragraph (m) of this section, including that they will be made within 14 days after the cancellation or substitution;

(o) The meaning of "major change", as set forth in § 380.33(a);

(p) That if the charter operator knows of a major change 10 or more days before scheduled departure, the operator will notify the participant of the change within 7 days after first knowing of it, but in any event at least 10 days before scheduled departure;

(q) That is the operator first knows of a major change less than 10 days before scheduled departure, the operator will get the message to the participant as soon as possible;

(r) That within 7 days after receiving a pre-departure notification of a major change but in no event later than departure, the participant may cancel, and that a full refund will be made to the participant within 14 days after canceling;

(s) That upon a post-departure notification of a major change, the participant may reject the substituted hotel or the changed date, origin, or destination of a flight leg and be sent, within 14 days after the return date named in the contract, a refund of the portion of his payment allocable to the hotel accommodations or air transportation not provided;

(t) That the participants rights and remedies set forth in the contract, including the procedures for major changes, shall be in addition to any other rights or remedies available under applicable law, although the operator may condition a refund on the participant's waiver of additional remedies;

(u) That trip cancellation, health, and accident insurance is available and that the operator will furnish details of the insurance to participants who check the space provided for this purpose on the contract form;

(v) The name and address of the surety company or bank issuing the security agreement; and that unless the charter participant files a claim with the charter operator or, if he is unavailable, with the securer, within 60 days after termination of the charter, the securer shall be released from all liability under the security agreement to that participant. Termination means the date of arrival (or in the case of a canceled charter, the intended date or arrival) of the return flight. If there is no return flight in a participant's itinerary, termination means the date or intended date of departure of the last flight in the participant's itinerary;

(w) For international flights only: That additional restrictions may be imposed on the flight by the foreign government involved, and that if landing rights are denied by a foreign government the flight will be canceled with a full refund to the participant. This statement need not be included in the contract if—

(1) The prospectus includes a certification by the charter operator and the direct air carrier that landing rights have been obtained from all the foreign governments involved, and

(2) All the foreign governments involved have adopted country-of-origin rules for charterworthiness;

(x) That the charter operator is the principal and is responsible to the participants for all services and accommodations offered in connection with the charter. However, the contract may expressly provide that the charter operator, unless negligent, is not responsible for personal injury or property damage caused by any direct air carrier, hotel or other supplier of services in connection with the charter.

§ 380.33 Major changes in itinerary or price; refunds.

(a) For the purposes of this section, "major change" means any of the following:

(1) A change in the departure or return date shown in the operator-participant contract, (or, if the contract states alternative dates, the date designated to the participant by the charter operator in accordance with § 380.33a(b)), unless the change results from a flight delay. In any event, however, a date change that the operator knows of more than 2 days before the scheduled flight date, and any delay of more than 48 hours, will be considered a major change.

(2) A change in the origin or destination city shown in the operator-participant contract for any flight leg (or, if the contract states alternative cities, the city designated to the participant by the operator in accordance with § 380.33a(b)), unless the change affects only the order in which cities named in a tour package are visited.

(3) A substitution of any hotel that is not named in the operator-participant contract; and

(4) A price increase to the participant that occurs 10 or more days before departure and results in an aggregate price increase of more than 10 percent.

(b) The charter operator shall not increase the price to any participant less than 10 days before departure.

(c) The charter operator shall notify all participants of major changes, as required by the operator-participant contracts. This notification shall include the participants' rights to refunds required to be described in the operator-participant contract. The operator shall, if applicable, also notify the participants that the acceptance of a refund constitutes a waiver of their legal rights.

(d) Except as otherwise specified, notifications and refunds required by this part are considered made at the time they are mailed or sent by an equivalent method.

(e) The charter operator shall make all refunds required to be described in the operator-participant contract within the time limits set forth in paragraphs (k), (n), (r), and (s) of § 380.32, as applicable.

§ 380.33a Operator's option plan.

(a) For the purposes of this part, an operator's option plan contract that states alternative dates for the outbound or return flights, or alternative origin or destination cities for any flight leg.

(b) Operator's option plan contracts shall state, in addition to the information required by § 380.32, that the selection of the actual dates or cities, as applicable, is at the charter operator's option and will not entitle the participant to a refund, and that the operator will notify the participant of the actual dates or cities at least 10 days before the earliest of any alternative dates for the outbound flight.

(c) Contract forms for all operator's option plan contracts shall be labeled "OPERATOR'S OPTION PLAN" in bold-faced capital letters at least ¼ inch high. The statement required by paragraph (b) of this section and the statement of alternative dates (§ 380.32(c)) or alternative cities (§ 380.32(d)), as applicable, shall be printed so as to contrast with the rest of the contract, as set forth in § 380.31(f).

(d) Any solicitation material that states a price per passenger for an operator's option plan contract shall clearly and conspicuously—

(1) Identify that price as being for the operator's option plan,

(2) Name all the possible dates or cities, as applicable, and

(3) State that the selection of the actual dates or cities is at the charter operator's option.

(e) Charter operators and their agents shall not misrepresent to prospective participants, orally, in solicitation materials, or otherwise, the probability that any particular city or date will be selected from among the alternatives named in an operator's option plan contract.

(f) The charter operator shall notify all participants with operator's option plan contracts of the actual dates or cities, as applicable, as required by contracts.

§ 380.34 Security and depository agreements.

(a) Except as provided in paragraph (b) of this section, the charter operator or foreign charter operator shall furnish a security agreement in an amount for not less than the charter price for the air transportation, if only air transportation is involved, or, if the charter involves land accommodations in addition to air transportation, a security agreement in one of the following amounts dependent upon the length of the charter or series of charters:

(1) For a charter or series of charters of 14 days or less, security in an amount of not less than the charter price for the air transportation to be furnished in connection with such charter or series of charters;

(2) For a charter or series of charters of more than 14 days but less than 28 days security in an amount of not less than twice the charter price; and

(3) For a charter or series of charters of 28 days or more, security in an amount of not less than three times the charter price: Provided, however, That the liability of the securer to any charter participant shall not exceed amounts paid by that participant to the charter operator with respect to the charter.

(b) The direct air carrier and the charter operator or foreign charter operator may elect, in lieu of furnishing a security agreement as provided under paragraph (a) of this section, to comply with the requirements of paragraphs (b)(1) and (b)(2) of this section, as follows:

(1) The charter operator shall furnish a security agreement in an amount of at least $10,000 times the number of flights, except that the amount need not be more than $200,000. The liability of the securer to any charter participant shall not exceed the amount paid by the participant to the charter operator for that charter.

(2) The direct air carrier and charter operator or foreign charter operator shall enter into an agreement with a designated bank, the terms of which shall provide that all payments by charter participants paid to charter operators or foreign charter operators and their retail travel agents shall be deposited with and maintained by the bank subject to the following conditions:

(i) On sales made to charter participants by charter operators or foreign charter operators the participant shall pay by check, money order, or credit card draft payable to the bank;[2] on sales made to charter participants by retail travel agents, the retail travel agent may deduct his commission and remit the balance to the designated bank by check, money order, or electronic transfer: Provided, That the travel agent agrees in writing with the charter operator or foreign charter operator that if the charter is canceled the travel agent shall remit to the bank the full amount of the commission previously deducted or received within 10 days after receipt of notification of cancellation of the charter; except for the credit card company's usual commission (not to exceed 3 percent), the charter operator shall not permit any portion of a charter participant's payments by credit cared to be "held back" by the credit card merchant bank;[3]

(ii) The bank shall pay the direct air carrier the charter price for the transportation not earlier than 60 days (including day of departure) prior to the scheduled day of departure of the originating or returning flight, upon certification of the departure date by the air carrier: Provided, That, in the case of a round trip charter contract to be performed by one carrier, the total round trip charter price shall be paid to the carrier not earlier than 60 days prior to the scheduled day of departure of the originating flight;

(iii) The bank shall reimburse the charter operator or foreign charter operator for refunds made by the latter to the charter participant upon written notification from the charter operator or foreign charter operator;

(iv) If the charter operator, foreign charter operator or the direct air carrier notifies the bank that a charter has been canceled, the bank shall make applicable refunds directly to the charter participants;

(v) After the charter price has been paid in full to the direct air carrier, the

[2] See also n.1, *supra*.

[3] "Holdback" is an amount in excess of usual commissions that a credit card merchant bank sometimes retains to cover potential charge-backs or other charges.

bank shall pay funds from the account directly to the hotels, sightseeing enterprises, or other persons or companies furnishing ground accommodations and services, if any, in connection with the charter or series of charters upon presentation to the bank of vendors' bills and upon certification by the charter operator or foreign charter operator of the amounts payable for such ground accommodations and services and the person or companies to whom payment is to be made: Provided, however, That the total amounts paid by the bank pursuant to paragraphs (b)(2) (ii) and (v) of this section shall not exceed either the total cost of the air transportation, or 80 percent of the total deposits received by the bank less any refunds made to charter participants pursuant to paragraphs (b)(2) (ii) and (iv) of this section, whichever is greater;

(vi) As used in this section, the term "bank" means a bank insured by the Federal Deposit Insurance Corporation;

(vii) The bank shall maintain a separate accounting for each charter group;

(viii) Notwithstanding any other provisions of this section, the amount of total cash deposits required to be maintained in the depository account of the bank may be reduced by one or both of the following: The amount of the security agreement in the form prescribed in this section in excess of the minimum coverage required by paragraph (b)(1) of this section; an escrow with the designated bank of Federal, State, or municipal bonds or other securities, consisting of certificates of deposit issued by banks having a stated policy of redeeming such certificates before maturity at the request of the holder (subject only to such interest penalties or other conditions as may be required by law), or negotiable securities which are publicly traded on a securities exchange, all such securities to be made payable to the escrow account: Provided, That such other securities shall be substituted in an amount no greater than 80 percent of the total market value of the escrow account at the time of such substitution: And provided, further, That should the market value of such other securities subsequently decrease, from time to time, then additional cash or securities qualified for investment hereunder shall promptly be added to the escrow account, in an amount equal to the amount of such decreased value; and

(ix) Except as provided in paragraph (b)(2)(i), (iii), (iv), (v), and (viii) of this section, the bank shall not pay out any funds from the account prior to 2 banking days after completion of each charter, when the balance in the account shall be paid the charter operator or foreign charter operator, upon certification of the completion date by the direct air carrier: Provided, however, That if the Charter involves air transportation only and the bank has paid the direct air carrier(s) the charter price for the originating flight, and the returning flight if any, and has paid all refunds due to participants, as provided in paragraph (b)(2)(ii) and (iii), respectively, of this section, then the bank may pay the balance in the account to the charter operator upon certification by the direct air carrier performing the originating flight that such flight has in fact departed.

(c)(1) The security agreement required under paragraphs (a) and (b) of this section shall insure the financial responsibility of the charter operator or foreign charter operator and the supplying of the transportation and all other accommodations, services, and facilities in accordance with the contract between the charter operator or foreign charter operator and the charter participants.

(2) The security agreement may be either:

(i) A surety bond in the form set forth as appendix A to this part;

(ii) A surety trust agreement in the form set forth as appendix B to this part; or

(iii) An arrangement with a bank (for instance, a standby letter of credit) that provides protection of charter participants' funds equivalent to or greater than that provided by the Bond in appendix A. An arrangement that furnishes a lesser degree of protection than would be provided under the bond shall be invalid to that extent, and instead the bank, the charter operator or foreign charter operator, and the charter participants shall have the same rights and liabilities as provided under a bond in the form of appendix A. If the arrangement does not give as much protection as a bond against the risk of the charter operator's bankruptcy, the bank shall be liable in the event of bankruptcy to the same extent as if it had entered into a bond.

(3) Any agreement under paragraph (c)(2)(iii) of this section shall include a statement that, in the event that the other provisions of the agreement do not provide protection to charter participants comparable to that provided under a bond in the form of appendix A, the bank shall assume, for the benefit of the charter participants, all the liabilities it would have if it entered into the bond.

(4) The security agreement shall be effective on or before the date the charter prospectus is filed with the Department.

(5) The security agreement shall be specifically identified by the issuing securer with a numbering system so that the Department can identify the security agreement with the specific charter or charters to which it relates. These data may be set forth in an addendum attached to the security agreement, which addendum must be signed by the charter operator or foreign charter operator and the securer.

(6) When security is provided by a surety bond, such bond shall be issued by a bonding or surety company that is listed in Best's Insurance Reports (Fire and Casualty) with a general policyholders' rating of "A" or better. The bonding or surety company shall be one legally authorized to issue bonds of that type in the State in which the charter originates. For purposes of this section the term "State" includes any territory or possession of the United States, or the District of Columbia.

(7) When security is provided by a security agreement other than a bond, the agreement shall be issued by a national bank complying with the provisions of 12 CFR 7.7010(a), or by a State bank complying with applicable State laws that give authority to issue such agreements, and all such banks must be insured by the Federal Deposit Insurance Corporation.

(d) The security agreement required by this section shall provide that unless the charter participant files a claim with the charter operator or foreign charter operator, or, if it is unavailable, with the securer, within 60 days after termination of the charter, the securer shall be released from all liability under the security agreement to such charter participant. Terminations means the date of arrival (or in the case of a canceled charter, the intended date of arrival) of the return flight. If there is no return flight in a participant's itinerary, termination means the date or intended date of departure of the last flight in the participant's itinerary.

§ 380.34a Substitution of direct air carrier's security or depository agreement.

(a) A direct air carrier may substitute its own security agreement and/or depository arrangements, as specified in this section, for those required of the charter operator under § 380.34, but only for charter trips in which all the air transportation is provided by one direct air carrier. Charter operators are relieved from § 380.34 to the extent that the direct carrier substitutes its own arrangements.

(b) The direct air carrier may substitute its security agreement for all of the arrangements required of the charter operator under § 380.34 (a) or (b). Alternatively, it may substitute its depository agreement for the depository agreement required of the charter operator under § 380.34(b)(2). If the direct carrier substitutes its depository agreement, it may also obtain and substitute a security agreement for the one otherwise required of the charter operator under § 380.34(b)(1). If the direct carrier substitutes its depository agreement only, the charter operator must supply the security agreement required under § 380.34(b)(1).

(c) If the direct carrier substitutes a security agreement for all the charter operator's requirements under § 380.34, the charter operator shall include in the charter prospectus, in place of the information in § 380.28(a)(2) regarding the charter operator's security agreement:

(1) A statement by the direct air carrier on OST Form 4535 that it will take responsibility for all charter participant payments (including those for

ground accommodations and services) and for the fulfillment of all the charter operator's contractual and regulatory obligations to the charter participants.

(2) A statement from the direct air carrier and its securer (under §212.12 of this chapter), OST Form 4533, that they have entered into a security agreement assuring the direct air carrier's responsibilities to charter participants under this section in an unlimited amount (except that the liability of the securer with respect to any charter participant may be limited to the charter price paid by or on behalf of such participant), and that the securer has received a copy of the proposed flight schedule identified by the schedule number assigned by the charter operator under this part.

(d) A substitute depository agreement under this section shall be signed by the direct air carrier, the charter operator, and the depository bank, and shall provide, in addition to existing requirements under §212.8 of this chapter, that:

(1) Payments by or on behalf of charter participants shall be allocated to the flight accounts matching the participant's itinerary in the following way: Each account shall have allocated to it the charter cost of the participant's air transportation on that flight. The portion of each payment not intended for air transportation services shall be allocated to the account for the return flight in the participant's itinerary. If there is only one flight in the itinerary, the entire payment shall be allocated to that account.

(2) The bank shall pay funds from a flight account directly to the hotels, sightseeing enterprises, or other persons or companies furnishing ground accommodations and services, if any, in connection with the charter flight, upon presentation to the bank of vendor's bills and upon certification by the person who contracted for the ground accommodations or services of the amounts payable and the persons or companies to whom payment is to be made, except that no disbursement shall be made that would reduce the balance in the account below the charter cost of the flight.

(3) On sales made to participants by a person other than a retail travel agent, the participant shall pay by check, money order, or credit card draft payable to the bank. On sales made to participants by a retail travel agent, payments shall be made in the same manner unless the agent deducts its commission and remits the balance to the bank by check, money order, or electronic transfer. The agent may deduct its commission only if it agrees in writing with its principal (the charter operator or direct air carrier, as applicable) that, if the charter is canceled, the agent shall remit to the bank the full amount of the commission previously deducted or received within 10 days after receipt of notification of the cancellation. The depository bank shall pay refunds directly to participants according to the terms of the operator-participant contract and the terms of this part.

(e) If the direct carrier substitutes a security agreement in addition to substituting a depository agreement, the charter prospectus information must include all the information required by paragraphs (c) and (d) of this section, except for the amount of the security agreement. That agreement shall be in an amount of at least $10,000 times the number of flights, except that the amount need not be more than $200,000.

(f) A copy of the depository agreement under paragraph (d) of this section shall be filed with the Department, and it shall not be effective until approved by the Department.

(g) A copy of the security agreement under paragraph (c) or paragraph (e) of this section shall be filed with the Department. It shall insure the financial responsibility of the direct air carrier for supplying the transportation and all other accommodations, services, and facilities in accordance with the contracts between the charter operator and the charter participants. Such security agreement shall meet all the other requirements of §380.34 (c) and (d).

§380.35 Disbursements from depository account.

No charter operator or direct air carrier shall cause its agents or the depository bank to make disbursements or payments from deposits except in accordance with the provisions of this part.

§ 380.36 Record retention.

Every charter operator conducting a charter pursuant to this part shall comply with the applicable record-retention provisions of part 249 of this chapter.

Subpart D—Requirements Applicable to Direct Air Carriers

§ 380.40 Charter not to be performed unless in compliance with this part 380.

(a) For all Public Charters other than foreign-originating charters organized by foreign charter operators: A direct air carrier shall not perform air transportation in connection with such a charter unless it has made a reasonable effort to verify that all provisions of this part have been complied with and that the charter operator's authority under this part has not been suspended by the Department.

(b) For foreign-originating Public Charters organized by foreign charter operators: A direct air carrier shall not perform air transportation in connection with such a charter unless—

(1) The charter is conducted in accordance with subpart B of this part and

(2) The charter operator conforms to all requirements of this part that are applicable to charter operators within the Department's jurisdiction, other than §§ 380.25, 380.28, 380.30 through 380.36, and 380.50.

§§ 380.41–380.42 [Reserved]

§ 380.43 Cancellations by direct air carriers.

The direct air carrier shall not cancel any charter under this part less than 10 days before the scheduled departure date, except for circumstances that make it physically impossible to perform the charter trip.

§ 380.45 Suspension of exemption authority.

The Department reserves the power to suspend the exemption authority of any air carrier, without hearing, if it finds that such action is necessary in order to protect the rights of the traveling public.

§ 380.46 Charter trip reporting.

The direct air carrier shall promptly notify the Office of Aviation Analysis, Special Authorities Division, regarding any charters covered by a prospectus filed under § 380.28 that are later canceled.

Subpart E—Registration of Foreign Charter Operators

§ 380.60 Purpose.

This subpart establishes registration procedures for foreign charter operators intending to engage in the formation of groups for transportation on Public Charters that originate in the United States.

§ 380.61 Operation by foreign charter operators.

(a) Each foreign charter operator shall be registered under this subpart and file a prospectus under § 380.25 before organizing groups for transportation on Public Charters that originate in the United States.

(b) Each foreign charter registered under this subpart shall comply with the other provisions of this part directed to charter operators.

§ 380.62 Registration applications.

(a) To be registered under this subpart, a foreign charter operator shall file two copies of an application for registration with the Office of Aviation Analysis, Special Authorities Division. The Department will list the names and nationalities of all persons applying for registration in its Weekly Summary of Filings.

(b) The application shall be made on OST Form 4530, which can be obtained from the Office of Aviation Analysis, Special Authorities Division.

(c) The applicant shall clearly indicate in its application for registration whether it requests authority to engage in foreign and/or interstate air transportation.

§380.63 Objections to registration applications.

Any person objecting to the registration application of a foreign charter operator or to a proposed change in the name or ownership of that operator shall file an objection with the Office of Aviation Analysis, Special Authorities Division, within 28 days after the Department receives the properly completed registration application.

§380.64 Department action on a registration application.

(a) After a registration is received, one of the following actions will be taken.

(1) The application will be approved by the stamping of the effective date of registration on OST Form 4530 and returning the duplicate copy of the form to the operator;

(2) Additional information will be requested for the applicant;

(3) The applicant will be notified that its application will require further analysis or procedures, or is being referred to the Department for formal action;

(4)The registration application will be rejected if it does not comply with the filing requirements of this subpart;

(5) The application will be approved subject to such terms, conditions, or limitations as may be required by the public interest; or

(6) The registration application will be rejected for reasons relating to the failure of effective reciprocity or if the Department finds that it would be in the public interest to do so.

(b) One of the actions described in paragraph (a) of this section will normally be taken within 60 days after the registration application is received. The Department will also consider requests for faster action that include a full explanation of the need for expedited action.

§380.65 Notification of change of operations or ownership.

(a) Not later than 30 days before any change in its name or address or before a temporary or permanent cessation of operations, each foreign charter operator registered under this subpart shall notify the Office of Aviation Analysis, Special Authorities Division, of the change by resubmitting OST Form 4530.

(b) A foreign charter operator registered under this subpart shall apply for an amendment to that registration not later than 30 days after either of the following events:

(1) A person listed on its existing registration as owning or holding beneficial interest in at least 10 percent of the operator or of the operator's stock reduces its holding to below 10 percent;

(2) A person not listed on the existing registration as owning or holding beneficial interest in at least 10 percent of the operator or of the operator's stock becomes an owner or holder of 10 percent or more of the company or of its stock.

(c) An application for an amendment shall be made by resubmitting OST Form 4530. The existing registration shall remain valid pending Department action on the amendment.

§380.66 Cancellation or conditioning of the registration.

The registration of a foreign charter operator may be canceled or subjected to additional terms, conditions, or limitations if any of the following occur:

(a) The operator files a written notice with the Department that it is discontinuing its charter operations;

(b) A substantial ownership interest is acquired by persons who are not citizens of the same country as the registrant; or

(c) The Department finds, after notice and an opportunity for responses, that it is in the public interest to do so. In making this finding, the Department will consider whether effective reciprocity exists between the United States and the government of the foreign charter operator.

§380.67 Waiver of sovereign immunity.

By accepting an approved registration form under this subpart, an operator waives any right it may have to assert any defense of sovereign immunity from suit in any proceeding against it, in any court or other tribunal of the United States, that is based upon a claim arising out of operations by the operator under this part.

APPENDIX A TO PART 380—PUBLIC CHARTER OPERATOR'S SURETY BOND UNDER PART 380 OF THE SPECIAL REGULATIONS OF THE DEPARTMENT OF TRANSPORTATION (14 CFR PART 380)

Know all men by these presents, that we ______ (name of charter operator) of ______, (city) ______ (state or country) as Principal (hereinafter called Principal), and ______ (name of surety) a corporation created and existing under the laws of the State of ______ (State) as Surety (hereinafter called Surety) are held and firmly bound unto the United States of America in the sum of $______ (see §380.34(f) of Part 380) for which payment, well and truly to be made, we bind ourselves and our heirs, executors, administrators, successors, and assigns, jointly and severally, firmly by these presents.

Whereas Principal intends to become a Public Charter operator pursuant to the provisions of part 380 of the Department's Special Regulations and other rules and regulations of the Department relating to insurance or other security for the protection of charter participants, and has elected to file with the Department of Transportation such a bond as will insure financial responsibility with respect to all moneys received from charter participants for services in connection with a Public Charter to be operated subject to Part 380 of the Department's Special Regulations in accordance with contracts, agreements, or arrangements therefor, and

Whereas this bond is written to assure compliance by Principal as an authorized charter operator with Part 380 of the Department's Special Regulations, and other rules and regulations of the Department relating to insurance and other security for the protection of charter participants, and shall inure to the benefit of any and all charter participants to whom Principal may be held legally liable for any damages herein described.

Now, therefor, the condition of this obligation is such that if Principal shall pay or cause to be paid to charter participants any sum or sums for which Principal may be held legally liable by reason of Principal's failure faithfully to perform, fulfill and carry out all contracts, agreements, and arrangements made by Principal while this bond is in effect with respect to the receipt of moneys from charter participants, and proper disbursement thereof pursuant to and in accordance with the provisions of Part 380 of the Department's Special Regulations, then this obligation shall be void, otherwise to remain in full force and effect.

The liability of Surety with respect to any charter participant shall not exceed the charter price paid by or on behalf of such participant.

The liability of Surety shall not be discharged by any payment or succession of payments hereunder, unless and until such payment or payments shall amount in the aggregate to the penalty of the bond, but in no event shall Surety's obligation hereunder exceed the amount of said penalty.

Surety agrees to furnish written notice to the Office of Aviation Analysis, Department of Transportation, forthwith of all suits or claims filed and judgments rendered, and payments made by Surety under this bond.

The bond shall cover the following charters:[1]

Surety company's bond No. ______

Date of flight departure ______

Place of flight departure ______

This bond is effective on the ______ day of ______, 12:01 a.m., standard time at the address of Principal as stated herein and as hereinafter provided. Principal or Surety may at any time terminate this bond by written notice to: "Special Authorities Division (P–57), Office of Aviation Analysis, U.S. Department of Transportation, Washington, DC 20590," such termination to become effective thirty (30) days after the actual receipt of said notice by the Department. Surety shall not be liable hereunder for the payment of any damages hereinbefore described which arise as a result of any contracts, agreements, undertakings, or arrangements for the supplying of transportation and other services made by Principal after the termination of this bond as herein provided, but such termination shall not affect the liability of the bond hereunder for the payment of any damages arising as a result of contracts, agreements, or arrangements for the supplying of transportation and other services made by Principal prior to the date that such termination becomes effective. Liability of Surety under this bond shall in all events be limited only to a charter participant or charter participants who shall within sixty (60) days after the termination of the particular charter described herein give written notice of claim to the charter operator or, if it is unavailable, to Surety, and all liability on this bond shall automatically terminate sixty (60) days after the termination date of each particular charter covered by this bond except for claims made in the time provided herein.

In witness whereof, the said Principal and Surety have executed this instrument on the ______ day of ______, ______.

[1] These data may be supplied in addendum attached to the bond.

Principal

Name ______________________________

By: Signature and title

Surety

Name ______________________________

By: Signature and title ______________

Only corporations may qualify to act as surety and they must meet the requirements set forth in §380.34(c)(6) of Part 380.

APPENDIX B TO PART 380—PUBLIC CHARTER SURETY TRUST AGREEMENT

This Trust Agreement is entered into between ______________ (charter operator) incorporated under the law of ______________ with the principal place of business being ______________ (hereinafter referred to as the Operator), and ______________ (Bank) with its principal place of business being ______________ (hereinafter referred to as the "Trustee"), for the purpose of creating a trust to become effective as of the ____ day of ______________, ______, which trust shall continue until terminated as hereinafter provided.

The Operator intends to become a Public Charter operator pursuant to the provisions of Part 380 of the Department's Special Regulations and other rules and regulations of the Department relating to insurance or other security for the protection of charter participants, and has elected to file with the Department of Transportation such a Surety Trust Agreements as will insure financial responsibility with respect to all moneys received from charter participants for services in connection with a Public Charter to be operated subject to Part 380 of the Department's Special Regulations in accordance with contracts, agreements, or arrangements therefor.

This Surety Trust Agreement is written to assure compliance by the Operator with the provisions of Part 380 of the Department's Special Regulations and other rules and regulations of the Department relating to insurance or other security for the protection of charter participants.

It shall inure to the benefit of any and all charter participants to whom the Operator may be held legally liable for any of the damages herein described.

It is mutually agreed by and between the operator and Trustee that the Trustee shall manage the corpus of the trust and carry out the purposes of the trust as hereinafter set forth during the term of the trust for the benefit of charter participants (who are hereinafter referred to as "Beneficiaries.")

Beneficiaries of the trust created by this Agreement shall be limited to those charter participants who meet the following requirements:

1. Those for whom Operator or Operator's agent has received payment toward participation in one or more charters operated by or proposed to be operated by Operator.

2. Who have legal claim or claims for money damages against the Operator by reason of the Operators' failure faithfully to perform, fulfill, and carry out all contracts, agreements, and arrangements made by the Operator while this trust is in respect to the receipt of moneys and proper disbursement thereof pursuant to Part 380 of the Department's Special Regulations; and

3. Who have given notice of such claim or claims in accordance with this Trust Agreement, but who have not been paid by the Operator.

The Operator shall convey to the Trustee legal title to the trust corpus, which has a value of $______________ by the time of the execution of this Agreement.

Trustee shall assume the responsibilities of the Trustee over the said trust corpus and shall distribute from the trust corpus to any and all Beneficiaries to whom the Operator, in its capacity as a Public Charter operator, may be held legally liable by reason of the Operator's failure faithfully to perform, fulfill, and carry out all contracts, agreements, and arrangements made by the Operator, while this trust is in effect with respect to the receipt of moneys and proper disbursement thereof pursuant to Part 380 of the Department's Special Regulations in connection with said charters, such damages as will discharge such liability while this trust is in effect; Provided, however, That the liability of the trust to any Beneficiary shall not exceed the charter price (as defined in Part 380 of the Department's Special Regulations) paid by or on behalf on any such Beneficiary; Provided, further, That there shall be on obligation of the trust to any Beneficiary if the Operator shall pay or cause to be paid to any Beneficiary any sum or sums for which the Operator may be held legally liable by reasons of its failure faithfully to perform, fulfill, and carry out all contracts, agreements, and arrangements made by the Operator in its capacity as charter operator while this trust is in effect with respect to the receipt of moneys and proper disbursement thereof pursuant to Part 380 of the Department's Special Regulations; And provided still further, That the liability of the trust as administered by the Trustee shall not be discharged by any payment or succession of payments hereunder, unless and until such payment or payments, shall amount in the aggregate to $______________. Notwithstanding anything herein to the contrary, in no event shall the obligation of the trust or the Trustee hereunder exceed the aggregate amount of $______________.

The Trustee agrees to furnish written notice to the Office of Aviation Analysis, Department of Transportation, forthwith of all suits of claims filed and judgments rendered (of which it has knowledge), and of payments made by the Trustee under the terms of this trust.

The Trust shall not be liable hereunder for the payment of any damages hereinbefore described which arise as a result of any contracts, agreements, undertakings, or arrangements for the supplying of transportation and other services made by the Operator after the termination of this trust as herein provided, but such termination shall not affect the liability of the trust hereunder for the payment of any damages arising as a result of contracts, agreements, or arrangements for the supplying of transportation and other services made by the Operator prior to the date that such termination becomes effective.

Liability of the trust shall in all events be limited only to a Beneficiary or Beneficiaries who shall within sixty days after the termination of the particular charter give written notice of claim to the Operator or, if it is unavailable, to the Trustee, and all liability of the trust with respect to participants in a charter shall automatically terminate sixty days after the termination date of each particular charter covered by this trust except for claims filed in the time provided herein. Sixty-one days after the completion of the last charter covered by this Trust Agreement, the trust shall automatically terminate except for claims of any Beneficiary or Beneficiaries previously made in accordance with this Agreement still pending on and after said sixty-first day. To the extent of such claims, the trust shall continue until those claims are discharged, dismissed, dropped, or otherwise terminated; the remainder of the trust corpus shall be conveyed forthwith to the Operator. After all remaining claims which are covered by this Trust Agreement pending on and after the said sixty-first day have been discharged, dismissed, dropped, or otherwise terminated, the Trustee shall convey forthwith the remainder of the trust corpus, if any, to the Operator.

Either the Operator or Trustee may at any time terminate this trust by written notice to: "Special Authorities Division (P–57), Office of Aviation Analysis, U.S. Department of Transportation, Washington, DC 20590," such termination to become effective thirty days after the actual receipt of said notice by the Department.

In the event of any controversy or claim arising hereunder, the Trustee shall not be required to determine same or take any other action with respect thereto, but may await the settlement of such controversy or claim by final appropriate legal proceedings, and in such event shall not be liable for interest or damages of any kind.

Any Successor to the Trustee by merger, consolidation, or otherwise, shall succeed to this trusteeship and shall have the powers and obligations set forth in this Agreement.

The trust created under this Agreement shall be operated and administered under the laws of the State of ________.

IN WITNESS WHEREOF, the Operator and Trustee have executed this instrument on the ____ day of ________, ____.

Trustee

Name ____________________

By: Signature and title

Charter Operator

Name ____________________

By: Signature and title

PART 381—SPECIAL EVENT TOURS

AUTHORITY: 49 U.S.C. 40113(a) and 41712.

SOURCE: Docket No. 49385, 59 FR 61514, Nov. 30, 1994, unless otherwise noted.

§ 381.1 Purpose.

The purpose of this part is ensure that air travelers who have purchased tours to special events will receive the promised admission to the event. This part expands the "Super Bowl rule" to other events.

§ 381.3 Applicability.

This part applies to Special Event Tours that are in interstate air transportation, or in foreign air transportation originating at a point in the United States. This part applies to U.S. and foreign operators of Special Event Tours, whether they be air carriers or ticket agents. This part applies to scheduled, charter, and other air transportation.

§ 381.5 Definition.

Special Event Tour means a tour that is organized for the purpose of attending a sporting, social, religious, educational, cultural, political or other event of a special nature and limited duration, which exists for reasons apart from the tour itself, and which is represented by the operator of the tour as including admission to that event. Examples of such events include, but are not limited to, college and professional sporting events, the Olympics, concerts, the Passion Play in Oberammergau, etc.

§381.7 Advertising.

No operator of a Special Event Tour or agent of such an operator shall conduct, or cause or allow to be conducted, any advertising, solicitation or other promotion for a Special Event Tour unless:

(a) The operator is in physical possession of enough tickets for admission to the event to provide such tickets for a substantial number of seats on the tour; or

(b) The operator has entered into a written contract with an organization that is the distributor of such tickets or an organization that receives such tickets directly from the distributor (e.g., a bowl committee; football conference, league or team; concert promoter or arena; etc.), the terms of which provide for that organization to furnish the operator enough admission tickets to provide such tickets for a substantial number of seats on the tour; or

(c) The operator has entered into a written contract with another person or organization that has a written contract or series of written contracts with the distributor of such tickets or with an organization that receives such tickets directly from the distributor, the terms of which provide for that organization (the organization with which the operator has contracted) to furnish the operator enough admission tickets to provide such tickets for a substantial number of seats on the tour.

§381.9 Sales.

(a) Except as provided in paragraph (b) of this section:

(1) No operator of a Special Event Tour shall accept money for a seat on a Special Event Tour, or authorize an agent to accept such money, unless the operator has physical possession of, or written contracts (in the manner described in §381.7) for, a ticket for admission to the event for that individual. To the extent that the operator receives an unsolicited booking for which the operator does not have physical possession of or written contracts for a ticket for admission to the event, any payment accompanying that booking must be returned within 3 business days.

(2) Upon acceptance of the money for a sale, the operator must reserve one event ticket for that individual. An operator may not sell more seats on the tour than it has event tickets in hand or under contract. (An operator need not continue to reserve an event ticket for an individual who withdraws from the tour by providing notice to the operator or by being notified by the operator that the individual's participation has been canceled due to failure to remit a required installment payment.)

(b) An operator of a Special Event Tour may accept a booking and payment from an individual for whom the operator does not have an event ticket in hand or under contract if that individual agrees in writing that he or she understands that no event ticket has been reserved for him or her. This agreement shall specify whether the person has agreed to participate in the tour without an event ticket and/or the operator has agreed to attempt to acquire an event ticket for this person. If the two parties agree that the operator will attempt to acquire an event ticket, the agreement shall specify any penalties that will apply if the individual later cancels because an event ticket did not become available. If the operator notifies this person that an event ticket has become available, that person shall enjoy all the other protections of this part from that time.

§381.11 Refunds.

If promised admission to the primary event for which a Special Event Tour was organized is not furnished by the tour operator, at the tour price agreed to before departure (including any increases that the participant has accepted pursuant to §381.13(a)), the operator must provide each tour participant affected in this way a refund of the total tour price. This refund is to be provided within 14 calendar days after the scheduled return date of the tour.

§ 381.13 Price increases.

(a) Should the tour operator increase a participant's tour price by more than 10 percent (aggregate of all increases to that participant), that participant shall have the option of canceling his or her participation in the tour and receiving a full refund within 14 days after the cancellation.

(b) The tour operator shall not increase the tour price to any participant less than ten days before departure.

PART 382—NONDISCRIMINATION ON THE BASIS OF DISABILITY IN AIR TRAVEL

Subpart A—General Provisions

Subpart B—Nondiscrimination and Access to Services and Information

Subpart C—Information for Passengers

Subpart D—Accessibility of Airport Facilities

Subpart E—Accessibility of Aircraft

Subpart F—Seating Accommodations

Subpart G—Boarding, Deplaning, and Connecting Assistance

Subpart H—Services on Aircraft

Subpart I—Stowage of Wheelchairs, Other Mobility Aids, and Other Assistive Devices

Subpart J—Training and Administrative Provisions

Subpart K—Complaints and Enforcement Procedures

AUTHORITY: 49 U.S.C. 41705.

SOURCE: Doc. No. DOT–OST–2004–19482, 73 FR 27665, May 13, 2008, unless otherwise noted.

Subpart A—General Provisions

§ 382.1 What is the purpose of this part?

The purpose of this part is to carry out the Air Carrier Access Act of 1986, as amended. This rule prohibits both U.S. and foreign carriers from discriminating against passengers on the basis of disability; requires carriers to make aircraft, other facilities, and services accessible; and requires carriers to take steps to accommodate passengers with a disability.

§ 382.3 What do the terms in this rule mean?

In this regulation, the terms listed in this section have the following meanings:

Air Carrier Access Act or ACAA means the Air Carrier Access Act of 1986, as amended, the statute that provides the principal authority for this part.

Air transportation means interstate or foreign air transportation or the transportation of mail by aircraft, as defined in 49 U.S.C. 40102. Generally this refers to transportation by aircraft within, to or from the United States.

Assistive device means any piece of equipment that assists a passenger with a disability to cope with the effects of his or her disability. Such devices are intended to assist a passenger with a disability to hear, see, communicate, maneuver, or perform other functions of daily life, and may include medical devices and medications.

Automated airport kiosk means a self-service transaction machine that a carrier owns, leases, or controls and makes available at a U.S. airport to enable customers to independently obtain flight-related services.

Battery-powered mobility aid means an assistive device that is used by individuals with mobility impairments such a wheelchair, a scooter, or a Segway when it is used as a mobility device by a person with a mobility-related disability.

Carrier means a U.S. citizen ("U.S. carrier") or foreign citizen ("foreign carrier") that undertakes, directly or indirectly, or by a lease or any other arrangement, to engage in air transportation.

Commuter carrier means an air taxi operator as defined in 14 CFR part 298 that carries passengers on at least 5 round trips per week on at least one route between two or more points according to its published flight schedules that specify the times, days of the week and places between which those flights are performed.

Conforming alternate version means a Web page that allows a corresponding non-conforming Web page on the primary Web site to be included within the scope of conformance as long as it meets the WCAG 2.0 Level AA success criteria, is up-to-date and contains the same information and functionality in the same language as the non-conforming page. At least one of the following applies to a conforming alternative version:

(1) The conforming version can be reached from the non-conforming page via an accessibility-supported mechanism; or

(2) The non-conforming version can only be reached from the conforming version; or

(3) The non-conforming version can only be reached from a conforming page that also provides a mechanism to reach the conforming version.

CPAP machine means a continuous positive airway pressure machine.

Department or DOT means the United States Department of Transportation.

Direct threat means a significant risk to the health or safety of others that cannot be eliminated by a modification of policies, practices, or procedures, or by the provision of auxiliary aids or services.

Equivalent alternative means a policy, practice, or other accommodation that provides substantially equivalent accessibility to passengers with disabilities, compared to compliance with a provision of this Part.

Expected maximum flight duration means the carrier's best estimate of the total duration of the flight from departure gate to arrival gate, including taxi time to and from the terminals, based on the scheduled flight time and factors such as (a) wind and other weather conditions forecast; (b) anticipated traffic delays; (c) one instrument approach and possible missed approach at destination; and (d) any other conditions that may delay arrival of the aircraft at the destination gate.

FAA means the Federal Aviation Administration, an operating administration of the Department of Transportation.

Facility means a carrier's aircraft and any portion of an airport that a carrier owns, leases, or controls (e.g., structures, roads, walks, parking lots, ticketing areas, baggage drop-off and retrieval sites, gates, other boarding locations, loading bridges) normally used by passengers or other members of the public.

Flight-related services mean functions related to air travel including, but not limited to, ticket purchase, rebooking cancelled flights, seat selection, and obtaining boarding passes or bag tags.

High-contrast captioning means captioning that is at least as easy to read as white letters on a consistent black background.

Indirect carrier means a person not directly involved in the operation of an aircraft who sells air transportation services to the general public other than as an authorized agent of a carrier.

Individual with a disability means any individual who has a physical or mental impairment that, on a permanent or temporary basis, substantially limits one or more major life activities, has a record of such an impairment, or is regarded as having such an impairment. As used in this definition, the phrase:

(a) *Physical or mental impairment* means:

(1) Any physiological disorder or condition, cosmetic disfigurement, or anatomical loss affecting one or more of the following body systems: neurological, musculoskeletal, special sense organs, respiratory including speech organs, cardio-vascular, reproductive, digestive, genito-urinary, hemic and lymphatic, skin, and endocrine; or

(2) Any mental or psychological disorder, such as mental retardation, organic brain syndrome, emotional or mental illness, and specific learning disabilities.

The term *physical or mental impairment* includes, but is not limited to, such diseases and conditions as orthopedic, visual, speech, and hearing impairments; cerebral palsy, epilepsy, muscular dystrophy, multiple sclerosis, cancer, heart disease, diabetes, mental retardation, emotional illness, drug addiction, and alcoholism.

(b) *Major life activities* means functions such as caring for one's self, performing manual tasks, walking, seeing, hearing, speaking, breathing, learning, and working.

(c) *Has a record of such impairment* means has a history of, or has been classified, or misclassified, as having a mental or physical impairment that substantially limits one or more major life activities.

(d) *Is regarded as having an impairment* means:

(1) Has a physical or mental impairment that does not substantially limit major life activities but that is treated by an air carrier as constituting such a limitation;

(2) Has a physical or mental impairment that substantially limits a major life activity only as a result of the attitudes of others toward such an impairment; or

(3) Has none of the impairments set forth in this definition but is treated by an air carrier as having such an impairment.

On-demand air taxi means an air taxi operator that carries passengers or property and is not a commuter carrier as defined in this section.

PHMSA means the Pipeline and Hazardous Materials Safety Administration, an operating administration of the Department of Transportation.

POC means portable oxygen concentrator.

Primary (or Main) Web site means the Web site that is accessed upon entering the uniform resource locator (e.g., *www.carriername.com*, www.airline designator code.com) in an Internet browser from a standard desktop or laptop computer where the carrier advertises or sells air transportation to the public.

Qualified individual with a disability means an individual with a disability—

(a) Who, as a passenger (referred to as a "passenger with a disability"),

(1) With respect to obtaining a ticket for air transportation on a carrier, offers, or makes a good faith attempt to offer, to purchase or otherwise validly to obtain such a ticket;

(2) With respect to obtaining air transportation, or other services or accommodations required by this Part,

(i) Buys or otherwise validly obtains, or makes a good faith effort to obtain, a ticket for air transportation on a carrier and presents himself or herself at the airport for the purpose of traveling on the flight to which the ticket pertains; and

(ii) Meets reasonable, nondiscriminatory contract of carriage requirements applicable to all passengers; or

(b) Who, with respect to accompanying or meeting a traveler, using ground transportation, using terminal facilities, or obtaining information about schedules, fares, reservations, or policies, takes those actions necessary to use facilities or services offered by an air carrier to the general public, with reasonable accommodations, as needed, provided by the carrier.

Scheduled service means any flight scheduled in the current edition of the Official Airline Guide, the carrier's published schedule, or the computer reservation system used by the carrier.

Shared-use automated airport kiosk means a self-service transaction machine that is jointly owned, controlled or leased by an airport operator and carriers and/or an independent service provider and that provides carrier software applications which enable customers to independently access flight-related services.

TSA means the Transportation Security Administration, an agency of the Department of Homeland Security.

United States or U.S. means the United States of America, including its territories and possessions.

[Doc. No. DOT–OST–2004–19482, 73 FR 27665, May 13, 2008, as amended at 78 FR 67914, Nov. 12, 2013]

§ 382.5 When are U.S. and foreign carriers required to begin complying with the provisions of this part?

As a U.S. or foreign carrier, you are required to comply with the requirements of this part on May 13, 2009, except as otherwise provided in individual sections of this part.

§ 382.7 To whom do the provisions of this part apply?

(a) If you are a U.S. carrier, this Part applies to you with respect to all your operations and aircraft, regardless of where your operations take place, except as otherwise provided in this part.

(b) If you are a foreign carrier, this part applies to you only with respect to flights you operate that begin or end at a U.S. airport and to aircraft used for these flights. For purposes of this part, a "flight" means a continuous journey in the same aircraft or with one flight number that begins or ends at a U.S. airport. The following are some examples of the application of this term:

Example 1 to paragraph (b): A passenger books a nonstop flight on a foreign carrier from New York to Frankfurt, or Frankfurt to New York. Each of these is a "flight" for purposes of this Part.

Example 2 to paragraph (b): A passenger books a journey on a foreign carrier from New York to Prague. The foreign carrier flies nonstop to Frankfurt. The passenger gets off the plane in Frankfurt and boards a connecting flight (with a different flight number), on the same foreign carrier or a different carrier, which goes to Prague. The New York-Frankfurt leg of the journey is a "flight" for purposes of this Part; the Frankfurt-Prague leg is not. On the reverse routing, the Prague-Frankfurt leg is not a covered flight for purposes of this Part, while the Frankfurt-New York leg is.

Example 3 to paragraph (b): A passenger books a journey on a foreign carrier from New York to Prague. The plane stops for refueling and a crew change in Frankfurt. If, after deplaning in Frankfurt, the passengers originating in New York reboard the aircraft (or a different aircraft, assuming the flight number remains the same) and continue to Prague, they remain on a covered flight for purposes of this Part. This is because their transportation takes place on a direct flight between New York and Prague, even though it had an interim stop in Frankfurt. This example would also apply in the opposite direction (Prague to New York via Frankfurt).

Example 4 to paragraph (b): In Example 3, the foreign carrier is not subject to coverage under this Part with respect to a Frankfurt-originating passenger who boards the aircraft and goes to Prague, or a Prague-originating passenger who gets off the plane in Frankfurt and does not continue to New York.

(c) As a foreign carrier, you are not subject to the requirements of this part with respect to flights between two foreign points, even with respect to flights involving code-sharing arrangements with U.S. carriers. As a U.S. carrier that participates in a code-sharing arrangement with a foreign carrier with respect to flights between two foreign points, you (as distinct from the foreign carrier) are responsible for ensuring compliance with the service provisions of subparts A through C, F through H, and K with respect to passengers traveling under your code on such a flight.

Example 1 to paragraph (c): A passenger buys a ticket from a U.S. carrier for a journey from New York to Prague. The ticket carries the U.S. carrier's code and flight number throughout the entire journey. There is a change of carrier and aircraft in Frankfurt, and a foreign carrier operates the Frankfurt-Prague segment. The foreign carrier is not subject to the provisions of Part

382 for the Frankfurt-Prague segment. However, the U.S. carrier must ensure compliance with the applicable provisions of Part 382 on the Frankfurt-Prague segment with respect to passengers flying under its code, and the Department could take enforcement action against the U.S. carrier for acts or omissions by the foreign carrier.

(d) As a foreign carrier, if you operate a charter flight from a foreign airport to a U.S. airport, and return to a foreign airport, and you do not pick up any passengers in the U.S., the charter flight is not a flight subject to the requirements of this part.

(e) Unless a provision of this Part specifies application to a U.S. carrier or a foreign carrier, the provision applies to both U.S. and foreign carriers.

(f) If you are an indirect carrier, §§382.1 through 382.15 of this part apply to you. §§382.17 through 382.157 of this part do not apply to you except insofar as provided by §382.11(b).

(g) Notwithstanding any provisions of this part, you must comply with all FAA safety regulations, TSA security regulations, and foreign safety and security regulations having legally mandatory effect that apply to you.

[Doc. No. DOT-OST-2004-19482, 73 FR 27665, May 13, 2008, as amended at 74 FR 11471, Mar. 18, 2009; 75 FR 44887, July 30, 2010]

§382.9 What may foreign carriers do if they believe a provision of a foreign nation's law conflicts with compliance with a provision of this part?

(a) If you are a foreign carrier, and you believe that an applicable provision of the law of a foreign nation precludes you from complying with a provision of this part, you may request a waiver of the provision of this Part.

(b) You must send such a waiver request to the following address: Assistant General Counsel for Aviation Enforcement and Proceedings, C-70 U.S. Department of Transportation, 1200 New Jersey Avenue, SE., Room W96-322, Washington, DC 20590.

(c) Your waiver request must be in English and include the following elements:

(1) A copy, in the English language, of the foreign law involved;

(2) A description of how the foreign law applies and how it precludes compliance with a provision of this part;

(3) A description of the alternative means the carrier will use, if the waiver is granted, to effectively achieve the objective of the provision of this part subject to the waiver or, if applicable, a justification of why it would be impossible to achieve this objective in any way.

(d) The Department may grant the waiver request, or grant the waiver request subject to conditions, if it determines that the foreign law applies, that it does preclude compliance with a provision of this part, and that the carrier has provided an effective alternative means of achieving the objective of the provisions of this part subject to the waiver or have demonstrated by clear and convincing evidence that it would be impossible to achieve this objective in any way.

(e)(1) If you submit a waiver request on or before September 10, 2008, the Department will, to the maximum extent feasible, respond to the request before May 13, 2009. If the Department does not respond to the waiver request by May 13, 2009, you may continue to implement the policy or practice that is the subject of your request until the Department does respond. The Department will not take enforcement action with respect to your implementation of the policy or practice during the time prior to the Department's response.

(2) If you submit a waiver request after September 10, 2008, the Department will, to the maximum extent feasible, respond to the request by May 13, 2009 or within 180 days of receiving it, whichever is later. If the Department does not respond to the waiver request by this date, you may continue to implement the policy or practice that is the subject of your request until the Department does respond. However, the Department may take enforcement action with respect to your implementation of the policy or practice during the time between May 13, 2009 and the date of the Department's response.

(3) If you submit a waiver request after September 10, 2008, and the request pertains to an applicable provision of the law of a foreign nation that did not exist on September 10, 2008, you may continue to implement the policy or practice that is the subject of your request until the Department responds

to the request. The Department will, to the maximum extent feasible, respond to such requests within 180 days of receiving them. The Department will not take enforcement action with respect to your implementation of the policy or practice during the time prior to the Department's response.

(f) Notwithstanding any other provision of this section, the Department may commence enforcement action at any time after May 13, 2009 with respect to the policy or practice that is the subject of the request if it finds the request to be frivolous or dilatory.

(g) If you have not submitted a request for a waiver under this section with respect to a provision of this part, or such a request has been denied, you cannot raise the alleged existence of such a conflict as a defense to an enforcement action.

§ 382.10 How does a U.S. or foreign carrier obtain a determination that it is providing an equivalent alternative to passengers with disabilities?

(a) As a U.S. or foreign carrier, you may apply to the Department for a determination that you are providing an equivalent alternative to passengers with disabilities.

(b) You must send your application for an equivalent alternative determination to the following address: Assistant General Counsel for Aviation Enforcement and Proceedings (C–70), U.S. Department of Transportation, 1200 New Jersey Avenue, SE., Room W96–322, Washington, DC 20590.

(c) Your application must be in English and include the following elements:

(1) A citation to the specific provision of this part concerning which you are proposing an equivalent alternative.

(2) A detailed description of the alternative policy, practice, or other accommodation you are proposing to use in place of compliance with the provision of this part that you cite, and an explanation of how it provides substantially equivalent accessibility to passengers with disabilities.

(d) The Department may grant the application, or grant the application subject to conditions, if it determines that the proposed facilitation does provide substantially equivalent accessibility to passengers with disabilities, compared to compliance with the provision of this part in question.

(e) If your application is granted, you will be deemed to be in compliance with this Part through implementing the equivalent alternative. If your application is denied, you must implement this part as written.

(f)(1) If you submit your application on or before September 10, 2008, the Department will respond to the request before May 13, 2009 to the maximum extent feasible. If the Department does not respond to the application by May 13, 2009, you may implement your policy or practice that is the subject of your application until the Department does respond.

(2) With respect to an application you make after September 10, 2008, you must comply with the provisions of this part without change from May 13, 2009 until the Department responds to your application.

Subpart B—Nondiscrimination and Access to Services and Information

§ 382.11 What is the general nondiscrimination requirement of this part?

(a) As a carrier, you must not do any of the following things, either directly or through a contractual, licensing, or other arrangement:

(1) You must not discriminate against any qualified individual with a disability, by reason of such disability, in the provision of air transportation;

(2) You must not require a qualified individual with a disability to accept special services (including, but not limited to, preboarding) that the individual does not request. However, you may require preboarding as a condition of receiving certain seating or in-cabin stowage accommodations, as specified in §§ 382.83(c), 382.85(b), and 382.123(a) of this part.

(3) You must not exclude a qualified individual with a disability from or deny the person the benefit of any air transportation or related services that are available to other persons, except where specifically permitted by this

Part. This is true even if there are separate or different services available for individuals with a disability, except when specifically permitted by another section of this Part; and

(4) You must not take any adverse action against an individual (e.g., refusing to provide transportation) because the individual asserts, on his or her own behalf or through or on behalf of others, rights protected by this part or the Air Carrier Access Act.

(b) As an indirect carrier, you must comply with §§382.17 through 382.157 of this part when providing facilities or services to passengers that would have otherwise been provided by a direct air carrier.

[Doc. No. DOT-OST-2004-19482, 73 FR 27665, May 13, 2008, as amended at 75 FR 44887, July 30, 2010]

§382.13 Do carriers have to modify policies, practices, and facilities to ensure nondiscrimination?

(a) As a carrier, you must modify your policies, practices, and facilities when needed to provide nondiscriminatory service to a particular individual with a disability, consistent with the standards of section 504 of the Rehabilitation Act, as amended.

(b) This requirement is part of your general nondiscrimination obligation, and is in addition to your duty to make the specific accommodations required by this part.

(c) However, you are not required to make modifications that would constitute an undue burden or would fundamentally alter your program.

§382.15 Do carriers have to make sure that contractors comply with the requirements of this Part?

(a) As a carrier, you must make sure that your contractors that provide services to the public (including airports where applicable) meet the requirements of this part that would apply to you if you provided the services yourself.

(b) As a carrier, you must include an assurance of compliance with this part in your contracts with any contractors that provide services to the public that are subject to the requirements of this part. Noncompliance with this assurance is a material breach of the contract on the contractor's part.

(1) This assurance must commit the contractor to compliance with all applicable provisions of this Part in activities performed on behalf of the carrier.

(2) The assurance must also commit the contractor to implementing directives issued by your CROs under §§382.151 through 382.153.

(c) As a U.S. carrier, you must also include such an assurance of compliance in your contracts or agreements of appointment with U.S. travel agents. You are not required to include such an assurance in contracts with foreign travel agents.

(d) You remain responsible for your contractors' compliance with this part and for enforcing the assurances in your contracts with them.

(e) It is not a defense against an enforcement action by the Department under this part that your noncompliance resulted from action or inaction by a contractor.

§382.17 May carriers limit the number of passengers with a disability on a flight?

As a carrier, you must not limit the number of passengers with a disability who travel on a flight. (See also §382.27(c)(6) of this part.)

[Doc. No. DOT-OST-2004-19482, 73 FR 27665, May 13, 2008, as amended at 74 FR 11471, Mar. 18, 2009]

§382.19 May carriers refuse to provide transportation on the basis of disability?

(a) As a carrier, you must not refuse to provide transportation to a passenger with a disability on the basis of his or her disability, except as specifically permitted by this part.

(b) You must not refuse to provide transportation to a passenger with a disability because the person's disability results in appearance or involuntary behavior that may offend, annoy, or inconvenience crewmembers or other passengers.

(c) You may refuse to provide transportation to any passenger on the basis of safety, as provided in 49 U.S.C. 44902 or 14 CFR 121.533, or to any passenger whose carriage would violate FAA or

TSA requirements or applicable requirements of a foreign government.

(1) You can determine that there is a disability-related safety basis for refusing to provide transportation to a passenger with a disability if you are able to demonstrate that the passenger poses a direct threat (see definition in § 382.3). In determining whether an individual poses a direct threat, you must make an individualized assessment, based on reasonable judgment that relies on current medical knowledge or on the best available objective evidence, to ascertain:

(i) The nature, duration, and severity of the risk;

(ii) The probability that the potential harm to the health and safety of others will actually occur; and

(iii) Whether reasonable modifications of policies, practices, or procedures will mitigate the risk.

(2) If you determine that the passenger does pose a direct threat, you must select the least restrictive response from the point of view of the passenger, consistent with protecting the health and safety of others. For example, you must not refuse transportation to the passenger if you can protect the health and safety of others by means short of a refusal.

(3) In exercising this authority, you must not act inconsistently with the provisions of this part.

(4) If your actions are inconsistent with any of the provisions of this part, you are subject to enforcement action under Subpart K of this part.

(d) If you refuse to provide transportation to a passenger on his or her originally-scheduled flight on a basis relating to the individual's disability, you must provide to the person a written statement of the reason for the refusal. This statement must include the specific basis for the carrier's opinion that the refusal meets the standards of paragraph (c) of this section or is otherwise specifically permitted by this part. You must provide this written statement to the person within 10 calendar days of the refusal of transportation.

§ 382.21 May carriers limit access to transportation on the basis that a passenger has a communicable disease or other medical condition?

(a) You must not do any of the following things on the basis that a passenger has a communicable disease or infection, unless you determine that the passenger's condition poses a direct threat:

(1) Refuse to provide transportation to the passenger;

(2) Delay the passenger's transportation (e.g., require the passenger to take a later flight);

(3) Impose on the passenger any condition, restriction, or requirement not imposed on other passengers; or

(4) Require the passenger to provide a medical certificate.

(b) In assessing whether the passenger's condition poses a direct threat, you must apply the provisions of § 382.19(c)(1)–(2) of this subpart.

(1) In making this assessment, you may rely on directives issued by public health authorities (e.g., the U.S. Centers for Disease Control or Public Health Service; comparable agencies in other countries; the World Health Organization).

(2) In making this assessment, you must consider the significance of the consequences of a communicable disease and the degree to which it can be readily transmitted by casual contact in an aircraft cabin environment.

Example 1 to paragraph (b)(2): The common cold is readily transmissible in an aircraft cabin environment but does not have severe health consequences. Someone with a cold would not pose a direct threat.

Example 2 to paragraph (b)(2): AIDS has very severe health consequences but is not readily transmissible in an aircraft cabin environment. Someone would not pose a direct threat because he or she is HIV-positive or has AIDS.

Example 3 to paragraph (b)(2): SARS may be readily transmissible in an aircraft cabin environment and has severe health consequences. Someone with SARS probably poses a direct threat.

(c) If a passenger with a communicable disease meeting the direct threat criteria of this section gives you a medical certificate of the kind outlined in § 382.23(c)(2) describing measures for preventing transmission of the disease during the normal course of the flight, you must provide transportation to the passenger, unless you are unable to carry out the measures.

(d) If your action under this section results in the postponement of a passenger's travel, you must permit the passenger to travel at a later time (up to 90 days from the date of the postponed travel) at the fare that would have applied to the passenger's originally scheduled trip without penalty or, at the passenger's discretion, provide a refund for any unused flights, including return flights.

(e) If you take any action under this section that restricts a passenger's travel, you must, on the passenger's request, provide a written explanation within 10 days of the request.

§ 382.23 May carriers require a passenger with a disability to provide a medical certificate?

(a) Except as provided in this section, you must not require a passenger with a disability to have a medical certificate as a condition for being provided transportation.

(b)(1) You may require a medical certificate for a passenger with a disability—

(i) Who is traveling in a stretcher or incubator;

(ii) Who needs medical oxygen during a flight; or

(iii) Whose medical condition is such that there is reasonable doubt that the individual can complete the flight safely, without requiring extraordinary medical assistance during the flight.

(2) For purposes of this paragraph, a medical certificate is a written statement from the passenger's physician saying that the passenger is capable of completing the flight safely, without requiring extraordinary medical assistance during the flight.

(3) To be valid, a medical certificate under this paragraph must be dated within 10 days of the scheduled date of the passenger's initial departing flight.

Example to paragraph (b)(3): A passenger who schedules a flight from New York to London on January 15 with a return on April 15 would have to show a medical certificate dated January 5 or later. The passenger would not have to show a second medical certificate dated April 5 or later.

(c)(1) You may also require a medical certificate for a passenger if he or she has a communicable disease or condition that could pose a direct threat to the health or safety of others on the flight.

(2) For purposes of this paragraph, a medical certificate is a written statement from the passenger's physician saying that the disease or infection would not, under the present conditions in the particular passenger's case, be communicable to other persons during the normal course of a flight. The medical certificate must state any conditions or precautions that would have to be observed to prevent the transmission of the disease or infection to other persons in the normal course of a flight. A medical certificate under this paragraph must be dated within 10 days of the date of the flight for which it is presented.

(d) As a carrier, you may require that a passenger with a medical certificate undergo additional medical review by you if there is a legitimate medical reason for believing that there has been a significant adverse change in the passenger's condition since the issuance of the medical certificate or that the certificate significantly understates the passenger's risk to the health of other persons on the flight. If the results of this medical review demonstrate that the passenger, notwithstanding the medical certificate, is likely to be unable to complete the flight without requiring extraordinary medical assistance (e.g., the passenger has apparent significant difficulty in breathing, appears to be in substantial pain, *etc.*) or would pose a direct threat to the health or safety of other persons on the flight, you may take an action otherwise prohibited under § 382.21(a) of this part.

[Doc. No. DOT–OST–2004–19482, 73 FR 27665, May 13, 2008, as amended at 75 FR 44887, July 30, 2010]

§ 382.25 May a carrier require a passenger with a disability to provide advance notice that he or she is traveling on a flight?

As a carrier, you must not require a passenger with a disability to provide advance notice of the fact that he or she is traveling on a flight.

§ 382.27 May a carrier require a passenger with a disability to provide advance notice in order to obtain certain specific services in connection with a flight?

(a) Except as provided in paragraph (b) of this section and § 382.133(e)(4) and (5) and (f)(5) and (6), as a carrier you must not require a passenger with a disability to provide advance notice in order to obtain services or accommodations required by this part.

(b) You may require a passenger with a disability to provide up to 72 hours' advance notice and check in one hour before the check-in time for the general public to receive carrier-supplied in-flight medical oxygen on international flights, 48 hours' advance notice and check-in one hour before the check-in time for the general public to receive carrier-supplied in-flight medical oxygen on domestic flights, and 48 hours' advance notice and check-in one hour before the check-in time for the general public to use his/her ventilator, respirator, CPAP machine or POC.

(c) You may require a passenger with a disability to provide up to 48 hours' advance notice and check in one hour before the check-in time for the general public to receive the following services and accommodations. The services listed in paragraphs (c)(1) through (c)(3) of this section are optional; you are not required to provide them, but you may choose to do so.

(1) Carriage of an incubator;

(2) Hook-up for a respirator, ventilator, CPAP machine or POC to the aircraft electrical power supply;

(3) Accommodation for a passenger who must travel in a stretcher;

(4) Transportation for an electric wheelchair on an aircraft with fewer than 60 seats;

(5) Provision of hazardous materials packaging for batteries or other assistive devices that are required to have such packaging;

(6) Accommodation for a group of ten or more qualified individuals with a disability, who make reservations and travel as a group; and

(7) Provision of an on-board wheelchair on an aircraft with more than 60 seats that does not have an accessible lavatory.

(8) Transportation of an emotional support or psychiatric service animal in the cabin;

(9) Transportation of a service animal on a flight segment scheduled to take 8 hours or more;

(10) Accommodation of a passenger who has both severe vision and hearing impairments (see § 382.29(b)(4)).

(d) If the passenger with a disability provides the advance notice you require, consistent with this section, for a service that you must provide (see paragraphs (c)(4) through (c)(10) of this section) or choose to provide (see paragraphs (c)(1) through (c)(3) of this section), you must provide the requested service or accommodation.

(e) Your reservation and other administrative systems must ensure that when passengers provide the advance notice that you require, consistent with this section, for services and accommodations, the notice is communicated, clearly and on time, to the people responsible for providing the requested service or accommodation.

(f) If a passenger with a disability provides the advance notice you require, consistent with this section, and the passenger is forced to change to another flight (e.g., because of a flight cancellation), you must, to the maximum extent feasible, provide the accommodation on the new flight. If the new flight is another carrier's flight, you must provide the maximum feasible assistance to the other carrier in providing the accommodation the passenger requested from you.

(g) If a passenger does not meet advance notice or check-in requirements you establish consistent with this section, you must still provide the service or accommodation if you can do so by making reasonable efforts, without delaying the flight.

[Doc. No. DOT–OST–2004–19482, 73 FR 27665, May 13, 2008, as amended at 74 FR 11471, Mar. 18, 2009; 75 FR 44887, July 30, 2010; Doc. No. FAA–2014–0554, 81 FR 33120, May 24, 2016]

§ 382.29 May a carrier require a passenger with a disability to travel with a safety assistant?

(a) Except as provided in paragraph (b) of this section, you must not require that a passenger with a disability travel with another person as a condition of being provided air transportation.

(b) You may require a passenger with a disability in one of the following categories to travel with a safety assistant as a condition of being provided air transportation, if you determine that a safety assistant is essential for safety:

(1) A passenger traveling in a stretcher or incubator. The safety assistant for such a person must be capable of attending to the passenger's in-flight medical needs;

(2) A passenger who, because of a mental disability, is unable to comprehend or respond appropriately to safety instructions from carrier personnel, including the safety briefing required by 14 CFR 121.571(a)(3) and (a)(4) or 14 CFR 135.117(b) or the safety regulations of a foreign carrier's government, as applicable;

(3) A passenger with a mobility impairment so severe that the person is unable to physically assist in his or her own evacuation of the aircraft;

(4) A passenger who has both severe hearing and severe vision impairments, if the passenger cannot establish some means of communication with carrier personnel that is adequate both to permit transmission of the safety briefing required by 14 CFR 121.57(a)(3) and (a)(4), 14 CFR 135,117(b) or the safety regulations of a foreign carrier's government, as applicable, and to enable the passenger to assist in his or her own evacuation of the aircraft in the event of an emergency. You may require a passenger with severe hearing and vision impairment who wishes to travel without a safety assistant to notify you at least 48 hours in advance to provide this explanation. If the passenger fails to meet this notice requirement, however, you must still accommodate him or her to the extent practicable.

(c)(1) If you determine that a person meeting the criteria of paragraph (b)(2), (b)(3) or (b)(4) of this section must travel with a safety assistant, contrary to the individual's self-assessment that he or she is capable of traveling independently, you must not charge for the transportation of the safety assistant. You are not required to find or provide the safety assistant, however.

(2) For purposes of paragraph (b)(4) of this section, you may require, contrary to the individual's self-assessment, that an individual with both severe hearing and vision impairments must travel with a safety assistant if you determine that—

(i) The means of communication that the individual has explained to you does not adequately satisfy the objectives identified in paragraph (b)(4) of this section; or

(ii) The individual proposes to establish communication by means of finger spelling and you cannot, within the time following the individual's notification, arrange for a flight crew member who can communicate using this method to serve the passenger's flight.

(3) If a passenger voluntarily chooses to travel with a personal care attendant or safety assistant that you do not require, you may charge for the transportation of that person.

(d) If, because there is not a seat available on a flight for a safety assistant whom the carrier has determined to be necessary, a passenger with a disability holding a confirmed reservation is unable to travel on the flight, you must compensate the passenger with a disability in an amount to be calculated as provided for instances of involuntary denied boarding under 14 CFR part 250, where part 250 applies.

(e) For purposes of determining whether a seat is available for a safety assistant, you must deem the safety assistant to have checked in at the same time as the passenger with a disability.

(f) Concern that a passenger with a disability may need personal care services (e.g., assistance in using lavatory facilities or with eating) is not a basis for requiring the passenger to travel with a safety assistant. You must explain this clearly in training or information you provide to your employees. You may advise passengers that your personnel are not required to provide such services.

§ 382.31 May carriers impose special charges on passengers with a disability for providing services and accommodations required by this rule?

(a) Except as otherwise provided in this part you must not, as a carrier, impose charges for providing facilities, equipment, or services that this rule requires to be provided to passengers with a disability. You may charge for services that this part does not require.

(b) You may charge a passenger for the use of more than one seat if the passenger's size or condition (e.g., use of a stretcher) causes him or her to occupy the space of more than one seat. This is not considered a special charge under this section.

[Doc. No. DOT–OST–2004–19482, 73 FR 27665, May 13, 2008, as amended at 78 FR 67914, Nov. 12, 2013]

§ 382.33 May carriers impose other restrictions on passengers with a disability that they do not impose on other passengers?

(a) As a carrier, you must not subject passengers with a disability to restrictions that do not apply to other passengers, except as otherwise permitted in this part (*e.g.*, advance notice requirements for certain services permitted by § 382.27).

(b) Restrictions you must not impose on passengers with a disability include, but are not limited to, the following:

(1) Restricting passengers'' movement within the terminal;

(2) Requiring passengers to remain in a holding area or other location in order to receive transportation, services, or accommodations;

(3) Making passengers sit on blankets on the aircraft;

(4) Making passengers wear badges or other special identification (*e.g.*, similar to badges worn by unaccompanied minors); or

(5) Otherwise mandating separate treatment for passengers with a disability, unless permitted or required by this part or other applicable Federal requirements.

§ 382.35 May carriers require passengers with a disability to sign waivers or releases?

(a) As a carrier, you must not require passengers with a disability to sign a release or waiver of liability in order to receive transportation or to receive services or accommodations for a disability.

(b) You must not require passengers with a disability to sign waivers of liability for damage to or loss of wheelchairs or other assistive devices, or for the loss of, death of, or injury to service animals. Carriers may note pre-existing damage to an assistive device to the same extent that carriers do this with respect to other checked baggage.

Subpart C—Information for Passengers

§ 382.41 What flight-related information must carriers provide to qualified individuals with a disability?

As a carrier, you must provide the following information, on request, to qualified individuals with a disability or persons making inquiries on their behalf concerning the accessibility of the aircraft expected to make a particular flight. The information you provide must be specific to the aircraft you expect to use for the flight unless it is unfeasible for you to do so (*e.g.*, because unpredictable circumstances such as weather or a mechanical problem require substitution of another aircraft that could affect the location or availability of an accommodation). The required information is:

(a) The specific location of seats, if any, with movable armrests (*i.e.*, by row and seat number);

(b) The specific location of seats (*i.e.*, by row and seat number) that the carrier, consistent with this part, does not make available to passengers with a disability (*e.g.*, exit row seats);

(c) Any aircraft-related, service-related or other limitations on the ability to accommodate passengers with a disability, including limitations on the availability of level-entry boarding to the aircraft at any airport involved with the flight. You must provide this information to any passenger who states that he or she uses a wheelchair for boarding, even if the passenger does not explicitly request the information.

(d) Any limitations on the availability of storage facilities, in the cabin or in the cargo bay, for mobility aids or other assistive devices commonly used by passengers with a disability, including storage in the cabin of a passenger's wheelchair as provided in §§382.67 and 382.123 of this part;

(e) Whether the aircraft has an accessible lavatory; and

(f) The types of services to passengers with a disability that are or are not available on the flight.

§382.43 Must information and reservation services of carriers be accessible to individuals with visual, hearing, and other disabilities?

(a) If, as a carrier, you provide telephone reservation and information service to the public, you must make this service available to individuals who use a text telephone (TTY), whether via your own TTY, voice relay, or other available technology, as follows:

(1) You must provide access to TTY users during the same hours as the telephone service is available to the general public.

(2) You must ensure that the response time for answering calls and the level of service provided to TTY users is substantially equivalent to the response time and level of service provided to the general public (*i.e.*, non-TTY users).

(3) You must not subject TTY users to charges exceeding those that apply to non-TTY users of telephone information and reservation service.

(4) In any medium in which you list the telephone number of your information and reservation service for the general public, you must also list your TTY number if you have one. If you do not have a TTY number, you must state how TTY users can reach your information and reservation service (*e.g.*, via a voice relay service).

(5) If you are a foreign carrier, you must meet this requirement by May 13, 2010.

(b) The requirements of paragraph (a) do not apply to you in any country in which the telecommunications infrastructure does not readily permit compliance.

(c) If you are a U.S. or foreign air carrier that operates at least one aircraft having a designed seating capacity of more than 60 passengers and owns or controls a primary Web site that markets passenger air transportation, or a tour (i.e., a combination of air transportation and ground or cruise accommodations), or tour component (e.g., a hotel stay) that must be purchased with air transportation, you must ensure the public-facing Web pages on your primary Web site are accessible to individuals with disabilities as provided in paragraphs (c)(1) through (4) of this section. Only Web sites that market air transportation to the general public in the United States must be accessible to individuals with disabilities. The following are among the characteristics of a primary Web site that markets to the general public in the U.S.: the content can be viewed in English, the site advertises or sells flights operating to, from, or within the United States, and the site displays fares in U.S. dollars.

(1) Your primary Web site must conform to all Success Criteria and all Conformance Requirements from the World Wide Web Consortium (W3C) Recommendation 11 December 2008, Web site Content Accessibility Guidelines (WCAG) 2.0 for Level AA as follows:

(i) Web pages associated with obtaining the following core air travel services and information that are offered on your primary Web site are conformant by December 12, 2015:

(A) Booking or changing a reservation, including all flight amenities;

(B) Checking in for a flight;

(C) Accessing a personal travel itinerary;

(D) Accessing the status of a flight;

(E) Accessing a personal frequent flyer account;

(F) Accessing flight schedules; and

(G) Accessing carrier contact information.

(ii) All remaining Web pages on your primary Web site are conformant by December 12, 2016.

(2) Your primary Web site must be tested in consultation with individuals with disabilities or members of disability organization(s) who use or want to use carrier Web sites to research or

book air transportation in order to obtain their feedback on the Web site's accessibility and usability before the dates specified in paragraph (c)(1) of this section. Collectively, such individuals must be able to provide feedback on the usability of the Web site by individuals with visual, auditory, tactile, and cognitive disabilities. Consultation is required to ensure that your Web site is usable by individuals with disabilities by the date specified in paragraph (c)(1).

(3) You are permitted to use a Level AA conforming alternate version only when conforming a public-facing Web page to all WCAG 2.0 Level AA success criteria would constitute an undue burden or fundamentally alter the information or functionality provided by that page.

(4) You must assist prospective passengers who indicate that they are unable to use your Web site due to a disability and contact you through other channels (e.g., by telephone or at the ticket counter) as follows:

(i) Disclose Web-based discount fares to the passenger if his or her itinerary qualifies for the discounted fare.

(ii) Provide Web-based amenities to the passenger, such as waiving any fee applicable to making a reservation or purchasing a ticket using a method other than your Web site (e.g., by telephone), unless the fee applies to other customers purchasing the same fare online.

(d) As a carrier covered under paragraph (c) of this section, you must provide a mechanism on your primary Web site for persons with disabilities to request disability accommodation services for future flights, including but not limited to wheelchair assistance, seating accommodation, escort assistance for a visually impaired passenger, and stowage of an assistive device no later than December 12, 2015. You may require individuals who request accommodations using this mechanism to provide contact information (e.g., name, daytime phone, evening phone, and email address) for follow-up by your customer service department or medical desk.

(e) As a carrier covered under paragraph (c) of this section, you must provide a disclaimer activated when a user clicks a link on your primary Web site to an external Web site or to third-party software informing the user that the Web site or software may not follow the same accessibility policies no later than December 12, 2016.

[Doc. No. DOT–OST–2004–19482, 73 FR 27665, May 13, 2008, as amended at 74 FR 11471, Mar. 18, 2009; 78 FR 67914, Nov. 12, 2013]

§ 382.45 Must carriers make copies of this Part available to passengers?

(a) As a carrier, you must keep a current copy of this part at each airport you serve. As a foreign carrier, you must keep a copy of this part at each airport serving a flight you operate that begins or ends at a U.S. airport. You must make this copy available for review by any member of the public on request.

(b) If you have a Web site, it must provide notice to consumers that they can obtain a copy of this part in an accessible format from the Department of Transportation by any of the following means:

(1) For calls made from within the United States, by telephone via the Toll-Free Hotline for Air Travelers with Disabilities at 1–800–778–4838 (voice) or 1–800–455–9880 (TTY),

(2) By telephone to the Aviation Consumer Protection Division at 202–366–2220 (voice) or 202–366–0511 (TTY),

(3) By mail to the Air Consumer Protection Division, C–75, U.S. Department of Transportation, 1200 New Jersey Ave., SE., West Building, Room W96–432, Washington, DC 20590, and

(4) On the Aviation Consumer Protection Division's Web site (*http://airconsumer.ost.dot.gov*).

Subpart D—Accessibility of Airport Facilities

§ 382.51 What requirements must carriers meet concerning the accessibility of airport facilities?

(a) As a carrier, you must comply with the following requirements with respect to all terminal facilities you own, lease, or control at a U.S. airport:

(1) You must ensure that terminal facilities providing access to air transportation are readily accessible to and usable by individuals with disabilities,

including individuals who use wheelchairs. You are deemed to comply with this obligation if the facilities meet requirements applying to places of public accommodation under Department of Justice (DOJ) regulations implementing Title III of the Americans with Disabilities Act (ADA).

(2) With respect to any situation in which boarding and deplaning by level-entry loading bridges or accessible passenger lounges to and from an aircraft is not available, you must ensure that there is an accessible route between the gate and the area from which aircraft are boarded (*e.g.*, the tarmac in a situation in which level-entry boarding is not available). An accessible route is one meeting the requirements of the Americans with Disabilities Act Accessibility Guidelines (ADAAG), sections 4.3.3 through 4.3.10.

(3) You must ensure that systems of intra- and inter-terminal transportation, including, but not limited to, moving sidewalks, shuttle vehicles and people movers, comply with applicable requirements of the Department of Transportation's ADA rules (49 CFR parts 37 and 38).

(4) Your contracts or leases with airport operators concerning the use of airport facilities must set forth your airport accessibility responsibility under this part and that of the airport operator under applicable section 504 and ADA rules of the Department of Transportation and Department of Justice.

(5) In cooperation with the airport operator and in consultation with local service animal training organization(s), you must provide animal relief areas for service animals that accompany passengers departing, connecting, or arriving at an airport on your flights.

(6) You must enable captioning at all times on all televisions and other audio-visual displays that are capable of displaying captions and that are located in any portion of the terminal to which any passengers have access on May 13, 2009. The captioning must be high-contrast insofar as is feasible.

(7) You must replace any televisions and other audio-visual displays providing passengers with safety briefings, information, or entertainment that do not have high-contrast captioning capability with equipment that does have such capability whenever such equipment is replaced in the normal course of operations and/or whenever areas of the terminal in which such equipment is located are undergoing substantial renovation or expansion.

(8) If you newly acquire televisions and other audio-visual displays for passenger safety briefings, information, or entertainment on or after May 13, 2009, such equipment must have high-contrast captioning capability.

(b) As a carrier, you must ensure that passengers with a disability can readily use all terminal facilities you own, lease, or control at a foreign airport. In the case of foreign carriers, this requirement applies only to terminal facilities that serve flights covered by §382.7 of this part.

(1) This means that passengers with a disability must be able to move readily through such terminal facilities to get to or from the gate and any other area from which passengers board the aircraft you use for such flights (*e.g.*, the tarmac in the case of flights that do not use level-entry boarding). This obligation is in addition to your obligation to provide enplaning, deplaning, and connecting assistance to passengers.

(2) You may meet this obligation through any combination of facility accessibility, auxiliary aids, equipment, the assistance of personnel, or other appropriate means consistent with the safety and dignity of passengers with a disability.

(c) As a foreign carrier, you must meet the requirements of this section by May 13, 2010, except as otherwise indicated in paragraph (a). As a U.S. carrier, you must meet the requirements of paragraph (b) of this section by May 13, 2010.

[Doc. No. DOT-OST-2004-19482, 73 FR 27665, May 13, 2008, as amended at 74 FR 11471, Mar. 18, 2009; 75 FR 44887, July 30, 2010]

§382.53 What information must carriers give individuals with a vision or hearing impairment at airports?

(a)(1) As a U.S. carrier, you must ensure that passengers with a disability who identify themselves as persons needing visual or hearing assistance have prompt access to the same information provided to other passengers at each gate, ticketing area, and customer service desk that you own, lease, or control at any U.S. or foreign airport, to the extent that this does not interfere with employees' safety and security duties as set forth in FAA, TSA, and applicable foreign regulations.

(2) As a foreign carrier, you must make this information available at each gate, ticketing area, and customer service desk that you own, lease, or control at any U.S. airport. At foreign airports, you must make this information available only at gates, ticketing areas, or customer service desks that you own, lease, or control and only for flights that begin or end in the U.S.

(3) As a U.S. or foreign carrier, at any U.S. airport covered by this paragraph where the airport has effective control over the covered gates, ticketing areas, and customer service desks, you and the airport are jointly responsible for compliance.

(b) The information you must provide under paragraph (a) of this section includes, but is not limited to, the following: Information concerning flight safety, ticketing, flight check-in, flight delays or cancellations, schedule changes, boarding information, connections, gate assignments, checking baggage, volunteer solicitation on oversold flights (*e.g.*, offers of compensation for surrendering a reservation), individuals being paged by airlines, aircraft changes that affect the travel of persons with disabilities, and emergencies (*e.g.*, fire, bomb threat).

(c) With respect to information on claiming baggage, you must provide the information to passengers who identify themselves as persons needing visual or hearing assistance no later than you provide this information to other passengers.

[Doc. No. DOT–OST–2004–19482, 73 FR 27665, May 13, 2008, as amended at 74 FR 11471, Mar. 18, 2009]

§ 382.55 May carriers impose security screening procedures for passengers with disabilities that go beyond TSA requirements or those of foreign governments?

(a) All passengers, including those with disabilities, are subject to TSA security screening requirements at U.S. airports. In addition, passengers at foreign airports, including those with disabilities, may be subject to security screening measures required by law of the country in which the airport is located.

(b) If, as a carrier, you impose security screening procedures for passengers with disabilities that go beyond those mandated by TSA (or, at a foreign airport, beyond the law of the country in which the airport is located), you must ensure that they meet the following requirements:

(1) You must use the same criteria for applying security screening procedures to passengers with disabilities as to other passengers.

(2) You must not subject a passenger with a disability to special screening procedures because the person is traveling with a mobility aid or other assistive device if the person using the aid or device clears the security system without activating it.

(i) However, your security personnel may examine a mobility aid or assistive device which, in their judgment, may conceal a weapon or other prohibited item.

(ii) You may conduct security searches of qualified individuals with a disability whose aids activate the security system in the same manner as for other passengers.

(3) You must not require private security screenings of passengers with a disability to a greater extent, or for any different reason, than for other passengers.

(c) Except as provided in paragraph (d) of this section, if a passenger with a disability requests a private screening in a timely manner, you must provide it in time for the passenger to enplane.

(d) If you use technology that can conduct an appropriate screening of a passenger with a disability without necessitating a physical search of the person, you are not required to provide a private screening.

[Doc. No. DOT–OST–2004–19482, 73 FR 27665, May 13, 2008, as amended at 74 FR 11471, Mar. 18, 2009]

§382.57 What accessibility requirements apply to automated airport kiosks?

(a) As a carrier, you must comply with the following requirements with respect to any automated airport kiosk you own, lease, or control at a U.S. airport with 10,000 or more enplanements per year.

(1) You must ensure that all automated airport kiosks installed on or after December 12, 2016, are models that meet the design specifications set forth in paragraph (c) of this section until at least 25 percent of automated kiosks provided in each location at the airport (i.e., each cluster of kiosks and all stand-alone kiosks at the airport) meets this specification.

(2) You must ensure that at least 25 percent of automated kiosks you own, lease, or control in each location at a U.S. airport meet the design specifications in paragraph (c) of this section by December 12, 2022.

(3) When the kiosks provided in a location at the airport perform more than one function (e.g., print boarding passes/bag tags, accept payment for flight amenities such as seating upgrades/meals/WiFi access, rebook tickets, etc.), you must ensure that the accessible kiosks provide all the same functions as the inaccessible kiosks in that location.

(4) You must ensure that a passenger with a disability who requests an accessible automated kiosk is given priority access to any available accessible kiosk you own, lease, or control in that location at the airport.

(5) You must ensure that each automated airport kiosk that meets the design specifications in paragraph (c) of this section is:

(i) Visually and tactilely identifiable to users as accessible (e.g., an international symbol of accessibility affixed to the front of the device).

(ii) Maintained in proper working condition.

(b) As a carrier, you must comply with the following requirements for any shared-use automated airport kiosks you jointly own, lease, or control at a U.S. airport with 10,000 or more enplanements per year.

(1) You must ensure that all shared-use automated airport kiosks you jointly own, lease, or control installed on or after December 12, 2016, meet the design specifications in paragraph (c) of this section until at least 25 percent of automated kiosks provided in each location at the airport (i.e., each cluster of kiosks and all stand-alone kiosks at an airport) meet this specification.

(2) You must ensure that at least 25 percent of shared-use automated kiosks you own, lease, or control in each location at the airport meet the design specifications in paragraph (c) of this section by December 12, 2022.

(3) When shared-use automated kiosks provided in a location at the airport perform more than one function (e.g., print boarding passes/bag tags, accept payment for flight amenities such as seating upgrades/meals/WiFi access, rebook tickets, etc.), you must ensure that the accessible kiosks provide all the same functions as the inaccessible kiosks in that location.

(4) You must ensure that each automated airport kiosk that meets the design specifications set forth in paragraph (c) of this section is:

(i) Visually and tactilely identifiable to users as accessible (e.g., an international symbol of accessibility affixed to the front of the device; and

(ii) Maintained in proper working condition.

(5) As a carrier, you are jointly and severally liable with airport operators and/or other participating carriers for ensuring that shared-use automated airport kiosks are compliant with the requirements of paragraphs (b) and (c) of this section.

(c) You must ensure that the automated airport kiosks provided in accordance with this section conform to the following technical accessibility standards with respect to their physical design and the functions they perform:

(1) *Self contained.* Except for personal headsets and audio loops, automated kiosks must be operable without requiring the user to attach assistive technology.

(2) *Clear floor or ground space.* A clear floor or ground space complying with section 305 of the U.S. Department of Justice's 2010 ADA Standards for Accessible Design, 28 CFR 35.104 (defining the "2010 Standards" for title II as the requirements set forth in appendices B and D to 36 CFR part 1191 and the requirements contained in 28 CFR 35.151) (hereinafter 2010 ADA Standards) must be provided.

(3) *Operable parts.* Operable parts must comply with section 309 of the 2010 ADA Standards, and the following requirements:

(i) *Identification.* Operable parts must be tactilely discernible without activation;

(ii) *Timing.* Where a timed response is required, the user must be alerted visually and by touch or sound and must be given the opportunity to indicate that more time is required;

(iii) *Status indicators.* Status indicators, including all locking or toggle controls or keys (e.g., Caps Lock and Num Lock keys), must be discernible visually and by touch or sound; and

(iv) *Color.* Color coding must not be used as the only means of conveying information, indicating an action, prompting a response, or distinguishing a visual element.

(4) *Privacy.* Automated airport kiosks must provide the opportunity for the same degree of privacy of input and output available to all individuals. However, if an option is provided to blank the screen in the speech output mode, the screen must blank when activated by the user, not automatically.

(5) *Output.* Automated airport kiosks must comply with paragraphs (c)(5)(i) through (iv) of this section.

(i) *Speech output enabled.* Automated airport kiosks must provide an option for speech output. Operating instructions and orientation, visible transaction prompts, user input verification, error messages, and all other visual information for full use must be accessible to and independently usable by individuals with vision impairments. Speech output must be delivered through a mechanism that is readily available to all users, including but not limited to, an industry standard connector or a telephone handset. Speech output must be recorded or digitized human, or synthesized. Speech output must be coordinated with information displayed on the screen. Speech output must comply with paragraphs (c)(5)(i)(A) through (F) of this section.

(A) When asterisks or other masking characters are used to represent personal identification numbers or other visual output that is not displayed for security purposes, the masking characters must be spoken ("*" spoken as "asterisk") rather than presented as beep tones or speech representing the concealed information.

(B) Advertisements and other similar information are not required to be audible unless they convey information that can be used in the transaction being conducted.

(C) Speech for any single function must be automatically interrupted when a transaction is selected or navigation controls are used. Speech must be capable of being repeated and paused by the user.

(D) Where receipts, tickets, or other outputs are provided as a result of a transaction, speech output must include all information necessary to complete or verify the transaction, except that—

(*1*) Automated airport kiosk location, date and time of transaction, customer account numbers, and the kiosk identifier are not required to be audible;

(*2*) Information that duplicates information available on-screen and already presented audibly is not required to be repeated; and

(*3*) Printed copies of a carrier's contract of carriage, applicable fare rules, itineraries and other similar supplemental information that may be included with a boarding pass are not required to be audible.

(ii) *Volume control.* Automated kiosks must provide volume control complying with paragraphs (c)(5)(ii)(A) and (B) of this section.

(A) *Private listening.* Where speech required by paragraph (c)(5)(i) of this section is delivered through a mechanism for private listening, the automated kiosk must provide a means for the user to control the volume. A function must be provided to automatically reset the volume to the default level after every use.

(B) *Speaker volume.* Where sound is delivered through speakers on the automated kiosk, incremental volume control must be provided with output amplification up to a level of at least 65 dB SPL. Where the ambient noise level of the environment is above 45 dB SPL, a volume gain of at least 20 dB above the ambient level must be user selectable. A function must be provided to automatically reset the volume to the default level after every use.

(iii) *Captioning.* Multimedia content that contains speech or other audio information necessary for the comprehension of the content must be open or closed captioned. Advertisements and other similar information are not required to be captioned unless they convey information that can be used in the transaction being conducted.

(iv) *Tickets and boarding passes.* Where tickets or boarding passes are provided, tickets and boarding passes must have an orientation that is tactilely discernible if orientation is important to further use of the ticket or boarding pass.

(6) *Input.* Input devices must comply with paragraphs (c)(6)(i) through (iv) of this section.

(i) *Input controls.* At least one input control that is tactilely discernible without activation must be provided for each function. Where provided, key surfaces not on active areas of display screens, must be raised above surrounding surfaces. Where touch or membrane keys are the only method of input, each must be tactilely discernible from surrounding surfaces and adjacent keys.

(ii) *Alphabetic keys.* Alphabetic keys must be arranged in a QWERTY keyboard layout. The "F" and "J" keys must be tactilely distinct from the other keys.

(iii) *Numeric keys.* Numeric keys must be arranged in a 12-key ascending or descending keypad layout or must be arranged in a row above the alphabetic keys on a QWERTY keyboard. The "5" key must be tactilely distinct from the other keys.

(iv) *Function keys.* Function keys must comply with paragraphs (c)(6)(iv)(A) and (B) of this section.

(A) *Contrast.* Function keys must contrast visually from background surfaces. Characters and symbols on key surfaces must contrast visually from key surfaces. Visual contrast must be either light-on-dark or dark-on-light. However, tactile symbols required by (c)(6)(iv)(B) are not required to comply with (c)(6)(iv)(A) of this section.

(B) *Tactile symbols.* Function key surfaces must have tactile symbols as follows: Enter or Proceed key: raised circle; Clear or Correct key: raised left arrow; Cancel key: raised letter ex; Add Value key: raised plus sign; Decrease Value key: raised minus sign.

(7) *Display screen.* The display screen must comply with paragraphs (c)(7)(i) and (ii) of this section.

(i) *Visibility.* The display screen must be visible from a point located 40 inches (1015 mm) above the center of the clear floor space in front of the automated kiosk.

(ii) *Characters.* Characters displayed on the screen must be in a sans serif font. Characters must be 3/16 inch (4.8 mm) high minimum based on the uppercase letter "I." Characters must contrast with their background with a minimum luminosity contrast ratio of 3:1.

(8) *Braille instructions.* Braille instructions for initiating the speech mode must be provided. Braille must comply with section 703.3 of the 2010 ADA Standards.

(9) *Biometrics.* Biometrics must not be the only means for user identification or control, unless at least two biometric options that use different biological characteristics are provided.

(d) You must provide equivalent service upon request to passengers with a disability who cannot readily use your automated airport kiosks (e.g., by directing a passenger who is blind to an accessible automated kiosk, assisting a passenger in using an inaccessible automated kiosk, assisting a passenger who due to his or her disability cannot use an accessible automated kiosk by allowing the passenger to come to the front of the line at the check-in counter).

[78 FR 67915, Nov. 12, 2013]

Subpart E—Accessibility of Aircraft

§ 382.61 What are the requirements for movable aisle armrests?

(a) As a carrier, you must ensure that aircraft with 30 or more passenger seats on which passenger aisle seats have armrests are equipped with movable aisle armrests on at least one-half of the aisle seats in rows in which passengers with mobility impairments are permitted to sit under FAA or applicable foreign government safety rules.

(b) You are not required to provide movable armrests on aisle seats of rows which a passenger with a mobility impairment is precluded from using by an FAA safety rule.

(c) You must ensure that these movable aisle armrests are provided proportionately in all classes of service in the cabin. For example, if 80 percent of the aisle seats in which passengers with mobility impairments may sit are in coach, and 20 percent are in first class, then 80 percent of the movable aisle armrests must be in coach, with 20 percent in first class.

(d) For aircraft equipped with movable aisle armrests, you must configure cabins, or establish administrative systems, to ensure that passengers with mobility impairments or other passengers with a disability can readily identify and obtain seating in rows with movable aisle armrests. You must provide this information by specific seat and row number.

(e) You are not required to retrofit cabin interiors of existing aircraft to comply with the requirements of this section. However, if you replace any of an aircraft's aisle seats with newly manufactured seats, the new seats must include movable aisle armrests as required by this section. However, an aircraft is never required to have movable aisle armrests on more than one half of the aisle seats.

(f) As a foreign carrier, you must comply with the requirements of paragraphs (a) through (d) of this section with respect to new aircraft you operate that were initially ordered after May 13, 2009 or which are delivered after May 13, 2010. As a U.S. carrier, the requirements of paragraphs (a), (b), (d), and (e) of this section applies to you with respect to new aircraft you operate that were initially ordered after April 5, 1990, or which are delivered after April 5, 1992. As a U.S. carrier, paragraph (c) of this section applies to you with respect to new aircraft you operate that were initially ordered after May 13, 2009 or which were delivered after May 13, 2010.

(g) As a foreign carrier, you must comply with the requirements of paragraph (e) of this section with respect to seats ordered after May 13, 2009.

§ 382.63 What are the requirements for accessible lavatories?

(a) As a carrier, you must ensure that aircraft with more than one aisle in which lavatories are provided shall include at least one accessible lavatory.

(1) The accessible lavatory must permit a qualified individual with a disability to enter, maneuver within as necessary to use all lavatory facilities, and leave, by means of the aircraft's on-board wheelchair.

(2) The accessible lavatory must afford privacy to persons using the on-board wheelchair equivalent to that afforded ambulatory users.

(3) The lavatory shall provide door locks, accessible call buttons, grab bars, faucets and other controls, and dispensers usable by qualified individuals with a disability, including wheelchair users and persons with manual impairments.

(b) With respect to aircraft with only one aisle in which lavatories are provided, you may, but are not required to, provide an accessible lavatory.

(c) You are not required to retrofit cabin interiors of existing aircraft to comply with the requirements of this section. However, if you replace a lavatory on an aircraft with more than one aisle, you must replace it with an accessible lavatory.

(d) As a foreign carrier, you must comply with the requirements of paragraph (a) of this section with respect to new aircraft you operate that were initially ordered after May 13, 2009 or which are delivered after May 13, 2010. As a U.S. carrier, this requirement applies to you with respect to new aircraft you operate that were initially ordered after April 5, 1990, or which were delivered after April 5, 1992.

(e) As a foreign carrier, you must comply with the requirements of paragraph (c) of this section beginning May 13, 2009. As a U.S. carrier, these requirements apply to you with respect to new aircraft you operate that were initially ordered after April 5, 1990, or which were delivered after April 5, 1992.

§382.65 What are the requirements concerning on-board wheelchairs?

(a) As a carrier, you must equip aircraft that have more than 60 passenger seats, and that have an accessible lavatory (whether or not having such a lavatory is required by §382.63 of this Part) with an on-board wheelchair. The Aerospatiale/Aeritalia ATR–72 and the British Aerospace Advanced Turboprop (ATP), in configurations having between 60 and 70 passenger seats, are exempt from this requirement.

(b) If a passenger asks you to provide an on-board wheelchair on a particular flight, you must provide it if the aircraft being used for the flight has more than 60 passenger seats, even if the aircraft does not have an accessible lavatory.

(1) The basis of the passenger's request must be that he or she can use an inaccessible lavatory but cannot reach it from a seat without using an on-board wheelchair.

(2) You may require the passenger to provide the advance notice specified in §382.27 to receive this service.

(c) You must ensure that on-board wheelchairs meet the following standards:

(1) On-board wheelchairs must include footrests, armrests which are movable or removable, adequate occupant restraint systems, a backrest height that permits assistance to passengers in transferring, structurally sound handles for maneuvering the occupied chair, and wheel locks or another adequate means to prevent chair movement during transfer or turbulence.

(2) The chair must be designed to be compatible with the maneuvering space, aisle width, and seat height of the aircraft on which it is to be used, and to be easily pushed, pulled, and turned in the cabin environment by carrier personnel.

(d) As a foreign carrier, you must meet this requirement as of May 13, 2010. As a U.S. carrier, you must meet this requirement by May 13, 2009.

§382.67 What is the requirement for priority space in the cabin to store passengers' wheelchairs?

(a) As a carrier, you must ensure that there is priority space (i.e., a closet, or a row of seats where a wheelchair may be strapped using a strap kit that complies with applicable Federal Aviation Administration or applicable foreign government regulations on the stowage of cargo in the cabin compartment) in the cabin of sufficient size to stow at least one typical adult-sized folding, collapsible, or break-down manual passenger wheelchair, the dimensions of which are 13 inches by 36 inches by 42 inches or less without having to remove the wheels or otherwise disassemble it. This section applies to any aircraft with 100 or more passenger seats and this space must be other than the overhead compartments and under-seat spaces routinely used for passengers' carry-on items.

(b) If you are a carrier that uses the seat-strapping method to stow a manual passenger wheelchair, you must ensure that there is priority space for at least two such wheelchairs, if stowing the second passenger wheelchair would not displace passengers.

(c) If you are a carrier that uses a closet as the priority space to stow a manual passenger wheelchair, you must install a sign or placard prominently on the closet indicating that such wheelchairs and other assistive devices are to be stowed in this area with priority over other items brought onto the aircraft by other passengers or crew, including crew luggage, as set forth in §382.123.

(d) If passengers holding confirmed reservations are not able to travel on a flight because their seats are being used to stow a passenger's wheelchair as required by paragraph (a) of this section, carriers must compensate those passengers in an amount to be calculated as provided for in instances of involuntary denied boarding under 14 CFR part 250, where part 250 applies.

(e) As a carrier, you must never request or suggest that a passenger not stow his or her wheelchair in the cabin to accommodate other passengers (e.g., informing a passenger that stowing his or her wheelchair in the cabin will require other passengers to be removed from the flight), or for any other non-safety related reason (e.g., that it is easier for the carrier if the wheelchair is stowed in the cargo compartment).

(f) As a carrier, you must offer preboarding to a passenger stowing his or her wheelchair in the cabin.

(g) As a foreign carrier, you must meet the requirement of this section for new aircraft ordered after May 13, 2009, or delivered after May 13, 2010. As a U.S. carrier, this section applies to you with respect to new aircraft you operate that were ordered after April 5, 1990, or which were delivered after April 5, 1992.

[78 FR 67923, Nov. 12, 2013]

§ 382.69 What requirements must carriers meet concerning the accessibility of videos, DVDs, and other audio-visual presentations shown on-aircraft to individuals who are deaf or hard of hearing?

(a) As a carrier, you must ensure that all new videos, DVDs, and other audio-visual displays played on aircraft for safety purposes, and all such new audio-visual displays played on aircraft for informational purposes that were created under your control, are high-contrast captioned. The captioning must be in the predominant language or languages in which you communicate with passengers on the flight.

(b) The requirements of paragraph (a) of this section go into effect with respect to audio-visual displays used for safety purposes on November 10, 2009.

(c) Between May 13, 2009 and November 9, 2009, U.S. carriers must ensure that all videos, DVDs, and other audio-visual displays played on aircraft for safety purposes have open captioning or an inset for a sign language interpreter, unless such captioning or inset either would interfere with the video presentation so as to render it ineffective or would not be large enough to be readable, in which case these carriers must use an equivalent non-video alternative for transmitting the briefing to passengers with hearing impairments.

(d) The requirements of paragraph (a) of this section go into effect with respect to informational displays on January 8, 2010.

§ 382.71 What other aircraft accessibility requirements apply to carriers?

(a) As a carrier, you must maintain all aircraft accessibility features in proper working order.

(b) You must ensure that any replacement or refurbishing of the aircraft cabin or its elements does not reduce the accessibility of that element to a level below that specified for new aircraft in this part.

[Doc. No. DOT–OST–2004–19482, 73 FR 27665, May 13, 2008, as amended at 74 FR 11471, Mar. 18, 2009]

Subpart F—Seating Accommodations

§ 382.81 For which passengers must carriers make seating accommodations?

As a carrier, you must provide the following seating accommodations to the following passengers on request, if the passenger self-identifies to you as having a disability specified in this section and the type of seating accommodation in question exists on the particular aircraft. Once the passenger self-identifies to you, you must ensure that the information is recorded and properly transmitted to personnel responsible for providing the accommodation.

(a) For a passenger who uses an aisle chair to access the aircraft and who cannot readily transfer over a fixed aisle armrest, you must provide a seat in a row with a movable aisle armrest. You must ensure that your personnel are trained in the location and proper use of movable aisle armrests, including appropriate transfer techniques. You must ensure that aisle seats with movable armrests are clearly identifiable.

(b) You must provide an adjoining seat for a person assisting a passenger with a disability in the following circumstances:

(1) When a passenger with a disability is traveling with a personal care attendant who will be performing

a function for the individual during the flight that airline personnel are not required to perform (*e.g.*, assistance with eating);

(2) When a passenger with a vision impairment is traveling with a reader/assistant who will be performing functions for the individual during the flight;

(3) When a passenger with a hearing impairment is traveling with an interpreter who will be performing functions for the individual during the flight; or

(4) When you require a passenger to travel with a safety assistant (see §382.29).

(c) For a passenger with a disability traveling with a service animal, you must provide, as the passenger requests, either a bulkhead seat or a seat other than a bulkhead seat.

(d) For a passenger with a fused or immobilized leg, you must provide a bulkhead seat or other seat that provides greater legroom than other seats, on the side of an aisle that better accommodates the individual's disability.

§382.83 Through what mechanisms do carriers make seating accommodations?

(a) If you are a carrier that provides advance seat assignments to passengers (*i.e.*, offer seat assignments to passengers before the day of the flight), you must comply with the requirements of §382.81 of this part by any of the following methods:

(1) You may "block" an adequate number of the seats used to provide the seating accommodations required by §382.81.

(i) You must not assign these seats to passengers who do not meet the criteria of §382.81 until 24 hours before the scheduled departure of the flight.

(ii) At any time up until 24 hours before the scheduled departure of the flight, you must assign a seat meeting the requirements of this section to a passenger with a disability meeting one or more of the requirements of §382.81 who requests it, at the time the passenger initially makes the request.

(iii) If a passenger with a disability specified in §382.81 does not make a request at least 24 hours before the scheduled departure of the flight, you must meet the passenger's request to the extent practicable, but you are not required to reassign a seat assigned to another passenger in order to do so.

(2) You may designate an adequate number of the seats used to provide seating accommodations required by §382.81 as "priority seats" for passengers with a disability.

(i) You must provide notice that all passengers assigned these seats (other than passengers with a disability listed in §382.81 of this part) are subject to being reassigned to another seat if necessary to provide a seating accommodation required by this section.

(ii) You may provide this notice through your computer reservation system, verbal information provided by reservation personnel, ticket notices, gate announcements, counter signs, seat cards or notices, frequent-flier literature, or other appropriate means.

(iii) You must assign a seat meeting the requirements of this section to a passenger with a disability listed in §382.81 of this part who requests the accommodation at the time the passenger makes the request. You may require such a passenger to check in and request the seating accommodation at least one hour before the standard check-in time for the flight. If all designated priority seats that would accommodate the passenger have been assigned to other passengers, you must reassign the seats of the other passengers as needed to provide the requested accommodation.

(iv) If a passenger with a disability listed in §382.81 does not check in at least an hour before the standard check-in time for the general public, you must meet the individual's request to the extent practicable, but you are not required to reassign a seat assigned to another passenger in order to do so.

(b) If you assign seats to passengers, but not until the date of the flight, you must use the "priority seating" approach of paragraph (a)(2) of this section.

(c) If you do not provide advance seat assignments to passengers, you must allow passengers specified in §382.81 to board the aircraft before other passengers, including other "preboarded" passengers, so that the passengers needing seating accommodations can select seats that best meet their needs.

(d) As a carrier, if you wish to use a different method of providing seating assignment accommodations to passengers with disabilities from those specified in this subpart, you must obtain the written concurrence of the Department of Transportation. Contact the Department at the address cited in § 382.159 of this part.

§ 382.85 What seating accommodations must carriers make to passengers in circumstances not covered by § 382.81 (a) through (d)?

As a carrier, you must provide the following seating accommodations to a passenger who self-identifies as having a disability other than one in the four categories listed in § 382.81 (a) through (d) of this part and as needing a seat assignment accommodation in order to readily access and use the carrier's air transportation services:

(a) As a carrier that assigns seats in advance, you must provide accommodations in the following ways:

(1) If you use the "seat-blocking" mechanism of § 382.83(a)(1) of this part, you must implement the requirements of this section as follows:

(i) When a passenger with a disability not described in § 382.81(a) through (d) of this part makes a reservation more than 24 hours before the scheduled departure time of the flight, you are not required to offer the passenger one of the seats blocked for the use of passengers with a disability listed under § 382.81.

(ii) However, you must assign to the passenger any seat, not already assigned to another passenger that accommodates the passenger's needs, even if that seat is not available for assignment to the general passenger population at the time of the request.

(2) If you use the "designated priority seats" mechanism of § 382.83(a)(2) of this part, you must implement the requirements of this section as follows:

(i) When a passenger with a disability not described in § 382.81 makes a reservation, you must assign to the passenger any seat, not already assigned to another passenger, that accommodates the passenger's needs, even if that seat is not available for assignment to the general passenger population at the time of the request. You may require a passenger making such a request to check in one hour before the standard check-in time for the flight.

(ii) If such a passenger is assigned to a designated priority seat, he or she is subject to being reassigned to another seat as provided in § 382.83(a)(2)(i) of this subpart.

(b) On flights where advance seat assignments are not offered, you must provide seating accommodations under this section by allowing passengers to board the aircraft before other passengers, including other "preboarded" passengers, so that the individuals needing seating accommodations can select seats that best meet their needs.

(c) If you assign seats to passengers, but not until the date of the flight, you must use the "priority seating" approach of section 382.83(a)(2).

§ 382.87 What other requirements pertain to seating for passengers with a disability?

(a) As a carrier, you must not exclude any passenger with a disability from any seat or require that a passenger with a disability sit in any particular seat, on the basis of disability, except to comply with FAA or applicable foreign government safety requirements.

(b) In responding to requests from individuals for accommodations under this subpart, you must comply with FAA and applicable foreign government safety requirements, including those pertaining to exit seating (see 14 CFR 121.585 and 135.129).

(c) If a passenger's disability results in involuntary active behavior that would result in the person properly being refused transportation under § 382.19, and the passenger could be transported safely if seated in another location, you must offer to let the passenger sit in that location as an alternative to being refused transportation.

(d) If you have already provided a seat to a passenger with a disability to furnish an accommodation required by this subpart, you must not (except in the circumstance described in § 382.85(a)(2)(ii)) reassign that passenger to another seat in response to a subsequent request from another passenger with a disability, without the first passenger's consent.

(e) You must never deny transportation to any passenger in order to provide accommodations required by this subpart.

(f) You are not required to furnish more than one seat per ticket or to provide a seat in a class of service other than the one the passenger has purchased in order to provide an accommodation required by this part.

Subpart G—Boarding, Deplaning, and Connecting Assistance

§382.91 What assistance must carriers provide to passengers with a disability in moving within the terminal?

(a) As a carrier, you must provide or ensure the provision of assistance requested by or on behalf of a passenger with a disability, or offered by carrier or airport operator personnel and accepted by a passenger with a disability, in transportation between gates to make a connection to another flight. If the arriving flight and the departing connecting flight are operated by different carriers, the carrier that operated the arriving flight (*i.e.*, the one that operates the first of the two flights that are connecting) is responsible for providing or ensuring the provision of this assistance, even if the passenger holds a separate ticket for the departing flight. It is permissible for the two carriers to mutually agree that the carrier operating the departing connecting flight (*i.e.*, the second flight of the two) will provide this assistance, but the carrier operating the arriving flight remains responsible under this section for ensuring that the assistance is provided.

(b) You must also provide or ensure the provision of assistance requested by or on behalf of a passenger with a disability, or offered by carrier or airport operator personnel and accepted by a passenger with a disability, in moving from the terminal entrance (or a vehicle drop-off point adjacent to the entrance) through the airport to the gate for a departing flight, or from the gate to the terminal entrance (or a vehicle pick-up point adjacent to the entrance after an arriving flight).

(1) This requirement includes assistance in accessing key functional areas of the terminal, such as ticket counters and baggage claim.

(2) This requirement also includes a brief stop upon the passenger's request at the entrance to a rest room (including an accessible rest room when requested). As a carrier, you are required to make such a stop only if the rest room is available on the route to the destination of the enplaning, deplaning, or connecting assistance and you can make the stop without unreasonable delay. To receive such assistance, the passenger must self-identify as being an individual with a disability needing the assistance.

(c) As a carrier at a U.S. airport, you must, on request, in cooperation with the airport operator, provide for escorting a passenger with a service animal to an animal relief area provided under §382.51(a)(5) of this part.

(d) As part of your obligation to provide or ensure the provision of assistance to passengers with disabilities in moving through the terminal (*e.g.*, between the terminal entrance and the gate, between gate and aircraft, from gate to a baggage claim area), you must assist passengers who are unable to carry their luggage because of a disability with transporting their gate-checked or carry-on luggage. You may request the credible verbal assurance that a passenger cannot carry the luggage in question. If a passenger is unable to provide credible assurance, you may require the passenger to provide documentation as a condition of providing this service.

§382.93 Must carriers offer preboarding to passengers with a disability?

As a carrier, you must offer preboarding to passengers with a disability who self-identify at the gate as needing additional time or assistance to board, stow accessibility equipment, or be seated.

§382.95 What are carriers' general obligations with respect to boarding and deplaning assistance?

(a) As a carrier, you must promptly provide or ensure the provision of assistance requested by or on behalf of passengers with a disability, or offered by carrier or airport operator personnel and accepted by passengers with a disability, in enplaning and deplaning. This assistance must include, as needed, the services of personnel and the use of ground wheelchairs, accessible motorized carts, boarding wheelchairs, and/or on-board wheelchairs where provided in accordance with this part, and ramps or mechanical lifts.

(b) As a carrier, you must, except as otherwise provided in this subpart, provide boarding and deplaning assistance through the use of lifts or ramps at any U.S. commercial service airport with 10,000 or more annual enplanements where boarding and deplaning by level-entry loading bridges or accessible passenger lounges is not available.

§ 382.97 To which aircraft does the requirement to provide boarding and deplaning assistance through the use of lifts apply?

The requirement of section 382.95(b) of this part to provide boarding and deplaning assistance through the use of lifts applies with respect to all aircraft with a passenger capacity of 19 or more, with the following exceptions:

(a) Float planes;

(b) The following 19-seat capacity aircraft models: the Fairchild Metro, the Jetstream 31 and 32, the Beech 1900 (C and D models), and the Embraer EMB–120;

(c) Any other aircraft model determined by the Department of Transportation to be unsuitable for boarding and deplaning assistance by lift, ramp, or other suitable device.

The Department will make such a determination if it concludes that—

(1) No existing boarding and deplaning assistance device on the market will accommodate the aircraft without a significant risk of serious damage to the aircraft or injury to passengers or employees, or

(2) Internal barriers are present in the aircraft that would preclude passengers who use a boarding or aisle chair from reaching a non-exit row seat.

§ 382.99 What agreements must carriers have with the airports they serve?

(a) As a carrier, you must negotiate in good faith with the airport operator of each U.S. airport described in § 382.95(b) to ensure the provision of lifts for boarding and deplaning where level-entry loading bridges are not available.

(b) You must have a written, signed agreement with the airport operator allocating responsibility for meeting the boarding and deplaning assistance requirements of this subpart between or among the parties. For foreign carriers, with respect to all covered aircraft, this requirement becomes effective May 13, 2010.

(c) For foreign carriers, the agreement with a U.S. airport must provide that all actions necessary to ensure accessible boarding and deplaning for passengers with a disability are completed as soon as practicable, but no later than May 13, 2011.

(d) Under the agreement, you may, as a carrier, require that passengers wishing to receive boarding and deplaning assistance requiring the use of a lift for a flight check in for the flight one hour before the standard check-in time for the flight. If the passenger checks in after this time, you must nonetheless provide the boarding and deplaning assistance by lift if you can do so by making a reasonable effort, without delaying the flight.

(e) The agreement must ensure that all lifts and other accessibility equipment are maintained in proper working condition.

(f) All carriers and airport operators involved are jointly and severally responsible for the timely and complete implementation of the agreement.

(g) You must make a copy of this agreement available, on request, to representatives of the Department of Transportation.

[Doc. No. DOT–OST–2004–19482, 73 FR 27665, May 13, 2008, as amended at 74 FR 11471, Mar. 18, 2009]

§ 382.101 What other boarding and deplaning assistance must carriers provide?

When level-entry boarding and deplaning assistance is not required to be provided under this subpart, you must, as a carrier, provide or ensure the provision of boarding and deplaning assistance by any available means to which the passenger consents. However, you must never use hand-carrying (*i.e.*, directly picking up the passenger's body in the arms of one or more carrier personnel to effect a level change the passenger needs to enter or leave the aircraft), even if the passenger consents, unless this is the only way of evacuating the individual in the event of an emergency. The situations in which level-entry boarding is not required but in which you must provide this boarding and deplaning assistance include, but are not limited to, the following:

(a) The boarding or deplaning process occurs at a U.S. airport that is not a commercial service airport that has 10,000 or more enplanements per year;

(b) The boarding or deplaning process occurs at a foreign airport;

(c) You are using an aircraft subject to an exception from the lift boarding and deplaning assistance requirements under § 382.97 (a)–(c) of this subpart;

(d) The deadlines established in § 382.99(c) have not yet passed; and

(e) Circumstances beyond your control (*e.g.*, unusually severe weather; unexpected mechanical problems) prevent the use of a lift.

§ 382.103 May a carrier leave a passenger unattended in a wheelchair or other device?

As a carrier, you must not leave a passenger who has requested assistance required by this subpart unattended by the personnel responsible for enplaning, deplaning, or connecting assistance in a ground wheelchair, boarding wheelchair, or other device, in which the passenger is not independently mobile, for more than 30 minutes. This requirement applies even if another person (*e.g.*, family member, personal care attendant) is accompanying the passenger, unless the passenger explicitly waives the obligation.

§ 382.105 What is the responsibility of carriers at foreign airports at which airport operators have responsibility for enplaning, deplaning, and connecting assistance?

At a foreign airport at which enplaning, deplaning, or connecting assistance is provided by the airport operator, rather than by carriers, as a carrier you may rely on the services provided by the airport operator to meet the requirements of this subpart. If the services provided by the airport operator are not sufficient to meet the requirements of this subpart, you must supplement the airport operator's services to ensure that these requirements are met. If you believe you are precluded by law from supplementing the airport operator's services, you may apply for a conflict of laws waiver under § 382.9 of this part.

Subpart H—Services on Aircraft

§ 382.111 What services must carriers provide to passengers with a disability on board the aircraft?

As a carrier, you must provide services within the aircraft cabin as requested by or on behalf of passengers with a disability, or when offered by carrier personnel and accepted by passengers with a disability, as follows:

(a) Assistance in moving to and from seats, as part of the enplaning and deplaning processes;

(b) Assistance in preparation for eating, such as opening packages and identifying food;

(c) If there is an on-board wheelchair on the aircraft, assistance with the use of the on-board wheelchair to enable the person to move to and from a lavatory;

(d) Assistance to a semi-ambulatory person in moving to and from the lavatory, not involving lifting or carrying the person; or

(e) Assistance in stowing and retrieving carry-on items, including mobility aids and other assistive devices stowed in the cabin (*see also* 382.91(d)). To receive such assistance, the passenger must self-identify as being an individual with a disability needing the assistance.

(f) Effective communication with passengers who have vision impairments or who are deaf or hard-of-hearing, so that these passengers have prompt access to information the carrier provides to other passengers (*e.g.* weather, on-board services, flight delays, connecting gates at the next airport).

[Doc. No. DOT–OST–2004–19482, 73 FR 27665, May 13, 2008, as amended at 75 FR 44887, July 30, 2010]

§ 382.113 What services are carriers not required to provide to passengers with a disability on board the aircraft?

As a carrier, you are not required to provide extensive special assistance to qualified individuals with a disability. For purposes of this section, extensive special assistance includes the following activities:

(a) Assistance in actual eating;

(b) Assistance within the restroom or assistance at the passenger's seat with elimination functions; and

(c) Provision of medical services.

§ 382.115 What requirements apply to on-board safety briefings?

As a carrier, you must comply with the following requirements with respect to on-board safety briefings:

(a) You must conduct an individual safety briefing for any passenger where required by 14 CFR 121.571(a)(3) and (a)(4), 14 CFR 135.117(b), or other FAA requirements.

(b) You may offer an individual briefing to any other passenger, but you may not require an individual to have such a briefing except as provided in paragraph (a) of this section.

(c) You must not require any passenger with a disability to demonstrate that he or she has listened to, read, or understood the information presented, except to the extent that carrier personnel impose such a requirement on all passengers with respect to the general safety briefing. You must not take any action adverse to a qualified individual with a disability on the basis that the person has not "accepted" the briefing.

(d) When you conduct an individual safety briefing for a passenger with a disability, you must do so as inconspicuously and discreetly as possible.

(e) The accessibility requirements for onboard video safety presentations that carriers must meet are outlined in section 382.69.

§ 382.117 Must carriers permit passengers with a disability to travel with service animals?

(a) As a carrier, you must permit a service animal to accompany a passenger with a disability.

(1) You must not deny transportation to a service animal on the basis that its carriage may offend or annoy carrier personnel or persons traveling on the aircraft.

(2) On a flight segment scheduled to take 8 hours or more, you may, as a condition of permitting a service animal to travel in the cabin, require the passenger using the service animal to provide documentation that the animal will not need to relieve itself on the flight or that the animal can relieve itself in a way that does not create a health or sanitation issue on the flight.

(b) You must permit the service animal to accompany the passenger with a disability at any seat in which the passenger sits, unless the animal obstructs an aisle or other area that must remain unobstructed to facilitate an emergency evacuation.

(c) If a service animal cannot be accommodated at the seat location of the passenger with a disability who is using the animal, you must offer the passenger the opportunity to move with the animal to another seat location, if present on the aircraft, where the animal can be accommodated.

(d) As evidence that an animal is a service animal, you must accept identification cards, other written documentation, presence of harnesses, tags, or the credible verbal assurances of a qualified individual with a disability using the animal.

(e) If a passenger seeks to travel with an animal that is used as an emotional support or psychiatric service animal, you are not required to accept the animal for transportation in the cabin unless the passenger provides you current documentation (*i.e.*, no older than one year from the date of the passenger's scheduled initial flight) on the letterhead of a licensed mental health professional (*e.g.*, psychiatrist, psychologist, licensed clinical social worker, including a medical doctor specifically treating the passenger's mental or emotional disability) stating the following:

(1) The passenger has a mental or emotional disability recognized in the Diagnostic and Statistical Manual of Mental Disorders—Fourth Edition (DSM IV);

(2) The passenger needs the emotional support or psychiatric service animal as an accommodation for air travel and/or for activity at the passenger's destination;

(3) The individual providing the assessment is a licensed mental health professional, and the passenger is under his or her professional care; and

(4) The date and type of the mental health professional's license and the state or other jurisdiction in which it was issued.

(f) You are never required to accommodate certain unusual service animals (*e.g.*, snakes, other reptiles, ferrets, rodents, and spiders) as service animals in the cabin. With respect to all other animals, including unusual or exotic animals that are presented as service animals (*e.g.*, miniature horses, pigs, monkeys), as a carrier you must determine whether any factors preclude their traveling in the cabin as service animals (*e.g.*, whether the animal is too large or heavy to be accommodated in the cabin, whether the animal would pose a direct threat to the health or safety of others, whether it would cause a significant disruption of cabin service, whether it would be prohibited from entering a foreign country that is the flight's destination). If no such factors preclude the animal from traveling in the cabin, you must permit it to do so. However, as a foreign carrier, you are not required to carry service animals other than dogs.

(g) Whenever you decide not to accept an animal as a service animal, you must explain the reason for your decision to the passenger and document it in writing. A copy of the explanation must be provided to the passenger either at the airport, or within 10 calendar days of the incident.

(h) You must promptly take all steps necessary to comply with foreign regulations (*e.g.*, animal health regulations) needed to permit the legal transportation of a passenger's service animal from the U.S. into a foreign airport.

(i) Guidance concerning the carriage of service animals generally is found in the preamble of this rule. Guidance on the steps necessary to legally transport service animals on flights from the U.S. into the United Kingdom is found in 72 FR 8268–8277, (February 26, 2007).

[Doc. No. DOT–OST–2004–19482, 73 FR 27665, May 13, 2008, as amended at 74 FR 11471, Mar. 18, 2009]

§ 382.119 What information must carriers give individuals with vision or hearing impairment on aircraft?

(a) As a carrier, you must ensure that passengers with a disability who identify themselves as needing visual or hearing assistance have prompt access to the same information provided to other passengers on the aircraft as described in paragraph (b) of this section, to the extent that it does not interfere with crewmembers' safety duties as set forth in FAA and applicable foreign regulations.

(b) The covered information includes but is not limited to the following: information concerning flight safety, procedures for takeoff and landing, flight delays, schedule or aircraft changes that affect the travel of persons with disabilities, diversion to a different airport, scheduled departure and arrival time, boarding information, weather conditions at the flight's destination, beverage and menu information, connecting gate assignments, baggage claim, individuals being paged by airlines, and emergencies (*e.g.*, fire or bomb threat).

Subpart I—Stowage of Wheelchairs, Other Mobility Aids, and Other Assistive Devices

§ 382.121 What mobility aids and other assistive devices may passengers with a disability bring into the aircraft cabin?

(a) As a carrier, you must permit passengers with a disability to bring the following kinds of items into the aircraft cabin, provided that they can be stowed in designated priority storage areas or in overhead compartments or under seats, consistent with FAA, PHMSA, TSA, or applicable foreign government requirements concerning security, safety, and hazardous materials with respect to the stowage of carry-on items.

(1) Manual wheelchairs, including folding or collapsible wheelchairs;

(2) Other mobility aids, such as canes (including those used by persons with impaired vision), crutches, and walkers; and

(3) Other assistive devices for stowage or use within the cabin (*e.g.*, prescription medications and any medical devices needed to administer them such as syringes or auto-injectors, vision-enhancing devices, and POCs, ventilators and respirators that use non-spillable batteries, as long as they comply with applicable safety, security and hazardous materials rules).

(b) In implementing your carry-on baggage policies, you must not count assistive devices (including the kinds of items listed in paragraph (a) of this section) toward a limit on carry-on baggage.

§ 382.123 What are the requirements concerning priority cabin stowage for wheelchairs and other assistive devices?

(a) The following rules apply to the stowage of passengers' wheelchairs or other assistive devices in the priority stowage area provided for in § 382.67 of this part:

(1) You must ensure that a passenger with a disability who uses a wheelchair and takes advantage of the opportunity to preboard the aircraft can stow his or her wheelchair in this area, with priority over other items brought onto the aircraft by other passengers or crew enplaning at the same airport, consistent with FAA, PHMSA, TSA, or applicable foreign government requirements concerning security, safety, and hazardous materials with respect to the stowage of carry-on items. You must move items that you or your personnel have placed in the priority stowage area (*e.g.*, crew luggage, an on-board wheelchair) to make room for the passenger's wheelchair, even if these items were stowed in the priority stowage area before the passenger seeking to stow a wheelchair boarded the aircraft (*e.g.*, the items were placed there on a previous leg of the flight).

(2) You must also ensure that a passenger with a disability who takes advantage of the opportunity to preboard the aircraft can stow other assistive devices in this area, with priority over other items (except wheelchairs) brought onto the aircraft by other passengers enplaning at the same airport consistent with FAA, PHMSA, TSA, or applicable foreign government requirements concerning security, safety, and hazardous materials with respect to the stowage of carry-on items.

(3) You must ensure that a passenger with a disability who does not take advantage of the opportunity to preboard is able to use the area to stow his or her wheelchair or other assistive device on a first-come, first-served basis along with all other passengers seeking to stow carry-on items in the area.

(b) If a wheelchair exceeds the space provided for in § 382.67 of this part while fully assembled but will fit if wheels or other components can be removed without the use of tools, you must remove the applicable components and stow the wheelchair in the designated space. In this case, you must stow the removed components in areas provided for stowage of carry-on luggage.

[Doc. No. DOT–OST–2004–19482, 73 FR 27665, May 13, 2008, as amended at 78 FR 67924, Nov. 12, 2013]

§ 382.125 What procedures do carriers follow when wheelchairs, other mobility aids, and other assistive devices must be stowed in the cargo compartment?

(a) As a carrier, you must stow wheelchairs, other mobility aids, or other assistive devices in the baggage compartment if an approved stowage area is not available in the cabin or the items cannot be transported in the cabin consistent with FAA, PHMSA, TSA, or applicable foreign government requirements concerning security, safety, and hazardous materials with respect to the stowage of carry-on items.

(b) You must give wheelchairs, other mobility aids, and other assistive devices priority for stowage in the baggage compartment over other cargo and baggage. Only items that fit into the baggage compartment and can be transported consistent with FAA, PHMSA, TSA, or applicable foreign government requirements concerning security, safety, and hazardous materials with respect to the stowage of items in the baggage compartment need be transported. Where this priority results in other passengers' baggage being unable to be carried on the flight, you must make your best efforts to ensure that the other baggage reaches the passengers' destination on the carrier's next flight to the destination.

(c) You must provide for the checking and timely return of passengers' wheelchairs, other mobility aids, and other assistive devices as close as possible to the door of the aircraft, so that passengers may use their own equipment to the extent possible, except

(1) Where this practice would be inconsistent with Federal regulations governing transportation security or the transportation of hazardous materials; or

(2) When the passenger requests the return of the items at the baggage claim area instead of at the door of the aircraft.

(d) In order to achieve the timely return of wheelchairs, you must ensure that passengers' wheelchairs, other mobility aids, and other assistive devices are among the first items retrieved from the baggage compartment.

§ 382.127 What procedures apply to stowage of battery-powered mobility aids?

(a) Whenever baggage compartment size and aircraft airworthiness considerations do not prohibit doing so, you must, as a carrier, accept a passenger's battery-powered wheelchair or other similar mobility device, including the battery, as checked baggage, consistent with the requirements of 49 CFR 175.10(a)(15) and (16) and the provisions of paragraphs (b) through (f) of this section.

(b) You may require that passengers with a disability wishing to have battery-powered wheelchairs or other similar mobility devices transported on a flight check in one hour before the check-in time for the general public. If the passenger checks in after this time, you must nonetheless carry the wheelchair or other similar mobility device if you can do so by making a reasonable effort, without delaying the flight.

(c) If the battery on the passenger's wheelchair or other similar mobility device has been labeled by the manufacturer as non-spillable as provided in 49 CFR 173.159(d)(2), or if a battery-powered wheelchair with a spillable battery can be loaded, stored, secured and unloaded in an upright position, you must not require the battery to be removed and separately packaged. Notwithstanding this requirement, you must remove and package separately any battery that is inadequately secured to a wheelchair or, for a spillable battery, is contained in a wheelchair that cannot be loaded, stowed, secured and unloaded in an upright position, in accordance with 49 CFR 175.10(a)(15) and (16). A damaged or leaking battery should not be transported.

(d) When it is necessary to detach the battery from the wheelchair, you must, upon request, provide packaging for the battery meeting the requirements of 49 CFR 175.10(a)(15) and (16) and package the battery. You may refuse to use packaging materials or devices other than those you normally use for this purpose.

(e) You must not disconnect the battery on wheelchairs or other mobility devices equipped with a non-spillable battery completely enclosed within a case or compartment integral to the design of the device unless an FAA or PHMSA safety regulation, or an applicable foreign safety regulation having mandatory legal effect, requires you to do so.

(f) You must not drain batteries.

§ 382.129 What other requirements apply when passengers' wheelchairs, other mobility aids, and other assistive devices must be disassembled for stowage?

(a) As a carrier, you must permit passengers with a disability to provide written directions concerning the disassembly and reassembly of their wheelchairs, other mobility aids, and other assistive devices. You must carry out these instructions to the greatest extent feasible, consistent with FAA, PHMSA, TSA, or applicable foreign government requirements concerning security, safety, and hazardous materials with respect to the stowage of carry-on items.

(b) When wheelchairs, other mobility aids, or other assistive devices are disassembled by the carrier for stowage, you must reassemble them and ensure their prompt return to the passenger. You must return wheelchairs, other mobility aids, and other assistive devices to the passenger in the condition in which you received them.

§ 382.131 Do baggage liability limits apply to mobility aids and other assistive devices?

With respect to transportation to which 14 CFR part 254 applies, the limits to liability for loss, damage, or delay concerning wheelchairs or other assistive devices provided in part 254 do not apply. The basis for calculating the compensation for a lost, damaged, or destroyed wheelchair or other assistive device shall be the original purchase price of the device.

§ 382.133 What are the requirements concerning the evaluation and use of passenger-supplied electronic devices that assist passengers with respiration in the cabin during flight?

(a) Except for on-demand air taxi operators, as a U.S. carrier conducting passenger service you must permit any individual with a disability to use in the passenger cabin during air transportation an electronic assistive device specified in paragraph (c) of this section on all aircraft originally designed to have a maximum passenger capacity of more than 19 seats unless:

(1) The device does not meet applicable FAA requirements for medical portable electronic device; or

(2) The device cannot be stowed and used in the passenger cabin consistent with applicable TSA, FAA, and PHMSA regulations.

(b) Except for foreign carriers conducting operations of a nature equivalent to on-demand air taxi operations by a U.S. carrier, as a foreign carrier conducting passenger service you must permit any individual with a disability to use in the passenger cabin during air transportation to, from or within the United States, an electronic assistive device specified in paragraph (d) of this section on all aircraft originally designed to have a maximum passenger capacity of more than 19 seats unless:

(1) The device does not meet requirements for medical portable electronic devices set by the foreign carrier's government if such requirements exist;

(2) The device does not meet requirements for medical portable electronic devices set by the FAA for U.S. carriers in circumstances where requirements for medical portable electronic devices have not been set by the foreign carrier's government and the foreign carrier elects to apply FAA requirements for medical portable electronic devices; or

(3) The device cannot be stowed and used in the passenger cabin consistent with applicable TSA, FAA and PHMSA regulations, and the safety or security regulations of the foreign carrier's government.

(c) Except as provided in paragraph (a) of this section, as a covered U.S. air carrier, you must accept the passenger supplied electronic assistive device in this paragraph (c):

(1) A portable oxygen concentrator (POC), a ventilator, a respirator or a continuous positive airway pressure machine that displays a manufacturer's label that indicates the device meets FAA requirements; and

(2) The following POC models whether or not they are labeled:

(i) AirSep Focus;

(ii) AirSep FreeStyle;

(iii) AirSep FreeStyle 5;

(iv) AirSep LifeStyle;

(v) Delphi RS–00400;

(vi) DeVilbiss Healthcare iGo;

(vii) Inogen One;

(viii) Inogen One G2;

(ix) Inogen One G3;

(x) Inova Labs LifeChoice;

(xi) Inova Labs LifeChoice Activox;

(xii) International Biophysics LifeChoice;

(xiii) Invacare Solo2;

(xiv) Invacare XPO2;

(xv) Oxlife Independence Oxygen Concentrator;

(xvi) Oxus RS–00400;

(xvii) Precision Medical EasyPulse;

(xviii) Respironics EverGo;

(xix) Respironics SimplyGo;

(xx) SeQual Eclipse;

(xxi) SeQual eQuinox Oxygen System (model 4000);

(xxii) SeQual Oxywell Oxygen System (model 4000);

(xxiii) SeQual SAROS; and

(xxiv) VBox Trooper Oxygen Concentrator.

(d) Except as provided in paragraph (b) of this section, as a covered foreign air carrier, you must accept the supplied electronic assistive devices in this paragraph (d):

(1) A POC, a ventilator, a respirator or a continuous positive airway pressure machine that displays a manufacturer's label according to FAA requirements in circumstances where requirements for labeling these devices have not been set by the foreign carrier's government; and

(2) The following POC models whether or not they are labeled:

(i) AirSep Focus;

(ii) AirSep FreeStyle;

(iii) AirSep FreeStyle 5;

(iv) AirSep LifeStyle;

(v) Delphi RS–00400;

(vi) DeVilbiss Healthcare iGo;

(vii) Inogen One;

(viii) Inogen One G2;

(ix) Inogen One G3;

(x) Inova Labs LifeChoice;

(xi) Inova Labs LifeChoice Activox;

(xii) International Biophysics LifeChoice;

(xiii) Invacare Solo2;

(xiv) Invacare XPO2;

(xv) Oxlife Independence Oxygen Concentrator;

(xvi) Oxus RS–00400;

(xvii) Precision Medical EasyPulse;

(xviii) Respironics EverGo;

(xix) Respironics SimplyGo;

(xx) SeQual Eclipse;

(xxi) SeQual eQuinox Oxygen System (model 4000);

(xxii) SeQual Oxywell Oxygen System (model 4000);

(xxiii) SeQual SAROS; and

(xxiv) VBox Trooper Oxygen Concentrator.

(e) As a U.S. carrier, you must provide information during the reservation process as indicated in paragraphs (e)(1) through (6) of this section upon inquiry from an individual concerning the use in the cabin during air transportation of a ventilator, respirator, continuous positive airway machine, or a POC. The information in this paragraph (e) must be provided:

(1) Any applicable requirement for a manufacturer-affixed label to reflect that the device has been tested to meet applicable FAA requirements for medical portable electronic devices;

(2) The maximum weight and dimensions (length, width, height) of the device to be used by an individual that can be accommodated in the aircraft cabin consistent with FAA safety requirements;

(3) The requirement to bring an adequate number of batteries as outlined in paragraph (h)(2) of this section and to ensure that extra batteries carried onboard to power the device are packaged and protected from short circuit and physical damage in accordance with applicable PHMSA regulations regarding spare batteries carried by passengers in an aircraft cabin;

(4) Any requirement, if applicable, that an individual contact the carrier operating the flight 48 hours before scheduled departure to learn the expected maximum duration of his/her flight in order to determine the required number of batteries for his/her particular ventilator, respirator, continuous positive airway pressure machine, or POC;

(5) Any requirement, if applicable, of the carrier operating the flight for an individual planning to use such a device to check-in up to one hour before that carrier's general check-in deadline; and

(6) For POCs, the requirement of § 382.23(b)(1)(ii) to present to the operating carrier at the airport a physician's statement (medical certificate).

(f) As a foreign carrier operating flights to, from or within the United States, you must provide the information during the reservation process as indicated in paragraphs (f)(1) through (7) of this section upon inquiry from an individual concerning the use in the cabin during air transportation on such a flight of a ventilator, respirator, continuous positive airway machine, or

POC. The information in this paragraph (f) must be provided:

(1) Any applicable requirement for a manufacturer-affixed label to reflect that the device has been tested to meet requirements for medical portable electronic devices set by the foreign carrier's government if such requirements exist;

(2) Any applicable requirement for a manufacturer-affixed label to reflect that the device has been tested to meet requirements for medical portable electronic devices set by the FAA for U.S. carriers if requirements for medical portable electronic devices have not been set by the foreign carrier's government and the foreign carrier elects to apply FAA requirements for medical portable electronic devices;

(3) The maximum weight and dimensions (length, width, height) of the device to be used by an individual that can be accommodated in the aircraft cabin consistent with the safety regulations of the foreign carrier's government;

(4) The requirement to bring an adequate number of batteries as outlined in paragraph (h)(2) of this section and to ensure that extra batteries carried onboard to power the device are packaged in accordance with applicable government safety regulations;

(5) Any requirement, if applicable, that an individual contact the carrier operating the flight 48 hours before scheduled departure to learn the expected maximum duration of his/her flight in order to determine the required number of batteries for his/her particular ventilator, respirator, continuous positive airway pressure machine, or POC;

(6) Any requirement, if applicable, of the carrier operating the flight for an individual planning to use such a device to check-in up to one hour before that carrier's general check-in deadline; and

(7) Any requirement, if applicable, that an individual who wishes to use a POC onboard an aircraft present to the operating carrier at the airport a physician's statement (medical certificate).

(g) In the case of a codeshare itinerary, the carrier whose code is used on the flight must either inform the individual inquiring about using a ventilator, respirator, CPAP machine or POC onboard an aircraft to contact the carrier operating the flight for information about its requirements for use of such devices in the cabin, or provide such information on behalf of the codeshare carrier operating the flight.

(h)(1) As a U.S. or foreign carrier subject to paragraph (a) or (b) of this section, you must inform any individual who has advised you that he or she plans to operate his/her device in the aircraft cabin, within 48 hours of his/her making a reservation or 24 hours before the scheduled departure date of his/her flight, whichever date is earlier, of the expected maximum flight duration of each segment of his/her flight itinerary.

(2) You may require an individual to bring an adequate number of fully charged batteries onboard, based on the battery manufacturer's estimate of the hours of battery life while the device is in use and the information provided in the physician's statement, to power the device for not less than 150% of the expected maximum flight duration.

(3) If an individual does not comply with the conditions for acceptance of a medical portable electronic device as outlined in this section, you may deny boarding to the individual in accordance with § 382.19(c) and in that event you must provide a written explanation to the individual in accordance with § 382.19(d).

[Doc. No. FAA–2014–0554, 81 FR 33120, May 24, 2016]

Subpart J—Training and Administrative Provisions

§ 382.141 What training are carriers required to provide for their personnel?

(a) As a carrier that operates aircraft with 19 or more passenger seats, you must provide training, meeting the requirements of this paragraph, for all personnel who deal with the traveling public, as appropriate to the duties of each employee.

(1) You must ensure training to proficiency concerning:

(i) The requirements of this part and other applicable Federal regulations affecting the provision of air travel to passengers with a disability;

(ii) Your procedures, consistent with this part, concerning the provision of air travel to passengers with a disability, including the proper and safe operation of any equipment used to accommodate passengers with a disability; and

(iii) For those personnel involved in providing boarding and deplaning assistance, the use of the boarding and deplaning assistance equipment used by the carrier and appropriate boarding and deplaning assistance procedures that safeguard the safety and dignity of passengers.

(2) You must also train such employees with respect to awareness and appropriate responses to passengers with a disability, including persons with physical, sensory, mental, and emotional disabilities, including how to distinguish among the differing abilities of individuals with a disability.

(3) You must also train these employees to recognize requests for communication accommodation from individuals whose hearing or vision is impaired and to use the most common methods for communicating with these individuals that are readily available, such as writing notes or taking care to enunciate clearly, for example. Training in sign language is not required. You must also train these employees to recognize requests for communication accommodation from deaf-blind passengers and to use established means of communicating with these passengers when they are available, such as passing out Braille cards if you have them, reading an information sheet that a passenger provides, or communicating with a passenger through an interpreter, for example.

(4) You must consult with organizations representing persons with disabilities in your home country when developing your training program and your policies and procedures. If such organizations are not available in your home country, you must consult with individuals with disabilities and/or international organizations representing individuals with disabilities.

(5) You must ensure that all personnel who are required to receive training receive refresher training on the matters covered by this section, as appropriate to the duties of each employee, as needed to maintain proficiency. You must develop a program that will result in each such employee receiving refresher training at least once every three years. The program must describe how employee proficiency will be maintained.

(6) You must provide, or ensure that your contractors provide, training to the contractors' employees concerning travel by passengers with a disability. This training is required only for those contractor employees who deal directly with the traveling public, and it must be tailored to the employees' functions. Training for contractor employees must meet the requirements of paragraphs (a)(1) through (a)(5) of this section.

(7) The employees you designate as CROs, for purposes of §382.151 of this part, must receive training concerning the requirements of this part and the duties of a CRO.

(8) Personnel subject to training required under this part, who are already employed on May 13, 2009, must be trained one time in the changes resulting from the reissuance of this part.

(b) If you are a carrier that operates only aircraft with fewer than 19 passenger seats, you must provide training for flight crewmembers and appropriate personnel to ensure that they are familiar with the matters listed in paragraphs (a)(1) and (a)(2) of this section and that they comply with the requirements of this part.

§382.143 When must carriers complete training for their personnel?

(a) As a U.S. carrier, you must meet the training requirements of §382.141 by the following times.

(1) Employees designated as CROs shall receive training concerning the requirements of this part and the duties of a CRO before assuming their duties under §382.151 (see §382.141(a)(7)). You must ensure that all employees performing the CRO function receive annual refresher training concerning their duties and the provisions of this regulation. The one-time training for CROs about the changes to Part 382 must take place by May 13, 2009. For employees who have already received

CRO training, this training may be limited to changes from the previous version of Part 382.

(2) The one-time training for existing employees about changes to Part 382 (see § 382.141(a)(8)) must take place for each such employee no later than the next scheduled recurrent training taking place after May 13, 2009 or within one year after May 13, 2009, whichever comes first.

(3) For crewmembers subject to training requirements under 14 CFR Part 121 or 135 whose employment in any given position commences after May 13, 2009, before they assume their duties; and

(4) For other personnel whose employment in any given position commences after May 13, 2009, within 60 days after the date on which they assume their duties.

(b) As a foreign carrier that operates aircraft with 19 or more passenger seats, you must provide training meeting the requirements of § 382.141(a) for all personnel who deal with the traveling public in connection with flights that begin or end at a U.S. airport, as appropriate to the duties of each employee. You must ensure that personnel required to receive training complete the training by the following times:

(1) Employees designated as CROs shall receive training in accordance with paragraph (a)(1) of this section, by May 13, 2009.

(2) For crewmembers and other personnel who are employed on May 13, 2009, within one year after that date;

(3) For crewmembers whose employment commences after May 13, 2010, before they assume their duties;

(4) For other personnel whose employment in any given position commences after May 13, 2010, or within 60 days after the date on which they assume their duties; and

(5) For crewmembers and other personnel whose employment in any given position commences after May 13, 2009, but before May 13, 2010, by May 13, 2010 or a date 60 days after the date of their employment, whichever is later.

[Doc. No. DOT–OST–2004–19482, 73 FR 27665, May 13, 2008, as amended at 74 FR 11472, Mar. 18, 2009]

§ 382.145 What records concerning training must carriers retain?

(a) As a carrier that operates aircraft with 19 or more passenger seats, you must incorporate procedures implementing the requirements of this part in the manuals or other guidance or instructional materials provided for the carrier and contract personnel who provide services to passengers, including, but not limited to, pilots, flight attendants, reservation and ticket counter personnel, gate agents, ramp and baggage handling personnel, and passenger service office personnel. You must retain these records for review by the Department on the Department's request. If, upon such review, the Department determines that any portion of these materials must be changed in order to comply with this part, DOT will direct you to make appropriate changes. You must incorporate and implement these changes.

(b) You must retain for three years individual employee training records demonstrating that all persons required to receive initial and refresher training have done so.

Subpart K—Complaints and Enforcement Procedures

§ 382.151 What are the requirements for providing Complaints Resolution Officials?

(a) As a carrier providing service using aircraft with 19 or more passenger seats, you must designate one or more CROs.

(b) As a U.S. carrier, you must make a CRO available at each airport you serve during all times you are operating at that airport. As a foreign carrier, you must make a CRO available at each airport serving flights you operate that begin or end at a U.S. airport. You may make the CRO available in person at the airport or via telephone, at no cost to the passenger. If a telephone link to the CRO is used, TTY service or a similarly effective technology must be available so that persons with hearing impairments may readily communicate with the CRO. You must make CRO service available in the language(s) in which you make your services available to the general public.

(c) You must make passengers with a disability aware of the availability of a CRO and how to contact the CRO in the following circumstances:

(1) In any situation in which any person complains or raises a concern with your personnel about discrimination, accommodations, or services with respect to passengers with a disability, and your personnel do not immediately resolve the issue to the customer's satisfaction or provide a requested accommodation, your personnel must immediately inform the passenger of the right to contact a CRO and then contact a CRO on the passenger's behalf or provide the passenger a means to do so (*e.g.*, a phone, a phone card plus the location and/or phone number of the CRO available at the airport). Your personnel must provide this information to the passenger in a format he or she can use.

(2) Your reservation agents, contractors, and Web sites must provide information equivalent to that required by paragraph (c)(1) of this section to passengers with a disability using those services who complain or raise a concern about a disability-related issue.

(d) Each CRO must be thoroughly familiar with the requirements of this part and the carrier's procedures with respect to passengers with a disability. The CRO is intended to be the carrier's "expert" in compliance with the requirements of this part.

(e) You must ensure that each of your CROs has the authority to make dispositive resolution of complaints on behalf of the carrier. This means that the CRO must have the power to overrule the decision of any other personnel, except that the CRO is not required to be given authority to countermand a decision of the pilot-in-command of an aircraft based on safety.

[Doc. No. DOT-OST-2004-19482, 73 FR 27665, May 13, 2008, as amended at 74 FR 11472, Mar. 18, 2009; 75 FR 44887, July 30, 2010]

§ 382.153 What actions do CROs take on complaints?

When a complaint is made directly to a CRO for a carrier providing service using aircraft with 19 or more passenger seats, the CRO must promptly take dispositive action as follows:

(a) If the complaint is made to a CRO before the action or proposed action of carrier personnel has resulted in a violation of a provision of this part, the CRO must take, or direct other carrier personnel to take, whatever action is necessary to ensure compliance with this part.

(b) If an alleged violation of a provision of this part has already occurred, and the CRO agrees that a violation has occurred, the CRO must provide to the complainant a written statement setting forth a summary of the facts and what steps, if any, the carrier proposes to take in response to the violation.

(c) If the CRO determines that the carrier's action does not violate a provision of this part, the CRO must provide to the complainant a written statement including a summary of the facts and the reasons, under this part, for the determination.

(d) The statements required to be provided under this section must inform the complainant of his or her right to pursue DOT enforcement action under this part. The CRO must provide the statement in person to the complainant at the airport if possible; otherwise, it must be forwarded to the complainant within 30 calendar days of the complaint.

[Doc. No. DOT-OST-2004-19482, 73 FR 27665, May 13, 2008, as amended at 75 FR 44887, July 30, 2010]

§ 382.155 How must carriers respond to written complaints?

(a) As a carrier providing service using aircraft with 19 or more passenger seats, you must respond to written complaints received by any means (*e.g.*, letter, fax, e-mail, electronic instant message) concerning matters covered buy this part.

(b) As a passenger making a written complaint, you must state whether you had contacted a CRO in the matter, provide the name of the CRO and the date of the contact, if available, and enclose any written response you received from the CRO.

(c) As a carrier, you are not required to respond to a complaint postmarked or transmitted more than 45 days after the date of the incident, except for complaints referred to you by the Department of Transportation.

(d) As a carrier, you must make a dispositive written response to a written disability complaint within 30 days of its receipt. The response must specifically admit or deny that a violation of this part has occurred.

(1) If you admit that a violation has occurred, you must provide to the complainant a written statement setting forth a summary of the facts and the steps, if any, you will take in response to the violation.

(2) If you deny that a violation has occurred, your response must include a summary of the facts and your reasons, under this part, for the determination.

(3) Your response must also inform the complainant of his or her right to pursue DOT enforcement action under this part.

[Doc. No. DOT–OST–2004–19482, 73 FR 27665, May 13, 2008, as amended at 75 FR 44887, July 30, 2010]

§ 382.157 What are carriers' obligations for recordkeeping and reporting on disability-related complaints?

(a) For the purposes of this section, a disability-related complaint means a specific written expression of dissatisfaction received from, or submitted on behalf, of an individual with a disability concerning a difficulty associated with the person's disability, which the person experienced when using or attempting to use an air carrier's or foreign carrier's services.

(b) If you are a carrier covered by this part, conducting passenger operations with at least one aircraft having a designed seating capacity of more than 60 passengers, this section applies to you. As a foreign carrier, you are covered by this section only with respect to disability-related complaints associated with any flight segment originating or terminating in the United States.

(c) You must categorize disability-related complaints that you receive according to the type of disability and nature of complaint. Data concerning a passenger's disability must be recorded separately in the following areas: vision impaired, hearing impaired, vision and hearing impaired, mentally impaired, communicable disease, allergies (*e.g.*, food allergies, chemical sensitivity), paraplegic, quadriplegic, other wheelchair, oxygen, stretcher, other assistive device (cane, respirator, etc.), and other disability. Data concerning the alleged discrimination or service problem related to the disability must be separately recorded in the following areas: refusal to board, refusal to board without an attendant, security issues concerning disability, aircraft not accessible, airport not accessible, advance notice dispute, seating accommodation, failure to provide adequate or timely assistance, damage to assistive device, storage and delay of assistive device, service animal problem, unsatisfactory information, and other.

(d) You must submit an annual report summarizing the disability-related complaints that you received during the prior calendar year using the form specified at the following internet address: *http://382reporting.ost.dot.gov*. You must submit this report by the last Monday in January of each year for complaints received during the prior calendar year. You must make submissions through the World Wide Web except for situations where you can demonstrate that you would suffer undue hardship if not permitted to submit the data via paper copies, disks, or e-mail, and DOT has approved an exception. All fields in the form must be completed; carriers are to enter "0" where there were no complaints in a given category. Each annual report must contain the following certification signed by your authorized representative: "I, the undersigned, do certify that this report has been prepared under my direction in accordance with the regulations in 14 CFR Part 382. I affirm that, to the best of my knowledge and belief, this is a true, correct, and complete report." Electronic signatures will be accepted.

(e) You must retain correspondence and record of action taken on all disability-related complaints for three years after receipt of the complaint or creation of the record of action taken. You must make these records available to Department of Transportation officials at their request.

(f)(1) As either carrier in a codeshare relationship, you must comply with paragraphs (c) through (e) of this section for—

(i) Disability-related complaints you receive from or on behalf of passengers with respect to difficulties encountered in connection with service you provide;

(ii) Disability-related complaints you receive from or on behalf of passengers when you are unable to reach agreement with your codeshare partner as to whether the complaint involves service you provide or service your codeshare partner provides; and

(iii) Disability-related complaints forwarded by another carrier or governmental agency with respect to difficulties encountered in connection with service you provide.

(2) As either carrier in a codeshare relationship, you must forward to your codeshare partner disability-related complaints you receive from or on behalf of passengers with respect to difficulties encountered in connection with service provided by your codesharing partner.

(g) Each carrier, except for carriers in codeshare situations, shall comply with paragraphs (c) through (e) of this section for disability-related complaints it receives from or on behalf of passengers as well as disability-related complaints forwarded by another carrier or governmental agency with respect to difficulties encountered in connection with service it provides.

(h) Carriers that do not submit their data via the Web shall use the disability-related complaint data form specified in appendix A to this part when filing their annual report summarizing the disability-related complaints they received. The report shall be mailed, by the date specified in paragraph (d) of this section, to the following address: U.S. Department of Transportation, Aviation Consumer Protection Division (C–75), 1200 New Jersey Avenue, SE., West Building, Room W96–432, Washington, DC 20590.

§ 382.159 How are complaints filed with DOT?

(a) Any person believing that a carrier has violated any provision of this part may seek assistance or file an informal complaint at the Department of Transportation no later than 6 months after the date of the incident by either:

(1) Going to the web site of the Department's Aviation Consumer Protection Division at *http://airconsumer.ost.dot.gov* and selecting "Air Travel Problems and Complaints," or

(2) Writing to Department of Transportation, Aviation Consumer Protection Division (C–75), 1200 New Jersey Avenue, SE., Washington, DC 20590.

(b) Any person believing that a carrier has violated any provision of this part may also file a formal complaint under the applicable procedures of 14 CFR part 302.

(c) You must file a formal complaint under this part within six months of the incident on which the complaint is based in order to ensure that the Department of Transportation will investigate the matter.

APPENDIX A TO PART 382—REPORT OF DISABILITY-RELATED COMPLAINT DATA

APPENDIX A TO PART 382 – REPORT OF DISABILITY-RELATED COMPLAINT DATA

Name of Carrier: ____________________ Submission Date: ____________________

Contact Person: Period of Data Collection: ____________________

Name: ____________________

Telephone # (include country code if outside the U.S.): ____________________

Email address: ____________________

Mailing address: ____________________

Total number of complaints (i.e., incidents): ____________________

REPORT OF DISABILITY-RELATED COMPLAINT DATA

	Vision Impaired	Hearing Impaired	Vision & Hearing Impaired	Paraplegic	Quadriplegic	Other wheelchair	Oxygen	Stretcher	Other Disability	Other Assistive Device	Mentally Impaired	Communicable Disease	Allergies
Refusal To Board Passenger													
Refusal to Board w/o Attendant													
Security Issues Regarding Disability													
Aircraft Not Accessible													
Airport Not Accessible													
Advance Notice Dispute													
Seating Accomm-odation													
Failure to Provide Assistance													

	Vision Impaired	Hearing Impaired	Vision & Hearing Impaired	Paraplegic	Quadriplegic	Other wheelchair	Oxygen	Stretcher	Other Disability	Other Assistive Device	Mentally Impaired	Communicable Disease	Allergies
Damage to Assistive Device													
Storage and Delay of Assistive Device													
Service Animal Problem													
Unsatisfac -tory Info													
Other													

Certification Statement: I, the undersigned, do certify that this report has been prepared under my direction in accordance with the regulations in 14 CFR Part 382. I affirm that, to the best of my knowledge and belief, this is a true, correct, and complete report

Signature: ______________________________

The valid OMB control number for this information collection is 2105-0551. The time required to complete this information is estimated to average 30 minutes per response.

Appendix B to Part 382—Cross-Reference Table

The Department is providing the following table to assist users familiar with the current Part 382 in finding material in the new, renumbered Part 382.

SECTION NUMBERS: OLD AND NEW RULES

Old section (382.x)	New section (382.x)	Subject
General provisions:		
1	1	Purpose.
3	7	Applicability.
5	3	Definitions.
7	11, 13	Non-discrimination generally.
9	15	Contractors.
Aircraft accessibility:		
21(a)(1)	61	Movable armrests.
21(a)(2)	67	Stowage space in cabin for passenger wheelchair.
21(a)(3)	63	Accessible lavatories.
21(a)(4)	65	Carrier-supplied on-board wheelchair.
21(e) and (f)	71	Aircraft accessibility: miscellaneous.
Airport accessibility:		
23	51	General.
(New)	53	Vision/hearing impairments.
Services and information:		
31	19	Refusal of transportation.
31(c)	17	Number limits.
33	25, 27	Advance notice requirements.
35	29	Safety assistants (formerly “attendants”).
37	87(a)	Seat assignments.
38	81 through 87	Seating accommodations.
39(a)	91 through 105	Enplaning, deplaning and connecting assistance.
39(b)	111 through 119	Assistance in cabin.
40 and 40a	95, 99	Mechanical lifts.
41	121 through 133	Stowage of assistive devices, POCs and other respiratory assistive devices.
43(a)	129(b)	Timely return of assistive devices.
43(b)	131	Liability limits.
43(c)	35	Liability waivers.
45(a)	41	Access to information (general).
45(b)	115	Individual safety briefings.
45(c)	119	Access to information in airport and aircraft.
45(d)	45	Availability of copy of rule.
47(a)	43	TTY's and reservations systems.
47(b)	69	Accessibility of videos on aircraft.
49	55	Security screening.
51	21	Communicable diseases.
53	23	Medical certificates.
55(a)	117	Service animals.
55(b)	33	Sitting on blankets.
55(c)	33	Restricting movement.
55	31	Charges for accommodations.
Administrative provisions:		
61	141, 143	Training.
63(c) and (d)	145	Manuals; directed changes.
65(a)	151, 153	Complaints Resolution Officials.
65(b)	155, 157	Written complaints to carriers.
65(c) and (d)	159	Complaints to DOT.

[Doc. No. DOT–OST–2004–19482, 73 FR 27665, May 13, 2008, as amended at 74 FR 11472, Mar. 18, 2009]

PART 383—CIVIL PENALTIES

Sec.
383.1 Purpose and periodic adjustment.
383.2 Amount of penalty.

AUTHORITY: Sec. 701, Pub. L. 114–74, 129 Stat. 584; Sec. 503, Pub. L. 108–176, 117 Stat. 2490; Pub. L. 101–410, 104 Stat. 890; Sec. 31001, Pub. L. 104–134.

SOURCE: 83 FR 60743, Nov. 27, 2018, unless otherwise noted.

§ 383.1 Purpose and periodic adjustment.

(a) *Purpose.* This part adjusts the civil penalty liability amounts prescribed in 49 U.S.C. 46301(a) for inflation in accordance with the Act cited in paragraph (b) of this section.

(b) *Periodic Adjustment.* DOT will periodically adjust the maximum civil penalties set forth in 49 U.S.C. 46301 and this part as required by the Federal Civil Penalties Inflation Adjustment Act of 1990 as amended by the Federal Civil Penalties Inflation Adjustment Act Improvements Act of 2015.

§ 383.2 Amount of penalty.

Civil penalties payable to the U.S. Government for violations of Title 49, Chapters 401 through 421, pursuant to 49 U.S.C. 46301(a), are as follows:

(a) A general civil penalty of not more than $33,333 (or $1,466 for individuals or small businesses) applies to violations of statutory provisions and rules or orders issued under those provisions, other than those listed in paragraph (b) of this section, (*see* 49 U.S.C. 46301(a)(1));

(b) With respect to small businesses and individuals, notwithstanding the general $1,466 civil penalty, the following civil penalty limits apply:

(1) A maximum civil penalty of $13,333 applies for violations of most provisions of Chapter 401, including the anti-discrimination provisions of sections 40127 (general provision), and 41705 (discrimination against the disabled) and rules and orders issued pursuant to those provisions (*see* 49 U.S.C. 46301(a)(5)(A));

(2) A maximum civil penalty of $6,666 applies for violations of section 41719 and rules and orders issued pursuant to that provision (*see* 49 U.S.C. 46301(a)(5)(C)); and

(3) A maximum civil penalty of $3,334 applies for violations of section 41712 or consumer protection rules or orders (*see* 49 U.S.C. 46301(a)(5)(D)).

SUBCHAPTER E—ORGANIZATION

PART 385—STAFF ASSIGNMENTS AND REVIEW OF ACTION UNDER ASSIGNMENTS

Subpart A—General Provisions

Subpart B—Assignment of Functions to Staff Members

Subpart C—Procedure on Review of Staff Action

AUTHORITY: 49 U.S.C. 329 and chapters 40101, 41101, 41301, and 41701.

SOURCE: Docket No. T-1, 49 FR 50985, Dec. 31, 1984, unless otherwise noted.

Subpart A—General Provisions

§ 385.1 Definitions.

Department means Department of Transportation.

Petition for review means a petition asking the appropriate Reviewing Official to exercise his or her discretionary right of review of staff action.

Precedent means applicable judicial decisions and decisions by the Department, or by the Board where consistent with Department policy.

Reviewing Official means the Assistant Secretary for Aviation and International Affairs, the General Counsel, or the Director of the Bureau of Transportation Statistics, as appropriate to the subject matter under review, but not with regard to Deputy General Counsel and Administrative Law Judge decisions made under this part.

Staff action means the exercise of a function under Subparts I, II and IV of Subtitle VII of Title 49 of the United States Code (Transportation) by a staff member pursuant to assignment under this part.

Staff members means officers and employees of the Department who are assigned authority under this part.

Statute means Subtitle VII of Title 49 of the United States Code (Transportation).

[Doc. No. T-1, 49 FR 50985, Dec. 31, 1984, as amended by Amdt. 1-261, 59 FR 10061, Mar. 3, 1994; 60 FR 66726, Dec. 26, 1995; Doc. No. OST-96-1268, 61 FR 19167, May 1, 1996]

§ 385.2 Applicability.

This part describes the organization of the Department insofar as, pursuant to authority conferred on it by section 40113 of the Statute, the Department has adopted rules herein or elsewhere which make continuing assignments of authority with respect to any of its functions of making orders or other determinations, many of which are not required to be made on an evidentiary record upon notice and hearing or which are not the subject of contest, and Department personnel have been assigned to perform such functions.

Delegations by the Secretary of Transportation to Secretarial Officers and the Director, Bureau of Transportation Statistics (BTS) of functions under Subparts I, II, and IV of the Statute appear in 49 CFR part 1. This part also sets forth the procedures governing discretionary review by the appropriate Reviewing Official of action taken under such assignments. Nothing in this part shall be construed as precluding the Department from issuing, by appropriate order, temporary delegations of authority with respect to any functions described in this part or with respect to any other functions which can be lawfully delegated.

[Doc. No. T–1, 49 FR 50985, Dec. 31, 1984, as amended at 60 FR 66726, Dec. 26, 1995; Doc. No. OST–96–1268, 61 FR 19167, May 1, 1996]

§385.3 Scope of staff action.

Applications for relief which, pursuant to this part, may be granted by staff members under assigned authority, and proceedings on such requests shall be governed by applicable rules in the same manner as if no assignment had been made (see §385.5). In such proceedings, each staff member may determine any procedural matters which may arise, including, inter alia, service of documents on additional persons; filing of otherwise unauthorized documents; waivers of procedural requirements; requests for hearing; requests for additional information; dismissal of applications upon the applicant's request, moot applications, or incomplete or otherwise defective applications; and extensions of time. Such determinations, except those which would terminate the matter, shall be subject to review only in connection with review of the staff member's decision on the merits. The dismissal of incomplete or otherwise defective applications under authority set forth in this part shall be without prejudice except where under otherwise applicable law the time for making application has run out or where the defect is not corrected within a reasonable time fixed by the staff member. Under the authority assigned to the staff as set forth in this part to approve, disapprove, grant, or deny, relief may be granted or denied in part and grants may be made subject to lawful and reasonable conditions. Moreover, where applicable, the authority to grant relief also includes authority to renew or extend an existing authorization.

[Doc. No. T–1, 49 FR 50985, Dec. 31, 1984; Amdt. 1, 50 FR 7170, Feb. 21, 1985]

§385.4 Form of staff action.

Unless otherwise specified, staff action shall be by order or informal writing (letters, telegrams, decision marked on copy of application form, etc.). Such orders or informal writings shall contain a recital that action is taken pursuant to authority assigned herein, shall, in cases where there are "parties or interveners," or where there may be an adverse effect upon a person with a substantial interest, contain a brief reference to the right of aggrieved parties to petition the Reviewing Official for review pursuant to applicable procedural rules, including a statement of the time within which petitions must be filed (§385.51); shall state whether the filing of a petition shall preclude the action from becoming effective; and shall be in the name of the person exercising the assigned function. They shall contain all findings, determinations and conclusions which would be required or appropriate if they were issued by the Secretary. Upon request, the appropriate Department Official shall attest as Departmental action orders or informal writings issued pursuant to this part which have become the action of the Department (§385.52).

[Doc. No. T–1, 49 FR 50985, Dec. 31, 1984; Amdt. 1, 50 FR 7170, Feb. 21, 1985]

§385.5 Procedures prescribed in other regulations.

Procedures set forth in this part do not supersede procedures applicable to matters on which decision has been assigned unless otherwise specifically provided herein: *Provided, however,* That any provisions in other regulations which provide for reconsideration of nonhearing determinations are not applicable to decisions made under authority assigned herein or to decisions made upon review thereof by the Reviewing Official.

§ 385.6 Referral to the Reviewing Official.

When the staff member finds that the public interest so requires, or that, with respect to other than matters requiring immediate action as hereafter specified, there will be insufficient time for discretionary review of his or her decision upon petition, the staff member shall, in lieu of exercising the authority, submit the matter to the Reviewing Official for decision. In any case in which the staff member finds that immediate action is required with respect to any matter assigned herein, the disposition of which is governed by prior precedent and policy, the staff member may take appropriate action and specify that the filing of a petition for review shall not preclude such action from becoming effective.

§ 385.7 Exercise of authority by superiors.

Any assignment of authority to a staff member other than the Chief Administrative Law Judge, the Administrative Law Judge, and the Deputy General Counsel, shall also be deemed to be made, severally, to each such staff member's respective superiors. In accordance with the Department's principle of management responsibility, the superior may choose to exercise the assigned power personally. Moreover, the Secretary may at any time exercise any authority assigned herein.

§ 385.8 Exercise of authority in "acting" capacity.

Unless the assignment provides otherwise, staff members serving in an "acting" capacity may exercise the authority assigned to the staff members for whom they are acting.

Subpart B—Assignment of Functions to Staff Members

§ 385.10 Authority of Chief Administrative Law Judge, Office of Hearings.

The Chief Administrative Law Judge has authority to:

(a) Consolidate, upon recommendation of the Director, Office of International Aviation (or such staff member of the Office of International Aviation as he or she may designate), into one proceeding cases involving the investigation of a tariff or of complaints concerned with related tariffs.

(b) With respect to matters to be decided after notice and hearing:

(1) Dismiss applications or complaints (except those falling under subpart D of part 302 of this chapter (Procedural Regulations)) when such dismissal is requested or consented to by the applicant or complainant, or where such party has failed to prosecute such application or complaint;

(2) Dismiss proceedings upon his or her finding that the proceeding has become moot or that no further basis for continuation exists; and

(3) Dismiss an application subject to dismissal as stale under part 302 of this chapter.

[49 FR 50985, Dec. 31, 1984, as amended at 55 FR 20448, May 17, 1990; 65 FR 6457, Feb. 9, 2000]

§ 385.11 Authority of the Administrative Law Judges, Office of Hearings.

The Administrative Law Judges, Office of Hearings, have authority to take the following actions in matters to which they are respectively assigned:

(a) Grant or deny intervention in formal proceedings.

(b) With respect to matters to be decided after notice and hearing, dismiss applications or complaints (except those falling under subpart D of part 302 of this chapter (Procedural Regulations)) when such dismissal is requested or consented to by the applicant or complainant, or where such party has failed to prosecute such application or complaint.

(c) Grant requests for consolidation of applications for route authority within the scope of the proceeding before him or her, and deny requests for consolidation of applications for route authority not within the scope of the proceeding.

(d) Approve or disapprove proposed settlements of enforcement proceedings submitted under § 302.215 of this chapter.

[Doc. No. T–1, 49 FR 50985, Dec. 31, 1984, as amended at 65 FR 6457, Feb. 9, 2000]

§385.12 Authority of the Director, Office of Aviation Analysis.

The Director, Office of Aviation Analysis, has authority:

(a) With respect to applications filed under section 41102 to engage in interstate or foreign scheduled or charter air transportation, section 41103 to engage in all-cargo air transportation, or section 41738 to engage in certain commuter air transportation:

(1) To issue an order stating the Department's intention to process the application through show-cause procedures or other expedited procedures, where that course of action is clear under current policy and precedent.

(2) To issue an order to show cause proposing to grant such application in those cases where no objections to the application have been filed, and where the Department has already found the applicant to be fit, willing and able to provide service of the same basic scope and character.

(3) To issue an order, subject to any Presidential review required under section 41307 of the Statute, making final an order to show cause issued under paragraph (a)(2) of this section, where no objections to the order to show cause have been filed.

(4) To issue an order dismissing an application:

(i) When dismissal is requested or consented to by the applicant;

(ii) For lack of prosecution; or

(iii) When the application has become moot.

(5) To review Air Carrier Certificates and Operations Specifications issued by the Federal Aviation Administration to carriers that have been granted certificate or commuter air carrier authority, and information concerning those carriers' fitness to operate under that authority that emerged following the issuance of orders establishing their fitness, and—

(i) To amend orders issuing the certificate or commuter air carrier authority to advance the effective dates of the authority if the review is satisfactory;

(ii) To stay the effectiveness of such orders for up to 30 days if the review is unsatisfactory;

(iii) To lift the stay of effectiveness imposed under paragraph (a)(5)(ii) of this section when the unsatisfactory conditions that required issuance of the stay have been resolved; or

(iv) To issue notices announcing the effective date of the certificate or commuter air carrier authority.

(b) To approve or deny applications of air carriers:

(1) For exemptions from section 41102 or 41103 of the Statute, and from orders issued thereunder, and from applicable regulations under this chapter where the course of action is clear under current policy or precedent.

(2) For waivers of the Department's filing fee requirements under part 389 of this chapter, in accordance with current policy or precedent.

(3) For relief under section 40109 of the Statute to hold out, arrange, and coordinate the operation of air ambulance flights as indirect air carriers in accordance with established precedent.

(c) To waive the deadlines in §377.10(c) of this chapter for filing applications for the renewal of temporary authorizations when, in the Director's judgment, the public interest would be served. The provisions of §377.10(d) of this chapter shall apply in the same manner as to a timely filed application.

(d) With respect to air carrier names:

(1) To register names and trade names of certificated and commuter air carriers pursuant to part 215 of this chapter.

(2) To reissue certificates issued under sections 41102 or 41103 of the Statute when revisions thereof are necessitated by a change in the name of a carrier, provided that no issue of substance concerning the operating authority of the carrier is involved.

(e) To approve, deny, or cancel registrations filed with the Department by air taxi operators pursuant to part 298 of this chapter.

(f) With respect to Canadian charter air taxi operations:

(1) To approve applications for registration, or require that a registrant submit additional information, or reject an application for registration for failure to comply with part 294 of this chapter.

(2) To cancel, revoke, or suspend the registration of any Canadian charter air taxi operator using small aircraft

registered under part 294 of this chapter that:

(i) Filed with the Department a written notice that it is discontinuing operations;

(ii) No longer is designated by its home government to operate the services contemplated by its registration;

(iii) Holds a foreign air carrier permit under section 41302 to operate large aircraft charters between the United States and Canada;

(iv) Fails to keep its filed certificate of insurance current;

(v) No longer is substantially owned or effectively controlled by persons who are:

(A) Citizens of Canada;

(B) The Government of Canada; or

(C) A combination of both; or

(vi) No longer holds current effective Operations Specifications issued by the FAA.

(3) To grant or deny requests for a waiver of part 294 of this chapter, where grant or denial of the request is in accordance with current policy or precedent.

(g) To approve certificates of insurance filed with the Department on behalf of U.S. and foreign air carriers in accordance with the provisions of part 205 of this chapter.

(h) With respect to foreign air freight forwarders:

(1) To approve applications for registration, or require that a registrant submit additional information, or reject an application for registration for failure to comply with part 297 of this chapter.

(2) To cancel the registration of any foreign air freight forwarder or foreign cooperative shippers association that files a written notice with the Department indicating the discontinuance of common carrier activities.

(3) To exempt the registrant from the requirement contained in § 297.20 of this chapter that substantial ownership and effective control reside in citizens of the country that the applicant claims as its country of citizenship, where the course of action is clear under current precedent or policies.

(i) With respect to charter operations:

(1) To grant or deny requests for waiver of parts 207, 208, 212, 372, and 380 of this chapter, where grant or denial of the request is in accordance with established precedent.

(2) To approve or disapprove direct air carrier escrow agreements filed pursuant to parts 207, 208, and 212 of this chapter.

(3) To reject or accept Public Charter prospectuses filed under part 380 of this chapter.

(4) With respect to the procedures for the registration of foreign charter operators under subpart F of part 380 of this chapter:

(i) To approve applications for registration, or require that a registrant submit additional information, or reject an application for registration for failure to comply with part 380 of this chapter.

(ii) To notify the applicant that its application will require further analysis or procedures, or is being referred to the Assistant Secretary for Aviation and International Affairs for formal action.

(iii) To cancel the registration of a foreign charter operator if it files a written notice with the Department that it is discontinuing its charter operations.

(iv) To waive provisions of subpart F of part 380 of this chapter.

(j) With respect to mail rates:

(1) To issue show-cause orders proposing to make modifications of a technical nature in the mail rate formula applicable to temporary or final service mail rate orders.

(2) To issue final orders establishing temporary and final service mail rates:

(i) In those cases where no objection has been filed following release of the show-cause order, and where the rates established are the same as those proposed in the show-cause order; and

(ii) In those cases where it is necessary to make modifications of a technical nature in the rates proposed in the show-cause order.

(3) To issue final orders amending mail rate orders of air carriers to reflect changes in the names of the carriers subject to the orders.

(4) To issue a letter, in the case of air mail contracts filed with the Department under part 302 of this chapter against which no complaints have been filed, stating that the contract will not

be disapproved by the Department and may become effective immediately.

(k) With respect to essential air service proceedings:

(1) To establish procedural dates.

(2) To issue orders setting interim rates of compensation for carriers required to provide essential air service.

(3) To issue orders approving a carrier's alternate service pattern if:

(i) The resulting level of service at the eligible place would be equal to or greater than the level of service earlier determined to be essential for that place;

(ii) The community concerned does not object to the carrier's implementation of the alternate service pattern; and

(iii) The carrier is not receiving a subsidy for the service or implementation of the alternate service pattern would not increase the carrier's subsidy.

(4) To issue orders adjusting the operational and/or financial unit rates of the payout formula for a carrier receiving subsidy under section 41732 of the Statute where the adjustment will not increase the total amount of compensation that the carrier will receive.

(5) To renew, up to five times in succession, an order under section 41734 of the Statute to an air carrier to continue providing essential air service while the Department attempts to find a replacement carrier.

(6) To request service and subsidy proposals from carriers interested in providing essential air service to an eligible place that is not receiving essential air service and for which no appeal of its essential air service determination is pending.

(7) To request service and subsidy proposals from carriers interested in providing essential air service when no proposals were filed in response to a previous request for proposals.

(8) To issue final orders establishing interim or final subsidy rates under section 41732 or final adjustments of compensation for continued service under section 41732 in those cases where no objection has been filed to a show-cause order, and where the rates established are the same as or less than those proposed in the approved show-cause order.

(9) With respect to provisions for terminations, suspensions, or reductions of service under part 323 of this chapter:

(i) To require any person who files a notice, objection, or answer to supply additional information.

(ii) To require service of a notice, objection, or answer upon any person.

(iii) To accept late-filed objections or answers, upon motion, for good cause shown.

(iv) To extend the time for filing objections for answers, when the initial notice has been filed earlier than required under §323.5.

[Doc. No. OST–96–1268, 61 FR 19167, May 1, 1996, as amended at 70 FR 25773, May 16, 2005]

§385.13 Authority of the Director, Office of International Aviation.

The Director, Office of International Aviation, has authority to:

(a) Approve or deny applications for exemptions, where the course of action is clear under current policy or precedent:

(1) For air carriers, from chapter 411 of the Statute and from certificates and orders issued under that chapter;

(2) For foreign air carriers, from section 41301 and from permits and related orders issued under chapter 413;

(3) For air carriers and foreign air carriers, from chapter 415 and from orders issued and tariffs filed under that chapter; and

(4) From orders and applicable regulations under this chapter.

(b) With respect to applications for certificates of public convenience and necessity under section 41102 and foreign air carrier permits under section 41302:

(1) Issue an order to show cause proposing to grant such application in those cases where no objections to the application have been filed, and the applicant has already been found fit, willing, and able by the Department to provide service of the same basic scope and character;

(2) Issue an order stating the Department's intention to process the application through show-cause procedures;

(3) Issue an order, subject to Presidential review under section 41307, to make final an order to show cause

issued under the circumstances of paragraph (b)(1) of this section, where no objections to the show-cause order have been filed; and

(4) Reissue certificates of public convenience and necessity and foreign air carrier permits when revisions are necessitated by a change in the name of the carrier or of points specified, provided that no issue of substance concerning the operating authority of a carrier is involved.

(c) With respect to an application under section 41102 for a certificate to engage in foreign scheduled air transportation, issue an order instituting an investigation of the applicant's fitness and other issues related to the application, where no person has already filed an objection to the application and the investigation will be conducted by oral hearing procedures.

(d) Issue an order to show cause why a foreign air carrier permit should not be revoked under section 41304 when:

(1) The government of the permit holder's home country represents that it does not object to revocation of the permit; and

(2) The permit holder—

(i) Has ceased operations; or

(ii) No longer holds valid authority from its own government to operate the services in its permit.

(e) Approve or disapprove requests by foreign air carriers for authorizations provided for, or waivers of restrictions contained, in any agreement or in any permit or order of the Department, when no person disclosing a substantial interest objects or where the course of action is clear under current policy or precedent.

(f) Waive the deadlines in § 377.10(c) of this chapter for filing applications for renewal of unexpired temporary authorizations when, in the Director's judgment, the public interest would be served. The provisions of § 377.10(d) of this chapter shall apply in the same manner as to a timely filed application.

(g) Extend the time allowed for action on a complaint of unfair or discriminatory practices, filed under section 41310, for an additional period or periods of 30 days each, not to exceed the 180th day after filing unless that deadline has been waived by the complainant.

(h) Grant or deny applications for statements of authorization under parts 207, 208, and 212 of this chapter, and requests for waivers of the requirements of parts 207, 208, and 212 of this chapter, where grant or denial of the request is in accordance with current policy or precedent.

(i) Approve or disapprove charter trips by foreign air carriers, and those by air carriers that are predominantly in foreign air transportation, when prior authorization is required by:

(1) Any provision of this chapter; or

(2) An order of the Department.

(j) Approve or disapprove requests by foreign air carriers for waivers of the 30-day advance filing requirement for proposed schedules whose filing the Department has ordered under part 213 of this chapter.

(k) Approve, when no person disclosing a substantial interest objects, or disapprove requests by foreign air carriers for special authorizations provided for in part 216 of this chapter.

(l) With respect to applications for statements of authorization to conduct intermodal cargo services under part 222 of this chapter:

(1) Approve applications under part 222 of this chapter where no person with a substantial interest raises objections citing specific facts of nonreciprocity or of restraints on competition by U.S. air carriers;

(2) Reject applications under part 222 of this chapter where there is no agreement by the United States permitting the proposed services; or

(3) Require that an applicant under part 222 of this chapter submit additional information.

(m) Approve or disapprove issuance of foreign aircraft permits provided for in part 375, subparts E and H, of this chapter.

(n) Grant or deny applications of foreign air carriers for renewal of emergency exemptions granted under 49 U.S.C. 40109(g).

(o) Grant or deny applications by air carriers and foreign air carriers under part 389 of this chapter for waivers of the Department's filing fee requirements, in accordance with current policy or precedent.

(p) Determine matters in proceedings under section 40109 and chapters 411, 413 and 415, that have not been set for oral evidentiary hearing, in addition to those authorized under §385.3, such matters to include, *inter alia*, filing times, service of documents, submissions of additional information, filing of otherwise unauthorized documents, access to information for which confidential treatment has been requested, rejection of incomplete or otherwise defective applications, and solicitation of applications for authority.

(q) Approve or disapprove applications under part 223 of this chapter for permission to furnish free or reduced-rate foreign air transportation.

(r) With respect to International Air Transport Association (IATA) agreements filed with the Department pursuant to sections 41309 and 41308 of the Statute, or pursuant to Civil Aeronautics Board Order E–9305 of June 15, 1955:

(1) Issue orders approving or disapproving IATA agreements relating to fare and rate matters under section 41309, and granting or denying antitrust immunity under section 41308, where the course of action is clear under current policy and precedent.

(2) Issue orders describing filed agreements, establishing procedural dates for submission of justification, comments and replies, which support or oppose agreements, and prescribing the particular types of data to be included in such submission.

(s) Reject any tariff, supplement, or revised page that is filed by any U.S. air carrier or foreign air carrier, and that is subject to rejection because it is not consistent with chapter 415 of the Statute or with part 221 or 222 of this chapter. Where a tariff, supplement or loose-leaf page is filed on more than 60 days' notice and is not rejected within the first 30 days (including the filing date), it shall not be rejected after such 30-day period under this authority unless the issuing carrier is given an opportunity to remove the cause for rejection by the effective date, by special tariff permission if necessary, and fails to take such corrective action.

(t) Approve or disapprove any application for special tariff permission under part 221, subpart P, of this chapter to make tariff changes upon less than statutory notice.

(u) Approve or disapprove applications for waiver of part 221 of this chapter.

(v) Institute an investigation of, or institute an investigation and suspend the effectiveness of, a tariff or change in a tariff which:

(1) Is substantially similar to a prior tariff under investigation or suspension; and

(2) Is filed by or on behalf of one or more of the parties to the prior tariff; and

(3) Is filed within 90 days after the expiration, modification, or cancellation of the prior tariff, or within 90 days after the effective date of an order requiring its cancellation or modification.

(w) In instances when an investigation of a tariff is pending, or the tariff is under suspension, or when a complaint requesting investigation or suspension of a tariff has been filed:

(1) Permit cancellation of the tariff; or

(2) If the grounds for the investigation or complaint have been removed through cancellation, expiration or modification of the tariff, either dismiss the investigation or complaint, or terminate the suspension.

(x) Extend the period of suspension of a tariff when the proceedings concerning the lawfulness of such tariff cannot be concluded before the expiration of the existing suspension period, provided that the aggregate of such extensions may not be for a longer period than permitted under section 41509.

(y) Cancel the suspension of and/or dismiss an investigation of a tariff relating to service predominantly in foreign air transportation where the course of action is clear under current policy and precedent.

[Doc. No. OST–96–1268, 61 FR 19169, May 1, 1996]

§385.14 Authority of the General Counsel.

(a) The General Counsel has authority to:

(1) Issue proposed or final regulations for the purpose of making editorial

changes or corrections in the Department's rules and regulations to carry out Titles IV and X of the Act, with the concurrence of the staff offices primarily responsible for the parts or sections involved: *Provided*, That any final regulation so issued shall have an effective date not less than 20 days after its date of publication in the FEDERAL REGISTER, and shall include a brief reference to the review procedures established in subpart C of this part.

(2) Where a petition for review is duly filed, reverse any rulemaking action taken by him or her pursuant to paragraph (a) of this section by withdrawing a proposed or final regulation issued thereunder, in which case the petition for review will not be submitted to the Reviewing Official involved. (Such a withdrawal is not subject to the review procedures of subpart C of this part.)

(3) Issue, upon request therefor, interpretations of facts bearing upon disqualifications of former members and employees, and Department employees under § 300.13 or § 300.14 of this chapter (Procedural Regulations).

(4) Issue orders deferring action until after oral argument on motions submitted by parties subsequent to the issuance of an Administrative Law Judge's initial or recommended decision.

(5) Reissue existing regulations for the purpose of incorporating prior amendments adopted by the Department.

(b) To the extent that a hearing case is involved, the authority assigned to the General Counsel in paragraph (a) of this section shall not be reassigned to the Deputy General Counsel or exercised by the Deputy General Counsel in the capacity of Acting General Counsel.

[Doc. No. T–1, 49 FR 50985, Dec. 31, 1984; Amdt. 1, 50 FR 7170, Feb. 21, 1985. Redesignated by Doc. No. OST–96–1268, 61 FR 19170, May 1, 1996]

§ 385.15 Authority of the Deputy General Counsel.

The Deputy General Counsel has authority to:

(a) Compromise any civil penalties being imposed in enforcement cases.

(b) Issue orders initiating and terminating informal nonpublic investigations under part 305 of this chapter (Procedural Regulations).

(c) Issue orders requiring air carriers to prepare and submit within a specified reasonable period, special reports, copies of agreements, records, accounts, papers, documents, and specific answers to questions upon which information is deemed necessary. Special reports shall be under oath whenever the Deputy General Counsel so requires.

(d) Institute and prosecute in the proper court, as agent of the Department, all necessary proceedings for the enforcement of the provisions of the act or any rule, regulation, requirement, or order thereunder, or any term, condition, or limitation of any certificate or permit, and for the punishment of all violations thereof. Any action taken by the Deputy General Counsel, pursuant to the authority of this section shall not be subject to the review procedures of this part.

(e) Make findings regarding the reasonable necessity for the application of the Department's authority to obtain access to lands, buildings and equipment, and to inspect, examine and make notes and copies of accounts, records, memorandums, documents, papers and correspondence of persons having control over, or affiliated with, any person subject to regulation under Titles IV or X of the Act, through issuance of an appropriate order, letter or other transmittal.

(f) Issue orders denying or granting conditional or complete confidential treatment of information supplied by any person to the Office of Aviation Enforcement and Proceedings. Confidential treatment may only be granted upon a finding that, if the information were in the Department's possession and a Freedom of Information Act (FOIA) request were made for the information:

(1) At the time of the confidentiality request, the FOIA request would be denied on the basis of one or more of the FOIA exemptions; and

(2) At any later time, the FOIA request would also be denied, absent a material change in circumstances (which may include a demonstration

that the asserted exemption does not apply).

[Doc. No. T-1, 49 FR 50985, Dec. 31, 1984. Redesignated by Doc. No. OST-96-1268, 61 FR 19170, May 1, 1996]

§ 385.16 Heads of Offices and Assistant General Counsels.

The heads of Offices and Assistant General Counsels have the authority to:

(a) Grant requests for permission to withdraw petitions, applications, motions, complaints, or other pleadings or documents which the respective Office has responsibility for processing where such authority has not otherwise been assigned in this regulation.

(b) Grant extensions of time for filing of documents or reports which are required to be filed by regulation or Department order and which reports or documents the respective Office has the responsibility for processing.

(c) Grant waivers of the environmental procedures set by Department order in any proceeding or portion of a proceeding dealing with environmental matters.

(d) Establish procedures on a case-by-case basis for environmental proceedings to ensure compliance with applicable law.

[Doc. No. T-1, 49 FR 50985, Dec. 31, 1984. Redesignated by Doc. No. OST-96-1268, 61 FR 19170, May 1, 1996]

§ 385.17 Authority of the Assistant General Counsel for Regulation and Enforcement.

The Assistant General Counsel for Regulation and Enforcement has authority to:

(a) Call public meetings in pending rulemaking proceedings,

(b) Issue a notice suspending the effective dates of final regulations issued by the General Counsel pending Departmental determination of review proceedings instituted thereon, whether by petition or upon order of the Department. (Such a notice is not subject to the review procedures of subpart C of this part.), and

(c) Approve or disapprove, for good cause shown, requests to extend the time for filing comments on all proposed or final new or amended regulations, and requests to extend comment periods following the issuance of final rules.

[Doc. No. T-1, 49 FR 50985, Dec. 31, 1984. Redesignated by Doc. No. OST-96-1268, 61 FR 19170, May 1, 1996]

§ 385.18 Authority of the Chief, Coordination Section, Documentary Services Division.

The Chief, Coordination Section, Documentary Services Division, has the authority to coordinate and perform all administrative functions of the Department provided for in sections 2, 3 and 5 of Executive Order 12597 issued May 13, 1987, except that this delegation shall not include the exercise of the authority delegated by the President to the Secretary by sections 2 and 5 of that Order to determine not to disapprove orders of the Department in certain cases.

[Amdt. 385-3, 52 FR 18905, May 20, 1987. Redesignated by Doc. No. OST-96-1268, 61 FR 19170, May 1, 1996]

§ 385.19 Authority of the Director, Office of Aviation Information, Bureau of Transportation Statistics.

The Director, Office of Aviation Information, Bureau of Transportation Statistics (BTS) has authority to:

(a) Conduct all rulemaking proceedings concerning accounting, reporting, and record retention requirements for carrying out Subparts I, II, and IV of the Statute, except the issuance of final rules and the disposition of petitions for reconsideration.

(b) Interpret the accounting, reporting, and record retention requirements used to carry out Subparts I, II, and IV of the Statute.

(c) Waive any of the accounting, reporting, and record retention requirements upon a showing of the existence of such facts, circumstances or other grounds, and subject to such limitations or conditions as may be prescribed for waivers in the applicable regulations, unless such authority is otherwise specifically assigned.

(d) Dismiss petitions for Department or BTS action with respect to accounting, reporting, and record retention matters when such dismissal is requested or consented to by the petitioner.

(e) Require special reports, documentation, or modifications to reports required by this chapter from any air carrier upon a determination that such reports or documentation or modifications are necessary to meet temporary information needs, assist in an evaluation of continued financial fitness, or comply with special information requests by Congress, Department officials, or another agency or component of the Federal Government.

(f) Grant or deny a request by an air carrier or foreign air carrier for an extension of a filing date for reports required by subchapters A and D of this chapter.

(g) Grant or deny requests by air carriers for substitution of their own forms, adaptation of Department forms, or use of ADP media to meet special needs where Department approval of such forms or ADP media is required by subchapter A of this chapter.

(h) Determine the data necessary to complete the International Civil Aviation Organization reports required by U.S. Treaty; as provided in Order 81–3–120, establish any necessary supplemental reporting requirements; and dispose of petitions for extensions of filing dates or waivers with respect to the data required for such reports.

(i) Grant or deny motions filed under §302.12 of this chapter requesting confidential treatment of aviation economic information or reports filed with BTS and place the decision in the motion's docket, which decision will be subject to review through a petition for reconsideration filed within ten days of issuance, to be acted upon by the Director, BTS.

(j) Grant or deny requests filed under §241.22 of this chapter for confidential treatment of preliminary year-end financial reports.

(k) Grant or deny requests filed under §248.5 of this chapter for confidential treatment of individual air carrier special reports.

(l) Grant or deny requests for use of domestic and international service segment and market data in accordance with the limitations on the availability of these data contained in §241.19–6 of this chapter and Order 81–12–9.

(m) Grant or deny requests for use of international Origin and Destination Survey statistics in accordance with the limitations on the availability of these data contained in §241.19–7 of this chapter.

(n) Grant or deny requests for individual air carrier fuel data in accordance with the limitations on the availability of these data contained in paragraph (k) of the reporting instructions for Schedule P–12(a), which are contained in §241.24 of this chapter.

(o) Grant or deny requests for individual air carrier financial data in accordance with the limitation on the availability of these data contained in paragraph (d) of the reporting instructions for Schedule F–1, which are contained in §298.62 of this chapter.

(p) Grant or deny requests for individual air carrier financial data as reported on Schedule P–1(a) in accordance with §241.22(b)(3) of this chapter.

[53 FR 51751, Dec. 23, 1988, as amended at 60 FR 66726, 66727, Dec. 26, 1995. Redesignated and amended by Doc. No. OST–96–1268, 61 FR 19170, May 1, 1996; 65 FR 6457, Feb. 9, 2000; 75 FR 41585, July 16, 2010]

§385.20 Authority of the Inspector General.

The Inspector General has authority to:

(a) Require special reports, including documentation, from any air carrier regarding audits and other examinations of carrier facilities, operations, and accounting and statistical records.

(b)(1) For accounting purpose, make findings regarding the reasonable necessity for the application of the Department authority to obtain access to lands, buildings, and equipment, and to inspect, examine, and make notes and copies of accounts, records, documents, papers, and correspondence of persons having control over, or affiliated with, any person subject to regulation used to carry out titles IV and X of the Act through issuance of an appropriate order, letter, or other transmittal;

(2) Authorize one or more auditors or special agents to conduct audits, inspections, and examinations and to make notes and copies in accordance with such findings.

(c) Release to the carrier that is the subject of a financial audit the audit report and other information developed during the audit.

(d) Require submission by carriers of special statements necessary to an explanation of any carrier accounting practice.

[Doc. No. T–1, 49 FR 50985, Dec. 31, 1984. Redesignated by Doc. No. OST–96–1268, 61 FR 19170, May 1, 1996]

§385.21 Authority of the Chief, Accounting Division, Office of Budget and Policy, Federal Transit Administration.

The Chief, Accounting Division, Office of Budget and Policy, Federal Transit Administration, has authority to:

(a) Approve and order the payment of refunds of filing fees paid under §389.27(b) of this chapter when such refunds have been authorized by either the Director, Office of Aviation Analysis, or the Director, Office of International Aviation.

(b) Pay from appropriated funds all properly documented claims consistent with Treasury, OMB, GAO, and DOT policies.

(c) Make minor or routine adjustments to payments based on audit reports prepared by the Inspector General, and through routine internal examinations of claims and vouchers.

(d) Design air carrier subsidy claim forms for small community service under 49 U.S.C. 41737.

[Doc. No. T–1, 49 FR 50985, Dec. 31, 1984; Amdt. 1, 50 FR 7170, Feb. 21, 1985. Redesignated and amended by Doc. No. OST–96–1268, 61 FR 19170, May 1, 1996]

Subpart C—Procedure on Review of Staff Action

§385.30 Persons who may petition for review.

Petitions for review may be filed by the applicant; by persons who have availed themselves of the opportunity, if any, to participate in the matter at the staff action level; and by persons who have not had opportunity to so participate or show good and sufficient cause for not having participated: *Provided*, That such persons, other than the applicant, disclose a substantial interest which would be adversely affected by the respective staff action.

[Doc. No. T–1, 49 FR 50985, Dec. 31, 1984. Redesignated by Doc. No. OST–96–1268, 61 FR 19171, May 1, 1996]

§385.31 Petitions for review.

(a) *Time for filing.* Petitions for review shall be filed and served within seven (7) days after the date of the staff action to which they relate, but a different period may be fixed in such staff action consistent with effective preservation of the right to petition for discretionary review and the exigencies of the situation.

(b) *Contents.* Petitions for review shall demonstrate that (1) a finding of material fact is clearly erroneous; (2) a legal conclusion is contrary to law, Department rules, or precedent; (3) a substantial and important question of policy is involved; (4) a prejudicial procedural error has occurred; or (5) the staff action is substantially deficient on its face. The petition shall briefly and specifically state the alleged grounds for review and the relief sought. If persons who participated at the staff action level set forth any new facts, arguments, or other new matter, an explanation must be furnished as to why said matter was not previously adduced at the staff action level. In the absence of a valid explanation, the Department may disregard such new matter.

(c) *Form and filing.* Petitions shall comply with the form and filing requirements of §§302.3 and 302.4 of this chapter. (Rules of practice in Economic Proceedings). Petitions shall not exceed 10 pages in length. A greater length, however, may be specified in the staff action taken. The petitions shall be accompanied by proof of required service. However, persons who seek review of a civil penalty proposed by the Assistant General Counsel for Aviation Enforcement and Proceedings pursuant to §385.15(a) may submit their request therefor by letter to the Department with a copy to the Assistant General Counsel for Aviation Enforcement and Proceedings and need not comply with the above form and filing requirements.

(d) *Service.* A petition filed by a person other than the applicant shall be served on the applicant. Petitions shall also be served on any persons who have served documents on the petitioner at the staff action level; and on such other persons as may be directed by the Department or the staff member who took the action to be reviewed.

(e) *Answers*. The applicant and such other persons as disclose a substantial interest which would be adversely affected by the relief sought in the petition may, within seven (7) days after filing the petition, file an answer thereto. A different period for the filing of answers may be fixed in the staff action. Such answers shall comply with the form and filing requirements applicable to petitions and shall be served on the applicant and any other person who has theretofore served a document in the matter on such respondent.

[Doc. No. T–1, 49 FR 50985, Dec. 31, 1984. Redesignated and amended by Doc. No. OST–96–1268, 61 FR 19171, May 1, 1996; 65 FR 6457, Feb. 9, 2000]

§ 385.32 Effective date of staff action.

Unless, within the time provided by or pursuant to this regulation, a petition for review is filed or the Department gives notice that it will review on its own motion, staff action shall, without further proceedings, be effective and become the action of the Department upon the expiration of such period. A timely petition for review filed in accordance with the provisions of this section, or notice given by the Department of review on its own motion, shall stay the staff action pending disposition by the Department, unless the Department determines otherwise or unless the staff action provides otherwise in accordance with subpart A of this part. However, in cases where the Department's regulations provide that permissions or approvals are granted, or that other legal effects result, within a stated period from the filing with the Department of a prescribed document, unless the Department gives notice to the contrary or takes other action within said period, such notice given or action taken by a staff member under delegated authority shall toll the running of such period. A timely petition for review of staff action which is not stayed by its filing which is received after or not acted upon before the effective date of the action shall be entertained and disposed of on its merits as a petition for reconsideration.

[Doc. No. T–1, 49 FR 50985, Dec. 31, 1984. Redesignated by Doc. No. OST–96–1268, 61 FR 19171, May 1, 1996]

§ 385.33 Review by the staff.

Where a petition for review is duly filed, the staff member may, upon consideration of all documents properly filed, reverse his or her decision. Except in the case of Administrative Law Judges, action taken by a staff member other than an office head or Assistant General Counsel may be reversed by the respective office head or Assistant General Counsel who is in the supervisory chain of command with respect to the staff member who took the initial action. If the initial action is reversed, the petition for review will not be submitted to the Reviewing Official. Staff action reversing the initial action shall be subject to petition for Department review as any other staff action.

[Doc. No. T–1, 49 FR 50985, Dec. 31, 1984. Redesignated by Doc. No. OST–96–1268, 61 FR 19171, May 1, 1996]

§ 385.34 Decision by the Reviewing Official.

(a) *Decline of right to review*. If the Reviewing Official declines the right to exercise discretionary review, the staff action stayed by the petition for review shall become effective on the second business day following the date of service of the order, unless the order provides otherwise.

(b) *Exercise of right to review*. The Reviewing Official will exercise his or her discretionary right of review either upon petition or on his or her own motion. The Reviewing official may by order provide for interlocutory relief pending his or her decision on the merits and may limit the issues on review. The Reviewing Official may affirm, modify or set aside the staff action, may order the matter remanded, or may order further submittals or other proceedings before making a decison on the merits. In case the Reviewing Official affirms the staff action, staff action stayed by the petition for review shall become effective on the second business day following the date of service of the Reviewing Official's order, unless the order provides otherwise. Decisions by the Reviewing Official under this part are final and are not subject to petitions for reconsideration.

[Doc. No. T-1, 49 FR 50985, Dec. 31, 1984; Amdt. 1, 50 FR 7170, Feb. 21, 1985. Redesignated by Doc. No. OST-96-1268, 61 FR 19171, May 1, 1996]

PART 389—FEES AND CHARGES FOR SPECIAL SERVICES

Subpart A—General Provisions

Subpart B—Fees for Special Services

Subpart C—Filing and Processing License Fees

AUTHORITY: Sec. 204, 1002, Pub. L. 85-726, as amended, 72 Stat. 743, 797; 49 U.S.C. 1324, 1502. Act of August 31, 1951, ch. 376, 65 Stat. 268; 31 U.S.C. 483a.

SOURCE: OR-27, 33 FR 70, Jan. 4, 1968, unless otherwise noted.

Subpart A—General Provisions

§ 389.1 Policy and scope.

Pursuant to the provisions of Title V of the Independent Offices Appropriation Act of 1952 (5 U.S.C. 140) as implemented by Bureau of Budget Circular A-25, dated September 23, 1959, the Board sets forth in this regulation the special services made available by the Board and prescribes the fees to be paid for these and various other services.

Subpart B—Fees for Special Services

§ 389.10 Applicability of subpart.

This subpart describes certain special services made available by the Board and prescribes the fees and charges for these services.

§ 389.11 Services available.

Upon request and payment of fees as provided in subsequent sections, there are available, with respect to documents subject to inspection, services as follows:

(a) Locating and copying records and documents.

(b) Certification of copies of documents under seal of the Board.

(c) Subscriptions to publications of the Board.

(d) Transcripts of hearings.

[OR-27, 33 FR 70, Jan. 4, 1968, as amended by OR-94, 40 FR 7242, Feb. 19, 1975]

§ 389.12 Payment of fees and charges.

The fees charged for special services may be paid by check, draft, or postal money order, payable to the Civil Aeronautics Board, except for charges for reporting services which are performed under competitive bid contracts with non-Government firms. Fees for reporting are payable to the firms providing the services.

§ 389.13 Fees for services.

Except for photocopy work, the basic fees set forth below provide for documents to be mailed with ordinary first class postage prepaid. If copy is to be transmitted by registered, certified, air, or special delivery mail, postal fees therefor will be added to the basic fee. Also, if special handling or packaging is required, costs therefor will be added to the basic fee. For photocopy work, postage will be in addition to the fee for copying.

§ 389.14 Locating and copying records and documents.

Public records and documents on file with the Civil Aeronautics Board will be located and copied upon request and payment of fees as set forth below:

(a) There shall be no charge in connection with searches for records or documents under this chapter.

(b) Photocopies of records or documents shall be made using the Board's facilities or by contractors.

(1) The fee for photocopying will be 15 cents per page.

(2) The fee for copying by contractors will be that established in the contracts with the Board and will be billed directly by those contractors.

(c) Copies of board data on magnetic tapes, or extractions of data from Board data tapes, will be made by the National Archives and Records Service (NARS) of the General Services Administration or by computer service bureaus.

(1) The Director, Bureau of Accounts and Statistics, furnishes many public records and documents contained on magnetic tape to NARS. Initial requests for data should be made directly to the Machine Readable Archives Division, National Archives and Records Services, General Services Administration, Washington, D.C. 20408, with the applicant directly reimbursing NARS for its copying or data extraction charges. When NARS does not have the requested data, the Director, Bureau of Accounts and Statistics, upon written request, will furnish the tapes for a reasonable length of time to a computer service bureau chosen by the applicant subject to the Director's approval. The computer service bureau shall assume the liability for the cost of replacing any tape that may be damaged or destroyed by it.

(2) The fee for data copying by NARS will be determined by NARS.

(3) The fee for data copying by a computer service bureau shall be established by agreement between the requesting party and the computer service bureau.

(d) Where the Board's fee for service requested will exceed $100, the service will not be performed until payment has been received. In such cases, the requester will be notified promptly of the amount of the fee, and the requested service will be performed as expeditiously as practicable following receipt of payment.

(e) Applications for waivers or modifications of any fees required to be paid to the Board under this section may be filed in accordance with the following:

(1) Each applicant shall set forth briefly and succinctly the relief that it seeks and the reasons why such relief should be granted. Waivers or modifications of stated fees shall be granted only where it is demonstrated that such action is in the public interest because furnishing of the information requested can be considered as primarily benefiting the general public.

(2) Applications requesting waivers or modifications of fees under this section shall be addressed to the Managing Director, who has been delegated authority by the Board to decide such applications in § 385.12 of this chapter, and shall accompany the request for service under this section.

(3) The Managing Director shall either rule on the application or, at his discretion, pass the matter on to the Board for its determination. In acting upon such applications the Managing Director and the Board, where applicable, shall be guided by the procedures and requirements of § 310.9(d) of this chapter.

(4) A decision by either the Managing Director or the Board pursuant to paragraph (d)(3) of this section is final and will not be subject to petitions for reconsideration.

[OR–94, 40 FR 7242, Feb. 19, 1975, as amended by OR–131, 43 FR 38574, Aug. 29, 1978]

§ 389.15 Certification of copies of documents.

The Secretary of the Board will provide, on request, certifications or validation (with the Civil Aeronautics Board seal) of documents filed with or issued by the Board. Copies of tariffs filed with the Board will be certified only when such copies have been made under the Board's supervision upon request of the applicant. Charges for this service are as follows:

(a) Certification of the Secretary, $2. This fee includes clerical services involved in checking the authenticity of records to be certified. If copying of the documents to be certified is required, the copying charges provided for in § 389.14 will be in addition to the charges specified in this section.

(b) [Reserved]

[OR–27, 33 FR 70, Jan. 4, 1968, as amended by OR–35, 34 FR 5598, Mar. 25, 1969]

§ 389.16 Board publications.

(a) *Charges for publications.* Charges have been established by the Superintendent of Documents for subscriptions to certain Board publications. A list of these publications together with information on how they can be ordered is contained in the "List of Publications", which is available on request from the Board's Publications Services Division, B–22, Washington, D.C., 20428.

(b) *Free services.* No charge will be made by the Board for notices, decisions, orders, etc., required by law to be served on a party to any proceeding or matter before the Board. No charge will be made for single copies of Board publications individually requested in person or by mail, except where a charge is specifically fixed for a publication at the time of its issuance.

(c) *Reciprocal services.* Arrangements may be made with the Board's Bureau of International Aviation for furnishing publications to a foreign country or to an international organization on a reciprocal basis.

[OR–178, 46 FR 8445, Jan. 27, 1981]

§ 389.17 Transcripts of proceedings.

Transcripts of testimony and oral argument are furnished to the Board by a non-Government contractor for any proceeding in which the presiding officer has determined that such transcript should be made, and copies thereof may be purchased directly from the reporting firm, at prices and upon other terms and conditions specified in the contract made between the Board and the reporting firm, and currently in effect, pursuant to section 11 of the Federal Advisory Committee Act (Pub. L. 92–463, 86 Stat. 770, 5 U.S.C. App. I). Any person may obtain from the Director, Office of Facilities and Operations, the name and address of the reporting firm with which the Board currently has such contract, as well as the contract prices then in effect for the various types of transcript and copying services covered by such contract.

[OR–84, 39 FR 22417, June 24, 1974]

Subpart C—Filing and Processing License Fees

§ 389.20 Applicability of subpart.

(a) This subpart applies to the filing of certain documents and records of the Department by non-government parties, and prescribes fees for their processing.

(b) For the purpose of this subpart, record means those electronic tariff records submitted to the Department under subpart W of 14 CFR part 221, and contains that set of information which describes one (1) tariff fare, or that set of information which describes one (1) related element associated with such tariff fare.

[Amdt. 389–37, 54 FR 2099, Jan. 19, 1989]

§ 389.21 Payment of fees.

(a) Any document or record for which a filing fee is requried by § 389.25 shall be accompanied by either (1) a check, draft, or postal money order, payable to the Civil Aeronautics Board, in the amount prescribed herein, or (2) a request for waiver or modification of the filing fee.

(b) [Reserved]

(c) Where a document seeks authority or relief in the alternative and therefore would otherwise be subject to more than one filing fee, only the highest fee shall be required.

(d) Where a document relating to a single transaction or matter seeks multiple authorities or relief and therefore would otherwise be subject to more than one filing fee, only the highest fee shall be required. Where a document relating to more than one transaction or matter seeks multiple authorities or relief, the requried filing fee shall be determiend by combining the highest fees for each transaction or matter. For purposes of this paragraph, a specific number of charters or inclusive tours described in one application will be regarded as a single transaction or matter.

(e) No fee shall be returned after the document has been filed with the

Board, except as provided in §§ 389.23 and 389.27.

[OR–27, 33 FR 70, Jan. 4, 1968, as amended by OR–27A, 33 FR 3633, Mar. 1, 1968; OR–50, 35 FR 15986, Oct. 10, 1970; 48 FR 642, Jan. 6, 1983; Amdt. 389–37, 54 FR 2099, Jan. 19, 1989]

§ 389.22 Failure to make proper payment.

(a)(1) Except as provided in § 389.23, documents (except tariff publications) which are not accompanied by filing fees shall be returned to the filing party, and such documents shall not be considered as filed by the Board.

(2) Except as provided in § 389.23, records which are not accompanied by the appropriate filing fees shall be retained and considered filed with the Department. The Department will notify the filer concerning the nonpayment or underpayment of the filing fees, and will also notify the filer that the records will not be processed until the fees are paid.

(b) The filing fee tendered by a filing party shall be accepted by the Board office to whom payment is made, subject to post audit by the Chief of the Board's Finance Division and notification to the filing party within 30 days of any additional amount due. Not more than 5 days after receipt of the notification, the determination of the Chief, Finance Division, may be appealed to the Managing Director of the Board, who has been delegated authority by the Board to decide such appeals in § 385.12 of this chapter. The filing party may submit to the Board a petition for review of the Managing Director's decision pursuant to § 385.50 of this chapter, and proceedings thereon will be governed by part 385, subpart C, of this chapter.

(c) The amount found due by the Chief, Finance Division, shall be paid within 10 days of notification except that (1) if that decision is appealed to the Managing Director, the amount due shall be paid within 10 days after the Managing Director notifies the filing party that he has affirmed or modified the decision of the Chief, Finance Division; and (2) if the decision of the Managing Director is appealed to the Board, the amount due shall be paid within 10 days after the Board notifies the filing party that it has affirmed or modified the staff decision. If the amount due is not paid, the document (except a tariff publication) shall be returned to the filing party along with the fee tendered, and such document shall be deemed to have been dismissed or withdrawn.

[OR–27, 33 FR 70, Jan. 4, 1968, as amended by OR–96, 40 FR 20613, May 12, 1975; Amdt. 389–37, 54 FR 2099, Jan. 19, 1989]

§ 389.23 Application for waiver or modification of fees.

(a) Applications may be filed asking for waiver or modification of any fee paid under this subpart. Each applicant shall set forth the reasons why a waiver or modification should be granted, and by what legal authority.

(b) Applications asking for a waiver or modification of fees shall be sent to the Managing Director of the Board, and shall accompany the document filed. Applicants may appeal the decision of the Managing Director to the Board under § 385.50 of this chapter. When no petition for review is filed with the Board, or when the Board reviews the Managing Director's decision, if the amount found due is not paid within 10 days after receipt of notification of the final determination, the document shall be returned to the filing party.

(Approved by the Office of Management and Budget under control number 3024–0071)

[48 FR 642, Jan. 6, 1983, as amended by OR–215, 49 FR 6884, Feb. 24, 1984]

§ 389.24 Foreign air carriers.

A foreign air carrier, or such carriers, if from the same country, acting jointly, may apply for a waiver of the requirements of this part based on reciprocity for U.S. air carriers contained in the requirement of their home governments, or as provided in a treaty or agreement with the United States. To apply for a waiver under this section, foreign air carriers shall send waiver requests to the Director, Bureau of International Aviation. The request should include applicable official government rules, decisions, statements of policy, or comparable evidence concerning filing fees for U.S. air carriers, or for all carriers serving that country. Once a waiver has been granted for a specific country, no further waiver applications need be filed for that country.

(Approved by the Office of Management and Budget under control number 3024–0071)

[OR–209, 48 FR 10628, Mar. 14, 1983, as amended by OR–215, 49 FR 6884, Feb. 24, 1984]

§ 389.25 Schedule of processing fees.

(a) *Document-filing fees.*

Code	Document	
	Interstate and Overseas Air Transportation	
	Certificate of Public Convenience and Necessity:	
	Application under sec. 401:	
1	Charter	850
2	Scheduled Service	850
3	Dormant Authority	290
4	All-Cargo under sec. 418	670
5	Transfer	290
6	Air Taxi Registration	8
7	Commuter Air Carrier Authorization	670
8	Change of Name (registration of trade name or reissuance of certificate)	56
9	Exemption Request (General):	
10	Section 403	53
11	Section 401 (domestic)	280
12	Section 419	120
13	Service Mail Rate Petition	420
	FOREIGN AIR TRANSPORTATION (U.S. AND AIR CARRIERS)	
	Certificate of Public Convenience and Necessity (sec. 401):	
14	Scheduled Service	900
15	Amendment to application	425
16	Charter Service	600
17	Amendment to application	200
18	Transfer	255
19	Change of Name (registration of trade name or reissuance of certificate)	56
	Foreign Air Carrier Permit (sec. 402):	
20	Initial	760
21	Amendment/Renewal of permit	475
22	Amendment to application for a permit	215
	Exemption:	
23	Section 403	53
	Section 401/402:	
24	10 or fewer flights	77
25	More than 10 flights	360
26	Filed less than 10 days before effective date requested	[1] 17
27	Other (U.S. and foreign air carriers)	360
28	Emergency cabotage (sec. 416(b)(7))	360
29	Relief for U.S. (sec. 101) and foreign (sec. 416) indirect air carriers	370
	Undocketed Items:	
30	Canadian Charter Air Taxi Registration	30
31	Foreign Freight Forwarder Registration	11
32	Foreign Tour Operator Registration	10
33	Foreign Aircraft Permit (part 375)	25
34	Special Authorization (part 375)	12
35	Charter Statement of Authorization	8
36	Intermodal Statement of Authorization	10
37	Special Authority (part 216)	37
38	Items 33–37 if filed less than time required before effective date	[1] 11
39	IATA resolutions	61
	OTHER (U.S. AND FOREIGN AIR CARRIERS)	
	Charters:	
40	Public Charter Prospectus	39
41	OMPC Operation Authorization	665
42	Waiver of Charter Regulations	39
	Tariffs:	
43	Pages	2
44	Special Tariff Permission	12
45	Waiver of Tariff Regulations	12
46	Approval of Interlocking Relationships	415
47	Merger or Acquisition of Control	1080
47a	Exemption request	371
	Agreements filed under section 412:	
48	Prior Approval (docketed)	1080
49	Routine (nondocketed)	64
50	Application for free and reduced-rate transportation	16

[1] Additional.

(b) *Electronic Tariff Filing Fees.* The filing fee for one (1) or more transactions proposed in any existing record, or for any new or canceled records, shall be 5 cents per record; *Provided:* That no fee shall be assessed for those records submitted to the Department pursuant to § 221.500(b)(1) of this subpart.

[48 FR 643, Jan. 6, 1983, as amended by OR–206, 48 FR 1941, Jan. 17, 1983; OR–210, 48 FR 15615, Apr. 12, 1983; 53 FR 17924, May 19, 1988; Amdt. 389–37, 54 FR 2099, Jan. 19, 1989; 70 FR 25773, May 16, 2005]

§ 389.26 Special rules for tariff page filings.

(a) *Tariffs issued by carriers.* The filing fee for tariff pages filed by U.S. air carriers will be charged even if the tariff includes matters involving participating foreign air carriers. It will also be charged if the tariff is issued by a foreign air carrier and includes matters involving participating U.S. air carriers, unless the foreign air carrier has obtained a waiver under § 389.24. The fee will not be charged for a blank looseleaf page unless it cancels matter in the preceding issue of the page.

(b) *Tariffs issued by publishing agents.* (1) If the tariff is issued for one or more air carriers exclusively, the fee will be charged for each page.

(2) If the tariff is issued for one or more air carriers and one or more foreign air carriers, the fee will be charged for each page, except for those pages that the issuing agent states contain only:

(i) Matters pertaining exclusively to foreign air carriers that have been granted a waiver, or

(ii) Changes in matters pertaining to foreign air carriers that have been granted a waiver and that are included on the same page with other matters that are reissued without change.

(3) The fee will not be charged for a blank looseleaf page unless it cancels matters in the preceding page.

(4) No fee will be charged when two pages are published back-to-back, one page is not subject to the fee under paragraph (b)(2), and the page on the reverse is issued without substantive change.

(5) The fee will be charged for two looseleaf pages containing a correction number check sheet unless all other pages of the tariff are exempt from the fee.

[48 FR 643, Jan. 6, 1983]

§ 389.27 Refund of fee.

(a) Any fee charged under this part may be refunded in full or in part upon request if the document for which it is charged is withdrawn before final action is taken. Such requests shall be filed in accordance with § 389.23.

(b) Any person may file an application for refund of a fee paid since April 28, 1977, on the grounds that such fee exceeded the Board's cost in providing the service. The application shall be filed with the Board's Comptroller and shall contain: the amount paid, the date paid, and the category of service.

(Approved by the Office of Management and Budget under control number 3024–0071)

[48 FR 643, Jan. 6, 1983, as amended by OR–215, 49 FR 6884, Feb. 24, 1984; 49 FR 32564, Aug. 15, 1984]

SUBCHAPTER F—POLICY STATEMENTS

PART 398—GUIDELINES FOR INDIVIDUAL DETERMINATIONS OF BASIC ESSENTIAL AIR SERVICE

AUTHORITY: 49 U.S.C. Chapters 401, 417; Airport and Airway Safety and Capacity Expansion Act of 1987 (Pub. L. 100–223, Dec. 30, 1987).

SOURCE: Docket No. OST–95–397, 60 FR 43529, Aug. 22, 1995, unless otherwise noted.

§ 398.1 Purpose.

The purpose of this part is to establish general guidelines for the determination of basic essential air service for each eligible place under 49 U.S.C. 41731 and 41732. Procedures for the determination of the essential air service level for a place are contained in part 325 of this chapter.

§ 398.2 Number and designation of hubs.

(a) *What is a hub?* The Department considers hubs as belonging to any one of three classifications:

(1) A *large* hub is a place accounting for at least 1.00 percent of the total enplanements in the United States;

(2) A *medium* hub is a place accounting for at least 0.25 percent but less than 1.00 percent of the total enplanements in the United States; and

(3) A *small* hub is a place accounting for at least 0.05 percent but less than 0.25 percent of the total enplanements in the United States.

(b) *How many hubs?* (1) As a general matter, the Department will require service to one large or medium hub.

(2) In Alaska or when the nearest large or medium hub is more than 400 miles from the eligible place, the Department may instead require service to a small hub or nonhub.

(3) In some cases, the Department may require service to two hubs, of which at least one will be a large or medium hub. The Department will require service to two hubs if an eligible place has close commercial, geographic, and political ties to both hubs and if there is sufficient traffic from the eligible place to support two round trips a day to both hubs. If traffic is not sufficient, the Department may require one round trip a day to both hubs if the community requests such service.

(4) In no event will essential air service consist of service to more than two hubs.

(c) *Which hub?* (1) In designating hubs, the Department will weigh all of the following factors:

(i) The extent to which candidate hubs provide access to the national air transportation system;

(ii) The commercial, geographic, and political ties of candidate hubs to the eligible place;

(iii) The traffic levels to candidate hubs, as shown by traffic studies and origin and designation data;

(iv) The distance of candidate hubs from the eligible place; and

(v) The size of candidate hubs. Large size will be a positive factor, but principally as substantiating the access and community-ties factors.

(2) For Alaska, rather than requiring service to a hub, the Department may instead require that service from an eligible place be provided to a nearby focal point for traffic which, in turn, has service to a hub.

§ 398.3 Specific airports.

(a) At an eligible place, essential air service may be specified as service to a particular airport. In the case of hyphenated places, essential air service will be specified as service to more than one airport only if clearly necessary and if the multi-airport service is economically feasible and justified on the basis of traffic levels at those airports.

(b) At a hub, essential air service is not usually specified as service to a particular airport.

§ 398.4 Equipment.

(a) Except in Alaska, service will be provided by aircraft offering at least 15 passenger seats, unless:

(1) Average daily enplanements at the place did not exceed 11 passengers for any fiscal year from 1976 through 1986;

(2) The requirement would necessitate the payment of compensation in a fiscal year for service at the place when compensation would otherwise not be necessary; or

(3) The affected community agrees in writing to the use of smaller aircraft to provide service at the place.

(b) The aircraft must have at least two engines and use two pilots, unless scheduled air transportation has not been provided to the place in aircraft with at least two engines and using two pilots for at least 60 consecutive operating days at any time since October 31, 1978.

(c) The aircraft must be pressurized when the service regularly involves flights above 8,000 feet in altitude.

(d) All aircraft must meet the applicable safety standards of the Federal Aviation Administration.

(e) The aircraft must be conveniently accessible to passengers by stairs rather than over the wing.

§ 398.5 Frequency of flights.

(a) Except in Alaska, at least two round trips each weekday and two round trips each weekend.

(b) In Alaska, a level of service at least equal to that provided in 1976, or two round trips each week, whichever is greater, except that the Department and the appropriate State authority of Alaska may agree to a different level of service after consulting with the affected community.

(c) An essential air service level may be set at more than that stated in paragraphs (a) and (b) of this section if:

(1) Historical traffic data and studies of traffic-generating potential for the place indicate that more frequent service is needed to accommodate passengers and accompanying baggage with the aircraft used at that place;

(2) More flights are needed because the capacity available to the eligible place is being shared with traffic destined for an intermediate stop or for a place beyond the eligible place;

(3) More flights are needed to accommodate passengers because smaller aircraft are being used at the place;

(4) More flights are needed in order to ensure adequate connecting opportunities as provided for by § 398.7; or

(5) For Alaska, the appropriate state agency agrees that more frequent service is needed to accommodate cargo traffic with the aircraft used at the eligible place.

(d) For eligible places where traffic levels vary substantially with the season, a two-tier level of essential air service may be established with required flight frequencies changing accordingly.

§ 398.6 Seat guarantees.

(a) The number of seats guaranteed at the eligible place will be sufficient to accommodate the estimated passenger traffic at an average load factor of 60 percent, except that an average load factor of 50 percent will be used when service is provided with aircraft having fewer than 15 passenger seats.

(b) Only under unusual circumstances will an eligible place's essential air service level be set at a number of flights that will accommodate more than 40 passengers a day in each direction (a total of 80 inbound and outbound passengers). Generally, 40 passengers can be accommodated by guaranteeing 67 seats a day in each direction (a total of 134 inbound and outbound seats).

(c) The Department may guarantee an eligible place more than 67 seats a day if:

(1) The number of stops between or beyond the eligible place and the hub results in available aircraft capacity being shared with passengers at those other places;

(2) The distance between the eligible place and the designated hub requires the use of large aircraft;

(3) The eligible place has suffered an abrupt and significant reduction in its service that warrants a temporary increase in the maximum guaranteed capacity; or

(4) Other unusual circumstances warrant guaranteeing the eligible place more than 67 seats a day.

§398.7 Timing of flights.

To qualify as essential air service, flights must depart at reasonable times, considering the needs of passengers with connecting flights at the hub. It is the policy of the Department to consider the reasonableness of the time in view of the purpose for which the local passengers are traveling. If travel is primarily to connect with other flights at the hub, local flight times should be designed to link with those flights. If travel is primarily local (*i.e.*, to and from the hub), there should be at least one morning flight in each direction and one late-afternoon or evening flight in each direction.

§398.8 Number of intermediate stops.

(a) Except in Alaska, no more than one intermediate stop is permitted in providing essential air service between the eligible place and its hub, unless otherwise agreed to with the community. In cases where an eligible place receives service to two hubs, however, more than one intermediate stop is permitted between that place and its secondary hub.

(b) In Alaska, more than one intermediate stop is permitted if required by low traffic levels at the eligible place or by the long distance between the eligible place and its hub.

(c) The Department may specify nonstop service when necessary to make the service viable.

(d) Where an eligible place normally is an intermediate stop that shares available capacity with another place, it is the policy of the Department either to require additional capacity (more flights or larger aircraft) between the eligible place and its hub or to specify some turnaround operations on that route segment.

§398.9 Load factor standards.

The load factor standards used in this part may be raised for individual eligible places under either of the following circumstances:

(a) The place is served by the carrier as part of a linear route; or

(b) It would be in the interest of the community, the carrier, or the general public to raise the load factor standard for that place.

§398.10 Overflights.

The Department considers it a violation of 49 U.S.C. 41732 and the air service guarantees provided under this part for an air carrier providing essential air service to an eligible place to overfly that place, except under one or more of the following circumstances:

(a) The carrier is not compensated for serving that place and another carrier is providing by its flights the service required by the Department's essential air service determination for that place;

(b) Circumstances beyond the carrier's control prevent it from landing at the eligible place;

(c) The flight involved is not in a market where the Department has determined air service to be essential; or

(d) The eligible place is a place in Alaska for which the Department's essential air service determination permits the overflight.

§398.11 Funding reductions.

(a) If, in any fiscal year, appropriations for payments to air carriers remain at or below the amounts estimated as necessary to maintain subsidy-supported essential air service at the places receiving such service, and Congress provides no statutory direction to the contrary, appropriations shall not be available for essential air service to otherwise eligible places within the 48 contiguous States and Puerto Rico that have a rate of subsidy per passenger in excess of $200.00, or are located:

(1) Less than 70 highway miles from the nearest large or medium hub airport;

(2) Less than 55 miles from the nearest small hub airport; or

(3) Less than 45 highway miles from the nearest nonhub airport that has enplaned, on certificated or commuter carriers, 100 or more passengers per day in the most recent year for which the Department has obtained complete data.

(b) The rate of subsidy per passenger shall be calculated by dividing the annual subsidy in effect as of July 1 of the prior fiscal year by the total origin-and-destination traffic during the most recent year for which the Department has obtained complete data.

PART 399—STATEMENTS OF GENERAL POLICY

Subpart A—Applicability and Effects of Policy Statements

Subpart B—Policies Relating to Operating Authority

Subpart C—Policies Relating to Rates and Tariffs

Subpart D [Reserved]

Subpart E—Policies Relating to Hearing Matters

Subpart F—Policies Relating to Rulemaking Proceedings

Subpart G—Policies Relating to Enforcement

Subpart H—Other Policies Relating to Interests, Activities, and Relationships of Air Carriers

Subpart I—Policies Relating to Disclosure of Information

Subpart J—Policies Relating to Federal Preemption of State Economic Regulations

Subpart K—Policies Relating to Certificate Duration

AUTHORITY: 49 U.S.C. 41712

SOURCE: PS-21, 29 FR 1446, Jan. 29, 1964, unless otherwise noted.

Subpart A—Applicability and Effects of Policy Statements

§ 399.1 Applicability.

All statements of general policy adopted by the Board for the guidance of the public will be published in this part, except as provided in § 399.2.

§ 399.2 Exclusions.

The following types of policies are generally not included in this part:

(a) Policies relating solely to the internal management of the Board;

(b) Policies requiring secrecy in the public interest or in the interest of national defense;

(c) Policies that are repetitive of section 102 of the Act;

(d) Policies that are fully expressed in a procedural or substantive rule of the Board, or in any opinion, decision, order, certificate, permit, exemption, or waiver of the Board;

(e) Expressions of encouragement or admonition to industry to follow a certain course of action;

(f) Positions on legislative items and on other matters that are outside the scope of the Board's current statutory powers and duties.

[PS-21, 29 FR 1446, Jan. 29, 1964, as amended by PS-63, 40 FR 6643, Feb. 13, 1975]

§ 399.3 Statements in other Board documents.

No statement contained in any Board opinion, decision, order, certificate, permit, exemption, or waiver shall be considered a statement of policy within the meaning of this part, even though such statements may constitute a precedent in future cases or declare future policy to be followed in like cases. Similarly, a denial by the Board or relief sought, or statements of the Board's reasons for failure to issue a rule upon which rulemaking proceedings have been commenced shall not be considered statements of policy, except to the extent that it is specifically stated that such denial or failure is based upon a policy thereafter to be followed.

§ 399.4 Nature and effect of policy statements.

Policy statements published in this part will be observed by the Board until rescinded, but any policy may be amended from time to time as experience or changing conditions may require. Changes in policy may be made with or without advance notice to the public and will become effective upon publication in the FEDERAL REGISTER unless otherwise provided. If it appears to the Board, in its consideration of any matter before it, that the application of a policy published in this part would run counter to an express provision of law or policy enunciated by Congress in the Act, the published policy shall not be applicable to such matter.

§ 399.5 Arrangement of policy statements.

The statements of general policy relating to the various duties and functions of the Board are grouped according to subject matter in the following subparts; the titles of the subparts indicate the general subject matter included therein.

Subpart B—Policies Relating to Operating Authority

§§ 399.10–399.11 [Reserved]

§ 399.12 Negotiation by air carriers for landing rights in foreign countries.

(a) It is the policy of the Board (jointly with the Department of State) that, as a general rule, landing rights abroad for United States flag air carriers will be acquired through negotiation by the U.S. Government with foreign governments rather than by direct negotiation between an air carrier and a foreign government.

(b) It is corollary to the foregoing policy that no United States air carrier may avail itself of representations by one foreign government to further its interest with another foreign government, especially with respect to landing rights, except insofar as such representations have been specifically authorized by the U.S. Government.

§§ 399.13–399.17 [Reserved]

§ 399.18 Maximum duration of fixed-term route authorization granted by exemption; renewal of such authority.

It is the policy of the Board to limit the duration of exemptions which authorize fixed-term route service to a maximum period of two years, and to entertain requests for renewal of such authority only when incorporated in a duly filed application for substantially equivalent certificate authority under section 401 of the Act. (See § 377.10(c) of this chapter (Special Regulations).)

[PS–21, 29 FR 1446, Jan. 29, 1964, as amended at 65 FR 6457, Feb. 9, 2000]

§ 399.19 [Reserved]

§ 399.21 Charter exemptions (except military).

In deciding applications for exemptions from section 41102 of Title 49 of the United States Code by air carriers seeking to perform charter service in air transportation, we will give primary weight to the chartering public's own assessment of the air carrier services that best meet its transportation needs. Therefore, we will not, as a general rule, consider as relevant to our decision on such applications, objections based upon (1) offers by the objectors to perform the charter service, and/or (2) estimates of revenue or traffic diversion, unless in the latter case the objectors demonstrate that the diversion resulting from grant of the exemption would threaten their ability to fulfill their certificate obligations.

[PS–78, 43 FR 31886, July 24, 1978, as amended at 60 FR 43531, Aug. 22, 1995]

Subpart C—Policies Relating to Rates and Tariffs

§ 399.30 Definitions.

As used in this subpart:

DPFI formula fare means the trunk coach formula fare on July 1, 1977, as established by the Board in Phase 9 of the Domestic Passenger Fares Investigation (Docket 21866–9).

SIFL means the standard industry fare level, as set forth in § 399.31.

[PS–92, 45 FR 24118, Apr. 9, 1980]

§ 399.31 Standard industry fare level.

(a) *Generally.* Except as set forth in paragraph (d) of this section, the standard industry fare level ("SIFL") for coach/standard service in a market is equal to the predominant fare in effect in that market on July 1, 1977, as adjusted by the Board for cost increases.

(b) *Predominant fare.* For each market, the predominant fare in effect on July 1, 1977, is presumed to be as set forth below. The presumption may be rebutted, however, by showing that more passengers used a higher fare.

(1) For U.S. Mainland-Puerto Rico/Virgin Islands markets where the Board has specified day-of-week fare differentials: the peak-season midweek fare appearing in tariffs in effect on July 1, 1977.

(2) For U.S. Mainland-Puerto Rico/Virgin Islands markets where the Board has specified only seasonal fare differentials: the off-peak-season fare appearing in tariffs in effect on July 1, 1977.

(3) For U.S. Mainland-Hawaii markets: the peak-season second class fare appearing in tariffs in effect on July 1, 1977.

(4) For all other interstate and overseas markets: the lowest unrestricted fare in effect on July 1, 1977.

(c) *Adjustments for cost increases.* The Board adjusts the SIFL at least once every 6 months by the percentage change, since the previous adjustment, in the actual operating cost per available seat-mile for interstate and overseas transportation combined. The method of adjustment is illustrated in the example set out at the end of this subpart.

(d) *Intrastate markets in California, Florida, and Texas.* For each of these markets, the SIFL is equal to the level that it would be if the market were an interstate one whose predominant fare on July 1, 1977, was the DPFI formula fare.

(e) *Intra-Hawaii markets.* For intra-Hawaii markets, the Board's flexibility zones are based not on the SIFL, but on the standard Hawaiian fare level ("SHFL"), which is equal to 110 percent of the first class fare in effect on July 1, 1977, as adjusted by the Board for cost increases.

[PS-92, 45 FR 24118, Apr. 9, 1980, as amended by PS-95, 45 FR 42255, June 24, 1980; PS-96, 45 FR 48604, July 21, 1980]

§399.32 Zone of limited suspension for domestic passenger fares.

(a) *Applicability.* This section sets forth the Board's policy on passenger fares for scheduled service by certificated air carriers in the following areas, except to the extent that greater flexibility is set forth in §399.33:

(1) Within the 48 contiguous States and the District of Columbia ("the Mainland"); and

(2) Between the Mainland and Puerto Rico, the Virgin Islands, Hawaii, or Alaska.

(b) *Downward flexibility.* Each carrier may set fares in each market at any amount below the SIFL. The Board will not suspend such a fare on the ground that its level is unreasonable, except in the following extraordinary circumstances:

(1) There is a high probability that the fare would be found to be unlawful after investigation;

(2) There is a substantial likelihood that the fare is predatory so that there would be an immediate and irreparable harm to competition if the fare were allowed to go into effect;

(3) The harm to competition is greater than the injury to the traveling public if the proposed fare were unavailable; and

(4) The suspension is in the public interest.

(c) [Reserved]

(d) *Upward flexibility.* Each carrier may set fares above the SIFL as follows, and where they are so set, the Board will not suspend them on the grounds that their level is unreasonable except upon a clear showing of abuse of market power that the Board does not expect to be corrected through marketplace forces:

(1) For service on the Mainland: Up to 30 percent above the sum of the SIFL plus $14. Each time after January 13, 1981, that the Board adjusts the SIFL for cost increases in accordance with §399.31(c), it will adjust the $14 figure by the same percentage rounded to the nearest whole dollar. The Board order announcing the adjustment will be published in the FEDERAL REGISTER and served on all certificated carriers, and copies will be available through the Domestic Fares and Rates Division, Bureau of Domestic Aviation, Civil Aeronautics Board, Washington, D.C. 20428.

(2) For service between the Mainland and Puerto Rico, the Virgin Islands, Hawaii, or Alaska: Up to 30 percent above the SIFL.

(e) *Fares above the zone.* Tariff filings that state fares above the applicable zone must include the data and information set forth in §221.165 of this chapter. For peak fares, this must include a description of the carrier's off-peak fares that are available in the market. The Board will suspend a fare above the zone that it finds not to be justified by cost or competitive factors.

[PS-94, 45 FR 40973, June 17, 1980, as amended by PS-96, 45 FR 48604, July 21, 1980; PS-101, 46 FR 11809, Feb. 11, 1981]

§399.33 Additional fare flexibility.

For scheduled service in the areas set forth in §399.32(a), certificated air carriers have the following fare flexibility in addition to that set forth in §399.32:

(a) *First class.* Carriers may without restriction set the level of first class fares.

(b) *Small aircraft.* Carriers may without restriction set the level of fares for service with aircraft designed to have a maximum passenger capacity of 60 or fewer seats.

(c) *Through service and on-line connecting service.* For through service and on-line connecting service, carriers may set their fares up to the sum of the local fares minus one tax-rounded coach ceiling terminal charge for each local fare after the first, if that level is higher than the ceiling set forth in §399.32(d). The Board will not suspend such a fare on the ground that its level is unreasonable except upon a clear showing of abuse of market power that the Board does not expect to be corrected through marketplace forces.

[PS–92, 45 FR 24119, Apr. 9, 1980, as amended by PS–94, 45 FR 40974, June 17, 1980; PS–96, 45 FR 48604, July 21, 1980]

§ 399.34 Intra-Hawaii and Intra-Puerto Rico/Virgin Islands fare flexibility.

For scheduled service within Hawaii, and within and between Puerto Rico and the Virgin Islands, certificated air carriers have the fare flexibility set forth in §§ 399.32 and 399.33, except that:

(a) Instead of the limits set forth in § 399.32(d), the upper limit of the zone for Puerto Rico/Virgin Islands is 30 percent above the SIFL, and for Hawaii is 30 percent above the SHFL; and

(b) The fare flexibility set forth in § 399.33(a) (first class) does not apply to service within Hawaii.

APPENDIX A TO § 399.34—UNITED STATES-PUERTO RICO ENTITY

[Normal fares in selected markets—comparison with SIFL]

Market	Rate-making mileage	DPFI formula fare July 1977	July 1977 normal fare level				DPFI formula May 1980	May 1980 normal fare level			
			Peak		Offpeak			Peak		Offpeak	
			Mid week	Week end	Mid week	Week end		Mid week	Week end	Mid week	Week end
San Juan:											
Atlanta	1,547	$130.81					$203.53				
Eastern			$113	$113	$107	$107		$176	$176	$166	$166
Boston	1,674	139.04					216.33				
American								209	218	199	209
Eastern			122	128	116	122		209	218	198	209
Chicago	2,072	164.83					256.45				
American			149	149	143	143		232	232	222	222
Eastern			149	149	143	143		232	232	222	222
Miami	1,045	97.09					151.06				
American								121	131	113	121
Delta								121	131	113	121
Eastern			78	84	72	78		121	131	112	121
Pan Am (National)			78	84	72	78		122	122	122	122
New York	1,597	134.05					208.57				
American			108	114	102	108		175	196	175	196
Eastern			108	114	102	108		175	196	175	196
Pan Am								147	147	147	147
Phildelaphia	1,576	132.69					206.45				
American			115	121	109	115		197	208	187	197
Eastern			115	121	109	115		175	196	175	196
Washington	1,565	131.97					205.34				
American			114	120	108	114		187	197	176	187
Eastern			114	120	108	114		195	206	184	195
Pan Am (National)								147	147	147	147

APPENDIX B TO § 399.34—SELECTED FARE AND SERVICE DATA FOR SEATTLE-ALASKA MARKETS

Market	Rate-making mileage	Actual July 1977 Y fare	DPFI formula fare May 1980 [1]	SIFL formula fare May 1980 [10]	Y fare as of June 1980 [2]		O. & D. passengers Y/E Aug. 30, 1979 [3]	Carriers providing single plane service June 1980 [4]
					Alaska Airlines	Wien Alaska		
Seattle:								
Anchorage	1,448	$119.00	$193.52	$185.14	$159	$159	196,630	AS/NW/WA/WC
Cordova	1,293	118.62	176.85	184.55	178		4,330	AS
Fairbanks	1,533	131.00	201.85	203.81	204	204	44,910	AS/NW/WC
Gustavus (Via JNU)	950	109.62	140.74	170.55	138		1,340	AS
Juneau	909	90.62	137.04	140.99	141	141	40,110	AS/WC
Ketchikan	680	71.62	112.96	111.43	112	112	34,970	AS/WC
Petersburg (Via KTN)	790	89.22	124.07	138.81	138		6,870	AS
Sitka	862	85.62	131.48	133	133.21		17,240	AS
Wrangell (Via KTN)	762	89.22	121.30	138.81	138		4,120	AS
Yakutat	1,092	117.62	155.56	182.99	175		1,500	AS
Kenai [5]	1,468	124.28	198.37	193.35		159	2,470	WC
King Salmon [6]	1,603	167.94	209.26	261.28		200	4,090	WC
Prudhoe Bay [7]	1,802	190.74	229.63	296.75		273	960	WC
Kodiak [8]	1,439	119.00	192.59	185.14		155	11,140	WC

APPENDIX B TO § 399.34—SELECTED FARE AND SERVICE DATA FOR SEATTLE-ALASKA MARKETS—Continued

Market	Rate-making mile-age	Actual July 1977 Y fare	DPFI formula fare May 1980 [1]	SIFL formula fare May 1980 [10]	Y fare as of June 1980 [2]		O. & D. pas-sengers Y/E Aug. 30, 1979 [3]	Carriers providing single plane serv-ice June 1980 [4]
					Alaska Airlines	Wien Alaska		
Homer [9]	1,449	143.40	193.52	223.10	....	159	1,250	WC

[1] $25.14 plus 13.75¢ per mile (0–500); 10.49¢ per mile (501–1500); 10.08¢ per mile (1501 and over). See Order 80–4–211.
[2] Domestic Tariffs.
[3] O. & D. Origin Destination Survey of Airline Passenger Traffic, Table 8, 12 months ended September 30, 1979.
[4] AS = Alaska Airlines; NW = Northwest Orient Airlines; WA = Western Airlines; WC = Wien Air Alaska.
[5] Via Anchorage ($15.28).
[6] Via Anchorage ($48.94).
[7] Via Fairbanks ($59.74).
[8] Local WA Fare.
[9] Via Kodiak ($24.40).
[10] July 1977 fare increased by cumulative adjustment factor of 1.5558% per Order 80–4–211.

APPENDIX C TO § 399.34—ADJUSTMENT OF THE INTRA-HAWAIIAN FARE LEVEL JULY 1, 1977, TO REFLECT COST AT 12.35 PERCENT RETURN

	Regulatory actual Y.E. March 1977			Cost inflation adjusted to July 1, 1977			July 1, 1977, at 12.35 pct R.O.I.
	Aloha	Hawaiian	Total	Aloha	Hawaiian	Total	
RPM's (000)	321,578	404,793	726,371	321,578	404,793	726,371	726,371
ASM's (000)	489,128	638,050	1,127,178	489,128	638,050	1,127,178	1,127,178
Load Factor (percent)	65.75	63.44	64.44	65.75	63.44	64.44	64.4
Yield (dollars) [2]	$0.1427	$0.1453	$0.1441	$0.1427	$0.1453	$0.1441	$0.1589
Operating Revenue—Total	$47,648	$71,599	$119,247	....	....	....	....
Passenger Related Revenue	$46,301	$59,942	$106,243	$46,301	$59,942	$106,243	$116,966
Operating Expense—Total	$45,195	$68,836	$114,031	....	....	....	....
Passenger Related Expenses	$43,858	$57,501	$101,359	[1] $45,937	$59,013	[1] $104,950	$104,950
Operating Profit—Passenger	$2,443	$2,441	$4,884	$364	$929	$1,293	$12,016
Interest Expense	$741	$2,583	$3,324	$741	$2,583	$3,324	$3,324
Earnings Before Tax	$1,702	$(142)	$1,560	$(377)	$(1,654)	$(2,031)	$8,692
Tax at 48 Percent	$817	$68	$749	$181	$794	$975	$4,172
Net Income	$885	$(74)	$811	$(196)	$(860)	$(1,056)	$4,520
Return Element	$1,626	$2,509	$4,135	$545	$1,723	$2,268	$7,844
Investment	$16,192	$47,326	$63,518	$16,192	$47,326	$63,518	$63,518
Return on Investment (percent)	10.04	5.30	6.51	3.37	3.64	3.57	12.35
Increase Factor [3]	....	....	....	....	....	....	10.27

[1] Cost inflation to July 1, 1977; 1.047 percent for Aloha, 1.026 for Hawaiian. The differing rates for the two carriers, having equivalent aircraft and duplicate route structures, is due primarily to a shift by Hawaiian to larger DC–9–50 aircraft starting in the fourth quarter of 1976.
[2] Passenger revenue divided by RPM's.
[3] Passenger yield at 12.35 percent return divided by actual passenger yield for the year ended March 1977.

[PS–96, 45 FR 48604, July 21, 1980]

§ 399.35 Special tariff permission.

(a) *Definition.* As used in this section, *to grant STP* means to approve a carrier's application for Special Tariff Permission to file a tariff on less than the statutory notice set forth in § 221.160(a) of this chapter.

(b) *Lower fares, rates, and charges.* It is the policy of the Board to grant STP for tariffs that state lower fares, rates, or charges and any rules affecting only those lower fares, rates, or charges, except that:

(1) The Board will not grant STP to match a tariff filed on statutory notice; and

(2) The Board will not grant STP if the proposed fares, rates, charges, or rules raise significant questions of lawfulness, that is, could reasonably be expected to be found unjust or unreasonable, unjustly discriminatory, unduly preferential, unduly prejudicial, or predatory, under current statutory or Board guidelines. In these situations, if the carrier files the tariff on statutory notice and at the same time applies for

STP to advance the tariff's effective date, the Board will use its best efforts to act within 15 days to grant or deny STP.

(c) *Higher fares or rates.* For tariffs that state higher fares or rates, and any rules affecting only those fares or rates, the Board's policy on STP is, except in unusual or emergency circumstances:

(1) To grant STP if the resulting fares or rates are within a statutory or Board-established zone of fare or rate flexibility; and

(2) Otherwise, to deny STP.

[PS–94, 45 FR 40974, June 17, 1980, as amended by PS–109, 48 FR 4279, Jan. 31, 1983]

§ 399.36 Unreasonable discrimination.

(a) As used in this section:

(1) *Unreasonable discrimination* means unjust discrimination or unreasonable preference or prejudice; and

(2) *Rate* means rate, fare, or charge.

(b) Except in unusual circumstances or as provided in paragraph (c) of this section, the Board will find a rate for domestic air transportation to constitute unreasonable discrimination only if:

(1) There is a reasonable probability that the rate will result in significant long-run economic injury to passengers or shippers;

(2) The rate is in fact discriminatory according to a reasonable cost allocation or other rational basis;

(3) The rate does not provide transportation or other statutorily recognized benefits that justify the discrimination; and

(4) Actual and potential competitive forces cannot reliably be expected to eliminate the undesirable effects of the discrimination within a reasonable period.

(c) A rate that discriminates on the basis of the status of the traffic carried will not be presumed to be unreasonably discriminatory, unless the use of the status categories in question is contrary to established national antidiscrimination policy.

[PS–93, 45 FR 36062, May 29, 1980]

§ 399.37 Joint fares.

There should be joint fares in all markets over all routings within the contiguous 48 states and the District of Columbia as follows:

(a) *Level.* The level shall not exceed the sum of the maximum local fares permitted by this subpart minus one tax-rounded coach ceiling terminal charge for each interline connection, and in any event shall not exceed the sum of the actual local fares.

(b) *Division.* Joint fares shall be divided according to the relative costs of the mileage flown by each carrier participating in the interline movement. However, where a joint fare is equal to the sum of the actual local fares, each carrier shall get the local fare as its share.

[PS–92, 45 FR 24119, Apr. 9, 1980, as amended by PS–95, 45 FR 42255, June 24, 1980]

§ 399.39 Equipment purchase deposits.

Equipment purchase deposits are advance payments made by air carriers to manufacturers for the purchase of equipment to be delivered in the future, or funds segregated by air carriers for this purpose. It is the policy of the Board not to recognize equipment purchase deposits in an air carrier's investment base for ratemaking purposes. When equipment is acquired by an air carrier and placed in air-transport service, the Board will recognize in the air carrier's investment base interest on purchase deposits on such equipment capitalized and amortized in accordance with the Uniform System of Accounts and Reports for Certificated Air Carriers (part 241 of this chapter).

[PS–32, 32 FR 5370, Mar. 30, 1967]

§ 399.40 Tariffs for domestic air transportation on or after January 1, 1983.

The Board will not approve or accept any tariff filings for interstate of overseas air transportation to be performed on or after January 1, 1983. Any tariffs for such transportation that do not specify an earlier expiration date shall expire at midnight on December 31, 1982.

[PS–107, 47 FR 14893, Apr. 7, 1982]

§399.41 Zones of limited suspension for international cargo rates.

(a) *Applicability.* This section states the Board's policy for suspending rate changes for the transportation of property in foreign air transportation. It does not affect the Board's authority to suspend any rate as unjustly discriminatory, unduly preferential, or unduly prejudicial. This section applies to rate changes by all direct air carriers and direct foreign air carriers.

(b) *Standard foreign rate levels.* For each market in foreign air transportation, the standard foreign rate level for the carriage of property shall be the bulk general commodity rates in effect in that market on April 1, 1982, as adjusted in accordance with paragraph (f) of this section. However, the general commodity rate for shipments larger than 500 kg. shall be deemed to be the same as the 500 kg. rate for the purposes of this paragraph, regardless of any different rate in effect in the market.

(c) *Ceilings of limited rate suspension.* Except as provided in paragraph (d) of this section, the Board will not suspend as unreasonable any proposed rate for foreign air transportation of property equal to or less than the following levels:

(1) For all bulk rates (GCR's and SCR's) in the Atlantic region, 20 percent above the standard foreign rate level.

(2) For all bulk rates (GCR's and SCR's) in the Pacific region, 15 percent above the standard foreign rate level.

(3) For all bulk rates (GCR's and SCR's) in the Western Hemisphere region (except Mexico and Canada), 5 percent above the standard foreign rate level.

(4) For all bulk rates (GCR's and SCR's) in Canada/Mexico transborder markets, 10 percent above the standard foreign rate level for the Western Hemisphere.

(5) For all container rates, no maximum level.

(d) *Extraordinary circumstances.* The Board may suspend any tariff if it finds that:

(1) The suspension is in the public interest because of unreasonable regulatory action by a foreign government with respect to rate proposals of an air carrier, or

(2) All of the following extraordinary circumstances are present:

(i) It is highly probable that the fare would be found unreasonable after investigation;

(ii) There is a substantial likelihood of immediate and irreparable harm to the public if the rate is allowed to go into effect; and

(iii) The suspension is required by the public interest.

(e) *Burden of proof.* Persons requesting tariff suspension under paragraph (d) of this section shall have the burden of producing convincing evidence that the conditions of that paragraph are present.

(f) *Standard foreign rate level adjustments.* (1) The Board will periodically adjust the standard foreign rate levels to reflect the percentage change in average operating costs per available ton-mile since the previous adjustment.

(2) Costs will be averaged for three regions—the Atlantic, the Pacific, and Western Hemisphere—and applied equally among all markets in each region.

(3) Cost computations will be based on scheduled freighter and combination service by U.S. air carriers.

(4) Adjustments will be made on April 1 and October 1 of each year, or more frequently as the Board finds appropriate.

(5) In computing costs under this section, the Board will make no adjustments for load factors, aircraft utilization, or other matters due to operational decisions made solely by carrier management. However, the Board retains the discretion to normalize costs for strikes, mandatory aircraft groundings, and other occurrences not solely due to management decisions.

(g) *Definitions.* For the purpose of this section:

(1) *GCR* means general commodity rate.

(2) *SCR* means specific commodity rate.

(3) *Container rate* means any rate specifically applicable to property tendered to the carrier in a unit load devise.

[PS-109, 48 FR 4279, Jan. 31, 1983]

§ 399.42 Flight equipment depreciation and residual values.

For rate-making purposes, for air carriers receiving subsidy under section 406 of the Act, it is the policy of the Board that flight equipment depreciation will be based on the conventional straight-line method of accrual, employing the service lives and residual values set forth below:

[In percent]

	Service life in years	Residual value as percent of cost
Turbofan equipment:		
4-engine	14	2
3-engine	14	2
2-engine	14	2
Turbojet equipment:		
4-engine	10	5
2-engine	10	5
Turboprop equipment:		
4-engine	12	5
2-engine	10	15
Wide-body equipment:		
4-engine	16	10
3-engine	16	10

[PS–54, 38 FR 24643, Sept. 10, 1973, as amended by PS–99, 45 FR 82625, Dec. 16, 1980]

§ 399.43 Treatment of leased aircraft.

In determining the appropriate treatment of leased aircraft for ratemaking purposes, it is the Board's policy to recognize actual rental expenses. In unusual circumstances where the leased aircraft value (determined on a constructive depreciated basis) in relation to net book value of owned aircraft operated by the same air carrier is significantly in excess of the ratio for the aggregate of the domestic trunklines and local service carriers (computed on the same basis), a reasonable profit element may be added which shall reflect the additional risks of operations with the leased aircraft, to the extent that such risks are not compensated by the return on investment. Such profit element would be determined by applying the standard rate of return, less 6 percentage points, to the value of the leased aircraft, on a constructive depreciated basis, to the extent the ratio of such value to depreciated cost of owned aircraft plus the value of leased aircraft exceeds the average for the domestic air carriers. Rental cost plus allowable profit, if any, will not be recognized in amounts exceeding depreciation plus return on investment computed as if the aircraft had been purchased by the carrier.

[PS–44, 36 FR 7229, Apr. 16, 1971]

§ 399.44 Treatment of deferred Federal income taxes for rate purposes.

For rate-making purposes other than the determination of subsidy under section 406(b), it is the policy of the Board that Federal income tax expense should be based on the normal taxes that would be paid under the depreciation standards used for rate making, and that accumulated reserves for deferred taxes should be excluded from the recognized capitalization for rate-base purposes.

[PS–46, 36 FR 7232, Apr. 16, 1971]

EXAMPLE OF SIFL ADJUSTMENT

[Methodology for determining change in operating expense per available seat-mile]

[See footnotes at end of table]

Year ended September 1979	Trunks	Locals	Trunks plus locals	Total passenger/cargo [16]
Total operating expense [1] (millions)	$16,455	$2,522	$18,977	$19,384
Less:				
All-cargo expenses [2]	269	....	269	269
Belly offset [3]	952	153	1,105	1,153
Nonscheduled [4]	141	46	187	205
Transport related [5]	379	31	410	416
Plus: Capitalized lease adjustment [10]	119	2	121	121
Passenger operating expense	14,833	2,294	17,127	17,462
Passenger fuel cost [11]	....	....	4,103	N.A.
Scheduled service ASM's (mils.)	281,671	33,051	314,722	318,459
Passenger nonfuel operating expense per ASM (dollars)	....	....	.04138	N.A.
Passenger fuel expense per ASM (dollars)	....	....	.01304	N.A.

[Methodology for determining change in operating expense per available seat-mile]
[See footnotes at end of table]

Year ended September 1979	Trunks	Locals	Trunks plus locals	Total passenger/cargo [16]
Total passenger expense per ASM (dollars)	....	....	.05442	.05483
Year ended September 1978				
Total operating expense [1] (millions)	14,081	2,033	16,114	16,448
Less:				
All-cargo expenses [2]	282	....	282	282
Belly offset [3]	869	152	1,021	1,065
Nonscheduled [4]	193	53	246	256
Transport related [5]	419	30	449	454
Plus: Capitalized lease adjustment [10]	78	1	79	79
Passenger operating expense	12,396	1,799	14,195	14,470
Passenger fuel cost [11]	....	....	3,129	N.A.
Scheduled service ASM's (mils.)	262,068	27,067	289,135	292,255
Passenger nonfuel operating expense per ASM (dollars)	....	....	.03827	N.A.
Passenger fuel expense per ASM (dollars)	....	....	.01082	N.A.
Total passenger expense per ASM (dollars)	....	....	.04909	.04951
Percent change in nonfuel operating expense per ASM (percent)	....	....	8.13	N.A.
Projected change in nonfuel expense from April 1, 1979 to April 1, 1980 [6]	....	....	8.13	N.A.
Estimated change in fuel cost, year ended September 1979 average to April 1, 1980 [14]	....	....	73.06	N.A.
Nonfuel operating expense per ASM at April 1, 1980 [7] (dollars)	....	....	.04474	N.A.
Fuel expense per ASM at April 1, 1980 [7] (dollars)	....	....	.02257	N.A.
Total expense per ASM at April 1, 1980 [7] (dollars)	....	....	.06731	[15] .06782
Year ended March 1977				
Total operating expense [1] (millions)	$11,726	$1,520	$13,316	$13,601
Less:				
All-cargo expense [2]	238	....	238	238
Belly offset [3]	729	96	825	865
Nonscheduled [4]	220	35	225	266
Transport related [5]	427	111	538	554
Passenger operating expense	10,112	1,348	11,460	11,678
Passenger fuel cost	2,190	230	2,420	N.A.
Scheduled service ASM's (mils.)	239,593	23,428	263,021	265,837
Operating expense per ASM (dollars)	.04221	.05754	.04357	.04393
Projected expense per ASM (dollars) as at July 1, 1977 [13]	....	....	....	.04593
Projected operating expense per ASM as at April 1, 1980 (page 1) (dollars)	....	....	....	.06782
Ceiling adjustment factor [8] (percent)	....	....	....	47.66

D.P.F.I. formula effective July 15, 1977 [12]:	
Terminal charge	$16.16
Plus	.0884/mile (0–500 miles).
Plus	.0674/mile (501–1,500 miles).
Plus	.0648/mile (over 1,500 miles).
Ceiling formula through April 30, 1980 [9]:	
Terminal charge	$23.86
Plus	.1305/mile (0–500 miles).
Plus	.0995/mile (501–1,500 miles).
Plus	.0957/mile (over 1,500 miles).

[1] Total operating expense for all operations and service (in millions).
[2] Scheduled all-cargo operations expense.
[3] Total scheduled-service cargo revenue, less scheduled all-cargo operations revenue, carried as a by-product in aircraft belly compartments. Includes freight, express, priority and non-priority U.S. mail, and excess baggage.
[4] Total non-scheduled revenues times 0.95, assuming charter operations would only be conducted at a profit.
[5] Total transport-related expense, less any excess of expense over total transport-related revenues.
[6] We here project costs from April 1, 1979 (the midpoint of the data year ended September 1979) to April 1, 1980 the resultant increase factor effective through April 30, 1980.
[7] Operating expense per ASM for year-ended September, 1979, times projected change.
[8] Projected operating expense per ASM on April 1, 1980 divided by the operating expense as at July 1, 1977.
[9] Adjustment results in a 2.5 percent increase in level over current January 1, 1980 factor.
[10] Additional rental expense that would have been incurred had leases not been capitalized under FASB–13, less actual amortization of capitalized lease expense.
[11] Total fuel cost, scheduled service, times complement of rate of All-Cargo expense to total Operating Expense.
[12] Order 77–7–26.

[13] Year ended March, 1977 cost per ASM, times cost escalation factor of 1.04543 (to July 5, 1977). See DPFI workpapers, Y.E. March, 1977.
[14] Estimated average cost per gallon for the trunk plus local service carriers at April 1, 1980, divided by the average for the year ended September, 1979 (48.33¢).
[15] Change in Trunks plus Locals cost per ASM as at April 1, 1980, to year ended September, 1979 times total Psgr/Cargo cost for the year ended September, 1979.
[16] Includes Alaskan, Hawaiian and other regional carriers.

[PS–92, 45 FR 24119, Apr. 9, 1980]

Subpart D [Reserved]

Subpart E—Policies Relating to Hearing Matters

§ 399.60 Standards for determining priorities of hearing.

(a) *General.* This policy statement describes the general standards which will be used by the Board in determining the order in which it will designate for hearing those matters on its docket which are to be decided after notice and hearing. Among such matters are applications for certificates of public convenience and necessity or for foreign air carrier permits; applications under section 408 of the Act for approval of consolidations or acquisitions of control; complaint cases; and various rate-making proceedings.

(b) *Standards.* Matters will be assigned for hearing in accordance with the degree of relative priority which each matter is entitled to on the basis of the comparative public interest involved therein. Among other things, the Board will take into account:

(1) Statutory requirements for preference or statutory limitations on the time within which the Board shall act;

(2) The impact of delay on the public or particular persons;

(3) The need for promptly securing compliance with the provisions of the Act;

(4) The time for which the matter has already been pending and which would be required to dispose of it;

(5) Whether the application requests renewal of an existing temporary authorization; and

(6) In matters relating to operating authority:

(i) Whether a proposal might reduce subsidy or increase economy of operations;

(ii) Whether an application proposes new service;

(iii) The volume of traffic that might be affected by the grant or denial of the proposal;

(iv) The period that has elapsed since the Board considered the service needs of the places or areas involved; and

(v) The relative availability of necessary staff members of the carriers, communities and the Board, in the light of other proceedings already in progress, to handle the processing of the case.

Interested persons may urge upon the Board such considerations as they believe should lead it to accord a particular application a priority different from that which the Board has given it.

§ 399.61 Presentations of public and civic bodies in route proceedings.

For the purpose of implementing the Board's policy to provide for the exclusion of irrelevant, immaterial, or unduly repetitious evidence and otherwise to expedite route proceedings, and in light of experience, the following guidelines are hereby established:

(a) Public and civic bodies which represent the same geographic area or community should consolidate their presentation of evidence, briefs or oral argument to the examiner and the Board;

(b) A public body or a civic organization, or several such bodies or organizations whose presentation of evidence is consolidated, should keep to a minimum the number of witnesses used to present the factual evidence in support of the community's position;

(c) Exhibits offered in evidence by a public body or civic organization should be limited to evidence of the economic characteristics of the community and area involved, data as to community of interest and traffic, evidence with respect to the sufficiency of existing service, and airport data, and should not include data relating to number of electricity, water and gas meters, telephones, schools, freight car loadings, building permits, sewer connections, or volume of bank deposits in the community.

§399.62 Target dates in hearing cases.

(a) *Applicability.* This section applies to initial and recommended decisions of administrative law judges, final decisions, and decisions on petitions for review or reconsideration in cases in which the Board has ordered a trial-type hearing before an administrative law judge.

(b) *Issuance of target dates.* In cases to which this section applies, the Board or the administrative law judge, as the situation calls for, shall issue a notice of the target date for the completion of the initial or recommended decision, final decision, or decision on a petition for review or reconsideration. The Board or the administrative law judge shall endeavor to render the pending decision not later than the target date.

(c) *Time for promulgating target dates.* (1) In the case of initial, recommended, or final decisions, notice of target dates shall be issued, served, and filed within 20 days of the submission of closing briefs, or the conclusion of oral argument to the administrative law judge or the Board, as may be appropriate.

(2) In the case of petitions for review or for reconsideration, notices of target dates shall be issued, served, and filed within 20 days of the date for the filing of answers: *Provided,* That, in the case of petitions for reconsideration of Board decisions awarding new route authority, the Board shall, in lieu of issuing individual target dates, endeavor to render its decision no later than the day preceding the effective date of the new authority awarded.

[PS–71, 41 FR 41407, Sept. 22, 1976, as amended by PS–73, 42 FR 21611, Apr. 28, 1977]

§399.63 Role of staff in route proceedings.

(a) *General.* This policy statement establishes the standards applicable to staff participation in oral hearing cases involving award of route authority.

(b) *Standards.* The staff's role during such hearings, primarily because it acts in the broad public interest, and not for a particular private or local interest, is to assure that essential evidence is introduced to resolve the public interest issues; that the evidence submitted by the parties is subject to adversary testing, and that decisional options are developed with the public interest in mind. In route cases designated by the Board that offer the opportunity for developing new policies to adapt to the administration of the Federal Aviation Act or that raise unusual evidentiary issues, a prehearing presentation by staff of decisional options will contribute to a better trial record, be consistent with traditional notions of fundamental fairness, better serve the Board's decisionmaking needs and ultimately serve the public interest. In any route case where the Board has not required the staff to participate by making a prehearing presentation, the staff shall present a prehearing presentation of decisional options if the administrative law judge finds that there exists unusual policy or evidentiary issues which clearly require such a presentation. We believe it is not desirable for the staff to advocate the adoption of a single decisional option at the outset of a case. Accordingly,

(1) In route cases designated by the Board that offer the opportunity for developing new policies, the staff shall make a prehearing presentation of the decisional options available, and describe the kinds of evidence needed or available to develop each option. The staff need not and should not be required to develop evidence on each option. In every case, after the close of the hearing, however, the staff shall advocate a position based upon one or more of the decisional options identified in its prehearing presentation or developed at trial.

(2) In any route case in which the administrative law judge finds that there exists unusual policy or evidentiary issues clearly requiring a prehearing presentation, the staff shall submit a prehearing statement of the decisional options available.

(3) To the extent possible, the Board, in its instituting orders, will identify or designate the cases which involve

the development of new policies or unusual evidentiary issues that will require the type of staff participation described in § 399.63(b)(1).

[PS–76, 43 FR 19354, May 5, 1978]

Subpart F—Policies Relating to Rulemaking Proceedings

§ 399.70 Cross-references to the Office of the Secretary's Rulemaking Procedures.

The rules and policies relating to the disposition of rulemaking petitions by the Department of Transportation Office of the Secretary are located in its rulemaking procedures contained in 49 CFR part 5. The criteria for identifying significant rules and determining whether a regulatory analysis will be performed are set forth in the Department's Regulatory Policies and Procedures, 44 FR 11034, February 26, 1979, and Executive Order 12866.

[Doc. No. OST–96–1429, 61 FR 29019, June 7, 1996]

§ 399.73 Definition of small business for Regulatory Flexibility Act.

For the purposes of the Department's implementation of chapter 6 of title 5, United States Code (Regulatory Flexibility Act), a direct air carrier or foreign air carrier is a small business if it provides air transportation only with small aircraft as defined in § 298.3 of this chapter (up to 60 seats/18,000 pound payload capacity).

[Doc. No. OST–96–1429, 61 FR 29019, June 7, 1996]

Subpart G—Policies Relating to Enforcement

§ 399.80 Unfair and deceptive practices of ticket agents.

It is the policy of the Department to regard as an unfair or deceptive practice or unfair method of competition the practices enumerated in paragraphs (a) through (m) of this section by a ticket agent of any size and the practice enumerated in paragraph (s) by a ticket agent that sells air transportation online and is not considered a small business under the Small Business Administration's size standards set forth in 13 CFR 121.201:

(a) Misrepresentations[1] which may induce members of the public to believe that the ticket agent is an air carrier.

(b) Using or displaying or permitting or suffering to be used or displayed the name, trade name, slogan or any abbreviation thereof, of the ticket agent, in advertisements, on or in places of business, or on aircraft in connection with the name of an air carrier with whom it does business, in such manner that it may mislead or confuse the traveling public with respect to the agency status of the ticket agent.

(c) Misrepresentations as to the quality or kind of service, type or size of aircraft, time of departure or arrival, points served, route to be flown, stops to be made, or total trip-time from point of departure to destination.

(d) Misrepresentation as to qualifications of pilots or safety record or certification of pilots, aircraft or air carriers.

(e) Misrepresentations that passengers are directly insured when they are not so insured; for example, where the only insurance in force is that protecting the air carrier in event of liability.

(f) Misrepresentations as to fares and charges for air transportation or services in connection therewith.

(g) Misrepresentation that special discounts or reductions are available, when such discounts or reductions are not specific in the lawful tariffs of the air carrier which is to perform the transportation.

(h) [Reserved]

(i) Misrepresentations that special priorities for reservations are available when such special considerations are not in fact granted to members of the public generally.

(j) Selling air transportation to persons on a reservation or charter basis for specified space, flight, or time, or representing that such definite reservation or charter is or will be available or has been arranged, without a binding

[1] The word "misrepresentation" used in this list includes any statement or representation made in advertising or made orally to members of the public which is false, fraudulent, deceptive or misleading, or which has the tendency or capacity to deceive or mislead.

commitment with an air carrier for the furnishing of such definite reservation or charter as represented or sold.

(k) Selling or issuing tickets or other documents to passengers to be exchanged or used for air transportation knowing or having reason to know or believe that such tickets or other documents will not be or cannot be legally honored by air carriers for air transportation.

(l) Failing or refusing to make proper refunds promptly when service cannot be performed as contracted or representing that such refunds are obtainable only at some other point, thus depriving persons of the immediate use of the money to arrange other transportation, or forcing them to suffer unnecessary inconveniences and delays or requiring them to accept transportation at higher cost, or under less desirable circumstances, or on less desirable aircraft than that represented at the time of sale.

(m) Misrepresentations regarding the handling, forwarding or routing of baggage or other property, or the loss or tracing thereof, or failing or refusing to honor proper claims for loss of or damage to baggage or other property.

(n) Misrepresentation as to the requirements that must be met by persons or organizations in order to qualify for charter or group fare flights.

(o)–(r) [Reserved]

(s) Failing to disclose and offer Web-based discount fares on or after June 10, 2014, to prospective passengers who contact the agent through other channels (e.g., by telephone or in the agent's place of business) and indicate they are unable to use the agent's Web site due to a disability.

[PS–21, 29 FR 1446, Jan. 29, 1964, as amended at 78 FR 67916, Nov. 12, 2013; Docket No. DOT–OST–2014–0056, 81 FR 76829, Nov. 3, 2016]

§ 399.81 Unrealistic or deceptive scheduling.

(a) The unrealistic scheduling of flights by any air carrier providing scheduled passenger air transportation is an unfair or deceptive practice and an unfair method of competition within the meaning of 49 U.S.C. 41712.

(b) With respect to the advertising of schedule performance, it is an unfair or deceptive practice and an unfair method of competition to use any figures purporting to reflect schedule or on-time performance without indicating the basis of the calculation, the time period involved, and the pairs of points or the percentage of system-wide operations thereby represented and whether the figures include all scheduled flights or only scheduled flights actually performed.

(c) *Chronically delayed flights.* (1) This section applies to any air carrier that is a "reporting carrier" as defined in Part 234 of Department regulations (14 CFR Part 234).

(2) For the purposes of this section, a chronically delayed flight means any domestic flight that is operated at least 10 times a month, and arrives more than 30 minutes late (including cancelled flights) more than 50 percent of the time during that month.

(3) For purposes of this paragraph, the Department considers all of a carrier's flights that are operated in a given city-pair market whose scheduled departure times are within 30 minutes of the most frequently occurring scheduled departure time to be one single flight.

(4) The holding out of a chronically delayed flight for more than four consecutive one-month periods represents one form of unrealistic scheduling and is an unfair or deceptive practice and an unfair method of competition within the meaning of 49 U.S.C. 41712.

[Doc. No. DOT–OST–2007–0022, 74 FR 69003, Dec. 30, 2009]

§ 399.82 Passing off of carrier identity by affiliation between carriers.

(a) *Applicability.* This policy shall apply to proceedings in which the Board, in exercising its regulatory powers with respect to air carriers and foreign air carriers, is required to determine whether carriers have engaged in unfair or deceptive practices, or unfair methods of competition. The standards herein shall not be construed to supersede any action previously taken by the Board in a particular proceeding dealing with the subject matter of this statement, but to the extent not inconsistent therewith shall provide standards which supplement, or implement such specific Board action. The limitation of this policy statement to certain affiliated carriers should not be construed as an indication that the Board will permit other carriers to pass off by means of activities which are inconsistent with the minimum safeguards set forth in paragraph (c) of this section. In such cases the Board may determine in an adjudicatory proceeding that the activities engaged in have a tendency to pass off and constitute an unfair or deceptive practice or an unfair method of competition.

(b) *Definition.* For the purpose of this statement, the term *affiliation*, as between an air carrier and a foreign air carrier, shall mean that one of the carriers directly or indirectly has one of the following relationships to the other:

(1) Owns or controls 10 percent or more of the securities of the other, with or without an accompanying power to vote;

(2) Is in control of the other within the meaning of section 408 of the Act;

(3) Has any of the interlocking relationships described in section 409 of the Act;

(4) Is jointly controlled with the other carrier, directly or indirectly by a third person;

(5) Provides general agency services for the other carrier.

For the purpose of this statement, *general agency services* shall mean services performed under an agreement between an air carrier and a foreign air carrier which provides for the general representation of one by the other in a specified area or point, in relation to services such as the following: Solicitation and sale of passenger, express, and cargo transportation; airport transportation and hotel accommodations; local advertising and publicity, local sales offices; passenger services; local government representation; purchase, lease or other acquisition of equipment; or aircraft and transit services, aircraft inspection, aircraft dispatch.

(c) *Minimum safeguards.* The minimum safeguards which the Board will consider as adequate to foreclose passing off by affiliated carriers are as follows:

(1) An air carrier and any affiliated foreign air carrier shall not engage in joint public relations activities at points served by both carriers which tend to pass off the services of one carrier as the services of the other carrier or as part of a unified system of which each is a part;

(2) Where one affiliated carrier provides general agency services for the other carrier, at points served by both carriers, it shall specifically identify all flights of the other carrier as flights of that carrier without reference to any relationship to the carrier performing the agency services;

(3) All forms of display (including aircraft insignia), scheduled publications, advertising, or printed matter employed by affiliated carriers shall not state or imply that the services of either carrier are performed in common with the other carrier or as part of a single system. In cases where it is necessary to indicate that any agency service is performed by one affiliated carrier for the other, the references to the carrier performing the agency should be sufficiently subordinated to the name of the other carrier as to emphasize the limited role of the agent;

(4) Telephone facilities at points served by both carriers should preserve the identity of the individual carriers;

(5) Where joint traffic or sales facilities are maintained by affiliated carriers, the separate identity of each carrier should be maintained by reasonably comparable use of display advertising, desk-space, personnel uniforms, and other facilities and activities;

(6) Where one carrier sells time payment tickets for travel over the other carrier (except interline travel), the application form should identify the carrier performing the transportation;

(7) The respective personnel of the affiliated carriers shall preserve the individual identity of the respective carriers in all public dealings.

(d) *Unfair and deceptive practice.* It is the policy of the Board to regard any joint activity of an affiliated air carrier and a foreign air carrier as an unfair or deceptive practice or unfair method of competition where such joint activity does not satisfy the minimum safeguards enumerated in the preceding subsection.

(e) *Exceptions.* Exceptions to a safeguard set forth in paragraph (c) of this section may be recognized for activities in a foreign country if the Board finds that special circumstances pertaining to the country render the safeguard inappropriate. Exceptions on other grounds may be recognized pursuant to § 399.4.

[PS-29, 30 FR 13781, Oct. 29, 1965]

§ 399.83 Unfair or deceptive practice of air carrier, foreign air carrier, or ticket agent in orally confirming to prospective passenger reserved space on scheduled flights.

It is the policy of the Board to consider the practice of an air carrier, foreign air carrier, or ticket agent, of stating to a prospective passenger by telephone or other means of communication that a reservation of space on a scheduled flight in air transportation is confirmed before a passenger has received a ticket specifying thereon his confirmed reserved space, to be an unfair or deceptive practice and an unfair method of competition in air transportation or the sale thereof within the meaning of section 411 of the Act, unless the tariff of the particular air carrier or foreign air carrier provides for confirmation of reserved space by the means so used.

[PS-58, 39 FR 38096, Oct. 29, 1974]

§ 399.84 Price advertising and opt-out provisions.

(a) The Department considers any advertising or solicitation by a direct air carrier, indirect air carrier, an agent of either, or a ticket agent, for passenger air transportation, a tour (*i.e.*, a combination of air transportation and ground or cruise accommodations) or tour component (e.g., a hotel stay) that must be purchased with air transportation that states a price for such air transportation, tour, or tour component to be an unfair and deceptive practice in violation of 49 U.S.C. 41712, unless the price stated is the entire price to be paid by the customer to the carrier, or agent, for such air transportation, tour, or tour component. Although charges included within the single total price listed (e.g., government taxes) may be stated separately or through links or "pop ups" on websites that display the total price, such charges may not be false or misleading, may not be displayed prominently, may not be presented in the same or larger size as the total price, and must provide cost information on a per passenger basis that accurately reflects the cost of the item covered by the charge.

(b) The Department considers any advertising by the entities listed in paragraph (a) of this section of an each-way airfare that is available only when purchased for round-trip travel to be an unfair and deceptive practice in violation of 49 U.S.C. 41712, unless such airfare is advertised as "each way" and in such a manner so that the disclosure of the round-trip purchase requirement is clearly and conspicuously noted in the advertisement and is stated prominently and proximately to the each-way fare amount. The Department considers it to be an unfair and deceptive practice to advertise each-way fares contingent on a round-trip purchase requirement as "one-way" fares, even if accompanied by prominent and proximate disclosure of the round trip purchase requirement.

(c) When offering a ticket for purchase by a consumer, for passenger air transportation or for a tour (*i.e.*, a combination of air transportation and ground or cruise accommodations) or tour component (e.g., a hotel stay) that must be purchased with air transportation, a direct air carrier, indirect air carrier, an agent of either, or a ticket agent, may not offer additional optional services in connection with air transportation, a tour, or tour component whereby the optional service is automatically added to the consumer's purchase if the consumer takes no other action, i.e., if the consumer does not opt out. The consumer must affirmatively "opt in" (*i.e.*, agree) to such a service and the fee for it before that fee is added to the total price for the air transportation-related purchase. The Department considers the use of "opt-out" provisions to be an unfair and deceptive practice in violation of 49 U.S.C. 41712.

[76 FR 23166, Apr. 25, 2011]

§ 399.85 Notice of baggage fees and other fees.

(a) If a U. S. or foreign air carrier has a website accessible for ticket purchases by the general public in the U.S., the carrier must promptly and prominently disclose any increase in its fee for carry-on or first and second checked bags and any change in the first and second checked bags or carry-on allowance for a passenger on the homepage of that website (e.g., provide a link that says "changed bag rules" or similarly descriptive language and takes the consumer from the homepage directly to a pop-up or a place on another webpage that details the change in baggage allowance or fees and the effective dates of such changes). Such notice must remain on the homepage for at least three months after the change becomes effective.

(b) If a U.S. carrier, a foreign air carrier, an agent of either, or a ticket agent has a website accessible for ticket purchases by the general public in the U.S., the carrier or agent must clearly and prominently disclose on the first screen in which the agent or carrier offers a fare quotation for a specific itinerary selected by a consumer that additional airline fees for baggage may apply and where consumers can see these baggage fees. An agent may refer consumers to the airline websites where specific baggage fee information may be obtained or to its own site if it displays airlines' baggage fees.

(c) On all e-ticket confirmations for air transportation within, to or from the United States, including the summary page at the completion of an online purchase and a post-purchase email confirmation, a U.S. carrier, a foreign air carrier, an agent of either, or a ticket agent that advertises or sells air transportation in the United States must include information regarding the passenger's free baggage allowance and/or the applicable fee for a carry-on bag and the first and second checked bag. Carriers must provide this information in text form in the e-ticket confirmation. Agents may provide this information in text form in the e-ticket confirmations or through a hyperlink to the specific location on airline websites or their own website where this information is displayed. The fee information provided for a carry-on bag and the first and second checked bag must be expressed as specific charges taking into account any factors (e.g., frequent flyer status, early purchase, and so forth) that affect those charges.

(d) If a U.S. or foreign air carrier has a website marketed to U.S. consumers where it advertises or sells air transportation, the carrier must prominently disclose on its website information on fees for all optional services that are available to a passenger purchasing air transportation. Such disclosure must be clear, with a conspicuous link from the carrier's homepage directly to a page or a place on a page where all such optional services and related fees are disclosed. For purposes of this section, the term "optional services" is defined as any service the airline provides, for a fee, beyond passenger air transportation. Such fees include, but are not limited to, charges for checked or carry-on baggage, advance seat selection, in-flight beverages, snacks and meals, pillows and blankets and seat upgrades. In general, fees for particular services may be expressed as a range; however, baggage fees must be expressed as specific charges taking into account any factors (e.g., frequent flyer status, early purchase, and so forth) that affect those charges.

(e) For air transportation within, to or from the United States, a carrier marketing a flight under its identity that is operated by a different carrier, otherwise known as a code-share flight, must through its website disclose to consumers booked on a code-share flight any differences between its optional services and related fees and those of the carrier operating the flight. This disclosure may be made through a conspicuous notice of the existence of such differences on the marketing carrier's website or a conspicuous hyperlink taking the reader directly to the operating carrier's fee listing or to a page on the marketing carrier's website that lists the differences in policies among code-share partners.

(f) The Department considers the failure to give the appropriate notice described in paragraphs (a) through (e) of this section to be an unfair and deceptive practice within the meaning of 49 U.S.C. 41712.

[Doc. No. DOT–OST–2010–0140, 76 FR 23166, Apr. 25, 2011]

§ 399.86 Payments for non-air transportation services for air cargo.

The Board considers that payments by air carriers and foreign air carriers to shippers, indirect air carriers, or foreign indirect air carriers for non-air transportation preparation of air cargo shipments are for services ancillary to the air transportation, and are not prohibited under section 403 of the Act.

[PS–86, 44 FR 45609, Aug. 3, 1979]

§ 399.87 Baggage allowances and fees.

For passengers whose ultimate ticketed origin or destination is a U.S. point, U.S. and foreign carriers must apply the baggage allowances and fees that apply at the beginning of a passenger's itinerary throughout his or her entire itinerary. In the case of code-share flights that form part of an itinerary whose ultimate ticketed origin or destination is a U.S. point, U.S. and foreign carriers must apply the baggage allowances and fees of the marketing carrier throughout the itinerary to the extent that they differ from those of any operating carrier.

[Doc. No. DOT–OST–2010–0140, 76 FR 23167, Apr. 25, 2011]

§ 399.88 Prohibition on post-purchase price increase.

(a) It is an unfair and deceptive practice within the meaning of 49 U.S.C. 41712 for any seller of scheduled air transportation within, to or from the United States, or of a tour (*i.e.*, a combination of air transportation and ground or cruise accommodations), or tour component (e.g., a hotel stay) that includes scheduled air transportation within, to or from the United States, to increase the price of that air transportation, tour or tour component to a consumer, including but not limited to an increase in the price of the seat, an increase in the price for the carriage of passenger baggage, or an increase in an applicable fuel surcharge, after the air transportation has been purchased by the consumer, except in the case of an increase in a government-imposed tax or fee. A purchase is deemed to have occurred when the full amount agreed upon has been paid by the consumer.

(b) A seller of scheduled air transportation within, to or from the United States or a tour (*i.e.*, a combination of air transportation and ground or cruise accommodations), or tour component (e.g., a hotel stay) that includes scheduled air transportation within, to or from the United States, must notify a consumer of the potential for a post-purchase price increase due to an increase in a government-imposed tax or fee and must obtain the consumer's written consent to the potential for such an increase prior to purchase of the scheduled air transportation, tour or tour component that includes scheduled air transportation. Imposition of any such increase without providing the consumer the appropriate notice and without obtaining his or her written consent of the potential increase constitutes an unfair and deceptive practice within the meaning of 49 U.S.C. 41712.

[Doc. No. DOT–OST–2010–0140, 76 FR 23167, Apr. 25, 2011]

§ 399.89 Disclosure of potential for price increase before payment.

Any seller of scheduled air transportation within, to or from the United States, or of a tour (*i.e.*, a combination of air transportation and ground or cruise accommodations), or tour component (e.g., a hotel stay) that includes scheduled air transportation within, to or from the United States, must notify a consumer of the potential for a price increase that could take place prior to the time that the full amount agreed upon has been paid by the consumer, including but not limited to an increase in the price of the seat, an increase in the price for the carriage of passenger baggage, an increase in an applicable fuel surcharge, or an increase in a government-imposed tax or fee and must obtain the consumer's written consent to the potential for such an increase prior to accepting any payment for the scheduled air transportation, or tour or tour component that includes scheduled air transportation. Imposition of any such increase without providing the consumer the appropriate notice and obtaining his or her written consent to the potential increase constitutes an unfair and deceptive practice within the meaning of 49 U.S.C. 41712.

[Doc. No. DOT–OST–2010–0140, 76 FR 23167, Apr. 25, 2011]

Subpart H—Other Policies Relating to Interests, Activities, and Relationships of Air Carriers

§ 399.91 Air carrier participation in programs of technical assistance to airlines of less developed countries.

(a) *Applicability.* This policy shall apply to proceedings under sections 408, 409, and 412 of the Act in which the Board is required to make any determination as to the public interest or consistency with the Act of any agreement or relationship sought to be entered into by an air carrier, or officer or director thereof, with a foreign airline in connection with the performance of some activity pursuant to a technical assistance contract financed by an agency of the U.S. Government.

(b) *Policy.* It is the policy of the Board that all U.S. air carriers interested in performing contracts for aviation technical assistance to foreign airlines should have equal access to information necessary to bid on such contracts, and should be given equal consideration thereafter in the award of such contracts based upon customary contracting criteria and subject to the considerations set forth below:

(1) The air carrier selected should possess the necessary technical and managerial skills and economic strength to perform the assigned task in the recipient country to the credit of the United States. Where familiarity with the particular language and culture of the recipient country are important to the success of the project, weight should be given to the capabilities of all interested carriers in this regard, including particularly those which a route carrier may have acquired through service to the country or area.

(2) Where a single U.S. route carrier is serving or is certificated to serve the recipient country or the region in which it is located, and where initiation or continued operation of the route by such carrier is an important national interest objective of the United States, weight should be given to any evidence that an award of the contract to the route carrier as opposed to any other U.S. carrier would be held to achieve this objective.

(3) An air carrier performing a technical assistance contract will necessarily occupy a close special relationship with the airline and government of the recipient country. Over and above the terms of any specific contract, there is latent in such relationship the possibility of a relative preference for such carrier over a competing U.S. air carrier in matters of interline traffic, governmental restrictions, etc. Accordingly, where more than one U.S. route carrier is certificated to serve the recipient country and more than one such carrier wishes to perform the technical assistance, none of such carriers should be awarded the contract over the objection of any other except under very unusual circumstances.

(4) Technical assistance contracts should contain realistic objectives and require competent performance at reasonable cost and within a reasonable period of time consistent with the ability of the foreign airline to become self-sufficient.

(5) Technical assistance contracts should not be awarded to a U.S. route carrier with major economic interests hostile to those of the U.S. route carrier serving the country.

(6) Technical assistance contracts should not be awarded to subsidized carriers except under special circumstances. Such circumstances should include at least a showing (i) that the subsidized carrier has special qualifications, the utilization of which is required in the national interest by the circumstances of a particular program, and (ii) that performance of the contract will not interfere with the primary business of the subsidized carrier which is to provide air transportation in the United States. In the latter connection, it is to be recognized that participation with maximum effectiveness in a technical assistance program would not only divert the attention of top management from certificated services but might also involve the assignment of the most competent senior

operational and technical personnel, the diversion of funds at least on a short-term basis, and the possible transfer from certificated services of aircraft and related equipment. Normally, therefore, unless substantial evidence and arguments are produced to the contrary, participation by subsidized carriers in technical assistance programs will be considered inconsistent with the public interest.

[PS-22, 29 FR 5788, May 1, 1964]

Subpart I—Policies Relating to Disclosure of Information

§399.101 Public release of Board decisions in cases where the action of the Board is subject to the review or approval of the President.

(a) By Executive Order 11920, 41 FR 23665 (June 11, 1976), effective July 11, 1976, the President has authorized the issuance for public inspection of decisions by the Board in cases where the action of the Board is subject to the review or approval of the President in accordance with section 801 of the Federal Aviation Act. In the interest of national security, and in order to allow for consideration of appropriate action under Executive Order 11652, Executive Order 11920 provides that decisions shall be withheld from public disclosure for five days after submission to the President but may be released on or after the sixth day following receipt by the President as to all unclassified portions of the text if the Board is not notified by the Assistant to the President for National Security Affairs or his designee that all or part of the decision shall be withheld from public disclosure.

(b) It is the policy of the Board to release to the public all decisions by the Board in section 801 cases as promptly as possible following submission of such decision to the President. Upon receipt of notice by the Assistant to the President for National Security Affairs as required by the Executive Order, the Board shall promptly provide one copy for public inspection in the Docket Section and one copy for public inspection and copying in the Public Reference Room, and shall promptly thereafter print and process the decision for more general distribution in accordance with Board procedures. Where the Board is required to withhold portions of the text of its decision it shall make public those portions of its decision which may be publicly released. Where the Board is required to withhold public release of its decision in its entirety it shall nonetheless publicly indicate that its decision has been transmitted to the President. The Board shall not publicly indicate that its decision has been transmitted to the President in those cases in which the Assistant to the President for National Security Affairs or his designee determines that classification of the existence of the decision is appropriate and so informs the Board. The provisions are also applicable to decisions submitted to the President for review pursuant to section 801(b) of the Act.

[PS-72, 41 FR 46291, Oct. 20, 1976]

Subpart J—Policies Relating to Federal Preemption of State Economic Regulations

AUTHORITY: Secs. 102, 105, 204, 401, 403, and 416 of the Federal Aviation Act of 1958, as amended; 72 Stat. 740, 743, 754, 758, 771; 49 U.S.C. 1302, 1305, 1324, 1371, 1373, and 1386.

SOURCE: PS-83, 44 FR 9951, Feb. 15, 1979, unless otherwise noted.

§399.111 All operations of federally authorized carriers to be regulated by the Board.

(a) All operations of Federally authorized carriers are subject to the requirements of Title IV of the Act, including certification and tariff-filing requirements, unless otherwise exempted from one or more of those requirements by Board order or regulation.

(b) When any intrastate air carrier that in August 1, 1977, was operating primarily in intrastate air transportation regulated by a State receives the authority to provide interstate air transportation, any authority received from such State shall be considered to be part of its authority to provide air transportation received from the Board under Title IV of the Act, until suspended, amended, or terminated as provided under such title.

Subpart K—Policies Relating to Certificate Duration

§ 399.120 Duration of certificates in limited-entry markets.

All certificate authority that the Department grants to U.S. air carriers in carrier selection proceedings will be awarded in the form of experimental certificates of five years' duration pursuant to section 401(d)(8) of the Federal Aviation Act. This provision does not alter or amend permanent certificates issued prior to January 1, 1985.

[Doc. No. 43403, 51 FR 43188, Dec. 1, 1986]

CHAPTER III—COMMERCIAL SPACE TRANSPORTATION, FEDERAL AVIATION ADMINISTRATION, DEPARTMENT OF TRANSPORTATION

SUBCHAPTER A—GENERAL

SUBCHAPTER B—PROCEDURE

SUBCHAPTER C—LICENSING

SUBCHAPTER A—GENERAL

PART 400—BASIS AND SCOPE

AUTHORITY: 51 U.S.C. 50901–50923.

SOURCE: Docket No. 43810, 53 FR 11013, Apr. 4, 1988, unless otherwise noted.

§ 400.1 Basis.

The basis for the regulations in this chapter is the Commercial Space Launch Act of 1984, and applicable treaties and international agreements to which the United States is party.

§ 400.2 Scope.

The regulations in this chapter set forth the procedures and requirements applicable to the authorization and supervision under 51 U.S.C. subtitle V, chapter 509, of commercial space transportation activities conducted in the United States or by a U.S. citizen. The regulations in this chapter do not apply to—

(a) Space activities carried out by the United States Government on behalf of the United States Government;

(b) The launch of an amateur rocket as defined in § 1.1 of chapter I of this title; or

(c) A launch of a tethered launch vehicle that meets all the following criteria:

(1) *Launch vehicle.* The launch vehicle must—

(i) Be unmanned;

(ii) Be powered by a liquid or hybrid rocket motor;

(iii) Not use any of the toxic propellants of Table I417–2 and Table I417–3 in Appendix I of part 417 of this chapter; and

(iv) Carry no more than 5,000 pounds of propellant.

(2) *Tether system.* The tether system must—

(i) Not yield or fail under—

(A) The maximum dynamic load on the system; or

(B) A load equivalent to two times the maximum potential engine thrust.

(ii) Have a minimum safety factor of 3.0 for yield stress and 5.0 for ultimate stress.

(iii) Constrain the launch vehicle within 75 feet above ground level as measured from the ground to the attachment point of the vehicle to the tether.

(iv) Display no damage prior to the launch.

(v) Be insulated or located such that it will not experience thermal damage due to the launch vehicle's exhaust.

(3) *Separation distances.* The launch operator must separate its launch from the public and the property of the public by a distance no less than that provided for each quantity of propellant listed in Table A of this section.

TABLE A—SEPARATION DISTANCES FOR TETHERED LAUNCHES

Propellant carried (lbs.)	Distance (ft.) of the public and property of the public from the launch point
1–500	900
501–1,000	1,200
1001–1,500	1,350
1,501–2,000	1,450
2,001–2,500	1,550
2,501–3,000	1,600
3,001–3,500	1,650
3,501–4,000	1,700
4,001–4,500	1,750
4,501–5,000	1,800

[Doc. No. FAA–2012–0045, 80 FR 31834, June 4, 2015]

PART 401—ORGANIZATION AND DEFINITIONS

AUTHORITY: 51 U.S.C. 50101–50923.

SOURCE: Docket No. 43810, 53 FR 11013, Apr. 4, 1988, unless otherwise noted.

§ 401.1 The Office of Commercial Space Transportation.

The Office of Commercial Space Transportation, referred to in these regulations as the "Office," is a line of business within the Federal Aviation Administration and is located in the Federal Aviation Administration Headquarters, 800 Independence Avenue, SW., Room 331, Washington, DC 20591.

[Amdt. 401–3, 68 FR 35289, June 13, 2003]

§ 401.3 The Associate Administrator for Commercial Space Transportation.

The Office is headed by an Associate Administrator to exercise the Secretary's authority to license or permit and otherwise regulate commercial space transportation and to discharge the Secretary's responsibility to encourage, facilitate, and promote commercial space transportation by the United States private sector.

[Doc. No. FAA–2006–24197, 72 FR 17016, Apr. 6, 2007]

§ 401.5 Definitions.

As used in this chapter—

Act means 51 U.S.C Subtitle V, Programs Targeting Commercial Opportunities, chapter 509—Commercial Space Launch Activities, 51 U.S.C. 50901–50923.

Associate Administrator means the Associate Administrator for Commercial Space Transportation, Federal Aviation Administration, or any person designated by the Associate Administrator to exercise the authority or discharge the responsibilities of the Associate Administrator.

Casualty means serious injury or death.

Contingency abort means cessation of vehicle flight during ascent or descent in a manner that does not jeopardize public health and safety and the safety of property, in accordance with mission rules and procedures. Contingency abort includes landing at an alternative location that has been designated as a contingency abort location in advance of vehicle flight.

Crew means any employee or independent contractor of a licensee, transferee, or permittee, or of a contractor or subcontractor of a licensee, transferee, or permittee, who performs activities in the course of that employment or contract directly relating to the launch, reentry, or other operation of or in a launch vehicle or reentry vehicle that carries human beings. A crew consists of flight crew and any remote operator.

Emergency abort means cessation of vehicle flight during ascent or descent in a manner that minimizes risk to public health and safety and the safety of property. Emergency abort involves failure of a vehicle, safety-critical system, or flight safety system such that contingency abort is not possible.

Equivalent level of safety means an approximately equal level of safety as determined by qualitative or quantitative means.

Expendable launch vehicle means a launch vehicle whose propulsive stages are flown only once.

Experimental permit or *permit* means an authorization by the FAA to a person to launch or reenter a reusable suborbital rocket.

Federal launch range means a launch site, from which launches routinely take place, that is owned and operated by the government of the United States.

Flight crew means crew that is on board a vehicle during a launch or reentry.

Flight safety system means a system designed to limit or restrict the hazards to public health and safety and the safety of property presented by a launch vehicle or reentry vehicle while in flight by initiating and accomplishing a controlled ending to vehicle flight. A flight safety system may be destructive resulting in intentional break up of a vehicle or nondestructive, such as engine thrust termination enabling vehicle landing or safe abort capability.

Hazardous materials means hazardous materials as defined in 49 CFR 172.101.

Human space flight incident means an unplanned event that poses a high risk of causing a serious or fatal injury to a space flight participant or crew.

Instantaneous impact point means an impact point, following thrust termination of a launch vehicle, calculated in the absence of atmospheric drag effects.

Launch means to place or try to place a launch vehicle or reentry vehicle and any payload from Earth in a suborbital trajectory, in Earth orbit in outer space, or otherwise in outer space, and includes preparing a launch vehicle for flight at a launch site in the United States. Launch includes the flight of a launch vehicle and includes pre- and post-flight ground operations as follows:

(1) *Beginning of launch.* (i) Under a license, launch begins with the arrival of a launch vehicle or payload at a U.S. launch site.

(ii) Under a permit, launch begins when any pre-flight ground operation at a U.S. launch site meets all of the following criteria:

(A) Is closely proximate in time to flight,

(B) Entails critical steps preparatory to initiating flight,

(C) Is unique to space launch, and

(D) Is inherently so hazardous as to warrant the FAA's regulatory oversight.

(2) *End of launch.* (i) For launch of an orbital expendable launch vehicle (ELV), launch ends after the licensee's last exercise of control over its launch vehicle.

(ii) For launch of an orbital reusable launch vehicle (RLV) with a payload, launch ends after deployment of the payload. For any other orbital RLV, launch ends upon completion of the first sustained, steady-state orbit of an RLV at its intended location.

(iii) For a suborbital ELV or RLV launch, launch ends after reaching apogee if the flight includes a reentry, or otherwise after vehicle landing or impact on Earth, and after activities necessary to return the vehicle to a safe condition on the ground.

Launch accident means

(1) An event that causes a fatality or serious injury (as defined in 49 CFR 830.2) to any person who is not associated with the flight;

(2) An event that causes damage estimated to exceed $25,000 to property not associated with the flight that is not located at the launch site or designated recovery area;

(3) An unplanned event occurring during the flight of a launch vehicle resulting in the impact of a launch vehicle, its payload or any component thereof:

(i) For an expendable launch vehicle, outside designated impact limit lines; and

(ii) For a reusable launch vehicle, outside a designated landing site.

(4) For a launch that takes place with a person on board, a fatality or serious injury to a space flight participant or crew member.

Launch incident means an unplanned event during the flight of a launch vehicle, other than a launch accident, involving a malfunction of a flight safety system or safety-critical system, or a failure of the licensee's or permittee's safety organization, design, or operations.

Launch operator means a person who conducts or who will conduct the launch of a launch vehicle and any payload.

Launch site means the location on Earth from which a launch takes place (as defined in a license the Secretary issues or transfers under this chapter) and necessary facilities at that location.

Launch site safety assessment means an FAA assessment of a Federal launch range to determine if the range meets FAA safety requirements. A difference between range practice and FAA requirements is documented in the LSSA.

Launch vehicle means a vehicle built to operate in, or place a payload in, outer space or a suborbital rocket.

Mishap means a launch or reentry accident, launch or reentry incident, launch site accident, failure to complete a launch or reentry as planned, or an unplanned event or series of events resulting in a fatality or serious injury (as defined in 49 CFR 830.2), or resulting in greater than $25,000 worth of damage to a payload, a launch or reentry vehicle, a launch or reentry support facility or government property located on the launch or reentry site.

Nominal means, in reference to launch vehicle performance, trajectory, or stage impact point, a launch vehicle flight where all vehicle aerodynamic parameters are as expected, all vehicle internal and external systems perform exactly as planned, and there are no external perturbing influences other than atmospheric drag and gravity.

Operation of a launch site means the conduct of approved safety operations at a permanent site to support the launching of vehicles and payloads.

Operation of a reentry site means the conduct of safety operations at a permanent site on Earth at which a reentry vehicle and its payload, if any, is intended to land.

Operator means a holder of a license or permit under 51 U.S.C. Subtitle V, chapter 509.

Payload means an object that a person undertakes to place in outer space by means of a launch vehicle, including components of the vehicle specifically designed or adapted for that object.

Person means an individual or an entity organized or existing under the laws of a state or country.

Physical electronic storage means a physical device that can store electronic documents and files including but not limited to an optical disc, a memory card, a USB flash drive, or an external hard drive.

Populated area means—

(1) An outdoor location, structure, or cluster of structures that may be occupied by people;

(2) Sections of roadways and waterways that are frequented by automobile and boat traffic; or

(3) Agricultural lands, if routinely occupied by field workers.

Pilot means a flight crew member who has the ability to control, in real time, a launch or reentry vehicle's flight path.

Public safety means, for a particular licensed launch, the safety of people and property that are not involved in supporting the launch and includes those people and property that may be located within the boundary of a launch site, such as visitors, individuals providing goods or services not related to launch processing or flight, and any other launch operator and its personnel.

Reenter; reentry means to return or attempt to return, purposefully, a reentry vehicle and its payload, if any, from Earth orbit or from outer space to Earth. The term "reenter; reentry" includes activities conducted in Earth orbit or outer space to determine reentry readiness and that are critical to ensuring public health and safety and the safety of property during reentry flight. The term "reenter; reentry" also includes activities conducted on the ground after vehicle landing on Earth to ensure the reentry vehicle does not pose a threat to public health and safety or the safety of property.

Reentry accident means

(1) Any unplanned event occurring during the reentry of a reentry vehicle resulting in the impact of the reentry vehicle, its payload, or any component thereof, outside a designated reentry site;

(2) An event that causes a fatality or serious injury (as defined in 49 CFR 830.2) to any person who is not associated with the reentry;

(3) An event that causes damage estimated to exceed $25,000 to property not associated with the reentry and not located within a designated reentry site; and

(4) For a reentry that takes place with a person on board, a fatality or serious injury to a space flight participant or crew member.

Reentry incident means any unplanned event occurring during the reentry of a reentry vehicle, other than a reentry accident, involving a malfunction of a reentry safety-critical system or failure of the licensee's or permittee's safety organization, procedures, or operations.

Reentry operator means a person responsible for conducting the reentry of a reentry vehicle as specified in a license issued by the FAA.

Reentry site means the location on Earth where a reentry vehicle is intended to return. It includes the area within three standard deviations of the intended landing point (the predicted three-sigma footprint).

Reentry vehicle means a vehicle designed to return from Earth orbit or outer space to Earth substantially intact. A reusable launch vehicle that is designed to return from Earth orbit or outer space to Earth substantially intact is a reentry vehicle.

Remote operator means a crew member who

(1) Has the ability to control, in real time, a launch or reentry vehicle's flight path, and

(2) Is not on board the controlled vehicle.

Reusable launch vehicle (RLV) means a launch vehicle that is designed to return to Earth substantially intact and therefore may be launched more than one time or that contains vehicle stages that may be recovered by a launch operator for future use in the operation of a substantially similar launch vehicle.

Risk means a measure that accounts for both the probability of occurrence of a hazardous event and the consequence of that event to persons or property.

Safety critical means essential to safe performance or operation. A safety critical system, subsystem, component, condition, event, operation, process, or item is one whose proper recognition, control, performance, or tolerance is essential to ensuring public safety. Something that is safety critical item creates a safety hazard or provide protection from a safety hazard.

Sigma means a single standard deviation from a fixed value, such as a mean.

Space flight participant means an individual, who is not crew, carried aboard a launch vehicle or reentry vehicle.

State and United States means, when used in a geographical sense, the several States, the District of Columbia, the Commonwealth of Puerto Rico, American Samoa, the United States Virgin Islands, Guam, and any other commonwealth, territory, or possession of the United States; and

Tether system means a device that contains launch vehicle hazards by physically constraining a launch vehicle in flight to a specified range from its launch point. A tether system includes all components, from the tether's point of attachment to the vehicle to a solid base, that experience load during a tethered launch.

United States citizen means:

(1) Any individual who is a citizen of the United States;

(2) Any corporation, partnership, joint venture, association, or other entity organized or existing under the laws of the United States or any State; and

(3) Any corporation, partnership, joint venture, association, or other entity which is organized or exists under the laws of a foreign nation, if the controlling interest in such entity is held by an individual or entity described in paragraph (1) or (2) of this definition. *Controlling interest* means ownership of an amount of equity in such entity sufficient to direct management of the entity or to void transactions entered into by management. Ownership of at least fifty-one percent of the equity in an entity by persons described in paragraph (1) or (2) of this definition creates a rebuttable presumption that such interest is controlling.

Suborbital rocket means a vehicle, rocket-propelled in whole or in part, intended for flight on a suborbital trajectory, and the thrust of which is greater than its lift for the majority of the rocket-powered portion of its ascent.

Suborbital trajectory means the intentional flight path of a launch vehicle, reentry vehicle, or any portion thereof, whose vacuum instantaneous impact point does not leave the surface of the Earth.

Validation means an evaluation to determine that each safety measure derived from a system safety process is correct, complete, consistent, unambiguous, verifiable, and technically feasible. Validation ensures that the right safety measure is implemented, and that the safety measure is well understood.

Vehicle safety operations personnel means those persons whose job performance is critical to public health and safety or the safety of property during RLV or reentry operations.

Verification means an evaluation to determine that safety measures derived from a system safety process are effective and have been properly implemented. Verification provides measurable evidence that a safety measure reduces risk to acceptable levels.

[Doc. No. FAA–1999–5535, 65 FR 56656, Sept. 19, 2000, as amended by Amdt. 401–2, 65 FR 62861, Oct. 19, 2000; Amdt. 401–4, 71 FR 50530, Aug. 25, 2006; 71 FR 75631, Dec. 15, 2006; Amdt. 401–5, 72 FR 17016, Apr. 6, 2007; Amdt. 401–6, 73 FR 73782, Dec. 4, 2008; Amdt. 401–7, 77 FR 20532, Apr. 5, 2012; 80 FR 30151, May 27, 2015; Amdt. 401–8, 80 FR 31834, June 4, 2015]

SUBCHAPTER B—PROCEDURE

PART 404— PETITION AND RULEMAKING PROCEDURES

AUTHORITY: 51 U.S.C. 50901–50923.

SOURCE: Docket No. 43810, 53 FR 11013, Apr. 4, 1988, unless otherwise noted.

§ 404.1 Scope.

This part establishes procedures for issuing regulations and for filing a petition for waiver or petition for rulemaking to the Associate Administrator for Commercial Space Transportation.

[Doc. No. FAA-2016-6761, Amdt. No. 404-6, 83 FR 28534, June 20, 2018]

§ 404.3 General.

(a) Any person may petition the Associate Administrator to:

(1) Issue, amend, or repeal a regulation to eliminate as a requirement for a license or permit any requirement of Federal law applicable to commercial space launch and reentry activities and the operation of launch and reentry sites;

(2) Waive any such requirement in the context of a specific application for a license or permit; or

(3) Waive the requirement for a license, except as provided in § 404.7(b).

(b) A petition filed under this section may request, under § 413.9 of this chapter, that the Associate Administrator withhold certain trade secrets or proprietary commercial or financial data from public disclosure.

(c) Each petitioner filing under this section must:

(1) For electronic submission, send one copy of the petition by email to the Office of Commercial Space Transportation at *ASTpetition@faa.gov;* or

(2) For paper submission, send one copy of the petition to the Office of Commercial Space Transportation, Federal Aviation Administration, 800 Independence Avenue SW, Room 331, Washington, DC 20591.

(d) Each petition filed under this section must include the petitioner's name, mailing address, telephone number and any other contact information, such as an email address or a fax number.

(e) *Notification.* When the Associate Administrator determines that a petition should be granted or denied, the Associate Administrator notifies the petitioner of the Associate Administrator's action and the reasons supporting the action.

(f) *Reconsideration.* Any person may petition the FAA to reconsider a denial of a petition the person filed. The petitioner must send a request for reconsideration within 60 days after being notified of the denial to the same address to which the original petition was filed. For the FAA to accept the reconsideration request, the petitioner must show—

(1) There is a significant additional fact and the reason it was not included in the original petition;

(2) The FAA made an important factual error in its denial of the original petition; or

(3) The denial is not in accordance with the applicable law and regulations.

(g) *Public hearing.* No public hearing, argument or other proceeding is held on a petition before its disposition under this section.

[Doc. No. FAA-2005-21234, 71 FR 51971, Aug. 31, 2006, as amended at 72 FR 68475, Dec. 5, 2007; Doc. No. FAA-2016-6761; Amdt. No. 404-6, 83 FR 28534, June 20, 2018]

§ 404.5 Filing a petition for waiver.

A petition for waiver must be submitted at least 60 days before the proposed effective date of the waiver unless the petitioner shows good cause for later submission in the petition, and the petition for waiver must—

(a) Include the specific section or sections of 14 CFR chapter III from which the petitioner seeks relief;

(b) Include the extent of the relief sought and the reason the relief is being sought;

(c) Include any facts, views, and data available to the petitioner to support the waiver request; and

(d) Show why granting the request for relief is in the public interest and will not jeopardize the public health and safety, safety of property, and national security and foreign policy interests of the United States.

[Doc. No. FAA–2016–6761, Amdt. No. 404–6, 83 FR 28534, June 20, 2018]

§ 404.7 Action on a petition for waiver.

(a) *Grant of waiver.* The Associate Administrator may grant a waiver, except as provided in paragraph (b) of this section, if the Associate Administrator determines that the waiver is in the public interest and will not jeopardize public health and safety, the safety of property, or any national security or foreign policy interest of the United States.

(b) *Waiver ineligibility.* The FAA may not grant a waiver that would permit the launch or reentry of a launch vehicle or a reentry vehicle without a license or permit if a human being will be on board.

(c) *Denial of waiver.* If the Associate Administrator determines that the petition does not justify granting a waiver, the Associate Administrator denies the petition.

[Doc. No. FAA–2016–6761, Amdt. No. 404–6, 83 FR 28534, June 20, 2018]

§ 404.9 Filing a petition for rulemaking.

A petition for rulemaking filed under this part must be made in accordance with 14 CFR 11.71.

[Doc. No. FAA–2016–6761, Amdt. No. 404–6, 83 FR 28534, June 20, 2018]

§ 404.11 Action on a petition for rulemaking.

The FAA will process petitions for rulemaking under this part in accordance with 14 CFR 11.73.

[Doc. No. FAA–2016–6761, Amdt. No. 404–6, 83 FR 28534, June 20, 2018]

§ 404.13 Rulemaking.

(a) The FAA's rulemaking procedures are located in subpart A of part 11 of this title, under the General, Written Comments, and Public Meetings and Other Proceedings headings.

(b) In addition to the rulemaking procedures referenced in paragraph (a) of this section, the provisions of §§ 404.17 and 404.19 also apply.

[Doc. No. FAA–2016–6761, Amdt. No. 404–6, 83 FR 28534, June 20, 2018]

§ 404.15 [Reserved]

§ 404.17 Additional rulemaking proceedings.

The FAA may initiate other rulemaking proceedings, if necessary or desirable. For example, it may invite interested people to present oral arguments, participate in conferences, appear at informal hearings, or participate in any other proceedings.

[Doc. No. FAA–2006–24197, 72 FR 17016, Apr. 6, 2007]

§ 404.19 Hearings.

(a) Sections 556 and 557 of Title 5, United States Code, do not apply to hearings held under this part. As a fact-finding forum, each hearing held under this part is nonadversarial and there are no formal pleadings or adverse parties. Any rule issued in a proceeding in which a hearing is held is not based exclusively on the record of the hearing, but on the entire record of the rulemaking proceeding.

(b) The Associate Administrator designates a representative to conduct any hearing held under this part. The FAA Chief Counsel designates a legal officer for the hearing.

[53 FR 11013, Apr. 4, 1988, as amended by Amdt. 404–2, 68 FR 35289, June 13, 2003]

PART 405—COMPLIANCE AND ENFORCEMENT

Sec.

AUTHORITY: 51 U.S.C. 50901–50923.

SOURCE: Docket No. 43810, 53 FR 11014, Apr. 4, 1988, unless otherwise noted.

§405.1 Monitoring of licensed, permitted, and other activities.

Each licensee or permittee must allow access by and cooperate with Federal officers or employees or other individuals authorized by the Associate Administrator to observe licensed facilities and activities, including launch sites and reentry sites, as well as manufacturing, production, testing, and training facilities, or assembly sites used by any contractor, licensee, or permittee to produce, assemble, or test a launch or reentry vehicle and to integrate a payload with its launch or reentry vehicle. Observations are conducted to monitor the activities of the licensee, permittee, or contractor at such time and to such extent as the Associate Administrator considers reasonable and necessary to determine compliance with the license or permit or to perform the Associate Administrator's responsibilities pertaining to payloads for which no Federal license, authorization, or permit is required.

[Doc. No. FAA-2006-24197, 72 FR 17016, Apr. 6, 2007]

§405.3 Authority to modify, suspend or revoke.

(a) The FAA may modify a license or permit issued under this chapter upon application by the licensee or permittee or upon the FAA's own initiative, if the FAA finds that the modification is consistent with the requirements of the Act.

(b) The FAA may suspend or revoke any license or permit issued to such licensee or permittee under this chapter if the FAA finds that a licensee or permittee has substantially failed to comply with any requirement of the Act, any regulation issued under the Act, the terms and conditions of a license or permit, or any other applicable requirement; or that public health and safety, the safety of property, or any national security or foreign policy interest of the United States so require.

(c) Unless otherwise specified by the Office, any modification, suspension or revocation made by the Office under this section:

(1) Takes effect immediately; and

(2) Continues in effect during any review of such action under Part 406 of this chapter.

(d) Whenever the FAA takes any action under this section, the FAA immediately notifies the licensee or permittee in writing of the FAA's finding and the action, which the FAA has taken or proposes to take regarding such finding.

[Doc. No. 43810, 53 FR 11014, Apr. 4, 1988, as amended by Amdt. 405-3, 72 FR 17016, Apr. 6, 2007]

§405.5 Emergency orders.

The Associate Administrator may immediately terminate, prohibit, or suspend a licensed or permitted launch, reentry, or operation of a launch or reentry site if the Associate Administrator determines that—

(a) The licensed or permitted launch, reentry, or operation of a launch or reentry site is detrimental to public health and safety, the safety of property, or any national security or foreign policy interest of the United States; and

(b) The detriment cannot be eliminated effectively through the exercise of other authority of the Office.

[53 FR 11014, Apr. 4, 1988, as amended by Amdt. 405-1, 65 FR 56657, Sept. 19, 2000; Amdt. 405-3, 72 FR 17017, Apr. 6, 2007]

PART 406—INVESTIGATIONS, ENFORCEMENT, AND ADMINISTRATIVE REVIEW

Subpart A—Investigations and Enforcement

Subpart B—Rules of Practice in FAA Space Transportation Adjudications

AUTHORITY: 51 U.S.C. 50901–50923.

SOURCE: Docket No. FAA–2001–8607, 66 FR 2180, Jan. 10, 2001, unless otherwise noted.

Subpart A—Investigations and Enforcement

§ 406.1 Hearings in license, permit, and payload actions.

(a) Pursuant to 51 U.S.C. 50912, the following are entitled to a determination on the record after an opportunity for a hearing in accordance with 5 U.S.C. 554.

(1) An applicant for a license and a proposed transferee of a license regarding any decision to issue or transfer a license with conditions or to deny the issuance or transfer of such license;

(2) An owner or operator of a payload regarding any decision to prevent the launch or reentry of the payload;

(3) A licensee regarding any decision to suspend, modify, or revoke a license or to terminate, prohibit, or suspend any licensed activity;

(4) An applicant for a permit regarding an FAA decision to issue a permit with conditions or to deny the issuance of the permit; and

(5) A permittee regarding any decision to suspend, modify, or revoke a permit or to terminate, prohibit, or suspend any permitted activity.

(b) An administrative law judge will be designated to preside over any hearing held under this part.

[Doc. No. FAA–2001–8607, 66 FR 2180, Jan. 10, 2001, as amended by Amdt. 406–4, 72 FR 17017, Apr. 6, 2007; Amdt. 406–7, 77 FR 20532, Apr. 5, 2012]

§ 406.3 Submissions; oral presentation in license, permit, and payload actions.

(a) The FAA will make decisions about license, permit, and payload actions under this subpart based on written submissions unless the administrative law judge requires an oral presentation.

(b) Submissions must include a detailed exposition of the evidence or arguments supporting the petition. Where an applicant must demonstrate an equivalent level of safety or fidelity, the applicant must make a clear and convincing demonstration.

(c) Petitions shall be filed as soon as practicable, but in no event more than 30 days after issuance of decision or finding under § 406.1.

[Doc. No. FAA–2001–8607, 66 FR 2180, Jan. 10, 2001, as amended by Amdt. 406–3, 71 FR 50530, Aug. 25, 2006; Amdt. 406–4, 72 FR 17017, Apr. 6, 2007]

§ 406.5 Administrative law judge's recommended decision in license, permit, and payload actions.

(a) The Associate Administrator, who shall make the final decision on the matter at issue, shall review the recommended decision of the administrative law judge. The Associate Administrator shall make such final decision within thirty days of issuance of the recommended decision.

(b) The authority and responsibility to review and decide rests solely with the Associate Administrator and may not be delegated.

§406.7 [Reserved]

§406.9 Civil penalties.

(a) *Civil penalty liability*. Under 51 U.S.C. 50917(c), a person found by the FAA to have violated a requirement of the Act, a regulation issued under the Act, or any term or condition of a license or permit issued or transferred under the Act, is liable to the United States for a civil penalty of not more than $234,247 for each violation. A separate violation occurs for each day the violation continues.

(b) *Delegations*. The authority to impose civil penalties is exercised by an agency attorney as described in §406.105.

(c) *Notice of proposed civil penalty*. A civil penalty action is initiated when the agency attorney advises a person, referred to as the respondent, of the charges or other reasons upon which the FAA bases the proposed action and allows the respondent to answer the charges and to be heard as to why the civil penalty should not be imposed. A notice of proposed civil penalty states the facts alleged; any requirement of the Act, a regulation issued under the Act, or any term or condition of a license or permit issued or transferred under the Act allegedly violated by the respondent; and the amount of the proposed civil penalty. Not later than 30 days after receipt of the notice of proposed civil penalty the respondent may elect to proceed by one or more of the following:

(1) Pay the amount of the proposed civil penalty or an agreed upon amount, in which case the agency attorney will issue either an order imposing civil penalty or a compromise order in that amount.

(2) Submit to the agency attorney one of the following:

(i) Written information, including documents and witnesses statements, demonstrating that a violation did not occur or that a penalty, or the amount of the proposed penalty, is not warranted by the circumstances.

(ii) A written request to reduce the proposed civil penalty, the amount of reduction, and the reasons and any document supporting a reduction of the proposed civil penalty, including records indicating a financial inability to pay or records showing that payment of the proposed civil penalty would prevent the person from continuing in business.

(iii) A written request for an informal conference to discuss the matter with the agency attorney and to submit relevant information.

(3) Request that a final notice of proposed civil penalty be issued so that the respondent may request a hearing in accordance with paragraph (g) of this section.

(d) *Final notice of proposed civil penalty*. A final notice of proposed civil penalty (final notice) provides the last opportunity for the respondent to request a hearing.

(1) The agency attorney issues a final notice if one of the following occurs:

(i) The respondent fails to respond to the notice of proposed civil penalty not later than 30 days after the date the respondent received the notice of proposed civil penalty.

(ii) The parties have not agreed to a resolution of the action after participating in informal procedures under paragraph (c)(2) of this section.

(iii) The respondent requests the issuance of a final notice in accordance with paragraph (c)(3) of this section.

(2) Not later than 15 days after the date the respondent received the final notice of proposed civil penalty, the respondent shall do one of the following:

(i) Submit the amount of the proposed civil penalty or an agreed-upon amount, in which case the agency attorney issues either an order imposing civil penalty or a compromise order in that amount.

(ii) Request a hearing in accordance with paragraph (g) of this section.

(e) *Order imposing civil penalty*. An order imposing civil penalty is the final order of the Secretary imposing a civil penalty. An order imposing civil penalty is issued for a violation described in paragraph (a) of this section after notice and an opportunity for a hearing.

(1) The agency attorney either issues an order imposing civil penalty, or another document becomes an order imposing civil penalty, as described below.

(i) The agency attorney issues an order imposing civil penalty if, in response to a notice of proposed civil penalty or a final notice of proposed civil penalty, the respondent pays or agrees to pay a civil penalty in the amount proposed or an agreed upon amount (other than an agreement for a compromise order under paragraph (f) of this section).

(ii) Unless the respondent requests a hearing not later than 15 days after the date the respondent received a final notice of proposed civil penalty, the final notice of proposed civil penalty becomes an order imposing civil penalty.

(iii) Unless an appeal is filed with the FAA decisionmaker in accordance with § 406.175, if the administrative law judge finds that a violation occurred and determines that a civil penalty, in an amount found appropriate by the administrative law judge, is warranted, an initial decision of an administrative law judge under subpart B of this part becomes an order imposing civil penalty.

(iv) Unless a complaint is filed with a United States district court in accordance with § 406.176, if the FAA decisionmaker finds that a violation occurred and determines that a civil penalty, in an amount found appropriate by the FAA decisionmaker, is warranted, a final decision and order of the FAA decisionmaker under subpart B of this part becomes an order imposing civil penalty. If a person seeks judicial review not later than 60 days after the final decision and order has been served on the respondent, the final decision and order is stayed.

(2) [Reserved]

(f) *Compromise order*. The agency attorney at any time may agree to compromise any civil penalty with no finding of violation. Under such agreement, the agency attorney issues a compromise order stating:

(1) The respondent agrees to pay a civil penalty.

(2) The FAA makes no finding of a violation.

(3) The compromise order may not be used as evidence of a prior violation in any subsequent civil penalty action, license, or permit action.

(g) *Request for hearing*. Any respondent who has been issued a final notice of proposed civil penalty may, not later than 15 days after the date the respondent received the final notice, request a hearing under subpart B of this part.

(1) The respondent must file a written request for hearing with the Federal Docket Management System (U.S. Department of Transportation, Docket Operations, West Building Ground Floor, Room W12–140, 1200 New Jersey Avenue, SE., Washington, DC 20590) and must serve a copy of the request on the agency attorney. Sections 406.113 and 406.115 state how filing and service must be done.

(2) The request for hearing must be dated and signed.

(h) *Method of payment*. A respondent must pay a civil penalty by check or money order, payable to the Federal Aviation Administration.

(i) *Collection of civil penalties*. If a respondent does not pay a civil penalty imposed by an order imposing civil penalty or a compromise order within 60 days after service of the final order, the FAA may refer the order to the United States Department of Treasury or Department of Justice to collect the civil penalty.

(j) *Exhaustion of administrative remedies*. A respondent may seek judicial review of a final decision and order of the FAA decisionmaker as provided in § 406.179. A respondent has not exhausted administrative remedies for purposes of judicial review if the final order is one of the following:

(1) An order imposing civil penalty issued by an agency attorney under paragraph (e)(1)(i) of this section.

(2) A final notice of proposed civil penalty that becomes an order imposing civil penalty under paragraph (e)(1)(ii) of this section.

(3) An initial decision of an administrative law judge that was not appealed to the FAA decisionmaker.

(4) A compromise order under paragraph (f) of this section.

(k) *Compromise.* The FAA may compromise or remit a civil penalty that has been proposed or imposed under this section.

[Doc. No. FAA-2001-8607, 66 FR 2180, Jan. 10, 2001, as amended by Amdt. 406-4, 72 FR 17017, Apr. 6, 2007; 72 FR 68475, Dec. 5, 2007; 75 FR 30693, June 2, 2010; Amdt. 406-7, 77 FR 20532, Apr. 5, 2012; 79 FR 61992, Oct. 16, 2014; Amdt. 406-10, 81 FR 43469, July 5, 2016; Doc. No. FAA-2016-7004, Amdt. 406-11, 82 FR 17101, Apr. 10, 2017; 83 FR 60743, Nov. 27, 2018]

§§ 406.10–406.100 [Reserved]

Subpart B—Rules of Practice in FAA Space Transportation Adjudications

§ 406.101 Applicability.

(a) *Adjudications to which these rules apply.* These rules apply to the following adjudications:

(1) A civil penalty action in which the respondent has requested a hearing under § 406.9.

(2) [Reserved]

(b) [Reserved]

§ 406.103 Definitions that apply in part 406.

For the purpose of this part:

Administrative law judge means an administrative law judge appointed pursuant to the provisions of 5 U.S.C. 3105.

Attorney means a person licensed by a state, the District of Columbia, or a territory of the United States to practice law or appear before the courts of that state or territory.

Complainant in a civil penalty action means the proponent of the civil penalty in the FAA.

FAA decisionmaker means the Associate Administrator for Commercial Space Transportation, or the Administrator of the Federal Aviation Administration, acting in the capacity of the decisionmaker on appeal; or a person who has been delegated the authority to act for the FAA decisionmaker. As used in this part, the FAA decisionmaker is the official authorized to issue a final decision and order of the Secretary in an action.

Mail means U.S. first class mail, U.S. certified mail, U.S. registered mail, or an express courier service.

Party means the respondent or the complainant.

Personal delivery includes hand-delivery or use of a same-day messenger service. "Personal delivery" does not include the use of Government interoffice mail service.

Properly addressed means using an address contained in agency records; a residential, business, or other address used by a person on any document submitted under this part; or any other address determined by other reasonable and available means.

Respondent means a person who has been charged with a violation.

§ 406.105 Separation of functions for prosecuting civil penalties and advising the FAA decisionmaker.

(a) *Agency attorney.* The authority to prosecute civil penalties within the FAA is exercised by an agency attorney in accordance with § 406.9.

(1) The following officials have the authority to act as the agency attorney under this part: The Deputy Chief Counsel; the Assistant Chief Counsel for Enforcement; the Assistant Chief Counsel for Regulations; the Assistant Chief Counsel for Europe, Africa, and Middle East Area Office; each Regional Counsel; and each Center Counsel. This authority may be delegated further.

(2) An agency attorney may not include:

(i) The Chief Counsel or the Assistant Chief Counsel for Litigation;

(ii) Any attorney on the staff of the Assistant Chief Counsel for Litigation who advises the FAA decisionmaker regarding an initial decision or any appeal to the FAA decisionmaker; or

(iii) Any attorney who is supervised in a civil penalty action by a person who provides such advice to the FAA decisionmaker in that action or a factually-related action.

(b) *Advisors to the FAA decisionmaker.* (1) The Chief Counsel, the Assistant Chief Counsel for Litigation or an attorney on the staff of the Assistant Chief Counsel for Litigation, will advise the FAA decisionmaker regarding an initial decision or any appeal of an action to the FAA decisionmaker.

(2) An agency employee engaged in the performance of investigative or prosecutorial functions must not, in

that case or a factually-related case, participate or give advice in a decision by the administrative law judge or by the FAA decisionmaker on appeal, except as counsel or a witness in the public proceedings.

§ 406.107 Appearances of parties, and attorneys and representatives.

(a) Any party may appear and be heard in person.

(b) Any party may be accompanied, represented, or advised by an attorney or representative designated by the party.

(1) An attorney or representative who represents a party must file a notice of appearance in the action with the Docket Management System and must serve a copy of the notice of appearance on each other party before participating in any proceeding governed by this subpart.

(2) The attorney or representative must include his or her name, address, and telephone number in the notice of appearance.

(3) That attorney or representative in any proceeding governed by this subpart may examine the party.

(4) Service of a document on the party's attorney or representative is considered to be service on the party.

(c) An agency attorney represents the complainant.

§ 406.109 Administrative law judges—powers and limitations.

(a) *Powers of an administrative law judge.* In accordance with the rules of this subpart, an administrative law judge may:

(1) Give notice of, and hold, prehearing conferences and hearings;

(2) Administer oaths and affirmations;

(3) Issue subpoenas authorized by law and requested by the parties;

(4) Rule on offers of proof;

(5) Receive relevant and material evidence;

(6) Regulate the course of the hearing in accordance with the rules of this subpart;

(7) Hold conferences to settle or to simplify the issues by consent of the parties;

(8) Dispose of procedural motions and requests; and

(9) Make findings of fact and conclusions of law, and issue an initial decision.

(b) *Duties to maintain the record.* (1) The administrative law judge must file with the FDMS, or instruct the party to file with the FDMS, a copy of each document that is submitted to the administrative law judge that has not bee filed with FDMS, except the portions of those documents that contain confidential information.

(2) The administrative law judge must file with the FDMS a copy of each ruling and order issued by the administrative law judge, except those portions that contain confidential information.

(3) The administrative law judge must file with the FDMS, or instruct the court reporter to file with the FDMS, a copy of each transcript and exhibit, except those portions that contain confidential information.

(4) The administrative law judge must maintain any confidential information filed in accordance with § 406.117 and deliver it to the Assistant Chief Counsel for Litigation when the administrative law judge no longer needs it.

(c) *Limitations on the power of the administrative law judge.* The administrative law judge may not issue an order of contempt, award costs to any party, or impose any sanction not specified in this subpart. If the administrative law judge imposes any sanction not specified in this subpart, a party may file an interlocutory appeal of right pursuant to § 406.173(c). This section does not preclude an administrative law judge from issuing an order that bars a person from a specific proceeding based on a finding of obstreperous or disruptive behavior in that specific proceeding.

(d) *Disqualification.* The administrative law judge may disqualify himself or herself at any time. A party may file a motion, pursuant to § 406.141(f)(8), requesting that an administrative law judge be disqualified from the proceedings.

[Doc. No. FAA–2001–8607, 66 FR 2180, Jan. 10, 2001, as amended at 72 FR 68475, Dec. 5, 2007]

§ 406.111 Signing documents.

(a) *Signature required.* The party, or the party's attorney or representative, must sign each document tendered for filing or served on each party.

(b) *Effect of signing a document.* By signing a document, the party, or the party's attorney or representative, certifies that he or she has read the document and, based on reasonable inquiry and to the best of that individual's knowledge, information, and belief, the document is—

(1) Consistent with these rules;

(2) Warranted by existing law or that a good faith argument exists for extension, modification, or reversal of existing law; and

(3) Not unreasonable or unduly burdensome or expensive, not made to harass any person, not made to cause unnecessary delay, not made to cause needless increase in the cost of the proceedings, or for any other improper purpose.

(c) *Sanctions.* If an individual signs a document in violation of this section, the administrative law judge or the FAA decisionmaker must:

(1) Strike the pleading signed in violation of this section;

(2) Strike the request for discovery or the discovery response signed in violation of this section and preclude further discovery by the party;

(3) Deny the motion or request signed in violation of this section;

(4) Exclude the document signed in violation of this section from the record;

(5) Dismiss the interlocutory appeal and preclude further appeal on that issue by the party who filed the appeal until an initial decision has been entered on the record; or

(6) Dismiss the appeal of the administrative law judge's initial decision to the FAA decisionmaker.

§406.113 Filing documents with the Docket Management System (DMS) and sending documents to the administrative law judge and Assistant Chief Counsel for Litigation.

(a) *The Federal Docket Management System (FDMS).* (1) Documents filed in a civil penalty adjudication are kept in the Federal Docket Management System (FDMS), except for documents that contain confidential information in accordance with 406.117. The FDMS is an electronic docket. Documents that are filed are scanned into the electronic docket and an index is made of all documents that have been filed so that any person may view the index and documents as provided in paragraph (f) of this section.

(2) A party is not required to file written interrogatories and responses, requests for production of documents or tangible items and responses, and requests for admission and responses with the Federal Docket Management System or submit them to administrative law judge, except as provided in 406.143.

(b) *Method of filing.* A person filing a document must mail or personally deliver the signed original and one copy of each document to the FDMS at the U.S. Department of Transportation, Docket Operations, West Building Ground Floor, Room W12–140, 1200 New Jersey Avenue, SE., Washington, DC 20590. A person must serve a copy of each document on each party in accordance with 406.115.

(c) *Date of filing.* The date of filing is the date of personal delivery, or if mailed, the mailing date shown on any certificate of service, the date shown on the postmark if there is no certificate of service, or other mailing data shown by other evidence if there is no certificate of service or postmark. The date shown in the FDMS index is not necessarily the date of service. It is the date the FDMS received the document.

(d) *Form.* FDMS scans the document into its electronic docket. To ensure that FDMS can scan the document and correctly identify it in the index, each person filing a document must comply with the following:

(1) Each document must be legible. It may be handwritten, typewritten, or printed from a computer.

(2) Each document must have a caption on its first page, clearly visible, with the following information:

(i) "FAA Space Adjudication."

(ii) Case name, such as "In the matter of X Corporation."

(iii) FAA Case Number and FDMS docket number, if assigned.

(iv) Name of the document being filed, including the party filing the document, such as "Respondent's Motion to Dismiss."

(v) "Confidential information filed with administrative law judge" or

"Confidential information filed with Assistant Chief Counsel for Litigation" if the party is filing confidential information under 406.117.

(3) The document must be capable of being scanned and be easy to read both in paper form and as scanned into the electronic docket. A document that meets the following specifications is capable of being scanned using automatic feeders and is easy to read both in paper form and as scanned into the electronic docket. Documents that do not meet these specifications may not be legible.

(i) On white paper.

(ii) On paper not larger than 8½ by 11 inches.

(iii) In black ink.

(iv) Text double-spaced. Footnotes and long quotes may be single spaced.

(v) At least 12 point type.

(vi) Margins at least 1 inch on each side.

(vii) The original not bound or hole-punched, only held together with removable metal clips or the like. The copy that is filed or sent to the administrative law judge or Assistant Chief Counsel for Litigation, and the copy served on another party, need not meet this specification.

(viii) The original has no tabs. The copy that is filed or sent to the administrative law judge or Assistant Chief Counsel for Litigation, and the copy served on another party, need not meet this specification.

(e) *Sending documents to the administrative law judge or Assistant Chief Counsel for Litigation.* Sending the document directly to the administrative law judge or to the Assistant Chief Counsel for Litigation is not a substitute for filing the original with the FDMS, except for confidential information under 406.117.

(f) *Viewing and copying the record.* Any person may view and copy the record, except for confidential information, as follows:

(1) During regular business hours at the U.S. Department of Transportation, Docket Operations, West Building Ground Floor, Room W12–140, 1200 New Jersey Avenue, SE., Washington, DC 20590.

(2) Through the Internet at *http://www.regulations.gov.*

(3) By requesting it from the FDMS and paying reasonable costs.

[Doc. No. FAA–2001–8607, 66 FR 2180, Jan. 10, 2001, as amended at 72 FR 68476, Dec. 5, 2007]

§406.115 Serving documents on other parties.

(a) *Service required.* A person must serve on each other party at the time of filing a copy of any document filed with the Federal Docket Management System. Service on a party's attorney or representative of record is adequate service on the party.

(b) *Method of service.* A person must serve documents by personal delivery or by mail.

(c) *Certificate of service.* A person may attach a certificate of service to a document filed with the FDMS. Any certificate of service must include a statement, dated and signed by the individual filing the document, that the document was served on each party, the method of service, and the date of service.

(d) *Date of service.* The date of service is the date of personal delivery; or if mailed, the mailing date shown on the certificate of service, the date shown on the postmark if there is no certificate of service, or other mailing date shown by other evidence if there is no certificate of service or postmark. The date shown in the FDMS index is not necessarily the date of service. It is the date the FDMS received the document.

(e) *Additional time after service by mail.* Whenever a party has a right or a duty to act or to make any response within a prescribed period after service by mail, or on a specified date after service by mail, 5 days is added to the prescribed period.

(f) *Service by the administrative law judge.* The administrative law judge must serve a copy of each document including, but not limited to, notices of pre-hearing conferences and hearings, rulings on motions, decisions, and orders, upon each party to the proceedings by personal delivery or by mail.

(g) *Service made.* A document is deemed served in accordance with this subpart if it was properly addressed; was sent in accordance with this subpart; and was returned, not claimed, or refused. Service is considered valid as of the date and the time that the document was mailed, or personal delivery of the document was refused.

(h) *Presumption of service*. There is a presumption of service where a party or a person, who customarily receives mail, or receives it in the ordinary course of business, at either the person's residence or the person's principal place of business, acknowledges receipt of the document.

[Doc. No. FAA-2001-8607, 66 FR 2180, Jan. 10, 2001, as amended at 72 FR 68476, Dec. 5, 2007]

§ 406.117 Confidential information.

(a) *Filing confidential information*. If a party wants certain information that the party is filing not made available to the public, the party must do the following:

(1) Place the information in a separate sealed envelope and clearly mark the envelope "CONFIDENTIAL." At least the first page of the document in the envelope also must be marked "CONFIDENTIAL."

(2) Attach to this envelope a cover document marked "Confidential information filed with administrative law judge" or "Confidential information filed with Assistant Chief Counsel for Litigation." The cover document must include, at the least, a short statement of what is being filed, such as "Respondent's motion for confidentiality order."

(3) Unless such a motion has already been granted, enclose a motion for confidentiality order in accordance with paragraph (c) of this section. The motion must be in the sealed envelope if it contains confidential information; otherwise the motion must be outside of the sealed envelope.

(b) *Marked information not made public*. If a party files a document in a sealed envelope clearly marked "CONFIDENTIAL" the document may not be made available to the public unless and until the administrative law judge or the FAA decisionmaker decides it may be made available to the public in accordance with 51 U.S.C. 50916.

(c) *Motion for confidentiality order*. If a party is filing, is requested to provide in discovery, or intends to offer at the hearing, information that the party does not wish to be available to the public, the party must file a motion for a confidentiality order.

(1) The party must state the specific grounds for withholding the information from the public.

(2) If the party claims that the information is protected under 51 U.S.C. 50916, and if both the complainant and the respondent agree that the information is protected under that section, the administrative law judge must grant the motion. If one party does not agree that the information is protected under 51 U.S.C. 50916 the administrative law judge must decide. Either party may file an interlocutory appeal of right under § 406.173(c).

(3) If the party claims that the information should be protected on grounds other than those provided by 51 U.S.C. 50916 the administrative law judge must grant the motion if, based on the motion and any response to the motion, the administrative law judge determines that disclosure would be detrimental to safety, disclosure would not be in the public interest, or that the information is not otherwise required to be made available to the public.

(4) If the administrative law judge determines that the information is not necessary to decide the case or would not otherwise lead to the discovery of relevant material, the administrative law judge must preclude any inquiry into the matter by any party.

(5) If the administrative law judge determines that the requested material may be disclosed during discovery, the administrative law judge may order that the material may be discovered and disclosed under limited conditions or may be used only under certain terms and conditions.

(6) If the administrative law judge determines that the requested material is necessary to decide the case, or would otherwise lead to the discovery of relevant material, and that a confidentiality order is warranted, the administrative law judge must—

(i) Provide an opportunity for review of the document by the attorneys of record off the record.

(ii) Provide procedures for excluding the information from the record, or order that portion of the record that includes confidential information be closed.

(iii) Order that the parties must not disclose the information in any manner and the parties must not use the information in any other proceeding.

(7) If an administrative law judge orders a record closed, in whole or in part:

(i) The closed record is not available to the public.

(ii) The closed record is available to the parties' attorneys of record.

(iii) The administrative law judge may determine whether the closed record is available to the parties, the parties' representatives, or other persons such as witnesses for a party.

(iv) No party, attorney of record, representative of record, or person who receives information from such persons, may disclose information that has been protected under this section except to a person authorized by this section or the administrative law judge to receive it.

(v) If a person other than one authorized by this section desires to view or copy a closed record, the person must file a motion to open the record.

[Doc. No. FAA–2001–8607, 66 FR 2180, Jan. 10, 2001, as amended by Amdt. 406–7, 77 FR 20532, Apr. 5, 2012]

§406.119 Computation of time.

(a) This section applies to any period of time prescribed or allowed by this subpart, by notice or order of the administrative law judge or the FAA decisionmaker, or by any applicable statute.

(b) The date of an act, event, or default, after which a designated time period begins to run, is not included in a computation of time under this subpart.

(c) The last day of a time period is included in a computation of time unless it is a Saturday, Sunday, or a legal holiday. If the last day of the time period is a Saturday, Sunday, or legal holiday, the time period runs until the end of the next day that is not a Saturday, Sunday, or legal holiday.

§406.121 Extension of time.

Before an appeal is filed with the FAA decisionmaker, the parties may seek an extension of time as follows:

(a) *Extension of time by agreement of the parties.* The parties may agree to extend for a reasonable period of time for filing a document under this subpart with the agreement of the administrative law judge. The party seeking the extension of time must submit a draft order to the administrative law judge for signature, file it with the Federal Docket Management System, and serve it on each party.

(b) *Motion for extension of time.* If the parties do not agree to an extension of time for filing a document, a party desiring an extension may file with the Federal Docket Management System and serve a written motion for an extension of time not later than 7 days before the document is due unless good cause for the late filing is shown. The administrative law judge may grant the extension of time if good cause for the extension is shown.

(c) *Failure to rule.* If the administrative law judge fails to rule on a written motion for an extension of time by the date the document is due, the motion for an extension of time is granted for no more than 20 days after the original date the document was to be filed.

[Doc. No. FAA–2001–8607, 66 FR 2180, Jan. 10, 2001, as amended at 72 FR 68476, Dec. 5, 2007]

§406.123 Waivers.

Waivers of any rights provided by statute or regulation must be in writing or by stipulation made at a hearing and entered into the record. The parties must set forth the precise terms of the waiver and any conditions.

§406.127 Complaint and answer in civil penalty adjudications.

(a) *Complaint*—(1) *Filing.* The complainant must file the original and one copy of the complaint with the Federal Docket Management System, or may file a written motion pursuant to 406.141(f)(1) instead of filling a complaint, not later than 20 days after receipt by the complainant of a request for hearing. The complainant should suggest a location for the hearing when filing the complaint.

(2) *Service.* The complainant must personally deliver or mail a copy of the complaint to the respondent, or the respondent's attorney or representative

who has filed a notice of appearance in accordance with §406.107.

(3) *Contents of complaint.* The final notice of proposed civil penalty issued under §406.9(d) may be filed as the complaint. A complaint must set forth the following in sufficient detail to provide notice:

(i) The facts alleged.

(ii) Any requirement of the Act, a regulation issued under the Act, or any term or condition of a license or permit issued or transferred under the Act allegedly violated by the respondent.

(iii) The proposed civil penalty.

(b) *Answer*—(1) *Time for filing.* The respondent must file an answer to the complaint, or may file a written motion pursuant to §406.141(f)(2) instead of filing an answer, not later than 30 days after service of the complaint.

(2) *Form.* The answer must be in writing. The answer may be in the form of a letter but must be dated and signed by the person responding to the complaint. The answer must be legible, and may be handwritten, typed, or printed from a computer.

(3) *Filing and service.* A respondent must file the answer with the Federal Docket Management System and serve a copy of the answer on the agency attorney who filed the complaint.

(4) *Contents of answer*—(i) *Specific denial of allegations required.* The respondent must admit, deny, or state that the respondent is without sufficient knowledge or information to admit or deny, each numbered paragraph of the complaint. Any statement or allegation contained in the complaint that is not specifically denied in the answer constitutes an admission of the truth of that allegation. An administrative law judge shall treat a general denial of the complaint as a failure to file an answer.

(ii) *Affirmative defenses.* The answer must specifically state any affirmative defense that the respondent asserts.

(iii) *Request for relief.* The answer may include a brief statement of any relief requested.

(iv) *Hearing location.* The respondent should suggest a location for the hearing when filing the answer.

(5) *Failure to file answer.* A respondent's failure to file an answer without good cause constitutes an admission of the truth of each allegation contained in the complaint.

[Doc. No. FAA-2001-8607, 66 FR 2180, Jan. 10, 2001, as amended by Amdt. 406-4, 72 FR 17017, Apr. 6, 2007; 72 FR 68476, Dec. 5, 2007]

§406.133 Amendment of pleadings.

(a) *Time.* A party must file with the Federal Docket Management System and serve on each other party any amendment to a complaint or an answer as follows:

(1) Not later than 15 days before the scheduled date of a hearing, a party may amend a complaint or an answer without the consent of the administrative law judge.

(2) Less than 15 days before the scheduled date of a hearing, the administrative law judge may allow amendment of a complaint or an answer only for good cause shown in a motion to amend.

(b) *Responses.* The administrative law judge must allow a reasonable time, but not more than 20 days from the date of filing, for other parties to respond to an amendment to a complaint or answer.

[Doc. No. FAA-2001-8607, 66 FR 2180, Jan. 10, 2001, as amended at 72 FR 68477, Dec. 5, 2007]

§406.135 Withdrawal of complaint or request for hearing.

At any time before or during a hearing, the complainant may withdraw a complaint or a party may withdraw a request for a hearing without the consent of the administrative law judge. If the complainant withdraws the complaint or a party withdraws the request for a hearing and the answer, the administrative law judge must dismiss the proceedings under this subpart with prejudice.

§406.137 Intervention.

(a) A person may file with the Federal Docket Management System and serve on each other party a motion for leave to intervene as party in an adjudication. Except for good cause shown, a motion for leave to intervene must be filed not later than 10 days before the hearing.

(b) The administrative law judge may grant a motion for leave to intervene if the administrative law judge finds that—

(1) Intervention will not unduly broaden the issues or delay the proceedings, and

(2) The intervener will be bound by any order or decision entered in the action or the intervener has a property, financial, or other legitimate interest that may not be addressed adequately by the parties.

(c) The administrative law judge may determine the extent to which an intervener may participate in the proceedings.

[Doc. No. FAA–2001–8607, 66 FR 2180, Jan. 10, 2001, as amended at 72 FR 68477, Dec. 5, 2007]

§ 406.139 Joint procedural or discovery schedule.

(a) *General.* The parties may agree to submit a schedule for filing all prehearing motions or for conducting discovery or both.

(b) *Form and content of schedule.* If the parties agree to a joint procedural or discovery schedule, one of the parties must file with the Federal Docket Management System and serve the joint schedule, setting forth the dates to which the parties have agreed. One of the parties must draft an order establishing a joint schedule for the administrative law judge.

(1) The joint schedule may include, but need not be limited to, times for requests for discovery, any objections to discovery requests, responses to discovery requests, submission of prehearing motions, responses to prehearing motions, exchange of exhibits to be introduced at the hearing, and lists of witnesses that may be called at the hearing.

(2) Each party must sign the original joint schedule.

(c) *Time.* The parties may agree to submit all prehearing motions and responses and may agree to close discovery in the proceedings under the joint schedule within a reasonable time before the date of the hearing, but not later than 15 days before the hearing.

(d) *Order establishing joint schedule.* The administrative law judge must approve the joint schedule filed by the parties by signing the joint schedule and filing it with the Federal Docket Management System.

(e) *Disputes.* The administrative law judge must resolve any dispute regarding discovery or regarding compliance with the joint schedule as soon as possible so that the parties may continue to comply with the joint schedule.

(f) *Sanctions for failure to comply with joint schedule.* If a party fails to comply with the order establishing a joint schedule, the administrative law judge may direct that party to comply with a motion to compel discovery; or, limited to the extent of the party's failure to comply with a motion or discovery request, the administrative law judge may:

(1) Strike that portion of a party's pleadings;

(2) Preclude prehearing or discovery motions by that party;

(3) Preclude admission of that portion of a party's evidence at the hearing; or

(4) Preclude that portion of the testimony of that party's witnesses at the hearing.

[Doc. No. FAA–2001–8607, 66 FR 2180, Jan. 10, 2001, as amended at 72 FR 68477, Dec. 5, 2007]

§ 406.141 Motions.

(a) *General.* A party applying for an order or ruling not specifically provided in this subpart must do so by motion. A party must comply with the requirements of this section when filing a motion for consideration by the administrative law judge or the FAA decisionmaker on appeal.

(b) *Contents.* A party must state the relief sought by the motion and the particular grounds supporting that relief. If a party has evidence in support of a motion, the party must attach any evidence, including affidavits, to the motion.

(c) *Form and time.* Except for oral motions heard on the record, a motion made prior to the hearing must be in writing. Unless otherwise agreed by the parties or for good cause shown, a party must file any prehearing motion with the Federal Docket Management System and serve each other party not later than 30 days before the hearing.

(d) *Answers to motions.* Any party may file and serve an answer, with affidavits or other evidence in support of the answer, not later than 10 days after service of a written motion on that party. When a motion is made during a hearing, the answer may be made at the hearing on the record, orally or in writing, within a reasonable time determined by the administrative law judge.

(e) *Rulings on motions.* The administrative law judge must rule on all motions as follows:

(1) *Discovery motions.* The administrative law judge must resolve all pending discovery motions not later than 10 days before the hearing.

(2) *Prehearing motions.* The administrative law judge must resolve all pending prehearing motions not later than 7 days before the hearing. If the administrative law judge issues a ruling or order orally, the administrative law judge must serve a written copy of the ruling or order, within 3 days, on each party. In all other cases, the administrative law judge must issue rulings and orders in writing and must serve a copy of the ruling or order on each party.

(3) *Motions made during the hearing.* The administrative law judge may issue rulings and orders on motions made during the hearing orally. Oral rulings or orders on motions must be made on the record.

(f) *Specific motions*—(1) *Complainant's motion to dismiss a request for a hearing as prematurely filed.* The complainant may file a motion to dismiss a request for a hearing as prematurely filed instead of filing a complaint. If the motion is not granted, the complainant must file the complaint and must serve a copy of the complaint on each party not later than 10 days after service of the administrative law judge's ruling or order on the motion to dismiss. If the motion to dismiss is granted and the proceedings are terminated without a hearing, the respondent may file an appeal in accordance with §406.175. If required by the decision on appeal, the complainant must file a complaint and must serve a copy of the complaint on each party not later than 10 days after service of the decision on appeal.

(2) *Respondent's motions instead of an answer.* A respondent may file one or more of the following motions instead of filing an answer. If the administrative law judge denies the motion, the respondent must file an answer not later than 10 days after service of the denial of the motion.

(i) *Respondent's motion to dismiss complaint for failure to state a claim for which a civil penalty may be imposed.* A respondent may file a motion to dismiss the complaint for failure to state a claim for which a civil penalty may be imposed instead of filing an answer. The motion must show that the complaint fails to state a violation of the Act, a regulation issued under the Act, or any term or condition of a license issued or transferred under the Act.

(ii) *Respondent's motion to dismiss allegations or complaint for staleness.* Instead of filing an answer to the complaint, a respondent may move to dismiss the complaint, or that part of the complaint that alleges a violation that occurred more than 5 years before an agency attorney issued a notice of proposed civil penalty to the respondent, as provided by 28 U.S.C. 2462.

(iii) *Respondent's motion for more definite statement.* A respondent may file a motion requesting a more definite statement of the allegations contained in the complaint instead of filing an answer. The respondent must set forth, in detail, the indefinite or uncertain allegations contained in a complaint or response to any pleading and must submit the details that the party believes would make the allegation or response definite and certain. If the administrative law judge grants the motion, the complainant must supply a more definite statement not later than 15 days after service of the ruling granting the motion. If the complainant fails to supply a more definite statement, the administrative law judge must strike the allegations in the complaint to which the motion is directed. If the administrative law judge denies the motion, the respondent must file an answer and must serve a copy of the answer on each party not later than 10 days after service of the order of denial.

(3) *Other motions to dismiss.* A party may file a motion to dismiss, specifying the grounds for dismissal.

(4) *Complainant's motion for more definite statement.* The complainant may file a motion requesting a more definite statement if an answer fails to respond clearly to the allegations in the complaint. The complainant must set

forth, in detail, the indefinite or uncertain allegations contained in the answer and must submit the details that the complainant believes would make the allegation or response definite and certain. If the administrative law judge grants the motion, the respondent must supply a more definite statement not later than 15 days after service of the ruling on the motion. If the respondent fails to supply a more definite statement, the administrative law judge must strike those statements in the answer to which the motion is directed. An administrative law judge shall treat a respondent's failure to supply a more definite statement as an admission of unanswered allegations in the complaint.

(5) *Other motions for more definite statement.* A party may file a motion for more definite statement of any pleading that requires or permits a response under this subpart. A party must set forth, in detail, each indefinite or uncertain allegation contained in a pleading or response and must submit the details that would make each allegation definite and certain.

(6) *Motion to strike.* Any party may make a motion to strike any insufficient allegation or defense, or any redundant, immaterial, or irrelevant matter in a pleading. A party must file a motion to strike and must serve a copy on each party before a response to that pleading is required under this subpart or, if a response is not required, not later than 10 days after service of the pleading.

(7) *Motion for decision.* A party may make a motion for decision, regarding all or any part of the proceedings, at any time before the administrative law judge has issued an initial decision in the proceedings. The administrative law judge must grant a party's motion for decision if the pleadings, depositions, answers to interrogatories, admissions, matters that the administrative law judge has officially noticed, or evidence introduced during the hearing show that there is no genuine issue of material fact and that the party making the motion is entitled to a decision as a matter of law. The party making the motion for decision has the burden of showing that there is no genuine issue of material fact disputed by the parties.

(8) *Motion for disqualification.* A party may file a motion for disqualification. A party may file the motion at any time after the administrative law judge has been assigned to the proceedings but must make the motion before the administrative law judge files an initial decision in the proceedings.

(i) *Motion and supporting affidavit.* A party must state the grounds for disqualification, including, but not limited to, personal bias, pecuniary interest, or other factors showing reason for disqualification, in the motion for disqualification. A party must submit an affidavit with the motion for disqualification that sets forth, in detail, the matters alleged to constitute grounds for disqualification.

(ii) *Answer.* A party may respond to the motion for disqualification not later than 5 days after service of the motion for disqualification.

(iii) *Decision on motion for disqualification.* The administrative law judge must issue a decision on the motion for disqualification not later than 15 days after the motion has been filed. If the administrative law judge finds that the motion for disqualification and supporting affidavit show a basis for disqualification, the administrative law judge must withdraw from the proceedings immediately. If the administrative law judge finds that disqualification is not warranted, the administrative law judge must deny the motion and state the grounds for the denial on the record. If the administrative law judge fails to rule on a party's motion for disqualification within 15 days after the motion has been filed, the motion is granted.

[Doc. No. FAA-2001-8607, 66 FR 2180, Jan. 10, 2001, as amended at 72 FR 68477, Dec. 5, 2007]

§ 406.143 Discovery.

(a) *Initiation of discovery.* Any party may initiate discovery described in this section, without the consent or approval of the administrative law judge, at any time after a complaint has been filed.

(b) *Methods of discovery.* The following methods of discovery are permitted under this section: depositions on oral examination or written questions of any person; written interrogatories directed to a party; requests for production of documents or tangible items to any person; and requests for admission by a party. A party is not required to file written interrogatories and responses, requests for production of documents or tangible items and responses, and requests for admission and responses with the Federal Docket Management System or submit any of them to the administrative law judge. In the event of a discovery dispute, a party must attach a copy of these documents in support of a motion filed under this section.

(c) *Service on the agency.* A party must serve each discovery request directed to the agency or any agency employee with the agency attorney.

(d) *Time for response to discovery request.* Unless otherwise directed by this subpart or agreed by the parties, a party must respond to a request for discovery, including filing objections to a request for discovery, not later than 30 days after service of the request.

(e) *Scope of discovery.* Subject to the limits on discovery set forth in paragraph (f) of this section, a party may discover any matter that is not privileged and that is relevant to the subject matter of the proceeding. A party may discover information that relates to the claim or defense of any party including the existence, description, nature, custody, condition, and location of any document or other tangible item and the identity and location of any person having knowledge of discoverable matter. A party may discover facts known, or opinions held, by an expert who any other party expects to call to testify at the hearing. A party has no ground to object to a discovery request on the basis that the information sought would not be admissible at the hearing if the information sought during discovery is reasonably calculated to lead to the discovery of admissible evidence.

(f) *Limiting discovery.* The administrative law judge must limit the frequency and extent of discovery permitted by this section if a party shows that—

(1) The information requested is cumulative or repetitious;

(2) The information requested can be obtained from another less burdensome and more convenient source;

(3) The party requesting the information has had ample opportunity to obtain the information through other discovery methods permitted under this section; or

(4) The method or scope of discovery requested by the party is unduly burdensome or expensive.

(g) *Confidentiality order.* A party or person who has received a discovery request for information that is related to a trade secret, confidential or sensitive material, competitive or commercial information, proprietary data, or information on research and development, may file and serve a motion for a confidentiality order in accordance with §406.117.

(h) *Protective order.* A party or a person who has received a request for discovery may file a motion for protective order and must serve a copy of the motion for protective order on each party. The party or person making the motion must show that the protective order is necessary to protect the party or the person from annoyance, embarrassment, oppression, or undue burden or expense. As part of the protective order, the administrative law judge may:

(1) Deny the discovery request;

(2) Order that discovery be conducted only on specified terms and conditions, including a designation of the time or place for discovery or a determination of the method of discovery; or

(3) Limit the scope of discovery or preclude any inquiry into certain matters during discovery.

(i) *Duty to supplement or amend response.* A party who has responded to a discovery request has a duty to supplement or amend the response, as soon as the information is known, as follows:

(1) A party must supplement or amend any response to a question requesting the identity and location of any person having knowledge of discoverable matters.

(2) A party must supplement or amend any response to a question requesting the identity of each person who will be called to testify at the

hearing as an expert witness and the subject matter and substance of that witness' testimony.

(3) A party must supplement or amend any response that was incorrect when made or any response that was correct when made but is no longer correct, accurate, or complete.

(j) *Depositions.* The following rules apply to all depositions taken pursuant to this section:

(1) *Form.* A deposition must be taken on the record and reduced to writing. The person being deposed must sign the deposition unless the parties agree to waive the requirement of a signature.

(2) *Administration of oaths.* Within the United States, or a territory or possession subject to the jurisdiction of the United States, a party must take a deposition before a person authorized to administer oaths by the laws of the United States or authorized by the law of the place where the examination is held. In a foreign country, a party must take a deposition in any manner allowed by the Federal Rules of Civil Procedure.

(3) *Notice of deposition.* A party must serve a notice of deposition, stating the time and place of the deposition and the name and address of each person to be examined, on the person to be deposed, must submit the notice to the administrative law judge, and must file the notice with the Federal Docket Management System, and must serve the notice on each party, not later than 7 days before the deposition. A party may serve a notice of deposition less than 7 days before the deposition only with consent of the administrative law judge. If a subpoena duces tecum is to be served on the person to be examined, the party must attach to the notice of deposition a copy of the subpoena duces tecum that describes the materials to be produced at the deposition.

(4) *Use of depositions.* A party may use any part or all of a deposition at a hearing authorized under this subpart only upon a showing of good cause. The deposition may be used against any party who was present or represented at the deposition or who had reasonable notice of the deposition.

(k) *Interrogatories.* (1) A party may not serve more than 30 interrogatories to each other party. Each subpart of an interrogatory must be counted as a separate interrogatory.

(2) A party must file a motion for leave to serve more than 30 interrogatories on a party before serving additional interrogatories on a party. The administrative law judge must grant the motion only if the party shows good cause for the party's failure to inquire about the information previously and that the information cannot reasonably be obtained using less burdensome discovery methods or be obtained from other sources.

(3) A party must answer each interrogatory separately and completely in writing.

(4) A party, or the party's attorney or representative of record, must sign the party's responses to interrogatories.

(5) If a party objects to an interrogatory, the party must state the objection and the reasons for the objection.

(6) An opposing party may offer into evidence any part or all of a party's responses to interrogatories at a hearing under this subpart to the extent that the response is relevant, material, and not repetitious.

(l) *Requests for admission.* A party may serve a written request for admission of the truth of any matter within the scope of discovery under this section or the authenticity of any document described in the request. A party must set forth each request for admission separately. A party must serve a copy of each document referenced in the request for admission unless the document has been provided or is reasonably available for inspection and copying.

(1) *Time.* A party's failure to respond to a request for admission is not later than 30 days after service of the request constitutes an admission of the truth of the statement or statements contained in the request for admission. The administrative law judge may determine that a failure to respond to a request for admission does not constitute an admission of the truth if a party shows that the failure was due to circumstances beyond the control of the party or the party's attorney or representative.

(2) *Response.* A party may object to a request for admission. The objection

must be in writing and signed by the party or the party's attorney or representative of record, and must state the reasons for objection. A party may specifically deny the truth of the matter or describe the reasons why the party is unable to truthfully deny or admit the matter. If a party is unable to deny or admit the truth of the matter, the party must show that the party has made reasonable inquiry into the matter or that the information known to, or readily obtainable by, the party is insufficient to enable the party to admit or deny the matter. A party may admit or deny any part of the request for admission. If an administrative law judge determines that a response does not comply with the requirements of this rule or that the response is insufficient, the matter is admitted.

(3) *Effect of admission.* Any matter admitted or treated as admitted under this section is conclusively established for the purpose of the hearing and appeal.

(m) *Motion to compel discovery.* A party may make a motion to compel discovery if a person refuses to answer a question during a deposition, a party fails or refuses to answer an interrogatory, a person gives an evasive or incomplete answer during a deposition or when responding to an interrogatory, or a party fails or refuses to produce documents or tangible items. During a deposition, the proponent of a question may complete the deposition or may adjourn the examination before making a motion to compel if a person refuses to answer.

(n) *Failure to comply with a discovery order or order to compel.* If a party fails to comply with a discovery order or an order to compel, the administrative law judge, limited to the extent of the party's failure to comply with the discovery order or motion to compel, may:

(1) Strike that portion of a party's pleadings;

(2) Preclude prehearing or discovery motions by that party;

(3) Preclude admission of that portion of a party's evidence at the hearing; or

(4) Preclude that portion of the testimony of that party's witnesses at the hearing.

[Doc. No. FAA-2001-8607, 66 FR 2180, Jan. 10, 2001, as amended at 72 FR 68477, Dec. 5, 2007]

§406.147 Notice of hearing.

(a) *Notice.* The administrative law judge must give each party at least 60 days notice of the date, time, and location of the hearing.

(b) *Date, time, and location of the hearing.* The administrative law judge must set a reasonable date, time, and location for the hearing within the United States. The administrative law judge must consider the need for discovery and any joint procedural or discovery schedule submitted by the parties when determining the hearing date. The administrative law judge must give due regard to the convenience of the parties, the location where the majority of the witnesses reside or work, and whether a scheduled air carrier serves the location.

(c) *Earlier hearing.* With the consent of the administrative law judge, the parties may agree to hold the hearing on an earlier date than the date specified in the notice of hearing.

(d) *Space hearing consolidated with aviation hearing under 14 CFR part 13 subpart G.* With the consent of the administrative law judge, the parties may agree to hold the hearing, or parts of the hearing, together with a hearing under 14 CFR part 13 subpart G if the cases involve some common issues of fact. If the hearings are consolidated, the administrative law judge may issue a consolidated initial decision covering both cases. The Administrator will serve as the FAA decisionmaker on appeal for both cases and will issue a consolidated decision, with the Associate Administrator for Commercial Space Transportation serving as an advisor to the FAA decisionmaker.

§406.149 Evidence.

(a) *General.* A party is entitled to present the party's case or defense by oral, documentary, or demonstrative evidence, to submit rebuttal evidence, and to conduct any cross-examination that may be required for a full and true disclosure of the facts.

(b) *Admissibility.* A party may introduce any oral, documentary, or demonstrative evidence in support of the party's case or defense. The administrative law judge must admit any oral, documentary, or demonstrative evidence introduced by a party but must exclude irrelevant, immaterial, or unduly repetitious evidence.

(c) *Hearsay evidence.* Hearsay evidence is admissible in proceedings governed by this subpart. The fact that evidence submitted by a party is hearsay goes only to the weight of the evidence and does not affect its admissibility.

§ 406.151 Standard of proof.

The administrative law judge must issue an initial decision or must rule in a party's favor only if the decision or ruling is supported by, and in accordance with, the reliable, probative, and substantial evidence contained in the record. In order to prevail, the party with the burden of proof must prove the party's case or defense by a preponderance of reliable, probative, and substantial evidence.

§ 406.153 Burden of proof.

(a) Except in the case of an affirmative defense, in a civil penalty adjudication the burden of proof is on the complainant.

(b) Except as otherwise provided by statute or rule, the proponent of a motion, request, or order has the burden of proof.

(c) A party who has asserted an affirmative defense has the burden of proving the affirmative defense.

§ 406.155 Offer of proof.

A party whose evidence has been excluded by a ruling of the administrative law judge may offer the evidence for the record on appeal.

§ 406.157 Expert or opinion witnesses.

An employee of the FAA may not be called as an expert or opinion witness for any party other than the agency, in any proceeding governed by this part. An employee of a respondent may not be called as an expert or opinion witness for the complainant in any proceeding governed by this part to which the respondent is a party.

§ 406.159 Subpoenas.

(a) *Request for subpoena.* A party may obtain from the administrative law judge a subpoena to compel the attendance of a witness at a deposition or hearing or to require the production of documents or tangible items. The administrative law judge must deliver the subpoena, signed by the administrative law judge but otherwise in blank, to the party. The party must complete the subpoena, stating the title of the action and the date and time for the witness' attendance or production of documents or items. The party who obtained the subpoena must serve the subpoena on the witness.

(b) *Motion to quash or modify the subpoena.* A party, or any person upon whom a subpoena has been served, may file a motion to quash or modify the subpoena at or before the time specified in the subpoena for compliance. The applicant must describe, in detail, the basis for the motion to quash or modify the subpoena including, but not limited to, a statement that the testimony, document, or tangible evidence is not relevant to the proceeding, that the subpoena is not reasonably tailored to the scope of the proceeding, or that the subpoena is unreasonable and oppressive. A motion to quash or modify the subpoena will stay the effect of the subpoena pending a decision by the administrative law judge on the motion.

(c) *Enforcement of subpoena.* Upon a showing that a person has failed or refused to comply with a subpoena, the Secretary may apply to the appropriate district court of the United States to seek enforcement of the subpoena in accordance with 51 U.S.C. 50917(c). A party may request the Secretary to seek such enforcement.

[Doc. No. FAA–2001–8607, 66 FR 2180, Jan. 10, 2001, as amended by Amdt. 406–7, 77 FR 20533, Apr. 5, 2012]

§ 406.161 Witness fees.

(a) *General.* Unless otherwise authorized by the administrative law judge, the party who applies for a subpoena to compel the attendance of a witness at a deposition or hearing, or the party at whose request a witness appears at a deposition or hearing, must pay the witness fees described in this section.

(b) *Amount.* Except for an employee of the agency who appears at the direction of the agency, a witness who appears at a deposition or hearing is entitled to the same fees and mileage expenses as are paid to a witness in a court of the United States in comparable circumstances.

§ 406.163 Record.

(a) *Exclusive record.* The transcript of all testimony in the hearing; all exhibits received into evidence; the complaint, answer, and amendments thereto; all motions, applications, and requests, and responses thereto; and all rulings constitute the exclusive record for decision of the proceedings and the basis for the issuance of any orders in the proceeding.

(b) A person may keep the original document, data, or other evidence, with the consent of the administrative law judge, by substituting a legible copy for the record.

§ 406.165 Argument before the administrative law judge.

(a) *Argument during the hearing.* During the hearing, the administrative law judge must give the parties a reasonable opportunity to present arguments on the record supporting or opposing motions, objections, and rulings if the parties request an opportunity for argument. The administrative law judge may request written arguments during the hearing if the administrative law judge finds that submission of written arguments would be reasonable.

(b) *Final oral argument.* At the conclusion of the hearing and before the administrative law judge issues an initial decision in the proceedings, the parties are entitled to submit oral proposed findings of fact and conclusions of law, exceptions to rulings of the administrative law judge, and supporting arguments for the findings, conclusions, or exceptions. At the conclusion of the hearing, a party may waive final oral argument.

(c) *Post-hearing briefs.* The administrative law judge may request written post-hearing briefs before the administrative law judge issues an initial decision if the administrative law judge finds that submission of written briefs would be reasonable. If a party files a written post-hearing brief, the party must include proposed findings of fact and conclusions of law, exceptions to rulings of the administrative law judge, and supporting arguments for the findings, conclusions, or exceptions. The administrative law judge must give the parties a reasonable opportunity, not more than 30 days after receipt of the transcript, to prepare and submit the briefs.

§ 406.167 Initial decision.

(a) *Contents.* The administrative law judge must issue an initial decision at the conclusion of the hearing. In each oral or written decision, the administrative law judge must include findings of fact and conclusions of law, and the grounds supporting those findings and conclusions, upon all material issues of fact, the credibility of witnesses, the applicable law, any exercise of the administrative law judge's discretion, the amount of any civil penalty found appropriate by the administrative law judge, and a discussion of the basis for any order issued in the proceedings. The administrative law judge is not required to provide a written explanation for rulings on objections, procedural motions, and other matters not directly relevant to the substance of the initial decision. If the administrative law judge refers to any previous unreported or unpublished initial decision, the administrative law judge must make copies of that initial decision available to all parties and the FAA decisionmaker.

(b) *Oral decision.* Except as provided in paragraph (c) of this section, at the conclusion of the hearing, the administrative law judge must issue the initial decision and order orally on the record.

(c) *Written decision.* The administrative law judge may issue a written initial decision not later than 30 days after the conclusion of the hearing or submission of the last posthearing brief if the administrative law judge finds that issuing a written initial decision is reasonable. The administrative law judge must serve a copy of any written initial decision on each party.

§ 406.173 Interlocutory appeals.

(a) *General.* Unless otherwise provided in this subpart, a party may not appeal a ruling or decision of the administrative law judge to the FAA decisionmaker until the initial decision has been entered on the record. A decision or order of the FAA decisionmaker on an interlocutory appeal does not constitute a final order of the Secretary for the purposes of judicial review under 5 U.S.C. chapter 7.

(b) *Interlocutory appeal for cause.* If a party files a written request for an interlocutory appeal for cause, or orally requests an interlocutory appeal for cause, the proceedings are stayed until the administrative law judge issues a decision on the request. If the administrative law judge grants the request, the proceedings are stayed until the FAA decisionmaker issues a decision on the interlocutory appeal. The administrative law judge must grant an interlocutory appeal for cause if a party shows that delay of the interlocutory appeal would be detrimental to the public interest or would result in undue prejudice to any party.

(c) *Interlocutory appeals of right.* If a party notifies the administrative law judge of an interlocutory appeal of right, the proceedings are stayed until the FAA decisionmaker issues a decision on the interlocutory appeal. A party may file an interlocutory appeal, without the consent of the administrative law judge, before an initial decision has been entered in the case of:

(1) A ruling or order by the administrative law judge barring a party, or a party's attorney or representative, from the proceedings.

(2) A ruling or order by the administrative law judge allegedly in violation of the limitations on the administrative law judge under § 406.109(c).

(3) Failure of the administrative law judge to grant a motion for a confidentiality order based on 51 U.S.C. 50916, under § 406.117(c)(2).

(4) Failure of the administrative law judge to dismiss the proceedings in accordance with § 406.135.

(d) *Procedure.* A party must file with the Federal Docket Management System and serve each other party a notice of interlocutory appeal, with supporting documents, not later than 10 days after the administrative law judge's decision forming the basis of an interlocutory appeal of right or not later than 10 days after the administrative law judge's decision granting an interlocutory appeal for cause. A party must file with the Federal Docket Management System a reply brief, if any, and serve a copy of the reply brief on each party, not later than 10 days after service of the appeal brief. The FAA decisionmaker must render a decision on the interlocutory appeal, on the record and as a part of the decision in the proceedings, within a reasonable time after receipt of the interlocutory appeal.

(e) *Rejection of interlocutory appeal.* The FAA decisionmaker may reject frivolous, repetitive, or dilatory appeals, and may issue an order precluding one or more parties from making further interlocutory appeals in a proceeding in which there have been frivolous, repetitive, or dilatory interlocutory appeals.

[Doc. No. FAA–2001–8607, 66 FR 2180, Jan. 10, 2001, as amended at 72 FR 68477, Dec. 5, 2007; Amdt. 406–7, 77 FR 20533, Apr. 5, 2012]

§ 406.175 Appeal from initial decision.

(a) *Notice of appeal.* A party may appeal the initial decision, and any decision not previously appealed pursuant to 406.173, by filing with the Federal Docket Management System and serving on each party a notice of appeal. A party must file the notice of appeal not later than 10 days after entry of the oral initial decision on the record or service of the written initial decision on the parties.

(b) *Issues on appeal.* A party may appeal only the following issues:

(1) Whether each finding of fact is supported by a preponderance of reliable, probative, and substantial evidence;

(2) Whether each conclusion of law is made in accordance with applicable law, precedent, and public policy; and

(3) Whether the administrative law judge committed any prejudicial errors during the hearing that support the appeal.

(c) *Perfecting an appeal.* Unless otherwise agreed by the parties, a party must perfect an appeal, not later than 50 days after entry of the oral initial decision on the record or service of the written initial decision on the party, by filing an appeal brief.

(1) *Extension of time by agreement of the parties.* The parties may agree to extend the time for perfecting the appeal with the consent of the FAA decisionmaker, who serves a letter confirming the extension of time on each party.

(2) *Motion for extension.* If the parties do not agree to an extension of time for perfecting an appeal, a party desiring an extension of time may file a motion for an extension and must serve a copy of the motion on each party. The FAA decisionmaker may grant an extension if good cause for the extension is shown in the motion.

(d) *Appeal briefs.* A party must file the appeal brief with the Federal Docket Management System and serve each party.

(1) A party must set forth, in detail, the party's specific objections to the initial decision or rulings in the appeal brief. A party also must set forth, in detail, the basis for the appeal, the reasons supporting the appeal, and the relief requested in the appeal. If the party relies on evidence contained in the record for the appeal, the party must specifically refer to the pertinent evidence contained in the record in the appeal brief.

(2) The FAA decisionmaker may dismiss an appeal, on the FAA decisionmaker's own initiative or upon motion of any other party, where a party has filed a notice of appeal but fails to perfect the appeal by timely filing an appeal brief.

(e) *Reply brief.* Unless otherwise agreed by the parties, any party may file a reply brief with the Federal Docket Management System and serve on each other party not later than 35 days after the appeal brief has been served on that party. If the party relies on evidence contained in the record for the reply, the party must specifically refer to the pertinent evidence contained in the record in the reply brief.

(1) *Extension of time by agreement of the parties.* The parties may agree to extend the time for filing a reply brief with the consent of the FAA decisionmaker, who will serve a letter confirming the extension of time on each party.

(2) *Motion for extension.* If the parties do not agree to an extension of time for filing a reply brief, a party desiring an extension of time may file and serve a motion for an extension and must serve a copy of the motion on each party. The FAA decisionmaker may grant an extension if good cause for the extension is shown in the motion.

(f) *Other briefs.* The FAA decisionmaker may allow any person to submit an amicus curiae brief in an appeal of an initial decision. A party may not file more than one appeal brief or reply brief without permission of the FAA decisionmaker. A party may file with the Federal Docket Management System a motion for permission to file an additional brief and must serve a copy of the motion on each other party. The party may not file the additional brief with the motion. The FAA decisionmaker may grant permission to file an additional brief if the party demonstrates good cause for allowing additional argument on the appeal. The FAA decisionmaker will allow a reasonable time for the party to file the additional brief.

(g) *Number of copies.* A party must file the original brief and two copies of the brief with the Federal Docket Management System and serve one copy on each other party.

(h) *Oral argument.* The FAA decisionmaker has sole discretion to permit oral argument on the appeal. On the FAA decisionmaker's own initiative or upon written motion by any party, the FAA decisionmaker may find that oral argument will contribute substantially to the development of the issues on appeal and may grant the parties an opportunity for oral argument.

(i) *Waiver of objections on appeal.* If a party fails to object to any alleged error regarding the proceedings in an appeal or a reply brief, the party waives any objection to the alleged error. The FAA decisionmaker is not required to consider any objection or argument in a brief if the party does not specifically refer in the brief to the pertinent evidence from the record.

(j) *FAA decisionmaker's decision on appeal.* The FAA decisionmaker will review the record, the briefs on appeal, and the oral argument, if any, to determine if the administrative law judge committed prejudicial error in the proceedings or that the initial decision should be affirmed, modified, or reversed. The FAA decisionmaker may affirm, modify, or reverse the initial decision, make any necessary findings, or may remand the case for any proceedings that the FAA decisionmaker determines may be necessary.

(1) The FAA decisionmaker may raise any issue, on the FAA decisionmaker's own initiative, that is required for proper disposition of the proceedings. The FAA decisionmaker will give the parties a reasonable opportunity to submit arguments on the new issues before making a decision on appeal. If an issue raised by the FAA decisionmaker requires the consideration of additional testimony or evidence, the FAA decisionmaker will remand the case to the administrative law judge for further proceedings and an initial decision related to that issue. If an issue raised by the FAA decisionmaker is solely an issue of law or the issue was addressed at the hearing but was not raised by a party in the briefs on appeal, a remand of the case to the administrative law judge for further proceedings is not required but may be provided in the discretion of the FAA decisionmaker.

(2) The FAA decisionmaker will issue the final decision and order of the Administrator on appeal in writing and will serve a copy of the decision and order on each party.

(3) A final decision and order of the FAA decisionmaker is precedent in any other civil penalty action under this part. Any issue, finding or conclusion, order, ruling, or initial decision of an administrative law judge that has not been appealed to the FAA decisionmaker is not precedent in any other civil penalty action.

[Doc. No. FAA–2001–8607, 66 FR 2180, Jan. 10, 2001, as amended at 72 FR 68477, Dec. 5, 2007]

§ 406.177 Petition to reconsider or modify a final decision and order of the FAA decisionmaker on appeal.

(a) *General.* Any party may petition the FAA decisionmaker to reconsider or modify a final decision and order issued by the FAA decisionmaker on appeal from an initial decision. A party must file a petition to reconsider or modify with the Federal Docket Management System not later than 30 days after service of the FAA decisionmaker's final decision and order on appeal and must serve a copy of the petition on each party. The FAA decisionmaker will not reconsider or modify an initial decision and order issued by an administrative law judge that has not been appealed by any party to the FAA decisionmaker.

(b) *Contents.* A party must state briefly and specifically the alleged errors in the final decision and order on appeal, the relief sought by the party, and the grounds that support, the petition to reconsider or modify.

(1) If the petition is based, in whole or in part, on allegations regarding the consequences of the FAA decisionmaker's decision, the party must describe these allegations and must describe, and support, the basis for the allegations.

(2) If the petition is based, in whole or in part, on new material not previously raised in the proceedings, the party must set forth the new material and include affidavits of prospective witnesses and authenticated documents that would be introduced in support of the new material. The party must explain, in detail, why the new material was not discovered through due diligence prior to the hearing.

(c) *Repetitious and frivolous petition.* The FAA decisionmaker will not consider a repetitious or frivolous petition. The FAA decisionmaker may summarily dismiss any repetitious or frivolous petition to reconsider or modify.

(d) *Reply to petition.* Any other party may reply to a petition to reconsider or modify, not later than 10 days after service of the petition on that party, by filing a reply. A party must serve a copy of the reply on each party.

(e) *Effect of filing petition.* Unless otherwise ordered by the FAA decisionmaker, filing a petition under this section stays the effective date of the FAA decisionmaker's final decision and order on appeal, and tolls the time allowed for judicial review.

(f) *FAA decisionmaker's decision on petition.* The FAA decisionmaker may affirm, modify, or reverse the final decision and order on appeal, or may remand the case for any proceedings that the FAA decisionmaker determines may be necessary.

[Doc. No. FAA-2001-8607, 66 FR 2180, Jan. 10, 2001, as amended at 72 FR 68477, Dec. 5, 2007]

§406.179 Judicial review of a final decision and order.

(a) A person may seek judicial review of a final decision and order of the FAA decisionmaker as provided in 5 U.S.C. chapter 7 and 28 U.S.C. 1331. A party seeking judicial review must file with a United States district court.

(b) In accordance with §406.9(e)(iv), if a person seeks judicial review not later than 60 days after the final decision and order has been served on the respondent, the final decision and order is stayed.

(c) In accordance with §406.9(i), if a respondent does not pay a civil penalty and does not file an appeal with the United States district court within 60 days after service of the final decision and order, the FAA may refer the order to the United States Department of Treasury or Department of Justice to collect the civil penalty.

SUBCHAPTER C—LICENSING

PART 411 [RESERVED]

PART 413—LICENSE APPLICATION PROCEDURES

AUTHORITY: 51 U.S.C. 50901–50923.

SOURCE: Amdt. 413–03, 64 FR 19614, Apr. 21, 1999, unless otherwise noted.

§ 413.1 Scope of this part.

(a) This part explains how to apply for a license or experimental permit. These procedures apply to all applications for issuing a license or permit, transferring a license, and renewing a license or permit.

(b) Use the following table to locate specific requirements:

Subject	Part
(1) Obtaining a Launch License	415
(2) License to Operate a Launch Site	420
(3) Launch and Reentry of a Reusable Launch Vehicle (RLV)	431
(4) License to Operate a Reentry Site	433
(5) Reentry of a Reentry Vehicle other than a Reusable Launch Vehicle (RLV)	435
(6) Experimental Permits	437

[Doc. No. FAA–2006–24197, 72 FR 17017, Apr. 6, 2007]

§ 413.3 Who must obtain a license or permit.

(a) A person must obtain a license in accordance with this section, unless eligible for an experimental permit under paragraph (f) of this section.

(b) A person must obtain a license to—

(1) Launch a launch vehicle from the United States;

(2) Operate a launch site within the United States;

(3) Reenter a reentry vehicle in the United States; or

(4) Operate a reentry site within the United States.

(c) A person who is a U.S. citizen or an entity organized under the laws of the United States or any State must obtain a license to—

(1) Launch a launch vehicle outside the United States;

(2) Operate a launch site outside the United States;

(3) Reenter a reentry vehicle outside the United States; or

(4) Operate a reentry site outside the United States.

(d) A foreign entity in which a United States citizen has a controlling interest must obtain a license to launch a launch vehicle from or to operate a launch site in—

(1) Any place that is outside the territory or territorial waters of any nation, unless there is an agreement in force between the United States and a foreign nation providing that such foreign nation has jurisdiction over the launch or the operation of the launch site; or

(2) The territory of any foreign nation, including its territorial waters, if there is an agreement in force between the United States and that foreign nation providing that the United States has jurisdiction over the launch or the operation of the launch site.

(e) A foreign entity in which a U.S. citizen has a controlling interest must obtain a license to reenter a reentry vehicle or to operate a reentry site in—

(1) Any place that is outside the territory or territorial waters of any nation, unless there is an agreement in force between the United States and a foreign nation providing that such foreign nation has jurisdiction over the reentry or the operation of the reentry site; or

(2) The territory of any foreign nation if there is an agreement in force between the United States and that foreign nation providing that the United States has jurisdiction over the reentry or the operation of the reentry site.

(f) A person, individual, or foreign entity otherwise requiring a license under this section may instead obtain an experimental permit to launch or reenter a reusable suborbital rocket under part 437 of this chapter.

[Doc. No. FAA-2006-24197, 72 FR 17017, Apr. 6, 2007]

§413.5 Pre-application consultation.

A prospective applicant must consult with the FAA before submitting an application to discuss the application process and possible issues relevant to the FAA's licensing or permitting decision. Early consultation helps an applicant to identify possible regulatory issues at the planning stage when changes to an application or to proposed licensed or permitted activities are less likely to result in significant delay or costs to the applicant.

[Doc. No. FAA-2006-24197, 72 FR 17018, Apr. 6, 2007]

§413.7 Application.

(a) An applicant must make an application in writing and in English. The applicant must file the application with the Federal Aviation Administration either by paper, by use of physical electronic storage, or by email in the following manner:

(1) For applications submitted on paper, an applicant must send two copies of the application to the Federal Aviation Administration, Associate Administrator for Commercial Space Transportation, Room 331, 800 Independence Avenue SW., Washington, DC 20591. Attention: Application Review.

(2) For an application submitted by use of physical electronic storage, the applicant must either mail the application to the address specified in paragraph (a)(1) of this section or hand-deliver the application to an authorized FAA representative. The application and the physical electronic storage containing the application must also satisfy all of the following criteria:

(i) The application must include a cover letter that is printed on paper and signed by the person who signed the application or by an authorized representative of the applicant;

(ii) The cover letter must identify each document that is included on the physical electronic storage; and

(iii) The physical electronic storage must be in a format such that its contents cannot be altered.

(3) For an application submitted by email, an applicant must send the application as an email attachment to *ASTApplications@faa.gov*. The application and the email to which the application is attached must also satisfy the following criteria:

(i) The email to which the application is attached must be sent from an email address controlled by the person who signed the application or by an authorized representative of the applicant; and

(ii) The application must be in a format that cannot be altered.

(b) *Administrative information.* An application must identify the following:

(1) The name and address of the applicant;

(2) The name, address, and telephone number of any person to whom inquiries and correspondence should be directed; and

(3) The type of license or permit for which the applicant is applying.

(c) *Signature and certification of accuracy.* An application must be legibly signed, dated, and certified as true, complete, and accurate by one of the following:

(1) For a corporation: An officer or other individual authorized to act for the corporation in licensing or permitting matters.

(2) *For a partnership or a sole proprietorship:* A general partner or proprietor, respectively.

(3) For a joint venture, association, or other entity: An officer or other individual authorized to act for the joint venture, association, or other entity in licensing or permitting matters.

(d) *Safety approval.* If the applicant proposes to include a safety element for which the FAA issued a safety approval under part 414 in the proposed license activity, the applicant must—

(1) Identify the safety approval in the application and explain the proposed use of the approved safety element.

(2) Show that the proposed use of the approved safety element is consistent

with the designated scope specified in the safety approval.

(3) Certify that the safety element will be used according to any terms and conditions of the issued safety approval.

(e) *Measurement system consistency.* For each analysis, an applicant must employ a consistent measurements system, whether English or metric, in its application and licensing information.

[Amdt. 413–03, 64 FR 19614, Apr. 21, 1999, as amended by Amdt. 413–6, 71 FR 46852, Aug. 15, 2006; Amdt. 413–8, 71 FR 51972, Aug. 31, 2006; Amdt. 413–7, 71 FR 56005, Sept. 26, 2006; Amdt. 413–9, 72 FR 17018, Apr. 6, 2007; Amdt. 413–11, 80 FR 30151, May 27, 2015]

§413.9 Confidentiality.

(a) Any person furnishing information or data to the FAA may request in writing that trade secrets or proprietary commercial or financial data be treated as confidential. The request must be made at the time the information or data is submitted, and state the period of time for which confidential treatment is desired.

(b) Information or data for which any person or agency requests confidentiality must be clearly marked with an identifying legend, such as "Proprietary Information," "Proprietary Commercial Information," "Trade Secret," or "Confidential Treatment Requested." Where this marking proves impracticable, a cover sheet containing the identifying legend must be securely attached to the compilation of information or data for which confidential treatment is requested.

(c) If a person requests that previously submitted information or data be treated confidentially, the FAA will do so to the extent practicable in light of any prior distribution of the information or data.

(d) Information or data for which confidential treatment has been requested or information or data that qualifies for exemption under section 552(b)(4) of Title 5, United States Code, will not be disclosed to the public unless the Associate Administrator determines that the withholding of the information or data is contrary to the public or national interest.

§413.11 Acceptance of an application.

The FAA will initially screen an application to determine whether it is complete enough for the FAA to start its review. After completing the initial screening, the FAA will notify the applicant in writing of one of the following:

(a) The FAA accepts the application and will initiate the reviews required to make a decision about the license or permit; or

(b) The application is so incomplete or indefinite that the FAA cannot start to evaluate it. The FAA will reject it and notify the applicant, stating each reason for rejecting it and what action the applicant must take for the FAA to accept the application. The FAA may return a rejected application to the applicant or may hold it until the applicant takes the required actions.

[Doc. No. FAA–2006–24197, 72 FR 17018, Apr. 6, 2007]

§413.13 Complete application.

The FAA's acceptance of an application does not mean it has determined that the application is complete. If, in addition to the information required by this chapter, the FAA requires other information necessary for a determination that public health and safety, safety of property, and national security and foreign policy interests of the United States are protected during the conduct of a licensed or permitted activity, an applicant must submit the additional information.

[Doc. No. FAA–2006–24197, 72 FR 17018, Apr. 6, 2007]

§413.15 Review period.

(a) *Review period duration.* Unless otherwise specified in this chapter, the FAA reviews and makes a decision on an application within 180 days of receiving an accepted license application or within 120 days of receiving an accepted permit application.

(b) *Review period tolled.* If an accepted application does not provide sufficient information to continue or complete the reviews or evaluations required by this chapter for a licensing or permitting determination, or an issue exists that would affect a determination, the FAA notifies the applicant, in writing, and informs the applicant of any information required to complete the application. If the FAA cannot review an accepted application because of lack of information or for any other reason, the FAA will toll the 180-day or 120-day review period until the FAA receives the information it needs or the applicant resolves the issue.

(c) *Notice*. If the FAA does not make a decision within 120 days of receiving an accepted license application or within 90 days of receiving an accepted permit application, the FAA informs the applicant, in writing, of any outstanding information needed to complete the review, or of any issues that would affect the decision.

[Doc. No. FAA–2006–24197, 72 FR 17018, Apr. 6, 2007]

§413.17 Continuing accuracy of application; supplemental information; amendment.

(a) An applicant must ensure the continuing accuracy and completeness of information furnished to the FAA as part of a pending license or permit application. If at any time the information an applicant provides is no longer accurate and complete in all material respects, the applicant must submit new or corrected information. As part of this submission, the applicant must recertify the accuracy and completeness of the application under §413.7. If an applicant does not comply with any of the requirements set forth in this paragraph, the FAA can deny the license or permit application.

(b) An applicant may amend or supplement a license or permit application at any time before the FAA issues or transfers the license or permit.

(c) Willful false statements made in any application or document relating to an application, license, or permit are punishable by fine and imprisonment under section 1001 of Title 18, United States Code, and by administrative sanctions in accordance with part 405 of this chapter.

[Doc. No. FAA–2006–24197, 72 FR 17018, Apr. 6, 2007]

§413.19 Issuing a license or permit.

After the FAA completes its reviews and makes the decisions required by this chapter, the FAA issues a license or permit to the applicant.

[Doc. No. FAA–2006–24197, 72 FR 17019, Apr. 6, 2007]

§413.21 Denial of a license application.

(a) The FAA informs an applicant, in writing, if it denies an application and states the reasons for denial.

(b) If the FAA has denied an application, the applicant may either:

(1) Attempt to correct any deficiencies identified and ask the FAA to reconsider the revised application. The FAA has 60 days or the number of days remaining in the review period, whichever is greater, within which to reconsider the decision; or

(2) Request a hearing in accordance with part 406 of this chapter, for the purpose of showing why the application should not be denied.

(c) An applicant whose license application is denied after reconsideration under paragraph (b)(1) of this section may request a hearing in accordance with paragraph (b)(2) of this section.

[Amdt. 413–03, 64 FR 19614, Apr. 21, 1999, as amended by Amdt. 413–9, 72 FR 17019, Apr. 6, 2007]

§413.23 License or permit renewal.

(a) *Eligibility*. A licensee or permittee may apply to renew its license or permit by submitting to the FAA a written application for renewal at least 90 days before the license expires or at least 60 days before the permit expires.

(b) *Application*. (1) A license or permit renewal application must satisfy the requirements set forth in this part and any other applicable part of this chapter.

(2) The application may incorporate by reference information provided as part of the application for the expiring license or permit, including any modifications to the license or permit.

(3) An applicant must describe any proposed changes in its conduct of licensed or permitted activities and provide any additional clarifying information required by the FAA.

(c) *Review of application*. The FAA reviews the application to determine whether to renew the license or permit for an additional term. The FAA may incorporate by reference any findings that are part of the record for the expiring license or permit.

(d) *Renewal of license or permit.* After the FAA finishes its reviews, the FAA issues an order modifying the expiration date of the license or permit. The FAA may impose additional or revised terms and conditions necessary to protect public health and safety and the safety of property and to protect U.S. national security and foreign policy interests.

(e) *Denial of license or permit renewal.* The FAA informs a licensee or permittee, in writing, if the FAA denies the application for renewal and states the reasons for denial. If the FAA denies an application, the licensee or permittee may follow the procedures of §413.21 of this part.

[Doc. No. FAA–2006–24197, 72 FR 17019, Apr. 6, 2007]

PART 414—SAFETY APPROVALS

Subpart A—General

AUTHORITY: 51 U.S.C. 50901–50923.

SOURCE: Docket No. FAA–2005–21332, 71 FR 46853, Aug. 15, 2006, unless otherwise noted.

Subpart A—General

§414.1 Scope.

This part establishes procedures for obtaining a safety approval and renewing and transferring an existing safety approval. Safety approvals issued under this part may be used to support the application review for one or more launch or reentry license requests under other parts of this chapter.

§414.3 Definitions.

Safety approval. For purposes of this part, a safety approval is an FAA document containing the FAA determination that one or more of the safety elements listed in paragraphs (1) and (2) of this definition, when used or employed within a defined envelope, parameter, or situation, will not jeopardize public health and safety or safety of property. A safety approval may be issued independent of a license, and it does not confer any authority to conduct activities for which a license is required under 14 CFR chapter III. A safety approval does not relieve its holder of the duty to comply with all applicable requirements of law or regulation that may apply to the holder's activities.

(1) Launch vehicle, reentry vehicle, safety system, process, service, or any identified component thereof; or

(2) Qualified and trained personnel, performing a process or function related to licensed launch activities or vehicles.

Safety element. For purposes of this part, a safety element is any one of the items or persons (personnel) listed in paragraphs (1) and (2) of the definition of "safety approval" in this section.

§414.5 Applicability.

This part applies to an applicant that wants to obtain a safety approval for any of the safety elements defined under this part and to persons granted a safety approval under this part. Any person eligible under this part may apply to become the holder of a safety approval.

§414.7 Eligibility.

(a) There is no citizenship requirement to obtain a safety approval.

(b) You may be eligible for a safety approval if you are—

(1) A manufacturer or designer of a launch or reentry vehicle or component thereof;

(2) The designer or developer of a safety system or process; or

(3) Personnel who perform safety critical functions in conducting a licensed launch or reentry.

(c) A safety approval applicant must have sufficient knowledge and expertise to show that the design and operation of the safety element for which safety approval is sought qualify for a safety approval.

(d) Only the safety elements defined under this part are eligible for a safety approval.

Subpart B—Application Procedures

§414.9 Pre-application consultation.

The applicant must consult with the FAA before submitting an application. Unless the applicant or the FAA requests another form of consultation, consultation is oral discussion with the FAA about the application process and the potential issues relevant to the FAA's safety approval decision.

§414.11 Application.

(a) An applicant must make an application in writing and in English. The applicant must file the application with the Federal Aviation Administration either by paper, by use of physical electronic storage, or by email in the following manner:

(1) For an application submitted on paper, an applicant must send two copies of the application to the Federal Aviation Administration, Associate Administrator for Commercial Space Transportation, Room 331, 800 Independence Avenue SW., Washington, DC 20591. Attention: Application Review.

(2) For an application submitted by use of physical electronic storage, the applicant must either mail the application to the address specified in paragraph (a)(1) of this section or hand-deliver the application to an authorized FAA representative. The application and the physical electronic storage containing the application must also satisfy all of the following criteria:

(i) The application must include a cover letter that is printed on paper and signed by the person who signed the application or by an authorized representative of the applicant;

(ii) The cover letter must identify each document that is included on the physical electronic storage; and

(iii) The physical electronic storage must be in a format such that its contents cannot be altered.

(3) For an application submitted by email, an applicant must send the application as an email attachment to *ASTApplications@faa.gov*. The application and the email to which the application is attached must also satisfy the following criteria:

(i) The email to which the application is attached must be sent from an email address controlled by the person who signed the application or by an authorized representative of the applicant; and

(ii) The application must be in a format that cannot be altered.

(b) The application must identify the following basic information:

(1) Name and address of the applicant.

(2) Name, address, and telephone number of any person to whom inquiries and correspondence should be directed.

(3) Safety element (*i.e.*, launch vehicle, reentry vehicle, safety system, process, service, or any identified component thereof; or personnel) for which the applicant seeks a safety approval.

(c) The application must contain the following technical information:

(1) A Statement of Conformance letter, describing the specific criteria the applicant used to show the adequacy of the safety element for which a safety approval is sought, and showing how the safety element complies with the specific criteria.

(2) The specific operating limits for which the safety approval is sought.

(3) The following as applicable:

(i) Information and analyses required under this chapter that may be applicable to demonstrating safe performance of the safety element for which the safety approval is sought.

(ii) Engineering design and analyses that show the adequacy of the proposed safety element for its intended use, such that the use in a licensed launch or reentry will not jeopardize public health or safety or the safety of property.

(iii) Relevant manufacturing processes.

(iv) Test and evaluation procedures.

(v) Test results.

(vi) Maintenance procedures.

(vii) Personnel qualifications and training procedures.

(d) The application must be in English, legibly signed, dated, and certified as true, complete, and accurate by one of the following:

(1) For a corporation, an officer or other individual authorized to act for the corporation in licensing or safety approval matters.

(2) For a partnership or a sole proprietorship, a general partner or proprietor, respectively.

(3) For a joint venture, association, or other entity, an officer or other individual duly authorized to act for the joint venture, association, or other entity in licensing matters.

(e) Failure to comply with any of the requirements set forth in this section is sufficient basis for denial of a safety approval application.

[Doc. No. FAA-2005-21332, 71 FR 46853, Aug. 15, 2006, as amended by Amdt. 414-3, 80 FR 30151, May 27, 2015]

§414.13 Confidentiality.

(a) To ensure confidentiality of data or information in the application, the applicant must—

(1) Send a written request with the application that trade secrets or proprietary commercial or financial data be treated as confidential, and include in the request the specific time frame confidential treatment is required.

(2) Mark data or information that require confidentiality with an identifying legend, such as "Proprietary Information," "Proprietary Commercial Information," "Trade Secret," or "Confidential Treatment Requested." Where this marking proves impracticable, attach a cover sheet that contains the identifying legend to the data or information for which confidential treatment is sought.

(b) If the applicant requests confidential treatment for previously submitted data or information, the FAA will honor that request to the extent practicable in case of any prior distribution of the data or information.

(c) Data or information for which confidential treatment is requested or data or information that qualifies for exemption under section 552(b)(4) of Title 5, U.S.C., will not be disclosed to the public unless the Associate Administrator determines that withholding the data or information is contrary to the public or national interest.

(d) If the proposed criteria for evaluating a safety approval is secret, as classified by the U.S. Government, or the applicant wants it to remain proprietary or confidential, it cannot be used as a basis for issuance of a safety approval.

§414.15 Processing the initial application.

(a) The FAA will initially screen an application to determine if the application is sufficiently complete to enable the FAA to initiate the reviews or evaluations required under this part.

(b) After completing the initial screening, the FAA will inform the applicant in writing of one of the following:

(1) The FAA accepts the application and will begin the reviews or evaluations required for a safety approval determination under this part.

(2) The FAA rejects the application because it is incomplete or indefinite making initiation of the reviews or evaluations required for a safety approval determination under this part inappropriate.

(c) The written notice will state the reason(s) for rejection and corrective actions necessary for the application to be accepted. The FAA may return a rejected application to the applicant or may hold it until the applicant provides more information.

(d) The applicant may withdraw, amend, or supplement an application anytime before the FAA makes a final determination on the safety approval application by making a written request to the Associate Administrator. If the applicant amends or supplements the initial application, the revised application must meet all the applicable requirements under this part.

§414.17 Maintaining the continued accuracy of the initial application.

The applicant is responsible for the continuing accuracy and completeness of information provided to the FAA as part of the safety approval application. If at any time after submitting the application, circumstances occur that cause the information to no longer be accurate and complete in any material respect, the applicant must submit a written statement to the Associate Administrator explaining the circumstances and providing the new or corrected information. The revised application must meet all requirements under §414.11.

Subpart C—Safety Approval Review and Issuance

§414.19 Technical criteria for reviewing a safety approval application.

(a) The FAA will determine whether a safety element is eligible for and may be issued a safety approval. We will base our determination on performance-based criteria, against which we may assess the effect on public health and safety and on safety of property, in the following hierarchy:

(1) FAA or other appropriate Federal regulations.

(2) Government-developed or adopted standards.

(3) Industry consensus performance-based criteria or standard.

(4) Applicant-developed criteria. Applicant-developed criteria are performance standards customized by the manufacturer that intends to produce the system, system component, or part. The applicant-developed criteria must define—

(i) Design and minimum performance;

(ii) Quality assurance system requirements;

(iii) Production acceptance test specifications; and

(iv) Continued operational safety monitoring system characteristics.

(b) The applicant must allow the FAA to make its proposed safety approval criteria available to the public as part of the approval process.

§414.21 Terms and conditions for issuing a safety approval; duration of a safety approval.

(a) The FAA will issue a safety approval to an applicant that meets all the requirements under this part.

(b) The scope of the safety approval will be limited by the scope of the safety demonstration contained in the application on which the FAA based the decision to grant the safety approval.

(c) The FAA will determine specific terms and conditions of a safety approval individually, limiting the safety approval to the scope for which the safety-approved launch or reentry element was approved. The terms and conditions will include reporting requirements tailored to the individual safety approval.

(d) A safety approval is valid for five years and may be renewed.

(e) If the FAA denies the application, the applicant may correct any deficiency the FAA identified and request a reconsideration of the revised application. The applicant also has the right to appeal a denial as set forth in subpart D of this part.

§414.23 Maintaining the continued accuracy of the safety approval application.

(a) The holder of a safety approval must ensure the continued accuracy and completeness of representations contained in the safety approval application, on which the approval was issued, for the entire term of the safety approval.

(b) If any representation contained in the application that is material to public health and safety or safety of property ceases to be accurate and complete, the safety approval holder must prepare and submit a revised application according to §414.11 under this part. The safety approval holder must point out any part of the safety approval or the associated application that would be changed or affected by a proposed modification. The FAA will review and make a determination on the revised application under the terms of this part.

(c) If the FAA approves the revised application, the FAA will provide written notice to the holder, stating the terms and conditions to which the approval is subject.

§ 414.25 Safety approval records.

The holder of a safety approval must maintain all records necessary to verify that the holder's activities are consistent with the representations contained in the application for which the approval was issued for the duration of the safety approval plus one year.

§ 414.27 Safety approval renewal.

(a) *Eligibility.* A holder of a safety approval may apply to renew it by sending the FAA a written application at least 90 days before the expiration date of the approval.

(b) *Application.* (1) A safety approval renewal application must meet all the requirements under § 414.11.

(2) The application may incorporate by reference information provided as part of the application for the expiring safety approval or any modification to that approval.

(3) Any proposed changes in the conduct of a safety element for which the FAA has issued a safety approval must be described and must include any added information necessary to support the fitness of the proposed changes to meet the criteria upon which the FAA evaluated the safety approval application.

(c) *Review of application.* The FAA conducts the reviews required under this part to determine whether the safety approval may be renewed. We may incorporate by reference any findings that are part of the record for the expiring safety approval.

(d) *Grant of safety approval renewal.* If the FAA makes a favorable safety approval determination, the FAA issues an order that amends the expiration date of the safety approval or issues a new safety approval. The FAA may impose added or revised terms and conditions necessary to protect public health and safety and the safety of property.

(e) *Written notice.* The FAA will provide written notice to the applicant of our determination on the safety approval renewal request.

(f) *Denial of a safety approval renewal.* If the FAA denies the renewal application, the applicant may correct any deficiency the FAA identified and request a reconsideration of the revised application. The applicant also has the right to appeal a denial as set forth in subpart D of this part.

§ 414.29 Safety approval transfer.

(a) Only the FAA may approve a transfer of a safety approval.

(b) Either the holder of a safety approval or the prospective transferee may request a safety approval transfer.

(c) Both the holder and prospective transferee must agree to the transfer.

(d) The person requesting the transfer must submit a safety approval application according to § 414.11, must meet the applicable requirements of this part, and may incorporate by reference relevant portions of the initial application.

(e) The FAA will approve a transfer of a safety approval only after all the approvals and determinations required under this chapter for a safety approval have been met. In conducting reviews and issuing approvals and determinations, the FAA may incorporate by reference any findings made part of the record to support the initial safety approval determination. The FAA may modify the terms and conditions of a safety approval to reflect any changes necessary because of a safety approval transfer.

(f) The FAA will provide written notice to the person requesting the safety approval transfer of our determination.

(g) If the FAA denies a transfer request, the applicant may correct any deficiency the FAA identified and request a reconsideration of the revised application. The applicant also has the right to appeal a denial as set forth in subpart D of this part.

§414.31 Monitoring compliance with the terms and conditions of a safety approval.

Each holder of a safety approval must allow access by, and cooperate with, Federal officers or employees or other individuals authorized by the Associate Administrator to inspect manufacturing, production, testing, or assembly performed by a holder of a safety approval or its contractor. The FAA may also inspect a safety approval process or service, including training programs and personnel qualifications.

§414.33 Modification, suspension, or revocation of a safety approval.

(a) *The safety approval holder.* The safety approval holder may submit an application to the FAA to modify the terms and conditions of the holder's safety approval. The application must meet all the applicable requirements under this part. The FAA will review and make a determination on the application using the same procedures under this part applicable to an initial safety approval application. If the FAA denies the request to modify a safety approval, the holder may correct any deficiency the FAA identified and request reconsideration. The holder also has the right to appeal a denial as set forth in subpart D of this part.

(b) *The FAA.* If the FAA finds it is in the interest of public health and safety, safety of property, or if the safety approval holder fails to comply with any applicable requirements of this part, any terms and conditions of the safety approval, or any other applicable requirement, the FAA may—

(1) Modify the terms and conditions of the safety approval; or

(2) Suspend or revoke the safety approval.

(c) *Effective Date.* Unless otherwise stated by the FAA, any modification, suspension, or revocation of a safety approval under paragraph (b)—

(1) Takes effect immediately; and

(2) Continues in effect during any reconsideration or appeal of such action under this part.

(d) *Notification and Right to Appeal.* If the FAA determines it is necessary to modify, suspend, or revoke a safety approval, we will notify the safety approval holder in writing. If the holder disagrees with the FAA's determination, the holder may correct any deficiency the FAA identified and request a reconsideration of the determination. The applicant also has the right to appeal the determination as set forth in subpart D of this part.

§414.35 Public notification of the criteria by which a safety approval was issued.

For each grant of a safety approval, the FAA will publish in the FEDERAL REGISTER a notice of the criteria that were used to evaluate the safety approval application, and a description of the criteria.

Subpart D—Appeal Procedures

§414.37 Hearings in safety approval actions.

(a) The FAA will give the safety approval applicant or holder, as appropriate, written notice stating the reason for issuing a denial or for modifying, suspending, or revoking a safety approval under this part.

(b) A safety approval applicant or holder is entitled to a determination on the record after an opportunity for a hearing.

(c) An administrative law judge will be designated to preside over any hearing held under this part.

§414.39 Submissions; oral presentations in safety approval actions.

(a) Determinations in safety approval actions under this part will be made on the basis of written submissions unless the administrative law judge, on petition or on his or her own initiative, determines that an oral presentation is required.

(b) Submissions must include a detailed exposition of the evidence or arguments supporting the petition.

(c) Petitions must be filed as soon as practicable, but in no event more than 30 days after issuance of decision or finding under §414.37.

§414.41 Administrative law judge's recommended decision in safety approval actions.

(a) The Associate Administrator, who will make the final decision on the matter at issue, will review the recommended decision of the administrative law judge. The Associate Administrator will make such final decision within 30 days of issuance of the recommended decision.

(b) The authority and responsibility to review and decide rests solely with the Associate Administrator and may not be delegated.

PART 415—LAUNCH LICENSE

Subpart A—General

Subpart B—Policy Review and Approval

Subpart C—Safety Review and Approval for Launch From a Federal Launch Range

Subpart D—Payload Review and Determination

Subpart E [Reserved]

Subpart F—Safety Review and Approval for Launch of an Expendable Launch Vehicle From a Non-Federal Launch Site

Subpart G—Environmental Review

AUTHORITY: 51 U.S.C. 50901–50923.

SOURCE: Amdt. 415–03, 64 FR 19616, Apr. 21, 1999, unless otherwise noted.

Subpart A—General

§ 415.1 Scope.

This part prescribes requirements for obtaining a license to launch a launch vehicle, other than a reusable launch vehicle (RLV), and post-licensing requirements with which a licensee must comply to remain licensed. Requirements for preparing a license application are in part 413 of this subchapter.

[Doc. No. FAA–2006–24197, 72 FR 17019, Apr. 6, 2007]

§ 415.3 Types of launch licenses.

(a) *Launch-specific license.* A launch-specific license authorizes a licensee to conduct one or more launches, having the same launch parameters, of one type of launch vehicle from one launch site. The license identifies, by name or mission, each launch authorized under the license. A licensee's authorization to launch terminates upon completion of all launches authorized by the license or the expiration date stated in the license, whichever occurs first.

(b) *Launch operator license*. A launch operator license authorizes a licensee to conduct launches from one launch site, within a range of launch parameters, of launch vehicles from the same family of vehicles transporting specified classes of payloads. A launch operator license remains in effect for five years from the date of issuance.

§415.5 Policy and safety approvals.

To obtain a launch license, an applicant must obtain policy and safety approvals from the FAA. Requirements for obtaining these approvals are contained in subparts B, C and F of this part. Only a launch license applicant may apply for the approvals, and may apply for either approval separately and in advance of submitting a complete license application, using the application procedures contained in part 413 of this subchapter.

§415.7 Payload determination.

A payload determination is required for a launch license unless the proposed payload is exempt from payload review under §415.53 of this part. The FAA conducts a payload review, as described in subpart D of this part, to make the determination. Either a launch license applicant or a payload owner or operator may request a review of its proposed payload using the application procedures contained in part 413 of this subchapter. Upon receipt of an application, the FAA may conduct a payload review independently of a launch license application.

§415.8 Human space flight.

To obtain a launch license, an applicant proposing to conduct a launch with flight crew or a space flight participant on board must demonstrate compliance with §§460.5, 460.7, 460.11, 460.13, 460.15, 460.17, 460.51 and 460.53 of this subchapter.

[Doc. No. FAA-2005-23449, 71 FR 75632, Dec. 15, 2006]

§415.9 Issuance of a launch license.

(a) The FAA issues a launch license to an applicant who has obtained all approvals and determinations required under this chapter for a license.

(b) A launch license authorizes a licensee to conduct a launch or launches in accordance with the representations contained in the licensee's application, subject to the licensee's compliance with terms and conditions contained in license orders accompanying the license, including financial responsibility requirements, and part 417 of this chapter.

[Amdt. 415-03, 64 FR 19616, Apr. 21, 1999, as amended by Amdt. 415-4, 71 FR 50531, Aug. 25, 2006]

§415.11 Additional license terms and conditions.

The FAA may modify a launch license at any time by modifying or adding license terms and conditions to ensure compliance with the Act and regulations.

§415.13 Transfer of a launch license.

(a) Only the FAA may transfer a launch license.

(b) An applicant for transfer of a launch license shall submit a license application in accordance with part 413 of this subchapter and shall meet the requirements of part 415 of this subchapter. The FAA will transfer a license to an applicant who has obtained all of the approvals and determinations required under this chapter for a license. In conducting its reviews and issuing approvals and determinations, the FAA may incorporate by reference any findings made part of the record to support the initial licensing determination. The FAA may modify a license to reflect any changes necessary as a result of a license transfer.

§415.15 Rights not conferred by launch license.

Issuance of a launch license does not relieve a licensee of its obligation to comply with all applicable requirements of law or regulation that may apply to its activities, nor does issuance confer any proprietary, property or exclusive right in the use of any federal launch range or related facilities, airspace, or outer space.

§§ 415.16–415.20 [Reserved]

Subpart B—Policy Review and Approval

§ 415.21 General.

The FAA issues a policy approval to a license applicant unless the FAA determines that a proposed launch would jeopardize U.S. national security or foreign policy interests, or international obligations of the United States. A policy approval is part of the licensing record on which the FAA's licensing determination is based.

§ 415.23 Policy review.

(a) The FAA reviews a license application to determine whether it presents any issues affecting U.S. national security or foreign policy interests, or international obligations of the United States.

(b) *Interagency consultation.* (1) The FAA consults with the Department of Defense to determine whether a license application presents any issues affecting U.S. national security.

(2) The FAA consults with the Department of State to determine whether a license application presents any issues affecting U.S. foreign policy interests or international obligations.

(3) The FAA consults with other federal agencies, including the National Aeronautics and Space Administration, authorized to address issues identified under paragraph (a) of this section, associated with an applicant's launch proposal.

(c) The FAA advises an applicant, in writing, of any issue raised during a policy review that would impede issuance of a policy approval. The applicant may respond, in writing, or revise its license application.

§ 415.25 Application requirements for policy review.

In its launch license application, an applicant shall—

(a) Identify the model and configuration of any launch vehicle proposed for launch by the applicant.

(b) Identify structural, pneumatic, propellant, propulsion, electrical and avionics systems used in the launch vehicle and all propellants.

(c) Identify foreign ownership of the applicant as follows:

(1) For a sole proprietorship or partnership, identify all foreign ownership;

(2) For a corporation, identify any foreign ownership interests of 10% or more; and

(3) For a joint venture, association, or other entity, identify any participating foreign entities.

(d) Identify proposed launch vehicle flight profile(s), including:

(1) Launch site;

(2) Flight azimuths, trajectories, and associated ground tracks and instantaneous impact points;

(3) Sequence of planned events or maneuvers during flight;

(4) Range of nominal impact areas for all spent motors and other discarded mission hardware, within three standard deviations of the mean impact point (a 3-sigma footprint); and

(5) For each orbital mission, the range of intermediate and final orbits of each vehicle upper stage, and their estimated orbital lifetimes.

§ 415.27 Denial of policy approval.

The FAA notifies an applicant, in writing, if it has denied policy approval for a license application. The notice states the reasons for the FAA's determination. The applicant may respond to the reasons for the determination and request reconsideration.

§§ 415.28–415.30 [Reserved]

Subpart C—Safety Review and Approval for Launch From a Federal Launch Range

§ 415.31 General.

(a) The FAA conducts a safety review to determine whether an applicant is capable of launching a launch vehicle and its payload without jeopardizing public health and safety and safety of property. The FAA issues a safety approval to a license applicant proposing to launch from a Federal launch range if the applicant satisfies the requirements of this subpart and has contracted with the Federal launch range for the provision of safety-related launch services and property, as long as an FAA launch site safety assessment shows that the range's launch services and launch property satisfy part 417 of this chapter. The FAA evaluates on an individual basis all other safety-related launch services and property associated with an applicant's proposal, in accordance with part 417 of this chapter. A safety approval is part of the licensing record on which the FAA's licensing determination is based.

(b) The FAA advises an applicant, in writing, of any issue raised during a safety review that would impede issuance of a safety approval. The applicant may respond, in writing, or revise its license application.

[Amdt. 415–03, 64 FR 19616, Apr. 21, 1999, as amended by Amdt. 415–4, 71 FR 50531, Aug. 25, 2006]

§415.33 Safety organization.

(a) An applicant shall maintain a safety organization and document it by identifying lines of communication and approval authority for all launch safety decisions. Lines of communication, both within the applicant's organization and between the applicant and any federal launch range providing launch services, shall be employed to ensure that personnel perform launch safety operations in accordance with range safety requirements and with plans and procedures required by this subpart. Approval authority shall be employed to ensure compliance with range safety requirements and with plans and procedures required by this subpart.

(b) *Safety official.* An applicant shall identify by name, title, and qualifications, a qualified safety official authorized to examine all aspects of the applicant's launch safety operations and to monitor independently personnel compliance with the applicant's safety policies and procedures. The safety official shall report directly to the person responsible for an applicant's licensed launches, who shall ensure that all of the safety official's concerns are addressed prior to launch.

§415.35 Acceptable flight risk.

(a) *Flight risk through orbital insertion or impact.* Acceptable flight risk through orbital insertion for an orbital launch vehicle, and through impact for a suborbital launch vehicle, is measured in terms of the expected average number of casualties (E_C) to the collective members of the public exposed to debris hazards from any one launch. To obtain safety approval, an applicant must demonstrate that the risk level associated with debris from an applicant's proposed launch meets the public risk criteria of §417.107(b)(1) of this chapter for impacting inert and impacting explosive debris.

(b) *Hazard identification and risk assessment.* To demonstrate compliance with paragraph (a) of this section, an applicant must file an analysis that identifies hazards and assesses risks to public health and safety and safety of property associated with nominal and non-nominal flight of its proposed launch.

(c) *Design.* A launch vehicle must be designed to ensure that flight risks meet the criteria of paragraph (a) of this section. An applicant must identify and describe the following:

(1) Launch vehicle structure, including physical dimensions and weight;

(2) Hazardous and safety critical systems, including propulsion systems; and

(3) Drawings and schematics for each system identified under paragraph (c)(2) of this section.

(d) *Operation.* A launch vehicle must be operated in a manner that ensures that flight risks meet the criteria of paragraph (a) of this section. An applicant must identify all launch operations and procedures that must be performed to ensure acceptable flight risk.

[Doc. No. FAA–2000–7953, 71 FR 50531, Aug. 25, 2006, as amended by Amdt. No. 415–6, 81 FR 59439, Aug. 30, 2016]

§415.37 Flight readiness and communications plan.

(a) *Flight readiness requirements.* An applicant must designate an individual responsible for flight readiness. The applicant must file the following procedures for verifying readiness for safe flight:

(1) Launch readiness review procedures involving the applicant's flight safety personnel and Federal launch range personnel involved in the launch, as required by §417.117(b)(3) of this chapter.

(2) Procedures that ensure mission constraints, rules and abort procedures are listed and consolidated in a safety directive or notebook approved by licensee flight safety and Federal launch range personnel.

(3) Procedures that ensure currency and consistency of licensee and Federal launch range countdown checklists.

(4) Dress rehearsal procedures that—

(i) Ensure crew readiness under nominal and non-nominal flight conditions;

(ii) Contain criteria for determining whether to dispense with one or more dress rehearsals; and

(iii) Verify currency and consistency of licensee and Federal launch range countdown checklists.

(5) Procedures for ensuring the licensee's flight safety personnel adhere to the crew rest rules of §417.113(f) of this chapter.

(b) *Communications plan requirements.* An applicant must file a communications plan that meets §417.111(k) of this chapter, and that provides licensee and Federal launch range personnel communications procedures during countdown and flight.

(c) An applicant must file procedures that ensure that licensee and Federal launch range personnel receive a copy of the communications plan required by paragraph (b) of this section, and that the Federal launch range concurs in the communications plan.

[Doc. No. FAA–2000–7953, 71 FR 50531, Aug. 25, 2006, as amended by Amdt. No. 415–6, 81 FR 59439, Aug. 30, 2016]

§415.39 Safety at end of launch.

To obtain safety approval, an applicant must demonstrate compliance with §417.129 of this chapter, for any proposed launch of a launch vehicle with a stage or component that will reach Earth orbit.

[Doc. No. FAA–2000–7953, 71 FR 50531, Aug. 25, 2006]

§415.41 Accident investigation plan.

An applicant must file an accident investigation plan (AIP), that satisfies §417.111(h) of this chapter, and contains the applicant's procedures for reporting and responding to launch accidents, launch incidents, or other mishaps, as defined by §401.5 of this chapter.

[Doc. No. FAA–2000–7953, 71 FR 50531, Aug. 25, 2006, as amended by Amdt. No. 415–6, 81 FR 59439, Aug. 30, 2016]

§415.43 Denial of safety approval.

The FAA notifies an applicant, in writing, if it has denied safety approval for a license application. The notice states the reasons for the FAA's determination. The applicant may respond to the reasons for the determination and request reconsideration.

§§415.44–415.50 [Reserved]

Subpart D—Payload Review and Determination

§415.51 General.

The FAA reviews a payload proposed for launch to determine whether a license applicant or payload owner or operator has obtained all required licenses, authorization, and permits, unless the payload is exempt from review under §415.53 of this subpart. If not otherwise exempt, the FAA reviews a payload proposed for launch to determine whether its launch would jeopardize public health and safety, safety of property, U.S. national security or foreign policy interests, or international obligations of the United States. A payload determination is part of the licensing record on which the FAA's licensing determination is based. The safety requirements of subpart C and F of this part and of part 417 of this chapter apply to all payloads, whether or not the payload is otherwise exempt.

[Amdt. 415–03, 64 FR 19616, Apr. 21, 1999, as amended by Amdt. 415–4, 71 FR 50531, Aug. 25, 2006]

§415.53 Payloads not subject to review.

The FAA does not review payloads that are—

(a) Subject to regulation by the Federal Communications Commission (FCC) or the Department of Commerce, National Oceanic and Atmospheric Administration (NOAA); or

(b) Owned or operated by the U.S. Government.

§415.55 Classes of payloads.

The FAA may review and issue findings regarding a proposed class of payload, e.g., communications, remote sensing or navigation. However, each payload is subject to compliance monitoring by the FAA before launch to determine whether its launch would jeopardize public health and safety, safety of property, U.S. national security or foreign policy interests, or international obligations of the United States. The licensee is responsible for providing current information, in accordance with §417.17(b)(2), regarding a payload proposed for launch not later than 60 days before a scheduled launch.

[Amdt. 415–03, 64 FR 19616, Apr. 21, 1999, as amended by Amdt. No. 415–6, 81 FR 59439, Aug. 30, 2016]

§415.57 Payload review.

(a) *Timing.* A payload review may be conducted as part of a license application review or may be requested by a payload owner or operator in advance of or apart from a license application.

(b) *Interagency consultation.* The FAA consults with other agencies to determine whether launch of a proposed payload or payload class would present any issues affecting public health and safety, safety of property, U.S. national security or foreign policy interests, or international obligations of the United States.

(1) The FAA consults with the Department of Defense to determine whether launch of a proposed payload or payload class would present any issues affecting U.S. national security.

(2) The FAA consults with the Department of State to determine whether launch of a proposed payload or payload class would present any issues affecting U.S. foreign policy interests or international obligations.

(3) The FAA consults with other federal agencies, including the National Aeronautics and Space Administration, authorized to address issues identified under paragraph (b) of this section associated with an applicant's launch proposal.

(c) The FAA advises a person requesting a payload determination, in writing, of any issue raised during a payload review that would impede issuance of a license to launch that payload or payload class. The person requesting payload review may respond, in writing, or revise its application.

§415.59 Information requirements for payload review.

(a) A person requesting review of a particular payload or payload class shall identify the following:

(1) Payload name;

(2) Payload class;

(3) Physical dimensions and weight of the payload;

(4) Payload owner and operator, if different from the person requesting payload review;

(5) Orbital parameters for parking, transfer and final orbits;

(6) Hazardous materials, as defined in §401.5 of this chapter, and radioactive materials, and the amounts of each;

(7) Intended payload operations during the life of the payload; and

(8) Delivery point in flight at which the payload will no longer be under the licensee's control.

(b) [Reserved]

§415.61 Issuance of payload determination.

(a) The FAA issues a favorable payload determination unless it determines that launch of the proposed payload would jeopardize public health and safety, safety of property, U.S. national security or foreign policy interests, or international obligations of the United States. The FAA advises any person who has requested a payload review of its determination, in writing. The notice states the reasons for the determination in the event of an unfavorable determination.

(b) Any person issued an unfavorable payload determination may respond to the reasons for the determination and request reconsideration.

§415.63 Incorporation of payload determination in license application.

A favorable payload determination issued for a payload or class of payload may be included by a license applicant as part of its application. However, any change in information provided under section 415.59 of this subpart must be reported in accordance with section 413.17 of this chapter. The FAA determines whether a favorable payload determination remains valid in light of reported changes and may conduct an additional payload review.

§§ 415.64–415.70 [Reserved]

Subpart E [Reserved]

Subpart F—Safety Review and Approval for Launch of an Expendable Launch Vehicle From a Non-Federal Launch Site

SOURCE: Docket No. FAA–2000–7953, 71 FR 50532, Aug. 25, 2006, unless otherwise noted.

§§ 415.91–415.100 [Reserved]

§ 415.101 Scope and applicability.

(a) This subpart F contains requirements that an applicant must meet to obtain a safety approval when applying for a license to launch an expendable launch vehicle from a non-Federal launch site. This subpart also contains administrative requirements for a safety review, such as when and how an applicant files the required information, and the requirements for the form and content of each submission.

(b) The requirements of this subpart apply to both orbital and suborbital expendable launch vehicles.

(c) An applicant must demonstrate, through the material filed with the FAA, its ability to comply with the requirements of part 417 of this chapter. To facilitate production of the information required by this subpart, an applicant should become familiar with the requirements of part 417 of this chapter.

(d) For a launch from an exclusive use launch site, where there is no licensed launch site operator, a launch operator must satisfy the requirements of this part and the public safety application requirements of part 420 of this chapter.

§ 415.102 Definitions.

For the purposes of this subpart, the definitions of §§ 417.3 and 401.5 of this chapter apply.

§ 415.103 General.

(a) The FAA conducts a safety review to determine whether an applicant is capable of conducting launch processing and flight without jeopardizing public health and safety and safety of property. The FAA issues a safety approval to a license applicant if the applicant satisfies the requirements of this subpart and demonstrates that it will meet the safety responsibilities and requirements of part 417 of this chapter.

(b) The FAA advises an applicant, in writing, of any issue raised during a safety review that would impede issuance of a safety approval. The applicant may respond, in writing, or amend its license application as required by § 413.17 of this chapter.

(c) An applicant must make available to the FAA upon request a copy of any information incorporated into a license application by reference.

(d) A safety approval is part of the licensing record on which the FAA bases its licensing determination.

§ 415.105 Pre-application consultation.

(a) An applicant must participate in a pre-application consultation meeting, as required by § 413.5 of this chapter, prior to an applicant's preparation of the initial flight safety analysis required by § 415.115.

(b) At a pre-application consultation meeting, an applicant must provide as complete a description of the planned launch or series of launches as available at the time. An applicant must provide the FAA the following information:

(1) *Launch vehicle.* Description of:

(i) Launch vehicle;

(ii) Any flight termination system; and

(iii) All hazards associated with the launch vehicle and any payload, including the type and amounts of all propellants, explosives, toxic materials and any radionuclides.

(2) *Proposed mission.* (i) For an applicant applying for a launch specific license under § 415.3(a), the apogee, perigee, and inclination of any orbital objects and each impact location of any stage or other component.

(ii) For an applicant applying for a launch operator license under § 415.3(b), the planned range of trajectories and flight azimuths, and the range of apogees, perigees, and inclinations of any orbital objects and each impact location of any stage or other component.

(3) *Potential launch site.* (i) Name and location of the proposed launch site, including latitude and longitude of the proposed launch point;

(ii) Identity of any launch site operator of that site; and

(iii) Identification of any facilities at the launch site that will be used for launch processing and flight.

§415.107 Safety review document.

(a) An applicant must file a safety review document that contains all the information required by §§415.109—415.133. An applicant must file the information for a safety review document as required by the outline in appendix B of this part. An applicant must file a sufficiently complete safety review document, except for the ground safety analysis report, no later than six months before the applicant brings any launch vehicle to the proposed launch site.

(b) A launch operator's safety review document must:

(1) Contain a glossary of unique terms and acronyms used in alphabetical order;

(2) Contain a listing of all referenced standards, codes, and publications;

(3) Be logically organized, with a clear and consistent page numbering system and must identify cross-referenced topics;

(4) Use equations and mathematical relationships derived from or referenced to a recognized standard or text, and must define all algebraic parameters;

(5) Include the units of all numerical values provided; and

(6) Include a legend or key that identifies all symbols used for any schematic diagrams.

(c) An applicant's safety review document may include sections not required by appendix B of this part. An applicant must identify each added section by using the word "added" in front of the title of the section. In the first paragraph of the section, an applicant must explain any addition to the outline in appendix B of this part.

(d) If a safety review document section required by appendix B of this part does not apply to an applicant's proposed launch, an applicant must identify the sections in the application by the words "not applicable" preceding the title of the section. In the first paragraph of the section, an applicant must describe and justify why the section does not apply.

(e) An applicant may reference documentation previously filed with the FAA.

§415.109 Launch description.

An applicant's safety review document must contain the following information:

(a) *Launch site description.* An applicant must identify the proposed launch site and include the following:

(1) Boundaries of the launch site;

(2) Launch point location, including latitude and longitude;

(3) Identity of any launch site operator of that proposed site; and

(4) Identification of any facilities at the launch site that will be used for launch processing and flight.

(b) *Launch vehicle description.* An applicant must provide the following:

(1) A written description of the launch vehicle. The description must include a table specifying the type and quantities of all hazardous materials on the launch vehicle and must include propellants, explosives, and toxic materials; and

(2) A drawing of the launch vehicle that identifies:

(i) Each stage, including strap-on motors;

(ii) Physical dimensions and weight;

(iii) Location of all safety critical systems, including any flight termination hardware, tracking aids, or telemetry systems;

(iv) Location of all major launch vehicle control systems, propulsion systems, pressure vessels, and any other hardware that contains potential hazardous energy or hazardous material; and

(v) For an unguided suborbital launch vehicle, the location of the rocket's center of pressure in relation to its center of gravity for the entire flight profile.

(c) *Payload description.* An applicant must include or reference documentation previously filed with the FAA that contains the payload information required by §415.59 for any payload or class of payload.

(d) *Trajectory.* An applicant must provide two drawings depicting trajectory information. An applicant must file additional trajectory information as part of the flight safety analysis data required by §415.115.

(1) One drawing must depict the proposed nominal flight profile with downrange depicted on the abscissa and altitude depicted on the ordinate axis. The nominal flight profile must be labeled to show each planned staging event and its time after liftoff from launch through orbital insertion or final impact; and

(2) The second drawing must depict instantaneous impact point ground traces for each of the nominal trajectory, the three-sigma left lateral trajectory and the three-sigma right lateral trajectory determined under §417.207 of this chapter. The trajectories must be depicted on a latitude/longitude grid, and the grid must include the outlines of any continents and islands.

(e) *Staging events.* An applicant must provide a table of nominal and ±three-sigma times for each major staging event and must describe each event, including the predicted impact point and dispersion of each spent stage.

(f) *Vehicle performance graphs.* An applicant must provide graphs of the nominal and ±three-sigma values as a function of time after liftoff for the following launch vehicle performance parameters: thrust, altitude, velocity, instantaneous impact point arc-range measured from the launch point, and present position arc-range measured from the launch point.

§415.111 Launch operator organization.

An applicant's safety review document must contain organizational charts and a description that shows that the launch operator's organization satisfies the requirements of §417.103 of this chapter. An applicant's safety review document must also identify all persons with whom the applicant has contracted to provide safety-related goods or services for the launch of the launch vehicle.

§415.113 Launch personnel certification program.

(a) A safety review document must describe how the applicant will satisfy the personnel certification program requirements of §417.105 of this chapter and identify by position those individuals who implement the program.

(b) An applicant's safety review document must contain a copy of its documentation that demonstrates how the launch operator implements the personnel certification program.

(c) An applicant's safety review document must contain a table listing each hazardous operation or safety critical task that certified personnel must perform. For each task, the table must identify by position the individual who reviews personnel qualifications and certifies personnel for performing the task.

§415.115 Flight safety.

(a) *Flight safety analysis.* An applicant's safety review document must describe each analysis method employed to meet the flight safety analysis requirements of part 417, subpart C, of this chapter. An applicant's safety review document must demonstrate how each analysis method satisfies the flight safety analysis requirements of part 417, subpart C, of this chapter. An applicant's safety review document must contain analysis products and other data that demonstrate the applicant's ability to meet the public risk criteria of §417.107 of this chapter and to establish launch safety rules as required by §417.113 of this chapter. An applicant's flight safety analysis must satisfy the following requirements:

(1) An applicant must file the proposed flight safety analysis methodology and the preliminary flight safety analysis products no later than 18 months for any orbital or guided suborbital launch vehicle, and nine months for any unguided suborbital launch vehicle, prior to bringing any launch vehicle to the proposed launch site.

(2) For a launch operator license, an applicant must file flight safety analysis products that account for the range of launch vehicles and flight trajectories applied for, or the worst case vehicle and trajectory under which flight will be attempted, no later than 6 months before the applicant brings any launch vehicle to the proposed launch site. For a launch specific license, an applicant must file flight safety analysis products that account for the actual flight conditions, no later than 6 months before the applicant brings any launch vehicle to the proposed launch site.

(3) The flight safety analysis performed by an applicant must be completed as required by subpart C of part 417 of this chapter. An applicant may identify those portions of the analysis that it expects to refine as the first proposed flight date approaches. An applicant must identify any analysis product subject to change, describe what needs to be done to finalize the product, and identify when before flight it will be finalized. If a license allows more than one launch, an applicant must demonstrate the applicability of the analysis methods to each of the proposed launches and identify any expected differences in the flight safety analysis methods among the proposed launches. Once licensed, a launch operator must perform a flight safety analysis for each launch using final launch vehicle performance and other data as required by subpart C of part 417 of this chapter and using the analysis methods approved by the FAA through the licensing process.

(b) *Radionuclides*. An applicant's safety review document must identify the type and quantity of any radionuclide on a launch vehicle or payload. For each radionuclide, an applicant must include a reference list of all documentation addressing the safety of its intended use and describe all approvals by the Nuclear Regulatory Commission for launch processing. An applicant must provide radionuclide information to the FAA at the pre-application consultation as required by §415.105. The FAA will evaluate launch of any radionuclide on a case-by-case basis, and issue an approval if the FAA finds that the launch is consistent with public health and safety.

(c) *Flight safety plan*. An applicant's safety review document must contain a flight safety plan that satisfies §417.111(b) of this chapter. The plan need not be restricted to public safety related issues and may combine other flight safety issues as well, such as employee safety, so as to be all-inclusive.

(d) *Natural and triggered lightning*. For any orbital or guided suborbital expendable launch vehicle, an applicant must demonstrate that it will satisfy the flight commit criteria of §417.113(c) of this chapter and appendix G of part 417 of this chapter for natural and triggered lightning. If an applicant's safety review document states that any flight commit criterion that is otherwise required by appendix G of part 417 of this chapter does not apply to a proposed launch or series of launches, the applicant's safety review document must demonstrate that the criterion does not apply.

§415.117 Ground safety.

(a) *General*. An applicant's safety review document must include a ground safety analysis report, and a ground safety plan for its launch processing and post-flight operations as required by this section, §417.109 of this chapter, and subpart E of part 417 of this chapter when launching from a launch point in the United States. Launch processing and post-launch operations at a launch point outside the United States may be subject to the requirements of the governing jurisdiction.

(b) *Ground safety analysis*. A ground safety analysis must review each system and operation used in launch processing and post-flight operations as required by §417.109 of this chapter, and subpart E of part 417 of this chapter.

(1) An applicant must file an initial ground safety analysis report no later than 12 months for any orbital or guided suborbital launch vehicle, and nine months for an unguided suborbital launch vehicle, before the applicant brings any launch vehicle to the proposed launch site. An initial ground safety analysis report must be in a proposed final or near final form and identify any incomplete items. An applicant must document any incomplete

items and track them to completion. An applicant must resolve any FAA comments on the initial report and file a complete ground safety analysis report, no later than two months before the applicant brings any launch vehicle to the proposed launch site. Furthermore, an applicant must keep its ground safety analysis report current. Any late developing change to a ground safety analysis report must be coordinated with the FAA as an application amendment as required by §413.17 of this chapter as soon as the applicant identifies the need for a change.

(2) An applicant must file a ground safety analysis report that satisfies the ground safety analysis requirements of §417.109 of this chapter, and subpart E of part 417 of this chapter.

(3) The person designated under §417.103(b)(1) of this chapter and the person designated under §417.103(b)(2) of this chapter must approve and sign the ground safety analysis report.

(c) *Ground safety plan.* An applicant's safety review document must contain a ground safety plan that satisfies §417.111(c) of this chapter. The applicant must file this plan with the FAA no later than six months prior to bringing the launch vehicle to the proposed launch site. This ground safety plan must describe implementation of the hazard controls identified by an applicant's ground safety analysis and implementation of the ground safety requirements of subpart E of part 417 of this chapter. A ground safety plan must address all public safety related issues and may include other ground safety issues if an applicant intends it to have a broader scope.

§415.119 Launch plans.

An applicant's safety review document must contain the plans required by §417.111 of this chapter, except for the countdown plan of §417.111(l) of this chapter. An applicant's launch plans do not have to be separate documents, and may be part of other applicant documentation. An applicant must incorporate each launch safety rule established under §417.113 of this chapter into a related launch safety plan.

§415.121 Launch schedule.

An applicant's safety review document must contain a generic launch processing schedule that identifies each review, rehearsal, and safety critical preflight operation to be conducted as required by §§417.117, 417.119, and 417.121 of this chapter. The launch schedule must also identify day of flight activities. The launch processing schedule must show each of these activities referenced to liftoff, such as liftoff minus three days.

§415.123 Computing systems and software.

(a) An applicant's safety review document must describe all computing systems and software that perform a safety-critical computer system function for any operation performed during launch processing or flight that could have a hazardous effect on the public as required by §417.123 of this chapter.

(b) An applicant's safety review document must list and describe all safety-critical computer system functions involved in a proposed launch, including associated hardware and software interfaces. For each system with a safety-critical computer system function, an applicant's safety review document must:

(1) Describe all safety-critical computer system functions, including each safety-critical interface with any other system;

(2) Describe all systems, including all hardware and software, and the layout of each operator console and display;

(3) Provide flow charts or diagrams that show all hardware data busses, hardware interfaces, software interfaces, data flow, and power systems, and all operations of each safety-critical computer system function;

(4) Provide all logic diagrams and software designs;

(5) List all operator user manuals and documentation by title and date;

(6) Describe the computing system and software system safety process as required by §417.123(a).

(7) Provide all results of computing system and software hazard analyses as required by §417.123(c).

(8) Provide all plans and results of computing systems and software validation and verification as required by §417.123(d).

(9) Provide all plans for software development as required by §417.123(e).

§415.125 Unique safety policies, requirements and practices.

An applicant's safety review document must identify any public safety-related policy, requirement, or practice that is unique to the proposed launch, or series of launches, as required by §417.127 of this chapter. An applicant's safety review document must describe how each unique safety policy, requirement, or practice ensures the safety of the public.

§415.127 Flight safety system design and operation data.

(a) *General.* This part applies to an applicant launching an orbital or guided sub-orbital expendable launch vehicle that uses a flight safety system to protect public safety as required by §417.107(a) of this chapter. An applicant's safety review document must contain the flight safety system data identified by this section. The applicant must file all data required by this section no later than 18 months before bringing any launch vehicle to a proposed launch site.

(b) *Flight safety system description.* A safety review document must describe an applicant's flight safety system and its operation. Part 417, subpart D of this chapter and appendices D, E, and F of part 417 of this chapter contain the flight safety system and subsystems design and operational requirements.

(c) *Flight safety system diagram.* An applicant's safety review document must contain a block diagram that identifies all flight safety system subsystems. The diagram must include the following subsystems defined in part 417, subpart D of this chapter: flight termination system; command control system; tracking; telemetry; communications; flight safety data processing, display, and recording system; and flight safety official console.

(d) *Subsystem design information.* An applicant's safety review document must contain all of the following data that applies to each subsystem identified in the block diagram required by paragraph (c) of this section:

(1) *Subsystem description.* A physical description of each subsystem and its components, its operation, and interfaces with other systems or subsystems.

(2) *Subsystem diagram.* A physical and functional diagram of each subsystem, including interfaces with other systems and subsystems.

(3) *Component location.* Drawings showing the location of all subsystem components, and the details of the mounting arrangements, as installed on the vehicle, and at the launch site.

(4) *Electronic components.* A physical description of each subsystem electronic component, including operating parameters and functions at the system and piece-part level. An applicant must also provide the name of the manufacturer and any model number of each component and identify whether the component is custom designed and built or off-the-shelf-equipment.

(5) *Mechanical components.* An illustrated parts breakdown of all mechanically operated components for each subsystem, including the name of the manufacturer and any model number.

(6) *Subsystem compatibility.* A demonstration of the compatibility of the onboard launch vehicle flight termination system with the command control system.

(7) *Flight termination system component storage, operating, and service life.* A listing of all flight termination system components that have a critical storage, operating, or service life and a summary of the applicant's procedures for ensuring that each component does not exceed its storage, operating, or service life before flight.

(8) *Flight termination system element location.* For a flight termination system, a description of where each subsystem element is located, where cables are routed, and identification of mounting attach points and access points.

(9) *Flight termination system electrical connectors and connections and wiring diagrams and schematics.* For a flight termination system, a description of all subsystem electrical connectors and connections, and any electrical isolation. The safety review document must

also contain flight termination system wiring diagrams and schematics and identify the test points used for integrated testing and checkout.

(10) *Flight termination system batteries.* A description of each flight termination system battery and cell, the name of the battery or cell manufacturer, and any model numbers.

(11) *Controls and displays.* For a flight safety official console, a description of all controls, displays, and charts depicting how real time vehicle data and flight safety limits are displayed. The description must identify the scales used for displays and charts.

(e) *System analyses.* An applicant must perform the reliability and other system analyses for a flight termination system and command control system of §417.309 of this chapter. An applicant's safety review document must contain the results of each analysis.

(f) *Environmental design.* An applicant must determine the flight termination system maximum predicted environment levels required by section D417.7 of appendix D of part 417 of this chapter, and the design environments and design margins of section D417.3 of appendix D of part 417 of this chapter. An applicant's safety review document must summarize the analyses and measurements used to derive the maximum predicted environment levels. The safety review document must contain a matrix that identifies the maximum predicted environment levels and the design environments.

(g) *Flight safety system compliance matrix.* An applicant's safety review document must contain a compliance matrix of the function, reliability, system, subsystem, and component requirements of part 417 of this chapter and appendix D of part 417 of this chapter. This matrix must identify each requirement and indicate compliance as follows:

(1) "Yes" if the applicant's system meets the requirement of part 417 of this chapter. The matrix must reference documentation that demonstrates compliance;

(2) "Not applicable" if the applicant's system design and operational environment are such that the requirement does not apply. For each such case, the applicant must demonstrate, in accordance with section 406.3(b), the non-applicability of that requirement as an attachment to the matrix; or

(3) "Equivalent level of safety" in each case where the applicant proposes to show that its system provides an equivalent level of safety through some means other than that required by part 417 of this chapter. For each such case, an applicant must clearly and convincingly demonstrate, as required by §406.3(b), through a technical rationale within the matrix, or as an attachment, that the proposed alternative provides a level of safety equivalent to satisfying the requirement that it would replace.

(h) *Flight termination system installation procedures.* An applicant's safety review document must contain a list of the flight termination system installation procedures and a synopsis of the procedures that demonstrates how each of those procedures meet the requirements of section D417.15 of appendix D of part 417 of this chapter. The list must reference each procedure by title, any document number, and date.

(i) *Tracking validation procedures.* An applicant's safety review document must contain the procedures identified by §417.121(h) of this chapter for validating the accuracy of the launch vehicle tracking data supplied to the flight safety crew.

§415.129 Flight safety system test data.

(a) *General.* An applicant's safety review document must contain the flight safety system test data required by this section for the launch of an orbital and guided suborbital expendable launch vehicle that uses a flight safety system to protect public safety as required by §417.107(a) of this chapter. This section applies to all testing required by part 417, subpart D of this chapter and its appendices, including qualification, acceptance, age surveillance, and preflight testing of a flight safety system and its subsystems and individual components. An applicant must file all required test data, no later than 12 months before the applicant brings any launch vehicle to the proposed launch site. An applicant may file test data earlier to allow greater time for addressing issues that the FAA may identify to avoid possible impact on the proposed launch date. Flight safety system testing need not be completed before the FAA issues a launch license. Prior to flight, a licensee must successfully complete all required flight safety system testing and file the completed test reports or the test report summaries required by §417.305(d) of this chapter and section E417.1(i) of appendix E of part 417 of this chapter.

(b) *Testing compliance matrix.* An applicant's safety review document must contain a compliance matrix of all the flight safety system, subsystem, and component testing requirements of part 417 of this chapter and appendix E to part 417 of this chapter. This matrix must identify each test requirement and indicate compliance as follows:

(1) "Yes" if the applicant performs the system or component testing required by part 417 of this chapter. The matrix must reference documentation that demonstrates compliance;

(2) "Not applicable" if the applicant's system design and operational environment are such that the test requirement does not apply. For each such case, an applicant must demonstrate, as required by §406.3(b), of the non-applicability of that requirement as an attachment to the matrix;

(3) "Similarity" if the test requirement applies to a component whose design is similar to a previously qualified component. For each such case, an applicant must demonstrate similarity by performing the analysis required by appendix E of part 417 of this chapter. The matrix, or an attachment, must contain the results of each analysis; or

(4) "Equivalent level of safety" in each case where the applicant proposes to show that its test program provides an equivalent level of safety through some means other than that required by part 417 of this chapter. For each such case, an applicant must clearly and convincingly demonstrate through a technical rationale, within the matrix or as an attachment, that the alternative provides a level of safety equivalent to satisfying the requirement that it replaces, as required by §406.3(c).

(c) *Test program overview and schedule.* A safety review document must contain a summary of the applicant's flight safety system test program that identifies the location of the testing and the personnel who ensure the validity of the results. A safety review document must contain a schedule for successfully completing each test before flight. The applicant must reference the schedule to the time of liftoff for the first proposed flight attempt.

(d) *Flight safety system test plans and procedures.* An applicant's safety review document must contain test plans that satisfy the flight safety system testing requirements of subpart D of part 417 of this chapter and appendix E of part 417 of this chapter. An applicant's safety review document must contain a list of all flight termination system test procedures and a synopsis of the procedures that demonstrates how they meet the test requirements of part 417 of this chapter. The list must reference each procedure by title, any document number, and date.

(e) *Test reports.* An applicant's safety review document must contain either the test reports, or a summary of the test report which captures the overall test results, including all test discrepancies and their resolution, prepared as required by §417.305(d) of this chapter and section E417.1(i) of appendix E of part 417 of this chapter, for each flight safety system test completed at the time of license application. An applicant must file any remaining test reports or summaries before flight as required by §417.305(d) and section E417.1(i) of appendix E of part 417 of this chapter. Upon request, the launch operator must file the complete test report with the FAA for review, if the launch operator previously filed test report summaries with the FAA.

(f) *Reuse of flight termination system components.* An applicant's safety review document must contain a reuse qualification test, refurbishment plan, and acceptance test plan for the use of any flight termination system component on more than one flight. This test plan must define the applicant's process for demonstrating that the component can satisfy all its performance specifications when subjected to the qualification test environmental levels plus the total number of exposures to the maximum expected environmental levels for each of the flights to be flown.

§415.131 Flight safety system crew data.

(a) An applicant's safety review document must identify each flight safety system crew position and the role of that crewmember during launch processing and flight of a launch vehicle.

(b) An applicant's safety review document must describe the certification program for flight safety system crewmembers established to ensure compliance with §§417.105 and 417.311 of this chapter.

§415.133 Safety at end of launch.

An applicant must demonstrate compliance with §417.129 of this chapter, for any proposed launch of a launch vehicle with a stage or component that will reach Earth orbit.

§415.135 Denial of safety approval.

The FAA notifies an applicant, in writing, if it has denied safety approval for a license application. The notice states the reasons for the FAA's determination. The applicant may respond to the reasons for the determination and request reconsideration.

§§415.136–415.200 [Reserved]

Subpart G—Environmental Review

§415.201 General.

An applicant shall provide the FAA with information for the FAA to analyze the environmental impacts associated with a proposed launch. The information provided by an applicant must be sufficient to enable the FAA to comply with the requirements of the National Environment Policy Act, 42 U.S.C. 4321 *et seq.* (NEPA), the Council on Environmental Quality Regulations for Implementing the Procedural Provisions of NEPA, 40 CFR parts 1500–1508, and the FAA's Procedures for Considering Environmental Impacts, FAA Order 1050.1D.

[Amdt. 415–03, 64 FR 19616, Apr. 21, 1999. Redesignated by Amdt. 415–4, 71 FR 50532, Aug. 25, 2006]

§415.203 Environmental information.

An applicant shall submit environmental information concerning:

(a) A proposed launch site not covered by existing environmental documentation;

(b) A proposed launch vehicle with characteristics falling measurably outside the parameters of existing environmental documentation;

(c) A proposed launch from an established launch site involving a vehicle with characteristics falling measurably outside the parameters of any existing environmental impact statement that applies to that site;

(d) A proposed payload that may have significant environmental impacts in the event of a mishap; and

(e) Other factors as determined by the FAA.

[Amdt. 415–03, 64 FR 19616, Apr. 21, 1999. Redesignated by Amdt. 415–4, 71 FR 50532, Aug. 25, 2006]

§§415.204–415.400 [Reserved]

APPENDIX A TO PART 415—FAA/USSPACECOM LAUNCH NOTIFICATION FORM

Form Approved OMB No. 2120-0608

U.S. Department of Transportation
Federal Aviation Administration

FAA/USSPACECOM Launch Notification

1) Launch Site & Launch Date:

2) Earliest and Latest possible Launch Time (GMT):

3) List of objects to achieve orbit - to include payload description, Rocket bodies, and all other objects:

4) Launch Booster, sustainer, and strap-on descriptions:

5) Launch operator POC - to include name, address, & phone numbers:

6) Orbital Parameters for all objects achieving orbit

a) inertial launch azimuth at liftoff:

b) inertial flight azimuth after liftoff:

c) epoch time:

d) nominal period (min):

e) inclination (deg):

f) eccentricity:

g) semimajor axis (km):

h) argument of perigee (deg):

i) right ascension of ascending node (deg):

j) mean anomaly (deg):

k) start time of orbit (hh:mm:ss after launch):

l) end time of orbit (hh:mm:ss after launch):

7) Injection data

a) injection point latitude (deg n or s) & longitude (deg e):

b) inertial azimuth at injection point:

c) height above earth (km):

FAA Form 8800-1 (7-98) PAGE 1

FAA/USSPACECOM Launch Notification

d) injection time (hh:mm:ss after liftoff):

8) Sequence of Events from liftoff to final injection. Give the times (hh:mm:ss after liftoff)

a) separation of each motor:

b) ignition of each motor:

c) cutoff of each motor:

d) jettison of pieces:

e) maneuvers:

f) reorientations:

g) deorbit:

h) ejection of special packages or other experiments:

9) Optional - Schedule for events (not included in no. 8), such as ejection or experiments, maneuvering (unclassified missions), jettison of parts, extension of antenna and solar arrays, venting, spinning or despinning attitude changes, reorientation, or anything which may affect the orbital characteristics:

10) A brief narrative description of the mission:

11) Transmitting frequencies and power (required only if space surveillance is required), including device, band, power (watts), frequency (mhz), and emission scheduled by fixed program, command, or transponder tracking:

12) Orbital objects cataloging instructions (include all orbital objects listed in no. 3, including common name, international designation, and country:

FAA Form 8800-1 (7-98) PAGE 2

APPENDIX B TO PART 415—SAFETY REVIEW DOCUMENT OUTLINE

This appendix contains the format and numbering scheme for a safety review document to be filed as part of an application for a launch license as required by subpart F of part 415. The applicable sections of parts 413, 415, and 417 of this chapter are referenced in the outline below.

SAFETY REVIEW DOCUMENT

1.0 Launch Description (§ 415.109)
1.1 Launch Site Description
1.2 Launch Vehicle Description
1.3 Payload Description
1.4 Trajectory
1.5 Staging Events
1.6 Vehicle Performance Graphs
2.0 Launch Operator Organization (§ 415.111)
2.1 Launch Operator Organization (§ 415.111 and § 417.103 of this chapter)
2.1.1 Organization Summary
2.1.3 Organization Charts
2.1.4 Office Descriptions and Safety Functions
3.0 Launch Personnel Certification Program (§ 415.113 and § 417.105 of this chapter)
3.1 Program Summary
3.2 Program Implementation Document(s)
3.3 Table of Safety Critical Tasks Performed by Certified Personnel
4.0 Flight Safety (§ 415.115)
4.1 Initial Flight Safety Analysis
4.1.1 Flight Safety Sub-Analyses, Methods, and Assumptions
4.1.2 Sample Calculation and Products
4.1.3 Launch Specific Updates and Final Flight Safety Analysis Data
4.2 Radionuclide Data (where applicable)
4.3 Flight Safety Plan
4.3.1 Flight Safety Personnel
4.3.2 Flight Safety Rules
4.3.3 Flight Safety System Summary and Preflight Tests
4.3.4 Trajectory and Debris Dispersion Data
4.3.5 Flight Hazard Areas and Safety Clear Zones
4.3.6 Support Systems and Services
4.3.7 Flight Safety Operations
4.3.8 Unguided Suborbital Launch Vehicles (where applicable)
5.0 Ground Safety (§ 415.117)
5.1 Ground Safety Analysis Report
5.2 Ground Safety Plan
6.0 Launch Plans (§ 415.119 and § 417.111 of this chapter)
6.1 Launch Support Equipment and Instrumentation Plan
6.2 Configuration Management and Control Plan
6.3 Frequency Management Plan
6.4 Flight Termination System Electronic Piece Parts Program Plan
6.5 Accident Investigation Plan
6.6 Local Agreements and Public Coordination Plan
6.7 Hazard Area Surveillance and Clearance Plan
6.8 Communications Plan
7.0 Launch Schedule (§ 415.121)
7.1 Launch Processing Schedule
8.0 Computing Systems and Software (§ 415.123)
8.1 Hardware and Software Descriptions
8.2 Flow Charts and Diagrams
8.3 Logic Diagrams and Software Design Descriptions
8.4 Operator User Manuals and Documentation
8.5 Software Hazard Analyses
8.6 Software Test Plans, Test Procedures, and Test Results
8.7 Software Development Plan
9.0 Unique Safety Policies, Requirements and Practices (§ 415.125)
10.0 Flight Safety System Design and Operation Data (§ 415.127)
10.1 Flight Safety System Description
10.2 Flight Safety System Diagram
10.3 Flight Safety System Subsystem Design Information
10.4 Flight Safety System Analyses
10.5 Flight Termination System Environmental Design
10.6 Flight Safety System Compliance Matrix
10.7 Flight Termination System Installation Procedures
10.8 Tracking System Validation Procedures
11.0 Flight Safety System Test Data (§ 415.129)
11.1 Testing Compliance Matrix
11.2 Test Program Overview and Schedule
11.3 Flight Safety System Test Plans and Procedures
11.4 Test Reports
11.5 Reuse of Flight Termination System Components
12.0 Flight Safety System Crew Data (§ 415.131)
12.1 Position Descriptions
12.2 Certification and Training Program Description
13.0 Safety at End of Launch (§ 415.133)

[Doc. No. FAA-2000-7953, 71 FR 50536, Aug. 25, 2006]

PART 417—LAUNCH SAFETY

Subpart A—General and License Terms and Conditions

Subpart B—Launch Safety Responsibilities

Subpart C—Flight Safety Analysis

Subpart D—Flight Safety System

Subpart E—Ground Safety

AUTHORITY: 51 U.S.C. 50901–50923.

SOURCE: Docket No. FAA–2000–7953, 71 FR 50537, Aug. 25, 2006, unless otherwise noted.

Subpart A—General and License Terms and Conditions

§417.1 General information.

(a) *Scope*. This part sets forth—

(1) The responsibilities of a launch operator conducting a licensed launch of an expendable launch vehicle; and

(2) The requirements for maintaining a launch license obtained under part 415 of this chapter. Parts 413 and 415 of this chapter contain requirements for preparing a license application to conduct a launch, including information

reviewed by the FAA to conduct a policy, safety, payload, and environmental review., and a payload determination.

(b) *Applicability.* (1) The administrative requirements for filing material with the FAA in subpart A of this part apply to all licensed launches from a Federal launch range or a non-Federal launch site, except where noted.

(2) The safety requirements of subparts B through E of this part apply to all licensed launches of expendable launch vehicles. See paragraphs (d) and (e) of this section for exceptions to this provision.

(c) *"Meets intent"* certification. For a licensed launch from a Federal launch range, a launch operator need not demonstrate to the FAA that an alternative means of satisfying a requirement of this part provides an equivalent level of safety for a launch if written evidence demonstrates that a Federal launch range has, by the effective date of this part, granted a "meets intent certification," including through "tailoring," that applies to the requirement and that launch. See paragraph (f) of this section for exceptions to this provision. Written evidence includes:

(1) Range flight plan approval,

(2) Missile system pre-launch safety package,

(3) Preliminary and final flight data packages,

(4) A tailored version of EWR 127–1,

(5) Range email to the FAA stating that the MIC was approved, or

(6) Operation approval.

(d) *Waiver.* For a licensed launch from a Federal launch range, a requirement of this part does not apply to a launch if written evidence demonstrates that a Federal launch range has, by the effective date of this part, granted a waiver that allows noncompliance with the requirement for that launch. See paragraph (f) of this section for exceptions to this provision. Written evidence includes:

(1) Range flight plan approval,

(2) Missile system pre-launch safety package,

(3) Preliminary and final flight data packages,

(4) A tailored version of EWR 127–1,

(5) Range email to the FAA stating that the waiver was approved, or

(6) Operation approval.

(e) *Grandfathering.* For a licensed launch from a Federal launch range, a requirement of this part does not apply to the launch if the Federal launch range's grandfathering criteria allow noncompliance with the requirement for that launch. See paragraph (f) of this section for exceptions to this provision.

(f) *Exceptions to Federal launch range meets intent certifications, waivers, and grandfathering.* Even if a licensed launch from a Federal launch range satisfies paragraph (c), (d), or (e) of this section for a requirement of this part, the requirement applies and a launch operator must satisfy the requirement, obtain FAA approval of any alternative, or obtain FAA approval for any further noncompliance if—

(1) The launch operator modifies the launch vehicle's operation or safety characteristics;

(2) The launch operator uses the launch vehicle, component, system, or subsystem in a new application;

(3) The FAA or the launch operator determines that a previously unforeseen or newly discovered safety hazard exists that is a source of significant risk to public safety; or

(4) The Federal launch range previously accepted a component, system, or subsystem, but did not then identify a noncompliance to a Federal launch range requirement.

(g) *Equivalent level of safety.* The requirements of this part apply to a launch operator and the launch operator's launch unless the launch operator clearly and convincingly demonstrates that an alternative approach provides an equivalent level of safety.

§417.3 Definitions and acronyms.

For the purpose of this part,

Command control system means the portion of a flight safety system that includes all components needed to send a flight termination control signal to an onboard vehicle flight termination system. A command control system starts with any flight termination activation switch at a flight safety crew console and ends at each command-transmitting antenna. It includes all intermediate equipment, linkages, and software and any auxiliary transmitter stations that ensure a command signal will reach the onboard vehicle flight termination system from liftoff until the launch vehicle achieves orbit or can no longer reach a populated or other protected area.

Command destruct system means a portion of a flight termination system that includes all components on board a launch vehicle that receive a flight termination control signal and achieve destruction of the launch vehicle. A command destruct system includes all receiving antennas, receiver decoders, explosive initiating and transmission devices, safe and arm devices and ordnance necessary to achieving destruction of the launch vehicle upon receipt of a destruct command.

Conjunction on launch means the approach of a launch vehicle or any launch vehicle component or payload within 200 kilometers of a manned or mannable orbiting object—

(1) During the flight of an unguided suborbital rocket; or

(2) For an orbital launch vehicle during—

(i) The ascent to initial orbital insertion and through at least one complete orbit; and

(ii) Each subsequent orbital maneuver or burn from initial park orbit, or direct ascent to a higher or interplanetary orbit.

Countdown means the timed sequence of events that must take place to initiate flight of a launch vehicle.

Crossrange means the distance measured along a line whose direction is either 90 degrees clockwise (right crossrange) or counter-clockwise (left crossrange) to the projection of a launch vehicle's planned nominal velocity vector azimuth onto a horizontal plane tangent to the ellipsoidal Earth model at the launch vehicle's sub-vehicle point. The terms right crossrange and left crossrange may also be used to indicate direction.

Data loss flight time means the shortest elapsed thrusting time during which a launch vehicle flown with a flight safety system can move from its normal trajectory to a condition where it is possible for the launch vehicle to endanger the public.

Destruct means the act of terminating the flight of a launch vehicle flown with a flight safety system in a way that destroys the launch vehicle and disperses or expends all remaining propellant and renders remaining energy sources non-propulsive before the launch vehicle or any launch vehicle component or payload impacts the Earth's surface.

Downrange means the distance measured along a line whose direction is parallel to the projection of a launch vehicle's planned nominal velocity vector azimuth into a horizontal plane tangent to the ellipsoidal Earth model at the launch vehicle sub-vehicle point. The term downrange may also be used to indicate direction.

Drag impact point means a launch vehicle instantaneous impact point corrected for atmospheric drag.

Dwell time means—

(1) The period during which a launch vehicle instantaneous impact point is over a populated or other protected area; or

(2) The period during which an object is subjected to a test condition.

Explosive debris means solid propellant fragments or other pieces of a launch vehicle or payload that result from break up of the launch vehicle during flight and that explode upon impact with the Earth's surface and cause overpressure.

Fail-over means a method of ensuring continuous or near continuous operation of a command transmitter system by automatically switching from a primary transmitter to a secondary transmitter when a condition exists that indicates potential failure of the primary transmitter.

Family performance data means—

(1) Results of launch vehicle component and system tests that represent similar characteristics for a launch vehicle component or system; and

(2) Data that is continuously updated as additional samples of a given component or system are tested.

Flight safety limit means criteria to ensure a set of impact limit lines established for the flight of a launch vehicle flown with a flight safety system bound the area where debris with a ballistic coefficient of three or more is allowed to impact when a flight safety system functions.

Flight safety system means the system that provides a means of control during flight for preventing a hazard from a launch vehicle, including any payload hazard, from reaching any populated or other protected area in the event of a launch vehicle failure. A flight safety system includes:

(1) All hardware and software used to protect the public in the event of a launch vehicle failure; and

(2) The functions of any flight safety crew.

Flight safety crew means the personnel, designated by a launch operator, who operate flight safety system hardware and software to monitor the flight of a launch vehicle and make a flight termination decision.

Flight termination system means all components, onboard a launch vehicle, that provide the ability to end a launch vehicle's flight in a controlled manner. A flight termination system consists of all command destruct systems, inadvertent separation destruct systems, or other systems or components that are onboard a launch vehicle and used to terminate flight.

Gate means the portion of a flight safety limit boundary through which the tracking icon of a launch vehicle flown with a flight safety system may pass without flight termination.

In-family means a launch vehicle component or system test result that indicates that the component or system's performance conforms to the family performance data that was established by previous test results.

Inadvertent separation destruct system means an automatic destruct system that uses mechanical means to trigger the destruction of a launch vehicle stage.

Launch azimuth means the horizontal angular direction initially taken by a launch vehicle at liftoff, measured clockwise in degrees from true north.

Launch crew means all personnel who control the countdown and flight of a launch vehicle or who make irrevocable operational decisions that have the potential for impacting public safety. A launch crew includes members of the flight safety crew.

Launch processing means all preflight preparation of a launch vehicle at a launch site, including buildup of the launch vehicle, integration of the payload, and fueling.

Launch wait means a relatively short period of time when launch is not permitted in order to avoid a conjunction on launch or to safely accommodate temporary intrusion into a flight hazard area. A launch wait can occur within a launch window, can delay the start of a launch window, or terminate a launch window early.

Launch window means a period of time during which the flight of a launch vehicle may be initiated.

"Meets intent" certification means a decision by a Federal launch range to accept a substitute means of satisfying a safety requirement where the substitute provides an equivalent level of safety to that of the original requirement.

Normal flight means the flight of a properly performing launch vehicle whose real-time instantaneous impact point does not deviate from the nominal instantaneous impact point by more than the sum of the wind effects and the three-sigma guidance and performance deviations in the uprange, downrange, left-crossrange, or right-crossrange directions.

Normal trajectory means a trajectory that describes normal flight.

Non-operating environment means an environment that a launch vehicle component experiences before flight and when not otherwise being subjected to acceptance tests. Non-operating environments include, but need not be limited to, storage, transportation, and installation.

Operating environment means an environment that a launch vehicle component will experience during acceptance testing, launch countdown, and flight. Operating environments include shock, vibration, thermal cycle, acceleration, humidity, and thermal vacuum.

Operating life means, for a flight safety system component, the period of time beginning with activation of the component or installation of the component on a launch vehicle, whichever is earlier, for which the component is capable of satisfying all its performance specifications through the end of flight.

Operation hazard means a hazard derived from an unsafe condition created by a system or operating environment or by an unsafe act.

Out-of-family means a component or system test result where the component or system's performance does not conform to the family performance data that was established by previous test results and is an indication of a potential problem with the component or system requiring further investigation and possible corrective action.

Passive component means a flight termination system component that does not contain active electronic piece parts.

Performance specification means a statement prescribing the particulars of how a component or part is expected to perform in relation to the system that contains the component or part. A performance specification includes specific values for the range of operation, input, output, or other parameters that define the component's or part's expected performance.

Protected area means an area of land not controlled by a launch operator that:

(1) Is a populated area;

(2) Is environmentally sensitive; or

(3) Contains a vital national asset.

Safety-critical computer system function means any computer system function that, if not performed, if performed out of sequence, or if performed incorrectly, may directly or indirectly cause a public safety hazard.

Service life means, for a flight termination system component, the sum total of the component's storage life and operating life.

Storage life means, for a flight termination system component, the period of time after manufacturing of the component is complete until the component is activated or installed on a launch vehicle, whichever is earlier, during which the component may be subjected to storage environments and must remain capable of satisfying all its performance specifications.

Sub-vehicle point means the location on an ellipsoidal Earth model where the normal to the ellipsoid passes through the launch vehicle's center of gravity. The term is the same as the weapon system term "sub-missile point."

System hazard means a hazard associated with a system and generally exists even when no operation is occurring.

Tracking icon means the representation of a launch vehicle's instantaneous impact point, debris footprint, or other vehicle performance metric that is displayed to a flight safety crew during real-time tracking of the launch vehicle's flight.

Uprange means the distance measured along a line that is 180 degrees to the downrange direction. The term uprange may also be used to indicate direction.

Waiver means a decision that allows a launch operator to continue with a launch despite not satisfying a specific safety requirement and where the launch operator is not able to demonstrate an equivalent level of safety.

§417.5 [Reserved]

§417.7 Public safety responsibility.

A launch operator is responsible for ensuring the safe conduct of a licensed launch and for ensuring public safety and safety of property at all times during the conduct of a licensed launch.

§417.9 Launch site responsibility.

(a) A launch operator must ensure that launch processing at a launch site in the United States satisfies the requirements of this part. Launch processing at a launch site outside the United States may be subject to the requirements of the governing jurisdiction.

(b) For a launch from a launch site licensed under part 420 of this chapter, a launch operator must—

(1) Conduct its operations as required by any agreements that the launch site operator has with any Federal and local authorities under part 420 of this chapter; and

(2) Coordinate with the launch site operator and provide any information on its activities and potential hazards necessary for the launch site operator to determine how to protect any other launch operator, person, or property at the launch site as required by the launch site operator's obligations under §420.55 of this chapter.

(c) For a launch from an exclusive-use site, where there is no licensed launch site operator, a launch operator must satisfy the requirements of this part and the public safety requirements of part 420 of this chapter. This subpart does not apply to licensed launches occurring from Federal launch ranges.

§417.11 Continuing accuracy of license application; application for modification of license.

(a) A launch operator must ensure the representations contained in its application are accurate for the entire term of the license. A launch operator must conduct a licensed launch and carry out launch safety procedures in accordance with its application.

(b) After the FAA issues a launch license, a launch operator must apply to the FAA for modification of a launch license if—

(1) A launch operator proposes to conduct a launch or carry out a launch safety procedure or operation in a manner that is not authorized by the license; or

(2) Any representation contained in the license application that is material to public health and safety or safety of property would no longer be accurate and complete or would not reflect the launch operator's procedures governing the actual conduct of a launch. A representation is material to public health and safety or safety of property if it alters or affects the launch operator's launch plans or procedures, class of payload, orbital destination, type of launch vehicle, flight path, launch site, launch point, or any safety system, policy, procedure, requirement, criteria or standard.

(c) A launch operator must prepare and file an application to modify a launch license under part 413 of this chapter. The launch operator must identify any part of its license or license application that a proposed modification would change or affect.

(d) The FAA reviews all approvals and determinations required by this chapter to determine whether they remain valid in light of a proposed modification. The FAA approves a modification that satisfies the requirements of this part.

(e) Upon approval of a modification, the FAA issues to a launch operator either a written approval or a license order modifying the license if a stated term or condition of the license is changed, added or deleted. A written approval has the full force and effect of a license order and is part of the licensing record.

§417.13 Agreement with Federal launch range.

Before conducting a licensed launch from a Federal launch range, a launch operator must—

(a) Enter into an agreement with a Federal launch range to provide access to and use of U.S. Government property and services required to support a licensed launch from the facility and for public safety related operations and support. The agreement must be in effect for the conduct of any licensed launch; and

(b) Comply with any requirements of the agreement with the Federal launch range that may affect public safety and safety of property during the conduct of a licensed launch, including flight safety procedures and requirements.

§417.15 Records.

(a) A launch operator must maintain all records necessary to verify that it conducts licensed launches according to representations contained in the licensee's application. A launch operator must retain records for three years after completion of all launches conducted under the license.

(b) If a launch accident or launch incident occurs, as defined by §401.5 of this chapter, a launch operator must preserve all records related to the event until completion of any Federal investigation and the FAA advises the licensee not to retain the records. The launch operator must make available to Federal officials for inspection and copying all records that these regulations require the launch operator to maintain.

[Docket No. FAA–2000–7953, 71 FR 50537, Aug. 25, 2006, as amended by Amdt. No. 417–5, 81 FR 59439, Aug. 30, 2016]

§417.17 Launch reporting requirements and launch specific updates.

(a) *General.* A launch operator must satisfy the launch reporting requirements and launch specific updates required by this section and by the terms of the launch operator's license. A launch operator must file any change to the information in the license application, not identified by this section, with the FAA as a request for license modification as required by §417.11.

(b) *Launch reporting requirements for a launch from a Federal launch range or a non-Federal launch site.* (1) *Launch schedule and point of contact.* For each launch, a launch operator must file a launch schedule that identifies each review, rehearsal, and safety critical launch processing. A launch operator must file a point of contact for the schedule. The launch schedule must be filed and updated in time to allow FAA personnel to participate in the reviews, rehearsals, and safety critical launch processing.

(2) *Sixty-day report.* Not later than 60 days before each flight conducted under a launch operator license, a launch operator must provide the FAA the following launch-specific information:

(i) Payload information required by §415.59 of this chapter; and

(ii) Flight information, including the launch vehicle, planned flight path, staging and impact locations, and any on-orbit activity of the launch vehicle, including each payload delivery point.

(3) *U.S. Space Command Launch Notification.* Not later than noon, EST, 15 days before each licensed flight, a launch operator must file a completed Federal Aviation Administration/U.S. Space Command (FAA/USSPACECOM) Launch Notification Form (OMB No. 2120–0608) with the FAA.

(c) *Launch specific updates for a launch from a non-Federal launch site.* A launch operator must file a launch specific update, required by this part, and any required by the terms of the launch license, for every substantive change to the information outlined in this part. For each launch, a launch operator must file the following launch specific updates:

(1) *Flight safety system test schedule.* For each launch of a launch vehicle flown with a flight safety system, a launch operator must file an updated flight safety system test schedule and points of contact no later than six months before flight. A launch operator must immediately file any later change to ensure that the FAA has the most current data.

(2) *Launch plans.* A launch operator must file any changes or additions to its launch plans required by §417.111 to the FAA no later than 15 days before the associated activity is to take place. A launch operator must file the countdown plan with the FAA no later than 15 days before the countdown is to take place. If a change involves the addition of a new public hazard or the elimination of any control for a previously identified public hazard, a launch operator must request a license modification under §417.11.

(3) *Thirty-day flight safety analysis update.* A launch operator must file updated flight safety analysis products, using previously approved methodologies, for each launch no later than 30 days before flight.

(i) The launch operator:

(A) Must account for vehicle and mission specific input data;

(B) May reference previously approved analysis products and data that are applicable to the launch or data that is applicable to a series of launches;

(C) Must account for potential variations in input data that may affect any analysis product within the final 30 days before flight;

(D) Must file the analysis products using the same format and organization used in its license application; and

(E) May not change an analysis product within the final 30 days before flight unless the launch operator identified a process for making a change in that period as part of the launch operator's flight safety analysis process and the FAA approved the process by grant of a license to the launch operator.

(ii) A launch operator need not file the 30-day analysis if the launch operator:

(A) Demonstrates that the analysis filed during the license application process satisfies all the requirements of this subpart; and

(B) Demonstrates the analysis does not need to be updated to account for launch specific factors.

(4) *Flight termination system qualification test reports.* For the launch of a launch vehicle flown with a flight safety system, a launch operator must file all flight termination system qualification test reports, or test report summaries, as required by section E417.1(i) of appendix E of this part, with the FAA no later than six months before the first flight attempt . The summary must identify when and where the tests were performed and provide the results. Complete qualification test reports must be made available to the FAA upon request.

(5) *Flight termination system acceptance and age surveillance test report summaries.* For the launch of a launch vehicle flown with a flight safety system, a launch operator must file a summary of the results of each flight termination system acceptance and age surveillance test, or the complete test report, as required by section E417.1(i) of appendix E of this part, no later than 30 days before the first flight attempt for each launch . The summary must identify when and where the tests were performed and provide the results. Complete acceptance and age surveillance test reports must be made available to the FAA upon request.

(6) *Command control system acceptance test reports.* For the launch of a launch vehicle flown with a flight safety system, a launch operator must file all command control system acceptance test reports, or test report summaries, as required by §417.305(d), with the FAA no later than 30 days before the first flight attempt. The summary must identify when and where the tests were performed and provide the results. Complete acceptance test reports must be made available to the FAA upon request.

(7) *Ground safety analysis report updates.* A launch operator must file ground safety analysis report updates with the FAA as soon as the need for the change is identified and at least 30 days before the associated activity takes place. A launch operator must file a license modification request with the FAA for each change that involves the addition of a hazard that can affect public safety or the elimination of a previously identified hazard control for a hazard that still exists.

§417.19 Registration of space objects.

(a) To assist the U.S. Government in implementing Article IV of the 1975 Convention on Registration of Objects Launched into Outer Space, each launch operator must provide to the FAA the information required by paragraph (b) of this section for all objects placed in space by a licensed launch, including a launch vehicle and any components, except:

(1) Any object owned and registered by the U.S. Government; and

(2) Any object owned by a foreign entity.

(b) For each object that must be registered in accordance with this section, not later than 30 days following the conduct of a licensed launch, an operator must file the following information:

(1) The international designator of the space object(s);

(2) Date and location of launch;

(3) General function of the space object; and

(4) Final orbital parameters, including:

(i) Nodal period;

(ii) Inclination;

(iii) Apogee; and

(iv) Perigee.

§417.21 Financial responsibility requirements.

A launch operator must comply with financial responsibility requirements as required by part 440 of this chapter and as specified in a license or license order.

§417.23 Compliance monitoring.

(a) A launch operator must allow access by, and cooperate with, Federal officers or employees or other individuals authorized by the FAA to observe any of its activities, or of its contractors or subcontractors, associated with the conduct of a licensed launch.

(b) For each licensed launch, a launch operator must provide the FAA with a console for monitoring the progress of the countdown and communication on all channels of the countdown communications network. A launch operator must also provide the FAA with the capability to communicate with the person designated by § 417.103(b)(1).

§ 417.25 Post launch report.

(a) For a launch operator launching from a Federal launch range, a launch operator must file a post launch report with the FAA no later than 90 days after the launch, unless an FAA launch site safety assessment shows that the Federal launch range creates a post launch report that contains the information required by this section.

(b) For a launch operator launching from a non-Federal launch site, a launch operator must file a post launch report with the FAA no later than 90 days after the launch.

(c) The post launch report must:

(1) Identify any discrepancy or anomaly that occurred during the launch countdown and flight;

(2) Identify any deviation from any term of the license or any event otherwise material to public safety, and each corrective action to be implemented before any future flight;

(3) For the launch of launch vehicle flown with a flight safety system, identify any flight environment not consistent with the maximum predicted environment as required by D 417.7(b) and any measured wind profiles not consistent with the predictions used for the launch, as required by § 417.7(g)(3); and

(4) For the launch of an unguided suborbital launch vehicle, identify the actual impact location of all impacting stages and any impacting components, and provide a comparison of actual and predicted nominal performance.

[Doc. No. FAA–2000–7953, 71 FR 50537, Aug. 25, 2006, as amended by Amdt. 417, 73 FR 63630, Oct. 27, 2008]

§§ 417.26–417.100 [Reserved]

Subpart B—Launch Safety Responsibilities

§ 417.101 Scope.

This subpart contains public safety requirements that apply to the launch of an orbital or suborbital expendable launch vehicle from a Federal launch range or other launch site. If the FAA has assessed the Federal launch range, through its launch site safety assessment, and found that an applicable range safety-related launch service or property satisfies the requirements of this subpart, then the FAA will treat the Federal launch range's launch service or property as that of a launch operator without need for further demonstration of compliance to the FAA if:

(a) A launch operator has contracted with a Federal launch range for the provision of the safety-related launch service or property; and

(b) The FAA has assessed the Federal launch range, through its launch site safety assessment, and found that the Federal launch range's safety-related launch service or property satisfy the requirements of this subpart. In this case, the FAA will treat the Federal launch range's process as that of a launch operator.

§ 417.103 Safety organization.

(a) A launch operator must maintain and document a safety organization. A launch operator must identify lines of communication and approval authority for all public safety decisions, including those regarding design, operations, and analysis. A launch operator must describe its lines of communication, both within the launch operator's organization and between the launch operator and any federal launch range or other launch site operator providing launch services, in writing. Documented approval authority shall also be employed by the launch operator throughout the life of the launch system to ensure public safety and compliance with this part.

(b) A launch operator's safety organization must include, but need not be limited to, the following launch management positions:

(1) An employee of the launch operator who has the launch operator's final approval authority for launch. This employee, referred to as the launch director in this part, must ensure compliance with this part.

(2) An employee of the launch operator who is authorized to examine all aspects of the launch operator's launch safety operations and to monitor independently personnel compliance with the launch operator's safety policies

and procedures. This employee, referred to as the safety official in this part, shall have direct access to the launch director, who shall ensure that all of the safety official's concerns are addressed prior to launch.

§417.105 Launch personnel qualifications and certification.

(a) *General.* A launch operator must employ a personnel certification program that documents the qualifications, including education, experience, and training, for each member of the launch crew.

(b) *Personnel certification program.* A launch operator's personnel certification program must:

(1) Conduct an annual personnel qualifications review and issue individual certifications to perform safety related tasks.

(2) Revoke individual certifications for negligence or failure to satisfy certification requirements.

§417.107 Flight safety.

(a) *Flight safety system.* For each launch vehicle, vehicle component, and payload, a launch operator must use a flight safety system that satisfies subpart D of this part as follows, unless §417.125 applies.

(1) *In the vicinity of the launch site.* For each launch vehicle, vehicle component, and payload, a launch operator must use a flight safety system in the vicinity of the launch site if the following exist:

(i) Any hazard from a launch vehicle, vehicle component, or payload can reach any protected area at any time during flight; or

(ii) A failure of the launch vehicle would have a high consequence to the public.

(2) *In the downrange area.* For each launch vehicle, vehicle component, and payload, a launch operator must provide a flight safety system downrange if the absence of a flight safety system would significantly increase the accumulated risk from debris impacts.

(b) *Public risk criteria.* A launch operator may initiate the flight of a launch vehicle only if flight safety analysis performed under paragraph (f) of this section demonstrates that any risk to the public satisfies the following public risk criteria:

(1) A launch operator may initiate the flight of a launch vehicle only if the total risk associated with the launch to all members of the public, excluding persons in water-borne vessels and aircraft, does not exceed an expected number of 1×10^{-4} casualties. The total risk consists of risk posed by impacting inert and explosive debris, toxic release, and far field blast overpressure. The FAA will determine whether to approve public risk due to any other hazard associated with the proposed flight of a launch vehicle on a case-by-case basis. The E_c criterion applies to each launch from lift-off through orbital insertion for an orbital launch, and through final impact for a suborbital launch.

(2) A launch operator may initiate flight only if the risk to any individual member of the public does not exceed a casualty expectation of 1×10^{-6} per launch for each hazard.

(3) A launch operator must establish any water borne vessel hazard areas necessary to ensure the probability of impact (P_i) with debris capable of causing a casualty for water borne vessels does not exceed 1×10^{-5}.

(4) A launch operator must establish any aircraft hazard areas necessary to ensure the probability of impact (P_i) with debris capable of causing a casualty for aircraft does not exceed 1×10^{-6}.

(c) *Debris thresholds.* A launch operator's flight safety analysis, performed as required by paragraph (f) of this section, must account for any inert debris impact with a mean expected kinetic energy at impact greater than or equal to 11 ft-lbs and, except for the far field blast overpressure effects analysis of §417.229, a peak incident overpressure greater than or equal to 1.0 psi due to any explosive debris impact.

(1) When using the 11 ft-lbs threshold to determine potential casualties due to blunt trauma from inert debris impacts, the analysis must:

(i) Incorporate a probabilistic model that accounts for the probability of casualty due to any debris expected to impact with kinetic energy of 11 ft-lbs or greater and satisfy paragraph (d) of this section; or

(ii) Count each expected impact with kinetic energy of 11 ft-lbs or greater to a person as a casualty.

(2) When applying the 1.0 psi threshold to determine potential casualties due to blast overpressure effects, the analysis must:

(i) Incorporate a probabilistic model that accounts for the probability of casualty due to any blast overpressures of 1.0 psi or greater and satisfy paragraph (d) of this section; or

(ii) Count each person within the 1.0 psi overpressure radius of the source explosion as a casualty. When using this approach, the analysis must compute the peak incident overpressure using the Kingery-Bulmash relationship and may not take into account sheltering, reflections, or atmospheric effects. For persons located in buildings, the analysis must compute the peak incident overpressure for the shortest distance between the building and the blast source. The analysis must count each person located anywhere in a building subjected to peak incident overpressure equal to or greater than 1.0 psi as a casualty.

(d) *Casualty modeling.* A probabilistic casualty model must be based on accurate data and scientific principles and must be statistically valid. A launch operator must obtain FAA approval of any probabilistic casualty model that is used in the flight safety analysis. If the launch takes place from a Federal launch range, the analysis may employ any probabilistic casualty model that the FAA accepts as part of the FAA's launch site safety assessment of the Federal launch range's safety process.

(e) *Collision avoidance.* (1) A launch operator must ensure that a launch vehicle, any jettisoned components, and its payload do not pass closer than 200 kilometers to a manned or mannable orbital object—

(i) Throughout a sub-orbital launch; or

(ii) For an orbital launch:

(A) During ascent to initial orbital insertion and through at least one complete orbit; and

(B) During each subsequent orbital maneuver or burn from initial park orbit, or direct ascent to a higher or interplanetary orbit or until clear of all manned or mannable objects, whichever occurs first.

(2) A launch operator must obtain a collision avoidance analysis for each launch from United States Strategic Command or from a Federal range having an approved launch site safety assessment. United States Strategic Command calls this analysis a conjunction on launch assessment. Sections 417.231 and A417.31 of appendix A of this part contain the requirements for obtaining a collision avoidance analysis. A launch operator must use the results of the collision avoidance analysis to develop flight commit criteria for collision avoidance as required by § 417.113(c).

(f) *Flight safety analysis.* A launch operator must perform and document a flight safety analysis as required by subpart C of this part. A launch operator must not initiate flight unless the flight safety analysis demonstrates that any risk to the public satisfies the public risk criteria of paragraph (b) of this section. For a licensed launch that involves a Federal launch range, the FAA will treat an analysis performed and documented by the Federal range, and which has an FAA approved launch site safety assessment, as that of the launch operator as provided in § 417.203(d) of subpart C of this part. A launch operator must use the flight safety analysis products to develop flight safety rules that govern a launch. Section 417.113 contains the requirements for flight safety rules.

[Docket No. FAA–2000–7953, 71 FR 50537, Aug. 25, 2006, as amended by Amdt. No. 417–5, 81 FR 59439, Aug. 30, 2016; Docket No. FAA–2014–0418, Amdt. No. 417–4, 81 FR 47026, July 20, 2016]

§ 417.109 Ground safety.

(a) Ground safety requirements apply to launch processing and post-launch operations at a launch site in the United States.

(b) A launch operator must protect the public from adverse effects of hazardous operations and systems associated with preparing a launch vehicle for flight at a launch site.

(c) §§ 417.111(c), 417.113(b), and 417.115(c), and subpart E of this part provide launch operator ground safety requirements.

§417.111 Launch plans.

(a) *General.* A launch operator must implement written launch plans that define how launch processing and flight of a launch vehicle will be conducted without adversely affecting public safety and how to respond to a launch mishap. A launch operator's launch plans must include those required by this section. A launch operator's launch plans do not have to be separate documents, and may be part of other applicant documentation. A launch operator must incorporate each launch safety rule established under §417.113 into a related launch safety plan. The launch operator must follow each launch plan.

(b) *Flight Safety Plan.* A launch operator must implement a plan that includes the following:

(1) *Flight safety personnel.* Identification of personnel by position who:

(i) Approve and implement each part of the flight safety plan and any modifications to the plan; and

(ii) Perform the flight safety analysis and ensure that the results, including the flight safety rules and establishment of flight hazard areas, are incorporated into the flight safety plan.

(2) *Flight safety rules.* All flight safety rules required by §417.113.

(3) *Flight safety system.* A description of any flight safety system and its operation, including any preflight safety tests that a launch operator will perform.

(4) *Trajectory and debris dispersion data.* A description of the launch trajectory. For an orbital expendable launch vehicle, the description must include each planned orbital parameter, stage burnout time and state vector, and all planned stage impact times, locations, and downrange and crossrange dispersions. For a guided or unguided suborbital launch vehicle, the description must include each planned stage impact time, location, and downrange and crossrange dispersion.

(5) *Flight hazard areas.* Identification and location of each flight hazard area established for each launch as required by §417.223, and identification of procedures for surveillance and clearance of these areas and zones as required by paragraph (j) of this section.

(6) *Support systems and services.* Identification of any support systems and services that are part of ensuring flight safety, including any aircraft or ship that a launch operator will use during flight.

(7) *Flight safety operations.* A description of the flight safety related tests, reviews, rehearsals, and other flight safety operations that a launch operator will conduct under §§417.115 through 417.121. A flight safety plan must contain or incorporate by reference written procedures for accomplishing all flight safety operations.

(8) *Unguided suborbital launch vehicles.* A launch operator's flight safety plan for the launch of an unguided suborbital rocket must meet the requirements of paragraph (b) of this section and provide the following data:

(i) Launch angle limits, as required by §417.125(c)(3); and

(ii) All procedures for measurement of launch day winds and for performing wind weighting as required by §§417.125 and 417.233.

(c) *Ground safety plan.* A launch operator must implement a ground safety plan that describes implementation of the hazard controls identified by a launch operator's ground safety analysis and implementation of the ground safety requirements of subpart E of this part. A ground safety plan must address all public safety related issues and may include other ground safety issues if a launch operator intends it to have a broader scope. A ground safety plan must include the following:

(1) A description of the launch vehicle and any payload, or class of payload, identifying each hazard, including explosives, propellants, toxics and other hazardous materials, radiation sources, and pressurized systems. A ground safety plan must include figures that show the location of each hazard on the launch vehicle, and indicate where at the launch site a launch operator performs hazardous operations during launch processing.

(2) Propellant and explosive information including:

(i) Total net explosive weight of each of the launch operator's liquid and solid propellants and other explosives for each explosive hazard facility as defined by part 420 of this chapter.

(ii) For each toxic propellant, any hazard controls and process constraints determined under the launch operator's toxic release hazard analysis for launch processing performed as required by § 417.229 and appendix I of this part.

(iii) The explosive and occupancy limits for each explosive hazard facility.

(iv) Individual explosive item information, including configuration (such as, solid motor, motor segment, or liquid propellant container), explosive material, net explosive weight, storage hazard classification and compatibility group as defined by part 420 of this chapter.

(3) A graphic depiction of the layout of a launch operator's launch complex and other launch processing facilities at the launch site. The depiction must show separation distances and any intervening barriers between explosive items that affect the total net explosive weight that each facility is sited to accommodate. A launch operator must identify any proposed facility modifications or operational changes that may affect a launch site operator's explosive site plan.

(4) A description of the process for ensuring that the person designated under § 417.103(b)(2) reviews and approves any procedures and procedure changes for safety implications.

(5) Procedures that launch personnel will follow when reporting a hazard or mishap to a launch operator's safety organization.

(6) Procedures for ensuring that personnel have the qualifications and certifications needed to perform a task involving a hazard that could affect public safety.

(7) A flow chart of launch processing activities, including a list of all major tasks. The flow chart must include all hazardous tasks and identify where and when, with respect to liftoff, each hazardous task will take place.

(8) Identification of each safety clear zone and hazard area established as required by §§ 417.411 and 417.413, respectively.

(9) A summary of the means for announcing when any hazardous operation is taking place, the means for making emergency announcements and alarms, and identification of the recipients of each type of announcement.

(10) A summary of the means of prohibiting access to each safety clear zone, and implementing access control to each hazard area, including any procedures for prohibiting or allowing public access to such areas.

(11) A description of the process for ensuring that all safety precautions and verifications are in place before, during, and after hazardous operations. This includes the process for verification that an area can be returned to a non-hazardous work status.

(12) Description of each hazard control required by the ground safety analysis for each task that creates a public or launch location hazard. The hazard control must satisfy § 417.407(b).

(13) A procedure for the use of any safety equipment that protects the public, for each task that creates a public hazard or a launch location hazard.

(14) The requirement and procedure for coordinating with any launch site operator and local authorities, for each task creating a public or launch location hazard.

(15) Generic emergency procedures that apply to all emergencies and the emergency procedures that apply to each specific task that may create a public hazard, including any task that involves hazardous material, as required by § 417.407.

(16) A listing of the ground safety plan references, by title and date, such as the ground safety analysis report, explosive quantity-distance site plan and other ground safety related documentation.

(d) *Launch support equipment and instrumentation plan.* A launch operator must implement a plan that ensures the reliability of the equipment and instrumentation involved in protecting public safety during launch processing and flight. A launch support equipment and instrumentation plan must:

(1) List and describe support equipment and instrumentation;

(2) Identify all certified personnel, by position, as required by § 417.105, who operate and maintain the support equipment and instrumentation;

(3) Contain, or incorporate by reference, written procedures for support

equipment and instrumentation operation, test, and maintenance that will be implemented for each launch;

(4) Identify equipment and instrumentation reliability; and

(5) Identify any contingencies that protect the public in the event of a malfunction.

(e) *Configuration management and control plan.* A launch operator must implement a plan that:

(1) Defines the launch operator's process for managing and controlling any change to a safety critical system to ensure its reliability;

(2) Identifies, for each system, each person by position who has authority to approve design changes and the personnel, by position, who maintain documentation of the most current approved design; and

(3) Contains, or incorporates by reference, all configuration management and control procedures that apply to the launch vehicle and each support system.

(f) *Frequency management plan.* A launch operator must implement a plan that:

(1) Identifies each frequency, all allowable frequency tolerances, and each frequency's intended use, operating power, and source;

(2) Provides for the monitoring of frequency usage and enforcement of frequency allocations; and

(3) Identifies agreements and procedures for coordinating use of radio frequencies with any launch site operator and any local and Federal authorities, including the Federal Communications Commission.

(g) *Flight termination system electronic piece parts program plan.* A launch operator must implement a plan that describes the launch operator's program for selecting and testing all electronic piece parts used in any flight termination system to ensure their reliability. This plan must—

(1) Demonstrate compliance with the requirements of §417.309(b)(2);

(2) Describe the program for selecting piece parts for use in a flight termination system;

(3) Identify performance of any derating, qualification, screening, lot acceptance testing, and lot destructive physical analysis for electronic piece parts;

(4) Identify all personnel, by position, who conduct the piece part tests;

(5) Identify the pass/fail criteria for each test for each piece part;

(6) Identify the levels to which each piece part specification will be derated; and

(7) Contain, or incorporate by reference, test procedures for each piece part.

(h) *Accident investigation plan (AIP).* A launch operator must implement a plan containing the launch operator's procedures for reporting and responding to launch accidents, launch incidents, or other mishaps, as defined by §401.5 of this chapter. An individual, authorized to sign and certify the application as required by §413.7(c) of this chapter, and the person designated under §417.103(b)(2) must sign the AIP.

(1) *Reporting requirements.* An AIP must provide for—

(i) Immediate notification to the Federal Aviation Administration (FAA) Washington Operations Center in case of a launch accident, a launch incident or a mishap that involves a fatality or serious injury (as defined by 49 CFR 830.2).

(ii) Notification within 24 hours to the Associate Administrator for Commercial Space Transportation or the Federal Aviation Administration (FAA) Washington Operations Center in the event of a mishap, other than those in §415.41 (b) (1) of this chapter, that does not involve a fatality or serious injury (as defined in 49 CFR 830.2).

(iii) Submission of a written preliminary report to the FAA, Associate Administrator for Commercial Space Transportation, in the event of a launch accident or launch incident, as defined by §401.5 of this chapter, within five days of the event. The report must identify the event as either a launch accident or launch incident, and must include the following information:

(A) Date and time of occurrence;

(B) Description of event;

(C) Location of launch;

(D) Launch vehicle;

(E) Any payload;

(F) Vehicle impact points outside designated impact lines, if applicable;

(G) Number and general description of any injuries;

(H) Property damage, if any, and an estimate of its value;

(I) Identification of hazardous materials, as defined by §401.5 of this chapter, involved in the event, whether on the launch vehicle, payload, or on the ground;

(J) Action taken by any person to contain the consequences of the event; and

(K) Weather conditions at the time of the event.

(2) *Response plan.* An AIP must—

(i) Contain procedures that ensure the containment and minimization of the consequences of a launch accident, launch incident or other mishap;

(ii) Contain procedures that ensure the preservation of the data and physical evidence;

(3) *Investigation plan.* An AIP must contain—

(i) Procedures for investigating the cause of a launch accident, launch incident or other mishap;

(ii) Procedures for reporting investigation results to the FAA; and

(iii) Delineated responsibilities, including reporting responsibilities for personnel assigned to conduct investigations and for any one retained by the licensee to conduct or participate in investigations.

(4) *Cooperation with FAA and NTSB.* An AIP must contain procedures that require the licensee to report to and cooperate with FAA and National Transportation Safety Board (NTSB) investigations and designate one or more points of contact for the FAA and NTSB.

(5) *Preventive measure.* An AIP must contain procedures that require the licensee to identify and adopt preventive measures for avoiding recurrence of the event.

(i) *Local agreements and public coordination plans.* (1) Where there is a licensed launch site operator, a launch operator must implement and satisfy the launch site operator's local agreements and plans with local authorities at or near a launch site whose support is needed to ensure public safety during all launch processing and flight, as required by part 420 of this chapter.

(2) For a launch from an exclusive-use site, where there is no licensed launch site operator, a launch operator must develop and implement any agreements and plans with local authorities at or near the launch site whose support is needed to ensure public safety during all launch processing and flight, as required by part 420 of this chapter.

(3) A launch operator must implement a schedule and procedures for the release of launch information before flight, after flight, and in the event of an mishap.

(4) A launch operator must develop and implement procedures for public access to any launch viewing areas that are under a launch operator's control.

(5) A launch operator must describe its procedures for and accomplish the following for each launch—

(i) Inform local authorities of each designated hazard areas near the launch site associated with a launch vehicle's planned trajectory and any planned impacts of launch vehicle components and debris as defined by the flight safety analysis required by subpart C of this part;

(ii) Provide any hazard area information prepared as required by §417.225 or §417.235 to the local United States Coast Guard or equivalent local authority for issuance of the notices to mariners;

(iii) Provide hazard area information prepared as required by §417.223 or §417.233 for each aircraft hazard area within a flight corridor to the FAA Air Traffic Control (ATC) office or equivalent local authority having jurisdiction over the airspace through which the launch will take place for the issuance of notices to airmen;

(iv) Communicate with the local Coast Guard and the FAA ATC office or equivalent local authorities, either directly or through any launch site operator, to ensure that notices to airmen and mariners are issued and in effect at the time of flight; and

(v) Coordinate with any other local agency that supports the launch, such as local law enforcement agencies, emergency response agencies, fire departments, National Park Service, and Mineral Management Service.

(j) *Hazard area surveillance and clearance plan.* A launch operator must implement a plan that defines the process for ensuring that any unauthorized persons, ships, trains, aircraft or other vehicles are not within any hazard areas identified by the flight safety analysis or the ground safety analysis. In the plan, the launch operator must—

(1) List each hazard area that requires surveillance under §§417.107 and 417.223;

(2) Describe how the launch operator will provide for day-of-flight surveillance of the flight hazard area to ensure that the presence of any member of the public in or near a flight hazard area is consistent with flight commit criteria developed for each launch as required by §417.113;

(3) Verify the accuracy of any radar or other equipment used for hazard area surveillance and account for any inaccuracies in the surveillance system when enforcing the flight commit criteria;

(4) Identify the number of security and surveillance personnel employed for each launch and the qualifications and training each must have;

(5) Identify the location of roadblocks and other security checkpoints, the times that each station must be manned, and any surveillance equipment used; and

(6) Contain, or incorporate by reference, all procedures for launch personnel control, handling of intruders, communications and coordination with launch personnel and other launch support entities, and implementation of any agreements with local authorities and any launch site operator.

(k) *Communications plan.* A launch operator must implement a plan providing licensee personnel and Federal launch range personnel, if applicable, communications procedures during countdown and flight. Effective issuance and communication of safety-critical information during countdown must include hold/resume, go/no go, and abort commands by licensee personnel and any Federal launch range personnel, during countdown. For all launches from Federal launch ranges, the Federal launch range must concur with the communications plan. The communications plan must:

(1) Describe the authority of licensee personnel and any Federal launch range personnel by individual or position title, to issue these commands;

(2) Ensure the assignment of communication networks, so that personnel identified under this paragraph have direct access to real-time safety-critical information required for issuing hold/resume, go/no go, and abort decisions and commands;

(3) Ensure personnel, identified under this paragraph, monitor each common intercom channel during countdown and flight; and

(4) Ensure the implementation of a protocol for using defined radio telephone communications terminology.

(l) *Countdown plan.* A launch operator must develop and implement a countdown plan that verifies that each launch safety rule and launch commit criterion is satisfied, verifies that personnel can communicate during the countdown and that the communication is available after the flight; and verifies that a launch operator will be able to recover from a launch abort or delay. A countdown plan must:

(1) Cover the period of time when any launch support personnel are to be at their designated stations through initiation of flight.

(2) Include procedures for handling anomalies that occur during a countdown and events and conditions that may result in a constraint to initiation of flight.

(3) Include procedures for delaying or holding a launch when necessary to allow for corrective actions, to await improved conditions, or to accommodate a launch wait.

(4) Describe a process for resolving issues that arise during a countdown and identify each person, by position, who approves corrective actions.

(5) Include a written countdown checklist that provides a formal decision process leading to flight initiation. A countdown checklist must include the flight day preflight tests of a flight safety system required by subpart D of this part and must contain:

(i) Identification of operations and specific actions completed, verification that there are no constraints to flight, and verification that a launch operator satisfied all launch safety rules and launch commit criteria;

(ii) Time of each event;

(iii) Identification of personnel, by position, who perform each operation or specific action, including reporting to the person designated under § 417.103(b)(3);

(iv) Identification of each communication channel that a launch operator uses for reporting each event;

(v) Identification of all communication and event reporting protocols;

(vi) Polling of personnel, by position, who oversee all safety critical systems and operations, to verify that the systems and the operations are ready to proceed with the launch; and

(vii) Record of all critical communications network channels that are used for voice, video, or data transmission that support the flight safety system, during each countdown.

(6) In case of a launch abort or delay:

(i) Identify each condition that must exist in order to make another launch attempt;

(ii) Include a schedule depicting the flow of tasks and events in relation to when the abort or delay occurred and the new planned launch time; and

(iii) Identify each interface and supporting entity needed to support recovery operations.

§ 417.113 Launch safety rules.

(a) *General.* For each launch, a launch operator must satisfy written launch safety rules that govern the conduct of the launch.

(1) The launch safety rules must identify the meteorological conditions and the status of the launch vehicle, launch support equipment, and personnel under which launch processing and flight may be conducted without adversely affecting public safety.

(2) The launch safety rules must satisfy the requirements of this section.

(3) A launch operator must follow all the launch safety rules.

(b) *Ground safety rules.* The launch safety rules must include ground safety rules that govern each preflight ground operation at a launch site that has the potential to adversely affect public safety. The ground safety rules must implement the ground safety analysis of subpart E of this part.

(c) *Flight-commit criteria.* The launch safety rules must include flight-commit criteria that identify each condition that must be met in order to initiate flight.

(1) The flight-commit criteria must implement the flight safety analysis of subpart C of this part. These must include criteria for:

(i) Surveillance of any region of land, sea, or air necessary to ensure the number and location of members of the public are consistent with the inputs used for the flight safety analysis of subpart C of this part;

(ii) Monitoring of any meteorological condition and implementing any flight constraint developed using appendix G of this part. The launch operator must have clear and convincing evidence that the lightning flight commit criteria of appendix G, which apply to the conditions present at the time of lift-off, are not violated. If any other hazardous conditions exist, other than those identified by appendix G, the launch weather team will report the hazardous condition to the official designated under § 417.103(b)(1), who will determine whether initiating flight would expose the launch vehicle to a lightning hazard and not initiate flight in the presence of the hazard; and

(iii) Implementation of any launch wait in the launch window for the purpose of collision avoidance.

(2) For a launch that uses a flight safety system, the flight-commit criteria must ensure that the flight safety system is ready for flight. This must include criteria for ensuring that:

(i) The flight safety system is operating to ensure the launch vehicle will launch within all flight safety limits;

(ii) Any command transmitter system required by section D417.9 has sufficient coverage from lift-off to the point in flight where the flight safety system is no longer required by § 417.107(a);

(iii) The launch vehicle tracking system has no less than two tracking sources prior to lift-off. The launch vehicle tracking system has no less than one verified tracking source at all times from lift-off to orbit insertion for an orbital launch, to the end of powered flight for a suborbital launch; and

(iv) The launch operator will employ its flight safety system as designed in accordance with this part.

(3) For each launch, a launch operator must document the actual conditions used for the flight-commit criteria at the time of lift-off and verify whether the flight-commit criteria are satisfied.

(d) *Flight termination rules.* For a launch that uses a flight safety system, the launch safety rules must identify the conditions under which the flight safety system, including the functions of the flight safety system crew, must terminate flight to ensure public safety. These flight termination rules must implement the flight safety analysis of subpart C of this part and include each of the following:

(1) The flight safety system must terminate flight when valid, real-time data indicate the launch vehicle has violated any flight safety limit of §417.213;

(2) The flight safety system must terminate flight at the straight-up-time required by §417.215 if the launch vehicle continues to fly a straight up trajectory and, therefore, does not turn downrange when it should;

(3) The flight safety system must terminate flight when all of the following conditions exist:

(i) Real-time data indicate that the performance of the launch vehicle is erratic;

(ii) The potential exists for the loss of flight safety system control of the launch vehicle and further flight has the potential to endanger the public.

(4) The flight termination rules must incorporate the data-loss flight times and planned safe flight state of §417.219, including each of the following:

(i) The flight safety system must terminate flight no later than the first data-loss flight time if, by that time, tracking of the launch vehicle is not established and vehicle position and status is unknown; and

(ii) Once launch vehicle tracking is established and there is a subsequent loss of verified tracking data before the planned safe flight state and verified tracking data is not received again, the flight safety system must terminate flight no later than the expiration of the data-loss flight time for the point in flight that the data was lost.

(5) For any gate established under §417.217, both of the following apply:

(i) The flight safety system must terminate flight if the launch vehicle is performing erratically immediately prior to entering the gate.

(ii) The flight termination rules may permit the instantaneous impact point or other tracking icon to cross the gate only if there is no indication that the launch vehicle's performance has become erratic and the launch vehicle is either flying parallel to the nominal trajectory or converging to the nominal trajectory.

(6) For any hold-and-resume gate established under §417.218;

(i) The flight safety system must terminate flight if the launch vehicle is performing erratically immediately prior to entering a hold gate.

(ii) The flight termination rules may permit the instantaneous impact point or other tracking icon to cross a hold gate only if there is no indication that the launch vehicle's performance has become erratic and the vehicle is either flying parallel to the nominal trajectory or converging to the nominal trajectory.

(iii) The flight termination rules of paragraphs (d)(1), (d)(3), and (d)(4) of this section apply after the instantaneous impact point or other tracking icon exits a resume gate.

(e) *Flight safety system safing.* For a launch that uses a flight safety system, the launch safety rules must ensure that any safing of the flight safety system occurs on or after the point in flight where the flight safety system is no longer required by §417.107(b).

(f) *Launch crew work shift and rest rules.* For any operation with the potential to have an adverse effect on public safety, the launch safety rules must ensure the launch crew is physically and mentally capable of performing all assigned tasks. These rules must govern the length, number, and frequency of work shifts, including the rest afforded the launch crew between shifts.

§ 417.115 Tests.

(a) *General.* All flight, communication, and ground systems and equipment that a launch operator uses to protect the public from any adverse effects of a launch, must undergo testing as required by this part, and any corrective action and re-testing necessary to ensure reliable operation. A launch operator must—

(1) Coordinate test plans and all associated test procedures with any launch site operator or local authorities, as required by local agreements, associated with the operation; and

(2) Make test results, test failure reports, information on any corrective actions implemented and the results of re-test available to the FAA upon request.

(b) *Flight safety system testing.* A launch operator must only use a flight safety system and all flight safety system components, including any onboard launch vehicle flight termination system, command control system, and support system that satisfy the test requirements of subpart D of this part.

(c) *Ground system testing.* A launch operator must only use a system or equipment used to support hazardous ground operations identified by the ground safety analysis required by § 417.405 that satisfies the test requirements of paragraph (a) of this section.

§ 417.117 Reviews.

(a) *General.* A launch operator must—

(1) Review the status of operations, systems, equipment, and personnel required by part 417;

(2) Maintain and implement documented criteria for successful completion of each review;

(3) Track to completion and document any corrective actions or issues identified during a review; and

(4) Ensure that launch operator personnel who oversee a review attest to successful completion of the review's criteria in writing.

(b) A launch operator must conduct the following reviews:

(1) *Hazardous operations safety readiness reviews.* A launch operator must conduct a review before performing any hazardous operation with the potential to adversely affect public safety. The review must determine a launch operator's readiness to perform the operation and ensure that safety provisions are in place. The review must determine the readiness status of safety systems and equipment and verify that the personnel involved satisfy certification and training requirements.

(2) *Launch safety review.* For each launch, a launch operator must conduct a launch safety review no later than 15 days before the planned day of flight, or as agreed to by the FAA during the application process. This review must determine the readiness of ground and flight safety systems, safety equipment, and safety personnel to support a flight attempt. Successful completion of a launch safety review must ensure satisfaction of the following criteria:

(i) A launch operator must verify that all safety requirements have been or will be satisfied before flight. The launch operator must resolve all safety related action items.

(ii) A launch operator must assign and certify flight safety personnel as required by § 417.105.

(iii) The flight safety rules and flight safety plan must incorporate a final flight safety analysis as required by subpart C of this part.

(iv) A launch operator must verify, at the time of the review, that the ground safety systems and personnel satisfy or will satisfy all requirements of the ground safety plan for support of flight.

(v) A launch operator must accomplish the safety related coordination with any launch site operator or local authorities as required by local agreements.

(vi) A launch operator must verify the filing of all safety related information for a specific launch with the FAA, as required by FAA regulations and any special terms of a license. A launch operator must verify that information filed with the FAA reflects the current status of safety-related systems and processes for each specific launch.

(3) *Launch readiness review for flight.* A launch operator must conduct a launch readiness review for flight as required by this section within 48 hours

of flight. A person, identified as required by §417.103(b)(1), must review all preflight testing and launch processing conducted up to the time of the review; and review the status of systems and support personnel to determine readiness to proceed with launch processing and the launch countdown. A decision to proceed must be in writing and signed by the person identified as required by §417.103(b)(1), and any launch site operator or Federal launch range. A launch operator, during the launch readiness review, must poll the FAA to verify that the FAA has identified no issues related to the launch operator's license. During a launch readiness review, the launch operator must account for the following information:

(i) Readiness of launch vehicle and payload.

(ii) Readiness of any flight safety system and personnel and the results of flight safety system testing.

(iii) Readiness of safety-related launch property and services to be provided by a Federal launch range.

(iv) Readiness of all other safety-related equipment and services.

(v) Readiness of launch safety rules and launch constraints.

(vi) Status of launch weather forecasts.

(vii) Readiness of abort, hold and recycle procedures.

(viii) Results of rehearsals conducted as required by §417.119.

(ix) Unresolved safety issues as of the time of the launch readiness review and plans for their resolution.

(x) Additional safety information that may be required to assess readiness for flight.

(xi) To review launch failure initial response actions and investigation roles and responsibilities.

§417.119 Rehearsals.

(a) *General.* A launch operator must rehearse its launch crew and systems to identify corrective actions needed to ensure public safety. The launch operator must conduct all rehearsals as follows:

(1) A launch operator must assess any anomalies identified by a rehearsal, and must incorporate any changes to launch processing and flight needed to correct any anomaly that is material to public safety.

(2) A launch operator must inform the FAA of any public safety related anomalies and related changes in operations performed during launch processing or flight resulting from a rehearsal.

(3) For each launch, each person with a public safety critical role who will participate in the launch processing or flight of a launch vehicle must participate in at least one related rehearsal that exercises his or her role during nominal and non-nominal conditions so that the launch vehicle will not harm the public.

(4) A launch operator must conduct the rehearsals identified in this section for each launch.

(5) At least one rehearsal must simulate normal and abnormal preflight and flight conditions to exercise the launch operator's launch plans.

(6) A launch operator may conduct rehearsals at the same time if joint rehearsals do not create hazardous conditions, such as changing a hardware configuration that affects public safety, during the rehearsal.

(b) *Countdown rehearsal.* A launch operator must conduct a rehearsal using the countdown plan, procedures, and checklist required by §417.111(l). A countdown rehearsal must familiarize launch personnel with all countdown activities, demonstrate that the planned sequence of events is correct, and demonstrate that there is adequate time allotted for each event. A launch operator must hold a countdown rehearsal after the assembly of the launch vehicle and any launch support systems into their final configuration for flight and before the launch readiness review required by §417.117.

(c) *Emergency response rehearsal.* A launch operator must conduct a rehearsal of the emergency response section of the accident investigation plan required by §417.111(h)(2). A launch operator must conduct an emergency response rehearsal for a first launch of a new vehicle, for any additional launch that involves a new safety hazard, or for any launch where more than a year has passed since the last rehearsal.

(d) *Communications rehearsal.* A launch operator must rehearse each part of the communications plan required by § 417.111(k), either as part of another rehearsal or during a communications rehearsal.

§ 417.121 Safety critical preflight operations.

(a) *General.* A launch operator must perform safety critical preflight operations that protect the public from the adverse effects of hazards associated with launch processing and flight of a launch vehicle. The launch operator must identify all safety critical preflight operations in the launch schedule required by § 417.17(b)(1). Safety critical preflight operations must include those defined in this section.

(b) *Countdown.* A launch operator must implement its countdown plan, of § 417.111(l), for each launch. A launch operator must disseminate a countdown plan to all personnel responsible for the countdown and flight of a launch vehicle, and each person must follow that plan.

(c) *Collision avoidance.* A launch operator must coordinate with United States Strategic Command to obtain a collision avoidance analysis, also referred to as a conjunction on launch assessment, as required by § 417.231. A launch operator must implement flight commit criteria as required by § 417.113(c) to ensure that each launch meets all the criteria of § 417.107(e).

(d) *Meteorological data.* A launch operator must conduct operations and coordinate with weather organizations, as needed, to obtain accurate meteorological data to support the flight safety analysis required by subpart C of this part and to ensure compliance with the flight commit criteria required by § 417.113.

(e) *Local notification.* A launch operator must implement its local agreements and public coordination plan of § 417.111(i).

(f) *Hazard area surveillance.* A launch operator must implement its hazard area surveillance and clearance plan, of § 417.111(j), to meet the public safety criteria of § 417.107(b) for each launch.

(g) *Flight safety system preflight tests.* A launch operator must conduct preflight tests of any flight safety system as required by section E417.41 of appendix E of this part.

(h) *Launch vehicle tracking data verification.* For each launch, a launch operator must implement written procedures for verifying the accuracy of any launch vehicle tracking data provided. For a launch vehicle flown with a flight safety system, any source of tracking data must satisfy the requirements of § 417.307(b).

(i) *Unguided suborbital rocket preflight operations.* For the launch of an unguided suborbital rocket, in addition to meeting the other requirements of this section, a launch operator must perform the preflight wind weighting and other preflight safety operations required by §§ 417.125, 417.233, and appendix C of this part.

[Docket No. FAA–2000–7953, 71 FR 50537, Aug. 25, 2006, as amended by Amdt. No. 417–5, 81 FR 59439, Aug. 30, 2016]

§ 417.123 Computing systems and software.

(a) A launch operator must document a system safety process that identifies the hazards and assesses the risks to public health and safety and the safety of property related to computing systems and software.

(b) A launch operator must identify all safety-critical functions associated with its computing systems and software. Safety-critical computing system and software functions must include the following:

(1) Software used to control or monitor safety-critical systems.

(2) Software that transmits safety-critical data, including time-critical data and data about hazardous conditions.

(3) Software used for fault detection in safety-critical computer hardware or software.

(4) Software that responds to the detection of a safety-critical fault.

(5) Software used in a flight safety system.

(6) Processor-interrupt software associated with previously designated safety-critical computer system functions.

(7) Software that computes safety-critical data.

(8) Software that accesses safety-critical data.

(9) Software used for wind weighting.

(c) A launch operator must conduct computing system and software hazard analyses for the integrated system.

(d) A launch operator must develop and implement computing system and software validation and verification plans.

(e) A launch operator must develop and implement software development plans, including descriptions of the following:

(1) Coding standards used;

(2) Configuration control;

(3) Programmable logic controllers;

(4) Policy on use of any commercial-off-the-shelf software; and

(5) Policy on software reuse.

§417.125 Launch of an unguided suborbital launch vehicle.

(a) *Applicability.* This section applies only to a launch operator conducting a launch of an unguided suborbital launch vehicle.

(b) *Need for flight safety system.* A launch operator must launch an unguided suborbital launch vehicle with a flight safety system in accordance with §417.107 (a) and subpart D of this part unless one of the following exceptions applies:

(1) The unguided suborbital launch vehicle, including any component or payload, does not have sufficient energy to reach any populated area in any direction from the launch point; or

(2) A launch operator demonstrates through the licensing process that the launch will be conducted using a wind weighting safety system that meets the requirements of paragraph (c) of this section.

(c) *Wind weighting safety system.* A launch operator's wind weighting safety system must consist of equipment, procedures, analysis and personnel functions used to determine the launcher elevation and azimuth settings that correct for the windcocking and wind drift that an unguided suborbital launch vehicle will experience during flight due to wind effects. The launch of an unguided suborbital launch vehicle that uses a wind weighting safety system must meet the following requirements:

(1) The unguided suborbital launch vehicle must not contain a guidance or directional control system.

(2) The launcher azimuth and elevation settings must be wind weighted to correct for the effects of wind conditions at the time of flight to provide a safe impact location. A launch operator must conduct the launch in accordance with the wind weighting analysis requirements and methods of §417.233 and appendix C of this part.

(3) A launch operator must use a launcher elevation angle setting that ensures the rocket will not fly uprange. A launch operator must set the launcher elevation angle in accordance with the following:

(i) The nominal launcher elevation angle must not exceed 85°. The wind corrected launcher elevation setting must not exceed 86°.

(ii) For an unproven unguided suborbital launch vehicle, the nominal launcher elevation angle must not exceed 80°. The wind corrected launcher elevation setting must not exceed 84°. A proven unguided suborbital launch vehicle is one that has demonstrated, by two or more launches, that flight performance errors are within all the three-sigma dispersion parameters modeled in the wind weighting safety system.

(d) *Public risk criteria.* A launch operator must conduct the launch of an unguided suborbital launch vehicle in accordance with the public risk criteria of §417.107(b). The risk to the public determined prior to the day of flight must satisfy the public risk criteria for the area defined by the range of nominal launch azimuths. A launch operator must not initiate flight until a launch operator has verified that the wind drifted impacts of all planned impacts and their five-sigma dispersion areas satisfy the public risk criteria after wind weighting on the day of flight.

(e) *Stability.* An unguided suborbital launch vehicle, in all configurations, must be stable in flexible body to 1.5 calibers and rigid body to 2.0 calibers throughout each stage of powered flight. A caliber, for a rocket configuration, is defined as the distance between the center of pressure and the center of gravity divided by the largest frontal diameter of the rocket configuration.

(f) *Tracking.* A launch operator must track the flight of an unguided suborbital launch vehicle. The tracking system must provide data to determine the actual impact locations of all stages and components, to verify the effectiveness of a launch operator's wind weighting safety system, and to obtain rocket performance data for comparison with the preflight performance predictions.

(g) *Post-launch review.* A launch operator must ensure that the post-launch report required by § 417.25 includes:

(1) Actual impact location of all impacting stages and each impacting component.

(2) A comparison of actual and predicted nominal performance.

(3) Investigation results of any launch anomaly. If flight performance deviates by more than a three-sigma dispersion from the nominal trajectory, a launch operator must conduct an investigation to determine the cause of the rocket's deviation from normal flight and take corrective action before the next launch. A launch operator must file any corrective actions with the FAA as a request for license modification before the next launch in accordance with § 417.11.

§ 417.127 Unique safety policies, requirements and practices.

For each launch, a launch operator must review operations, system designs, analysis, and testing, and identify any unique hazards not otherwise addressed by this part. A launch operator must implement any unique safety policy, requirement, or practice needed to protect the public from the unique hazard. A launch operator must demonstrate through the licensing process that any unique safety policy, requirement, or practice ensures the safety of the public. For any change to a unique safety policy, requirement, or practice, with the exception of a launch specific update, the launch operator must file a request for license modification as required by § 417.11. The FAA may identify and impose a unique safety policy, requirement, or practice as needed to protect the public.

§ 417.129 Safety at end of launch.

A launch operator must ensure for any proposed launch that for all launch vehicle stages or components that reach Earth orbit—

(a) There is no unplanned physical contact between the vehicle or any of its components and the payload after payload separation;

(b) Debris generation does not result from the conversion of energy sources into energy that fragments the vehicle or its components. Energy sources include chemical, pressure, and kinetic energy; and

(c) Stored energy is removed by depleting residual fuel and leaving all fuel line valves open, venting any pressurized system, leaving all batteries in a permanent discharge state, and removing any remaining source of stored energy.

§§ 417.130–417.200 [Reserved]

Subpart C—Flight Safety Analysis

§ 417.201 Scope and applicability.

(a) This subpart contains requirements for performing the flight safety analysis required by § 417.107(f).

(b) The flight safety analysis requirements of this subpart apply to the flight of any launch vehicle that must use a flight safety system as required by § 417.107(a), except as permitted by paragraph (d) of this section.

(c) The flight safety analysis requirements of §§ 417.203, 417.205, 417.207, 417.211, 417.223, 417.224, 417.225, 417.227, 417.229, 417.231, and 417.233 apply to the flight of any unguided suborbital launch vehicle that uses a wind-weighting safety system. Appendices B, C, and I of this part also apply.

(d) For any alternative flight safety system approved by the FAA under § 417.301(b), the FAA will determine during the licensing process which of the analyses required by this subpart apply.

§ 417.203 Compliance.

(a) *General.* A launch operator's flight safety analysis must satisfy the performance requirements of this subpart. The flight safety analysis must also meet the requirements for methods of analysis contained in appendices A and

B of this part for a launch vehicle flown with a flight safety system and appendices B and C of this part for an unguided suborbital launch vehicle that uses a wind-weighting safety system except as otherwise permitted by this section. A flight safety analysis for a launch may rely on an earlier analysis from an identical or similar launch if the analysis still applies to the later launch.

(b) *Method of analysis.* (1) For each launch, a launch operator's flight safety analysis must use—

(i) A method approved by the FAA during the licensing process;

(ii) A method approved as a license modification by the FAA; or,

(iii) If the launch takes place from a Federal launch range, a method approved as part of the FAA's launch site safety assessment of the Federal range's processes.

(2) Appendix A of this part contains requirements that apply to all methods of flight safety analysis. A licensee must notify the FAA for any change to the flight safety analysis method. A licensee must file any material change with the FAA as a request for license modification before the launch to which the proposed change would apply. Section 417.11 contains requirements governing a license modification.

(c) *Alternate analysis method.* The FAA will approve an alternate flight safety analysis method if a launch operator demonstrates, in accordance with §406.3(b), that its proposed analysis method provides an equivalent level of fidelity to that required by this subpart. A launch operator must demonstrate that an alternate flight safety analysis method is based on accurate data and scientific principles and is statistically valid. The FAA will not find a launch operator's application for a license or license modification sufficiently complete to begin review under §413.11 of this chapter until the FAA approves the alternate flight safety analysis method.

(d) *Analyses performed by a Federal launch range.* This provision applies to all sections of this subpart. The FAA will accept a flight safety analysis used by a Federal launch range without need for further demonstration of compliance to the FAA, if:

(1) A launch operator has contracted with a Federal launch range for the provision of flight safety analysis; and

(2) The FAA has assessed the Federal launch range, through its launch site safety assessment, and found that the range's analysis methods satisfy the requirements of this subpart. In this case, the FAA will treat the Federal launch range's analysis as that of a launch operator.

(e) *Analysis products.* For a licensed launch that does not satisfy paragraph (d) of this section, a launch operator must demonstrate to the FAA compliance with the requirements of this subpart, and must include in its demonstration the analysis products required by part 415 subpart F of this chapter, part 417 subpart A, and appendices A, B, C, and I of this part, depending on whether the launch vehicle uses a flight safety system or a wind-weighting safety system.

§417.205 General.

(a) *Public risk management.* A flight safety analysis must demonstrate that a launch operator will, for each launch, control the risk to the public from hazards associated with normal and malfunctioning launch vehicle flight. The analysis must employ risk assessment, hazard isolation, or a combination of risk assessment and partial isolation of the hazards, to demonstrate control of the risk to the public.

(1) *Risk assessment.* When demonstrating control of risk through risk assessment, the analysis must demonstrate that any risk to the public satisfies the public risk criteria of §417.107(b). The analysis must account for the variability associated with:

(i) Each source of a hazard during flight;

(ii) Normal flight and each failure response mode of the launch vehicle;

(iii) Each external and launch vehicle flight environment;

(iv) Populations potentially exposed to the flight; and

(v) The performance of any flight safety system, including time delays associated with the system.

(2) *Hazard isolation.* When demonstrating control of risk through hazard isolation, the analysis must establish the geographical areas from which the public must be excluded during flight and any operational controls needed to isolate all hazards from the public.

(3) *Combination of risk assessment and partial isolation of hazards.* When demonstrating control of risk through a combination of risk assessment and partial isolation of the hazards from the public, the analysis must demonstrate that the residual public risk due to any hazard not isolated from the public under paragraph (a)(2) of this section satisfies the public risk criteria of § 417.107(b).

(b) *Dependent analyses.* Because some analyses required by this subpart are inherently dependent on one another, the data output of any one analysis must be compatible in form and content with the data input requirements of any other analysis that depends on that output. Figure 417.205–1 illustrates the flight safety analyses that might be performed for a launch flown with a flight safety system and the typical dependencies that might exist among the analyses.

Data Source Analyses (These analyses provide data to the dependent analyses indicated with an X.)	**Dependent Analyses** (These analyses use data from the data source analyses indicated as input.)									
	Malfunction Turn	Flight Safety Limits	Straight Up Time	No-Longer Terminate Gate	Data Loss Flight Time	Flight Hazard Areas	Debris Risk Analysis	Toxic Release Hazard Analysis	Far Field Overpressure Blast Effects Analysis	
Trajectory Analysis	X	X	X	X	X	X	X	X	X	X
Malfunction Turn Analysis		X	X		X	X	X	X	X	
Debris Analysis		X	X	X	X	X	X	X	X	X
Flight Safety Limits			X	X	X	X	X	X	X	
Straight-Up Time								X	X	
Planned Safe Flight State					X		X	X	X	
Data Loss Flight Time	X									
Time-Delay Analysis	X	X	X	X	X	X	X	X	X	X

Figure 417.205-1, Illustration of dependent flight safety analyses that might be performed for a launch that uses a flight safety system

§ 417.207 Trajectory analysis.

(a) *General.* A flight safety analysis must include a trajectory analysis that establishes:

(1) For any time after lift-off, the limits of a launch vehicle's normal flight, as defined by the nominal trajectory and potential three-sigma trajectory dispersions about the nominal trajectory.

(2) A fuel exhaustion trajectory that produces instantaneous impact points with the greatest range for any given time after liftoff for any stage that has the potential to impact the Earth and does not burn to propellant depletion before a programmed thrust termination.

(3) For launch vehicles flown with a flight safety system, a straight-up trajectory for any time after lift-off until the straight-up time that would result if the launch vehicle malfunctioned and flew in a vertical or near vertical direction above the launch point.

(b) *Trajectory model.* A final trajectory analysis must use a six-degree of freedom trajectory model to satisfy the requirements of paragraph (a) of this section.

(c) *Wind effects.* A trajectory analysis must account for all wind effects, including profiles of winds that are no less severe than the worst wind conditions under which flight might be attempted, and must account for uncertainty in the wind conditions.

§ 417.209 Malfunction turn analysis.

(a) *General.* A flight safety analysis must include a malfunction turn analysis that establishes the launch vehicle's turning capability in the event of a malfunction during flight. A malfunction turn analysis must account for each cause of a malfunction turn, such as thrust vector offsets or nozzle burn-through. For each cause of a malfunction turn, the analysis must establish the launch vehicle's turning capability using a set of turn curves. The analysis must account for:

(1) All trajectory times during the thrusting phases of flight.

(2) When a malfunction begins to cause each turn throughout the thrusting phases of flight. The analysis must account for trajectory time intervals between malfunction turn start times that are sufficient to establish flight safety limits and hazard areas that are smooth and continuous.

(3) The relative probability of occurrence of each malfunction turn of which the launch vehicle is capable.

(4) The time, as a single value or a probability time distribution, when each malfunction turn will terminate due to vehicle breakup.

(5) What terminates each malfunction turn, such as, aerodynamic breakup or inertial breakup.

(6) The launch vehicle's turning behavior from the time when a malfunction begins to cause a turn until aerodynamic breakup, inertial breakup, or ground impact. The analysis must account for trajectory time intervals during the malfunction turn that are sufficient to establish turn curves that are smooth and continuous.

(7) For each malfunction turn, the launch vehicle velocity vector turn angle from the nominal launch vehicle velocity vector.

(8) For each malfunction turn, the launch vehicle velocity turn magnitude from the nominal velocity magnitude that corresponds to the velocity vector turn angle.

(9) For each malfunction turn, the orientation of the launch vehicle longitudinal axis measured relative to the nominal launch vehicle longitudinal axis or Earth relative velocity vector at the start of the turn.

(b) *Set of turn curves for each malfunction turn cause.* For each cause of a malfunction turn, the analysis must establish a set of turn curves that satisfies paragraph (a) of this section and must establish the associated envelope of the set of turn curves. Each set of turn curves must describe the variation in the malfunction turn characteristics for each cause of a turn. The envelope of each set of curves must define the limits of the launch vehicle's malfunction turn behavior for each cause of a malfunction turn. For each malfunction turn envelope, the analysis must establish the launch vehicle velocity vector turn angle from the nominal launch vehicle velocity vector. For each malfunction turn envelope, the analysis must establish the vehicle velocity turn magnitude from the nominal velocity magnitude that corresponds to the velocity vector turn angle envelope.

§417.211 Debris analysis.

(a) *General.* A flight safety analysis must include a debris analysis. For an orbital or suborbital launch, a debris analysis must identify the inert, explosive, and other hazardous launch vehicle debris that results from normal and malfunctioning launch vehicle flight.

(b) *Launch vehicle breakup.* A debris analysis must account for each cause of launch vehicle breakup, including at a minimum:

(1) Any flight termination system activation;

(2) Launch vehicle explosion;

(3) Aerodynamic loads;

(4) Inertial loads;

(5) Atmospheric reentry heating; and

(6) Impact of intact vehicle.

(c) *Debris fragment lists.* A debris analysis must produce lists of debris fragments for each cause of breakup and any planned jettison of debris, launch vehicle components, or payload. The lists must account for all launch vehicle debris fragments, individually or in groupings of fragments whose characteristics are similar enough to be described by a single set of characteristics. The debris lists must describe the physical, aerodynamic, and harmful characteristics of each debris fragment, including at a minimum:

(1) Origin on the vehicle, by vehicle stage or component, from which each fragment originated;

(2) Whether it is inert or explosive;

(3) Weight, dimensions, and shape;

(4) Lift and drag characteristics;

(5) Properties of the incremental velocity distribution imparted by breakup; and

(6) Axial, transverse, and tumbling area.

§417.213 Flight safety limits analysis.

(a) *General.* A flight safety analysis must identify the location of populated or other protected areas, and establish flight safety limits that define when a flight safety system must terminate a launch vehicle's flight to prevent the hazardous effects of the resulting debris impacts from reaching any populated or other protected area and ensure that the launch satisfies the public risk criteria of §417.107(b).

(b) *Flight safety limits.* The analysis must establish flight safety limits for use in establishing flight termination rules. Section 417.113(c) contains requirements for flight termination rules. The flight safety limits must account for all temporal and geometric extents on the Earth's surface of a launch vehicle's hazardous debris impact dispersion resulting from any planned or unplanned event for all times during flight. Flight safety limits must account for all potential contributions to the debris impact dispersions, including at a minimum:

(1) All time delays, as established by the time delay analysis of §417.221;

(2) Residual thrust remaining after flight termination implementation or vehicle breakup due to aerodynamic and inertial loads;

(3) All wind effects;

(4) Velocity imparted to vehicle fragments by breakup;

(5) All lift and drag forces on the malfunctioning vehicle and falling debris;

(6) All launch vehicle guidance and performance errors;

(7) All launch vehicle malfunction turn capabilities; and

(8) Any uncertainty due to map errors and launch vehicle tracking errors.

(c) *Gates.* If a launch involves flight over any populated or other protected area, the flight safety analysis must establish a gate as required by §§417.217 and 417.218.

(d) *Designated debris impact limits.* The analysis must establish designated impact limit lines to bound the area where debris with a ballistic coefficient of three or more is allowed to impact if the flight safety system functions properly.

§417.215 Straight-up time analysis.

A flight safety analysis must establish the straight-up time for a launch for use as a flight termination rule. Section 417.113(c) contains requirements for flight termination rules. The analysis must establish the straight-up time as the latest time after liftoff, assuming a launch vehicle malfunctioned and flew in a vertical or near vertical direction above the launch point, at which activation of the launch vehicle's flight termination system or breakup of the launch vehicle would not cause hazardous debris or critical overpressure to affect any populated or other protected area.

§417.217 Overflight gate analysis.

For a launch that involves flight over a populated or other protected area, the flight safety analysis must include an overflight gate analysis. The analysis must establish the portion of a flight safety limit, a gate, through which a normally performing launch vehicle's tracking icon will be allowed to proceed. A tracking icon must enable the flight safety crew to determine whether the launch vehicle's flight is in compliance with the flight safety rules established under §417.113. When establishing that portion of a flight safety limit, the analysis must demonstrate that the launch vehicle flight satisfies the flight safety requirements of §417.107.

§417.218 Hold-and-resume gate analysis.

(a) For a launch that involves overflight or near overflight of a populated or otherwise protected area prior to the planned safe flight state calculated as required by §417.219, the flight safety analysis must construct a hold-and-resume gate for each populated or otherwise protected area. After a vehicle's tracking icon crosses a hold-and-resume gate, flight termination must occur as required by sections 417.113(d)(6).

(b) The hold-and-resume gate analysis must account for:

(1) *Overflight of a wholly contained populated or otherwise protected area.* A hold-and-resume gate must be a closed, continuous contour that encompasses any populated or otherwise protected area located wholly within the impact limit lines. The hold-and-resume gate must encompass a populated or otherwise protected area such that flight termination or breakup of the launch vehicle while the tracking icon is outside the gate would not cause hazardous debris or overpressure to endanger the populated or otherwise protected area.

(2) *Overflight of an uncontained populated or otherwise protected area.* A hold-and-resume gate must be a closed, continuous contour that encompasses any area in which flight termination is allowed to occur. The hold-and-resume gate must encompass all hazard areas such that flight termination or breakup of the launch vehicle while the vehicle's tracking icon is inside the gate would not cause hazardous debris or critical overpressure to endanger any populated or otherwise protected area.

§417.219 Data loss flight time and planned safe flight state analyses.

(a) *General.* For each launch, a flight safety analysis must establish data loss flight times, as identified by paragraph (b) of this section, and a planned safe flight state to establish each flight termination rule that applies when launch vehicle tracking data is not available for use by the flight safety crew. Section 417.113(d) contains requirements for flight termination rules.

(b) *Data loss flight times.* A flight safety analysis must establish the shortest elapsed thrusting time during which a launch vehicle can move from normal flight to a condition where the launch vehicle's hazardous debris impact dispersion extends to any protected area as a data loss flight time. The analysis must establish a data loss flight time for all times along the nominal trajectory from liftoff through that point during nominal flight when the minimum elapsed thrusting time is no greater than the time it would take for a normal vehicle to reach the overflight gate, or the planned safe flight state established under paragraph (c) of this section, whichever occurs earlier.

(c) *Planned safe flight state.* For a launch vehicle that performs normally during all portions of flight, the planned safe flight state is the point during the nominal flight of a launch vehicle where:

(1) No launch vehicle component, debris, or hazard can impact or affect a populated or otherwise protected area for the remainder of the launch;

(2) The launch vehicle achieves orbital insertion; or

(3) The launch vehicle's state vector reaches a state where the absence of a

flight safety system would not significantly increase the accumulated risk from debris impacts and maintains positive flight safety system control to the maximum extent feasible.

§417.221 Time delay analysis.

(a) *General.* A flight safety analysis must include a time delay analysis that establishes the mean elapsed time between the violation of a flight termination rule and the time when the flight safety system is capable of terminating flight for use in establishing flight safety limits as required by §417.213.

(b) *Analysis constraints.* A time delay analyses must determine a time delay distribution that accounts for the following:

(1) The variance of all time delays for each potential failure scenario, including but not limited to, the range of malfunction turn characteristics and the time of flight when the malfunction occurs;

(2) A flight safety official's decision and reaction time, including variation in human response time; and

(3) Flight termination hardware and software delays including all delays inherent in:

(i) Tracking systems;

(ii) Data processing systems, including all filter delays;

(iii) Display systems;

(iv) Command control systems; and

(v) Flight termination systems.

§417.223 Flight hazard area analysis.

(a) *General.* A flight safety analysis must include a flight hazard area analysis that identifies any regions of land, sea, or air that must be surveyed, publicized, controlled, or evacuated in order to control the risk to the public from debris impact hazards. The risk management requirements of §417.205(a) apply. The analysis must account for, at a minimum:

(1) All trajectory times from liftoff to the planned safe flight state of §417.219(c), including each planned impact, for an orbital launch, and through final impact for a suborbital launch;

(2) Regions of land potentially exposed to debris resulting from normal flight events and events resulting from any potential malfunction;

(3) Regions of sea and air potentially exposed to debris from normal flight events, including planned impacts;

(4) In the vicinity of the launch site, any waterborne vessels, populated offshore structures, or aircraft exposed to debris from events resulting from any potential abnormal flight events, including launch vehicle malfunction;

(5) Any operational controls implemented to control risk to the public from debris hazards;

(6) Debris identified by the debris analysis of §417.211; and

(7) All launch vehicle trajectory dispersion effects in the surface impact domain.

(b) Public notices. A flight hazard areas analysis must establish the ship hazard areas for notices to mariners that encompass the three-sigma impact dispersion area for each planned debris impact. A flight hazard areas analysis must establish the aircraft hazard areas for notices to airmen that encompass the 3-sigma impact dispersion volume for each planned debris impact. Section 417.121(e) contains procedural requirements for issuing notices to mariners and airmen.

§417.224 Probability of failure analysis.

(a) *General.* All flight safety analyses for a launch, regardless of hazard or phase of flight, must account for launch vehicle failure probability in a consistent manner. A launch vehicle failure probability estimate must use accurate data, scientific principles, and a method that is statistically or probabilistically valid. For a launch vehicle with fewer than two flights, the failure probability estimate must account for the outcome of all previous launches of vehicles developed and launched in similar circumstances. For a launch vehicle with two or more flights, launch vehicle failure probability estimates must account for the outcomes of all previous flights of the vehicle in a statistically valid manner.

(b) *Failure.* For flight safety analysis purposes, a failure occurs when a launch vehicle does not complete any phase of normal flight or when any anomalous condition exhibits the potential for a stage or its debris to impact the Earth or reenter the atmosphere during the mission or any future mission of similar launch vehicle capability. Also, either a launch incident or launch accident constitutes a failure.

(c) *Previous flight.* For flight analysis purposes, flight begins at a time in which a launch vehicle normally or inadvertently lifts off from a launch platform. Lift-off occurs with any motion of the launch vehicle with respect to the launch platform.

§417.225 Debris risk analysis.

A flight safety analysis must demonstrate that the risk to the public potentially exposed to inert and explosive debris hazards from any one flight of a launch vehicle satisfies the public risk criterion of §417.107(b) for debris. A debris risk analysis must account for risk to populations on land, including regions of launch vehicle flight following passage through any gate in a flight safety limit established as required by §417.217. A debris risk analysis must account for any potential casualties to the public as required by the debris thresholds and requirements of §417.107(c).

§417.227 Toxic release hazard analysis.

A flight safety analysis must establish flight commit criteria that protect the public from any hazard associated with toxic release and demonstrate compliance with the public risk criterion of §417.107(b). The analysis must account for any toxic release that will occur during the proposed flight of a launch vehicle or that would occur in the event of a flight mishap. The analysis must account for any operational constraints and emergency procedures that provide protection from toxic release. The analysis must account for all members of the public that may be exposed to the toxic release, including all members of the public on land and on any waterborne vessels, populated offshore structures, and aircraft that are not operated in direct support of the launch.

§417.229 Far-field overpressure blast effects analysis.

(a) *General.* A flight safety analysis must establish flight commit criteria that protect the public from any hazard associated with far field blast overpressure effects due to potential explosions during launch vehicle flight and demonstrate compliance with the public risk criterion of §417.107(b).

(b) *Analysis constraints.* The analysis must account for:

(1) The potential for distant focus overpressure or overpressure enhancement given current meteorological conditions and terrain characteristics;

(2) The potential for broken windows due to peak incident overpressures below 1.0 psi and related casualties;

(3) The explosive capability of the launch vehicle at impact and at altitude and potential explosions resulting from debris impacts, including the potential for mixing of liquid propellants;

(4) Characteristics of the launch vehicle flight and the surroundings that would affect the population's susceptibility to injury, such as, shelter types and time of day of the proposed launch;

(5) Characteristics of the potentially affected windows, including their size, location, orientation, glazing material, and condition; and

(6) The hazard characteristics of the potential glass shards, such as falling from upper building stories or being propelled into or out of a shelter toward potentially occupied spaces.

§417.231 Collision avoidance analysis.

(a) *General.* A flight safety analysis must include a collision avoidance analysis that establishes each launch wait in a planned launch window during which a launch operator must not initiate flight, in order to protect any maned or mannable orbiting object. A launch operator must account for uncertainties associated with launch vehicle performance and timing and ensure that any calculated launch waits incorporate all additional time periods associated with such uncertainties. A launch operator must implement any launch waits as flight commit criteria according to §417.113(c).

(b) *Orbital launch.* For an orbital launch, the analysis must establish any launch waits needed to ensure that the launch vehicle, any jettisoned components, and its payload do not pass closer than 200 kilometers to a manned or mannable orbiting object during ascent to initial orbital insertion through at least one complete orbit.

(c) *Suborbital launch.* For a suborbital launch, the analysis must establish any launch waits needed to ensure that the launch vehicle, any jettisoned components, and any payload do not pass closer than 200 kilometers to a manned or mannable orbital object throughout the flight.

(d) *Analysis not required.* A collision avoidance analysis is not required if the maximum altitude attainable by a launch operator's unguided suborbital launch vehicle is less than the altitude of the lowest manned or mannable orbiting object. The maximum altitude attainable must be obtained using an optimized trajectory, assuming 3-sigma maximum performance.

[Docket No. FAA–2000–7953, 71 FR 50537, Aug. 25, 2006, as amended by Amdt. No. 417–5, 81 FR 59439, Aug. 30, 2016]

§ 417.233 Analysis for an unguided suborbital launch vehicle flown with a wind weighting safety system.

For each launch of an unguided suborbital launch vehicle flown with a wind weighting safety system, in addition to the other requirements in this subpart outlined in § 417.201(c), the flight safety analysis must:

(a) Establish flight commit criteria and other launch safety rules that a launch operator must implement to control the risk to the public from potential adverse effects resulting from normal and malfunctioning flight;

(b) Establish any wind constraints under which launch may occur; and

(c) Include a wind weighting analysis that establishes the launcher azimuth and elevation settings that correct for the windcocking and wind-drift effects on the unguided suborbital launch vehicle.

Subpart D—Flight Safety System

§ 417.301 General.

(a) *Applicability.* This subpart applies to any flight safety system that a launch operator uses. The requirements of § 417.107(a) define when a launch operator must use a flight safety system. A launch operator must ensure that its flight safety system satisfies all the requirements of this subpart, including the referenced appendices. Paragraph (b) of this section provides an exception to this.

(b) *Alternate flight safety system.* A flight safety system need not satisfy one or more of the requirements of this subpart for a launch if a launch operator demonstrates, in accordance with § 406.3(b), that the launch achieves an equivalent level of safety as a launch that satisfies all the requirements of this part. The flight safety system must undergo analysis and testing that is comparable to that required by this part to demonstrate that the system's reliability to perform each intended function is comparable to that required by this subpart.

(c) *Functions, subsystems, and components.* When initiated in the event of a launch vehicle failure, a flight safety system must prevent any launch vehicle hazard, including any payload hazard, from reaching a populated or other protected area. A flight safety system must consist of all of the following:

(1) A flight termination system that satisfies appendices D, E, and F of this part;

(2) A command control system that satisfies §§ 417.303 and 417.305;

(3) Each support system required by § 417.307; and

(4) The functions of any personnel who operate flight safety system hardware or software including a flight safety crew that satisfies § 417.311.

(d) *Compliance*—(1) *Non-Federal launch site.* For launch from a non-Federal launch site, any flight safety system, including all components, must:

(i) Comply with a launch operator's flight safety system compliance matrix of § 415.127(g) that accounts for all the design, installation, and monitoring requirements of this subpart, including the referenced appendices; and

(ii) Comply with a launch operator's testing compliance matrix of § 415.129(b) that accounts for all the test requirements of this subpart, including the referenced appendices.

(2) *Federal launch range.* This provision applies to all sections of this subpart. The FAA will accept a flight safety system used or approved on a Federal launch range without need for further demonstration of compliance to the FAA if:

(i) A launch operator has contracted with a Federal launch range for the provision of flight safety system property and services; and

(ii) The FAA has assessed the Federal launch range, through its launch site safety assessment, and found that the Federal launch range's flight safety system property and services satisfy the requirements of this subpart. In this case, the FAA will treat the Federal launch range's flight safety system property and services as that of a launch operator.

[Docket No. FAA–2000–7953, 71 FR 50537, Aug. 25, 2006, as amended by Amdt. No. 417–5, 81 FR 59439, Aug. 30, 2016]

§417.303 Command control system requirements.

(a) *General.* When initiated by a flight safety official, a command control system must transmit a command signal that has the radio frequency characteristics and power needed for receipt of the signal by the onboard vehicle flight termination system. A command control system must include all of the following:

(1) All flight termination system activation switches;

(2) All intermediate equipment, linkages, and software;

(3) Any auxiliary stations;

(4) Each command transmitter and transmitting antenna; and

(5) All support equipment that is critical for reliable operation, such as power, communications, and air conditioning systems.

(b) *Performance specifications.* A command control system and each subsystem, component, and part that can affect the reliability of a component must have written performance specifications that demonstrate, and contain the details of, how each satisfies the requirements of this section.

(c) *Reliability prediction.* A command control system must have a predicted reliability of 0.999 at the 95 percent confidence level when operating, starting with completion of the preflight testing and system verification of §417.305(c) through initiation of flight and until the planned safe flight state for each launch. Any demonstration of the system's predicted reliability must satisfy §417.309(b).

(d) *Fault tolerance.* A command control system must not contain any single-failure-point that, upon failure, would inhibit the required functioning of the system or cause the transmission of an undesired flight termination message. A command control system's design must ensure that the probability of transmitting an undesired or inadvertent command during flight is less than 1×10^{-7}.

(e) *Configuration control.* A command control system must undergo configuration control to ensure its reliability and compatibility with the flight termination system used for each launch.

(f) *Electromagnetic interference.* Each command control system component must function within the electromagnetic environment to which it is exposed. A command control system must include protection to prevent interference from inhibiting the required functioning of the system or causing the transmission of an undesired or inadvertent flight termination command. Any susceptible remote control data processing or transmitting system that is part of the command control system must prevent electromagnetic interference.

(g) *Command transmitter failover.* A command control system must include independent, redundant transmitter systems that automatically switch, or "fail-over," from a primary transmitter to a secondary transmitter when a condition exists that indicates potential failure of the primary transmitter. The switch must be automatic and provide all the same command control system capabilities through the secondary transmitter system. The secondary transmitter system must respond to any transmitter system configuration and radio message orders established for the launch. The fail-over criteria that trigger automatic switching from the primary transmitter to the secondary transmitter must account for each of the following transmitter performance parameters and failure indicators:

(1) Low transmitter power;

(2) Center frequency shift;

(3) Out of tolerance tone frequency;

(4) Out of tolerance message timing;

(5) Loss of communication between central control and transmitter site;

(6) Central control commanded status and site status disagree;

(7) Transmitter site fails to respond to a configuration or radiation order within a specified period of time; and

(8) For a tone-based system, tone deviation and tone imbalance.

(h) *Switching between transmitter systems.* Any manual or automatic switching between transmitter systems, including fail-over, must not result in the radio carrier being off the air long enough for any command destruct system to be captured by an unauthorized transmitter. The time the radio carrier is off the air must account for any loss of carrier and any simultaneous multiple radio carrier transmissions from two transmitter sites during switching.

(i) *Radio carrier.* For each launch, a command control system must provide all of the following:

(1) The radio frequency signal and radiated power density that each command destruct system needs to activate during flight;

(2) The 12-dB power density margin required by section D417.9(d) of appendix D of this part under nominal conditions; and

(3) A 6-dB power density margin under worst-case conditions.

(j) *Command control system monitoring and control.* A command control system must provide for monitoring and control of the system from the flight safety system displays and controls required by §417.307(f), including real-time selection of a transmitter, transmitter site, communication circuits, and antenna configuration.

(k) *Command transmitter system.* For each launch, a command transmitter system must:

(1) Transmit signals that are compatible with any command destruct system's radio frequency receiving system of section D417.25 and command receiver decoder of section D417.29 of appendix D of this part;

(2) Ensure that all arm and destruct commands transmitted to a flight termination system have priority over any other commands transmitted;

(3) Employ an authorized radio carrier frequency and bandwidth with a guard band that provides the radio frequency separation needed to ensure that the system does not interfere with any other flight safety system that is required to operate at the same time;

(4) Transmit an output bandwidth that is consistent with the signal spectrum power used in the link analysis of §417.309(f); and

(5) Not transmit other frequencies that could degrade the airborne flight termination system's performance.

(l) *Command control system antennas.* A command control system antenna or antenna system must satisfy all of the following:

(1) The antenna system must provide two or more command signals to any command destruct system throughout normal flight and in the event of a launch vehicle failure regardless of launch vehicle orientation;

(2) Each antenna beam-width must:

(i) Allow for complete transmission of the command destruct sequence of signal tones before a malfunctioning launch vehicle can exit the 3-dB point of the antenna pattern;

(ii) When the vehicle is centered in the antenna pattern at the beginning of the malfunction, account for the launch vehicle's malfunction turn capability determined by the analysis of §417.209, the data loss flight times of §417.219, and the time delay of §417.221.

(iii) Encompass the boundaries of normal flight for the portion of flight that the antenna is scheduled to support; and

(iv) Account for any error associated with launch vehicle tracking and pointing of the antenna;

(3) The location of each antenna must provide for an unobstructed line of site between the antenna and the launch vehicle;

(4) The antenna system must provide a continuous omni-directional radio carrier pattern that covers the launch vehicle's flight from the launch point to no less than an altitude of 50,000 feet

above sea level, unless the system uses a steerable antenna that satisfies paragraphs (l)(1) and (2) of this section for the worst-case launch vehicle malfunction that could occur during that portion of flight;

(5) An antenna must radiate circularly polarized radio waves that are compatible with the flight termination system antennas on the launch vehicle; and

(6) Any steerable antenna must allow for control of the antenna manually at the antenna site or by remote slaving data from a launch vehicle tracking source. A steerable antenna's positioning lag, accuracy, and slew rates must allow for tracking a nominally performing launch vehicle within one half of the antenna's beam-width and for tracking a malfunctioning launch vehicle to satisfy paragraph (l)(2) of this section.

[Docket No. FAA–2000–7953, 71 FR 50537, Aug. 25, 2006, as amended by Amdt. No. 417–5, 81 FR 59439, Aug. 30, 2016]

§ 417.305 Command control system testing.

(a) *General.* (1) A command control system, including its subsystems and components must undergo the acceptance testing of paragraph (b) of this section when new or modified. For each launch, a command control system must undergo the preflight testing of paragraph (c) of this section.

(2) Each acceptance and preflight test must follow a written test plan that specifies the procedures and test parameters for the test and the testing sequence. A test plan must include instructions on how to handle procedural deviations and how to react to test failures.

(3) If hardware or software is redesigned or replaced with a different hardware or software that is not identical to the original, the system must undergo all acceptance testing and analysis with the new hardware or software and all preflight testing for each launch with the new hardware or software.

(4) After a command control system passes all acceptance tests, if a component is replaced with an identical component, the system must undergo testing to ensure that the new component is installed properly and is operational.

(b) *Acceptance testing.* (1) All new or modified command control system hardware and software must undergo acceptance testing to verify that the system satisfies the requirements of § 417.303.

(2) Acceptance testing must include functional testing, system interface validation testing, and integrated system-wide validation testing.

(3) Each acceptance test must measure the performance parameters that demonstrate whether the requirements of § 417.303 are satisfied.

(4) Any computing system, software, or firmware that performs a software safety critical function must undergo validation testing and satisfy § 417.123. If command control system hardware interfaces with software, the interface must undergo validation testing.

(c) *Preflight testing*—(1) *General.* For each launch, a command control system must undergo preflight testing to verify that the system satisfies the requirements of § 417.303 for the launch.

(2) *Coordinated command control system and flight termination system testing.* For each launch, a command control system must undergo preflight testing during the preflight testing of the associated flight termination system under section E417.41 of appendix E of this part.

(3) *Command transmitter system carrier switching tests.* A command transmitter system must undergo a test of its carrier switching system no earlier than 24 hours before a scheduled flight. The test must satisfy all of the following:

(i) *Automatic carrier switching.* For any automatic carrier switching system, the test must verify that the switching algorithm selects and enables the proper transmitter site for each portion of the planned flight; and

(ii) *Manual carrier switching.* For any manual carrier switching, the test must verify that the flight safety system crew can select and enable each transmitter site planned to support the launch.

(4) *Independent radio frequency open loop verification tests.* A command control system must undergo an open loop end-to-end verification test for each launch as close to the planned flight as

operationally feasible and after any modification to the system or break in the system configuration. The test must:

(i) Verify the performance of each element of the system from the flight safety system displays and controls to each command transmitter site;

(ii) Measure all system performance parameters received and transmitted using measuring equipment that does not physically interface with any elements of the operational command control system;

(iii) Verify the performance of each flight safety system display and control and remote command transmitter site combination by repeating all measurements for each combination, for all strings and all operational configurations of cross-strapped equipment; and

(iv) Verify that all critical command control system performance parameters satisfy all their performance specifications. These parameters must include:

(A) Transmitter power output;

(B) Center frequency stability;

(C) Tone deviation;

(D) Tone frequency;

(E) Message timing;

(F) Status of each communication circuit between the flight safety system display and controls and any supporting command transmitter sites;

(G) Status agreement between the flight safety system display and controls and each and any supporting command transmitter sites;

(H) Fail-over conditions;

(I) Tone balance; and

(J) Time delay from initiation of a command at each flight safety system control to transmitter output of the command signal.

(d) *Test reports.* If a Federal launch range oversees the safety of a launch, the range's requirements are consistent with this subpart, and the range provides and tests the command control system, a launch operator need only obtain the range's verification that the system satisfies all the test requirements. For any other case a launch operator must prepare or obtain one or more written reports that:

(1) Verify that the command control system satisfies all the test requirements;

(2) Describe all command control system test results and test conditions;

(3) Describe any analysis performed instead of testing;

(4) Identify by serial number or other identification each test result that applies to each system or component;

(5) Describe any test failure or anomaly, including any variation from an established performance baseline, each corrective action taken, and all results of any additional tests; and

(6) Identify any test failure trends.

[Docket No. FAA–2000–7953, 71 FR 50537, Aug. 25, 2006, as amended by Amdt. No. 417–5, 81 FR 59439, Aug. 30, 2016]

§417.307 Support systems.

(a) *General.* (1) A flight safety system must include the systems required by this section to support the functions of the flight safety system crew, including making a flight termination decision.

(2) Each support system and each subsystem, component, and part that can affect the reliability of the support system must have written performance specifications that demonstrate, and contain the details of, how each satisfies the requirements of this section.

(3) For each launch, each support system must undergo testing to ensure it functions according to its performance specifications.

(b) *Launch vehicle tracking.* (1) A flight safety system must include a launch vehicle tracking system that provides launch vehicle position and status data to the flight safety crew from the first data loss flight time until the planned safe flight state for the launch.

(2) The tracking system must consist of at least two sources of launch vehicle position data. The data sources must be independent of one another, and at least one source must be independent of any vehicle guidance system.

(3) All ground tracking systems and components must be compatible with any tracking system components onboard the launch vehicle.

(4) If a tracking system uses radar as one of the independent tracking sources, the system must:

(i) Include a tracking beacon onboard the launch vehicle; or

(ii) If the system relies on skin tracking, it must maintain a tracking margin of no less than 6 dB above noise throughout the period of flight that the radar is used. The flight safety limits must account for the larger tracking errors associated with skin tracking.

(5) The tracking system must provide real-time data to the flight safety data processing, display, and recording system required by paragraph (e) of this section.

(6) For each launch, each tracking source must undergo validation of its accuracy. For each stage of flight that a launch vehicle guidance system is used as a tracking source, a tracking source that is independent of any system used to aid the guidance system must validate the guidance system data before the data is used in the flight termination decision process.

(7) The launch vehicle tracking error from all sources, including data latency and any possible gaps or dropouts in tracking coverage, must be consistent with the flight safety limits of § 417.213 and the flight safety system time delay of § 417.221.

(8) Any planned gap in tracking coverage must not occur at the same time as any planned switching of command transmitters.

(c) *Telemetry.* (1) A flight safety system must include a telemetry system that provides the flight safety crew with accurate flight safety data during preflight operations and during flight until the planned safe flight state.

(2) The onboard telemetry system must monitor and transmit the flight termination system monitoring data of section D417.17 and any launch vehicle tracking data used to satisfy paragraph (b) of this section.

(3) The telemetry receiving system must acquire, store, and provide real-time data to the flight safety data processing, display, and recording system required by paragraph (e) of this section.

(d) *Communications network.* A flight safety system must include a communications network that connects all flight safety functions with all launch control centers and any down-range tracking and command transmitter sites. The system must provide for recording all required data and all voice communications channels during launch countdown and flight.

(e) *Data processing, display, and recording.* A flight safety system must include one or more subsystems that process, display, and record flight safety data to support the flight safety crew's monitoring of the launch, including the data that the crew uses to make a flight termination decision. The system must:

(1) Satisfy § 417.123 for any computing system, software, or firmware that must operate properly to ensure the accuracy of the data;

(2) Receive vehicle status data from tracking and telemetry, evaluate the data for validity, and provide valid data for display and recording;

(3) Perform any reformatting of the data as appropriate and forward it to display and recording devices;

(4) Display real-time data against background displays of the nominal trajectory and flight safety limits established in accordance with the flight safety analysis required by subpart C of this part;

(5) Display and record raw input and processed data at a rate that maintains the validity of the data and at no less than 0.1-second intervals;

(6) Record the timing of when flight safety system commands are input by the flight safety crew; and

(7) Record all health and status parameters of the command control system, including the transmitter failover parameters, command outputs, check channel or pilot tone monitor, and status of communications.

(f) *Displays and controls.* (1) A flight safety system must include the displays of real-time data and controls that the flight safety crew needs to perform all its functions, such as to monitor and evaluate launch vehicle performance, communicate with other flight safety and launch personnel, and initiate flight termination.

(2) A flight safety system must present all data that the flight safety crew needs to ensure that all flight

commit criteria are satisfied for each launch, such as hazard area surveillance, any aircraft and ship traffic information, meteorological conditions, and the flight termination system monitoring data of section D417.17.

(3) The real-time displays must include all data that the flight safety crew needs to ensure the operational functionality of the flight safety system, including availability and quality, and that all flight termination rules are satisfied for each launch, such as:

(i) Launch vehicle tracking data, such as instantaneous vacuum impact point, drag corrected debris footprint, or present launch vehicle position and velocities as a function of time;

(ii) Vehicle status data from telemetry, including yaw, pitch, roll, and motor chamber pressure;

(iii) The flight termination system monitoring data of section D417.17;

(iv) Background displays of nominal trajectory, flight safety limits, data loss flight times, planned safe flight state, and any overflight gate through a flight safety limit all as determined by the flight safety analysis required by subpart C of this part; and

(v) Any video data when required by the flight safety crew to perform its functions, such as video from optical program and flight line cameras.

(4) The controls must allow the flight safety crew to turn a command transmitter on and off, manually switch from primary to backup transmitter antenna, and switch between each transmitter site. These functions may be accomplished through controls available to command transmitter support personnel and communications between those personnel and the flight safety crew.

(5) Each set of command transmitter system controls must include a means of identifying when it has primary control of the system.

(6) The displays must include a means of immediately notifying the flight safety system crew of any automatic fail-over of the system transmitters.

(7) All flight safety system controls must be dedicated to the flight safety system and must not rely on time or equipment shared with other systems.

(8) All data transmission links between any control, transmitter, or antenna must consist of two or more complete and independent duplex circuits. The routing of these circuits must ensure that they are physically separated from each other to eliminate any potential single failure point in the command control system in accordance with §417.303(d).

(9) The system must include hardware or procedural security provisions for controlling access to all controls and other related hardware. These security provisions must ensure that only the flight safety crew can initiate a flight safety system transmission.

(10) The system must include two independent means for the flight safety crew to initiate arm and destruct messages. The location and functioning of the controls must provide the crew easy access to the controls and prevent inadvertent activation.

(11) The system must include a digital countdown for use in implementing the flight termination rules of §417.113 that apply data loss flight times and the planned safe flight state. The system must also include a manual method of applying the data loss flight times in the event that the digital countdown malfunctions.

(g) *Support equipment calibration.* Each support system and any equipment used to test flight safety system components must undergo calibration to ensure that measurement and monitoring devices that support a launch provide accurate indications.

(h) *Destruct initiator simulator.* A flight safety system must include one or more destruct initiator simulators that simulate each destruct initiator during the flight termination system preflight tests. Each destruct initiator simulator must:

(1) Have electrical and operational characteristics matching those of the actual destruct initiator;

(2) Monitor the firing circuit output current, voltage, or energy, and indicate whether the firing output occurs. The indication that the output occurred must remain after the output is removed;

(3) Have the ability to remain connected throughout ground processing

until the electrical connection of the actual initiators is accomplished;

(4) Include a capability that permits the issuance of destruct commands by test equipment only if the simulator is installed and connected to the firing lines; and

(5) For any low voltage initiator, provide a stray current monitoring device in the firing line. The stray current monitoring device, such as a fuse or automatic recording system, must be capable of indicating a minimum of one-tenth of the maximum no-fire current.

(i) *Timing.* A flight safety system must include a timing system that is synchronized to a universal time coordinate. The system must:

(1) Initiate first motion signals;

(2) Synchronize flight safety system instrumentation, including countdown clocks; and

(3) Identify when, during countdown or flight, a data measurement or voice communication occurs.

§ 417.309 Flight safety system analysis.

(a) *General.* (1) Each flight termination system and command control system, including each of their components, must satisfy the analysis requirements of this section.

(2) Each analysis must follow an FAA approved system safety and reliability analysis methodology.

(b) *System reliability.* Each flight termination system and command control system must undergo an analysis that demonstrates the system's predicted reliability. Each analysis must:

(1) Account for the probability of a flight safety system anomaly occurring and all of its effects as determined by the single failure point analysis and the sneak circuit analysis required by paragraphs (c) and (g) of this section;

(2) Demonstrate that each system satisfies the predicted reliability requirement of 0.999 at the 95 percent confidence level;

(3) Use a reliability model that is statistically valid and accurately represents the system;

(4) Account for the actual or predicted reliability of all subsystems and components;

(5) Account for the effects of storage, transportation, handling, maintenance, and operating environments on component predicted reliability; and

(6) Account for the interface between the launch vehicle systems and the flight termination system.

(c) *Single failure point.* A command control system must undergo an analysis that demonstrates that the system satisfies the fault tolerance requirements of § 417.303(d). A flight termination system must undergo an analysis that demonstrates that the system satisfies the fault tolerance requirements of section D417.5(b). Each analysis must:

(1) Follow a standard industry methodology such as a fault tree analysis or a failure modes effects and criticality analysis;

(2) Identify all possible failure modes and undesired events, their probability of occurrence, and their effects on system performance;

(3) Identify single point failure modes;

(4) Identify areas of design where redundancy is required and account for any failure mode where a component and its backup could fail at the same time due to a single cause;

(5) Identify functions, including redundancy, which are not or cannot be tested;

(6) Account for any potential system failures due to hardware, software, test equipment, or procedural or human errors;

(7) Account for any single failure point on another system that could disable a command control system or flight termination system, such as any launch vehicle system that could trigger safing of a flight termination system; and

(8) Provide input to the reliability analysis of paragraph (b) of this section.

(d) *Fratricide.* A flight termination system must undergo an analysis that demonstrates that the flight termination of any stage, at any time during flight, will not sever interconnecting flight termination system circuitry or ordnance to other stages until flight termination on all the other stages has been initiated.

(e) *Bent pin.* Each component of a flight termination system and command control system must undergo an analysis that demonstrates that any single short circuit occurring as a result of a bent electrical connection pin will not result in inadvertent system activation or inhibiting the proper operation of the system.

(f) *Radio frequency link.* (1) The flight safety system must undergo a radio frequency link analysis to demonstrate that it satisfies the required 12-dB margin for nominal system performance and 6-dB margin for worst-case system performance.

(2) When demonstrating the 12-dB margin, each link analysis must account for the following nominal system performance and attenuation factors:

(i) Path losses due to plume or flame attenuation;

(ii) Vehicle trajectory;

(iii) Ground system and airborne system radio frequency characteristics; and

(iv) The antenna gain value that ensures that the margin is satisfied over 95% of the antenna radiation sphere surrounding the launch vehicle.

(3) When demonstrating the 6-dB margin, each link analysis must account for the following worst-case system performance and attenuation factors:

(i) The system performance and attenuation factors of paragraph (f)(2) of this section;

(ii) The command transmitter failover criteria of §417.303(g) including the lowest output power provided by the transmitter system;

(iii) Worst-case power loss due to antenna pointing inaccuracies; and

(iv) Any other attenuation factors.

(g) *Sneak circuit.* Each electronic component that contains an electronic inhibit that could inhibit the functioning, or cause inadvertent functioning of a flight termination system or command control system, must undergo a sneak circuit analysis. The analysis must demonstrate that there are no latent paths of an unwanted command that could, when all components otherwise function properly, cause the occurrence of an undesired, unplanned, or inhibited function that could cause a system anomaly. The analysis must determine the probability of an anomaly occurring for input to the system reliability analysis of paragraph (b) of this section.

(h) *Software and firmware.* Any computing system, software, or firmware that performs a software safety critical function must undergo the analysis needed to ensure reliable operation and satisfy §417.123.

(i) *Battery capacity.* A flight termination system must undergo an analysis that demonstrates that each flight termination system battery has a total amp hour capacity of no less than 150% of the capacity needed during flight plus the capacity needed for load and activation checks, preflight and launch countdown checks, and any potential launch hold time. For a launch vehicle that uses any solid propellant, the analysis must demonstrate that the battery capacity allows for an additional 30-minute hang-fire hold time. The battery analysis must also demonstrate each flight termination system battery's ability to meet the charging temperature and current control requirements of appendix D of this part.

(j) *Survivability.* A flight termination system must undergo an analysis that demonstrates that each subsystem and component, including their location on the launch vehicle, provides for the flight termination system to complete all its required functions when exposed to:

(1) Breakup of the launch vehicle due to aerodynamic loading effects at high angle of attack trajectories during early stages of flight, including the effects of any automatic or inadvertent destruct system;

(2) An engine hard-over nozzle induced tumble during each phase of flight for each stage; or

(3) Launch vehicle staging, ignition, or any other normal or abnormal event that, when it occurs, could damage flight termination system hardware or inhibit the functionality of any subsystem or component, including any inadvertent separation destruct system.

§417.311 Flight safety crew roles and qualifications.

(a) A flight safety crew must operate the flight safety system hardware. A flight safety crew must document each flight safety crew position description and maintain documentation on individual crew qualifications, including education, experience, and training as part of the personnel certification program required by § 417.105.

(b) A flight safety crew must be able to demonstrate the knowledge, skills, and abilities needed to operate the flight safety system hardware in accordance with § 417.113.

(1) A flight safety crew must have knowledge of:

(i) All flight safety system assets and responsibilities, including:

(A) Communications systems and launch operations procedures;

(B) Both voice and data systems;

(C) Graphical data systems;

(D) Tracking; and

(E) Telemetry real time data;

(ii) Flight termination systems; and

(iii) Contingency operations, including hold, recycle and abort procedures.

(2) An individual who monitors vehicle performance and performs flight termination must have knowledge of and be capable of resolving malfunctions in:

(i) The application of safety support systems such as position tracking sources;

(ii) Digital computers;

(iii) Displays;

(iv) Command destruct;

(v) Communications;

(vi) Telemetry;

(vii) All electrical functions of a flight termination system;

(viii) The principles of radio frequency transmission and attenuation;

(ix) The behavior of ballistic and aerodynamic vehicles in flight under the influence of aerodynamic forces; and

(x) The application of flight termination rules.

(3) An individual who operates flight safety support systems must have knowledge of and be capable of resolving malfunctions in:

(i) The design and assembly of the flight safety support system hardware;

(ii) The operation of electromechanical systems; and

(iii) The nature and inherent tendencies of the flight safety system hardware being operated.

(4) An individual who performs flight safety analysis must have knowledge of orbital mechanics and be proficient in the calculation and production of range safety displays, impact probabilities, and casualty expectations.

(c) Flight safety crew members must complete a training and certification program to ensure launch site familiarization, launch vehicle familiarization, flight safety system functions, equipment, and procedures related to a launch before being called upon to support that launch. Each flight safety crew member must complete a preflight readiness training and certification program. This preflight readiness training and certification program must include:

(1) Mission specific training programs to ensure team readiness.

(2) Launch simulation exercises of system failure modes, including nominal and failure modes, that test crew performance, flight termination criteria, and flight safety data display integrity.

Subpart E—Ground Safety

§ 417.401 Scope.

This subpart contains public safety requirements that apply to launch processing and post-launch operations at a launch site in the United States. Ground safety requirements in this subpart apply to activities performed by, or on behalf of, a launch operator at a launch site in the United States. A licensed launch site operator must satisfy the requirements of part 420 of this chapter.

§ 417.402 Compliance.

(a) *General.* A launch operator's ground safety process must satisfy this subpart.

(b) *Ground safety analysis conducted for launch at a Federal launch range.* This provision applies to all sections of this subpart. The FAA will accept a ground safety process conducted for a launch from a Federal launch range without need for further demonstration of compliance to the FAA if:

(1) A launch operator has contracted with a Federal launch range for the provision of the ground safety process; and

(2) The FAA has assessed the Federal launch range, through its launch site

safety assessment, and found that the Federal launch range's ground safety process satisfies the requirements of this subpart. In this case, the FAA will treat the Federal launch range's process as that of a launch operator.

(c) *Toxic release hazard analysis conducted for launch processing at a Federal launch range.* The FAA will accept a toxic release hazard analysis conducted for launch processing from a Federal launch range provided the toxic release analysis satisfies the Federal launch range's requirements, and the FAA has assessed the Federal launch range, through its launch site safety assessment, and found that the applicable Federal launch range safety-related launch services and property satisfy the requirements of this subpart.

(d) *Demonstration of compliance.* For a licensed launch that does not satisfy paragraphs (b) and (c) of this section, a launch operator must demonstrate compliance to the FAA with the requirements of this subpart, and must include in its demonstration the analysis products required by subparts A and E of this part, and appendices I and J of this part.

(e) *Alternate methods.* The FAA will approve an alternate hazard control method if a launch operator demonstrates, in accordance with § 406.3(b), that its proposed hazard control method provides an equivalent level of safety to that required by this subpart.

§ 417.403 General.

(a) *Public safety.* A launch operator must ensure that each hazard control is in place to protect the public from each potential hazard associated with launch processing and post-launch operations.

(b) *Ground safety analysis.* A launch operator must perform and document a ground safety analysis that satisfies § 417.405 and appendix J of this part.

(c) *Local agreements.* A launch operator must coordinate and perform launch processing and post-launch operations that satisfy local agreements to ensure the responsibilities and requirements in this part and § 420.57 of this chapter are met. A launch operator, when using a launch site of a licensed launch site operator, must coordinate the launch operator's operations with the launch site operator and with any agreements that the launch site operator has with local authorities that form a basis for the launch site operator's license.

(d) *Launch operator's exclusive use of a launch site.* For a launch conducted from a launch site exclusive to its own use, a launch operator must satisfy the requirements of this subpart and of part 420 of this chapter, including subpart D of part 420.

§ 417.405 Ground safety analysis.

(a) A launch operator must perform a ground safety analysis for launch vehicle hardware, ground hardware including launch site and ground support equipment, launch processing, and post-launch operations at a launch site in the United States. The requirements of this section apply to the performance of the ground safety analysis and to the ground safety analysis products that a launch operator must file with the FAA as required by § 417.402(d). This analysis must identify each potential hazard, each associated cause, and each hazard control that a launch operator must establish and maintain to keep each identified hazard from affecting the public. A launch operator must incorporate the launch site operator's systems and operations involved in ensuring public safety into the ground safety analysis.

(b) Technical personnel who are knowledgeable of launch vehicle systems, launch processing, ground systems, operations, and their associated hazards must prepare the ground safety analysis. These individuals must be qualified to perform the ground safety analysis through training, education, and experience.

(c) A launch operator must ensure personnel performing a ground safety analysis or preparing a ground safety analysis report will have the cooperation of the entire launch operator's organization. A launch operator must maintain supporting documentation and it must be available upon request.

(d) A launch operator must:

(1) Begin a ground safety analysis by identifying the systems and operations to be analyzed;

(2) Define the extent of each system and operation being assessed to ensure

there is no miscommunication as to what the hazards are, and who, in a launch operator's organization or other organization supporting the launch, controls those hazards; and

(3) Ensure that the ground safety analysis accounts for each launch vehicle system and operation involved in launch processing and post-launch operations, even if only to show that no hazard exists.

(e) A ground safety analysis need not account for potential hazards of a component if a launch operator demonstrates that no hazard to the public exists at the system level. A ground safety analysis need not account for an operation's individual task or subtask level if a launch operator demonstrates that no hazard to the public exists at the operation level. A launch operator must provide verifiable controls for hazards that are confined within the boundaries of a launch operator's facility to ensure the public will not have access to the associated hazard area while the hazard exists.

(f) A launch operator must identify each potential hazard, including non-credible hazards. The probability of occurrence is not relevant with respect to identifying a hazard. Where an assertion is made that no hazard exists for a particular system or operation, the ground safety analysis must provide the rationale. A launch operator must identify the following hazards of each launch vehicle system, launch site and ground support equipment, launch processing, and post-launch operations:

(1) System hazards, including explosives and other ordnance, solid and liquid propellants, toxic and radioactive materials, asphyxiants, cryogens, and high pressure. System hazards generally exist even when no operation is occurring, and

(2) Operation hazards derived from an unsafe condition created by a system, operating environment, or an unsafe act.

(g) A launch operator must categorize identified system and operation hazards as follows:

(1) *Public hazard.* A hazard that extends beyond the launch location under the control of a launch operator. Public hazards include the following:

(i) Blast overpressure and fragmentation resulting from an explosion;

(ii) Fire and deflagration, including hazardous materials such as radioactive material, beryllium, carbon fibers, and propellants. A launch operator must assume that in the event of a fire, hazardous smoke from systems containing hazardous materials will reach the public;

(iii) Sudden release of a hazardous material into the air, water, or ground; and

(iv) Inadvertent ignition of a propulsive launch vehicle payload, stage, or motor.

(2) *Launch location hazard.* A hazard that stays within the confines of the location under the control of a launch operator but extends beyond individuals doing the work. The confines may be bounded by a wall or a fence line of a facility or launch complex, or by a fenced or unfenced boundary of an entire industrial complex or multi-user launch site. A launch location hazard may affect the public depending on public access controls. Launch location hazards that may affect the public include the hazards listed in paragraphs (g)(1)(i)–(iv) of this section and additional hazards in potentially unsafe locations accessible to the public such as:

(i) Unguarded electrical circuits or machinery;

(ii) Oxygen deficient environments;

(iii) Falling objects;

(iv) Potential falls into unguarded pits or from unguarded elevated work platforms; and

(v) Sources of ionizing and non-ionizing radiation such as x-rays, radio transmitters, and lasers.

(3) *Employee hazard.* A hazard to individuals performing a launch operator's work, but not to other people in the area. A launch operator must comply with all applicable Federal, state, and local employee safety regulations. A launch operator's ground safety analysis must identify employee hazards and demonstrate that there are no associated public safety issues.

(4) *Non-credible hazard.* A hazard for which possible adverse effects on people or property would be negligible and where the possibility of adverse effects on people or property is remote. A

launch operator's ground safety analysis must identify non-credible hazards and demonstrate that the hazard is non-credible.

(h) A ground safety analysis must identify each hazard cause for each public hazard and launch location hazard. The ground safety analysis must account for conditions, acts, or chain of events that can result in a hazard. The ground safety analysis must account for the possible failure of any control or monitoring circuitry within hardware systems that can cause a hazard.

(i) A ground safety analysis must identify the hazard controls to be established by a launch operator for each hazard cause identified in paragraph (h) of this section. A launch operator's hazard controls include the use of engineering controls for the containment of hazards within defined areas and the control of public access to those areas.

(j) A launch operator must verify all information in a ground safety analysis, including design margins, fault tolerance and successful completion of tests. A launch operator must:

(1) Trace any identified hardware to an engineering drawing or other document that describes hardware configuration;

(2) Trace any test or analysis used in developing the ground safety analysis to a report or memorandum that describes how the test or analysis was performed;

(3) Ensure the accuracy of the test or analysis and the associated results;

(4) Trace any procedural hazard control identified to a written procedure, and approved by the person designated under §417.103(b)(2) or the person's designee, with the paragraph or step number of the procedure specified;

(5) Identify a verifiable hazard control for each hazard; if a hazard control is not verifiable, a launch operator may include it as an informational note on the hazard analysis form;

(6) For each hazard control, reference a released drawing, report, procedure or other document that verifies the existence of the hazard control; and

(7) Maintain records, as required by §417.15, of the documentation that verifies the information in the ground safety analysis.

(k) A launch operator must ensure the continuing accuracy of its ground safety analysis. The analysis of systems and operations must not end upon submission of a ground safety analysis report to the FAA during the license application process. A launch operator must analyze each new or modified system or operation for potential hazards that can affect the public. A launch operator must ensure that each existing system and operation is subject to continual scrutiny and that the information in a ground safety analysis report is kept current.

§417.407 Hazard control implementation.

(a) *General.* A launch operator must establish and maintain the hazard controls identified by the ground safety analysis including:

(1) System hazard controls that satisfy §417.409;

(2) Safety clear zones for hazardous operations that satisfy §417.411;

(3) Hazard areas and controls for allowing public access that satisfy §417.413;

(4) Hazard controls after launch or an attempt to launch that satisfy §417.415; and

(5) Controls for propellant and explosive hazards that satisfy §417.417.

(b) *Hazard control verification.* A launch operator must establish a hazard tracking process to ensure that each identified hazard has a verifiable hazard control. Verification status must remain "open" for an individual hazard control until the hazard control is verified to exist in a released drawing, report, procedure, or similar document.

(c) *Hazard control configuration control.* A launch operator must establish and maintain a configuration control process for safety critical hardware. Procedural steps to verify hazard controls, and their associated documentation, cannot be changed without coordination with the person designated in §417.103(b)(2).

(d) *Inspections.* When a potential hazard exists, a launch operator must conduct periodic inspections of related hardware, software, and facilities. A launch operator must ensure qualified and certified personnel, as required by

§417.105, conduct the inspection. A launch operator must demonstrate that the time interval between inspections is sufficient to ensure satisfaction of this subpart. A launch operator must ensure safety devices and other hazard controls must remain in place for that hazard, and that safety devices and other hazard controls must remain in working order so that no unsafe conditions exist.

(e) *Procedures.* A launch operator must conduct each launch processing or post-launch operation involving a public hazard or a launch location hazard pursuant to written procedures that incorporate the hazard controls identified by a launch operator's ground safety analysis and as required by this subpart. The person designated in §417.103(b)(2) must approve the procedures. A launch operator must maintain an "as-run" copy of each procedure. The "as-run" procedure copy must include changes, start and stop dates, and times that each procedure was performed and observations made during the operations.

(f) *Hazardous materials.* A launch operator must establish procedures for the receipt, storage, handling, use, and disposal of hazardous materials, including toxic substances and sources of ionizing radiation. A launch operator must establish procedures for responding to hazardous material emergencies and protecting the public that complies with the accident investigation plan as defined in §417.111(h)(2). These procedures must include:

(1) Identification of each hazard and its effects;

(2) Actions to be taken in response to release of a hazardous material;

(3) Identification of protective gear and other safety equipment that must be available in order to respond to a release;

(4) Evacuation and rescue procedures;

(5) Chain of command; and

(6) Communication both on-site and off-site to surrounding communities and local authorities.

(g) *Toxic release hazard notifications and evacuations.* A launch operator must perform a toxic release hazard analysis for launch processing performed at the launch site that satisfies section I417.7 of this part. A launch operator must apply toxic plume modeling techniques that satisfy section I417.7 of this part and ensure that notifications and evacuations are accomplished to protect the public from potential toxic release.

§417.409 System hazard controls.

(a) *General.* A launch operator must establish and maintain hazard controls for each system that presents a public hazard as identified by the ground safety analysis and satisfy the requirements of this section. A launch operator must:

(1) Ensure a system be at least single fault tolerant to creating a public hazard unless other hazard control criteria are specified for the system by the requirements of this part. A system capable of creating a catastrophic public hazard must be at least dual fault tolerant. Dual fault tolerant system hazard controls include: Switches, valves, or similar components that prevent an unwanted transfer or release of energy or hazardous materials;

(2) Ensure each hazard control used to provide fault tolerance is independent from other hazard controls so that no single action or event can remove more than one inhibit. A launch operator must prevent inadvertent activation of hazard control devices such as switches and valves;

(3) Provide at least two fully redundant safety devices if a safety device must function in order to control a public hazard. A single action or event must not be capable of disabling both safety devices; and

(4) Ensure computing systems and software used to control a public hazard satisfy the requirements of §417.123.

(b) *Structures and material handling equipment.* A launch operator must ensure safety factors applied in the design of a structure or material handling equipment account for static and dynamic loads, environmental stresses, expected wear, and duty cycles. A launch operator must:

(1) Inspect structures and material handling equipment to verify workmanship, proper operations, and maintenance;

(2) Prepare plans to ensure proper operations and maintenance of structures and material handling equipment;

(3) Assess structures and material handling equipment for potential single point failure;

(4) Eliminate single point failures from structures and material handling equipment or subject the structures and material handling equipment to specific inspection and testing to ensure proper operation. Single point failure welds must undergo both surface and volumetric non-destructive inspection to verify that no rejectable discontinuities exist;

(5) Establish other non-destructive inspection techniques if a volumetric inspection cannot be performed. A launch operator, in such a case, must demonstrate through the licensing process that the inspection processes used accurately verify the absence of rejectable discontinuities; and

(6) Ensure qualified and certified personnel, as defined in §417.105, conduct the inspections.

(c) *Pressure vessels and pressurized systems.* A launch operator must apply the following hazard controls to a pressurized flight or ground pressure vessel, component, or systems:

(1) Qualified and certified personnel, as defined in §417.105, must test each pressure vessel, component, or system upon installation and before being placed into service, and periodically inspect to ensure that no rejectable discontinuities exists;

(2) Safety factors applied in the design of a pressure vessel, component, or system must account for static and dynamic loads, environmental stresses, and expected wear;

(3) Pressurized system flow-paths, except for pressure relief and emergency venting, must be single fault tolerant to causing pressure ruptures and material releases during launch processing; and

(4) Provide pressure relief and emergency venting capability to protect against pressure ruptures. Pressure relief devices must provide the flow rate necessary to prevent a rupture in the event a pressure vessel is exposed to fire.

(d) *Electrical and mechanical systems.* A launch operator must apply the following hazard controls to electrical or mechanical systems that can release electrical or mechanical energy during launch processing:

(1) A launch operator must ensure electrical and mechanical systems, including systems that generate ionizing or non-ionizing radiation, are single fault tolerant to providing or releasing electrical or mechanical energy;

(2) In areas where flammable material exists, a launch operator must ensure electrical systems and equipment are hermetically sealed, explosion proof, intrinsically safe, purged, or otherwise designed so as not to provide an ignition source. A launch operator must assess each electrical system as a possible source of thermal energy and ensure that the electrical system can not act as an ignition source; and

(3) A launch operator must prevent unintentionally conducted or radiated energy due to possible bent pins in a connector, a mismated connector, shorted wires, or unshielded wires within electrical power and signal circuits that interface with hazardous subsystems.

(e) *Propulsion systems.* A propulsion system must be dual fault tolerant to inadvertently becoming propulsive. Propulsion systems must be single fault tolerant to inadvertent mixing of fuel and oxidizer. Each material in a propulsion system must be compatible with other materials that may contact the propulsion system during launch processing including materials used to assemble and clean the system. A launch operator must use engineering controls, including procedures, to prevent connecting incompatible systems. A launch operator must comply with §417.417 for hazard controls applicable to propellants and explosives.

(f) *Ordnance systems.* An ordnance system must be at least single fault tolerant to prevent a hazard caused by inadvertent actuation of the ordnance system. A launch operator must comply with §417.417 for hazard controls applicable to ordnance. In addition, an ordnance system must satisfy the following requirements;

(1) A launch operator must ensure ordnance electrical connections are disconnected until final preparations for flight;

(2) An ordnance system must provide for safing and arming of the ordnance. An electrically initiated ordnance system must include ordnance initiation devices and arming devices, also referred to as safe and arm devices, that provide a removable and replaceable mechanical barrier or other positive means of interrupting power to each ordnance firing circuit to prevent inadvertent initiation of ordnance. A mechanical safe and arm device must have a safing pin that locks the mechanical barrier in a safe position. A mechanical actuated ordnance device must also have a safing pin that prevents mechanical movement within the device. A launch operator must comply with section D417.13 of this part for specific safing and arming requirements for a flight termination system;

(3) Protect ordnance systems from stray energy through grounding, bonding, and shielding; and

(4) Current limit any monitoring or test circuitry that interfaces with an ordnance system to protect against inadvertent initiation of ordnance. Equipment used to measure bridgewire resistance on electro-explosive devices must be special purpose ordnance system instrumentation with features that limit current.

§417.411 Safety clear zones for hazardous operations.

(a) A launch operator must define a safety clear zone that confines the adverse effects of each operation involving a public hazard or launch location hazard. A launch operator's safety clear zones must satisfy the following:

(1) A launch operator must establish a safety clear zone that accounts for the potential blast, fragment, fire or heat, toxic and other hazardous energy or material potential of the associated systems and operations. A launch operator must base a safety clear zone on the following criteria:

(i) For a possible explosive event, base a safety clear zone on the worst case event, regardless of the fault tolerance of the system;

(ii) For a possible toxic event, base a safety clear zone on the worst case event. A launch operator must have procedures in place to maintain public safety in the event toxic releases reach beyond the safety clear zone; and

(iii) For a material handling operation, base a safety clear zone on a worst case event for that operation.

(2) A launch operator must establish a safety clear zone when the launch vehicle is in a launch command configuration with the flight safety systems fully operational and on internal power.

(b) A launch operator must establish restrictions that prohibit public access to a safety clear zone during a hazardous operation. A safety clear zone may extend to areas beyond the launch location boundaries if local agreements provide for restricting public access to such areas and a launch operator verifies that the safety clear zone is clear of the public during the hazardous operation.

(c) A launch operator's procedures must verify that the public is outside of a safety clear zone prior to a launch operator beginning a hazardous operation.

(d) A launch operator must control a safety clear zone to ensure no public access during the hazardous operation. Safety clear zone controls include:

(1) Use of security guards and equipment;

(2) Physical barriers; and

(3) Warning signs, and other types of warning devices.

§417.413 Hazard areas.

(a) *General.* A launch operator must define a hazard area that confines the adverse effects of a hardware system should an event occur that presents a public hazard or launch location hazard. A launch operator must prohibit public access to the hazard area whenever a hazard is present unless the requirements for public access of paragraph (b) of this section are met.

(b) *Public access.* A launch operator must establish a process for authorizing public access if visitors or members of the public must have access to a launch operator's facility or launch location. The process must ensure that each member of the public is briefed on the hazards within the facility and related safety warnings, procedures, and rules that provide protection, or a launch operator must ensure that each member of the public is accompanied by a knowledgeable escort.

(c) *Hazard controls during public access.* A launch operator must establish procedural controls that prevent hazardous operations from taking place while members of the public have access to the launch location and must verify that system hazard controls are in place that prevent initiation of a hazardous event. Hazard controls and procedures that prevent initiation of a hazardous event include the following:

(1) Use of lockout devices or other restraints on system actuation switches or other controls to eliminate the possibility of inadvertent actuation of a hazardous system.

(2) Disconnect ordnance systems from power sources, incorporate the use of safing plugs, or have safety devices in place that prevent inadvertent initiation. Activity involving the control circuitry of electrically activated safety devices must not be ongoing while the public has access to the hazard area. Install safing pins on safe and arm devices and mechanically actuated devices. Disconnect explosive transfer lines, not protected by a safe and arm device or a mechanically actuated device or equivalent.

(3) When systems or tanks are loaded with hypergols or other toxic materials, close the system or tank and verify it is leak-tight with two verifiable closures, such as a valve and a cap, to every external flow path or fitting. Such a system must also be in a steady-state condition.

(4) Keep each pressurized system below its maximum allowable working pressure and do not allow it to be in a dynamic state. Activity involving the control circuitry of electrically activated pressure system valves must not be ongoing while the public has access to the associated hazard area. Launch vehicle systems must not be pressurized to more than 25% of the system's design burst pressure, when the public has access to the associated hazard area.

(5) Do not allow sources of ionizing or non-ionizing radiation, such as, x-rays, nuclear power sources, high-energy radio transmitters, radar, and lasers to be present or verify they are to be inactive when the public has access to the associated hazard area.

(6) Guard physical hazards to prevent potential physical injury to visiting members of the public. Physical hazards include the following:

(i) Potential falling objects;

(ii) Falls from an elevated height; and

(iii) Protection from potentially hazardous vents, such as pressure relief discharge vents.

(7) Maintain and verify that safety devices or safety critical systems are operating properly prior to permitting public access.

§417.415 Post-launch and post-flight-attempt hazard controls.

(a) A launch operator must establish, maintain and perform procedures for controlling hazards and returning the launch facility to a safe condition after a successful launch. Procedural hazard controls must include:

(1) Provisions for extinguishing fires;

(2) Re-establishing full operational capability of safety devices, barriers, and platforms; and

(3) Access control.

(b) A launch operator must establish procedures for controlling hazards associated with a failed flight attempt where a solid or liquid launch vehicle engine start command was sent, but the launch vehicle did not liftoff. These procedures must include the following:

(1) Maintaining and verifying that each flight termination system remains operational until verification that the launch vehicle does not represent a risk of inadvertent liftoff. If an ignition signal has been sent to a solid rocket motor, the flight termination system must remain armed and active for a period of no less than 30 minutes. During this time, flight termination system batteries must maintain sufficient voltage and current capacity for flight termination system operation. The flight termination system receivers must remain captured by the command control system transmitter's carrier signal;

(2) Assuring that the vehicle is in a safe configuration, including its propulsion and ordnance systems. The flight safety system crew must have

access to the vehicle status. Re-establish safety devices and bring each pressurized system down to safe pressure levels; and

(3) Prohibiting launch complex entry until the launch pad area safing procedures are complete.

(c) A launch operator must establish procedural controls for hazards associated with an unsuccessful flight where the launch vehicle has a land or water impact. These procedures must include the following provisions:

(1) Evacuation and rescue of members of the public, to include modeling the dispersion and movement of toxic plumes, identification of areas at risk, and communication with local government authorities;

(2) Extinguishing fires;

(3) Securing impact areas to ensure that personnel and the public are evacuated, and ensure that no unauthorized personnel or members of the public enter, and to preserve evidence; and

(4) Ensuring public safety from hazardous debris, such as plans for recovery and salvage of launch vehicle debris and safe disposal of hazardous materials.

§ 417.417 Propellants and explosives.

(a) A launch operator must comply with the explosive safety criteria in part 420 of this chapter.

(b) A launch operator must ensure that:

(1) The explosive site plan satisfies part 420 of this chapter;

(2) Only those explosive facilities and launch points addressed in the explosive site plan are used and only for their intended purpose; and

(3) The total net explosive weight for each explosive hazard facility and launch point must not exceed the maximum net explosive weight limit indicated on the explosive site plan for each location.

(c) A launch operator must establish, maintain, and perform procedures that ensure public safety for the receipt, storage, handling, inspection, test, and disposal of explosives.

(d) A launch operator must establish and maintain each procedural system control to prevent inadvertent initiation of propellants and explosives. These controls must include the following:

(1) Protect ordnance systems from stray energy through methods of bonding, grounding, and shielding, and controlling radio frequency radiation sources in a radio frequency radiation exclusion area. A launch operator must determine the vulnerability of its electro-explosive devices and systems to radio frequency radiation and establish radio frequency radiation power limits or radio frequency radiation exclusion areas as required by the launch site operator or to ensure safety.

(2) Keep ordnance safety devices, as required by § 417.409, in place until the launch complex is cleared as part of the final launch countdown. No members of the public may re-enter the complex until each safety device is reestablished.

(3) Do not allow heat and spark or flame producing devices in an explosive or propellant facility without written approval and oversight from a launch operator's safety organization.

(4) Do not allow static producing materials in close proximity to solid or liquid propellants, electro-explosive devices, or systems containing flammable liquids.

(5) Use fire safety measures including:

(i) Elimination or reduction of flammable and combustible materials;

(ii) Elimination or reduction of ignition sources;

(iii) Fire and smoke detection systems;

(iv) Safe means of egress; and

(v) Timely fire suppression response.

(6) Include lightning protection on each facility used to store or process explosives to prevent inadvertent initiation of propellants and explosives due to lightning unless the facility complies with the lightning protection criteria of § 420.71 of this part.

(e) A launch operator, in the event of an emergency, must perform the accident investigation plan as defined in § 417.111(h).

APPENDIX A TO PART 417—FLIGHT SAFETY ANALYSIS METHODOLOGIES AND PRODUCTS FOR A LAUNCH VEHICLE FLOWN WITH A FLIGHT SAFETY SYSTEM

A417.1 SCOPE

The requirements of this appendix apply to the methods for performing the flight safety analysis required by §417.107(f) and subpart C of this part. The methodologies contained in this appendix provide an acceptable means of satisfying the requirements of subpart C and provide a standard and a measure of fidelity against which the FAA will measure any proposed alternative analysis approach. This appendix also identifies the analysis products that a launch operator must file with the FAA as required by §417.203(e).

A417.3 APPLICABILITY

The requirements of this appendix apply to a launch operator and the launch operator's flight safety analysis unless the launch operator clearly and convincingly demonstrates that an alternative approach provides an equivalent level of safety. If a Federal launch range performs the launch operator's analysis, §417.203(d) applies. Section A417.33 applies to the flight of any unguided suborbital launch vehicle that uses a wind-weighting safety system. All other sections of this appendix apply to the flight of any launch vehicle required to use a flight safety system as required by §417.107(a). For any alternative flight safety system approved by the FAA as required by §417.301(b), the FAA will determine the applicability of this appendix during the licensing process.

A417.5 GENERAL

A launch operator's flight safety analysis must satisfy the requirements for public risk management and the requirements for the compatibility of the input and output of dependent analyses of §417.205.

A417.7 TRAJECTORY

(a) *General.* A flight safety analysis must include a trajectory analysis that satisfies the requirements of §417.207. This section applies to the computation of each of the trajectories required by §417.207 and to each trajectory analysis product that a launch operator must file with the FAA as required by §417.203(e).

(b) *Wind standards.* A trajectory analysis must incorporate wind data in accordance with the following:

(1) For each launch, a trajectory analysis must produce "with-wind" launch vehicle trajectories pursuant to paragraph (f)(6) of this section and do so using composite wind profiles for the month that the launch will take place or composite wind profiles that are as severe or more severe than the winds for the month that the launch will take place.

(2) A composite wind profile used for the trajectory analysis must have a cumulative percentile frequency that represents wind conditions that are at least as severe as the worst wind conditions under which flight would be attempted for purposes of achieving the launch operator's mission. These worst wind conditions must account for the launch vehicle's ability to operate normally in the presence of wind and accommodate any flight safety limit constraints.

(c) *Nominal trajectory.* A trajectory analysis must produce a nominal trajectory that describes a launch vehicle's flight path, position and velocity, where all vehicle aerodynamic parameters are as expected, all vehicle internal and external systems perform exactly as planned, and no external perturbing influences other than atmospheric drag and gravity affect the launch vehicle.

(d) *Dispersed trajectories.* A trajectory analysis must produce the following dispersed trajectories and describe the distribution of a launch vehicle's position and velocity as a function of winds and performance error parameters in the uprange, downrange, left-crossrange and right-crossrange directions.

(1) *Three-sigma maximum and minimum performance trajectories.* A trajectory analysis must produce a three-sigma maximum performance trajectory that provides the maximum downrange distance of the instantaneous impact point for any given time after lift-off. A trajectory analysis must produce a three-sigma minimum performance trajectory that provides the minimum downrange distance of the instantaneous impact point for any given time after lift-off. For any time after lift-off, the instantaneous impact point dispersion of a normally performing launch vehicle must lie between the extremes achieved at that time after lift-off by the three-sigma maximum and three-sigma minimum performance trajectories. The three-sigma maximum and minimum performance trajectories must account for wind and performance error parameter distributions as follows:

(i) For each three-sigma maximum and minimum performance trajectory, the analysis must use composite head wind and composite tail wind profiles that represent the worst wind conditions under which a launch would be attempted as required by paragraph (b) of this section.

(ii) Each three-sigma maximum and minimum performance trajectory must account for all launch vehicle performance error parameters identified as required by paragraph (f)(1) of this section that have an effect upon instantaneous impact point range.

(2) *Three-sigma left and right lateral trajectories.* A trajectory analysis must produce a

three-sigma left lateral trajectory that provides the maximum left crossrange distance of the instantaneous impact point for any time after lift-off. A trajectory analysis must produce a three-sigma right lateral trajectory that provides the maximum right crossrange distance of the instantaneous impact point for any time after lift-off. For any time after lift-off, the instantaneous impact point dispersion of a normally performing launch vehicle must lie between the extremes achieved at that time after liftoff by the three-sigma left lateral and three-sigma right lateral performance trajectories. The three-sigma lateral performance trajectories must account for wind and performance error parameter distributions as follows:

(i) In producing each left and right lateral trajectory, the analysis must use composite left and composite right lateral-wind profiles that represent the worst wind conditions under which a launch would be attempted as required by paragraph (b) of this section.

(ii) The three-sigma left and right lateral trajectories must account for all launch vehicle performance error parameters identified as required by paragraph (f)(1) of this section that have an effect on the lateral deviation of the instantaneous impact point.

(3) *Fuel-exhaustion trajectory.* A trajectory analysis must produce a fuel-exhaustion trajectory for the launch of any launch vehicle with a final suborbital stage that will terminate thrust nominally without burning to fuel exhaustion. The analysis must produce the trajectory that would occur if the planned thrust termination of the final suborbital stage did not occur. The analysis must produce a fuel-exhaustion trajectory that extends either the nominal trajectory taken through fuel exhaustion of the last suborbital stage or the three-sigma maximum trajectory taken through fuel exhaustion of the last suborbital stage, whichever produces an instantaneous impact point with the greatest range for any time after liftoff.

(e) *Straight-up trajectory.* A trajectory analysis must produce a straight-up trajectory that begins at the planned time of ignition, and that simulates a malfunction that causes the launch vehicle to fly in a vertical or near vertical direction above the launch point. A straight up trajectory must last no less than the sum of the straight-up time determined as required by section A417.15 plus the duration of a potential malfunction turn determined as required by section A417.9(b)(2).

(f) *Analysis process and computations.* A trajectory analysis must produce each three-sigma trajectory required by this appendix using a six-degree-of-freedom trajectory model and an analysis method, such as root sum-square or Monte Carlo, that accounts for all individual launch vehicle performance error parameters that contribute to the dispersion of the launch vehicle's instantaneous impact point.

(1) A trajectory analysis must identify all launch vehicle performance error parameters and each parameter's distribution to account for all launch vehicle performance variations and any external forces that can cause offsets from the nominal trajectory during normal flight. A trajectory analysis must account for, but need not be limited to, the following performance error parameters:

(i) Thrust;

(ii) Thrust misalignment;

(iii) Specific impulse;

(iv) Weight;

(v) Variation in firing times of the stages;

(vi) Fuel flow rates;

(vii) Contributions from the guidance, navigation, and control systems;

(ix) Steering misalignment; and

(x) Winds.

(2) Each three-sigma trajectory must account for the effects of wind from liftoff through the point in flight where the launch vehicle attains an altitude where wind no longer affects the launch vehicle.

(g) *Trajectory analysis products.* The products of a trajectory analysis that a launch operator must file with the FAA include the following:

(1) *Assumptions and procedures.* A description of all assumptions, procedures and models, including the six-degrees-of-freedom model, used in deriving each trajectory.

(2) *Three-sigma launch vehicle performance error parameters.* A description of each three-sigma performance error parameter accounted for by the trajectory analysis and a description of each parameter's distribution determined as required by paragraph (f)(1) of this section.

(3) *Wind profile.* A graph and tabular listing of each wind profile used in performing the trajectory analysis as required by paragraph (b)(1) of this section and the worst case winds required by paragraph (b)(2) of this section. The graph and tabular wind data must provide wind magnitude and direction as a function of altitude for the air space regions from the Earth's surface to 100,000 feet in altitude for the area intersected by the launch vehicle trajectory. Altitude intervals must not exceed 5000 feet.

(4) *Launch azimuth.* The azimuthal direction of the trajectory's ''X-axis'' at liftoff measured clockwise in degrees from true north.

(5) *Launch point.* Identification and location of the proposed launch point, including its name, geodetic latitude, geodetic longitude, and geodetic height.

(6) *Reference ellipsoid.* The name of the reference ellipsoid used by the trajectory analysis to approximate the average curvature of the Earth and the following information about the model:

(i) Length of semi-major axis;

(ii) Length of semi-minor axis;

(iii) Flattening parameter;

(iv) Eccentricity;

(v) Gravitational parameter;

(vi) Angular velocity of the Earth at the equator; and

(vii) If the reference ellipsoid is not a WGS–84 ellipsoidal Earth model, the equations that convert the filed ellipsoid information to the WGS–84 ellipsoid.

(7) *Temporal trajectory items.* A launch operator must provide the following temporal trajectory data for time intervals not in excess of one second and for the discrete time points that correspond to each jettison, ignition, burnout, and thrust termination of each stage. If any stage burn time lasts less than four seconds, the time intervals must not exceed 0.2 seconds. The launch operator must provide the temporal trajectory data from launch up to a point in flight when effective thrust of the final stage terminates, or to thrust termination of the stage or burn that places the vehicle in orbit. For an unguided sub-orbital launch vehicle flown with a flight safety system, the launch operator must provide these data for each nominal quadrant launcher elevation angle and payload weight. The launch operator must provide these data on paper in text format and electronically in ASCII text, space delimited format. The launch operator must provide an electronic "read-me" file that identifies the data and their units of measure in the individual disk files.

(i) *Trajectory time-after-liftoff.* A launch operator must provide trajectory time-after liftoff measured from first motion of the first thrusting stage of the launch vehicle. The tabulated data must identify the first motion time as T–0 and as the "0.0" time point on the trajectory.

(ii) *Launch vehicle direction cosines.* A launch operator must provide the direction cosines of the roll axis, pitch axis, and yaw axis of the launch vehicle. The roll axis is a line identical to the launch vehicle's longitudinal axis with its origin at the nominal center of gravity positive towards the vehicle nose. The roll plane is normal to the roll axis at the vehicle's nominal center of gravity. The yaw axis and the pitch axis are any two orthogonal axes lying in the roll plane. The launch operator must provide roll, pitch and yaw axes of right-handed systems so that, when looking along the roll axis toward the nose, a clockwise rotation around the roll axis will send the pitch axis toward the yaw axis. The right-handed system must be oriented so that the yaw axis is positive in the downrange direction while in the vertical position (roll axis upward from surface) or positive at an angle of 180 degrees to the downrange direction. The axis may be related to the vehicle's normal orientation with respect to the vehicle's trajectory but, once defined, remain fixed with respect to the vehicle's body. The launch operator must indicate the positive direction of the yaw axis chosen. The analysis products must present the direction cosines using the EFG reference system described in paragraph (g)(7)(iv) of this section.

(iii) *X, Y, Z, XD, YD, ZD trajectory coordinates.* A launch operator must provide the launch vehicle position coordinates (X, Y, Z) and velocity magnitudes (XD, YD, ZD) referenced to an orthogonal, Earth-fixed, right-handed coordinate system. The XY plane must be tangent to the ellipsoidal Earth at the origin, which must coincide with the launch point. The positive X-axis must coincide with the launch azimuth. The positive Z-axis must be directed away from the ellipsoidal Earth. The Y-axis must be positive to the left looking downrange.

(iv) *E, F, G, ED, FD, GD trajectory coordinates.* A launch operator must provide the launch vehicle position coordinates (E, F, G) and velocity magnitudes (ED, FD, GD) referenced to an orthogonal, Earth fixed, Earth centered, right-handed coordinate system. The origin of the EFG system must be at the center of the reference ellipsoid. The E and F axes must lie in the plane of the equator and the G-axis coincides with the rotational axis of the Earth. The E-axis must be positive through 0° East longitude (Greenwich Meridian), the F-axis positive through 90' East longitude, and the G-axis positive through the North Pole. This system must be non-inertial and rotate with the Earth.

(v) *Resultant Earth-fixed velocity.* A launch operator must provide the square root of the sum of the squares of the XD, YD, and ZD components of the trajectory state vector.

(vi) *Path angle of velocity vector.* A launch operator must provide the angle between the local horizontal plane and the velocity vector measured positive upward from the local horizontal. The local horizontal must be a plane tangent to the ellipsoidal Earth at the sub-vehicle point.

(vii) *Sub-vehicle point.* A launch operator must provide sub-vehicle point coordinates that include present position geodetic latitude and present position longitude. These coordinates must be at each trajectory time on the surface of the ellipsoidal Earth model and located at the intersection of the line normal to the ellipsoid and passing through the launch vehicle center of gravity.

(viii) *Altitude.* A launch operator must provide the distance from the sub-vehicle point to the launch vehicle's center of gravity.

(ix) *Present position arc-range.* A launch operator must provide the distance measured along the surface of the reference ellipsoid, from the launch point to the sub-vehicle point.

(x) *Total weight.* A launch operator must provide the sum of the inert and propellant weights for each time point on the trajectory.

(xi) *Total vacuum thrust.* A launch operator must provide the total vacuum thrust for each time point on the trajectory.

(xii) *Instantaneous impact point data.* A launch operator must provide instantaneous impact point geodetic latitude, instantaneous impact point longitude, instantaneous impact point arc-range, and time to instantaneous impact. The instantaneous impact point arc-range must consist of the distance, measured along the surface of the reference ellipsoid, from the launch point to the instantaneous impact point. For each point on the trajectory, the time to instantaneous impact must consist of the vacuum flight time remaining until impact if all thrust were terminated at the time point on the trajectory.

(xiii) *Normal trajectory distribution.* A launch operator must provide a description of the distribution of the dispersed trajectories required under paragraph (d) of this section, such as the elements of covariance matrices for the launch vehicle position coordinates and velocity component magnitudes.

A417.9 MALFUNCTION TURN

(a) *General.* A flight safety analysis must include a malfunction turn analysis that satisfies the requirements of §417.209. This section applies to the computation of the malfunction turns and the production of turn data required by §417.209 and to the malfunction turn analysis products that a launch operator must file with the FAA as required by §417.203(e).

(b) *Malfunction turn analysis constraints.* The following constraints apply to a malfunction turn analysis:

(1) The analysis must produce malfunction turns that start at a given malfunction start time. The turn must last no less than 12 seconds. These duration limits apply regardless of whether or not the vehicle would breakup or tumble before the prescribed duration of the turn.

(2) A malfunction turn analysis must account for the thrusting periods of flight along a nominal trajectory beginning at first motion until thrust termination of the final thrusting stage or until the launch vehicle achieves orbit, whichever occurs first.

(3) A malfunction turn must consist of a 90-degree turn or a turn in both the pitch and yaw planes that would produce the largest deviation from the nominal instantaneous impact point of which the launch vehicle is capable at any time during the malfunction turn as required by paragraph (d) of this section.

(4) The first malfunction turn must start at liftoff. The analysis must account for subsequent malfunction turns initiated at regular nominal trajectory time intervals not to exceed four seconds.

(5) A malfunction turn analysis must produce malfunction turn data for time intervals of no less than one second over the duration of each malfunction turn.

(6) The analysis must assume that the launch vehicle performance is nominal up to the point of the malfunction that produces the turn.

(7) A malfunction turn analysis must not account for the effects of gravity.

(8) A malfunction turn analysis must ensure the tumble turn envelope curve maintains a positive slope throughout the malfunction turn duration as illustrated in figure A417.9–1. When calculating a tumble turn for an aerodynamically unstable launch vehicle, in the high aerodynamic region it often turns out that no matter how small the initial deflection of the rocket engine, the airframe tumbles through 180 degrees, or one-half cycle, in less time than the required turn duration period. In such a case, the analysis must use a 90-degree turn as the malfunction turn.

(c) *Failure modes.* A malfunction turn analysis must account for the significant failure modes that result in a thrust vector offset from the nominal state. If a malfunction turn at a malfunction start time can occur as a function of more than one failure mode, the analysis must account for the failure mode that causes the most rapid and largest launch vehicle instantaneous impact point deviation.

(d) *Type of malfunction turn.* A malfunction turn analysis must establish the maximum turning capability of a launch vehicle's velocity vector during each malfunction turn by accounting for a 90-degree turn to estimate the vehicle's turning capability or by accounting for trim turns and tumble turns in both the pitch and yaw planes to establish the vehicle's turning capability. When establishing the turning capability of a launch vehicle's velocity vector, the analysis must account for each turn as follows:

(1) *90-degree turn.* A 90-degree turn must constitute a turn produced at the malfunction start time by instantaneously re-directing and maintaining the vehicle's thrust at 90 degrees to the velocity vector, without regard for how this situation can be brought about.

(2) *Pitch turn.* A pitch turn must constitute the angle turned by the launch vehicle's total velocity vector in the pitch-plane. The velocity vector's pitch-plane must be the two dimensional surface that includes the launch vehicle's yaw-axis and the launch vehicle's roll-axis.

(3) *Yaw turn.* A yaw turn must constitute the angle turned by the launch vehicle's total velocity vector in the lateral plane. The velocity vector's lateral plane must be the two dimensional surface that includes the launch vehicle's pitch axis and the launch vehicle's total velocity.

(4) *Trim turn.* A trim turn must constitute a turn where a launch vehicle's thrust moment balances the aerodynamic moment while a constant rotation rate is imparted to the launch vehicle's longitudinal axis. The analysis must account for a maximum-rate trim turn made at or near the greatest angle of attack that can be maintained while the aerodynamic moment is balanced by the thrust moment, whether the vehicle is stable or unstable.

(5) *Tumble turn.* A tumble turn must constitute a turn that results if the launch vehicle's airframe rotates in an uncontrolled fashion, at an angular rate that is brought about by a thrust vector offset angle, and if the offset angle is held constant throughout the turn. The analysis must account for a series of tumble turns, each turn with a different thrust vector offset angle, that are plotted on the same graph for each malfunction start time.

(6) *Turn envelope.* A turn envelope must constitute a curve on a tumble turn graph that has tangent points to each individual tumble turn curve computed for each malfunction start time. The curve must envelope the actual tumble turn curves to predict tumble turn angles for each area between the calculated turn curves. Figure A417.9–1 depicts a series of tumble turn curves and the tumble turn envelope curve.

(7) *Malfunction turn capabilities.* When not using a 90-degree turn, a malfunction turn analysis must establish the launch vehicle maximum turning capability as required by the following malfunction turn constraints:

(i) *Launch vehicle stable at all angles of attack.* If a launch vehicle is so stable that the maximum thrust moment that the vehicle could experience cannot produce tumbling, but produces a maximum-rate trim turn at some angle of attack less than 90 degrees, the analysis must produce a series of trim turns, including the maximum-rate trim turn, by varying the initial thrust vector offset at the beginning of the turn. If the maximum thrust moment results in a maximum-rate trim turn at some angle of attack greater than 90 degrees, the analysis must produce a series of trim turns for angles of attack up to and including 90 degrees.

(ii) *Launch vehicle aerodynamically unstable at all angles of attack.* If flying a trim turn is not possible even for a period of only a few seconds, the malfunction turn analysis need only establish tumble turns. Otherwise, the malfunction turn analysis must establish a series of trim turns, including the maximum-rate trim turn, and the family of tumble turns.

(iii) *Launch vehicle unstable at low angles of attack but stable at some higher angles of attack.* If large engine deflections result in tumbling, and small engine deflections do not, the analysis must produce a series of trim and tumble turns as required by paragraph (d)(7)(ii) of this section for launch vehicles aerodynamically unstable at all angles of attack. If both large and small constant engine deflections result in tumbling, regardless of how small the deflection might be, the analysis must account for the malfunction turn capabilities achieved at the stability angle of attack, assuming no upsetting thrust moment, and must account for the turns achieved by a tumbling vehicle.

(e) *Malfunction turn analysis products.* The products of a malfunction turn analysis that a launch operator must file with the FAA include:

(1) A description of the assumptions, techniques, and equations used in deriving the malfunction turns.

(2) A set of sample calculations for at least one flight hazard area malfunction start time and one downrange malfunction start time. The sample computation for the downrange malfunction must start at a time at least 50 seconds after the flight hazard area malfunction start time or at the time of nominal thrust termination of the final stage minus the malfunction turn duration.

(3) A launch operator must file malfunction turn data in electronic tabular and graphic formats. The graphs must use scale factors such that the plotting and reading accuracy do not degrade the accuracy of the data. For each malfunction turn start time, a graph must use the same time scales for the malfunction velocity vector turn angle and malfunction velocity magnitude plot pairs. A launch operator must provide tabular listings of the data used to generate the graphs in digital ASCII file format. A launch operator must file the data items required in this paragraph for each malfunction start time and for time intervals that do not exceed one second for the duration of each malfunction turn.

(i) *Velocity turn angle graphs.* A launch operator must file a velocity turn angle graph for each malfunction start time. For each velocity turn angle graph, the ordinate axis must represent the total angle turned by the velocity vector, and the abscissa axis must represent the time duration of the turn and must show increments not to exceed one second. The series of tumble turns must include the envelope of all tumble turn curves. The tumble turn envelope must represent the tumble turn capability for all possible constant thrust vector offset angles. Each tumble turn curve selected to define the envelope must appear on the same graph as the envelope. A launch operator must file a series of trim turn curves for representative values of thrust vector offset. The series of trim turn curves must include the maximum rate trim turn. Figure A417.9–1 depicts an example family of tumble turn curves and the tumble turn velocity vector envelope.

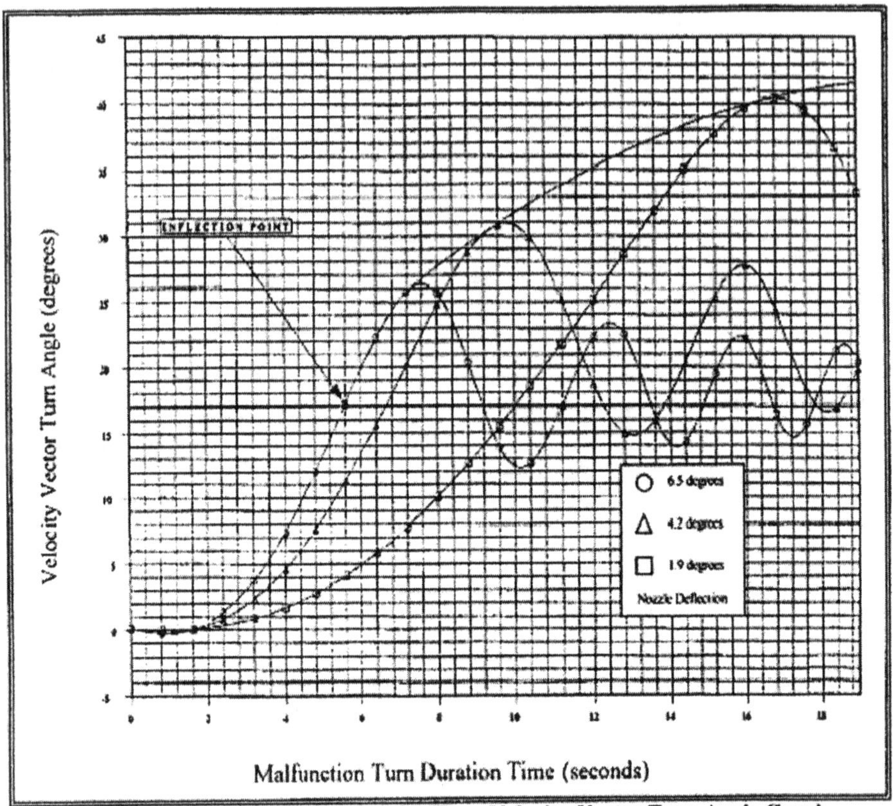

Figure A417.9-1, Example Tumble Turn Velocity Vector Turn Angle Graph.

(ii) *Velocity magnitude graphs.* A launch operator must file a velocity magnitude graph for each malfunction start time. For each malfunction velocity magnitude graph, the ordinate axis must represent the magnitude of the velocity vector and the abscissa axis must represent the time duration of the turn. Each graph must show the abscissa divided into increments not to exceed one second. Each graph must show the total velocity magnitude plotted as a function of time starting with the malfunction start time for each thrust vector offset used to define the corresponding velocity turn-angle curve. A launch operator must provide a corresponding velocity magnitude curve for each velocity tumble turn angle curve and each velocity trim-turn angle curve. For each individual tumble turn curve selected to define the tumble turn envelope, the corresponding velocity magnitude graph must show the individual tumble turn curve's point of tangency to the envelope. The point of tangency must consist of the point where the tumble turn envelope is tangent to an individual tumble turn curve produced with a discrete thrust vector offset angle. A launch operator must transpose the points of tangency to the velocity magnitude curves by plotting a point on the velocity magnitude curve at the same time point where tangency occurs on the corresponding velocity tumble-turn angle curve. Figure A417.9–2 depicts an example tumble turn velocity magnitude curve.

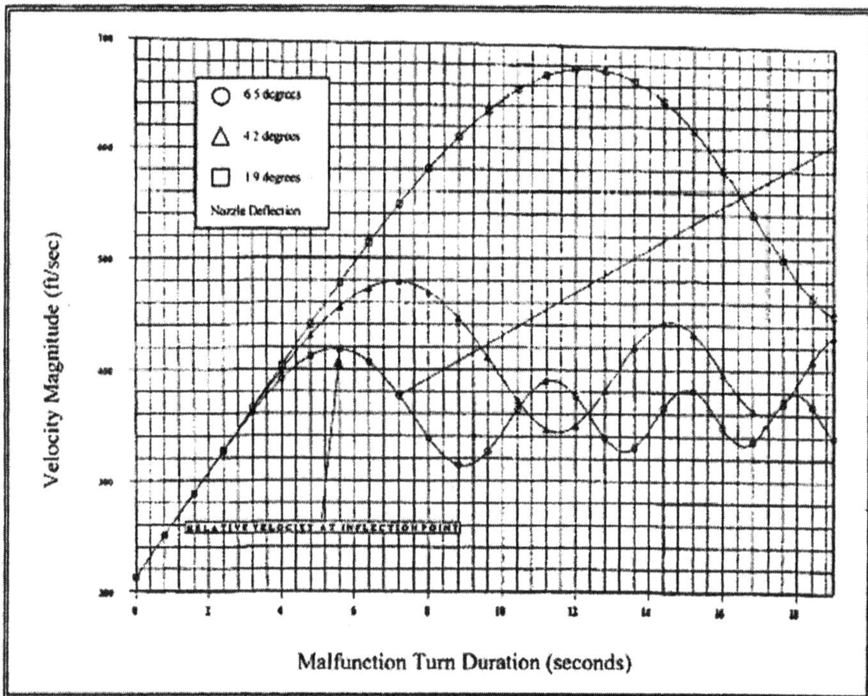

Figure A417.9-2, Illustrative Tumble Turn Velocity Magnitude Graph.

(iii) *Vehicle orientation.* The launch operator must file tabular or graphical data for the vehicle orientation in the form of roll, pitch, and yaw angular orientation of the vehicle longitudinal axis as a function of time into the turn for each turn initiation time. Angular orientation of a launch vehicle's longitudinal axis is illustrated in figures A417.9–3 and A417.9–4.

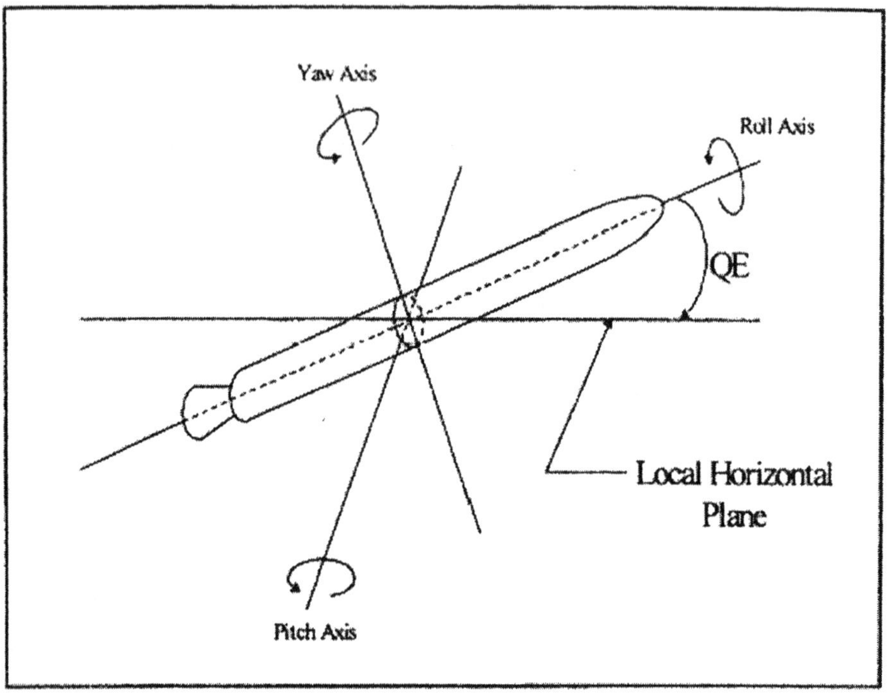

Figure A417.9-3, Illustrative Longitudinal Axis Quadrant Elevation (QE)

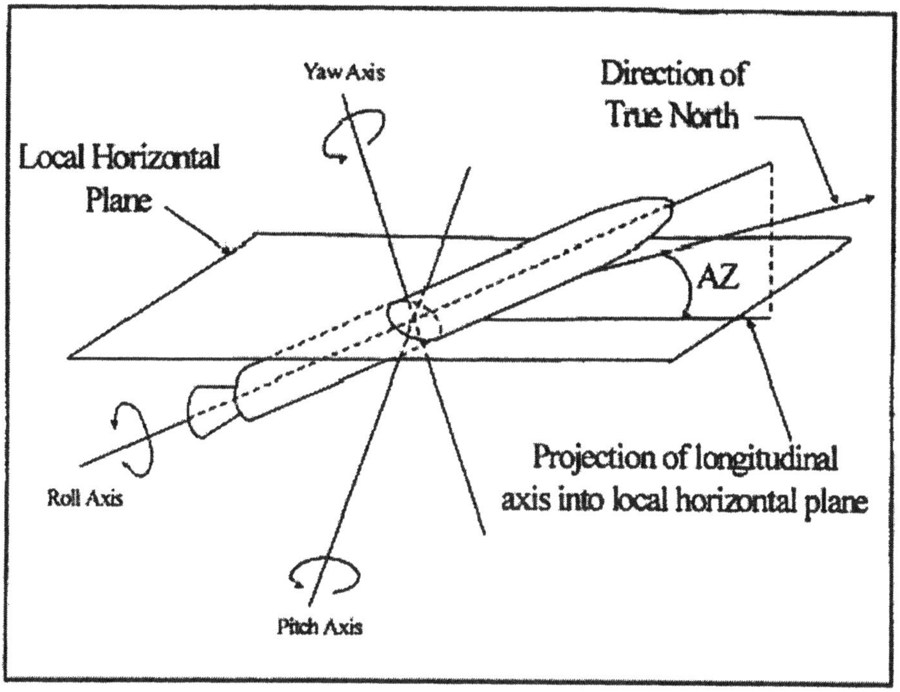

Figure A417.9-4, Illustrative Longitudinal Axis Azimuth (AZ)

(iv) *Onset conditions.* A launch operator must provide launch vehicle state information for each malfunction start time. This state data must include the launch vehicle thrust, weight, velocity magnitude and pad-centered topocentric X, Y, Z, XD, YD, ZD state vector.

(v) *Breakup information.* A launch operator must specify whether its launch vehicle will remain intact throughout each malfunction turn. If the launch vehicle will break up during a turn, the launch operator must identify the time for launch vehicle breakup on each velocity magnitude graph. The launch operator must show the time into the turn at which vehicle breakup would occur as either a specific value or a probability distribution for time until breakup.

(vi) *Inflection point.* A launch operator must identify the inflection point on each tumble turn envelope curve and maximum rate trim turn curve for each malfunction start time as illustrated in figure A417.9–1. The inflection point marks the point in time during the turn where the slope of the curve stops increasing and begins to decrease or, in other words, the point were the concavity of the curve changes from concave up to concave down. The inflection point on a malfunction turn curve must identify the time in the malfunction turn that the launch vehicle body achieves a 90-degree rotation from the nominal position. On a tumble turn curve the inflection point must represent the start of the launch vehicle tumble.

A417.11 DEBRIS

(a) *General.* A flight safety analysis must include a debris analysis that satisfies the requirements of § 417.211. This section applies to the debris data required by § 417.211 and the debris analysis products that a launch operator must file with the FAA as required by § 417.203(e).

(b) *Debris analysis constraints.* A debris analysis must produce the debris model described in paragraph (c) of this section. The analysis must account for all launch vehicle debris fragments, individually or in groupings of fragments called classes. The characteristics of each debris fragment represented by a class must be similar enough to the characteristics of all the other debris fragments represented by that class that all the debris fragments of the class can be described by a single set of characteristics. Paragraph (c)(10) of this section applies when establishing a debris class. A debris model must describe the physical, aerodynamic, and harmful characteristics of each debris fragment either individually or as a member of a class. A debris model must consist of lists of individual debris or debris classes for each cause of breakup and any planned jettison of debris, launch vehicle components, or payload. A debris analysis must account for:

(1) Launch vehicle breakup caused by the activation of any flight termination system. The analysis must account for:

(i) The effects of debris produced when flight termination system activation destroys an intact malfunctioning vehicle.

(ii) Spontaneous breakup of the launch vehicle, if the breakup is assisted by the action of any inadvertent separation destruct system.

(iii) The effects of debris produced by the activation of any flight termination system after inadvertent breakup of the launch vehicle.

(2) Debris due to any malfunction where forces on the launch vehicle may exceed the launch vehicle's structural integrity limits.

(3) The immediate post-breakup or jettison environment of the launch vehicle debris, and any change in debris characteristics over time from launch vehicle breakup or jettison until debris impact.

(4) The impact overpressure, fragmentation, and secondary debris effects of any confined or unconfined solid propellant chunks and fueled components containing either liquid or solid propellants that could survive to impact, as a function of vehicle malfunction time.

(5) The effects of impact of the intact vehicle as a function of failure time. The intact impact debris analysis must identify the trinitrotoluene (TNT) yield of impact explosions, and the numbers of fragments projected from all such explosions, including non-launch vehicle ejecta and the blast overpressure radius. The analysis must use a model for TNT yield of impact explosion that accounts for the propellant weight at impact, the impact speed, the orientation of the propellant, and the impacted surface material.

(c) *Debris model.* A debris analysis must produce a model of the debris resulting from planned jettison and from unplanned breakup of a launch vehicle for use as input to other analyses, such as establishing flight safety limits and hazard areas and performing debris risk, toxic, and blast analyses. A launch operator's debris model must satisfy the following:

(1) *Debris fragments.* A debris model must provide the debris fragment data required by this section for the launch vehicle flight from the planned ignition time until the launch vehicle achieves orbital velocity for an orbital launch. For a sub-orbital launch, the debris model must provide the debris fragment data required by this section for the launch vehicle flight from the planned ignition time until impact of the last thrusting stage. A debris model must provide debris fragment data for the number of time periods sufficient to meet the requirements for smooth and continuous contours used to define hazard areas as required by section A417.23.

(2) *Inert fragments.* A debris model must identify all inert fragments that are not volatile and that do not burn or explode under normal and malfunction conditions. A debris model must identify all inert fragments for each breakup time during flight corresponding to a critical event when the fragment catalog is significantly changed by the event. Critical events include staging, payload fairing jettison, and other normal hardware jettison activities.

(3) *Explosive and non-explosive propellant fragments.* A debris model must identify all propellant fragments that are explosive or non-explosive upon impact. The debris model must describe each propellant fragment as a function of time, from the time of breakup through ballistic free-fall to impact. The debris model must describe the characteristics of each fragment, including its origin on the launch vehicle, representative dimensions and weight at the time of breakup and at the time of impact. For any fragment identified as an un-contained or contained propellant fragment, whether explosive or non-explosive, the debris model must identify whether or not it burns during free fall, and provide the consumption rate during free fall. The debris model must identify:

(i) Solid propellant that is exposed directly to the atmosphere and that burns but does not explode upon impact as "un-contained non-explosive solid propellant."

(ii) Solid or liquid propellant that is enclosed in a container, such as a motor case or pressure vessel, and that burns but does not explode upon impact as "contained non-explosive propellant."

(iii) Solid or liquid propellant that is enclosed in a container, such as a motor case or pressure vessel, and that explodes upon impact as "contained explosive propellant fragment."

(iv) Solid propellant that is exposed directly to the atmosphere and that explodes upon impact as "un-contained explosive solid propellant fragment."

(4) *Other non-inert debris fragments.* In addition to the explosive and flammable fragments required by paragraph (c)(3) of this section, a debris model must identify any other non-inert debris fragments, such as toxic or radioactive fragments, that present any other hazards to the public.

(5) *Fragment weight.* At each modeled breakup time, the individual fragment weights must approximately add up to the

sum total weight of inert material in the vehicle and the weight of contained liquid propellants and solid propellants that are not consumed in the initial breakup or conflagration.

(6) *Fragment imparted velocity.* A debris model must identify the maximum velocity imparted to each fragment due to potential explosion or pressure rupture. When accounting for imparted velocity, a debris model must:

(i) Use a Maxwellian distribution with the specified maximum value equal to the 97th percentile; or

(ii) Identify the distribution, and must state whether or not the specified maximum value is a fixed value with no uncertainty.

(7) *Fragment projected area.* A debris model must include each of the axial, transverse, and mean tumbling areas of each fragment. If the fragment may stabilize under normal or malfunction conditions, the debris model must also provide the projected area normal to the drag force.

(8) *Fragment ballistic coefficient.* A debris model must include the axial, transverse, and tumble orientation ballistic coefficient for each fragment's projected area as required by paragraph (c)(7) of this section.

(9) *Debris fragment count.* A debris model must include the total number of each type of fragment required by paragraphs (c)(2), (c)(3), and (c)(4) of this section and created by a malfunction.

(10) *Fragment classes.* A debris model must categorize each malfunction debris fragment into classes where the characteristics of the mean fragment in each class conservatively represent every fragment in the class. The model must define fragment classes for fragments whose characteristics are similar enough to be described and treated by a single average set of characteristics. A debris class must categorize debris by each of the following characteristics, and may include any other useful characteristics:

(i) The type of fragment, defined by paragraphs (c)(2), (c)(3), and (c)(4) of this section. All fragments within a class must be the same type, such as inert or explosive.

(ii) Debris subsonic ballistic coefficient (β_{sub}). The difference between the smallest $\log10(\beta_{sub})$ value and the largest $\log10(\beta_{sub})$ value in a class must not exceed 0.5, except for fragments with β_{sub} less than or equal to three. Fragments with β_{sub} less than or equal to three may be grouped within a class.

(iii) Breakup-imparted velocity (ΔV). A debris model must categorize fragments as a function of the range of ΔV for the fragments within a class and the class's median subsonic ballistic coefficient. For each class, the debris model must keep the ratio of the maximum breakup-imparted velocity (ΔV_{max}) to minimum breakup-imparted velocity (ΔV_{min}) within the following bound:

$$\frac{\Delta V_{max}}{\Delta V_{min}} < \frac{5}{2 + \log_{10}(\beta'_{sub})}$$

Where: β'_{sub} is the median subsonic ballistic coefficient for the fragments in a class.

(d) *Debris analysis products.* The products of a debris analysis that a launch operator must file with the FAA include:

(1) *Debris model.* The launch operator's debris model that satisfies the requirements of this section.

(2) *Fragment description.* A description of the fragments contained in the launch operator's debris model. The description must identify the fragment as a launch vehicle part or component, describe its shape, representative dimensions, and may include drawings of the fragment.

(3) *Intact impact TNT yield.* For an intact impact of a launch vehicle, for each failure time, a launch operator must identify the TNT yield of each impact explosion and blast overpressure hazard radius.

(4) *Fragment class data.* The class name, the range of values for each parameter used to categorize fragments within a fragment class, and the number of fragments in any fragment class established as required by paragraph (c)(10) of this section.

(5) *Ballistic coefficient.* The mean ballistic coefficient (β) and plus and minus three-sigma values of the β for each fragment class. A launch operator must provide graphs of the coefficient of drag (C_d) as a function of Mach number for the nominal and three-sigma β variations for each fragment shape. The launch operator must label each graph with the shape represented by the curve and reference area used to develop the curve. A launch operator must provide a C_d vs. Mach curve for any axial, transverse, and tumble orientations for any fragment that will not stabilize during free-fall conditions. For any fragment that may stabilize during free-fall, a launch operator must provide C_d vs. Mach curves for the stability angle of attack. If the angle of attack where the fragment stabilizes is other than zero degrees, a launch operator must provide both the coefficient of lift (C_L) vs. Mach number and the C_d vs. Mach number curves. The launch operator must provide the equations for each C_d vs. Mach curve.

(6) *Pre-flight propellant weight.* The initial preflight weight of solid and liquid propellant for each launch vehicle component that contains solid or liquid propellant.

(7) *Normal propellant consumption.* The nominal and plus and minus three-sigma solid and liquid propellant consumption rate, and pre-malfunction consumption rate for each component that contains solid or liquid propellant.

(8) *Fragment weight.* The mean and plus and minus three-sigma weight of each fragment or fragment class.

(9) *Projected area.* The mean and plus and minus three-sigma axial, transverse, and tumbling areas for each fragment or fragment class. This information is not required for those fragment classes classified as burning propellant classes under section A417.25(b)(8).

(10) *Imparted velocities.* The maximum incremental velocity imparted to each fragment class created by flight termination system activation, or explosive or overpressure loads at breakup. The launch operator must identify the velocity distribution as Maxwellian or must define the distribution, including whether or not the specified maximum value is a fixed value with no uncertainty.

(11) *Fragment type.* The fragment type for each fragment established as required by paragraphs (c)(2), (c)(3), and (c)(4) of this section.

(12) *Origin.* The part of the launch vehicle from which each fragment originated.

(13) *Burning propellant classes.* The propellant consumption rate for those fragments that burn during free-fall.

(14) *Contained propellant fragments, explosive or non-explosive.* For contained propellant fragments, whether explosive or non-explosive, a launch operator must provide the initial weight of contained propellant and the consumption rate during free-fall. The initial weight of the propellant in a contained propellant fragment is the weight of the propellant before any of the propellant is consumed by normal vehicle operation or failure of the launch vehicle.

(15) *Solid propellant fragment snuff-out pressure.* The ambient pressure and the pressure at the surface of a solid propellant fragment, in pounds per square inch, required to sustain a solid propellant fragment's combustion during free-fall.

(16) *Other non-inert debris fragments.* For each non-inert debris fragment identified as required by paragraph (c)(4) of this section, a launch operator must describe the diffusion, dispersion, deposition, radiation, and other hazard exposure characteristics used to determine the effective casualty area required by paragraph (d)(10) of this section.

(17) *Residual thrust dispersion.* For each thrusting or non-thrusting stage having residual thrust capability following a launch vehicle malfunction, a launch operator must provide either the total residual impulse imparted or the full-residual thrust as a function of breakup time. For any stage not capable of thrust after a launch vehicle malfunction, a launch operator must provide the conditions under which the stage is no longer capable of thrust. For each stage that can be ignited as a result of a launch vehicle malfunction on a lower stage, a launch operator must identify the effects and duration of the potential thrust, and the maximum deviation of the instantaneous impact point, which can be brought about by the thrust. A launch operator must provide the explosion effects of all remaining fuels, pressurized tanks, and remaining stages, particularly with respect to ignition or detonation of upper stages if the flight termination system is activated during the burning period of a lower stage.

A417.13 FLIGHT SAFETY LIMITS.

(a) *General.* A flight safety analysis must include a flight safety limits analysis that satisfies the requirements of § 417.213. This section applies to the computation of the flight safety limits and identifying the location of populated or other protected areas as required by § 417.213 and to the analysis products that the launch operator must file with the FAA as required by § 417.203(e).

(b) *Flight safety limits constraints.* The analysis must establish flight safety limits as follows:

(1) Flight safety limits must account for potential malfunction of a launch vehicle during the time from launch vehicle first motion through flight until the planned safe flight state determined as required by section A417.19.

(2) For a flight termination at any time during launch vehicle flight, the impact limit lines must:

(i) Represent no less than the extent of the debris impact dispersion for all debris fragments with a ballistic coefficient greater than or equal to three; and

(ii) Ensure that the debris impact area on the Earth's surface that is bounded by the debris impact dispersion in the uprange, downrange and crossrange directions does not extend to any populated or other protected area.

(3) Each debris impact area determined by a flight safety limits analysis must be offset in a direction away from populated or other protected areas. The size of the offset must account for all parameters that may contribute to the impact dispersion. The parameters must include:

(i) Launch vehicle malfunction turn capabilities.

(ii) Effective casualty area produced as required by section A417.25(b)(8).

(iii) All delays in the identification of a launch vehicle malfunction.

(iv) Malfunction imparted velocities, including any velocity imparted to vehicle fragments by breakup.

(v) Wind effects on the malfunctioning vehicle and falling debris.

(vi) Residual thrust remaining after flight termination.

(vii) Launch vehicle guidance and performance errors.

(viii) Lift and drag forces on the malfunctioning vehicle and falling debris including variations in drag predictions of fragments and debris.

(ix) All hardware and software delays during implementation of flight termination.

(x) All debris impact location uncertainties caused by conditions prior to, and after, activation of the flight termination system.

(xi) Any other impact dispersion parameters peculiar to the launch vehicle.

(xii) All uncertainty due to map error and launch vehicle tracking error.

(c) *Risk management.* The requirements for public risk management of § 417.205(a) apply to a flight safety limits analysis. When employing risk assessment, the analysis must establish flight safety limits that satisfy paragraph (b) of this section, account for the products of the debris risk analysis performed as required by section A417.25, and ensure that any risk to the public satisfies the public risk criteria of § 417.107(b). When employing hazard isolation, the analysis must establish flight safety limits in accordance with the following:

(1) The flight safety limits must account for the maximum deviation impact locations for the most wind sensitive debris fragment with a minimum of 11 ft-lbs of kinetic energy at impact.

(2) The maximum deviation impact location of the debris identified in paragraph (c)(1) of this section for each trajectory time must account for the three-sigma impact location for the maximum deviation flight, and the launch day wind conditions that produce the maximum ballistic wind for that debris.

(3) The maximum deviation flight must account for the instantaneous impact point, of the debris identified in paragraph (c)(1) of this section at breakup, that is closest to a protected area and the maximum ballistic wind directed from the breakup point toward that protected area.

(d) *Flight safety limits analysis products.* The products of a flight safety limits analysis that a launch operator must file with the FAA include:

(1) A description of each method used to develop and implement the flight safety limits. The description must include equations and example computations used in the flight safety limits analysis.

(2) A description of how each analysis method meets the analysis requirements and constraints of this section, including how the method produces a worst-case scenario for each impact dispersion area.

(3) A description of how the results of the analysis are used to protect populated and other protected areas.

(4) A graphic depiction or series of depictions of the flight safety limits, the launch point, all launch site boundaries, surrounding geographic area, all protected area boundaries, and the nominal and three-sigma launch vehicle instantaneous impact point ground traces from liftoff to orbital insertion or the end of flight. Each depiction must have labeled geodetic latitude and longitude lines. Each depiction must show the flight safety limits at trajectory time intervals sufficient to depict the mission success margin between the flight safety limits and the protected areas. The launch vehicle trajectory instantaneous impact points must be plotted with sufficient frequency to provide a conformal representation of the launch vehicle's instantaneous impact point ground trace curvature.

(5) A tabular description of the flight safety limits, including the geodetic latitude and longitude for any flight safety limit. The table must contain quantitative values that define flight safety limits. Each quantitative value must be rounded to the number of significant digits that can be determined from the uncertainty of the measurement device used to determine the flight safety limits and must be limited to a maximum of six decimal places.

(6) A map error table of direction and scale distortions as a function of distance from the point of tangency from a parallel of true scale and true direction or from a meridian of true scale and true direction. A launch operator must provide a table of tracking error as a function of downrange distance from the launch point for each tracking station used to make flight safety control decisions. A launch operator must file a description of the method, showing equations and sample calculations, used to determine the tracking error. The table must contain the map and tracking error data points within 100 nautical miles of the reference point at an interval of one data point every 10 nautical miles, including the reference point. The table must contain map and tracking error data points beyond 100 nautical miles from the reference point at an interval of one data point every 100 nautical miles out to a distance that includes all populated or other areas protected by the flight safety limits.

(7) A launch operator must provide the equations used for geodetic datum conversions and one sample calculation for converting the geodetic latitude and longitude coordinates between the datum ellipsoids used. A launch operator must provide any equations used for range and bearing computations between geodetic coordinates and one sample calculation.

A417.15 STRAIGHT-UP TIME

(a) *General.* A flight safety analysis must include a straight-up time analysis that satisfies the requirements of § 417.215. This section applies to the computation of straight-up time as required by § 417.215 and to the analysis products that the launch operator must file with the FAA as required by

§417.203(e). The analysis must establish a straight-up time as the latest time-after-liftoff, assuming a launch vehicle malfunctioned and flew in a vertical or near vertical direction above the launch point, at which activation of the launch vehicle's flight termination system or breakup of the launch vehicle would not cause hazardous debris or critical overpressure to affect any populated or other protected area.

(b) *Straight-up time constraints.* A straight-up time analysis must account for the following:

(1) Launch vehicle trajectory. The analysis must use the straight-up trajectory determined as required by section A417.7(e).

(2) Sources of debris impact dispersion. The analysis must use the sources described in section A417.13(b)(3)(iii) through (xii).

(c) *Straight-up time analysis products.* The products of a straight-up-time analysis that a launch operator must file with the FAA include:

(1) The straight-up-time.

(2) A description of the methodology used to determine straight-up time.

A417.17 OVERFLIGHT GATE

(a) *General.* The flight safety analysis for a launch that involves flight over a populated or other protected area must include an overflight gate analysis that satisfies the requirements of §417.217. This section applies to determining a gate as required by §417.217 and the analysis products that the launch operator must file with the FAA as required by §417.203(e). The analysis must determine the portion, referred to as a gate, of a flight safety limit, through which a launch vehicle's tracking representation will be allowed to proceed without flight termination.

(b) *Overflight gate analysis constraints.* The following analysis constraints apply to a gate analysis.

(1) For each gate in a flight safety limit, all the criteria used for determining whether to allow passage through the gate or to terminate flight at the gate must use all the same launch vehicle flight status parameters as the criteria used for determining whether to terminate flight at a flight safety limit. For example, if the flight safety limits are a function of instantaneous impact point location, the criteria for determining whether to allow passage through a gate in the flight safety limit must also be a function of instantaneous impact point location. Likewise, if the flight safety limits are a function of drag impact point, the gate criteria must also be a function of drag impact point.

(2) When establishing a gate in a flight safety limit, the analysis must ensure that the launch vehicle flight satisfies the flight safety requirements of §417.107.

(3) For each established gate, the analysis must account for:

(i) All launch vehicle tracking and map errors.

(ii) All launch vehicle plus and minus three-sigma trajectory limits.

(iii) All debris impact dispersions.

(4) The width of a gate must restrict a launch vehicle's normal trajectory ground trace.

(c) *Overflight gate analysis products.* The products of a gate analysis that a launch operator must file with the FAA include:

(1) A description of the methodology used to establish each gate.

(2) A description of the tracking representation.

(3) A tabular description of the input data.

(4) Example analysis computations performed to determine a gate. If a launch involves more than one gate and the same methodology is used to determine each gate, the launch operator need only file the computations for one of the gates.

(5) A graphic depiction of each gate. A launch operator must provide a depiction or depictions showing flight safety limits, protected area outlines, nominal and 3-sigma left and right trajectory ground traces, protected area overflight regions, and predicted impact dispersion about the three-sigma trajectories within the gate. Each depiction must show latitude and longitude grid lines, gate latitude and longitude labels, and the map scale.

A417.19 DATA LOSS FLIGHT TIME AND PLANNED SAFE FLIGHT STATE

(a) *General.* A flight safety analysis must include a data loss flight time analysis that satisfies the requirements of §417.219. This section applies to the computation of data loss flight times and the planned safe flight state required by §417.219, and to the analysis products that the launch operator must file with the FAA as required by §417.203(e).

(b) *Planned safe flight state.* The analysis must establish a planned safe flight state for a launch as follows:

(1) For a suborbital launch, the analysis must determine a planned safe flight state as the nominal state vector after liftoff that a launch vehicle's hazardous debris impact dispersion can no longer reach any protected area.

(2) For an orbital launch where the launch vehicle's instantaneous impact point does not traverse a protected area prior to reaching orbit, the analysis must establish the planned safe flight state as the time after liftoff that the launch vehicle's hazardous debris impact dispersion can no longer reach any protected area or orbital insertion, whichever occurs first.

(3) For an orbital launch where a gate permits overflight of a protected area and where orbital insertion occurs after reaching the gate, the analysis must determine the planned safe flight state as the time after

liftoff when the time for the launch vehicle's instantaneous impact point to reach the gate is less than the time for the instantaneous impact point to reach any flight safety limit.

(4) The analysis must account for a malfunction that causes the launch vehicle to proceed from its position at the trajectory time being evaluated toward the closest flight safety limit and protected area.

(5) The analysis must account for the launch vehicle thrust vector that produces the highest instantaneous impact point range rate that the vehicle is capable of producing at the trajectory time being evaluated.

(c) *Data loss flight times.* For each launch vehicle trajectory time, from the predicted earliest launch vehicle tracking acquisition time until the planned safe flight state, the analysis must determine the data loss flight time as follows:

(1) The analysis must determine each data loss flight time as the minimum thrusting time for a launch vehicle to move from a normal trajectory position to a position where a flight termination would cause the malfunction debris impact dispersion to reach any protected area.

(2) A data loss flight time analysis must account for a malfunction that causes the launch vehicle to proceed from its position at the trajectory time being evaluated toward the closest flight safety limit and protected area.

(3) The analysis must account for the launch vehicle thrust vector that produces the highest instantaneous impact point range rate that the vehicle is capable of producing at the trajectory time being evaluated.

(4) Each data loss flight time must account for the system delays at the time of flight.

(5) The analysis must determine a data loss flight time for time increments that do not exceed one second along the launch vehicle nominal trajectory.

(d) *Products.* The products of a data loss flight time and planned safe flight state analysis that a launch operator must file include:

(1) A launch operator must describe the methodology used in its analysis, and identify all assumptions, techniques, input data, and equations used. A launch operator must file calculations performed for one data loss flight time in the vicinity of the launch site and one data loss flight time that is no less than 50 seconds later in the downrange area.

(2) A launch operator must file a graphical description or depictions of the flight safety limits, the launch point, the launch site boundaries, the surrounding geographic area, any protected areas, the planned safe flight state within any applicable scale requirements, latitude and longitude grid lines, and launch vehicle nominal and three-sigma instantaneous impact point ground traces from liftoff through orbital insertion for an orbital launch, and through final impact for a suborbital launch. Each graph must show any launch vehicle trajectory instantaneous impact points plotted with sufficient frequency to provide a conformal estimate of the launch vehicle's instantaneous impact point ground trace curvature. A launch operator must provide labeled latitude and longitude lines and the map scale on the depiction.

(3) A launch operator must provide a tabular description of each data loss flight time. The tabular description must include the malfunction start time and the geodetic latitude (positive north of the equator) and longitude (positive east of the Greenwich Meridian) coordinates of the intersection of the launch vehicle instantaneous impact point trajectory with the flight safety limit. The table must identify the first data lost flight time and planned safe flight state. The tabular description must include data loss flight times for trajectory time increments not to exceed one second.

A417.21 TIME DELAY

(a) *General.* A flight safety analysis must include a time delay analysis that satisfies the requirements of § 417.221. This section applies to the computation of time delays associated with a flight safety system and other launch vehicle systems and operations as required by § 417.221 and to the analysis products that the launch operator must file with the FAA as required by § 417.203(e).

(b) *Time delay analysis constraints.* The analysis must account for all significant causes of time delay between the violation of a flight termination rule and the time when a flight safety system is capable of terminating flight as follows:

(1) The analysis must account for decision and reaction times, including variation in human response time, for flight safety official and other personnel that are part of a launch operator's flight safety system as defined by subpart D of this part.

(2) The analyses must determine the time delay inherent in any data, from any source, used by a flight safety official for making flight termination decisions.

(3) A time delay analysis must account for all significant causes of time delay, including data flow rates and reaction times, for hardware and software, including, but not limited to the following:

(i) *Tracking system.* A time delay analysis must account for time delays between the launch vehicle's current location and last known location and that are associated with the hardware and software that make up the launch vehicle tracking system, whether or not it is located on the launch vehicle, such as transmitters, receivers, decoders, encoders, modulators, circuitry and any encryption and decryption of data.

(ii) *Display systems.* A time delay analysis must account for delays associated with hardware and software that make up any display system used by a flight safety official to aid in making flight control decisions. A time delay analysis must also account for any manual operations requirements, tracking source selection, tracking data processing, flight safety limit computations, inherent display delays, meteorological data processing, automated or manual system configuration control, automated or manual process control, automated or manual mission discrete control, and automated or manual fail over decision control.

(iii) *Flight termination system and command control system.* A time delay analysis must account for delays and response times associated with flight termination system and command control system hardware and software, such as transmitters, decoders, encoders, modulators, relays and shutdown, arming and destruct devices, circuitry and any encryption and decryption of data.

(iv) *Software specific time delays.* A delay analysis must account for delays associated with any correlation of data performed by software, such as timing and sequencing; data filtering delays such as error correction, smoothing, editing, or tracking source selection; data transformation delays; and computation cycle time.

(4) A time delay analysis must determine the time delay plus and minus three-sigma values relative to the mean time delay.

(5) For use in any risk analysis, a time delay analysis must determine time delay distributions that account for the variance of time delays for potential launch vehicle failure, including but not limited to, the range of malfunction turn characteristics and the time of flight when the malfunction occurs.

(c) *Time delay analysis products.* The products of a time delay analysis that a launch operator must file include:

(1) A description of the methodology used to produce the time delay analysis.

(2) A schematic drawing that maps the flight safety official's data flow time delays from the start of a launch vehicle malfunction through the final commanded flight termination on the launch vehicle, including the flight safety official's decision and reaction time. The drawings must indicate major systems, subsystems, major software functions, and data routing.

(3) A tabular listing of each time delay source and its individual mean and plus and minus three-sigma contribution to the overall time delay. The table must provide all time delay values in milliseconds.

(4) The mean delay time and the plus and minus three-sigma values of the delay time relative to the mean value.

A417.23 FLIGHT HAZARD AREAS

(a) *General.* A flight safety analysis must include a flight hazard area analysis that satisfies the requirements of §417.223. This section applies to the determination of flight hazard areas for orbital and suborbital launch vehicles that use a flight termination system to protect the public as required by §417.223 and to the analysis products that the launch operator must file with the FAA as required by §417.203(e). Requirements that apply to determining flight hazard areas for an unguided suborbital rocket that uses a wind-weighting safety system are contained in appendix C of this part.

(b) *Launch site flight hazard area.* A flight hazard area analysis must establish a launch site flight hazard area that encompasses the launch point and:

(1) If the flight safety analysis employs hazard isolation to establish flight safety limits as required by section A417.13(c), the launch site flight hazard area must encompass the flight safety limits.

(2) If the flight safety analysis does not employ hazard isolation to establish the flight safety limits, the launch site flight hazard area must encompass all hazard areas established as required by paragraphs (c) through (e) of this section.

(c) *Debris impact hazard area.* The analysis must establish a debris impact hazard area that accounts for the effects of impacting debris resulting from normal and malfunctioning launch vehicle flight, except for toxic effects, and accounts for potential impact locations of all debris fragments. The analysis must establish a debris hazard area as follows:

(1) An individual casualty contour that defines where the risk to an individual would exceed an expected casualty (Ec) criteria of 1×10^{-6} if one person were assumed to be in the open and inside the contour during launch vehicle flight must bound a debris hazard area. The analysis must produce an individual casualty contour as follows:

(i) The analysis must account for the location of a hypothetical person, and must vary the location of the person to determine when the risk would exceed the Ec criteria of 1×10^{-6}. The analysis must count a person as a casualty when the person's location is subjected to any inert debris impact with a mean expected kinetic energy greater than or equal to 11 ft-lbs or a peak incident overpressure equal to or greater than 1.0 psi due to explosive debris impact. The analysis must determine the peak incident overpressure using the Kingery-Bulmash relationship, without regard to sheltering, reflections, or atmospheric effects.

(ii) The analysis must account for person locations that are no more than 1000 feet apart in the downrange direction and no more than 1000 feet apart in the crossrange direction to produce an individual casualty contour. For each person location, the analysis must sum the probabilities of casualty over all flight times for all debris groups.

(iii) An individual casualty contour must consist of curves that are smooth and continuous. To accomplish this, the analysis must vary the time interval between the trajectory times assessed so that each location of a debris impact point is less than one-half sigma of the downrange dispersion distance.

(2) The input for determining a debris impact hazard area must account for the results of the trajectory analysis required by section A417.7, the malfunction turn analysis required by section A417.9, and the debris analysis required by section A417.11 to define the impact locations of each class of debris established by the debris analysis, and the time delay analysis required by section A417.21.

(3) The analysis must account for the extent of the impact debris dispersions for each debris class produced by normal and malfunctioning launch vehicle flight at each trajectory time. The analysis must also account for how the vehicle breaks up, either by the flight termination system or by aerodynamic forces, if the different breakup may result in a different probability of existence for each debris class. A debris impact hazard area must account for each impacting debris fragment classified as required by section A417.11(c).

(4) The analysis must account for launch vehicle flight that exceeds a flight safety limit. The analysis must also account for trajectory conditions that maximize the mean debris impact distance during the flight safety system delay time determined as required by section A417.21 and account for a debris model that is representative of a flight termination or aerodynamic breakup. For each launch vehicle breakup event, the analysis must account for trajectory and breakup dispersions, variations in debris class characteristics, and debris dispersion due to any wind condition under which a launch would be attempted.

(5) The analysis must account for the probability of failure of each launch vehicle stage and the probability of existence of each debris class. The analysis must account for the probability of occurrence of each type of launch vehicle failure. The analysis must account for vehicle failure probabilities that vary depending on the time of flight.

(6) In addition to failure debris, the analysis must account for nominal jettisoned body debris impacts and the corresponding debris impact dispersions. The analysis must use a probability of occurrence of 1.0 for the planned debris fragments produced by normal separation events during flight.

(d) *Near-launch-point blast hazard area.* A flight hazard area analysis must define a blast overpressure hazard area as a circle extending from the launch point with a radius equal to the 1.0 psi overpressure distance produced by the equivalent TNT weight of the explosive capability of the vehicle. In addition, the analysis must establish a minimum near-pad blast hazard area to provide protection from hazardous fragments potentially propelled by an explosion. The analysis must account for the maximum possible total solid and liquid propellant explosive potential of the launch vehicle and any payload. The analysis must define a blast overpressure hazard area using the following equations:

$$R_{op} = 45 \cdot (NEW)^{1/3}$$

Where:

R_{op} is the over pressure distance in feet.
$NEW = W_E \cdot C$ (pounds).
W_E is the weight of the explosive in pounds.
C is the TNT equivalency coefficient of the propellant being evaluated. A launch operator must identify the TNT equivalency of each propellant on its launch vehicle including any payload. TNT equivalency data for common liquid propellants is provided in tables A417–1. Table A417–2 provides factors for converting gallons of specified liquid propellants to pounds.

(e) *Other hazards.* A flight hazard area analysis must identify any additional hazards, such as radioactive material, that may exist on the launch vehicle or payload. For each such hazard, the analysis must determine a hazard area that encompasses any debris impact point and its dispersion and includes an additional hazard radius that accounts for potential casualty due to the additional hazard. Analysis requirements for toxic release and far field blast overpressure are provided in §417.27 and section A417.29, respectively.

(1) *Aircraft hazard areas.* The analysis must establish an aircraft hazard area for each planned debris impact for the issuance of notices to airmen as required by §417.121(e). Each aircraft hazard area must encompass an air space region, from an altitude of 60,000 feet to impact on the Earth's surface, that contains the three-sigma drag impact dispersion.

(2) *Ship hazard areas.* The analysis must establish a ship hazard area for each planned debris impact for the issuance of notices to mariners as required by §417.121(e). Each ship hazard area must encompass a surface region that contains the three-sigma drag impact dispersion.

(f) *Flight hazard area analysis products.* The products of a flight hazard area analysis that a launch operator must file with the FAA include:

(1) A chart that depicts the launch site flight hazard area, including its size and location.

(2) A chart that depicts each hazard area required by this section.

(3) A description of each hazard for which analysis was performed; the methodology used to compute each hazard area; and the debris classes for aerodynamic breakup of the launch vehicle and for flight termination. For each debris class, the launch operator must identify the number of debris fragments, the variation in ballistic coefficient, and the standard deviation of the debris dispersion.

(4) A chart that depicts each of the individual casualty contour.

(5) A description of the aircraft hazard area for each planned debris impact, the information to be published in a Notice to Airmen, and all information required as part of any agreement with the FAA ATC office having jurisdiction over the airspace through which flight will take place.

(6) A description of any ship hazard area for each planned debris impact and all information required in a Notice to Mariners.

(7) A description of the methodology used for determining each hazard area.

(8) A description of the hazard area operational controls and procedures to be implemented for flight.

TABLE A417-1. LIQUID PROPELLANT EXPLOSIVE EQUIVALENTS

Propellant combinations	TNT equivalents
LO_2/LH_2	The larger of $8W^{2/3}$ or 14% of W. Where W is the weight of LO_2/LH_2.
LO_2/LH_2 + LO_2/RP-1	Sum of (20% for LO_2/RP-1) the larger of $8W^{2/3}$ or 14% of W. Where W is the weight of LO_2/LH_2.
LO_2/RP-1	20% of W up to 500,000 pounds + 10% of W over 500,000 pounds. Where W is the weight of LO_2/RP-1.
N_2O_4/N_2H_4 (or UDMH or UDMH/N_2H_4 Mixture)	10% of W. Where W is the weight of the propellant.

TABLE A417-2. PROPELLANT HAZARD AND COMPATIBILITY GROUPINGS AND FACTORS TO BE USED WHEN CONVERTING GALLONS OF PROPELLANT INTO POUNDS

Propellant	Hazard group	Compatibility group	Pounds/gallon	^{0}F
Hydrogen Peroxide	II	A	11.6	68
Hydrazine	III	C	8.4	68
Liquid Hydrogen	III	C	0.59	-423
Liquid Oxygen	II	A	9.5	-297
Nitrogen Tetroxide	I	A	12.1	68
RP-1	I	C	6.8	68
UDMH	III	C	6.6	68
UDMH/Hydrazine	III	C	7.5	68

A417.25 DEBRIS RISK

(a) *General.* A flight safety analysis must include a debris risk analysis that satisfies the requirements of §417.225. This section applies to the computation of the average number of casualties (E_c) to the collective members of debris hazards from the proposed flight of a launch vehicle as required by §417.225 and to the analysis products that the launch operator must file with the FAA as required by §417.203(e).

(b) *Debris risk analysis constraints.* The following constraints apply to a debris risk:

(1) A debris risk analysis must use valid risk analysis models that compute E_c as the summation over all trajectory time intervals from lift-off through orbital insertion of the products of the probability of each possible event and the casualty consequences due to debris impacts for each possible event.

(2) A debris risk analysis must account for the following populations:

(i) The overflight of populations located inside any flight safety limits.

(ii) All populations located within five-sigma left and right crossrange of a nominal trajectory instantaneous impact point ground trace and within five-sigma of each planned nominal debris impact.

(iii) Any planned overflight of the public within any gate overflight areas.

(iv) Any populations outside the flight safety limits identified as required by paragraph (b)(10) of this section.

(3) A debris risk analysis must account for both inert and explosive debris hazards produced from any impacting debris caused by normal and malfunctioning launch vehicle flight. The analysis must account for the debris classes determined by the debris analysis required by section A417.11. A debris risk analysis must account for any inert debris impact with mean expected kinetic energy at impact greater than or equal to 11 ft-lbs and peak incident overpressure of greater than or equal to 1.0 psi due to any explosive debris impact. The analysis must account for all debris hazards as a function of flight time.

(4) A debris risk analysis must account for debris impact points and dispersion for each class of debris as follows:

(i) A debris risk analysis must account for drag corrected impact points and dispersions for each class of impacting debris resulting from normal and malfunctioning launch vehicle flight as a function of trajectory time from lift-off through orbital insertion, including each planned impact, for an orbital launch, and through final impact for a suborbital launch.

(ii) The dispersion for each debris class must account for the position and velocity state vector dispersions at breakup, the variance produced by breakup imparted velocities, the effect of winds on both the ascent trajectory state vector at breakup and the descending debris piece impact location the variance produced by aerodynamic properties for each debris class, and any other dispersion variances.

(iii) A debris risk analysis must account for the survivability of debris fragments that are subject to reentry aerodynamic forces or heating. A debris class may be eliminated from the debris risk analysis if the launch operator demonstrates that the debris will not survive to impact.

(5) A debris risk analysis must account for launch vehicle failure probability. The following constraints apply:

(i) For flight safety analysis purposes, a failure occurs when a vehicle does not complete any phase of normal flight or exhibits the potential for the stage or its debris to impact the Earth or reenter the atmosphere during the mission or any future mission of similar vehicle capability. Also, either a launch incident or launch accident constitutes a failure.

(ii) For a launch vehicle with fewer than 2 flights completed, the analysis must use a reference value for the launch vehicle failure probability estimate equal to the upper limit of the 60% two-sided confidence limits of the binomial distribution for outcomes of all previous launches of vehicles developed and launched in similar circumstances. The FAA may adjust the failure probability estimate to account for the level of experience demonstrated by the launch operator and other factors that affects the probability of failure. The FAA may adjust the failure probability estimate for the second launch based on evidence obtained from the first flight of the vehicle.

(iii) For a launch vehicle with at least 2 flights completed, the analysis must use the reference value for the launch vehicle failure probability of Table A417–3 based on the outcomes of all previous launches of the vehicle. The FAA may adjust the failure probability estimate to account for evidence obtained from the flight history of the vehicle. The FAA may adjust the failure probability estimate to account for the nature of launch outcomes in the flight history of the vehicle, corrective actions taken in response to a failure of the vehicle, or other vehicle modifications that may affect reliability. The FAA may adjust the failure probability estimate to account for the demonstrated quality of the engineering approach to launch vehicle processing, meeting safety requirements in this part, and associated hazard mitigation. The analysis must use a final failure estimate within the confidence limits of Table A417–3.

(A) Values listed on the far left of Table A417–3 apply when no launch failures are experienced. Values on the far right apply when only launch failures are experienced. Values in between apply for flight histories that include both failures and successes.

(B) Reference values in Table A417–3 are shown in bold. The reference values are the median values between 60% two-sided confidence limits of the binomial distribution. For the special cases of zero or N failures in N launch attempts, the reference values may also be recognized as the median value between the 80% one-sided confidence limit of the binomial distribution and zero or one, respectively.

(C) Upper and lower confidence bounds in Table A417–3 are shown directly above and below each reference value. These confidence bounds are based on 60% two-sided confidence limits of the binomial distribution. For the special cases of zero or N failures in N launch attempts, the upper and lower confidence bounds are based on the 80% one-sided confidence limit, respectively.

Table A417-3. LAUNCH VEHICLE FAILURE PROBABILITY REFERENCE ESTIMATES AND CONFIDENCE BOUNDS of with Two or More Flights

Launch #									<--------Success			Failure ------->									
									.553		.894		1.00								
3									**.276**		**.50**		**.724**								
									.00		.106		.447								
								.415		.713		.928		1.00							
4								**.208**		**.392**		**.608**		**.792**							
								.00		.072		.287		.585							
							.331		.582		.788		.946		1.00						
5							**.166**		**.318**		**.50**		**.682**		**.834**						
							.00		.054		.212		.418		.669						
						.275		.49		.673		.831		.956		1.00					
6						**.138**		**.267**		**.421**		**.579**		**.733**		**.862**					
						.00		.044		.169		.327		.51		.725					
					.235		.422		.585		.731		.86		.963		1.00				
7					**.118**		**.229**		**.363**		**.50**		**.637**		**.771**		**.882**				
					.00		.037		.14		.269		.415		.578		.765				
				.205		.371		.517		.65		.772		.88		.969		1.00			
8				**.103**		**.201**		**.318**		**.439**		**.561**		**.682**		**.799**		**.897**			
				.00		.031		.12		.228		.35		.483		.629		.795			
			.182		.33		.462		.584		.697		.801		.896		.972		1.00		
9			**.091**		**.179**		**.283**		**.391**		**.50**		**.609**		**.717**		**.821**		**.909**		
			.00		.028		.104		.199		.303		.416		.538		.67		.818		
		.164		.298		.418		.529		.634		.732		.824		.907		.976		1.00	
10		**.082**		**.161**		**.255**		**.352**		**.451**		**.549**		**.648**		**.745**		**.839**		**.918**	
		.00		.024		.093		.176		.268		.366		.471		.582		.702		.836	
	.149		.271		.381		.484		.581		.673		.761		.842		.917		.978		1.00
11	**.074**		**.147**		**.232**		**.321**		**.41**		**.50**		**.59**		**.679**		**.768**		**.853**		**.926**
	.00		.022		.083		.158		.239		.327		.419		.516		.619		.729		.851

(6) A debris risk analysis must account for the dwell time of the instantaneous impact point ground trace over each populated or protected area being evaluated.

(7) A debris risk analysis must account for the three-sigma instantaneous impact point trajectory variations in left-crossrange, right-crossrange, uprange, and downrange as

a function of trajectory time, due to launch vehicle performance variations as determined by the trajectory analysis performed as required by section A417.7.

(8) A debris risk analysis must account for the effective casualty area as a function of launch vehicle flight time for all impacting debris generated from a catastrophic launch vehicle malfunction event or a planned impact event. The effective casualty area must account for both payload and vehicle systems and subsystems debris. The effective casualty area must account for all debris fragments determined as part of a launch operator's debris analysis as required by section A417.11. The effective casualty area for each explosive debris fragment must account for a 1.0 psi blast overpressure radius and the projected debris effects for all potentially explosive debris. The effective casualty area for each inert debris fragment must:

(i) Account for bounce, skip, slide, and splatter effects; or

(ii) Equal seven times the maximum projected area of the fragment.

(9) A debris risk analysis must account for current population density data obtained from a current population database for the region being evaluated or by estimating the current population using exponential population growth rate equations applied to the most current historical data available. The population model must define population centers that are similar enough to be described and treated as a single average set of characteristics without degrading the accuracy of the debris risk estimate.

(10) For a launch vehicle that uses a flight safety system, a debris risk analysis must account for the collective risk to any populations outside the flight safety limits during flight, including people who will be at any public launch viewing area during flight. For such populations, in addition to the constraints of paragraphs (b)(1) through (b)(9) of this section, a launch operator's debris risk analysis must account for the following:

(i) The probability of a launch vehicle failure that would result in debris impact in protected areas outside the flight safety limits.

(ii) The failure probability of the launch operator's flight safety system. A flight safety system failure rate of 0.002 may be used if the flight safety system complies with the flight safety system requirements of subpart D of this part. For an alternate flight safety system approved as required by § 417.107(a)(3), the launch operator must demonstrate the validity of the probability of failure through the licensing process.

(iii) Current population density data and population projections for the day and time of flight for the areas outside the flight safety limits.

(c) *Debris risk analysis products.* The products of a debris risk analysis that a launch operator must file with the FAA include:

(1) A debris risk analysis report that provides the analysis input data, probabilistic risk determination methods, sample computations, and text or graphical charts that characterize the public risk to geographical areas for each launch.

(2) Geographic data showing:

(i) The launch vehicle nominal, five-sigma left-crossrange and five-sigma right-crossrange instantaneous impact point ground traces;

(ii) All exclusion zones relative to the instantaneous impact point ground traces; and

(iii) All populated areas included in the debris risk analysis.

(3) A discussion of each launch vehicle failure scenario accounted for in the analysis and the probability of occurrence, which may vary with flight time, for each failure scenario. This information must include failure scenarios where a launch vehicle:

(i) Flies within normal limits until some malfunction causes spontaneous breakup or results in a commanded flight termination;

(ii) Experiences malfunction turns; and

(iii) Flight safety system fails to function.

(4) A population model applicable to the launch overflight regions that contains the following: region identification, location of the center of each population center by geodetic latitude and longitude, total area, number of persons in each population center, and a description of the shelter characteristics within the population center.

(5) A description of the launch vehicle, including general information concerning the nature and purpose of the launch and an overview of the launch vehicle, including a scaled diagram of the general arrangement and dimensions of the vehicle. A launch operator's debris risk analysis products may reference other documentation filed with the FAA containing this information. The description must include:

(i) Weights and dimensions of each stage.

(ii) Weights and dimensions of any booster motors attached.

(iii) The types of fuel used in each stage and booster.

(iv) Weights and dimensions of all interstage adapters and skirts.

(v) Payload dimensions, materials, construction, and any payload fuel; payload fairing construction, materials, and dimensions; and any non-inert components or materials that add to the effective casualty area of the debris, such as radioactive or toxic materials or high-pressure vessels.

(6) A typical sequence of events showing times of ignition, cutoff, burnout, and jettison of each stage, firing of any ullage rockets, and starting and ending times of coast periods and control modes.

(7) The following information for each launch vehicle motor:

(i) Propellant type and composition;

(ii) Thrust profile;

(iii) Propellant weight and total motor weight as a function of time;

(iv) A description of each nozzle and steering mechanism;

(v) For solid rocket motors, internal pressure and average propellant thickness, or borehole radius, as a function of time;

(vi) Maximum impact point deviations as a function of failure time during destruct system delays. Burn rate as a function of ambient pressure;

(vii) A discussion of whether a commanded destruct could ignite a non-thrusting motor, and if so, under what conditions; and

(viii) Nozzle exit and entrance areas.

(8) The launch vehicle's launch and failure history, including a summary of past vehicle performance. For a new vehicle with little or no flight history, a launch operator must provide all known data on similar vehicles that include:

(i) Identification of the launches that have occurred;

(ii) Launch date, location, and direction of each launch;

(iii) The number of launches that performed normally;

(iv) Behavior and impact location of each abnormal experience;

(v) The time, altitude, and nature of each malfunction; and

(vi) Descriptions of corrective actions taken, including changes in vehicle design, flight termination, and guidance and control hardware and software.

(9) The values of probability of impact (P_I) and expected casualty (E_c) for each populated area.

A417.27 TOXIC RELEASE HAZARD ANALYSIS

A flight safety analysis must include a toxic release hazard analysis that satisfies the requirements of §417.227. A launch operator's toxic release hazard analysis must satisfy the methodology requirements of appendix I of this part. A launch operator must file the analysis products identified in appendix I of this part as required by §417.203(e).

A417.29 FAR FIELD BLAST OVERPRESSURE EFFECTS ANALYSIS

(a) *General.* A flight safety analysis must include a far field blast overpressure effects hazard analysis that satisfies the requirements of §417.229. This section applies to the computation of far field blast overpressure effects from the proposed flight of a launch vehicle as required by §417.229 and to the analysis products that the launch operator must file with the FAA as required by §417.203(e). The analysis must account for distant focus overpressure and any overpressure enhancement to establish the potential for broken windows due to peak incident overpressures below 1.0 psi and related casualties due to falling or projected glass shards. The analysis must employ either paragraph (b) of this section or the risk analysis of paragraph (c) of this section.

(b) *Far field blast overpressure hazard analysis.* Unless an analysis satisfies the requirements of paragraph (c) of this section a far field blast overpressure hazard analysis must satisfy the following:

(1) Explosive yield factors. The analysis must use explosive yield factor curves for each type or class of solid or liquid propellant used by the launch vehicle. Each explosive yield factor curve must be based on the most accurate explosive yield data for the corresponding type or class of solid or liquid propellant based on empirical data or computational modeling.

(2) Establish the maximum credible explosive yield. The analysis must establish the maximum credible explosive yield resulting from normal and malfunctioning launch vehicle flight. The explosive yield must account for impact mass and velocity of impact on the Earth's surface. The analysis must account for explosive yield expressed as a TNT equivalent for peak overpressure.

(3) Characterize the population exposed to the hazard. The analysis must demonstrate whether any population centers are vulnerable to a distant focus overpressure hazard using the methodology provided by section 6.3.2.4 of the American National Standard Institute's ANSI S2.20–1983, "Estimating Air Blast Characteristics for Single Point Explosions in Air with a Guide to Evaluation of Atmospheric Propagation and Effects" and as follows:

(i) For the purposes of this analysis, a population center must include any area outside the launch site and not under the launch operator's control that contains an exposed site. An exposed site includes any structure that may be occupied by human beings, and that has at least one window, but does not include automobiles, airplanes, and waterborne vessels. The analysis must account for the most recent census information on each population center. The analysis must treat any exposed site for which no census information is available, or the census information indicates a population equal to or less than four persons, as a 'single residence.'

(ii) The analysis must identify the distance between the location of the maximum credible impact explosion and the location of each population center potentially exposed. Unless the location of the potential explosion site is limited to a defined region, the analysis must account for the distance between the potential explosion site and a population center as the minimum distance between any point within the region contained by the flight safety limits and the nearest exposed site within the population center.

(iii) The analysis must account for all weather conditions optimized for a distant focus overpressure hazard by applying an atmospheric blast "focus factor" (F) of 5.

(iv) The analysis must determine, using the methodology of section 6.3.2.4 of ANSI S2.20–1983, for each a population center, whether the maximum credible explosive yield of a launch meets, exceeds or is less than the "no damage yield limit," of the population center. If the maximum credible explosive yield is less than the "no damage yield limit" for all exposed sites, the remaining requirements of this section do not apply. If the maximum credible explosive yield meets or exceeds the "no damage yield limit" for a population center then that population center is vulnerable to far field blast overpressure from the launch and the requirements of paragraphs (b)(4) and (b)(5) of this section apply.

(4) Estimate the quantity of broken windows. The analysis must use a focus factor of 5 and the methods provided by ANSI S2.20–1983 to estimate the number of potential broken windows within each population center determined to be vulnerable to the distant focus overpressure hazard as required by paragraph (b)(3) of this section.

(5) Determine and implement measures necessary to prevent distant focus overpressure from breaking windows. For each population center that is vulnerable to far field blast overpressure from a launch, the analysis must identify mitigation measures to protect the public from serious injury from broken windows and the flight commit criteria of §417.113(c) needed to enforce the mitigation measures. A launch operator's mitigation measures must include one or more of the following:

(i) Apply a minimum 4-millimeter thick anti-shatter film to all exposed sites where the maximum credible yield exceeds the "no damage yield limit."

(ii) Evacuate the exposed public to a location that is not vulnerable to the distant focus overpressure hazard at least two hours prior to the planned flight time.

(iii) If, as required by paragraph (b)(4) of this section, the analysis predicts that less than 20 windows will break, advise the public of the potential for glass breakage.

(c) *Far field blast overpressure risk analysis.* If a launch operator does not employ paragraph (b) of this section to perform a far field overpressure hazard analysis, the launch operator must conduct a risk analysis that demonstrates that the launch will be conducted in accordance with the public risk criteria of §417.107(b).

(d) *Far field blast overpressure effect products.* The products of a far field blast overpressure analysis that a launch operator must file with the FAA include:

(1) A description of the methodology used to produce the far field blast overpressure analysis results, a tabular description of the analysis input data, and a description of any far field blast overpressure mitigation measures implemented.

(2) For any far field blast overpressure risk analysis, an example set of the analysis computations.

(3) The values for the maximum credible explosive yield as a function of time of flight.

(4) The distance between the potential explosion location and any population center vulnerable to the far field blast overpressure hazard. For each population center, the launch operator must identify the exposed populations by location and number of people.

(5) Any mitigation measures established to protect the public from far field blast overpressure hazards and any flight commit criteria established to ensure the mitigation measures are enforced.

A417.31 COLLISION AVOIDANCE

(a) *General.* A flight safety analysis must include a collision avoidance analysis that satisfies the requirements of §417.231. This section applies to a launch operator obtaining a collision avoidance assessment from United States Strategic Command as required by §417.231 and to the analysis products that the launch operator must file with the FAA as required by §417.203(e). United States Strategic Command refers to a collision avoidance analysis for a space launch as a conjunction on launch assessment.

(b) *Analysis constraints.* A launch operator must satisfy the following when obtaining and implementing the results of a collision avoidance analysis:

(1) A launch operator must provide United States Strategic Command with the launch window and trajectory data needed to perform a collision avoidance analysis for a launch as required by paragraph (c) of this section, at least 15 days before the first attempt at flight. The FAA will identify a launch operator to United States Strategic Command as part of issuing a license and provide a launch operator with current United States Strategic Command contact information.

(2) A launch operator must obtain a collision avoidance analysis performed by United States Strategic Command 6 hours before the beginning of a launch window.

(3) A launch operator may use a collision avoidance analysis for 12 hours from the time that United States Strategic Command determines the state vectors of the manned or mannable orbiting objects. If a launch operator needs an updated collision avoidance analysis due to a launch delay, the launch operator must file the request with United States Strategic Command at least 12 hours

prior to the beginning of the new launch window.

(4) For every 90 minutes, or portion of 90 minutes, that pass between the time United States Strategic Command last determined the state vectors of the orbiting objects, a launch operator must expand each wait in a launch window by subtracting 15 seconds from the start of the wait in the launch window and adding 15 seconds to the end of the wait in the launch window. A launch operator must incorporate all the resulting waits in the launch window into its flight commit criteria established as required by §417.113.

(c) *Information required.* A launch operator must prepare a collision avoidance analysis worksheet for each launch using a standardized format that contains the input data required by this paragraph. A launch operator must file the input data with United States Strategic Command for the purposes of completing a collision avoidance analysis. A launch operator must file the input data with the FAA as part of the license application process as required by §415.115 of this chapter.

(1) *Launch information.* A launch operator must file the following launch information:

(i) *Mission name.* A mnemonic given to the launch vehicle/payload combination identifying the launch mission from all others.

(ii) *Segment number.* A segment is defined as a launch vehicle stage or payload after the thrusting portion of its flight has ended. This includes the jettison or deployment of any stage or payload. A launch operator must provide a separate worksheet for each segment. For each segment, a launch operator must determine the "vector at injection" as defined by paragraph (c)(5) of this section. The data must present each segment number as a sequence number relative to the total number of segments for a launch, such as "1 of 5."

(iii) *Launch window.* The launch window opening and closing times in Greenwich Mean Time (referred to as ZULU time) and the Julian dates for each scheduled launch attempt.

(2) *Point of contact.* The person or office within a launch operator's organization that collects, analyzes, and distributes collision avoidance analysis results.

(3) *Collision avoidance analysis analysis results transmission medium.* A launch operator must identify the transmission medium, such as voice, FAX, or e-mail, for receiving results from United States Strategic Command.

(4) *Requestor launch operator needs.* A launch operator must indicate the types of analysis output formats required for establishing flight commit criteria for a launch:

(i) *Waits.* All the times within the launch window during which flight must not be initiated.

(ii) *Windows.* All the times within an overall launch window during which flight may be initiated.

(5) *Vector at injection.* A launch operator must identify the vector at injection for each segment. "Vector at injection" identifies the position and velocity of all orbital or suborbital segments after the thrust for a segment has ended.

(i) *Epoch.* The epoch time, in Greenwich Mean Time (GMT), of the expected launch vehicle liftoff time.

(ii) *Position and velocity.* The position coordinates in the EFG coordinate system measured in kilometers and the EFG components measured in kilometers per second, of each launch vehicle stage or payload after any burnout, jettison, or deployment.

(6) *Time of powered flight.* The elapsed time in seconds, from liftoff to arrival at the launch vehicle vector at injection. The input data must include the time of powered flight for each stage or jettisoned component measured from liftoff.

(7) *Time span for launch window file (LWF).* A launch operator must provide the following information regarding its launch window:

(i) *Launch window.* The launch window measured in minutes from the initial proposed liftoff time.

(ii) *Time of powered flight.* The time provided as required by paragraph (c)(6) of this section measured in minutes rounded up to the nearest integer minute.

(iii) *Screen duration.* The time duration, after all thrusting periods of flight have ended, that a collision avoidance analysis must screen for potential conjunctions with manned or mannable orbital objects. Screen duration is measured in minutes and must be greater than or equal to 100 minutes for an orbital launch.

(iv) *Extra pad.* An additional period of time for collision avoidance analysis screening to ensure the entire first orbit is screened for potential conjunctions with manned or mannable orbital objects. This time must be 10 minutes unless otherwise specified by United States Strategic Command.

(v) *Total.* The summation total of the time spans provided as required by paragraphs (c)(7)(i) through (c)(7)(iv) expressed in minutes.

(8) *Screening.* A launch operator must select spherical or ellipsoidal screening as defined in this paragraph for determining any conjunction. The default must be the spherical screening method using an avoidance radius of 200 kilometers for manned or mannable orbiting objects. If the launch operator requests screening for any unmanned or unmannable objects, the default must be the spherical screening method using a miss distance of 25 kilometers.

(i) *Spherical screening.* Spherical screening utilizes an impact exclusion sphere centered on each orbiting object's center-of-mass to determine any conjunction. A launch operator must specify the avoidance radius for manned or mannable objects and for any unmanned or unmannable objects if the launch operator elects to perform the analysis for unmanned or unmannable objects.

(ii) *Ellipsoidal screening.* Ellipsoidal screening utilizes an impact exclusion ellipsoid of revolution centered on the orbiting object's center-of-mass to determine any conjunction. A launch operator must provide input in the UVW coordinate system in kilometers. The launch operator must provide delta–U measured in the radial-track direction, delta–V measured in the in-track direction, and delta–W measured in the cross-track direction.

(9) *Orbiting objects to evaluate.* A launch operator must identify the orbiting objects to be included in the analysis.

(10) *Deliverable schedule/need dates.* A launch operator must identify the times before flight, referred to as "L-times," for which the launch operator requests a collision avoidance analysis.

(d) *Collision avoidance assessment products.* A launch operator must file its collision avoidance analysis products as required by § 417.203(e) and must include the input data required by paragraph (c) of this section. A launch operator must incorporate the result of the collision avoidance analysis into its flight commit criteria established as required by § 417.113.

[Docket No. FAA-2000-7953, 71 FR 50537, Aug. 25, 2006, as amended by Amdt. No. 417-5, 81 FR 59439, Aug. 30, 2016]

APPENDIX B TO PART 417—FLIGHT HAZARD AREA ANALYSIS FOR AIRCRAFT AND SHIP PROTECTION

B417.1 SCOPE

This appendix contains requirements to establish aircraft hazard areas, ship hazard areas, and land impact hazard areas. The methodologies contained in this appendix represent an acceptable means of satisfying the requirements of § 417.107 and § 417.223 as they pertain to ship, aircraft, and land hazard areas. This appendix provides a standard and a measure of fidelity against which the FAA will measure any proposed alternative approaches. Requirements for a launch operator's implementation of a hazard area are contained in §§ 417.121(e) and (f).

B417.3 HAZARD AREA NOTIFICATIONS AND SURVEILLANCE

(a) A launch operator must ensure the following notifications have been made and adhered to at launch:

(1) A Notice to Airmen (NOTAM) must be issued for every aircraft hazard area identified as required by sections B417.5 and B417.7. The NOTAM must be effective no less than thirty minutes prior to flight and effective until no sooner than thirty minutes after the air space volume requested by the NOTAM can no longer be affected by the launch vehicle or its potential hazardous effects.

(2) A Notice to Mariners (NOTMAR) must be issued for every ship hazard area identified as required by sections B417.5 and B417.7. The NOTMAR must be effective no less than thirty minutes prior to flight and effective until no sooner than thirty minutes after the area requested by the NOTMAR can no longer be affected by the launch vehicle or its potential hazardous effects.

(3) All local officials and landowners adjacent to any hazard area must be notified of the flight schedule no less than two days prior to the flight of the launch vehicle.

(b) A launch operator must survey each of the following hazard areas:

(1) Each launch site hazard area;

(2) Each aircraft hazard area in the vicinity of the launch site; and

(3) Each ship hazard area in the vicinity of the launch site.

B417.5 LAUNCH SITE HAZARD AREA

(a) *General.* A launch operator must perform a launch site hazard area analysis that protects the public, aircraft, and ships from the hazardous activities in the vicinity of the launch site. The launch operator must evacuate and monitor each launch site hazard area to ensure compliance with §§ 417.107(b)(2) and (b)(3).

(b) *Launch site hazard area analysis input.* A launch site hazard area must encompass no less than the following:

(1) Each land hazard area in the vicinity of the launch site calculated as required by section B417.13;

(2) Each ship hazard area in the vicinity of the launch site calculated as required by section B417.11(c); and

(3) The aircraft hazard area in the vicinity of the launch site calculated as required by section B417.9(c).

B417.7 DOWNRANGE HAZARD AREAS

(a) *General.* A launch operator must perform a downrange hazard area analysis that protects the public, aircraft, and ships from the hazardous activities in the vicinity of each scheduled impact location.

(b) *Downrange hazard areas analysis input.* A launch hazard area must bound no less than the following:

(1) The aircraft hazard area in the vicinity of each planned impact location calculated as required by section B417.9(d);

(2) The ship hazard area in the vicinity of each planned water impact location calculated as required by section B417.11(d); and

(3) The land hazard area in the vicinity of each planned land impact location calculated as required by section B417.13.

B417.9 AIRCRAFT HAZARD AREAS ANALYSIS

(a) *General.* A launch operator must perform an aircraft hazard areas analysis as required by § 417.223(b). A launch operator's aircraft hazard areas analysis must determine the aircraft hazard area in the vicinity of the launch site and the aircraft hazard area in the vicinity of each planned impact location as required by this section.

(b) *Aircraft hazard areas analysis input.* A launch operator must account for the following inputs to determine the aircraft hazard areas:

(1) The trajectory analysis performed as required by section A417.7 or section C417.3; and

(2) The debris risk analysis performed as required by section A417.25 or section C417.9.

(c) *Methodology for computing an aircraft hazard area in the vicinity of the launch site.* An aircraft hazard area analysis must determine an aircraft hazard area that encompasses the launch point from the surface of the Earth to an altitude of 100,000 ft MSL and wholly contains the launch vehicle's normal trajectory plus five nautical miles in every radial direction. A launch operator must calculate an aircraft hazard area in the vicinity of the launch site as follows:

(1) Using the trajectory analysis performed as required by section A417.7 or section C417.3, select all data locations where the vehicle's nominal altitude, or positional component on the z-axis, is less than and equal to 100,000 ft MSL.

(2) From the data locations representing the dispersed trajectories calculated as required by section A417.7(d) or section C417.3(f) and modified to incorporate a 5 nm buffer as required by paragraph (c)(1) of this section for the data locations selected below a nominal altitude of 100,000 ft MSL as required by paragraph (c)(1) of this section, select the location that is the farthest left-hand crossrange, the location that is the farthest right-hand crossrange, the location that is the farthest downrange, and the location that is the farthest uprange.

(3) Construct a box in the xy plane that includes two lines parallel to the azimuth, two lines perpendicular to the azimuth, and contains the four locations selected as required by paragraph (c)(2) of this section.

(4) Extend the box constructed as required by paragraph (c)(3) of this section from the surface of the Earth to an infinite altitude.

(d) *Methodology for computing an aircraft hazard area in the vicinity of each planned impact location.* A launch operator must determine an aircraft hazard area in the vicinity of each planned impact location from the surface of the Earth to an altitude of 100,000 ft MSL that wholly contains the launch vehicle's calculated impact dispersion with a 5 nm buffer and the normal trajectory. A launch operator must compute an aircraft hazard area in the vicinity of each planned impact location as follows:

(1) The analysis must calculate a three-sigma dispersion ellipse by determining the three-sigma impact limit around a planned impact location.

(2) Taking the three-sigma dispersion ellipse calculated as required by paragraph (d)(1) of this section, plot a co-centric ellipse in the xy plane where the major and minor axes are 10nm longer than the major and minor axes of the three-sigma dispersion ellipse.

(3) Extend the ellipse calculated as required by paragraph (d)(2) of this section from the surface to an infinite altitude.

(4) Using the trajectory that predicts the instantaneous impact locations required in section A417.7(g)(7)(xii) or section C417.3(d), find the location on the trajectory where the vehicle's nominal altitude is predicted to be 100,000 ft MSL.

(5) At the trajectory time where the altitude is represented as 100,000 ft MSL, select the corresponding points from the normal trajectory dispersion that are the farthest uprange, downrange, right crossrange, and left crossrange relative to the nominal trajectory.

(6) Construct a box in the xy plane that includes two lines parallel to the azimuth, two lines perpendicular to the azimuth, and contains the points selected as required by paragraph (d)(5) of this section and the nominal impact point.

(7) Extend the box constructed as required by paragraph (d)(6) of this section from the surface of the Earth to an infinite altitude.

(8) Construct a volume, the aircraft hazard area, that encompasses the volumes calculated as required by paragraphs (d)(3) and (d)(7) of this section.

B417.11 SHIP HAZARD AREAS ANALYSIS

(a) *General.* A flight hazard area analysis must establish ship hazard areas bound by the 1×10^{-5} ship impact contour in the vicinity of the launch site and the vehicle's three-sigma dispersion limit plus a 5 nm buffer in the vicinity of a planned, downrange impact location.

(b) *Ship hazard area analysis input.* A launch operator must account for the following inputs to determine the ship hazard areas:

(1) The trajectory analysis performed as required by section A417.7 or section C417.3;

(2) For a launch vehicle flown with a flight safety system, the malfunction turn analysis required by section A417.9;

(3) The debris analysis required by section A417.11 or section C417.7 to define the impact locations of each class of debris established by the debris analysis;

(4) For a launch vehicle flown with a flight safety system, the time delay analysis required by section A417.21; and

(5) The debris risk analysis performed as required by section A417.25 or section C417.9.

(c) *Methodology for computing ship hazard areas in the vicinity of the launch site.* The analysis must establish the ship-hit contours as follows:

(1) A ship-hit contour must account for the size of the largest ship that could be located in the ship hazard area. The analysis must demonstrate that the ship size used represents the largest ship that could be present in the ship hazard area or, if the ship size is unknown, the analysis must use a ship size of 120,000 square feet.

(2) The analysis must first calculate the probability of impacting the reference ship selected as required by paragraph (c)(1) of this section at the location of interest. From the location of interest, move the ship away from the launch location along a single radial until the probability that debris is present at that location multiplied by the probability that a ship is at that location is less than or equal to 1×10^{-5}. When calculating the probability of impacting a ship, an impact occurs when:

(i) The analysis predicts that inert debris will directly impact the vessel with a mean expected kinetic energy at impact greater than or equal to 11 ft-lbs; or

(ii) The analysis predicts the peak incident overpressure at the reference vessel will be greater than or equal to 1.0 psi due to any explosive debris impact.

(3) The analysis must account for:

(i) The variance in winds;

(ii) The aerodynamic properties of the debris;

(iii) The variance in velocity of the debris;

(iv) Guidance and performance errors;

(v) The type of vehicle breakup, either by any flight termination system or by aerodynamic forces that may result in different debris characteristics; and

(vi) Debris impact dispersion resulting from vehicle breakup and the malfunction turn capabilities of the launch vehicle.

(4) Repeat the process outlined in paragraph (c)(2) of this section while varying the radial direction until enough locations are found where the reference ship's probability of impact is less than or equal to 1×10^{-5} such that connecting each location will result in a smooth and continuous contour.

(d) *Methodology for computing ship hazard areas in the vicinity of each planned water impact location.* A launch operator must compute a ship hazard area in the vicinity of each planned impact location as required by the following:

(1) The analysis must calculate a three-sigma dispersion ellipse by determining the three-sigma impact limit around a planned impact location.

(2) Taking the three-sigma dispersion ellipse calculated as required by paragraph (d)(1) of this section, plot a co-centric ellipse in the xy plane where the major and minor axes are 10 nm longer than the major and minor axes of the three-sigma dispersion ellipse.

B417.13 LAND HAZARD AREAS ANALYSIS

(a) *General.* A flight hazard area analysis must establish land hazard areas in the vicinity of the launch site and land hazard areas in the vicinity of each land impact location to ensure that the probability of a member of the public being struck by debris satisfies the probability threshold of 1×10^{-6} required by § 417.107(b) and to determine exclusion areas that may require entry control and surveillance prior to initiation of flight. The analysis must establish a land impact hazard area that accounts for the effects of impacting debris resulting from normal and malfunctioning launch vehicle flight, except for toxic effects, and accounts for potential impact locations of all debris fragments. The land hazard area must encompass all individual casualty contours and the near-launch-point blast hazard area calculated as required by paragraph (c) of this section. A launch operator may initiate flight only if no member of the public is present within the land hazard area.

(b) *Land hazard areas analysis input.* A land hazard analysis must account for the following inputs to determine the land hazard area:

(1) The trajectory analysis performed as required by section A417.7 or section C417.3;

(2) For a launch vehicle flown with a flight safety system, the malfunction turn analysis required by section A417.9;

(3) The debris analysis required by section A417.11 or section C417.7 to define the impact locations of each class of debris established by the debris analysis;

(4) For a launch vehicle flown with a flight safety system, the time delay analysis required by section A417.21; and

(5) The debris risk analysis performed as required by section A417.25 or section C417.9.

(c) *Methodology for computing land hazard areas in the vicinity of the launch site and in the vicinity of each planned land impact location.* The analysis must establish a land hazard area as follows:

(1) Each land hazard area must completely encompass all individual casualty contours that define where the risk to an individual would exceed the expected casualty (E_c) criteria of 1×10^{-6} if one person were assumed to be in the open and inside the contour during launch vehicle flight. The analysis must produce an individual casualty contour as follows:

(i) The analysis must account for the location of a hypothetical person, and must vary the location of the person to determine when the risk would exceed the E_c criteria of 1 × 10^{-6}. The analysis must count a person as a casualty when the person's location is subjected to any inert debris impact with a mean expected kinetic energy greater than or equal to 11 ft-lbs or a peak incident overpressure equal to or greater than 1.0 psi due to explosive debris impact. The analysis must determine the peak incident overpressure using the Kingery-Bulmash relationship, without regard to sheltering, reflections, or atmospheric effects.

(ii) The analysis must account for all person locations that are no more than 1000 feet apart in the downrange direction and no more than 1000 feet apart in the crossrange direction to produce an individual casualty contour. For each person location, the analysis must sum all the probabilities of casualty over all flight times for all debris groups.

(iii) An individual casualty contour must consist of curves that are smooth and continuous. To accomplish this, the analysis must vary the time interval between each trajectory time assessed so that each location of a debris impact point is less than one-half sigma of the downrange dispersion distance.

(2) The input for determining a land impact hazard area must account for the following in order to define the impact locations of each class of debris established by the debris analysis and the time delay analysis required by section A417.21 for a launch vehicle flown with a flight safety system:

(i) The results of the trajectory analysis required by section A417.7 or section C417.3;

(ii) The malfunction turn analysis required by section A417.9 for a launch vehicle flown with a flight safety system; and

(iii) The debris analysis required by section A417.11 or section C417.7.

(3) The analysis must account for the extent of the impact debris dispersions for each debris class produced by normal and malfunctioning launch vehicle flight at each trajectory time. The analysis must also account for how the vehicle breaks up, either by any flight termination system or by aerodynamic forces, if the different breakup may result in a different probability of existence for each debris class. A land impact hazard area must account for each impacting debris fragment classified as required by section A417.11(c) or section C417.7.

(4) For a launch vehicle flown with a flight safety system, the analysis must account for launch vehicle flight that exceeds a flight safety limit. The analysis must also account for trajectory conditions that maximize the mean debris impact distance during the flight safety system delay time determined as required by section A417.21 and account for a debris model that is representative of a flight termination or aerodynamic breakup.

(5) For each launch vehicle breakup event, the analysis must account for trajectory and breakup dispersions, variations in debris class characteristics, and debris dispersion due to any wind condition under which a launch would be attempted.

(6) The analysis must account for the probability of failure of each launch vehicle stage and the probability of existence of each debris class. The analysis must account for the probability of occurrence of each type of launch vehicle failure. The analysis must account for each vehicle failure probabilities that vary depending on the time of flight.

(7) In addition to failure debris, the analysis must account for nominal jettisoned body debris impacts and the corresponding debris impact dispersions. The analysis must use a probability of occurrence of 1.0 for the planned debris fragments produced by normal separation events during flight.

(d) *Near-launch-point blast hazard area.* A land hazard area analysis must define a blast overpressure hazard area as a circle extending from the launch point with a radius equal to the 1.0 psi overpressure distance produced by the equivalent TNT weight of the explosive capability of the vehicle. In addition, the analysis must establish a minimum near-launch point blast hazard area to provide protection from hazardous fragments potentially propelled by an explosion. The analysis must account for the maximum possible total solid and liquid propellant explosive potential of the launch vehicle and any payload. The analysis must define a blast overpressure hazard area using the following equations:

$$R_{op} = 45 \cdot (NEW)^{1/3}$$

Where:

R_{op} is the over pressure distance in feet.

$NEW = W_E \cdot C$ (pounds).

W_E is the weight of the explosive in pounds.

C is the TNT equivalency coefficient of the propellant being evaluated. A launch operator must identify the TNT equivalency of each propellant on its launch vehicle including any payload. TNT equivalency data for common liquid propellants is provided in tables A417–1. Table A417–2 provides factors for converting gallons of specified liquid propellants to pounds.

(e) *Other hazards.* A flight hazard area analysis must identify any additional hazards, such as radioactive material, that may exist on the launch vehicle or payload. For each such hazard, the analysis must determine a hazard area that encompasses any debris impact point and its dispersion and includes an additional hazard radius that accounts for potential casualty due to the additional hazard. Analysis requirements for toxic release and far field blast overpressure are provided in sections A417.27 and A417.29, respectively.

(f) *Land impact dispersion ellipses.* A land impact hazard area must contain the land impact dispersion ellipse for each planned land impact. A launch operator must compute a land impact dispersion ellipse in the vicinity of each planned land impact location as follows:

(1) The analysis must calculate a one-sigma dispersion ellipse by determining the one-sigma impact limit around a planned impact location.

(2) Taking the one-sigma dispersion ellipse calculated as required by paragraph (f)(1) of this section, plot a co-centric ellipse in the xy plane where the major and minor axes are 10nm longer than the major and minor axes of the one-sigma dispersion ellipse.

APPENDIX C TO PART 417—FLIGHT SAFETY ANALYSIS METHODOLOGIES AND PRODUCTS FOR AN UNGUIDED SUBORBITAL LAUNCH VEHICLE FLOWN WITH A WIND WEIGHTING SAFETY SYSTEM

C417.1 GENERAL

(a) This appendix contains methodologies for performing the flight safety analysis required for the launch of an unguided suborbital launch vehicle flown with a wind weighting safety system, except for the hazard area analysis required by § 417.107, which is covered in appendix B of this part. This appendix includes methodologies for a trajectory analysis, wind weighting analysis, debris analysis, debris risk analysis, and a collision avoidance analysis.

(b) The requirements of this appendix apply to a launch operator and the launch operator's flight safety analysis unless the launch operator clearly and convincingly demonstrates that an alternative approach provides an equivalent level of safety.

(c) A launch operator must:

(1) Perform a flight safety analysis to determine the launch parameters and conditions under which an unguided suborbital launch vehicle may be flown using a wind weighting safety system as required by § 417.233.

(2) When conducting the flight safety analysis, comply with the safety criteria and operational requirements contained in § 417.125; and

(3) Conduct the flight safety analysis for an unguided suborbital launch vehicle using the methodologies of this appendix and appendix B of this part unless the launch operator demonstrates, in accordance with § 406.3(b), through the licensing process, that an alternate method provides an equivalent level of fidelity.

C417.3 TRAJECTORY ANALYSIS

(a) *General.* A launch operator must perform a trajectory analysis for the flight of an unguided suborbital launch vehicle to determine:

(1) The launch vehicle's nominal trajectory;

(2) Each nominal drag impact point; and

(3) Each potential three-sigma dispersion about each nominal drag impact point.

(b) *Definitions.* A launch operator must employ the following definitions when determining an unguided suborbital launch vehicle's trajectory and drag impact points:

(1) *Drag impact point* means the intersection of a predicted ballistic trajectory of an unguided suborbital launch vehicle stage or other impacting component with the Earth's surface. A drag impact point reflects the effects of atmospheric influences as a function of drag forces and mach number.

(2) *Maximum range trajectory* means an optimized trajectory, extended through fuel exhaustion of each stage, to achieve a maximum downrange drag impact point.

(3) *Nominal trajectory* means the trajectory that an unguided suborbital launch vehicle will fly if all rocket aerodynamic parameters are as expected without error, all rocket internal and external systems perform exactly as planned, and there are no external perturbing influences, such as winds, other than atmospheric drag and gravity.

(4) *Normal flight* means all possible trajectories of a properly performing unguided suborbital launch vehicle whose drag impact point location does not deviate from its nominal location more than three sigma in each of the uprange, downrange, left crossrange, or right crossrange directions.

(5) *Performance error parameter* means a quantifiable perturbing force that contributes to the dispersion of a drag impact point in the uprange, downrange, and cross-range directions of an unguided suborbital launch vehicle stage or other impacting launch vehicle component. Performance error parameters for the launch of an unguided suborbital launch vehicle reflect rocket performance variations and any external forces that can cause offsets from the nominal trajectory during normal flight. Performance error parameters include thrust, thrust misalignment, specific impulse, weight, variation in firing times of the stages, fuel flow rates, contributions from the wind weighting safety system employed, and winds.

(c) *Input.* A trajectory analysis requires the input necessary to produce a six-degree-of-freedom trajectory. A launch operator must use each of the following as inputs to the trajectory computations:

(1) Launcher data, as follows—

(i) Geodetic latitude and longitude;

(ii) Height above sea level;

(iii) All location errors; and

(iv) Launch azimuth and elevation.

(2) Reference ellipsoidal Earth model, as follows—

(i) Name of the Earth model employed;

(ii) Semi-major axis;

(iii) Semi-minor axis;

(iv) Eccentricity;

(v) Flattening parameter;

(vi) Gravitational parameter;

(vii) Rotation angular velocity;

(viii) Gravitational harmonic constants; and

(ix) Mass of the Earth.

(3) *Vehicle characteristics for each stage.* A launch operator must identify the following for each stage of an unguided suborbital launch vehicle's flight:

(i) Nozzle exit area of each stage.

(ii) Distance from the rocket nose-tip to the nozzle exit for each stage.

(iii) Reference drag area and reference diameter of the rocket including any payload for each stage of flight.

(iv) Thrust as a function of time.

(v) Propellant weight as a function of time.

(vi) Coefficient of drag as a function of mach number.

(vii) Distance from the rocket nose-tip to center of gravity as a function of time.

(viii) Yaw moment of inertia as a function of time.

(ix) Pitch moment of inertia as a function of time.

(x) Pitch damping coefficient as a function of mach number.

(xi) Aerodynamic damping coefficient as a function of mach number.

(xii) Normal force coefficient as a function of mach number.

(xiii) Distance from the rocket nose-tip to center of pressure as a function of mach number.

(xiv) Axial force coefficient as a function of mach number.

(xv) Roll rate as a function of time.

(xvi) Gross mass of each stage.

(xvii) Burnout mass of each stage.

(xviii) Vacuum thrust.

(xix) Vacuum specific impulse.

(xx) Stage dimensions.

(xxi) Weight of each spent stage.

(xxii) Payload mass properties.

(xxiii) Nominal launch elevation and azimuth.

(4) *Launch events.* Each stage ignition times, each stage burn time, and each stage separation time, referenced to ignition time of first stage.

(5) *Atmosphere.* Density as a function of altitude, pressure as a function of altitude, speed of sound as a function of altitude, temperature as a function of altitude.

(6) *Wind errors.* Error in measurement of wind direction as a function of altitude and wind magnitude as a function of altitude, wind forecast error, such as error due to time delay from wind measurement to launch.

(d) *Methodology for determining the nominal trajectory and nominal drag impact points.* A launch operator must employ the steps in paragraphs (d)(1)–(d)(3) of this section to determine the nominal trajectory and the nominal drag impact point locations for each impacting rocket stage and component:

(1) A launch operator must identify each performance error parameter associated with the unguided suborbital launch vehicle's design and operation and the value for each parameter that reflect nominal rocket performance. A launch operator must identify each performance error parameter's distribution to account for all launch vehicle performance variations and any external forces that can cause offsets from the nominal trajectory during normal flight. These performance error parameters include thrust misalignment, thrust variation, weight variation, fin misalignment, impulse variation, aerodynamic drag variation, staging timing variation, stage separation-force variation, drag error, uncompensated wind, launcher elevation angle error, launcher azimuth angle error, launcher tip-off, and launcher location error.

(2) A launch operator must perform a no-wind trajectory simulation using a six-degrees-of-freedom (6–DOF) trajectory simulation with all performance error parameters set to their nominal values to determine the impact point of each stage or component. The 6–DOF trajectory simulation must provide rocket position translation along three axes of an orthogonal Earth-centered coordinate system and rocket orientation in roll, pitch and yaw. The 6–DOF trajectory simulation must compute each translation and orientation in response to forces and moments internal and external to the rocket including all the effects of the input data required by paragraph (c) of this section. A launch operator may incorporate the following assumptions in a 6–DOF trajectory simulation:

(i) The airframe may be treated as a rigid body.

(ii) The airframe may have a plane of symmetry coinciding with the vertical plane of reference.

(iii) The vehicle may have aerodynamic symmetry in roll.

(iv) The airframe may have six degrees-of-freedom.

(v) The aerodynamic forces and moments may be functions of mach number and may be linear with small flow incidence angles of attack.

(3) A launch operator must tabulate the geodetic latitude and longitude of the launch vehicle's nominal drag impact point as a function of trajectory time and the final nominal drag impact point of each planned impacting stage or component.

(e) *Methodology for determining maximum downrange drag impact points.* A launch operator must compute the maximum possible downrange drag impact point for each launch vehicle stage and impacting component. A launch operator must use the nominal drag impact point methodology, as defined by paragraph (d) of this section, modified to optimize the unguided suborbital launch vehicle's performance and flight profile to create the conditions for a maximum downrange drag impact point, including fuel exhaustion for each stage and impacting component.

(f) *Methodology for computing drag impact point dispersions.* A launch operator must employ the steps in paragraphs (f)(1)–(f)(3) of this section when determining the dispersions in terms of drag impact point distance standard deviations in uprange, downrange, and crossrange direction from the nominal drag impact point location for each stage and impacting component:

(1) For each stage of flight, a launch operator must identify the plus and minus one-sigma values for each performance error parameter identified as required by paragraph (d)(1) of this section (*i.e.*, nominal value plus one standard deviation and nominal value minus one standard deviation). A launch operator must determine the dispersion in downrange, uprange, and left and right crossrange for each impacting stage and component. A launch operator may either perform a Monte Carlo analysis that accounts for the distribution of each performance error parameter or determine the dispersion by a root-sum-square method under paragraph (f)(2) of this section.

(2) When using a root-sum-square method to determine dispersion, a launch operator must determine the deviations for a given stage by evaluating the deviations produced in that stage due to the performance errors in that stage and all preceding stages of the launch vehicle as illustrated in Table C417-1, and by computing the square root of the sum of the squares of each deviation caused by each performance error parameter's one sigma dispersion for each stage in each of the right crossrange, left crossrange, uprange and downrange directions. A launch operator must evaluate the performance errors for one stage at a time, with the performance of all subsequent stages assumed to be nominal. A launch operator's root-sum-square method must incorporate the following requirements:

Table C417-1, Illustrative simulation runs required to determine drag impact point dispersions for a three stage launch vehicle.

Trajectory Simulation Runs Stage Performance Error Parameters	Dispersion Being Determined		
	Stage 1	Stage 2	Stage 3
Stage 1 errors	X[1]	-	-
Stage 1 errors, Stage 2 nominal	-	X	-
Stage 1 nominal, Stage 2 errors	-	X	-
Stage 1 errors, Stage 2 nominal, Stage 3 nominal	-	-	X
Stage 1 nominal, Stage 2 errors, Stage 3 nominal	-	-	X
Stage 1 nominal, Stage 2 nominal, Stage 3 errors	-	-	X

[1] An X in a given stage column means that the noted simulation runs are required to determine the dispersion for that stage.

(i) With the 6-DOF trajectory simulation used to determine nominal drag impact points as required by paragraph (d) of this section, perform a series of trajectory simulation runs for each stage and planned ejected debris, such as a fairing, payload, or other component, and, for each simulation, model only one performance error parameter set to either its plus or minus one-sigma value. For a given simulation run, set all other performance error parameters to their nominal values. Continue until achieving a trajectory simulation run for each plus one-sigma performance error parameter value and each minus one-sigma performance error parameter value for the stage or the planned ejected debris being evaluated. For each trajectory simulation run and for each impact being evaluated, tabulate the downrange, uprange, left crossrange, and right crossrange drag impact point distance deviations measured from the nominal drag impact point location for that stage or planned debris.

(ii) For uprange, downrange, right crossrange, and left crossrange, compute the square root of the sum of the squares of the distance deviations in each direction. The square root of the sum of the squares distance value for each direction represents the one-sigma drag impact point dispersion in that direction. For a multiple stage rocket, perform the first stage series of simulation runs with all subsequent stage performance error parameters set to their nominal value. Tabulate the uprange, downrange, right crossrange, and left crossrange distance deviations from the nominal impact for each subsequent drag impact point location caused by the first stage one-sigma performance error parameter. Use these deviations in determining the total drag impact point dispersions for the subsequent stage impacts as described in paragraph (f)(2)(iii) of this section.

(iii) For each subsequent stage impact of an unguided suborbital launch vehicle, determine the one-sigma impact dispersions by first determining the one-sigma distance deviations for that stage impact caused by each preceding stage as described in paragraph (f)(2)(ii) of this section. Then perform a series of simulation runs and tabulate the uprange, downrange, right crossrange, and left crossrange drag impact point distance deviations as described in paragraph (f)(2)(i) of this section for that stage's one-sigma performance error parameter values with the preceding stage performance parameters set to nominal values. For each uprange, downrange, right crossrange, and left crossrange direction, compute the square root of the sum of the squares of the stage impact distance deviations due to that stage's and each preceding stage's one-sigma performance error parameter values. This square root of the sum of the squares distance value for each direction represents the total one-sigma drag impact point dispersion in that direction for the nominal drag impact point location of that stage. Use these deviations when determining the total drag impact point dispersions for the subsequent stage impacts.

(3) A launch operator must determine a three-sigma dispersion area for each impacting stage or component as an ellipse that is centered at the nominal drag impact point location and has semi-major and semi-minor axes along the uprange, downrange, left crossrange, and right crossrange axes. The length of each axis must be three times as large as the total one-sigma drag impact point dispersions in each direction.

(g) *Trajectory analysis products for a suborbital launch vehicle.* A launch operator must file the following products of a trajectory analysis for an unguided suborbital launch vehicle with the FAA as required by § 417.203(e):

(1) A description of the process that the launch operator used for performing the trajectory analysis, including the number of simulation runs and the process for any Monte Carlo analysis performed.

(2) A description of all assumptions and procedures the launch operator used in deriving each of the performance error parameters and their standard deviations.

(3) Launch point origin data: name, geodetic latitude (+N), longitude (+E), geodetic height, and launch azimuth measured clockwise from true north.

(4) Name of reference ellipsoid Earth model used. If a launch operator employs a reference ellipsoid Earth model other than WGS–84, Department of Defense World Geodetic System, Military Standard 2401 (Jan. 11, 1994), the launch operator must identify the semi-major axis, semi-minor axis, eccentricity, flattening parameter, gravitational parameter, rotation angular velocity, gravitational harmonic constants (e.g., J2, J3, J4), and mass of Earth.

(5) If a launch operator converts latitude and longitude coordinates between different ellipsoidal Earth models to complete a trajectory analysis, the launch operator must file the equations for geodetic datum conversions and a sample calculation for converting the geodetic latitude and longitude coordinates between the models employed.

(6) A launch operator must file tabular data that lists each performance error parameter used in the trajectory computations and each performance error parameter's plus and minus one-sigma values. If the launch operator employs a Monte Carlo analysis method for determining the dispersions about the nominal drag impact point, the tabular data must list the total one-sigma drag impact point distance deviations in each direction for each impacting stage and component. If the launch operator employs

the square root of the sum of the squares method of paragraph (f)(2) of this section, the tabular data must include the one-sigma drag impact point distance deviations in each direction due to each one-sigma performance error parameter value for each impacting stage and component.

(7) A launch operator must file a graphical depiction showing geographical landmasses and the nominal and maximum range trajectories from liftoff until impact of the final stage. The graphical depiction must plot trajectory points in time intervals of no greater than one second during thrusting flight and for times corresponding to ignition, thrust termination or burnout, and separation of each stage or impacting body. If there are less than four seconds between stage separation or other jettison events, a launch operator must reduce the time intervals between plotted trajectory points to 0.2 seconds or less. The graphical depiction must show total launch vehicle velocity as a function of time, present-position ground-range as a function of time, altitude above the reference ellipsoid as a function of time, and the static stability margin as a function of time.

(8) A launch operator must file tabular data that describes the nominal and maximum range trajectories from liftoff until impact of the final stage. The tabular data must include the time after liftoff, altitude above the reference ellipsoid, present position ground range, and total launch vehicle velocity for ignition, burnout, separation, booster apogee, and booster impact of each stage or impacting body. The launch operator must file the tabular data for the same time intervals required by paragraph (g)(7) of this section.

(9) A launch operator must file a graphical depiction showing all geographical landmasses and the unguided suborbital launch vehicle's drag impact point for the nominal trajectory, the maximum impact range boundary, and the three-sigma drag impact point dispersion area for each impacting stage or component. The graphical depiction must show the following in relationship to each other: The nominal trajectory, a circle whose radius represents the range to the farthest downrange impact point that results from the maximum range trajectory, and the three-sigma drag impact point dispersions for each impacting stage and component.

(10) A launch operator must file tabular data that describes the nominal trajectory, the maximum impact range boundary, and each three-sigma drag impact point dispersion area. The tabular data must include the geodetic latitude (positive north of the equator) and longitude (positive east of the Greenwich Meridian) of each point describing the nominal drag impact point positions, the maximum range circle, and each three-sigma impact dispersion area boundary. Each three-sigma dispersion area must be described by no less than 20 coordinate pairs. All coordinates must be rounded to the fourth decimal point.

C417.5 WIND WEIGHTING ANALYSIS

(a) *General.* As part of a wind weighting safety system, a launch operator must perform a wind weighting analysis to determine launcher azimuth and elevation settings that correct for the windcocking and wind-drift effects on an unguided suborbital launch vehicle due to forecasted winds in the airspace region of flight. A launch operator's wind weighting safety system and its operation must comply with §417.125(c). The launch azimuth and elevation settings resulting from a launch operator's wind weighting analysis must produce a trajectory, under actual wind conditions, that results in a final stage drag impact point that is the same as the final stage's nominal drag impact point determined according to section C417.3(d).

(b) *Wind weighting analysis constraints.* (1) A launch operator's wind weighting analysis must:

(i) Account for the winds in the airspace region through which the rocket will fly. A launch operator's wind weighting safety system must include an operational method of determining the wind direction and wind magnitude at all altitudes that the rocket will reach up to the maximum altitude defined by dispersion analysis as required by section C417.3.

(ii) Account for all errors due to the methods used to measure the winds in the airspace region of the launch, delay associated with wind measurement, and the method used to model the effects of winds. The resulting sum of these error components must be no greater than those used as the wind error dispersion parameter in the launch vehicle trajectory analysis performed as required by section C417.3.

(iii) Account for the dispersion of all impacting debris, including any uncorrected wind error accounted for in the trajectory analysis performed as required by section C417.3.

(iv) Establish flight commit criteria that are a function of the analysis and operational methods employed and reflect the maximum wind velocities and wind variability for which the results of the wind weighting analysis are valid.

(v) Account for the wind effects during each thrusting phase of an unguided suborbital launch vehicle's flight and each ballistic phase of each rocket stage and component until burnout of the last stage.

(vi) Determine the impact point location for any parachute recovery of a stage or component or the launch operator must perform a wind drift analysis to determine the parachute impact point location.

(2) A launch operator must perform a wind weighting analysis using a six-degrees-of-freedom (6–DOF) trajectory simulation that targets an impact point using an iterative process. The 6–DOF simulation must account for launch day wind direction and wind magnitude as a function of altitude.

(3) A launch operator must perform a wind weighting analysis using a computer program or other method of editing wind data, recording the time the data was obtained, and recording the balloon number or identification of any other measurement device used for each wind altitude layer.

(c) *Methodology for performing a wind weighting analysis.* A launch operator's method for performing a wind weighting analysis on the day of flight must account for the following:

(1) A launch operator must measure the winds on the day of flight to determine wind velocity and direction. A launch operator's process for measuring winds must provide wind data that is consistent with any assumptions made in the launch operator's trajectory and drag impact point dispersion analysis, as required by section C417.3, regarding the actual wind data available on the day of flight. Wind measurements must be made at altitude increments such that the maximum correction between any two measurements does not exceed 5%. Winds must be measured from the ground level at the launch point to a maximum altitude that is consistent with the launch operator's drag impact point dispersion analysis. The maximum wind measurement altitude must be that necessary to account for 99% of the wind effect on the impact dispersion point. A launch operator's wind measuring process must employ the use of balloons and radar tracking or balloons fitted with a Global Positioning System transceiver, and must account for the following:

(i) Measure winds from ground level to an altitude of at least that necessary to account for 99% of the wind effect on the impact dispersion point within six hours before flight and after any weather front passes the launch site before liftoff. Repeat a wind measurement up to the maximum altitude whenever a wind measurement, for any given altitude, from a later balloon release is not consistent with a wind measurement, for the same altitude, from an earlier balloon release.

(ii) Measure winds from ground level to an altitude of at least that necessary to account for 95% of the wind effect on the impact dispersion point within four hours before flight and after any weather front passes the launch site before liftoff. Repeat a wind measurement to the 95% wind effect altitude whenever a wind measurement, for any given altitude, from a later lower altitude balloon release is not consistent with the wind measurement, for the same altitude, from the 95% wind effect altitude balloon release.

(iii) Measure winds from ground level to an altitude of no less than that necessary to account for 80% of the wind effect on the impact dispersion point twice within 30 minutes of liftoff. Use the first measurement to set launcher azimuth and elevation, and the second measurement to verify the first measurement data.

(2) A launch operator must perform runs of the 6–DOF trajectory simulation using the flight day measured winds as input and targeting for the nominal final stage drag impact point. In an iterative process, vary the launcher elevation angle and azimuth angle settings for each simulation run until the nominal final stage impact point is achieved. The launch operator must use the resulting launcher elevation angle and azimuth angle settings to correct for the flight day winds. The launch operator must not initiate flight unless the launcher elevation angle and azimuth angle settings after wind weighting are in accordance with the following:

(i) The launcher elevation angle setting resulting from the wind weighting analysis must not exceed ±5° from the nominal launcher elevation angle setting and must not exceed a total of 86° for a proven launch vehicle, and 84° for an unproven launch vehicle. A launch operator's nominal launcher elevation angle setting must be as required by §417.125(c)(3).

(ii) The launcher azimuth angle setting resulting from the wind weighting analysis must not exceed + 30° from the nominal launcher azimuth angle setting unless the launch operator demonstrates clearly and convincingly, through the licensing process, that its unguided suborbital launch vehicle has a low sensitivity to high wind speeds, and the launch operator's wind weighting analysis and wind measuring process provide an equivalent level of safety.

(3) Using the trajectory produced in paragraph (c)(2) of this section, for each intermediate stage and planned ejected component, a launch operator must compute the impact point that results from wind drift by performing a run of the 6-DOF trajectory simulation with the launcher angles determined in paragraph (c)(2) of this section and the flight day winds from liftoff until the burnout time or ejection time of the stage or ejected component. The resulting impact point(s) must be accounted for when performing flight day ship-hit operations defined in section B417.11(c).

(4) If a parachute is used for any stage or component, a launch operator must determine the wind drifted impact point of the stage or component using a trajectory simulation that incorporates modeling for the

change in aerodynamics at parachute ejection. Perform this simulation run in addition to any simulation of spent stages without parachutes.

(5) A launch operator must verify that the launcher elevation angle and azimuth angle settings at the time of liftoff are the same as required by the wind weighting analysis.

(6) A launch operator must monitor and verify that any wind variations and maximum wind limits at the time of liftoff are within the flight commit criteria established according to § 417.113(c).

(7) A launch operator must generate output data from its wind weighting analysis for each impacting stage or component in printed, plotted, or computer medium format. This data must include:

(i) Launch day wind measurement data, including magnitude and direction.

(ii) The results of each computer run made using the launch day wind measurement data, including but not limited to, launcher settings, and impact locations for each stage or component.

(iii) Final launcher settings recorded.

(d) *Wind weighting analysis products.* The products of a launch operator's wind weighting analysis filed with the FAA as required by § 417.203(e) must include the following:

(1) A launch operator must file a description of its wind weighting analysis methods, including its method and schedule of determining wind speed and wind direction for each altitude layer.

(2) A launch operator must file a description of its wind weighting safety system and identify all equipment used to perform the wind weighting analysis, such as any wind towers, balloons, or Global Positioning System wind measurement system employed and the type of trajectory simulation employed.

(3) A launch operator must file a sample wind weighting analysis using actual or statistical winds for the launch area and provide samples of the output required by paragraph (c)(7) of this section.

C417.7 DEBRIS ANALYSIS

(a) *General.* A flight safety analysis must include a debris analysis that satisfies the requirements of § 417.211. This section applies to the debris data required by § 417.211 and the debris analysis products that a launch operator must file with the FAA as required by § 417.203(e).

(b) *Debris analysis constraints.* A debris analysis must produce the debris model described in paragraph (c) of this section. The analysis must account for all launch vehicle debris fragments, individually or in groupings of fragments called classes. The characteristics of each debris fragment represented by a class must be similar enough to the characteristics of all the other debris fragments represented by that class that all the debris fragments of the class can be described by a single set of characteristics. Paragraph (c)(10) of this section applies when establishing a debris class. A debris model must describe the physical, aerodynamic, and harmful characteristics of each debris fragment either individually or as a member of a class. A debris model must consist of lists of individual debris or debris classes for each cause of breakup and any planned jettison of debris, launch vehicle components, or payload. A debris analysis must account for:

(1) Debris due to any malfunction where forces on the launch vehicle may exceed the launch vehicle's structural integrity limits.

(2) The immediate post-breakup or jettison environment of the launch vehicle debris, and any change in debris characteristics over time from launch vehicle breakup or jettison until debris impact.

(3) The impact overpressure, fragmentation, and secondary debris effects of any confined or unconfined solid propellant chunks and fueled components containing either liquid or solid propellants that could survive to impact, as a function of vehicle malfunction time.

(4) The effects of impact of the intact vehicle as a function of failure time. The intact impact debris analysis must identify the trinitrotoluene (TNT) yield of impact explosions, and the numbers of fragments projected from all such explosions, including non-launch vehicle ejecta and the blast overpressure radius. The analysis must use a model for TNT yield of impact explosion that accounts for the propellant weight at impact, the impact speed, the orientation of the propellant, and the impacted surface material.

(c) *Debris model.* A debris analysis must produce a model of the debris resulting from planned jettison and from unplanned breakup of a launch vehicle for use as input to other analyses, such as establishing hazard areas and performing debris risk and toxic analyses. A launch operator's debris model must satisfy the following:

(1) *Debris fragments.* A debris model must provide the debris fragment data required by this section for the launch vehicle flight from the planned ignition time until thrust termination of the last thrusting stage. A debris model must provide debris fragment data for the number of time periods sufficient to meet the requirements for smooth and continuous contours used to define hazard areas as required by appendix B of this part.

(2) *Inert fragments.* A debris model must identify all inert fragments that are not volatile and that do not burn or explode under normal and malfunction conditions. A debris model must identify all inert fragments for each breakup time during flight

corresponding to a critical event when the fragment catalog is significantly changed by the event. Critical events include staging, payload fairing jettison, and other normal hardware jettison activities.

(3) *Explosive and non-explosive propellant fragments.* A debris model must identify all propellant fragments that are explosive or non-explosive upon impact. The debris model must describe each propellant fragment as a function of time, from the time of breakup through ballistic free-fall to impact. The debris model must describe the characteristics of each fragment, including its origin on the launch vehicle, representative dimensions and weight at the time of breakup and at the time of impact. For any fragment identified as an un-contained or contained propellant fragment, whether explosive or non-explosive, the debris model must identify whether or not it burns during free fall, and provide the consumption rate during free fall. The debris model must identify:

(i) Solid propellant that is exposed directly to the atmosphere and that burns but does not explode upon impact as "un-contained non-explosive solid propellant."

(ii) Solid or liquid propellant that is enclosed in a container, such as a motor case or pressure vessel, and that burns but does not explode upon impact as "contained non-explosive propellant."

(iii) Solid or liquid propellant that is enclosed in a container, such as a motor case or pressure vessel, and that explodes upon impact as "contained explosive propellant fragment."

(iv) Solid propellant that is exposed directly to the atmosphere and that explodes upon impact as "un-contained explosive solid propellant fragment."

(4) *Other non-inert debris fragments.* In addition to the explosive and flammable fragments identified under paragraph (c)(3) of this section, a debris model must identify any other non-inert debris fragments, such as toxic or radioactive fragments, that present any other hazards to the public.

(5) *Fragment weight.* At each modeled breakup time, the individual fragment weights must approximately add up to the sum total weight of inert material in the vehicle and the weight of contained liquid propellants and solid propellants that are not consumed in the initial breakup or conflagration.

(6) *Fragment imparted velocity.* A debris model must identify the maximum velocity imparted to each fragment due to potential explosion or pressure rupture. When accounting for imparted velocity, a debris model must:

(i) Use a Maxwellian distribution with the specified maximum value equal to the 97th percentile; or

(ii) Identify the distribution, and state whether or not the specified maximum value is a fixed value with no uncertainty.

(7) *Fragment projected area.* A debris model must include each of the axial, transverse, and mean tumbling areas of each fragment. If the fragment may stabilize under normal or malfunction conditions, the debris model must also provide the projected area normal to the drag force.

(8) *Fragment ballistic coefficient.* A debris model must include the axial, transverse, and tumble orientation ballistic coefficient for each fragment's projected area as required by paragraph (c)(7) of this section.

(9) *Debris fragment count.* A debris model must include the total number of each type of fragment required by paragraphs (c)(2), (c)(3), and (c)(4) of this section and created by a malfunction.

(10) *Fragment classes.* A debris model must categorize malfunction debris fragments into classes where the characteristics of the mean fragment in each class conservatively represent every fragment in the class. The model must define fragment classes for fragments whose characteristics are similar enough to be described and treated by a single average set of characteristics. A debris class must categorize debris by each of the following characteristics, and may include any other useful characteristics:

(i) The type of fragment, defined by paragraphs (c)(2), (c)(3), and (c)(4) of this section. All fragments within a class must be the same type, such as inert or explosive.

(ii) Debris subsonic ballistic coefficient (β_{sub}). The difference between the smallest $\log_{10}(\beta_{sub})$ value and the largest $\log_{10}(\beta_{sub})$ value in a class must not exceed 0.5, except for fragments with β_{sub} less than or equal to three. Fragments with β_{sub} less than or equal to three may be grouped within a class.

(iii) Breakup-imparted velocity (ΔV). A debris model must categorize fragments as a function of the range of ΔV for the fragments within a class and the class's median subsonic ballistic coefficient. For each class, the debris model must keep the ratio of the maximum breakup-imparted velocity (ΔV_{max}) to minimum breakup-imparted velocity (ΔV_{min}) within the following bound:

$$\frac{\Delta V_{max}}{\Delta V_{min}} < \frac{5}{2 + \log_{10}\left(\beta'_{sub}\right)}$$

Where:

β'_{sub} is the median subsonic ballistic coefficient for the fragments in a class.

(d) *Debris analysis products.* The products of a debris analysis that a launch operator must file with the FAA as required by §417.203(e) must include:

(1) *Debris model.* The launch operator's debris model that satisfies the requirements of this section.

(2) *Fragment description.* A description of the fragments contained in the launch operator's debris model. The description must identify the fragment as a launch vehicle part or component, describe its shape, representative dimensions, and may include drawings of the fragment.

(3) *Intact impact TNT yield.* For an intact impact of a launch vehicle, for each failure time, a launch operator must identify the TNT yield of each impact explosion and blast overpressure hazard radius.

(4) *Fragment class data.* The class name, the range of values for each parameter used to categorize fragments within a fragment class, and the number of fragments in any fragment class established as required by paragraph (c)(10) of this section.

(5) *Ballistic coefficient.* The mean ballistic coefficient (β) and plus and minus three-sigma values of the β for each fragment class. A launch operator must provide graphs of the coefficient of drag (C_d) as a function of Mach number for the nominal and three-sigma β variations for each fragment shape. The launch operator must label each graph with the shape represented by the curve and reference area used to develop the curve. A launch operator must provide a C_d vs. Mach curve for any axial, transverse, and tumble orientations for any fragment that will not stabilize during free-fall conditions. For any fragment that may stabilize during free-fall, a launch operator must provide C_d vs. Mach curves for the stability angle of attack. If the angle of attack where the fragment stabilizes is other than zero degrees, a launch operator must provide both the coefficient of lift (C_L) vs. Mach number and the C_d vs. Mach number curves. The launch operator must provide the equations for each C_d vs. Mach curve.

(6) *Pre-flight propellant weight.* The initial preflight weight of solid and liquid propellant for each launch vehicle component that contains solid or liquid propellant.

(7) *Normal propellant consumption.* The nominal and plus and minus three-sigma solid and liquid propellant consumption rate, and pre-malfunction consumption rate for each component that contains solid or liquid propellant.

(8) *Fragment weight.* The mean and plus and minus three-sigma weight of each fragment or fragment class.

(9) *Projected area.* The mean and plus and minus three-sigma axial, transverse, and tumbling areas for each fragment or fragment class. This information is not required for those fragment classes classified as burning propellant classes under section A417.25(b)(8).

(10) *Imparted velocities.* The maximum incremental velocity imparted to each fragment class created by explosive or overpressure loads at breakup. The launch operator must identify the velocity distribution as Maxwellian or must define the distribution, including whether or not the specified maximum value is a fixed value with no uncertainty.

(11) *Fragment type.* The fragment type for each fragment established as required by paragraphs (c)(2), (c)(3), and (c)(4) of this section.

(12) *Origin.* The part of the launch vehicle from which each fragment originated.

(13) *Burning propellant classes.* The propellant consumption rate for those fragments that burn during free-fall.

(14) *Contained propellant fragments, explosive or non-explosive.* For contained propellant fragments, whether explosive or non-explosive, a launch operator must provide the initial weight of contained propellant and the consumption rate during free-fall. The initial weight of the propellant in a contained propellant fragment is the weight of the propellant before any of the propellant is consumed by normal vehicle operation or failure of the launch vehicle.

(15) *Solid propellant fragment snuff-out pressure.* The ambient pressure and the pressure at the surface of a solid propellant fragment, in pounds per square inch, required to sustain a solid propellant fragment's combustion during free-fall.

(16) *Other non-inert debris fragments.* For each non-inert debris fragment identified as required by paragraph (c)(4) of this section, a launch operator must describe the diffusion, dispersion, deposition, radiation, and other hazard exposure characteristics used to determine the effective casualty area required by paragraph (c)(9) of this section.

(17) *Residual thrust dispersion.* For each thrusting or non-thrusting stage having residual thrust capability following a launch vehicle malfunction, a launch operator must provide either the total residual impulse imparted or the full-residual thrust in foot-pounds as a function of breakup time. For any stage not capable of thrust after a launch vehicle malfunction, a launch operator must provide the conditions under which the stage is no longer capable of thrust. For each stage that can be ignited as a result of a launch vehicle malfunction on a lower stage, a launch operator must identify the effects and duration of the potential thrust, and the maximum deviation of the instantaneous impact point which can be brought about by the thrust.

C417.9 DEBRIS RISK

(a) *General.* A launch operator must perform a debris risk analysis that satisfies the requirements of §417.225. This section applies to the computation of the average number of casualties (E_c) to the collective members of the public exposed to inert and explosive debris hazards from the proposed flight of an unguided suborbital launch vehicle as required by § 417.225 and to the analysis products that the launch operator must file with the FAA as required by § 417.203(e).

(b) *Debris risk analysis constraints.* The following constraints apply to debris risk:

(1) A debris risk analysis must use valid risk analysis models that compute E_c as the summation over all trajectory time intervals from lift-off through impact of the products of the probability of each possible event and the casualty consequences due to debris impacts for each possible event.

(2) A debris risk analysis must account for the following populations:

(i) The overflight of populations located inside any flight hazard area.

(ii) All populations located within five-sigma left and right crossrange of a nominal trajectory instantaneous impact point ground trace and within five-sigma of each planned nominal debris impact.

(3) A debris risk analysis must account for both inert and explosive debris hazards produced from any impacting debris caused by normal and malfunctioning launch vehicle flight. The analysis must account for the debris classes determined by the debris analysis required by section A417.11. A debris risk analysis must account for any inert debris impact with mean expected kinetic energy at impact greater than or equal to 11 ft-lbs and peak incident overpressure of greater than or equal to 1.0 psi due to any explosive debris impact. The analysis must account for all debris hazards as a function of flight time.

(4) A debris risk analysis must account for debris impact points and dispersion for each class of debris in accordance with the following:

(i) A debris risk analysis must account for drag corrected impact points and dispersions for each class of impacting debris resulting from normal and malfunctioning launch vehicle flight as a function of trajectory time from lift-off through final impact.

(ii) The dispersion for each debris class must account for the position and velocity state vector dispersions at breakup, the variance produced by breakup imparted velocities, the effects of winds on both the ascent trajectory state vector at breakup and the descending debris piece impact location, the variance produced by aerodynamic properties for each debris class, and any other dispersion variances.

(iii) A debris risk analysis must account for the survivability of debris fragments that are subject to reentry aerodynamic forces or heating. A debris class may be eliminated from the debris risk analysis if the launch operator demonstrates that the debris will not survive to impact.

(5) A debris risk analysis must account for launch vehicle failure probability. The following constraints apply:

(i) For flight safety analysis purposes, a failure occurs when a vehicle does not complete any phase of normal flight or exhibits the potential for the stage or its debris to impact the Earth or reenter the atmosphere during the mission or any future mission of similar vehicle capability. Also, either a launch incident or launch accident constitutes a failure.

(ii) For a launch vehicle with fewer than 2 flights completed, the analysis must use a reference value for the launch vehicle failure probability estimate equal to the upper limit of the 60% two-sided confidence limits of the binomial distribution for outcomes of all previous launches of vehicles developed and launched in similar circumstances. The FAA may adjust the failure probability estimate to account for the level of experience demonstrated by the launch operator and other factors that affects the probability of failure. The FAA may adjust the failure probability estimate for the second launch based on evidence obtained from the first flight of the vehicle.

(iii) For a launch vehicle with at least 2 flights completed, the analysis must use the reference value for the launch vehicle failure probability of Table C417–2 based on the outcomes of all previous launches of the vehicle. The FAA may adjust the failure probability estimate to account for evidence obtained from the flight history of the vehicle. Failure probability estimate adjustments to the reference value may account for the nature of launch outcomes in the flight history of the vehicle, corrective actions taken in response to a failure of the vehicle, or other vehicle modifications that may affect reliability. The FAA may adjust the failure probability estimate to account for the demonstrated quality of the engineering approach to launch vehicle processing. The analysis must use a final failure estimate within the confidence limits of Table C417–2.

(A) Values listed on the far left of Table C417–2 apply when no launch failures are experienced. Values on the far right apply when only launch failures are experienced. Values in between apply for flight histories that include both failures and successes.

(B) Reference values in Table C417–2 are shown in bold. The reference values are the median values between 60% two-sided confidence limits of the binomial distribution. For the special cases of zero or N failures in N launch attempts, the reference values may also be recognized as the median value between the 80% one-sided confidence limit of the binomial distribution and zero or one, respectively.

(C) Upper and lower confidence bounds in Table C417–2 are shown directly above and below each reference value. These confidence bounds are based on 60% two-sided confidence limits of the binomial distribution. For the special cases of zero or N failures in N launch attempts, the upper and lower confidence bounds are based on the 80% one-sided confidence limit, respectively.

Table C417-2, Launch Vehicle Failure Probability Reference Estimates and Confidence Bounds of Launch Vehicles with Two or More Flights

Launch #	<------Success										Failure ------>
3	.553 **.276** .00	.894 **.50** .106	1.00 **.724** .447								
4	.415 **.208** .00	.713 **.392** .072	.928 **.608** .287	1.00 **.792** .585							
5	.331 **.166** .00	.582 **.318** .054	.788 **.50** .212	.946 **.682** .418	1.00 **.834** .669						
6	.275 **.138** .00	.49 **.267** .044	.673 **.421** .169	.831 **.579** .327	.956 **.733** .51	1.00 **.862** .725					
7	.235 **.118** .00	.422 **.229** .037	.585 **.363** .14	.731 **.50** .269	.86 **.637** .415	.963 **.771** .578	1.00 **.882** .765				
8	.205 **.103** .00	.371 **.201** .031	.517 **.318** .12	.65 **.439** .228	.772 **.561** .35	.88 **.682** .483	.969 **.799** .629	1.00 **.897** .795			
9	.182 **.091** .00	.33 **.179** .028	.462 **.283** .104	.584 **.391** .199	.697 **.50** .303	.801 **.609** .416	.896 **.717** .538	.972 **.821** .67	1.00 **.909** .818		
10	.164 **.082** .00	.298 **.161** .024	.418 **.255** .093	.529 **.352** .176	.634 **.451** .268	.732 **.549** .366	.824 **.648** .471	.907 **.745** .582	.976 **.839** .702	1.00 **.918** .836	
11	.149 **.074** .00	.271 **.147** .022	.381 **.232** .083	.484 **.321** .158	.581 **.41** .239	.673 **.50** .327	.761 **.59** .419	.842 **.679** .516	.917 **.768** .619	.978 **.853** .729	1.00 **.926** .851

(6) A debris risk analysis must account for the dwell time of the instantaneous impact point ground trace over each populated or protected area being evaluated.

(7) A debris risk analysis must account for the three-sigma instantaneous impact point trajectory variations in left-crossrange, right-crossrange, uprange, and downrange as a function of trajectory time, due to launch vehicle performance variations as determined by the trajectory analysis performed as required by section C417.3.

(8) A debris risk analysis must account for the effective casualty area as a function of launch vehicle flight time for all impacting debris generated from a catastrophic launch vehicle malfunction event or a planned impact event. The effective casualty area must:

(i) Account for both payload and vehicle systems and subsystems debris;

(ii) Account for all debris fragments determined as part of a launch operator's debris analysis as required by section A417.11;

(iii) For each explosive debris fragment, account for a 1.0 psi blast overpressure radius and the projected debris effects for all potentially explosive debris; and

(iv) For each inert debris fragment, account for bounce, skip, slide, and splatter effects; or equal seven times the maximum projected area of the fragment.

(9) A debris risk analysis must account for current population density data obtained from a current population database for the region being evaluated or by estimating the current population using exponential population growth rate equations applied to the most current historical data available. The population model must define population centers that are similar enough to be described and treated as a single average set of characteristics without degrading the accuracy of the debris risk estimate.

(c) *Debris risk analysis products.* The products of a debris risk analysis that a launch operator must file with the FAA must include:

(1) A debris risk analysis report that provides the analysis input data, probabilistic risk determination methods, sample computations, and text or graphical charts that characterize the public risk to geographical areas for each launch.

(2) Geographic data showing:

(i) The launch vehicle nominal, five-sigma left-crossrange and five-sigma right-crossrange instantaneous impact point ground traces;

(ii) All exclusion zones relative to the instantaneous impact point ground traces; and

(iii) All populated areas included in the debris risk analysis.

(3) A discussion of each launch vehicle failure scenario accounted for in the analysis and the probability of occurrence, which may vary with flight time, for each failure scenario. This information must include failure scenarios where a launch vehicle:

(i) Flies within normal limits until some malfunction causes spontaneous breakup; and

(ii) Experiences malfunction turns.

(4) A population model applicable to the launch overflight regions that contains the following: Region identification, location of the center of each population center by geodetic latitude and longitude, total area, number of persons in each population center, and a description of the shelter characteristics within the population center.

(5) A description of the launch vehicle, including general information concerning the nature and purpose of the launch and an overview of the launch vehicle, including a scaled diagram of the general arrangement and dimensions of the vehicle. A launch operator's debris risk analysis products may reference other documentation filed with the FAA containing this information. The description must include:

(i) Weights and dimensions of each stage.

(ii) Weights and dimensions of any booster motors attached.

(iii) The types of fuel used in each stage and booster.

(iv) Weights and dimensions of all interstage adapters and skirts.

(v) Payload dimensions, materials, construction, and any payload fuel; payload fairing construction, materials, and dimensions; and any non-inert components or materials that add to the effective casualty area of the debris, such as radioactive or toxic materials or high-pressure vessels.

(6) A typical sequence of events showing times of ignition, cutoff, burnout, and jettison of each stage, firing of any ullage rockets, and starting and ending times of coast periods and control modes.

(7) The following information for each launch vehicle motor:

(i) Propellant type and composition;

(ii) Vacuum thrust profile;

(iii) Propellant weight and total motor weight as a function of time;

(iv) A description of each nozzle and steering mechanism;

(v) For solid rocket motors, internal pressure and average propellant thickness, or borehole radius, as a function of time;

(vi) Burn rate; and

(vii) Nozzle exit and entrance areas.

(8) The launch vehicle's launch and failure history, including a summary of past vehicle performance. For a new vehicle with little or no flight history, a launch operator must provide all known data on similar vehicles that include:

(i) Identification of the launches that have occurred;

(ii) Launch date, location, and direction of each launch;

(iii) The number of launches that performed normally;

(iv) Behavior and impact location of each abnormal experience;

(v) The time, altitude, and nature of each malfunction; and

(vi) Descriptions of corrective actions taken, including changes in vehicle design, flight termination, and guidance and control hardware and software.

(9) The values of probability of impact (PI) and expected casualty (Ec) for each populated area.

C417.11 COLLISION AVOIDANCE

(a) *General.* A flight safety analysis must include a collision avoidance analysis that satisfies the requirements of §417.231. This section applies to a launch operator obtaining a collision avoidance assessment from United States Strategic Command as required by §417.231 and to the analysis products that the launch operator must file with the FAA as required by §417.203(e). United States Strategic Command refers to a collision avoidance analysis for a space launch as a conjunction on launch assessment.

(b) *Analysis not required.* A collision avoidance analysis is not required if the maximum altitude attainable by the launch operator's unguided suborbital launch vehicle is less than the altitude of the lowest manned or mannable orbiting object. The maximum altitude attainable means an optimized trajectory, assuming 3-sigma maximum performance, extended through fuel exhaustion of each stage, to achieve a maximum altitude.

(c) *Analysis constraints.* A launch operator must satisfy the following when obtaining and implementing the results of a collision avoidance analysis:

(1) A launch operator must provide United States Strategic Command with the launch window and trajectory data needed to perform a collision avoidance analysis for a launch as required by paragraph (d) of this section, at least 15 days before the first attempt at flight. The FAA will identify a launch operator to United States Strategic Command as part of issuing a license and provide a launch operator with current United States Strategic Command contact information.

(2) A launch operator must obtain a collision avoidance analysis performed by United States Strategic Command 6 hours before the beginning of a launch window.

(3) A launch operator may use a collision avoidance analysis for 12 hours from the time that United States Strategic Command

determines the state vectors of the manned or mannable orbiting objects. If a launch operator needs an updated collision avoidance analysis due to a launch delay, the launch operator must file the request with United States Strategic Command at least 12 hours prior to the beginning of the new launch window.

(4) For every 90 minutes, or portion of 90 minutes, that pass between the time United States Strategic Command last determined the state vectors of the orbiting objects, a launch operator must expand each wait in a launch window by subtracting 15 seconds from the start of the wait in the launch window and adding 15 seconds to the end of the wait in the launch window. A launch operator must incorporate all the resulting waits in the launch window into its flight commit criteria established as required by §417.113.

(d) *Information required.* A launch operator must prepare a collision avoidance analysis worksheet for each launch using a standardized format that contains the input data required by this paragraph. A launch operator must file the input data with United States Strategic Command for the purposes of completing a collision avoidance analysis.

(1) *Launch information.* A launch operator must file the following launch information:

(i) *Mission name.* A mnemonic given to the launch vehicle/payload combination identifying the launch mission from all others.

(ii) *Segment number.* A segment is defined as a launch vehicle stage or payload after the thrusting portion of its flight has ended. This includes the jettison or deployment of any stage or payload. A launch operator must provide a separate worksheet for each segment. For each segment, a launch operator must determine the "vector at injection" as defined by paragraph (d)(5) of this section. The data must present each segment number as a sequence number relative to the total number of segments for a launch, such as "1 of 5."

(iii) *Launch window.* The launch window opening and closing times in Greenwich Mean Time (referred to as ZULU time) and the Julian dates for each scheduled launch attempt.

(2) *Point of contact.* The person or office within a launch operator's organization that collects, analyzes, and distributes collision avoidance analysis results.

(3) *Collision avoidance analysis results transmission medium.* A launch operator must identify the transmission medium, such as voice, FAX, or e-mail, for receiving results from United States Strategic Command.

(4) *Requestor launch operator needs.* A launch operator must indicate the types of analysis output formats required for establishing flight commit criteria for a launch:

(i) *Waits.* All the times within the launch window during which flight must not be initiated.

(ii) *Windows.* All the times within an overall launch window during which flight may be initiated.

(5) *Vector at injection.* A launch operator must identify the vector at injection for each segment. "Vector at injection" identifies the position and velocity of all orbital or suborbital segments after the thrust for a segment has ended.

(i) *Epoch.* The epoch time, in Greenwich Mean Time (GMT), of the expected launch vehicle liftoff time.

(ii) *Position and velocity.* The position coordinates in the EFG coordinate system measured in kilometers and the EFG components measured in kilometers per second, of each launch vehicle stage or payload after any burnout, jettison, or deployment.

(6) *Time of powered flight.* The elapsed time in seconds, from liftoff to arrival at the launch vehicle vector at injection. The input data must include the time of powered flight for each stage or jettisoned component measured from liftoff.

(7) *Time span for launch window file (LWF).* A launch operator must provide the following information regarding its launch window:

(i) *Launch window.* The launch window measured in minutes from the initial proposed liftoff time.

(ii) *Time of powered flight.* The time provided as required by paragraph (d)(6) of this section measured in minutes rounded up to the nearest integer minute.

(iii) *Screen duration.* The time duration, after all thrusting periods of flight have ended, that a collision avoidance analysis must screen for potential conjunctions with manned or mannable orbital objects. Screen duration is measured in minutes.

(iv) *Extra pad.* An additional period of time for collision avoidance analysis screening to ensure the entire trajectory time is screened for potential conjunctions with manned or mannable orbital objects. This time must be 10 minutes unless otherwise specified by United States Strategic Command.

(v) *Total.* The summation total of the time spans provided as required by paragraphs (d)(7)(i) through (d)(7)(iv) expressed in minutes.

(8) *Screening.* A launch operator must select spherical or ellipsoidal screening as defined in this paragraph for determining any conjunction. The default must be the spherical screening method using an avoidance radius of 200 kilometers for manned or mannable orbiting objects. If the launch operator requests screening for any unmanned or unmannable objects, the default must be the spherical screening method using a miss-distance of 25 kilometers.

(i) *Spherical screening.* Spherical screening utilizes an impact exclusion sphere centered on each orbiting object's center-of-mass to determine any conjunction. A launch operator must specify the avoidance radius for manned or mannable objects and for any unmanned or unmannable objects if the launch operator elects to perform the analysis for unmanned or unmannable objects.

(ii) *Ellipsoidal screening.* Ellipsoidal screening utilizes an impact exclusion ellipsoid of revolution centered on the orbiting object's center-of-mass to determine any conjunction. A launch operator must provide input in the UVW coordinate system in kilometers. The launch operator must provide delta-U measured in the radial-track direction, delta-V measured in the in-track direction, and delta-W measured in the cross-range direction.

(9) *Deliverable schedule/need dates.* A launch operator must identify the times before flight, referred to as "L-times," for which the launch operator requests a collision avoidance analysis.

(e) *Collision avoidance assessment products.* A launch operator must file its collision avoidance analysis products as required by §417.203(e) and must include the input data required by paragraph (d) of this section. A launch operator must incorporate the result of the collision avoidance analysis into its flight commit criteria established as required by §417.113.

APPENDIX D TO PART 417—FLIGHT TERMINATION SYSTEMS, COMPONENTS, INSTALLATION, AND MONITORING

D417.1 GENERAL

This appendix applies to each flight termination system and the components that make up the system for each launch. Section 417.301 requires that a launch operator's flight safety system include a flight termination system that complies with this appendix. Section 417.301 also contains requirements that apply to a launch operator's demonstration of compliance with the requirements of this appendix.

D417.3 FLIGHT TERMINATION SYSTEM FUNCTIONAL REQUIREMENTS

(a) When a flight safety system terminates the flight of a vehicle because it has either violated a flight safety rule as defined in §417.113 or the vehicle inadvertently separates or destructs as described in section D417.11, a flight termination system must:

(1) Render each propulsion system that has the capability of reaching a populated or other protected area, incapable of propulsion, without significant lateral or longitudinal deviation in the impact point. This includes each stage and any strap on motor or propulsion system that is part of any payload;

(2) Terminate the flight of any inadvertently or prematurely separated propulsion system capable of reaching a populated or other protected area;

(3) Destroy the pressure integrity of any solid propellant system to terminate all thrust or ensure that any residual thrust causes the propulsion system to tumble without significant lateral or longitudinal deviation in the impact point; and

(4) Disperse any liquid propellant, whether by rupturing the propellant tank or other equivalent method, and initiate burning of any toxic liquid propellant.

(b) A flight termination system must not cause any solid or liquid propellant to detonate.

(c) The flight termination of a propulsion system must not interfere with the flight termination of any other propulsion system.

D417.5 FLIGHT TERMINATION SYSTEM DESIGN

(a) *Reliability prediction.* A flight termination system must have a predicted reliability of 0.999 at a confidence level of 95 percent. A launch operator must demonstrate the system's predicted reliability by satisfying the requirements for system reliability analysis of §417.309(b).

(b) *Single fault tolerance.* A flight termination system, including monitoring and checkout circuits, must not have a single failure point that would:

(1) Inhibit functioning of the system during flight; or

(2) Produce an inadvertent initiation of the system that would endanger the public.

(c) *Redundancy.* A flight termination system must use redundant components that are structurally, electrically, and mechanically separated. Each redundant component's mounting on a launch vehicle, including location or orientation, must ensure that any failure that will damage, destroy or otherwise inhibit the operation of one redundant component will not inhibit the operation of the other redundant component and will not inhibit functioning of the system. Each of the following exceptions applies:

(1) Any linear shaped charge need not be redundant if it initiates at both ends, and the initiation source for one end is not the same as the initiation source for the other end; or

(2) Any passive component such as an antenna or radio frequency coupler need not be redundant if it satisfies the requirements of this appendix.

(d) *System independence.* A flight termination system must operate independently of any other launch vehicle system. The failure of another launch vehicle system must not inhibit the functioning of a flight termination system. A flight termination system may share a component with another launch vehicle system, only if the launch operator demonstrates that sharing the component will not degrade the flight termination system's reliability. A flight termination system may share a connection with another system if the connection must exist to satisfy a flight termination system requirement, such as any connection needed to:

(1) Accomplish flight termination system arming and safing;

(2) Provide data to the telemetry system; or

(3) Accomplish any engine shut-down.

(e) *Performance specifications for components and parts.* Each flight termination system component and each part that can affect the reliability of a flight termination component during flight must have written performance specifications that show, and contain the details of, how the component or part satisfies the requirements of this appendix.

(f) *Ability to test.* A flight termination system, including each component and associated ground support and monitoring equipment, must satisfy the tests required by appendix E of this part.

(g) *Software safety critical functions.* The requirements of § 417.123 apply to any computing system, software or firmware that is associated with a flight termination system and performs a software safety critical function as defined in § 417.123.

(h) *Component storage, operating, and service life.* Each flight termination system component must have a specified storage life, operating life, and service life and must satisfy all of the following:

(1) Each component must satisfy all its performance specifications when subjected to the full length of its specified storage life, operating life, and service life; and

(2) A component's storage, operating, or service life must not expire before flight. A launch operator may extend an ordnance component's service life by satisfying the service life extension tests of appendix E of this part.

(i) *Consistency of components.* A launch operator must ensure that each flight component sample is manufactured using parts, materials, processes, quality controls, and procedures that are each consistent with the manufacture of each qualification test sample.

D417.7 FLIGHT TERMINATION SYSTEM ENVIRONMENT SURVIVABILITY

(a) *General.* A flight termination system, including all of its components, mounting hardware, cables, and wires, must each satisfy all of their performance specifications when subjected to each maximum predicted operating and non-operating environment and environmental design margin required by this appendix. As an alternative to subjecting the flight termination system to the maximum predicted environments and margin for each dynamic operating environment, such as vibration or shock, a flight termination system need only satisfy all its performance specifications when subjected to an environmental level greater than the level that would cause structural breakup of the launch vehicle.

(b) *Maximum predicted environments.* A launch operator must determine all maximum predicted non-operating and operating environments that a flight termination system, including each component, will experience before its safe flight state. This determination must be based on analysis, modeling, testing, or monitoring. Non-operating and operating environments include temperature, vibration, shock, acceleration, acoustic, and other environments that apply to a specific launch vehicle and launch site, such as humidity, salt fog, dust, fungus, explosive atmosphere, and electromagnetic energy. Both of the following apply:

(1) Each maximum predicted vibration, shock, and thermal environment for a flight termination system component must include a margin that accounts for the uncertainty due to flight-to-flight variability and any analytical uncertainty. For a launch vehicle configuration for which there have been fewer than three flights, the margin must be no less than plus 3 dB for vibration, plus 4.5 dB for shock, and plus and minus 11 °C for thermal range; and

(2) For a launch vehicle configuration for which there have been fewer than three flights, a launch operator must monitor flight environments at as many locations within the launch vehicle as needed to verify the maximum predicted flight environments for each flight termination system component. An exception is that the launch operator may obtain empirical shock environment data through ground testing. A launch operator must adjust each maximum predicted flight environment for any future launch to account for all data obtained through monitoring.

(c) *Thermal environment.* A component must satisfy all its performance specifications when exposed to preflight and flight thermal cycle environments. A thermal cycle must begin with the component at ambient temperature. The cycle must continue as the component is heated or cooled to achieve the required dwell time at one extreme of the required thermal range, then to achieve the required dwell time at the other extreme, and then back to ambient temperature. Each cycle, including all dwell times, must be continuous without interruption by any other period of heating or cooling. Paragraphs (c)(2) through (c)(6) of this section identify the required thermal range for each component. A thermal cycle must include no less than a one-hour dwell time at each temperature extreme. The thermal rate of change between the extremes must be no less than the maximum predicted thermal rate of change or 1 °C per minute, whichever is greater. For an ordnance device, the thermal cycle must include no less than a two-hour dwell time at each temperature extreme. The thermal rate of change between the extremes for an ordnance device must be no less than the maximum predicted thermal rate of change or 3 °C per minute, whichever is greater.

(1) *Acceptance-number of thermal cycles.* For each component, the acceptance-number of thermal cycles must be no less than eight thermal cycles or 1.5 times the maximum number of thermal cycles that the component could experience during launch processing and flight, including all launch delays and recycling, rounded up to the nearest whole number, whichever is greater.

(2) *Passive components.* A passive component must satisfy all its performance specifications when subjected to:

(i) The acceptance-number of thermal cycles from one extreme of the maximum predicted thermal range to the other extreme; and

(ii) Three times the acceptance-number of thermal cycles from the lower of −34 °C or the predicted lowest temperature minus 10 °C, to the higher of 71 °C or the predicted highest temperature plus 10 °C.

(3) *Electronic components.* An electronic flight termination system component, including any component that contains an active electronic piece-part such as a microcircuit, transistor, or diode must satisfy all its performance specifications when subjected to:

(i) The sum of ten thermal cycles and the acceptance-number of thermal cycles from one extreme of the maximum predicted thermal range to the other extreme; and

(ii) Three times the acceptance-number of thermal cycles from the lower of −34 °C or the predicted lowest temperature minus 10 °C, to the higher of 71 °C or the predicted highest temperature plus 10 °C.

(4) *Power source thermal design.* A flight termination system power source, including any battery, must satisfy all its performance specifications when exposed to preflight and flight thermal environments. The power source must satisfy the following:

(i) A silver zinc battery must satisfy all its performance specifications when subjected to the acceptance-number of thermal cycles from 10 °C lower than the lowest temperature of the battery's maximum predicted temperature range to 10 °C higher than the highest temperature of the range. An exception is that each thermal cycle may range from 5.5 °C lower than the lowest temperature of the battery's maximum predicted temperature range to 10 °C higher than the highest temperature of the range if the launch operator monitors the battery's operating temperature on the launch vehicle with an accuracy of no less than ±1.5 °C.

(ii) A nickel cadmium battery must satisfy all its performance specifications when subjected to three times the acceptance-number of thermal cycles from the lower of −20 °C or the predicted lowest temperature minus 10 °C, to the higher of 40 °C or the predicted highest temperature plus 10 °C.

(iii) Any other power source must satisfy all its performance specifications when subjected to three times the acceptance-number of thermal cycles from 10 °C lower than the lowest temperature of the maximum predicted temperature range to 10 °C higher the highest temperature of the range.

(5) *Electro-mechanical safe-and-arm devices with internal explosives.* A safe-and-arm device must satisfy all its performance specifications when subjected to:

(i) The acceptance-number of thermal cycles from one extreme of the maximum predicted thermal range to the other extreme; and

(ii) Three times the acceptance-number of thermal cycles from the lower of −34 °C or the predicted lowest temperature minus 10 °C, to the higher of 71 °C or the predicted highest temperature plus 10 °C.

(6) *Ordnance thermal design.* An ordnance device and any associated hardware must satisfy all its performance specifications when subjected to the acceptance-number of thermal cycles from the lower of −54 °C or the predicted lowest temperature minus 10 °C, to the higher of 71 °C or the predicted highest temperature plus 10 °C. Each cycle must include a two-hour dwell time at each temperature extreme and a thermal rate of change between the extremes must be no less than the maximum predicted thermal rate of change or 3 °C per minute, whichever is greater.

(d) *Random vibration.* A component must satisfy all its performance specifications when exposed to a composite vibration level profile consisting of the higher of 6 dB above the maximum predicted flight random vibration level or a 12.2Grms workmanship screening level, across the 20 Hz to 2000 Hz spectrum of the two levels. The component must satisfy all its performance specifications when exposed to three times the maximum predicted random vibration duration time or three minutes per axis, whichever is greater, on each of three mutually perpendicular axes and for all frequencies from 20 Hz to 2000 Hz.

(e) *Sinusoidal vibration.* A component must satisfy all its performance specifications when exposed to 6 dB above the maximum predicted flight sinusoidal vibration level. The component must satisfy all its performance specifications when exposed to three times the maximum predicted sinusoidal vibration duration time on each of three mutually perpendicular axes and for all frequencies from 50% lower than the predicted lowest frequency to 50% higher than the predicted highest frequency. The sweep rate must be no greater than one-third the maximum predicted sweep rate on each of the three axes.

(f) *Transportation vibration.* A component must satisfy all its performance specifications when exposed to 6 dB above the maximum predicted transportation vibration level to be experienced when the component is in the configuration in which it is transported, for three times the maximum predicted transportation exposure time. A component must also satisfy all its performance specifications when exposed to the workmanship screening vibration levels and duration required by section E417.9(f).

(g) *Pyrotechnic shock.* (1) A flight termination system component must satisfy all its performance specifications when exposed to the greater of:

(i) A force of 6 dB above the maximum predicted pyrotechnic shock level to be experienced during flight with a shock frequency response range from 100 Hz to 10,000 Hz; or

(ii) The minimum breakup qualification shock levels and frequencies required by Table E417.11–2 of appendix E of this part.

(2) A component must satisfy all its performance specifications after it experiences a total of 18 shocks consisting of three shocks in each direction, positive and negative, for each of three mutually perpendicular axes.

(h) *Transportation shock.* A flight termination system component must satisfy all its performance specifications after being exposed to the maximum predicted shock to be experienced during transportation while in the configuration in which it is packed for transport.

(i) *Bench handling shock.* A flight termination system component must satisfy all its performance specifications after being exposed to the maximum predicted shock to be experienced during handling in its unpacked configuration.

(j) *Acceleration environment.* A flight termination system component must satisfy all its performance specifications when exposed to launch vehicle breakup acceleration levels or twice the maximum predicted flight acceleration levels, whichever is greater. The component must satisfy all its performance specifications when exposed to three times the maximum predicted acceleration duration for each of three mutually perpendicular axes.

(k) *Acoustic environment.* A flight termination system component must satisfy all its performance specifications when exposed to 6 dB above the maximum predicted sound pressure level. The component must satisfy all its performance specifications when exposed to three times the maximum predicted sound pressure duration time or three minutes, whichever is greater for each of three mutually perpendicular axes. The frequency must range from 20 Hz to 2000 Hz.

(l) *Other environments.* A flight termination system component must satisfy all its performance specifications after experiencing any other environment that it could experience during transportation, storage, preflight processing, or preflight system testing. Such environments include storage temperature, humidity, salt fog, fine sand, fungus, explosive atmosphere, and electromagnetic energy environments.

D417.9 COMMAND DESTRUCT SYSTEM

(a) A flight termination system must include a command destruct system that is initiated by radio command and satisfies the requirements of this section.

(b) A command destruct system must have its radio frequency components on or above the last launch vehicle stage capable of reaching a populated or other protected area before the planned safe flight state for the launch.

(c) The initiation of a command destruct system must result in accomplishing all the flight termination system functions of section D417.3.

(d) At any point along the nominal trajectory from liftoff until no longer required by §417.107, a command destruct system must operate with a radio frequency input signal that has an electromagnetic field intensity of 12 dB below the intensity provided by the command transmitter system under nominal conditions over 95 percent of the radiation sphere surrounding the launch vehicle.

(e) A command destruct system must survive the breakup of the launch vehicle until the system accomplishes all its flight termination functions or until breakup of the vehicle, including the use of any automatic or inadvertent separation destruct system, accomplishes the required flight termination.

(f) A command destruct system must receive and process a valid flight termination system arm command before accepting a flight termination system destruct command.

(g) For any liquid propellant, a command destruct system must allow a flight safety official to non-destructively shut down any thrusting liquid engine by command before destroying the launch vehicle.

D417.11 AUTOMATIC OR INADVERTENT SEPARATION DESTRUCT SYSTEM

(a) A flight termination system must include an automatic or inadvertent separation destruct system for each stage or strap-on motor capable of reaching a protected area before the planned safe flight state for each launch if the stage or strap-on motor does not possess a complete command destruct system. Any automatic or inadvertent separation destruct system must satisfy the requirements of this section.

(b) The initiation of an automatic or inadvertent separation destruct system must accomplish all flight termination system functions of section D417.3 that apply to the stage or strap-on motor on which it is installed.

(c) An inadvertent separation destruct system must activate when it senses any launch vehicle breakup or premature separation of the stage or strap-on motor on which the inadvertent separation destruct system is located.

(d) A launch operator must locate an automatic or inadvertent separation destruct system so that it will survive launch vehicle breakup until the system activates and accomplishes all its flight termination functions.

(e) For any electrically initiated automatic or inadvertent separation destruct system, each power source that supplies energy to initiate the destruct ordnance must be on the same stage or strap-on motor as the system.

D417.13 FLIGHT TERMINATION SYSTEM SAFING AND ARMING

(a) *General.* A flight termination system must provide for safing and arming of all flight termination system ordnance through the use of a mechanical barrier or other positive means of interrupting power to each of the ordnance firing circuits to prevent inadvertent initiation of ordnance.

(b) *Flight termination system arming.* A flight termination system must provide for each flight termination system ordnance initiation device or arming device to be armed and all electronic flight termination system components to be turned on before arming any launch vehicle or payload propulsion ignition circuits. For a launch where propulsive ignition occurs after first motion of the launch vehicle, the system must include an ignition interlock that prevents the arming of any launch vehicle or payload propulsion ignition circuit unless all flight termination system ordnance initiation devices and arming devices are armed and all electronic flight termination system components are turned on.

(c) *Preflight safing.* A flight termination system must provide for remote and redundant safing of all flight termination system ordnance before flight and during any launch abort or recycle operation.

(d) *In-flight safing.* Any safing of flight termination system ordnance during flight must satisfy all of the following:

(1) Any onboard launch vehicle hardware or software used to automatically safe flight termination system ordnance must be single fault tolerant against inadvertent safing. Any automatic safing must satisfy all of the following:

(i) Any automatic safing must occur only when the flight of the launch vehicle satisfies the safing criteria for no less than two different safing parameters or conditions, such as time of flight, propellant depletion, acceleration, or altitude. The safing criteria for each different safing parameter or condition must ensure that the flight termination system on a stage or strap-on-motor can only be safed once the stage or strap-on motor attains orbit or can no longer reach a populated or other protected area;

(ii) Any automatic safing must ensure that all flight termination system ordnance initiation devices and arming devices remain armed and all electronic flight termination system components remain powered during flight until the requirements of paragraph (d)(1)(i) of this section are satisfied and the system is safed; and

(iii) If operation of the launch vehicle could result in satisfaction of the safing criteria for one of the two safing parameters or conditions before normal thrust termination of the stage or strap-on motor to which the parameter or condition applies, the launch operator must demonstrate that the greatest remaining thrust, assuming a three-sigma maximum engine performance, cannot result in the stage or strap-on motor reaching a populated or other protected area;

(2) If a radio command safes a flight termination system, the command control system used for in-flight safing must be single fault tolerant against inadvertent transmission of a safing command under § 417.303(d).

D417.15 FLIGHT TERMINATION SYSTEM INSTALLATION

(a) A launch operator must establish and implement written procedures to ensure that all flight termination system components are installed on a launch vehicle according to the qualified flight termination system design. The procedures must ensure that:

(1) The installation of all flight termination system mechanical interfaces is complete;

(2) Installation personnel use calibrated tools to install ordnance when a specific standoff distance is necessary to ensure that the ordnance has the desired effect on the material it is designed to cut or otherwise destroy; and

(3) Each person involved is qualified for each task that person is to perform.

(b) Flight termination system installation procedures must include:

(1) A description of each task to be performed, each facility to be used, and each hazard involved;

(2) A checklist of tools and equipment required;

(3) A list of personnel required for performing each task;

(4) Step-by-step directions written with sufficient detail for a qualified person to perform each task;

(5) Identification of any tolerances that must be met during the installation; and

(6) Steps for inspection of installed flight termination system components, including quality assurance oversight procedures.

(c) The personnel performing a flight termination system installation procedure must signify that the procedure is accomplished, and record the outcome and any data verifying successful installation.

D417.17 FLIGHT TERMINATION SYSTEM MONITORING

(a) A flight termination system must interface with the launch vehicle's telemetry system to provide the data that the flight safety system crew needs to evaluate the health and status of the flight termination system prior to and during flight.

(b) The telemetry data must include:

(1) Signal strength for each command destruct receiver;

(2) Whether the power to each electronic flight termination system component is on or off;

(3) Status of output commands for each command destruct receiver and each automatic or inadvertent separation destruct system;

(4) Safe or arm status of each safe-and-arm device of sections D417.35 and D417.39;

(5) Voltage for each flight termination system battery;

(6) Current for each flight termination system battery;

(7) Status of any electrical inhibit at the system level that is critical to the operation of a flight termination system and is not otherwise identified by this appendix;

(8) Status of any exploding bridgewire firing unit, including arm input, power level, firing capacitor charge level, and trigger capacitor charge level;

(9) Temperature of each flight termination system battery, whether monitored at each battery or in the immediate vicinity of each battery so that each battery's temperature can be derived; and

(10) Status of each switch used to provide power to a flight termination system, including any switch used to change from an external power source to an internal power source.

D417.19 FLIGHT TERMINATION SYSTEM ELECTRICAL COMPONENTS AND ELECTRONIC CIRCUITRY

(a) *General.* All flight termination system electrical components and electronic circuitry must satisfy the requirements of this section.

(b) *Electronic piece-parts.* Each electronic piece-part that can affect the reliability of an electrical component or electronic circuitry during flight must satisfy §417.309(b)(2) of this part.

(c) *Over and under input voltage protection.* A flight termination system component must satisfy all its performance specifications and not sustain any damage when subjected to a maximum input voltage of no less than the maximum open circuit voltage of the component's power source. The component must satisfy all its performance specifications and not sustain any damage when subjected to a minimum input voltage of no greater than the minimum loaded voltage of the component's power source.

(d) *Series-redundant circuit.* A flight termination system component that uses a series-redundant branch in a firing circuit to satisfy the prohibition against a single failure point must possess one or more monitoring circuits or test points for verifying the integrity of each series-redundant branch after assembly and during testing.

(e) *Power control and switching.* In the event of an input power dropout, a power control or switching circuit, including any solid-state power transfer switch and arm-and-enable circuit must not change state for 50 milliseconds or more. Any electromechanical, solid-state, or relay component used in a flight termination system firing circuit must be capable of delivering the maximum firing current for no less than 10 times the duration of the intended firing pulse.

(f) *Circuit isolation, shielding, and grounding.* The circuitry of a flight termination system component must be shielded, filtered, grounded, or otherwise isolated to preclude any energy sources, internal or external to the launch vehicle, such as electromagnetic energy, static electricity, or stray electrical currents, from causing interference that would inhibit the flight termination system from functioning or cause an undesired output of the system. An electrical firing circuit must have a single-point ground connection directly to the power source only.

(g) *Circuit protection.* Any circuit protection provided within a flight termination system must satisfy all of the following:

(1) Electronic circuitry must not contain protection devices, such as fuses, except as allowed by paragraph (g)(2) of this section. A destruct circuit may employ current limiting resistors;

(2) Any electronic circuit designed to shut down or disable a launch vehicle engine and that interfaces with a launch vehicle function must use one or more devices, such as fuses, circuit breakers, or limiting resistors, to protect against over-current, including any direct short; and

(3) The design of a flight termination system output circuit that interfaces with another launch vehicle circuit must prevent any launch vehicle circuit failure from disabling or degrading the flight termination system's performance.

(h) *Repetitive functioning.* Each circuit, element, component, and subsystem of a flight termination system must satisfy all its performance specifications when subjected to repetitive functioning for five times the expected number of cycles required for all acceptance testing, checkout, and operations, including re-tests caused by schedule or other delays.

(i) *Watchdog circuits.* A flight termination system or component must not use a watchdog circuit that automatically shuts down or disables circuitry during flight.

(j) *Self-test capability.* If a flight termination system component uses a microprocessor, the component and the microprocessor must perform self-tests, detect errors, and relay the results through telemetry during flight to the launch operator. The execution of a self-test must not inhibit the intended processing function of the unit or cause any output to change.

(k) *Electromagnetic interference protection.* The design of a flight termination system component must eliminate the possibility of the maximum predicted electromagnetic interference emissions or susceptibilities, whether conducted or radiated, from affecting the component's performance. A component's electromagnetic interference susceptibility level must ensure that the component satisfies all its performance specifications when subjected to the maximum predicted emission levels of all other launch vehicle components and external sources to which the component would be exposed.

(l) *Ordnance initiator circuits.* An ordnance initiator circuit that is part of a flight termination system must satisfy all of the following:

(1) An ordnance initiator circuit must deliver an operating current of no less than 150% of the initiator's all-fire qualification current level when operating at the lowest battery voltage and under the worse case system tolerances allowed by the system design limits;

(2) For a low voltage ordnance initiator with an electro-explosive device that initiates at less than 50 volts, the initiator's circuitry must limit the power at each associated electro-explosive device that could be produced by an electromagnetic environment to a level at least 20 dB below the pin-to-pin direct current no-fire power of the electro-explosive device; and

(3) For a high voltage ordnance initiator that initiates ordnance at greater than 1,000 volts, the initiator must include safe-and-arm plugs that interrupt power to the main initiator's charging circuits, such as the trigger and output capacitors. A high voltage initiator's circuitry must ensure that the power that could be produced at the initiator's command input by an electromagnetic environment is no greater than 20 dB below the initiator's firing level.

D417.21 FLIGHT TERMINATION SYSTEM MONITOR CIRCUITS

(a) Each parameter measurement made by a monitor circuit must show the status of the parameter.

(b) Each monitor circuit must be independent of any firing circuit. A monitor, control, or checkout circuit must not share a connector with a firing circuit.

(c) A monitor circuit must not route through a safe-and-arm plug.

(d) Any monitor current in an electro-explosive device system firing line must not exceed one-tenth of the no-fire current of the electro-explosive device.

(e) Resolution, accuracy, and data rates for each monitoring circuit must provide for detecting whether performance specifications are satisfied and detecting any out-of-family conditions.

D417.23 FLIGHT TERMINATION SYSTEM ORDNANCE TRAIN

(a) An ordnance train must consist of all components responsible for initiation, transfer, and output of an explosive charge. Ordnance train components must include, initiators, energy transfer lines, boosters, explosive manifolds, and destruct charges.

(b) The reliability of an ordnance train to initiate ordnance, including the ability to propagate a charge across any ordnance interface, must be 0.999 at a 95% confidence level.

(c) The decomposition, cook-off, sublimation, auto-ignition, and melting temperatures of all flight termination system ordnance must be no less than 30(C higher than the maximum predicted environmental temperature to which the material will be exposed during storage, handling, installation, transportation, and flight.

(d) An ordnance train must include initiation devices that can be connected or removed from the destruct charge. The design of an ordnance train must provide for easy access to the initiation devices.

D417.25 RADIO FREQUENCY RECEIVING SYSTEM

(a) *General.* A radio frequency receiving system must include each flight termination system antenna, radio frequency coupler, any radio frequency cable, or other passive device used to connect a flight termination system antenna to a command receiver decoder. The system must deliver command control system radio frequency energy that satisfies all its performance specifications to each flight termination system command receiver decoder when subjected to performance degradation caused by command control system transmitter variations, launch vehicle flight conditions, and flight termination system hardware performance variations.

(b) *Sensitivity.* A radio frequency receiving system must provide command signals to each command receiver decoder at an electromagnetic field intensity of no less than 12dB above the level required for reliable receiver operation. The system must satisfy the 12-dB margin over 95% of the antenna radiation sphere surrounding the launch vehicle and must account for command control system radio frequency transmitter characteristics, airborne system characteristics including antenna gain, path loses due to plume or flame attenuation, and vehicle trajectory. For each launch, the system must satisfy the 12-dB margin at any point along the nominal trajectory until the planned safe flight state for the launch.

(c) *Antenna.* All of the following apply to each flight termination system antenna:

(1) A flight termination system antenna must have a radio frequency bandwidth that is no less than two times the total combined maximum tolerances of all applicable radio frequency performance factors. The performance factors must include frequency modulation deviation, command control transmitter inaccuracies, and variations in hardware performance during thermal and dynamic environments;

(2) A launch operator must treat any thermal protection used on a flight termination system antenna as part of the antenna; and

(3) A flight termination system antenna must be compatible with the command control system transmitting equipment.

(d) *Radio frequency coupler.* A flight termination system must use a passive radio frequency coupler to combine radio frequency signals inputs from each flight termination system antenna and distribute the required signal level to each command receiver. A radio frequency coupler must satisfy all of the following:

(1) A radio frequency coupler must prevent any single point failure in one redundant command receiver or antenna from affecting any other redundant command receiver or antenna by providing isolation between each port. An open or short circuit in one redundant command destruct receiver or antenna path must not prevent the functioning of the other command destruct receiver or antenna path;

(2) Each input port must be isolated from all other input ports;

(3) Each output port must be isolated from all other output ports; and

(4) A radio frequency coupler must provide for a radio frequency bandwidth that exceeds two times the total combined maximum tolerances of all applicable radio frequency performance factors. The performance factors must include frequency modulation deviation of multiple tones, command control transmitter inaccuracies, and variations in hardware performance during thermal and dynamic environments.

D417.27 ELECTRONIC COMPONENTS

(a) *General.* The requirements in this section apply to each electronic component that contains piece-part circuitry and is part of a flight termination system, including each command receiver decoder. Each piece-part used in an electronic component must satisfy § 417.309(b)(2) of this part.

(b) *Response time.* Each electronic component's response time must be such that the total flight termination system response time, from receipt of a destruct command sequence to initiation of destruct output, is less than or equal to the response time used in the time delay analysis required by § 417.221.

(c) *Wire and connectors.* All wire and connectors used in an electronic component must satisfy section D417.31.

(d) *Adjustment.* An electronic component must not require any adjustment after successful completion of acceptance testing.

(e) *Self-test.* The design of an electronic component that uses a microprocessor must provide for the component to perform a self-test, detect errors, and relay the results through telemetry during flight to the launch operator. The execution of a self-test must not inhibit the intended processing function of the unit or cause any output to change state.

(f) *Electronic component repetitive functioning.* An electronic component, including all its circuitry and parts, must satisfy all its performance specifications when subjected to repetitive functioning for five times the total expected number of cycles required for acceptance tests, preflight tests, and flight operations, including potential retests due to schedule delays.

(g) *Acquisition of test data.* The test requirements of appendix E of this part apply to all electronic components. Each electronic component must allow for separate component testing and the recording of parameters that verify its functional performance, including the status of any command output, during testing.

(h) *Warm-up time.* The warm-up time that an electronic component needs to ensure reliable operation must be no greater than the warm-up time that is incorporated into the preflight testing of appendix E of this part.

(i) *Electronic component circuit protection.* An electronic component must include circuit protection for power and control circuitry, including switching circuitry. The circuit protection must ensure that the component satisfies all its performance specifications when subjected to launch processing and flight environments. An electronic component's circuit protection must satisfy all of the following:

(1) Circuit protection must provide for an electronic component to satisfy all its performance specifications when subjected to

the open circuit voltage of the component's power source for no less than twice the expected duration and when subjected to the minimum input voltage of the loaded voltage of the power source for no less than twice the expected duration;

(2) In the event of an input power dropout, any control or switching circuit critical to the reliable operation of a component, including solid-state power transfer switches, must not change state for at least 50 milliseconds;

(3) An electronic component must not use a watchdog circuit that automatically shuts down or disables the component during flight;

(4) An electronic component must satisfy all its performance specifications when any of its monitoring circuits or nondestruct output ports are subjected to a short circuit or the highest positive or negative voltage capable of being supplied by the monitor batteries or other power supplies where the voltage lasts for no less than five minutes; and

(5) An electronic component must satisfy all its performance specifications when subjected to any undetectable reverse polarity voltage that can occur during launch processing for no less than five minutes.

(j) *Electromagnetic interference susceptibility.* The design of an electronic component must eliminate the possibility of electromagnetic interference or modulated or unmodulated radio frequency emissions from affecting the component's performance. These electromagnetic interference and radio frequency environments include emissions or susceptibilities, whether conducted or radiated.

(1) The susceptibility level of an electronic component must be below the emissions of all other launch vehicle components and external transmitters.

(2) Any electromagnetic emissions from an electronic component must not be at a level that would affect the performance of other flight termination system components.

(3) An electronic component must not produce any inadvertent command output and must satisfy all its performance specifications when subjected to external radio frequency sources and modulation schemes to which the component could be subjected prior to and during flight.

(k) *Output functions and monitoring.* An electronic component must provide for all of the following output functions and monitoring:

(1) Each series redundant branch in any firing circuit of an electronic component that prevents a single failure point from issuing a destruct output must include a monitoring circuit or test points that verify the integrity of each redundant branch after assembly;

(2) Any piece-part used in a firing circuit must have the capacity to output at least 1.5 times the maximum firing current for no less than 10 times the duration of the maximum firing pulse;

(3) An electronic component's destruct output circuit and all its parts must deliver the required output power to the intended output load while operating with any input voltage that is within the component's input power operational design limits;

(4) An electronic component must include monitoring circuits that provide for monitoring the health and performance of the component including the status of any command output; and

(5) The maximum leakage current through an electronic component's destruct output port must:

(i) Not degrade the performance of downstream circuitry;

(ii) Be 20 dB lower than the level that could degrade the performance of any downstream ordnance initiation system or component, such as any electro-explosive device; and

(iii) Be 20 dB lower than the level that could result in inadvertent initiation of any downstream ordnance.

D417.29 COMMAND RECEIVER DECODER

(a) *General.* Each command receiver decoder must:

(1) Receive radio frequency energy from the command control system through the radio frequency receiving system and interpret, process, and send commands to the flight termination system;

(2) Be compatible with the command control system transmitting equipment;

(3) Satisfy the requirements of section D417.27 for all electronic components;

(4) Satisfy all its performance specifications and reliably process a command signal when subjected to command control system transmitting equipment tolerances and flight generated signal degradation, including:

(i) Locally induced radio frequency noise sources;

(ii) Vehicle plume;

(iii) The maximum predicted noise-floor;

(iv) Command transmitter performance variations; and

(v) Launch vehicle trajectory.

(b) *Tone-based radio frequency processing.* Each tone-based command receiver decoder must satisfy all of the following for all preflight and flight environments:

(1) *Decoder channel deviation.* A receiver decoder must reliably process the intended tone deviated signal at the minimum and maximum number of expected tones. The receiver decoder must satisfy all its performance specifications when subjected to:

(i) Plus and minus 3 KHz per tone; or

(ii) A nominal tone deviation plus twice the maximum and minus half the minimum of the total combined tolerances of all applicable radio frequency performance factors, whichever range is greater.

(2) *Operational bandwidth.*

(i) The receiver decoder's operational bandwidth must be no less than plus and minus 45 KHz and must ensure that the receiver decoder satisfies all its performance specifications at:

(A) Twice the worst-case command control system transmitter radio frequency shift;

(B) Doppler shifts of the carrier center frequency; and

(C) Shifts in flight hardware center frequency during flight at the manufacturer guaranteed receiver sensitivity.

(ii) The operational bandwidth must account for tone deviation and the receiver sensitivity must not vary by more than 3dB across the bandwidth.

(3) *Radio frequency dynamic range.* The receiver decoder must satisfy all its performance specifications when subjected to the variations of the radio frequency input signal level that will occur during checkout and flight. The receiver decoder must output all commands with input from the radio frequency threshold level up to:

(i) The maximum radio frequency level that it will experience from the command control system transmitter during checkout and flight plus a 3-dB margin; or

(ii) 13 dBm, whichever is greater.

(4) *Capture ratio.* For each launch, the receiver decoder's design must ensure that no transmitter with less than 80% of the power of the command transmitter system for the launch, could capture or interfere with the receiver decoder.

(5) *Radio frequency level monitor.* (i) The receiver decoder must include a monitoring circuit that accurately monitors and outputs the strength of the radio frequency input signal during flight.

(ii) The output of the monitor circuit must be directly related and proportional to the strength of the radio frequency input signal from the threshold level to saturation.

(iii) The dynamic range of the radio frequency input from threshold to saturation must be no less than 50 dB. The monitor circuit output amplitude from threshold to saturation must have a corresponding range of 18 dB or greater.

(iv) The monitor output signal level must be compatible with vehicle telemetry system interfaces and provide a maximum response time of 100 ms.

(v) The slope of the monitor circuit output must not change polarity.

(6) *Radio frequency threshold sensitivity.* The receiver decoder's threshold sensitivity must satisfy its performance specifications and be repeatable within a tolerance of plus and minus 3 dB, to demonstrate in-family performance.

(7) *Noise level margin.* The receiver decoder's guaranteed input sensitivity must be no less than 6 dB higher than the maximum predicted noise-floor.

(8) *Voltage standing wave ratio.* All radio frequency losses within the receiver decoder interface to the antenna system must satisfy the 12–dB margin of §417.9(d) and be repeatable to demonstrate in-family performance. The radio frequency receiving system and the impedance of the receiver decoder must match.

(9) *Decoder channel bandwidth.* The receiver decoder must provide for reliable recognition of the command signal when subjected to variations in ground transmitter tone frequency and frequency modulation deviation variations. The command receiver must satisfy all its performance specifications within the specified tone filter frequency bandwidth using a frequency modulation tone deviation from 2 dB to 20 dB above the measured threshold level.

(10) *Tone balance.* Any secure receiver decoder must reliably decode a valid command with an amplitude imbalance between two tones within the same message.

(11) *Message timing.* Any secure receiver decoder must function reliably when subjected to errors in timing caused by ground transmitter tolerances. The receiver decoder must process commands at twice the maximum and one-half the minimum timing specification of the ground system.

(12) *Check tone.* The receiver decoder must decode a tone, such as a pilot tone or check tone, which is representative of link and command closure and provide a telemetry output indicating whether the tone is decoded. The presence or absence of this tone signal must have no effect on a command receiver decoder's command processing and output capability.

(c) *Inadvertent command output.* A command receiver decoder must satisfy all of the following to ensure that it does not provide an output other than when it receives a valid command.

(1) *Dynamic stability.* The receiver decoder must not produce an inadvertent output when subjected to a radio frequency input short-circuit, open-circuit, or changes in input voltage standing wave ratio.

(2) *Out of band rejection.* The receiver decoder must not degrade in performance nor respond when subjected to any out-of-band vehicle or ground transmitter source that could be encountered from liftoff to the no-longer endanger time. The receiver decoder must not respond to frequencies, from 10 MHz to 1000 MHz except at the receiver specified operational bandwidth. The receiver decoder's radio frequency rejection of out of band signals must provide a minimum of 60

dB beyond eight times the maximum specified operational bandwidth. These frequencies must include all expected interfering transmitting sources using a minimum bandwidth of 20% of each transmitter center frequency, receiver image frequencies and harmonics of the assigned center frequency.

(3) *Decoder channel bandwidth rejection.* The receiver decoder must distinguish between tones that are capable of inhibiting or inadvertently issuing an output command. Each tone filter must not respond to another tone outside the specified tone filter frequency bandwidth using an FM tone deviation from 2 dB to 20 dB above the measured threshold level.

(4) *Adjacent tone decoder channel rejection.* The receiver decoder must not be inhibited or inadvertently issue an output command when subjected to any over-modulation of adjacent tones. The tone decoder channels must not respond to adjacent frequency modulation-modulated tone channels when they are modulated with a minimum of 150% of the expected tone deviation.

(5) *Logic sequence.* Each tone sequence used for arm and destruct must protect against inadvertent or unintentional destruct actions.

(6) *Destruct sequence.* The receiver decoder must provide a Destruct command only if preceded by a valid Arm command.

(7) *Receiver abnormal logic.* The receiver decoder must not respond to any combination of tones or tone pairs other than the correct command sequence.

(8) *Noise immunity.* The receiver decoder must not respond to a frequency modulated white noise radio frequency input that has a minimum frequency modulated deviation of 12 dB above the measured threshold deviation.

(9) *Tone drop.* The receiver decoder must not respond to a valid command output when one tone in the sequence is dropped.

(10) *Amplitude modulation rejection.* The receiver decoder must not respond to any tone or modulated input at 50% and 100% amplitude modulated noise when subjected to the maximum pre-flight and flight input power levels.

(11) *Decoder channel deviation rejection.* The receiver decoder must not inadvertently trigger on frequency modulated noise. The receiver decoder must not respond to tone modulations 10 dB below the nominal tone modulation or lower.

D417.31 WIRING AND CONNECTORS

(a) All wiring, including any cable and all connectors, that interface with any flight termination system component must provide for the component, wiring, and connectors to satisfy the qualification tests required by appendix E of this part.

(b) Each connector that interfaces with a flight termination system component must protect against electrical dropout and ensure electrical continuity as needed to ensure the component satisfies all its performance specifications.

(c) All wiring and connectors must have shielding that ensures the flight termination system satisfies all its performance specifications and will not experience an inadvertent destruct output when subjected to electromagnetic interference levels 20 dB greater than the greatest electromagnetic interference induced by launch vehicle and launch site systems.

(d) The dielectric withstanding voltage between mutually insulated portions of any component part must provide for the component to function at the component's rated voltage and satisfy all its performance specifications when subjected to any momentary over-potentials that could normally occur, such as due to switching or surge.

(e) The insulation resistance between mutually insulated portions of any component must provide for the component to function at its rated voltage. Any insulation material must satisfy all its performance specifications when subjected to workmanship, heat, dirt, oxidation, or loss of volatile material.

(f) The insulation resistance between wire shields and conductors, and between each connector pin must withstand a minimum workmanship voltage of at least 1,500 volts, direct current, or 150 percent of the rated output voltage, whichever is greater.

(g) If any wiring or connector will experience loads with continuous duty cycles of 100 seconds or greater, that wiring or connector, including each connector pin, must have a capacity of 150% of the design load. If any wiring or connector will experience loads that last less than 100 seconds, all wiring and insulation must provide a design margin greater than the wire insulation temperature specification.

(h) All wiring, including any cable or connector, must satisfy all its performance specifications when subjected to the pull force required by section E417.9(j) and any additional handling environment that the component could experience undetected.

(i) Redundant circuits that can affect a flight termination system's reliability during flight must not share any wiring harness or connector with each other.

(j) For any connector or pin connection that is not functionally tested once connected as part of a flight termination system or component, the design of the connector or pin connection must eliminate the possibility of a bent pin, mismating, or misalignment.

(k) The design of a flight termination system component must prevent undetectable damage or overstress from occurring as the result of a bent connector pin. An inadvertent initiation must not occur if a bent connector pin:

(1) Makes unintended contact with another pin;

(2) Makes unintended contact with the case of the connector or component; or

(3) Produces an open circuit.

(l) Each connector that can affect a flight termination system component's reliability during flight must satisfy the requirements of §417.309(b)(2) of this part.

(m) All connectors must positively lock to prevent inadvertent disconnection during launch vehicle processing and flight.

(n) The installation of all wiring, including any cable, must protect against abrasion and crimping of the wiring.

D417.33 BATTERIES

(a) *Capacity*. A flight termination system battery must have a manufacturer-specified capacity of no less than the sum total amp-hour and pulse capacity needed for:

(1) Any self discharge;

(2) All load and activation checks;

(3) All launch countdown checks;

(4) Any potential hold time;

(5) Any potential number of preflight retests due to potential schedule delays including the number of potential launch attempts that the battery could experience before it would have to be replaced;

(6) Two arm and two destruct command loads at the end of the flight; and

(7) A flight capacity of no less than 150% of the capacity needed to support a normal flight from liftoff to the planned safe flight state. For a launch vehicle that uses solid propellant, the flight capacity must be no less than a 30-minute hang-fire hold time.

(b) *Electrical characteristics*. A flight termination system battery, under all load conditions, including line loss, must have all the following electrical characteristics:

(1) The manufacturer specified minimum voltage must be no less than the minimum acceptance test voltage that satisfies the electrical component acceptance tests of appendix E of this part. For a battery used in a pulse application to fire an electro-explosive device, the manufacturer specified minimum voltage must be no less than the minimum qualification test voltage that satisfies the electro-explosive device qualification tests of appendix E of this part;

(2) A battery that provides power to an electro-explosive device initiator, including to any initiator fired simultaneously with another initiator, must:

(i) Deliver 150% of each electro-explosive device's all-fire current at the qualification test level. The battery must deliver the current to each ordnance initiator at the lowest system battery voltage;

(ii) Have a current pulse that lasts ten times longer than the duration required to initiate the electro-explosive device or a minimum workmanship screening level of 200 milliseconds, whichever is greater; and

(iii) Have a pulse capacity of no less than twice the expected number of arm and destruct command sets planned to occur during launch vehicle processing, preflight flight termination system end-to-end tests, plus flight commands including load checks, conditioning, and firing of initiators;

(3) The design of a battery and any activation procedures must ensure uniform cell voltage after activation. Activation must include any battery conditioning needed to ensure uniform cell voltage, such as peroxide removal or nickel cadmium preparation; and

(4) The design of a battery or the system using the battery must protect against undetectable damage to the battery from any reverse polarity, shorting, overcharging, thermal runaway, or overpressure.

(c) *Service and storage life*. The service and storage life of a flight termination system battery must satisfy all of the following:

(1) A flight termination system battery must have a total activated service life that provides for the battery to meet the capacity and electrical characteristics required by paragraphs (a) and (b) of this section; and

(2) A flight termination system battery must have a specified storage life. The battery must satisfy the activated service life requirement of paragraph (c)(1) of this section after experiencing its storage life, whether stored in an activated or inactivated state.

(d) *Monitoring capability*. A battery or the system that uses the battery must provide for monitoring the status of the battery voltage and current. The monitoring must be sufficient to detect the smallest change in voltage or current that would indicate any health problem with each battery. Monitoring accuracy must be consistent with the minimum and maximum voltage and current limits used for launch countdown. The design of a battery that requires heating or cooling to sustain performance must provide for monitoring the battery's temperature with a resolution of 0.5 °C.

(e) *Battery identification*. Each battery must have an attached permanent label with the component name, type of construction (including chemistry), manufacturer identification, part number, lot and serial number, date of manufacture, and storage life.

(f) *Battery temperature control*. Any battery heater must ensure even temperature regulation of all battery cells.

(g) *Silver zinc batteries*. Any silver zinc battery that is part of a flight termination system must satisfy all of the following:

(1) A silver zinc battery must consist of cells assembled from electrode plates that are manufactured together and without interruption;

(2) The design of a silver zinc battery must allow activation of each individual cell within the battery;

(3) For any silver zinc battery that may vent electrolyte mist as part of normal operations, the battery must satisfy all its performance specifications for pin-to-case and pin-to-pin resistances after the battery experiences the maximum normal venting;

(4) The design of a silver zinc battery and its cells must allow for the qualification, acceptance, and storage life extension testing required by appendix E of this part. A launch operator must ensure sufficient batteries and cells are available from the same lot to accomplish the required testing;

(5) Each silver zinc battery must have attached, no less than one additional cell from the same production lot, with the same lot date code, as the cells in the battery for use in cell acceptance verification tests. The cell must remain attached to the battery from the time of assembly until performance of the acceptance tests to ensure that the additional cell is subjected to all the same environments as the complete battery;

(6) The design of a silver zinc battery must permit voltage monitoring of each cell during open circuit voltage and load tests of the battery; and

(7) All cell and battery parts and materials and manufacturing parts, materials, and processes must undergo configuration control that ensures that each cell and battery has repeatable in-family performance unless each cell and battery undergoes lot testing that demonstrates repeatable in-family performance. The launch operator must identify and implement any lot testing that replaces configuration control.

(h) *Rechargeable cells and batteries.* (1) Any rechargeable battery or cell that is part of a flight termination system must satisfy all the requirements of this section for each charge-discharge cycle.

(2) With the exception of any silver zinc battery, a rechargeable battery must satisfy all its performance specifications for five times the number of operating charge and discharge cycles expected of the battery throughout its life, including all acceptance testing, preflight testing, and flight. A silver zinc rechargeable battery must satisfy all its performance specifications for each operating charge-discharge cycle expected of the battery throughout its life, including all acceptance testing, preflight testing, and flight.

(3) A rechargeable battery must consist of cells from the same production lot. For a battery that consists of commercially produced nickel cadmium cells, each cell must be from the same production lot of no less than three thousand cells that are manufactured without interruption.

(4) The design of a silver zinc or commercial nickel cadmium battery and each of its cells must allow for the qualification and acceptance tests required by appendix E of this part. A launch operator must ensure sufficient batteries and cells are available to accomplish the required testing. A launch operator must identify and implement design and test requirements for any other type of rechargeable battery proposed for use as part of a flight safety system.

(i) *Commercial nickel cadmium cells and batteries.* Any nickel cadmium battery that uses one or more commercially produced nickel cadmium cells and is part of a flight termination system must satisfy each of the following to demonstrate that each cell or battery satisfies all its performance specifications:

(1) The battery or cell must have repeatable capacity and voltage performance. Capacity must be repeatable within one percent for each charge and discharge cycle.

(2) Any battery or cell venting device must ensure that the battery or cell does not experience a loss of structural integrity or create a hazardous condition when subjected to electrical discharge, charging and short-circuit conditions.

(3) The battery or cell must retain its charge and provide its required capacity, including the required capacity margin, from the final charge used prior to launch to the planned safe flight state during flight at the maximum pre-launch and flight temperature. The cell or battery must not self-discharge more than 10% of its fully charged capacity after 72 hours at ambient temperature.

(4) The design of the battery must prevent current leakage from pin-to-pin or pin-to-case from creating undesired events or battery self-discharge. Pin-to-pin and pin-to-case resistances must be repeatable so that measurements of pin-to-pin and pin-to-case resistances can establish in-family performance and determine whether all battery wiring and connectors are installed according to the manufacturer's design specifications.

(5) The battery or battery case must be sealed to the required leak rate and not loose structural integrity or create a hazardous condition when subjected to the predicted operating conditions plus all required margins including any battery short-circuit. The battery or battery case must maintain its structural integrity when subjected to no less than 1.5 times the greatest operating pressure differential that could occur under qualification testing, preflight, or flight conditions.

(6) Any battery voltage, current, or temperature monitoring circuit that is part of the battery must have resolution, accuracy, and data rates that all for detecting whether the performance specifications are satisfied and detecting any out-of-family conditions.

(7) Any battery heater circuit, including any thermostat must ensure that all cells

are heated uniformly and must allow for repeatable battery performance that satisfies all the battery's performance specifications. Any heating must ensure that cells are not overstressed due to excessive temperature. The thermostat tolerances must ensure that the battery remains within its thermal design limits.

(8) The battery or cell must satisfy all its electrical performance specifications and be in-family while subjected to all pre-flight and flight environments, including hot and cold temperature, and all required electrical loads at the beginning, middle, and end of its manufacturer specified capacity.

D417.35 ELECTRO-MECHANICAL SAFE-AND-ARM DEVICES WITH AN INTERNAL ELECTRO-EXPLOSIVE DEVICE

(a) This section applies to any electro-mechanical safe-and-arm device that has an internal electro-explosive device and is part of a flight termination system. A safe-and-arm device must provide for safing and arming of the flight termination system ordnance to satisfy section D417.13.

(b) A safe-and-arm device in the arm position must remain in the arm position and satisfy all its performance specifications when subjected to the design environmental levels determined under section D417.7.

(c) All wiring and connectors used in a safe-and-arm device must satisfy section D417.31.

(d) Each piece-part that is used in the firing circuit of a safe-and-arm device and that can affect the reliability of the device during flight must satisfy §417.309(b)(2) of this part.

(e) A safe-and-arm device's internal electro-explosive device must satisfy the requirements for an ordnance initiator of section D417.41.

(f) A safe-and-arm device must not require any adjustment throughout its service life.

(g) A safe-and-arm device's internal electrical firing circuitry, such as wiring, connectors, and switch deck contacts, must satisfy all its performance specifications when subjected to an electrical current pulse with an energy level of no less than 150% of the internal electro-explosive device's all-fire energy level for 10 times as long as the all-fire pulse lasts. A safe-and-arm device must deliver this firing pulse to the internal electro-explosive device without any dropout that could affect the electro-explosive device's performance when subjected to the design environmental levels.

(h) A safe-and-arm device must satisfy all its performance specifications after being exposed to the handling drop required by section E417.9(k) and any additional transportation, handling, or installation environment that the device could experience undetected.

(i) A safe-and-arm device must not initiate and must allow for safe disposal after experiencing the abnormal drop required by section E417.9(l).

(j) When a safe-and-arm device's electro-explosive device is initiated, the safe- and arm-device's body must not fragment, regardless of whether the explosive transfer system is connected or not.

(k) When dual electro-explosive devices are used within a single safe-and-arm device, the design must ensure that one electro-explosive device does not affect the performance of the other electro-explosive device.

(l) A safe-and-arm device must satisfy all its performance specifications when subjected to no less than five times the total number of safe and arm cycles required for the combination of all acceptance tests, preflight tests, and flight operations, including an allowance for potential re-tests due to schedule changes.

(m) The design of a safe-and-arm device must allow for separate component testing and recording of parameters that verify its functional performance , and the status of any command output during the tests required by section E417.25.

(n) A safe-and-arm device must be environmentally sealed to the equivalent of 10^{-4} scc/sec of helium at one atmosphere differential or the device must provide other means of withstanding non-operating environments, such as salt-fog and humidity, experienced during storage, transportation and preflight testing.

(o) The safing of a safe-and-arm device must satisfy all of the following:

(1) While in the safe position, a safe-and-arm device must protect each internal electro-explosive device from any condition that could degrade the electro-explosive device's performance and prevent inadvertent initiation during transportation, storage, preflight testing, and any preflight fault conditions.

(2) While in the safe position, a safe-and-arm device's electrical input firing circuit must prevent degradation in performance or inadvertent initiation of the electro-explosive device when the safe-and-arm device is subjected to any external energy source, such as static discharge, radio frequency energy, or firing voltage.

(3) While in the safe position, a safe-and-arm device must prevent the initiation of its internal electro-explosive device and any other ordnance train component, with a reliability of 0.999 at a 95% confidence level.

(4) A safe-and-arm device must satisfy all its performance specifications when in the safe position and subjected to the continuous operational arming voltage required by section E417.25(d).

(5) A safe-and-arm device must not initiate its electro-explosive device or any other ordnance train component when locked in the safe position and subjected to the continuous

operational arming voltage required by section E417.25(e)(3).

(6) A safe-and-arm device must have a visual display of its status on the device and remote display of the status when the device is in the safe position. When transitioning from the arm to safe position, the safe indication must not appear unless the position of the safe-and-arm device has progressed more than 50% beyond the no-fire transition motion.

(7) A safe-and-arm device must have a remote means of moving its rotor or barrier to the safe position from any rotor or barrier position.

(8) A safe-and-arm device must have a manual means of moving its rotor or barrier to the safe position.

(9) A safe-and-arm device must have a safing interlock that prevents movement from the safe position to the arm position while operational arming current is being applied. The interlock must have a means of positively locking into place and must allow for verification of proper functioning. The interlock removal design or procedure must eliminate the possibility of accidental disconnection of the interlock.

(p) The arming of a safe-and-arm device must satisfy all of the following:

(1) When a safe-and-arm device is in the arm position, all ordnance interfaces, such as electro-explosive device, rotor charge, and explosive transfer system components must align with one another to ensure propagation of the explosive charge with a reliability of 0.999 at a 95% confidence level;

(2) When in the arm position, the greatest energy supplied to a safe-and-arm device's electro-explosive device from electronic circuit leakage and radio frequency energy must be no greater than 20 dB below the guaranteed no-fire level of the electro-explosive device;

(3) A safe-and-arm device must have a visual display of its status on the device and provide for remote display of the status when the device is in the arm position. The arm indication must not appear unless the safe-and-arm device is armed as required by paragraph (o)(1) of this section; and

(4) A safe-and-arm device must provide for remote arming of the device.

D417.37 Exploding bridgewire firing unit

(a) *General.* This section applies to any exploding bridgewire firing unit that is part of a flight termination system. An exploding bridgewire firing unit must provide for safing and arming of the flight termination system ordnance to satisfy section D417.13. An exploding bridgewire firing unit must satisfy the requirements for electronic components of section D417.29.

(b) *Charging and discharging.* An exploding bridgewire firing unit must have a remote means of charging and discharging of the unit's firing capacitor and an external means of positively interrupting the firing capacitor charging voltage.

(c) *Input command processing.* An exploding bridgewire firing unit's electrical input processing circuitry must satisfy all of the following:

(1) An exploding bridgewire firing unit's input circuitry must function, when subjected to the greatest potential electromagnetic interference noise environments, without inadvertently triggering;

(2) In the firing circuit of an exploding bridgewire firing unit, all series redundant branches that prevent any single failure point from issuing a destruct output must include monitoring circuits or test points for verifying the integrity of each redundant branch after assembly;

(3) The unit input trigger circuitry of an exploding bridgewire firing unit must maintain a minimum 20 dB margin between the threshold trigger level and the worst-case noise environment;

(4) An exploding bridgewire firing unit must have a minimum trigger sensitivity that provides for the unit to fire at 6 dB lower in amplitude and one-half the duration of the worst-case trigger signal that the unit could receive during flight;

(5) In the event of a power dropout, any control or switching circuit critical to the reliable operation of an exploding bridgewire firing unit, including solid-state power transfer switches, must not change state for 50 milliseconds or more; and

(6) An exploding bridgewire firing unit's response time must satisfy all its performance specifications for the range of input trigger signals from the specified minimum trigger signal amplitude and duration to the specified maximum trigger signal amplitude and duration.

(d) *High voltage output.* An exploding bridgewire firing unit's high voltage discharge circuit must satisfy all of the following:

(1) An exploding bridgewire firing unit must include circuits for capacitor charging, bleeding, charge interruption, and triggering;

(2) An exploding bridgewire firing unit must have a single fault tolerant capacitor discharge capability;

(3) An exploding bridgewire firing unit must deliver a voltage to the exploding bridgewire that is no less than 50% greater than the exploding bridgewire's minimum all-fire voltage, not including transmission losses, at the unit's worst-case high and low arming voltages;

(4) The design of an exploding bridgewire firing unit must prevent corona and arcing on internal and external high voltage circuitry;

(5) An exploding bridgewire firing unit must satisfy all its performance specifications at the worst-case high and low arm voltages that could be delivered during flight; and

(6) Any high energy trigger circuit used to initiate exploding bridgewire firing unit's main firing capacitor must deliver an output signal of no less than a 50% voltage margin above the nominal voltage threshold level.

(e) *Output monitors*. The monitoring circuits of an exploding bridgewire firing unit must provide the data for real-time checkout and determination of the firing unit's acceptability for flight. The monitored data must include the voltage level of all high voltage capacitors and the arming power to the firing unit.

D417.39 ORDNANCE INTERRUPTER SAFE-AND-ARM DEVICE WITHOUT AN ELECTRO-EXPLOSIVE DEVICE

(a) This section applies to any ordnance interrupter safe-and-arm device that does not have an internal electro-explosive device and is part of a flight termination system. An ordnance interrupter must provide for safing and arming of the flight termination system ordnance to satisfy section D417.13.

(b) An ordnance interrupter must remain in the armed position and satisfy all its performance specifications when subjected to the design environmental levels determined according to section D417.7.

(c) An ordnance interrupter must not require adjustment throughout its service life.

(d) An ordnance interrupter must satisfy all its performance specifications after experiencing any transportation, handling, or installation environment that the device could experience undetected.

(e) An ordnance interrupter that uses ordnance rotor leads must not initiate and must allow for safe disposal after experiencing the worst-case drop and resulting impact that it could experience during storage, transportation, or installation.

(f) An ordnance interrupter must satisfy all of its performance specifications when subjected to repetitive functioning for five times the expected number of arming cycles required for acceptance testing, preflight checkout, and flight operations, including an allowance for re-tests due to potential schedule delays.

(g) An ordnance interrupter must not fragment during ordnance initiation.

(h) The design of a flight termination system must protect an ordnance interrupter from conditions that could degrade its performance or cause inadvertent initiation during transportation, storage, installation, preflight testing, and potential preflight fault conditions. Safing of an ordnance interrupter must satisfy all of the following:

(1) While in the safe position, an ordnance interrupter must prevent the functioning of an ordnance train with a reliability of 0.999 at a 95% confidence level;

(2) When locked in the safe position, an ordnance interrupter must prevent initiation of an ordnance train. The ordnance interrupter must satisfy all its performance specification when locked in the safe position and subjected to the continuous operational arming voltage required by section E417.29(j);

(3) An ordnance interrupter must not initiate its electro-explosive device or any other ordnance train component when locked in the safe position and subjected to the continuous operational arming voltage required by section E417.29(e)(3);

(4) An ordnance interrupter must have a manual and a remote means of safing from any rotor or barrier position;

(5) An ordnance interrupter must have a visual display of the status on the device and provide for remote display of the status when the ordnance interrupter is in the safe position; and

(6) An ordnance interrupter must include a safing interlock that prevents the interrupter from moving from the safe position to the arm position when subjected to an operational arming current. A safing interlock must have a means of positively locking into place and a means of verifying proper function of the interlock. A safing interlock and any related operation procedure must eliminate the possibility of inadvertent disconnection of the interlock.

(i) Arming of an ordnance interrupter must satisfy all of the following:

(1) An ordnance interrupter is armed when all ordnance interfaces, such as a donor explosive transfer system, rotor charge, and acceptor explosive transfer system are aligned with one another to propagate the explosive charge with a reliability of 0.999 at a 95% confidence level;

(2) An ordnance interrupter must have a visual display of the status on the device and provide for remote display of the status when the ordnance interrupter is in the arm position; and

(3) An ordnance interrupter must provide for remote arming of the interrupter.

D417.41 ORDNANCE INITIATORS

(a) This section applies to any low-voltage electro-explosive device that is part of a flight termination system or high-voltage exploding bridgewire ordnance initiator that is part of a flight termination system. An ordnance initiator must use electrical energy to trigger an explosive charge that initiates the flight termination system ordnance.

(b) An ordnance initiator must have a manufacturer-specified all-fire energy level. When the all-fire energy level is applied, the ordnance initiator must fire with a reliability of no less than 0.999 at a 95 percent confidence level.

(c) An ordnance initiator must have a specified no-fire energy level. An ordnance initiator must not fire when exposed to continuous application of the no-fire energy level, with a reliability of no less than 0.999 at a 95 percent confidence level. An ordnance initiator must satisfy all its performance specifications when subjected to continuous application of the no-fire energy level.

(d) The lowest temperature at which an ordnance initiator would experience autoignition, sublimation, or melting or in any other way experience degradation in performance must be no less than 30 °C higher than the highest temperature that the initiator could experience prior to or during flight.

(e) An ordnance initiator must not fire, and must satisfy all its performance specifications when subjected to the maximum expected electrostatic discharge that it could experience from personnel or conductive surfaces. An ordnance initiator must not fire, and must satisfy all its performance specifications when subjected to workmanship discharges of no less than a 25-kV, 500-pF pin-to-pin discharge through a 5-kΩ resistor and a 25-kV, 500-pF pin-to-case discharge with no resistor.

(f) An ordnance initiator must not initiate and must satisfy all its performance specifications when exposed to stray electrical current that is at a 20-dB margin greater than the greatest stray electrical current that the ordnance initiator could experience prior to or during flight. When determining the 20-dB margin, a launch operator must account for all potential sources of stray electrical current, including leakage current from other electronic components and radio frequency induced electrical current.

(g) An ordnance initiator must satisfy all its performance specification after being exposed to the tensile load required by section E417.9(j), the handling drop required by section E417.9(k), and any additional transportation, handling, or installation environment that the device could experience undetected.

(h) An ordnance initiator must not initiate and must allow for safe disposal after experiencing the abnormal drop required by section E417.9(l).

(i) An ordnance initiator must be hermetically sealed to the equivalent of 5×10^{-6} scc/sec of helium at one atmosphere pressure differential.

(j) The insulation resistance between mutually insulated points must ensure that an ordnance initiator satisfies all its performance specifications when subjected to the greater of twice the maximum applied voltage during testing and flight or a workmanship voltage of no less than 500 volts. The insulation material must satisfy all its performance specifications when exposed to workmanship, heat, dirt, oxidation, and any additional expected environment.

D417.43 EXPLODING BRIDGEWIRE

(a) This section applies to any exploding bridgewire that is part of a flight termination system. An exploding bridgewire must use high-voltage electrical energy of 50 volts or greater to trigger an explosive charge that initiates the flight termination system ordnance.

(b) An exploding bridgewire must satisfy the ordnance initiator requirements of section D417.41.

(c) An exploding bridgewire's electrical circuitry, such as connectors, pins, wiring and header assembly, must transmit an all-fire pulse at a level 50% greater than the lowest exploding bridgewire firing unit's operational firing voltage. This must include allowances for effects such as corona and arcing of a flight configured exploding bridgewire exposed to altitude, thermal vacuum, salt-fog, and humidity environments.

(d) An exploding bridgewire must not fragment during ordnance initiation.

(e) All exploding bridgewire connector pins must withstand the tension and compression loads required by section E417.9(j).

D417.45 PERCUSSION-ACTIVATED DEVICE

(a) This section applies to any percussion-activated device that is part of a flight termination system. A percussion-activated device must use mechanical energy to trigger an explosive charge that initiates the flight termination system ordnance.

(b) A percussion-activated device's lanyard pull system must have a protective cover or other feature that prevents inadvertent pulling of the lanyard.

(c) A percussion-activated device must not fragment upon initiation.

(d) A percussion-activated device must have a guaranteed no-fire pull force of no less than twice the largest inadvertent pull force that the device could experience:

(1) Any time prior to flight that the safing interlock of paragraph (o) of this section is not in place; or

(2) During flight.

(e) A percussion-activated device must not initiate when pulled with its maximum no-fire pull force and then released with a reliability of no less than 0.999 at a 95% confidence level.

(f) A percussion-activated device must have a primer all-fire energy level, including spring constant and pull distance that ensures initiation, with a reliability of no less than 0.999 at a 95% confidence level when subjected to preflight and flight environments.

(g) A percussion-activated device must deliver an operational impact force to the primer of no less than twice the all-fire energy level.

(h) A percussion-activated device's primer must initiate and must satisfy all its performance specifications when subjected to two times the operational impact energy or four times the all-fire impact energy level.

(i) A percussion-activated device's reliability must satisfy its performance specifications when subjected to a no-fire pull force and then released.

(j) The lowest temperature at which a percussion-activated device would experience autoignition, sublimation, or melting, or in any other way not satisfy its performance specifications, must be no less than 30 °C higher than the highest temperature that the percussion-activated device could experience prior to or during flight.

(k) A percussion-activated device must satisfy all its performance specifications after experiencing the handling drop required by section E417.9(k) and any additional transportation, handling, or installation environment that the device could experience undetected.

(l) A percussion-activated device's ordnance must be hermetically sealed to the equivalent of 5×10^{-6} scc/sec of helium at one atmosphere differential.

(m) A percussion-activated device's structural and firing components must withstand 500 percent of the largest pull or jerk force that the device could experience during breakup of the launch vehicle.

(n) A percussion-activated device must not initiate and must allow for safe disposal after experiencing the abnormal drop required by section E417.9(l).

(o) A percussion-activated device must include a safing interlock, such as a safing pin, that provides a physical means of preventing the percussion-activated device assembly from pulling more than 50% of the guaranteed no-fire pull distance. The following apply to a safing interlock:

(1) A safing interlock must positively lock into place and must have a means of verifying proper function of the interlock.

(2) A safing interlock must eliminate the possibility of inadvertent disconnection or removal of the interlock should a pre-load condition exist on the lanyard unless the device provides a visual or other means of verifying that there is no load on the lanyard.

(3) A safing interlock, when in place, must prevent initiation of the percussion actuated device when subjected to twice the greatest possible inadvertent pull force that could be experienced during launch processing.

D417.47 EXPLOSIVE TRANSFER SYSTEM

(a) This section applies to any explosive transfer system that is part of a flight termination system. An explosive transfer system must transmit an explosive charge from an initiation source, such as an ordnance initiator, to other flight termination system ordnance such as a destruct charge.

(b) Ordnance used in an explosive transfer system must consist of a secondary explosive. An exception to this is any transition component that contains a primary explosive that is fully contained within the transition component. Any transition component that contains a primary explosive must be no more sensitive to inadvertent detonation than a secondary explosive.

(c) An explosive transfer system, including all donor, acceptor, and transition charges and components must transfer an explosive charge with a reliability of no less than 0.999 at a 95% confidence level.

(d) An explosive transfer system must satisfy all its performance specifications with the smallest bend radius that it is subjected to when installed in its flight configuration.

(e) All explosive transfer connectors must positively lock in place and provide for verification of proper connection through visual inspection.

(f) Each explosive transfer system component must satisfy all its performance specifications when subjected to the tensile load required by section E417.9(j).

(g) An explosive transfer system must satisfy all its performance specifications after experiencing the handling drop required by section E417.9(k) and any additional transportation, handling, or installation environment that the system could experience undetected.

(h) An explosive transfer system must not initiate and must allow for safe disposal after experiencing the abnormal drop required by section E417.9(l).

(i) An explosive transfer system must be hermetically sealed to the equivalent of 5×10^{-6} scc/sec of helium at one atmosphere pressure differential.

D417.49 DESTRUCT CHARGE

(a) This section applies to any destruct charge that is part of a flight termination system. A destruct charge must sever or penetrate a launch vehicle component or payload, such as a propellant tank or motor casing, to accomplish a flight termination function.

(b) A destruct charge must use a secondary explosive.

(c) When initiated, a destruct charge acceptor, where applicable, or main charge must ensure the transfer of the explosive charge with a reliability of 0.999 at a 95% confidence level.

(d) Initiation of a destruct charge must result in a flight termination system action in accordance with the flight termination system functional requirements of § 417.303.

(e) A destruct charge must sever or penetrate 150% of the thickness of the material that must be severed or penetrated in order for the destruct charge to accomplish its intended flight termination function. A destruct charge, when initiated to terminate the flight of a launch vehicle, must not detonate any launch vehicle or payload propellant.

(f) Each destruct charge and associated fitting must satisfy all its performance specifications when subjected to the tensile load required by section E417.9(j).

(g) A destruct charge must satisfy all its performance specifications after experiencing the handling drop required by section E417.9(k) and any additional transportation, handling, or installation environment that the charge could experience undetected.

(h) A destruct charge must not initiate and must allow for safe disposal after experiencing the abnormal drop required by section E417.9(l).

(i) A destruct charge must be hermetically sealed to the equivalent of 5×10^{-6} scc/sec of helium at one atmosphere pressure differential.

D417.51 VIBRATION AND SHOCK ISOLATORS

(a) This section applies to any vibration or shock isolator that is part of a flight safety system. A vibration or shock isolator must ensure the environmental survivability of a flight termination system component by reducing the vibration or shock levels that the component experiences during flight.

(b) A vibration or shock isolator must have repeatable natural frequency and resonant amplification parameters when subjected to flight environments.

(c) An isolator must account for all effects that could cause variations in repeatability, including acceleration preloads, temperature, component mass, and vibration level variations.

(d) A vibration or shock isolator must satisfy all of its performance specifications when subjected to the qualification test environments for each component that is mounted on the isolator.

(e) All components mounted on a vibration or shock isolator must withstand the environments introduced by isolator amplification. In addition, all component interface hardware, such as connectors, cables, and grounding straps, must withstand any added deflection introduced by an isolator.

D417.53 MISCELLANEOUS COMPONENTS

(a) This section applies to any miscellaneous flight termination system component that is not specifically identified by this appendix.

(b) A miscellaneous component must satisfy all its performance specifications when subjected to the non-operating and operating environments of section D417.3.

(c) The design of a miscellaneous component must provide for the component to be tested in accordance with appendix E of this part.

(d) A launch operator must identify any additional requirements that apply to any new or unique component and demonstrate that those requirements ensure the reliability of the component.

APPENDIX E TO PART 417—FLIGHT TERMINATION SYSTEM TESTING AND ANALYSIS

E417.1 GENERAL

(a) *Scope and compliance.* This appendix contains requirements for tests and analyses that apply to all flight termination systems and the components that make up each flight termination system. Section 417.301 requires that a launch operator's flight safety system employ a flight termination system that complies with this appendix. Section 417.301 also contains requirements that apply to a launch operator's demonstration of compliance with the requirement of this appendix. A launch operator must employ on its launch vehicle only those flight termination system components that satisfy the requirements of this appendix.

(b) *Component tests and analyses.* A component must satisfy each test or analysis required by any table of this appendix to demonstrate that the component satisfies all its performance specifications when subjected to non-operating and operating environments. A launch operator must identify and implement any additional test or analysis for any new technology or any unique application of an existing technology.

(c) *Test plans.* Each test of a component, subsystem, or system must follow a written plan that specifies the test parameters, including pass/fail criteria, and a testing sequence that satisfy the requirements of this appendix. For any component that is used for more than one flight, the test plan must provide for component reuse qualification, refurbishment, and acceptance as required by section E417.7(g). The test plan must include any alternate procedures for testing a component when it is in place on the launch vehicle.

(d) *Test failures.* If a test of a component results in a failure, the component does not satisfy the test requirement. Each of the following is a test failure:

(1) Any component sample that does not satisfy a performance specification;

(2) Any failure to accomplish a test objective;

(3) Any component sample with a test result that indicates that the component is out-of-family when compared to other samples of the component, even if the component satisfies other test criteria;

(4) Any unexpected change in the performance of a component sample occurring at any time during testing;

(5) Any component sample that exhibits any sign that a part is stressed beyond its design limit, such as a cracked circuit board, bent clamps, worn part, or loose connector or screw, even if the component passes the final functional test;

(6) When component examination shows any defect that could adversely affect the component's performance;

(7) Any discontinuity or dropout in a measured performance parameter that could prevent the component from satisfying a performance specification;

(8) Any inadvertent output; or

(9) Any indication of internal component damage.

(e) *Failure analysis.* In the event of a test failure, the test item, procedures and equipment must undergo a written failure analysis. The failure analysis must identify the cause of the failure, the mechanism of the failure, and isolate the failure to the smallest replaceable item or items and ensure that there are no generic design, workmanship, or process problems with other flight components of similar configuration.

(f) *Test tolerances.* Each test must apply to the nominal values specified by this appendix tolerances that satisfy the following:

(1) The tolerance of any measurement taken during a functional test must provide the accuracy needed to detect any out-of-family or out-of-specification anomaly.

(2) An environmental level, such as for vibration or temperature, used to satisfy a component test requirement of this appendix must include the environment design margin required by appendix D of this part. The environmental level must account for any test equipment tolerance to ensure that the component experiences the required margin.

(g) *Test equipment.* All equipment used during environmental testing must provide for the test item to experience the required environmental test levels. Any test fixture used to simultaneously test multiple component samples must ensure that each component sample, at each mounting location on the fixture experiences each required environmental test level. Any difference in a qualification or acceptance test fixture or cable must undergo an evaluation to ensure that flight hardware is not subjected to stresses greater than that which the unit experiences during qualification.

(h) *Rework and repair of components.* Components that fail a test may undergo rework and repair and must then complete the failed test and each remaining test. If a repair requires disassembly of the component or soldering operations, the component must repeat any test necessary to demonstrate that the repair corrected the original anomaly and did not cause other damage. The total number of acceptance tests experienced by a repaired component must not exceed the environments for which the component is qualified.

(i) *Test and analysis reports.* A launch operator must prepare or obtain one or more written reports that:

(1) Describe all flight termination system test results and test conditions;

(2) Describe any analysis performed instead of testing;

(3) Identify, by serial number or other identification, each test result that applies to each system or component;

(4) Describe any family performance data to be used for comparison to any subsequent test of a component or system;

(5) Describe all performance parameter measurements made during component testing for comparison to each previous and subsequent test to identify any performance variations that may indicate a potential workmanship or other defect that could lead to a failure of the component during flight; and

(6) Identify any test failure or anomaly, including any variation from an established performance baseline, with a description of the failure or anomaly, each corrective action taken, and all results of additional tests.

E417.3 Component Test and Analysis Tables

(a) *General.* This section applies to each test and analysis table of this appendix. Each component or system that is identified by a table must satisfy each test or analysis identified by the table. Each component or system must satisfy a test by undergoing and passing the test as described in the paragraph that the table lists. In cases where the listed paragraph allows a test or analysis, any analysis must satisfy any specific requirement listed in the paragraph and must demonstrate one of the following:

(1) The test environment does not apply to the component;

(2) The test environment does not degrade the component's performance; or

(3) Another test or combination of tests that the component undergoes places equal or greater stress on the component than the test in question.

(b) *Test sequence.* A component or system must undergo each test in the same order as the table identifies the test. A launch operator may deviate from the test sequence if the launch operator demonstrates that another order will detect any component anomaly that could occur during testing.

(c) *Quantity of sample components tested.* (1) For a new component, each table identifies the quantity of component samples that must undergo each test identified by the table.

(2) A launch operator may test fewer samples than the quantity identified for a new component if the launch operator demonstrates one of the following:

(i) That the component has experienced comparable environmental tests; or

(ii) The component is similar to a design that has experienced comparable environmental tests.

(3) Any component that a launch operator uses for any comparison to a new component must have undergone all the environmental tests required for the new component to develop cumulative effects.

(d) *Performance verification tests.* Each performance verification test identified by any table of this appendix must satisfy all of the following:

(1) Each test must measure one or more of a component or system's performance parameters to demonstrate that the component or system satisfies all its performance specifications;

(2) The component must undergo each test:

(i) Before the component is exposed to each test environment; and

(ii) After the component is exposed to the test environment to identify any performance degradation due to the environment; and

(3) Any electronic component must undergo each performance verification test at:

(i) The lowest operating voltage;

(ii) Nominal operating voltage; and

(iii) Highest operating voltage that the component could experience during preflight and flight operations.

(e) *Abbreviated performance verification tests.* Each abbreviated performance verification test required by any table of this appendix must satisfy all of the following:

(1) Each test must exercise all of a component's functions that are critical to a flight termination system's performance during flight

(i) while the component is subjected to each test environment; or,

(ii) for short duration environments such as shock, before and after each test;

(2) Each test must measure a sampling of the component's critical performance parameters while the component is subjected to each test environment to demonstrate that the component satisfies all its performance specifications; and

(3) Any electronic component must undergo each abbreviated performance verification test at the component's nominal operating voltage.

(f) *Status-of-health tests.* Each status-of-health test required by any table of this appendix must satisfy all of the following:

(1) Each test must measure one or more critical performance parameter to demonstrate that a component or system satisfies all its performance specifications;

(2) The critical performance parameters must include those parameters that act as an indicator of an internal anomaly that a functional performance test might not detect; and

(3) Each test must compare the results to any previous test results to identify any degradation in performance.

E417.5 COMPONENT EXAMINATION

(a) *General.* This section applies to each component examination identified by any table of this appendix. Each component examination must identify any manufacturing defect that the performance tests might not detect. The presence of a defect that could adversely affect the component's performance constitutes a failure.

(b) *Visual examination.* A visual examination must verify that good workmanship was employed during manufacture of a component and that the component is free of any physical defect that could adversely affect performance. A visual examination may include the use of optical magnification, mirrors, or specific lighting, such as ultraviolet illumination.

(c) *Dimension measurement.* A dimension measurement of a component must verify that the component satisfies all its dimensional specifications.

(d) *Weight measurement.* A weight measurement of a component must verify that the component satisfies its weight specification.

(e) *Identification check.* An identification check of a component must verify that the component has one or more identification tags that contain information that allows for configuration control and tracing of the component.

(f) *X-ray and N-ray examination.* An X-ray or N-ray examination of a component must have a resolution that allows detailed inspection of the internal parts of the component and must identify any internal anomalous condition. The examination must include enough photographs, taken from different angles, to allow complete coverage of the component's internal parts. When utilized as a recurring inspection technique to accept production hardware, the examination must use the same set of angles for each sample of a component to allow for comparison. A certified technician must evaluate X-ray and N-ray photographs.

(g) *Internal inspection.* An internal inspection of a component must demonstrate that there is no wear or damage, including any internal wear or damage, to the component that could adversely affect its performance after exposure to any test environment. An internal inspection must satisfy all of the following:

(1) All internal components and subassemblies, such as circuit board traces, internal connectors, welds, screws, clamps, electronic

piece parts, battery cell plates and separators, and mechanical subassemblies must undergo examination to satisfy this paragraph using an inspection method such as a magnifying lens or radiographic inspection;

(2) For a component that can be disassembled, the component must undergo complete disassembly to the point needed to satisfy this paragraph; and

(3) For a component that cannot be disassembled, such as an antenna, potted component, or welded structure, the component must undergo any special procedures needed to satisfy this paragraph, such as depotting the component, cutting the component into cross-sections, or radiographic inspection.

(h) *Leakage.* A leakage test must demonstrate that a component's seal satisfies all its performance specifications before and after the component is subjected to any test environment as follows:

(1) The test must have the resolution and sample rate to demonstrate that the component's leak rate is no greater than its design limit.

(2) For an electronic component, the test must demonstrate a leak rate of no greater than the equivalent of 10^{-4} standard cubic centimeters/second (scc/sec) of helium.

(3) For an ordnance component, the test must demonstrate a leak rate of no greater than the equivalent of 5×10^{-6} scc/sec of helium.

E417.7 QUALIFICATION TESTING AND ANALYSIS

(a) This section applies to each qualification non-operating and operating test or analysis identified by any table of this appendix. A qualification test or analysis must demonstrate that a component will satisfy all its performance specifications when subjected to the design environmental levels required by section D417.7.

(b) Before a component sample undergoes a qualification environmental test, the component sample must pass all the required acceptance tests.

(c) A component must undergo each qualification test in a flight representative configuration, with all flight representative hardware such as connectors, cables, and any cable clamps, and with all attachment hardware, such as dynamic isolators, brackets and bolts, as part of that flight representative configuration.

(d) A component must undergo re-qualification tests if there is a change in the design of the component or if the environmental levels to which it will be exposed exceed the levels for which the component is qualified. A component must undergo re-qualification if the manufacturer's location, parts, materials, or processes have changed since the previous qualification. A change in the name of the manufacturer as a result of a sale does not require re-qualification if the personnel, factory location or the parts, material and processes remain unchanged since the last component qualification. The extent of any re-qualification tests must be the same as the initial qualification tests except where paragraph (f) of this section applies.

(e) A launch operator must not use for flight any component sample that has been subjected to a qualification test environment.

(f) A launch operator may reduce the testing required to qualify or re-qualify a component's design through qualification by similarity to tests performed on identical or similar hardware. To qualify component "A" based on similarity to component "B" that has already been qualified for use, a launch operator must demonstrate that all of the following conditions are satisfied:

(1) "B" must have been qualified through testing, not by similarity;

(2) The environments encountered by "B" during its qualification or flight history must have been equal to or more severe than the qualification environments required for "A;"

(3) "A" must be a minor variation of "B." The demonstration that A is a minor variation of B must account for all of the following:

(i) Any difference in weight, mechanical configuration, thermal effects, or dynamic response;

(ii) Any change in piece-part quality level; and

(iii) Any addition or subtraction of an electronic piece-part, moving part, ceramic or glass part, crystal, magnetic device, or power conversion or distribution equipment;

(4) "A" and "B" must perform the same functions, with "A" having equivalent or better capability; and

(5) The same manufacturer must produce "A" and "B" in the same location using identical tools and manufacturing processes;

(g) For any flight termination system component used for more than one flight, the component qualification tests must demonstrate that the component satisfies all its performance specifications when subjected to:

(1) Each qualification test environment; and

(2) The total number of exposures to each maximum predicted environment for the total number of flights.

E417.9 QUALIFICATION NON-OPERATING ENVIRONMENTS

(a) *General.* This section applies to each qualification non-operating environment test or analysis identified by any table of this appendix. A qualification non-operating test or analysis must demonstrate that a component satisfies all its performance specifications when subjected to each maximum predicted non-operating environment that the component could experience, including all storage, transportation, and installation environments.

(b) *Storage temperature.* A storage temperature test or analysis must demonstrate that a component will satisfy all its performance specifications when subjected to the maximum predicted high and low temperatures, thermal cycles, and dwell-times at the high and low temperatures that the component could experience under storage conditions as follows:

(1) Any storage temperature test must subject the component to the range of temperatures from 10 °C lower than the maximum predicted storage thermal range to 10 °C higher. The rate of change from one thermal extreme to the other must be no less than the maximum predicted thermal rate of change. All thermal dwell-times and thermal cycles must be no less than those of the maximum predicted storage environment.

(2) Any analysis must demonstrate that the qualification operating thermal cycle environment is more severe than the storage thermal environment by satisfying one of the following:

(i) The analysis must include thermal fatigue equivalence calculations that demonstrate that the large change in temperature for a few thermal cycles experienced during flight is a more severe environment than the relatively small change in temperature for many thermal cycles that would be experienced during storage; or

(ii) The analysis must demonstrate that the component's operating qualification thermal cycle range encompasses −34 °C to 71 °C and that any temperature variation that the component experiences during storage does not exceed 22 °C.

(c) *High-temperature storage of ordnance.* A component may undergo a high-temperature storage test to extend the service-life of an ordnance component production lot from one year to three or five years as permitted by any test table of this appendix. The test must demonstrate that each component sample satisfies all its performance specifications after being subjected to + 71 °C and 40 to 60 percent relative humidity for no less than 30 days each.

(d) *Transportation shock.* A transportation shock test or analysis must demonstrate that a component satisfies all its performance specifications after being subjected to the maximum predicted transportation induced shock levels that the component could experience when transported in its transported configuration. Any analysis must demonstrate that the qualification operating shock environment is more severe than the transportation shock environment.

(e) *Bench handling shock.* A bench handling shock test must demonstrate that a component satisfies all its performance specifications after being subjected to maximum predicted bench handling induced shock levels. The test must include, for each orientation that could occur during servicing; a drop from the maximum predicted handling height onto a representative surface.

(f) *Transportation vibration.* A transportation vibration test or analysis must demonstrate that a component satisfies all its performance specifications after being subjected to a maximum predicted transportation-induced vibration level when transported in its transportation configuration as follows:

(1) Any transportation vibration test must subject a component to vibration in three mutually perpendicular axes for 60 minutes per axis. The test must subject each axis to the following vibration profile:

(i) 0.01500 g^2/Hz at 10 Hz to 40 Hz;

(ii) 0.01500 g^2/Hz at 40 Hz to 0.00015 g^2/Hz at 500 Hz; and

(iii) If the component is resonant below 10 Hz, the test vibration profile must extend to the lowest resonant frequency.

(2) Any analysis must demonstrate that the qualification operating vibration environment is more severe than the transportation vibration environment. The analysis must include vibration fatigue equivalence calculations that demonstrate that the high vibration levels with short duration experienced during flight creates a more severe environment than the relatively low-vibration levels with long duration that would be experienced during transportation.

(g) *Fungus resistance.* A fungus resistance test or analysis must demonstrate that a component satisfies all its performance specifications after being subjected to a fungal growth environment. Any analysis must demonstrate that all unsealed and exposed surfaces do not contain nutrient materials for fungus.

(h) *Salt fog.* For a component that will be exposed to salt fog, a salt fog test or analysis must demonstrate that the component satisfies all its performance specifications after being subjected to the effects of a moist, salt-laden atmosphere. The test or analysis must demonstrate the ability of all externally exposed surfaces to withstand a salt-fog environment. The test or analysis must demonstrate the ability of each internal part of a component to withstand a salt-fog environment unless the component is environmentally sealed, and acceptance testing verifies that the seal works.

(i) *Fine sand.* For a component that will be exposed to fine sand or dust, a fine sand test or analysis must demonstrate that the component satisfies all its performance specifications after being subjected to the effects of dust or fine sand particles that may penetrate into cracks, crevices, bearings and joints. The test or analysis must demonstrate the ability of all externally exposed surfaces to withstand a fine sand environment. The test or analysis must demonstrate the ability of each internal part of a component to withstand a fine sand environment unless the component is environmentally sealed and acceptance testing verifies that the seal works.

(j) *Tensile load.* A tensile load test must demonstrate that a component satisfies all its performance specifications after being exposed to tensile and compression loads of no less than twice the maximum predicted level during transportation and installation. In addition, the test load must satisfy one of the following where applicable:

(1) For an explosive transfer system and its associated fittings, a pull of no less than 100 pounds unless the launch operator establishes procedural controls or tests that prevent or detect mishandling;

(2) For a destruct charge and its associated fittings, a pull of no less than 50 pounds;

(3) For a flight radio frequency connector, a pull of no less than one-half the manufacturer specified limit;

(4) For an electro-explosive device wire, a pull of no less than 18 pounds; or

(5) For an electrical pin of an exploding bridgewire device, no less than an 18-pound force in axial and compression modes.

(k) *Handling drop of ordnance.* A handling drop test must demonstrate that an ordnance component satisfies all its performance specifications after experiencing the more severe of the following:

(1) The maximum predicted drop and resulting impact that could occur and go undetected during storage, transportation, or installation; or

(2) A six-foot drop onto a representative surface in any orientation that could occur during storage, transportation, or installation.

(l) *Abnormal drop of ordnance.* An abnormal drop test must demonstrate that an ordnance component does not initiate and allows for safe disposal after experiencing the maximum predicted drop and resulting impact onto a representative surface in any orientation, that could occur during storage, transportation, or installation. The component need not function after this drop.

E417.11 QUALIFICATION OPERATING ENVIRONMENTS

(a) *General.* This section applies to each qualification operating environment test or analysis identified by any table of this appendix. A qualification operating environment test must demonstrate that a component satisfies all of its performance specifications when subjected to each qualification operating environment including each physical environment that the component will experience during acceptance testing, launch countdown, and flight. The test must employ each margin required by this section.

(b) *Qualification sinusoidal vibration.* (1) A qualification sinusoidal vibration test or analysis of a component must demonstrate that the component and each connection to any item that attaches to the component satisfy all their performance specifications when subjected to the qualification sinusoidal vibration environment. The attached items must include any vibration or shock isolator, grounding strap, bracket, explosive transfer system, or cable to the first tie-down. Any cable that interfaces with the component during any test must be representative of the cable used for flight.

(2) The qualification sinusoidal vibration environment must be no less than 6dB greater than the maximum predicted sinusoidal vibration environment for no less than three times the maximum predicted duration.

(3) The sinusoidal frequency must range from 50% lower than the maximum predicted frequency range to 50% higher than the maximum predicted frequency range.

(4) Any test must satisfy all of the following:

(i) The test must subject each of three mutually perpendicular axes of the component to the qualification sinusoidal vibration environment, one axis at a time. For each axis, the duration of the vibration must be no less than three times the maximum predicted sinusoidal vibration duration.

(ii) The sinusoidal sweep rate must be no greater than one-third the maximum predicted sweep rate;

(iii) The sinusoidal vibration test amplitude must have an accuracy of ±10%; and

(iv) For any component that uses one or more shock or vibration isolators, the component must undergo the test mounted on its isolator or isolators as a unit. Each isolator must satisfy the requirements of section E417.35.

(5) Any analysis must demonstrate that the qualification random vibration environment of paragraph (c) of this section encompasses the qualification sinusoidal vibration environment.

(c) *Qualification random vibration.* (1) A qualification random vibration test of a component must demonstrate that the component and each connection to any item that attaches to the component satisfy all their performance specifications when subjected to the qualification random vibration environment. The attached items must include any isolator, grounding strap, bracket, explosive transfer system, or cable to the first tie-down. Any cable that interfaces with the component during any test must be representative of the cable used for flight.

(2) For each component required by this appendix to undergo 100% acceptance testing, the minimum qualification random vibration environment must be no less than a 3 dB margin greater than the maximum acceptance random vibration test environment for all frequencies from 20 Hz to 2,000 Hz. The minimum and maximum test environments

must account for all the test tolerances to ensure that the test maintains the 3 dB margin.

(3) For each component that is not required by this appendix to undergo 100% acceptance testing, the minimum qualification random vibration environment must be no less than a 4.5–dB margin greater than the greater of the maximum predicted random vibration environment or the minimum workmanship test levels of table E417.11–1 for all frequencies from 20 Hz to 2000 Hz. The minimum qualification test environment must account for all the test tolerances to ensure that the test maintains the 4.5 dB margin.

(4) If a component is mounted on one or more shock or vibration isolators during flight, the component must undergo the qualification random vibration test while hard-mounted or isolator-mounted as follows:

(i) Any qualification random vibration test with the component hard-mounted must subject the component to a qualification random vibration environment that:

(A) Accounts for the isolator attenuation and amplification due to the maximum predicted operating random vibration environment, including any thermal effects and acceleration pre-load performance variability, and adds a 1.5 dB margin to account for any isolator attenuation variability;

(B) Adds the required qualification random vibration margin of paragraph (c)(1) or (c)(2) of this section after accounting for the isolator effects of paragraph (c)(4)(i)(A) of this section and accounts for all tolerances that apply to the isolator's performance specifications to ensure that the qualification test margin is maintained; and

(C) Is no less than the minimum workmanship screening qualification random vibration level of table E417.11–1.

(ii) Any qualification random vibration test with the component isolator-mounted must:

(A) Use an isolator or isolators that passed the tests required by section E417.35;

(B) Have an input to each isolator of no less than the required qualification random vibration environment of paragraph (c)(1) or (c)(2) of this section; and

(C) Subject the component to no less than the minimum workmanship screening qualification random vibration level of table E417.11–1. If the isolator or isolators prevent the component from experiencing the minimum workmanship level, the component must undergo a test while hard-mounted that subjects the component to the workmanship level.

(5) The test must subject each component sample to the qualification random vibration environment in each of three mutually perpendicular axes. For each axis, the test must last three times as long as the acceptance test duration or a minimum workmanship qualification duration of 180 seconds, whichever is greater.

(6) For a component sample that must experience the acceptance random vibration environment before it experiences the qualification random vibration environment, such as a command receiver decoder, the test must use the same configuration and methods for the acceptance and qualification environments.

(7) If the duration of the qualification random vibration environment leaves insufficient time to complete any required performance verification test while the component is subjected to the full qualification environment, the test must continue at no less than the acceptance random vibration environment. The test need only continue for the additional time needed to complete the performance verification test.

(8) The test must continuously monitor and record all performance and status-of-health parameters while the component is subjected to the qualification environment. This monitoring must have a sample rate that will detect any component performance degradation. Any electrical component must undergo the test while subjected to its nominal operating voltage.

(9) A launch operator may substitute a random vibration test for another required dynamic test, such as acceleration, acoustic, or sinusoidal vibration if the launch operator demonstrates that the forces, displacements, and test duration imparted on a component during the random vibration test are no less severe than the other test environment.

Table E417.11-1, Minimum Workmanship

Power Spectral Density for Qualification Random Vibration Testing

Frequency Range (Hz)	Minimum Power Spectral Density
20	0.021 g^2/Hz
20-150	3 dB/octave slope
150-600	0.16 g^2/Hz
600-2000	-6 dB/octave slope
2000	0.014 g^2/Hz
Overall G_{rms} = 12.2	

(d) *Qualification acoustic.* (1) A qualification acoustic vibration test or analysis of a component must demonstrate that the component and each connection to any item that attaches to the component satisfy all their performance specifications when subjected to the qualification acoustic vibration environment. The attached items must include any isolator, grounding strap, bracket, explosive transfer system, or cable to the first tie-down. Any cable that interfaces with the component during any test must be representative of the cable used for flight.

(2) For each component required by this appendix to undergo 100% acoustic acceptance testing, the minimum qualification acoustic vibration environment must be greater than the maximum acceptance acoustic vibration test environment for all frequencies from 20 Hz to 2000 Hz. The minimum and maximum test environments must account for all the test tolerances to ensure that the test maintains a positive margin between the minimum qualification environment and the maximum acceptance environment. For each acoustic vibration test required by this appendix to have a tolerance of ±3 dB, the qualification test level must be 6 dB greater than the acceptance test level.

(3) For each component that is not required by this appendix to undergo 100% acceptance testing, such as ordnance, the minimum qualification acoustic vibration environment must be no less than a 3 dB margin greater than the maximum predicted acoustic vibration environment or a minimum workmanship screening test level of 144 dBA for all frequencies from 20 Hz to 2000 Hz. The minimum qualification test environment must account for all the test tolerances to ensure that the test maintains the 3 dB margin. For each acoustic vibration test required by this appendix to have a tolerance of ±3.0 dB, the qualification test level must be 6 dB greater than the greater of the maximum predicted environment or the minimum workmanship test level.

(4) For any component that uses one or more shock or vibration isolators during flight, the component must undergo any qualification acoustic vibration test mounted on its isolator or isolators as a unit. Each isolator must satisfy the test requirements of section E417.35.

(5) Any test must continuously monitor and record all performance and status-of-health parameters while the component is subjected to the qualification environment. This monitoring must have a sample rate that will detect any component performance degradation.

(6) Any analysis must demonstrate that the qualification random vibration test environment of paragraph (c) of this section encompasses the qualification acoustic vibration environment. The analysis must demonstrate that the qualification random vibration environment is more severe than the

qualification acoustic vibration environment. The analysis must account for all peak vibration levels and durations.

(e) *Qualification shock.* (1) A qualification shock test of a component must demonstrate that the component and each connection to any item that attaches to the component satisfies all their performance specifications when subjected to the qualification shock environment. The attached items must include any isolator, grounding strap, bracket, explosive transfer system, or cable to the first tie-down. Any cable that interfaces with the component during the test must be representative of the cable used for flight.

(2) The minimum qualification shock environment must be no less than a 3 dB margin plus the greater of the maximum predicted environment or the minimum breakup levels identified in table E417.11–2 for all frequencies from 100 Hz to 10000 Hz. The minimum qualification test environment must account for all the test tolerances to ensure that the test maintains the 3dB margin. For a shock test required by this appendix to have a ±3 dB tolerance, the qualification test environment must be 6 dB greater than the greater of the maximum predicted shock environment or the minimum breakup test level.

(3) The test must subject the component simultaneously to a shock transient and all the required frequencies.

(4) The test must subject each component to three shocks in each direction along each of the three orthogonal axes.

(5) The shock must last as long as the maximum predicted shock event.

(6) The test must continuously monitor each component's critical performance parameters for any discontinuity or inadvertent output while the component is subjected to the shock environment.

(7) The test must continuously monitor and record all performance and status-of-health parameters while the component is subjected to the qualification environment. This monitoring must have a sample rate of once every millisecond or better.

(8) For any component that uses one or more shock or vibration isolators during flight, the component must undergo the qualification shock test mounted on its isolator or isolators. Each isolator must satisfy the test requirements of section E417.35.

Table E417.11-2, Minimum Breakup Qualification Shock Levels

Frequency Range (Hz)	Minimum Acceleration Spectral Density
100	100 G
2000	1300 G
10000	1300 G
Q (Resonant Amplification Factor) = 10	

(f) *Qualification acceleration.* (1) A qualification acceleration test or analysis of a component must demonstrate that the component and each connection to any item that attaches to the component satisfy all their performance specifications when subjected to the qualification acceleration environment. The attached items must include any isolator, grounding strap, bracket, explosive transfer system, or cable to the first tie-down. Any cable that interfaces with the component during any test must be representative of the cable used for flight.

(2) The qualification acceleration test environment must be no less than 200% greater than the maximum predicted acceleration environment.

(3) The qualification acceleration must last three times as long as the maximum predicted environment lasts in each direction for each of the three orthogonal axes.

(4) For any test, if the test tolerance is more than ±10%, the qualification acceleration test environment of paragraph (f)(1) of this section must account for the test tolerance to ensure that the test maintains the

200% margin between the minimum qualification acceleration test and the maximum predicted environment.

(5) Any analysis must demonstrate that the qualification operating random vibration test required by paragraph (c) of this section encompasses the qualification acceleration environment. The analysis must demonstrate that the qualification random vibration environment is equal to or more severe than the qualification acceleration environment. The analysis must account for the peak vibration and acceleration levels and durations.

(6) Any test must continuously monitor and record all performance and status-of-health parameters while the component is subjected to the qualification environment. This monitoring must have a sample rate that will detect any component performance degradation.

(7) For any component that uses one or more shock and vibration isolators during flight, the component must undergo any qualification acceleration test mounted on its isolator or isolators. Each isolator must satisfy the test requirements of section E417.35.

(g) *Qualification humidity.* A qualification humidity test or analysis must demonstrate that a component satisfies all its performance specifications when subjected to the maximum predicted relative humidity environment that the component could experience when stored, transported, or installed as follows:

(1) The test or analysis must demonstrate the ability of all externally exposed surfaces to withstand the maximum predicted relative humidity environment.

(2) The test or analysis must demonstrate the ability of each internal part of a component to withstand the maximum predicted relative humidity environment unless the component is environmentally sealed and an acceptance test demonstrates that the seal works.

(3) Each test must satisfy all of the following:

(i) The test must subject the component to no less than four thermal cycles while the component is exposed to a relative humidity of no less than 95%;

(ii) The test must measure each electrical performance parameter at the cold and hot temperatures during the first, middle and last thermal cycles; and

(iii) The test must continuously measure and record all performance and status-of-health parameters with a resolution and sample rate that will detect any component performance degradation throughout each thermal cycle.

(h) *Qualification thermal cycle.* A qualification thermal cycle test must demonstrate that a component satisfies all its performance specifications when subjected to the qualification thermal cycle environment as follows:

(1) *Electronic components.* For any command receiver decoder or other electronic component that contains piece-part circuitry, such as microcircuits, transistors, diodes and relays, a qualification thermal cycle test must satisfy all of the following:

(i) The qualification thermal cycle environment must range from 10 °C above the acceptance test high temperature to 10 °C below the acceptance test low temperature;

(ii) The test must subject a component to no less than three times the acceptance-number of thermal cycles. For each component, the acceptance-number of thermal cycles must satisfy section E417.13(d)(1). For each cycle, the dwell-time at each of the high and low temperatures must last long enough for the component to achieve internal thermal equilibrium and must last no less than one hour. The test must begin each dwell-time at each high and low temperature with the component turned off. The component must remain off until the temperature stabilizes. Once the temperature stabilizes, the component must be turned on and the test must complete each dwell-time with the component turned on;

(iii) When heating or cooling the component, the temperature must change at an average rate of 1 °C per minute or the maximum predicted rate, whichever is greater;

(iv) The test must measure all performance parameters with the component powered at its low and high operating voltages when the component is at ambient temperature before beginning the first thermal cycle and after completing the last cycle. The test must measure all performance parameters with the component powered at its low and high operating voltages when the component is at the high and low temperatures during the first, middle, and last thermal dwell cycles; and

(v) The test must continuously monitor and record all critical performance and status-of-health parameters during all cycles and thermal transitions and with the component operating at its nominal operating voltage. The monitoring and recording must have a resolution and sample rate that will detect any component performance degradation.

(2) *Passive components.* For any passive component that does not contain an active electronic piece-part, such as a radio frequency antenna, coupler, or cable, a qualification thermal cycle test must satisfy all of the following:

(i) The qualification thermal cycle environment must range from 10 °C above the acceptance test high temperature to 10 °C below the acceptance test low temperature;

(ii) The test must subject a component to no less than three times the acceptance-number of thermal cycles. For each component, the acceptance-number of thermal cycles must satisfy section E417.13(d)(1). For each cycle, the dwell-time at each high and low temperature must last long enough for the component to achieve internal thermal equilibrium and must last no less than one hour;

(iii) When heating or cooling the component, the temperature must change at an average rate of 1 °C per minute or the maximum predicted rate, whichever is greater;

(iv) The test must measure all performance parameters when the component is at ambient temperature before beginning the first thermal cycle and after completing the last cycle. The test must measure all performance parameters when the component is at the high and low temperatures during the first, middle, and last thermal cycles; and

(v) The test must continuously monitor and record all critical performance and status-of-health parameters with a resolution and sample rate that will detect any component performance degradation during all cycles and thermal transitions.

(3) *Safe-and-Arm Devices.* For any electromechanical safe-and-arm device with an internal explosive, a qualification thermal cycle test must satisfy all of the following:

(i) The qualification thermal cycle must range from 10 °C above the acceptance test high temperature to 10 °C below the acceptance test low temperature;

(ii) The test must subject the component to no less than three times the acceptance-number of thermal cycles. For each component, the acceptance-number of thermal cycles must satisfy section E417.13(d)(1). For each cycle, the dwell-time at each high and low temperature must last long enough for the component to achieve internal thermal equilibrium and must last no less than one hour;

(iii) When heating or cooling the component, the temperature must change at an average rate of 1 °C per minute or the maximum predicted rate, whichever is greater;

(iv) The test must measure all performance parameters when the component is at ambient temperature before beginning the first thermal cycle. The test must measure all performance parameters when the component is at the high and low temperatures during the first, middle, and last thermal cycles. The test must measure all performance parameters when the component is at ambient temperature after completing the last cycle; and

(v) The test must continuously monitor and record all critical performance and status-of-health parameters during all temperature cycles and transitions using a resolution and sample rate that will detect any component performance degradation.

(4) *Ordnance components.* For any ordnance component, a qualification thermal cycle test must satisfy all of the following:

(i) The qualification thermal cycle must range from 10 °C above the predicted highest temperature, or 71 °C, whichever is higher, to 10 °C below the predicted lowest temperature, or −54 °C, whichever is lower;

(ii) The test must subject each ordnance component to no less than the acceptance-number of thermal cycles. For each component, the acceptance-number of thermal cycles must satisfy section E417.13(d)(1). For an ordnance component that is used inside a safe-and-arm device, the test must subject the component to three times the acceptance-number of thermal cycles. For each cycle, the dwell-time at each high and low temperature must last long enough for the component to achieve internal thermal equilibrium and must last no less than two hours; and

(iii) When heating or cooling the component, the temperature must change at an average rate of 3 °C per minute or the maximum predicted rate, whichever is greater.

(i) *Qualification thermal vacuum.* A qualification thermal vacuum test or analysis must demonstrate that a component satisfies all its performance specifications, including structural integrity, when subjected to the qualification thermal vacuum environment as follows:

(1) The qualification thermal vacuum environment must satisfy all of the following:

(i) The thermal vacuum pressure gradient must equal or exceed the maximum predicted rate of altitude change that the component will experience during flight;

(ii) The final vacuum dwell-time must last long enough for the component to achieve pressure equilibrium and equal or exceed the greater of the maximum predicted dwell-time or 12 hours;

(iii) During the final vacuum dwell-time, the environment must include no less than three times the maximum predicted number of thermal cycles; and

(iv) Each thermal cycle must range from 10 °C above the acceptance thermal vacuum range, to 10 °C below the acceptance thermal vacuum range. The acceptance thermal vacuum temperature range is described in section E417.13(e);

(2) Any test must satisfy all of the following:

(i) The test must measure all performance parameters with the component powered at its low and high operating voltages when the component is at ambient temperature before beginning the first thermal cycle and after completing the last cycle;

(ii) The test must measure all performance parameters while the component is powered at its low and high operating voltages when the component is at the high and low temperatures during the first, middle and last thermal cycles;

(iii) The test must continuously monitor and record all critical performance and status-of-health parameters during chamber pressure reduction and the final vacuum dwell-time, with the component at its high operating voltage and using a resolution and sample rate that will detect any component performance degradation; and

(3) Any analysis must satisfy all of the following:

(i) For any low voltage component of less than 50 volts, the analysis must demonstrate that the component is not susceptible to corona, arcing, or structural failure; and

(ii) For any high voltage component of 50 volts or greater, the component must undergo a thermal vacuum test unless the component is environmentally sealed and the analysis demonstrates that any low voltage externally exposed part is not susceptible to corona, arcing, or structural failure. A component with any high voltage externally exposed part of 50 volts or greater must undergo a thermal vacuum test.

(j) *Electromagnetic interference and electromagnetic compatibility.* An electromagnetic interference and electromagnetic compatibility test must demonstrate that a component satisfies all its performance specifications when subjected to radiated or conducted emissions from all flight vehicle systems and external ground transmitter sources. In addition, the test must demonstrate that the component does not radiate or conduct electromagnetic interference that would degrade the performance of any other flight termination system component.

(k) *Explosive atmosphere.* An explosive atmosphere test or analysis must demonstrate that a component is capable of operating in an explosive atmosphere without creating an explosion or that the component is not used in an explosive environment.

E417.13 ACCEPTANCE TESTING AND ANALYSIS

(a) *General.* This section applies to each acceptance test or analysis identified by any table of this appendix. An acceptance test or analysis must demonstrate that a component does not have any material or workmanship defect that could adversely affect the component's performance and that the component satisfies all its performance specifications when subjected to each acceptance environment, including each workmanship and maximum predicted operating environment.

(1) An acceptance test of a component must subject the component to one or more of the component's maximum predicted environments as determined under section D417.7. An acceptance test must not subject a component to a force or environment that is not tested during qualification testing.

(2) Each component sample that is intended for flight must undergo each acceptance test identified by any table of this appendix. A single-use component, such as ordnance or a battery, must undergo the production lot sample acceptance tests identified by any tables of this appendix.

(3) If a launch vehicle uses a previously flown and recovered flight termination system component, the component must undergo one or more reuse acceptance tests before each next flight to demonstrate that the component still satisfies all its performance specifications when subjected to each maximum predicted environment. Each reuse acceptance test must be the same as the initial acceptance test for the component's first flight. Each reuse acceptance test must follow a written component reuse qualification, refurbishment, and acceptance plan and procedures. Each acceptance reuse test must compare performance parameter measurements taken during the test to all previous acceptance test measurements to ensure that the data show no trends that indicate any degradation in performance that could prevent the component from satisfying all its performance specifications during flight.

(4) Each acceptance test of a component must use test tolerances that are consistent with the test tolerances used by each qualification test of the component.

(b) *Acceptance random vibration.* An acceptance random vibration test must demonstrate that a component satisfies all its performance specifications when exposed to the acceptance random vibration environment as follows:

(1) The acceptance random vibration environment must equal or exceed the greater of the maximum predicted random vibration level or the minimum workmanship acceptance test level of table E417.13–1, for all frequencies from 20 Hz to 2000 Hz, in each of three mutually perpendicular axes.

(2) For each axis, the vibration must last the greater of three times the maximum predicted duration or a minimum workmanship screening level of 60 seconds.

(3) For a component sample that undergoes qualification testing and must experience the acceptance environment before it experiences the qualification environment, such as a command receiver decoder, the test must use the same configuration and methods for the acceptance and qualification random vibration environments. An acceptance random vibration test of a flight component sample must use a configuration and method that is representative of the component's qualification tests to ensure that the requirements of paragraph (a) of this section are satisfied.

(4) For any component that is mounted on one or more vibration or shock isolators during flight, the component must undergo the acceptance random vibration test in the

same isolator-mounted configuration or hard-mounted configuration as the component's qualification random vibration test as follows:

(i) Any hard-mounted acceptance random vibration test must subject the component to an acceptance random vibration environment that:

(A) Accounts for the isolator attenuation and amplification due to the maximum predicted operating random vibration environment, including any thermal effects and acceleration pre-load performance variability, and adds a 1.5 dB margin to account for any isolator attenuation variability; and

(B) Is no less than the minimum workmanship screening acceptance random vibration level of table E417.13–1.

(ii) Any isolator-mounted acceptance random vibration test must:

(A) Use an isolator or isolators that passed the tests required by section E417.35;

(B) Have an input to each isolator of no less than the required acceptance random vibration environment of paragraphs (b)(1) and (b)(2) of this section; and

(C) Subject the component to no less than the minimum workmanship screening acceptance random vibration level of table E417.13–1. If the isolator or isolators prevent the component from experiencing the minimum workmanship level, the component must undergo a hard-mount test that subjects the component to the workmanship level.

(5) If the duration of the acceptance random vibration environment leaves insufficient time to complete any required performance verification test while the component is subjected to the full acceptance environment, the test must continue at no lower than 6 dB below the acceptance environment. The test need only continue for the additional time needed to complete the performance verification test.

(6) The test must continuously monitor all performance and status-of-health parameters with any electrical component at its nominal operating voltage. This monitoring must have a sample rate that will detect any component performance degradation.

Table E417.13-1, Minimum Workmanship

Power Spectral Density for Acceptance Random Vibration

Frequency Range	Minimum Power Spectral Density
20	0.0053 g^2/Hz
20-150	3 dB/Octave Slope
150-600	0.04 g^2/Hz
600-2000	-6 dB/Octave Slope
2000	0.0036 g^2/Hz
Overall G_{rms} = 6.1	

(c) *Acceptance acoustic vibration.* An acceptance acoustic vibration test or analysis must demonstrate that a component satisfies all its performance specifications when exposed to the acceptance acoustic vibration environment as follows:

(1) The acceptance acoustic vibration environment must satisfy all of the following:

(i) The vibration level must equal or exceed the maximum predicted acoustic level for all frequencies from 20 Hz to 2,000 Hz in each of three mutually perpendicular axes; and

(ii) For each axis, the vibration must last the maximum predicted duration or 60 seconds, whichever is greater.

(2) Any test must satisfy all of the following:

(i) The test must continuously monitor all performance and status-of-health parameters with any electrical component at its nominal operating voltage. This monitoring must have a sample rate that will detect any component performance degradation; and

(ii) If the duration of the acceptance acoustic vibration environment leaves insufficient time to complete any required performance verification test while the component is subjected to the full acceptance environment, the test must continue at no lower than 6 dB below the acceptance environment. The test need only continue for the additional time needed to complete the performance verification test.

(3) Any analysis must demonstrate that the acceptance random vibration environment of paragraph (b) of this section encompasses the acceptance acoustic vibration environment. The analysis must demonstrate that the peak acceptance random vibration levels and duration are equal to or are more severe than the acceptance acoustic vibration environment.

(d) *Acceptance thermal cycle.* An acceptance thermal cycle test of a component must demonstrate that the component satisfies all its performance specifications when exposed to the acceptance thermal cycle environment as follows:

(1) *Acceptance-number of thermal cycles.* The acceptance-number of thermal cycles for a component means the number of thermal cycles that the component must experience during the test. The test must subject each component to no less than the greater of eight thermal cycles or 1.5 times the maximum number of thermal cycles that the component could experience during launch processing and flight, including all launch delays and recycling, rounded up to the nearest whole number.

(2) *Electronic components.* For any electronic component, an acceptance thermal cycle test must satisfy all of the following:

(i) The acceptance thermal cycle environment must range from the higher of the maximum predicted environment high temperature or 61 °C workmanship screening level, to the lower of the predicted low temperature or a −24 °C workmanship screening level.

(ii) The test must subject a component to no fewer than 10 plus the acceptance-number of thermal cycles. For each component, the acceptance-number of thermal cycles must satisfy this paragraph. For each cycle, the dwell-time at each high and low temperature must last long enough for the component to achieve internal thermal equilibrium and must last no less than one hour. The test must begin each dwell-time at each high and low temperature with the component turned off. The component must remain off until the temperature stabilizes. Once the temperature stabilizes, the test must complete each dwell-time with the component turned on.

(iii) When heating or cooling the component, the temperature must change at an average rate of 1 °C per minute or the maximum predicted rate, whichever is greater.

(iv) The test must measure all performance parameters with the component powered at its low and high operating voltages when the component is at ambient temperature before beginning the first thermal cycle and after completing the last cycle.

(v) The test must measure all performance parameters with the component at its low and high operating voltages when the component is at the high and low temperatures during the first, middle, and last thermal cycles.

(vi) The test must continuously monitor and record all critical performance and status-of-health parameters during all cycles and thermal transitions and with the component at its nominal operating voltage. The monitoring and recording must have a resolution and sample rate that will detect any component performance degradation.

(3) *Passive components.* For any passive component that does not contain any active electronic piece-part, such as any radio frequency antenna, coupler, or cable, an acceptance thermal cycle test must satisfy all of the following:

(i) Unless otherwise noted, the acceptance thermal cycle environment must range from the higher of the maximum predicted environment high temperature or a 61 °C workmanship screening temperature, to the lower of the predicted lowest temperature or a −24 °C workmanship screening temperature;

(ii) The test must subject a component to no fewer than the acceptance-number of thermal cycles. For each component, the acceptance-number of thermal cycles must satisfy this paragraph. For each cycle, the dwell-time at each high and low temperature must last long enough for the component to achieve internal thermal equilibrium and must last no less than one hour;

(iii) When heating or cooling the component, the temperature must change at an average rate of 1 °C per minute or the maximum predicted rate, whichever is greater;

(iv) The test must measure all performance parameters when the component is at ambient temperature before beginning the first thermal cycle and after completing the last cycle;

(v) The test must measure all performance parameters when the component is at the high and low temperatures during the first, middle, and last thermal cycles; and

(vi) The test must continuously monitor and record all critical performance and status-of-health parameters throughout each thermal cycle with a resolution and sample rate that will detect any component performance degradation.

(4) *Safe-and-arm devices.* For any electromechanical safe-and-arm device with an internal explosive, an acceptance thermal cycle test must satisfy all of the following:

(i) The acceptance thermal cycle environment must range from the higher of the maximum predicted environment high temperature or the minimum workmanship screening temperature of 61 °C to the lower of the predicted lowest temperature or the minimum workmanship screening temperature of −24 °C.

(ii) The test must subject a component to no fewer than the acceptance-number of thermal cycles. For each component, the acceptance-number of thermal cycles must satisfy this paragraph. For each cycle, the dwell-time at each high and low temperature must last long enough for the component to achieve internal thermal equilibrium and must last no less than one hour.

(iii) When heating or cooling the component, the temperature must change at an average rate of 1 °C per minute or the maximum predicted rate, whichever is greater.

(iv) The test must measure all performance parameters when the component is at ambient temperature before beginning the first thermal cycle and after completing the last cycle.

(v) The test must measure all performance parameters including each critical electrical parameter, when the component is at the high and low temperatures during the first, middle, and last thermal cycles.

(vi) The test must continuously monitor and record all critical performance and status-of-health parameters throughout each thermal cycle with a resolution and sample rate that will detect whether the component satisfies all its performance specifications.

(e) *Acceptance thermal vacuum.* An acceptance thermal vacuum test or analysis must demonstrate that a component satisfies all its performance specifications when exposed to the acceptance thermal vacuum environment as follows:

(1) The acceptance thermal vacuum environment must satisfy all of the following:

(i) The thermal vacuum pressure gradient must equal or exceed the maximum predicted rate of altitude change that the component will experience during flight. The pressure gradient must allow for no less than ten minutes for reduction of chamber pressure at the pressure zone from ambient pressure to 20 Pascal;

(ii) The final vacuum dwell-time must last long enough for the component to achieve pressure equilibrium and must last no less than the maximum predicted dwell-time or 12 hours, whichever is greater;

(iii) During the final vacuum dwell-time, the environment must include no less than the maximum predicted number of thermal cycles; and

(iv) Each thermal cycle must range from the higher of the maximum predicted environment high temperature or the workmanship screening high temperature of 61 °C, to the lower of the predicted low temperature or the workmanship screening low temperature of −24 °C.

(2) Any test must satisfy all of the following:

(i) The test must measure all performance parameters with the component powered at its low and high operating voltages when the component is at ambient temperature before beginning the first thermal cycle and after completing the last cycle.

(ii) The test must measure all performance parameters with the component powered at its low and high operating voltages when the component is at the high and low temperatures during the first, middle, and last thermal cycles; and

(iii) The test must continuously monitor all critical performance and status-of-health parameters during chamber pressure reduction and during the final vacuum dwell-time with the component at its high operating voltage. This monitoring must have a resolution and sample rate that will detect any component performance degradation.

(3) Any analysis must satisfy all of the following:

(i) For any low voltage component of less than 50 volts, any analysis must demonstrate that the component is not susceptible to corona, arcing, or structural failure; and

(ii) Any high voltage component of 50 volts or greater must undergo a thermal vacuum test unless the component is environmentally sealed and the analysis demonstrates that any low voltage externally exposed part of less than 50 volts is not susceptible to corona, arcing, or structural failure. A component with any high voltage externally exposed part must undergo an acceptance thermal vacuum test.

(f) *Tensile loads.* An acceptance tensile load test of a component must demonstrate that the component is not damaged and satisfies all its performance specifications after experiencing twice the maximum predicted pull-force that the component could experience before, during, or after installation.

E417.15 ORDNANCE SERVICE-LIFE EXTENSION TESTING

(a) *General.* This section applies to each service-life extension test of an ordnance component that is identified by any table of this appendix. A service-life extension test must demonstrate that an ordnance component will satisfy all its performance specifications when subjected to non-operating and operating environments throughout its initial service-life and throughout any extension to the service-life. An ordnance component must undergo a service-life extension test to extend its service-life if its initial service-life and any previous extension will expire before the component is used for flight.

(b) *Service-life.* An ordnance component must undergo any service-life extension test before the component's initial service-life expires and again before each service-life extension expires. The initial service-life of an ordnance component, including any component that contains ordnance or is used to directly initiate ordnance, must start upon completion of the initial production lot sample acceptance tests and must include both storage time and time after installation until completion of flight. The test tables of this appendix identify the options for the length of any service-life extension for each type of ordnance component.

(c) *Test samples.* The tables of this appendix identify the number of ordnance component samples that must undergo any service-life extension test. Each component sample must be:

(i) From the same production lot;

(ii) Consist of identical parts and materials;

(iii) Manufactured through identical processes; and

(iv) Stored with the flight ordnance component or in an environment that duplicates the storage conditions of the flight ordnance component.

E417.17 RADIO FREQUENCY RECEIVING SYSTEM

(a) *General.* (1) This section applies to a radio frequency receiving system, which includes each flight termination system antenna and radio frequency coupler and any radio frequency cable or other passive device used to connect a flight termination system antenna to a command receiver.

(2) The components of a radio frequency receiving system must satisfy each test or analysis identified by any table of this section to demonstrate that:

(i) The system is capable of delivering command control system radio frequency energy to each flight termination system receiver; and

(ii) The system satisfies all its performance specifications when subjected to each non-operating and operating environment and any performance degradation source. Such sources include any command control system transmitter variation, non-nominal launch vehicle flight condition, and flight termination system performance variation.

Table E417.17-1

Radio frequency receiving system Acceptance	Section E417.13	Quantity Tested		
		Cable	Coupler	Antenna
Component Examination:	E417.5			
Visual Examination	E417.5(b)	100%	100%	100%
Dimension Measurement	E417.5(c)	100%	100%	100%
Identification Check	E417.5(e)	100%	100%	100%
Performance Verification:	E417.3(d)			
Status-of-Health [(1)]	E417.17(b)	-	-	100%
Link Performance [(1)]	E417.17(c)	100%	100%	-
Isolation [(1)]	E417.17(d)	-	100%	-
Abbreviated Antenna Pattern	E417.17(g)	-	-	100%
Abbreviated Performance Verification:	E417.3(e)			
Abbreviated Status-of-health [(2)]	E417.17(e)	100%	100%	100%
Operating Environment Tests:	E417.13			
Thermal Cycling	E417.13(d)	100%	100%	100%
Acoustic	E417.13(c)	-	100%	100%
Random Vibration	E417.13(b)	-	100%	100%
Tensile Load	E417.13(f)	100%	-	-
Abbreviated Antenna Pattern	E417.17(g)	-	-	100%

(1) A component must undergo this test before the first and after the last operating environment test.

(2) A component must undergo this test during each operating environment test.

Table E417.17-2

Radio frequency receiving system Qualification	Section E417.7	Quantity Tested [6]		
		Cable X=3	Coupler X=3	Antenna X=3
Acceptance Tests [1]	Table E417.17-1	X	X	X
Antenna Pattern [2]	E417.17(f)	X	X	X
Abbreviated Antenna Pattern	E417.17(g)	-	-	X
Performance Verification:	E417.3(d)			
Status-of-Health [3]	E417.17(b)	-	-	X
Link Performance [3]	E417.17(c)	X	X	-
Isolation [3]	E417.17(d)	-	X	-
Non-Operating Environment Tests:	E417.9			
Storage Temperature	E417.9(b)	X	X	X
Transportation Shock	E417.9(d)	X	X	X
Bench Handling Shock	E417.9(e)	X	X	X
Transportation Vibration	E417.9(f)	X	X	X
Fungus Resistance	E417.9(g)	1	1	1
Salt Fog	E417.9(h)	1	1	1
Fine Sand	E417.9(i)	1	1	1
Abbreviated Performance Verification:	E417.3(e)			
Abbreviated Status-of-Health [4]	E417.17(e)	X	X	X
Operating Environment Tests:	E417.11			

Thermal Cycling [5]	E417.11(h)	X	X	X
Humidity [5]	E417.11(g)	X	X	X
Acceleration [5]	E417.11(f)	X	X	X
Shock [5]	E417.11(e)	X	X	X
Sinusoidal Vibration [5]	E417.11(b)	X	X	X
Acoustic [5]	E417.11(d)	X	X	X
Random Vibration [5]	E417.11(c)	X	X	X
Tensile Load	E417.9(j)	X	-	-
Abbreviated Antenna Pattern	E417.17(g)	-	-	X
Internal Inspection	E417.5(g)	-	X	X

(1) Each sample component to undergo qualification testing must first successfully complete all acceptance tests identified by table E417.17-1 of this section.

(2) The radio frequency receiving system, including the antenna, radio frequency cables, and radio frequency coupler must undergo this test.

(3) A component must undergo this test before the first and after the last non-operating environment test and before the first and after the last operating environment test.

(4) A component must undergo this test during the operating environment tests.

(5) A component must undergo this test with flight radio frequency cables attached in the flight representative configuration.

(6) The same three sample components must undergo each test designated with an X. For a test designated with a quantity of less than three, each sample component tested must be one of the original three sample components.

(b) *Status-of-health.* A status-of-health test of a radio frequency receiving system must satisfy section E417.3(f) and include antenna voltage standing wave ratio testing that measures the assigned operating frequency at the high and low frequencies of the operating bandwidth to verify that the antenna satisfies all its performance specifications.

(c) *Link performance.* A link performance test of a radio frequency component or subsystem must demonstrate that the component or subsystem satisfies all its performance specifications when subjected to performance degradation caused by ground transmitter variations and non-nominal vehicle flight. This must include demonstrating all of the following:

(1) The radio frequency receiving system provides command signals to each command destruct receiver at an electromagnetic field intensity of 12 dB above the level required for reliable receiver operation over 95% of the antenna radiation sphere surrounding the launch vehicle;

(2) The radio frequency coupler insertion loss and voltage standing wave ratio at the assigned operating frequency and at the high and low frequencies of the operating bandwidth satisfy all their performance specifications; and

(3) The cable insertion loss at the assigned operating frequency and at the high and low frequencies of the operating bandwidth satisfies all its performance specifications.

(d) *Isolation.* An isolation test of a radio frequency receiving system must demonstrate that each of the system's radio frequency couplers isolate the redundant antennas and receiver decoders from one another. The test must demonstrate that an open or short-circuit in one string of the redundant system, antenna or receiver decoder, will not prevent functioning of the other side of the redundant system. The test must demonstrate that the system satisfies all its performance specifications for isolation and is in-family.

(e) *Abbreviated status-of-health.* An abbreviated status-of health test of a radio frequency receiving system component must determine any internal anomaly while the component is under environmental stress conditions. The test must include continuous monitoring of the voltage standing wave ratio and any other critical performance parameter that indicates an internal anomaly during environmental testing to detect any variations in amplitude. Any amplitude variation constitutes a test failure. The monitoring must have a sample rate that will detect any component performance degradation.

(f) *Antenna pattern.* An antenna pattern test must demonstrate that the radiation gain pattern of the entire radio frequency receiving system, including the antenna, radio frequency cables, and radio frequency coupler will satisfy all the system's performance specifications during vehicle flight. This must include all of the following:

(1) The test must determine the radiation gain pattern around the launch vehicle and demonstrate that the system is capable of providing command signals to each command receiver decoder with electromagnetic field intensity at a 12 dB link margin above the level required for reliable receiver operation. The test must demonstrate the 12–dB margin over 95 percent of the antenna radiation sphere surrounding the launch vehicle.

(2) All test conditions must emulate flight conditions, including ground transmitter polarization, using a simulated flight vehicle and a flight configured radio frequency command destruct system.

(3) The test must measure the radiation gain for 360 degrees around the launch vehicle in degree increments that are small enough to identify any deep pattern null and to verify that the required 12 dB link margin is maintained throughout flight. Each degree increment must not exceed two degrees.

(4) The test must generate each antenna pattern in a data format that is compatible with the format needed to perform the flight safety system radio frequency link analysis required by § 417.329(h).

(g) *Abbreviated antenna pattern.* An abbreviated antenna pattern test must determine any antenna pattern changes that might have occurred due to damage to an antenna resulting from exposure to test environments. This must include all of the following:

(1) The antenna must undergo the test before and after exposure to the qualification or acceptance test environments.

(2) The test must use a standard ground plane test fixture. The test configuration need not generate antenna pattern data that is representative of the actual system-level patterns.

(3) The test must include gain measurements in the 0° and 90° plane vectors and a conical cut at 80°.

E417.19 COMMAND RECEIVER DECODER

(a) *General.* A command receiver decoder must satisfy each test or analysis identified by any table of this section to demonstrate that the receiver decoder satisfies all its performance specifications when subjected to each non-operating and operating environment and any command control system transmitter variation.

Table E417.19-1

Command Receiver Decoder Acceptance	**Section E417.13**	**Quantity Tested**
Component Examination:	E417.5	
Visual Examination	E417.5(b)	100%
Dimension Measurement	E417.5(c)	100%
Identification Check	E417.5(e)	100%
Performance Verification:	E417.3(d)	
Status-of-health [(1)]	E417.19(b)	100%
Functional Performance [(1)]	E417.19(c)	100%
Radio Frequency Processing [(1)]	E417.19(e)	100%
Inadvertent Command Output	E417.19(f)	
Logic Sequence [(1)]	E417.19(f)(5)	100%
Destruct Sequence [(1)]	E417.19(f)(6)	100%
Receiver Abnormal Logic [(1)]	E417.19(f)(7)	100%
Tone Drop [(1)]	E417.19(f)(9)	100%
AM Rejection [(1)]	E417.19(f)(10)	100%
Decoder Channel Deviation Rejection [(1)]	E417.19(f)(11)	100%
Abbreviated Performance Verification:	E417.3(e)	
Input Current Monitor [(2)]	E417.19(g)	100%
Output Functions [(2)]	E417.19(h)	100%
Radio Frequency Level Monitor [(2)]	E417.19(i)	100%
Thermal Performance [(3)]	E417.19(j)	100%
Operating Environment Tests:	E417.13	

Thermal Cycling	E417.13(d)	100%
Thermal Vacuum	E417.13(e)	100%
Acoustic	E417.13(c)	100%
Random Vibration	E417.13(b)	100%
Leakage [(4)]	E417.5(h)	100%

(1) A component must undergo this test before the first and after the last operating environment test.

(2) A component must undergo this test during the vibration and acoustic operating environments.

(3) A component must undergo this test during the operating thermal cycle and thermal vacuum environments.

(4) An unsealed component that has successfully completed salt-fog, humidity, fungus resistance, and fine sand qualification tests need not undergo a leakage test.

Table E417.19-2

Command Receiver Decoder Qualification	Section E417.7	Quantity [5] Tested X=3
Acceptance Tests and Analyses [1]	Table E417.19-1	X
Performance Verification:	E417.3(d)	
Status-of-health [2]	E417.19(b)	X
Functional Performance [2]	E417.19(c)	X
Radio Frequency Processing [2]	E417.19(e)	X
Inadvertent Command Output [2]	E417.19(f)(1)-(11)	X
Non-Operating Environment Tests:	E417.9	
Storage Temperature	E417.9(b)	X
Transportation Shock	E417.9(d)	X
Bench Handling Shock	E417.9(e)	X
Transportation Vibration	E417.9(f)	X
Fungus Resistance	E417.9(g)	1
Salt Fog	E417.9(h)	1
Fine Sand	E417.9(i)	1
Abbreviated Performance Verification:	E417.3(e)	
Input Current Monitor [3]	E417.19(g)	X
Output Functions [3]	E417.19(h)	X
Radio Frequency Level Monitor [3]	E417.19(i)	X
Thermal Performance [4]	E417.19(j)	X
Operating Environment Tests:	E417.11	

Thermal Cycling	E417.11(h)	X
Humidity	E417.11(g)	X
Thermal Vacuum	E417.11(i)	X
Acceleration	E417.11(f)	X
Shock	E417.11(e)	X
Sinusoidal Vibration	E417.11(b)	X
Acoustic	E417.11(d)	X
Random Vibration	E417.11(c)	X
Electromagnetic Interference and Compatibility	E417.11(j)	2
Explosive Atmosphere	E417.11(k)	1
Leakage [(6)]	E417.5(h)	X
Circuit Protection Test	E417.19(d)	X
Internal Inspection	E417.5(g)	X

(1) Each sample component to undergo qualification testing must first successfully complete all applicable acceptance tests.

(2) A component must undergo this test before the first and after the last non-operating environment test and before the first and after the last operating environment test.

(3) A component must undergo this test during shock, acceleration, and vibration testing.

(4) A component must undergo this test during operating thermal cycle and thermal vacuum testing.

(5) The same three sample components must undergo each test designated with an X. For a test designated with a quantity of less than three, each sample component tested must be one of the original three sample components.

(6) An unsealed component that has successfully completed salt-fog, humidity, fungus resistance, and fine sand qualification tests need not undergo a leakage test.

(b) *Status-of-health.* A status-of-health test of a command receiver decoder must satisfy section E417.3(f) and must measure each pin-to-pin and pin-to-case resistance, input current, voltage standing wave ratio, and radio frequency threshold sensitivity. Each measurement must demonstrate that all wiring and connectors are installed according to the manufacturer's design. The test must demonstrate that each pin-to-pin and pin-to-case resistance satisfies its performance specification and is in-family.

(c) *Functional performance.* A functional performance test must demonstrate that a command receiver decoder satisfies all the requirements for an electronic component of section D417.27 that apply to the receiver decoder. This test must:

(1) *Response time.* Demonstrate that the receiver decoder satisfies all its performance specifications for response time, from receipt of destruct sequence to initiation of destruct output;

(2) *Input current.* Monitor the input current into the receiver decoder to demonstrate reliable functioning of all internal components. The test must demonstrate that the receiver decoder's electrical characteristics satisfy all its performance specifications and are in-family;

(3) *Leakage current.* Demonstrate that the maximum leakage current through any command output port is at a level that cannot degrade performance of down-string electrical or ordnance initiation systems or result in an unsafe condition. The test must demonstrate no less than a 20–dB safety margin between the receiver leakage output and the lowest level that could degrade performance of down-string electrical or ordnance initiation systems or result in an unsafe condition;

(4) *Output Functions.* Function all receiver outputs to demonstrate that all the output performance specifications are satisfied. The test must include drawing the expected current at the receiver's low, nominal and high input specified voltages using output impedances that simulate the flight-configured load. The test must demonstrate that a command receiver is capable of simultaneously outputting arm, destruct, and check channel signals; and

(5) *Warm Up Time.* Demonstrate that the receiver decoder satisfies all its performance specifications after being powered for the manufacturer specified warm-up time.

(d) *Circuit protection.* A circuit protection test must demonstrate that a receiver decoder's circuit protection provides for the receiver decoder to satisfy all its performance specifications when subjected to any improper launch processing, abnormal flight condition, or any non-flight termination system vehicle component failure. This test must:

(1) *Abnormal voltage.* Demonstrate that any circuit protection allows the receiver decoder to satisfy all its performance specifications when powered with the open circuit voltage of the receiver decoder's power source for no less than twice the expected duration of the open circuit voltage and then when powered with the minimum input voltage of the loaded voltage of the power source for no less than twice the expected duration of the loaded voltage. The test must also demonstrate that the receiver decoder satisfies all its performance specifications when subjected to increasing voltage from zero volts to the nominal voltage and then decreasing voltage from nominal back to zero;

(2) *Power dropout.* Demonstrate that, in the event of an input power dropout, any control or switching circuit that contributes to the reliable operation of a receiver decoder, including solid-state power transfer switches, does not change state for 50 milliseconds or more;

(3) *Watchdog circuits.* Demonstrate that any watchdog circuit satisfies all its performance specifications;

(4) *Output circuit protection.* Demonstrate that the receiver decoder's performance does not degrade when any of its monitoring circuits or non-destruct output ports are subjected to a short circuit or the highest positive or negative voltage capable of being supplied by the monitor batteries or other power supplies, for no less than five minutes;

(5) *Reverse polarity.* Demonstrate that the receiver decoder satisfies all of its performance specifications when subjected to a reverse polarity voltage that could occur before flight, for no less than five minutes; and

(6) *Memory.* Demonstrate by test or analysis that any memory device that is part of the receiver decoder satisfies all its performance specifications. The test or analysis must demonstrate that the data stored in memory is retained in accordance with the performance specifications. For any secure receiver decoder, the test or analysis must demonstrate that the command codes remain in memory for the specified time interval while the receiver decoder is not powered.

(e) *Radio frequency processing.* (1) *General.* A radio frequency processing test must demonstrate that a receiver decoder's radio frequency processing satisfies all its performance specifications when subjected to command control system transmitting equipment tolerances and flight generated signal degradation. The environment must include locally induced radio frequency noise sources, vehicle plume, the maximum predicted noise-floor, ground transmitter performance variations, and abnormal launch vehicle flight.

(2) *Tone-based system.* For any tone-based system, a radio frequency processing test must demonstrate that the receiver decoder satisfies all the design requirements of section D417.29(b) of appendix D of this part and must satisfy all of the following;

(i) *Decoder channel deviation.* The test must demonstrate that the receiver decoder reliably processes the intended tone deviated signal at the minimum and maximum number of expected tones. The test must demonstrate that the receiver decoder satisfies all its performance specifications when subjected to a nominal tone deviation plus twice the maximum and minus half the minimum of the total combined tolerances of all applicable radio frequency performance factors. The tone deviation must be no less than ±3 KHz per tone.

(ii) *Operational bandwidth.* The testing must demonstrate that the receiver decoder satisfies all its performance specifications at twice the worst-case command control system transmitter radio frequency shift, Doppler shifts of the carrier center frequency, and shifts in flight hardware center frequency during flight at the manufacturer guaranteed receiver sensitivity. The test must demonstrate an operational bandwidth of no less than ±45KHz. The test must demonstrate that the operational bandwidth accounts for any tone deviation and that the receiver sensitivity does not vary by more than 3dB across the bandwidth.

(iii) *Radio frequency dynamic range.* The test must demonstrate that the receiver decoder satisfies all its performance specifications when subjected to variations of the radio frequency input signal level that it will experience during checkout and flight. The test must subject the receiver decoder to no less than five uniformly distributed radio frequency input levels. The test must demonstrate that the receiver outputs the destruct command from the radio frequency threshold level up to:

(A) The maximum radio frequency level that it will experience from the command control system transmitter during checkout and flight plus a 3 dB margin; or

(B) 13 dBm, whichever is greater.

(iv) *Capture ratio.* The test must demonstrate that the receiver cannot be captured by another transmitter with less than 80% of the power of the command transmitter system for the launch. The test must show that the application of any unmodulated radio frequency at a power level of up to 80% of the command control system transmitter's modulated carrier signal does not capture the receiver or interfere with a signal from the command control system.

(v) *Radio frequency monitor.* The test must demonstrate that the receiver decoder's monitoring circuit accurately monitors and outputs the strength of the radio frequency input signal and must satisfy all of the following:

(A) The test must show that the output of the monitor circuit is directly related and proportional to the strength of the radio frequency input signal from the threshold level to saturation.

(B) The dynamic range of the radio frequency input from the threshold level to saturation must be no less than 50 dB. The monitor circuit output from threshold to saturation must have a corresponding range that is greater than 18 dB.

(C) The test must perform periodic samples sufficient to demonstrate that the monitor satisfies all its performance specifications.

(D) The test must include the following radio frequency input levels: Quiescent; threshold; manufacturer guaranteed; beginning of saturation; and 13 dBm.

(E) The test must demonstrate that the slope of the monitor circuit output does not change polarity.

(vi) *Radio frequency threshold sensitivity.* The test must determine the radio frequency threshold sensitivity or each receiver decoder output command to demonstrate reliable radio frequency processing capability. The threshold sensitivity values must satisfy all their performance specifications, be repeatable, and be in-family. In-family performance may be met with a tolerance of ±3 dB.

(vii) *Noise level margin.* The test must demonstrate that the receiver decoder's guaranteed input sensitivity is no less than 6 dB higher than the maximum predicted noise-floor.

(viii) *Voltage standing wave ratio.* The test must demonstrate that any radio frequency losses within the receiver decoder interface to the antenna system satisfy the required 12 dB margin. The test must determine the radio frequency voltage standing wave ratio at the high, low, and assigned operating frequencies of the operating bandwidth and demonstrate that it satisfies its performance specifications and is in-family. The test must also demonstrate that the impedance of the radio frequency receiving system and the impedance of the receiver decoder are matched closely enough to ensure that the receiver decoder satisfies all its performance specifications.

(ix) *Decoder channel bandwidth.* The test must demonstrate that the receiver decoder provides for reliable recognition of any command signal when subjected to variations in ground transmitter tone frequency and frequency modulation deviation variations. The test must demonstrate that the receiver decoder satisfies all its performance specifications within the specified tone filter frequency bandwidth using a frequency modulated tone deviation from 2 dB to 20 dB above the measured threshold level.

(x) *Tone balance.* For any secure receiver decoder, the test must demonstrate that the receiver decoder can reliably decode a valid command with an amplitude imbalance between two tones within the same message.

(xi) *Message timing.* For any secure receiver decoder, the test must demonstrate that the receiver decoder functions reliably during any errors in timing caused by any ground transmitter tolerances. The test must demonstrate that the receiver decoder can process commands at twice the maximum and one-half the minimum timing specification of the ground system. These tolerances must include character dead-time, character on-time and inter-message dead-time.

(xii) *Check tone.* The test must demonstrate that the decoding and output of a tone, such as a pilot tone or check tone, is representative of link and command closure. The test must also demonstrate that the presence or absence of the tone signal will have no effect on the receiver decoder's command processing and output capability.

(xiii) *Self-test.* The test must demonstrate that the receiver decoder's self-test capability functions and satisfies all its performance specifications and does not inhibit functionality of the command destruct output. The test must include initiating the self-test while issuing valid command outputs.

(xiv) *Reset.* For any receiver decoder with a reset capability, the test must demonstrate that the reset will unlatch any command output that has been latched by a previous command.

(f) *Inadvertent command output.* Each of the following inadvertent command output tests must demonstrate that the receiver decoder does not provide an output other than when it receives a valid command.

(1) *Dynamic stability.* The test must demonstrate that the receiver decoder does not produce an inadvertent output when subjected to any radio frequency input short-circuit, open-circuit, or change in input voltage standing wave ratio.

(2) *Out of band rejection.* The test must demonstrate that the receiver decoder does not degrade in performance when subjected to any out-of-band vehicle or ground transmitter source that it could encounter from liftoff to the planned safe flight state. The test must ensure the receiver decoder does not respond to frequencies, from 10 MHz to 1000 MHz except at the receiver specified operational bandwidth. The test must demonstrate that the radio frequency rejection of out of band signals provides a minimum of 60 dB beyond eight times the maximum specified operational bandwidth. The test frequencies must include all expected interfering transmitting sources using a minimum bandwidth of 20% of each transmitter center frequency, receiver image frequencies and harmonics of the assigned center frequency.

(3) *Decoder channel bandwidth rejection.* The test must demonstrate that the receiver decoder rejects any out-of-band command tone frequency. The test must demonstrate that each tone filter will not respond to another tone outside the specified tone filter frequency bandwidth using a frequency modulated tone deviation from 2 dB to 20 dB above the measured threshold level.

(4) *Adjacent tone decoder channel rejection.* The test must demonstrate that none of the tone decoder channels responds to any adjacent frequency modulated tone channel when they are frequency modulated with a minimum of 150% of the expected tone deviation.

(5) *Logic sequence.* The test must demonstrate that the receiver issues the required commands when commanded and does not issue false commands during any abnormal logic sequence including issuing a destruct command prior to the arm command.

(6) *Destruct sequence.* The test must demonstrate that the receiver decoder requires two commanded steps to issue a destruct command. The test must demonstrate that the receiver processes an arm command as a prerequisite for the destruct command.

(7) *Receiver abnormal logic.* The test must demonstrate that the receiver decoder will not respond to any combination of tones or tone pairs other than the correct command sequence.

(8) *Noise immunity.* The test must demonstrate that a receiver decoder will not respond to a white noise frequency modulated radio frequency input at a minimum frequency modulated deviation of 12 dB above the measured threshold deviation.

(9) *Tone drop.* The test must demonstrate that the receiver decoder will not respond to a valid command output when one tone in the sequence is dropped.

(10) *Amplitude modulation rejection.* The test must demonstrate that the receiver decoder will not respond to any tone or amplitude modulated noise when subjected to maximum pre-flight and flight input power levels. An acceptance test must subject the receiver decoder to 50% amplitude modulation. A qualification test must subject the receiver decoder to 100% amplitude modulation.

(11) *Decoder channel deviation rejection.* The test must demonstrate that the receiver decoder does not inadvertently trigger on frequency-modulated noise. The test must demonstrate that the receiver decoder does not respond to tone modulations 10 dB below the nominal tone modulation.

(g) *Input current monitor.* An input current monitor test must continuously monitor command receiver decoder power input current during environmental stress conditions to detect any variation in amplitude. Any variation in input current indicates internal component damage and constitutes a test failure. Any fluctuation in nominal current draw when the command receiver decoder is in the steady state indicates internal component damage and constitutes a test failure.

(h) *Output functions.* An output functions test must subject the receiver decoder to the arm and destruct commands during environmental stress conditions and continuously monitor all command outputs to detect any variation in amplitude. Any variation in output level indicates internal component damage and constitutes a test failure.

(i) *Radio frequency level monitor.* A radio frequency level monitor test must subject a receiver decoder to the guaranteed radio frequency input power level during environmental stress conditions and continuously monitor the radio frequency level monitor, also known as radio frequency signal strength, signal strength telemetry output, or automatic gain control. Any unexpected fluctuations or dropout constitutes a test failure.

(j) *Thermal performance.* A thermal performance test must demonstrate that the receiver decoder satisfies all its performance specifications when subjected to operating and workmanship thermal environments. The receiver decoder must undergo the thermal performance test during a thermal cycle test and during a thermal vacuum test. The receiver decoder must undergo the thermal performance test at its low and high operating voltage while the receiver decoder is at the high and low temperatures during the first, middle, and last thermal cycles. The thermal performance test at each high and low temperature must include each of the following sub-tests of this section:

(1) Response time, paragraph (c)(1) of this section;

(2) Input current, paragraph (c)(2) of this section;

(3) Output functions, paragraph (c)(4) of this section;

(4) Decoder channel deviation, paragraph (e)(2)(i) of this section;

(5) Operational bandwidth, paragraph (e)(2)(ii) of this section;

(6) Radio frequency dynamic range, paragraph (e)(2)(iii) of this section;

(7) Capture ratio, paragraph (e)(2)(iv) of this section;

(8) Radio frequency monitor, paragraph (e)(2)(v) of this section;

(9) Message timing, paragraph (e)(2)(xi) of this section;

(10) Check tone, paragraph (e)(2)(xii) of this section; and

(11) Self test, paragraph (e)(2)(xiii) of this section.

E417.21 SILVER-ZINC BATTERIES

(a) *General.* This section applies to any silver-zinc battery that is part of a flight termination system. Any silver-zinc battery must satisfy each test or analysis identified by any table of this section to demonstrate that the battery satisfies all its performance specifications when subjected to each non-operating and operating environment.

Table E417.21-1

Manually Activated Silver-Zinc Battery Acceptance	**Section E417.13(a)**	**Quantity Tested X= 100% of Batteries**
Cell Capacity	E417.21(b)	Cell Sample [3]
500-Volt Insulation	E417.21(c)(1)	X
Proof Pressure	E417.21(d)	X
Electrolyte	E417.21(e)	X
Battery Mounting and Case Integrity [1]	E417.21(f)	X
Component Examination:	E417.5	
Visual Examination [2]	E417.5(b)	X
Dimension Measurement [2]	E417.5(c)	X
Identification Check [2]	E417.5(e)	X
Weight Measurement [2]	E417.5(d)	X
Pre-Activation [2]	E417.21(g)	X
Continuity and Isolation [2]	E417.21(c)(2)	X
Performance Verification:	E417.3(d)	
Monitoring Capability [2]	E417.21(h)	X
Heater Circuit Verification [2]	E417.21(i)	X
Coupon Cell Acceptance [2]	E417.21(r)	1 cell per flight battery
Activation [2]	E417.21(j)	X
No-load Voltage [2]	E417.21(c)(3)	X
Pin-to-case Isolation [2]	E417.21(c)(4)	X
Electrical Performance [2]	E417.21(k)	X
Pin-to-case Isolation [2]	E417.21(c)(4)	X
Battery Case Proof Pressure [2]	E417.21(d)(2)	X

(1) This test applies only to any battery with a mounting or case that contains a weld.

(2) A battery must undergo this test at the launch site just before installation.

(3) For each battery, no less than one cell that is representative of the cells that make up the battery must undergo this test. This test need not take place at the launch site.

Table E417.21-2

Manually Activated Silver-Zinc Battery Qualification	Section E417.7	Quantity Tested [4] Batteries X=3	Cells X=12
Cell Capacity	E417.21(b)	Cell Sample [7]	-
500-Volt Insulation	E417.21(c)(1)	X	-
Proof Pressure	E417.21(d)	X	X
Electrolyte	E417.21(e)	X	X
Battery Mounting and Case Integrity [1]	E417.21(f)	X	-
Component Examination:	E417.5		
Visual Examination	E417.5(b)	X	X
Dimension Measurement	E417.5(c)	X	X
Identification Check	E417.5(e)	X	X
Weight Measurement	E417.5(d)	X	X
Pre-Activation	E417.21(g)	X	X
Continuity and Isolation	E417.21(c)(2)	X	-
Non-Operating Environment Tests:	E417.9		
Storage Temperature	E417.9(b)	X	X
Transportation Shock	E417.9(d)	X	-
Bench Handling Shock	E417.9(e)	X	-
Transportation Vibration	E417.9(f)	X	-
Fungus Resistance	E417.9(g)	X	-
Salt Fog	E417.9(h)	X	-
Fine Sand	E417.9(i)	X	-
Performance Verification:	E417.3(d)		

Manually Activated Silver-Zinc Battery Qualification	Section E417.7	Quantity Tested (4)	
		Batteries X=3	Cells X=12
Monitoring Capability	E417.21(h)	X	X
Heater Circuit Verification	E417.21(i)	X	-
Activation	E417.21(j)	X	X
No-load Voltage	E417.21(c)(3)	X	X
Pin-to-case Isolation	E417.21(c)(4)	X	-
Electrical Performance	E417.21(k)	X	X
Battery Case Proof Pressure	E417.21(d)(2)	X	-

Operating Environment Tests:	E417.11		
Activated Stand Time	E417.21(l)	X	X
Pin-to-case Isolation	E417.21(c)(4)	X	-
Overcharge (6)	E417.21(m)	X	-
Charge-Discharge Cycles (6)	E417.21(n)	X	X
Humidity (5)	E417.11(g)	X	-
Acoustic (2) (3) (5)	E417.11(d)	X	-
Shock (3) (5)	E417.11(e)	X	-
Thermal Vacuum (2) (3) (5)	E417.11(i)	X	-
Acceleration (2) (3) (5)	E417.11(f)	X	-
Sinusoidal Vibration (2) (3) (5)	E417.11(b)	X	-
Random Vibration (2) (3) (5)	E417.11(c)	X	-
Thermal Cycle (2) (5)	E417.21(o)	X	X
Pin-to-case Isolation	E417.21(c)(4)	X	-
Electromagnetic Interference and Compatibility (5)	E417.11(j)	1	-
Explosive Atmosphere (5)	E417.11(k)	1	-
Performance Verification:	E417.3(d)		
Monitoring Capability	E417.21(h)	X	X
Heater Circuit Verification	E417.21(i)	X	-
Discharge and Pulse Capacity (5)	E417.21(p)	X	X
Pin-to-case Isolation	E417.21(c)(4)	X	X
Proof Pressure (5)	E417.21(d)	X	X
Internal Inspection (5)	E417.21(q)	X	X

(1) This test applies only to any battery that has a mounting or case that contains a weld.

(2) A battery or cell must undergo the electrical performance test of paragraph (k) of this section while the battery is under ambient conditions before the battery undergoes this operating environment test and again while the battery is subjected to the operating environment.

(3) This test must include continuous monitoring of the battery to verify that the required voltage regulation is maintained while supplying the required operating steady-state current. The monitoring must have a sample rate of once every 0.1 millisecond or better. Any dropout constitutes a test failure.

(4) The same three sample batteries must undergo each test designated with an X in that column and the same 12 sample cells must undergo each test designated with an X in that column. For tests designated with a quantity of less than three, each battery tested must be one of the original three sample batteries.

(5) Each battery or cell sample must undergo this test at the end of the wet stand time after the last operating charge.

(6) This test only applies if normal operation of the battery includes charging.

(7) For each of the three battery samples, no less than one cell that is representative of the cells that make up the battery must undergo this test. These cells, no less than three, are in addition to the 12 cells of the far right column.

Table E417.21-3

Silver-Zinc Battery Storage Life	Section	Quantity Tested X=2 Cells Per Year (1)
Proof Pressure	E417.21(d)	X
Electrolyte	E417.21(e)	X
Component Examination:	E417.5	
Visual Examination	E417.5(b)	X
Dimension Measurement	E417.5(c)	X
Identification Check	E417.5(e)	X
Weight Measurement	E417.5(d)	X
Performance Verification:	E417.3(d)	
Monitoring Capability	E417.21(h)	X
Activation	E417.21(j)	X
No-load Voltage	E417.21(c)(3)	X
Electrical Performance	E417.21(k)	X
Operating Environment Tests:	E417.11	
Activated Stand Time	E417.21(l)	X
Charge-Discharge Cycles (2)	E417.21(n)	X
Thermal Cycling (3) (4)	E417.21(o)	X
Discharge and Pulse Capacity (4)	E417.21(p)	X
Proof Pressure (4)	E417.21(d)	X
Internal Inspection (4)	E417.21(q)	X

(1) Two silver-zinc cells from the production lot used for qualification testing must undergo each test designated with an X, each year of the manufacturer's specified storage life, to demonstrate that they still satisfy their performance specifications.

(2) This test only applies if normal operation of the battery includes charging.

(3) Each cell must undergo the electrical performance test of paragraph (k) of this section under ambient conditions before the cell undergoes this operating environment test and again while the cell is subjected to the operating environment.

(4) Each cell sample must undergo this test at the end of the wet stand time after the last operating charge.

(b) *Cell capacity.* (1) *Single electrical cycle.* For a sample silver-zinc cell from a battery that has only one charge-discharge cycle, a capacity test must satisfy all of the following:

(i) The cell must undergo activation that satisfies paragraph (j) of this section;

(ii) At the end of the manufacturer-specified wet stand time, the cell must undergo a discharge of the nameplate capacity;

(iii) The test must then subject the cell to the electrical performance test of paragraph (k) of this section using the qualification electrical load profile described in paragraph (k)(7)(ii) of this section;

(iv) The cell must then undergo a final discharge to determine the positive and negative plate capacity; and

(v) The test must demonstrate that each capacity satisfies the manufacturer's specification and is in-family.

(2) *Multiple electrical cycles.* For a silver-zinc cell from a battery that has more than one charge-discharge cycle, a capacity test must satisfy all of the following:

(i) The cell must undergo activation that satisfies paragraph (j) of this section;

(ii) The test must subject the cell to the maximum predicted number of charge-discharge cycles that the battery will experience during normal operations;

(iii) At the end of each cycle life after each charge, the test must satisfy all of the following:

(A) The cell must undergo a discharge of the manufacturer's nameplate capacity;

(B) The cell must then undergo the electrical performance test of paragraph (k) of this section using the qualification electrical load profile described in paragraph (k)(7)(ii) of this section; and

(C) The cell must then undergo a discharge to determine the positive plate capacity;

(iv) At the end of the cycle life of the last charge-discharge cycle, in addition to determining the positive plate capacity, the cell must undergo a discharge to determine the negative plate capacity; and

(v) The test must demonstrate that each capacity for each cycle satisfies the manufacturer's specification and is in-family.

(c) *Silver-zinc battery status-of-health tests.* (1) *500-volt insulation.* A 500-volt insulation test of a silver-zinc battery must satisfy the status-of-health test requirements of section E417.3(f). The test must measure insulation resistance between mutually insulated pin-to-pin and pin-to-case points using a minimum 500-volt workmanship voltage prior to connecting any battery harness to the cells. The test must measure the continuity of the battery harness after completion of all wiring, but before battery activation to demonstrate that the insulation and continuity resistances satisfy their performance specifications.

(2) *Continuity and isolation.* A continuity and isolation test of a silver zinc battery must satisfy the status-of-health test requirements of section E417.3(f). The test must demonstrate that all battery wiring and connectors are installed according to the

manufacturer's specifications. The test must measure all pin-to-pin and pin-to-case resistances and demonstrate that each satisfies all its performance specifications and are in-family.

(3) *No-load voltage.* A no-load voltage test must satisfy the status-of-health test requirements of section E417.3(f). The test must demonstrate that each battery cell satisfies its performance specification for voltage without any load applied. A battery must undergo this test just after introduction of electrolyte to each cell, after electrical conditioning of the battery, before and after each electrical performance test and, for a flight battery, just before installation into the launch vehicle.

(4) *Pin-to-case isolation.* A pin-to-case isolation test must satisfy the status-of-health test requirements of section E417.3(f). The test must measure voltage isolation between each pin and the battery case to demonstrate that no current leakage path exists as a result of electrolyte leakage. This measurement must use a voltmeter with an internal resistance of no less than 100K ohms and have a resolution that detects any leakage current of 0.1 milliamps or greater.

(d) *Proof pressure.* (1) *Cells.* Each individual cell or each cell within a battery must undergo pressurization to 1.5 times the worst case operating differential pressure or highest setting of the cell vent valve for no less than 15 seconds. The test must demonstrate that the leak rate satisfies its performance specification. After pressurization, each cell must remain sealed until activation. For a battery, the test must demonstrate the integrity of each cell seal when in the battery configuration.

(2) *Battery cases.* Each battery case must undergo pressurization to 1.5 times the worst case operating differential pressure for no less than 15 minutes. The test must demonstrate no loss of structural integrity and no hazardous condition. For any sealed battery, the test must demonstrate that the leak rate satisfies its performance specification.

(e) *Electrolyte.* A test of each electrolyte lot for battery activation must demonstrate that the electrolyte satisfies the manufacturer's specifications, including volume and concentration.

(f) *Battery mounting and case integrity.* A battery mounting and case integrity test must demonstrate that any welds in the battery's mounting hardware or case are free of workmanship defects using X-ray examination that satisfies section E417.5(f).

(g) *Pre-activation.* A pre-activation test must demonstrate that a battery or cell will not experience a loss of structural integrity or create a hazardous condition when subjected to predicted operating conditions and all required margins. This must include all of the following:

(1) The test must demonstrate that any battery or cell pressure relief device satisfies all its performance specifications;

(2) The test must exercise 100% of all pressure relief devices that can function repeatedly without degradation; and

(3) The test must demonstrate that each pressure relief device opens within ±10% of its performance specification.

(h) *Monitoring capability.* A monitoring capability test must demonstrate that each device that monitors a silver-zinc battery's voltage, current, or temperature satisfies all its performance specifications.

(i) *Heater circuit verification.* A heater circuit verification test must demonstrate that any battery heater, including its control circuitry, satisfies all its performance specifications.

(j) *Activation.* (1) The activation of a battery or cell must follow a procedure that is approved by the manufacturer and includes the manufacturer's activation steps.

(2) The activation procedure and equipment for acceptance testing must be equivalent to those used for qualification and storage life testing.

(3) The activation procedure must include verification that the electrolyte satisfies the manufacturer's specification for percentage of potassium hydroxide.

(4) The quantity of electrolyte for activation of the batteries and cells for any qualification test must satisfy all of the following:

(i) One of the three required qualification battery samples and six of the 12 required individual qualification cell samples must undergo activation with no less than the manufacturer specified maximum amount of electrolyte; and

(ii) One of the three required qualification battery samples and six of the 12 required individual qualification cell samples must undergo activation with no greater than the manufacturer specified minimum amount of electrolyte.

(k) *Electrical performance.* An electrical performance test must demonstrate that a battery or cell satisfies all its performance specifications and is in-family while the battery is subjected to the electrical load profile described in paragraph (k)(7) of this section and include all of the following:

(1) The test must demonstrate that the battery or cell supplies the required current while maintaining the required voltage regulation that satisfies the manufacturer's specifications and is in family with previous test results;

(2) The test must monitor each of the battery or cell's critical electrical performance parameters; including voltage, current, and temperature, with a resolution and sample rate that detects any failure to satisfy a performance specification. For a battery, the test must monitor the battery's performance

parameters and the voltage of each cell within the battery. During the current pulse portion of the load profile, the voltage monitoring must have a sample rate of once every 0.1 millisecond or better;

(3) The test must measure a battery or cell's no-load voltage before and after the application of any load to the battery or cell;

(4) A silver-zinc battery or cell must undergo this test after the battery or cell is activated and after the manufacturer's specified soak period;

(5) The test must demonstrate that the battery or cell voltage does not fall below the voltage needed to provide the minimum acceptance voltage of each electronic component that the battery powers while the battery or cell is subjected to the steady state portion of the load profile;

(6) The test must demonstrate that the battery or cell voltage does not fall below the voltage needed to provide the minimum qualification voltage of each electronic component that the battery powers while the battery or cell is subjected to the pulse portion of the load profile; and

(7) The test load profile must satisfy one of the following:

(i) For acceptance testing, the load profile must begin with a steady-state flight load that lasts for no less than 180 seconds followed without interruption by a current pulse. The pulse width must be no less than 1.5 times the ordnance initiator qualification pulse width or a minimum workmanship screening pulse width of 100 milliseconds, whichever is greater. The pulse amplitude must be no less than 1.5 times the ordnance initiator qualification pulse amplitude. After the pulse, the acceptance load profile must end with the application of a steady-state flight load that lasts for no less than 15 seconds; or

(ii) For qualification testing or any storage life testing, the load profile must begin with a steady-state flight load that lasts for no less than 180 seconds followed by a current pulse. The pulse width must be no less than three times the ordnance initiator qualification pulse width or a minimum workmanship screening pulse width of 200 milliseconds, whichever is greater. The pulse amplitude must be no less than 1.5 times the ordnance initiator qualification pulse amplitude. After the pulse, the qualification load profile must end with a steady-state flight load that lasts for no less than 15 seconds.

(l) *Activated stand time.* An activated stand time test must demonstrate that a silver-zinc battery or cell satisfies all its performance specifications after it is activated and subjected to the environments that the battery or cell will experience from the time it is activated until flight. This must include all of the following:

(1) The test environment must simulate the pre-flight battery or cell conditioning environments, including the launch vehicle installation environment;

(2) The test environment must simulate the worst case temperature exposure and any thermal cycling, such as due to any freezer storage, and any diurnal cycling on the launch vehicle;

(3) The test must measure the battery or cell's open-circuit voltage at the beginning and again at the end of the activated stand time to demonstrate that it satisfies its performance specifications; and

(4) The test must apply an electrical load to the battery or cell at the end of the activated stand time to demonstrate whether the battery or cell is in a peroxide or monoxide chemical state that satisfies its performance specifications before undergoing any other operating environmental test.

(m) *Overcharge.* An overcharge test only applies to a battery or cell that undergoes charging during normal operations. The test must demonstrate that the battery or cell satisfies all its performance specifications when subjected to an overcharge of no less than the manufacturer's specified overcharge limit using the nominal charging rate.

(n) *Charge-discharge cycles.* This test only applies to a battery or cell that undergoes charging during normal operations. The test must satisfy all of the following:

(1) The test must subject the battery or cell sample to the maximum predicted number of charge-discharge cycles that the battery or cell will experience during normal operations;

(2) After activation, each battery or cell sample must undergo three thermal cycles at the end of the first cycle life and three thermal cycles at the end of each cycle life after each intermediate charge before the final charge;

(3) During each set of three thermal cycles for each charge-discharge cycle, the test must satisfy the thermal cycle test requirements of paragraphs (o)(2)–(o)(5) of this section;

(4) For a battery, after the three thermal cycles for each charge-discharge cycle, the battery must undergo a pin-to-case isolation test that satisfies paragraph (c)(4) of this section;

(5) Each battery or cell must undergo a discharge of its nameplate capacity before each charge; and

(6) The battery or cell must undergo any further operating environment tests only after the final charge.

(o) *Thermal cycle.* A thermal cycle test must demonstrate that a silver-zinc battery or cell satisfies all its performance specifications when subjected to pre-flight thermal cycle environments, including acceptance testing, and flight thermal cycle environments. This must include all of the following:

(1) The test must subject the battery or cell to no less than the acceptance-number of thermal cycles that satisfies section E417.13(d)(1);

(2) The thermal cycle environment must satisfy all of the following:

(i) Each thermal cycle must range from 10 °C above the maximum predicted temperature range to 5.5 °C below. If the launch vehicle's telemetry system does not provide the battery's temperature before and during flight as described in section D417.17(b)(9), each thermal cycle must range from 10 °C above the maximum predicted temperature range to 10 °C below;

(ii) For each cycle, the dwell-time at each high and low temperature must last long enough for the battery or cell to achieve internal thermal equilibrium and must last no less than one hour; and

(iii) When heating and cooling the battery or cell, the temperature change at a rate that averages 1 °C per minute or the maximum predicted rate, whichever is greater;

(3) Each battery or cell must undergo the electrical performance test of paragraph (k) of this section when the battery or cell is at ambient temperature before beginning the first thermal cycle and after completing the last cycle;

(4) Each battery or cell must undergo the electrical performance test of paragraph (k) of this section, at the high and low temperatures during the first, middle and last thermal cycles; and

(5) The test must continuously monitor and record all critical performance and status-of-health parameters, including the battery or cell's open circuit voltage, during all thermal cycle dwell times and transitions with a resolution and sample rate that will detect any performance degradation.

(p) *Discharge and pulse capacity.* A discharge and pulse capacity test must demonstrate that a silver zinc battery or cell satisfies all its electrical performance specifications at the end of its specified capacity limit for the last operating charge and discharge cycle. The test must include all of the following:

(1) The battery or cell must undergo discharge at flight loads until the total capacity consumed during this discharge and during all previous qualification tests reaches the manufacturer's specified capacity.

(2) The test must demonstrate that the total amount of capacity consumed during the discharge test and all previous qualification tests satisfies the battery or cell's minimum performance specification.

(3) After satisfying paragraphs (p)(1) and (p)(2) of this section, the test must measure the battery or cell's no-load voltage and then apply a qualification load profile that satisfies all of the following:

(i) The load profile must begin with a steady state flight load for no less than 180 seconds followed by a current pulse;

(ii) The pulse width must be no less than three times the ordnance initiator qualification pulse width or a minimum workmanship screening pulse width of 200 milliseconds; whichever is greater;

(iii) The pulse amplitude must be no less than 1.5 times the ordnance initiator qualification pulse amplitude; and

(iv) After the pulse, the qualification load profile must end with a steady state flight load that lasts for no less than 15 seconds.

(4) The test must monitor each of the battery or cell's critical electrical performance parameters; including voltage, current, and temperature, with a resolution and sample rate that detects any failure to satisfy a performance specification. For a battery, the test must monitor the battery's performance parameters and the voltage of each cell within the battery. During the current pulse portion of the load profile, the voltage monitoring must have sample rate that will detect any component performance degradation.

(5) The test must demonstrate that the battery or cell voltage does not fall below the voltage needed to provide the minimum acceptance voltage of each electronic component that the battery powers while the battery or cell is subjected to the steady state portion of the load profile.

(6) The test must demonstrate that the battery or cell voltage does not fall below the voltage needed to provide the minimum qualification voltage of each electronic component that the battery powers while the battery or cell is subjected to the pulse portion of the load profile.

(7) After satisfying paragraphs (p)(1) through (p)(6) of this section, the battery or cell must undergo a complete discharge and the test must demonstrate that the total silver plate capacity is in-family.

(q) *Internal inspection.* An internal inspection must identify any excessive wear or damage to a silver-zinc battery, including any of its cells, or an individual cell after the battery or cell is exposed to all the qualification test environments. An internal inspection must satisfy section E417.5(g) and include all of the following:

(1) An internal examination of any battery to verify that there was no movement of any component within the battery that could stress that component beyond its design limit during flight:

(2) An examination to verify the integrity of all cell and wiring interconnects.

(3) An examination to verify the integrity of all potting and shimming materials.

(4) The removal of all cells from the battery and examination of each cell for any physical damage.

(5) A destructive physical analysis to verify the integrity of all plate tab to cell terminal connections and the integrity of each plate and separator. For each battery sample required to undergo all the qualification tests, one cell from each corner and two cells from the middle of the battery must undergo the destructive physical analysis. For storage life testing, one of the two cells required to undergo all the storage life tests must undergo destructive physical analysis. The inspection must verify the integrity of each plate tab, identify any anomaly in each plate, including its color or shape, and identify any anomaly in each separator, including its condition, silver migration, and any oxalate crystals.

(6) A test that demonstrates that the zinc plate capacity of the cells satisfies the manufacturer's specification. For each battery sample required to undergo all the qualification tests, the test must determine the zinc plate capacity for three cells from the battery, other than the cells of paragraph (q)(5) of this section. For storage life testing, the test must determine the zinc plate capacity for one cell that is required to undergo all the storage life tests, other than the cell of paragraph (q)(5) of this section.

(r) *Coupon cell acceptance.* A coupon cell acceptance test must demonstrate that the silver zinc cells that make up a flight battery were manufactured the same as the qualification battery cells and satisfy all their performance specifications after being subjected to the environments that the battery experiences from the time of manufacture until activation and installation. This must include all of the following:

(1) One test cell that is from the same production lot as the flight battery, with the same lot date code as the cells in the flight battery, must undergo the test.

(2) The test cell must have been attached to the battery from the time of the manufacturer's acceptance test and have experienced the same non-operating environments as the battery.

(3) The test must occur immediately before activation of the flight battery.

(4) The test cell must undergo activation that satisfies paragraph (j) of this section.

(5) The test cell must undergo discharge at a moderate rate, using the manufacturer's specification, undergo two qualification load profiles of paragraph (k)(7)(ii) of this section at the nameplate capacity, and then undergo further discharge until the minimum manufacturer specified voltage is achieved. The test must demonstrate that the cell's amp-hour capacity and voltage characteristics satisfy all their performance specifications and are in-family.

(6) For a silver-zinc battery that will undergo charging during normal operations, the test cell must undergo the requirements of paragraph (r)(5) of this section for each qualification charge-discharge cycle. The test must demonstrate that the cell capacity and electrical characteristics satisfy all their performance specifications and are in family for each charge-discharge cycle.

E417.22 COMMERCIAL NICKEL-CADMIUM BATTERIES

(a) *General.* This section applies to any nickel-cadmium battery that uses one or more commercially produced nickel-cadmium cells and is part of a flight termination system.

(1) *Compliance.* Any commercial nickel-cadmium battery must satisfy each test or analysis identified by any table of this section to demonstrate that the battery satisfies all its performance specifications when subjected to each non-operating and operating environment.

(2) *Charging and discharging of nickel-cadmium batteries and cells.* Each test required by any table of this section that requires a nickel-cadmium battery or cell to undergo a charge or discharge must include all of the following:

(i) The rate of each charge or discharge must prevent any damage to the battery or cell and provide for the battery or cell's electrical characteristics to remain consistent. Unless otherwise specified, the charge or discharge rate used for qualification testing must be identical to the rate that the flight battery experiences during acceptance and preflight testing;

(ii) A discharge of a cell must subject the cell to the discharge rate until the cell voltage reaches no greater than 0.9 volt. A discharge of a battery, must subject the battery to the discharge rate until the battery voltage reaches no greater than 0.9 volt times the number of cells in the battery. Any discharge that results in a cell voltage below 0.9 volt must use a discharge rate that is slow enough to prevent cell damage or cell reversal. Each discharge must include monitoring of voltage, current, and time with sufficient resolution and sample rate to determine capacity and demonstrate that the battery or cell is in-family;

(iii) A charge of a battery or cell must satisfy the manufacturer's charging specifications and procedures. The charging input to the battery or cell must be no less than 160% of the manufacturer's specified capacity. The charge rate must not exceed C/10 unless the launch operator demonstrates that a higher charge rate does not damage the battery or cell and results in repeatable battery or cell performance. The cell voltage must not exceed 1.55 volts during charging to avoid creating a hydrogen gas explosion hazard; and

(iv) The test must monitor each of the battery or cell's critical electrical performance parameters with a resolution and sample rate to detect any failure to satisfy a performance specification. For a battery, the test must monitor the battery's performance parameters and those of each cell within the battery. During the current pulse portion of the load profile, the monitoring must have a resolution and sample rate that will detect any component performance degradation.

Table E417.22-1

Nickel-cadmium Cell Lot Acceptance [(1)]	Section	Quantity Tested
Cell Lot Acceptance: [(2)]		
Component Examination:	E417.5	
Visual Examination [(3)]	E417.5(b)	100%
Dimension Measurement [(3)]	E417.5(c)	100%
Identification Check [(3)]	E417.5(e)	100%
Cell Screening:		
Cell Reusable Venting Devices [(3)]	E417.22(b)(1)	100%
Cell Inspection and Preparation [(3)]	E417.22(c)	100%
Cell Conditioning [(3)]	E417.22(d)	100%
Cell Characterization [(3)]	E417.22(e)	100%
Charge Retention [(3)]	E417.22(f)	100%
Capacity and Overcharge at 0°C [(3)]	E417.22(g)	100%
Electrical Performance	E417.22(n)	100%
Cell leakage	E417.22(s)	100%
Lot Sample Tests:		
X-ray Inspection [(4)] [(5)]	E417.5(f)	Lot Sample [(6)]
Cell Non-Reusable Venting Devices [(4)]	E417.22(b)(2)	Lot Sample [(6)]
Post Acceptance Discharge and Storage	E417.22(h)	100% of Lot Remainder

(1) Each test that requires a nickel-cadmium cell to undergo a charge or discharge must satisfy paragraph (a)(2) of this section. Unless otherwise specified, each test must begin with the cell fully charged.

(2) All nickel-cadmium cells used in a qualification or flight battery must be from a production lot that has successfully passed each cell lot acceptance test required

by this table. A production lot must consist of cells that were manufactured in a single continuous production run using identical parts, materials, and processes. Each production lot must undergo the tests required by this table to ensure that the cells are consistent and will provide the required performance and to detect any manufacturer variation introduced into the lot of cells. A launch operator must ensure that all the results of the tests executed on each lot are entered into an engineering database to establish family characteristics and that those characteristics satisfy all the cell's performance specifications.

(3) For any cell sample that fails to pass this test, a launch operator may not use that cell sample in any further test or flight, but such a failure does not disqualify the remainder of the lot for use.

(4) If any cell sample fails to pass this test, a launch operator may not use the entire lot.

(5) This test only applies to any cell with multiple internal tabs. Any X-ray inspection must demonstrate tab integrity at 0^0 and 90^0.

(6) The lot sample quantity must be no less than five samples or 10% of the production lot; whichever is greater.

Table E417.22-2

Nickel-cadmium Battery Acceptance	Section E417.13(a)	Quantity Tested
Cell Lot Acceptance and Qualification Tests [2]	Table E417.22-1	100% of Cells
Component Examination (Complete Battery):	E417.5	
Visual Examination	E417.5(b)	100%
Weight Measurement	E417.5(d)	100%
Dimension Measurement	E417.5(c)	100%
Identification Check	E417.5(e)	100%
Battery Case Integrity [3]	E417.22(k)	100%
Charge Retention (Battery)	E417.22(f)	100%
Status-of-health	E417.22(j)	100%
Electrical Performance [4]	E417.22(n)	100%
Reusable Venting Devices (Battery Only)	E417.22(b)(1)	100%
Non-Reusable Venting Devices (Battery Only)	E417.22(b)(2)	Lot Sample [6]
Monitoring Capability	E417.22(l)	100%
Heater Circuit Verification	E417.22(m)	100%
Operating Environment Tests:	E417.11	
Acceptance Thermal Cycle	E417.22(o)	100%
Random Vibration [5]	E417.13(b)	100%
Charge Retention (Battery)	E417.22(f)	100%
Status-of-health	E417.22(j)	100%
Electrical Performance [4]	E417.22(n)	100%

Component Examination (Complete Battery):	E417.5	
Visual Examination	E417.5(b)	100%
Battery Case Integrity [(3)]	E417.22(k)	100%
Post acceptance discharge and storage	E417.22(h)	100%

(1) Each test that requires a nickel-cadmium battery to undergo a charge or discharge must satisfy paragraph (a)(2) of this section. Unless otherwise specified, each test must begin with the battery fully charged.

(2) All cells used in each qualification or flight battery must be from a production lot that has successfully passed the cell lot acceptance tests required by Table E417.22-1.

(3) This test is required only for any sealed battery.

(4) The battery must undergo an electrical performance test under ambient conditions before the first operating environment test and while the battery is subjected to each environment as required by each operating environment test.

(5) The battery must undergo continuous monitoring of its voltage while subjected to the expected steady-state flight load during the random vibration environment. The monitoring must have a sample rate of once every 0.1-millisecond or better, and demonstrate that the voltage does not does experience any dropout.

(6) The lot sample quantity must be no less than five samples or 10% of the production lot, whichever is greater. The sample venting devices need not undergo this test in the battery assembly.

Table E417.22-3

Nickel-cadmium Battery and Cell Qualification [1] [2]	Section E417.7	Quantity Tested X = 3 Batteries
Battery Acceptance Tests [3]	Table E417.22-2	X
Non-Operating Environment Tests:	E417.9	
Storage Temperature	E417.9(b)	X
Transportation Shock	E417.9(d)	X
Bench Shock	E417.9(e)	1
Transportation Vibration	E417.9(f)	X
Fungus Resistance	E417.9(g)	1
Salt Fog	E417.9(h)	X
Charge Retention (Battery)	E417.22(f)	X
Electrical Performance [4]	E417.22(n)	X
Operating Environment Tests:	E417.11	
Sinusoidal Vibration [5]	E417.11(b)	X
Acoustic [5]	E417.11(d)	X
Shock [5]	E417.11(e)	X
Acceleration [5]	E417.11(f)	X
Humidity [6]	E417.11(g)	X
Qualification Thermal Cycle	E417.22(p)	X
Random Vibration [5]	E417.11(c)	X
Electromagnetic Interference and Compatibility	E417.11(j)	1

Status-of-health	E417.22(j)	X
Cycle Life	E417.22(i)	X
Electrical Performance (7)	E417.22(n)	X
Charge Retention	E417.22(f)	X
Operational Stand Time	E417.22(q)	2
Battery Case Integrity (8)	E417.22(k)	X
Explosive Atmosphere	E417.11(k)	1
Internal Inspection	E417.22(r)	X
X-ray Inspection (9)	E417.5(f)	5 cells

(1) Each new production lot of nickel-cadmium cells must satisfy all the qualification tests required by this table to demonstrate that any variation in parts, material, or processes between each production lot does not adversely affect cell performance. For each new cell production lot, three battery assemblies that are made up of cells from the lot must undergo each test required by this table to demonstrate that each battery and each cell satisfy all their performance specifications when in their packaged flight configuration.

(2) Each test that requires a nickel-cadmium battery to undergo a charge or discharge must satisfy paragraph (a)(2) of this section. Unless otherwise specified, each test must begin with the battery fully charged.

(3) Each qualification test battery must pass all the acceptance tests of table E417.22-2.

(4) The battery must undergo an electrical performance test under ambient conditions before the first operating environment test and while the battery is subjected to each environment as required by each operating environment test.

(5) The battery must undergo continuous monitoring of its voltage while subjected to the expected steady-state flight load during the dynamic environment. The monitoring must have a sample rate of once every 0.1 millisecond or better; and demonstrate that the voltage does not experience any dropout.

(6) A battery must undergo a charge retention test that satisfies paragraph (f) of this section while the battery is exposed to the humidity environment and the test results must undergo comparison to previous charge retention test results to demonstrate that the humidity environment does not degrade battery capacity.

(7) Each battery must undergo an electrical performance test during the first three charge and discharge cycles, during every tenth cycle thereafter, and during the last three cycles.

(8) This test is only required for any sealed battery.

(9) This test is only required for any cell with multiple internal tabs. The test must demonstrate tab integrity at 0^0 and 90^0.

(b) *Venting devices.* A test of a battery or cell venting device must demonstrate that the battery or cell will not experience a loss of structural integrity or create a hazardous condition when subjected to any electrical discharge, charging, or short-circuit condition and satisfy the following paragraphs:

(1) *Reusable venting devices.* For a venting device that is capable of functioning repeatedly without degradation, such as a vent valve, the test must exercise the device and demonstrate that it satisfies all its performance specifications.

(2) *Non-reusable venting devices.* For a venting device that does not function repeatedly without degradation, such as a burst disc, the test must exercise a lot sample to demonstrate that the venting device satisfies all its performance specifications. The test must demonstrate that each device sample vents within ±10% of the manufacturer specified average vent pressure with a maximum vent pressure no higher than 350 pounds per square inch.

(c) *Cell inspection and preparation.* A cell inspection and preparation must:

(1) Record the manufacturer's lot-code;

(2) Demonstrate that the cell is clean and free of manufacturing defects;

(3) Use a chemical indicator to demonstrate that the cell has no leak; and

(4) Discharge each cell to no greater than 0.9 volt using a discharge rate that will not cause damage to the cell.

(d) *Cell conditioning.* Conditioning of a nickel-cadmium cell must stabilize the cell and ensure repeatable electrical performance throughout the cell's service-life. Conditioning of a cell must include both of the following:

(1) Before any testing, each cell must age for no less than 11 months after the manufacturer's lot date code to ensure consistent electrical performance of the cell for its entire service-life; and

(2) After aging, each cell must undergo a first charge at a charging rate of no greater than its capacity divided by 20 (C/20), to initialize the chemistry within the cell. Any battery stored for over one month after the first charge must undergo recharging at the same rate.

(e) *Cell characterization.* Characterization of a nickel-cadmium cell must stabilize the cell chemistry and determine the cell's capacity. A cell characterization must satisfy both of the following:

(1) Each cell must repeatedly undergo charge and discharge cycles until the capacities for three consecutive cycles agree to within 1% of each other; and

(2) During characterization, each cell must remain at a temperature of 20 °C ±2 °C to ensure that the cell is not overstressed and to allow repeatable performance.

(f) *Charge retention.* A charge retention test must demonstrate that a nickel-cadmium battery or cell consistently retains its charge and provides its required capacity, including the required capacity margin, from the final charge used prior to flight to the end of flight. The test must satisfy the status-of-heath test requirements of § E417.3(f) and satisfy all of the following steps in the following order:

(1) The test must begin with the battery or cell fully charged. The battery or cell must undergo an immediate capacity discharge to develop a baseline capacity for comparison to its charge retention performance;

(2) The battery or cell must undergo complete charging and then storage at 20 °C ±2 °C for 72 hours;

(3) The battery or cell must undergo discharging to determine its capacity; and

(4) The test must demonstrate that each cell or battery's capacity is greater than 90% of the baseline capacity of paragraph (f)(1) of this section and the test must demonstrate that the capacity retention is in-family.

(g) *Capacity and overcharge at 0 °C.* A 0 °C test of a nickel-cadmium cell must validate the cell's chemistry status-of-health and determine the cell's capacity when subjected to a high charge efficiency temperature. The test must include all of the following:

(1) Each cell must undergo repeated charge and discharge cycles at 0 °C ±2 °C until all the capacities for three consecutive cycles agree to within 1% of each other; and

(2) After the charge and discharge cycles of paragraph (g)(1) of this section, each cell must undergo an inspection to demonstrate that it is not cracked.

(h) *Post acceptance discharge and storage.* Post acceptance discharge and storage of a nickel-cadmium battery or cell must prevent any damage that could affect electrical performance. This must include all of the following:

(1) Any battery must undergo discharge to a voltage between 0.05 volts and 0.9 volts to prevent cell reversal, allow safe handling, and minimize any aging degradation;

(2) Any individual cell must undergo discharge to no greater than 0.05 volts to allow safe handling and minimize any aging degradation;

(3) After the discharge, each battery or cell must undergo storage in an open circuit configuration and under storage conditions that protect against any performance degradation and are consistent with the qualification tests. This must include a storage temperature of no greater than 5 °C.

(i) *Cycle life.* A cycle life test of a nickel-cadmium cell or battery must demonstrate that the cell or battery satisfies all its performance specifications for no less than five times the number of operating charge and discharge cycles expected of the flight battery, including acceptance testing, pre-flight checkout, and flight.

(j) *Status-of-health.* A status-of-health test of a nickel-cadmium battery must satisfy section E417.3(f) and include continuity and isolation measurements that demonstrate that all battery wiring and connectors are installed according to the manufacturer's specifications. The test must also measure all pin-to-pin and pin-to-case resistances to demonstrate that each satisfies all its performance specifications and are in-family.

(k) *Battery case integrity.* A battery case integrity test of a sealed nickel-cadmium battery must demonstrate that the battery will not lose structural integrity or create a hazardous condition when subjected to all predicted operating conditions and all required margins and that the battery's leak rate satisfies all its performance specifications. This must include all of the following:

(1) The test must monitor the battery's pressure while subjecting the battery case to no less than 1.5 times the greatest operating pressure differential that could occur under qualification testing, pre-flight, or flight conditions;

(2) The pressure monitoring must have a resolution and sample rate that allows accurate determination of the battery's leak rate;

(3) The test must demonstrate that the battery's leak rate is no greater than the equivalent of 10^{-4} scc/sec of helium; and

(4) The battery must undergo examination to identify any condition that indicates that

the battery might loose structural integrity or create a hazardous condition.

(l) *Monitoring capability.* A monitoring capability test must demonstrate that each device that monitors a nickel-cadmium battery's voltage, current, or temperature satisfies all its performance specifications.

(m) *Heater circuit verification.* A heater circuit verification test must demonstrate that any battery heater, including its control circuitry, satisfies all its performance specifications.

(n) *Electrical performance.* An electrical performance test of a nickel-cadmium battery or cell must demonstrate that the battery or cell satisfies all its performance specifications and is in-family while the battery or cell is subjected to an acceptance or qualification electrical load profile. The test must also demonstrate that the battery or cell satisfies all its electrical performance specifications at the beginning, middle, and end of its specified preflight and flight capacity plus the required margin. The test must include and satisfy each of the following:

(1) The test must measure a battery or cell's no-load voltage before applying any load to ensure it is within the manufacturer's specification limits.

(2) The test must demonstrate that the battery or cell voltage does not violate the manufacturer's specification limits while the battery or cell is subjected to the steady-state flight load. The test must also demonstrate that the battery provides the minimum acceptance voltage of each electronic component that the battery powers.

(3) The test must demonstrate that the battery or cell supplies the required current while maintaining the required voltage regulation that satisfies the manufacturer's specification. The test must demonstrate that the battery or cell voltage does not fall below the voltage needed to provide the minimum qualification voltage of each electronic component that the battery powers while the battery or cell is subjected to the pulse portion of the load profile. The test must subject the battery or cell to one of the following load profiles:

(i) For acceptance testing, the test load profile must satisfy all of the following:

(A) The load profile must begin with a steady-state flight load that lasts for no less than 180 seconds followed without interruption by a current pulse;

(B) The pulse width must be no less than 1.5 times the ordnance initiator qualification pulse width or a minimum workmanship screening pulse width of 100 milliseconds, whichever is greater;

(C) The pulse amplitude must be no less than 1.5 times the ordnance initiator qualification pulse amplitude; and

(D) After the pulse, the acceptance load profile must end with a steady state flight load that lasts for no less than 15 seconds.

(ii) For qualification testing, the test load profile must satisfy all of the following:

(A) The load profile must begin with a steady-state flight load that lasts for no less than 180 seconds followed by a current pulse;

(B) The pulse width must be no less than three times the ordnance initiator qualification pulse width or a minimum workmanship screening pulse width of 200 milliseconds, whichever is greater;

(C) The pulse amplitude must be no less than 1.5 times the ordnance initiator qualification pulse amplitude; and

(D) After the pulse, the qualification load profile must end with a steady-state flight load that lasts for no less than 15 seconds.

(4) The test must repeat, satisfy, and accomplish paragraphs (n)(1)–(n)(3) of this section with the battery or cell at each of the following levels of charge-discharge and in the following order:

(A) Fully charged;

(B) After the battery or cell undergoes a discharge that removes 50% of the capacity required for launch and all required margins; and

(C) After the battery or cell undergoes a discharge that removes an additional 50% of the capacity required for launch.

(5) The test must subject the battery or cell the a final discharge that determines the remaining capacity. The test must demonstrate that the total capacity removed from the battery during all testing, including this final discharge, satisfies all the battery's performance specifications and is in-family.

(o) *Acceptance thermal cycle.* An acceptance thermal cycle test must demonstrate that a nickel-cadmium battery satisfies all it performance specifications when subjected to workmanship and maximum predicted thermal cycle environments. This must include each of the following:

(1) The acceptance-number of thermal cycles for a component means the number of thermal cycles that the component must experience during the acceptance thermal cycle test. The test must subject each component to no less than eight thermal cycles or 1.5 times the maximum number of thermal cycles that the component could experience during launch processing and flight, including all launch delays and recycling, rounded up to the nearest whole number, whichever is greater.

(2) The acceptance thermal cycle high temperature must be a 30 °C workmanship screening level or the maximum predicted environment high temperature, whichever is higher. The acceptance thermal cycle low temperature must be a −24 °C workmanship screening temperature or the predicted environment low temperature, whichever is lower;

(3) When heating or cooling the battery during each cycle, the temperature must

change at an average rate of 1 °C per minute or the maximum predicted rate, whichever is greater. The dwell time at each high and low temperature must be long enough for the battery to achieve internal thermal equilibrium and must be no less than one hour.

(4) The test must measure all of a battery's critical status-of-health parameters at the thermal extremes on all cycles and during thermal transition to demonstrate that the battery satisfies all its performance specifications. The battery must undergo monitoring of its open circuit voltage throughout the test to demonstrate that it satisfies all its performance specifications throughout testing. The sample rate must be once every 10 seconds or more often.

(5) The battery must undergo an electrical performance test that satisfies paragraph (n) of this section while the battery is at the high, ambient, and low temperatures, during the first, middle, and last thermal cycles.

(6) If either the workmanship high or low temperature exceeds the battery's maximum predicted operating temperature range and the battery is not capable of passing the electrical performance test at the workmanship temperature, the battery may undergo the electrical performance test at an interim temperature during the cycle. This must include all of the following:

(i) Any interim high temperature must be no less than the maximum predicted high temperature;

(ii) Any interim low temperature must be no greater than the maximum predicted low temperature;

(iii) The dwell-time at any interim temperature must be long enough for the battery to reach thermal equilibrium; and

(iv) After any electrical performance test at an interim temperature, the thermal cycle must continue until the battery reaches its workmanship temperature.

(p) *Qualification thermal cycle.* A qualification thermal cycle test must demonstrate that a nickel-cadmium battery satisfies all its performance specifications when subjected to pre-flight, acceptance test, and flight thermal cycle environments. This must include each of the following:

(1) The test must subject the fully charged battery to no less than three times the acceptance-number of thermal cycles of paragraph (o)(1) of this section.

(2) The qualification thermal cycle high temperature must be a 40 °C workmanship screening level or the maximum predicted environment high temperature plus 10 °C, whichever is higher. The qualification thermal cycle low temperature must be a −34 °C workmanship screening temperature or the predicted environment low temperature minus 10 °C, whichever is lower.

(3) When heating or cooling the battery during each cycle, the temperature must change at an average rate of 1 °C per minute or the maximum predicted rate, whichever is greater. The dwell time at each high and low temperature must be long enough for the battery to achieve internal thermal equilibrium and must be no less than one hour.

(4) The test must measure the battery's critical status-of-health parameters at the thermal extremes on all cycles and during thermal transition to demonstrate that the battery satisfies all its performance specifications. The battery must undergo monitoring of its open circuit voltage throughout the test to demonstrate that it satisfies all it performance specifications. The sample rate must be once every 10 seconds or more often.

(5) The battery must undergo an electrical performance test that satisfies paragraph (n) of this section while the battery is at the high, ambient, and low temperatures, during the first, middle, and last thermal cycles.

(6) If either the workmanship high or low temperature exceeds the battery's maximum predicted operating temperature range and the battery is not capable of passing the electrical performance test at the workmanship temperature, the battery may undergo the discharge and pulse capacity test at an interim temperature during the cycle. This must include all of the following:

(i) Any interim high temperature must be no less than the maximum predicted high temperature plus 10 °C;

(ii) Any interim low temperature must be no greater than the maximum predicted low temperature minus 10 °C;

(iii) The dwell-time at any interim temperature must last long enough for the battery to reach thermal equilibrium; and

(iv) After any electrical performance test at an interim temperature, the thermal cycle must continue to the workmanship temperature.

(q) *Operational stand time.* An operational stand time test must demonstrate that a nickel-cadmium battery will maintain its required capacity, including all required margins, from the final charge that the battery receives before flight until the planned safe flight state. This must include each of the following:

(1) The battery must undergo a charge to full capacity and then an immediate capacity discharge to establish a baseline capacity for comparison to the capacity after the battery experiences the operational stand time.

(2) The battery must undergo a charge to full capacity. The test must then subject the battery to the maximum predicted pre-flight temperature for the maximum operating stand time between final battery charging to the planned safe flight state while in an open circuit configuration. The maximum operating stand time must account for all launch processing and launch delay contingencies that could occur after the battery receives its final charge.

(3) After the maximum operating stand time has elapsed, the battery must undergo a capacity discharge to determine any capacity loss due to any self-discharge by comparing the operational stand time capacity with the baseline capacity in paragraph (q)(1) of this section.

(4) The test must demonstrate that the battery's capacity, including all required margins, and any loss in capacity due to the operational stand time satisfy all associated performance specifications.

(r) *Internal inspection.* An internal inspection of a nickel-cadmium battery must identify any excessive wear or damage to the battery, including any of its cells, after the battery is exposed to all the qualification test environments. An internal inspection must satisfy section E417.5(g) and include all of the following:

(1) An internal examination to verify that there was no movement of any component within the battery that stresses that component beyond its design limit;

(2) An examination to verify the integrity of all cell and wiring interconnects;

(3) An examination to verify the integrity of all potting and shimming materials;

(4) The removal of all cells from the battery and examination of each cell for any physical damage;

(5) A test with a chemical indicator to demonstrate that none of the cells leaked; and

(6) Destructive physical analysis of one cell from each corner and one cell from the middle of each battery that undergoes all the qualification tests. The destructive physical analysis must verify the integrity of all connections between all plate tabs and cell terminals, and the integrity of each plate and separator.

(s) *Cell leakage.* A leakage test of a cell must demonstrate the integrity of the cell case seal using one of the following approaches:

(1) *Leak test 1:*

(i) The test must measure each cell's weight to 0.001 grams to create a baseline for comparison.

(ii) The test must subject each cell, fully charged, to a vacuum of less than 10^{-2} torr for no less than 20 hours. While under vacuum, the cell must undergo charging at a C/20 rate. The test must control each cell's temperature to ensure that its does not exceed the cell's maximum predicted thermal environment.

(iii) The test must measure each cell's weight after the 20-hour vacuum and demonstrate that the cell does not experience a weight loss greater than three-sigma from the average weight loss for each cell in the lot.

(iv) Any cell that fails the weight-loss test of paragraph (h)(3) of this section must undergo cleaning and discharge. The cell must then undergo a full charge and then inspection with a chemical indicator. If the chemical indicator shows that the cell has a leak, a launch operator may not use the cell in any further test or flight.

(2) *Leak test 2:*

(i) The cell must develop greater than one atmosphere differential pressure during the 0 °C capacity and overcharge test of paragraph (g) of this section.

(ii) After the 0 °C capacity and overcharge test of paragraph (g) of this section, the cell must undergo a full charge and then inspection with a chemical indicator. If the chemical indicator shows that the cell has a leak, a launch operator may not use the cell in any further test or flight.

E417.23 MISCELLANEOUS COMPONENTS

This section applies to any component that is critical to the reliability of a flight termination system and is not otherwise identified by this appendix. This includes any new technology or any component that may be unique to the design of a launch vehicle, such as any auto-destruct box, current limiter, or timer. A miscellaneous component must satisfy each test or analysis identified by any table of this section to demonstrate that the component satisfies all its performance specifications when subjected to each non-operating and operating environment. For any new or unique component, the launch operator must identify any additional test requirements necessary to ensure its reliability.

Table E417.23-1

Miscellaneous Component Acceptance	Section E417.13(a)	Quantity Tested
Component Examination:	E417.5	
Visual Examination	E417.5(b)	100%
Dimension Measurement	E417.5(c)	100%
Identification Check	E417.5(e)	100%
Performance Verification [(1)]	E417.3(d)	100%
Abbreviated Performance Verification [(2)]	E417.3(e)	100%
Operating Environment Tests:	E417.13	
Thermal Cycling	E417.13(d)	100%
Thermal Vacuum	E417.13(e)	100%
Acoustic	E417.13(c)	100%
Random Vibration	E417.13(b)	100%
Leakage[(3)]	E417.5(h)	100%

(1) A component must undergo this test before the first and after the last operating environment test.

(2) A component must undergo this test during each operating environment test.

(3) An unsealed component that has successfully completed salt-fog, humidity, fungus resistance, and fine sand qualification tests need not undergo a leakage test.

Table E417.23-2

Miscellaneous Component Qualification	Section E417.11	Quantity [4] Tested X=3
Acceptance Tests [1]	Table E417.23-1	X
Performance Verification [2]	E417.3(d)	X
Non-Operating Environment Tests:	E417.9	
Storage Temperature	E417.9(b)	X
Transportation Shock	E417.9(d)	X
Bench Handling Shock	E417.9(e)	X
Transportation Vibration	E417.9(f)	X
Fungus Resistance	E417.9(g)	1
Salt Fog	E417.9(h)	1
Fine Sand	E417.9(I)	1
Abbreviated Performance Verification [3]	E417.3(e)	X
Operating Environment Tests:	E417.11	

Thermal Cycling	E417.11(h)	X
Humidity	E417.11(g)	X
Thermal Vacuum	E417.11(i)	X
Acceleration	E417.11(f)	X
Shock	E417.11(e)	X
Sinusoidal Vibration	E417.11(b)	X
Acoustic	E417.11(d)	X
Random Vibration	E417.11(c)	X
Electromagnetic Interference and Compatibility	E417.11(j)	1
Explosive Atmosphere	E417.11(k)	1
Leakage [(5)]	E417.5(h)	X
Internal Inspection	E417.5(g)	X

(1) Each sample component to undergo qualification testing must first successfully complete all acceptance tests required by table E417.23-1.

(2) A component must undergo this test before the first and again after the last non-operating environment test and before the first and again after the last operating environment test.

(3) A component must undergo this test during each operating environment test.

(4) The same three sample components must undergo each test designated with an X. For a test designated with a quantity of less than three, each component tested must be one of the original three sample components.

(5) An unsealed component that has successfully completed salt-fog, humidity, fungus resistance, and fine sand qualification tests need not undergo a leakage test.

E417.25 SAFE-AND-ARM DEVICES, ELECTRO-EXPLOSIVE DEVICES, ROTOR LEADS, AND BOOSTER CHARGES

(a) *General.* This section applies to any safe-and-arm device that is part of a flight termination system, including each electro-explosive device, rotor lead, or booster charge used by the safe-and-arm device. Any safe-and-arm device, electro-explosive device, rotor lead, or booster charge must satisfy each test or analysis identified by any table of this section to demonstrate that it satisfies all its performance specifications when subjected to each non-operating and operating environment.

Table E417.25-1

Safe-and-Arm Device Acceptance	Section E417.13(a)	Quantity Tested
Component Examination:	E417.5	
Visual Examination	E417.5(b)	100%
Dimension Measurement	E417.5(c)	100%
Identification Check	E417.5(e)	100%
Performance Verification:	E417.3(d)	
Safe-and-Arm Device Status-of-Health [(1)]	E417.25(b)	100%
Safety Tests:	E417.25(e)	
Manual Safing	E417.25 (e)(4)	100%
Safing-interlock test	E417.25 (e)(5)	100%
Abbreviated Performance Verification:	E417.3(e)	
Dynamic Performance [(2)]	E417.25(g)	100%
Thermal Performance [(2)]	E417.25(f)	100%
Operating Environment Tests:	E417.13	
Thermal Cycling	E417.13(d)	100%
Random Vibration	E417.13(b)	100%
X-ray	E417.5(f)	100%
Leakage [(3)]	E417.5(h)	100%

(1) A component must undergo this test before the first and after the last operating environment test.

(2) A component must undergo this test while it is subjected to each operating environment test.

(3) An unsealed component that has successfully completed salt-fog, humidity, fungus resistance, and fine sand qualification tests need not undergo a leakage test.

Table E417.25-2

Safe-and-Arm Device Qualification	Section E417.7	Quantity Tested		
		X=1 [4]	X=6 [5]	X=3 [6]
Barrier Alignment	E417.25(o)			
Acceptance Tests [1]	Table E417.25-1	X	X	-
Safety Tests:	E417.25(e)			
Extended Stall	E417.25(e)(3)	X	-	-
Abnormal Drop	E417.9(l)	X	-	-
Containment	E417.25(e)(1)	-	-	1
Barrier Functionality	E417.25(e)(2)	-	-	2
Safing Verification	E417.25(e)(6)	-	X	-
Non-Operating Environment Tests:	E417.9			
Storage Temperature	E417.9(b)	-	X	-
Transportation Shock	E417.9(d)	-	X	-
Bench Handling shock	E417.9(e)	-	X	-
Transportation Vibration	E417.9(f)	-	X	-
Fungus Resistance	E417.9(g)	-	1	-
Salt Fog	E417.9(h)	-	1	-
Fine Sand	E417.9(I)	-	1	-
Handling Drop	E417.9(k)	-	X	-
Performance Verification:	E417.3(d)			
Safe-and-Arm Device Status-of-Health [2]	E417.25(b)		X	
Abbreviated Performance Verification:	E417.3(e)			

Safe-and-Arm Device	**Section**	**Quantity Tested**		
Qualification	**E417.7**	**X=1 (4)**	**X=6 (5)**	**X=3 (6)**
Dynamic Performance (3)	E417.25(g)	-	X	-
Thermal Performance (3)	E417.25(f)	-	X	-
Operating Environment Tests:	E417.11			
Thermal Cycling	E417.11(h)	-	X	-
Humidity	E417.11(g)	-	X	-
Acceleration	E417.11(f)	-	X	-
Shock	E417.11(e)	-	X	-
Sinusoidal Vibration	E417.11(b)	-	X	-
Acoustic	E417.11(d)	-	X	-
Random Vibration	E417.11(c)	-	X	-
Explosive Atmosphere	E417.11(k)	-	X	-
Safe-and-Arm Transition	E417.25(c)	-	X	-
Stall	E417.25(d)	-	X	-

X-ray	E417.5(f)	-	X	-
Leakage [7]	E417.5(h)	-	X	-
Internal Inspection	E417.5(g)	-	2	-
Firing Tests:	E417.25(j)(1)			
Operating Current:	E417.25(j)(3)			
High-temperature	E417.25(j)(6)	-	2	-
Low-temperature	E417.25(j)(7)	-	2	-

(1) Each sample safe-and-arm device to undergo qualification testing must first successfully complete all acceptance tests required by table E417.25-1.

(2) A component must undergo this test before the first and after the last operating environment test.

(3) A component must undergo this test during each operating environment test.

(4) One safe-and-arm device must undergo the extended stall and abnormal drop tests designated with an X.

(5) The same six sample safe-and-arm devices must undergo each test designated with an X. For a test designated with a quantity of less than six, each safe-and-arm device tested must be one of the original six sample components.

(6) One safe-and-arm device must undergo the containment test and two safe-and-arm devices must under go the barrier functionality test. The safe-and-arm device samples used for these tests need not be flight safe-and-arm devices. The test samples must duplicate all dimensions of a flight safe-and-arm device, including gaps between explosive components, free-volume, and diaphragm thickness.

(7) An unsealed component that has successfully completed salt-fog, humidity, fungus resistance, and fine sand qualification tests need not undergo a leakage test.

Table E417.25-3

Electro-explosive Device Lot Acceptance	Section	Quantity Tested
Component Examination:	E417.5	
Visual Examination	E417.5(b)	100%
Dimension Measurement	E417.5(c)	100%
Leakage	E417.5(h)	100%
X-ray and N-ray	E417.5(f)	100%
Performance Verification:	E417.3(d)	
Static Discharge	E417.25(i)	100%
Electro-explosive Device Status-of-Health	E417.25(h)	100%
Non-Operating Environment Tests and	E417.9	
Operating Environment Tests:	E417.11	
Thermal Cycling (1)	E417.11(h)	Lot Sample (3)
High-temperature Storage (2)	E417.9(c)	Lot Sample
Shock (1)	E417.11(e)	Lot Sample
Random Vibration (1)	E417.11(c)	Lot Sample
No Fire Verification	E417.25(p)	Lot Sample
Performance Verification:	E417.3(d)	
Status-of-Health	E417.25(h)	Lot Sample
Component Examination:	E415.5	
Visual Examination	E417.5(b)	Lot Sample
Leakage	E417.5(h)	Lot Sample
X-ray and N-ray	E417.5(f)	Lot Sample

Firing Tests:	E417.25(j)(1)	
Ambient-temperature:	E417.25(j)(5)	
All-Fire Current	E417.25(j)(2)	1/6 Lot Sample
Operating Current	E417.25(j)(3)	1/6 Lot Sample
High-temperature:	E417.25(j)(6)	
All-Fire Current	E417.25(j)(2)	1/6 Lot Sample
Operating Current	E417.25(j)(3)	1/6 Lot Sample
Low-temperature:	E417.25(j)(7)	
All-Fire Current	E417.25(j)(2)	1/6 Lot Sample
Operating Current	E417.25(j)(3)	1/6 Lot Sample

(1) This test must subject each electro-explosive device sample to the qualification environmental test level. For an electro-explosive device that is internal to a safe-and-arm device, the test level must be no less than the environment that the electro-explosive device experiences when installed and the safe-and-arm device is subjected to its qualification environment.

(2) A high-temperature storage test is optional. A lot will have an initial service-life of three years if it passes this test and all the required tests. A lot will have an initial service-life of one year if it passes all the required tests, but does not undergo this test.

(3) The lot sample quantity must be no less than 10 percent of the production lot or 30 sample electro-explosive devices, whichever is greater.

Table E417.25-4

Electro-explosive Device	Section	Quantity Tested (5) X=				
		5	SS (6)	SS (7)	SS (8)	105
Component Examination:	E417.5					
Visual Examination	E417.5(b)	X	X	X	X	X
Dimension Measurement	E417.5(c)	X	X	X	X	X
Leakage	E417.5(h)	X	X	X	X	X
X-ray and N-ray	E417.5(f)	X	X	X	X	X
Performance Verification:	E417.3(d)					
Static Discharge	E417.25(i)	X	X	X	X	X
Electro-expl. Dev. Status-of-Health	E417.25(h)	X	X	X	X	X
Component Examination:	E417.5	X	X	X	X	X
Visual Examination	E417.5(b)	X	X	X	X	X
Dimension Measurement	E417.5(c)	X	X	X	X	X
Leakage	E417.5(h)	X	X	X	X	X
X-ray and N-ray	E417.5(f)	X	X	X	X	X
Radio Frequency Impedance	E417.25(k)	-	10	-	-	-
Radio Frequency Sensitivity	E417.25(l)	-	X	-	-	-
No-Fire Level	E417.25(m)	-	-	X	-	-
All-Fire Level	E417.25(n)	-	-	-	X	-
Non-Operating Environment Tests and	E417.9					

Electro-explosive Device Qualification [1]	**Section E417.7**	**Quantity Tested** [5] **X=**				
		5	**SS** [6]	**SS** [7]	**SS** [8]	**105**
Operating Environment Tests:	E417.11	-	-	-	-	X
Thermal Cycling [2]	E417.11(h)	-	-	-	-	30
High-temperature Storage [3]	E417.9(c)	-	-	-	-	X
Shock [2]	E417.11(e)	-	-	-	-	X
Random Vibration [2]	E417.11(c)	-	-	-	-	30
No-Fire Verification	E417.25(p)	-	-	-	-	30
Tensile Load [4]	E417.9(j)	X	-	-	-	-
Auto Ignition	E417.25(q)					
Performance Verification	E417.3(d)					
Static Discharge	E417.25(i)	-	-	-	-	X
Status-of-Health	E417.25(h)	-	-	-	-	X
Component Examination	E415.5					
Visual Examination	E417.5(b)	---	-	-	-	X
Leakage	E417.5(h)		-	-	-	X
X-ray and N-ray	E417.5(f)		-	-	-	X

Firing Tests:	E417.25(j)(1)					
Ambient-temperature:	E417.25(j)(5)					
All-Fire Current [9]	E417.25(j)(2)	-	-	-	-	15
Operating Current [9]	E417.25(j)(3)	-	-	-	-	15
22-Amps Current	E417.25(j)(4)	-	-	-	-	5
High-temperature:	E417.25(j)(6)					
All-Fire Current [9]	E417.25(j)(2)	-	-	-	-	15
Operating Current [9]	E417.25(j)(3)	-	-	-	-	15
22-Amps Current	E417.25(j)(4)	-	-	-	-	5
Low-temperature:	E417.25(j)(7)					
All-Fire Current [9]	E417.25(j)(2)	-	-	-	-	15
Operating Current [9]	E417.25(j)(3)	-	-	-	-	15
22-Amps Current	E417.25(j)(4)	-	-	-	-	5

(1) All sample electro-explosive devices to undergo qualification testing must be from a production lot that has passed the lot acceptance tests required by Table E417.25-3.

(2) This test must subject each electro-explosive device sample to the qualification environmental test level. For an electro-explosive device that is internal to a safe-and-arm device, the test level must be no less than the environment that the electro-explosive device experiences when installed in a safe-and-arm device subjected to the safe-and-arm device's qualification environment.

(3) A high-temperature storage test is optional. A lot will have an initial service-life of three years if it passes this test and all the required tests. A lot will have an

initial service-life of one year if it passes all the required tests, but does not undergo this test.

(4) This test is not required if any other test verifies that each electro-explosive device is not damaged during installation.

(5) For each column, the quantity required at the top of the column must be from the same production lot and must be subjected to each test designated with an X. For a test designated with a lessor quantity, each sample tested must be one of the original samples for that column.

(6) For the designated column, SS (statistical sample) must be the quantity of sample components needed to perform a statistical firing series to determine the radio frequency sensitivity of the electro-explosive device and must be no less than 10 samples. Each sample component must undergo each test designated with an X.

(7) For the designated column, SS must be the quantity of sample components needed to perform a statistical firing series to determine the electro-explosive device's no-fire energy level. Each sample component must undergo each test designated with an X.

(8) For the designated column, SS must be the quantity of sample components needed to perform a statistical firing series to determine the electro-explosive device's all-fire energy level. Each sample component must undergo each test designated with an X.

(9) All the electro-explosive device samples that undergo the high-temperature storage test, no-fire verification test, or tensile load test must be evenly distributed between each all-fire current and operating current firing test.

Table E417.25-5

Electro-explosive Device Service-life Extension [5]	Section E417.15	Quantity Tested [2]	
		1 Year [3] X=5	3 Years [4] X=10
Component Examination:	E417.5		
Visual Examination	E417.5(b)	X	X
Dimension Measurement	E417.5(c)	X	X
Leakage	E417.5(h)	X	X
X-ray and N-ray	E417.5(f)	X	X
Performance Verification:	E417.3(d)		
Static Discharge	E417.25(i)	X	X
Electro-explosive Device Status-of-Health	E417.25(h)	X	X
Non-Operating Environment Tests and	E417.9		
Operating Environment Tests:	E417.11		
Thermal Cycling [1]	E417.11(h)	X	X
High-temperature Storage	E417.9(c)	-	X
Shock [1]	E417.11(e)	X	X
Random Vibration [1]	E417.11(c)	X	X
Performance Verification:	E417.3(d)		
Electro-explosive Device Status-of-Health	E417.25(h)	X	X
Component Examination:	E417.5		
Visual Examination	E417.5(b)	X	X
Leakage	E417.5(h)	X	X
X-ray and N-ray	E417.5(f)	X	X

Firing Tests:	E417.25(j)(1)		
All-Fire Current:	E417.25(j)(2)		
Ambient-temperature	E417.25(j)(5)	1	3
High-temperature	E417.25(j)(6)	2	3
Low-temperature	E417.25(j)(7)	2	4

(1) This test must subject each electro-explosive device sample to the qualification environmental test level. For an electro-explosive device that is internal to a safe-and-arm device, the test level must be no less than the environment that the electro-explosive device experiences when installed in a safe-and-arm device subjected to the safe-and-arm device's qualification environment.

(2) For each column, the quantity of sample electro-explosive devices required at the top of the column must be from the same production lot and must undergo each test designated with an X. For a test designated with a lessor quantity, each electro-explosive device tested must be one of the original samples for that column.

(3) Five electro-explosive devices from the same lot must undergo the tests required by this column to extend the service-life of the remaining electro-explosive devices from the same lot for one year.

(4) Ten electro-explosive devices from the same lot must undergo the tests required by this column to extend the service-life of the remaining electro-explosive devices from the same lot for three years.

(5) In order to extend the service-life of an electro-explosive device, the device must undergo the tests required by the one-year column or the three-year column before the device's initial service-life or any previous service-life extension expires.

Table E417.25-6

Safe-and-Arm Rotor Lead and Booster Charge Lot Acceptance [(1)]	Section E417.13(a)	Quantity Tested
Component Examination:	E417.5	
Visual Examination	E417.5(b)	100%
Dimension Measurement	E417.5(c)	100%
Leakage	E417.5(h)	100%
X-ray and N-ray	E417.5(f)	100%
Non-Operating Environment Tests and	E417.9	
Operating Environment Tests:	E417.11	
Thermal Cycling [(2)]	E417.11(h)	Lot Sample [(4)]
High-temperature Storage [(3)]	E417.9(c)	Lot Sample
Component Examination:	E417.5	
Leakage	E417.5(h)	Lot Sample
X-ray and N-ray	E417.5(f)	Lot Sample
Firing Tests:	E417.25(j)(1)	
High-temperature	E417.25(j)(6)	½ Lot Sample [(5)]
Low-temperature	E417.25(j)(7)	½ Lot Sample [(6)]

(1) This table applies to any rotor lead or booster charge that is used by a safe-and-arm device.

(2) This test must subject each ordnance sample to the qualification environmental test level. For ordnance that is internal to a safe-and-arm device, the test level must be no less than the environment that the ordnance experiences when installed and the safe-and-arm device is subjected to its qualification environment.

(3) A lot will have an initial service-life of five years if it passes this test and all the required tests. A lot will have an initial service-life of one year if it passes all the required tests, but does not undergo this test.

(4) The lot sample quantity must be no less than 10 percent of the lot or nine sample units from the lot, whichever is greater.

(5) For this test, the quantity must be no less than one half the lot sample quantity rounded down to the nearest whole number.

(6) For this test, the quantity must be no less than one half the lot sample quantity rounded up to the nearest whole number.

Table E417.25-7

Safe-and-Arm Rotor Lead and Booster Charge Qualification [1]	Section E417.7	Quantity [4] Tested X=21
Component Examination:	E417.5	
Visual Examination	E417.5(b)	X
Dimension Measurement	E417.5(c)	X
Leakage	E417.5(h)	X
X-ray and N-ray	E417.5(f)	X
Non-Operating and	E417.9	
Operating Environment Tests:	E417.11	
Thermal Cycling [2]	E417.11(h)	X
High-temperature Storage [3]	E417.9(c)	10
Shock [2]	E417.11(e)	X
Random Vibration [2]	E417.11(c)	X
Component Examination:	E417.5	
X-ray and N-ray	E417.5(f)	X
Leakage	E417.5(h)	X
Firing Tests:	E417.25(j)(1)	
Ambient-temperature	E417.25(j)(5)	7
High-temperature	E417.25(j)(6)	7
Low-temperature	E417.25(j)(7)	7

(1) This table applies to any rotor lead or booster charge that is used by a safe-and-arm device.

(2) This test must subject each ordnance sample to the qualification environmental test level. For ordnance that is internal to a safe-and-arm device, the test level must be no less than the actual environment that the ordnance experiences when installed and the safe-and-arm device is subjected to its qualification environment.

(3) A lot will have an initial service-life of five years if it passes this test and all the required tests. A lot will have an initial service-life of one year if it passes all the required tests, but does not undergo this test.

(4) The same 21 sample components, from the same production lot, must undergo each test designated with an X. For a test designated with a quantity of less than 21, each component sample tested must be one of the original 21 samples.

Table E417.25-8

Safe-and-Arm Rotor Lead and Booster Charge Service-life Extension [(1)]	Section E417.15	Quantity Tested [(3)] 1 Year [(4)] X=5	Quantity Tested [(3)] 5 Years [(5)] X=10
Component Examination:	E417.5		
Visual Examination	E417.5(b)	X	X
Dimension Measurement	E417.5(c)	X	X
Leakage	E417.5(h)	X	X
X-ray and N-ray	E417.5(f)	X	X
Non-Operating and Operating Environment Tests:	E417.9 E417.11		
Thermal Cycling [(2)]	E417.11(h)	X	X
High-temperature Storage	E417.9(c)	-	X
Component Examination:	E417.5		
Leakage	E417.5(h)	X	X
X-ray and N-ray	E417.5(f)	X	X
Firing Tests:	E417.25(j)(1)		
High-temperature	E417.25(j)(6)	2	5
Low-temperature	E417.25(j)(7)	3	5

[(1)] This table applies to any rotor lead or booster charge that is used by a safe-and-arm device. In order to extend the service-life of a rotor lead or booster charge, the rotor lead or charge must undergo each test required by the one-year column or the five-year column before its initial service-life or any previous service-life extension expires.

(2) This test must subject each ordnance sample to the qualification environmental test level. For ordnance that is internal to a safe-and-arm device, the test level must be no less than the actual environment that the ordnance experiences when installed and the safe-and-arm device is subjected to its qualification environment.

(3) For each column, the quantity of sample components required at the top of the column must be from the same production lot and must undergo each test designated with an X. For a test designated with a lessor quantity, each component tested must be one of the original samples for that column.

(4) Five ordnance samples from the same lot must undergo the tests required by this column to extend the service-life of the remaining ordnance from the same lot for one year.

(5) Ten ordnance samples from the same lot must undergo the tests required by this column to extend the service-life of the remaining ordnance from the same lot for five years.

(b) *Safe-and-arm device status-of-health.* A safe-and-arm device status-of-health test must satisfy section E417.3(f). This must include measuring insulation resistance from pin-to-pin and pin-to-case, safe-and-arm transition time, and bridgewire resistance consistency through more than one safe-and-arm transition cycle.

(c) *Safe-and-arm transition.* This test must demonstrate that the safe-and-arm transition, such as rotational or sliding operation, satisfies all its performance specifications. This must include all of the following:

(1) The test must demonstrate that the safe-and-arm monitors accurately determine safe-and-arm transition and whether the safe-and-arm device is in the proper configuration;

(2) The test must demonstrate that a safe-and-arm device is not susceptible to inadvertent initiation or degradation in performance of the electro-explosive device during pre-flight processing; and

(3) The test must demonstrate the ability of a safe-and-arm device to satisfy all its performance specifications when subjected to five times the maximum predicted number of safe-to-arm and arm-to-safe cycles.

(d) *Stall.* A stall test must demonstrate that a safe-and-arm device satisfies all its performance specifications after being locked in its safe position and subjected to an operating arming voltage for the greater of:

(i) Five minutes; or

(ii) The maximum time that could occur inadvertently and the device still be used for flight.

(e) *Safety tests.* The following safety tests must demonstrate that a safe-and-arm device can be handled safely:

(1) *Containment.* A containment test must demonstrate that a safe-and-arm device will not fragment when any internal electro-explosive device or rotor charge is initiated. A safe-and-arm device must undergo the test in

the arm position and with any shipping cap or plug installed in each output port.

(2) *Barrier functionality.* A barrier functionality test must demonstrate that, when in the safe position, if a safe-and-arm device's internal electro-explosive device is initiated, the ordnance output will not propagate to an explosive transfer system. This demonstration must include all of the following:

(i) The test must consist of firings at high and low temperature extremes, the explosive transfer system must be configured for flight;

(ii) Each high-temperature firing must be initiated at the manufacturer specified high temperature or a 71 °C workmanship screening level, whichever is higher; and

(iii) Each low-temperature firing must be initiated at the manufacturer specified low temperature or a −54 °C workmanship screening level, whichever is lower.

(3) *Extended stall.* An extended stall test must demonstrate that a safe-and-arm device does not initiate when locked in its safe position and is subjected to a continuous operating arming voltage for the maximum predicted time that could occur accidentally or one hour, whichever is greater.

(4) *Manual safing.* A manual safing test must demonstrate that a safe-and-arm device can be manually safed in accordance with all its performance specifications.

(5) *Safing-interlock.* A safing-interlock test must demonstrate that when a safe-and-arm device's safing-interlock is in place and operational arming current is applied, the interlock prevents arming in accordance with all the interlock's performance specifications.

(6) *Safing verification.* A safing verification test must demonstrate that, while a safe-and-arm device is in the safe position, any internal electro-explosive device will not initiate if the safe-and-arm device input circuit is accidentally subjected to a firing voltage, such as from a command receiver or inadvertent separation destruct system output.

(f) *Thermal performance.* A thermal performance test must demonstrate that a safe-and-arm device satisfies all its performance specifications when subjected to operating and workmanship thermal environments. This demonstration must include all of the following:

(1) The safe-and-arm device must undergo the test while subjected to each required thermal environment;

(2) The test must continuously monitor the bridgewire continuity with the safe-and-arm device in its arm position to detect each and any variation in amplitude. Any variation in amplitude constitutes a test failure;

(3) The test must measure the bridgewire resistance for the first and last thermal cycle during the high and low temperature dwell times to demonstrate that the bridgewire resistance satisfies the manufacturer specification;

(4) The test must subject the safe-and-arm device to five safe-and-arm cycles and measure the bridgewire continuity during each cycle to demonstrate that the continuity is consistent; and

(5) The test must measure the safe-and-arm cycle time to demonstrate that it satisfies the manufacturer specification.

(g) *Dynamic performance.* A dynamic performance test must demonstrate that a safe-and-arm device satisfies all its performance specifications when subjected to the dynamic operational environments, such as vibration and shock. This demonstration must include all of the following:

(1) The safe-and-arm device must undergo the test while subjected to each required dynamic operational environment;

(2) The test must continuously monitor the bridgewire continuity with the safe-and-arm device in the arm position to detect each and any variation in amplitude. Any amplitude variation constitutes a test failure. The monitoring must have a sample rate that will detect any component performance degradation;

(3) The test must continuously monitor each safe-and-arm device monitor circuit to detect each and any variation in amplitude. Any variation in amplitude constitutes a test failure. This monitoring must have a sample rate that will detect any component performance degradation; and

(4) The test must continuously monitor the safe-and-arm device to demonstrate that it remains in the fully armed position throughout all dynamic environment testing.

(h) *Electro-explosive device status-of-health.* An electro-explosive device status of health test must satisfy section E417.3(f). The test must include measuring insulation resistance and bridgewire continuity.

(i) *Static discharge.* A static discharge test must demonstrate that an electro-explosive device can withstand an electrostatic discharge that it could experience from personnel or conductive surfaces without firing and still satisfy all its performance specifications. The test must subject the electro-explosive device to the greater of:

(1) A 25k-volt, 500-picofarad pin-to-pin discharge through a 5k ohm resistor and a 25k-volt, 500-picofarad pin-to-case discharge with no resistor; or

(2) The maximum predicted pin-to-pin and pin-to-case electrostatic discharges.

(j) *Firing tests.* (1) *General.* Each firing test of a safe-and-arm device, electro-explosive device, rotor lead, or booster charge must satisfy all of the following:

(i) The test must demonstrate the initiation and transfer of all ordnance charges and that the component does not fragment. For a safe-and-arm device that has more than one internal electro-explosive device, each firing test must also demonstrate that the initiation of one internal electro-explosive device does not adversely affect the performance of any other internal electro-explosive device;

(ii) The number of component samples that the test must fire and the test conditions, including firing current and temperature must satisfy each table of this section;

(iii) Before initiation, each component sample must experience the required temperature for enough time to achieve thermal equilibrium;

(iv) Each test must measure ordnance output using a measuring device, such as a swell cap or dent block, to demonstrate that the output satisfies all its performance specifications; and

(v) Each test of a safe-and-arm device or electro-explosive device must subject each sample device to a current source that duplicates the operating output waveform and impedance of the flight current source. Each test of a rotor lead or booster charge must subject the component to an energy source that simulates the flight energy source.

(2) *All-fire current.* Each all-fire current test must subject each component sample to the manufacturer's specified all-fire current value.

(3) *Operating current.* Each operating current test must subject each component sample to the launch vehicle operating current value if known at the time of testing. If the operating current is unknown, the test must use no less than 200% of the all-fire current value.

(4) *22-amps current.* This test must subject each component sample to a firing current of 22 amps.

(5) *Ambient-temperature.* This test must initiate each ordnance sample while it is subjected to ambient-temperature.

(6) *High-temperature.* Each high-temperature test must initiate each ordnance sample while it is subjected to the qualification high-temperature level or a + 71 °C workmanship screening level, whichever is higher.

(7) *Low-temperature.* Each low-temperature test must initiate each ordnance sample while it is subjected to the qualification low-temperature level or a −54 °C workmanship screening level, whichever is lower.

(k) *Radio frequency impedance.* This test must determine the radio frequency impedance of an electro-explosive device for use in any flight termination system radio frequency susceptibility analysis.

(l) *Radio frequency sensitivity.* This test must consist of a statistical firing series of electro-explosive device lot samples to determine the radio frequency no-fire energy level for the remainder of the lot. The firing series must determine the highest continuous radio frequency energy level to which the device can be subjected and not fire with a reliability of 0.999 at a 95% confidence level. Any demonstrated radio frequency no-fire energy level that is less than the level used in the flight termination system design and analysis constitutes a test failure.

(m) *No-fire energy level.* This test must consist of a statistical firing series of electro-explosive device lot samples to determine the no-fire energy level for the remainder of the lot. The firing series must determine the highest electrical energy level at which the device will not fire with a reliability of 0.999 at a 95% confidence level when subjected to a continuous current pulse. Any demonstrated no-fire energy level that is less than the no-fire energy level used in the flight termination system design and analysis constitutes a test failure.

(n) *All-fire energy level.* This test must consist of a statistical firing series of electro-explosive device lot samples to determine the all-fire energy level for the remainder of the lot. This firing series must determine the lowest electrical energy level at which the device will fire with a reliability of 0.999 at a 95% confidence level when subjected to a current pulse that simulates the launch vehicle flight termination system firing characteristics. Any demonstrated all-fire energy level that exceeds the all-fire energy level used in the flight termination system design and analysis constitutes a test failure.

(o) *Barrier alignment.* A barrier alignment test must consist of a statistical firing series of safe-and-arm device samples. The test must demonstrate that the device's safe to arm transition motion provides for ordnance initiation with a reliability of 0.999 at a 95% confidence level. The test must also demonstrate that the device's arm to safe transition motion provides for no ordnance initiation with a reliability of 0.999 at a 95% confidence level. This test may employ a reusable safe-and-arm subassembly that simulates the flight configuration.

(p) *No-fire verification.* This test must demonstrate that a flight configured electro-explosive device will not inadvertently initiate when exposed to the maximum predicted circuit leakage current and will still satisfy all its performance specifications. The test must subject each sample electro-explosive device to the greater of:

(1) The worst-case leakage current level and duration that could occur in an operating condition; or

(2) One amp/one watt for five minutes.

(q) *Auto-ignition.* This test must demonstrate that an electro-explosive device does not experience auto-ignition, sublimation, or melting when subjected to any high-temperature environment during handling, testing, storage, transportation, installation, or flight. The test must include all of the following:

(1) The test environment must be no less than 30 °C higher than the highest non-operating or operating temperature that the device could experience;

(2) The test must last the maximum predicted high-temperature duration or one hour, whichever is greater; and

(3) After exposure to the test environment, each sample device must undergo external and internal examination, including any dissection needed to identify any auto-ignition, sublimation, or melting.

E417.27 EXPLODING BRIDGEWIRE FIRING UNITS AND EXPLODING BRIDGEWIRES

(a) *General.* This section applies to any exploding bridgewire firing unit that is part of a flight termination system, including each exploding bridgewire that is used by the firing unit. Any firing unit or exploding bridgewire must satisfy each test or analysis identified by any table of this section to demonstrate that it satisfies all its performance specifications when subjected to each non-operating and operating environment.

Table E417.27-1

Exploding Bridgewire Firing Unit Acceptance	Section E417.13	Quantity Tested
Component Examination:	E417.5	
Visual Examination	E417.5(b)	100%
Dimension Measurement	E417.5(c)	100%
Identification Check	E417.5(e)	100%
Performance Verification:	E417.3(d)	
Firing Unit Status-of-Health [(1)]	E417.27(b)	100%
Input Command Processing [(1)]	E417.27(c)	100%
High Voltage Circuitry [(1)]	E417.27(d)	100%
Output Monitoring [(1)]	E417.27(e)(1)	100%
Abbreviated Performance Verification:	E417.3(e)	
Abbreviated Status-of-Health [(2)]	E417.27(f)	100%
Abbreviated Command Processing [(2)]	E417.27(g)	100%
Output Monitoring [(2)]	E417.27(e)(2)	100%
Operating Environment Tests:	E417.13	
Thermal Cycling [(3)]	E417.13(d)	100%
Thermal Vacuum [(3)]	E417.13(e)	100%
Acoustic	E417.13(c)	100%
Random Vibration	E417.13(b)	100%
Leakage[(4)]	E417.5(h)	100%

(1) A component must undergo this test before the first and again after the last operating environment test.

(2) A component must undergo this test during each operating environment test.

(3) This test must include continuous monitoring of all abbreviated status-of-health parameters and output monitors during all thermal cycles and transitions.

(4) An unsealed component that has successfully completed salt-fog, humidity, fungus resistance, and fine sand qualification tests need not undergo a leakage test.

Table E417.27-2

Exploding Bridgewire Firing Unit Qualification	Section E417.7	Quantity Tested		
		X=1	X=1	X=1
Acceptance Tests [1]	*Table E417.27-1*	X	X	X
Performance Verification:	E417.3(d)			
Firing Unit Status-of-Health [2]	E417.27(b)	X	X	X
Input Command Processing [2]	E417.27(c)	X	X	X
High Voltage Circuitry [2]	E417.27(d)	X	X	X
Abbreviated Performance Verification:	E417.3(e)			
Abbreviated Status-of-Health [3]	E417.27(f)	X	X	X
Abbreviated Command Processing [3]	E417.27(g)	X	X	X
Output Monitoring [3]	E417.27(e)(2)	X	X	X
Non-Operating Environment Tests:	E417.9			
Storage Temperature	E417.9(b)	X	X	X
Transportation Shock	E417.9(d)	X	X	X
Bench Handling Shock	E417.9(e)	X	X	X
Transportation Vibration	E417.9(f)	X	X	X
Fungus Resistance	E417.9(g)	X	-	-
Salt Fog	E417.9(h)	X	-	-
Fine Sand	E417.9(I)	X	-	-
Operating Environment Tests:	E417.11			

Thermal Cycling [4]	E417.11(h)	X	X	X
Humidity	E417.11(g)	X	X	X
Thermal Vacuum [4]	E417.11(i)	X	X	X
Acceleration	E417.11(f)	X	X	X
Shock	E417.11(e)	X	X	X
Sinusoidal Vibration	E417.11(b)	X	X	X
Acoustic	E417.11(d)	X	X	X
Random Vibration	E417.11(c)	X	X	X
Electromagnetic Interference and Compatibility	E417.11(j)	X	X	-
Explosive Atmosphere	E417.11(k)	-	X	-
Repetitive functioning	E417.27(i)	X	X	X
Circuit Protection	E417.27(h)	X	-	-
Leakage [5]	E417.5(h)	X	X	X
Internal Inspection	E417.5(g)	X	X	X

(1) Each qualification test component sample must successfully complete all acceptance tests before undergoing qualification testing.

(2) A component sample must undergo this test before the first and after the last environmental test.

(3) A component sample must undergo this test during each operating environment test.

(4) While undergoing this test, a component sample must undergo an abbreviated status-of-health test and output monitor test during all thermal cycles and transitions.

(5) An unsealed component that has successfully completed salt-fog, humidity, fungus resistance, and fine sand qualification tests need not undergo a leakage test.

Table E417.27-3

Exploding Bridgewire Lot Acceptance	Section	Quantity Tested
Component Examination and	E417.5	
Performance Verification:	E417.3(d)	
Visual Examination	E417.5(b)	100%
Dimension Measurement	E417.5(c)	100%
Static Discharge	E417.27(j)	100%
Exploding Bridgewire Status-of-Health	E417.27(k)	100%
Safety Devices (1)	E417.27(l)	100%
Leakage	E417.5(h)	100%
X-ray and N-ray	E417.5(f)	100%
Non Operating Environment Tests and	E417.9	
Operating Environment Tests:	E417.11	
Thermal Cycling (2)	E417.11(h)	Lot Sample (4)
High-temperature Storage (3)	E417.9(c)	Lot Sample
Shock (2)	E417.11(e)	Lot Sample
Random Vibration (2)	E417.11(c)	Lot Sample
Component Examination and	E417.5	
Performance Verification:	E417.3(d)	
Exploding Bridgewire Status-of-health	E417.27(k)	Lot Sample
Safety Devices (1)	E417.27(l)	Lot Sample
Leakage	E417.5(h)	Lot Sample
X-ray and N-ray	E417.5(f)	Lot Sample

Firing Tests:	E417.27(m)(1)	
Ambient-temperature:	E417.27(m)(5)	
All-Fire Voltage	E417.27(m)(2)	1/6 Lot Sample
Operating Voltage	E417.27(m)(3)	1/6 Lot Sample
High-temperature:	E417.27(m)(6)	
All-Fire Voltage	E417.27(m)(2)	1/6 Lot Sample
Operating Voltage	E417.27(m)(3)	1/6 Lot Sample
Low-temperature:	E417.27(m)(7)	
All-Fire Voltage	E417.27(m)(2)	1/6 Lot Sample
Operating Voltage	E417.27(m)(3)	1/6 Lot Sample

(1) An exploding bridgewire must undergo this test only if it contains internal protection circuitry such as a spark gap.

(2) This test must subject a component sample to the qualification test environmental level.

(3) A high-temperature storage test is optional. A lot will have an initial service-life of three years if it passes this test and all the required tests. A lot will have an initial service-life of one year if it passes all the required tests, but does not undergo this test.

(4) The lot sample quantity must be no less than 10 percent of the production lot or 30 sample exploding bridgewires; whichever is greater.

Table E417.27-4

Exploding Bridgewire Qualification	Section	Quantity Tested [4] X=				
		5	SS [5]	SS [6]	SS [7]	105
Lot Acceptance Tests [1]	Table E417.27-3					
Component Examination and	E417.5					
Performance Verification:	E417.3(d)	X	X	X	X	X
Visual Examination	E417.5(b)	X	X	X	X	X
Dimension Measurement	E417.5(c)	X	X	X	X	X
Static Discharge	E417.27(j)	X	X	X	X	X
Expl. Bridgewire Status-of-Health	E417.27(k)	X	X	X	X	X
Safety Devices [2]	E417.27(l)	X	X	X	X	X
Leakage	E417.5(h)	X	X	X	X	X
X-ray and N-ray	E417.5(f)					
Radio Frequency Impedance	E417.27(n)	-	10	-	-	-
Radio Frequency Sensitivity	E417.27(o)	-	X	-	-	-
No-Fire Energy Level	E417.27(p)	-	-	X	-	-
All-Fire Energy Level	E417.27(q)	-	-	-	X	-
Non-Operating Environment Tests and	E417.9					
Operating Environment Tests:	E417.11					

Exploding Bridgewire Qualification	Section	Quantity Tested [4] X=				
		5	SS [5]	SS [6]	SS [7]	105
Storage Temperature	E417.9(b)	-	-	-	-	X
Transportation Shock	E417.9(d)	-	-	-	-	X
Bench Handling Shock	E417.9(e)	-	-	-	-	X
Transportation Vibration	E417.9(f)	-	-	-	-	X
Fungus Resistance	E417.9(g)	-	-	-	-	5
Salt Fog	E417.9(h)	-	-	-	-	5
Fine Sand	E417.9(I)	-	-	-	-	5
Thermal Cycling	E417.11(h)	-	-	-	-	X
High-temperature Storage [3]	E417.9(c)	-	-	-	-	30
Shock	E417.11(e)	-	-	-	-	X
Random Vibration	E417.11(c)	-	-	-	-	X
Handling Drop	E417.9(k)	-	-	-	-	X
Tensile Load	E417.9(j)	X	-	-	-	-
Abnormal Drop	E417.9(l)	X	-	-	-	-
Auto Ignition	E417.27(r)	X	-	-	-	-
Component Examination and Performance Verification:	E417.5 E417.3(d)					
Expl. Bridgewire Status-of-health	E417.27(k)	-	-	-	-	X
Safety Devices [2]	E417.27(l)	-	-	-	-	X
Leakage	E417.5(h)	-	-	-	-	X
X-ray and N-ray	E417.5(f)	-	-	-	-	X

Firing Tests:	E417.27(m)(1)					
Ambient-temperature:	E417.27(m)(5)					
All-Fire Voltage	E417.27(m)(2)	-	-	-	-	15
Operating Voltage	E417.27(m)(3)	-	-	-	-	15
Twice-Operating Voltage	E417.27(m)(4)	-	-	-	-	5
High-temperature:	E417.27(m)(6)					
All-Fire Voltage	E417.27(m)(2)	-	-	-	-	15
Operating Voltage	E417.27(m)(3)	-	-	-	-	15
Twice-Operating Voltage	E417.27(m)(4)	-	-	-	-	5
Low-temperature:	E417.27(m)(7)					
All-Fire Voltage	E417.27(m)(2)	-	-	-	-	15
Operating Voltage	E417.27(m)(3)	-	-	-	-	15
Twice-Operating Voltage	E417.27(m)(4)	-	-	-	-	5

(1) All sample-exploding bridgewire samples used in qualification testing must be from a production lot that has passed the lot acceptance tests required by table E417.27-3.

(2) An exploding bridgewire must undergo this test only if it contains internal protection circuitry such as a spark gap.

(3) A high-temperature storage test is optional. A lot will have an initial service-life of three years if it passes this test and all the required tests. A lot will have an initial service-life of one year if it passes all the required tests, but does not undergo this test.

(4) For each column, the quantity required at the top of the column must be from the same production lot and must undergo each test designated with an X. For a test

designated with a lessor quantity, each sample exploding bridgewire tested must be one of the original samples for the column.

(5) The statistical sample (SS) must be the quantity of sample components needed to perform a statistical firing series to determine the radio frequency sensitivity of the exploding bridgewire. Each sample component must undergo each test designated with an X. The statistical sample quantity must be no less than 10 sample components, which is the minimum required to undergo the radio frequency impedance test.

(6) The statistical sample (SS) must be the quantity of sample components needed to perform a statistical firing series to determine the electro exploding bridgewire's no-fire energy level. Each sample component must undergo each test designated with an X.

(7) The statistical sample (SS) must be the quantity of sample components needed to perform a statistical firing series to determine the exploding bridgewire's all-fire energy level. Each sample component must undergo each test designated with an X.

Table E417.27-5

Exploding Bridgewire Service-life Extension [6]	Section E417.15	Quantity Tested [3] 1 Year [4] X=5	3 Years [5] X=10
Component examination and Performance Verification:	E417.5 E417.3(d)		
Visual Examination	E417.5(b)	X	X
Dimension Measurement	E417.5(c)	X	X
Static Discharge	E417.27(j)	X	X
Exploding Bridgewire Status-of-Health	E417.27(k)	X	X
Safety Devices [2]	E417.27(l)	X	X
Leakage	E417.5(h)	X	X
X-ray and N-ray	E417.5(f)	X	X
Non-Operating Environment Tests and Operating Environment Tests:	E417.9 E417.11		
Thermal Cycling [1]	E417.11(h)	X	X
High-temperature Storage	E417.9(c)	-	X
Shock [1]	E417.11(e)	X	X
Random Vibration [1]	E417.11(c)	X	X
Component examination and Performance Verification:	E417.5 E417.3(d)		
X-ray and N-ray	E417.5(f)	X	X
Exploding Bridgewire Status-of-Health	E417.27(k)	X	X
Safety Devices [2]	E417.27(l)	X	X
Leakage	E417.5(h)	X	X

Firing Tests:	E417.27(m)(1)		
All-Fire Voltage:	E417.27(m)(2)		
Ambient-temperature	E417.27(m)(5)	1	3
High-temperature	E417.27(m)(6)	2	3
Low-temperature	E417.27(m)(7)	2	4

(1) This test must subject each component sample to the qualification environmental level.

(2) An exploding bridgewire must undergo this test only it contains internal protection circuitry such as a spark gap.

(3) For each column, the component samples required at the top of the column must be from the same production lot and each component sample must undergo each test designated with an X. For a test designated with a lessor quantity, each sample exploding bridgewire tested must be one of the original samples for the column.

(4) Five exploding bridgewires from the same lot must undergo each test designated with an X to extend the service-life of the remaining exploding bridgewires from the same lot for one year.

(5) Ten exploding bridgewires from the same lot must undergo each test designated with an X to extend the service-life of the remaining exploding bridgewires from the same lot for three years.

(6) In order to extend an exploding bridgewire's service-life, the bridgewire must undergo the tests required by the one-year column or the three-year column before its initial service-life or any previous service-life extension expires.

(b) *Firing unit status-of-health.* A firing unit status-of-health test must satisfy section E417.3(f). This must include measuring input current, all pin-to-pin and pin-to-case resistances, trigger circuit threshold, capacitor charge time and arming time.

(c) *Input command processing.* An input command processing test must demonstrate that an exploding bridgewire firing unit's input trigger circuit satisfies all its performance specifications when subjected to any variation in input that it could experience during flight. The firing unit must undergo this test before the first and after the last environmental test to identify any degradation in performance due to any of the test environments. The test must demonstrate all of the following:

(1) The amplitude sensitivity of the firing unit trigger circuit provides margin over the worst-case trigger signal that could be delivered on the launch vehicle as follows:

(i) The firing unit triggers at 50% of the amplitude and 50% of the pulse duration of the lowest trigger signal that could be delivered during flight; and

(ii) The firing unit triggers at 120% amplitude and 120% of the pulse duration of the highest trigger signal that could be delivered during flight;

(2) The firing unit satisfies all its performance specifications when subjected to the maximum input voltage of the open circuit voltage of the power source, ground or airborne, and the minimum input voltage of the loaded voltage of the power source;

(3) Each control and switching circuit that is critical to the reliable operation of an exploding bridgewire firing unit does not change state when subjected to a minimum input power drop-out for a period of 50 milliseconds;

(4) The firing unit's response time satisfies all its performance specifications with input at the specified minimum and maximum vehicle supplied trigger signal; and

(5) If the firing unit has differential input, the unit satisfies all its performance specifications with all input combinations at the specified trigger amplitude input signals.

(d) *High voltage circuitry.* This test must demonstrate that a firing unit's high voltage circuitry satisfies all its performance specifications for initiating the exploding bridgewire when subjected to any variation in input that the circuitry could experience during flight. The firing unit must undergo the test before the first and after the last environmental test to identify any degradation in performance due to any of the test environments. The test must demonstrate all of the following:

(1) The firing unit satisfies all its performance specifications when subjected to the worst-case high and low arm voltages that it could experience during flight;

(2) The firing unit's charging and output circuitry has an output waveform, rise-time, and amplitude that delivers no less than a 50% voltage margin to the exploding bridgewire. The test must use the identical parameters, such as capacitor values and circuit and load impedance, as those used to provide the exploding bridgewire all-fire energy level;

(3) The firing unit does not experience any arcing or corona during high voltage discharge; and

(4) Each high-energy trigger circuit used to initiate the main firing capacitor has an output signal that delivers no less than a 50% voltage margin with an input to the circuit at the nominal trigger threshold level.

(e) *Output monitoring.* (1) An output monitoring test must measure the voltage of each high voltage capacitor and the arm power to a firing unit and demonstrate that it satisfies all its performance specifications.

(2) An output monitoring test conducted while the firing unit is subjected to an operating environment, must continuously monitor the voltage of each high voltage capacitor and the arm power to the firing unit to detect any variation in amplitude. Any amplitude variation constitutes a test failure. The monitoring must use a sample rate that will detect any component performance degradation.

(f) *Abbreviated status-of-health.* An abbreviated status-of-health test must measure all a firing unit's critical performance parameters while the unit is subjected to each required operating environment to identify any degradation in performance while exposed to each environment. This must include continuous monitoring of the firing unit's input to detect any variation in amplitude. Any amplitude variation constitutes a test failure. The monitoring must have a sample rate that will detect any component performance degradation.

(g) *Abbreviated command processing.* An abbreviated command processing test must exercise all of a firing unit's flight critical functions while the unit is subjected to each required operating environment. This must include subjecting the firing unit to the fire command throughout each environment while monitoring function time and the high voltage output waveform to demonstrate that each satisfies all its performance specifications.

(h) *Circuit protection.* A circuit protection test must demonstrate that any circuit protection allows a firing unit to satisfy all its performance specifications, when subjected to any improper launch processing, abnormal flight condition, or any failure of another launch vehicle component. The demonstration must include all of the following:

(1) Any circuit protection allows an exploding bridgewire firing unit to satisfy all its performance specifications when subjected to the maximum input voltage of the open circuit voltage of the unit's power source and when subjected to the minimum input voltage of the loaded voltage of the power source;

(2) In the event of an input power dropout, any control or switching circuit that contributes to the reliable operation of an exploding bridgewire firing unit, including solid-state power transfer switches, does not change state for at least 50 milliseconds;

(3) Any watchdog circuit satisfies all its performance specifications;

(4) The firing unit satisfies all its performance specifications when any of its monitoring circuits' output ports are subjected to

a short circuit or the highest positive or negative voltage capable of being supplied by the monitor batteries or other power supplies; and

(5) The firing unit satisfies all its performance specifications when subjected to any reverse polarity voltage that could occur during launch processing.

(i) *Repetitive functioning.* This test must demonstrate that a firing unit satisfies all its performance specifications when subjected to repetitive functioning for five times the worst-case number of cycles required for acceptance, checkout and operations, including any retest due to schedule delays.

(j) *Static discharge.* A static discharge test must demonstrate that an exploding bridgewire will not fire and satisfies all its performance specifications when subjected to any electrostatic discharge that it could experience from personnel or conductive surfaces. The test must subject an exploding bridgewire to the greater of:

(1) A 25k-volt, 500-picofarad pin-to-pin discharge through a 5k-ohm resistor and a 25k-volt, 500-picofarad pin-to-case discharge with no resistor; or

(2) The maximum predicted pin-to-pin and pin-to-case electrostatic discharge.

(k) *Exploding bridgewire status-of-health.* An exploding bridgewire status-of-health test must satisfy section E417.3(f). This must include measuring the bridgewire insulation resistance at operating voltage.

(l) *Safety devices.* This test must demonstrate that any protection circuitry that is internal to an exploding bridgewire, such as a spark gap, satisfies all its performance specifications and will not degrade the bridgewire's performance or reliability when exposed to the qualification environments. The test must include static gap breakdown, dynamic gap breakdown, and specification hold-off voltage under sustained exposure.

(m) *Firing tests*—(1) *General.* Each firing test of an exploding bridgewire must satisfy all of the following:

(i) Each test must demonstrate that the exploding bridgewire satisfies all its performance specifications when subjected to qualification stress conditions;

(ii) The number of exploding bridgewire samples that each test must fire and the test conditions, including firing voltage and temperature, must satisfy each table of this section;

(iii) Before initiation, each component sample must experience the required temperature for enough time to achieve thermal equilibrium;

(iv) Each test must subject each exploding bridgewire sample to a high voltage initiation source that duplicates the exploding bridgewire firing unit output waveform and impedance, including high voltage cabling; and

(v) Each test must measure ordnance output using a measuring device, such as a swell cap or dent block, to demonstrate that the ordnance output satisfies all its performance specifications.

(2) *All-fire voltage.* Each all-fire voltage test must subject each exploding bridgewire sample to the manufacturer specified all-fire energy level for voltage, current, and pulse duration.

(3) *Operating voltage.* Each operating voltage test must subject each exploding bridgewire sample to the firing unit's manufacturer specified operating voltage, current, and pulse duration. If the operating energy is unknown, the test must use no less than 200% of the all-fire voltage.

(4) *Twice-operating voltage.* This test must subject each exploding bridgewire sample to 200% of the operating voltage.

(5) *Ambient-temperature.* This test must initiate each exploding bridgewire sample while at ambient temperature.

(6) *High-temperature.* Each high-temperature test must initiate each exploding bridgewire sample while it is subjected to the manufacturer specified high-temperature level or at a + 71 °C workmanship screening level, whichever is higher.

(7) *Low-temperature.* Each low-temperature test must initiate each exploding bridgewire sample while it is subjected to the manufacturer specified low-temperature level or at a −54 °C workmanship screening level, whichever is lower.

(n) *Radio frequency impedance.* A radio frequency impedance test must determine an exploding bridgewire's radio frequency impedance for use in any system radio frequency susceptibility analysis.

(o) *Radio frequency sensitivity.* A radio frequency sensitivity test must consist of a statistical firing series of exploding bridgewire lot samples to determine the radio frequency sensitivity of the exploding bridgewire. The test must demonstrate that the radio frequency no-fire energy level does not exceed the level used in the flight termination system design and analysis.

(p) *No-fire energy level.* A no-fire energy level test must consist of a statistical firing series of exploding bridgewire lot samples to determine the highest electrical energy level at which the exploding bridgewire will not fire with a reliability of 0.999 with a 95% confidence level when subjected to a continuous current pulse. The test must demonstrate that the no-fire energy level is no less than the no-fire energy level used in the flight termination system design and analysis.

(q) *All-fire energy level.* An all-fire energy level test must consist of a statistical firing series of exploding bridgewire lot samples to determine the lowest electrical energy level at which the exploding bridgewire will fire with a reliability of 0.999 with a 95% confidence level when subjected to a current pulse simulating the firing unit output waveform and impedance characteristics. Each exploding bridgewire sample must be in its flight configuration, and must possess any internal safety devices, such as a spark gap, employed in the flight configuration. The test must demonstrate that the all-fire energy level does not exceed the all-fire energy level used in the flight termination system design and analysis.

(r) *Auto-ignition.* This test must demonstrate that an exploding bridgewire does not experience auto-ignition, sublimation, or melting when subjected to any high-temperature environment during handling, testing, storage, transportation, installation, or flight. The test must include all of the following:

(1) The test environment must be no less than 30 °C higher than the highest non-operating or operating temperature that the device could experience;

(2) The test duration must be the maximum predicted high-temperature duration or one hour, whichever is greater; and

(3) After exposure to the test environment, each exploding bridgewire sample must undergo external and internal examination, including any dissection needed to identify any auto-ignition, sublimation, or melting.

E417.29 Ordnance interrupter

(a) *General.* This section applies to any ordnance interrupter that is part of a flight termination system, including any rotor lead or booster charge that is used by the interrupter. Any ordnance interrupter, rotor lead, or booster charge must satisfy each test or analysis identified by any table of this section to demonstrate that it satisfies all its performance specifications when subjected to each non-operating and operating environment.

Table E417.29-1

Ordnance Interrupter Acceptance	Section	Quantity Tested
Component Examination:	E417.5	
Visual Examination	E417.5(b)	100%
Dimension Measurement	E417.5(c)	100%
Identification Check	E417.5(e)	100%
Performance Verification:	E417.3(d)	
Status-of-Health [(1)]	E417.29(b)	100%
Safe-and-arm position monitor [(1)]	E417.29(c)	100%
Safety Tests:	E417.29(d)(1)	
Manual Safing	E417.29(d)(5)	100%
Safing-interlock	E417.29(d)(6)	100%
Abbreviated Performance Verification:	E417.3(e)	
Interrupter Abbreviated Performance [(2)]	E417.29(e)	100%
Operating Environment Tests:	E417.13	
Thermal Cycling	E417.13(d)	100%
Random Vibration	E417.13(b)	100%
X-ray	E417.5(f)	100%
Leakage [(3)]	E417.5(h)	100%

(1) A component must undergo this test before the first and again after the last environmental test.

(2) A component must undergo this test during each operating environment test.

(3) An unsealed component that has successfully completed salt-fog, humidity, fungus resistance, and fine sand qualification tests need not undergo a leakage test.

Table E417.29-2

Ordnance Interrupter Qualification	Section	Quantity Tested X=		
		1	6	3
Barrier Alignment	E417.29(g)			
Acceptance Tests	Table E417.29-1	X	X	-
Safety Tests:	E417.29(d)(1)			
Extended Stall [(1)]	E417.29(d)(4)	X	-	-
Abnormal Drop [(1)]	E417.9(1)	X	-	-
Containment	E417.29(d)(2)	-	-	1
Barrier Functionality	E417.29(d)(3)			
High-temperature	E417.29(d)(3)(i)	-	-	1
Low-temperature	E417.29(d)(3)(ii)	-	-	1
Non-Operating Environment Tests:	E417.9			
Storage Temperature	E417.9(b)	-	X	-
Transportation Shock	E417.9(d)	-	X	-
Bench Handling	E417.9(e)	-	X	-
Transportation Vibration	E417.9 (f)	-	X	-
Fungus Resistance	E417.9(g)	-	1	-
Salt Fog	E417.9(h)	-	1	-
Fine Sand	E417.9(i)	-	1	-
Handling Drop	E417.9(k)	-	X	-
Performance Verification:	E417.3(d)			
Status-of-Health [(2)]	E417.29(b)		X	
Abbreviated Performance Verification:	E417.3(e)			

Interrupter Abbreviated Performance [3]	E417.29(e)		X	
Operating Environment Tests:	E417.11			
Thermal Cycling	E417.11(h)	-	X	-
Humidity	E417.11(g)	-	X	-
Acceleration	E417.11(f)	-	X	-
Shock	E417.11(e)	-	X	-
Sinusoidal Vibration	E417.11(b)	-	X	-
Acoustic	E417.11(d)	-	X	-
Random Vibration	E417.11(c)	-	X	-
Explosive Atmosphere	E417.11(k)	-	X	-
Repetitive Function	E417.29(h)	-	X	-
Stall	E417.29(I)	-	X	-
X-ray	E417.5(f)	-	X	-
Leakage [4]	E417.5(h)	-	X	-
Internal Inspection	E417.5(g)	-	2	-
Firing Tests:	E417.29(f)(1)			
High-temperature	E417.29(f)(3)	-	2	-
Low-temperature	E417.29(f)(4)	-	2	-
	I			

(1) This test is only required for an ordnance interrupter that uses a rotor or booster charge.

(2) A component must undergo this test before the first and again after the last operating environment test.

(3) A component must undergo this test during each operating environment test.

(4) An unsealed component that has successfully completed salt-fog, humidity, fungus resistance, and fine sand qualification tests need not undergo a leakage test.

Table E417.29-3

Ordnance Interrupter Rotor Lead and Booster Charge Acceptance [(1)]	Section	Quantity Tested
Non-Destructive Component Examination:	E417.5	
Visual Examination	E417.5(b)	100%
Dimension Measurement	E417.5(c)	100%
Leakage	E417.5(h)	100%
X-ray and N-ray	E417.5(f)	100%
Non-Operating Environment Tests and	E417.9	
Operating Environment Tests:	E417.11	
Thermal Cycling [(2)]	E417.11(h)	Lot Sample [(4)]
High-temperature Storage [(3)]	E417.9(c)	Lot Sample
Component Examination:	E417.5	
Leakage	E417.5(h)	Lot Sample
X-ray and N-ray	E417.5(f)	Lot Sample
Firing Tests:	E417.29(f)(1)	
High-temperature	E417.29(f)(3)	½ Lot Sample
Low-temperature	E417.29(f)(4)	½ Lot Sample

(1) This table applies to any rotor lead or booster charge that is used by an ordnance interrupter.

(2) This test must subject the component to the qualification environmental test level. For a rotor lead or booster charge that is internal to an ordnance interrupter, the test level must be no less than the environment that the rotor lead or booster charge experiences when installed and the ordnance interrupter is subjected to the ordnance interrupter's qualification environment.

(3) A high-temperature storage test is optional. A lot will have an initial service-life of five years if it passes this test and all the required tests. A lot will have an initial service-life of one year if it passes all the required tests, but does not undergo this test.

(4) The lot sample quantity must be no less than 10 percent of the lot or 10 sample units, whichever is greater.

Table E417.29-4

Ordnance Interrupter Rotor Lead and Booster Charge Qualification [1]	**Section E417.7**	**Quantity Tested X=21** [4]
Component Examination:	E417.5	
Visual Examination	E417.5(b)	X
Dimension Measurement	E417.5(c)	X
Leakage	E417.5(h)	X
X-ray and N-ray	E417.5(f)	X
Non-Operating and	E417.9	
Operating Environment Tests:	E417.11	
Thermal Cycling [2]	E417.11(h)	X
High-temperature Storage [3]	E417.9(c)	10
Shock [2]	E417.11(e)	X
Random Vibration [2]	E417.11(c)	X
Component Examination:	E417.5	
X-ray and N-ray	E417.5(f)	X
Leakage	E417.5(h)	X
Firing Tests:	E417.29(f)(1)	
Ambient-temperature	E417.29(f)(2)	7
High-temperature	E417.29(f)(3)	7
Low-temperature	E417.29(f)(4)	7

(1) This table applies to any rotor lead or booster charge that is used by an ordnance interrupter.

(2) This test must subject the component to the qualification environmental test level. For a rotor lead or booster charge that is internal to an ordnance interrupter, the

test level must be no less than the environment that the rotor lead or booster charge experiences when installed and the ordnance interrupter is subjected to the ordnance interrupter's qualification environment.

(3) A high-temperature storage test is optional. A lot will have an initial service-life of five years if it passes this test and all the required tests. A lot will have an initial service-life of one year if it passes all the required tests, but does not undergo this test.

(4) The same 21 sample components, from the same lot, must be subjected to each test designated with an X. For tests designated with a lessor quantity, each component tested must be one of the original 21 sample components.

Table E417.29-5

Ordnance Interrupter Rotor Lead and Booster Charge Service-life Extension [1]	Section E417.15	Quantity Tested [3] 1 Year [4] X=5	5 Years [5] X=10
Component Examination:	E417.5		
Visual Examination	E417.5(b)	X	X
Dimension Measurement	E417.5(c)	X	X
Leakage	E417.5(h)	X	X
X-ray and N-ray	E417.5(f)	X	X
Non-Operating Environment Tests and	E417.9		
Operating Environment Tests:	E417.11		
Thermal Cycling [2]	E417.11(h)	X	X
High-temperature Storage	E417.9(c)	-	X
Component Examination:	E417.5		
Leakage	E417.5(h)	X	X
X-ray and N-ray	E417.5(f)	X	X
Firing Tests:	E417.29(f)(1)		
High-temperature	E417.29(f)(3)	2	5
Low-temperature	E417.29(f)(4)	3	5

(1) This table applies to any rotor lead or booster charge that is used by an ordnance interrupter. In order to extend a rotor lead or booster charge service live, the rotor lead or charge must undergo the tests required by the one-year column or the five-year column before its initial service-life or any previous service-life extension expires.

(2) This test must subject the component to the qualification environmental test levels. For a rotor lead or booster charge that is internal to an ordnance interrupter, the test level must be no less than the environment that the rotor lead or booster charge experiences when installed and the ordnance interrupter is subjected to ordnance interrupter's qualification environment.

(3) For each column, the quantity of sample components required at the top of the column must be from the same production lot and must undergo each test designated with an X. For a test designated with a lessor quantity, each component must be one of the original samples for that column.

(4) Five sample components from the same lot must undergo each test required by this column to extend the service-life of the remaining components from the same lot for one year.

(5) Ten components from the same lot must undergo each test required by this column to extend the service-life of the remaining components from the same lot for five years.

(b) *Status-of-health.* An ordnance interrupter status-of-health test must satisfy section E45417.3(f). This must include measuring the interrupter's safe-and-arm transition time.

(c) *Safe-and-arm position monitor.* This test must demonstrate all of the following:

(1) That an ordnance interrupter's safe-and-arm transition operation, such as rotation or sliding, satisfies all its performance specifications;

(2) That any ordnance interrupter-monitoring device can determine, before flight, if the ordnance interrupter is in the proper flight configuration;

(3) The presence of the arm indication when the ordnance interrupter is armed; and

(4) The presence of the safe indication when the ordnance interrupter is safed.

(d) *Safety tests*—(1) *General.* Each safety test must demonstrate that an ordnance interrupter is safe to handle and use on the launch vehicle.

(2) *Containment.* For any ordnance interrupter that has an internal rotor charge, a containment test must demonstrate that the interrupter will not fragment when the internal charge is initiated.

(3) *Barrier functionality.* A barrier functionality test must demonstrate that, when the ordnance interrupter is in the safe position, if the donor transfer line or the internal rotor charge is initiated, the ordnance output will not propagate to an explosive transfer system. The test must consist of firing tests at high- and low-temperature extremes with an explosive transfer system that simulates the flight configuration. The number of samples that the test must fire and the test conditions must satisfy each table of this section and all of the following:

(i) *High-temperature.* A high-temperature test must initiate each ordnance sample while it is subjected to no lower than the qualification high-temperature level or a 71 °C workmanship screening level, whichever is higher; and

(ii) *Low-temperature.* A low-temperature test must initiate each ordnance sample while it is subjected to no higher than the qualification low-temperature level or a −54 °C workmanship screening level, whichever is lower.

(4) *Extended stall.* For an ordnance interrupter with an internal rotor or booster charge, an extended stall test must demonstrate that the interrupter does not initiate when:

(i) Locked in its safe position; and

(ii) Subjected to a continuous operating arming voltage for the maximum predicted time that could occur accidentally or one hour, whichever is greater.

(5) *Manual safing.* A manual safing test must demonstrate that an ordnance interrupter can be manually safed.

(6) *Safing-interlock.* A safing-interlock test must demonstrate that when an ordnance interrupter's safing-interlock is in place and operating arming current is applied, the interlock prevents arming and satisfies any other performance specification of the interlock.

(e) *Interrupter abbreviated performance.* An interrupter abbreviated performance test must satisfy section E417.3(e). This must include continuous monitoring of the interrupter's arm monitoring circuit. An ordnance interrupter must undergo this test while armed.

(f) *Firing tests.* (1) General. A firing test of an ordnance interrupter, rotor lead, or booster charge must satisfy all of the following:

(i) The test must demonstrate that the initiation and output energy transfer of each ordnance charge satisfies all its performance specifications and that the component does not fragment;

(ii) The number of samples that the test must fire and the test conditions, including firing current and temperature, must satisfy each table of this section;

(iii) Before initiation, each component sample must experience the required temperature for enough time to achieve thermal equilibrium;

(iv) The test of an ordnance interrupter must simulate the flight configuration, including the explosive transfer system lines on the input and output;

(v) Each test of a rotor lead or booster charge must subject the component to an energy source that simulates the flight energy source;

(vi) Each test must measure each ordnance output using a measuring device, such as a swell cap or dent block, to demonstrate that the output satisfies all its performance specifications; and

(vii) For a single interrupter that contains more than one firing path, the test must demonstrate that the initiation of one firing path does not adversely affect the performance of any other path.

(2) *Ambient-temperature.* This test must initiate each ordnance sample while it is at ambient temperature.

(3) *High-temperature.* A high-temperature test must initiate each ordnance sample while it is subjected to no lower than the qualification high-temperature level or a + 71 °C workmanship level, whichever is higher.

(4) *Low-temperature.* A low-temperature test must initiate each ordnance sample while it is subjected to no higher than the qualification low-temperature level or a − 54 °C workmanship level, whichever is lower.

(g) *Barrier alignment.* A barrier alignment test must consist of a statistical firing series of ordnance interrupter samples. The test must demonstrate that the interrupter's safe to arm transition motion provides for ordnance initiation with a reliability of 0.999 at a 95% confidence level. The test must also demonstrate that the interrupter's arm to safe transition motion provides for no ordnance initiation with a reliability of 0.999 at a 95% confidence level. The test may employ a reusable ordnance interrupter subassembly that simulates the flight configuration.

(h) *Repetitive function.* A repetitive function test must demonstrate the ability of an ordnance interrupter to satisfy all its performance specifications when subjected to five times the maximum predicted number of safe-to-arm and arm-to-safe cycles.

(i) *Stall.* A stall test must demonstrate that an ordnance interrupter satisfies all its performance specifications after being locked in its safe position and subjected to an operating arming voltage for the greater of:

(1) Five minutes; or

(2) The maximum predicted time that could occur inadvertently and the interrupter would still be used for flight.

E417.31 PERCUSSION-ACTIVATED DEVICE (PAD)

(a) *General.* This section applies to any percussion-activated device that is part of a flight termination system, including any primer charge it uses. Any percussion-activated device or primer charge must satisfy each test or analysis identified by any table of this section to demonstrate that it satisfies all its performance specifications when subjected to each non-operating and operating environment.

Table E417.31-1

Percussion-activated Device Lot Acceptance [1]	Section	Quantity Tested
Component Examination:	E417.5	
Visual Examination	E417.5(b)	100%
Dimension Measurement	E417.5(c)	100%
Identification Check	E417.5(e)	100%
Status-of-health	E417.31(c)	100%
Leakage	E417.5(h)	100%
X-ray and N-ray	E417.5(f)	100%
Non-Operating Environment Tests and	E417.9	
Operating Environment Tests:	E417.11	
Thermal Cycling [2]	E417.11(h)	Lot Sample[4]
High-temperature Storage: [3]	E417.9(c)	Lot Sample
Shock [2]	E417.11(e)	Lot Sample
Random Vibration [2]	E417.11(c)	Lot Sample
Component Examination:	E417.5	
Leakage	E417.5(h)	Lot Sample
Safety Tests	E417.31(b)	Lot Sample
X-ray and N-ray	E417.5(f)	Lot Sample
Percussion-activated Device Firing Tests:	E417.31(d)(1)	
Ambient-temperature	E417.31(d)(2)	1/3 of Lot Sample
High-temperature	E417.31(d)(3)	1/3 of Lot Sample
Low-temperature	E417.31(d)(4)	1/3 of Lot Sample

(1) The tests required by this table apply to a fully assembled percussion-activated device including all internal ordnance.

(2) This test must subject each percussion-activated device sample to the qualification environmental test level.

(3) A high-temperature storage test is optional. A lot will have an initial service-life of three years if it passes this test and all the required tests. A lot will have an initial service-life of one year if it passes all the required tests, but does not undergo this test.

(4) The lot sample quantity must be no less than the greater of 10% of the lot or nine sample units.

Table E417.31-2

Percussion-activated Device Qualification	Section	Quantity Tested [2]	
		X=5	X=21
Component Examination:	E417.5		
Visual Examination	E417.5(b)	X	X
Dimension Measurement	E417.5(c)	X	X
Identification Check	E417.5(e)	X	X
Status-of-health	E417.31(c)	X	X
Leakage	E417.5(h)	X	X
X-ray and N-ray	E417.5(f)	X	X
Safety Tests:	E417.31(b)(1)		
No-fire impact	E417.31(b)(2)	-	X
Safing-interlock Locking	E417.31(b)(3)	-	X
Safing-interlock Retention	E417.31(b)(4)	-	X
Non-Operating Environment Tests and	E417.9		
Operating Environment Tests:	E417.11		

Storage Temperature	E417.9(b)	-	X
Transportation Shock	E417.9(d)	-	X
Bench Handling	E417.9(e)	-	X
Transportation Vibration	E417.9(f)	-	X
Fungus Resistance	E417.9(g)	-	4
Salt Fog	E417.9(h)	-	4
Fine Sand	E417.9(I)'	-	4
Handling Drop	E417.9(k)	-	X
Thermal Cycling	E417.11(h)	-	X
High-temperature Storage (1)	E417.9(c)	-	X
Humidity	E417.11(g)	-	4
Acceleration	E417.11(f)	-	X
Shock	E417.11(e)	-	X
Sinusoidal Vibration	E417.11(b)	-	X
Random Vibration	E417.11(c)	-	X
Abnormal Drop	E417.9(l)	1	-
Auto Ignition (4)	E417.31(g)	X	-
Component Examination:	E417.5		
Leakage	E417.5(h)	-	X
X-ray and N-ray	E417.5(f)	-	X
Internal Inspection	E417.5(g)	-	3 (3)
Percussion-activated Device Firing Tests:	E417.31(d)(1)		
Ambient-temperature	E417.31(d)(2)	-	6
High-temperature	E417.31(d)(3)	-	6
Low-temperature	E417.31(d)(4)	-	6

(1) A high-temperature storage test is optional. A lot will have an initial service-life of three years if it passes this test and all the required tests. A lot will have an initial service-life of one year if it passes all the required tests, but does not undergo this test.

(2) For each column, the required quantity of sample components from the same lot must undergo each test designated with an X. For a test designated with a lessor quantity, each component tested must be one of the original samples for that column.

(3) One of the three disassembled sample components must be a sample that was subjected to all non-operating environment tests required by this table except for the abnormal drop test.

(4) An auto ignition test applies to any ordnance internal to a percussion-activated device. The ordnance may undergo the test in a subassembly.

Table E417.31-3

Percussion-activated Device Primer Charge Lot Acceptance [1]	Section	Quantity Tested	
Component Examination:	E417.5		
Visual Examination	E417.5(b)	100%	
Dimension Measurement	E417.5(c)	100%	
Leakage	E417.5(h)	100%	
X-ray and N-ray	E417.5(f)	100%	
Operating Environment Tests:	E417.11		
Thermal Cycle	E417.11(h)	Lot Sample [4]	-
Component Examination:	E417.5		
Visual Examination	E417.5(b)	Lot Sample	-
Dimension Measurement	E417.5(c)	Lot Sample	-
Leakage	E417.5(h)	Lot Sample	-
X-ray and N-ray	E417.5(f)	Lot Sample	-
Primer Charge Firing Tests:	E417.31(f)(1)		
All-Fire Impact:	E417.31(f)(2)		
High-temperature [2]	E417.31(f)(6)	½ Lot Sample	-
Low-temperature [2]	E417.31(f)(7)	½ Lot Sample	-
All-Fire [3]	E417.31(e)	-	Statistical Sample

(1) Each test required by this table applies to a primer charge before its installation in a percussion-activated device.

(2) This test must subject each sample primer charge to the all-fire impact determined by the statistical all-fire impact series required during the qualification testing of table E417.31-4.

(3) This test must demonstrate that the production lot is a representative sample of the all-fire baseline established during the qualification testing required by table E417.31-4.

(4) The lot sample quantity must be no less than the greater of 10% of the lot or 30 sample units.

Table E417.31-4

Percussion-activated Device Primer Charge Qualification	Section	Quantity Tested X=	
		Statistical Sample	105
Component Examination	E417.5		
Visual Examination	E417.5(b)	X	X
Dimension Measurement	E417.5(c)	X	X
Leakage	E417.5(h)	X	X
X-ray and N-ray	E417.5(f)	X	X
All-Fire Energy Level	E417.31(e)	X	-
Operating Environmental Tests:	E417.11		
Thermal Cycling	E417.11(h)	-	X
Component Examination:	E417.5		
Leakage	E417.5(h)	-	X
X-ray and N-ray	E417.5(f)	-	X
Primer Charge Firing Tests:	E417.31(f)(1)		
Ambient-temperature:	E417.31(f)(5)		
All-Fire Impact (1)	E417.31(f)(2)	-	15
Operational Impact (2)	E417.31(f)(3)	-	15
200% Operational Impact	E417.31(f)(4)	-	5
High-temperature:	E417.31(f)(6)		
All-Fire Impact (1)	E417.31(f)(2)	-	15
Operational Impact (2)	E417.31(f)(3)	-	15
200% Operational Impact	E417.31(f)(4)	-	5

Low-temperature:	E417.31(f)(7)		
All-Fire Impact [1]	E417.31(f)(2)	-	15
Operational Impact [2]	E417.31(f)(3)	-	15
200% Operational Impact	E417.31(f)(4)	-	5

(1) This test must subject each sample primer charge to the all-fire impact determined by the statistical all-fire impact series required by this table.

(2) This test must subject each sample primer charge to no less than the operational impact that it would receive from the percussion-activated device assembly according to the device's performance specifications, or 200% of the all-fire impact; whichever is greater.

Table E417.31-5

Percussion-activated Device Service-life Extension [(1)]	Section	Quantity Tested [(3)]	
		1 Year [(4)] X=5	3 Years [(5)] X=10
Component Examination:	E417.5		
Visual Examination	E417.5(b)	X	X
Dimension Measurement	E417.5(c)	X	X
Leakage	E417.5(h)	X	X
X-ray and N-ray	E417.5(f)	X	X
Non-Operating Environmental Tests and	E417.9		
Operating Environmental Tests:	E417.11		
Thermal Cycling [(2)]	E417.11(h)	X	X
High-temperature Storage	E417.9(c)	-	X
Shock [(2)]	E417.11(e)	X	X
Random Vibration [(2)]	E417.11(c)	X	X
Component Examination:	E417.5		
Leakage	E417.5(h)	X	X
X-ray and N-ray	E417.5(f)	X	X
Percussion-activated Device Firing Tests:	E417.31(d)(1)		
High-temperature	E417.31(d)(3)	2	5
Low-temperature	E417.31(d)(4)	3	5

[(1)] Each test required by this table applies to a fully assembled percussion-activated device including all internal ordnance. In order to extend a percussion-activated device's service-life, the device must undergo the tests required by the one-year column or the three-year column before its initial service-life or any previous service-life extension expires.

(2) This test must subject each sample percussion-activated device to the qualification environmental level.

(3) For each column, the quantity of sample components required at the top of the column must be from the same production lot and must undergo each test designated with an X. For a test designated with a lessor quantity, each sample component tested must be one of the original samples for that column.

(4) Five sample percussion-activated devices from the same lot must undergo each test required by this column to extend the service-life of remaining percussion-activated devices from the same lot for one year.

(5) Ten sample percussion-activated devices from the same lot must undergo each test required by this column to extend the service-life of remaining percussion-activated devices from the same lot for three years.

(b) *Safety tests*—(1) *General.* Each safety test must demonstrate that a percussion-activated device is safe to handle and use on the launch vehicle.

(2) *No-fire impact.* A no-fire impact test must demonstrate that a percussion-activated device, when pulled with the guaranteed no-fire pull force:

(i) Will not fire;

(ii) The device's primer initiation assembly will not disengage; and

(iii) The device will continue to satisfy all its performance specifications.

(3) *Safing-interlock locking.* A safing-interlock test must demonstrate that, a percussion-activated device, with its safing-interlock in place, will continue to satisfy all its performance specifications and the device's firing assembly will not move more than half the no-fire pull distance when subjected to the greater of:

(i) A 200-pound pull force;

(ii) The device's all-fire pull-force; or

(iii) Twice the worst-case pull force that the device can experience after it is installed on the vehicle.

(4) *Safing-interlock retention test.* A safing-interlock retention test must demonstrate that a percussion-activated device's safing-interlock is not removable when a no-fire pull or greater force is applied to the percussion-activated device lanyard. The test must also demonstrate that the force needed to remove the safing-interlock with the lanyard in an unloaded condition satisfies its performance specification.

(c) *Status-of-health.* A status-of-health test of a percussion-activated device must satisfy section E417.3(f). This test must include measuring the spring constant and firing pull distance.

(d) *Percussion-activated-device firing tests*—(1) *General.* Each firing test of a percussion-activated device must satisfy all of the following:

(i) The test must demonstrate that the device satisfies all its performance specifications when subjected to all qualification stress conditions;

(ii) The number of samples that the test must fire and the test conditions, including temperature, must satisfy each table of this section;

(iii) Before initiation, each component sample must experience the required temperature for enough time to achieve thermal equilibrium;

(iv) The test must subject the device to the manufacturer specified pull-force;

(v) The test must simulate the flight configuration, including the explosive transfer system lines on the output; and

(vi) The test must measure each ordnance output using a measuring device, such as a swell cap or dent block, to demonstrate that the output satisfies all its performance specifications.

(2) *Ambient-temperature.* This test must initiate each ordnance sample while it is subjected to ambient temperature.

(3) *High-temperature.* A high-temperature test must initiate each ordnance sample while it is subjected to no lower than the qualification high-temperature level or a + 71 °C workmanship screening level, whichever is higher.

(4) *Low-temperature.* A low-temperature test must initiate each ordnance sample while it is subjected to no higher than the qualification low-temperature level or a −54 °C workmanship screening level, whichever is lower.

(e) *All-fire energy level.* An all-fire energy level test must consist of a statistical firing series of primer charge lot samples to determine the lowest energy impact at which the primer will fire with a reliability of 0.999 at a 95% confidence level. The test must use a firing pin and configuration that is representative of the flight configuration.

(f) *Primer charge firing tests.* (1) *General.* Each firing test of a primer charge must satisfy all of the following:

(i) The test must demonstrate that the primer charge, including any booster charge or ordnance delay as an integral unit, satisfies all its performance specifications when subjected to all qualification stress conditions;

(ii) The number of samples that the test must fire and the test conditions, including impact energy and temperature, must satisfy each table of this section;

(iii) Before initiation, each component sample must experience the required temperature for enough time to achieve thermal equilibrium;

(iv) The test must use a firing pin and configuration that is representative of the flight configuration; and

(v) The test must measure ordnance output using a measuring device, such as a swell cap or dent block, to demonstrate that the ordnance output satisfies all its performance specifications.

(2) *Ambient-temperature.* This test must initiate each ordnance sample while it is subjected to ambient temperature.

(3) *High-temperature.* A high-temperature test must initiate each ordnance sample while it is subjected to no lower than the qualification high-temperature level or a + 71 °C workmanship screening level, whichever is higher.

(4) *Low-temperature.* A low-temperature test must initiate each ordnance sample while it is subjected to no higher than the qualification low-temperature level or a −54 °C workmanship screening level, whichever is lower.

(g) *Auto-ignition.* This test must demonstrate that any ordnance internal to a percussion-activated device does not experience auto-ignition, sublimation, or melting when subjected to any high-temperature environment during handling, testing, storage, transportation, installation, or flight. The test must include all of the following:

(1) The test environment must be no less than 30 °C higher than the highest non-operating or operating temperature that the device could experience;

(2) The test duration must be the maximum predicted high-temperature duration or one hour, whichever is greater; and

(3) After exposure to the test environment, each ordnance component must undergo external and internal examination, including any dissection needed to identify any auto-ignition, sublimation, or melting.

E417.33 Explosive transfer system, ordnance manifold, and destruct charge

(a) *General.* This section applies to any explosive transfer system, ordnance manifold, or destruct charge that is part of a flight termination system. Any explosive transfer system, ordnance manifold, or destruct charge must satisfy each test or analysis identified by any table of this section to demonstrate that it satisfies all its performance specifications when subjected to each non-operating and operating environment.

Table E417.33-1

Explosive Transfer System, Ordnance Manifold and Destruct Charge Lot Acceptance	Section	Quantity Tested		
		Ordnance Manifolds [3] [4]	Explosive Transfer System [5]	Destruct Charges
Component Examination:	E417.5			
Visual Examination	E417.5(b)	100%	100%	100%
Dimension Measurement	E417.5(c)	100%	100%	100%
Leakage	E417.5(h)	100%	100%	100%
X-ray and N-ray	E417.5(f)	100%	100%	100%
Non-operating and Operating Environments:	E417.9 E417.11			
Thermal Cycling [1]	E417.9(c)	Lot Sample [6]	Lot Sample [6]	Lot Sample [6]
High-temperature Storage [2]	E417.11(h)	Lot Sample	Lot Sample	Lot Sample
Shock [1]	E417.11(e)	Lot Sample	Lot Sample	Lot Sample
Random Vibration [1]	E417.11(c)	Lot Sample	Lot Sample	Lot Sample
Tensile Load [7]	E417.9(j)	-	Lot Sample	Lot Sample
Component Examination:	E417.5			
X-ray and N-ray	E417.5(f)	Lot Sample	Lot Sample	Lot Sample
Leakage	E417.5(h)	Lot Sample	Lot Sample	Lot Sample
Firing Tests:	E417.33(b)(1)			
Ambient-temperature	E417.33(b)(2)	1/3 Lot Sample	1/3 Lot Sample	1/3 Lot Sample
High-temperature	E417.33(b)(3)	1/3 Lot Sample	1/3 Lot Sample	1/3 Lot Sample
Low-temperature	E417.33(b)(4)	1/3 Lot Sample	1/3 Lot Sample	1/3 Lot Sample

(1) This test must subject each sample component to the qualification environment.

(2) A high-temperature storage test is optional. A lot will have an initial service-life of five years if it passes this test and all the required tests. A lot will have an initial service-life of one year if it passes all the required tests, but does not undergo this test.

(3) Any inert manifold need only undergo visual examination and dimension measurement.

(4) The tests required by this column apply to any manifold that contains a booster charge. A fully assembled manifold, including any internal ordnance must undergo each test.

(5) The required quantity applies to each configuration of explosive transfer line end-tip.

(6) The lot sample quantity must be no less than 10 percent of the lot or nine sample units, whichever is greater.

(7) No less than one half the lot sample quantity must undergo a tensile load test after the operational environment tests. The remainder of the lot sample quantity may undergo the tensile load test before the operational environmental tests.

Table E417.33-2

Destruct Charge Qualification	Section	Quantity Tested			
		X=5	X=2	X=1	X=21
Component Examination:	E417.5				
Visual Examination	E417.5(b)	-	-	X	X
Dimension Measurement	E417.5(c)	-	-	X	X
Leakage	E417.5(h)	-	-	X	X
X-ray and N-ray	E417.5(f)	-	-	X	X
Non-Operating Environment Tests and Operating Environment Tests:	E417.9 E417.11				
Storage Temperature	E417.9(b)	-	-	-	4
Transportation Shock	E417.9(d)	-	-	-	4
Bench Handling	E417.9(e)	-	-	-	4
Transportation Vibration	E417.9(f)	-	-	-	4
Fungus Resistance	E417.9(g)	-	-	-	4
Salt Fog	E417.9(h)	-	-	-	4
Fine Sand	E417.9(i)	-	-	-	4
Thermal Cycling	E417.11(h)	-	-	-	X
High-temperature Storage (1)	E417.9(c)	-	-	-	10
Humidity	E417.11(g)	-	-	-	4
Acceleration	E417.11(f)	-	-	-	X
Shock	E417.11(e)	-	-	-	X
Sinusoidal Vibration	E417.11(b)	-	-	-	X
Random Vibration	E417.11(c)	-	-	-	X
Handling Drop	E417.9(k)	-	-	-	X
Abnormal Drop	E417.9(l)	-	-	X	-
Tensile Load	E417.9(j)	-	-	-	X

Component Examination:	E417.5				
Leakage	E417.5(h)	-	-	-	X
X-ray and N-ray	E417.5(f)	-	-	-	X
Penetration Margin Test	E417.33(c)	X	-	-	-
Propellant Detonation	E417.33(d)	-	X	-	-
Firing Tests:	E417.33(b)(1)				
Ambient-temperature	E417.33(b)(2)	-	-	-	7
High-temperature	E417.33(b)(3)	-	-	-	7
Low-temperature	E417.33(b)(4)	-	-	-	7

(1) A high-temperature storage test is optional. A lot will have an initial service-life of five years if it passes this test and all the required tests. A lot will have an initial service-life of one year if it passes all the required tests, but does not undergo this test.

Table E417.33-3

Explosive Transfer System and Ordnance Manifold Qualification	Section	Quantity [3] [4] Tested	
		X=1	X=21
Component Examination	E417.5		
Visual Examination	E417.5(b)	X	X
Dimension Measurement	E417.5(c)	X	X
Leakage	E417.5(h)	X	X
X-ray and N-ray	E417.5(f)	X	X
Non-Operating Environment Test and Operating Environment Tests:	E417.9 E417.11		
Storage Temperature	E417.9(b)	-	4
Transportation Shock	E417.9(d)	-	4
Bench Handling	E417.9(e)	-	4
Transportation Vibration	E417.9(f)	-	4
Fungus Resistance	E417.9(g)	-	4
Salt Fog	E417.9(h)	-	4
Fine Sand	E417.9(I)	-	4
Thermal Cycling	E417.11(h)	-	X
High-temperature Storage [1]	E417.9(c)	-	10
Humidity	E417.11(g)	-	4
Acceleration [5]	E417.11(f)	-	X
Shock [2] [5]	E417.11(e)	-	X
Sinusoidal Vibration [2] [5]	E417.11(b)	-	X
Random Vibration [2] [5]	E417.11(c)	-	X
Handling Drop	E417.9(k)	-	X
Abnormal Drop	E417.9(l)	X	-
Tensile Load	E417.9(j)	-	X

Component Examination:	E417.5		
Leakage	E417.5(h)	-	X
X-ray and N-ray	E417.5(f)	-	X
Firing Tests:	E417.33(b)(1)		
Ambient-temperature	E417.33(b)(2)	-	7
High-temperature	E417.33(b)(3)	-	7
Low-temperature	E417.33(b)(4)	-	7

(1) A high-temperature storage test is optional. A lot will have an initial service-life of five years if it passes this test and all the required tests. A lot will have an initial service-life of one year if it passes all the required tests, but does not undergo this test.

(2) Any explosive transfer system must undergo this test attached to a dynamically equivalent test fixture that simulates each flight configured interface.

(3) The quantity of test samples required by the column applies to explosive transfer lines and explosive manifolds with internal ordnance.

(4) The required quantity applies for each configuration of explosive transfer line end-tip.

(5) Any explosive transfer system manifold must undergo this test with its explosive transfer system assembly attached.

Table E417.33-4

Explosive Transfer System, Explosive Manifold, and Destruct Charge Service-life Extension [1]	Section	Quantity Tested [3]	
		1 Year [4]	5 Years [5]
		X=5	X=10
Component Examination:	E417.5		
Visual Examination	E417.5(b)	X	X
Dimension Measurement	E417.5(c)	X	X
Leakage	E417.5(h)	X	X
X-ray and N-ray	E417.5(f)	X	X
Non-Operating Environment Test and	E417.9		
Operating Environment Tests:	E417.11		
Thermal Cycling [2]	E417.11(h)	X	X
High-temperature Storage	E417.9(c)	-	X
Shock [2]	E417.11(e)	X	X
Random Vibration [2]	E417.11(c)	X	X
Tensile load	E417.9(j)	X	X
Component Examination:	E417.5		
Leakage	E417.5(h)	X	X
X-ray and N-ray	E417.5(f)	X	X
Firing Tests:	E417.33(b)(1)		
High-temperature	E417.33(b)(3)	2	5
Low-temperature	E417.33(b)(4)	3	5

(1) In order to extent an explosive transfer system, manifold, or destruct charge service-life, the component must undergo the tests required by the one-year column or the five-year column before its initial service-life or any previous service-life extension expires. For any explosive manifold with internal ordnance, the ordnance may undergo each test installed in the manifold or separately.

(2) This test must subject each sample component to the qualification environmental level.

(3) The quantity required by each column applies for each configuration of explosive transfer line end-tip. For each column, the quantity of sample components required at the top of the column must be from the same production lot and must undergo each test designated with an X. For a test designated with a lessor quantity, each sample component tested must be one of the original samples for that column.

(4) Five sample ordnance components from the same lot must undergo each test required by this column to extend the service-life of the remaining components from the same lot for one year.

(5) Ten sample ordnance components from the same lot must undergo each test required by this column to extend the service-life of the remaining components from the same lot for five years.

(b) *Firing tests*—(1) *General.* A firing test of an explosive transfer system, explosive manifold, or destruct charge must satisfy all of the following:

(i) The test must demonstrate that each ordnance sample satisfies all its performance specifications when subjected to all qualification stress conditions;

(ii) The number of samples that the test must fire and the test conditions, including temperature, must satisfy each table of this section;

(iii) Before initiation, each ordnance sample must experience the required temperature for enough time to achieve thermal equilibrium;

(iv) For any destruct charge, the test must initiate the charge against a witness plate to demonstrate that the charge satisfies all its performance specifications and is in-family;

(v) For any explosive transfer system component, the test must measure ordnance output using a measuring device, such as a swell cap or dent block, to demonstrate that the ordnance output satisfies all its performance specifications; and

(vi) For any explosive manifold that contains ordnance, the test must initiate the ordnance using an explosive transfer system in a flight representative configuration.

(2) *Ambient-temperature.* This test must initiate each ordnance sample while it is subjected to ambient temperature.

(3) *High-temperature.* A high-temperature test must initiate each ordnance sample while it is subjected to no lower than the qualification high-temperature level or a +71 °C workmanship screening level, whichever is higher.

(4) *Low-temperature.* A low-temperature test must initiate each ordnance sample while it is subjected to no higher than the qualification low-temperature level or a −54 °C workmanship screening level, whichever is lower.

(c) *Penetration margin.* A penetration margin test must demonstrate a destruct charge's ability to accomplish its intended flight termination function, such as to destroy the pressure integrity of any solid propellant stage or motor or rupture any propellant tank. This must include penetrating no less than 150% of the thickness of the target material. Each test must also demonstrate that the charge is in-family by correlating equivalent penetration depth into a witness plate and comparing the results from each test.

(d) *Propellant detonation.* A propellant detonation test or analysis must demonstrate that a destruct charge will not detonate the propellant of its intended target.

E417.35 SHOCK AND VIBRATION ISOLATORS

(a) *General.* This section applies to any shock or vibration isolator that is part of a flight termination system. Any isolator must satisfy each test or analysis identified by table E417.35–1 to demonstrate that it has repeatable performance and is free of any workmanship defects.

Table E417.35-1

Shock and Vibration Isolator Acceptance [(1)]	Section	Quantity Tested
Component Examination:	E417.5	
Visual Examination	E417.5(b)	100%
Dimension Measurement	E417.5(c)	100%
Performance Verification Tests:	E417.3	
Load Deflection	E417.35(b)	100%
Status-of-Health	E417.35(c)	100%

(1) Each isolator must undergo the tests required by this table in a configuration that demonstrates whether isolator satisfies all its performance specifications. The test configuration need not be the flight configuration.

(b) *Load deflection.* A load deflection test must demonstrate the ability of a shock or vibration isolator to withstand the full-scale deflection expected during flight while satisfying all its performance specifications and that the isolator is in-family. This must include subjecting each isolator to varying deflection increments from the null position to the full-scale flight deflection and measuring the isolator's spring constant at each deflection increment.

(c) *Status-of-health.* A status-of-health test of a shock or vibration isolator must satisfy section E417.3(f). The test must include all of the following:

(1) The test must measure the isolator's natural frequency while the isolator is subjected to a random vibration or sinusoidal sweep vibration with amplitudes that are representative of the maximum predicted operating environment; and

(2) The test must measure the isolator's dynamic amplification value while the isolator is subjected to a random vibration or sinusoidal sweep vibration with amplitudes that are representative of the maximum predicted operating environment.

E417.37 ELECTRICAL CONNECTORS AND HARNESSES

(a) *General.* This section applies to any electrical connector or harness that is critical to the functioning of a flight termination system during flight, but is not otherwise part of a flight termination system component. Any electrical connector or harness must satisfy each test or analysis identified by table E417.37–1 of this section to demonstrate that it satisfies all its performance specifications when subjected to each non-operating and operating environment.

Table E417-37-1

Electrical Connector and Harness Qualification	Section	Quantity Tested X=2
Non Operating Environments:	E417.9	
Salt Fog [(1)]	E417.9(h)	X
Status-of-health	E417.37(b)	X
Operating Environments:	E417.11	
Humidity [(1)]	E417.11(g)	X
Shock [(2)]	E417.11(e)	X
Sinusoidal Vibration [(2)]	E417.11(b)	X
Random Vibration [(2)]	E417.11(c)	X
Status-of-health	E417.37(b)	X

(1) This test must measure each connector and cable pin to pin and pin-to-case resistance immediately after the connector or harness is subjected to the test environment.

(2) This test must continuously monitor connector and cable continuity using a sample rate of no less than once every millisecond.

(b) *Status-of-health.* A status-of-health test of a harness or connector must satisfy section E417.3(f). The test must include all of the following:

(1) The test must measure the dielectric withstanding voltage between mutually insulated portions of the harness or connector to demonstrate that the harness or connector satisfies all its performance specifications at its rated voltage and withstands any momentary over-potential due to switching, surge, or any other similar phenomena;

(2) The test must demonstrate that the insulation resistance between mutually insulated points is sufficient to ensure that the harness or connector satisfies all its performance specifications at its rated voltage and the insulation material is not damaged after the harness or connector is subjected to the qualification environments;

(3) The test must demonstrate the ability of the insulation resistance between each wire shield and harness or conductor and the insulation between each harness or connector pin to every other pin to withstand a minimum workmanship voltage of 500 VDC or 150% of the rated output voltage, whichever is greater; and

(4) The test must measure the resistance of any wire and harness insulation to demonstrate that it satisfies all its performance specifications.

E417.39 Ordnance Interfaces and Manifold Qualification

(a) *General.* This section applies to any ordnance interface or manifold that is part of a flight termination system. Each ordnance interface or manifold must undergo a qualification test that demonstrates that the interface or manifold satisfies its performance specifications with a reliability of 0.999 at a 95% confidence level.

(b) *Interfaces.* A qualification test of an ordnance interface must demonstrate the interface's reliability. This must include all of the following:

(1) The test must use a simulated flight configured interface and test hardware that duplicate the geometry and volume of the firing system used on the launch vehicle; and

(2) The test must account for performance variability due to manufacturing and workmanship tolerances such as minimum gap, maximum gap, and axial and angular offset.

(c) *Detonation flier plate ordnance transfer systems.* A qualification test of a detonation flier plate ordnance transfer system composed of any component that has a charge or initiates a charge such as; electro-explosive devices, exploding bridgewires, ordnance delays, explosive transfer systems, destruct charges, and percussion-activated devices; must demonstrate the system's reliability using one of the following:

(1) A statistical firing series that varies critical performance parameters, including gap and axial and angular alignment, to ensure that ordnance initiation occurs across each flight configured interface with a reliability of 0.999 at a 95% confidence level;

(2) Firing 2994 flight units in a flight representative configuration to demonstrate that ordnance initiation occurs across each flight configured interface with a reliability of 0.999 at a 95% confidence level; or

(3) Firing all of the following units to demonstrate a gap margin that ensures ordnance initiation:

(i) Five units at four times the combined maximum system gap;

(ii) Five units at four times the combined maximum system axial misalignment;

(iii) Five units at four times the combined maximum system angular misalignment; and

(iv) Five units at 50% of the combined minimum system gap.

(d) *Deflagration and pressure sensitive ordnance transfer systems.* A qualification test of a deflagration or pressure sensitive ordnance transfer system composed of devices such as ordnance delays, electro-explosive system low energy end-tips, and percussion-activated device primers must demonstrate the system's reliability using one of the following:

(1) A statistical firing series that varies critical performance parameters, including gap interface, to ensure that ordnance initiation occurs across each flight configured interface;

(2) Firing 2994 flight units in a flight representative configuration to demonstrate that ordnance initiation occurs across each flight configured interface; or

(3) Firing all of the following units to demonstrate a significant gap margin:

(i) Five units using a 75% downloaded donor charge across the maximum gap; and

(ii) Five units using a 120% overloaded donor charge across the minimum gap.

E417.41 FLIGHT TERMINATION SYSTEM PRE-FLIGHT TESTING

(a) *General.* A flight termination system, its subsystems, and components must undergo the pre-flight tests required by this section to demonstrate that the system will satisfy all its performance specifications during the countdown and launch vehicle flight. After successful completion of any pre-flight test, if the integrity of the system, subsystem, or component is compromised due to a configuration change or other event, such as a lightning strike or connector demate, the system, subsystem, or component must repeat the pre-flight test.

(b) *Pre-flight component tests.* A component must undergo one or more pre-flight tests at the launch site to detect any change in performance due to any shipping, storage, or other environments that may have affected performance after the component passed the acceptance tests. Each test must measure all the component's performance parameters and compare the measurements to the acceptance test performance baseline to identify any performance variations, including any out-of-family results, which may indicate potential defects that could result in an in-flight failure.

(c) *Silver-zinc batteries.* Any silver-zinc battery that is part of a flight termination system, must undergo the pre-flight activation and tests that table E417.21–1 identifies must take place just before installation on the launch vehicle. The time interval between pre-flight activation and flight must not exceed the battery's performance specification for activated stand time capability.

(d) *Nickel-cadmium batteries.* Any nickel-cadmium flight termination system battery must undergo pre-flight processing and testing before installation on the launch vehicle and the processing and testing must satisfy all of the following:

(1) Any pre-flight processing must be equivalent to that used during qualification testing to ensure the flight battery's performance is equivalent to that of the battery samples that passed the qualification tests;

(2) Each battery must undergo all of the following tests at ambient temperature no later than one year before the intended flight date and again no earlier than two weeks before the first flight attempt:

(i) A status-of-health test that satisfies section E417.22(j);

(ii) A charge retention test that satisfies section E417.22(f); and

(iii) An electrical performance test that satisfies section E417.22(n); and

(3) The test results from the battery acceptance tests of section E417.22 and the one-year and two-week pre-flight tests of paragraph (d)(2) of this section must undergo a comparison to demonstrate that the battery satisfies all its performance specifications.

The flight battery test data must undergo an evaluation to identify any out-of-family performance and to ensure that there is no degradation in electrical performance that indicates an age-related problem.

(4) In the event of a launch schedule slip, after six weeks has elapsed from a preflight test, the battery must undergo the test again no earlier than two weeks before the next launch attempt.

(e) *Pre-flight testing of a safe-and-arm device that has an internal electro-explosive device.* An internal electro-explosive device in a safe-and-arm device must undergo a pre-flight test that satisfies all of the following:

(1) The test must take place no earlier than 10 calendar days before the first flight attempt. If the flight is delayed more than 14 calendar days or the flight termination system configuration is broken or modified for any reason, such as to replace batteries, the device must undergo the test again no earlier than 10 calendar days before the next flight attempt. A launch operator may extend the time between the test and flight if the launch operator demonstrates that the electro-explosive device and its firing circuit will each satisfy all their performance specifications when subjected to the expected environments for the extended period of time;

(2) The test must include visual checks for signs of any physical defect or corrosion; and

(3) The test must include a continuity and resistance check of the electro-explosive device circuit while the safe-and-arm device is in the arm position and again while the device is in the safe position.

(f) *Pre-flight testing of an external electro-explosive device.* An external electro-explosive device that is part of a safe-and-arm device must undergo a pre-flight test that satisfies all of the following:

(1) The test must take place no earlier than 10 calendar days before the first flight attempt. If the flight is delayed more than 14 calendar days or the flight termination system configuration is broken or modified for any reason, such as to replace batteries, the device must undergo the test again no earlier than 10 calendar days before the next flight attempt. A launch operator may extend the time between the test and flight if the launch operator demonstrates that the electro-explosive device and its firing circuit will satisfy all their performance specifications when subjected to the expected environments for the extended period of time; and

(2) The test must include visual checks for signs of any physical defect or corrosion and a resistance check of the electro-explosive device.

(g) *Pre-flight testing of an exploding bridgewire.* An exploding bridgewire must undergo a pre-flight test that satisfies all of the following:

(1) The test must take place no earlier than 10 calendar days before the first flight attempt. If the flight is delayed more than 14 calendar days or the flight termination system configuration is broken or modified for any reason, such as to replace batteries, the exploding bridgewire must undergo the test again no earlier than 10 calendar days before the next flight attempt. A launch operator may extend the time between the test and flight if the launch operator demonstrates that the exploding bridgewire will satisfy all its performance specifications when subjected to the expected environments for the extended period of time.

(2) The test must verify the continuity of each bridgewire.

(3) Where applicable, the test must include a high voltage static test and a dynamic gap breakdown voltage test to demonstrate that any spark gap satisfies all its performance specifications.

(h) *Pre-flight testing for command receiver decoders and other electronic components.* (1) An electronic component, including any component that contains piece part circuitry, such as a command receiver decoder, must undergo a pre-flight test that satisfies all of the following:

(i) The test must take place no earlier than 180 calendar days before flight. If the 180-day period expires before flight, the launch operator must replace the component with one that meets the 180-day requirement or test the component in place on the launch vehicle. The test must satisfy the alternate procedures for testing the component on the launch vehicle contained in the test plan and procedures required by section E417.1(c); and

(ii) The component must undergo the test at ambient temperature. The test must measure all performance parameters measured during acceptance testing.

(2) A launch operator may substitute an acceptance test for a pre-flight test if the acceptance test is performed no earlier than 180 calendar days before flight.

(i) *Pre-flight subsystem and system level test.* A flight termination system must undergo the pre-flight subsystem and system level tests required by this paragraph after the system's components are installed on a launch vehicle to ensure proper operation of the final subsystem and system configurations. Each test must compare data obtained from the test to data from the pre-flight component tests and acceptance tests to demonstrate that there are no discrepancies indicating a flight reliability concern.

(1) *Radio frequency system pre-flight test.* All radio frequency systems must undergo a pre-flight test that satisfies all of the following:

(i) The test must demonstrate that the flight termination system antennas and associated radio frequency systems satisfy all their performance specifications once installed in their final flight configuration;

(ii) The test must measure the system's voltage standing wave ratio and demonstrate that any insertion losses are within the design limits;

(iii) The test must demonstrate that the radio frequency system, from each command control system transmitter antenna used for the first stage of flight to each command receiver satisfies all its performance specifications;

(iv) The test must occur no earlier than 90 days before flight; and

(v) The test must demonstrate the functions of each command receiver decoder and calibrate the automatic gain control signal strength curves, verify the threshold sensitivity for each command, and verify the operational bandwidth.

(2) *End-to-end test of a non-secure command receiver decoder system.* Any flight termination system that uses a non-secure command receiver decoder must undergo an end-to-end test of all flight termination system subsystems, including command destruct systems and inadvertent separation destruct systems. The test must satisfy all of the following:

(i) The test must take place no earlier than 72 hours before the first flight attempt. After the test, if the flight is delayed more than 14 calendar days or the flight termination system configuration is broken or modified for any reason, such as to replace batteries, the system must undergo the end-to-end test again no earlier than 72 hours before the next flight attempt;

(ii) The flight termination system, except for all ordnance initiation devices, must undergo the test in its final onboard launch vehicle configuration;

(iii) The test must use a destruct initiator simulator that satisfies §417.307(h) in place of each flight initiator to demonstrate that the command destruct and inadvertent separation destruct systems deliver the required energy to initiate the flight termination system ordnance;

(iv) The flight termination system must undergo the test while powered by the batteries that the launch vehicle will use for flight. A flight termination system battery must not undergo recharging at any time during or after the end-to-end test. If the battery is recharged at any time before flight the system must undergo the end-to-end test again;

(v) The end-to-end test must exercise all command receiver decoder functions critical to flight termination system operation during flight, including the pilot or check tone, using the command control system transmitters in their flight configuration or other representative equipment;

(vi) The test must demonstrate that all primary and redundant flight termination system components, flight termination system circuits, and command control system transmitting equipment are operational; and

(vii) The test must exercise the triggering mechanism of all electrically initiated inadvertent separation destruct systems to demonstrate that each is operational.

(3) *Open-loop test of a non-secure command destruct system.* For each flight attempt, any flight termination system that uses a non-secure command receiver decoder must undergo an open-loop radio frequency test, no earlier than 60 minutes before the start of the launch window, to validate the entire radio frequency command destruct link. For each flight attempt, the flight safety system must undergo the test again after any break or change in the system configuration. The test must satisfy all of the following:

(i) The system must undergo the test with all flight termination system ordnance initiation devices in a safe condition;

(ii) Flight batteries must power all receiver decoders and other electronic components. The test must account for any warm-up time needed to ensure the reliable operation of electronic components;

(iii) The test must exercise the command receiver decoder arm function, including the pilot or check tone, using a command control transmitter in its flight configuration;

(iv) The test must demonstrate that each receiver decoder is operational and is compatible with the command control transmitter system; and

(v) Following successful completion of the open-loop test, if any receiver decoder is turned off or the transmitter system fails to continuously transmit the pilot or check tone, the flight termination system must undergo the open-loop test again before flight.

(4) *Initial open-loop test of a secure high-alphabet command destruct system.* Any flight termination system that uses a secure high-alphabet command receiver decoder must undergo an open-loop radio frequency test to demonstrate the integrity of the system between the command control transmitter system and launch vehicle radio frequency system from the antenna to the command receiver decoders. The test must satisfy all of the following:

(i) The test must occur before loading the secure flight code on to the command transmitting system and the command receiver decoders;

(ii) The test must use a non-secure code, also known as a maintenance code, loaded on to the command control transmitting system and the command receiver decoders;

(iii) Each command receiver decoder must be powered by either the ground or launch vehicle power sources;

(iv) The command control transmitter system must transmit, open-loop, all receiver decoder commands required for the flight termination system functions, including pilot or check tone to the vehicle;

(v) The test must demonstrate that each command receiver decoder receives, decodes and outputs each command sent by the command control system; and

(vi) The testing must demonstrate that all primary and redundant flight termination system components, flight termination system circuits, and command control system transmitting equipment are operational.

(5) *End-to-end test of a secure high-alphabet command destruct system.* Any flight termination system that uses a secure high-alphabet command receiver decoder must undergo an end-to-end test of all flight termination system subsystems, including command destruct systems and inadvertent separation destruct systems. The test must satisfy all of the following:

(i) The system must undergo the test no earlier than 72 hours before the first flight attempt. After the test, if the flight is delayed more than 14 calendar days or the flight termination system configuration is broken or modified for any reason, such as to replace batteries, the system must undergo the end-to-end tests again no earlier than 72 hours before the next flight attempt;

(ii) The system must undergo the test in a closed-loop configuration using the secure flight code;

(iii) The flight termination system, except for the ordnance initiation devices, must undergo the test in its final onboard launch vehicle configuration;

(iv) The test must use a destruct initiator simulator that satisfies §417.307(h) in place of each flight initiator to demonstrate that the command destruct and inadvertent separation destruct systems deliver the energy required to initiate the flight termination system ordnance;

(v) The flight termination system must undergo the test while powered by the batteries that the launch vehicle will use for flight. A flight termination system battery must not undergo recharging at any time during or after the end-to-end test. If the battery is recharged at any time before flight the system must undergo the end-to-end test again;

(vi) The test must exercise all command receiver decoder functions critical to flight termination system operation during flight, including the pilot or check tone, in a closed-loop test configuration using ground support testing equipment hardwired to the launch vehicle radio frequency receiving system;

(vii) The test must demonstrate that all primary and redundant launch vehicle flight termination system components and circuits are operational; and

(viii) The test must exercise the triggering mechanism of all electrically initiated inadvertent separation destruct systems to demonstrate that they are operational.

(6) *Abbreviated closed-loop test of a secure high-alphabet command destruct system.* Any flight termination system that uses a secure high-alphabet command receiver decoder must undergo an abbreviated closed-loop test if, due to a launch scrub or delay, more than 72 hours pass since the end-to-end test of paragraph (h)(5) of this section. The test must satisfy all of the following:

(i) The flight termination system must undergo the test in its final flight configuration with all flight destruct initiators connected and in a safe condition;

(ii) The test must occur just before launch support tower rollback or other similar final countdown event that suspends access to the launch vehicle;

(iii) Each command receiver decoder must undergo the test powered by the flight batteries;

(iv) The test must exercise all command receiver decoder functions critical to flight termination system operation during flight except the destruct function, including the pilot or check tone, in a closed-loop test configuration using ground support testing equipment hardwired to the launch vehicle radio frequency receiving system; and

(v) The test must demonstrate that the launch vehicle command destruct system, including each command receiver decoder and all batteries, is functioning properly.

(7) *Final open-loop test of a secure high-alphabet command destruct system.* Any flight termination system that uses a secure high-alphabet command receiver decoder must undergo a final open-loop radio frequency test no earlier than 60 minutes before flight, to validate the entire radio frequency command destruct link from the command control transmitting system to launch vehicle antenna. The test must satisfy all of the following:

(i) The flight termination system must undergo the test in its final flight configuration with all flight destruct initiators connected and in a safe condition;

(ii) Flight batteries must power all receiver decoders and other electronic components. The test must account for any warm-up time needed for reliable operation of the electronic components;

(iii) The test must exercise each command receiver decoder's self-test function including pilot or check tone using the command control system transmitters in their flight configuration;

(iv) The test must demonstrate that each receiver decoder is operational and compatible with the command control transmitter system; and

(v) Following successful completion of the open-loop test, if any command receiver decoder is turned off or the transmitter system fails to continuously transmit the pilot or check tone, the flight termination system must undergo the final open-loop test again before flight.

[Docket No. FAA–2000–7953, 71 FR 50537, Aug. 25, 2006, as amended by Amdt. No. 417–5, 81 FR 59439, Aug. 30, 2016]

APPENDIX F TO PART 417 [RESERVED]

APPENDIX G TO PART 417—NATURAL AND TRIGGERED LIGHTNING FLIGHT COMMIT CRITERIA

G417.1 GENERAL

This appendix provides flight commit criteria for mitigating against natural lightning strikes and lightning triggered by the flight of a launch vehicle through or near an electrified environment. A launch operator may not initiate flight unless the weather conditions at the time of launch satisfy all lightning flight commit criteria of this appendix.

(a) In order to meet the lightning flight commit criteria, a launch operator must employ any:

(1) Weather monitoring and measuring equipment needed, and

(2) Procedures needed to verify compliance.

(b) When equipment or procedures, such as a field mill or calculation of the volume-averaged, height-integrated radar reflectivity (VAHIRR) of clouds, are used with the lightning flight commit criteria to increase launch opportunities, a launch operator must evaluate all applicable measurements to determine whether the measurements satisfy the criteria. A launch operator may not turn off available instrumentation to create the appearance of meeting a requirement and must use all radar reflectivity measurements within a specified volume for a VAHIRR calculation.

(c) If a launch operator proposes any alternative lightning flight commit criteria, the launch operator must clearly and convincingly demonstrate that the alternative provides an equivalent level of safety to that required by this appendix.

G417.3 DEFINITIONS

For the purpose of this appendix:

Anvil cloud means a stratiform or fibrous cloud formed by the upper-level outflow or blow-off from a thunderstorm or convective cloud.

Associated means two or more clouds are caused by the same disturbed weather or are physically connected.

Bright band means an enhancement of radar reflectivity caused by frozen hydrometeors falling and beginning to melt at any altitude where the temperature is 0 degrees Celsius or warmer.

Cloud means a visible mass of suspended water droplets or ice crystals, or a combination of water droplets and ice crystals. The cloud is the entire volume containing such particles.

Cloud layer means a vertically continuous array of clouds, not necessarily of the same type, whose bases are approximately at the same altitude.

Cone of silence means the volume within which a radar cannot detect any object, and is an inverted circular cone centered on the radar antenna. A cone of silence consists of all elevation angles greater than the maximum elevation angle reached by the radar.

Debris cloud means any cloud, except an anvil cloud, that has become detached from a parent cumulonimbus cloud or thunderstorm, or that results from the decay of a parent cumulonimbus cloud or thunderstorm.

Disturbed weather means a weather system where a dynamical process destabilizes the air on a scale larger than the individual clouds or cells. Examples of disturbed weather include fronts, troughs, and squall lines.

Electric field means a vertical electric field (Ez) at the surface of the Earth.

Field mill means an electric-field sensor that uses a moving, grounded conductor to induce a time-varying electric charge on one or more sensing elements in proportion to the ambient electrostatic field.

Flight path means a launch vehicle's planned flight trajectory, and includes the trajectory's vertical and horizontal uncertainties resulting from all three-sigma guidance and performance deviations.

Horizontal distance means a distance that is measured horizontally between a field mill or electric field measurement point and the nearest part of the vertical projection of an object or flight path onto the surface of the Earth.

Moderate precipitation means a precipitation rate of 0.1 inches/hr or a radar reflectivity of 30 dBZ.

Non-transparent means that one or more of the following conditions apply:

(1) Objects above, including higher clouds, blue sky, and stars, are blurred, indistinct, or obscured when viewed from below when looking through a cloud at visible wavelengths; or objects below, including terrain, buildings, and lights on the ground are blurred, indistinct, or obscured when viewed from above when looking through a cloud at visible wavelengths;

(2) Objects above an observer are seen distinctly only through breaks in a cloud; or

(3) The cloud has a radar reflectivity of 0 dBZ or greater.

Precipitation means detectable rain, snow, hail, graupel, or sleet at the ground; virga; or a radar reflectivity greater than 18 dBZ.

Radar reflectivity means the radar reflectivity factor due to hydrometeors, in dBZ.

Slant distance means the shortest distance between two ports, whether horizontal, vertical, or inclined, in three dimensional space.

Thick cloud layer means one or more cloud layers whose combined vertical extent from the base of the bottom cloud layer to the top of the uppermost cloud layer exceeds 4,500 feet. Cloud layers are combined with neighboring layers for determining total thickness only when they are physically connected by vertically continuous clouds.

Thunderstorm means any convective cloud that produces lightning.

Transparent means that any of the following conditions apply:

(1) Objects above, including higher clouds, blue sky, and stars, are not blurred, are distinct and are not obscured when viewed at visible wavelengths; or objects below, including terrain, buildings, and lights on the ground, are clear, distinct, and not obscured when viewed at visible wavelengths; (2) Objects identified in paragraph (1) of this definition are seen distinctly not only through breaks in a cloud; and (3) The cloud has a radar reflectivity of less than 0 dBZ.

Triboelectrification means the transfer of electrical charge between ice particles and a launch vehicle when the ice particles collide with the vehicle during flight.

Volume-averaged, height integrated radar reflectivity (VAHIRR) means the product, expressed in units of dBZ-km or dBZ-kft, of a volume-averaged radar reflectivity and an average cloud thickness in a specified volume corresponding to a point.

G417.5 LIGHTNING

(a) A launch operator must wait 30 minutes to initiate flight after any type of lightning occurs in a thunderstorm if the flight path will carry the launch vehicle at a slant distance of less than or equal to 10 nautical miles from that thunderstorm. This paragraph does not apply to an anvil cloud that is attached to a parent thunderstorm.

(b) A launch operator must wait 30 minutes to initiate flight after any type of lightning occurs at a slant distance of less than or equal to 10 nautical miles from the flight path, unless:

(1) The non-transparent part of the cloud that produced the lightning is at a slant distance of greater than 10 nautical miles from the flight path;

(2) There is at least one working field mill at a horizontal distance of less than or equal to 5 nautical miles from each such lightning discharge; and

(3) The absolute values of all electric field measurements at a horizontal distance of less than or equal to 5 nautical miles from the flight path and at each field mill specified in paragraph (b)(2) of this section have been less than 1000 volts/meter for at least 15 minutes.

G417.7 CUMULUS CLOUDS

(a) This section applies to non-transparent cumulus clouds, except for cirrocumulus, altocumulus, or stratocumulus clouds. This section does not apply to an anvil cloud that is attached to a parent cumulus cloud.

(b) A launch operator may not initiate flight if the slant distance to the flight path is less than or equal to 10 nautical miles from any cumulus cloud that has a top at an altitude where the temperature is colder than or equal to −20 degrees Celsius.

(c) A launch operator may not initiate flight if the slant distance to the flight path is less than or equal to 5 nautical miles from any cumulus cloud that has a top at an altitude where the temperature is colder than or equal to −10 degrees Celsius.

(d) A launch operator may not initiate flight if the flight path will carry the launch vehicle through any cumulus cloud with its top at an altitude where the temperature is colder than or equal to −5 degrees Celsius.

(e) A launch operator may not initiate flight if the flight path will carry the launch vehicle through any cumulus cloud that has a top at an altitude where the temperature is colder than or equal to + 5, and warmer than −5 degrees Celsius unless:

(1) The cloud is not producing precipitation;

(2) The horizontal distance from the center of the cloud top to at least one working field mill is less than 2 nautical miles; and

(3) All electric field measurements at a horizontal distance of less than or equal to 5 nautical miles of the flight path and at each field mill specified in paragraph (e)(2) of this section have been between −100 volts/meter and + 500 volts/meter for at least 15 minutes.

G417.9 ATTACHED ANVIL CLOUDS

(a) This section applies to any non-transparent anvil cloud formed from a parent cloud that has a top at an altitude where the temperature is colder than or equal to −10 degrees Celsius.

(b) Flight path through cloud: If a flight path will carry a launch vehicle through any attached anvil cloud, the launch operator may not initiate flight unless:

(1) The portion of the attached anvil cloud at a slant distance of less than or equal to 5 nautical miles from the flight path is located entirely at altitudes where the temperature is colder than 0 degrees Celsius; and

(2) The volume-averaged, height-integrated radar reflectivity is less than + 10 dBZ-km (+33 dBZ-kft) at every point at a slant distance of less than or equal to 1 nautical mile from the flight path.

(c) Flight path between 0 and 3 nautical miles from cloud: If a flight path will carry a launch vehicle at a slant distance of greater than 0, but less than or equal to 3, nautical miles from any attached anvil cloud, a launch operator must wait 3 hours to initiate flight after a lightning discharge in or from the parent cloud or anvil cloud, unless:

(1) The portion of the attached anvil cloud at a slant distance of less than or equal to 5 nautical miles from the flight path is located entirely at altitudes where the temperature is colder than 0 degrees Celsius; and

(2) The volume-averaged, height-integrated radar reflectivity is less than + 10 dBZ-km (+33 dBZ-kft) at every point at a slant distance of less than or equal to 1 nautical mile from the flight path.

(d) Flight path between 3 and 5 nautical miles from cloud: If a flight path will carry a launch vehicle at a slant distance of greater than 3 and less than or equal to 5 nautical miles from any attached anvil cloud, a launch operator must wait 3 hours to initiate flight after every lightning discharge in or from the parent cloud or anvil cloud, unless the portion of the attached anvil cloud at a slant distance of less than or equal to 5 nautical miles from the flight path is located entirely at altitudes where the temperature is colder than 0 degrees Celsius.

(e) Flight path between 5 and 10 nautical miles from cloud: If the flight path will carry the launch vehicle at a slant distance of greater than 5 and less than or equal to 10 nautical miles from any attached anvil cloud, the launch operator must wait to initiate flight for 30 minutes after every lightning discharge in or from the parent cloud or anvil cloud, unless the portion of the attached anvil cloud at a slant distance of less than or equal to 10 nautical miles from the flight path is located entirely at altitudes where the temperature is colder than 0 degrees Celsius.

G417.11 DETACHED ANVIL CLOUDS

(a) This section applies to any non-transparent anvil cloud formed from a parent cloud that had a top at an altitude where the temperature was colder than or equal to −10 degrees Celsius.

(b) Flight path through cloud: If the flight path will carry the launch vehicle through a detached anvil cloud, the launch operator may not initiate flight unless:

(1) The launch operator waits 4 hours after every lightning discharge in or from the detached anvil cloud; and observation shows that 3 hours have passed since the anvil cloud detached from the parent cloud; or

(2) Each of the following conditions exists:

(i) Any portion of the detached anvil cloud at a slant distance of less than or equal to 5 nautical miles from the flight path is located entirely at altitudes where the temperature is colder than 0 degrees Celsius; and

(ii) The VAHIRR is less than +10 dBZ-km (+33 dBZ-kft) everywhere in the flight path.

(c) Flight path between 0 and 3 nautical miles from cloud: If a flight path will carry a launch vehicle at a slant distance of greater than 0 and less than or equal to 3 nautical miles from a detached anvil cloud, the launch operator must accomplish both of the following:

(1) Wait 30 minutes to initiate flight after every lightning discharge in or from the parent cloud or anvil cloud before detachment of the anvil cloud, and after every lightning discharge in or from the detached anvil cloud after detachment, unless:

(i) The portion of the detached anvil cloud less than or equal to 5 nautical miles from the flight path is located entirely at altitudes where the temperature is colder than 0 degrees Celsius; and

(ii) The VAHIRR is less than + 10 dBZ-km (+33 dBZ-kft) at every point at a slant distance of less than or equal to 1 nautical mile from the flight path; and

(2) If a launch operator is unable to initiate flight in the first 30 minutes under paragraph (c)(1) of this section, the launch operator must wait to initiate flight for 3 hours after every lightning discharge in or from the parent cloud or anvil cloud before detachment of the anvil cloud, and after every lightning discharge in or from the detached anvil cloud after detachment, unless:

(i) All of the following are true:

(A) There is at least one working field mill at a horizontal distance of less than or equal to 5 nautical miles from the detached anvil cloud;

(B) The absolute values of all electric field measurements at a horizontal distance of less than or equal to 5 nautical miles from the flight path and at each field mill specified in paragraph (c)(2)(i)(A) of this section have been less than 1000 V/m for at least 15 minutes; and

(C) The maximum radar reflectivity from any part of the detached anvil cloud at a slant distance of less than or equal to 5 nautical miles from the flight path has been less than +10 dBZ for at least 15 minutes; or

(ii) Both of the following are true:

(A) The portion of the detached anvil cloud at a slant distance of less than or equal to 5 nautical miles from the flight path is located entirely at altitudes where the temperature is colder than 0 degrees Celsius; and

(B) The volume-averaged, height-integrated radar reflectivity is less than +10 dBZ-km (+33 dBZ-kft) at every point at a slant distance of less than or equal to 1 nautical mile from the flight path.

(d) Flight path between 3 and 10 nautical miles from cloud: If a flight path will carry a launch vehicle at a slant distance of greater than 3 and less than or equal to 10 nautical miles from a detached anvil cloud, the launch operator must wait 30 minutes to initiate flight after every lightning discharge in or from the parent cloud or anvil cloud before detachment, and after every lightning discharge in or from the detached anvil cloud after detachment, unless the portion of the detached anvil cloud at a slant distance of less than or equal to 10 nautical miles from the flight path is located entirely at altitudes where the temperature is colder than 0 degrees Celsius.

G417.13 DEBRIS CLOUDS

(a) This section applies to any non-transparent debris cloud whose parent cumuliform cloud has had any part at an altitude where the temperature was colder than −20 degrees Celsius or to any debris cloud formed by a thunderstorm. This section does not apply to a detached anvil cloud.

(b) A launch operator must calculate a "3-hour period" as starting at the latest of the following times:

(1) The debris cloud is observed to be detached from the parent cloud;

(2) The debris cloud is observed to have formed by the collapse of the parent cloud top to an altitude where the temperature is warmer than −10 degrees Celsius; or

(3) Any lightning discharge occurs in or from the debris cloud.

(c) Flight path through cloud: If a flight path will carry a launch vehicle through a debris cloud, the launch operator may not initiate flight during the "3-hour period," of paragraph (b) of this section, unless:

(1) The portion of the debris cloud at a slant distance of less than or equal to 5 nautical miles from the flight path is located entirely at altitudes where the temperature is colder than 0 degrees Celsius; and

(2) The VAHIRR is less than +10 dBZ-km (+33 dBZ-kft) everywhere in the flight path.

(d) Flight path between 0 and 3 nautical miles from cloud: If the flight path will carry the launch vehicle at a slant distance of greater than or equal to 0 and less than or equal to 3 nautical miles from the debris cloud, the launch operator may not initiate flight during the "3-hour period," unless one of the following applies:

(1) A launch operator may initiate flight during the "3-hour period," of paragraph (b) of this section if:

(i) There is at least one working field mill at a horizontal distance of less than or equal to 5 nautical miles from the debris cloud;

(ii) The absolute values of all electric field measurements at a horizontal distance of less than or equal to 5 nautical miles from the flight path and at each field mill specified in paragraph (d)(1)(i) of this section have been less than 1000 volts/meter for at least 15 minutes; and

(ii) The maximum radar reflectivity from any part of the debris cloud less than or equal to a slant distance of 5 nautical miles from the flight path has been less than + 10 dBZ for at least 15 minutes; or

(2) A launch operator may initiate flight during the "3-hour period," of paragraph (b) of this section if:

(i) The portion of the debris cloud at a slant distance of less than or equal to 5 nautical miles from the flight path is located entirely at altitudes where the temperature is colder than 0 degrees Celsius; and

(ii) The VAHIRR is less than +10 dBZ-km (+33 dBZ-kft) at every point at a slant distance of less than or equal to 1 nautical mile from the flight path.

G417.15 DISTURBED WEATHER

A launch operator may not initiate flight if the flight path will carry the launch vehicle through a non-transparent cloud associated with disturbed weather that has clouds with tops at altitudes where the temperature is colder than 0 degrees Celsius and that contains, at a slant distance of less than or equal to 5 nautical miles from the flight path, either:

(a) Moderate or greater precipitation; or

(b) Evidence of melting precipitation such as a radar bright band.

G417.17 THICK CLOUD LAYERS

(a) This section does not apply to either attached or detached anvil clouds.

(b) A launch operator may not initiate flight if the flight path will carry the launch vehicle through a non-transparent cloud layer that is:

(1) Greater than or equal to 4,500 feet thick and any part of the cloud layer in the flight path is located at an altitude where the temperature is between 0 degrees Celsius and −20 degrees Celsius, inclusive; or

(2) Connected to a thick cloud layer that, at a slant distance of less than or equal to 5 nautical miles from the flight path, is greater than or equal to 4,500 feet thick and has any part located at any altitude where the temperature is between 0 degrees Celsius and −20 degrees Celsius, inclusive.

(c) A launch operator may initiate flight despite paragraphs (a)(1) and (a)(2) of this section if the thick cloud layer:

(1) Is a cirriform cloud layer that has never been associated with convective clouds,

(2) Is located entirely at altitudes where the temperature is colder than or equal to −15 degrees Celsius, and

(3) Shows no evidence of containing liquid water.

G417.19 SMOKE PLUMES

(a) A launch operator may not initiate flight if the flight path will carry the launch vehicle through any non-transparent cumulus cloud that has developed from a smoke plume while the cloud is attached to the smoke plume, or for the first 60 minutes after the cumulus cloud is observed to be detached from the smoke plume.

(b) This section does not apply to non-transparent cumulus clouds that have formed above a fire but have been detached from the smoke plume for more than 60 minutes. Section G417.7 applies.

G417.21 SURFACE ELECTRIC FIELDS

(a) A launch operator must wait 15 minutes to initiate flight after the absolute value of any electric field measurement at a horizontal distance of less than or equal to 5 nautical miles from the flight path has been greater than or equal to 1500 volts/meter.

(b) A launch operator must wait 15 minutes to initiate flight after the absolute value of any electric field measurement at a horizontal distance of less than or equal to 5 nautical miles from the flight path has been greater than or equal to 1000 volts/meter, unless:

(1) All clouds at a slant distance of less than or equal to 10 nautical miles from the flight path are transparent; or

(2) All non-transparent clouds at a slant distance less than or equal to 10 nautical miles from the flight path:

(i) Have tops at altitudes where the temperature is warmer than or equal to + 5 degrees Celsius, and

(ii) Have not been part of convective clouds with cloud tops at altitudes where the temperature was colder than or equal to −10 degrees Celsius for 3 hours.

G417.23 TRIBOELECTRIFICATION

(a) A launch operator may not initiate flight if the flight path will carry the launch vehicle through any part of a cloud at any altitude where:

(1) The temperature is colder than or equal to −10 degrees Celsius; and

(2) The launch vehicle's velocity is less than or equal to 3000 feet/second,

(b) Paragraph (a) of this section does not apply if either:

(1) The launch vehicle is treated for surface electrification so that:

(i) All surfaces of the launch vehicle susceptible to ice particle impact are such that the surface resistivity is less than 10^9 Ohms per square; and

(ii) All conductors on surfaces, including dielectric surfaces that have been coated with conductive materials, are bonded to the launch vehicle by a resistance that is less than 10^5 ohms; or

(2) A launch operator demonstrates by test or analysis that electrostatic discharges on the surface of the launch vehicle caused by triboelectrification will not be hazardous to the launch vehicle or the spacecraft.

G417.25 MEASUREMENT OF CLOUD RADAR REFLECTIVITY, COMPUTATION OF VAHIRR, AND MEASUREMENT OF ELECTRIC FIELD

(a) *Radar reflectivity measurement.* A launch operator who measures radar reflectivity to comply with this appendix must employ a meteorological radar and ensure that—

(1) The radar wavelength is greater than or equal to 5 cm;

(2) A reflectivity measurement is due to a meteorological target;

(3) The spatial accuracy and resolution of a reflectivity measurement is 1 kilometer or better;

(4) Any attenuation caused by intervening precipitation or by an accumulation of water or ice on the radome is less than or equal to 1 dBZ; and

(5) A reflectivity measurement contains no portion of the cone of silence above the radar antenna, nor any portion of any sector that is blocked out for payload safety reasons.

(b) *Computation of VAHIRR.* A launch operator who measures VAHIRR to comply with this appendix must ensure that—

(1) A digital signal processor provides radar reflectivity measurements on a three-dimensional Cartesian grid having a maximum grid-point-to-grid-point spacing of one kilometer in each of the three dimensions;

(2) The specified volume is the volume bounded in the horizontal by vertical, plane, perpendicular sides located 5.5 kilometers (3 nautical miles) north, east, south, and west of the point where VAHIRR is to be evaluated; on the bottom by the 0 degree Celsius level; and on the top by an altitude of 20 kilometers;

(3) Volume-averaged radar reflectivity is the arithmetic average of the radar reflectivity measurements in dBZ at grid points within the specified volume. A launch operator must include each grid point within the specified volume in the average if and only if that grid point has a radar reflectivity measurement equal to or greater than 0 dBZ. If fewer than 10% of the grid points in the specified volume have radar reflectivity measurements equal to or greater than 0 dBZ, then the volume-averaged radar reflectivity is either the maximum radar reflectivity measurement in the specified volume, or 0 dBZ, whichever is greater.

(4) Average cloud thickness is the difference in kilometers or thousands of feet between an average top and an average base of all clouds in the specified volume, computed as follows:

(i) The cloud base to be averaged is the higher, at each horizontal position, of either

(A) The 0 degree Celsius altitude, or

(B) The lowest altitude of all radar reflectivity measurements of 0 dBZ or greater.

(ii) The cloud top to be averaged is the highest altitude of all radar reflectivity measurements of 0 dBZ or greater at each horizontal position.

(iii) A launch operator must—

(A) Take the cloud base at any horizontal position as the altitude of the corresponding base grid point minus half of the grid-point vertical separation;

(B) Take the cloud top at that horizontal position as the altitude of the corresponding top grid point plus half of this vertical separation.

(5) All VAHIRR-evaluation points in the flight path itself are:

(i) Greater than a slant distance of 10 nautical miles from any radar reflectivity of 35 dBZ or greater at altitudes of 4 kilometers or greater above mean sea level; and

(ii) Greater than a slant distance of 10 nautical miles from any type of lightning that has occurred in the previous 5 minutes.

(iii) A launch operator need not apply paragraph (b)(5) of this section to VAHIRR evaluation points outside the flight path but within one nautical mile of the flight path.

(6) VAHIRR is the product, expressed in units of dBZ-km or dBZ-kft, of the volume-averaged radar reflectivity defined in paragraph (b)(3) of this section and the average cloud thickness defined in paragraph (b)(4) of this section in the specified volume defined in paragraph (b)(2) of this section.

(c) *Electric field measurement.* A launch operator who measures an electric field to comply with this appendix must—

(1) Employ a ground-based field mill,

(2) Use only the one-minute arithmetic average of the instantaneous readings from that field mill,

(3) Ensure that all field mills are calibrated so that the polarity of the electric field measurements is the same as the polarity of a voltage placed on a test plate above the sensor,

(4) Ensure that the altitude of the flight path of the launch vehicle is equal to or less than 20 kilometers (66 thousand feet) everywhere above a horizontal circle of 5 nautical miles centered on the field mill being used,

(5) Use only direct measurements from a field mill, and

(6) Not interpolate based on electric-field contours.

[Amdt. 417–2, 76 FR 33149, June 8, 2011]

APPENDIX H TO PART 417 [RESERVED]

APPENDIX I TO PART 417—METHODOLOGIES FOR TOXIC RELEASE HAZARD ANALYSIS AND OPERATIONAL PROCEDURES

I417.1 GENERAL

This appendix provides methodologies for performing toxic release hazard analysis for the flight of a launch vehicle as required by §417.227 and for launch processing at a launch site in the United States as required by §417.407(f). The requirements of this appendix apply to a launch operator and the launch operator's toxic release hazard analysis unless the launch operator clearly and convincingly demonstrates that an alternative approach provides an equivalent level of safety.

I417.3 IDENTIFICATION OF NON-TOXIC AND TOXIC PROPELLANTS

(a) *General.* A launch operator's toxic release hazard analysis for launch vehicle flight (section I417.5) and for launch processing (section I417.7) must identify all propellants used for each launch and identify whether each propellant is toxic or non-toxic as required by this section.

(b) *Non-toxic exclusion.* A launch operator need not conduct a toxic release hazard analysis under this appendix for flight or launch processing if its launch vehicle, including all launch vehicle components and payloads, uses only those propellants listed in Table I417–1.

Table I417-1, Commonly Used Non-Toxic Propellants

Item	Chemical Name	Formula
1	Liquid Hydrogen	H_2
2	Liquid Oxygen	O_2
3	Kerosene (RP-1)	$CH_{1.96}$

(c) *Identification of toxic propellants.* A launch operator's toxic release hazard analysis for flight and for launch processing must identify all toxic propellants used for each launch, including all toxic propellants on all launch vehicle components and payloads. Table I417–2 lists commonly used toxic propellants and the associated toxic concentration thresholds used by the Federal launch ranges for controlling potential public exposure. The toxic concentration thresholds contained in Table I417–2 are peak exposure concentrations in parts per million (ppm). A launch operator must perform a toxic release hazard analysis to ensure that the public is not exposed to concentrations above the toxic concentration thresholds for each toxicant involved in a launch. A launch operator must use the toxic concentration thresholds contained in table I417–2 for those propellants. Any propellant not identified in table I417–1 or table I417–2 falls into the category of unique or uncommon propellants, such as those identified in table I417–3, which are toxic or produce toxic combustion by-products. Table I417.3 is not an exhaustive list of possible toxic propellants and combustion by-products. For a launch that uses any propellant listed in table I417–3 or any other unique propellant not listed, a launch operator must identify the chemical composition of the propellant and all combustion by-products and the release scenarios. A launch operator must determine the toxic concentration threshold in ppm for any uncommon toxic propellant or combustion by-product in accordance with the following:

(1) For a toxicant that has a level of concern (LOC) established by the U.S. Environmental Protection Agency (EPA), Federal Emergency Management Agency (FEMA), or Department of Transportation (DOT), a launch operator must use the LOC as the toxic concentration threshold for the toxic release hazard analysis except as required by paragraph (c)(2) of this section.

(2) If an EPA acute emergency guidance level (AEGL) exists for a toxicant and is more conservative than the LOC (that is, lower after reduction for duration of exposure), a launch operator must use the AEGL instead of the LOC as the toxic concentration threshold.

(3) A launch operator must use the EPA's Hazard Quotient/Hazard Index (HQ/HI) formulation to determine the toxic concentration threshold for mixtures of two or more toxicants.

(4) If a launch operator must determine a toxic concentration threshold for a toxicant for which an LOC has not been established, the launch operator must clearly and convincingly demonstrate through the licensing process that public exposure at the proposed toxic concentration threshold will not cause a casualty.

Table I417-2, Commonly Used Toxic Propellants

Chemical Name	Formula	Toxic Concentration Threshold (ppm)
Nitrogen Tetroxide	N_2O_4	4
Mixed Oxides of Nitrogen (MON)	NO, NO_2, N_2O_4	4
Nitric Acid	HNO_3	4
Hydrazine	N_2H_4	8
Monomethylhydrazine (MMH)	CH_3NHNH_2	5
Unsymmetrical Dimethylhydrazine (UDMH)	$(CH_3)_2NNH_2$	5
Ammonium Perchlorate/Aluminum	NH_3ClO_4/Al	10

Table I417-3, Uncommon Toxic Propellants and Combustion By-products

Item	Chemical Name	Formula	Toxic Concentration Threshold (ppm)
1	Fluorine	F_2	Determined according to section I417.3(c).
2	Hydrogen Fluoride	HF	
3	Potassium Perchlorate	$KClO_4$	
4	Lithium Perchlorate	$LiClO_4$	
5	Chlorine Oxides	Cl_2O, ClO_2, CL_2O_6, Cl_2O_7	
6	Chlorine Trifluoride	ClF_3	
7	Beryllium	Be	
8	Beryllium Borohydride	$Be(BH_4)_2$	
9	Boron	B	
10	Boron Trifluoride	BF_3	
11	Diborane	B_2H_6	
12	Pentaborane	B_5H_9	
13	Hexaborane	B_6H_{10}	
14	Aluminum Borohydride	$Al(BH_4)_3$	
15	Lithium Borohydride	$Li(BH_4)_2$	
16	Ammonia	NH_3	
17	Ammonium Nitrate	NH_4NO_3	
18	Ozone	O_3	
19	Methylamine	CH_3NH_2	

20	Ethylamine	$CH_3CH_2NHH_2$	
21	Triethylamine	$(C_2H_5)_3N$	
22	Ethylenediamine	$NH_2CH_2CH_2NH_2$	
23	Diethylenetriamine	$NH_2C_2H_4NHC_2H_4NH_2$	
24	Aniline	$C_6H_5NH_2$	
25	Monoethylaniline	$C_6H_5NHC_2H_5$	
26	Xylidine	$(CH_3)_2C_6H_3NH_3$	
27	Trimethylaluminum	$Al(CH_3)_3$	
28	Dimethylberyllium	$Be(CH_3)_2$	
29	Nitromethane	CH_3NO_2	
30	Tetranitromethane	$C(NO_2)_4$	
31	Nitroglycerine	$C_3H_5(ONO_2)_3$	
32	Butyl Mercaptan	$CH_3(CH_2)_2CH_2SH$	
33	Dimethyl Sulfide	$(CH_3)_2S$	
34	Tetraethyl Silicate	$(C_2H_5)_4SiO_4$	

I417.5 TOXIC RELEASE HAZARD ANALYSIS FOR LAUNCH VEHICLE FLIGHT

(a) *General.* For each launch, a launch operator's toxic release hazard analysis must determine all hazards to the public from any toxic release that will occur during the proposed flight of a launch vehicle or that would occur in the event of a flight mishap. A launch operator must use the results of the toxic release hazard analysis to establish for each launch, in accordance with §417.113(c), flight commit criteria that protect the public from a casualty arising out of any potential toxic release. A launch operator's toxic release hazard analysis must determine if toxic release can occur based on an evaluation of the propellants, launch vehicle materials, and estimated combustion products. This evaluation must account for both normal combustion products and the chemical composition of any unreacted propellants.

(b) *Evaluating toxic hazards for launch vehicle flight.* Each launch must satisfy either the exclusion requirements of section I417.3(b), the containment requirements of paragraph (c) of this section, or the statistical risk management requirements of paragraph (d) of this section, to prevent any casualty that could arise out of exposure to any toxic release.

(c) *Toxic containment for launch vehicle flight.* For a launch that uses any toxic propellant, a launch operator's toxic release hazard analysis must determine a hazard distance for each toxicant and a toxic hazard area for the launch. A hazard distance for a toxicant is the furthest distance from the launch point where toxic concentrations may be greater than the toxicant's toxic concentration threshold in the event of a release during flight. A launch operator must determine the toxic hazard distance for each toxicant as required by paragraphs (c)(1) and (c)(2) of this section. A toxic hazard area defines the region on the Earth's surface that may be exposed to toxic concentrations greater than any toxic concentration threshold of any toxicant involved in a launch in the event of a release during flight. A launch operator must determine a toxic hazard area in accordance with paragraph (c)(3) of this section. In order to achieve containment, a launch operator must evacuate the public from a toxic hazard area as required by paragraph (c)(4) of this section or employ meteorological constraints as required by paragraph (c)(5) of this section. A launch operator must determine the hazard distance for a quantity of toxic propellant and determine and implement a toxic hazard area for a launch as follows:

(1) *Hazard distances for common propellants.* Table I417–4 lists toxic hazard distances as a function of propellant quantity and toxic concentration threshold for commonly used propellants released from a catastrophic launch vehicle failure. Tables I417–10 and I417–11 list the hazard distance as a function of solid propellant mass for HC1 emissions during a launch vehicle failure and during normal flight for ammonium perchlorate based solid propellants. A launch operator must use the hazard distances corresponding to the toxic concentration thresholds established for a launch to determine the toxic hazard area for the launch in accordance with paragraph (c)(3) of this section.

(2) *Hazard distances for uncommon or unique propellants.* For a launch that involves any uncommon or unique propellant, a launch operator must determine the toxic hazard distance for each such propellant using an analysis methodology that accounts for the following worst case conditions:

(i) Surface wind speed of 2.9 knots with a wind speed increase of 1.0 knot per 1000 feet of altitude.

(ii) Surface temperature of 32 degrees Fahrenheit with a dry bulb temperature lapse rate of 13.7 degrees Fahrenheit per 1000 feet over the first 500 feet of altitude and a lapse rate of 3.0 degrees F per 1000 feet above 500 feet.

(iii) Directional wind shear of 2 degrees per 1000 feet of altitude.

(iv) Relative humidity of 50 percent.

(v) Capping temperature inversion at the thermally stabilized exhaust cloud center of mass altitude.

(vi) Worst case initial source term assuming instantaneous release of fully loaded propellant storage tanks or pressurized motor segments.

(vii) Worst case combustion or mixing ratios such that production of toxic chemical species is maximized within the bounds of reasonable uncertainties.

(viii) Evaluation of toxic hazards for both normal launch and vehicle abort failure modes.

Table I417-4

Hazard Distances from the Launch Point							
Quantity	Concentrations [ppm] and Hazard Distances [km]						
	NO_2 4 ppm[1]	UDMH 5 ppm[1]	N_2H_4 8 ppm[1]	MMH 5 ppm[1]	NO 4 ppm[1]	HNO_3 4 ppm[1]	HCl[2] 10 ppm[1]
[pounds]	[km]	[km]	[km]	[km]	[km]	[km]	[km]
100	8	4	3	5	9	8	0
300	14	8	7	9	17	15	0
500	18	10	8	12	20	19	0
1000	26	15	11	17	26	24	0
2000	36	19	13	21	33	31	0
3000	44	22	15	24	39	35	1
4000	47	24	16	27	42	39	2
5000	50	26	17	29	45	42	2
7500	58	30	20	35	52	48	2
10000	64	34	22	37	58	52	3
20000	78	42	27	47	71	66	4
30000	91	47	29	55	81	76	5
40000	99	52	31	59	88	81	5
50000	105	56	34	64	100	87	6
60000	111	59	35	67	104	92	7
70000	116	62	36	72	109	100	8
80000	123	64	37	74	114	104	9
90000	126	68	38	77	118	108	9
100000	130	69	39	79	122	111	10

125000	138	74	42	85	131	119	12
150000	145	78	44	95	138	125	13
175000	151	81	45	99	144	131	14
200000	160	88	47	103	156	136	16
250000	167	94	49	110	163	148	18
300000	175	99	50	117	171	155	21
350000	182	103	52	122	179	161	22
400000	189	107	53	128	186	167	25
450000	203	110	54	132	193	173	27
500000	207	114	57	136	196	178	28
750000	230	127	61	157	206	184	37
1000000	247	140	64	170	220	195	43

1 Indicates a toxic concentration threshold from Table I417-2.

2 HCL emissions from catastrophic launch vehicle failure.

(3) *Toxic hazard area.* Having determined the toxic hazard distance for each toxicant, a launch operator must determine the toxic hazard area for a launch as a circle centered at the launch point with a radius equal to the greatest toxic hazard distance determined as required by paragraphs (c)(1) and (c)(2) of this section, of all the toxicants involved in the launch. A launch operator does not have to satisfy paragraph (c)(3) of this section if:

(i) The launch operator demonstrates that there are no populated areas contained or partially contained within the toxic hazard area; and

(ii) The launch operator ensures that no member of the public is present within the toxic hazard area during preflight fueling, launch countdown, flight and immediate postflight operations at the launch site. To ensure the absence of the public, a launch operator must develop flight commit criteria and related provisions for implementation as part of the launch operator's flight safety plan and hazard area surveillance and clearance plan developed under §§417.111(b) and 417.111(j), respectively.

(4) *Evacuation of populated areas within a toxic hazard area.* For a launch where there is a populated area that is contained or partially contained within a toxic hazard area, the launch operator does not have to satisfy paragraph (c)(5) of this section if the launch operator evacuates all people from all populated areas at risk and ensures that no member of the public is present within the toxic hazard area during preflight fueling and flight. A launch operator must develop flight commit criteria and provisions for implementation of the evacuations as part of the launch operator's flight safety plan, hazard area surveillance and clearance plan, and local agreements and public coordination plan developed according to §§417.111(b), 417.111(j) and 417.111(i), respectively.

(5) *Flight meteorological constraints.* For a launch where there is a populated area that is contained or partially contained within a toxic hazard area and that will not be evacuated under paragraph (c)(4) of this section, the launch is exempt from any further requirements of this section if the launch operator constrains the flight of a launch vehicle to favorable wind conditions or during times when atmospheric conditions result in reduced toxic hazard distances such that any potentially affected populated area is outside the toxic hazard area. A launch operator must employ wind and other meteorological constraints as follows:

(i) When employing wind constraints, a launch operator must re-define the toxic hazard area by reducing the circular toxic hazard area determined under paragraph (c)(3) of this section to one or more arc segments that do not contain any populated area. Each arc segment toxic hazard area must have the same radius as the circular toxic hazard area and must be defined by a range of downwind bearings.

(ii) The launch operator must demonstrate that there are no populated areas within any arc segment toxic hazard area and that no member of the public is present within an arc segment toxic hazard area during preflight fueling, launch countdown, and immediate postflight operations at the launch site.

(iii) A launch operator must establish wind constraints to ensure that any winds present at the time of flight will transport any toxicant into an arc segment toxic hazard area and away from any populated area. For each arc segment toxic hazard area, the wind constraints must consist of a range of downwind bearings that are within the arc segment toxic hazard area and that provide a safety buffer, in both the clockwise and counterclockwise directions, that accounts for any uncertainty in the spatial and temporal variations of the transport winds. When determining the wind uncertainty, a launch operator must account for the variance of the mean wind directions derived from measurements of the winds through the first 6000 feet in altitude at the launch point. Each clockwise and counterclockwise safety buffer must be no less than 20 degrees of arc width within the arc segment toxic hazard area. A launch operator must ensure that the wind conditions at the time of flight satisfy the wind constraints. To accomplish this, a launch operator must monitor the launch site vertical profile of winds from the altitude of the launch point to no less than 6,000 feet above ground level. The launch operator must proceed with a launch only if all wind vectors within this vertical range satisfy the wind constraints. A launch operator must develop wind constraint flight commit criteria and implementation provisions as part of the launch operator's flight safety plan and its hazard area surveillance and clearance plan developed according to §§417.111(b) and 417.111(j), respectively.

(iv) A launch operator may reduce the radius of the circular toxic hazard area determined in accordance with paragraph (c)(3) of this section by imposing operational meteorological restrictions on specific parameters that mitigate potential toxic downwind concentrations levels at any potentially affected populated area to levels below the toxic concentration threshold of each toxicant in question. The launch operator must establish meteorological constraints to ensure that flight will be allowed to occur only if the specific meteorological conditions that would reduce the toxic hazard area exist and will continue to exist throughout the flight.

(d) *Statistical toxic risk management for flight.* If a launch that involves the use of a toxic propellant does not satisfy the containment requirements of paragraph (c) of this section, the launch operator must use statistical toxic risk management to protect public safety. For each such case, a launch operator must perform a toxic risk assessment and develop launch commit criteria that protect the public from unacceptable risk due to planned and potential toxic release. A launch operator must ensure that the resultant toxic risk meets the collective and individual risk criteria requirements contained in §417.107(b). A launch operator's toxic risk assessment must account for the following:

(1) All credible vehicle failure and non-failure modes, along with the consequent release and combustion of propellants and other vehicle combustible materials.

(2) All vehicle failure rates.

(3) The effect of positive or negative buoyancy on the rise or descent of each released toxicant.

(4) The influence of atmospheric physics on the transport and diffusion of each toxicant.

(5) Meteorological conditions at the time of launch.

(6) Population density, location, susceptibility (health categories) and sheltering for all populations within each potential toxic hazard area.

(7) Exposure duration and toxic propellant concentration or dosage that would result in casualty for all populations.

(e) *Flight toxic release hazard analysis products.* The products of a launch operator's toxic release hazard analysis for launch vehicle flight to be filed in accordance with §417.203(e) must include the following:

(1) For each launch, a listing of all propellants used on all launch vehicle components and any payloads.

(2) The chemical composition of each toxic propellant and all toxic combustion products.

(3) The quantities of each toxic propellant and all toxic combustion products involved in the launch.

(4) For each toxic propellant and combustion product, identification of the toxic concentration threshold used in the toxic risk analysis and a description of how the toxic concentration threshold was determined if other than specified in table I417.2.

(5) When using the toxic containment approach of paragraph (c) of this section:

(i) The hazard distance for each toxic propellant and combustion product and a description of how it was determined.

(ii) A graphic depiction of the toxic hazard area or areas.

(iii) A listing of any wind or other constraints on flight, and any plans for evacuation.

(iv) A description of how the launch operator determines real-time wind direction in relation to the launch site and any populated area and any other meteorological condition in order to implement constraints on flight or to implement evacuation plans.

(6) When using the statistical toxic risk management approach of paragraph (d) of this section:

(i) A description of the launch operator's toxic risk management process, including an explanation of how the launch operator ensures that any toxic risk from launch meets the toxic risk criteria of §417.107(b).

(ii) A listing of all models used.

(iii) A listing of all flight commit criteria that protect the public from unacceptable risk due to planned and potential toxic release.

(iv) A description of how the launch operator measures and displays real-time meteorological conditions in order to determine whether conditions at the time of flight are within the envelope of those used by the launch operator for toxic risk assessment and to develop flight commit criteria, or for use in any real-time physics models used to ensure compliance with the toxic flight commit criteria.

I417.7 TOXIC RELEASE HAZARD ANALYSIS FOR LAUNCH PROCESSING

(a) *General.* A launch operator must perform a toxic release hazard analysis to determine potential public hazards from toxic releases that will occur during normal launch processing and that will occur in the event of a mishap during launch processing. This section implements the ground safety requirements of §417.407(g). A launch operator must use the results of the toxic release hazard analysis to establish hazard controls for protecting the public. A launch operator must include the toxic release hazard analysis results in the ground safety plan as required by §417.111(c).

(b) *Process hazards analysis.* A launch operator must perform an analysis on all processes to identify toxic hazards and determine the potential for release of a toxic propellant. The analysis must account for the complexity of the process and must identify and evaluate the hazards and each hazard control involved in the process. An analysis that complies with 29 CFR 1910.119(e) satisfies paragraphs (b)(1) and (b)(2) of this section. A launch operator's process hazards analysis must include the following:

(1) Identify and evaluate each hazard of a process involving a toxic propellant using an analysis method, such as a failure mode and effects analysis or fault tree analysis.

(2) Describe:

(i) Each toxic hazard associated with the process and the potential for release of toxic propellants;

(ii) Each mishap or incident experienced which has a potential for catastrophic consequences;

(iii) Each engineering and administrative control applicable to each hazard and their interrelationships, such as application of detection methodologies to provide early warning of releases and evacuation of toxic hazard areas prior to conducting an operation that involves a toxicant;

(iv) Consequences of failure of engineering and administrative controls;

(v) Location of the source of the release;

(vi) All human factors;

(vii) Each opportunity for equipment malfunction or human error that can cause an accidental release;

(viii) Each safeguard used or needed to control each hazard or prevent equipment malfunctions or human error;

(ix) Each step or procedure needed to detect or monitor releases; and

(x) A qualitative evaluation of a range of the possible safety and health effects of failure of controls.

(3) The process hazards analysis must be updated for each launch. The launch operator must conduct a review of all the hazards associated with each process involving a toxic propellant for launch processing. The review must include inspection of equipment to determine whether the process is designed, fabricated, maintained, and operated according to the current process hazards analysis. A launch operator must revise a process hazards analysis to reflect changes in processes, types of toxic propellants stored or handled, or other aspects of a source of a potential toxic release that can affect the results of overall toxic release hazard analysis.

(4) The personnel who perform a process hazard analysis must possess expertise in engineering and process operations, and at least one person must have experience and knowledge specific to the process being evaluated. At least one person must be knowledgeable in the specific process hazard analysis methodology being used.

(5) A launch operator must resolve all recommendations resulting from a process hazards analysis in a timely manner prior to launch processing and the resolution must be documented. The documentation must identify each corrective action and include a written schedule of when any such actions are to be completed.

(c) *Evaluating toxic hazards of launch processing.* A launch operator must protect the public from each potential toxic hazard identified by the process hazards analysis required by paragraph (b) of this section, the exclusion requirements of section I417.3(b), the containment requirements of paragraph

(d) of this section, or the statistical risk management requirements of paragraph (l) of this section, to prevent any casualty that could arise out of exposure to any toxic release.

(d) *Toxic containment for launch processing.* A launch operator's toxic release hazard analysis must determine a toxic hazard area surrounding the potential release site for each toxic propellant based on the amount and toxicity of the propellant and the meteorological conditions involved. A launch operator must determine whether there are populated areas located within a toxic hazard area that satisfy paragraph (h) of this section. If necessary to achieve toxic containment, a launch operator must evacuate the public in order to satisfy paragraph (i) of this section or employ meteorological constraints that satisfy paragraph (j) of this section. A launch operator, in determining a toxic hazard area, must first perform a worst-case release scenario analysis that satisfies paragraph (e) of this section or a worst-case alternative release scenario analysis that satisfies paragraph (f) of this section for each process that involves a toxic propellant. The launch operator must then determine a toxic hazard distance for each process that satisfies paragraph (g) of this section.

(e) *Worst-case release scenario analysis.* A launch operator's worst-case release scenario analysis must account for the following:

(1) *Determination of worst-case release quantity.* A launch operator must determine the worst-case release quantity of a toxic propellant by selecting the greater of the following:

(i) For substances in a vessel, the greatest amount held in a single vessel, accounting for administrative controls that limit the maximum quantity; or

(ii) For toxic propellants in pipes, the greatest amount in a pipe, accounting for administrative controls that limit the maximum quantity.

(2) *Worst-case release scenario for toxic liquids.* A launch operator must determine the worst-case release scenario for a toxic liquid propellant as follows:

(i) A launch operator must assume that for toxic propellants that are normally liquids at ambient temperature, the quantity in the vessel or pipe, as determined in paragraph (e)(1) of this section, is spilled instantaneously to form a liquid pool.

(ii) The launch operator must determine surface area of the pool by assuming that the liquid spreads to one centimeter deep unless passive mitigation systems are in place that serve to contain the spill and limit the surface area. Where passive mitigation is in place, the launch operator must use the surface area of the contained liquid to calculate the volatilization rate.

(iii) If the release occurs on a surface that is not paved or smooth, the launch operator may account for actual surface characteristics.

(iv) The volatilization rate must account for the highest daily maximum temperature occurring in the past three years, the temperature of the substance in the vessel, and the concentration of the toxic propellants if the liquid spilled is a mixture or solution.

(v) The launch operator must determine rate of release to the air from the volatilization rate of the liquid pool. A launch operator must use either the methodology provided in the Risk Management Plan (RMP) Offsite Consequence Analysis Guidance, dated April 1999, available at *http://www.epa.gov/swercepp/ap-ocgu.htm*, or an air dispersion modeling technique that satisfies paragraph (g) of this section.

(3) *Worst-case release scenario for toxic gases.* A launch operator must determine the worst-case release scenario for a toxic gas as follows:

(i) For toxic propellants that are normally gases at ambient temperature and handled as a gas or as a liquid under pressure, the launch operator must assume that the quantity in the vessel, or pipe, as determined in paragraph (e)(1) of this section, is released as a gas over 10 minutes. The launch operator must assume a release rate that is the total quantity divided by 10 unless passive mitigation systems are in place.

(ii) For gases handled as refrigerated liquids at ambient pressure, if the released toxic propellant is not contained by passive mitigation systems or if the contained pool would have a depth of 1 cm or less, the launch operator must assume that the toxic propellant is released as a gas in 10 minutes.

(iii) For gases handled as refrigerated liquids at ambient pressure, if the released toxic propellant is contained by passive mitigation systems in a pool with a depth greater than 1 cm, the launch operator must assume that the quantity in the vessel or pipe, as defined in paragraph (e)(1) of this section, is spilled instantaneously to form a liquid pool. The launch operator must calculate the volatilization rate at the boiling point of the toxic propellant and at the conditions defined in paragraph (e)(2) of this section.

(4) *Consideration of passive mitigation.* The launch operator must account for passive mitigation systems in the analysis of a worst case release scenario if the passive mitigation system is capable of withstanding the release event triggering the scenario and would function as intended.

(5) *Additional factors in selecting a worst-case scenario.* A launch operator's worst-case release scenario for a toxic propellant must account for each factor that would result in a greater toxic hazard distance, such as a smaller quantity of the toxic propellant than

required by paragraph (e)(1) of this section, that is handled at a higher process temperature or pressure.

(f) *Worst-case alternative release scenario analysis.* A launch operator's worst-case alternative release scenario analysis must account for the following:

(1) The worst-case release scenario for each toxic propellant and for each toxic propellant handling process;

(2) Each release event that is more likely to occur than the worst-case release scenario that is determined in paragraph (e) of this section;

(3) Each release scenario that exceeds a toxic concentration threshold at a distance that reaches the general public;

(4) Each potential transfer hose release due to splits or sudden hose uncoupling;

(5) Each potential process piping release from failures at flanges, joints, welds, valves, valve seals, and drain bleeds;

(6) Each potential process vessel or pump release due to cracks, seal failure, or drain, bleed, or plug failure;

(7) Each vessel overfilling and spill, or over pressurization and venting through relief valves or rupture disks;

(8) Shipping container mishandling and breakage or puncturing leading to a spill;

(9) Mishandling or dropping flight or ground hardware that contains toxic commodities;

(10) Each active and passive mitigation system provided they are capable of withstanding the event that triggered the release and would still be functional;

(11) History of each accident experienced by the launch operator involving the release of a toxic propellant; and

(12) Each failure scenario.

(g) *Toxic hazard distances for launch processing.* For each process involving a toxic propellant, a launch operator must perform an air dispersion analysis to determine the hazard distance for the worst-case release scenario or the worst-case alternative release scenario as determined under paragraphs (e) and (f) of this section. A launch operator must use either the methodology provided in the RMP Offsite Consequence Analysis Guidance, dated April 1999, or an air dispersion modeling technique that is applicable to the proposed launch. A launch operator's air dispersion modeling technique must account for the following analysis parameters:

(1) *Toxic concentration thresholds.* A launch operator must use the toxic concentration thresholds defined by section I417.3(c).

(2) *Wind speed and atmospheric stability class.* A launch operator, for the worst-case release analysis, must use a wind speed of 1.5 meters per second and atmospheric stability class F. If the launch operator demonstrates that local meteorological data applicable to the source of a toxic release show a higher wind minimum wind speed or less stable atmosphere during the three previous years, the launch operator may use these minimums. The launch operator, for analysis of the worst-case alternative scenario, must use statistical meteorological conditions for the location of the source.

(3) *Ambient temperature and humidity.* For a worst-case release scenario analysis of a toxic propellant, the launch operator must use the highest daily maximum temperature from the last three years and average humidity for the site, based on temperature and humidity data gathered at the source location or at a local meteorological station. For analysis of a worst-case alternative release scenario, the launch operator must use typical temperature and humidity data gathered at the source location or at a local meteorological station.

(4) *Height of release.* The launch operator must analyze the worst-case release of a toxic propellant assuming a ground level release. For a worst-case alternative scenario analysis of a toxic propellant, the release scenario may determine release height.

(5) *Surface roughness.* The launch operator must use either an urban or rural topography, as appropriate. Urban means that there are many obstacles in the immediate area; obstacles include buildings or trees. Rural means there are no buildings in the immediate area and the terrain is generally flat and unobstructed.

(6) *Dense or neutrally buoyant gases.* Models or tables used for dispersion analysis of a toxic propellant must account for gas density.

(7) *Temperature of release substance.* For a worst-case release scenario, the launch operator must account for the release of liquids other than gases liquefied by refrigeration at the highest daily maximum temperature, based on data for the previous three years appropriate to the source of the potential toxic release, or at process temperature, whichever is higher. For a worst-case alternative scenario, the launch operator may consider toxic propellants released at a process or ambient temperature that is appropriate for the scenario.

(h) *Toxic hazard areas for launch processing.* A launch operator, having determined the toxic hazard distance for the toxic concentration threshold for each toxic propellant involved in a process using either a worst-case release scenario or a worst-case alternative release scenario, must determine the toxic hazard area for the process as a circle centered at the potential release point with a radius equal to the greatest toxic hazard distance for the toxic propellants involved in the process. A launch operator does not have to satisfy this section if:

(1) There are no populated areas contained or partially contained within the toxic hazard area; and

(2) There is no member of the public present within the toxic hazard area during the process.

(i) *Evacuation of populated areas within a toxic hazard area.* For a process where there is a populated area that is contained or partially contained within the toxic hazard area, the launch processing operation does not have to satisfy this section if the launch operator evacuates the public from the populated area and ensures that no member of the public is present within the toxic hazard area during the operation. A launch operator must coordinate notification and evacuation procedures with the Local Emergency Planning Committee (LEPC) and ensure that notification and evacuation occurs according to its launch plans, including the launch operator's ground safety plan, hazard area surveillance and clearance plan, accident investigation plan, and local agreements and public coordination plan.

(j) *Meteorological constraints for launch processing.* For a launch processing operation with the potential for a toxic release where there is a populated area that is contained or partially contained within the toxic hazard area and that will not be evacuated as required by paragraph (i) of this section, the operation is exempt from further requirements in this section if the launch operator constrains the process to favorable wind conditions or during times when atmospheric conditions result in reduced toxic hazard distances such that the potentially affected populated area is outside the toxic hazard area. A launch operator must employ wind and other meteorological constraints that satisfy the following:

(1) A launch operator must limit a launch processing operation to times during which prevailing winds will transport a toxic release away from populated areas that would otherwise be at risk. If the mean wind speed during the operation is equal to or greater than four knots, the launch operator must re-define the toxic hazard area by reducing the circular toxic hazard area as determined in paragraph (h) of this section to one or more arc segments that do not contain a populated area. Each arc segment toxic hazard area must have the same radius as the circular toxic hazard area and must be defined by a range of downwind bearings. If the mean wind speed during the operation is less than four knots, the toxic hazard area for the operation must be the full 360-degree toxic hazard area as defined by paragraph (h) of this section. The total arc width of an arc segment hazard area for launch processing must be greater than or equal to 30 degrees. If the launch operator determines the standard deviation of the measured wind direction, the total arc width of an arc segment hazard area must include all azimuths within the mean measured wind direction plus three sigma and the mean measured wind direction minus three sigma; otherwise, the following apply for the conditions defined by the Pasquil-Gifford meteorological stability classes:

(i) For stable classes D–F, if the mean wind speed is less than 10 knots, the total arc width of the arc segment toxic hazard area must be no less than 90 degrees;

(ii) For stable classes D–F, if the mean wind speed is greater than or equal to 10 knots, the total arc width of the arc segment toxic hazard area must be no less than 45 degrees;

(iii) For neutral class C, the total arc width of the arc segment toxic hazard area must be no less than 60 degrees;

(iv) For slightly unstable class B, the total arc width of the arc segment toxic hazard area must be no less than 105 degrees; and

(v) For mostly unstable class A, the total arc width of the arc segment toxic hazard area must be no less than 150 degrees.

(2) The launch operator must ensure that there are no populated areas within an arc segment toxic hazard area and that no member of the public is present within an arc segment toxic hazard area during the process as defined by paragraph (i) of this section.

(3) A launch operator must establish wind constraints to ensure that winds present at the time of an operation will transport toxicants into an arc segment toxic hazard area and away from populated areas. For each arc segment toxic hazard area, the wind constraints must consist of a range of downwind bearings that are within the arc segment toxic hazard area and that provide a safety buffer, in both the clockwise and counterclockwise directions, that accounts for uncertainty in the spatial and temporal variations of the transport winds.

(4) A launch operator may reduce the radius of the circular toxic hazard area as determined under paragraph (h) of this section by imposing operational meteorological restrictions on specific parameters that mitigate potential toxic downwind concentrations levels at a potentially affected populated area to levels below the toxic concentration threshold of the toxicant in question. The launch operator must establish meteorological constraints to ensure that the operation will be allowed to occur only if the specific meteorological conditions that would reduce the toxic hazard area exist and will continue to exist throughout the operation, or the operation will be terminated.

(k) *Implementation of meteorological constraints.* A launch operator must use one or more of the following approaches to determine wind direction or other meteorological conditions in order to establish constraints on a launch processing operation or evacuate the populated area in a potential toxic hazard area:

(1) The launch operator must ensure that the wind conditions at the time of the process comply with the wind constraints used to define each arc segment toxic hazard area. The launch operator must monitor the vertical profile of winds at the potential toxic release site from ground level to an altitude of 10 meters or the maximum height above ground of the potential release, whichever is larger. The launch operator may proceed with a launch processing operation only if wind vectors meet the wind constraints used to define each arc segment toxic hazard area.

(2) A launch operator must monitor the specific meteorological parameters that affect toxic downwind concentrations at a potential toxic release site for a process and for the sphere of influence out to each populated area within the potential toxic hazard area as defined by paragraph (h) of this section. The launch operator must monitor spatial variations in the wind field that could affect the transport of toxic material between the potential release site and populated areas. The launch operator must acquire real-time meteorological data from sites between the potential release site and each populated area sufficient to demonstrate that the toxic hazard area, when adjusted to the spatial wind field variations, excludes populated areas. Meteorological parameters that affect toxic downwind concentrations from the potential release site and covering the sphere of influence out to the populated areas must fall within the conditions as determined in paragraph (j)(4) of this section. A launch operator must use one of the following methods to determine the meteorological conditions that will constrain a launch processing operation:

(i) A launch operator may employ real-time air dispersion models to determine the toxic hazard distance for the toxic concentration threshold and proximity of a toxicant to populated areas. A launch operator, when employing this method, must proceed with a launch processing operation only if real-time modeling of the potential release demonstrates that the toxic hazard distance would not reach populated areas. The launch operator's process for carrying out this method must include the use of an air dispersion modeling technique that complies with paragraph (g) of this section and providing real-time meteorological data for the sphere of influence around a potential toxic release site as input to the air dispersion model. The launch operator's process must also include a review of the meteorological conditions to identify changing conditions that could affect the toxic hazard distance for a toxic concentration threshold prior to proceeding with the operation.

(ii) A launch operator may use air dispersion modeling techniques to define the meteorological conditions that, when present, would prevent a toxic hazard distance for a toxic concentration threshold from reaching populated areas. The launch operator, when employing this method, must constrain the associated launch processing operation to be conducted only when the prescribed meteorological conditions exist. A launch operator's air dispersion modeling technique must comply with paragraph (g) of this section.

(l) *Statistical toxic risk management for launch processing*. The launch operator must use statistical toxic risk management to protect public safety if a process that involves the use of a toxic propellant does not satisfy the containment requirements of paragraph (d) of this section. A launch operator, for each such case, must perform a toxic risk assessment and develop criteria that protect the public from risks due to planned and potential toxic release. A launch operator must ensure that the resultant toxic risk meets the collective and individual risk criteria requirements defined in §417.107(b). A launch operator's toxic risk assessment must account for the following:

(1) All credible equipment failure and non-failure modes, along with the consequent release and combustion of toxic propellants;

(2) Equipment failure rates;

(3) The effect of positive or negative buoyancy on the rise or descent of the released toxic propellants;

(4) The influence of atmospheric physics on the transport and diffusion of toxic propellants released;

(5) Meteorological conditions at the time of the process;

(6) Population density, location, susceptibility (health categories) and sheltering for populations within each potential toxic hazard area; and

(7) Exposure duration and toxic propellant concentration or dosage that would result in casualty for populations.

(m) *Launch processing toxic release hazard analysis products*. The products of a launch operator's toxic release hazards analysis for launch processing must include the following:

(1) For each worst-case release scenario, a description of the vessel or pipeline and toxic propellant selected as the worst case for each process, assumptions and parameters used, and the rationale for selection of that scenario. Assumptions must include use of administrative controls and passive mitigation that were assumed to limit the quantity that could be released. The description must include the anticipated effect of the controls and mitigation on the release quantity and rate;

(2) For each worst-case alternative release scenario, a description of the scenario identified for each process, assumptions and parameters used, and the rationale for the selection of that scenario. Assumptions must include use of administrative controls and

passive mitigation that were assumed to limit the quantity that could be released. The description must include the anticipated effect of the controls and mitigation on the release quantity and rate;

(3) Estimated quantity released, release rate, and duration of release for each worst-case scenario and worst-case alternative scenario for each process;

(4) A description of the methodology used to determine the toxic hazard distance for each toxic concentration threshold;

(5) Data used to estimate off-site population receptors potentially affected; and

(6) The following data for each worst-case scenario and worst-case alternative release scenario:

(i) Chemical name;

(ii) Physical state;

(iii) Basis of results (provide model name if used, or other methodology);

(iv) Scenario (explosion, fire, toxic gas release, or liquid spill and vaporization);

(v) Quantity released in pounds;

(vi) Release rate;

(vii) Release duration;

(viii) Wind speed and atmospheric stability class;

(ix) Topography;

(x) Toxic hazard distance;

(xi) All members of the public within the toxic hazard distance;

(xii) Any passive mitigation considered; and

(xiii) Active mitigation considered (worst-case alternative release scenario only).

[Docket No. FAA-2000-7953, 71 FR 50537, Aug. 25, 2006, as amended by Amdt. No. 417-5, 81 FR 59439, Aug. 30, 2016]

APPENDIX J TO PART 417—GROUND SAFETY ANALYSIS REPORT

J417.1 GENERAL

(a) This appendix provides the content and format requirements for a ground safety analysis report. A launch operator must perform a ground safety analysis as required by subpart E of part 417 and document the analysis in a ground safety analysis report that satisfies this appendix, as required by § 417.402(d).

(b) A ground safety analysis report must contain hazard analyses that describe each hazard control, and describe a launch operator's hardware, software, and operations so that the FAA can assess the adequacy of the hazard analysis. A launch operator must document each hazard analysis on hazard analysis forms as required by § J417.3(d) and file each system and operation descriptions as a separate volume of the report.

(c) A ground safety analysis report must include a table of contents and provide definitions of any acronyms and unique terms used in the report.

(d) A launch operator's ground safety analysis report may reference other documents filed with the FAA that contain the information required by this appendix.

J417.3 GROUND SAFETY ANALYSIS REPORT CHAPTERS

(a) *Introduction.* A ground safety analysis report must include an introductory chapter that describes all administrative matters, such as purpose, scope, safety certification of personnel who performed any part of the analysis, and each special interest issue, such as a high-risk situation or potential non-compliance with any applicable FAA requirement.

(b) *Launch vehicle and operations summary.* A ground safety analysis report must include a chapter that provides general safety information about the vehicle and operations, including the payload and flight termination system. This chapter must serve as an executive summary of detailed information contained within the report.

(c) *Systems, subsystems, and operations information.* A ground safety analysis report must include a chapter that provides detailed safety information about each launch vehicle system, subsystem and operation and each associated interface. The data in this chapter must include the following:

(1) *Introduction.* A launch operator's ground safety analysis report must contain an introduction to its systems, subsystems, and operations information that serves as a roadmap and checklist to ensure all applicable items are covered. All flight and ground hardware must be identified with a reference to where the items are discussed in the document. All interfacing hardware and operations must be identified with a reference to where the items are discussed in the document. The introduction must identify interfaces between systems and operations and the boundaries that describe a system or operation.

(2) *Subsystem description.* For each hardware system identified in a ground safety analysis report as falling under one of the hazardous systems listed in paragraphs (c)(3), (c)(4) and (c)(5) of this section, the report must identify each of the hardware system's subsystems. A ground safety analysis report must describe each hazardous subsystem using the following format:

(i) General description including nomenclature, function, and a pictorial overview;

(ii) Technical operating description including text and figures describing how a subsystem works and any safety features and fault tolerance levels;

(iii) Each safety critical parameter, including those that demonstrate established system safety approaches that are not evident in the technical operating description or figures, such as factors of safety for structures and pressure vessels;

(iv) Each major component, including any part of a subsystem that must be technically described in order to understand the subsystem hazards. For a complex subsystem such as a propulsion subsystem, the ground safety analysis report must provide a majority of the detail of the subsystem including any figures at the major component level such as tanks, engines and vents. The presentation of figures in the report must progress in detail from broad overviews to narrowly focused figures. Each figure must have supporting text that explains what the figure is intended to illustrate;

(v) Ground operations and interfaces including interfaces with other launch vehicle and launch site subsystems. A ground safety analysis report must identify a launch operator's and launch site operator's hazard controls for all operations that are potentially hazardous to the public. The report must contain facility figures that illustrate where hazardous operations take place and must identify all areas where controlled access is employed as a hazard control; and

(vi) Hazard analysis summary of subsystem hazards that identifies each specific hazard and the threat to public safety. This summary must provide cross-references to the hazard analysis form required by paragraph (d) of this section and indicate the nature of the control, such as design margin, fault tolerance, or procedure.

(3) *Flight hardware.* For each stage of a launch vehicle, a ground safety analysis report must identify all flight hardware systems, using the following sectional format:

(i) Structural and mechanical systems;

(ii) Ordnance systems;

(iii) Propulsion and pressure systems;

(iv) Electrical and non-ionizing radiation systems; and

(v) Ionizing radiation sources and systems.

(4) *Ground hardware.* A ground safety analysis report must identify the launch operator's and launch site operator's ground hardware, including launch site and ground support equipment, that contains hazardous energy or materials, or that can affect flight hardware that contains hazardous energy or materials. A launch operator must identify all ground hardware by using the following sectional format:

(i) Structural and mechanical ground support and checkout systems;

(ii) Ordnance ground support and checkout systems;

(iii) Propulsion and pressure ground support and checkout systems;

(iv) Electrical and non-ionizing radiation ground support and checkout systems;

(v) Ionizing radiation ground support and checkout systems;

(vi) Hazardous materials; and

(vii) Support and checkout systems and any other safety equipment used to monitor or control a potential hazard not otherwise addressed above.

(5) *Flight safety system.* A ground safety analysis report must describe each hazard of inadvertent actuation of the launch operator's flight safety system, potential damage to the flight safety system during ground operations, and each hazard control that the launch operator will implement.

(6) *Hazardous materials.* A ground safety analysis report must:

(i) Identify each hazardous material used in all the launch operator's flight and ground systems, including the quantity and location of each material;

(ii) Contain a summary of the launch operator's approach for protecting the public from toxic plumes, including the toxic concentration thresholds used to control public exposure and a description of any related local agreements;

(iii) Describe any toxic plume model used to protect public safety and contain any algorithms used by the model; and

(iv) Include the products of the launch operator's toxic release hazard analysis for launch processing as defined by section I417.7(m) of appendix I of this part for each launch that involves the use of any toxic propellants.

(d) *Hazard analysis.* A ground safety analysis report must include a chapter containing a hazard analysis of the launch vehicle and launch vehicle processing and interfaces. The hazard analysis must identify each hazard and all hazard controls that the launch operator will implement. A ground safety analysis report must contain the results of the launch operator's hazard analysis of each system, subsystem, and operation using a standardized format that includes the items listed on the example hazard analysis form provided in figure J417–1 and that satisfies the following:

(1) *Introduction.* A ground safety analysis report must contain an introduction that serves as a roadmap and checklist to the launch operator's hazard analysis forms. A launch operator must identify all flight hardware, ground hardware, interfacing hardware, and operations with a reference to where the items are discussed in the ground safety analysis report. The introduction must explain how a launch operator presents its hazard analysis in terms of hazard identification numbers as identified in figure J417–1.

(2) *Analysis.* A launch operator may present each hazard on a separate form or consolidate hazards of a specific system, subsystem, component, or operation onto a single form. There must be at least one form for each hazardous subsystem and each hazardous subsystem operation. A launch operator must state which approach it has chosen in

the introduction to the hazard analysis section. A launch operator must track each identified hazard control separately.

(3) *Numbering*. A launch operator must number each hazard analysis form with the applicable system or subsystem identified. A launch operator must number each line item on a hazard analysis form with numbers and letters provided for multiple entries against an individual line item. A line item consists of a hardware or operation description and a hazard.

(4) *Hazard analysis data*. A hazard analysis form must contain or reference all information necessary to understand the relationship of a system, subsystem, component, or operation with a hazard cause, control, and verification.

(e) *Hazard analysis supporting data*. A ground safety analysis report must include data that supports the hazard analysis. If such data does not fit onto the hazard analysis form, a launch operator must provide the data in a supporting data chapter. This chapter must contain a table of contents and may reference other documents that contain supporting data.

PARTS 418–419 [RESERVED]

PART 420—LICENSE TO OPERATE A LAUNCH SITE

Subpart A—General

Sec.

Subpart B—Criteria and Information Requirements for Obtaining a License

Subpart C—License Terms and Conditions

Subpart D—Responsibilities of a Licensee

AUTHORITY: 51 U.S.C. 50901–50923.

SOURCE: Docket No. FAA–1999–5833, 65 FR 62861, Oct. 19, 2000, unless otherwise noted.

Subpart A—General

§420.1 General.

(a) *Scope*. This part prescribes the information and demonstrations that must be provided to the FAA as part of a license application, the bases for license approval, license terms and conditions, and post-licensing requirements with which a licensee shall comply to remain licensed. Requirements for preparing a license application are contained in part 413 of this subchapter.

(b) *Equivalent level of safety*. Each requirement of this part applies unless the applicant or licensee clearly and convincingly demonstrates that an alternative approach provides an equivalent level of safety to the requirement of this part.

[Doc. No. FAA–2016–6761, Amdt. No. 420–8, 83 FR 28535, June 20, 2018]

§ 420.3 Applicability.

This part applies to any person seeking a license to operate a launch site or to a person licensed under this part. A person operating a site that only supports amateur rocket activities as defined in 14 CFR 1.1, does not need a license under this part to operate the site.

[Doc. No. FAA–2007–27390, 73 FR 73782, Dec. 4, 2008]

§ 420.5 Definitions.

For the purpose of this part.

Ballistic coefficient means the weight of an object divided by the quantity product of the coefficient of drag of the object and the area of the object.

Compatibility means the chemical property of materials that may be located together without increasing the probability of an accident or, for a given quantity, the magnitude of the effects of such an accident.

Debris dispersion radius (D_{max}) means the estimated maximum distance from a launch point that debris travels given a worst-case launch vehicle failure and flight termination early in flight. For an expendable launch vehicle, flight termination is assumed to occur at 10 seconds into flight.

Downrange area means a portion of a flight corridor beginning where a launch area ends and ending 5,000 nautical miles from the launch point, or where the IIP leaves the surface of the Earth, whichever is shorter, for an orbital launch vehicle; and ending with an impact dispersion area for a guided sub-orbital launch vehicle.

E,F,G coordinate system means an orthogonal, Earth-fixed, geocentric, right-handed system. The origin of the coordinate system is at the center of an ellipsoidal Earth model. The E-axis is positive directed through the Greenwich meridian. The F-axis is positive directed though 90 degrees east longitude. The EF-plane is coincident with the ellipsoidal Earth model's equatorial plane. The G-axis is normal to the EF-plane and positive directed through the north pole.

E,N,U coordinate system means an orthogonal, Earth-fixed, topocentric, right-handed system. The origin of the coordinate system is at a launch point. The E-axis is positive directed east. The N-axis is positive directed north. The EN-plane is tangent to an ellipsoidal Earth model's surface at the origin and perpendicular to the geodetic vertical. The U-axis is normal to the EN-plane and positive directed away from the Earth.

Effective casualty area (A_c) means the aggregate casualty area of each piece of debris created by a launch vehicle failure at a particular point on its trajectory. The effective casualty area for each piece of debris is the area within which 100 percent of the unprotected population on the ground are assumed to be a casualty, and outside of which 100 percent of the population are assumed not to be a casualty. An effective casualty area accounts for the characteristics of the debris piece, including its size, the path angle of its trajectory, impact explosions, and debris skip, splatter, and bounce. An effective casualty area also accounts for the size of a person.

Energetic liquid means a liquid, slurry, or gel, consisting of, or containing an explosive, oxidizer, fuel, or combination of the above, that may undergo, contribute to, or cause rapid exothermic decomposition, deflagration, or detonation.

Explosive means any chemical compound or mechanical mixture that, when subjected to heat, impact, friction, detonation or other suitable initiation, undergoes a rapid chemical change that releases large volumes of highly heated gases that exert pressure in the surrounding medium. The term applies to materials that either detonate or deflagrate.

Explosive division means the division within hazard class 1 of an explosive as defined in the United Nations Organization classification system for transport of dangerous goods, and as determined in accordance with 49 CFR part 173, subpart C.

Explosive equivalent means a measure of the blast effects from explosion of a given quantity of material expressed in terms of the weight of trinitrotoluene (TNT) that would produce the same blast effects when detonated.

Explosive hazard facility means a facility or location at a launch site where solid propellants, energetic liquids, or other explosives are stored or handled.

Flight azimuth means the initial direction in which a launch vehicle flies relative to true north expressed in degrees-decimal-degrees.

Flight corridor means an area on the Earth's surface estimated to contain the hazardous debris from nominal flight of a launch vehicle, and non-nominal flight of a launch vehicle assuming a perfectly functioning flight termination system or other flight safety system.

Guided suborbital launch vehicle means a suborbital rocket that employs an active guidance system.

Hazard class means the class of an explosive as defined by the United Nations Organization classification system for transport of dangerous goods, and as determined in accordance with 49 CFR part 173, subpart C.

Impact dispersion area means an area representing an estimated three standard deviation dispersion about a nominal impact point of an intermediate or final stage of a suborbital launch vehicle.

Impact dispersion factor means a constant used to estimate, using a stage apogee, a three standard deviation dispersion about a nominal impact point of an intermediate or final stage of a suborbital launch vehicle.

Impact dispersion radius (R_i) means a radius that defines an impact dispersion area.

Impact range means the distance between a launch point and the impact point of a suborbital launch vehicle stage.

Impact range factor means a constant used to estimate, when multiplied by a stage apogee, the nominal impact point of an intermediate or final stage of a suborbital launch vehicle.

Instantaneous impact point (IIP) means an impact point, following thrust termination of a launch vehicle. IIP may be calculated with or without atmospheric drag effects.

Instantaneous impact point (IIP) range rate means a launch vehicle's estimated IIP velocity along the Earth's surface.

Intraline distance means the minimum distance permitted between any two explosive hazard facilities in the ownership, possession or control of one launch site customer.

Launch area means, for a flight corridor defined in accordance with appendix A of this part, the portion of a flight corridor from the launch point to a point 100 nautical miles in the direction of the flight azimuth. For a flight corridor defined in accordance with appendix B of this part, a launch area is the portion of a flight corridor from the launch point to the enveloping line enclosing the outer boundary of the last debris dispersion circle.

Launch point means a point on the Earth from which the flight of a launch vehicle begins, and is defined by its geodetic latitude, longitude and height on an ellipsoidal Earth model.

Launch site accident means an unplanned event occurring during a ground activity at a launch site resulting in a fatality or serious injury (as defined in 49 CFR 830.2) to any person who is not associated with the activity, or any damage estimated to exceed $25,000 to property not associated with the activity.

Liquid propellant means:

(1) A monopropellant on a launch vehicle or related device; or

(2) Incompatible energetic liquids co-located for purposes of serving as propellants on a launch vehicle or a related device where the incompatible energetic liquids are housed in tanks connected by piping for purposes of mixing.

Maximum credible event means a hypothesized worst-case accidental explosion, fire, or agent release that is likely to occur from a given quantity and disposition of explosives, chemical agents, or reactive material.

Net explosive weight (NEW) means the total weight, expressed in pounds, of explosive material or explosive equivalency contained in an item.

Nominal means, in reference to launch vehicle performance, trajectory, or stage impact point, a launch vehicle flight where all launch vehicle aerodynamic parameters are as expected, all vehicle internal and external systems perform as planned, and there are no external perturbing influences (e.g., winds) other than atmospheric drag and gravity.

Overflight dwell time means the period of time it takes for a launch vehicle's IIP to move past a populated area. For a given populated area, the overflight dwell time is the time period measured along the nominal trajectory IIP ground trace from the time point whose normal with the trajectory intersects the most uprange part of the populated area to the time point whose normal with the trajectory intersects the most downrange part of the populated area.

Overflight exclusion zone means a portion of a flight corridor which must remain clear of the public during the flight of a launch vehicle.

Populated area means a land area with population.

Population density means the number of people per unit area in a populated area.

Position data means data referring to the current position of a launch vehicle with respect to flight time expressed through the X, Y, Z coordinate system.

Public means people and property that are not involved in supporting a licensed or permitted launch, and includes those people and property that may be located within the boundary of a launch site, such as visitors, any individual providing goods or services not related to launch processing or flight, and any other launch operator and its personnel.

Public area means any area outside a hazard area and is an area that is not in the possession, ownership or other control of a launch site operator or of a launch site customer who possesses, owns or otherwise controls that hazard area.

Public area distance means the minimum distance permitted between a public area and an explosive hazard facility.

Public traffic route means any highway or railroad that the general public may use.

Public traffic route distance means the minimum distance permitted between a public highway or railroad line and an explosive hazard facility.

Trajectory means the position and velocity components as a function of time of a launch vehicle relative to an x, y, z coordinate system, expressed in $x, y, z, \dot{x}, \dot{y}, \dot{z}$.

Unguided sub-orbital launch vehicle means a sub-orbital rocket that does not have a guidance system.

X, Y, Z coordinate system means an orthogonal, Earth-fixed, topocentric, right-handed system. The origin of the coordinate system is at a launch point. The x-axis coincides with the initial launch azimuth and is positive in the downrange direction. The y-axis is positive to the left looking downrange. The xy-plane is tangent to the ellipsoidal earth model's surface at the origin and perpendicular to the geodetic vertical. The z-axis is normal to the xy-plane and positive directed away from the earth.

φ_O, λ_O, h_O means a latitude, longitude, height system where φ_0 is the geodetic latitude of a launch point, λ_0 is the east longitude of the launch point, and h_0 is the height of the launch point above the reference ellipsoid. φ_0 and λ_0 are expressed in degrees-decimal-degrees.

[Doc. No. FAA–1999–5833, 65 FR 62861, Oct. 19, 2000, as amended by Amdt. 420–3, 72 FR 17019, Apr. 6, 2007; Amdt. 420–6, 77 FR 55113, Sept. 7, 2012]

§§ 420.6–420.14 [Reserved]

Subpart B—Criteria and Information Requirements for Obtaining a License

§ 420.15 Information requirements.

(a) *General*—(1) *Launch site operator.* An applicant shall identify the name and address of the applicant, and the name, address, and telephone number of any person to whom inquiries and correspondence should be directed.

(2) *Launch site.* An applicant shall provide the name and location of the proposed launch site and include the following information:

(i) A list of downrange equipment;

(ii) A description of the layout of the launch site, including launch points;

(iii) The types of launch vehicles to be supported at each launch point;

(iv) The range of launch azimuths planned from each launch point; and

(v) The scheduled operational date.

(3) *Foreign ownership.* Identify foreign ownership of the applicant, as follows:

(i) For a sole proprietorship or partnership, all foreign owners or partners;

(ii) For a corporation, any foreign ownership interest of 10 percent or more; and

(iii) For a joint venture, association, or other entity, any foreign entities participating in the entity.

(b) *Environmental.* An applicant shall provide the FAA with information for the FAA to analyze the environmental impacts associated with the operation of the proposed launch site. The information provided by an applicant must be sufficient to enable the FAA to comply with the requirements of the National Environment Policy Act, 42 U.S.C. 4321 *et seq.* (NEPA), the Council on Environmental Quality Regulations for Implementing the Procedural Provisions of NEPA, 40 CFR parts 1500–1508, and the FAA's Procedures for Considering Environmental Impacts, FAA Order 1050.1D. An applicant shall submit environmental information concerning a proposed launch site not covered by existing environmental documentation, and other factors as determined by the FAA.

(c) *Launch site location.* (1) Except as provided by paragraph (c)(2) of this section, an applicant shall provide the information necessary to demonstrate compliance with §§420.19–420.29.

(2) An applicant who is proposing to locate a launch site at an existing launch point at a federal launch range is not required to comply with paragraph (c)(1) of this section if a launch vehicle of the same type and class as proposed for the launch point has been safely launched from the launch point.

(d) *Explosive site plan.* (1) Except as provided by paragraph (d)(2) of this section, an applicant shall submit an explosive site plan that complies with §§420.63, 420.65, 420.67, and 420.69.

(2) If an applicant plans to operate a launch site located on a federal launch range, and if the applicant is required by the federal launch range to comply with the federal launch range's explosive safety requirements, the applicant shall submit the explosive site plan submitted to the federal launch range.

(e) *Launch site operations.* An applicant shall provide the information necessary to demonstrate compliance with the requirements of §§420.53, 420.55, 420.57, 420.59, 420.61, and 420.71.

§420.17 Bases for issuance of a license.

(a) The FAA will issue a license under this part when the FAA determines that:

(1) The application provides the information required by §420.15;

(2) The FAA has completed an analysis of the environmental impacts associated with the proposed operation of the launch site, in accordance with NEPA, 40 CFR parts 1500–1508, and FAA Order 1050.1D;

(3) The launch site location meets the requirements of §§420.19, 420.21, 420.23, 420.25, 420.27, and 420.29;

(4) The applicant has completed the agreements required by §420.31;

(5) The application demonstrates that the applicant shall satisfy the requirements of §§420.53, 420.55, 420.57, 420.59, 420.61 and 420.71;

(6) The explosive site plan meets the criteria of §§420.63, 420.65, 420.67 and 420.69; and

(7) Issuing a license would not jeopardize foreign policy or national security interests of the United States.

(b) The FAA advises an applicant, in writing, of any issue arising during an application review that would lead to denial. The applicant may respond in writing, submit additional information, or amend its license application.

§420.19 Launch site location review—general.

(a) To gain approval for a launch site location, an applicant shall demonstrate that for each launch point proposed for the launch site, at least one type of expendable or reusable launch vehicle can be flown from the launch point safely. For purposes of the launch site location review:

(1) A safe launch must possess a risk level estimated, in accordance with the requirements of this part, not to exceed an expected number of 1×10^{-4}

casualties (E_c) to the collective members of the public exposed to hazards from the flight.

(2) Types of launch vehicles include orbital expendable launch vehicles, guided sub-orbital expendable launch vehicles, unguided sub-orbital expendable launch vehicles, and reusable launch vehicles. Orbital expendable launch vehicles are further classified by weight class, based on the weight of payload the launch vehicle can place in a 100-nm orbit, as defined in table 1.

(b) If an applicant proposes to have more than one type of launch vehicle flown from a launch point, the applicant shall demonstrate that each type of expendable or reusable launch vehicle planned to be flown from the launch point can be flown from the launch point safely.

(c) If an applicant proposes to have more than one weight class of orbital expendable launch vehicles flown from a launch point, the applicant shall demonstrate that the heaviest weight class planned to be flown from the launch point can be flown from the launch point safely.

TABLE 1 OF § 420.19—ORBITAL EXPENDABLE LAUNCH VEHICLE CLASSES BY PAYLOAD WEIGHT (LBS)

100 nm orbit	Weight class			
	Small	Medium	Medium large	Large
28 degrees inclination *	≤4400	>4400 to ≤11100	>11100 to ≤18500	>18500
90 degrees inclination	≤3300	>3300 to ≤8400	>8400 to ≤15000	>15000

* 28 degrees inclination orbit from a launch point at 28 degrees latitude.

[Docket No. FAA–1999–5833, 65 FR 62861, Oct. 19, 2000, as amended by Docket No. FAA–2014–0418, Amdt. No. 420–7, 81 FR 47026, July 20, 2016]

§ 420.21 Launch site location review—launch site boundary.

(a) The distance from any proposed launch point to the closest launch site boundary must be at least as great as the debris dispersion radius of the largest launch vehicle type and weight class proposed for the launch point.

(b) For a launch site supporting any expendable launch vehicle, an applicant shall use the largest distance provided by table 2 for the type and weight class of any launch vehicle proposed for the launch point.

(c) For a launch site supporting any reusable launch vehicle, an applicant shall determine the debris dispersion radius that represents the maximum distance from a launch point that debris travels given a worst-case launch vehicle failure in the launch area. An applicant must clearly and convincingly demonstrate the validity of its proposed debris dispersion radius.

TABLE 2 OF § 420.21—MINIMUM DISTANCE FROM LAUNCH POINT TO LAUNCH SITE BOUNDARY (FEET)

Orbital expendable launch vehicle class			Type of suborbital launch vehicle		
Small	Medium	Medium large	Large	Guided	Unguided
7300	9300	10600	13000	8000	1600

§ 420.23 Launch site location review—flight corridor.

(a) *Guided orbital expendable launch vehicle.* For a guided orbital expendable launch vehicle, an applicant shall define a flight corridor that:

(1) Encompasses an area that the applicant estimates, in accordance with the requirements of this part, to contain debris with a ballistic coefficient of ≥3 pounds per square foot, from any non-nominal flight of a guided orbital expendable launch vehicle from the launch point to a point 5000 nm downrange, or where the IIP leaves the surface of the Earth, whichever is shorter;

(2) Includes an overflight exclusion zone where the public risk criteria of 1

$\times 10^{-4}$ would be exceeded if one person were present in the open; and

(3) Uses one of the methodologies provided in appendix A or B of this part.

(b) *Guided sub-orbital expendable launch vehicle.* For a guided sub-orbital expendable launch vehicle, an applicant shall define a flight corridor that:

(1) Encompasses an area that the applicant estimates, in accordance with the requirements of this part, to contain debris with a ballistic coefficient of ≥3 pounds per square foot, from any non-nominal flight of a guided sub-orbital expendable launch vehicle from the launch point to impact with the earth's surface;

(2) Includes an impact dispersion area for the launch vehicle's last stage;

(3) Includes an overflight exclusion zone where the public risk criteria of 1×10^{-4} would be exceeded if one person were present in the open; and

(4) Uses one of the methodologies provided in appendix A or B to this part.

(c) *Unguided sub-orbital expendable launch vehicle.* (1) For an unguided sub-orbital expendable launch vehicle, an applicant shall define the following using the methodology provided by appendix D of this part:

(i) Impact dispersion areas that the applicant estimates, in accordance with the requirements of this part, to contain the impact of launch vehicle stages from nominal flight of an unguided sub-orbital expendable launch vehicle from the launch point to impact with the earth's surface; and

(ii) An overflight exclusion zone where the public risk criteria of 1×10^{-4} would be exceeded if one person were present in the open.

(2) An applicant shall base its analysis on an unguided suborbital launch vehicle whose final launch vehicle stage apogee represents the intended use of the launch point.

(d) *Reusable launch vehicle.* For a reusable launch vehicle, an applicant shall define a flight corridor that contains the hazardous debris from nominal and non-nominal flight of a reusable launch vehicle. The applicant must provide a clear and convincing demonstration of the validity of its flight corridor.

[Docket No. FAA–1999–5833, 65 FR 62861, Oct. 19, 2000, as amended by Docket No. FAA–2014–0418, Amdt. No. 420–7, 81 FR 47026, July 20, 2016; Doc. No. FAA–2016–6761, Amdt. No. 420–8, 83 FR 28535, June 20, 2018]

§ 420.25 Launch site location review—risk analysis.

(a) If a flight corridor or impact dispersion area defined by § 420.23 contains a populated area, the applicant shall estimate the casualty expectation associated with the flight corridor or impact dispersion area. An applicant shall use the methodology provided in appendix C to this part for guided orbital or suborbital expendable launch vehicles and appendix D for unguided suborbital launch vehicles.

(b) For licensed launches, the FAA will not approve the location of the proposed launch point if the estimated expected casualty exceeds 1×10^{-4}.

[Doc. No. FAA–1999–5833, 65 FR 62861, Oct. 19, 2000, as amended by Amdt. 420–3, 72 FR 17019, Apr. 6, 2007; Docket No. FAA–2014–0418, Amdt. No. 420–7, 81 FR 47027, July 20, 2016; Doc. No. FAA–2016–6761, Amdt. No. 420–8, 83 FR 28535, June 20, 2018]

§ 420.27 Launch site location review—information requirements.

An applicant shall provide the following launch site location review information in its application:

(a) A map or maps showing the location of each launch point proposed, and the flight azimuth, IIP, flight corridor, and each impact range and impact dispersion area for each launch point;

(b) Each launch vehicle type and any launch vehicle class proposed for each launch point;

(c) Trajectory data;

(d) Wind data, including each month and any percent wind data used in the analysis;

(e) Any launch vehicle apogee used in the analysis;

(f) Each populated area located within a flight corridor or impact dispersion area;

(g) The estimated casualty expectancy calculated for each populated area within a flight corridor or impact dispersion area;

(h) The effective casualty areas used in the analysis;

(i) The estimated casualty expectancy for each flight corridor or set of impact dispersion areas; and

(j) If populated areas are located within an overflight exclusion zone, a demonstration that there are times when the public is not present or that the applicant has an agreement in place to evacuate the public from the overflight exclusion zone during a launch.

§ 420.29 Launch site location review for unproven launch vehicles.

An applicant for a license to operate a launch site for an unproven launch vehicle shall provide a clear and convincing demonstration that its proposed launch site location provides an equivalent level of safety to that required by this part.

§ 420.30 Launch site location review for permitted launch vehicles.

If an applicant plans to use its proposed launch site solely for launches conducted under an experimental permit, the FAA will approve a launch site location if the FAA has approved an operating area under part 437 for launches from that site.

[Doc. No. FAA–2006–24197, 72 FR 17019, Apr. 6, 2007]

§ 420.31 Agreements.

(a) Except as provided by paragraph (c) of this section, an applicant shall complete an agreement with the local U.S. Coast Guard district to establish procedures for the issuance of a Notice to Mariners prior to a launch and other such measures as the Coast Guard deems necessary to protect public health and safety.

(b) Except as provided by paragraph (c) of this section, an applicant shall complete an agreement with the FAA Air Traffic Control (ATC) office having jurisdiction over the airspace through which launches will take place, to establish procedures for the issuance of a Notice to Airmen prior to a launch and for closing of air routes during the launch window and other such measures as the FAA ATC office deems necessary to protect public health and safety.

(c) An applicant that plans to operate a launch site located on a federal launch range does not have to comply with section 420.31 if the applicant is using existing federal launch range agreements with the U.S. Coast Guard and the FAA ATC office having jurisdiction over the airspace through which launches will take place.

§§ 420.32–420.40 [Reserved]

Subpart C—License Terms and Conditions

§ 420.41 License to operate a launch site—general.

(a) A license to operate a launch site authorizes a licensee to operate a launch site in accordance with the representations contained in the licensee's application, with terms and conditions contained in any license order accompanying the license, and subject to the licensee's compliance with 51 U.S.C. Subtitle V, chapter 509 and this chapter.

(b) A license to operate a launch site authorizes a licensee to offer its launch site to a launch operator for each launch point for the type and any weight class of launch vehicle identified in the license application and upon which the licensing determination is based.

(c) Issuance of a license to operate a launch site does not relieve a licensee of its obligation to comply with any other laws or regulations; nor does it confer any proprietary, property, or exclusive right in the use of airspace or outer space.

[Doc. No. FAA–1999–5833, 65 FR 62861, Oct. 19, 2000, as amended by Amdt. 420–5, 77 FR 20533, Apr. 5, 2012]

§ 420.43 Duration.

A license to operate a launch site remains in effect for five years from the date of issuance unless surrendered, suspended, or revoked before the expiration of the term and is renewable upon application by the licensee.

§ 420.45 Transfer of a license to operate a launch site.

(a) Only the FAA may transfer a license to operate a launch site.

(b) The FAA will transfer a license to an applicant who has submitted an application in accordance with 14 CFR part 413, satisfied the requirements of § 420.15, and obtained each approval required by § 420.17 for a license.

(c) The FAA may incorporate by reference any findings made part of the record that supported a prior related licensing determination.

§ 420.47 License modification.

(a) Upon application or upon its own initiative, the FAA may modify a license to operate a launch site at any time by issuing a license order that adds, removes, or modifies a license term or condition to ensure compliance with the Act and the requirements of this chapter.

(b) After a license to operate a launch site has been issued, a licensee shall apply to the FAA for modification of its license if:

(1) The licensee proposes to operate the launch site in a manner that is not authorized by the license; or

(2) The licensee proposes to operate the launch site in a manner that would make any representation contained in the license application that is material to public health and safety or safety of property no longer accurate and complete.

(c) An application to modify a license shall be prepared and submitted in accordance with part 413 of this chapter. The licensee shall indicate any part of its license or license application that would be changed or affected by a proposed modification.

(d) The FAA approves a modification request that satisfies the requirements of this part.

(e) Upon approval of a license modification, the FAA issues either a written approval to the licensee or a license order modifying the license if a stated term or condition of the license is changed, added, or deleted. A written approval has the full force and effect of a license order and is part of the licensing record.

§ 420.49 Compliance monitoring.

A licensee shall allow access by and cooperate with federal officers or employees or other individuals authorized by the FAA to observe any activities of the licensee, its customers, its contractors, or subcontractors, associated with licensed operation of the licensee's launch site.

Subpart D—Responsibilities of a Licensee

§ 420.51 Responsibilities—general.

(a) A licensee shall operate its launch site in accordance with the representations in the application upon which the licensing determination is based.

(b) A licensee is responsible for compliance with 51 U.S.C. Subtitle V, chapter 509 and for meeting the requirements of this chapter.

[Doc. No. FAA–1999–5833, 65 FR 62861, Oct. 19, 2000, as amended by Amdt. 420–5, 77 FR 20533, Apr. 5, 2012]

§ 420.53 Control of public access.

(a) A licensee shall prevent unauthorized access to the launch site, and unauthorized, unescorted access to explosive hazard facilities or other hazard areas not otherwise controlled by a launch operator, through the use of security personnel, surveillance systems, physical barriers, or other means approved as part of the licensing process.

(b) A licensee shall notify anyone entering the launch site of safety rules and emergency and evacuation procedures prior to that person's entry unless that person has received a briefing on those rules and procedures within the previous year.

(c) A licensee shall employ warning signals or alarms to notify any persons at the launch site of any emergency.

§ 420.55 Scheduling of launch site operations.

(a) A licensee shall develop and implement procedures to schedule operations to ensure that each operation carried out by a customer at the launch site does not create the potential for a mishap that could result in harm to the public because of the proximity of the operations, in time or place, to operations of any other customer. A customer includes any launch operator, and any contractor, subcontractor or customer of the launch site operator's customer at the launch site.

(b) A licensee shall provide its launch site scheduling requirements to each customer before the customer begins operations at the launch site.

§ 420.57 Notifications.

(a) A licensee shall notify each launch operator and any other customer of any limitations on the use of the launch site. A licensee shall also communicate limitations on the use of facilities provided to customers by the launch site operator.

(b) A licensee shall maintain its agreement, made in accordance with § 420.31(a), with the local U.S. Coast Guard district.

(c) A licensee shall maintain its agreement, made in accordance with § 420.31(b), with the FAA ATC office having jurisdiction over the airspace through which launches will take place.

(d) At least two days prior to flight of a launch vehicle, the licensee shall notify local officials and all owners of land adjacent to the launch site of the flight schedule.

§ 420.59 Launch site accident investigation plan.

(a) *General.* A licensee shall develop and implement a launch site accident investigation plan that contains the licensee's procedures for reporting, responding to, and investigating launch site accidents, as defined by § 420.5, and for cooperating with federal officials in case of a launch accident. The launch site accident investigation plan must be signed by an individual authorized to sign and certify the application in accordance with § 413.7(c) of this chapter.

(b) *Reporting requirements.* A launch site accident investigation plan shall provide for—

(1) Immediate notification to the Federal Aviation Administration (FAA) Washington Operations Center in the event of a launch site accident.

(2) Submission of a written preliminary report to the FAA, Associate Administrator for Commercial Space Transportation, within five days of any launch site accident. The report must include the following information:

(i) Date and time of occurrence;

(ii) Location of the event;

(iii) Description of the event;

(iv) Number of injuries, if any, and general description of types of injuries suffered;

(v) Property damage, if any, and an estimate of its value;

(vi) Identification of hazardous materials, as defined by § 401.5 of this chapter, involved in the event;

(vii) Any action taken to contain the consequences of the event; and

(viii) Weather conditions at the time of the event.

(c) *Response plan.* A launch site accident investigation plan shall contain procedures that—

(1) Ensure the consequences of a launch site accident are contained and minimized;

(2) Ensure data and physical evidence are preserved;

(3) Require the licensee to report to and cooperate with FAA or National Transportation Safety Board (NTSB) investigations and designate one or more points of contact for the FAA or NTSB; and

(4) Require the licensee to identify and adopt preventive measures for avoiding recurrence of the event.

(d) *Investigation plan.* A launch site accident investigation plan must contain—

(1) Procedures for investigating the cause of a launch site accident;

(2) Procedures for reporting launch site accident investigation results to the FAA; and

(3) Delineated responsibilities, including reporting responsibilities for personnel assigned to conduct investigations and for any one retained by the licensee to conduct or participate in investigations.

(e) *Launch accidents.* A launch site accident investigation plan shall contain—

(1) Procedures for participating in an investigation of a launch accident for launches launched from the launch site;

(2) Require the licensee to cooperate with FAA or National Transportation Safety Board (NTSB) investigations of a launch accident for launches launched from the launch site.

(f) *Applicability of other accident investigation procedures.* Accident investigation procedures developed in accordance with 29 CFR 1910.119 and 40 CFR part 68 will satisfy the requirements of paragraphs (c) and (d) of this section to the extent that they include the elements required by paragraphs (c) and (d) of this section.

§ 420.61 Records.

(a) A licensee shall maintain all records, data, and other material needed to verify that its operations are conducted in accordance with representations contained in the licensee's application. A licensee shall retain records for three years.

(b) In the event of a launch or launch site accident, a licensee shall preserve all records related to the event. Records shall be retained until completion of any federal investigation and the FAA advises the licensee that the records need not be retained.

(c) A licensee shall make available to federal officials for inspection and copying all records required to be maintained under the regulations.

§ 420.63 Explosive siting.

(a) Except as otherwise provided by paragraph (b) of this section, a licensee must ensure the configuration of the launch site follows its explosive site plan, and the licensee's explosive site plan complies with the requirements of §§ 420.65 through 420.70. The explosive site plan must include:

(1) A scaled map that shows the location of all explosive hazard facilities at the launch site and that shows actual and minimal allowable distances between each explosive hazard facility and all other explosive hazard facilities, each public traffic route, and each public area, including the launch site boundary;

(2) A list of the maximum quantity of energetic liquids, solid propellants and other explosives to be located at each explosive hazard facility, including explosive class and division;

(3) A description of each activity to be conducted at each explosive hazard facility; and

(4) An explosive site map using a scale sufficient to show whether distances and structural relationships satisfy the requirements of this part.

(b) A licensee operating a launch site located on a federal launch range does not have to comply with the requirements in §§ 420.65 through 420.70 if the licensee complies with the federal launch range's explosive safety requirements.

(c) For explosive siting issues not addressed by the requirements of §§ 420.65 through 420.70, a launch site operator must clearly and convincingly demonstrate a level of safety equivalent to that otherwise required by this part.

(d) A launch site operator may separate an explosive hazard facility from another explosive hazard facility, public area, or public traffic route by a distance different from one required by this part only if the launch site operator clearly and convincingly demonstrates a level of safety equivalent to that required by this part.

[Doc. No. FAA–2011–0105, 77 FR 55113, Sept. 7, 2012]

§ 420.65 Separation distance requirements for handling division 1.1 and 1.3 explosives.

(a) *Quantity.* For each explosive hazard facility, a launch site operator must determine the total quantity of division 1.1 and 1.3 explosives as follows:

(1) A launch site operator must determine the maximum total quantity of division 1.1 and 1.3 explosives by class and division, in accordance with 49 CFR part 173, Subpart C, to be located in each explosive hazard facility where division 1.1 and 1.3 explosives will be handled.

(2) When division 1.1 and 1.3 explosives are located in the same explosive hazard facility, the total quantity of explosive must be treated as division 1.1 for determining separation distances; or, a launch site operator may add the net explosive weight of the division 1.3 items to the net explosive weight of division 1.1 items to determine the total quantity of explosives.

(b) *Separation of division 1.1 and 1.3 explosives and determination of distances.* A launch site operator must separate each explosive hazard facility where division 1.1 and 1.3 explosives are handled from all other explosive hazard facilities, all public traffic routes, and each public area, including the launch site boundary, by a distance no less than that provided for each quantity and explosive division in appendix E of this part as follows:

(1) For division 1.1 explosives, the launch site operator must use tables E–1, E–2, and E–3 of appendix E of this part to determine the distance to each public area and public traffic route, and to determine each intraline distance.

(2) For division 1.3 explosives, the launch site operator must use table E–4 of appendix E of this part to determine the distance to each public area and public traffic route, and to determine each intraline distance.

(c) *Separation distance by weight and table.* A launch site operator must:

(1) Employ no less than the public area distance, calculated under paragraph (b) of this section, to separate an explosive hazard facility from each public area, including the launch site boundary.

(2) Employ no less than an intraline distance to separate an explosive hazard facility from all other explosive hazard facilities used by a single customer. For explosive hazard facilities used by different customers a launch site operator must use the greater public area distance to separate the facilities from each other.

(3) Separate each public area containing any member of the public in the open by a distance equal to −1133.9 + [389 *ln(NEW)], where the NEW is greater than 450 pounds and less than 501,500 pounds.

(d) *NEW Quantities that Fall between Table Entries.* A launch site operator must, when determining a separation distance for NEW quantities that fall between table entries, use the equation provided by tables E–1, E–3, or E–4 of appendix E of this part.

(e) *Calculating Maximum Permissible NEW Given a Distance. A launch site operator must, when determining* a permissible quantity of explosives, calculate maximum permissible NEW using the equation of tables E–1, E–3, or E–4 of appendix E of this part.

[Doc. No. FAA–2011–0105, 77 FR 55114, Sept. 7, 2012]

§ 420.66 Separation distance requirements for storage of hydrogen peroxide, hydrazine, and liquid hydrogen and any incompatible energetic liquids stored within an intraline distance.

(a) *Separation of energetic liquids and determination of distances.* A launch site operator must separate each explosive hazard facility from each other explosive hazard facility, each public area, and each public traffic route in accordance with the minimum separation distance determined under this section for each explosive hazard facility storing:

(1) Hydrogen peroxide in concentrations of greater than 91 percent;

(2) Hydrazine;

(3) Liquid hydrogen; or

(4) Any energetic liquid that is:

(i) Incompatible with any of the energetic liquids of paragraph (a)(1) through (3) of this section; and

(ii) Stored within an intraline distance of any of them.

(b) *Quantity.* For each explosive hazard facility, a launch site operator must determine the total quantity of all energetic liquids in paragraph (a)(1) through (4) of this section as follows:

(1) The quantity of energetic liquid in a tank, drum, cylinder, or other container is the net weight in pounds of the energetic liquid in the container. The determination of quantity must include any energetic liquid in associated piping to any point where positive means exist for:

(i) Interrupting the flow through the pipe, or

(ii) Interrupting a reaction in the pipe in the event of a mishap.

(2) A launch site operator must convert the quantity of each energetic liquid from gallons to pounds using the conversion factors provided in table E–6 of appendix E of this part and the following equation:

Pounds of energetic liquid = gallons × density of energetic liquid (pounds per gallon).

(3) Where two or more containers of compatible energetic liquids are stored in the same explosive hazard facility, the total quantity of energetic liquids is the total quantity of energetic liquids in all containers, unless:

(i) The containers are each separated from each other by the distance required by paragraph (c) of this section; or

(ii) The containers are subdivided by intervening barriers that prevent mixing, such as diking.

(4) Where two or more containers of incompatible energetic liquids are stored within an intraline distance of each other, paragraph (d) of this section applies.

(c) *Determination of separation distances for compatible energetic liquids.* A launch site operator must determine separation distances for compatible energetic liquids as follows:

(1) To determine each intraline, public area, and public traffic route distance, a launch site operator must use the following tables in appendix E of this part:

(i) Table E–7 for hydrogen peroxide in concentrations of greater than 91 percent; and

(ii) Table E–8 for hydrazine and liquid hydrogen.

(2) For liquid hydrogen and hydrazine, a launch site operator must use the "intraline distance to compatible energetic liquids" for the energetic liquid that requires the greater distance under table E–8 of appendix E of this part as the minimum separation distance between compatible energetic liquids.

(d) *Determination of separation distances for incompatible energetic liquids.* If incompatible energetic liquids are stored within an intraline distance of each other, a launch site operator must determine the explosive equivalent in pounds of the combined liquids as provided by paragraph (d)(2) of this section unless intervening barriers prevent mixing.

(1) If intervening barriers prevent mixing, a launch site operator must separate the incompatible energetic liquids by no less than the intraline distance that tables E–7 and E–8 of appendix E of this part apply to compatible energetic liquids using the quantity or energetic liquid requiring the greater separation distance.

(2) A launch site operator must use the formulas provided in table E–5 of appendix E of this part, to determine the explosive equivalent in pounds of the combined incompatible energetic liquids. A launch site operator must then use the explosive equivalent in pounds requiring the greatest separation distance to determine the minimum separation distance between each explosive hazard facility and all other explosive hazard facilities and each public area and public traffic route as required by tables E–1, E–2 and E–3 of appendix E of this part.

[Doc. No. FAA–2011–0105, 77 FR 55114, Sept. 7, 2012]

§420.67 Separation distance requirements for handling incompatible energetic liquids that are co-located.

(a) *Separation of energetic liquids and determination of distances.* Where incompatible energetic liquids are co-located in a launch or reentry vehicle tank or other vessel, a launch site operator must separate each explosive hazard facility from each other explosive hazard facility, each public area, and each public traffic route in accordance with the minimum separation distance determined under this section for each explosive hazard facility.

(b) *Quantity.* For each explosive hazard facility, a launch site operator must determine the total quantity of all energetic liquids as follows:

(1) The quantity of energetic liquid in a launch or reentry vehicle tank is the net weight in pounds of the energetic liquid. The determination of quantity must include any energetic liquid in associated piping to any point where positive means exist for:

(i) Interrupting the flow through the pipe; or

(ii) Interrupting a reaction in the pipe in the event of a mishap.

(2) A launch site operator must convert each energetic liquid's quantity from gallons to pounds using the conversion factors provided by table E–6 of appendix E of this part and the following equation:

Pounds of energetic liquid = gallons × density of energetic liquid (pounds per gallon).

(c) *Determination of separation distances for incompatible energetic liquids.* A launch site operator must determine separation distances for incompatible energetic liquids as follows:

(1) A launch site operator must use the formulas provided in table E–5 of appendix E of this part, to determine the explosive equivalent in pounds of the combined incompatible energetic liquids; and

(2) A launch site operator must then use the explosive equivalent in pounds to determine the minimum separation distance between each explosive hazard facility and all other explosive hazard facilities and each public area and public traffic route as required by tables E–1, E–2 and E–3 of appendix E of this part. Where two explosive hazard facilities contain different quantities, the launch site operator must use the quantity of liquid propellant requiring the greatest separation distance to determine the minimum separation distance between the two explosive hazard facilities.

(d) *Separation distance by weight and table.* For each explosive hazard facility, a launch site operator must:

(1) For an explosive equivalent weight from one pound through and including 450 pounds, determine the distance to any public area and public traffic route following table E–1 of appendix E of this part;

(2) For explosive equivalent weight greater than 450 pounds, determine the distance to any public area and public traffic route following table E–2 of appendix E of this part;

(3) Separate each public area containing any member of the public in the open by a distance equal to −1133.9 + [389 *ln(NEW)], where the NEW is greater than 450 pounds and less than 501,500 pounds;

(4) Separate each explosive hazard facility from all other explosive hazard facilities of a single customer using the intraline distance provided by table E–3 of appendix E of this part; and

(5) For explosive hazard facilities used by different customers, use the greater public area distance to separate the facilities from each other.

[Doc. No. FAA–2011–0105, 77 FR 55115, Sept. 7, 2012]

§ 420.69 Separation distance requirements for co-location of division 1.1 and 1.3 explosives with liquid propellants.

(a) *Separation of energetic liquids and explosives and determination of distances.* A launch site operator must separate each explosive hazard facility from each other explosive hazard facility, each public traffic route, and each public area in accordance with the minimum separation distance determined under this section for each explosive hazard facility where division 1.1 and 1.3 explosives are co-located with liquid propellants. A launch site operator must determine each minimum separation distance from an explosive hazard facility where division 1.1 and 1.3 explosives and liquid propellants are to be located together, to each other explosive hazard facility, public traffic route, and public area as described in paragraphs (b) through (e) of this section.

(b) *Liquid propellants and division 1.1 explosives located together.* For liquid propellants and division 1.1 explosives located together, a launch site operator must:

(1) Determine the explosive equivalent weight of the liquid propellants by following § 420.67(c);

(2) Add the explosive equivalent weight of the liquid propellants and the net explosive weight of division 1.1 explosives to determine the combined net explosive weight;

(3) Use the combined net explosive weight to determine the distance to each public area, public traffic route, and each other explosive hazard facility by following tables E–1, E–2, and E–3 of appendix E of this part; and

(4) Separate each public area containing any member of the public in the open by a distance equal to −1133.9 + [389 *ln(NEW)], where the net explosive weight is greater than 450 pounds and less than 501,500 pounds.

(c) *Liquid propellants and division 1.3 explosives located together.* For liquid propellants and division 1.3 explosives located together, a launch site operator must separate each explosive hazard facility from each other explosive hazard facility, public area, and public traffic route using either of the following two methods:

(1) *Method 1.* (i) Determine the explosive equivalent weight of the liquid propellants by following §420.67(c);

(ii) Add to the explosive equivalent weight of the liquid propellants, the net explosive weight of each division 1.3 explosive, treating division 1.3 explosives as division 1.1 explosives;

(iii) Use the combined net explosive weight to determine the minimum separation distance to each public area, public traffic route, and each other explosive hazard facility by following tables E–1, E–2, and E–3 of appendix E of this part; and

(iv) Separate each public area containing any member of the public in the open by a distance equal to −1133.9 + [389 *ln(NEW)], where the net explosive weight is greater than 450 pounds and less than 501,500 pounds.

(2) *Method 2.* (i) Determine the explosive equivalent weight of each liquid propellant by following §420.67(c);

(ii) Add to the explosive equivalent weight of the liquid propellants, the net explosive weight of each division 1.3 explosive to determine the combined net explosive weight;

(iii) Use the combined net explosive weight to determine the minimum separation distance to each public area, public traffic route, and each other explosive hazard facility by following tables E–1, E–2, and E–3 of appendix E of this part; and

(iv) Separate each public area containing any member of the public in the open by a distance equal to −1133.9 + [389 *ln(NEW)], where the net explosive weight is greater than 450 pounds and less than 501,500 pounds.

(d) *Liquid propellants and division 1.1 and 1.3 explosives located together.* For liquid propellants and division 1.1 and 1.3 explosives located together, a launch site operator must:

(1) Determine the explosive equivalent weight of the liquid propellants by following §420.67(c);

(2) Determine the total explosive quantity of each division 1.1 and 1.3 explosive by following §420.65(a)(2);

(3) Add the explosive equivalent weight of the liquid propellants to the total explosive quantity of division 1.1 and 1.3 explosives together to determine the combined net explosive weight;

(4) Use the combined net explosive weight to determine the distance to each public area, public traffic route, and each other explosive hazard facility by following tables E–1, E–2, and E–3 of appendix E of this part; and

(5) Separate each public area containing any member of the public in the open by a distance equal to −1133.9 + [389 *ln(NEW)], where the net explosive weight is greater than 450 pounds and less than 501,500 pounds

(e) *Use of maximum credible event analysis.* If a launch site operator does not want to employ paragraphs (b), (c), or (d) of this section, the launch site operator must analyze the maximum credible event (MCE) or the worst case explosion expected to occur. If the MCE shows there will be no simultaneous explosion reaction of the liquid propellant tanks and the solid propellant motors, the minimum distance between the explosive hazard facility and all other explosive hazard facilities and public areas must be based on the MCE.

[Doc. No. FAA–2011–0105, 77 FR 55115, Sept. 7, 2012]

§420.70 Separation distance measurement requirements.

(a) This section applies to all measurements of distances performed under §§420.63 through 420.69.

(b) A launch site operator must measure each separation distance along straight lines. For large intervening topographical features such as hills, the launch site operator must measure over or around the feature, whichever is the shorter.

(c) A launch site operator must measure each minimum separation distance from the closest hazard source, such as a container, building, segment, or positive cut-off point in piping, in an explosive hazard facility. When measuring, a launch site operator must:

(1) For a public traffic route distance, measure from the nearest side of the public traffic route to the closest point of the hazard source; and

(2) For an intraline distance, measure from the nearest point of one hazard source to the nearest point of the next hazard source. The minimum separation distance must be the distance for the quantity of energetic liquids or net

explosive weight that requires the greater distance.

[Doc. No. FAA–2011–0105, 77 FR 55116, Sept. 7, 2012]

§ 420.71 Lightning protection.

(a) *Lightning protection.* A licensee shall ensure that the public is not exposed to hazards due to the initiation of explosives by lightning.

(1) *Elements of a lighting protection system.* Unless an explosive hazard facility meets the conditions of paragraph (a)(3) of this section, all explosive hazard facilities shall have a lightning protection system to ensure explosives are not initiated by lightning. A lightning protection system shall meet the requirements of this paragraph and include the following:

(i) *Air terminal.* An air terminal to intentionally attract a lightning strike.

(ii) *Down conductor.* A low impedance path connecting an air terminal to an earth electrode system.

(iii) *Earth electrode system.* An earth electrode system to dissipate the current from a lightning strike to ground.

(2) *Bonding and surge protection.* A lightning protection system must meet the requirements of this paragraph and include the following:

(i) *Bonding.* All metallic bodies shall be bonded to ensure that voltage potentials due to lightning are equal everywhere in the explosive hazard facility. Any fence within six feet of a lightning protection system shall have a bond across each gate and other discontinuations and shall be bonded to the lightning protection system. Railroad tracks that run within six feet of the lightning protection system shall be bonded to the lightning protection system.

(ii) *Surge protection.* A lightning protection system shall include surge protection to reduce transient voltages due to lightning to a harmless level for all metallic power, communication, and instrumentation lines entering an explosive hazard facility.

(3) *Circumstances where no lightning protection system is required.* No lightning protection system is required for an explosive hazard facility when a lightning warning system is available to permit termination of operations and withdrawal of the public to public area distance prior to an electrical storm, or for an explosive hazard facility containing explosives that cannot be initiated by lightning. If no lightning protection system is required, a licensee must ensure the withdrawal of the public to a public area distance prior to an electrical storm.

(4) *Testing and inspection.* Lightning protection systems shall be visually inspected semiannually and shall be tested once each year for electrical continuity and adequacy of grounding. A licensee shall maintain at the explosive hazard facility a record of results obtained from the tests, including any action taken to correct deficiencies noted.

(b) *Electrical power lines.* A licensee shall ensure that electric power lines at its launch site meet the following requirements:

(1) Electric power lines shall be no closer to an explosive hazard facility than the length of the lines between the poles or towers that support the lines unless an effective means is provided to ensure that energized lines cannot, on breaking, come in contact with the explosive hazard facility.

(2) Towers or poles supporting electrical distribution lines that carry between 15 and 69 KV, and unmanned electrical substations shall be no closer to an explosive hazard facility than the public area distance for that explosive hazard facility.

(3) Towers or poles supporting electrical transmission lines that carry 69 KV or more, shall be no closer to an explosive hazard facility than the public area distance for that explosive hazard facility.

APPENDIX A TO PART 420—METHOD FOR DEFINING A FLIGHT CORRIDOR

(a) Introduction

(1) This appendix provides a method for constructing a flight corridor from a launch point for a guided suborbital launch vehicle or any one of the four classes of guided orbital launch vehicles from table 1, § 420.19, without the use of local meteorological data or a launch vehicle trajectory.

(2) A flight corridor includes an overflight exclusion zone in a launch area and, for a guided suborbital launch vehicle, an impact

dispersion area in a downrange area. A flight corridor for a guided suborbital launch vehicle ends with the impact dispersion area, and, for the four classes of guided orbital launch vehicles, 5000 nautical miles (nm) from the launch point.

(b) Data requirements

(1) Maps. An applicant shall use any map for the launch site region with a scale not less than 1:250,000 inches per inch in the launch area and 1:20,000,000 inches per inch in the downrange area. As described in paragraph (b)(2), an applicant shall use a mechanical method, a semi-automated method, or a fully-automated method to plot a flight corridor on maps. A source for paper maps acceptable to the FAA is the U.S. Dept. of Commerce, National Oceanic and Atmospheric Administration, National Ocean Service.

(i) Projections for mechanical plotting method. An applicant shall use a conic projection. The FAA will accept a "Lambert-Conformal" conic projection. A polar aspect of a plane-azimuthal projection may also be used for far northern launch sites.

(ii) Projections for semi-automated plotting method. An applicant shall use cylindrical, conic, or plane projections for semi-automated plotting. The FAA will accept "Mercator" and "Oblique Mercator" cylindrical projections. The FAA will accept "Lambert-Conformal" and "Albers Equal-Area" conic projections. The FAA will accept "Lambert Azimuthal Equal-Area" and "Azimuthal Equidistant" plane projections.

(iii) Projections for fully-automated plotting method. The FAA will accept map projections used by geographical information system software scaleable pursuant to the requirements of paragraph (b)(1).

(2) Plotting Methods.

(i) Mechanical method. An applicant may use mechanical drafting equipment such as pencil, straight edge, ruler, protractor, and compass to plot the location of a flight corridor on a map. The FAA will accept straight lines for distances less than or equal to 7.5 times the map scale on map scales greater than or equal to 1:1,000,000 inches per inch (in/in); or straight lines representing 100 nm or less on map scales less than 1:1,000,000 in/in.

(ii) Semi-automated method. An applicant may employ the range and bearing techniques in paragraph (b)(3) to create latitude and longitude points on a map. The FAA will accept straight lines for distances less than or equal to 7.5 times the map scale on map scales greater than or equal to 1:1,000,000 inches per inch (in/in); or straight lines representing 100 nm or less on map scales less than 1:1,000,000 in/in.

(iii) Fully-automated method. An applicant may use geographical information system software with global mapping data scaleable in accordance with paragraph (b)(1).

(3) Range and bearing computations on an ellipsoidal Earth model.

(i) To create latitude and longitude pairs on an ellipsoidal Earth model, an applicant shall use the following equations to calculate geodetic latitude (+N) and longitude (+E) given the launch point geodetic latitude (+N), longitude (+E), range (nm), and bearing (degrees, positive clockwise from North).

(A) Input. An applicant shall use the following input in making range and bearing computations. Angle units must be in radians.

$$\phi_1 = \text{Geodetic latitude of launch point (radians)}$$

$$= \phi_1\ (\text{DDD}) \cdot \frac{\pi}{180}\ (\text{radians per degree})$$

$$\lambda_1 = \text{Longitude of launch point (DDD)}$$

$$= \lambda\ (\text{DDD}) \cdot \frac{\pi}{180}\ (\text{radians per degree})$$

$$S = \text{Range from launch point (nm)}$$

$$= S\ (\text{DDD}) \cdot \frac{\pi}{180}\ (\text{radians per degree})$$

$$\alpha_{12} = \text{Azimuth bearing from launch point (deg)}$$

$$= \alpha_{12}(\text{DDD}) \cdot \frac{\pi}{180}\ (\text{radians per degree})$$

(B) Computations. An applicant shall use the following equations to determine the latitude (φ_2) and longitude (λ_2) of a target point situated "S" nm from the launch point on an azimuth bearing (α_{12}) degrees.

$$f = 1 - \frac{b}{a} \quad \text{(Equation A1)}$$

where:

a = WGS–84 semi-major axis (3443.91846652 nmi)

b = WGS–84 semi-minor axis (3432.37165994 nmi)

$$\varepsilon^2 = \frac{\left(a^2 - b^2\right)}{b^2} \quad \text{(Equation A2)}$$

$$\theta = \frac{S}{b} \text{ (radians)} \quad \text{(Equation A3)}$$

$$\beta_1 = \tan^{-1}\left[\frac{\left(b \cdot \sin\phi_1\right)}{\left(a \cdot \cos\phi_1\right)}\right] \quad \text{(Equation A4)}$$

$$g = \left(\cos\beta_1\right)\left(\cos\alpha_{12}\right) \quad \text{(Equation A5)}$$

$$h = \left(\cos\beta_1\right)\left(\sin\alpha_{12}\right) \quad \text{(Equation A6)}$$

$$m = \frac{\left[1 + \left(\frac{\varepsilon^2}{2}\right)\sin^2\beta_1\right]\left[1 - h^2\right]}{2} \quad \text{(Equation A7)}$$

$$n = \frac{\left[1 + \left(\frac{\varepsilon^2}{2}\right)\sin^2\beta_1\right]\left[\left(\sin^2\beta_1\right)(\cos\theta) + g\cdot\left(\sin\beta_1\right)(\sin\theta)\right]}{2} \quad \text{(Equation A8)}$$

$$L = h\cdot\left[-f\cdot\theta + 3\cdot f^2\cdot n\cdot\sin\theta + \frac{3\cdot f^2\cdot m\cdot(\theta - \sin\theta\cdot\cos\theta)}{2}\right] \text{(radians)} \quad \text{(Equation A9)}$$

$$M = m\cdot\varepsilon^2 \quad \text{(Equation A10)}$$

$$N = n\cdot\varepsilon^2 \quad \text{(Equation A11)}$$

$$A_1 = N\cdot\sin\theta \quad \text{(Equation A12)}$$

$$A_2 = \left(\frac{M}{2}\right)(\sin\theta\cdot\cos\theta - \theta) \quad \text{(Equation A13)}$$

$$A_3 = \left(\frac{5}{2}\right)\left(N^2\cdot\sin\theta\cdot\cos\theta\right) \quad \text{(Equation A14)}$$

$$A_4 = \left(\frac{M^2}{16}\right)\left(11\cdot\theta - 13\cdot\sin\theta\cdot\cos\theta - 8\cdot\theta\cdot\cos^2\theta + 10\cdot\sin\theta\cdot\cos^3\theta\right) \quad \text{(Equation A15)}$$

$$A_5 = \left(\frac{M\cdot N}{2}\right)\left(3\cdot\sin\theta + 2\cdot\theta\cdot\cos\theta - 5\cdot\sin\theta\cdot\cos^2\theta\right) \quad \text{(Equation A16)}$$

$$\delta = \theta - A_1 + A_2 + A_3 + A_4 + XA_5(\text{radians}) \quad \text{(Equation A17)}$$

$$\sin\beta_2 = \sin\beta_1\cdot\cos\delta + g\cdot\sin\delta \quad \text{(Equation A18)}$$

$$\cos\beta_2 = \left[h^2 + \left(g\cdot\cos\delta - \sin\beta_1\cdot\sin\delta\right)^2\right]^{\frac{1}{2}} \quad \text{(Equation A19)}$$

$$\phi_2 = \left\{\tan^{-1}\left[\frac{(a\cdot\sin\beta_2)}{(b\cdot\cos\beta_2)}\right]\right\}\cdot\left(\frac{180}{\pi}\right)(\text{geodetic latitude of target point, DDD}) \quad \text{(Equation A20)}$$

$$\Lambda = \tan^{-1}\left[\frac{(\sin\delta\cdot\sin\alpha_{12})}{(\cos\beta_1\cdot\cos\delta - \sin\beta_1\cdot\sin\delta\cdot\cos\alpha_{12})}\right] \quad \text{(Equation A21)}$$

$$\lambda_2 = (\lambda_1 + \Lambda + L)\left(\frac{180}{\pi}\right)(\text{longitude of target point, DDD}) \quad \text{(Equation A22)}$$

(ii) To create latitude and longitude pairs on an ellipsoidal Earth model, an applicant shall use the following equations to calculate the distance (S) of the geodesic between two points (P_1 and P_2), the forward azimuth (α_{12}) of the geodesic at P_1, and the back azimuth (α_{21}) of the geodesic at P_2, given the geodetic latitude (+N), longitude (+E) of P_1 and P_2. Azimuth is measured positively clockwise from North.

(A) Input. An applicant shall use the following input. Units must be in radians.

$$\phi_1 = \text{Geodetic latitude of launch point (radians)}$$
$$= \phi_1(\text{DDD})\cdot\frac{\pi}{180}(\text{radians per degree})$$
$$\lambda_1 = \text{Longitude of launch point (DDD)}$$
$$= \lambda_1(\text{DDD})\cdot\frac{\pi}{180}(\text{radians per degree})$$
$$S = \text{Range from launch point (nm)}$$
$$= S(\text{DDD})\cdot\frac{\pi}{180}(\text{radians per degree})$$
$$\alpha_{12} = \text{Azimuth bearing from launch point (deg)}$$
$$= \alpha_{12}(\text{DDD})\cdot\frac{\pi}{180}(\text{radians per degree})$$

(B) Computations. An applicant shall use the following equations to determine the distance (S), the forward azimuth (α_{12}) of the geodesic at P_1, and the back azimuth (α_{12}) of the geodesic at P_2.

$$f = 1 - \frac{b}{a} \qquad \text{(Equation A23)}$$

where:

a = WGS–84 semi-major axis (3443.91846652 nmi)

b = WGS–84 semi-minor axis (3432.37165994 nmi)

$$L = \lambda_2 - \lambda_1 \qquad \text{(Equation A24)}$$

$$\beta_1 = \tan^{-1}\left[\frac{(b \cdot \sin\phi_1)}{\alpha \cdot \cos\phi_1}\right] \qquad \text{(Equation A25)}$$

$$\beta_2 = \tan^{-1}\left[\frac{(b \cdot \sin\phi_2)}{\alpha \cdot \cos\phi_2}\right] \qquad \text{(Equation A26)}$$

$$A = \sin\beta_1 \cdot \sin\beta_2 \qquad \text{(Equation A27)}$$

$$B = \cos\beta_1 \cdot \cos\beta_2 \qquad \text{(Equation A28)}$$

$$\cos\delta = A + B \cdot \cos L \qquad \text{(Equation A29)}$$

$$n = \frac{(a-b)}{(a+b)} \qquad \text{(Equation A30)}$$

$$(\beta_2 - \beta_1) = (\phi_2 - \phi_1) + 2 \cdot \left\lfloor A \cdot (n + n^2 + n^3) - B \cdot (n - n^2 + n^3) \right\rfloor \cdot \sin(\phi_2 - \phi_1) \text{ radians} \qquad \text{(Equation A31)}$$

$$\sin\delta = \left\{(\sin L \cdot \cos\beta_2)^2 + \left[\sin(\beta_2 - \beta_1) + 2 \cdot \cos\beta_2 \cdot \sin\beta_1 \cdot \sin^2(L/2)\right]^2\right\}^{\frac{1}{2}} \qquad \text{(Equation A32)}$$

$$\delta = \tan^{-1}\left(\frac{\sin\delta}{\cos\delta}\right) \text{evaluated in positive radians} \le \pi \qquad \text{(Equation A33)}$$

$$c = \frac{B \cdot \sin L}{\sin\delta} \qquad \text{(Equation A34)}$$

$$m = 1 - c^2 \qquad \text{(Equation A35)}$$

$$S = b \cdot \left\{ \begin{array}{l} \delta \cdot \left[1+f+f^2\right] + A \cdot \left[\left(f+f^2\right) \cdot \sin\delta - \left(f^2 \cdot \delta^2\right)/(2 \cdot \sin\delta)\right] \\ -(m/2)\left[\left(f+f^2\right)(\delta + \sin\delta \cdot \cos\delta) - \left(f^2 \cdot \delta^2\right)/(\tan\delta)\right] \\ -\left(A^2 \cdot f^2/2\right) \cdot \sin\delta \cdot \cos\delta \\ +\left(f^2 \cdot m^2/16\right)\left[\delta + \sin\delta \cdot \cos\delta - 2 \cdot \sin\delta \cdot \cos^3\delta - 8\delta^2/(\tan\delta)\right] \\ +\left(A^2 \cdot m \cdot f^2/2\right)\left[\sin\delta \cdot \cos^2 + \delta + \delta^2/(\sin\delta)\right] \text{ in the same units as "a" and "b"} \end{array} \right\} \quad \text{(Equation A36)}$$

$$\Lambda = L + c \cdot \left\{ \begin{array}{l} \delta \cdot \left(f+f^2\right) - \left(A \cdot f^2/2\right)\left[\sin\delta + 2\delta^2/(\sin\delta)\right] \\ +\left(m \cdot f^2/4\right)\left[\sin\delta\cos\delta - 5\delta + 4\delta^2/(\tan\delta)\right] \end{array} \right\} \text{radians} \quad \text{(Equation A37)}$$

$$\alpha_{12} = \tan^{-1}\left\{ \frac{\left(\cos\beta_2 \cdot \sin\Lambda\right)}{\left[\sin\left(\beta_2 - \beta_1\right) + 2 \cdot \cos\beta_2 \cdot \sin\beta_1 \cdot \sin^2(\Lambda/2)\right]} \right\} \cdot \left(\frac{180}{\pi}\right) \text{degrees} \quad \text{(Equation A38)}$$

$$\alpha_{21} = \tan^{-1}\left\{ \frac{\left(-\cos\beta_1 \cdot \sin\Lambda\right)}{\left[2 \cdot \cos\beta_1 \cdot \sin\beta_2 \cdot \sin^2(\Lambda/2) - \sin\left(\beta_2 - \beta_1\right)\right]} \right\} \cdot \left(\frac{180}{\pi}\right) \text{degrees} \quad \text{(Equation A39)}$$

(c) Creation of a Flight Corridor

(1) To define a flight corridor, an applicant shall:

(i) Select a guided suborbital or orbital launch vehicle, and, for an orbital launch vehicle, select from table 1 of §420.19 a launch vehicle weight class that best represents the launch vehicle the applicant plans to support at its launch point;

(ii) Select a debris dispersion radius (D_{max}) from table A–1 corresponding to the guided suborbital launch vehicle or orbital launch vehicle class selected in paragraph (c)(1)(i);

(iii) Select a launch point geodetic latitude and longitude; and

(iv) Select a flight azimuth.

(2) An applicant shall define and map an overflight exclusion zone using the following method:

(i) Select a debris dispersion radius (D_{max}) from table A–1 and a downrange distance (D_{OEZ}) from table A–2 to define an overflight exclusion zone for the guided suborbital launch vehicle or orbital launch vehicle class selected in paragraph (c)(1)(i).

(ii) An overflight exclusion zone is described by the intersection of the following boundaries, which are depicted in figure A–1:

(A) An applicant shall define an uprange boundary with a half-circle arc of radius D_{max} and a chord of length twice D_{max} connecting the half-circle arc endpoints. The uprange boundary placement on a map has the chord midpoint positioned on the launch point with the chord oriented along an azimuth ±90°from the launch azimuth and the half-circle arc located uprange from the launch point.

(B) An applicant shall define the downrange boundary with a half-circle arc of radius D_{max} and a chord of length twice D_{max} connecting the half-circle arc endpoints. The downrange boundary placement on a map has the chord midpoint intersecting the nominal flight azimuth line at a distance D_{OEZ} inches downrange with the chord oriented along an azimuth ±90°from the launch azimuth and the half-circle arc located downrange from the intersection of the chord and the flight azimuth line.

(C) Crossrange boundaries of an overflight exclusion zone are defined by two lines segments. Each is parallel to the flight azimuth with one to the left side and one to the right side of the flight azimuth line. Each line connects an uprange half-circle arc endpoint to a downrange half-circle arc endpoint as shown in figure A–1.

(iii) An applicant shall identify the overflight exclusion zone on a map that meets the requirements of paragraph (b).

(3) An applicant shall define and map a flight corridor using the following method:

(i) In accordance with paragraph (b), an applicant shall draw a flight corridor on one or more maps with the D_{max} origin centered on the intended launch point and the flight corridor centerline (in the downrange direction) aligned with the initial flight azimuth. The flight corridor is depicted in figure A–2 and its line segment lengths are tabulated in table A–3.

(ii) An applicant shall define the flight corridor using the following boundary definitions:

(A) An applicant shall draw an uprange boundary, which is defined by an arc-line GB (figure A–2), directly uprange from and centered on the intended launch point with radius D_{max}.

(B) An applicant shall draw line CF perpendicular to and centered on the flight azimuth line, and positioned 10 nm downrange from the launch point. The applicant shall use the length of line CF provided in table A–3 corresponding to the guided suborbital launch vehicle or orbital launch vehicle class selected in paragraph (c)(1)(i).

(C) An applicant shall draw line DE perpendicular to and centered on the flight azimuth line, and positioned 100 nm downrange from the launch point. The applicant shall use the length of line DE provided in table A–3 corresponding to the guided suborbital launch vehicle or orbital launch vehicle class selected in paragraph (c)(1)(i).

(D) Except for a guided suborbital launch vehicle, an applicant shall draw a downrange boundary, which is defined by line HI and is drawn perpendicular to and centered on the flight azimuth line, and positioned 5,000 nm downrange from the launch point. The applicant shall use the length of line HI provided in table A–3 corresponding to the orbital launch vehicle class selected in paragraph (c)(1)(i).

(E) An applicant shall draw crossrange boundaries, which are defined by three lines on the left side and three lines on the right side of the flight azimuth. An applicant shall construct the left flight corridor boundary according to the following, and as depicted in figure A–3 :

(*1*) The first line (line BC in figure A–3) is tangent to the uprange boundary arc, and ends at endpoint C of line CF, as depicted in figure A–3;

(*2*) The second line (line CD in figure A–3) begins at endpoint C of line BC and ends at endpoint D of line DH, as depicted in figure A–3;

(*3*) For all orbital launch vehicles, the third line (line DH in figure A–3) begins at endpoint D of line CD and ends at endpoint H of line HI, as depicted in figure A–3; and

(*4*) For a guided suborbital launch vehicle, the line DH begins at endpoint D of line CD and ends at a point tangent to the impact dispersion area drawn in accordance with paragraph (c)(4) and as depicted in figure A–4.

(F) An applicant shall repeat the procedure in paragraph (c)(3)(ii)(E) for the right side boundary.

(iii) An applicant shall identify the flight corridor on a map that meets the requirements of paragraph (b).

(4) For a guided suborbital launch vehicle, an applicant shall define a final stage impact dispersion area as part of the flight corridor and show the impact dispersion area on a map, as depicted in figure A–4, in accordance with the following:

(i) An applicant shall select an apogee altitude (H_{ap}) for the launch vehicle final stage. The apogee altitude should equal the highest altitude intended to be reached by a guided suborbital launch vehicle launched from the launch point.

(ii) An applicant shall define the impact dispersion area by using an impact range factor $[IP(H_{ap})]$ and a dispersion factor $[DISP(H_{ap})]$ as shown below:

(A) An applicant shall calculate the impact range (D) for the final launch vehicle stage. An applicant shall set D equal to the maximum apogee altitude (H_{ap}) multiplied by the impact range factor as shown below:

$$D = H_{ap} \cdot IP(H_{ap}) \qquad \text{(Equation A40)}$$

where: $IP(H_{ap})$ = 0.4 for an apogee less than 100 km; and $IP(H_{ap})$ = 0.7 for an apogee 100 km or greater.

(B) An applicant shall calculate the impact dispersion radius (R) for the final launch vehicle stage. An applicant shall set R equal to the maximum apogee altitude (H_{ap}) multiplied by the dispersion factor as shown below:

$$R = H_{ap} \cdot DISP(H_{ap}) \qquad \text{(Equation A41)}$$

where: $DISP(H_{ap})$ = 0.05

(iii) An applicant shall draw the impact dispersion area on a map with its center on the predicted impact point. An applicant shall then draw line DH in accordance with paragraph (c)(3)(ii)(E)(*4*).

(d) Evaluate the Flight Corridor

(1) An applicant shall evaluate the flight corridor for the presence of any populated areas. If an applicant determines that no populated area is located within the flight corridor, then no additional steps are necessary.

(2) If a populated area is located in an overflight exclusion zone, an applicant may modify its proposal or demonstrate that there are times when no people are present or that the applicant has an agreement in place to evacuate the public from the overflight exclusion zone during a launch.

(3) If a populated area is located within the flight corridor, an applicant may modify its proposal and create another flight corridor pursuant to appendix A, use appendix B to narrow the flight corridor, or complete a risk analysis in accordance with appendix C.

TABLE A–1—DEBRIS DISPERSION RADIUS (D_{max}) (IN)

Orbital launch vehicles				Suborbital launch vehicles
Small	Medium	Medium large	Large	Guided
87,600 (1.20 nm)	111,600 (1.53 nm)	127,200 (1.74 nm)	156,000 (2.14 nm)	96,000 (1.32 nm)

TABLE A–2—OVERFLIGHT EXCLUSION ZONE DOWNRANGE DISTANCE (D_{oez}) (IN)

Orbital launch vehicles				Suborbital launch vehicles
Small	Medium	Medium large	Large	Guided
240,500 (3.30 nm)	253,000 (3.47 nm)	310,300 (4.26 nm)	937,700 (12.86 nm)	232,100 (3.18 nm)

Table A-3: Flight Corridor Line Segment Lengths

D_{max} (in)		Line Segment Lengths (x 10^6 inches)		
Orbital Launch Vehicles		$\overline{CF}$	$\overline{DE}$	$\overline{HI}$
Small	87600 (1.20 nm)	2.87620 (39.45 nm)	8.59452 (117.87 nm)	128.566 (1763.27 nm)
Medium	111,600 (1.53 nm)	2.97220 (40.76 nm)	8.64252 (118.53 nm)	128.566 (1763.27 nm)
Med-Large	127,200 (1.74 nm)	3.03460 (41.62 nm)	8.67372 (118.96 nm)	128.566 (1763.27 nm)
Large	156,000 (2.14 nm)	3.14979 (43.20 nm)	8.73131 (119.75 nm)	128.566 (1763.27 nm)
Suborbital Launch Vehicles		$\overline{CF}$	$\overline{DE}$	$\overline{HI}$
Guided	96,000 (1.32 nm)	2.90980 (39.91 nm)	8.61132 (118.10 nm)	N/A

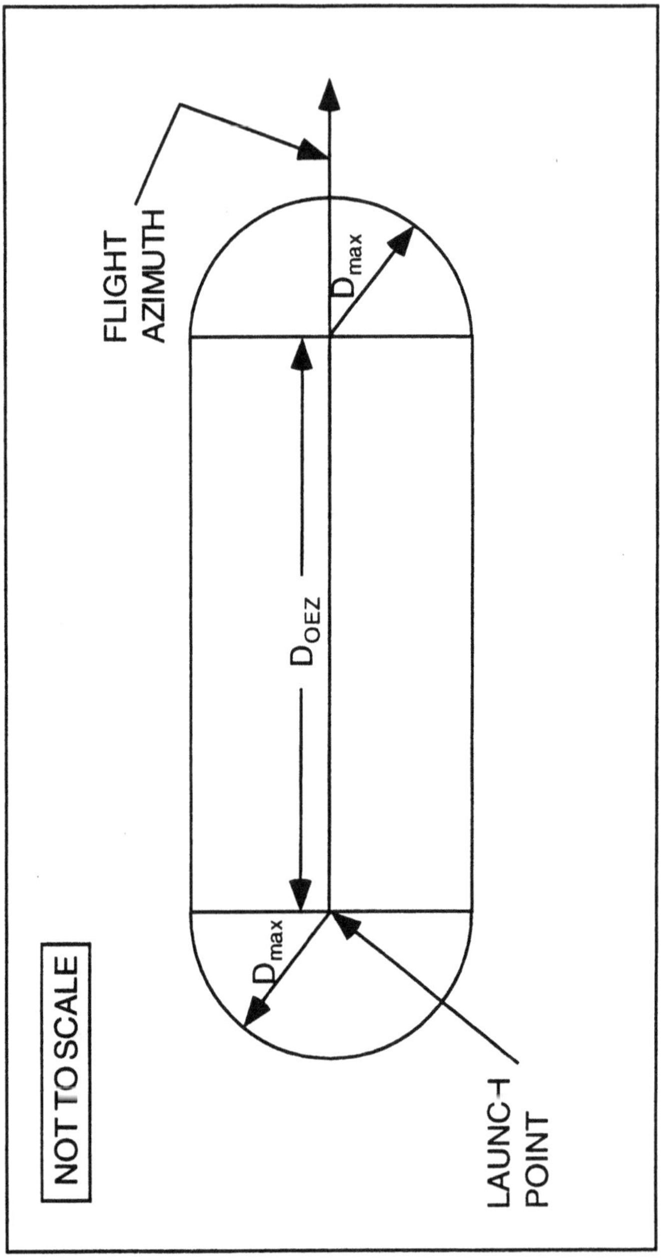

Figure A-1
Overflight Exclusion Zone

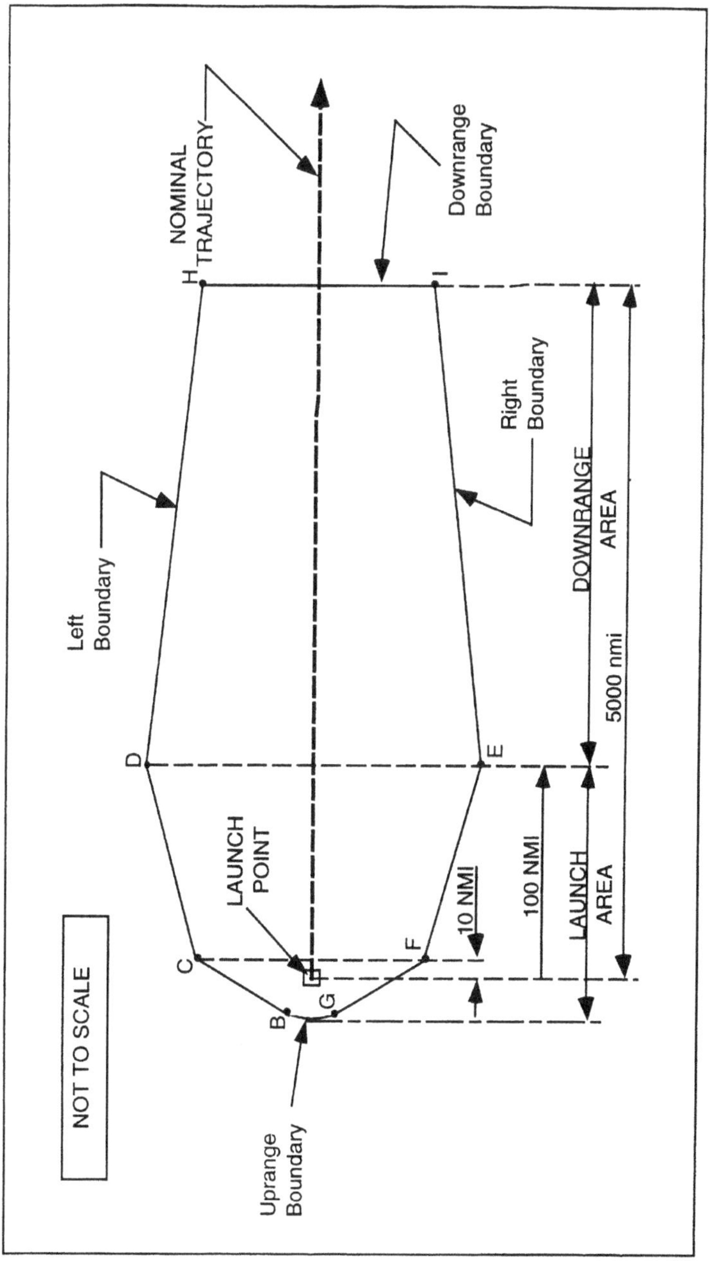

Figure A-2
Flight Corridor

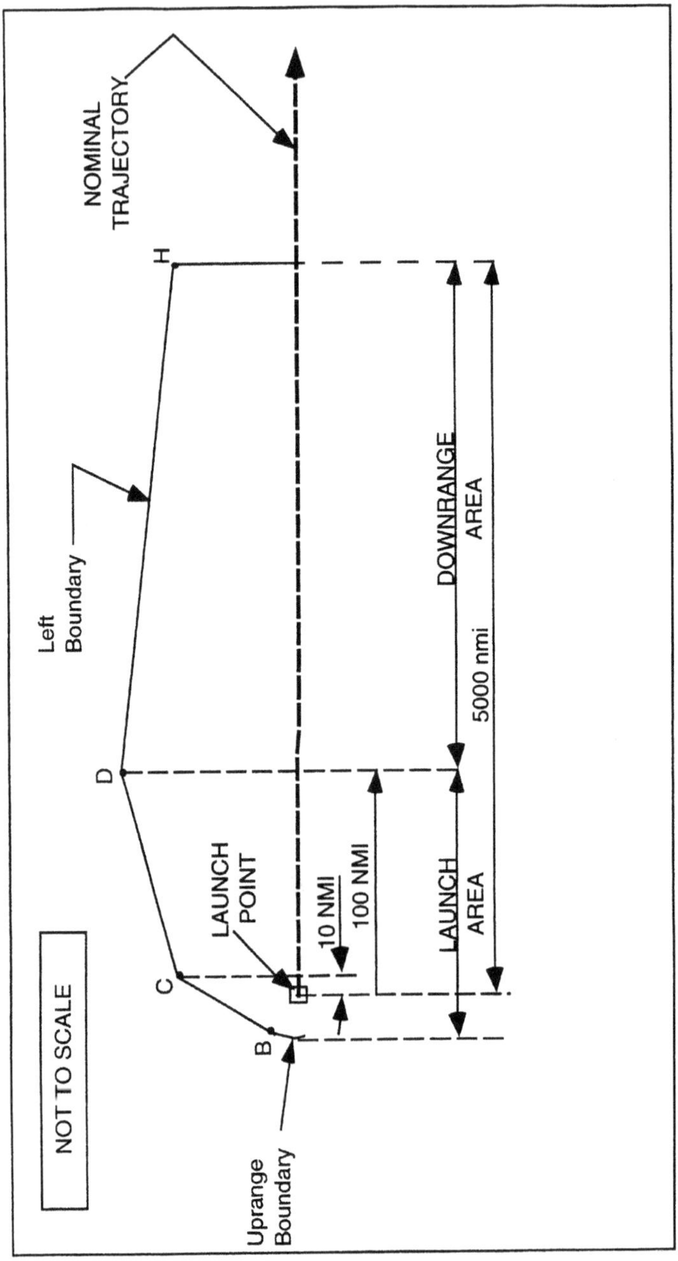

Figure A-3
Construction of Left Boundary of Flight Corridor

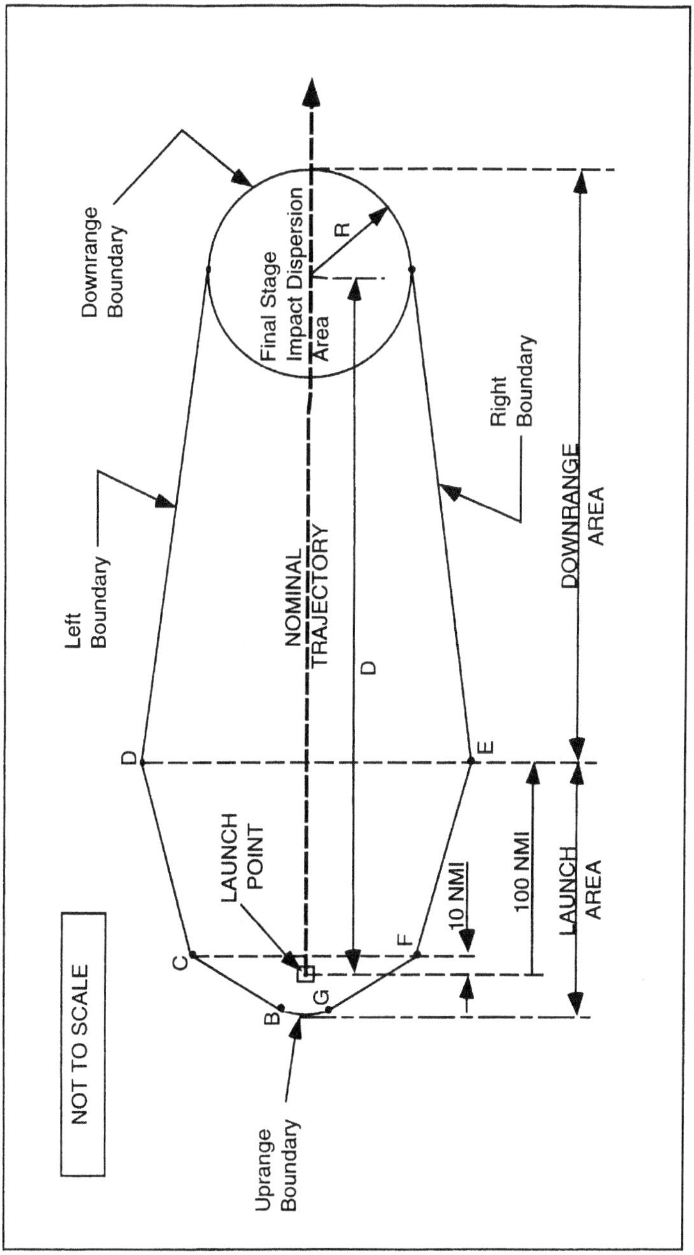

Figure A-4
Flight Corridor for Guided Sub-Orbital Launch Vehicles

APPENDIX B TO PART 420—METHOD FOR DEFINING A FLIGHT CORRIDOR

(a) Introduction

(1) This appendix provides a method to construct a flight corridor from a launch point for a guided suborbital launch vehicle or any one of the four weight classes of guided orbital launch vehicles from table 1, § 420.19, using local meteorological data and a launch vehicle trajectory.

(2) A flight corridor is constructed in two sections—one section comprising a launch area and one section comprising a downrange area. The launch area of a flight corridor reflects the extent of launch vehicle debris impacts in the event of a launch vehicle failure and applying local meteorological conditions. The downrange area reflects the extent of launch vehicle debris impacts in the event of a launch vehicle failure and applying vehicle imparted velocity, malfunctions turns, and vehicle guidance and performance dispersions.

(3) A flight corridor includes an overflight exclusion zone in the launch area and, for a guided suborbital launch vehicle, an impact dispersion area in the downrange area. A flight corridor for a guided suborbital launch vehicle ends with an impact dispersion area and, for the four classes of guided orbital launch vehicles, 5,000 nautical miles (nm) from the launch point, or where the IIP leaves the surface of the Earth, whichever is shorter.

(b) Data Requirements

(1) Launch area data requirements. An applicant shall satisfy the following data requirements to perform the launch area analysis of this appendix. The data requirements are identified in table B–1 along with sources where data acceptable to the FAA may be obtained.

(i) An applicant must select meteorological data that meet the specifications in table B–1 for the proposed launch site.

TABLE B–1—LAUNCH AREA DATA REQUIREMENTS

Data category	Data item	Data source
Meteorological Data	Local statistical wind data as a function of altitude up to 50,000 feet. Required data include: altitude (ft), atmospheric density (slugs/ft^3), mean East/West meridianal (u) and North/South zonal (v) wind (ft/sec), standard deviation of u and v wind (ft/sec), correlation coefficient, number of observations and wind percentile (%).	These data may be obtained from: Global Gridded Upper Air Statistics, Climate Applications Branch National Climatic Data Center.
Nominal Trajectory Data	State vector data as function of time after liftoff in topocentric launch point centered X,Y,Z,X,Y,Z coordinates with the X-axis aligned with the flight azimuth. Trajectory time intervals shall not be greater than one second. XYZ units are in feet and X,Y,Z units are in ft/sec.	Actual launch vehicle trajectory data; or trajectory generation software that meets the requirements of paragraph (b)(1)(ii).
Debris Data	A fixed ballistic coefficient equal to 3 lbs/ft^2 is used for the launch area.	N/A.
Geographical Data	Launch point geodetic latitude on a WGS–84 ellipsoidal Earth model.	Geographical surveys or Global Positioning System.
	Launch point longitude on an ellipsoidal Earth model.	
	Maps using scales of not less than 1:250,000 inches per inch within 100 nm of a launch point and 1:20,000,000 inches per inch for distances greater than 100 nm from a launch point.	Map types with scale and projection information are listed in the Defense Mapping Agency, Public Sale, Aeronautical Charts and Publications Catalog. The catalog and maps may be ordered through the U.S. Dept. of Commerce, National Oceanic and Atmospheric Administration, National Ocean Service.

(ii) For a guided orbital launch vehicle, an applicant shall obtain or create a launch vehicle nominal trajectory. An applicant may use trajectory data from a launch vehicle manufacturer or generate a trajectory using trajectory simulation software. Trajectory time intervals shall be no greater than one second. If an applicant uses a trajectory computed with commercially available software, the software must calculate the trajectory using the following parameters, or clearly and convincingly demonstrated equivalents:

(A) Launch location:

(*1*) Launch point, using geodetic latitude and longitude to four decimal places; and

(*2*) Launch point height above sea level.

(B) Ellipsoidal Earth:

(*1*) Mass of Earth;

(*2*) Radius of Earth;

(*3*) Earth flattening factor; and

(*4*) Gravitational harmonic constants (J2, J3, J4).

(C) Vehicle characteristics:

(*1*) Mass as a function of time;

(*2*) Thrust as a function of time;

(*3*) Specific impulse (I_{SP}) as a function of time; and

(*4*) Stage dimensions.

(D) Launch events:

(*1*) Stage burn times; and

(*2*) Stage drop-off times.

(E) Atmosphere:

(*1*) Density as a function of altitude;

(*2*) Pressure as a function of altitude;

(*3*) Speed of sound as a function of altitude; and

(*4*) Temperature as a function of altitude.

(F) Winds:

(1) Wind direction as a function of altitude; and

(2) Wind magnitude as a function of altitude.

(I) Aerodynamics: drag coefficient as a function of mach number for each stage of flight showing subsonic, transonic and supersonic mach regions for each stage.

(iii) An applicant shall use a ballistic coefficient (β) of 3 lbs/ft² for debris impact computations.

(iv) An applicant shall satisfy the map and plotting requirements for a launch area of appendix A, paragraph (b).

(2) Downrange area data requirements. An applicant shall satisfy the following data requirements to perform the downrange area analysis of this appendix.

(i) The launch vehicle weight class and method of generating a trajectory used in the launch area shall be used by an applicant in the downrange area as well. Trajectory time intervals must not be greater than one second.

(ii) An applicant shall satisfy the map and plotting data requirements for a downrange area of appendix A, paragraph (b).

(c) Construction of a Launch Area of a Flight Corridor

(1) An applicant shall construct a launch area of a flight corridor using the processes and equations of this paragraph for each trajectory position. An applicant shall repeat these processes at time points on the launch vehicle trajectory for time intervals of no greater than one second. When choosing wind data, an applicant shall use a time period of between one and 12 months.

(2) A launch area analysis must include all trajectory positions whose Z-values are less than or equal to 50,000 ft.

(3) Each trajectory time is denoted by the subscript "i". Height intervals for a given atmospheric pressure level are denoted by the subscript "j".

(4) Using data from the GGUAS CD-ROM, an applicant shall estimate the mean atmospheric density, maximum wind speed, height interval fall times and height interval debris dispersions for 15 mean geometric height intervals.

(i) The height intervals in the GGUAS source data vary as a function of the following 15 atmospheric pressure levels expressed in millibars: surface, 1000, 850, 700, 500, 400, 300, 250, 200, 150, 100, 70, 50, 30, 10. The actual geometric height associated with each pressure level varies depending on the time of year. An applicant shall estimate the mean geometric height over the period of months selected in subparagraph (1) of this paragraph for each of the 15 pressure levels as shown in equation B1.

$$\bar{H}_j = \frac{\sum_{m=1}^{k} h_m \cdot n_m}{\sum_{m=1}^{k} n_m} \qquad \text{(Equation B1)}$$

where:

$\bar{H}_j$ = mean geometric height h_m = geometric height for a given month n_m = number of observations for a given month

k = number of wind months of interest

(ii) The atmospheric densities in the source data also vary as a function of the 15 atmospheric pressure levels. The actual atmospheric density associated with each pressure level varies depending on the time of year. An applicant shall estimate the mean atmospheric density over the period of months selected in accordance with subparagraph (1) of this paragraph for each of the 15 pressure levels as shown in equation B2.

$$\bar{\rho}_j \frac{\sum_{m=1}^{k} \rho_m \cdot n_m}{\sum_{m=1}^{k} n_m} \qquad \text{(Equation B2)}$$

where:

ρ_j = mean atmospheric density

ρ_m = atmospheric density for a given month

n_m = number of observations for a given month

k = number of wind months of interest

(iii) An applicant shall estimate the algebraic maximum wind speed at a given pressure level as follows and shall repeat the process for each pressure level.

(A) For each month, an applicant shall calculate the monthly mean wind speed ($\bar{W}_{az}$) for 360 azimuths using equation B3;

(B) An applicant shall select the maximum monthly mean wind speed from the 360 azimuths;

(C) An applicant shall repeat subparagraphs (c)(4)(iii)(A) and (B) for each month of interest; and

(D) An applicant shall select the maximum mean wind speed from the range of months. The absolute value of this wind is designated W_{max} for the current pressure level.

(iv) An applicant shall calculate wind speed using the means for winds from the West (u) and winds from the North (v). An applicant shall use equation B3 to resolve the winds to a specific azimuth bearing.

$$\overline{W}_{az} = u \cdot \cos(90 - az) + v \cdot \sin(90 - az) \qquad \text{(Equation B3)}$$

where:

az = wind azimuth
u = West zonal wind component
v = North zonal wind component
$\bar{W}_{az}$ = mean wind speed at azimuth for each month

(v) An applicant shall estimate the interval fall time over a height interval assuming the initial descent velocity is equal to the terminal velocity (V_T). An applicant shall use equations B4 through B6 to estimate the fall time over a given height interval.

$$\Delta H_j = \overline{H}_{j+1} - \overline{H}_j \qquad \text{(Equation B4)}$$

$$V_{Tj} = \left[\frac{\dfrac{2 \cdot \beta}{\left(\overline{\rho}_{j+1} + \overline{\rho}_j\right)}}{2} \right]^{0.5} \qquad \text{(Equation B5)}$$

$$t_j = \frac{\Delta H_j}{V_{Tj}} \qquad \text{(Equation B6)}$$

where:

ΔH_{Tj} = height difference between two mean geometric heights
β = ballistic coefficient
$\overline{\rho x}$ = mean atmospheric density for the corresponding mean geometric heights
V_{Tj} = terminal velocity

(vi) An applicant shall estimate the interval debris dispersion (D_j) by multiplying the interval fall time by the algebraic maximum mean wind speed (W_{max}) as shown in equation B7.

$$D_j = t_j \cdot W_{max} \qquad \text{(Equation B7)}$$

(5) Once the Dj are estimated for each height interval, an applicant shall determine the total debris dispersion (D_i) for each Z_i using a linear interpolation and summation exercise, as shown below in equation B8. An applicant shall use a launch point height of zero equal to the surface level of the nearest GGUAS grid location.

$$D_i = D_j \cdot \left(\frac{Z_i - \overline{H}_i}{H_{j+1} - \overline{H}_i} \right) + \sum_{n=1}^{j-1} D_n \qquad \text{(Equation B8)}$$

where:

n = number of height intervals below jth height interval

(6) Once all the D_i radii have been calculated, an applicant shall produce a launch area flight corridor in accordance with the requirements of subparagraphs (c)(6)(i)–(iv).

(i) On a map meeting the requirements of appendix A, paragraph (b), an applicant shall plot the X_i position location on the flight azimuth for the corresponding Z_i position;

(ii) An applicant shall draw a circle of radius D_i centered on the corresponding X_i position; and

(iii) An applicant shall repeat the instructions in subparagraphs (c)(6)(i)–(ii) for each D_i radius.

(iv) The launch area of a flight corridor is the enveloping line that encloses the outer boundary of the D_i circles as shown in Fig. B–1. The uprange portion of a flight corridor is described by a semi-circle arc that is a portion of either the most uprange D_i dispersion circle, or the overflight exclusion zone (defined by subparagraph (c)(7)), whichever is further uprange.

(7) An applicant shall define an overflight exclusion zone in the launch area in accordance with the requirements of appendix A, subparagraph (c)(2).

(8) An applicant shall draw the launch area flight corridor and overflight exclusion zone on a map or maps that meet the requirements of table B–1.

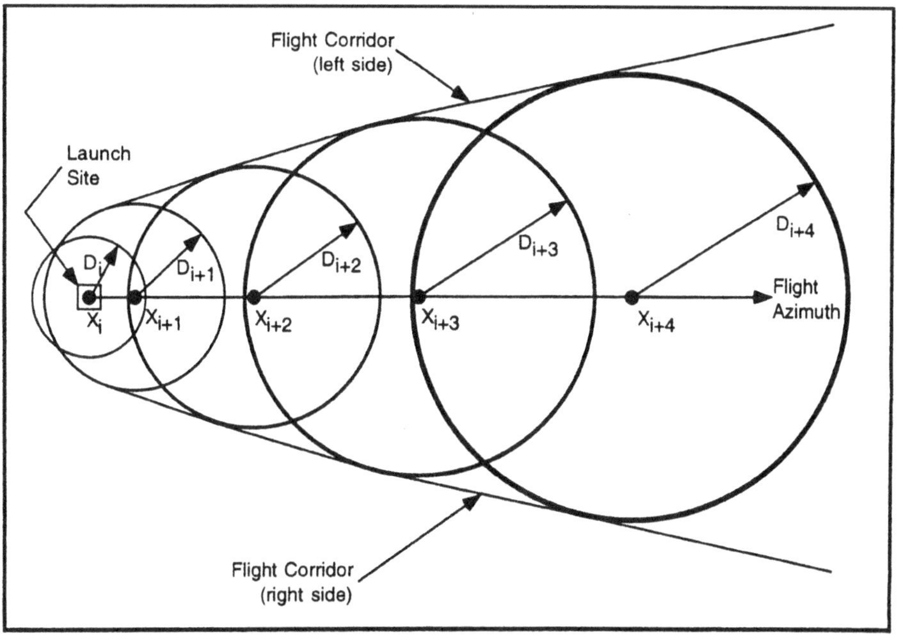

Figure B - 1: Launch Area of a Flight Corridor

(d) Construction of a Downrange Area of a Flight Corridor

(1) The downrange area analysis estimates the debris dispersion for the downrange time points on a launch vehicle trajectory. An applicant shall perform the downrange area analysis using the processes and equations of this paragraph.

(2) The downrange area analysis shall include trajectory positions at a height (the Z_i-values) greater than 50,000 feet and nominal trajectory IIP values less than or equal to 5,000 nm. For a guided suborbital launch vehicle, the final IIP value for which an applicant must account is the launch vehicle final stage impact point. Each trajectory time shall be one second or less and is denoted by the subscript ''i'.

(3) An applicant shall compute the downrange area of a flight corridor boundary in four steps, from each trajectory time increment: determine a reduction ratio factor; calculate the launch vehicle position after simulating a malfunction turn; rotate the state vector after the malfunction turn in the range of three degrees to one degree as a function of X_i distance downrange; and compute the IIP of the resulting trajectory. The locus of IIPs describes the boundary of the downrange area of a flight corridor. An applicant shall use the following subparagraphs, (d)(3)(i)–(v), to compute the downrange area of the flight corridor boundary:

(i) Compute the downrange Distance to the final IIP position for a nominal trajectory as follows:

(A) Using equations B30 through B69, determine the IIP coordinates (φ_{max}, λ_{max}) for the nominal state vector before the launch vehicle enters orbit where α in equation B30 is the nominal flight azimuth angle measured from True North.

(B) Using the range and bearing equations of appendix A, paragraph (b)(3), determine the distance (S_{max}) from the launch point coordinates (φ_{lp}, λ_{lp}) to the IIP coordinates (φ_{max}, λ_{max}) computed in accordance with (3)(i)(A) of this paragraph.

(C) The distance for S_{max} may not exceed 5000 nm. In cases when the actual value exceeds 5000 nm the applicant shall use 5000 nm for S_{max}.

(ii) Compute the reduction ratio factor (F_n) for each trajectory time increment as follows:

(A) Using equations B30 through B69, determine the IIP coordinates (φ_i, λ_i) for the nominal state vector where α in equation B30 is the nominal flight azimuth angle measured from True North.

(B) Using the range and bearing equations of appendix A, paragraph (b)(3), determine the distance (S_i) from the launch point coordinates (φ_{lp}, λ_{lp}) to the IIP coordinates (φ_i, λ_i) computed in (3)(ii)(A) of this paragraph.

(C) The reduction ratio factor is:

$$F_{ri} = \left(1 - \frac{S_i}{S_{max}}\right) \qquad \text{(Equation B9)}$$

(iii) An applicant shall compute the launch vehicle position and velocity components after a simulated malfunction turn for each X_i using the following method.

(A) Turn duration (Δt) = 4 sec.

(B) Turn angle (θ)

$$\theta = \left(F_{ri}\right) * 45 \text{ degrees.} \qquad \text{(Equation B10)}$$

The turn angle equations perform a turn in the launch vehicle's yaw plane, as depicted in figure B–2.

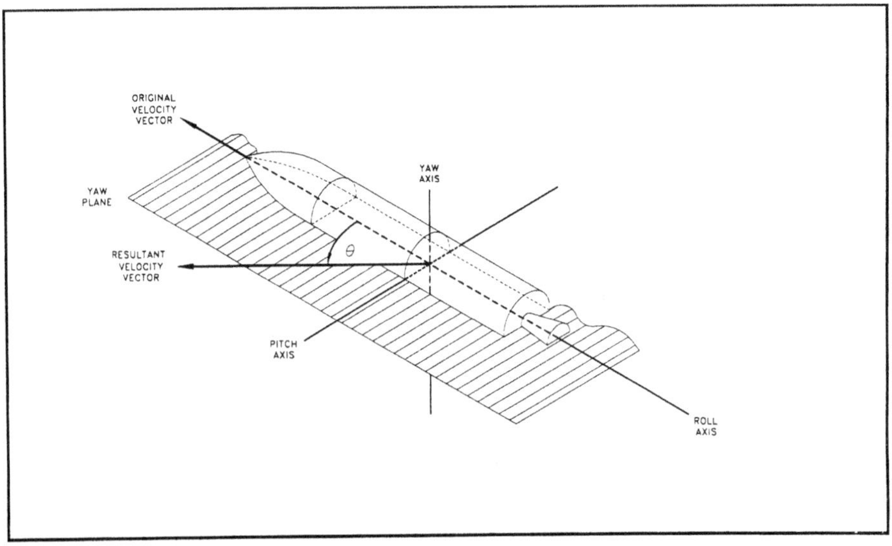

Figure B-2: Velocity Vector Turn Angle in Yaw Plane

(C) Launch vehicle velocity magnitude at the beginning of the turn (V_b) and velocity magnitude at the end of the turn (V_e)

$$V_b = \left(\dot{X}_1{}^2 + \dot{Y}_i{}^2 + \dot{Z}_i{}^2\right)^{0.5} \text{ ft/sec} \qquad \text{(Equation B11)}$$

$$V_e = \left(\dot{X}_{i+5}^2 + \dot{Y}_{i+5}^2 + \dot{X}_{i+5}^2\right)^{0.5} \text{ ft/sec} \qquad \text{(Equation B12)}$$

(D) Average velocity magnitude over the turn duration ($\bar{V}$)

$$\overline{V}_i = \frac{(V_b + V_e)}{2}\text{ ft/sec} \qquad \text{(Equation B13)}$$

(E) Velocity vector path angle (γ_i) at turn epoch

$$\gamma_i = \tan^{-1}\left[\frac{\dot{Z}_i}{\left(\dot{X}_i^2 + \dot{Y}_i^2\right)^{0.5}}\right] \qquad \text{(Equation B14)}$$

(F) Launch vehicle position components at the end of turn duration

$$X_{90L} = X_i + \overline{V}_i \cdot \Delta t \cdot \cos\left(\frac{-\theta}{2}\right) \cdot \cos(\gamma_i)$$

$$X_{90R} = X_i + \overline{V}_i \cdot \Delta t \cdot \cos\left(\frac{\theta}{2}\right) \cdot \cos(\gamma_i)$$

$$Y_{90L} = Y_i + \overline{V}_i \cdot \Delta t \cdot \sin\left(\frac{-\theta}{2}\right)$$

$$Y_{90R} = Y_i + \overline{V}_i \cdot \Delta t \cdot \sin\left(\frac{\theta}{2}\right)$$

$$Z_{90L} = Z_i + \overline{V}_i \cdot \Delta t \cdot \cos\left(\frac{-\theta}{2}\right) \cdot \sin(\gamma_i) - \left(\frac{1}{2}\right) \cdot g_1 \cdot \Delta t^2 \qquad \text{(Equations B15-B20)}$$

$$Z_{90R} = Z_i + \overline{V}_i \cdot \Delta t \cdot \cos\left(\frac{\theta}{2}\right) \cdot \sin(\gamma_i) - \left(\frac{1}{2}\right) \cdot g_1 \cdot \Delta t^2$$

where: g_1 = 32.17405 ft/sec^2

(G) Launch vehicle velocity components at the end of turn duration

$$\dot{X}_{90L} = \left(X_{90L} - X_i\right)/\Delta t$$

$$\dot{X}_{90R} = \left(X_{90R} - X_i\right)/\Delta t$$

$$\dot{Y}_{90L} = \left|\left(Y_{90L} - Y_i\right)/\Delta t\right|$$

$$\dot{Y}_{90R} = (-1)\cdot\left|\left(Y_{90R} - Y_i\right)/\Delta t\right| \qquad \text{(Equations B21 - B26)}$$

$$\dot{Z}_{90L} = \left(Z_{90L} - Z_i\right)/\Delta t$$

$$\dot{Z}_{90R} = \left(Z_{90R} - Z_i\right)/\Delta t$$

(iv) An applicant shall rotate the trajectory state vector at the end of the turn duration to the right and left to define the right-lateral flight corridor boundary and the left-lateral flight corridor boundary, respectively. An applicant shall perform the trajectory rotation in conjunction with a trajectory transformation from the X_{90}, Y_{90}, Z_{90}, $\dot{X}_{90}$, $\dot{Y}_{90}$, $\dot{Z}_{90}$, components to E, N, U, $\dot{E}$, $\dot{N}$, $\dot{U}$. The trajectory subscripts "R" and "L" from equations B15 through B26 have been discarded to reduce the number of equations. An applicant shall transform from to E,N,U,$\dot{E}$,$\dot{N}$,$\dot{U}$ to E,F,G,$\dot{E}$,$\dot{F}$,$\dot{G}$. An applicant shall use the equations of paragraph (d)(3)(iv)(A)–(F) to produce the EFG components necessary to estimate each instantaneous impact point.

(A) An applicant must calculate the flight angle (α)

$$\Delta\alpha_i = 3 - 2\cdot f_1\cdot\left(1 - F_{ri}\right) \qquad \text{(Equation B27)}$$

$$\alpha_{Li} = \left(\text{Flight Azimuth} - \Delta\alpha_i\right)$$

for left lateral boundary computations (Equation B28)

- OR

$$\alpha_{Ri} = \left(\text{Flight Azimuth} - \Delta\alpha_i\right)$$

for right lateral boundary computations (Equation B29)

where: $$f_1 = \begin{Bmatrix} 0.0\text{:}\ F_{ri} \geq 0.8 \\ 1.0\text{:}\ F_{ri} < 0.8 \end{Bmatrix}$$

(B) An applicant shall transform X_{90},Y_{90},Z_{90} to E,N,U

$$\begin{aligned} E &= X_{90}\sin(\alpha) - Y_{90}\cos(\alpha) \\ N &= X_{90}\cos(\alpha) + Y_{90}\sin(\alpha) \qquad \text{(Equations B30 - B32)} \\ U &= Z_{90} \end{aligned}$$

(C) An applicant shall transform to $\dot{X}_{90}$, $\dot{Y}_{90}$, $\dot{Z}_{90}$ to $\dot{E}$, $\dot{N}$, $\dot{U}$.

$$\dot{E} = \dot{X}_{90}\sin(\alpha) - \dot{Y}_{90}\cos(\alpha)$$
$$\dot{N} = \dot{X}_{90}\cos(\alpha) + \dot{Y}_{90}\sin(\alpha) \qquad \text{(Equations B33 - B35)}$$
$$\dot{U} = \dot{Z}_{90}$$

(D) An applicant shall transform the launch point coordinates ($\phi_0\lambda_0$,h_0) to E_0,F_0,G_0

$$R = a_E\left\{1 - e^2\left[\sin^2(\phi_0)\right]\right\}^{-0.5}$$

where: $a_E = 20925646.3255$ ft

$$e^2 = 0.00669437999013$$
$$E_0 = (R + h_0)\cos(\phi_0)\cos(\lambda_0) \qquad \text{(Equations B36 - B39)}$$
$$F_0 = (R + h_0)\cos(\phi_0)\sin(\lambda_0)$$
$$G_0 = \left[R(1 - e^2) + h_0\right]\sin(\phi_0)$$

(E) An applicant shall transform E,N,U to E_{90},F_{90},G_{90}

$$E_{90} = E\cos(270 - \lambda_0) + N\cos(90 - \phi_0)\sin(270 - \lambda_0) - U\sin(90 - \phi_0)\sin(270 - \lambda_0) \qquad \text{(Equations B40 - B42)}$$
$$F_{90} = E\sin(270 - \lambda_0) + N\cos(90 - \phi_0)\cos(270 - \lambda_0) - U\sin(90 - \phi_0)\cos(270 - \lambda_0)$$
$$G_{90} = N\sin(90 - \phi_0) + U\cos(90 - \phi_0) + G_0$$

(F) An applicant shall transform to $\dot{E}$,$\dot{N}$,$\dot{U}$ TO $\dot{E}$,$\dot{F}$,$\dot{G}$

$$\dot{E}_{90} = \dot{E}\cos(270 - \lambda_0) + \dot{N}\cos(90 - \phi_0)\sin(270 - \lambda_0) - \dot{U}\sin(90 - \phi_0)\sin(270 - \lambda_0) \qquad \text{(Equations B43 - B45)}$$
$$\dot{F}_{90} = \dot{E}\sin(270 - \lambda_0) + \dot{N}\cos(90 - \phi_0)\cos(270 - \lambda_0) - \dot{U}\sin(90 - \phi_0)\cos(270 - \lambda_0)$$
$$\dot{G}_{90} = \dot{N}\sin(90 - \phi_0) + \dot{U}\cos(90 - \phi_0)$$

(v) The IIP computation implements an iterative solution to the impact point problem. An applicant shall solve equations B46 through B69, with the appropriate substitutions, up to a maximum of five times. Each repetition of the equations provides a more accurate prediction of the IIP. An applicant shall use the required IIP computations of paragraphs (d)(3)(v)(A)–(W) below. An applicant shall use this IIP computation for both the left-and right-lateral offsets. The IIP computations will result in latitude and longitude pairs for the left-lateral flight corridor boundary and the right-lateral flight corridor boundary. An applicant shall use the lines connecting the latitude and longitude pairs to describe the entire downrange area boundary of the flight corridor up to 5000 nm or a final stage impact dispersion area.

(A) An applicant shall approximate the radial distance ($r_{k,l}$) from the geocenter to the IIP. The distance from the center of the Earth ellipsoid to the launch point shall be used for the initial approximation of $r_{k,l}$ as shown in equation B46.

$$r_{k,1} = \left(E_0^2 + F_0^2 + G_0^2\right)^{0.5} \qquad \text{(Equation B46)}$$

(B) An applicant shall compute the radial distance (r) from the geocenter to the launch vehicle position.

$$r = \left(E_{90}^2 + F_{90}^2 + G_{90}^2\right)^{0.5} \qquad \text{(Equation B47)}$$

If r <$r_{k,l}$ then the launch vehicle position is below the Earth's surface and an impact point cannot be computed. An applicant must restart the calculations with the next trajectory state vector.

(C) An applicant shall compute the inertial velocity components.

$$\begin{aligned} \dot{E}I_{90} &= \dot{E}_{90} - \omega \cdot F_{90} \\ \dot{F}I_{90} &= \dot{F}_{90} + \omega \cdot E_{90} \end{aligned} \qquad \text{(Equations B48-B49)}$$

where: $\omega = 4.178074 \times 10^{-3}$ deg/sec

(D) An applicant shall compute the magnitude of the inertial velocity vector.

$$v_0\left(\dot{E}I_{90}^2 + \dot{F}I_{90}^2 + \dot{G}_{90}^2\right)^{0.5} \qquad \text{(Equation B50)}$$

(E) An applicant shall compute the eccentricity of the trajectory ellipse multiplied by the cosine of the eccentric anomaly at epoch ε_c).

$$\varepsilon_c = \left(\frac{r \cdot v_0^2}{K}\right) - 1 \qquad \text{(Equation B51)}$$

where: $K = 1.407644 \times 10^{16}$ ft^3/sec^2

(F) An applicant shall compute the semi-major axis of the trajectory ellipse (a^t).

$$a_t = \frac{r}{1 - \varepsilon_c} \qquad \text{(Equation B52)}$$

If a_t 0 or a_t then the trajectory orbit is not elliptical, but is hyperbolic or parabolic, and an impact point cannot be computed. The launch vehicle has achieved escape velocity and the applicant may terminate computations.

(G) An applicant shall compute the eccentricity of the trajectory ellipse multiplied by the sine of the eccentric anomaly at epoch ε_s).

$$\varepsilon_s = \frac{\left(E_{90}\dot{E}I_{90} + F_{90}\dot{F}I_{90} + G_{90}\dot{G}_{90}\right)}{\left(K \cdot a_t\right)^{0.5}} \quad \text{(Equation B53)}$$

(H) An applicant shall compute the eccentricity of the trajectory ellipse squared ε^2).

$$\varepsilon^2 = \left(\varepsilon_c^2 + \varepsilon_s^2\right) \quad \text{(Equation B54)}$$

If $a_t(1-\varepsilon)-a_E]$ >0 and $\varepsilon \geq 0$ then the trajectory perigee height is positive and an impact point cannot be computed. The launch vehicle has achieved Earth orbit and the applicant may terminate computations.

(I) An applicant shall compute the eccentricity of the trajectory ellipse multiplied by the cosine of the eccentric anomaly at impact (ε_{c_k}).

$$\varepsilon_{c_k} = \frac{\left(a_t - r_{k,1}\right)}{a_t} \quad \text{(Equation B55)}$$

(J) An applicant shall compute the eccentricity of the trajectory ellipse multiplied by the sine of the eccentric anomaly at impact (ε_{s_k}).

$$\varepsilon_{s_k} = -\left(\varepsilon^2 - {\varepsilon^2}_{c_k}\right)^{0.5} \quad \text{(Equation B56)}$$

If ε_{s_k} <0 then the trajectory orbit does not intersect the Earth's surface and an impact point cannot be computed. The launch vehicle has achieved Earth orbit and the applicant may terminate computations.

(K) An applicant shall compute the cosine of the difference between the eccentric anomaly at impact and the eccentric anomaly at epoch ($\Delta\varepsilon_{c_k}$).

$$\Delta\varepsilon_{c_k} = \frac{\left(\varepsilon_{c_k} \cdot \varepsilon_c\right) + \left(\varepsilon_{s_k} \cdot \varepsilon_s\right)}{\varepsilon^2} \quad \text{(Equation B57)}$$

(L) An applicant shall compute the sine of the difference between the eccentric anomaly at impact and the eccentric anomaly at epoch ($\Delta\varepsilon_{s_k}$).

$$\Delta\varepsilon_{s_k} = \frac{\left(\varepsilon_{s_k} \cdot \varepsilon_c\right) - \left(\varepsilon_{c_k} \cdot \varepsilon_s\right)}{\varepsilon^2} \quad \text{(Equation B58)}$$

(M) An applicant shall compute the f-series expansion of Kepler's equations.

$$f_2 = \frac{\left(\Delta\varepsilon_{c_k} - \varepsilon_c\right)}{\left(1 - \varepsilon_c\right)} \quad \text{(Equation B59)}$$

(N) An applicant shall compute the g-series expansion of Kepler's equations.

$$g_2 = \left(\Delta\varepsilon_{s_k} + \varepsilon_s - \varepsilon_{s_k}\right)\left(\frac{a_t^3}{K}\right)^{0.5} \quad \text{(Equation B60)}$$

(O) An applicant shall compute the E,F,G coordinates at impact (E_i,F_i,G_i).

$$E_k = f_2 \cdot E_{90} + g_2 \cdot \dot{E}l_{90}$$
$$F_k = f_2 \cdot F_{90} + g_2 \cdot \dot{F}l_{90} \qquad \text{(Equations B61-B63)}$$
$$G_k = f_2 \cdot G_{90} + g_2 \cdot \dot{G}_{90}$$

(P) An applicant shall approximate the distance from the geocenter to the launch vehicle position at impact ($r_{k,2}$).

$$r_{k,2} = \frac{a_E}{\left[\left(\frac{e^2}{1-e^2}\right)\left(\frac{G_k}{r_{k,1}}\right)^2 + 1\right]^{0.5}} \qquad \text{(Equation B64)}$$

where:

a_E = 20925646.3255 ft
e^2 = 0.00669437999013

(Q) An applicant shall let $r_{k+1,1} = r_{k,2}$, substitute $r_{k+1,1}$ for $r_{k,1}$ in equation B55 and repeat equations B55—B64 up to four more times increasing "k" by an increment of one on each loop (e.g. $k\varepsilon\{1, 2, 3, 4, 5\}$). If $|r_{5,1} - r_{5,2}|$ >1 then the iterative solution does not converge and an impact point does not meet the accuracy tolerance of plus or minus one foot. An applicant must try more iterations, or restart the calculations with the next trajectory state vector.

(R) An applicant shall compute the difference between the eccentric anomaly at impact and the eccentric anomaly at epoch ($\Delta\varepsilon$).

$$\Delta\varepsilon = \tan^{-1}\left(\frac{\Delta\varepsilon_{s_5}}{\Delta\varepsilon_{c_5}}\right) \qquad \text{(Equation B65)}$$

(S) An applicant shall compute the time of flight from epoch to impact (t).

$$t = \left(\Delta\varepsilon + \varepsilon_s - \varepsilon_{s_5}\right)\left(\frac{a_t^3}{K}\right)^{0.5} \qquad \text{(Equation B66)}$$

(T) An applicant shall compute the geocentric latitude at impact (φ').

$$\phi_i' = \sin^{-1}\left(\frac{G_5}{r_{5,2}}\right) \qquad \text{(Equation B67)}$$

Where: $+90° > \varphi'_i > -90°$

(U) An applicant shall compute the geodetic latitude at impact (φ).

$$\phi_i = \tan^{-1}\left[\frac{\tan\left(\phi_i'\right)}{\left(1-e^2\right)}\right] \qquad \text{(Equation B68)}$$

Where: $+90° > \varphi_i > -90°$

(V) An applicant shall compute the East longitude at impact (λ).

$$\lambda_i = \tan^{-1}\left(\frac{F_5}{E_5}\right) - \omega t \qquad \text{(Equation B69)}$$

(W) If the range from the launch point to the impact point is equal to or greater than 5000 nm, an applicant shall terminate IIP computations.

(4) For a guided suborbital launch vehicle, an applicant shall define a final stage impact dispersion area as part of the flight corridor and show the area on a map using the following procedure:

(i) For equation B70 below, an applicant shall use an apogee altitude (H_{ap}) corresponding to the highest altitude reached by the launch vehicle final stage in the applicant's launch vehicle trajectory analysis done in accordance with paragraph (b)(1)(ii).

(ii) An applicant shall define the final stage impact dispersion area by using a dispersion factor [DISP(H_{ap})] as shown below. An applicant shall calculate the impact dispersion radius (R) for the final launch vehicle stage. An applicant shall set R equal to the maximum apogee altitude (H_{ap}) multiplied by the dispersion factor as shown below:

$$R = H_{ap} \cdot DISP(H_{ap}) \qquad \text{(Equation B70)}$$

where: DISP(H_{ap}) = 0.05

(5) An applicant shall combine the launch area and downrange area flight corridor and any final stage impact dispersion area for a guided suborbital launch vehicle.

(i) On the same map with the launch area flight corridor, an applicant shall plot the latitude and longitude positions of the left and right sides of the downrange area of the flight corridor calculated in accordance with subparagraph (d)(3).

(ii) An applicant shall connect the latitude and longitude positions of the left side of the downrange area of the flight corridor sequentially starting with the last IIP calculated on the left side and ending with the first IIP calculated on the left side. An applicant shall repeat this procedure for the right side.

(iii) An applicant shall connect the left sides of the launch area and downrange portions of the flight corridor. An applicant shall repeat this procedure for the right side.

(iv) An applicant shall plot the overflight exclusion zone defined in subparagraph (c)(7).

(v) An applicant shall draw any impact dispersion area on the downrange map with the center of the impact dispersion area on the launch vehicle final stage impact point obtained from the applicant's launch vehicle trajectory analysis done in accordance with subparagraph (b)(1)(ii).

(e) Evaluate the Launch Site

(1) An applicant shall evaluate the flight corridor for the presence of populated areas. If no populated area is located within the flight corridor, then no additional steps are necessary.

(2) If a populated area is located in an overflight exclusion zone, an applicant may modify its proposal or demonstrate that there are times when no people are present or that the applicant has an agreement in place to evacuate the public from the overflight exclusion zone during a launch.

(3) If a populated area is located within the flight corridor, an applicant may modify its proposal or complete an overflight risk analysis in accordance with appendix C.

APPENDIX C TO PART 420—RISK ANALYSIS

(a) Introduction

(1) This appendix provides a method for an applicant to estimate the expected casualty (E_c) for a launch of a guided expendable launch vehicle using a flight corridor generated either by appendix A or appendix B. This appendix also provides an applicant options to simplify the method where population at risk is minimal.

(2) An applicant shall perform a risk analysis when a populated area is located within a flight corridor defined by either appendix A or appendix B. If the estimated expected casualty exceeds 1×10^{-4}, an applicant may either modify its proposal, or if the flight corridor used was generated by the appendix A method, use the appendix B method to narrow the flight corridor and then redo the overflight risk analysis pursuant to this appendix. If the estimated expected casualty still exceeds 1×10^{-4}, the FAA will not approve the location of the proposed launch point.

(b) Data Requirements

(1) An applicant shall obtain the data specified by subparagraphs (b)(2) and (3) and summarized in table C–1. Table C–1 provides sources where an applicant may obtain data acceptable to the FAA. An applicant must also employ the flight corridor information from appendix A or B, including flight azimuth and, for an appendix B flight corridor, trajectory information.

(2) Population data. Total population (N) and the total landmass area within a populated area (A) are required. Population data up to and including 100 nm from the launch point are required at the U.S. census block group level. Population data downrange from 100 nm are required at no greater than $1^\circ \times 1^\circ$ latitude/longitude grid coordinates.

(3) Launch vehicle data. Launch vehicle data consist of the launch vehicle failure probability (P_f), the launch vehicle effective casualty area (A_c), trajectory position data, and the overflight dwell time (t_d). The failure probability is a constant (P_f = 0.10) for a guided orbital or suborbital expendable launch vehicle. Table C–3 provides effective casualty area data based on IIP range. Trajectory position information is provided from distance computations provided by this appendix for an appendix A flight corridor, or trajectory data used in appendix B for an appendix B flight corridor. The dwell time (t_d) may be determined from trajectory data produced when creating an appendix B flight corridor.

TABLE C–1—OVERFLIGHT ANALYSIS DATA REQUIREMENTS

Data category	Data item	Data source
Population Data	Total population within a populated area (N)	Within 100 nm of the launch point: U.S. census data at the census block-group level. Downrange from 100 nm beyond the launch point, world population data are available from:
	Total landmass area within the populated area (A).	Carbon Dioxide Information Analysis Center (CDIAC) Oak Ridge National Laboratory Database—Global Population Distribution (1990), Terrestrial Area and Country Name Information on a One by One Degree Grid Cell Basis (DB1016 (8–1996)
Launch Vehicle Data	Failure probability—P_f = 0.10	N/A.
	Effective casualty area (A_c)	See table C–3.
	Overflight dwell time	Determined by range from the launch point or trajectory used by applicant.
	Nominal trajectory data (for an appendix B flight corridor only).	See appendix B, table B–1.

(c) Estimating Corridor Casualty Expectation

(1) A corridor casualty expectation [E_C(Corridor)] estimate is the sum of the expected casualty measurement of each populated area inside a flight corridor.

(2) An applicant shall identify and locate each populated area in the proposed flight corridor.

(3) An applicant shall determine the probability of impact in each populated area using the procedures in subparagraphs (5) or (6) of this paragraph. Figures C–1 and C–2 illustrate an area considered for probability of impact (P_i) computations by the dashed-lined box around the populated area within a flight corridor, and figure C–3 illustrates a populated area in a final stage impact dispersion area. An applicant shall then estimate the E_C for each populated area in accordance with subparagraphs (7) and (8) of this paragraph.

(4) The P_i computations do not directly account for populated areas whose areas are bisected by an appendix A flight corridor centerline or an appendix B nominal trajectory ground trace. Accordingly, an applicant must evaluate P_i for each of the bi-sections as two separate populated areas, as shown in figure C–4, which shows one bi-section to the left of an appendix A flight corridor's centerline and one to its right.

(5) Probability of impact (P_i) computations for a populated area in an appendix A flight corridor. An applicant shall compute P_i for each populated area using the following method:

(i) For the launch and downrange areas, but not for a final stage impact dispersion area for a guided suborbital launch vehicle, an applicant shall compute P_i for each populated area using the following equation:

$$P_i = \frac{\left(\frac{|y_2 - y_1|}{\sigma_y}\right)}{6\sqrt{2\pi}} \cdot \left(\exp\left(\frac{-\left(y_1/\sigma_y\right)^2}{2}\right) + 4\cdot\exp\left[\frac{-\left(\frac{y_1+y_2}{2\sigma_y}\right)^2}{2}\right] + \exp\left(\frac{-\left(y_2/\sigma_y\right)^2}{2}\right)\right) \cdot \left[\frac{P_f}{C}\cdot\frac{(x_2 - x_1)}{\dot{R}}\right] \quad \text{(Equation C1)}$$

where:

x_1, x_2 = closest and farthest downrange distance (nm) along the flight corridor centerline to the populated area (see figure C–1)

y_1, y_2 = closest and farthest cross range distance (nm) to the populated area measured from the flight corridor centerline (see figure C–1)

σ_y = one-third of the cross range distance from the centerline to the flight corridor boundary (see figure C–1)

exp = exponential function (e^x)

P_f = probability of failure = 0.10

$\dot{R}$ = IIP range rate (nm/sec) (see table C–2)

C = 643 seconds (constant)

TABLE C–2—IIP RANGE RATE VS. IIP RANGE

IIP range (nm)	IIP range rate (nm/s)
0–75	0.75
76–300	1.73
301–900	4.25
901–1700	8.85
1701–2600	19.75
2601–3500	42.45
3501–4500	84.85
4501–5250	154.95

(ii) For each populated area within a final stage impact dispersion area, an applicant shall compute P_i using the following method:

(A) An applicant shall estimate the probability of final stage impact in the x and y sectors of each populated area within the final stage impact dispersion area using equations C2 and C3:

$$P_x = \frac{\left(\frac{|x_2 - x_1|}{\sigma_x}\right)}{6\sqrt{2\pi}} \cdot \left(\exp\left(\frac{-\left(x_1/\sigma_x\right)^2}{2}\right) + 4 \cdot \exp\left[\frac{-\left(\frac{x_1 + x_2}{2\sigma_x}\right)^2}{2}\right] + \exp\left(\frac{-\left(x_2/\sigma_x\right)^2}{2}\right) \right) \quad \text{(Equation C2)}$$

where:

X_1, X_2 = closest and farthest downrange distance, measured along the flight corridor centerline, measured from the nominal impact point to the populated area (see figure C–3)

σ_x = one-third of the impact dispersion radius (see figure C–3)

exp = exponential function (e^x)

$$P_y = \frac{\left(\frac{|y_2 - y_1|}{\sigma_y}\right)}{6\sqrt{2\pi}} \cdot \left(\exp\left(\frac{-\left(y_1/\sigma_y\right)^2}{2}\right) + 4 \cdot \exp\left[\frac{-\left(\frac{y_1 + y_2}{2\sigma_y}\right)^2}{2}\right] + \exp\left(\frac{-\left(y_2/\sigma_y\right)^2}{2}\right) \right) \quad \text{(Equation C3)}$$

where:

y_1, y_2 = closest and farthest cross range distance to the populated area measured from the flight corridor centerline (see figure C–3)

σ_y = one-third of the impact dispersion radius (see figure C–3)

exp = exponential function (e^x)

(B) If a populated area intersects the impact dispersion area boundary so that the x_2 or y_2 distance would otherwise extend outside the impact dispersion area, the x_2 or y_2 distance should be set equal to the impact dispersion area radius. The x_2 distance for populated area A in figure C–3 is an example. If a populated area intersects the flight azimuth, an applicant shall solve equation C3 by obtaining the solution in two parts. An applicant shall determine, first, the probability between $y_1 = 0$ and $y_2 = a$ and, second, the probability between $y_1 = 0$ and $y_2 = b$, as depicted in figure C–4. The probability P_y is then equal to the sum of the probabilities of the two parts. If a populated area intersects the line that is normal to the flight azimuth on the impact point, an applicant shall solve equation C2 by obtaining the solution in two parts in the same manner as with the values of x.

(C) An applicant shall calculate the probability of impact for each populated area using equation C4 below:

$$P_I = P_s \cdot P_x \cdot P_y \quad \text{(Equation C4)}$$

where: $P_s = 1 - P_f = 0.90$

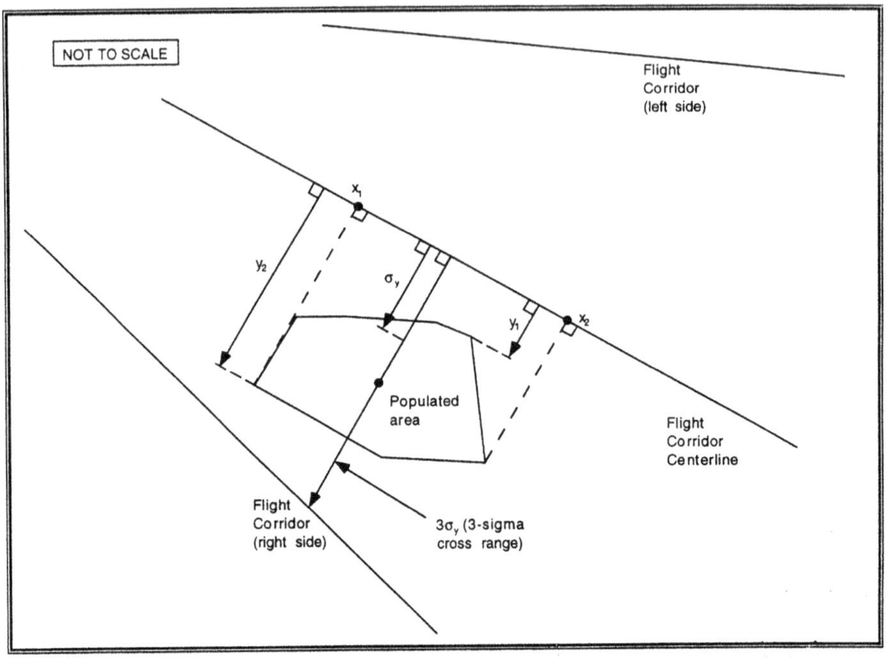

Figure C-1: Analysis of an Appendix A Flight Corridor

(6) Probability of impact computations for a populated area in an appendix B flight corridor. An applicant shall compute P_i using the following method:

(i) For the launch and downrange areas, but not for a final stage impact dispersion area for a guided suborbital launch vehicle, an applicant shall compute P_i for each populated area using the following equation:

$$P_i = \frac{\left(\frac{|y_2 - y_1|}{\sigma_y}\right)}{6\sqrt{2\pi}} \cdot \left(\exp\left(\frac{-\left(y_1/\sigma_y\right)^2}{2}\right) + 4\cdot\exp\left[\frac{-\left(\frac{y_1+y_2}{2\sigma_y}\right)^2}{2}\right] + \exp\left(\frac{-\left(y_2/\sigma_y\right)^2}{2}\right)\right)\cdot\left(\frac{P_f}{t}\cdot t_d\right) \quad \text{(Equation C5)}$$

where:

y_1, y_2 = closest and farthest cross range distance (nm) to a populated area measured from the nominal trajectory IIP ground trace (see figure C–2)

σ_y = one-third of the cross range distance (nm) from nominal trajectory to the flight corridor boundary (see figure C–2)

exp = exponential function (e^x)

P_f = probability of failure = 0.10

t = flight time from lift-off to orbital insertion (seconds)

t_d = overflight dwell time (seconds)

(ii) For each populated area within a final stage impact dispersion area, an applicant shall compute P_i using the following method:

(A) An applicant shall estimate the probability of final stage impact in the x and y sectors of each populated area within the final stage impact dispersion area using equations C6 and C7:

$$P_x = \frac{\left(\frac{|x_2 - x_1|}{\sigma_x}\right)}{6\sqrt{2\pi}} \cdot \left(\exp\left(\frac{-\left(\frac{x_1}{\sigma_x}\right)^2}{2}\right) + 4 \cdot \exp\left[\frac{-\left(\frac{x_1 + x_2}{2\sigma_x}\right)^2}{2}\right] + \exp\left(\frac{-\left(\frac{x_2}{\sigma_x}\right)^2}{2}\right) \right) \qquad \text{(Equation C6)}$$

where:

x_1, x_2 = closest and farthest downrange distance, measured along nominal trajectory IIP ground trace, measured from the nominal impact point to the populated area (see figure C–3)

σ_x = one-third of the impact dispersion radius (see figure C–3)

exp = exponential function (e^x)

$$P_y = \frac{\left(\frac{|y_2 - y_1|}{\sigma_y}\right)}{6\sqrt{2\pi}} \cdot \left(\exp\left(\frac{-\left(\frac{y_1}{\sigma_y}\right)^2}{2}\right) + 4 \cdot \exp\left[\frac{-\left(\frac{y_1 + y_2}{2\sigma_y}\right)^2}{2}\right] + \exp\left(\frac{-\left(\frac{y_2}{\sigma_y}\right)^2}{2}\right) \right) \qquad \text{(Equation C7)}$$

where:

y_1, y_2 = closest and farthest cross range distance to the populated area measured from the nominal trajectory IIP ground trace (see figure C–3)

σ_y = one-third of the impact dispersion radius (see figure C–3)

exp = exponential function (e^x)

(B) If a populated area intersects the impact dispersion area boundary so that the x_2 or y_2 distance would otherwise extend outside the impact dispersion area, the x_2 or y_2 distance should be set equal to the impact dispersion area radius. The x_2 distance for populated area A in figure C–3 is an example. If a populated area intersects the flight azimuth, an applicant shall solve equation C7 by obtaining the solution in two parts. An applicant shall determine, first, the probability between $y_1 = 0$ and $y_2 = a$ and, second, the probability between $y_1 = 0$ and $y_2 = b$, as depicted in figure C–4. The probability P_y is then equal to the sum of the probabilities of the two parts. If a populated area intersects the line that is normal to the flight azimuth on the impact point, an applicant shall solve equation C6 by obtaining the solution in two parts in a similar manner with the values of x.

(C) An applicant shall calculate the probability of impact for each populated area using equation C8 below:

$$P_I = P_s \cdot P_x \cdot P_y \qquad \text{(Equation C8)}$$

where: $P_s = 1 - P_f = 0.90$

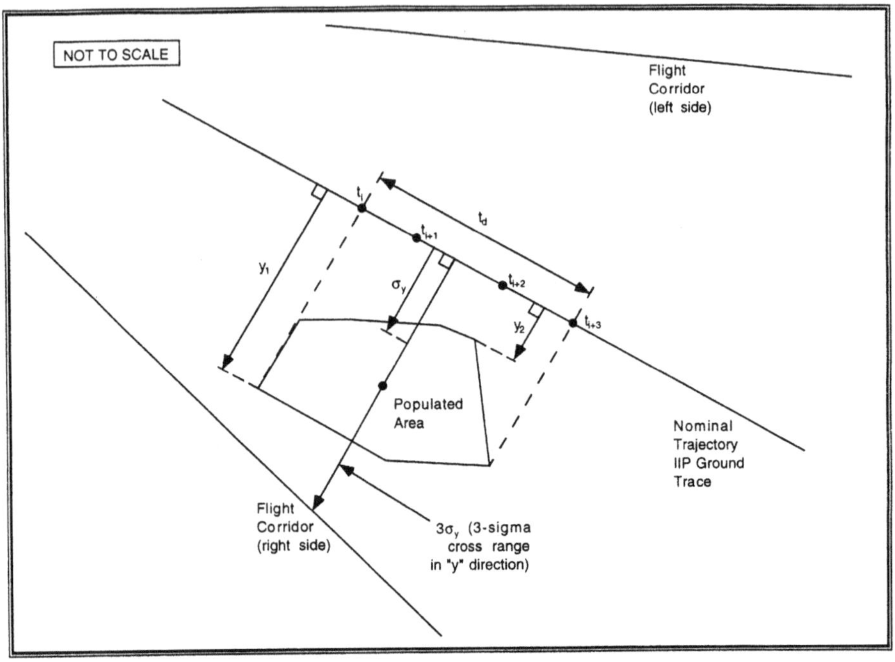

Figure C-2: Analysis of an Appendix B Flight Corridor

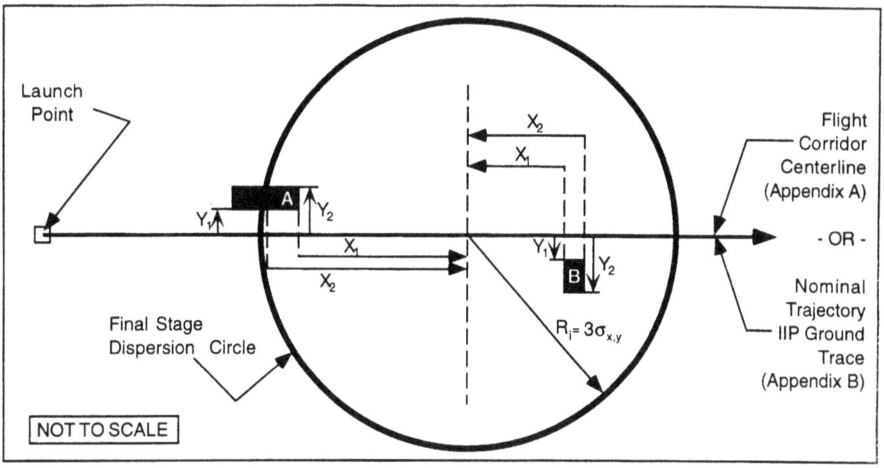

Figure C-3: Appendix A and B Final Stage Impact Risk Analysis

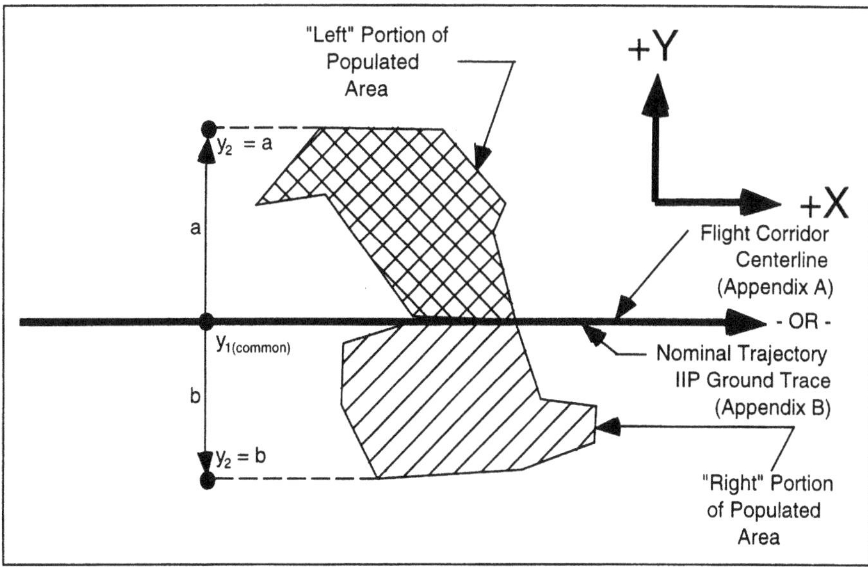

Figure C-4: Flight Azimuth Intersecting a Populated Area

(7) Using the P_i calculated in either subparagraph (c)(5) or (6) of this paragraph, an applicant shall calculate the casualty expectancy for each populated area within the flight corridor in accordance with equation C9. E_{ck} is the casualty expectancy for a given populated area as shown in equation C9, where individual populated areas are designated with the subscript "k".

$$E_{ck} = P_i \cdot \left(\frac{A_c}{A_k} \right) \cdot N_k \qquad \text{(Equation C9)}$$

where:

A_c = casualty area (from table C–3)
A_k = populated area
N_k = population in A_k

TABLE C–3—EFFECTIVE CASUALTY AREA (MILES²) AS A FUNCTION OF IIP RANGE (NM)

Instantaneous impact point range (nautical miles)	Orbital launch vehicles				Suborbital launch vehicles
	Small	Medium	Medium large	Large	Guided
0–49	3.14×10^{-2}	1.28×10^{-1}	4.71×10^{-2}	8.59×10^{-2}	4.3×10^{-1}
50–1749	2.47×10^{-2}	2.98×10^{-2}	9.82×10^{-3}	2.45×10^{-2}	1.3×10^{-1}
1750–5000	3.01×10^{-4}	5.52×10^{-3}	7.82×10^{-3}	1.14×10^{-2}	3.59×10^{-6}

(8) An applicant shall estimate the total corridor risk using the following summation of risk:

$$\mathrm{Ec(Corridor)} = \left(\sum_{k=1}^{n} E_{c_k} \right) \quad \text{(Equation C10)}$$

(9) Alternative casualty expectancy (E_C) analyses. An applicant may employ specified variations to the analysis defined by subparagraphs (c)(1)–(8). Those variations are identified in subparagraphs (9)(i) through (vi) of this paragraph. Subparagraphs (i) through (iv) permit an applicant to make conservative assumptions that would lead to an overestimation of the corridor E_C compared with the analysis defined by subparagraphs (c)(1)–(8). In subparagraphs (v) and (vi), an applicant that would otherwise fail the analysis prescribed by subparagraphs (c)(1)–(8) may avoid (c)(1)–(8)'s overestimation of the probability of impact in each populated area. An applicant employing a variation shall identify the variation used, show and discuss the specific assumptions made to modify the analysis defined by subparagraphs (c)(1)–(8), and demonstrate how each assumption leads to overestimation of the corridor E_C compared with the analysis defined by subparagraphs (c)(1)–(c)(8).

(i) Assume that P_x and P_y have a value of 1.0 for all populated areas.

(ii) Combine populated areas into one or more larger populated areas, and use a population density for the combined area or areas equal to the most densely populated area.

(iii) For any given populated area, assume P_y has a value of one.

(iv) For any given P_x sector (an area spanning the width of a flight corridor and bounded by two time points on the trajectory IIP ground trace) assume P_y has a value of one and use a population density for the sector equal to the most densely populated area.

(v) For a given populated area, divide the populated area into smaller rectangles, determine P_i for each individual rectangle, and sum the individual impact probabilities to determine P_i for the entire populated area.

(vi) For a given populated area, use the ratio of the populated area to the area of the P_i rectangle from the subparagraph (c)(1)–(8) analysis.

(d) Evaluation of Results

(1) If the estimated expected casualty does not exceed 1×10^{-4}, the FAA will approve the launch site location.

(2) If the estimated expected casualty exceeds 1×10^{-4}, then an applicant may either modify its proposal, or, if the flight corridor used was generated by the appendix A method, use the appendix B method to narrow the flight corridor and then perform another appendix C risk analysis.

[Doc. No. FAA–1999–5833, 65 FR 62861, Oct. 19, 2000, as amended by Amdt. 420–2, 71 FR 51972, Aug. 31, 2006; Docket No. FAA–2014–0418, Amdt. No. 420–7, 81 FR 47027, July 20, 2016]

APPENDIX D TO PART 420—IMPACT DISPERSION AREAS AND CASUALTY EXPECTANCY ESTIMATE FOR AN UNGUIDED SUBORBITAL LAUNCH VEHICLE

(a) Introduction

(1) This appendix provides a method for determining the acceptability of the location of a launch point from which an unguided suborbital launch vehicle would be launched. The appendix describes how to define an overflight exclusion zone and impact dispersion areas, and how to evaluate whether the

public risk presented by the launch of an unguided suborbital launch vehicle remains at acceptable levels.

(2) An applicant shall base its analysis on an unguided suborbital launch vehicle whose final launch vehicle stage apogee represents the intended use of the launch point.

(3) An applicant shall use the apogee of each stage of an existing unguided suborbital launch vehicle with a final launch vehicle stage apogee equal to the one proposed, and calculate each impact range and dispersion area using the equations provided.

(4) This appendix also provides a method for performing an impact risk analysis that estimates the expected casualty (E_c) within each impact dispersion area. This appendix provides an applicant options to simplify the method where population at risk is minimal.

(5) If the estimated E_c is less than or equal to 1×10^{-4}, the FAA will approve the launch point for unguided suborbital launch vehicles. If the estimated E_c exceeds 1×10^{-4}, the proposed launch point will fail the launch site location review.

(b) Data Requirements

(1) An applicant shall employ the apogee of each stage of an existing unguided suborbital launch vehicle whose final stage apogee represents the maximum altitude to be reached by unguided suborbital launch vehicles launched from the launch point. The apogee shall be obtained from one or more actual flights of an unguided suborbital launch vehicle launched at an 84 degree elevation.

(2) An applicant shall satisfy the map and plotting data requirements of appendix A, paragraph (b).

(3) Population data. An applicant shall use total population (N) and the total landmass area within a populated area (A) for all populated areas within an impact dispersion area. Population data up to and including 100 nm from the launch point are required at the U.S. census block group level. Population data downrange from 100 nm are required at no greater than $1° \times 1°$ latitude/longitude grid coordinates.

(c) Overflight Exclusion Zone and Impact Dispersion Areas

(1) An applicant shall choose a flight azimuth from a launch point.

(2) An applicant shall define an overflight exclusion zone as a circle with a radius of 1600 feet centered on the launch point.

(3) An applicant shall define an impact dispersion area for each stage of the suborbital launch vehicle chosen in accordance with subparagraph (b)(1) in accordance with the following:

(i) An applicant shall calculate the impact range for the final launch vehicle stage (D_n). An applicant shall set D_n equal to the last stage apogee altitude (H_n) multiplied by an impact range factor [$IP(H_n)$] in accordance with the following:

$$D_n = H_n \cdot IP(H_n) \qquad \text{(Equation D1)}$$

where:

$IP(H_n)$ = 0.4 for an apogee less than 100 km, and

$IP(H_n)$ = 0.7 for an apogee of 100 km or greater.

(ii) An applicant shall calculate the impact range for each intermediate stage (D_i), where $i \in \{1, 2, 3, \ldots (n-1)\}$, and where n is the total number of launch vehicle stages. Using the apogee altitude (H_i) of each intermediate stage, an applicant shall use equation D1 to compute the impact range of each stage by substituting H_i for H_n. An applicant shall use the impact range factors provided by equation D1.

(iii) An applicant shall calculate the impact dispersion radius for the final launch vehicle stage (R_n). An applicant shall set R_n equal to the last stage apogee altitude (H_n) multiplied by an impact dispersion factor [$DISP(H_n)$] in accordance with the following:

$$R_n = H_n \cdot DISP(H_n) \qquad \text{(Equation D2)}$$

where:

$DISP(H_n)$ = 0.4 for an apogee less than 100 km, and

DISP(Hn) = 0.7 for an apogee of 100 km or greater.

(iv) An applicant shall calculate the impact dispersion radius for each intermediate stage (R_i), where $i \in \{1, 2, 3, \ldots (n-1)\}$ and where n is the total number of launch vehicle stages. Using the apogee altitude (H_i) of each intermediate stage, an applicant shall use equation D2 to compute an impact dispersion radius of each stage by substituting H_i for H_n. An applicant shall use the dispersion factors provided by equation D2.

(4) An applicant shall display an overflight exclusion zone, each intermediate and final stage impact point (D_i through D_n), and each impact dispersion area for the intermediate and final launch vehicle stages on maps in accordance with paragraph (b)(2).

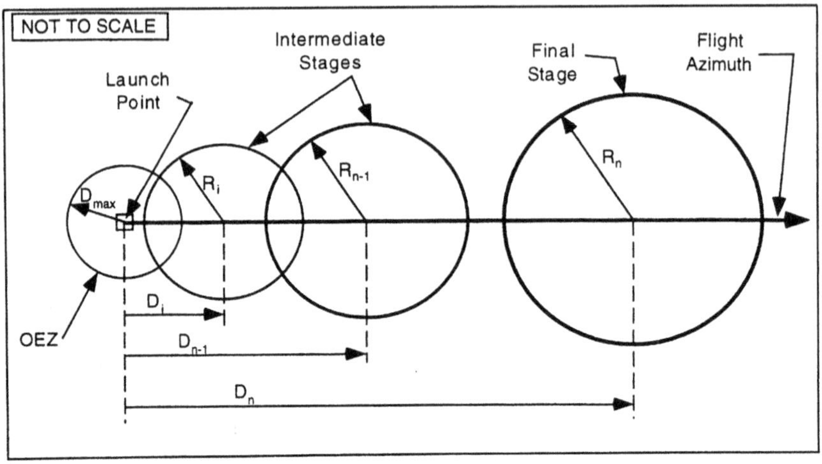

Figure D-1
Unguided Suborbital Launch Vehicle Overflight Exclusion Zone and Impact Dispersion Areas

(d) Evaluate the Overflight Exclusion Zone and Impact Dispersion Areas

(1) An applicant shall evaluate the overflight exclusion zone and each impact dispersion area for the presence of any populated areas. If an applicant determines that no populated area is located within the overflight exclusion zone or any impact dispersion area, then no additional steps are necessary.

(2) If a populated area is located in an overflight exclusion zone, an applicant may modify its proposal or demonstrate that there are times when no people are present or that the applicant has an agreement in place to evacuate the public from the overflight exclusion zone during a launch.

(3) If a populated area is located within any impact dispersion area, an applicant may modify its proposal and define a new overflight exclusion zone and new impact dispersion areas, or perform an impact risk analysis in accordance with paragraph (e).

(e) Impact Risk Analysis

(1) An applicant shall estimate the expected average number of casualties, E_C, within the impact dispersion areas according to the following method:

(i) An applicant shall calculate the E_c by summing the impact risk for the impact dispersion areas of the final launch vehicle stage and all intermediate stages. An applicant shall estimate E_c for the impact dispersion area of each stage by using equations D3 through D7 for each of the populated areas located within the impact dispersion areas.

(ii) An applicant shall estimate the probability of impacting inside the X and Y sectors of each populated area within each impact dispersion area using equations D3 and D4:

$$P_x = \frac{\left(\frac{x_2}{\sigma_x} - \frac{x_1}{\sigma_x}\right)}{6\sqrt{2\pi}} \cdot \left(\exp\left(\frac{-\left(\frac{x_1}{\sigma_x}\right)^2}{2} \right) + 4 \cdot \exp\left[\frac{-\left(\frac{x_1 + x_2}{2\sigma_x}\right)^2}{2} \right] + \exp\left(\frac{-\left(\frac{x_2}{\sigma_x}\right)^2}{2} \right) \right) \qquad \text{(Equation D3)}$$

where:

x_1, x_2 = closest and farthest downrange distance to populated area (see figure D–2)

σ_x = one-third of the impact dispersion radius (see figure D–2)

exp = exponential function (e^x)

$$P_y = \frac{\left(\frac{|y_2|}{\sigma_y} - \frac{|y_1|}{\sigma_y}\right)}{6\sqrt{2\pi}} \cdot \left(\exp\left(\frac{-\left(\frac{y_1}{\sigma_y}\right)^2}{2}\right) + 4 \cdot \exp\left[\frac{-\left(\frac{y_1 + y_2}{2\sigma_y}\right)^2}{2}\right] + \exp\left(\frac{-\left(\frac{y_2}{\sigma_y}\right)^2}{2}\right) \right) \quad \text{(Equation D4)}$$

where:

y_1, y_2 = closest and farthest cross range distance to the populated area (see figure D–2)

σ_y = one-third of the impact dispersion radius (see figure D–2)

exp = exponential function (e^x)

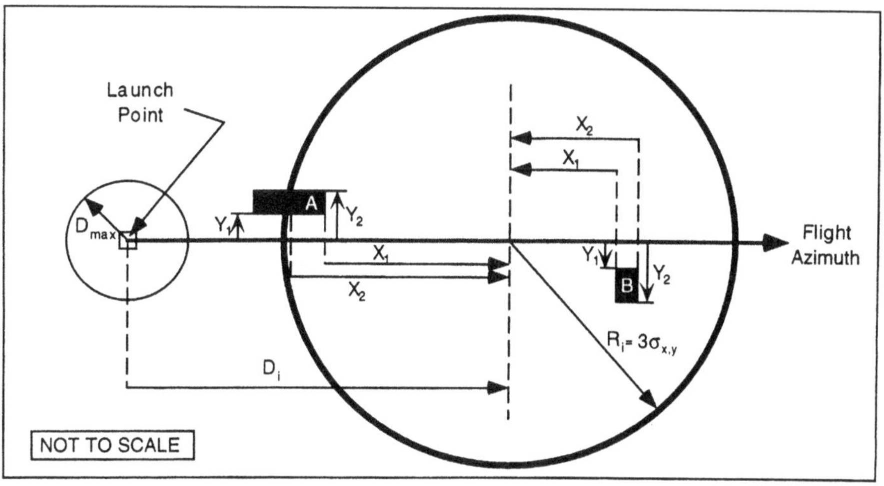

Figure D-2
Intermediate and Final Stage Impact Risk Analysis

(iii) If a populated area intersects the impact dispersion area boundary so that the x_2 or y_2 distance would otherwise extend outside the impact dispersion area, the x_2 or y_2 distance should be set equal to the impact dispersion area radius. The x_2 distance for populated area A in figure D–2 is an example.

(iv) If a populated area intersects the flight azimuth, an applicant shall solve equation D4 by obtaining the solution in two parts. An applicant shall determine, first, the probability between $y_1 = 0$ and $y_2 = a$ and, second, the probability between $y_1 = 0$ and $y_2 = b$, as depicted in figure D–3. The probability P_y is then equal to the sum of the probabilities of the two parts. If a populated area intersects the line that is normal to the flight azimuth on the impact point, an applicant shall solve equation D3 by obtaining the solution in two parts in the same manner as with the values of x.

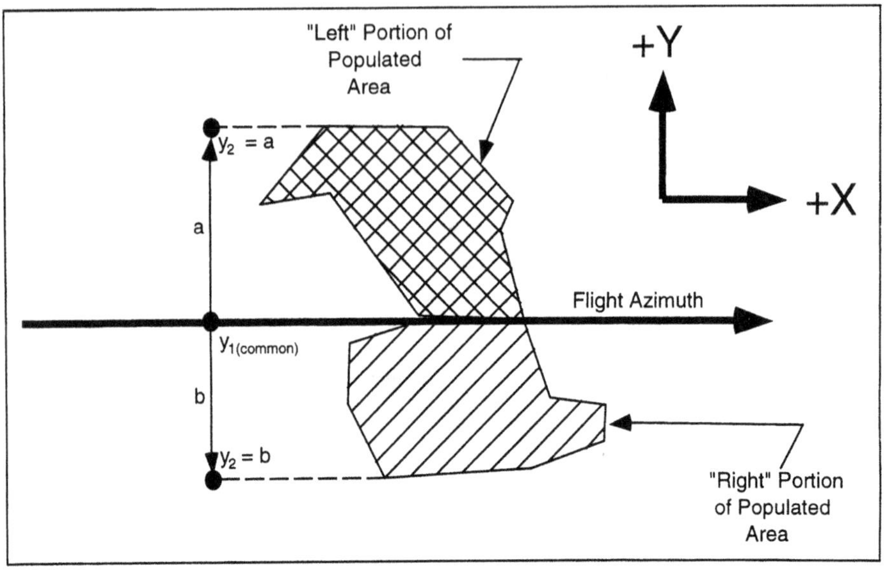

Figure D-3
Flight Azimuth Intersecting a Populated Area

(v) An applicant shall calculate the probability of impact (P_i) for each populated area using the following equation:

$$P_i = P_s \cdot P_x \cdot P_y \qquad \text{(Equation D5)}$$

where:

P_s = probability of success = 0.98

(vi) An applicant shall calculate the casualty expectancy for each populated area. E_{ck} is the casualty expectancy for a given populated area as shown in equation D6, where individual populated areas are designated with the subscript "k".

$$E_{ck} = P_i \cdot \left(\frac{A_c}{A_k} \right) \cdot N_k \qquad \text{(Equation D6)}$$

where:

k { {1, 2, 3, . . . , n}
A_c = casualty area (from table D–1)
A_k = populated area
N_k = population in A_k

TABLE D–1—EFFECTIVE CASUALTY AREA (A_c) VS. IMPACT RANGE

Impact range (nm)	Effective casualty area (miles²)
0–4	9×10^{-3}
5–49	9×10^{-3}
50–1,749	1.1×10^{-5}
1,750–4,999	3.6×10^{-6}
5,000–more	3.6×10^{-6}

(vii) An applicant shall estimate the total risk using the following summation of risk:

$$Ec(\text{Corridor}) = \left(\sum_{k=1}^{n} E_{c_k}\right) \quad \text{(Equation D7)}$$

(viii) Alternative casualty expectancy (E_c) analysis. An applicant may employ specified variations to the analysis defined by subparagraphs (d)(1)(i)–(vii). Those variations are identified in subparagraphs (viii)(A) through (F) of this paragraph. Subparagraphs (A) through (D) permit an applicant to make conservative assumptions that would lead to an overestimation of E_c compared with the analysis defined by subparagraphs (d)(1)(i)–(vii). In subparagraphs (E) and (F), an applicant that would otherwise fail the analysis prescribed by subparagraphs (d)(1)(i)–(vii) may avoid (d)(1)(i)–(vii)'s overestimation of the probability of impact in each populated area. An applicant employing a variation shall identify the variation used, show and discuss the specific assumptions made to modify the analysis defined by subparagraphs (d)(1)(i)–(vii), and demonstrate how each assumption leads to overestimation of the corridor E_c compared with the analysis defined by subparagraphs (d)(1)(i)–(vii).

(A) Assume that P_x and P_y have a value of 1.0 for all populated areas.

(B) Combine populated areas into one or more larger populated areas, and use a population density for the combined area or areas equal to the most densely populated area.

(C) For any given populated area, assume P_x has a value of one.

(D) For any given populated area, assume P_y has a value of one.

(E) For a given populated area, divide the populated area into smaller rectangles, determine P_i for each individual rectangle, and sum the individual impact probabilities to determine P_i for the entire populated area.

(F) For a given populated area, use the ratio of the populated area to the area of the P_i rectangle used in the subparagraph (d)(1)(i)–(vii) analysis.

(2) If the estimated expected casualty does not exceed 1×10^{-4}, the FAA will approve the launch point.

(3) If the estimated expected casualty exceeds 1×10^{-4}, then an applicant may modify its proposal and then repeat the impact risk analysis in accordance with this appendix D. If no set of impact dispersion areas exist which satisfy the FAA's risk threshold, the applicant's proposed launch site will fail the launch site location review.

[Docket No. FAA–1999–5833, 65 FR 62861, Oct. 19, 2000, as amended by Docket No. FAA–2014–0418, Amdt. No. 420–7, 81 FR 47027, July 20, 2016]

APPENDIX E TO PART 420—TABLES FOR EXPLOSIVE SITE PLAN

TABLE E–1—DIVISION 1.1 DISTANCES TO A PUBLIC AREA OR PUBLIC TRAFFIC ROUTE FOR NEW >450 LBS

NEW (lbs.)	Distance to public area (ft) [1] [2]	Distance to public traffic route distance (ft) [2]
≤0.5	236	142
0.7	263	158
1	291	175
2	346	208
3	378	227
5	419	251
7	445	267
10	474	284
15	506	304
20	529	317
30	561	337
31	563	338
50	601	361
70	628	377
100	658	395
150	815	489
200	927	556
300	1085	651
450	1243	746

[1] To calculate distance d to a public area from NEW:
NEW ≤0.5 lbs: d = 236
0.5 lbs <NEW <100 lbs: d = 291.3 + [79.2 *ln(NEW)]
100 lbs ≤NEW ≤450 lbs: d = −1133.9 + [389 *ln(NEW)]
NEW is in lbs; d is in ft; ln is natural logarithm.
To calculate maximum NEW given distance d (noting that d can never be less than 236 ft):
0 ≤d <236 ft: Not allowed (d cannot be less than 236 ft)
236 ft ≤d <658 ft: NEW = exp [(d/79.2)-3.678]
658 ft ≤d <1250 ft: NEW = exp [(d/389) + 2.914]
NEW is in lbs; d is in ft; exp[x] is e^x.

[2] The public traffic route distance is 60 percent of the distance to a public area.

TABLE E–2—DIVISION 1.1 DISTANCE TO PUBLIC AREA AND PUBLIC TRAFFIC ROUTE FOR NEW >450 LBS

NEW (lbs)	Distance to public area (ft) [1]	Distance to public traffic route (ft)
450 lbs<NEW ≤30,000 lbs	1,250	750.
30,000 lbs<NEW ≤100,000 lbs	$40 \times NEW^{1/3}$	0.60*(Distance to Public Area).
100,000 lbs<NEW ≤250,000 lbs	$2.42 \times NEW^{0.577}$	0.60*(Distance to Public Area).

TABLE E–2—DIVISION 1.1 DISTANCE TO PUBLIC AREA AND PUBLIC TRAFFIC ROUTE FOR NEW >450 LBS—Continued

NEW (lbs)	Distance to public area (ft) [1]	Distance to public traffic route (ft)
250,000 lbs<NEW	50*NEW $^{1/3}$	0.60*(Distance to Public Area).

[1] To calculate NEW from distance d to a public area:
1, 243 ft<d ≤1,857 ft: NEW = d^3/64,000
1, 857 ft<d ≤3,150 ft: NEW = 0.2162 * d $^{1.7331}$
3,150 ft<d: NEW = d^3/125,000
NEW is in lbs; d is in ft.

TABLE E–3—DIVISION 1.1 INTRALINE DISTANCES [1 2 3]

NEW (lbs)	Intraline Distance (ft)
50	66
70	74
100	84
150	96
200	105
300	120
500	143
700	160
1,000	180
1,500	206
2,000	227
3,000	260
5,000	308
7,000	344
10,000	388
15,000	444
20,000	489
30,000	559
50,000	663
70,000	742
100,000	835
150,000	956
200,000	1,053
300,000	1,205
500,000 [3]	1,429
700,000	1,598
1,000,000	1,800
1,500,000	2,060
2,000,000	2,268
3,000,000	2,596
5,000,000	3,078

[1] To calculate intraline distance d from NEW:
d = 18*NEW $^{1/3}$
NEW is in pounds; d is in feet

[2] To calculate maximum NEW from given intraline distance d:
NEW = d^3/5,832
NEW is in pounds; d is in feet.

[3] NEW values of more than 500,000 lbs only apply to liquid propellants with TNT equivalents equal to those NEW values. The intraline distances for NEW greater than 500,000 pounds do not apply to division 1.1 explosives.

TABLE E–4—DIVISION 1.3 SEPARATION DISTANCES

NEW (lbs)	Distance to public area or public traffic route (ft) [1]	Intraline distance (ft) [2]
≤1000	75	50
1,500	82	56
2,000	89	61
3,000	101	68
5,000	117	80
7,000	130	88
10,000	145	98
15,000	164	112
20,000	180	122
30,000	204	138
50,000	240	163
70,000	268	181
100,000	300	204
150,000	346	234
200,000	385	260
300,000	454	303
500,000	569	372
700,000	668	428
1,000,000	800	500
1,500,000	936	577
2,000,000	1,008	630

[1] To calculate distance d to a public area or traffic route from NEW:
NEW ≤1,000lbs
d= 75 ft
1,000 lbs<NEW ≤96,000 lbs
d = exp[2.47 + 0.2368*(ln(NEW)) + 0.00384*(ln(NEW))^2]
96,000 lbs<NEW ≤1,000,000 lbs
d = exp[7.2297 − 0.5984*(ln(NEW)) + 0.04046*(ln(NEW))^2]
NEW >1,000,000 lbs

$d = 8*NEW^{1/3}$
NEW is in pounds; d is in feet; exp[x] is e^x; ln is natural logarithm.
To calculate NEW from distance d to a public area or traffic route (noting that d cannot be less than 75 ft):
$0 \le d < 75$ ft:
Not allowed (d cannot be less than 75 ft) for NEW ≤1000 lbs
75 ft $\le d \le$ 296 ft
$NEW = \exp[-30.833 + (307.465 + 260.417*(\ln(d)))^{1/2}]$
296 ft$<d\le$800 ft
$NEW = \exp[7.395 + (-124.002 + 24.716*(\ln(d)))^{1/2}]$
800 ft$<d$
$NEW = d^3/512$
NEW is in lbs; d is in ft; exp[x] is e^x; ln is natural logarithm
[2] To calculate intraline distance d from NEW:
NEW ≤1,000 lbs
$d = 50$ ft
1,000 lbs<NEW ≤84,000 lbs
$d = \exp[2.0325 + 0.2488*(\ln(NEW)) + 0.00313*(\ln(NEW))^2]$
84,000 lbs<NEW ≤1,000,000 lbs
$d = \exp[4.338 - 0.1695*(\ln(NEW)) + 0.0221*(\ln(NEW))^2]$
1,000,000 lbs<NEW
$d = 5*NEW^{1/3}$
NEW is in pounds; d is in feet; exp[x] is e^x; ln is natural logarithm
To calculate NEW from an intraline distance d:
$0 \le d < 50$ ft:
Not allowed (d cannot be less than 50 ft) for NEW ≤1000 lbs
50 ft $\le d \le$ 192 ft
$NEW = \exp[-39.744 + (930.257 + 319.49*(\ln(d)))^{1/2}]$
192 ft$<d\le$500 ft
$NEW = \exp[3.834 + (-181.58 + 45.249*(\ln(d)))^{1/2}]$
500 ft$\le d$
$NEW = d^3/125$
NEW is in pounds; d is in feet; exp[x] is e^x; ln is natural logarithm

TABLE E–5—ENERGETIC LIQUID EXPLOSIVE EQUIVALENTS[1,2,3]

Energetic liquids	TNT Equivalence	TNT Equivalence
	Static Test Stands	Launch Pads.
LO_2/LH_2	See Note 3	See Note 3.
$LO_2/LH_2 + LO_2/RP\text{–}1$	Sum of (see Note 3 for LO_2/LH_2) + (10% for LO_2/RP1).	Sum of (see Note 3 for LO_2/LH_2) + (20% for LO_2/RP1).
LO_2/RP–1	10%	20% up to 500,000 lbs Plus 10% over 500,000 lbs
IRFNA/UDMH	10%	10%.
$N_2O_4/UDMH + N_2H_4$	5%	10%.

[1] A launch site operator must use the percentage factors of table E–5 to determine TNT equivalencies of incompatible energetic liquids that are within an intraline distance of each other.
[2] A launch site operator may substitute the following energetic liquids to determine TNT equivalency under this table as follows:
Alcohols or other hydrocarbon for RP–1
H_2O_2 for LO_2 (only when H_2O_2 is in combination with RP–1 or equivalent hydrocarbon fuel)
MMH for N_2H_4, UDMH, or combinations of the two.
[3] TNT equivalency for LO_2/LH_2 is the larger of:
(a) TNT equivalency of $8*W^{2/3}$, where W is the weight of LO_2/LH_2 in lbs; or
(b) 14 percent of the LO_2/LH_2 weight.

TABLE E–6—FACTORS TO USE WHEN CONVERTING ENERGETIC LIQUID DENSITIES

Item	Density (lb/gal)	Temperature (°F)
Ethyl alcohol	6.6	68
Hydrazine	8.4	68
Hydrogen peroxide (90 percent)	11.6	68
Liquid hydrogen	0.59	−423
Liquid oxygen	9.5	−297
Red fuming nitric acid (IRFNA)	12.9	77
RP–1	6.8	68
UDMH	6.6	68
UDMH/Hydrazine	7.5	68

TABLE E–7—SEPARATION DISTANCE CRITERIA FOR STORAGE OF HYDROGEN PEROXIDE IN CONCENTRATIONS OF MORE THAN 91 PERCENT[1,2]

Quantity (lbs)	Intraline distance or distance to public area or distance to public traffic route (ft)
10,000	510
15,000	592
20,000	651
30,000	746
50,000	884
70,000	989
100,000	1114
150,000	1275
200,000	1404
300,000	1607

TABLE E–7—SEPARATION DISTANCE CRITERIA FOR STORAGE OF HYDROGEN PEROXIDE IN CONCENTRATIONS OF MORE THAN 91 PERCENT[1 2]—Continued

Quantity (lbs)	Intraline distance or distance to public area or distance to public traffic route (ft)
500,000	1905

[1] Multiple tanks containing hydrogen peroxide in concentrations of greater than 91 percent may be located at distances less than those required by table E–7; however, if the tanks are not separated from each other by 10 percent of the distance specified for the largest tank, then the launch site operator must use the total contents of all tanks to calculate each intraline distance and the distance to each public area and each public traffic route.

[2] A launch site operator may use the equations below to determine permissible distance or quantity between the entries of table E–7:

W >10,000 lbs Distance = $24 * W^{1/3}$

Where Distance is in ft and W is in lbs.

To calculate weight of hydrogen peroxide from a distance d:

d >75 ft

$W = \exp[-134.286 + 71.998*(\ln(d)) - 12.363*(\ln(d))^2 + 0.7229*(\ln(d))^3]$

TABLE E–8—SEPARATION DISTANCE CRITERIA FOR STORAGE OF LIQUID HYDROGEN AND BULK QUANTITIES OF HYDRAZINE

Pounds of energetic liquid	Pounds of energetic liquid	Public area and intraline distance to incompatible energetic liquids	Intraline distance to compatible energetic liquids	Pounds of energetic liquid	Pounds of energetic liquid	Public area and intraline distance to incompatible energetic liquids	Intraline distance to compatible energetic liquids
Over	Not Over	Distance in feet	Distance in feet	Over	Not Over	Distance in feet	Distance in feet
				60,000	70,000	1,200	130
100	200	600	35	70,000	80,000	1,200	130
200	300	600	40	80,000	90,000	1,200	135
300	400	600	45	90,000	100,000	1,200	135
400	500	600	50	100,000	125,000	1,800	140
500	600	600	50	125,000	150,000	1,800	145
600	700	600	55	150,000	175,000	1,800	150
700	800	600	55	175,000	200,000	1,800	155
800	900	600	60	200,000	250,000	1,800	160
900	1,000	600	60	250,000	300,000	1,800	165
1,000	2,000	600	65	300,000	350,000	1,800	170
2,000	3,000	600	70	350,000	400,000	1,800	175
3,000	4,000	600	75	400,000	450,000	1,800	180
4,000	5,000	600	80	450,000	500,000	1,800	180
5,000	6,000	600	80	500,000	600,000	1,800	185
6,000	7,000	600	85	600,000	700,000	1,800	190
7,000	8,000	600	85	700,000	800,000	1,800	195
8,000	9,000	600	90	800,000	900,000	1,800	200
9,000	10,000	600	90	900,000	1,000,000	1,800	205
10,000	15,000	1,200	95	1,000,000	2,000,000	1,800	235
15,000	20,000	1,200	100	2,000,000	3,000,000	1,800	255
20,000	25,000	1,200	105	3,000,000	4,000,000	1,800	265
25,000	30,000	1,200	110	4,000,000	5,000,000	1,800	275
30,000	35,000	1,200	110	5,000,000	6,000,000	1,800	285
35,000	40,000	1,200	115	6,000,000	7,000,000	1,800	295
40,000	45,000	1,200	120	7,000,000	8,000,000	1,800	300
45,000	50,000	1,200	120	8,000,000	9,000,000	1,800	305
50,000	60,000	1,200	125	9,000,000	10,000,000	1,800	310

[Doc. No. FAA–2011–0105, 77 FR 55116, Sept. 7, 2012]

PARTS 421–430 [RESERVED]

PART 431—LAUNCH AND REENTRY OF A REUSABLE LAUNCH VEHICLE (RLV)

Subpart A—General

Subpart B—Policy Review and Approval for Launch and Reentry of a Reusable Launch Vehicle

Subpart C—Safety Review and Approval for Launch and Reentry of a Reusable Launch Vehicle

Subpart D—Payload Reentry Review and Determination

Subpart E—Post-Licensing Requirements—Reusable Launch Vehicle Mission License Terms and Conditions

Subpart F—Environmental Review

AUTHORITY: 51 U.S.C. 50901–50923.

SOURCE: Docket No. FAA–1999–5535, 65 FR 56658, Sept. 19, 2000, unless otherwise noted.

Subpart A—General

§431.1 General.

(a) *Scope.* This part prescribes requirements for obtaining a reusable launch vehicle (RLV) mission license and post-licensing requirements with which a licensee must comply to remain licensed. Requirements for preparing a license application are contained in part 413 of this subchapter.

(b) *Equivalent level of safety.* Each requirement of this part applies unless the applicant or licensee clearly and convincingly demonstrates that an alternative approach provides an equivalent level of safety to the requirement of this part.

[Doc. No. FAA–2016–6761, Amdt. No. 431–6, 83 FR 28535, June 20, 2018]

§431.3 Types of reusable launch vehicle mission licenses.

(a) *Mission-specific license.* A mission-specific license authorizing an RLV mission authorizes a licensee to launch and reenter, or otherwise land, one model or type of RLV from a launch site approved for the mission to a reentry site or other location approved for the mission. A mission-specific license authorizing an RLV mission may authorize more than one RLV mission and identifies each flight of an RLV authorized under the license. A licensee's authorization to conduct RLV missions terminates upon completion of all activities authorized by the license or the expiration date stated in the reentry license, whichever occurs first.

(b) *Operator license.* An operator license for RLV missions authorizes a licensee to launch and reenter, or otherwise land, any of a designated family of RLVs within authorized parameters, including launch sites and trajectories, transporting specified classes of payloads to any reentry site or other location designated in the license. An operator license for RLV missions is valid for a two-year renewable term.

§ 431.5 Policy and safety approvals.

To obtain either type of RLV mission license, an applicant must obtain policy and safety approvals from the FAA. Requirements for obtaining these approvals are contained in subparts B and C of this part. Only the license applicant may apply for the approvals, and may apply for either approval separately and in advance of submitting a complete license application, using the application procedures contained in part 413 of this subchapter.

§ 431.7 Payload and payload reentry determinations.

(a) A payload determination is required to launch a payload unless the proposed payload is exempt from payload review under § 415.53 of this chapter. Requirements for obtaining a payload determination are set forth in part 415, subpart D of this chapter.

(b) A payload reentry determination is required to reenter a payload to Earth on an RLV unless the proposed payload is exempt from payload reentry review.

(c) A payload reentry determination made under a previous license application under this subchapter may satisfy the requirements of paragraph (b) of this section.

(d) The FAA conducts a review, as described in subpart D of this part, to make a payload reentry determination. Either an RLV mission license applicant or a payload owner or operator may request a review of the proposed payload using the application procedures contained in part 413 of this subchapter. Upon receipt of an application, the FAA may conduct a payload reentry review independently of an RLV mission license application.

§ 431.8 Human space flight.

To obtain a license, an applicant proposing to conduct a reusable launch vehicle mission with flight crew or a space flight participant on board must demonstrate compliance with §§ 460.5, 460.7, 460.11, 460.13, 460.15, 460.17, 460.51 and 460.53 of this subchapter.

[Doc. No. FAA–2005–23449, 71 FR 75632, Dec. 15, 2006]

§ 431.9 Issuance of a reusable launch vehicle mission license.

(a) The FAA issues either a mission-specific or operator license authorizing RLV missions to an applicant who has obtained all approvals and determinations required under this chapter for the license.

(b) An RLV mission license authorizes a licensee to launch and reenter, or otherwise land, an RLV and payload, if any, in accordance with the representations contained in the licensee's application, subject to the licensee's compliance with terms and conditions contained in license orders accompanying the license, including financial responsibility requirements.

§ 431.11 Additional license terms and conditions.

The FAA may amend an RLV mission license at any time by modifying or adding license terms and conditions to ensure compliance with 51 U.S.C. Subtitle V, chapter 509, and applicable regulations.

[Doc. No. FAA–2012–0232, 77 FR 20533, Apr. 5, 2012]

§ 431.13 Transfer of a reusable launch vehicle mission license.

(a) Only the FAA may transfer an RLV mission license.

(b) An applicant for transfer of an RLV mission license shall submit a license application in accordance with part 413 of this subchapter and satisfy the applicable requirements of this part. The FAA will transfer an RLV mission license to an applicant who has obtained all of the approvals and determinations required under this chapter for an RLV mission license. In conducting its reviews and issuing approvals and determinations, the FAA may incorporate any findings made part of the record to support the initial licensing determination. The FAA may modify an RLV mission license to reflect any changes necessary as a result of a license transfer.

§431.15 Rights not conferred by a reusable launch vehicle mission license.

Issuance of an RLV mission license does not relieve a licensee of its obligation to comply with requirements of law that may apply to its activities.

§§431.16–431.20 [Reserved]

Subpart B—Policy Review and Approval for Launch and Reentry of a Reusable Launch Vehicle

§431.21 General.

The FAA issues a policy approval to an RLV mission license applicant upon completion of a favorable policy review. A policy approval is part of the licensing record on which the licensing determination is based.

§431.23 Policy review.

(a) The FAA reviews an RLV mission license application to determine whether the proposed mission presents any issues, other than those issues addressed in the safety review, that would adversely affect U.S. national security or foreign policy interests, would jeopardize public health and safety or the safety of property, or would not be consistent with international obligations of the United States.

(b) Interagency consultation is conducted as follows:

(1) The FAA consults with the Department of Defense to determine whether an RLV mission license application presents any issues adversely affecting U.S. national security.

(2) The FAA consults with the Department of State to determine whether an RLV mission license application presents any issues adversely affecting U.S. foreign policy interests or international obligations.

(3) The FAA consults with other Federal agencies, including the National Aeronautics and Space Administration, authorized to address issues identified under paragraph (a) of this section, associated with an applicant's RLV mission proposal.

(c) The FAA advises an applicant, in writing, of any issue raised during a policy review that would impede issuance of a policy approval. The applicant may respond, in writing, or revise its license application.

§431.25 Application requirements for policy review.

In its RLV mission license application, an applicant must—

(a) Identify the model, type, and configuration of any RLV proposed for launch and reentry, or otherwise landing on Earth, by the applicant.

(b) Identify all vehicle systems, including structural, thermal, pneumatic, propulsion, electrical, and avionics and guidance systems used in the vehicle(s), and all propellants.

(c) Identify foreign ownership of the applicant as follows:

(1) For a sole proprietorship or partnership, identify all foreign ownership;

(2) For a corporation, identify any foreign ownership interests of 10% or more; and

(3) For a joint venture, association, or other entity, identify any participating foreign entities.

(d) Identify proposed launch and reentry flight profile(s), including—

(1) Launch and reentry site(s), including planned contingency abort locations, if any;

(2) Flight trajectories, reentry trajectories, associated ground tracks, and instantaneous impact points for nominal operations, and contingency abort profiles, if any;

(3) Sequence of planned events or maneuvers during the mission; and for an orbital mission, the range of intermediate and final orbits of the vehicle and upper stages, if any, and their estimated orbital life times.

§431.27 Denial of policy approval.

The FAA notifies an applicant, in writing, if the FAA has denied policy approval for an RLV mission license application. The notice states the reasons for the FAA's determination. The applicant may respond to the reasons for the determination and request reconsideration.

§§ 431.28–431.30 [Reserved]

Subpart C—Safety Review and Approval for Launch and Reentry of a Reusable Launch Vehicle

§ 431.31 General.

(a) The FAA conducts a safety review to determine whether an applicant is capable of launching an RLV and payload, if any, from a designated launch site, and reentering the RLV and payload, if any, to a designated reentry site or location, or otherwise landing it on Earth, without jeopardizing public health and safety and the safety of property.

(b) The FAA issues a safety approval to an RLV mission license applicant that satisfies the requirements of this Subpart. The FAA evaluates on an individual basis all public safety aspects of a proposed RLV mission to ensure they are sufficient to support safe conduct of the mission. A safety approval is part of the licensing record on which the FAA's licensing determination is based.

(c) The FAA advises an applicant, in writing, of any issue raised during a safety review that would impede issuance of a safety approval. The applicant may respond, in writing, or revise its license application.

§ 431.33 Safety organization.

(a) An applicant shall maintain a safety organization and document it by identifying lines of communication and approval authority for all mission decisions that may affect public safety. Lines of communication within the applicant's organization, between the applicant and the launch site, and between the applicant and the reentry site, shall be employed to ensure that personnel perform RLV mission operations in accordance with plans and procedures required by this subpart. Approval authority shall be employed to ensure compliance with terms and conditions stated in an RLV mission license and with the plans and procedures required by this subpart.

(b) An applicant must designate a person responsible for the conduct of all licensed RLV mission activities.

(c) An applicant shall designate by name, title, and qualifications, a qualified safety official authorized by the applicant to examine all aspects of the applicant's operations with respect to safety of RLV mission activities and to monitor independently compliance by vehicle safety operations personnel with the applicant's safety policies and procedures. The safety official shall report directly to the person responsible for an applicant's licensed RLV mission activities, who shall ensure that all of the safety official's concerns are addressed both before a mission is initiated and before reentry or descent flight of an RLV is initiated. The safety official is responsible for—

(1) Monitoring and evaluating operational dress rehearsals to ensure they are conducted in accordance with procedures required by § 431.37(a)(4) and under § 431.37(a)(1)(iv) to ensure the readiness of vehicle safety operations personnel to conduct a safe mission under nominal and non-nominal conditions; and

(2) Completing a mission readiness determination as required by § 431.37 before an RLV mission is initiated. The safety official must monitor and report to the person responsible for the conduct of licensed RLV mission activities any non-compliance with procedures listed in §§ 431.37 and 431.43, or any representation contained in the application, and the readiness of the licensee to conduct mission operations in accordance with the license and this part. The safety official is responsible for compliance with §§ 431.37 and 431.43, and with representations contained in the application.

§ 431.35 Acceptable reusable launch vehicle mission risk.

(a) To obtain safety approval for an RLV mission, an applicant must demonstrate that the proposed mission does not exceed acceptable risk as defined in this subpart. For purposes of this section, the mission commences upon initiation of the launch phase of flight and consists of launch flight through orbital insertion of an RLV or vehicle stage or flight to outer space, whichever is applicable, and reentry or descent flight, and concludes upon landing on Earth of the RLV.

(b) Acceptable risk for a proposed mission is measured in terms of the expected average number of casualties (E_c).

(1) To obtain safety approval, an applicant must demonstrate the following for public risk:

(i) The risk to the collective members of the public from the proposed launch meets the public risk criteria of §417.107(b)(1) of this chapter;

(ii) The risk level to the collective members of the public, excluding persons in water-borne vessels and aircraft, from each proposed reentry does not exceed an expected number of 1×10^{-4} casualties from impacting inert and explosive debris and toxic release associated with the reentry; and

(iii) The risk level to an individual does not exceed 1×10^{-6} probability of casualty per mission.

(2) [Reserved]

(c) To demonstrate compliance with acceptable risk criteria in this section, an applicant shall employ a system safety process to identify the hazards and assess the risks to public health and safety and the safety of property associated with the mission, including nominal and non-nominal operation and flight of the vehicle and payload, if any. An acceptable system safety analysis identifies and assesses the probability and consequences of any reasonably foreseeable hazardous event, and safety-critical system failures during launch flight or reentry that could result in a casualty to the public.

(d) As part of the demonstration required under paragraph (c) of this section, an applicant must—

(1) Identify and describe the structure of the RLV, including physical dimensions and weight;

(2) Identify and describe any hazardous materials, including radioactive materials, and their container on the RLV;

(3) Identify and describe safety-critical systems;

(4) Identify and describe all safety-critical failure modes and their consequences;

(5) Provide drawings and schematics for eachsafety-critical system identified under paragraph (d)(3) of this section;

(6) Provide a timeline identifying all safety-critical events;

(7) Provide data that verifies the risk elimination and mitigation measures resulting from the applicant's system safety analyses required by paragraph (c) of this section; and

(8) Provide flight trajectory analyses covering launch or ascent of the vehicle through orbital insertion and reentry or descent of the vehicle through landing, including its three-sigma dispersion.

[Doc. No. FAA-1999-5535, 65 FR 56658, Sept. 19, 2000, as amended by Amdt. 431-2, 72 FR 17019, Apr. 6, 2007; Docket No. FAA-2014-0418, Amdt. No. 431-4, 81 FR 47027, July 20, 2016]

§431.37 Mission readiness.

(a) *Mission readiness requirements.* An applicant shall submit the following procedures for verifying mission readiness:

(1) Mission readiness review procedures that involve the applicant's vehicle safety operations personnel, and launch site and reentry site personnel involved in the mission. The procedures shall ensure a mission readiness review is conducted during which the designated individual responsible for the conduct of licensed activities under §431.33(b) is provided with the following information to make a judgment as to mission readiness—

(i) Readiness of the RLV including safety-critical systems and payload for launch and reentry flight;

(ii) Readiness of the launch site, personnel, and safety-related launch property and launch services to be provided by the launch site;

(iii) Readiness of the reentry site, personnel, and safety-related property and services for reentry flight and vehicle recovery;

(iv) Readiness of vehicle safety operations personnel to support mission flight, including results of dress rehearsals and simulations conducted in accordance with paragraph (a)(4) of this section;

(v) Mission rules and constraints, including contingency abort plans and procedures, if any, as required under §431.39;

(vi) Unresolved safety issues identified during the mission readiness review and plans for addressing them; and

(vii) Any additional safety information required by the individual designated under § 431.33(b) to determine launch and reentry readiness.

(2) Procedures that ensure mission constraints, rules, contingency abort and emergency abort procedures are listed and consolidated in a safety directive or notebook approved by the person designated by the applicant under § 431.33(b), the launch site operator, and the reentry site operator, if any;

(3) Procedures that ensure currency and consistency of licensee, launch site operator, and reentry site operator checklists;

(4) Dress rehearsal procedures that—

(i) Ensure crew readiness under nominal and non-nominal flight conditions;

(ii) Contain criteria for determining whether to dispense with or add one or more dress rehearsals; and

(iii) Verify currency and consistency of licensee, launch site operator, and reentry site operator checklists; and

(5) Procedures for ensuring the licensee's vehicle safety operations personnel adhere to crew rest rules of this part.

(b) [Reserved]

§ 431.39 Mission rules, procedures, contingency plans, and checklists.

(a) An applicant shall submit mission rules, procedures, checklists, emergency plans, and contingency abort plans, if any, that ensure safe conduct of mission operations during nominal and non-nominal vehicle flight.

(b) Mission rules, procedures, checklists, emergency plans, and contingency abort plans must be contained in a safety directive, notebook, or other compilation that is approved by the safety official designated under § 431.33(c) and concurred in by the launch site operator and reentry site operator, if any.

(c) Vehicle safety operations personnel must have current and consistent mission checklists.

§ 431.41 Communications plan.

(a) An applicant shall submit a plan providing vehicle safety operations personnel communications procedures during the mission. Procedures for effective issuance and communication of safety-critical information during the mission shall include hold/resume, go/no go, contingency abort, if any, and emergency abort commands by vehicle safety operations personnel. The communications plan shall describe the authority of vehicle safety operations personnel, by individual or position title, to issue these commands. The communications plan shall ensure that—

(1) Communication networks are assigned so that personnel identified under this section have direct access to real-time, safety-critical information required for making decisions and issuing commands;

(2) Personnel identified under this section monitor a common intercom channel for safety-critical communications during launch and reentry;

(3) A protocol is established for utilizing defined radio communications terminology; and

(4) Communications affecting the safety of the mission are recorded in a manner that accurately reflects communications made on individual channels, synchronized time coding, and sequence of communications.

(b) An applicant shall submit procedures to ensure that licensee and reentry site personnel, if any, receive a copy of the communications plan required by this section and that the reentry site operator, if any, concurs with the communications plan.

§ 431.43 Reusable launch vehicle mission operational requirements and restrictions.

(a) An applicant for RLV mission safety approval shall submit procedures—

(1) That ensure RLV mission risks do not exceed the criteria set forth in § 431.35 for nominal and non-nominal operations;

(2) That ensure conformance with the system safety process and associated hazard identification and risk assessment required under § 431.35(c);

(3) That ensure conformance with operational restrictions listed in paragraphs (c) through (e) of this section;

(4) To monitor and verify the status of RLV safety-critical systems sufficiently before enabling both launch and reentry flight to ensure public safety and during mission flight unless technically infeasible; and

(5) For human activation or initiation of a flight safety system that safely aborts the launch of an RLV if the vehicle is not operating within approved mission parameters and the vehicle poses risk to public health and safety and the safety of property in excess of acceptable flight risk as defined in §431.35.

(b) To satisfy risk criteria set forth in §431.35(b)(1), an applicant for RLV mission safety approval shall identify suitable and attainable locations for nominal landing and vehicle staging impact or landing, if any. An application shall identify such locations for a contingency abort if necessary to satisfy risk criteria contained in §431.35(b)(1) during launch of an RLV. A nominal landing, vehicle staging impact and contingency abort location are suitable for launch or reentry if—

(1) For any vehicle or vehicle stage, the area of the predicted three-sigma dispersion of the vehicle or vehicle stage can be wholly contained within the designated location; and

(2) The location is of sufficient size to contain landing impacts, including debris dispersion upon impact and any toxic release.

(c) For an RLV mission—

(1) A collision avoidance analysis shall be performed in order to maintain at least a 200-kilometer separation from any inhabitable orbiting object during launch and reentry. The analysis shall address:

(i) For launch, closures in a planned launch window for ascent to outer space or, for an orbital RLV, to initial orbit through at least one complete orbit;

(ii) For reentry, the reentry trajectory;

(iii) Expansions of the closure period by subtracting 15 seconds from the closure start-time and adding 15 seconds to the closure end-time for each sequential 90 minutes elapsed time period, or portion there of, beginning at the time the state vectors of the orbiting objects were determined;

(2) The projected instantaneous impact point (IIP) of the vehicle shall not have substantial dwell time over densely populated areas during any segment of mission flight;

(3) There will be no unplanned physical contact between the vehicle or its components and payload after payload separation and debris generation will not result from conversion of energy sources into energy that fragments the vehicle or its payload. Energy sources include, but are not limited to, chemical, pneumatic, and kinetic energy; and

(4) Vehicle safety operations personnel shall adhere to the following work and rest standards:

(i) A maximum 12-hour work shift with at least 8 hours of rest after 12 hours of work, preceding initiation of an RLV reentry mission or during the conduct of a mission;

(ii) A maximum of 60 hours worked in the 7 days, preceding initiation of an RLV mission;

(iii) A maximum of 14 consecutive work days; and

(iv) A minimum 48-hour rest period after 5 consecutive days of 12-hour shifts.

(d) In addition to requirements of paragraph (c) of this section, any unproven RLV may only be operated so that during any portion of flight—

(1) The projected instantaneous impact point (IIP) of the vehicle does not have substantial dwell time over populated areas; or

(2) The expected number of casualties to members of the public does not exceed 1×10^{-4} given a probability of vehicle failure equal to 1 (pf=1) at any time the IIP is over a populated area;

(e) Any RLV that enters Earth orbit may only be operated such that the vehicle operator is able to—

(1) Monitor and verify the status of safety-critical systems before enabling reentry flight to assure the vehicle can reenter safely to Earth; and

(2) Issue a command enabling reentry flight of the vehicle. Reentry flight cannot be initiated autonomously

under nominal circumstances without prior enable.

[Docket No. FAA–1999–5535, 65 FR 56658, Sept. 19, 2000, as amended by Docket No. FAA–2014–0418, Amdt. No. 431–4, 81 FR 47027, July 20, 2016]

§ 431.45 Mishap investigation plan and emergency response plan.

(a) *Mishap investigation plan and emergency response plan.* An applicant shall submit a mishap investigation plan (MIP) containing the applicant's procedures for reporting and responding to launch and reentry accidents, launch and reentry incidents, or other mishaps, as defined in § 401.5 of this chapter, that occur during the conduct of an RLV mission. An acceptable MIP satisfies the requirements of paragraphs (b)–(d) of this section. An applicant shall also submit an emergency response plan (ERP) that contains procedures for informing the affected public of a planned RLV mission. An acceptable ERP satisfies the requirements of paragraph (e) of this section. The MIP and ERP shall be signed by an individual authorized to sign and certify the application in accordance with § 413.7(c) of this chapter, the person responsible for the conduct of all licensed RLV mission activities designated under § 431.33(b) of this subpart, and the safety official designated under § 431.33(c) of this subpart.

(b) *Report requirements.* A MIP shall provide for—

(1) Immediate notification to the FAA Washington Operations Center in case of a launch or reentry accident, launch or reentry incident, or a mishap that involves a fatality or serious injury (as defined in 49 CFR 830.2);

(2) Notification within 24 hours to the Associate Administrator for Commercial Space Transportation in the event of a mishap that does not involve a fatality or serious injury, as defined in 49 CFR 830.2; and

(3) Submission of a written preliminary report to the FAA Associate Administrator for Commercial Space Transportation in the event of a launch accident or launch incident occurring in the conduct of an RLV mission, or reentry accident or reentry incident, occurring in the conduct of an RLV mission, within 5 days of the event. The report shall identify the event as either a launch or reentry accident or incident and must include the following information:

(i) Date and time of occurrence;

(ii) Description of the event and sequence of events leading to the accident or incident, to the extent known;

(iii) Intended and actual location of launch and reentry or other landing on Earth;

(iv) Identification of the vehicle;

(v) Identification of the payload, if applicable;

(vi) Number and general description of any fatalities and injuries;

(vii) Property damage, if any, and an estimate of its value;

(viii) Identification of hazardous materials, as defined in § 401.5 of this chapter, involved in the event, whether on the vehicle, payload, or on the ground;

(ix) Action taken by any person to contain the consequences of the event;

(x) Weather conditions at the time of the event; and

(xi) Potential consequences for other vehicles or systems of similar type and proposed operations.

(c) *Response plan.* A MIP must contain procedures to—

(1) Ensure the consequences of a launch accident, launch incident, reentry accident, reentry incident, or other mishap occurring in the conduct of an RLV mission are contained and minimized;

(2) Ensure data and physical evidence are preserved;

(3) Require the licensee to report and to cooperate with FAA and the National Transportation Safety Board investigations and designate one or more points of contact for the FAA or NTSB; and;

(4) Require the licensee to identify and adopt preventive measures for avoiding recurrence of the event.

(d) *Investigation plan.* A MIP shall contain—

(1) Procedures for investigating the cause of an event described in paragraph (c)(1) of this section;

(2) Procedures for reporting investigation results to the FAA;

(3) Delineated responsibilities, including reporting responsibilities, for personnel assigned to conduct investigations and for any unrelated entities

retained by the licensee to conduct or participate in investigations.

(e) *Emergency response plan.* An ERP shall provide for—

(1) Notification to local officials in the event of an off-site or unplanned landing so that vehicle recovery can be conducted safely and effectively and with minimal risk to public safety. The plan must provide for the quick dissemination of up to date information to the public, and for doing so in advance of reentry or other landing on Earth to the extent practicable; and

(2) A public information dissemination plan for informing the potentially affected public, in laymen's terms and in advance of a planned reentry, of the estimated date, time and landing location for the reentry activity.

§431.47 Denial of safety approval.

The FAA notifies an applicant, in writing, if the FAA has denied safety approval for an RLV mission license application. The notice states the reasons for the FAA's determination. The applicant may respond to the reasons for the determination and request reconsideration.

§§431.48–431.50 [Reserved]

Subpart D—Payload Reentry Review and Determination

§431.51 General.

(a) A payload reentry review is conducted to examine the policy and safety issues related to the proposed reentry of a payload, other than a U.S. Government payload or a payload whose reentry is subject to regulation by another Federal agency, to determine whether the FAA will approve reentry of the payload.

(b) A payload reentry review may be conducted as part of an RLV mission license application review or may be requested by a payload owner or operator in advance of or separate from an RLV mission license application.

(c) A payload reentry determination will be made part of the licensing record on which the FAA's licensing determination is based.

§431.53 Classes of payloads.

(a) The FAA may approve the return of a type or class of payload (for example, communications or microgravity/scientific satellites).

(b) The RLV mission licensee that will return a payload approved for reentry under this section, is responsible for providing current information in accordance with §431.57 regarding the payload proposed for reentry no later than 60 days before a scheduled RLV mission involving that payload.

§431.55 Payload reentry review.

(a) In conducting a payload reentry review to decide if the FAA should approve reentry of a payload, the FAA determines whether its reentry presents any issues that would adversely affect U.S. national security or foreign policy interests, would jeopardize public health and safety or the safety of property, or would not be consistent with international obligations of the United States.

(b) The FAA consults with the Department of Defense to determine whether reentry of a proposed payload presents any issues adversely affecting U.S. national security.

(c) The FAA consults with the Department of State to determine whether reentry of a proposed payload presents any issues adversely affecting U.S. foreign policy interests or international obligations.

(d) The FAA consults with other Federal agencies, including the National Aeronautics and Space Administration, authorized to address issues identified under paragraph (a) of this section.

(e) The FAA advises a person requesting a payload reentry determination, in writing, of any issue raised during a payload reentry review that would impede the issuance of a favorable determination to reenter that payload. The person requesting a payload reentry review may respond, in writing, or revise its application.

§431.57 Information requirements for payload reentry review.

A person requesting reentry review of a particular payload or payload class must identify the following:

(a) Payload name or class and function;

(b) Physical characteristics, dimensions, and weight of the payload;

(c) Payload owner and operator, if different from the person requesting the payload reentry review;

(d) Type, amount, and container of hazardous materials, as defined in § 401.5 of this chapter, and radioactive materials in the payload;

(e) Explosive potential of payload materials, alone and in combination with other materials found on the payload or RLV during reentry;

(f) Designated reentry site(s); and

(g) Method for securing the payload on the RLV.

§ 431.59 Issuance of payload reentry determination.

(a) The FAA issues a favorable payload reentry determination unless it determines that reentry of the proposed payload would adversely affect U.S. national security or foreign policy interests, would jeopardize public health and safety or the safety of property, or would not be consistent with international obligations of the United States. The FAA responds to any person who has requested a payload reentry review of its determination in writing. The notice states the reasons for the determination in the event of an unfavorable determination.

(b) Any person issued an unfavorable payload reentry determination may respond to the reasons for the determination and request reconsideration.

§ 431.61 Incorporation of payload reentry determination in license application.

A favorable payload reentry determination issued for a payload or class of payload may be included by an RLV mission license applicant as part of its application. Before the conduct of an RLV mission involving a payload approved for reentry, any change in information provided under § 431.57 must be reported by the licensee in accordance with § 413.17 of this chapter. The FAA determines whether a favorable payload reentry determination remains valid and may conduct an additional payload reentry review.

§§ 431.62–431.70 [Reserved]

Subpart E—Post-Licensing Requirements—Reusable Launch Vehicle Mission License Terms and Conditions

§ 431.71 Public safety responsibility.

(a) A licensee is responsible for ensuring the safe conduct of an RLV mission and for protecting public health and safety and the safety of property during the conduct of the mission.

(b) A licensee must conduct a licensed RLV mission and perform RLV safety procedures in accordance with representations made in its license application. A licensee's failure to perform safety procedures in accordance with the representations made in the license application or comply with any license condition is sufficient basis for the revocation of a license or other appropriate nforcement action.

§ 431.73 Continuing accuracy of license application; application for modification of license.

(a) A licensee is responsible for the continuing accuracy of representations contained in its application for the entire term of the license.

(b) After a license has been issued, a licensee must apply to the FAA for modification of the license if—

(1) The licensee proposes to conduct an RLV mission or perform a safety-critical operation in a manner not authorized by the license; or

(2) Any representation contained in the license application that is material to public health and safety or the safety of property is no longer accurate and complete or does not reflect the licensee's procedures governing the actual conduct of an RLV mission. A change is material to public health and safety or the safety of property if it alters or affects the—

(i) Mission rules, procedures, checklists, emergency plans, and contingency abort plans, if any, submitted in accordance with § 431.39

(ii) Class of payload;

(iii) Type of RLV;

(iv) Any safety-critical system;

(v) Type and container of the hazardous material carried by the vehicle;

(vi) Flight trajectory;

(vii) Launch site or reentry site or other landing location; or

(viii) Any safety system, policy, procedure, requirement, criteria, or standard.

(c) An application to modify an RLV mission license must be prepared and submitted in accordance with part 413 of this chapter. The licensee must indicate any part of its license or license application that would be changed or affected by a proposed modification.

(d) The FAA reviews determinations and approvals required by this chapter to determine whether they remain valid after submission of a proposed modification.

(e) Upon approval of a modification, the FAA issues either a written approval to the licensee or a license order amending the license if a stated term or condition of the license is changed, added, or deleted. An approval has the full force and effect of a license order and is part of the licensing record.

§431.75 Agreements.

(a) *Launch and reentry site use agreements.* Before conducting a licensed RLV mission using property and services of a Federal launch range or licensed launch or reentry site operator, a licensee or applicant shall enter into an agreement with the Federal launch range and/or licensed site operator that provides for access to and use of property and services required to support a licensed RLV mission or reentry and for public safety related operations and support. The agreement shall be in effect before any licensed RLV mission or reentry. A licensee shall comply with any requirements of the agreement that may affect public health and safety and the safety of property during the conduct of its licensed activity.

(b) *Agreements for notices to mariners and airmen.* Unless otherwise addressed in agreements between a licensed launch site operator and the U.S. Coast Guard and the FAA, respectively, a licensee authorized to conduct an RLV mission using a launch site or reentry site other than a Federal launch range shall complete the following:

(1) An agreement between the licensee and the local U.S. Coast Guard district to establish procedures for the issuance of a Notice to Mariners prior to a launch or reentry and other measures as the Coast Guard deems necessary to protect public health and safety; and

(2) An agreement between the licensee and the FAA regional office having jurisdiction over the airspace through which a launch and reentry will take place, to establish procedures for the issuance of a Notice to Airmen prior to the conduct of a licensed launch or reentry and for closing of air routes during the respective launch and reentry windows and other measures deemed necessary by the FAA regional office in order to protect public health and safety.

§431.77 Records.

(a) Except as specified in paragraph (b) of this section, a licensee shall maintain for 3 years all records, data, and other material necessary to verify that a licensed RLV mission is conducted in accordance with representations contained in the licensee's application.

(b) In the event of a launch accident, reentry accident, launch incident or reentry incident, as defined in §401.5 of this chapter, a licensee shall preserve all records related to the event. Records must be retained until completion of any Federal investigation and the FAA advises the licensee that the records need not be retained. The licensee shall make all records required to be maintained under the regulations available to Federal officials for inspection and copying.

§431.79 Reusable launch vehicle mission reporting requirements.

(a) Not less than 60 days before each RLV mission conducted under a license, a licensee shall provide the FAA with the following information:

(1) Payload information in accordance with 14 CFR §415.59 of this chapter and §431.57; and

(2) Flight information, including the vehicle, launch site, planned launch and reentry flight path, and intended landing sites including contingency abort sites.

(3) Launch or reentry waivers, approved or pending, from a Federal range from which the launch or reentry

will take place, that are unique and may affect public safety.

(b) Not later than 15 days before each licensed RLV mission, a licensee must notify the FAA, in writing, of the time and date of the intended launch and reentry or other landing on Earth of the RLV and may utilize the FAA/U.S. Space Command Launch Notification Form, contained in part 415, Appendix A, of this subchapter for doing so.

(c) A licensee must report a launch accident, launch incident, reentry accident, reentry incident, or other mishap immediately to the FAA Washington Operations Center and provide a written preliminary report in the event of a launch accident, launch incident, reentry accident, or reentry incident, in accordance with the mishap investigation and emergency response plan submitted as part of its license application under § 431.45.

[Docket No. FAA–1999–5535, 65 FR 56658, Sept. 19, 2000, as amended by Amdt. No. 431–5, 81 FR 59440, Aug. 30, 2016]

§ 431.81 Financial responsibility requirements.

A licensee under this part must comply with financial responsibility requirements specified in its license.

§ 431.83 Compliance monitoring.

A licensee shall allow access by, and cooperate with, Federal officers or employees or other individuals authorized by the FAA to observe any activities of the licensee, or of the licensee's contractors or subcontractors, associated with the conduct of a licensed RLV mission.

§ 431.85 Registration of space objects.

(a) To assist the U.S. Government in implementing Article IV of the 1975 Convention on Registration of Objects Launched into Outer Space, each licensee shall provide to the FAA the information required by paragraph (b) of this section for all objects placed in space by a licensed RLV mission, including an RLV and any components, except:

(1) Any object owned and registered by the U.S. Government; and

(2) Any object owned by a foreign entity.

(b) For each object that must be registered in accordance with this section, a licensee shall submit the following information not later than thirty (30) days following the conduct of a licensed RLV mission :

(1) The international designator of the space object(s);

(2) Date and location of the RLV mission initiation;

(3) General function of the space object; and

(4) Final orbital parameters, including:

(i) Nodal period;

(ii) Inclination;

(iii) Apogee; and

(iv) Perigee.

(c) A licensee shall notify the FAA when it removes an object that it has previously placed in space.

§§ 431.86–431.90 [Reserved]

Subpart F—Environmental Review

§ 431.91 General.

An applicant shall provide the FAA with sufficient information to analyze the environmental impacts associated with proposed operation of an RLV, including the impacts of anticipated activities to be performed at its reentry site. The information provided by an applicant must be sufficient to enable the FAA to comply with the requirements of the National Environmental Policy Act, 42 U.S.C. 4321 *et seq.*, the Council on Environmental Quality Regulations for Implementing the Procedural Provisions of the National Environmental Policy Act, 40 CFR parts 1500–1508, and the FAA's Procedures for Considering Environmental Impacts, FAA Order 1050.1D. Copies of FAA Order 1050.1D may be obtained from the Office of Environment and Energy, AEE–300, Federal Aviation Administration, 800 Independence Avenue SW., Washington, DC 20591, (202) 267–3553. Copies of FAA Order 1050.1D may be inspected in the Rules Docket at the Federal Aviation Administration, Office of the Chief Counsel, AGC–200, Room 915G, 800 Independence Avenue SW., Washington, DC 20591 weekdays between 8:30 a.m. and 5:00 p.m.

§ 431.93 Environmental information.

An applicant shall submit environmental information concerning—

(a) A designated launch and reentry site, including contingency abort locations, if any, not covered by existing FAA or other Federal environmental documentation;

(b) A proposed new RLV with characteristics falling measurably outside the parameters of existing environmental documentation;

(c) A proposed reentry to an established reentry site involving an RLV with characteristics falling measurably outside the parameters of existing environmental impact statements covering that site;

(d) A proposed payload that may have significant environmental impacts in the event of a reentry accident; and

(e) Other factors as necessary to comply with the National Environmental Policy Act.

PART 432 [RESERVED]

PART 433—LICENSE TO OPERATE A REENTRY SITE

Sec.

AUTHORITY: 51 U.S.C. 50901-50923.

SOURCE: Docket No. FAA-1999-5535, 65 FR 56665, Sept. 19, 2000, unless otherwise noted.

§ 433.1 General.

The FAA evaluates on an individual basis an applicant's proposal to operate a reentry site.

§ 433.3 Issuance of a license to operate a reentry site.

(a) The FAA issues a license to operate a reentry site when it determines that an applicant's operation of the reentry site does not jeopardize public health and safety, the safety of property, U.S. national security or foreign policy interests, or international obligations of the United States.

(b) A license to operate a reentry site authorizes a licensee to operate a reentry site in accordance with the representations contained in the licensee's application, subject to the licensee's compliance with terms and conditions contained in any license order accompanying the license.

§ 433.5 Operational restrictions on a reentry site.

A license to operate a reentry site authorizes the licensee to offer use of the site to support reentry of a reentry vehicle for which the three-sigma footprint of the vehicle upon reentry is wholly contained within the site.

§ 433.7 Environmental.

An applicant shall provide the FAA with information for the FAA to analyze the environmental impacts associated with proposed operation of a reentry site. The information provided by an applicant must be sufficient to enable the FAA to comply with the requirements of the National Environmental Policy Act, 42 U.S.C. 4321 *et seq.* (NEPA), the Council on Environmental Quality Regulations for Implementing the Procedural Provisions of NEPA, 40 CFR Parts 1500–1508, and the FAA's Procedures for Consideration Environmental Impacts, FAA Order 1050.1D.

§ 433.9 Environmental information.

An applicant shall submit environmental information concerning a proposed reentry site not covered by existing environmental documentation for purposes of assessing reentry impacts.

PART 434 [RESERVED]

PART 435—REENTRY OF A REENTRY VEHICLE OTHER THAN A REUSABLE LAUNCH VEHICLE (RLV)

Subpart A—General

Sec.

AUTHORITY: 51 U.S.C. 50901–50923.

SOURCE: Docket No. FAA–1999–5535, 65 FR 56665, Sept. 19, 2000, unless otherwise noted.

Subpart A—General

§ 435.1 General.

(a) *Scope.* This part prescribes requirements for obtaining a license to reenter a reentry vehicle other than a reusable launch vehicle (RLV), and postlicensing requirements with which a licensee must comply to remain licensed. Requirements for preparing a license application are contained in part 413 of this subchapter.

(b) *Equivalent level of safety.* Each requirement of this part applies unless the applicant or licensee clearly and convincingly demonstrates that an alternative approach provides an equivalent level of safety to the requirement of this part.

[Doc. No. FAA–2016–6761, Amdt. No. 435–4, 83 FR 28535, June 20, 2018]

§ 435.3 Types of reentry licenses.

(a) *Reentry-specific license.* A reentry-specific license authorizes a licensee to reenter one model or type of reentry vehicle, other than an RLV, to a reentry site or other location approved for the reentry. A reentry-specific license may authorize more than one reentry and identifies each reentry authorized under the license. A licensee's authorization to reenter terminates upon completion of all activities authorized by the license or the expiration date stated in the reentry license, whichever occurs first.

(b) *Reentry-operator license.* A reentry operator license authorizes a licensee to reenter any of a designated family of reentry vehicles, other than an RLV, within authorized parameters, including trajectories, transporting specified classes of payloads to any reentry site designated in the license. A reentry operator license is valid for a 2-year renewable term.

§ 435.5 Policy and safety approvals.

To obtain a reentry license, an applicant must obtain policy and safety approvals from the FAA. Requirements for obtaining these approvals are contained in subparts B and C of this part. Only a reentry license applicant may apply for the approvals, and may apply for either approval separately and in advance of submitting a complete license application, using the application procedures contained in part 413 of this subchapter.

§ 435.7 Payload reentry determination.

(a) A payload reentry determination is required to transport a payload to Earth on a reentry vehicle unless the proposed payload is exempt from payload review.

(b) A payload reentry determination made under a previous license application under this subchapter may satisfy the requirements of paragraph (a) of this section.

(c) The FAA conducts a review, as described in subpart D of this part, to make a payload reentry determination.

Either a reentry license applicant or a payload owner or operator may request a review of the proposed payload using the application procedures contained in part 413 of this subchapter. Upon receipt of an application, the FAA may conduct a payload reentry review independently of a reentry license application.

§435.8 Human space flight.

An applicant for a license to conduct a reentry with flight crew or a space flight participant on board the vehicle must demonstrate compliance with §§460.5, 460.7, 460.11, 460.13, 460.15, 460.17, 460.51 and 460.53 of this subchapter.

[Doc. No. FAA-2005-23449, 71 FR 75632, Dec. 15, 2006]

§435.9 Issuance of a reentry license.

(a) The FAA issues a reentry license to an applicant who has obtained all approvals and determinations required under this chapter for a reentry license.

(b) A reentry license authorizes a licensee to reenter a reentry vehicle and payload, if any, in accordance with the representations contained in the reentry licensee's application, subject to the licensee's compliance with terms and conditions contained in license orders accompanying the reentry license, including financial responsibility requirements.

§435.11 Additional license terms and conditions.

The FAA may amend a reentry license at any time by modifying or adding license terms and conditions to ensure compliance with 51 U.S.C. Subtitle V, chapter 509, and applicable regulations.

[Doc. No. FAA-2012-0232, 77 FR 20533, Apr. 5, 2012]

§435.13 Transfer of a reentry license.

(a) Only the FAA may transfer a reentry license.

(b) An applicant for transfer of a reentry license shall submit a reentry license application in accordance with part 413 of this subchapter and satisfy the applicable requirements of this part. The FAA will transfer a reentry license to an applicant who has obtained all of the approvals and determinations required under this chapter for a reentry license. In conducting its reviews and issuing approvals and determinations, the FAA may incorporate any findings made part of the record to support the initial licensing determination. The FAA may modify a reentry license to reflect any changes necessary as a result of a reentry license transfer.

§435.15 Rights not conferred by reentry license.

Issuance of a reentry license does not relieve a licensee of its obligation to comply with requirements of law that may apply to its activities.

§§435.16–431.20 [Reserved]

Subpart B—Policy Review and Approval for Reentry of a Reentry Vehicle

§435.21 General.

The FAA issues a policy approval to a reentry license applicant upon completion of a favorable policy review. A policy approval is part of the licensing record on which the licensing determination is based.

§435.23 Policy review requirements and procedures.

Unless otherwise indicated in this subpart, regulations applicable to policy review and approval of the reentry of an RLV contained in part 431, subpart B of this subchapter shall apply to the policy review conducted for a license to reenter a reentry vehicle under this part.

§§435.24–435.30 [Reserved]

Subpart C—Safety Review and Approval for Reentry of a Reentry Vehicle

§435.31 General.

The FAA conducts a safety review to determine whether an applicant is capable of reentering a reentry vehicle and payload, if any, to a designated reentry site without jeopardizing public health and safety and the safety of property. A safety approval is part of the licensing record on which the licensing determination is based.

§ 435.33 Safety review requirements and procedures.

Unless otherwise stated in this subpart, regulations applicable to safety review and approval of the reentry of an RLV contained in part 431, subpart C of this subchapter shall apply to the safety review conducted for a license to reenter a reentry vehicle under this part.

§ 435.35 Acceptable reusable launch vehicle risk.

To obtain safety approval for reentry, an applicant must demonstrate the following for public risk:

(a) The risk to the collective members of the public from the proposed launch meets the public risk criteria of § 417.107(b)(1) of this chapter;

(b) The risk level to the collective members of the public, excluding persons in water-borne vessels and aircraft, from each proposed reentry does not exceed an expected number of 1×10^{-4} casualties from impacting inert and explosive debris and toxic release associated with the reentry; and

(c) The risk level to an individual does not exceed 1×10^{-6} probability of casualty per mission.

[Docket No. FAA–2014–0418, Amdt. No. 435–3, 81 FR 47027, July 20, 2016]

§§ 435.36–435.40 [Reserved]

Subpart D—Payload Reentry Review and Determination

§ 435.41 General.

The FAA conducts a payload reentry review to examine the policy and safety issues related to the proposed reentry of a payload, except a U.S. Government payload, to determine whether the FAA will approve the reentry of the payload.

§ 435.43 Payload reentry review requirements and procedures.

Unless otherwise indicated in this subpart, regulations contained in part 431, subpart D of this subchapter applicable to a payload reentry review and determination for reentering a payload using an RLV shall apply to the payload reentry review conducted for a license to reenter a reentry vehicle under this part.

§§ 435.44–435.50 [Reserved]

Subpart E—Post-Licensing Requirements—Reentry License Terms and Conditions

§ 435.51 General.

Unless otherwise indicated in this subpart, post-licensing requirements contained in part 431 subpart E, of this subchapter applicable to a license to reenter an RLV shall apply to a license issued under this part.

§§ 435.52–435.60 [Reserved]

Subpart F—Environmental Review

§ 435.61 General.

Unless otherwise indicated in this subpart, environmental review requirements contained in part 431 subpart F, applicable to a license to reenter an RLV shall apply to an application for a reentry license under this part.

§§ 435.62–435.70 [Reserved]

PART 436 [RESERVED]

PART 437—EXPERIMENTAL PERMITS

Subpart A—General Information

Sec.

Subpart B—Requirements to Obtain an Experimental Permit

PROGRAM DESCRIPTION

FLIGHT TEST PLAN

AUTHORITY: 51 U.S.C. 50901–50923.

SOURCE: Docket No. FAA–2006–24197, 72 FR 17019, Apr. 6, 2007, unless otherwise noted.

Subpart A—General Information

§ 437.1 Scope and organization of this part.

(a) *Scope.* This part prescribes requirements for obtaining an experimental permit. It also prescribes post-permitting requirements with which a permittee must comply to maintain its permit. Part 413 of this subchapter contains procedures for applying for an experimental permit.

(b) *Equivalent level of safety.* Each requirement of this part applies unless the applicant or permittee clearly and convincingly demonstrates that an alternative approach provides an equivalent level of safety to the requirement of this part.

(c) *Organization of this part.* Subpart A contains general information about an experimental permit. Subpart B contains requirements to obtain an experimental permit. Subpart C contains the safety requirements with which a permittee must comply while conducting permitted activities. Subpart D contains terms and conditions of an experimental permit.

[Doc. No. FAA–2016–6761, Amdt. No. 437–2, 83 FR 28535, June 20, 2018]

§ 437.3 Definitions.

Anomaly means a problem that occurs during verification or operation of a system, subsystem, process, facility, or support equipment.

Envelope expansion means any portion of a flight where planned operations will subject a reusable suborbital rocket to the effects of altitude, velocity, acceleration, or burn duration that exceed a level or duration successfully verified during an earlier flight.

Exclusion area means an area, within an operating area, that a reusable suborbital rocket's instantaneous impact point may not traverse.

Key flight-safety event means a permitted flight activity that has an increased likelihood of causing a launch accident compared with other portions of flight.

Operating area means a three-dimensional region where permitted flights may take place.

Permitted vehicle means a reusable suborbital rocket operated by a launch or reentry operator under an experimental permit.

Reentry impact point means the location of a reusable suborbital rocket's instantaneous impact point during its unpowered exoatmospheric suborbital flight.

§ 437.5 Eligibility for an experimental permit.

The FAA will issue an experimental permit to a person to launch or reenter a reusable suborbital rocket only for—

(a) Research and development to test new design concepts, new equipment, or new operating techniques;

(b) A showing of compliance with requirements for obtaining a license under this subchapter; or

(c) Crew training before obtaining a license for a launch or reentry using the design of the rocket for which the permit would be issued.

§ 437.7 Scope of an experimental permit.

An experimental permit authorizes launch or reentry of a reusable suborbital rocket. The authorization includes pre- and post-flight ground operations as defined in this section.

(a) A pre-flight ground operation includes each operation that—

(1) Takes place at a U.S. launch site; and

(2) Meets the following criteria:

(i) Is closely proximate in time to flight,

(ii) Entails critical steps preparatory to initiating flight,

(iii) Is unique to space launch, and

(iv) Is inherently so hazardous as to warrant the FAA's regulatory oversight.

(b) A post-flight ground operation includes each operation necessary to return the reusable suborbital rocket to a safe condition after it lands or impacts.

§ 437.9 Issuance of an experimental permit.

The FAA issues an experimental permit authorizing an unlimited number of launches or reentries for a suborbital rocket design for the uses described in § 437.5.

§ 437.11 Duration of an experimental permit.

An experimental permit lasts for one year from the date it is issued. A permittee may apply to renew a permit yearly under part 413 of this subchapter.

§ 437.13 Additional experimental permit terms and conditions.

The FAA may modify an experimental permit at any time by modifying or adding permit terms and conditions to ensure compliance with 51 U.S.C. Subtitle V, chapter 509.

[Doc. No. FAA–2012–0232, 77 FR 20533, Apr. 5, 2012]

§ 437.15 Transfer of an experimental permit.

An experimental permit is not transferable.

§ 437.17 Rights not conferred by an experimental permit.

Issuance of an experimental permit does not relieve a permittee of its obligation to comply with any requirement of law that applies to its activities.

Subpart B—Requirements to Obtain an Experimental Permit

§ 437.21 General.

To obtain an experimental permit an applicant must make the demonstrations and provide the information required by this section.

(a) *This subpart.* An applicant must provide a program description, a flight test plan, and operational safety documentation as required by this subpart.

(b) *Other regulations*—(1) *Environmental.* An applicant must provide enough information for the FAA to analyze the environmental impacts associated with proposed reusable suborbital rocket launches or reentries. The information provided by an applicant must be sufficient to enable the FAA to comply with the requirements of the National Environmental Policy Act, 42 U.S.C. 4321 *et seq.*, and the Council on Environmental Quality Regulations for Implementing the Procedural Provisions of the National Environmental Policy Act, 40 CFR parts 1500–1508.

(2) *Financial responsibility.* An applicant must provide the information required by part 3 of appendix A of part 440 for the FAA to conduct a maximum probable loss analysis.

(3) *Human space flight.* An applicant proposing launch or reentry with flight crew or a space flight participant on board a reusable suborbital rocket must demonstrate compliance with §§ 460.5, 460.7, 460.11, 460.13, 460.15, 460.17, 460.51 and 460.53 of this subchapter.

(c) *Use of a safety approval.* If an applicant proposes to use any reusable suborbital rocket, safety system, process, service, or personnel for which the FAA has issued a safety approval under part 414 of this subchapter, the FAA will not reevaluate that safety element to the extent its use is within its approved envelope. As part of the application process, the FAA will evaluate the integration of that safety element into vehicle systems or operations.

(d) *Inspection before issuing a permit.* Before the FAA issues an experimental permit, an applicant must make each reusable suborbital rocket planned to be flown available to the FAA for inspection. The FAA will determine whether each reusable suborbital rocket is built as represented in the application.

(e) *Other requirements.* The FAA may require additional analyses, information, or agreements if necessary to protect public health and safety, safety of property, and national security and foreign policy interests of the United States.

PROGRAM DESCRIPTION

§437.23 Program description.

(a) An applicant must provide—

(1) Dimensioned three-view drawings or photographs of the reusable suborbital rocket; and

(2) Gross liftoff weight and thrust profile of the reusable suborbital rocket.

(b) An applicant must describe—

(1) All reusable suborbital rocket systems, including any structural, flight control, thermal, pneumatic, hydraulic, propulsion, electrical, environmental control, software and computing systems, avionics, and guidance systems used in the reusable suborbital rocket;

(2) The types and quantities of all propellants used in the reusable suborbital rocket;

(3) The types and quantities of any hazardous materials used in the reusable suborbital rocket;

(4) The purpose for which a reusable suborbital rocket is to be flown; and

(5) Each payload or payload class planned to be flown.

(c) An applicant must identify any foreign ownership of the applicant as follows:

(1) For a sole proprietorship or partnership, identify all foreign ownership,

(2) For a corporation, identify any foreign ownership interests of 10% or more, and

(3) For a joint venture, association, or other entity, identify any participating foreign entities.

FLIGHT TEST PLAN

§437.25 Flight test plan.

An applicant must—

(a) Describe any flight test program, including estimated number of flights and key flight-safety events.

(b) Identify and describe the geographic coordinates of the boundaries of one or more proposed operating areas where it plans to perform its flights and that satisfy §437.57(b) of subpart C. The FAA may designate one or more exclusion areas in accordance with §437.57(c) of subpart C.

(c) For each operating area, provide the planned maximum altitude of the reusable suborbital rocket.

OPERATIONAL SAFETY DOCUMENTATION

§437.27 Pre-flight and post-flight operations.

An applicant must demonstrate how it will meet the requirements of §437.53(a) and (b) to establish a safety clear zone and verify that the public is outside that zone before and during any hazardous operation.

§437.29 Hazard analysis.

(a) An applicant must perform a hazard analysis that complies with §437.55(a).

(b) An applicant must provide to the FAA all the results of each step of the hazard analysis required by paragraph (a) of this section.

§437.31 Verification of operating area containment and key flight-safety event limitations.

(a) An applicant must identify, describe, and provide verification evidence of the methods and systems used to meet the requirement of §437.57(a) to contain its reusable suborbital rocket's instantaneous impact point within an operating area and outside any exclusion area. The description must include, at a minimum—

(1) Proof of physical limits on the ability of the reusable suborbital rocket to leave the operating area; or

(2) Abort procedures and other safety measures derived from a system safety engineering process.

(b) An applicant must identify, describe, and provide verification evidence of the methods and systems used to meet the requirements of § 437.59 to conduct any key flight-safety event so that the reusable suborbital rocket's instantaneous impact point, including its expected dispersions, is over unpopulated or sparsely populated areas, and to conduct each reusable suborbital rocket flight so that the reentry impact point does not loiter over a populated area.

§ 437.33 Landing and impact locations.

An applicant must demonstrate that each location for nominal landing or any contingency abort landing of the reusable suborbital rocket, and each location for any nominal or contingency impact or landing of a component of that rocket, satisfies § 437.61.

§ 437.35 Agreements.

An applicant must enter into the agreements required by § 437.63, and provide a copy to the FAA.

§ 437.37 Tracking.

An applicant must identify and describe each method or system used to meet the tracking requirements of § 437.67.

§ 437.39 Flight rules.

An applicant must provide flight rules as required by § 437.71.

§ 437.41 Mishap response plan.

An applicant must provide a mishap response plan that meets the requirements of § 437.75(b).

Subpart C—Safety Requirements

§ 437.51 Rest rules for vehicle safety operations personnel.

A permittee must ensure that all vehicle safety operations personnel adhere to the work and rest standards in this section during permitted activities.

(a) No vehicle safety operations personnel may work more than:

(1) 12 consecutive hours,

(2) 60 hours in the 7 days preceding a permitted activity, or

(3) 14 consecutive work days.

(b) All vehicle safety operations personnel must have at least 8 hours of rest after 12 hours of work.

(c) All vehicle safety operations personnel must receive a minimum 48-hour rest period after 5 consecutive days of 12-hour shifts.

§ 437.53 Pre-flight and post-flight operations.

A permittee must protect the public from adverse effects of hazardous operations and systems in preparing a reusable suborbital rocket for flight at a launch site in the United States and returning the reusable suborbital rocket and any support equipment to a safe condition after flight. At a minimum, a permittee must—

(a) Establish a safety clear zone that will contain the adverse effects of each operation involving a hazard; and

(b) Verify that the public is outside of the safety clear zone before and during any hazardous operation.

§ 437.55 Hazard analysis.

(a) A permittee must identify and characterize each of the hazards and assess the risk to public health and safety and the safety of property resulting from each permitted flight. This hazard analysis must—

(1) Identify and describe hazards, including but not limited to each of those that result from—

(i) Component, subsystem, or system failures or faults;

(ii) Software errors;

(iii) Environmental conditions;

(iv) Human errors;

(v) Design inadequacies; or

(vi) Procedural deficiencies.

(2) Determine the likelihood of occurrence and consequence for each hazard before risk elimination or mitigation.

(3) Ensure that the likelihood and consequence of each hazard meet the following criteria through risk elimination and mitigation measures:

(i) The likelihood of any hazardous condition that may cause death or serious injury to the public must be extremely remote.

(ii) The likelihood of any hazardous condition that may cause major property damage to the public, major safety-critical system damage or reduced capability, a significant reduction in safety margins, or a significant increase in crew workload must be remote.

(4) Identify and describe the risk elimination and mitigation measures required to satisfy paragraph (a)(3) of this section. The measures must include one or more of the following:

(i) Designing for minimum risk,

(ii) Incorporating safety devices,

(iii) Providing warning devices, or

(iv) Implementing procedures and training.

(5) Demonstrate that the risk elimination and mitigation measures achieve the risk levels of paragraph (a)(3)(i) of this section through validation and verification. Verification includes:

(i) Test data,

(ii) Inspection results, or

(iii) Analysis.

(b) A permittee must carry out the risk elimination and mitigation measures derived from its hazard analysis.

(c) A permittee must ensure the continued accuracy and validity of its hazard analysis throughout the term of its permit.

§437.57 Operating area containment.

(a) During each permitted flight, a permittee must contain its reusable suborbital rocket's instantaneous impact point within an operating area determined in accordance with paragraph (b) and outside any exclusion area defined by the FAA in accordance with paragraph (c) of this section.

(b) An operating area—

(1) Must be large enough to contain each planned trajectory and all expected vehicle dispersions;

(2) Must contain enough unpopulated or sparsely populated area to perform key flight-safety events as required by §437.59;

(3) May not contain or be adjacent to a densely populated area or large concentrations of members of the public; and

(4) May not contain or be adjacent to significant automobile traffic, railway traffic, or waterborne vessel traffic.

(c) The FAA may prohibit a reusable suborbital rocket's instantaneous impact point from traversing certain areas within an operating area by designating one or more areas as exclusion areas, if necessary to protect public health and safety, safety of property, or foreign policy or national security interests of the United States. An exclusion area may be confined to a specific phase of flight.

§437.59 Key flight-safety event limitations.

(a) A permittee must conduct any key flight-safety event so that the reusable suborbital rocket's instantaneous impact point, including its expected dispersion, is over an unpopulated or sparsely populated area. At a minimum, a key flight-safety event includes:

(1) Ignition of any primary rocket engine,

(2) Any staging event, or

(3) Any envelope expansion.

(b) A permittee must conduct each reusable suborbital rocket flight so that the reentry impact point does not loiter over a populated area.

§437.61 Landing and impact locations.

For a nominal or any contingency abort landing of a reusable suborbital rocket, or for any nominal or contingency impact or landing of a component of that rocket, a permittee must use a location that—

(a) Is big enough to contain an impact, including debris dispersion upon impact; and

(b) At the time of landing or impact, does not contain any members of the public.

§437.63 Agreements with other entities involved in a launch or reentry.

A permittee must comply with the agreements required by this section.

(a) A permittee must have an agreement in writing with a Federal launch range operator, a licensed launch site operator, or any other party that provides access to or use of property and services required to support the safe launch or reentry under a permit.

(b) Unless otherwise addressed in agreements with a licensed launch site operator or a Federal launch range, a permittee must have an agreement in writing with the following:

(1) For overflight of navigable water, a written agreement between the applicant and the local United States Coast Guard district to establish procedures for issuing a Notice to Mariners before a permitted flight, and

(2) A written agreement between the applicant and responsible Air Traffic Control authority having jurisdiction over the airspace through which a permitted launch or reentry is to take place, for measures necessary to ensure the safety of aircraft. The agreement must, at a minimum, demonstrate satisfaction of §§ 437.69(a) and 437.71(d).

§ 437.65 Collision avoidance analysis.

(a) For a permitted flight with a planned maximum altitude greater than 150 kilometers, a permittee must obtain a collision avoidance analysis from United States Strategic Command.

(b) The collision avoidance analysis must establish each period during which a permittee may not initiate flight to ensure that a permitted vehicle and any jettisoned components do not pass closer than 200 kilometers to a manned or mannable orbital object.

[Docket No. FAA-2006-24197, 72 FR 17019, Apr. 6, 2007, as amended by Doc. No. FAA-2016-6761, Amdt. No. 437-2, 83 FR 28535, June 20, 2018]

§ 437.67 Tracking a reusable suborbital rocket.

A permittee must—

(a) During permitted flight, measure in real time the position and velocity of its reusable suborbital rocket; and

(b) Provide position and velocity data to the FAA for post-flight use.

§ 437.69 Communications.

(a) A permittee must be in communication with Air Traffic Control during all phases of flight.

(b) A permittee must record communications affecting the safety of the flight.

§ 437.71 Flight rules.

(a) Before initiating rocket-powered flight, a permittee must confirm that all systems and operations necessary to ensure that safety measures derived from §§ 437.55, 437.57, 437.59, 437.61, 437.63, 437.65, 437.67, and 437.69 are within acceptable limits.

(b) During all phases of flight, a permittee must—

(1) Follow flight rules that ensure compliance with §§ 437.55, 437.57, 437.59, and 437.61; and

(2) Abort the flight if it would endanger the public.

(c) A permittee may not operate a reusable suborbital rocket in a careless or reckless manner that would endanger any member of the public during any phase of flight.

(d) A permittee may not operate a reusable suborbital rocket in areas designated in a Notice to Airmen under § 91.137, § 91.138, § 91.141, or § 91.145 of this title, unless authorized by:

(1) Air Traffic Control; or

(2) A Flight Standards Certificate of Waiver or Authorization.

(e) For any phase of flight where a permittee operates a reusable suborbital rocket like an aircraft in the National Airspace System, a permittee must comply with the provisions of part 91 of this title specified in an experimental permit issued under this part.

§ 437.73 Anomaly recording, reporting and implementation of corrective actions.

(a) A permittee must record each anomaly that affects a safety-critical system, subsystem, process, facility, or support equipment.

(b) A permittee must identify all root causes of each anomaly, and implement all corrective actions for each anomaly.

(c) A permittee must report to the FAA any anomaly of any system that is necessary for complying with §§ 437.55(a)(3), 437.57, and 437.59, and must report the corrective action for each reported anomaly.

(d) A permittee must implement each corrective action before the next flight.

§437.75 Mishap reporting, responding, and investigating.

A permittee must report, respond to, and investigate mishaps that occur during permitted activities, in accordance with this section.

(a) *Reporting requirements.* A permittee must—

(1) Immediately notify the FAA Washington Operations Center if there is a launch or reentry accident or incident or a mishap that involves a fatality or serious injury, as defined in 49 CFR 830.2;

(2) Notify within 24 hours the FAA's Office of Commercial Space Transportation if there is a mishap that does not involve a fatality or serious injury, as defined in 49 CFR 830.2; and

(3) Submit within 5 days of the event a written preliminary report to the FAA's Office of Commercial Space Transportation if there is a launch or reentry accident or incident during a permitted flight. The report must identify the event as a launch or reentry accident or incident, and must include:

(i) The date and time of occurrence,

(ii) A description of the event and sequence of events leading to the launch or reentry accident, or launch or reentry incident, to the extent known,

(iii) The intended and actual location of launch or reentry, including landing or impact on Earth,

(iv) A description of any payload,

(v) The number and general description of any fatalities and injuries,

(vi) Property damage, if any, and an estimate of its value,

(vii) A description of any hazardous materials involved in the event, whether on the reusable suborbital rocket or on the ground,

(viii) Action taken by any person to contain the consequences of the event, and

(ix) Weather conditions at the time of the event.

(b) *Response requirements.* A permittee must—

(1) Immediately—

(i) Ensure the consequences of a mishap are contained and minimized; and

(ii) Ensure data and physical evidence are preserved.

(2) Report to and cooperate with FAA and National Transportation Safety Board (NTSB) investigations and designate one or more points of contact for the FAA or NTSB; and

(3) Identify and adopt preventive measures for avoiding a recurrence of the event.

(c) *Investigation requirements.* A permittee must—

(1) Investigate the root cause of an event described in paragraph (a) of this section;

(2) Report investigation results to the FAA upon completion; and

(3) Identify responsibilities, including reporting responsibilities, for personnel assigned to conduct investigations and for any unrelated persons that the permittee retains to conduct or participate in investigations.

§437.77 Additional safety requirements.

The FAA may impose additional safety requirements on an applicant or permittee proposing an activity with a hazard not otherwise addressed in this part. This may include a toxic hazard or the use of solid propellants. The FAA may also require the permittee to conduct additional analyses of the cause of any anomaly and corrective actions.

Subpart D—Terms and Conditions of an Experimental Permit

§437.81 Public safety responsibility.

A permittee must ensure that a launch or reentry conducted under an experimental permit is safe, and must protect public health and safety and the safety of property.

§437.83 Compliance with experimental permit.

A permittee must conduct any launch or reentry under an experimental permit in accordance with representations made in its permit application, with subparts C and D of this part, and with terms and conditions contained in the permit.

§437.85 Allowable design changes; modification of an experimental permit.

(a) The FAA will identify in the experimental permit the type of changes that the permittee may make to the reusable suborbital rocket design without invalidating the permit.

(b) Except for design changes made under paragraph (a) of this section, a permittee must ask the FAA to modify the experimental permit if—

(1) It proposes to conduct permitted activities in a manner not authorized by the permit; or

(2) Any representation in its permit application that is material to public health and safety or the safety of property is no longer accurate or complete.

(c) A permittee must prepare an application to modify an experimental permit and submit it in accordance with part 413 of this subchapter. If requested during the application process, the FAA may approve an alternate method for requesting permit modifications. The permittee must indicate any part of its permit that would be changed or affected by a proposed modification.

(d) When a permittee proposes a modification, the FAA reviews the determinations made on the experimental permit to decide whether they remain valid.

(e) When the FAA approves a modification, it issues the permittee either a written approval or a permit order modifying the permit if a stated term or condition of the permit is changed, added, or deleted. An approval has the full force and effect of a permit order and is part of the permit record.

§ 437.87 Records.

(a) Except as required by paragraph (b) of this section, a permittee must maintain for 3 years all records, data, and other material necessary to verify that a permittee conducted its launch or reentry in accordance with its permit.

(b) If there is a launch or reentry accident or incident, a permittee must preserve all records related to the event. A permittee must keep the records until after any Federal investigation and the FAA advises the permittee that it may dispose of them.

(c) A permittee must make all records that it must maintain under this section available to Federal officials for inspection and copying.

§ 437.89 Pre-flight reporting.

(a) Not later than 30 days before each flight or series of flights conducted under an experimental permit, a permittee must provide the FAA with the following information:

(1) Any payload to be flown, including any payload operations during the flight,

(2) When the flight or series of flights are planned,

(3) The operating area for each flight, and

(4) The planned maximum altitude for each flight.

(b) Not later than 15 days before each permitted flight planned to reach greater than 150 km altitude, a permittee must provide the FAA its planned trajectory for a collision avoidance analysis.

§ 437.91 For-hire prohibition.

No permittee may carry any property or human being for compensation or hire on a reusable suborbital rocket.

§ 437.93 Compliance monitoring.

A permittee must allow access by, and cooperate with, federal officers or employees or other individuals authorized by the FAA to observe any activities of the permittee, or of its contractors or subcontractors, associated with the conduct of permitted activities.

§ 437.95 Inspection of additional reusable suborbital rockets.

A permittee may launch or reenter additional reusable suborbital rockets of the same design under the permit after the FAA inspects each additional reusable suborbital rocket.

PARTS 438–439 [RESERVED]

PART 440—FINANCIAL RESPONSIBILITY

Subpart A—Financial Responsibility for Licensed and Permitted Activities

AUTHORITY: 51 U.S.C. 50901–50923.

SOURCE: Docket No. FAA–2005–23449, 71 FR 75632, Dec. 15, 2006, unless otherwise noted.

Subpart A—Financial Responsibility for Licensed and Permitted Activities

§440.1 Scope of part.

This part establishes financial responsibility and allocation of risk requirements for any launch or reentry authorized by a license or permit issued under this subchapter.

§440.3 Definitions.

Except as otherwise provided in this section, any term used in this part and defined in 51 U.S.C. 50901–50923, or in §401.5 of this chapter shall have the meaning contained therein. For purposes of this part—

Bodily injury means physical injury, sickness, disease, disability, shock, mental anguish, or mental injury sustained by any person, including death.

Contractors and subcontractors means those entities that are involved at any level, directly or indirectly, in licensed or permitted activities, and includes suppliers of property and services, and the component manufacturers of a launch vehicle, reentry vehicle, or payload.

Customer means.

(1) Any person:

(i) Who procures launch or reentry services from a licensee or permittee;

(ii) With rights in the payload (or any part of the payload) to be launched or reentered by the licensee or permittee, including a conditional sale, lease, assignment, or transfer of rights;

(iii) Who has placed property on board the payload for launch, reentry, or payload services; or

(iv) To whom the customer has transferred its rights to the launch or reentry services.

(2) A space flight participant, for the purposes of this part, is not a customer.

Federal range facility means a U.S. Government-owned installation at which a launch or reentry takes place.

Financial responsibility means capable of satisfying a liability obligation as required by 51 U.S.C Subtitle V, chapter 509.

First-tier customer means a customer as defined in this section, and who has a contractual relationship with a license or permit holder to obtain launch or reentry services.

Government personnel means employees of the United States, its agencies, and its contractors and subcontractors, involved in launch or reentry services for an activity authorized by an FAA license or permit. Employees of the United States include members of the Armed Forces of the United States.

Hazardous operations means activities, processes, and procedures that, because of the nature of the equipment, facilities, personnel, environment involved or function being performed, may result in bodily injury or property damage.

Liability means a legal obligation to pay a claim for bodily injury or property damage resulting from a licensed or permitted activity.

License means an authorization the FAA issues under this subchapter to launch or reenter a launch or reentry vehicle.

Licensed activity means the launch of a launch vehicle or the reentry of a reentry vehicle conducted under a license the FAA issues.

Maximum probable loss (MPL) means the greatest dollar amount of loss for bodily injury or property damage that is reasonably expected to result from a licensed or permitted activity;

(1) Losses to third parties, excluding Government personnel and other launch or reentry participants' employees involved in licensed or permitted activities, that are reasonably expected to result from a licensed or permitted activity are those that have a probability of occurrence of no less than one in ten million.

(2) Losses to Government property and Government personnel involved in licensed or permitted activities that are reasonably expected to result from licensed or permitted activities are those that have a probability of occurrence of no less than one in one hundred thousand.

Part 440 customer means a customer as defined in this section, other than a first-tier customer.

Permit means an authorization the FAA issues under this subchapter for the launch or reentry of a reusable suborbital rocket.

Permitted activity means the launch or reentry of a reusable suborbital rocket conducted under a permit issued by the FAA.

Property damage means partial or total destruction, impairment, or loss of tangible property, real or personal.

Regulations mean the Commercial Space Transportation Licensing Regulations codified at 14 CFR Ch. III.

Third party means

(1) Any person other than:

(i) The United States, any of its agencies, and its contractors and subcontractors involved in launch or reentry services for a licensed or permitted activity;

(ii) A licensee, permittee, and its contractors and subcontractors involved in launch or reentry services for a licensed or permitted activity;

(iii) A customer and its contractors and subcontractors involved in launch or reentry services for a licensed or permitted activity;

(iv) A member of a crew; and

(v) A space flight participant.

(2) Government personnel, as defined in this section, are third parties.

United States means the United States Government, including each of its agencies.

[Doc. No. FAA–2005–23449, 71 FR 75632, Dec. 15, 2006, as amended by Amdt. 440–3, 77 FR 20533, Apr. 5, 2012; Doc. No. FAA–2014–1012, Amdt. 440–4, 81 FR 55122, Aug. 18, 2016]

§440.5 General.

(a) No person may commence or conduct any launch or reentry activity that requires a license or permit unless that person has demonstrated compliance with the requirements of this part.

(b) The FAA will prescribe the amount of financial responsibility a licensee or permittee must obtain and any adjustments of the amount in a license or permit order issued concurrent with or subsequent to the issuance of a license or a permit.

(c) Demonstration of financial responsibility under this part shall not relieve a licensee of ultimate responsibility for liability, loss, or damage sustained by the United States resulting from a licensed activity, except to the extent that:

(1) Liability, loss, or damage sustained by the United States results from willful misconduct of the United States or its agents;

(2) Any covered claim of a third party for bodily injury or property damage arising out of any particular licensed activity exceeds the amount of financial responsibility required under §440.9(c) of this part and does not exceed $1,500,000,000 (as adjusted for inflation occurring after January 1, 1989) above such amount, and are payable pursuant to 51 U.S.C. 50915 and §440.19 of this part. A claim of an employee of any entity listed in paragraphs (1)(ii) through (1)(iii) in the Third party definition in §440.3 of this part for bodily injury or property damage is not a covered claim;

(3) A covered claim for property loss or damage exceeds the amount of financial responsibility required under §440.9(e) of this part and does not result from willful misconduct of the licensee; or

(4) The licensee has no liability for covered claims by third parties for bodily injury or property damage arising out of any particular launch or reentry that exceeds $1,500,000,000 (as adjusted for inflation) above the amount of financial responsibility required under §440.9(c).

(d) Demonstration of financial responsibility under this part does not relieve a permittee of ultimate responsibility for liability, loss, or damage sustained by the United States resulting from a permitted activity, except to the extent that:

(1) Liability, loss, or damage sustained by the United States results from willful misconduct of the United States or its agents; or

(2) A covered claim for property loss or damage to the United States exceeds the amount of financial responsibility required under §440.9(e) and does not result from willful misconduct of the permittee.

(e) A licensee's or permittee's failure to comply with any requirement of this part may result in suspension or revocation of a license or permit, and subject the licensee or permittee to civil penalties as provided in part 405 of this chapter.

[Doc. No. FAA-2005-23449, 71 FR 75632, Dec. 15, 2006, as amended by Amdt. 440-3, 77 FR 20533, Apr. 5, 2012]

§440.7 Determination of maximum probable loss.

(a) The FAA will determine the maximum probable loss (MPL) from covered claims by a third party for bodily injury or property damage, and the United States, its agencies, and its contractors and subcontractors for covered property damage or loss, resulting from a permitted or licensed activity. The maximum probable loss determination forms the basis for financial responsibility requirements issued in a license or permit order.

(b) The FAA issues its determination of maximum probable loss no later than ninety days after a licensee or permittee has requested a determination and submitted all information required by the FAA to make the determination. The FAA will consult with Federal agencies that are involved in, or whose personnel or property are exposed to risk of damage or loss as a result of, a licensed or permitted activity before issuing a license or permit order prescribing financial responsibility requirements, and shall notify the licensee, or permittee, if interagency consultation may delay issuance of the MPL determination.

(c) Appendix A of this part contains information requirements for obtaining a maximum probable loss determination. Any person requesting a determination of maximum probable loss must submit the information required by Appendix A, unless the FAA has waived a requirement. In lieu of submitting required information, a person requesting a maximum probable loss determination may designate and certify certain information previously submitted for a prior determination as complete, valid, and equally applicable to its current request. The requester is responsible for the continuing accuracy and completeness of information submitted under this part and must promptly report any changes in writing.

(d) The FAA will amend a determination of maximum probable loss required under this section at any time prior to completion of licensed or permitted activities as warranted by supplementary information provided to or obtained by the FAA after the MPL determination is issued. Any change in financial responsibility requirements as a result of an amended MPL determination shall be set forth in a license or permit order.

(e) The FAA may make a determination of maximum probable loss at any time other than as set forth in paragraph (b) of this section upon request by any person.

§440.9 Insurance requirements for licensed or permitted activities.

(a) As a condition of each license or permit, a licensee or permittee must comply with all insurance requirements of this section and of a license or permit issued by the FAA, or otherwise demonstrate the required amount of financial responsibility.

(b) A licensee or permittee must obtain and maintain in effect a policy or policies of liability insurance, in an amount determined by the FAA under paragraph (c) of this section, that protects the following persons as additional insureds to the extent of their respective potential liabilities against covered claims by a third party for bodily injury or property damage resulting from a licensed or permitted activity:

(1) The licensee or permittee, its customer, and their respective contractors and subcontractors, and the employees of each, involved in a licensed or permitted activity;

(2) The United States, its agencies, and its contractors and subcontractors involved in a licensed or permitted activity; and

(3) Government personnel.

(c) The FAA will prescribe for each licensee or permittee the amount of insurance required to compensate the total of covered third-party claims for bodily injury or property damage resulting from a licensed or permitted activity in connection with any particular launch or reentry. A covered third-party claim includes a claim by the United States, its agencies, and its contractors and subcontractors for damage or loss to property other than property for which insurance is required under paragraph (d) of this section. The amount of insurance required is based upon the FAA's determination of maximum probable loss; however, it will not exceed the lesser of:

(1) $500 million; or

(2) The maximum liability insurance available on the world market at a reasonable cost, as determined by the FAA.

(d) The licensee or permittee must obtain and maintain in effect a policy or policies of insurance, in an amount determined by the FAA under paragraph (e) of this section, that covers claims by the United States, its agencies, and its contractors and subcontractors involved in a licensed or permitted activity for property damage or loss resulting from a licensed or permitted activity. Property covered by this insurance must include all property owned, leased, or occupied by, or within the care, custody, or control of, the United States and its agencies, and its contractors and subcontractors involved in a licensed or permitted activity, at a Federal range facility. Insurance must protect the United States and its agencies, and its contractors and subcontractors involved in a licensed or permitted activity.

(e) The FAA will prescribe for each licensee or permittee the amount of insurance required to compensate claims for property damage under paragraph (d) of this section resulting from a licensed or permitted activity in connection with any particular launch or reentry. The amount of insurance is based upon a determination of maximum probable loss; however, it will not exceed the lesser of:

(1) $100 million; or

(2) The maximum available on the world market at a reasonable cost, as determined by the FAA.

(f) In lieu of a policy of insurance, a licensee or permittee may demonstrate financial responsibility in another manner meeting the terms and conditions for insurance of this part. The licensee or permittee must describe in detail the method proposed for demonstrating financial responsibility and how it ensures that the licensee or permittee is able to cover claims as required under this part.

§ 440.11 Duration of coverage for licensed launch, including suborbital launch, or permitted activities; modifications.

(a) Insurance coverage required under § 440.9, or other form of financial responsibility, shall attach when a licensed launch or permitted activity starts, and remain in full force and effect as follows:

(1) Until completion of licensed launch or permitted activities at a launch or reentry site; and

(2) For orbital launch, until the later of—

(i) Thirty days following payload separation, or attempted payload separation in the event of a payload separation anomaly; or

(ii) Thirty days from ignition of the launch vehicle.

(3) For a suborbital launch, until the later of—

(i) Motor impact and payload recovery; or

(ii) The FAA's determination that risk to third parties and Government property as a result of licensed launch or permitted activities is sufficiently small that financial responsibility is no longer necessary. That determination is made through the risk analysis conducted before the launch to determine MPL and specified in a license or permit order.

(b) Financial responsibility required under this part may not be replaced, canceled, changed, withdrawn, or in any way modified to reduce the limits of liability or the extent of coverage, nor expire by its own terms, prior to the time specified in a license or permit order, unless the FAA is notified at least 30 days in advance and expressly approves the modification.

§440.12 Duration of coverage for licensed reentry; modifications.

(a) For reentry, insurance coverage required under §440.9, or other form of financial responsibility, shall attach upon commencement of licensed reentry, and remain in full force and effect as follows:

(1) For ground operations, until completion of licensed reentry at the reentry site; and

(2) For other licensed reentry activities, 30 days from initiation of reentry flight; however, in the event of an abort that results in the reentry vehicle remaining on orbit, insurance shall remain in place until the FAA's determination that risk to third parties and Government property as a result of licensed reentry is sufficiently small that financial responsibility is no longer necessary, as determined by the FAA through the risk analysis conducted to determine MPL and specified in a license order.

(b) Financial responsibility required under this part may not be replaced, canceled, changed, withdrawn, or in any way modified to reduce the limits of liability or the extent of coverage, nor expire by its own terms, prior to the time specified in a license order, unless the FAA is notified at least 30 days in advance and expressly approves the modification.

§440.13 Standard conditions of insurance coverage.

(a) Insurance obtained under §440.9 must comply with each of the following terms and conditions of coverage:

(1) Bankruptcy or insolvency of an insured, including any additional insured, shall not relieve an insurer of any of its obligations under any policy.

(2) Policy limits shall apply separately to each occurrence and, for each occurrence to the total of claims arising out of a licensed or permitted activity in connection with any particular launch or reentry.

(3) Except as provided in this section, each policy must pay claims from the first dollar of loss, without regard to any deductible, to the limits of the policy. A licensee or permittee may obtain a policy containing a deductible amount if the amount of the deductible is placed in an escrow account or otherwise demonstrated to be unobligated, unencumbered funds of the licensee or permittee, available to compensate claims at any time claims may arise.

(4) No policy may be invalidated by any action or inaction of the licensee or permittee or any additional insured, even by nonpayment by the licensee or permittee of the policy premium, and each policy must insure the licensee or permittee and each additional insured regardless of any breach or violation of any warranties, declarations, or conditions contained in the policies by the licensee or permittee or any additional insured (other than a breach or violation by the licensee, permittee or an additional insured, and then only as against that licensee, permittee or additional insured).

(5) Each exclusion from coverage must be specified.

(6) Insurance shall be primary without right of contribution from any other insurance that is carried by the licensee or permittee or any additional insured.

(7) Each policy must expressly provide that all of its provisions, except the policy limits, operate in the same manner as if there were a separate policy with and covering the licensee or permittee and each additional insured.

(8) Each policy must be placed with an insurer of recognized reputation and responsibility that either:

(i) Is licensed to do business in any State, territory, possession of the United States, or the District of Columbia; or

(ii) Includes in each of its policies or insurance obtained under this part a contract clause in which the insurer agrees to submit to the jurisdiction of a court of competent jurisdiction within the United States and designates an authorized agent within the United States for service of legal process on the insurer.

(9) Except as to claims resulting from the willful misconduct of the United States or any of its agents, the insurer shall waive any and all rights of subrogation against each of the parties protected by required insurance.

(b) [Reserved]

§ 440.15 Demonstration of compliance.

(a) A licensee or permittee must submit to the FAA evidence of financial responsibility and compliance with allocation of risk requirements under this part, as follows, unless a license or permit order specifies otherwise due to the proximity of the intended date for commencement of licensed or permitted activities:

(1) All reciprocal waiver of claims agreements required under § 440.17(c) must be submitted at least 30 days before the start of any licensed or permitted activity involving a customer, crew member, or space flight participant;

(2) Evidence of insurance must be submitted at least 30 days before commencement of any licensed launch or permitted activity, and for licensed reentry no less than 30 days before commencement of launch activities involving the reentry licensee;

(3) Evidence of financial responsibility in a form other than insurance, as provided under § 440.9(f), must be submitted at least 60 days before commencement of a licensed or permitted activity; and

(4) Evidence of renewal of insurance or other form of financial responsibility must be submitted at least 30 days in advance of its expiration date.

(b) Upon a complete demonstration of compliance with financial responsibility and allocation of risk requirements under this part, the requirements of this part shall preempt each and any provision in any agreement between the licensee or permittee and an agency of the United States governing access to or use of United States launch or reentry property or launch or reentry services for a licensed or permitted activity which addresses financial responsibility, allocation of risk and related matters covered by 51 U.S.C. 50914, 50915.

(c) A licensee or permittee must demonstrate compliance as follows:

(1) The licensee or permittee must provide proof of the existence of the insurance required by § 440.9 by:

(i) Certifying to the FAA that it has obtained insurance in compliance with the requirements of this part and any applicable license or permit order;

(ii) Filing with the FAA one or more certificates of insurance evidencing insurance coverage by one or more insurers under a currently effective and properly endorsed policy or policies of insurance, applicable to a licensed or permitted activity, on terms and conditions and in amounts prescribed under this part, and specifying policy exclusions;

(iii) In the event of any policy exclusions or limitations of coverage that may be considered usual under § 440.19(c), or for purposes of implementing the Government's waiver of claims for property damage under 51 U.S.C. 50914(b), certifying that insurance covering the excluded risks is not commercially available at reasonable cost; and

(iv) Submitting to the FAA, for signature by the Department on behalf of the United States Government, the waiver of claims and assumption of responsibility agreement required by § 440.17(c), executed by the licensee or permittee and its customer.

(v) Submitting to the FAA, for signature by the Department on behalf of the United States Government, an agreement to waive claims and assume responsibility required by § 440.17(e), executed by each space flight participant.

(vi) Submitting to the FAA, for signature by the Department on behalf of the United States Government, an agreement to waive claims and assume responsibility required by § 440.17(f), executed by each member of the crew.

(2) Any certification required by this section must be signed by a duly authorized officer of the licensee or permittee.

(d) Each certificate of insurance required by paragraph (c)(1)(ii) of this section must be signed by the insurer issuing the policy and accompanied by an opinion of the insurance broker that the insurance obtained by the licensee or permittee complies with all the requirements for insurance of this part and any applicable license or permit order.

(e) The licensee or permittee must maintain, and make available for inspection by the FAA upon request, all required policies of insurance and other documents necessary to demonstrate compliance with this part.

(f) In the event the licensee or permittee demonstrates financial responsibility using means other than insurance, as provided under §440.9(f), the licensee or permittee must provide proof that it has met the requirements of this part and of a FAA issued license or permit order.

[Doc. No. FAA–2005–23449, 71 FR 75632, Dec. 15, 2006, as amended by Amdt. 440–3, 77 FR 20533, Apr. 5, 2012]

§440.17 Reciprocal waiver of claims requirements.

(a) As a condition of each license or permit, the licensee or permittee must comply with the reciprocal waiver of claims requirements of this section.

(b) The licensee or permittee and each of its contractors and subcontractors, each customer, and each customer's contractors and subcontractors, must enter into a reciprocal waiver of claims agreement under which each party waives and releases claims against all the other parties to the waiver and against any other customer, and agrees to assume financial responsibility for property damage it sustains and for bodily injury or property damage sustained by its own employees, and to hold harmless and indemnify each other from bodily injury or property damage sustained by its employees, resulting from a licensed or permitted activity, regardless of fault.

(1) The licensee or permittee must extend the reciprocal waiver of claims requirements to each of its contractors and subcontractors involved in launch or reentry services, and each of its first-tier customers.

(2) Any first-tier customer must extend the reciprocal waiver of claims requirements to each of its contractors and subcontractors involved in launch or reentry services, and each of its customers.

(3) Any part 440 customer must extend the reciprocal waiver of claims requirements to each of its contractors and subcontractors involved in launch or reentry services, and each of its customers.

(c) For each licensed or permitted activity in which the United States, or its contractors and subcontractors, is involved or where property insurance is required under §440.9(d), the Federal Aviation Administration of the Department of Transportation, the licensee or permittee, and each first-tier customer must enter into a reciprocal waiver of claims agreement. The reciprocal waiver of claims must be in the form set forth in appendix B of this part for a licensed activity, in appendix C of this part for a permitted activity, or in a form that otherwise provides all the same obligations and benefits. The reciprocal waiver of claims must provide that:

(1) Each party to the reciprocal waiver of claims, including the United States but only to the extent provided in legislation:

(i) Waives and releases claims it may have against each other party to the reciprocal waiver of claims, any customer, and against their respective contractors and subcontractors, for property damage it sustains and for bodily injury or property damage sustained by its own employees, resulting from licensed or permitted activities, regardless of fault;

(ii) Assumes responsibility for property damage it sustains and for bodily injury or property damage sustained by its own employees, resulting from licensed or permitted activities, regardless of fault. A licensee or permittee and each first-tier customer shall each hold harmless and indemnify each other, the United States, any other customer, and the contractors and subcontractors of each for bodily injury or property damage sustained by its own employees, resulting from licensed or permitted activities, regardless of fault; and

(iii) Extends the requirements of the waiver and release of claims, and the assumption of responsibility, hold harmless, and indemnification, to its contractors and subcontractors involved in launch and reentry services, and, for each customer, to its contractors and subcontractors involved in launch and reentry services, and customers, by requiring them to waive and release all claims as follows:

(A) For each contractor and subcontractor of the licensee or permittee, all claims against any customer, the United States, and each of their respective contractors and subcontractors, and to agree to be responsible for property damage they sustain and to be responsible, hold harmless and indemnify any customer, the United States, and each of their respective contractors and subcontractors, for bodily injury or property damage sustained by their own employees, resulting from licensed activities, regardless of fault;

(B) For each contractor and subcontractor of any customer, all claims against the licensee or permittee, any other customer, the United States, and each of their respective contractors and subcontractors, and to agree to be responsible for property damage they sustain and to be responsible, hold harmless and indemnify the licensee or permittee, any other customer, the United States, and each of their respective contractors and subcontractors, for bodily injury or property damage sustained by their own employees, resulting from licensed activities, regardless of fault;

(C) For each contractor and subcontractor of the United States, all claims against the licensee or permittee, any customer, and each of their respective contractors and subcontractors, and to agree to be responsible for property damage they sustain and to be responsible, hold harmless and indemnify the licensee or permittee, any other customer, the United States, and each of their respective contractors and subcontractors, for bodily injury or property damage sustained by their own employees, resulting from licensed activities, regardless of fault to the extent that claims they would otherwise have for such damage or injury exceed the amount of insurance or demonstration of financial responsibility required under § 440.9(c) and (e);

(D) For each part 440 customer, all claims against the licensee or permittee, any other customer, the United States, and each of their respective contractors and subcontractors; and to agree to be responsible for property damage they sustain and to be responsible, hold harmless and indemnify the licensee or permittee, any other customer, the United States, and each of their respective contractors and subcontractors, for bodily injury or property damage sustained by their own employees, resulting from licensed activities, regardless of fault; and

(2) For the following parties—

(i) The licensee or permittee must hold harmless and indemnify each first-tier customer and its directors, officers, servants, agents, subsidiaries, employees and assignees, or any of them; the United States and its servants, agents, subsidiaries, employees and assignees, or any of them; and any part 440 customer and its directors, officers, servants, agents, subsidiaries, employees and assignees, or any of them from and against liability, loss or damage arising out of claims that any of licensee's or permittee's contractors and subcontractors may have for property damage sustained by them and for bodily injury or property damage sustained by their employees, resulting from licensed or permitted activities and arising out of the indemnifying party's failure to implement properly the waiver requirement. The requirement of paragraph (c)(2)(i) of this section to hold harmless and indemnify the United States and its servants, agents, subsidiaries, employees and assignees, or any of them, does not apply when:

(A) Claims result from willful misconduct of the United States or its agents;

(B) Claims for property damage sustained by the United States or its contractors and subcontractors exceed the amount of insurance or demonstration of financial responsibility required under § 440.9(e);

(C) For licensed activity, claims by a third party for bodily injury or property damage exceed the amount of insurance or demonstration of financial responsibility required under §440.9(c), and do not exceed $1,500,000,000 (as adjusted for inflation after January 1, 1989) above such amount, and are payable pursuant to the provisions of 51 U.S.C. 50915 and §440.19; or

(D) The licensee has no liability for claims exceeding $1,500,000,000 (as adjusted for inflation after January 1, 1989) above the amount of insurance or demonstration of financial responsibility required under §440.9(c).

(ii) Each first-tier customer must hold harmless and indemnify the licensee or permittee and its directors, officers, servants, agents, subsidiaries, employees and assignees, or any of them; the United States and its servants, agents, subsidiaries, employees and assignees, or any of them; and any part 440 customer and its directors, officers, servants, agents, subsidiaries, employees and assignees, or any of them, from and against liability, loss or damage arising out of claims that any of each first-tier customer's customers, contractors, or subcontractors, may have for property damage sustained by them and for bodily injury or property damage sustained by their employees, resulting from licensed or permitted activities and arising out of the indemnifying party's failure to implement properly the waiver requirement.

(iii) The Federal Aviation Administration of the Department of Transportation on behalf of the United States, but only to the extent provided in legislation, must hold harmless and indemnify the licensee or permittee, each first-tier customer, any part 440 customer, and their respective directors, officers, servants, agents, subsidiaries, employees and assignees, or any of them, from and against liability, loss or damage arising out of claims that contractors and subcontractors of the United States may have for property damage sustained by them and for bodily injury or property damage sustained by their employees, resulting from licensed or permitted activities and arising out of the indemnifying party's failure to implement properly the waiver requirement to the extent that claims they would otherwise have for such damage or injury exceed the amount of insurance or demonstration of financial responsibility required under §440.9(c) and (e).

(d) For each licensed or permitted activity in which the United States or its contractors and subcontractors are involved, the Federal Aviation Administration of the Department of Transportation and each space flight participant must enter into or have in place a reciprocal waiver of claims agreement. The reciprocal waiver of claims must be in the form set forth in appendix E of this part, or in a form that otherwise provides all the same obligations and benefits.

(1) The reciprocal waiver of claims must provide that each space flight participant:

(i) Waive and release claims he or she may have against the United States, and against each of its contractors and subcontractors, for bodily injury or property damage sustained by the space flight participant, resulting from licensed or permitted activities, regardless of fault;

(ii) Assume responsibility for bodily injury or property damage, sustained by the space flight participant, resulting from licensed or permitted activities, regardless of fault;

(iii) Hold harmless the United States, and its contractors and subcontractors, for bodily injury or property damage, sustained by the space flight participant, resulting from licensed or permitted activities, regardless of fault; and

(iv) Hold harmless and indemnify the United States and its servants, agents, subsidiaries, employees and assignees, or any of them, from and against liability, loss, or damage arising out of claims brought by anyone for property damage or bodily injury sustained by the space flight participant, resulting from licensed or permitted activities.

(2) The reciprocal waiver of claims must provide that the United States:

(i) Waive and release claims it may have against the space flight participant for property damage it sustains, and for bodily injury or property damage sustained by its own employees, resulting from licensed or permitted activities, regardless of fault;

(ii) Assume responsibility for property damage it sustains, and for bodily injury or property damage sustained by its own employees, resulting from licensed activities, regardless of fault, to the extent that claims it would otherwise have for such damage or injury exceed the amount of insurance or demonstration of financial responsibility required under § 440.9(c) and (e), respectively;

(iii) Assume responsibility for property damage it sustains, resulting from permitted activities, regardless of fault, to the extent that claims it would otherwise have for such damage exceed the amount of insurance or demonstration of financial responsibility required under § 440.9(e);

(iv) Extend the requirements of the waiver and release of claims, and the assumption of responsibility to its contractors and subcontractors by requiring them to waive and release all claims they may have against the space flight participant, and to agree to be responsible, for any property damage they sustain and for any bodily injury or property damage sustained by their own employees, resulting from licensed activities, regardless of fault; and

(v) Extend the requirements of the waiver and release of claims, and the assumption of responsibility to its contractors and subcontractors by requiring them to waive and release all claims they may have against the space flight participant, and to agree to be responsible, for any property damage they sustain, resulting from permitted activities, regardless of fault.

(e) For each licensed or permitted activity in which the United States or its contractors and subcontractors is involved, the Federal Aviation Administration of the Department of Transportation and each crew member must enter into or have in place a reciprocal waiver of claims agreement. The reciprocal waiver of claims must be in the form set forth in appendix D of this part, or in a form that otherwise provides all the same obligations and benefits.

(1) The reciprocal waiver of claims must provide that each crew member:

(i) Waive and release claims he or she may have against the United States, and against each of its contractors and subcontractors, for bodily injury or property damage sustained by the crew member, resulting from licensed or permitted activities, regardless of fault;

(ii) Assume responsibility for bodily injury or property damage, sustained by the crew member, resulting from licensed or permitted activities, regardless of fault;

(iii) Hold harmless the United States, and its contractors and subcontractors, for bodily injury or property damage, sustained by the crew member, resulting from licensed or permitted activities, regardless of fault; and

(iv) Hold harmless and indemnify the United States and its agencies, servants, agents, subsidiaries, employees and assignees, or any of them, from and against liability, loss, or damage arising out of claims brought by anyone for property damage or bodily injury sustained by the crew member, resulting from licensed or permitted activities.

(2) The reciprocal waiver of claims must provide that the United States:

(i) Waive and release claims it may have against the crew member for property damage it sustains, and for bodily injury, including death, or property damage sustained by its own employees, resulting from licensed or permitted activities, regardless of fault;

(ii) Assume responsibility for property damage it sustains, and for bodily injury or property damage sustained by its own employees, resulting from licensed activities, regardless of fault, to the extent that claims it would otherwise have for such damage or injury exceed the amount of insurance or demonstration of financial responsibility required under § 440.9(c) and (e), respectively;

(iii) Assume responsibility for property damage it sustains, resulting from permitted activities, regardless of fault, to the extent that claims it would otherwise have for such damage exceed the amount of insurance or demonstration of financial responsibility required under §440.9(e);

(iv) Extend the requirements of the waiver and release of claims, and the assumption of responsibility to its contractors and subcontractors by requiring them to waive and release all claims they may have against the crew member and to agree to be responsible, for any property damage they sustain and for any bodily injury or property damage sustained by their own employees, resulting from licensed activities, regardless of fault; and

(v) Extend the requirements of the waiver and release of claims, and the assumption of responsibility to its contractors and subcontractors by requiring them to waive and release all claims they may have against the crew member and to agree to be responsible, for any property damage they sustain, resulting from permitted activities, regardless of fault.

(f) Any waiver, release, assumption of responsibility or agreement to hold harmless and indemnify pursuant to this section does not apply to claims for bodily injury or property damage resulting from willful misconduct of any of the parties to the reciprocal waiver of claims, the contractors and subcontractors of any of the parties to the reciprocal waiver of claims, and in the case of licensee or permittee and customers and the contractors and subcontractors of each of them, the directors, officers, agents and employees of any of the foregoing, and in the case of the United States, its agents.

[Doc. No. FAA-2005-23449, 71 FR 75632, Dec. 15, 2006, as amended by Amdt. 440-2, 76 FR 8630, Feb. 15, 2011; Doc. No. FAA-2014-1012, Amdt. 440-4, 81 FR 55122, Aug. 18, 2016]

§440.19 United States payment of excess third-party liability claims.

(a) The United States pays successful covered claims (including reasonable expenses of litigation or settlement) of a third party against a licensee, a customer, and the contractors and subcontractors of the licensee and the customer, and the employees of each involved in licensed activities, and the contractors and subcontractors of the United States and its agencies, and their employees, involved in licensed activities to the extent provided in an appropriation law or other legislative authority providing for payment of claims in accordance with 51 U.S.C. 50915, and to the extent the total amount of such covered claims arising out of any particular launch or reentry:

(b) Payment by the United States under paragraph (a) of this section shall not be made for any part of such claims for which bodily injury or property damage results from willful misconduct by the party seeking payment.

(c) The United States shall provide for payment of claims by third parties for bodily injury or property damage that are payable under 49 U.S.C. 70113 and not covered by required insurance under §440.9(b), without regard to the limitation under paragraph (a)(1) of this section, because of an insurance policy exclusion that is usual. A policy exclusion is considered usual only if insurance covering the excluded risk is not commercially available at reasonable rates. The licensee must submit a certification in accordance with §440.15(c)(1)(iii) of this part for the United States to cover the claims.

(d) Upon the expiration of the policy period prescribed in accordance with §440.11(a), the United States shall provide for payment of claims that are payable under 51 U.S.C. 50915 from the first dollar of loss up to $1,500,000,000 (as adjusted for inflation occurring after January 1, 1989).

(e) Payment by the United States of excess third-party claims under 51 U.S.C. 50915 shall be subject to:

(1) Prompt notice by the licensee to the FAA that the total amount of claims arising out of licensed activities exceeds, or is likely to exceed, the required amount of financial responsibility. For each claim, the notice must specify the nature, cause, and amount of the claim or lawsuit associated with the claim, and the party or parties who may otherwise be liable for payment of the claim;

(2) Participation or assistance in the defense of the claim or lawsuit by the United States, at its election;

(3) Approval by the FAA of any settlement, or part of a settlement, to be paid by the United States; and

(4) Approval by Congress of a compensation plan prepared by the FAA and submitted by the President.

(f) The FAA will:

(1) Prepare a compensation plan outlining the total amount of claims and meeting the requirements set forth in 51 U.S.C. 50915;

(2) Recommend sources of funds to pay the claims; and

(3) Propose legislation as required to implement the plan.

(g) The FAA may withhold payment of a claim if it finds that the amount is unreasonable, unless it is the final order of a court that has jurisdiction over the matter.

[Doc. No. FAA–2005–23449, 71 FR 75632, Dec. 15, 2006, as amended by Amdt. 440–3, 77 FR 20534, Apr. 5, 2012]

APPENDIX A TO PART 440—INFORMATION REQUIREMENTS FOR OBTAINING A MAXIMUM PROBABLE LOSS DETERMINATION FOR LICENSED OR PERMITTED ACTIVITIES

Any person requesting a maximum probable loss determination shall submit the following information to the FAA, unless the FAA has waived a particular information requirement under 14 CFR 440.7(c):

Part 1: Information Requirements for Licensed Launch, Including Suborbital Launch

I. GENERAL INFORMATION

A. Mission description.

1. A description of mission parameters, including:

a. Launch trajectory;

b. Orbital inclination; and

c. Orbit altitudes (apogee and perigee).

2. Flight sequence.

3. Staging events and the time for each event.

4. Impact locations.

5. Identification of the launch site facility, including the launch complex on the site, planned date of launch, and launch windows.

6. If the applicant has previously been issued a license or permit to conduct activities using the same vehicle from the same launch site, a description of any differences planned in the conduct of proposed activities.

B. Launch vehicle description.

1. General description of the launch vehicle and its stages, including dimensions.

2. Description of major systems, including safety systems.

3. Description of rocket motors and type of fuel used.

4. Identification of all propellants to be used and their hazard classification under the Hazardous Materials Table, 49 CFR 172.101.

5. Description of hazardous components.

C. Payload.

1. General description of the payload, including type (e.g., telecommunications, remote sensing), propellants, and hazardous components or materials, such as toxic or radioactive substances.

D. Flight safety system.

1. Identification of any flight safety system on the vehicle, including a description of operations and component location on the vehicle.

II. PRE-FLIGHT PROCESSING OPERATIONS

A. General description of pre-flight operations including vehicle processing consisting of an operational flow diagram showing the overall sequence and location of operations, commencing with arrival of vehicle components at the launch site facility through final safety checks and countdown sequence, and designation of hazardous operations, as defined in 14 CFR 440.3. For purposes of these information requirements, payload processing, as opposed to integration, is not a hazardous operation.

B. For each hazardous operation, including but not limited to fueling, solid rocket motor build-up, ordnance installation, ordnance checkout, movement of hazardous materials, and payload integration:

1. Identification of location where each operation will be performed, including each building or facility identified by name or number.

2. Identification of facilities adjacent to the location where each operation will be performed and therefore exposed to risk, identified by name or number.

3. Maximum number of Government personnel and individuals not involved in licensed activities who may be exposed to risk during each operation. For Government personnel, identification of his or her employer.

4. Identification of launch site policies or requirements applicable to the conduct of operations.

III. FLIGHT OPERATIONS

A. Identification of launch site facilities exposed to risk during licensed flight.

B. Identification of accident failure scenarios, probability assessments for each, and estimation of risks to Government personnel, individuals not involved in licensed activities, and Government property, due to property damage or bodily injury. The estimation of risks for each scenario shall take into account the number of such individuals at risk as a result of lift-off and flight of a launch vehicle (on-range, off-range, and down-range) and specific, unique facilities exposed to risk. Scenarios shall cover the range of launch trajectories, inclinations and orbits for which authorization is sought in the license application.

C. On-orbit risk analysis assessing risks posed by a launch vehicle to operational satellites.

D. Reentry risk analysis assessing risks to Government personnel and individuals not involved in licensed activities as a result of reentering debris or reentry of the launch vehicle or its components.

E. Trajectory data as follows: Nominal and 3-sigma lateral trajectory data in x, y, z and x (dot), y (dot), z (dot) coordinates in one-second intervals, data to be pad-centered with x being along the initial launch azimuth and continuing through impact for suborbital flights, and continuing through orbital insertion or the end of powered flight for orbital flights.

F. Tumble-turn data for guided vehicles only, as follows: For vehicles with gimbaled nozzles, tumble turn data with zeta angles and velocity magnitudes stated. A separate table is required for each combination of fail times (every two to four seconds), and significant nozzle angles (two or more small angles, generally between one and five degrees).

G. Identification of debris lethal areas and the projected number and ballistic coefficient of fragments expected to result from flight termination, initiated either by command or self-destruct mechanism, for lift-off, land overflight, and reentry.

IV. Post-Flight Processing Operations

A. General description of post-flight ground operations including overall sequence and location of operations for removal of vehicle components and processing equipment from the launch site facility and for handling of hazardous materials, and designation of hazardous operations.

B. Identification of all facilities used in conducting post-flight processing operations.

C. For each hazardous operation:

1. Identification of location where each operation is performed, including each building or facility identified by name or number.

2. Identification of facilities adjacent to location where each operation is performed and exposed to risk, identified by name or number.

3. Maximum number of Government personnel and individuals not involved in licensed launch activities that may be exposed to risk during each operation. For Government personnel, identification of his or her employer.

4. Identification of launch site facility policies or requirements applicable to the conduct of operations.

Part 2: Information Requirements for Licensed Reentry

I. General Information

A. Reentry mission description.

1. A description of mission parameters, including:

a. Orbital inclination; and

b. Orbit altitudes (apogee and perigee).

c. Reentry trajectories.

2. Reentry flight sequences.

3. Reentry initiation events and the time for each event.

4. Nominal landing location, alternative landing sites and contingency abort sites.

5. Identification of landing facilities, (planned date of reentry), and reentry windows.

6. If the applicant has previously been issued a license or permit to conduct reentry activities using the same reentry vehicle to the same reentry site facility, a description of any differences planned in the conduct of proposed activities.

B. Reentry vehicle description.

1. General description of the reentry vehicle, including dimensions.

2. Description of major systems, including safety systems.

3. Description of propulsion system (reentry initiation system) and type of fuel used.

4. Identification of all propellants to be used and their hazard classification under the Hazardous Materials Table, 49 CFR 172.101.

5. Description of hazardous components.

C. Payload.

1. General description of any payload, including type (e.g., telecommunications, remote sensing), propellants, and hazardous components or materials, such as toxic or radioactive substances.

D. Flight Safety System.

1. Identification of any flight safety system on the reentry vehicle, including a description of operations and component location on the vehicle.

II. Flight Operations

A. Identification of reentry site facilities exposed to risk during vehicle reentry and landing.

B. Identification of accident failure scenarios, probability assessments for each, and estimation of risks to Government personnel, individuals not involved in licensed reentry, and Government property, due to property damage or bodily injury. The estimation of risks for each scenario shall take into account the number of such individuals at risk as a result of reentry (flight) and landing of a reentry vehicle (on-range, off-range, and down-range) and specific, unique facilities exposed to risk. Scenarios shall cover the range of reentry trajectories for which authorization is sought.

C. On-orbit risk analysis assessing risks posed by a reentry vehicle to operational satellites during reentry.

D. Reentry risk analysis assessing risks to Government personnel and individuals not involved in licensed activities as a result of inadvertent or random reentry of the launch vehicle or its components.

E. Nominal and 3-sigma dispersed trajectories in one-second intervals, from reentry initiation through landing or impact. (Coordinate system will be specified on a case-by-case basis)

F. Three-sigma landing or impact dispersion area in downrange (±) and crossrange (±) measured from the nominal and contingency landing or impact target. The applicant is responsible for including all significant landing or impact dispersion constituents in the computations of landing or impact dispersion areas. The dispersion constituents should include, but not be limited to: Variation in orbital position and velocity at the reentry initiation time; variation in re-entry initiation time offsets, either early or late; variation in the bodies' ballistic coefficient; position and velocity variation due to winds; and variations in re-entry retro-maneuvers.

G. Malfunction turn data (tumble, trim) for guided (controllable) vehicles. The malfunction turn data shall include the total angle turned by the velocity vector versus turn duration time at one second intervals; the magnitude of the velocity vector versus turn duration time at one second intervals; and an indication on the data where the reentry body will impact the Earth, or breakup due to aerodynamic loads. A malfunction turn data set is required for each malfunction time. Malfunction turn start times shall not exceed four-second intervals along the trajectory.

H. Identification of debris casualty areas and the projected number and ballistic coefficient of fragments expected to result from each failure mode during reentry, including random reentry.

III. POST-FLIGHT PROCESSING OPERATIONS

A. General description of post flight ground operations including overall sequence and location of operations for removal of vehicle and components and processing equipment from the reentry site facility and for handling of hazardous materials, and designation of hazardous operations.

B. Identification of all facilities used in conducting post-flight processing operations.

C. For each hazardous operation:

1. Identification of location where each operation is performed, including each building or facility identified by name or number.

2. Identification of facilities adjacent to location where each operation is performed and exposed to risk, identified by name or number.

3. Maximum number of Government personnel and individuals not involved in licensed reentry activities who may be exposed to risk during each operation. For Government personnel, identification of his or her employer.

4. Identify and provide reentry site facility policies or requirements applicable to the conduct of operations.

Part 3: Information Requirements for Permitted Activities

In addition to the information required in part 437 subpart B, an applicant for an experimental permit must provide, for each permitted pre-flight and post-flight operation, the following information to the FAA:

A. Identification of location where each operation will be performed, including any U.S. Government or third party facilities identified by name or number.

B. Identification of any U.S. Government or third party facilities adjacent to the location where each operation will be performed and therefore exposed to risk, identified by name or number.

C. Maximum number of Government personnel and individuals not involved in permitted activities that may be exposed to risk during each operation. For Government personnel, identification of his or her employer.

APPENDIX B TO PART 440—AGREEMENT FOR WAIVER OF CLAIMS AND ASSUMPTION OF RESPONSIBILITY FOR LICENSED ACTIVITIES

PART 1—WAIVER OF CLAIMS AND ASSUMPTION OF RESPONSIBILITY FOR LICENSED LAUNCH, INCLUDING SUBORBITAL LAUNCH

Subpart A—Waiver of Claims and Assumption of Responsibility for Licensed Launch, Including Suborbital Launch, With One Customer

This agreement is entered into this____day of________, by and among [Licensee] (the "Licensee"), [Customer] (the "Customer") and the Federal Aviation Administration of the Department of Transportation, on behalf of the United States Government (collectively, the "Parties"), to implement the provisions of § 440.17(c) of the Commercial Space Transportation Licensing Regulations, 14 CFR Ch. III (the "Regulations"). This agreement applies to the launch of [Payload] payload on a [Launch Vehicle] vehicle at [Location of Launch Site]. In consideration of the mutual releases and promises contained herein, the Parties hereby agree as follows:

1. Definitions

Contractors and Subcontractors means entities defined by § 440.3 of the Regulations.

Customer means the above-named Customer.

Part 440 Customer means a customer defined by § 440.3 of the Regulations, other than the above-named Customer.

License means License No.____issued on________, by the Associate Administrator for Commercial Space Transportation, Federal Aviation Administration, Department of Transportation, to the Licensee, including all license orders issued in connection with the License.

Licensee means the Licensee and any transferee of the Licensee under 51 U.S.C. Subtitle V, ch. 509.

United States means the United States and its agencies involved in Licensed Activities. Except as otherwise defined herein, terms used in this Agreement and defined in 51 U.S.C. Subtitle V, ch. 509—Commercial Space Launch Activities, or in the Regulations, shall have the same meaning as contained in 51 U.S.C. Subtitle V, ch. 509, or the Regulations, respectively.

2. Waiver and Release of Claims

(a) Licensee hereby waives and releases claims it may have against Customer, the United States, any Part 440 Customer, and each of their respective Contractors and Subcontractors, for Property Damage it sustains and for Bodily Injury or Property Damage sustained by its own employees, resulting from Licensed Activities, regardless of fault.

(b) Customer hereby waives and releases claims it may have against Licensee, the United States, any other customer, and each of their respective Contractors and Subcontractors, for Property Damage it sustains and for Bodily Injury or Property Damage sustained by its own employees, resulting from Licensed Activities, regardless of fault.

(c) The United States hereby waives and releases claims it may have against Licensee, Customer, any Part 440 Customer, and each of their respective Contractors and Subcontractors, for Property Damage it sustains, and for Bodily Injury or Property Damage sustained by its own employees, resulting from Licensed Activities, regardless of fault, to the extent that claims it would otherwise have for such damage or injury exceed the amount of insurance or demonstration of financial responsibility required under § 440.9(c) and (e), respectively, of the Regulations.

3. Assumption of Responsibility

(a) Licensee and Customer shall each be responsible for Property Damage it sustains and for Bodily Injury or Property Damage sustained by its own employees, resulting from Licensed Activities, regardless of fault. Licensee and Customer shall each hold harmless and indemnify each other, the United States, any other customer, and the Contractors and Subcontractors of each, for Bodily Injury or Property Damage sustained by its own employees, resulting from Licensed Activities, regardless of fault.

(b) The United States shall be responsible for Property Damage it sustains, and for Bodily Injury or Property Damage sustained by its own employees, resulting from Licensed Activities, regardless of fault, to the extent that claims it would otherwise have for such damage or injury exceed the amount of insurance or demonstration of financial responsibility required under § 440.9(c) and (e), respectively, of the Regulations.

4. Extension of Assumption of Responsibility and Waiver and Release of Claims

(a) Licensee shall extend the requirements of the waiver and release of claims, and the assumption of responsibility, hold harmless, and indemnification, as set forth in paragraphs 2(a) and 3(a), respectively, to its Contractors and Subcontractors by requiring them to waive and release all claims they may have against Customer, the United States, any Part 440 Customer, and each of their respective Contractors and Subcontractors, and to agree to be responsible, for Property Damage they sustain and to be responsible, hold harmless and indemnify Customer, the United States, any Part 440 Customer, and each of their respective Contractors and Subcontractors, for Bodily Injury or Property Damage sustained by their own employees, resulting from Licensed Activities, regardless of fault.

(b) Customer shall extend the requirements of the waiver and release of claims, and the assumption of responsibility, hold harmless, and indemnification, as set forth in paragraphs 2(b) and 3(a), respectively, to its customers, Contractors, and Subcontractors, by requiring them to waive and release all claims they may have against Licensee, the United States, and any other customer, and each of their respective Contractors and Subcontractors, and to agree to be responsible, for Property Damage they sustain and to be responsible, hold harmless and indemnify Licensee, the United States, and any other customer, and each of their respective Contractors and Subcontractors for Bodily Injury or Property Damage sustained by their own employees, resulting from Licensed Activities, regardless of fault.

(c) The United States shall extend the requirements of the waiver and release of claims, and the assumption of responsibility as set forth in paragraphs 2(c) and 3(b), respectively, to its Contractors and Subcontractors by requiring them to waive and release all claims they may have against Licensee, Customer, any Part 440 Customer, and each of their respective Contractors and Subcontractors, and to agree to be responsible, for any Property Damage they sustain and for any Bodily Injury or Property Damage sustained by their own employees, resulting from Licensed Activities, regardless of fault, to the extent that claims they would otherwise have for such damage or injury exceed the amount of insurance or demonstration of financial responsibility required under § 440.9(c) and (e), respectively, of the Regulations.

5. Indemnification

(a) Licensee shall hold harmless and indemnify Customer and its directors, officers, servants, agents, subsidiaries, employees and assignees, or any of them; the United States and its agencies, servants, agents, subsidiaries, employees and assignees, or any of them; and any Part 440 Customer and its directors, officers, servants, agents, subsidiaries, employees and assignees, or any of them, from and against liability, loss or damage arising out of claims that Licensee's Contractors and Subcontractors may have for Property Damage sustained by them and for Bodily Injury or Property Damage sustained by their employees, resulting from Licensed Activities and arising out of the indemnifying party's failure to implement properly the waiver requirement.

(b) Customer shall hold harmless and indemnify Licensee and its directors, officers, servants, agents, subsidiaries, employees and assignees, or any of them; the United States and its agencies, servants, agents, subsidiaries, employees and assignees, or any of them; and any other customer and its directors, officers, servants, agents, subsidiaries, employees and assignees, or any of them, from and against liability, loss or damage arising out of claims that Customer's Contractors, Subcontractors, or customers, may have for Property Damage sustained by them and for Bodily Injury or Property Damage sustained by their employees, resulting from Licensed Activities and arising out of the indemnifying party's failure to implement properly the waiver requirement.

(c) To the extent provided in advance in an appropriations law or to the extent there is enacted additional legislative authority providing for the payment of claims, the United States shall hold harmless and indemnify Licensee, Customer, any Part 440 Customer, and their respective directors, officers, servants, agents, subsidiaries, employees and assignees, or any of them, from and against liability, loss or damage arising out of claims that Contractors and Subcontractors of the United States may have for Property Damage sustained by them, and for Bodily Injury or Property Damage sustained by their employees, resulting from Licensed Activities and arising out of the indemnifying party's failure to implement properly the waiver requirement, to the extent that claims they would otherwise have for such damage or injury exceed the amount of insurance or demonstration of financial responsibility required under § 440.9(c) and (e), respectively, of the Regulations.

6. Assurances Under 51 U.S.C. 50914(e)

Notwithstanding any provision of this Agreement to the contrary, Licensee shall hold harmless and indemnify the United States and its agencies, servants, agents, employees and assignees, or any of them, from and against liability, loss or damage arising out of claims for Bodily Injury or Property Damage, resulting from Licensed Activities, regardless of fault, except to the extent that: (i) As provided in paragraph 7(b) of this Agreement, claims result from willful misconduct of the United States or its agents; (ii) claims for Property Damage sustained by the United States or its Contractors and Subcontractors exceed the amount of insurance or demonstration of financial responsibility required under § 440.9(e) of the Regulations; (iii) claims by a Third Party for Bodily Injury or Property Damage exceed the amount of insurance or demonstration of financial responsibility required under § 440.9(c) of the Regulations, and do not exceed $1,500,000,000 (as adjusted for inflation after January 1, 1989) above such amount, and are payable pursuant to the provisions of 51 U.S.C. 50915 and § 440.19 of the Regulations; or (iv) Licensee has no liability for claims exceeding $1,500,000,000 (as adjusted for inflation after January 1, 1989) above the amount of insurance or demonstration of financial responsibility required under § 440.9(c) of the Regulations.

7. Miscellaneous

(a) Nothing contained herein shall be construed as a waiver or release by Licensee, Customer or the United States of any claim by an employee of the Licensee, Customer or the United States, respectively, including a member of the Armed Forces of the United States, for Bodily Injury or Property Damage, resulting from Licensed Activities.

(b) Notwithstanding any provision of this Agreement to the contrary, any waiver, release, assumption of responsibility or agreement to hold harmless and indemnify herein shall not apply to claims for Bodily Injury or Property Damage resulting from willful misconduct of any of the Parties, the Contractors and Subcontractors of any of the Parties, any Part 440 Customer, the Contractors and Subcontractors of any Part 440 Customer, and in the case of Licensee, Customer, any Part 440 Customer, and the Contractors and Subcontractors of each of them, the directors, officers, agents and employees of any of the foregoing, and in the case of the United States, its agents.

(c) This Agreement shall be governed by and construed in accordance with United States Federal law.

In witness whereof, the Parties to this Agreement have caused the Agreement to be duly executed by their respective duly authorized representatives as of the date written above.

Licensee

By: ______

Its: ______

Customer

By: ______

Its: ______

Federal Aviation Administration of the Department of Transportation on Behalf of the United States Government

By: ______

Its: ______

Associate Administrator for Commercial Space Transportation

SUBPART B—WAIVER OF CLAIMS AND ASSUMPTION OF RESPONSIBILITY FOR LICENSED LAUNCH, INCLUDING SUBORBITAL LAUNCH, WITH MORE THAN ONE CUSTOMER

This agreement is entered into this___day of_______, by and among [Licensee] (the "Licensee"); [List of Customers]; (with [List of Customers] hereinafter referred to in their individual capacity as "Customer"); and the Federal Aviation Administration of the Department of Transportation, on behalf of the United States Government (collectively, the "Parties"), to implement the provisions of §440.17(c) of the Commercial Space Transportation Licensing Regulations, 14 CFR Ch. III (the "Regulations"). This agreement applies to the launch of [Payload] payload on a [Launch Vehicle] vehicle at [Location of Launch Site].

In consideration of the mutual releases and promises contained herein, the Parties hereby agree as follows:

1. Definitions

Contractors and Subcontractors means entities defined by §440.3 of the Regulations.

Customer means each above-named Customer.

Part 440 Customer means a customer defined by §440.3 of the Regulations, other than the above-named Customer.

License means License No.___issued on_______, by the Associate Administrator for Commercial Space Transportation, Federal Aviation Administration, Department of Transportation, to the Licensee, including all license orders issued in connection with the License.

Licensee means the Licensee and any transferee of the Licensee under 51 U.S.C. Subtitle V, ch. 509.

United States means the United States and its agencies involved in Licensed Activities. Except as otherwise defined herein, terms used in this Agreement and defined in 51 U.S.C. Subtitle V, ch. 509—Commercial Space Launch Activities, or in the Regulations, shall have the same meaning as contained in 51 U.S.C. Subtitle V, ch. 509, or the Regulations, respectively.

2. Waiver and Release of Claims

(a) Licensee hereby waives and releases claims it may have against each Customer, the United States, any Part 440 Customer, and each of their respective Contractors and Subcontractors, for Property Damage it sustains and for Bodily Injury or Property Damage sustained by its own employees, resulting from Licensed Activities, regardless of fault.

(b) Each Customer hereby waives and releases claims it may have against Licensee, the United States, any other customer, and each of their respective Contractors and Subcontractors for Property Damage it sustains and for Bodily Injury or Property Damage sustained by its own employees, resulting from Licensed Activities, regardless of fault.

(c) The United States hereby waives and releases claims it may have against Licensee, each Customer, any Part 440 Customer, and each of their respective Contractors and Subcontractors, for Property Damage it sustains, and for Bodily Injury or Property Damage sustained by its own employees, resulting from Licensed Activities, regardless of fault, to the extent that claims it would otherwise have for such damage or injury exceed the amount of insurance or demonstration of financial responsibility required under §440.9(c) and (e), respectively, of the Regulations.

3. Assumption of Responsibility

(a) Licensee and each Customer shall each be responsible for Property Damage it sustains and for Bodily Injury or Property Damage sustained by its own employees, resulting from Licensed Activities, regardless of fault. Licensee and each Customer shall each hold harmless and indemnify each other, the United States, any other customer, and the Contractors and Subcontractors of each, for Bodily Injury or Property Damage sustained by its own employees, resulting from Licensed Activities, regardless of fault.

(b) The United States shall be responsible for Property Damage it sustains, and for Bodily Injury or Property Damage sustained by its own employees, resulting from Licensed Activities, regardless of fault, to the extent that claims it would otherwise have for such damage or injury exceed the amount of insurance or demonstration of financial responsibility required under §440.9(c) and (e), respectively, of the Regulations.

4. Extension of Assumption of Responsibility and Waiver and Release of Claims

(a) Licensee shall extend the requirements of the waiver and release of claims, and the assumption of responsibility, hold harmless, and indemnification, as set forth in paragraphs 2(a) and 3(a), respectively, to its Contractors and Subcontractors by requiring them to waive and release all claims they may have against each Customer, the United States, any Part 440 Customer, and each of their respective Contractors and Subcontractors, and to agree to be responsible, for Property Damage they sustain and to be responsible, hold harmless and indemnify each Customer, the United States, any Part 440 Customer, and each of their respective Contractors and Subcontractors, for Bodily Injury or Property Damage sustained by their own employees, resulting from Licensed Activities, regardless of fault.

(b) Each Customer shall extend the requirements of the waiver and release of claims, and the assumption of responsibility, hold harmless, and indemnification, as set forth in paragraphs 2(b) and 3(a), respectively, to its customers, Contractors, and Subcontractors, by requiring them to waive and release all claims they may have against Licensee, the United States, and any other customer, and each of their respective Contractors and Subcontractors, and to agree to be responsible, for Property Damage they sustain and to be responsible, hold harmless and indemnify Licensee, the United States, and any other customer, and each of their respective Contractors and Subcontractors, for Bodily Injury or Property Damage sustained by their own employees, resulting from Licensed Activities, regardless of fault.

(c) The United States shall extend the requirements of the waiver and release of claims, and the assumption of responsibility as set forth in paragraphs 2(c) and 3(b), respectively, to its Contractors and Subcontractors by requiring them to waive and release all claims they may have against Licensee, each Customer, any Part 440 Customer, and each of their respective Contractors and Subcontractors, and to agree to be responsible, for any Property Damage they sustain and for any Bodily Injury or Property Damage sustained by their own employees, resulting from Licensed Activities, regardless of fault, to the extent that claims they would otherwise have for such damage or injury exceed the amount of insurance or demonstration of financial responsibility required under §440.9(c) and (e), respectively, of the Regulations.

5. Indemnification

(a) Licensee shall hold harmless and indemnify each Customer and its directors, officers, servants, agents, subsidiaries, employees and assignees, or any of them; the United States and its agencies, servants, agents, subsidiaries, employees and assignees, or any of them; and any part 440 customer and its directors, officers, servants, agents, subsidiaries, employees and assignees, or any of them, from and against liability, loss or damage arising out of claims that Licensee's Contractors and Subcontractors may have for Property Damage sustained by them and for Bodily Injury or Property Damage sustained by their employees, resulting from Licensed Activities and arising out of the indemnifying party's failure to implement properly the waiver requirement.

(b) Each Customer shall hold harmless and indemnify Licensee and its directors, officers, servants, agents, subsidiaries, employees and assignees, or any of them; the United States and its agencies, servants, agents, subsidiaries, employees and assignees, or any of them; and any other customer and its directors, officers, servants, agents, subsidiaries, employees and assignees, or any of them, from and against liability, loss or damage arising out of claims that each Customer's Contractors, Subcontractors, or customers, may have for Property Damage sustained by them and for Bodily Injury or Property Damage sustained by their employees, resulting from Licensed Activities and arising out of the indemnifying party's failure to implement properly the waiver requirement.

(c) To the extent provided in advance in an appropriations law or to the extent there is enacted additional legislative authority providing for the payment of claims, the United States shall hold harmless and indemnify Licensee, each Customer, any Part 440 Customer, and their respective directors, officers, servants, agents, subsidiaries, employees and assignees, or any of them, from and against liability, loss or damage arising out of claims that Contractors and Subcontractors of the United States may have for Property Damage sustained by them, and for Bodily Injury or Property Damage sustained by their employees, resulting from Licensed Activities and arising out of the indemnifying party's failure to implement properly the waiver requirement, to the extent that claims they would otherwise have for such damage or injury exceed the amount of insurance or demonstration of financial responsibility required under §440.9(c) and (e), respectively, of the Regulations.

6. Assurances Under 51 U.S.C. 50914(e)

Notwithstanding any provision of this Agreement to the contrary, Licensee shall hold harmless and indemnify the United

States and its agencies, servants, agents, employees and assignees, or any of them, from and against liability, loss or damage arising out of claims for Bodily Injury or Property Damage, resulting from Licensed Activities, regardless of fault, except to the extent that: (i) As provided in paragraph 7(b) of this Agreement, claims result from willful misconduct of the United States or its agents; (ii) claims for Property Damage sustained by the United States or its Contractors and Subcontractors exceed the amount of insurance or demonstration of financial responsibility required under §440.9(e) of the Regulations; (iii) claims by a Third Party for Bodily Injury or Property Damage exceed the amount of insurance or demonstration of financial responsibility required under §440.9(c) of the Regulations, and do not exceed $1,500,000,000 (as adjusted for inflation after January 1, 1989) above such amount, and are payable pursuant to the provisions of 51 U.S.C. 50915 and §440.19 of the Regulations; or (iv) Licensee has no liability for claims exceeding $1,500,000,000 (as adjusted for inflation after January 1, 1989) above the amount of insurance or demonstration of financial responsibility required under §440.9(c) of the Regulations.

7. Miscellaneous

(a) Nothing contained herein shall be construed as a waiver or release by Licensee, any Customer or the United States of any claim by an employee of the Licensee, any Customer or the United States, respectively, including a member of the Armed Forces of the United States, for Bodily Injury or Property Damage, resulting from Licensed Activities.

(b) Notwithstanding any provision of this Agreement to the contrary, any waiver, release, assumption of responsibility or agreement to hold harmless and indemnify herein shall not apply to claims for Bodily Injury or Property Damage resulting from willful misconduct of any of the Parties, the Contractors and Subcontractors of any of the Parties, any Part 440 Customer, the Contractors and Subcontractors of any Part 440 Customer, and in the case of Licensee, each Customer, any Part 440 Customer, and the Contractors and Subcontractors of each of them, the directors, officers, agents and employees of any of the foregoing, and in the case of the United States, its agents.

(c) References herein to Customer shall apply to, and be deemed to include, each such customer severally and not jointly.

(d) This Agreement shall be governed by and construed in accordance with United States Federal law.

In witness whereof, the Parties to this Agreement have caused the Agreement to be duly executed by their respective duly authorized representatives as of the date written above.

Licensee

By: ____________________
Its: ____________________

Customer 1

By: ____________________
Its: ____________________

[Signature lines for each additional customer]

Federal Aviation Administration of the Department of Transportation on Behalf of the United States Government

By: ____________________
Its: ____________________

Associate Administrator for Commercial Space Transportation

PART 2—WAIVER OF CLAIMS AND ASSUMPTION OF RESPONSIBILITY FOR LICENSED REENTRY

SUBPART A—WAIVER OF CLAIMS AND ASSUMPTION OF RESPONSIBILITY FOR LICENSED REENTRY WITH ONE CUSTOMER

This Agreement is entered into this ___ day of ______, by and among [Licensee] (the "Licensee"), [Customer] (the "Customer"), and the Federal Aviation Administration of the Department of Transportation, on behalf of the United States Government (collectively, the "Parties"), to implement the provisions of §440.17(c) of the Commercial Space Transportation Licensing Regulations, 14 CFR Ch. III (the "Regulations"). This agreement applies to the reentry of the [Payload] payload on a [Reentry Vehicle] vehicle.

In consideration of the mutual releases and promises contained herein, the Parties hereby agree as follows:

1. Definitions

Contractors and Subcontractors means entities defined by §440.3 of the Regulations.

Customer means the above-named Customer.

Part 440 Customer means a customer defined by §440.3 of the Regulations, other than the above named Customer.

License means License No. ___ issued on ______, by the Associate Administrator for Commercial Space Transportation, Federal Aviation Administration, Department of Transportation, to the Licensee, including all license orders issued in connection with the License.

Licensee means the Licensee and any transferee of the Licensee under 51 U.S.C. Subtitle V, ch. 509.

United States means the United States and its agencies involved in Licensed Activities.

Except as otherwise defined herein, terms used in this Agreement and defined in 51 U.S.C. Subtitle V, ch. 509—Commercial

Space Launch Activities, or in the Regulations, shall have the same meaning as contained in 51 U.S.C. Subtitle V, ch. 509, or the Regulations, respectively.

2. Waiver and Release of Claims

(a) Licensee hereby waives and releases claims it may have against Customer, the United States, any Part 440 Customer, and each of their respective Contractors and Subcontractors, for Property Damage it sustains and for Bodily Injury or Property Damage sustained by its own employees, resulting from Licensed Activities, regardless of fault.

(b) Customer hereby waives and releases claims it may have against Licensee, the United States, any other customer, and each of their respective Contractors and Subcontractors, for Property Damage it sustains and for Bodily Injury or Property Damage sustained by its own employees, resulting from Licensed Activities, regardless of fault.

(c) The United States hereby waives and releases claims it may have against Licensee, Customer, any Part 440 Customer, and each of their respective Contractors and Subcontractors, for Property Damage it sustains, and for Bodily Injury or Property Damage sustained by its own employees, resulting from Licensed Activities, regardless of fault, to the extent that claims it would otherwise have for such damage or injury exceed the amount of insurance or demonstration of financial responsibility required under §440.9(c) and (e), respectively, of the Regulations.

3. Assumption of Responsibility

(a) Licensee and Customer shall each be responsible for Property Damage it sustains and for Bodily Injury or Property Damage sustained by its own employees, resulting from Licensed Activities, regardless of fault. Licensee and Customer shall each hold harmless and indemnify each other, the United States, any other customer, and the Contractors and Subcontractors of each, for Bodily Injury or Property Damage sustained by its own employees, resulting from Licensed Activities, regardless of fault.

(b) The United States shall be responsible for Property Damage it sustains, and for Bodily Injury or Property Damage sustained by its own employees, resulting from Licensed Activities, regardless of fault, to the extent that claims it would otherwise have for such damage or injury exceed the amount of insurance or demonstration of financial responsibility required under §440.9(c) and (e) of the Regulations.

4. Extension of Assumption of Responsibility and Waiver and Release of Claims

(a) Licensee shall extend the requirements of the waiver and release of claims, and the assumption of responsibility, hold harmless, and indemnification, as set forth in paragraphs 2(a) and 3(a), respectively, to its Contractors and Subcontractors by requiring them to waive and release all claims they may have against Customer, the United States, any Part 440 Customer, and each of their respective Contractors and Subcontractors, and to agree to be responsible, for Property Damage they sustain and to be responsible, hold harmless and indemnify Customer, the United States, any Part 440 Customer, and each of their respective Contractors and Subcontractors, for Bodily Injury or Property Damage sustained by their own employees, resulting from Licensed Activities, regardless of fault.

(b) Customer shall extend the requirements of the waiver and release of claims, and the assumption of responsibility, hold harmless, and indemnification, as set forth in paragraphs 2(b) and 3(a), respectively, to its customers, Contractors, and Subcontractors, by requiring them to waive and release all claims they may have against Licensee, the United States, and any other customer, and each of their respective Contractors and Subcontractors, and to agree to be responsible, for Property Damage they sustain and to be responsible, hold harmless and indemnify Licensee, the United States, and any other customer, and each of their respective Contractors and Subcontractors, for Bodily Injury or Property Damage sustained by their own employees, resulting from Licensed Activities, regardless of fault.

(c) The United States shall extend the requirements of the waiver and release of claims, and the assumption of responsibility as set forth in paragraphs 2(c) and 3(b), respectively, to its Contractors and Subcontractors by requiring them to waive and release all claims they may have against Licensee, Customer, any Part 440 Customer, and each of their respective Contractors and Subcontractors, and to agree to be responsible, for any Property Damage they sustain and for any Bodily Injury or Property Damage sustained by their own employees, resulting from Licensed Activities, regardless of fault, to the extent that claims they would otherwise have for such damage or injury exceed the amount of insurance or demonstration of financial responsibility required under §440.9(c) and (e), respectively, of the Regulations.

5. Indemnification

(a) Licensee shall hold harmless and indemnify Customer and its directors, officers, servants, agents, subsidiaries, employees and assignees, or any of them; the United States and its agencies, servants, agents, subsidiaries, employees and assignees, or any of them; and any Part 440 Customer and its directors, officers, servants, agents, subsidiaries, employees and assignees, or any of them from and against liability, loss or damage arising out of claims that Licensee's Contractors and Subcontractors may have for Property Damage sustained by them and for Bodily Injury or Property Damage sustained by their employees, resulting from Licensed Activities and arising out of the indemnifying party's failure to implement properly the waiver requirement.

(b) Customer shall hold harmless and indemnify Licensee and its directors, officers, servants, agents, subsidiaries, employees and assignees, or any of them; the United States and its agencies, servants, agents, subsidiaries, employees and assignees, or any of them; and any other customer and its directors, officers, servants, agents, subsidiaries, employees and assignees, or any of them from and against liability, loss or damage arising out of claims that Customer's Contractors, Subcontractors, or customers may have for Property Damage sustained by them and for Bodily Injury or Property Damage sustained by their employees, resulting from Licensed Activities and arising out of the indemnifying party's failure to implement properly the waiver requirement.

(c) To the extent provided in advance in an appropriations law or to the extent there is enacted additional legislative authority providing for the payment of claims, the United States shall hold harmless and indemnify Licensee, Customer, any Part 440 Customer, and their respective directors, officers, servants, agents, subsidiaries, employees and assignees, or any of them, from and against liability, loss or damage arising out of claims that Contractors and Subcontractors of the United States may have for Property Damage sustained by them, and for Bodily Injury or Property Damage sustained by their employees, resulting from Licensed Activities and arising out of the indemnifying party's failure to implement properly the waiver requirement, to the extent that claims they would otherwise have for such damage or injury exceed the amount of insurance or demonstration of financial responsibility required under §440.9(c) and (e) of the Regulations.

6. Assurances Under 51 U.S.C. 50914(e)

Notwithstanding any provision of this Agreement to the contrary, Licensee shall hold harmless and indemnify the United States and its agencies, servants, agents, employees and assignees, or any of them, from and against liability, loss or damage arising out of claims for Bodily Injury or Property Damage, resulting from Licensed Activities, regardless of fault, except to the extent that: (i) As provided in paragraph 7(b) of this Agreement, claims result from willful misconduct of the United States or its agents; (ii) claims for Property Damage sustained by the United States or its Contractors and Subcontractors exceed the amount of insurance or demonstration of financial responsibility required under §440.9(e) of the Regulations; (iii) claims by a Third Party for Bodily Injury or Property Damage exceed the amount of insurance or demonstration of financial responsibility required under §440.9(c) of the Regulations, and do not exceed $1,500,000,000 (as adjusted for inflation after January 1, 1989) above such amount, and are payable pursuant to the provisions of 51 U.S.C. 50915 and §440.19 of the Regulations; or (iv) Licensee has no liability for claims exceeding $1,500,000,000 (as adjusted for inflation after January 1, 1989) above the amount of insurance or demonstration of financial responsibility required under §440.9(c) of the Regulations.

7. Miscellaneous

(a) Nothing contained herein shall be construed as a waiver or release by Licensee, Customer or the United States of any claim by an employee of the Licensee, Customer or the United States, respectively, including a member of the Armed Forces of the United States, for Bodily Injury or Property Damage, resulting from Licensed Activities.

(b) Notwithstanding any provision of this Agreement to the contrary, any waiver, release, assumption of responsibility or agreement to hold harmless and indemnify herein shall not apply to claims for Bodily Injury or Property Damage resulting from willful misconduct of any of the Parties, the Contractors and Subcontractors of any of the Parties, any Part 440 Customer, the Contractors and Subcontractors of any Part 440 Customer, and in the case of Licensee, Customer, any Part 440 Customer, and the Contractors and Subcontractors of each of them, the directors, officers, agents and employees of any of the foregoing, and in the case of the United States, its agents.

(c) This Agreement shall be governed by and construed in accordance with United States Federal law.

In Witness Whereof, the Parties to this Agreement have caused the Agreement to be duly executed by their respective duly authorized representatives as of the date written above.

Licensee

By: __________

Its: __________

Customer

By: __________

Its: __________

Federal Aviation Administration of the Department of Transportation on Behalf of the United States Government

By: __________

Its: __________

Associate Administrator for Commercial Space Transportation

SUBPART B—WAIVER OF CLAIMS AND ASSUMPTION OF RESPONSIBILITY FOR LICENSED REENTRY WITH MORE THAN ONE CUSTOMER

This agreement is entered into this ___ day of ______, by and among [Licensee] (the "Licensee"); [List of Customers] (with [List of Customers] hereinafter referred to in their individual capacity as "Customer"); and the Federal Aviation Administration of the Department of Transportation, on behalf of the United States Government (collectively, the "Parties"), to implement the provisions of §440.17(c) of the Commercial Space Transportation Licensing Regulations, 14 CFR Ch. III (the "Regulations"). This agreement applies to the reentry of [Payload] payload on a [Reentry Vehicle] vehicle.

In consideration of the mutual releases and promises contained herein, the Parties hereby agree as follows:

1. Definitions

Contractors and Subcontractors means entities described in §440.3 of the Regulations.

Customer means each above-named Customer.

Part 440 Customer means a customer defined by §440.3 of the Regulations, other than the above-named customer.

License means License No. ___ issued on ______, by the Associate Administrator for Commercial Space Transportation, Federal Aviation Administration, Department of Transportation, to the Licensee, including all license orders issued in connection with the License.

Licensee means the Licensee and any transferee of the Licensee under 51 U.S.C. Subtitle V, ch. 509.

United States means the United States and its agencies involved in Licensed Activities. Except as otherwise defined herein, terms used in this Agreement and defined in 51 U.S.C. Subtitle V, ch. 509—Commercial Space Launch Activities, or in the Regulations, shall have the same meaning as contained in 51 U.S.C. Subtitle V, ch. 509, or the Regulations, respectively.

2. Waiver and Release of Claims

(a) Licensee hereby waives and releases claims it may have against each Customer, the United States, any Part 440 Customer, and each of their respective Contractors and Subcontractors, for Property Damage it sustains and for Bodily Injury or Property Damage sustained by its own employees, resulting from Licensed Activities, regardless of fault.

(b) Each Customer hereby waives and releases claims it may have against Licensee, the United States, any other customer, and each of their respective Contractors and Subcontractors, for Property Damage it sustains and for Bodily Injury or Property Damage sustained by its own employees, resulting from Licensed Activities, regardless of fault.

(c) The United States hereby waives and releases claims it may have against Licensee, each Customer, any Part 440 Customer, and each of their respective Contractors and Subcontractors, for Property Damage it sustains, and for Bodily Injury or Property Damage sustained by its own employees, resulting from Licensed Activities, regardless of fault, to the extent that claims it would otherwise have for such damage or injury exceed the amount of insurance or demonstration of financial responsibility required under §440.9(c) and (e), respectively, of the Regulations.

3. Assumption of Responsibility

(a) Licensee and each Customer shall each be responsible for Property Damage it sustains and for Bodily Injury or Property Damage sustained by its own employees, resulting from Licensed Activities, regardless of fault. Licensee and each Customer shall each hold harmless and indemnify each other, the United States, any other customer, and the Contractors and Subcontractors of each, for Bodily Injury or Property Damage sustained by its own employees, resulting from Licensed Activities, regardless of fault.

(b) The United States shall be responsible for Property Damage it sustains, and for Bodily Injury or Property Damage sustained by its own employees, resulting from Licensed Activities, regardless of fault, to the extent that claims it would otherwise have for such damage or injury exceed the amount of insurance or demonstration of financial responsibility required under §440.9(c) and (e), respectively, of the Regulations.

4. Extension of Assumption of Responsibility and Waiver and Release of Claims

(a) Licensee shall extend the requirements of the waiver and release of claims, and the assumption of responsibility, hold harmless, and indemnification, as set forth in paragraphs 2(a) and 3(a), respectively, to its Contractors and Subcontractors by requiring them to waive and release all claims they may have against each Customer, the United States, any Part 440 Customer, and each of their respective Contractors and Subcontractors, and to agree to be responsible, for Property Damage they sustain and to be responsible, hold harmless and indemnify each Customer, the United States, any Part 440 Customer, and each of their respective Contractors and Subcontractors, for Bodily Injury or Property Damage sustained by their own employees, resulting from Licensed Activities, regardless of fault.

(b) Each Customer shall extend the requirements of the waiver and release of claims, and the assumption of responsibility, hold harmless, and indemnification, as set forth in paragraphs 2(b) and 3(a), respectively, to its customers, Contractors, and Subcontractors, by requiring them to waive and release all claims they may have against Licensee, the United States, and any other customer, and each of their respective Contractors and Subcontractors, and to agree to be responsible, for Property Damage they sustain and to be responsible, hold harmless and indemnify Licensee, the United States, and any other customer, and each of their respective Contractors and Subcontractors, for Bodily Injury or Property Damage sustained by their own employees, resulting from Licensed Activities, regardless of fault.

(c) The United States shall extend the requirements of the waiver and release of claims, and the assumption of responsibility as set forth in paragraphs 2(c) and 3(b), respectively, to its Contractors and Subcontractors by requiring them to waive and release all claims they may have against Licensee, each Customer, any Part 440 Customer, and each of their respective Contractors and Subcontractors, and to agree to be responsible, for any Property Damage they sustain and for any Bodily Injury or Property Damage sustained by their own employees, resulting from Licensed Activities, regardless of fault, to the extent that claims they would otherwise have for such damage or injury exceed the amount of insurance or demonstration of financial responsibility required under §440.9(c) and (e), respectively, of the Regulations.

5. Indemnification

(a) Licensee shall hold harmless and indemnify each Customer and its directors, officers, servants, agents, subsidiaries, employees and assignees, or any of them; the United States and its agencies, servants, agents, subsidiaries, employees and assignees, or any of them; and any Part 440 Customer and its directors, officers, servants, agents, subsidiaries, employees and assignees, or any of them, from and against liability, loss or damage arising out of claims that Licensee's Contractors and Subcontractors may have for Property Damage sustained by them and for Bodily Injury or Property Damage sustained by their employees, resulting from Licensed Activities and arising out of the indemnifying party's failure to implement properly the waiver requirement.

(b) Each Customer shall hold harmless and indemnify Licensee and its directors, officers, servants, agents, subsidiaries, employees and assignees, or any of them; and the United States and any other customer as defined by §440.3 its agencies, servants, agents, subsidiaries, employees and assignees, or any of them; and any other customer and its directors, officers, servants, agents, subsidiaries, employees and assignees, or any of them, from and against liability, loss or damage arising out of claims that each Customer's Contractors, Subcontractors, and customers, may have for Property Damage sustained by them and for Bodily Injury or Property Damage sustained by their employees, resulting from Licensed Activities and arising out of the indemnifying party's failure to implement properly the waiver requirement.

(c) To the extent provided in advance in an appropriations law or to the extent there is enacted additional legislative authority providing for the payment of claims, the United States shall hold harmless and indemnify Licensee, each Customer, any Part 440 Customer, and their respective directors, officers, servants, agents, subsidiaries, employees and assignees, or any of them, from and against liability, loss or damage arising out of claims that Contractors and Subcontractors of the United States may have for Property Damage sustained by them, and for Bodily Injury or Property Damage sustained by their employees, resulting from Licensed Activities and arising out of the indemnifying party's failure to implement properly the waiver requirement, to the extent that claims they would otherwise have for such damage or injury exceed the amount of insurance or demonstration of financial responsibility required under §440.9(c) and (e), respectively, of the Regulations.

6. Assurances Under 51 U.S.C. 50914(e)

Notwithstanding any provision of this Agreement to the contrary, Licensee shall hold harmless and indemnify the United States and its agencies, servants, agents, employees and assignees, or any of them, from and against liability, loss or damage arising out of claims for Bodily Injury or Property Damage, resulting from Licensed Activities, regardless of fault, except to the extent that: (i) As provided in paragraph 7(b) of this Agreement, claims result from willful misconduct of the United States or its agents; (ii) claims for Property Damage sustained by the United States or its Contractors and Subcontractors exceed the amount of insurance or demonstration of financial responsibility required under §440.9(e) of the Regulations; (iii) claims by a Third Party for Bodily Injury or Property Damage exceed the amount of insurance or demonstration of financial responsibility required under §440.9(c) of the Regulations, and do not exceed $1,500,000,000 (as adjusted for inflation after January 1, 1989) above such amount, and are payable pursuant to the provisions of 51 U.S.C. 50915 and §440.19 of the Regulations; or (iv) Licensee has no liability for claims exceeding $1,500,000,000 (as adjusted for inflation after January 1, 1989) above the amount of insurance or demonstration of financial responsibility required under §440.9(c) of the Regulations.

7. Miscellaneous

(a) Nothing contained herein shall be construed as a waiver or release by Licensee, any Customer or the United States of any claim by an employee of the Licensee, any Customer or the United States, respectively, including a member of the Armed Forces of the United States, for Bodily Injury or Property Damage, resulting from Licensed Activities.

(b) Notwithstanding any provision of this Agreement to the contrary, any waiver, release, assumption of responsibility or agreement to hold harmless and indemnify herein shall not apply to claims for Bodily Injury or Property Damage resulting from willful misconduct of any of the Parties, the Contractors and Subcontractors of any of the Parties, any Part 440 Customers, the Contractors and Subcontractors of any Part 440 Customer, and in the case of Licensee, each Customer, any Part 440 Customer, and the Contractors and Subcontractors of each of them, the directors, officers, agents and employees of any of the foregoing, and in the case of the United States, its agents.

(c) References herein to Customer shall apply to, and be deemed to include, each such customer severally and not jointly.

(d) This Agreement shall be governed by and construed in accordance with United States Federal law.

In witness whereof, the Parties to this Agreement have caused the Agreement to be duly executed by their respective duly authorized representatives as of the date written above.

Licensee

By: ____________________

Its: ____________________

Customer 1

By: ____________________

Its: ____________________

[Signature lines for each additional customer]

Federal Aviation Administration of the Department of Transportation on Behalf of the United States Government

By: ____________________

Its: ____________________

Associate Administrator for Commercial Space Transportation

[Doc. No. FAA–2014–1012, Amdt. 440–4, 81 FR 55124, Aug. 18, 2016]

Appendix C to Part 440—Agreement for Waiver of Claims and Assumption of Responsibility for Permitted Activities

Part 1—Waiver of Claims and Assumption of Responsibility for Permitted Activities With No Customer

This agreement is entered into this ____ day of ________, by and between [Permittee] (the "Permittee") and the Federal Aviation Administration of the Department of Transportation, on behalf of the United States Government (collectively, the "Parties"), to implement the provisions of §440.17(c) of the Commercial Space Transportation Licensing Regulations, 14 CFR Ch. III (the "Regulations"). This agreement applies to [describe permitted activity]. In consideration of the mutual releases and promises contained herein, the Parties hereby agree as follows:

1. Definitions

Contractors and Subcontractors means entities defined by §440.3 of the Regulations.

Permit means Permit No.____________ issued on ____________________, by the Associate Administrator for Commercial Space Transportation, Federal Aviation Administration, Department of Transportation, to the Permittee, including all permit orders issued in connection with the Permit.

Permittee means the holder of the Permit issued under 51 U.S.C. Subtitle V, ch. 509.

United States means the United States and its agencies involved in Permitted Activities. Except as otherwise defined herein, terms used in this Agreement and defined in 51 U.S.C. Subtitle V, ch. 509—Commercial Space Launch Activities, or in the Regulations, shall have the same meaning as contained in 51 U.S.C. Subtitle V, ch. 509, or the Regulations, respectively.

2. Waiver and Release of Claims

(a) Permittee hereby waives and releases claims it may have against the United States, and against its Contractors and Subcontractors, for Property Damage it sustains and for Bodily Injury or Property Damage sustained by its own employees, resulting from Permitted Activities, regardless of fault.

(b) The United States hereby waives and releases claims it may have against Permittee and against its Contractors and Subcontractors, for Property Damage it sustains resulting from Permitted Activities, regardless of fault, to the extent that claims it would otherwise have for such damage exceed the amount of insurance or demonstration of financial responsibility required under §440.9(e) of the Regulations.

3. Assumption of Responsibility

(a) Permittee shall be responsible for Property Damage it sustains and for Bodily Injury or Property Damage sustained by its own employees, resulting from Permitted Activities, regardless of fault. Permittee shall hold harmless and indemnify the United States, and the Contractors and Subcontractors of the United States, for Bodily Injury or Property Damage sustained by its own employees, resulting from Permitted Activities, regardless of fault.

(b) The United States shall be responsible for Property Damage it sustains, resulting from Permitted Activities, regardless of fault, to the extent that claims it would otherwise have for such damage exceed the amount of insurance or demonstration of financial responsibility required under §440.9(e) of the Regulations.

4. Extension of Assumption of Responsibility and Waiver and Release of Claims

(a) Permittee shall extend the requirements of the waiver and release of claims, and the assumption of responsibility, hold harmless, and indemnification, as set forth in paragraphs 2(a) and 3(a), respectively, to its Contractors and Subcontractors by requiring them to waive and release all claims they may have against the United States, and against the Contractors and Subcontractors of the United States, and to agree to be responsible for Property Damage they sustain and to be responsible, hold harmless, and indemnify the United States, and the Contractors and Subcontractors of the United States, for Bodily Injury or Property Damage sustained by their own employees, resulting from Permitted Activities, regardless of fault.

(b) The United States shall extend the requirements of the waiver and release of claims, and the assumption of responsibility as set forth in paragraphs 2(b) and 3(b), respectively, to its Contractors and Subcontractors by requiring them to waive and release all claims they may have against Permittee, and against the Contractors and Subcontractors of Permittee, and to agree to be responsible, for any Property Damage they sustain, resulting from Permitted Activities, regardless of fault, to the extent that claims they would otherwise have for such damage exceed the amount of insurance or demonstration of financial responsibility required under §440.9(e) of the Regulations.

5. Indemnification

Permittee shall hold harmless and indemnify the United States and its agencies, servants, agents, subsidiaries, employees and assignees, or any of them, from and against liability, loss, or damage arising out of claims that Permittee's Contractors and Subcontractors may have for Property Damage sustained by them and for Bodily Injury or Property Damage sustained by their employees, resulting from Permitted Activities and arising out of the indemnifying party's failure to implement properly the waiver requirement.

6. Assurances Under 51 U.S.C. 50914(e)

(a) Permittee shall hold harmless and indemnify Customer and its directors, officers, servants, agents, subsidiaries, employees and assignees, or any of them; the United States and its agencies, servants, agents, subsidiaries, employees and assignees, or any of them; and any Part 440 Customer and its directors, officers, servants, agents, subsidiaries, employees and assignees, or any of them, from and against liability, loss or damage arising out of claims that Permittee's Contractors and Subcontractors may have for Property Damage sustained by them and for Bodily Injury or Property Damage sustained by their employees, resulting from Permitted Activities.

(b) Customer shall hold harmless and indemnify Permittee and its directors, officers, servants, agents, subsidiaries, employees and assignees, or any of them; the United States and its agencies, servants, agents, subsidiaries, employees and assignees, or any of them; and any other customer and its directors, officers, servants, agents, subsidiaries, employees and assignees, or any of them, from and against liability, loss or damage arising out of claims that Customer's Contractors, Subcontractors, and customers, may have for Property Damage sustained by them and for Bodily Injury or Property Damage sustained by their employees, resulting from Permitted Activities.

7. Miscellaneous

(a) Nothing contained herein shall be construed as a waiver or release by Permittee or the United States of any claim by an employee of the Permittee or the United States, respectively, including a member of the Armed Forces of the United States, for Bodily Injury or Property Damage, resulting from Permitted Activities.

(b) Notwithstanding any provision of this Agreement to the contrary, any waiver, release, assumption of responsibility, or agreement to hold harmless and indemnify herein shall not apply to claims for Bodily Injury or Property Damage resulting from willful misconduct of any of the Parties, the Contractors and Subcontractors of any of the Parties, and in the case of Permittee and its Contractors and Subcontractors, the directors, officers, agents, and employees of any of the foregoing, and in the case of the United States, its agents.

(c) This Agreement shall be governed by and construed in accordance with United States Federal law.

In witness whereof, the Parties to this Agreement have caused the Agreement to be duly executed by their respective duly authorized representatives as of the date written above.

Permittee

By: ______________________
Its: ______________________

Federal Aviation Administration of the Department of Transportation on Behalf of the United States Government

By: ______________________
Its: ______________________

Associate Administrator for Commercial Space Transportation

PART 2—WAIVER OF CLAIMS AND ASSUMPTION OF RESPONSIBILITY FOR PERMITTED ACTIVITIES WITH ONE CUSTOMER

This agreement is entered into this ____ day of ______, by and among [Permittee] (the "Permittee"), [Customer] (the "Customer") and the Federal Aviation Administration of the Department of Transportation, on behalf of the United States Government (collectively, the "Parties"), to implement the provisions of § 440.17(c) of the Commercial Space Transportation Licensing Regulations, 14 CFR Ch. III (the "Regulations"). This agreement applies to [describe permitted activity]. In consideration of the mutual releases and promises contained herein, the Parties hereby agree as follows:

1. Definitions

Contractors and Subcontractors means entities defined by § 440.3 of the Regulations.

Customer means the above-named Customer.

Part 440 Customer means a customer defined by § 440.3 of the Regulations, other than the above-named customer.

Permit means Permit No. ____ issued on ______, by the Associate Administrator for Commercial Space Transportation, Federal Aviation Administration, Department of Transportation, to the Permittee, including all permit orders issued in connection with the Permit.

Permittee means the holder of the Permit issued under 51 U.S.C. Subtitle V, ch. 509.

United States means the United States and its agencies involved in Permitted Activities.

Except as otherwise defined herein, terms used in this Agreement and defined in 51 U.S.C. Subtitle V, ch. 509—Commercial Space Launch Activities, or in the Regulations, shall have the same meaning as contained in 51 U.S.C. Subtitle V, ch. 509, or the Regulations, respectively.

2. Waiver and Release of Claims

(a) Permittee hereby waives and releases claims it may have against Customer, the United States, any Part 440 Customer, and each of their respective Contractors and Subcontractors, for Property Damage it sustains and for Bodily Injury or Property Damage sustained by its own employees, resulting from Permitted Activities, regardless of fault.

(b) Customer hereby waives and releases claims it may have against Permittee, the United States, any other customer, and each of their respective Contractors and Subcontractors, for Bodily Injury or Property Damage sustained by its own employees, resulting from Permitted Activities, regardless of fault.

(c) The United States hereby waives and releases claims it may have against Permittee, Customer, any Part 440 Customer, and each of their respective Contractors and Subcontractors, for Property Damage it sustains, and for Bodily Injury or Property Damage sustained by its own employees, resulting from Permitted Activities, regardless of fault, to the extent that claims it would otherwise have for such damage or injury exceed the amount of insurance or demonstration of financial responsibility required under § 440.9(c) and (e), respectively, of the Regulations.

3. Assumption of Responsibility

(a) Permittee and Customer shall each be responsible for Property Damage it sustains and for Bodily Injury or Property Damage sustained by its own employees, resulting from Permitted Activities, regardless of fault. Permittee and Customer shall each hold harmless and indemnify each other, the United States, any other customer, and the Contractors and Subcontractors of each, for Bodily Injury or Property Damage sustained by its own employees, resulting from Permitted Activities, regardless of fault.

(b) The United States shall be responsible for Property Damage it sustains, resulting from Permitted Activities, regardless of fault, to the extent that claims it would otherwise have for such damage exceed the amount of insurance or demonstration of financial responsibility required under § 440.9(e) of the Regulations.

4. Extension of Assumption of Responsibility and Waiver and Release of Claims

(a) Permittee shall extend the requirements of the waiver and release of claims, and the assumption of responsibility, hold harmless, and indemnification, as set forth in paragraphs 2(a) and 3(a), respectively, to its Contractors and Subcontractors by requiring them to waive and release all claims they may have against Customer, the United States, any Part 440 Customer, and each of their respective Contractors and Subcontractors, and to agree to be responsible, for Property Damage they sustain and to be responsible, hold harmless and indemnify Customer, the United States, any Part 440 Customer, and each of their respective Contractors and Subcontractors, for Bodily Injury or Property Damage sustained by their own employees, resulting from Permitted Activities, regardless of fault.

(b) Customer shall extend the requirements of the waiver and release of claims, and the assumption of responsibility, hold harmless, and indemnification, as set forth in paragraphs 2(b) and 3(a), respectively, to its customers, Contractors, and Subcontractors, by requiring them to waive and release all claims they may have against Permittee, the United States, any other customer, and each of their respective Contractors and Subcontractors, and to agree to be responsible, for Property Damage they sustain and to be responsible, hold harmless and indemnify Permittee, the United States, any other customer, and each of their respective Contractors and Subcontractors, for Bodily Injury or Property Damage sustained by their own employees, resulting from Permitted Activities, regardless of fault.

(c) The United States shall extend the requirements of the waiver and release of claims, and the assumption of responsibility as set forth in paragraphs 2(c) and 3(b), respectively, to its Contractors and Subcontractors by requiring them to waive and release all claims they may have against Permittee, Customer, any Part 440 Customer, and each of their respective Contractors and Subcontractors, and to agree to be responsible, for any Property Damage they sustain and for any Bodily Injury or Property Damage sustained by their own employees, resulting from Permitted Activities, regardless of fault, to the extent that claims they would otherwise have for such damage or injury exceed the amount of insurance or demonstration of financial responsibility required under §440.9(c) and (e), respectively, of the Regulations.

5. Indemnification

(a) Permittee shall hold harmless and indemnify Customer and its directors, officers, servants, agents, subsidiaries, employees and assignees, or any of them; the United States and its agencies, servants, agents, subsidiaries, employees and assignees, or any of them; and any Part 440 Customer and its directors, officers, servants, agents, subsidiaries, employees and assignees, or any of them, from and against liability, loss or damage arising out of claims that Permittee's Contractors and Subcontractors may have for Property Damage sustained by them and for Bodily Injury or Property Damage sustained by their employees, resulting from Permitted Activities and arising out of the indemnifying party's failure to implement properly the waiver requirement.

(b) Customer shall hold harmless and indemnify Permittee and its directors, officers, servants, agents, subsidiaries, employees and assignees, or any of them; the United States and its agencies, servants, agents, subsidiaries, employees and assignees, or any of them; and any other customer and its directors, officers, servants, agents, subsidiaries, employees and assignees, or any of them, from and against liability, loss or damage arising out of claims that Customer's Contractors, Subcontractors, and customers, may have for Property Damage sustained by them and for Bodily Injury or Property Damage sustained by their employees, resulting from Permitted Activities and arising out of the indemnifying party's failure to implement properly the waiver requirement.

6. Assurances Under 51 U.S.C. 50914(e)

Notwithstanding any provision of this Agreement to the contrary, Permittee shall hold harmless and indemnify the United States and its agencies, servants, agents, employees and assignees, or any of them, from and against liability, loss or damage arising out of claims for Bodily Injury or Property Damage, resulting from Permitted Activities, regardless of fault, except to the extent that: (i) As provided in paragraph 7(b) of this Agreement, claims result from willful misconduct of the United States or its agents; (ii) claims for Property Damage sustained by the United States or its Contractors and Subcontractors exceed the amount of insurance or demonstration of financial responsibility required under §440.9(e) of the Regulations; (iii) claims by a Third Party for Bodily Injury or Property Damage exceed the amount of insurance or demonstration of financial responsibility required under §440.9(c) of the Regulations, and do not exceed $1,500,000,000 (as adjusted for inflation after January 1, 1989) above such amount, and are payable pursuant to the provisions of 51 U.S.C. 50915 and §440.19 of the Regulations; or (iv) Licensee has no liability for claims exceeding $1,500,000,000 (as adjusted for inflation after January 1, 1989) above the amount of insurance or demonstration of financial responsibility required under §440.9(c) of the Regulations.

7. Miscellaneous

(a) Nothing contained herein shall be construed as a waiver or release by Permittee, Customer or the United States of any claim by an employee of the Permittee, Customer or the United States, respectively, including a member of the Armed Forces of the United States, for Bodily Injury or Property Damage, resulting from Permitted Activities.

(b) Notwithstanding any provision of this Agreement to the contrary, any waiver, release, assumption of responsibility or agreement to hold harmless and indemnify herein shall not apply to claims for Bodily Injury or Property Damage resulting from willful misconduct of any of the Parties, the Contractors and Subcontractors of any of the Parties, any Part 440 Customer, the Contractors and Subcontractors of any Part 440 Customer, and in the case of Permittee, Customer, any Part 440 Customer, and the Contractors and Subcontractors of each of them, the directors, officers, agents and employees of any of the foregoing, and in the case of the United States, its agents.

(c) This Agreement shall be governed by and construed in accordance with United States Federal law.

In witness whereof, the Parties to this Agreement have caused the Agreement to be duly executed by their respective duly authorized representatives as of the date written above.

Permittee

By: ____________________
Its: ____________________

Customer

By: ____________________
Its: ____________________

Federal Aviation Administration of the Department of Transportation on Behalf of the United States Government

By: ____________________
Its: ____________________

Associate Administrator for Commercial Space Transportation

PART 3—WAIVER OF CLAIMS AND ASSUMPTION OF RESPONSIBILITY FOR PERMITTED ACTIVITIES WITH MORE THAN ONE CUSTOMER

This agreement is entered into this ____ day of ________, by and among [Permittee] (the "Permittee"); [List of Customers]; (with [List of Customers] hereinafter referred to in their individual capacity as "Customer"); and the Federal Aviation Administration of the Department of Transportation, on behalf of the United States Government (collectively, the "Parties"), to implement the provisions of § 440.17(c) of the Commercial Space Transportation Licensing Regulations, 14 CFR Ch. III (the "Regulations"). This agreement applies to [describe permitted activity].

In consideration of the mutual releases and promises contained herein, the Parties hereby agree as follows:

1. Definitions

Contractors and Subcontractors means entities defined by § 440.3 of the Regulations.

Customer means each above-named Customer.

Part 440 Customer means a customer defined by § 440.3 of the Regulations, other than the above-named Customer.

Permit means Permit No. ____ issued on ________, by the Associate Administrator for Commercial Space Transportation, Federal Aviation Administration, Department of Transportation, to the Permittee, including all permit orders issued in connection with the Permit.

Permittee means the holder of the Permit issued under 51 U.S.C. Subtitle V, ch. 509.

United States means the United States and its agencies involved in Permitted Activities.Except as otherwise defined herein, terms used in this Agreement and defined in 51 U.S.C. Subtitle V, ch. 509—Commercial Space Launch Activities, or in the Regulations, shall have the same meaning as contained in 51 U.S.C. Subtitle V, ch. 509, or the Regulations, respectively.

2. Waiver and Release of Claims

(a) Permittee hereby waives and releases claims it may have against each Customer, the United States, any Part 440 Customer, and each of their respective Contractors and Subcontractors, for Property Damage it sustains and for Bodily Injury or Property Damage sustained by its own employees, resulting from Permitted Activities, regardless of fault.

(b) Each Customer hereby waives and releases claims it may have against Permittee, the United States, any other customer, and each of their Contractors and Subcontractors, for Property Damage it sustains and for Bodily Injury or Property Damage sustained by its own employees, resulting from Permitted Activities, regardless of fault.

(c) The United States hereby waives and releases claims it may have against Permittee, each Customer, any Part 440 Customer, and each of their respective Contractors and Subcontractors, for Property Damage it sustains, and for Bodily Injury or Property Damage sustained by its own employees, resulting from Permitted Activities, regardless of fault, to the extent that claims it would otherwise have for such damage or injury exceed the amount of insurance or demonstration of financial responsibility required under § 440.9(c) and (e), respectively, of the Regulations.

3. Assumption of Responsibility

(a) Permittee and each Customer shall each be responsible for Property Damage it sustains and for Bodily Injury or Property Damage sustained by its own employees, resulting from Permitted Activities, regardless of fault. Permittee and each Customer shall each hold harmless and indemnify each other, the United States, any other customer, and the Contractors and Subcontractors of each, for Bodily Injury or Property Damage sustained by its own employees, resulting from Permitted Activities, regardless of fault.

(b) The United States shall be responsible for Property Damage it sustains, resulting from Permitted Activities, regardless of fault, to the extent that claims it would otherwise have for such damage or injury exceed the amount of insurance or demonstration of financial responsibility required under § 440.9(e) of the Regulations.

4. Extension of Assumption of Responsibility and Waiver and Release of Claims

(a) Permittee shall extend the requirements of the waiver and release of claims, and the assumption of responsibility, hold harmless, and indemnification, as set forth in paragraphs 2(a) and 3(a), respectively, to its Contractors and Subcontractors by requiring them to waive and release all claims they may have against each Customer, the United States, any Part 440 Customer, and each of their respective Contractors and Subcontractors, and to agree to be responsible, for Property Damage they sustain and to be responsible, hold harmless and indemnify each Customer, the United States, any Part 440 Customer, and each of their respective Contractors and Subcontractors, for Bodily Injury or Property Damage sustained by their own employees, resulting from Permitted Activities, regardless of fault.

(b) Each Customer shall extend the requirements of the waiver and release of claims, and the assumption of responsibility, hold harmless, and indemnification, as set forth in paragraphs 2(b) and 3(a), respectively, to its customers, Contractors, and Subcontractors, by requiring them to waive and release all claims they may have against Permittee, the United States, any other customer, and each of their respective Contractors and Subcontractors, and to agree to be responsible, for Property Damage they sustain and to be responsible, hold harmless and indemnify Permittee, the United States, any other customer, and each of their respective Contractors and Subcontractors, for Bodily Injury or Property Damage sustained by their own employees, resulting from Permitted Activities, regardless of fault.

(c) The United States shall extend the requirements of the waiver and release of claims, and the assumption of responsibility as set forth in paragraphs 2(c) and 3(b), respectively, to its Contractors and Subcontractors by requiring them to waive and release all claims they may have against Permittee, each Customer, any Part 440 Customer, and each of their respective Contractors and Subcontractors, and to agree to be responsible, for any Property Damage they sustain and for any Bodily Injury or Property Damage sustained by their own employees, resulting from Permitted Activities, regardless of fault, to the extent that claims they would otherwise have for such damage or injury exceed the amount of insurance or demonstration of financial responsibility required under § 440.9(c) and (e), respectively, of the Regulations.

5. Indemnification

(a) Permittee shall hold harmless and indemnify each Customer and its directors, officers, servants, agents, subsidiaries, employees and assignees, or any of them; the United States and its agencies, servants, agents, subsidiaries, employees and assignees, or any of them; and any Part 440 Customer and its directors, officers, servants, agents, subsidiaries, employees and assignees, or any of them, from and against liability, loss or damage arising out of claims that Permittee's Contractors and Subcontractors may have for Property Damage sustained by them and for Bodily Injury *or Property Damage sustained by their employees, resulting from Permitted Activities* and arising out of the indemnifying party's failure to implement properly the waiver requirement.

(b) Each Customer shall hold harmless and indemnify Permittee and its directors, officers, servants, agents, subsidiaries, employees and assignees, or any of them; the United States and its agencies, servants, agents, subsidiaries, employees and assignees, or any of them; and any other customer and its directors, officers, servants, agents, subsidiaries, employees and assignees, or any of them, from and against liability, loss or damage arising out of claims that each Customer's Contractors, Subcontractors, and customers, may have for Property Damage sustained by them and for Bodily Injury or Property Damage sustained by their employees, resulting from Permitted Activities and arising out of the indemnifying party's failure to implement properly the waiver requirement.

6. Assurances Under 51 U.S.C. 50914(e)

Notwithstanding any provision of this Agreement to the contrary, Permittee shall hold harmless and indemnify the United States and its agencies, servants, agents, employees and assignees, or any of them, from and against liability, loss or damage arising out of claims for Bodily Injury or Property Damage, resulting from Permitted Activities, regardless of fault, except to the extent that: (i) As provided in paragraph 7(b) of this Agreement, claims result from willful misconduct of the United States or its agents; (ii) claims for Property Damage sustained by the United States or its Contractors and Subcontractors exceed the amount of insurance or demonstration of financial responsibility required under § 440.9(e) of the

Regulations; (iii) claims by a Third Party for Bodily Injury or Property Damage exceed the amount of insurance or demonstration of financial responsibility required under §440.9(c) of the Regulations, and do not exceed $1,500,000,000 (as adjusted for inflation after January 1, 1989) above such amount, and are payable pursuant to the provisions of 51 U.S.C. 50915 and §440.19 of the Regulations; or (iv) Licensee has no liability for claims exceeding $1,500,000,000 (as adjusted for inflation after January 1, 1989) above the amount of insurance or demonstration of financial responsibility required under §440.9(c) of the Regulations.

7. Miscellaneous

(a) Nothing contained herein shall be construed as a waiver or release by Permittee, any Customer or the United States of any claim by an employee of the Permittee, any Customer or the United States, respectively, including a member of the Armed Forces of the United States, for Bodily Injury or Property Damage, resulting from Permitted Activities.

(b) Notwithstanding any provision of this Agreement to the contrary, any waiver, release, assumption of responsibility or agreement to hold harmless and indemnify herein shall not apply to claims for Bodily Injury or Property Damage resulting from willful misconduct of any of the Parties, the Contractors and Subcontractors of any of the Parties, any Part 440 Customer, the Contractors and Subcontractors of any Part 440 Customer, and in the case of Permittee, each Customer, any Part 440 Customer, and the Contractors and Subcontractors of each of them, the directors, officers, agents and employees of any of the foregoing, and in the case of the United States, its agents.

(c) References herein to Customer shall apply to, and be deemed to include, each such customer severally and not jointly.

(d) This Agreement shall be governed by and construed in accordance with United States Federal law.

In witness whereof, the Parties to this Agreement have caused the Agreement to be duly executed by their respective duly authorized representatives as of the date written above.

Permittee

By: ________________
Its: ________________

Customer 1

By: ________________
Its: ________________

[Signature lines for each additional customer]

Federal Aviation Administration of the Department of Transportation on Behalf of the United States Government

By: ________________
Its: ________________

[Doc. No. FAA–2014–1012, Amdt. 440–4, 81 FR 55130, Aug. 18, 2016]

APPENDIX D TO PART 440—AGREEMENT FOR WAIVER OF CLAIMS AND ASSUMPTION OF RESPONSIBILITY FOR A CREW MEMBER

THIS AGREEMENT is entered into this ___ day of ______, by and among [name of Crew Member] (the "Crew Member") and the Federal Aviation Administration of the Department of Transportation, on behalf of the United States Government (collectively, the "Parties"), to implement the provisions of section 440.17(f) of the Commercial Space Transportation Licensing Regulations, 14 CFR chapter III (the "Regulations"). This agreement applies to the Crew Member's participation in activities that the FAA has authorized by license or permit during the Crew Member's employment with [Name of licensee or permittee].

In consideration of the mutual releases and promises contained herein, the Parties hereby agree as follows:

1. Definitions

Crew Member means:

(a) The above-named Crew Member,

(b) All the heirs, administrators, executors, assignees, next of kin, and estate of the above-named Crew Member, and

(c) Anyone who attempts to bring a claim on behalf of the Crew Member or for damage or harm arising out of the Bodily Injury, including Death, of the Crew Member.

License/Permit means License/Permit No. ______ issued on ______, by the Associate Administrator for Commercial Space Transportation, Federal Aviation Administration, Department of Transportation, to the Licensee/Permittee, including all license/permit orders issued in connection with the License/Permit.

Licensee/Permittee means the Licensee/Permittee and any transferee of the Licensee under 51 U.S.C. Subtitle V, chapter 509.

United States means the United States and its agencies involved in Licensed/Permitted Activities.

Except as otherwise defined herein, terms used in this Agreement and defined in 51 U.S.C. Subtitle V, chapter 509—Commercial Space Launch Activities, or in the Regulations, shall have the same meaning as contained in 51 U.S.C. Subtitle V, chapter 509, or the Regulations, respectively.

2. Waiver and Release of Claims

(a) Crew Member hereby waives and releases claims it may have against the United States, and against its respective Contractors and Subcontractors, for Bodily Injury, including Death, or Property Damage sustained by Crew Member, resulting from Licensed/Permitted Activities, regardless of fault.

(b) The United States hereby waives and releases claims it may have against the Crew Member for Property Damage it sustains, and for Bodily Injury, including Death, or Property Damage sustained by its own employees, resulting from Licensed/Permitted Activities, regardless of fault.

3. Assumption of Responsibility

(a) The Crew Member shall be responsible for Bodily Injury, including Death, or Property Damage sustained by Crew Member, resulting from Licensed/Permitted Activities, regardless of fault. The Crew Member shall hold harmless the United States, and the Contractors and Subcontractors of each Party, for Bodily Injury, including Death, or Property Damage sustained by Crew Member, resulting from Licensed/Permitted Activities, regardless of fault.

(b) The United States shall be responsible for Property Damage it sustains, and for Bodily Injury, including Death, or Property Damage sustained by its own employees, resulting from Licensed Activities, regardless of fault, to the extent that claims it would otherwise have for such damage or injury exceed the amount of insurance or demonstration of financial responsibility required under sections 440.9(c) and (e), respectively, of the Regulations.

(c) The United States shall be responsible for Property Damage it sustains, resulting from Permitted Activities, regardless of fault, to the extent that claims it would otherwise have for such damage exceed the amount of insurance or demonstration of financial responsibility required under section 440.9(e) of the Regulations.

4. Extension of Assumption of Responsibility and Waiver and Release of Claims

(a) The United States shall extend the requirements of the waiver and release of claims, and the assumption of responsibility as set forth in paragraphs 2(b) and 3(b), respectively, to its Contractors and Subcontractors by requiring them to waive and release all claims they may have against Crew Member and to agree to be responsible, for any Property Damage the Contractors and Subcontractors sustain and for any Bodily Injury, including Death, or Property Damage sustained by their own employees, resulting from Licensed Activities, regardless of fault.

(b) The United States shall extend the requirements of the waiver and release of claims, and the assumption of responsibility as set forth in paragraphs 2(b) and 3(c), respectively, to its Contractors and Subcontractors by requiring them to waive and release all claims the Contractors and Subcontractors may have against Crew Member and to agree to be responsible, for any Property Damage they sustain, resulting from Permitted Activities, regardless of fault.

5. Indemnification

Crew Member shall hold harmless and indemnify the United States and its agencies, servants, agents, subsidiaries, employees and assignees, or any of them, from and against liability, loss, or damage arising out of claims brought by anyone for Property Damage or Bodily Injury, including Death, sustained by Crew Member, resulting from Licensed/Permitted Activities.

6. Assurances Under 51 U.S.C. 50914(e)

Notwithstanding any provision of this Agreement to the contrary, Crew Member shall hold harmless the United States and its agencies, servants, agents, employees and assignees, or any of them, from and against liability, loss or damage arising out of claims for Bodily Injury, including Death, or Property Damage, sustained by Crew Member, resulting from Licensed/Permitted Activities, regardless of fault, except to the extent that, as provided in section 6(b) of this Agreement, claims result from willful misconduct of the United States or its agents.

7. Miscellaneous

(a) Nothing contained herein shall be construed as a waiver or release by the United States of any claim by an employee of the United States, respectively, including a member of the Armed Forces of the United States, for Bodily Injury or Property Damage, resulting from Licensed/Permitted Activities.

(b) Notwithstanding any provision of this Agreement to the contrary, any waiver, release, assumption of responsibility or agreement to hold harmless herein shall not apply to claims for Bodily Injury, including Death, or Property Damage resulting from willful misconduct of any of the Parties, the Contractors and Subcontractors of any of the Parties, and in the case of the United States, its agents.

(c) This Agreement shall be governed by and construed in accordance with United States Federal law.

In witness whereof, the Parties to this Agreement have caused the Agreement to be duly executed by their respective duly authorized representatives as of the date written above.

I [name of Crew Member] have read and understand this agreement and agree that I am bound by it.

Crew Member

Signature: ______________________

Printed Name: ______________________

Federal Aviation Administration of the Department of Transportation on Behalf of the United States Government

By: ______________________

Its: ______________________

Associate Administrator for Commercial Space Transportation

[Doc. No. FAA–2012–0232, 77 FR 20534, Apr. 5, 2012]

APPENDIX E TO PART 440—AGREEMENT FOR WAIVER OF CLAIMS AND ASSUMPTION OF RESPONSIBILITY FOR A SPACE FLIGHT PARTICIPANT

This agreement is entered into this ____ day of ______, by and among [name of Space Flight Participant] (the "Space Flight Participant") and the Federal Aviation Administration of the Department of Transportation, on behalf of the United States Government (collectively, the "Parties"), to implement the provisions of section 440.17(e) of the Commercial Space Transportation Licensing Regulations, 14 CFR chapter III (the "Regulations"). This agreement applies to Space Flight Participant's travel on [name of launch or reentry vehicle] of [name of Licensee or Permittee]. In consideration of the mutual releases and promises contained herein, the Parties hereby agree as follows:

1. Definitions

Space Flight Participant means

(a) The above-named Space Flight Participant,

(b) All the heirs, administrators, executors, assignees, next of kin, and estate of the above-named Space Flight Participant, and

(c) Anyone who attempts to bring a claim on behalf of the Space Flight Participant or for damage or harm arising out of the Bodily Injury, including Death, of the Space Flight Participant.

License/Permit means License/Permit No. ______ issued on ______, by the Associate Administrator for Commercial Space Transportation, Federal Aviation Administration, Department of Transportation, to the Licensee/Permittee, including all license/permit orders issued in connection with the License/Permit.

Licensee/Permittee means the Licensee/Permittee and any transferee of the Licensee under 51 U.S.C. Subtitle V, chapter 509.

United States means the United States and its agencies involved in Licensed/Permitted Activities.

Except as otherwise defined herein, terms used in this Agreement and defined in 51 U.S.C. Subtitle V, chapter 509—Commercial Space Launch Activities, or in the Regulations, shall have the same meaning as contained in 51 U.S.C. Subtitle V, chapter 509, or the Regulations, respectively.

2. Waiver and Release of Claims

(a) Space Flight Participant hereby waives and releases claims it may have against the United States, and against its respective Contractors and Subcontractors, for Bodily Injury, including Death, or Property Damage sustained by Space Flight Participant, resulting from Licensed/Permitted Activities, regardless of fault.

(b) The United States hereby waives and releases claims it may have against Space Flight Participant for Property Damage it sustains, and for Bodily Injury, including Death, or Property Damage sustained by its own employees, resulting from Licensed/Permitted Activities, regardless of fault.

3. Assumption of Responsibility

(a) Space Flight Participant shall be responsible for Bodily Injury, including Death, or Property Damage sustained by the Space Flight Participant resulting from Licensed/Permitted Activities, regardless of fault. Space Flight Participant shall hold harmless the United States, and its Contractors and Subcontractors, for Bodily Injury, including Death, or Property Damage sustained by Space Flight Participant from Licensed/Permitted Activities, regardless of fault.

(b) The United States shall be responsible for Property Damage it sustains, and for Bodily Injury, including Death, or Property Damage sustained by its own employees, resulting from Licensed Activities, regardless of fault, to the extent that claims it would otherwise have for such damage or injury exceed the amount of insurance or demonstration of financial responsibility required under sections 440.9(c) and (e), respectively, of the Regulations.

(c) The United States shall be responsible for Property Damage it sustains, resulting from Permitted Activities, regardless of fault, to the extent that claims it would otherwise have for such damage exceed the amount of insurance or demonstration of financial responsibility required under section 440.9(e) of the Regulations.

4. Extension of Assumption of Responsibility and Waiver and Release of Claims

(a) The United States shall extend the requirements of the waiver and release of claims, and the assumption of responsibility as set forth in paragraphs 2(b) and 3(b), respectively, to its Contractors and Subcontractors by requiring them to waive and release all claims they may have against

Space Flight Participant, and to agree to be responsible, for any Property Damage they sustain and for any Bodily Injury, including Death, or Property Damage sustained by their own employees, resulting from Licensed Activities, regardless of fault.

(b) The United States shall extend the requirements of the waiver and release of claims, and the assumption of responsibility as set forth in paragraphs 2(b) and 3(c), respectively, to its Contractors and Subcontractors by requiring them to waive and release all claims they may have against Space Flight Participant, and to agree to be responsible, for any Property Damage the Contractors and Subcontractors sustain, resulting from Permitted Activities, regardless of fault.

5. Indemnification

Space Flight Participant shall hold harmless and indemnify the United States and its agencies, servants, agents, subsidiaries, employees and assignees, or any of them, from and against liability, loss or damage arising out of claims brought by anyone for Property Damage or Bodily Injury, including Death, sustained by Space Flight Participant, resulting from Licensed/Permitted Activities.

6. Assurances Under 51 U.S.C. 50914(e)

Notwithstanding any provision of this Agreement to the contrary, Space Flight Participant shall hold harmless the United States and its agencies, servants, agents, employees and assignees, or any of them, from and against liability, loss or damage arising out of claims for Bodily Injury, including Death, or Property Damage, sustained by Space Flight Participant, resulting from Licensed/Permitted Activities, regardless of fault, except to the extent that, as provided in section 6(b) of this Agreement, claims result from willful misconduct of the United States or its agents.

7. Miscellaneous

(a) Nothing contained herein shall be construed as a waiver or release by the United States of any claim by an employee of the United States, respectively, including a member of the Armed Forces of the United States, for Bodily Injury or Property Damage, resulting from Licensed/Permitted Activities.

(b) Notwithstanding any provision of this Agreement to the contrary, any waiver, release, assumption of responsibility or agreement to hold harmless herein shall not apply to claims for Bodily Injury, including Death, or Property Damage resulting from willful misconduct of any of the Parties, the Contractors, Subcontractors, and agents of the United States, and Space Flight Participant.

(c) This Agreement shall be governed by and construed in accordance with United States Federal law.

In witness whereof, the Parties to this Agreement have caused the Agreement to be duly executed by their respective duly authorized representatives as of the date written above.

I [name of Space Flight Participant] have read and understand this agreement and agree that I am bound by it.

Space Flight Participant

Signature: ____________________

Printed Name: ____________________

Federal Aviation Administration of the Department of Transportation on Behalf of the United States Government

By: ____________________

Its: ____________________

Associate Administrator for Commercial Space Transportation

[Doc. No. FAA-2012-0232, 77 FR 20535, Apr. 5, 2012]

PARTS 441–459 [RESERVED]

PART 460—HUMAN SPACE FLIGHT REQUIREMENTS

Subpart A—Launch and Reentry with Crew

Subpart B—Launch and Reentry with a Space Flight Participant

AUTHORITY: 51 U.S.C. 50901–50923.

SOURCE: Docket No. FAA-2005-23449, 71 FR 75632, Dec. 15, 2006, unless otherwise noted.

Subpart A—Launch and Reentry with Crew

§ 460.1 Scope.

This subpart establishes requirements for crew of a vehicle whose operator is licensed or permitted under this chapter.

§ 460.3 Applicability.

(a) This subpart applies to:

(1) An applicant for a license or permit under this chapter who proposes to have flight crew on board a vehicle or proposes to employ a remote operator of a vehicle with a human on board.

(2) An operator licensed or permitted under this chapter who has flight crew on board a vehicle or who employs a remote operator of a vehicle with a human on board.

(3) A crew member participating in an activity authorized under this chapter.

(b) Each member of the crew must comply with all requirements of the laws of the United States that apply to crew.

§ 460.5 Crew qualifications and training.

(a) Each crew member must—

(1) Complete training on how to carry out his or her role on board or on the ground so that the vehicle will not harm the public; and

(2) Train for his or her role in nominal and non-nominal conditions. The conditions must include—

(i) Abort scenarios; and

(ii) Emergency operations.

(b) Each member of a flight crew must demonstrate an ability to withstand the stresses of space flight, which may include high acceleration or deceleration, microgravity, and vibration, in sufficient condition to safely carry out his or her duties so that the vehicle will not harm the public.

(c) A pilot and a remote operator must—

(1) Possess and carry an FAA pilot certificate with an instrument rating.

(2) Possess aeronautical knowledge, experience, and skills necessary to pilot and control the launch or reentry vehicle that will operate in the National Airspace System (NAS). Aeronautical experience may include hours in flight, ratings, and training.

(3) Receive vehicle and mission-specific training for each phase of flight by using one or more of the following—

(i) A method or device that simulates the flight;

(ii) An aircraft whose characteristics are similar to the vehicle or that has similar phases of flight to the vehicle ;

(iii) Flight testing; or

(iv) An equivalent method of training approved by the FAA through the license or permit process.

(4) Train in procedures that direct the vehicle away from the public in the event the flight crew abandons the vehicle during flight; and

(5) Train for each mode of control or propulsion, including any transition between modes, such that the pilot or remote operator is able to control the vehicle.

(d) A pilot or a remote operator may demonstrate an equivalent level of safety to paragraph (c)(1) of this section through the license or permit process.

(e) Each crew member with a safety-critical role must possess and carry an FAA second-class airman medical certificate issued in accordance with 14 CFR part 67, no more than 12 months prior to the month of launch and reentry.

[Docket No. FAA–2005–23449, 71 FR 75632, Dec. 15, 2006, as amended by Doc. No. FAA–2016–6761, Amdt. No. 460–2, 83 FR 28535, June 20, 2018]

§ 460.7 Operator training of crew.

(a) *Implementation of training.* An operator must train each member of its crew and define standards for successful completion in accordance with § 460.5.

(b) *Training device fidelity.* An operator must

(1) Ensure that any crew-training device used to meet the training requirements realistically represents the vehicle's configuration and mission, or

(2) Inform the crew member being trained of the differences between the two.

(c) *Maintenance of training records.* An operator must continually update the crew training to ensure that it incorporates lessons learned from training and operational missions. An operator must—

(1) Track each revision and update in writing; and

(2) Document the completed training for each crew member and maintain the documentation for each active crew member.

(d) *Current qualifications and training.* An operator must establish a recurrent training schedule and ensure that all crew qualifications and training required by §460.5 are current before launch and reentry.

§460.9 Informing crew of risk.

An operator must inform in writing any individual serving as crew that the United States Government has not certified the launch vehicle and any reentry vehicle as safe for carrying flight crew or space flight participants. An operator must provide this information—

(a) Before entering into any contract or other arrangement to employ that individual; or

(b) For any crew member employed as of December 23, 2004, as early as possible and prior to any launch in which that individual will participate as crew.

§460.11 Environmental control and life support systems.

(a) An operator must provide atmospheric conditions adequate to sustain life and consciousness for all inhabited areas within a vehicle. The operator or flight crew must monitor and control the following atmospheric conditions in the inhabited areas or demonstrate through the license or permit process that an alternate means provides an equivalent level of safety—

(1) Composition of the atmosphere, which includes oxygen and carbon dioxide, and any revitalization;

(2) Pressure, temperature and humidity;

(3) Contaminants that include particulates and any harmful or hazardous concentrations of gases, or vapors; and

(4) Ventilation and circulation.

(b) An operator must provide an adequate redundant or secondary oxygen supply for the flight crew.

(c) An operator must

(1) Provide a redundant means of preventing cabin depressurization; or

(2) Prevent incapacitation of any of the flight crew in the event of loss of cabin pressure.

§460.13 Smoke detection and fire suppression.

An operator or crew must have the ability to detect smoke and suppress a cabin fire to prevent incapacitation of the flight crew.

§460.15 Human factors.

An operator must take the precautions necessary to account for human factors that can affect a crew's ability to perform safety-critical roles, including in the following safety critical areas—

(a) Design and layout of displays and controls;

(b) Mission planning, which includes analyzing tasks and allocating functions between humans and equipment;

(c) Restraint or stowage of all individuals and objects in a vehicle; and

(d) Vehicle operation, so that the vehicle will be operated in a manner that flight crew can withstand any physical stress factors, such as acceleration, vibration, and noise.

§460.17 Verification program.

An operator must successfully verify the integrated performance of a vehicle's hardware and any software in an operational flight environment before allowing any space flight participant on board during a flight. Verification must include flight testing.

§460.19 Crew waiver of claims against U.S. Government.

Each member of a flight crew and any remote operator must execute a reciprocal waiver of claims with the Federal Aviation Administration of the Department of Transportation in accordance with the requirements of part 440.

§§ 460.20–460.40 [Reserved]

Subpart B—Launch and Reentry with a Space Flight participant

§ 460.41 Scope.

This subpart establishes requirements for space flight participants on board a vehicle whose operator is licensed or permitted under this chapter.

§ 460.43 Applicability.

This subpart applies to:

(a) An applicant for a license or permit under this chapter who proposes to have a space flight participant on board a vehicle;

(b) An operator licensed or permitted under this chapter who has a space flight participant on board a vehicle; and

(c) A space flight participant in an activity authorized under this chapter.

§ 460.45 Operator informing space flight participant of risk.

(a) Before receiving compensation or making an agreement to fly a space flight participant, an operator must satisfy the requirements of this section. An operator must inform each space flight participant in writing about the risks of the launch and reentry, including the safety record of the launch or reentry vehicle type. An operator must present this information in a manner that can be readily understood by a space flight participant with no specialized education or training, and must disclose in writing—

(1) For each mission, each known hazard and risk that could result in a serious injury, death, disability, or total or partial loss of physical and mental function;

(2) That there are hazards that are not known; and

(3) That participation in space flight may result in death, serious injury, or total or partial loss of physical or mental function.

(b) An operator must inform each space flight participant that the United States Government has not certified the launch vehicle and any reentry vehicle as safe for carrying crew or space flight participants.

(c) An operator must inform each space flight participant of the safety record of all launch or reentry vehicles that have carried one or more persons on board, including both U.S. government and private sector vehicles. This information must include—

(1) The total number of people who have been on a suborbital or orbital space flight and the total number of people who have died or been seriously injured on these flights; and

(2) The total number of launches and reentries conducted with people on board and the number of catastrophic failures of those launches and reentries.

(d) An operator must describe the safety record of its vehicle to each space flight participant. The operator's safety record must cover launch and reentry accidents and human space flight incidents that occurred during and after vehicle verification performed in accordance with § 460.17, and include—

(1) The number of vehicle flights;

(2) The number of accidents and human space flight incidents as defined by section 401.5; and

(3) Whether any corrective actions were taken to resolve these accidents and human space flight incidents.

(e) An operator must inform a space flight participant that he or she may request additional information regarding any accidents and human space flight incidents reported.

(f) Before flight, an operator must provide each space flight participant an opportunity to ask questions orally to acquire a better understanding of the hazards and risks of the mission, and each space flight participant must then provide consent in writing to participate in a launch or reentry. The consent must—

(1) Identify the specific launch vehicle the consent covers;

(2) State that the space flight participant understands the risk, and his or her presence on board the launch vehicle is voluntary; and

(3) Be signed and dated by the space flight participant.

§460.47 [Reserved]

§460.49 Space flight participant waiver of claims against U.S. Government.

Each space flight participant must execute a reciprocal waiver of claims with the Federal Aviation Administration of the Department of Transportation in accordance with the requirements of part 440 of this chapter.

§460.51 Space flight participant training.

An operator must train each space flight participant before flight on how to respond to emergency situations, including smoke, fire, loss of cabin pressure, and emergency exit.

§460.53 Security.

An operator must implement security requirements to prevent any space flight participant from jeopardizing the safety of the flight crew or the public. A space flight participant may not carry on board any explosives, firearms, knives, or other weapons.

PARTS 461–1199 [RESERVED]

FINDING AIDS

A list of CFR titles, subtitles, chapters, subchapters and parts and an alphabetical list of agencies publishing in the CFR are included in the CFR Index and Finding Aids volume to the Code of Federal Regulations which is published separately and revised annually.

Table of CFR Titles and Chapters
Alphabetical List of Agencies Appearing in the CFR
List of CFR Sections Affected

Table of CFR Titles and Chapters

(Revised as of January 1, 2019)

Title 1—General Provisions

Title 2—Grants and Agreements

Title 2—Grants and Agreements—Continued

Chap.	
XXVII	Small Business Administration (Parts 2700—2799)
XXVIII	Department of Justice (Parts 2800—2899)
XXIX	Department of Labor (Parts 2900—2999)
XXX	Department of Homeland Security (Parts 3000—3099)
XXXI	Institute of Museum and Library Services (Parts 3100—3199)
XXXII	National Endowment for the Arts (Parts 3200—3299)
XXXIII	National Endowment for the Humanities (Parts 3300—3399)
XXXIV	Department of Education (Parts 3400—3499)
XXXV	Export-Import Bank of the United States (Parts 3500—3599)
XXXVI	Office of National Drug Control Policy, Executive Office of the President (Parts 3600—3699)
XXXVII	Peace Corps (Parts 3700—3799)
LVIII	Election Assistance Commission (Parts 5800—5899)
LIX	Gulf Coast Ecosystem Restoration Council (Parts 5900—5999)

Title 3—The President

I	Executive Office of the President (Parts 100—199)

Title 4—Accounts

I	Government Accountability Office (Parts 1—199)

Title 5—Administrative Personnel

I	Office of Personnel Management (Parts 1—1199)
II	Merit Systems Protection Board (Parts 1200—1299)
III	Office of Management and Budget (Parts 1300—1399)
IV	Office of Personnel Management and Office of the Director of National Intelligence (Parts 1400—1499)
V	The International Organizations Employees Loyalty Board (Parts 1500—1599)
VI	Federal Retirement Thrift Investment Board (Parts 1600—1699)
VIII	Office of Special Counsel (Parts 1800—1899)
IX	Appalachian Regional Commission (Parts 1900—1999)
XI	Armed Forces Retirement Home (Parts 2100—2199)
XIV	Federal Labor Relations Authority, General Counsel of the Federal Labor Relations Authority and Federal Service Impasses Panel (Parts 2400—2499)
XVI	Office of Government Ethics (Parts 2600—2699)
XXI	Department of the Treasury (Parts 3100—3199)
XXII	Federal Deposit Insurance Corporation (Parts 3200—3299)
XXIII	Department of Energy (Parts 3300—3399)
XXIV	Federal Energy Regulatory Commission (Parts 3400—3499)
XXV	Department of the Interior (Parts 3500—3599)
XXVI	Department of Defense (Parts 3600—3699)

Chap.	
XXVIII	Department of Justice (Parts 3800—3899)
XXIX	Federal Communications Commission (Parts 3900—3999)
XXX	Farm Credit System Insurance Corporation (Parts 4000—4099)
XXXI	Farm Credit Administration (Parts 4100—4199)
XXXIII	Overseas Private Investment Corporation (Parts 4300—4399)
XXXIV	Securities and Exchange Commission (Parts 4400—4499)
XXXV	Office of Personnel Management (Parts 4500—4599)
XXXVI	Department of Homeland Security (Parts 4600—4699)
XXXVII	Federal Election Commission (Parts 4700—4799)
XL	Interstate Commerce Commission (Parts 5000—5099)
XLI	Commodity Futures Trading Commission (Parts 5100—5199)
XLII	Department of Labor (Parts 5200—5299)
XLIII	National Science Foundation (Parts 5300—5399)
XLV	Department of Health and Human Services (Parts 5500—5599)
XLVI	Postal Rate Commission (Parts 5600—5699)
XLVII	Federal Trade Commission (Parts 5700—5799)
XLVIII	Nuclear Regulatory Commission (Parts 5800—5899)
XLIX	Federal Labor Relations Authority (Parts 5900—5999)
L	Department of Transportation (Parts 6000—6099)
LII	Export-Import Bank of the United States (Parts 6200—6299)
LIII	Department of Education (Parts 6300—6399)
LIV	Environmental Protection Agency (Parts 6400—6499)
LV	National Endowment for the Arts (Parts 6500—6599)
LVI	National Endowment for the Humanities (Parts 6600—6699)
LVII	General Services Administration (Parts 6700—6799)
LVIII	Board of Governors of the Federal Reserve System (Parts 6800—6899)
LIX	National Aeronautics and Space Administration (Parts 6900—6999)
LX	United States Postal Service (Parts 7000—7099)
LXI	National Labor Relations Board (Parts 7100—7199)
LXII	Equal Employment Opportunity Commission (Parts 7200—7299)
LXIII	Inter-American Foundation (Parts 7300—7399)
LXIV	Merit Systems Protection Board (Parts 7400—7499)
LXV	Department of Housing and Urban Development (Parts 7500—7599)
LXVI	National Archives and Records Administration (Parts 7600—7699)
LXVII	Institute of Museum and Library Services (Parts 7700—7799)
LXVIII	Commission on Civil Rights (Parts 7800—7899)
LXIX	Tennessee Valley Authority (Parts 7900—7999)
LXX	Court Services and Offender Supervision Agency for the District of Columbia (Parts 8000—8099)
LXXI	Consumer Product Safety Commission (Parts 8100—8199)
LXXIII	Department of Agriculture (Parts 8300—8399)

Title 5—Administrative Personnel—Continued

Chap.	
LXXIV	Federal Mine Safety and Health Review Commission (Parts 8400—8499)
LXXVI	Federal Retirement Thrift Investment Board (Parts 8600—8699)
LXXVII	Office of Management and Budget (Parts 8700—8799)
LXXX	Federal Housing Finance Agency (Parts 9000—9099)
LXXXIII	Special Inspector General for Afghanistan Reconstruction (Parts 9300—9399)
LXXXIV	Bureau of Consumer Financial Protection (Parts 9400—9499)
LXXXVI	National Credit Union Administration (Parts 9600—9699)
XCVII	Department of Homeland Security Human Resources Management System (Department of Homeland Security—Office of Personnel Management) (Parts 9700—9799)
XCVIII	Council of the Inspectors General on Integrity and Efficiency (Parts 9800—9899)
XCIX	Military Compensation and Retirement Modernization Commission (Parts 9900—9999)
C	National Council on Disability (Parts 10000—10049)
CI	National Mediation Board (Part 10101)

Title 6—Domestic Security

I	Department of Homeland Security, Office of the Secretary (Parts 1—199)
X	Privacy and Civil Liberties Oversight Board (Parts 1000—1099)

Title 7—Agriculture

	SUBTITLE A—OFFICE OF THE SECRETARY OF AGRICULTURE (PARTS 0—26)
	SUBTITLE B—REGULATIONS OF THE DEPARTMENT OF AGRICULTURE
I	Agricultural Marketing Service (Standards, Inspections, Marketing Practices), Department of Agriculture (Parts 27—209)
II	Food and Nutrition Service, Department of Agriculture (Parts 210—299)
III	Animal and Plant Health Inspection Service, Department of Agriculture (Parts 300—399)
IV	Federal Crop Insurance Corporation, Department of Agriculture (Parts 400—499)
V	Agricultural Research Service, Department of Agriculture (Parts 500—599)
VI	Natural Resources Conservation Service, Department of Agriculture (Parts 600—699)
VII	Farm Service Agency, Department of Agriculture (Parts 700—799)
VIII	Grain Inspection, Packers and Stockyards Administration (Federal Grain Inspection Service), Department of Agriculture (Parts 800—899)

Title 8—Aliens and Nationality

Chap.

I Department of Homeland Security (Immigration and Naturalization) (Parts 1—499)

V Executive Office for Immigration Review, Department of Justice (Parts 1000—1399)

Title 9—Animals and Animal Products

I Animal and Plant Health Inspection Service, Department of Agriculture (Parts 1—199)

II Grain Inspection, Packers and Stockyards Administration (Packers and Stockyards Programs), Department of Agriculture (Parts 200—299)

III Food Safety and Inspection Service, Department of Agriculture (Parts 300—599)

Title 10—Energy

I Nuclear Regulatory Commission (Parts 0—199)

II Department of Energy (Parts 200—699)

III Department of Energy (Parts 700—999)

X Department of Energy (General Provisions) (Parts 1000—1099)

XIII Nuclear Waste Technical Review Board (Parts 1300—1399)

XVII Defense Nuclear Facilities Safety Board (Parts 1700—1799)

XVIII Northeast Interstate Low-Level Radioactive Waste Commission (Parts 1800—1899)

Title 11—Federal Elections

I Federal Election Commission (Parts 1—9099)

II Election Assistance Commission (Parts 9400—9499)

Title 12—Banks and Banking

I Comptroller of the Currency, Department of the Treasury (Parts 1—199)

II Federal Reserve System (Parts 200—299)

III Federal Deposit Insurance Corporation (Parts 300—399)

IV Export-Import Bank of the United States (Parts 400—499)

V (Parts 500—599) [Reserved]

VI Farm Credit Administration (Parts 600—699)

VII National Credit Union Administration (Parts 700—799)

VIII Federal Financing Bank (Parts 800—899)

IX Federal Housing Finance Board (Parts 900—999)

X Bureau of Consumer Financial Protection (Parts 1000—1099)

XI Federal Financial Institutions Examination Council (Parts 1100—1199)

XII Federal Housing Finance Agency (Parts 1200—1299)

XIII Financial Stability Oversight Council (Parts 1300—1399)

Title 12—Banks and Banking—Continued

Chap.

XIV Farm Credit System Insurance Corporation (Parts 1400—1499)

XV Department of the Treasury (Parts 1500—1599)

XVI Office of Financial Research (Parts 1600—1699)

XVII Office of Federal Housing Enterprise Oversight, Department of Housing and Urban Development (Parts 1700—1799)

XVIII Community Development Financial Institutions Fund, Department of the Treasury (Parts 1800—1899)

Title 13—Business Credit and Assistance

I Small Business Administration (Parts 1—199)

III Economic Development Administration, Department of Commerce (Parts 300—399)

IV Emergency Steel Guarantee Loan Board (Parts 400—499)

V Emergency Oil and Gas Guaranteed Loan Board (Parts 500—599)

Title 14—Aeronautics and Space

I Federal Aviation Administration, Department of Transportation (Parts 1—199)

II Office of the Secretary, Department of Transportation (Aviation Proceedings) (Parts 200—399)

III Commercial Space Transportation, Federal Aviation Administration, Department of Transportation (Parts 400—1199)

V National Aeronautics and Space Administration (Parts 1200—1299)

VI Air Transportation System Stabilization (Parts 1300—1399)

Title 15—Commerce and Foreign Trade

SUBTITLE A—OFFICE OF THE SECRETARY OF COMMERCE (PARTS 0—29)

SUBTITLE B—REGULATIONS RELATING TO COMMERCE AND FOREIGN TRADE

I Bureau of the Census, Department of Commerce (Parts 30—199)

II National Institute of Standards and Technology, Department of Commerce (Parts 200—299)

III International Trade Administration, Department of Commerce (Parts 300—399)

IV Foreign-Trade Zones Board, Department of Commerce (Parts 400—499)

VII Bureau of Industry and Security, Department of Commerce (Parts 700—799)

VIII Bureau of Economic Analysis, Department of Commerce (Parts 800—899)

IX National Oceanic and Atmospheric Administration, Department of Commerce (Parts 900—999)

XI National Technical Information Service, Department of Commerce (Parts 1100—1199)

Title 15—Commerce and Foreign Trade—Continued

Title 16—Commercial Practices

Title 17—Commodity and Securities Exchanges

Title 18—Conservation of Power and Water Resources

Title 19—Customs Duties

Title 20—Employees' Benefits

Title 20—Employees' Benefits—Continued

Chap.

IV Employees' Compensation Appeals Board, Department of Labor (Parts 500—599)

V Employment and Training Administration, Department of Labor (Parts 600—699)

VI Office of Workers' Compensation Programs, Department of Labor (Parts 700—799)

VII Benefits Review Board, Department of Labor (Parts 800—899)

VIII Joint Board for the Enrollment of Actuaries (Parts 900—999)

IX Office of the Assistant Secretary for Veterans' Employment and Training Service, Department of Labor (Parts 1000—1099)

Title 21—Food and Drugs

I Food and Drug Administration, Department of Health and Human Services (Parts 1—1299)

II Drug Enforcement Administration, Department of Justice (Parts 1300—1399)

III Office of National Drug Control Policy (Parts 1400—1499)

Title 22—Foreign Relations

I Department of State (Parts 1—199)

II Agency for International Development (Parts 200—299)

III Peace Corps (Parts 300—399)

IV International Joint Commission, United States and Canada (Parts 400—499)

V Broadcasting Board of Governors (Parts 500—599)

VII Overseas Private Investment Corporation (Parts 700—799)

IX Foreign Service Grievance Board (Parts 900—999)

X Inter-American Foundation (Parts 1000—1099)

XI International Boundary and Water Commission, United States and Mexico, United States Section (Parts 1100—1199)

XII United States International Development Cooperation Agency (Parts 1200—1299)

XIII Millennium Challenge Corporation (Parts 1300—1399)

XIV Foreign Service Labor Relations Board; Federal Labor Relations Authority; General Counsel of the Federal Labor Relations Authority; and the Foreign Service Impasse Disputes Panel (Parts 1400—1499)

XV African Development Foundation (Parts 1500—1599)

XVI Japan-United States Friendship Commission (Parts 1600—1699)

XVII United States Institute of Peace (Parts 1700—1799)

Title 23—Highways

I Federal Highway Administration, Department of Transportation (Parts 1—999)

Title 23—Highways—Continued

Chap.

II National Highway Traffic Safety Administration and Federal Highway Administration, Department of Transportation (Parts 1200—1299)

III National Highway Traffic Safety Administration, Department of Transportation (Parts 1300—1399)

Title 24—Housing and Urban Development

SUBTITLE A—OFFICE OF THE SECRETARY, DEPARTMENT OF HOUSING AND URBAN DEVELOPMENT (PARTS 0—99)

SUBTITLE B—REGULATIONS RELATING TO HOUSING AND URBAN DEVELOPMENT

I Office of Assistant Secretary for Equal Opportunity, Department of Housing and Urban Development (Parts 100—199)

II Office of Assistant Secretary for Housing-Federal Housing Commissioner, Department of Housing and Urban Development (Parts 200—299)

III Government National Mortgage Association, Department of Housing and Urban Development (Parts 300—399)

IV Office of Housing and Office of Multifamily Housing Assistance Restructuring, Department of Housing and Urban Development (Parts 400—499)

V Office of Assistant Secretary for Community Planning and Development, Department of Housing and Urban Development (Parts 500—599)

VI Office of Assistant Secretary for Community Planning and Development, Department of Housing and Urban Development (Parts 600—699) [Reserved]

VII Office of the Secretary, Department of Housing and Urban Development (Housing Assistance Programs and Public and Indian Housing Programs) (Parts 700—799)

VIII Office of the Assistant Secretary for Housing—Federal Housing Commissioner, Department of Housing and Urban Development (Section 8 Housing Assistance Programs, Section 202 Direct Loan Program, Section 202 Supportive Housing for the Elderly Program and Section 811 Supportive Housing for Persons With Disabilities Program) (Parts 800—899)

IX Office of Assistant Secretary for Public and Indian Housing, Department of Housing and Urban Development (Parts 900—1699)

XII Office of Inspector General, Department of Housing and Urban Development (Parts 2000—2099)

XV Emergency Mortgage Insurance and Loan Programs, Department of Housing and Urban Development (Parts 2700—2799) [Reserved]

XX Office of Assistant Secretary for Housing—Federal Housing Commissioner, Department of Housing and Urban Development (Parts 3200—3899)

XXIV Board of Directors of the HOPE for Homeowners Program (Parts 4000—4099) [Reserved]

XXV Neighborhood Reinvestment Corporation (Parts 4100—4199)

Title 25—Indians

Chap.

I Bureau of Indian Affairs, Department of the Interior (Parts 1—299)

II Indian Arts and Crafts Board, Department of the Interior (Parts 300—399)

III National Indian Gaming Commission, Department of the Interior (Parts 500—599)

IV Office of Navajo and Hopi Indian Relocation (Parts 700—899)

V Bureau of Indian Affairs, Department of the Interior, and Indian Health Service, Department of Health and Human Services (Part 900—999)

VI Office of the Assistant Secretary, Indian Affairs, Department of the Interior (Parts 1000—1199)

VII Office of the Special Trustee for American Indians, Department of the Interior (Parts 1200—1299)

Title 26—Internal Revenue

I Internal Revenue Service, Department of the Treasury (Parts 1—End)

Title 27—Alcohol, Tobacco Products and Firearms

I Alcohol and Tobacco Tax and Trade Bureau, Department of the Treasury (Parts 1—399)

II Bureau of Alcohol, Tobacco, Firearms, and Explosives, Department of Justice (Parts 400—699)

Title 28—Judicial Administration

I Department of Justice (Parts 0—299)

III Federal Prison Industries, Inc., Department of Justice (Parts 300—399)

V Bureau of Prisons, Department of Justice (Parts 500—599)

VI Offices of Independent Counsel, Department of Justice (Parts 600—699)

VII Office of Independent Counsel (Parts 700—799)

VIII Court Services and Offender Supervision Agency for the District of Columbia (Parts 800—899)

IX National Crime Prevention and Privacy Compact Council (Parts 900—999)

XI Department of Justice and Department of State (Parts 1100—1199)

Title 29—Labor

SUBTITLE A—OFFICE OF THE SECRETARY OF LABOR (PARTS 0—99)

SUBTITLE B—REGULATIONS RELATING TO LABOR

I National Labor Relations Board (Parts 100—199)

Title 29—Labor—Continued

Chap.

II Office of Labor-Management Standards, Department of Labor (Parts 200—299)

III National Railroad Adjustment Board (Parts 300—399)

IV Office of Labor-Management Standards, Department of Labor (Parts 400—499)

V Wage and Hour Division, Department of Labor (Parts 500—899)

IX Construction Industry Collective Bargaining Commission (Parts 900—999)

X National Mediation Board (Parts 1200—1299)

XII Federal Mediation and Conciliation Service (Parts 1400—1499)

XIV Equal Employment Opportunity Commission (Parts 1600—1699)

XVII Occupational Safety and Health Administration, Department of Labor (Parts 1900—1999)

XX Occupational Safety and Health Review Commission (Parts 2200—2499)

XXV Employee Benefits Security Administration, Department of Labor (Parts 2500—2599)

XXVII Federal Mine Safety and Health Review Commission (Parts 2700—2799)

XL Pension Benefit Guaranty Corporation (Parts 4000—4999)

Title 30—Mineral Resources

I Mine Safety and Health Administration, Department of Labor (Parts 1—199)

II Bureau of Safety and Environmental Enforcement, Department of the Interior (Parts 200—299)

IV Geological Survey, Department of the Interior (Parts 400—499)

V Bureau of Ocean Energy Management, Department of the Interior (Parts 500—599)

VII Office of Surface Mining Reclamation and Enforcement, Department of the Interior (Parts 700—999)

XII Office of Natural Resources Revenue, Department of the Interior (Parts 1200—1299)

Title 31—Money and Finance: Treasury

SUBTITLE A—OFFICE OF THE SECRETARY OF THE TREASURY (PARTS 0 50)

SUBTITLE B—REGULATIONS RELATING TO MONEY AND FINANCE

I Monetary Offices, Department of the Treasury (Parts 51—199)

II Fiscal Service, Department of the Treasury (Parts 200—399)

IV Secret Service, Department of the Treasury (Parts 400—499)

V Office of Foreign Assets Control, Department of the Treasury (Parts 500—599)

VI Bureau of Engraving and Printing, Department of the Treasury (Parts 600—699)

VII Federal Law Enforcement Training Center, Department of the Treasury (Parts 700—799)

Title 31—Money and Finance: Treasury—Continued

Title 32—National Defense

Title 33—Navigation and Navigable Waters

Title 34—Education

Title 34—Education—Continued

Chap.

IV Office of Career, Technical and Adult Education, Department of Education (Parts 400—499)

V Office of Bilingual Education and Minority Languages Affairs, Department of Education (Parts 500—599) [Reserved]

VI Office of Postsecondary Education, Department of Education (Parts 600—699)

VII Office of Educational Research and Improvement, Department of Education (Parts 700—799) [Reserved]

SUBTITLE C—REGULATIONS RELATING TO EDUCATION

XI (Parts 1100—1199) [Reserved]

XII National Council on Disability (Parts 1200—1299)

Title 35 [Reserved]

Title 36—Parks, Forests, and Public Property

I National Park Service, Department of the Interior (Parts 1—199)

II Forest Service, Department of Agriculture (Parts 200—299)

III Corps of Engineers, Department of the Army (Parts 300—399)

IV American Battle Monuments Commission (Parts 400—499)

V Smithsonian Institution (Parts 500—599)

VI [Reserved]

VII Library of Congress (Parts 700—799)

VIII Advisory Council on Historic Preservation (Parts 800—899)

IX Pennsylvania Avenue Development Corporation (Parts 900—999)

X Presidio Trust (Parts 1000—1099)

XI Architectural and Transportation Barriers Compliance Board (Parts 1100—1199)

XII National Archives and Records Administration (Parts 1200—1299)

XV Oklahoma City National Memorial Trust (Parts 1500—1599)

XVI Morris K. Udall Scholarship and Excellence in National Environmental Policy Foundation (Parts 1600—1699)

Title 37—Patents, Trademarks, and Copyrights

I United States Patent and Trademark Office, Department of Commerce (Parts 1—199)

II U.S. Copyright Office, Library of Congress (Parts 200—299)

III Copyright Royalty Board, Library of Congress (Parts 300—399)

IV National Institute of Standards and Technology, Department of Commerce (Parts 400—599)

Title 38—Pensions, Bonuses, and Veterans' Relief

I Department of Veterans Affairs (Parts 0—199)

II Armed Forces Retirement Home (Parts 200—299)

Title 39—Postal Service

Title 40—Protection of Environment

Title 41—Public Contracts and Property Management

Title 42—Public Health

Title 43—Public Lands: Interior

Title 44—Emergency Management and Assistance

Title 45—Public Welfare

Title 45—Public Welfare—Continued

Chap.	
V	Foreign Claims Settlement Commission of the United States, Department of Justice (Parts 500—599)
VI	National Science Foundation (Parts 600—699)
VII	Commission on Civil Rights (Parts 700—799)
VIII	Office of Personnel Management (Parts 800—899)
IX	Denali Commission (Parts 900—999)
X	Office of Community Services, Administration for Children and Families, Department of Health and Human Services (Parts 1000—1099)
XI	National Foundation on the Arts and the Humanities (Parts 1100—1199)
XII	Corporation for National and Community Service (Parts 1200—1299)
XIII	Administration for Children and Families, Department of Health and Human Services (Parts 1300—1399)
XVI	Legal Services Corporation (Parts 1600—1699)
XVII	National Commission on Libraries and Information Science (Parts 1700—1799)
XVIII	Harry S. Truman Scholarship Foundation (Parts 1800—1899)
XXI	Commission of Fine Arts (Parts 2100—2199)
XXIII	Arctic Research Commission (Parts 2300—2399)
XXIV	James Madison Memorial Fellowship Foundation (Parts 2400—2499)
XXV	Corporation for National and Community Service (Parts 2500—2599)

Title 46—Shipping

I	Coast Guard, Department of Homeland Security (Parts 1—199)
II	Maritime Administration, Department of Transportation (Parts 200—399)
III	Coast Guard (Great Lakes Pilotage), Department of Homeland Security (Parts 400—499)
IV	Federal Maritime Commission (Parts 500—599)

Title 47—Telecommunication

I	Federal Communications Commission (Parts 0—199)
II	Office of Science and Technology Policy and National Security Council (Parts 200—299)
III	National Telecommunications and Information Administration, Department of Commerce (Parts 300—399)
IV	National Telecommunications and Information Administration, Department of Commerce, and National Highway Traffic Safety Administration, Department of Transportation (Parts 400—499)
V	The First Responder Network Authority (Parts 500—599)

Title 48—Federal Acquisition Regulations System

Chap.

1 Federal Acquisition Regulation (Parts 1—99)

2 Defense Acquisition Regulations System, Department of Defense (Parts 200—299)

3 Department of Health and Human Services (Parts 300—399)

4 Department of Agriculture (Parts 400—499)

5 General Services Administration (Parts 500—599)

6 Department of State (Parts 600—699)

7 Agency for International Development (Parts 700—799)

8 Department of Veterans Affairs (Parts 800—899)

9 Department of Energy (Parts 900—999)

10 Department of the Treasury (Parts 1000—1099)

12 Department of Transportation (Parts 1200—1299)

13 Department of Commerce (Parts 1300—1399)

14 Department of the Interior (Parts 1400—1499)

15 Environmental Protection Agency (Parts 1500—1599)

16 Office of Personnel Management, Federal Employees Health Benefits Acquisition Regulation (Parts 1600—1699)

17 Office of Personnel Management (Parts 1700—1799)

18 National Aeronautics and Space Administration (Parts 1800—1899)

19 Broadcasting Board of Governors (Parts 1900—1999)

20 Nuclear Regulatory Commission (Parts 2000—2099)

21 Office of Personnel Management, Federal Employees Group Life Insurance Federal Acquisition Regulation (Parts 2100—2199)

23 Social Security Administration (Parts 2300—2399)

24 Department of Housing and Urban Development (Parts 2400—2499)

25 National Science Foundation (Parts 2500—2599)

28 Department of Justice (Parts 2800—2899)

29 Department of Labor (Parts 2900—2999)

30 Department of Homeland Security, Homeland Security Acquisition Regulation (HSAR) (Parts 3000—3099)

34 Department of Education Acquisition Regulation (Parts 3400—3499)

51 Department of the Army Acquisition Regulations (Parts 5100—5199)

52 Department of the Navy Acquisition Regulations (Parts 5200—5299)

53 Department of the Air Force Federal Acquisition Regulation Supplement (Parts 5300—5399) [Reserved]

54 Defense Logistics Agency, Department of Defense (Parts 5400—5499)

57 African Development Foundation (Parts 5700—5799)

61 Civilian Board of Contract Appeals, General Services Administration (Parts 6100—6199)

99 Cost Accounting Standards Board, Office of Federal Procurement Policy, Office of Management and Budget (Parts 9900—9999)

Title 49—Transportation

Title 50—Wildlife and Fisheries

Alphabetical List of Agencies Appearing in the CFR

(Revised as of January 1, 2019)

Agency	CFR Title, Subtitle or Chapter
Administrative Conference of the United States	1, III
Advisory Council on Historic Preservation	36, VIII
Advocacy and Outreach, Office of	7, XXV
Afghanistan Reconstruction, Special Inspector General for	5, LXXXIII
African Development Foundation	22, XV
Federal Acquisition Regulation	48, 57
Agency for International Development	2, VII; 22, II
Federal Acquisition Regulation	48, 7
Agricultural Marketing Service	7, I, IX, X, XI
Agricultural Research Service	7, V
Agriculture, Department of	2, IV; 5, LXXIII
Advocacy and Outreach, Office of	7, XXV
Agricultural Marketing Service	7, I, IX, X, XI
Agricultural Research Service	7, V
Animal and Plant Health Inspection Service	7, III; 9, I
Chief Financial Officer, Office of	7, XXX
Commodity Credit Corporation	7, XIV
Economic Research Service	7, XXXVII
Energy Policy and New Uses, Office of	2, IX; 7, XXIX
Environmental Quality, Office of	7, XXXI
Farm Service Agency	7, VII, XVIII
Federal Acquisition Regulation	48, 4
Federal Crop Insurance Corporation	7, IV
Food and Nutrition Service	7, II
Food Safety and Inspection Service	9, III
Foreign Agricultural Service	7, XV
Forest Service	36, II
Grain Inspection, Packers and Stockyards Administration	7, VIII; 9, II
Information Resources Management, Office of	7, XXVII
Inspector General, Office of	7, XXVI
National Agricultural Library	7, XLI
National Agricultural Statistics Service	7, XXXVI
National Institute of Food and Agriculture	7, XXXIV
Natural Resources Conservation Service	7, VI
Operations, Office of	7, XXVIII
Procurement and Property Management, Office of	7, XXXII
Rural Business-Cooperative Service	7, XVIII, XLII
Rural Development Administration	7, XLII
Rural Housing Service	7, XVIII, XXXV
Rural Telephone Bank	7, XVI
Rural Utilities Service	7, XVII, XVIII, XLII
Secretary of Agriculture, Office of	7, Subtitle A
Transportation, Office of	7, XXXIII
World Agricultural Outlook Board	7, XXXVIII
Air Force, Department of	32, VII
Federal Acquisition Regulation Supplement	48, 53
Air Transportation Stabilization Board	14, VI
Alcohol and Tobacco Tax and Trade Bureau	27, I
Alcohol, Tobacco, Firearms, and Explosives, Bureau of	27, II
AMTRAK	49, VII
American Battle Monuments Commission	36, IV
American Indians, Office of the Special Trustee	25, VII
Animal and Plant Health Inspection Service	7, III; 9, I

Agency	CFR Title, Subtitle or Chapter
Appalachian Regional Commission	5, IX
Architectural and Transportation Barriers Compliance Board	36, XI
Arctic Research Commission	45, XXIII
Armed Forces Retirement Home	5, XI
Army, Department of	32, V
Engineers, Corps of	33, II; 36, III
Federal Acquisition Regulation	48, 51
Bilingual Education and Minority Languages Affairs, Office of	34, V
Blind or Severely Disabled, Committee for Purchase from People Who Are	41, 51
Broadcasting Board of Governors	22, V
Federal Acquisition Regulation	48, 19
Career, Technical, and Adult Education, Office of	34, IV
Census Bureau	15, I
Centers for Medicare & Medicaid Services	42, IV
Central Intelligence Agency	32, XIX
Chemical Safety and Hazardous Investigation Board	40, VI
Chief Financial Officer, Office of	7, XXX
Child Support Enforcement, Office of	45, III
Children and Families, Administration for	45, II, III, IV, X, XIII
Civil Rights, Commission on	5, LXVIII; 45, VII
Civil Rights, Office for	34, I
Council of the Inspectors General on Integrity and Efficiency	5, XCVIII
Court Services and Offender Supervision Agency for the District of Columbia	5, LXX
Coast Guard	33, I; 46, I; 49, IV
Coast Guard (Great Lakes Pilotage)	46, III
Commerce, Department of	2, XIII; 44, IV; 50, VI
Census Bureau	15, I
Economic Analysis, Bureau of	15, VIII
Economic Development Administration	13, III
Emergency Management and Assistance	44, IV
Federal Acquisition Regulation	48, 13
Foreign-Trade Zones Board	15, IV
Industry and Security, Bureau of	15, VII
International Trade Administration	15, III; 19, III
National Institute of Standards and Technology	15, II; 37, IV
National Marine Fisheries Service	50, II, IV
National Oceanic and Atmospheric Administration	15, IX; 50, II, III, IV, VI
National Technical Information Service	15, XI
National Telecommunications and Information Administration	15, XXIII; 47, III, IV
National Weather Service	15, IX
Patent and Trademark Office, United States	37, I
Secretary of Commerce, Office of	15, Subtitle A
Commercial Space Transportation	14, III
Commodity Credit Corporation	7, XIV
Commodity Futures Trading Commission	5, XLI; 17, I
Community Planning and Development, Office of Assistant Secretary for	24, V, VI
Community Services, Office of	45, X
Comptroller of the Currency	12, I
Construction Industry Collective Bargaining Commission	29, IX
Consumer Financial Protection Bureau	5, LXXXIV; 12, X
Consumer Product Safety Commission	5, LXXI; 16, II
Copyright Royalty Board	37, III
Corporation for National and Community Service	2, XXII; 45, XII, XXV
Cost Accounting Standards Board	48, 99
Council on Environmental Quality	40, V
Court Services and Offender Supervision Agency for the District of Columbia	5, LXX; 28, VIII
Customs and Border Protection	19, I
Defense Contract Audit Agency	32, I
Defense, Department of	2, XI; 5, XXVI; 32, Subtitle A; 40, VII
Advanced Research Projects Agency	32, I
Air Force Department	32, VII

Agency	CFR Title, Subtitle or Chapter
Army Department	32, V; 33, II; 36, III; 48, 51
Defense Acquisition Regulations System	48, 2
Defense Intelligence Agency	32, I
Defense Logistics Agency	32, I, XII; 48, 54
Engineers, Corps of	33, II; 36, III
National Imagery and Mapping Agency	32, I
Navy Department	32, VI; 48, 52
Secretary of Defense, Office of	2, XI; 32, I
Defense Contract Audit Agency	32, I
Defense Intelligence Agency	32, I
Defense Logistics Agency	32, XII; 48, 54
Defense Nuclear Facilities Safety Board	10, XVII
Delaware River Basin Commission	18, III
Denali Commission	45, IX
Disability, National Council on	5, C; 34, XII
District of Columbia, Court Services and Offender Supervision Agency for the	5, LXX; 28, VIII
Drug Enforcement Administration	21, II
East-West Foreign Trade Board	15, XIII
Economic Analysis, Bureau of	15, VIII
Economic Development Administration	13, III
Economic Research Service	7, XXXVII
Education, Department of	2, XXXIV; 5, LIII
Bilingual Education and Minority Languages Affairs, Office of	34, V
Career, Technical, and Adult Education, Office of	34, IV
Civil Rights, Office for	34, I
Educational Research and Improvement, Office of	34, VII
Elementary and Secondary Education, Office of	34, II
Federal Acquisition Regulation	48, 34
Postsecondary Education, Office of	34, VI
Secretary of Education, Office of	34, Subtitle A
Special Education and Rehabilitative Services, Office of	34, III
Educational Research and Improvement, Office of	34, VII
Election Assistance Commission	2, LVIII; 11, II
Elementary and Secondary Education, Office of	34, II
Emergency Oil and Gas Guaranteed Loan Board	13, V
Emergency Steel Guarantee Loan Board	13, IV
Employee Benefits Security Administration	29, XXV
Employees' Compensation Appeals Board	20, IV
Employees Loyalty Board	5, V
Employment and Training Administration	20, V
Employment Policy, National Commission for	1, IV
Employment Standards Administration	20, VI
Endangered Species Committee	50, IV
Energy, Department of	2, IX; 5, XXIII; 10, II, III, X
Federal Acquisition Regulation	48, 9
Federal Energy Regulatory Commission	5, XXIV; 18, I
Property Management Regulations	41, 109
Energy, Office of	7, XXIX
Engineers, Corps of	33, II; 36, III
Engraving and Printing, Bureau of	31, VI
Environmental Protection Agency	2, XV; 5, LIV; 40, I, IV, VII
Federal Acquisition Regulation	48, 15
Property Management Regulations	41, 115
Environmental Quality, Office of	7, XXXI
Equal Employment Opportunity Commission	5, LXII; 29, XIV
Equal Opportunity, Office of Assistant Secretary for	24, I
Executive Office of the President	3, I
Environmental Quality, Council on	40, V
Management and Budget, Office of	2, Subtitle A; 5, III, LXXVII; 14, VI; 48, 99
National Drug Control Policy, Office of	2, XXXVI; 21, III
National Security Council	32, XXI; 47, 2

Agency	CFR Title, Subtitle or Chapter
Presidential Documents	3
Science and Technology Policy, Office of	32, XXIV; 47, II
Trade Representative, Office of the United States	15, XX
Export-Import Bank of the United States	2, XXXV; 5, LII; 12, IV
Family Assistance, Office of	45, II
Farm Credit Administration	5, XXXI; 12, VI
Farm Credit System Insurance Corporation	5, XXX; 12, XIV
Farm Service Agency	7, VII, XVIII
Federal Acquisition Regulation	48, 1
Federal Aviation Administration	14, I
Commercial Space Transportation	14, III
Federal Claims Collection Standards	31, IX
Federal Communications Commission	5, XXIX; 47, I
Federal Contract Compliance Programs, Office of	41, 60
Federal Crop Insurance Corporation	7, IV
Federal Deposit Insurance Corporation	5, XXII; 12, III
Federal Election Commission	5, XXXVII; 11, I
Federal Emergency Management Agency	44, I
Federal Employees Group Life Insurance Federal Acquisition Regulation	48, 21
Federal Employees Health Benefits Acquisition Regulation	48, 16
Federal Energy Regulatory Commission	5, XXIV; 18, I
Federal Financial Institutions Examination Council	12, XI
Federal Financing Bank	12, VIII
Federal Highway Administration	23, I, II
Federal Home Loan Mortgage Corporation	1, IV
Federal Housing Enterprise Oversight Office	12, XVII
Federal Housing Finance Agency	5, LXXX; 12, XII
Federal Housing Finance Board	12, IX
Federal Labor Relations Authority	5, XIV, XLIX; 22, XIV
Federal Law Enforcement Training Center	31, VII
Federal Management Regulation	41, 102
Federal Maritime Commission	46, IV
Federal Mediation and Conciliation Service	29, XII
Federal Mine Safety and Health Review Commission	5, LXXIV; 29, XXVII
Federal Motor Carrier Safety Administration	49, III
Federal Prison Industries, Inc.	28, III
Federal Procurement Policy Office	48, 99
Federal Property Management Regulations	41, 101
Federal Railroad Administration	49, II
Federal Register, Administrative Committee of	1, I
Federal Register, Office of	1, II
Federal Reserve System	12, II
Board of Governors	5, LVIII
Federal Retirement Thrift Investment Board	5, VI, LXXVI
Federal Service Impasses Panel	5, XIV
Federal Trade Commission	5, XLVII; 16, I
Federal Transit Administration	49, VI
Federal Travel Regulation System	41, Subtitle F
Financial Crimes Enforcement Network	31, X
Financial Research Office	12, XVI
Financial Stability Oversight Council	12, XIII
Fine Arts, Commission of	45, XXI
Fiscal Service	31, II
Fish and Wildlife Service, United States	50, I, IV
Food and Drug Administration	21, I
Food and Nutrition Service	7, II
Food Safety and Inspection Service	9, III
Foreign Agricultural Service	7, XV
Foreign Assets Control, Office of	31, V
Foreign Claims Settlement Commission of the United States	45, V
Foreign Service Grievance Board	22, IX
Foreign Service Impasse Disputes Panel	22, XIV
Foreign Service Labor Relations Board	22, XIV
Foreign-Trade Zones Board	15, IV
Forest Service	36, II
General Services Administration	5, LVII; 41, 105

Agency	CFR Title, Subtitle or Chapter
Contract Appeals, Board of	48, 61
Federal Acquisition Regulation	48, 5
Federal Management Regulation	41, 102
Federal Property Management Regulations	41, 101
Federal Travel Regulation System	41, Subtitle F
General	41, 300
Payment From a Non-Federal Source for Travel Expenses	41, 304
Payment of Expenses Connected With the Death of Certain Employees	41, 303
Relocation Allowances	41, 302
Temporary Duty (TDY) Travel Allowances	41, 301
Geological Survey	30, IV
Government Accountability Office	4, I
Government Ethics, Office of	5, XVI
Government National Mortgage Association	24, III
Grain Inspection, Packers and Stockyards Administration	7, VIII; 9, II
Gulf Coast Ecosystem Restoration Council	2, LIX; 40, VIII
Harry S. Truman Scholarship Foundation	45, XVIII
Health and Human Services, Department of	2, III; 5, XLV; 45, Subtitle A
Centers for Medicare & Medicaid Services	42, IV
Child Support Enforcement, Office of	45, III
Children and Families, Administration for	45, II, III, IV, X, XIII
Community Services, Office of	45, X
Family Assistance, Office of	45, II
Federal Acquisition Regulation	48, 3
Food and Drug Administration	21, I
Indian Health Service	25, V
Inspector General (Health Care), Office of	42, V
Public Health Service	42, I
Refugee Resettlement, Office of	45, IV
Homeland Security, Department of	2, XXX; 5, XXXVI; 6, I; 8, I
Coast Guard	33, I; 46, I; 49, IV
Coast Guard (Great Lakes Pilotage)	46, III
Customs and Border Protection	19, I
Federal Emergency Management Agency	44, I
Human Resources Management and Labor Relations Systems	5, XCVII
Immigration and Customs Enforcement Bureau	19, IV
Transportation Security Administration	49, XII
HOPE for Homeowners Program, Board of Directors of	24, XXIV
Housing and Urban Development, Department of	2, XXIV; 5, LXV; 24, Subtitle B
Community Planning and Development, Office of Assistant Secretary for	24, V, VI
Equal Opportunity, Office of Assistant Secretary for	24, I
Federal Acquisition Regulation	48, 24
Federal Housing Enterprise Oversight, Office of	12, XVII
Government National Mortgage Association	24, III
Housing—Federal Housing Commissioner, Office of Assistant Secretary for	24, II, VIII, X, XX
Housing, Office of, and Multifamily Housing Assistance Restructuring, Office of	24, IV
Inspector General, Office of	24, XII
Public and Indian Housing, Office of Assistant Secretary for	24, IX
Secretary, Office of	24, Subtitle A, VII
Housing—Federal Housing Commissioner, Office of Assistant Secretary for	24, II, VIII, X, XX
Housing, Office of, and Multifamily Housing Assistance Restructuring, Office of	24, IV
Immigration and Customs Enforcement Bureau	19, IV
Immigration Review, Executive Office for	8, V
Independent Counsel, Office of	28, VII
Independent Counsel, Offices of	28, VI
Indian Affairs, Bureau of	25, I, V
Indian Affairs, Office of the Assistant Secretary	25, VI

Agency	CFR Title, Subtitle or Chapter
Indian Arts and Crafts Board	25, II
Indian Health Service	25, V
Industry and Security, Bureau of	15, VII
Information Resources Management, Office of	7, XXVII
Information Security Oversight Office, National Archives and Records Administration	32, XX
Inspector General	
Agriculture Department	7, XXVI
Health and Human Services Department	42, V
Housing and Urban Development Department	24, XII, XV
Institute of Peace, United States	22, XVII
Inter-American Foundation	5, LXIII; 22, X
Interior, Department of	2, XIV
American Indians, Office of the Special Trustee	25, VII
Endangered Species Committee	50, IV
Federal Acquisition Regulation	48, 14
Federal Property Management Regulations System	41, 114
Fish and Wildlife Service, United States	50, I, IV
Geological Survey	30, IV
Indian Affairs, Bureau of	25, I, V
Indian Affairs, Office of the Assistant Secretary	25, VI
Indian Arts and Crafts Board	25, II
Land Management, Bureau of	43, II
National Indian Gaming Commission	25, III
National Park Service	36, I
Natural Resource Revenue, Office of	30, XII
Ocean Energy Management, Bureau of	30, V
Reclamation, Bureau of	43, I
Safety and Enforcement Bureau, Bureau of	30, II
Secretary of the Interior, Office of	2, XIV; 43, Subtitle A
Surface Mining Reclamation and Enforcement, Office of	30, VII
Internal Revenue Service	26, I
International Boundary and Water Commission, United States and Mexico, United States Section	22, XI
International Development, United States Agency for	22, II
Federal Acquisition Regulation	48, 7
International Development Cooperation Agency, United States	22, XII
International Joint Commission, United States and Canada	22, IV
International Organizations Employees Loyalty Board	5, V
International Trade Administration	15, III; 19, III
International Trade Commission, United States	19, II
Interstate Commerce Commission	5, XL
Investment Security, Office of	31, VIII
James Madison Memorial Fellowship Foundation	45, XXIV
Japan–United States Friendship Commission	22, XVI
Joint Board for the Enrollment of Actuaries	20, VIII
Justice, Department of	2, XXVIII; 5, XXVIII; 28, I, XI; 40, IV
Alcohol, Tobacco, Firearms, and Explosives, Bureau of	27, II
Drug Enforcement Administration	21, II
Federal Acquisition Regulation	48, 28
Federal Claims Collection Standards	31, IX
Federal Prison Industries, Inc.	28, III
Foreign Claims Settlement Commission of the United States	45, V
Immigration Review, Executive Office for	8, V
Independent Counsel, Offices of	28, VI
Prisons, Bureau of	28, V
Property Management Regulations	41, 128
Labor, Department of	2, XXIX; 5, XLII
Employee Benefits Security Administration	29, XXV
Employees' Compensation Appeals Board	20, IV
Employment and Training Administration	20, V
Employment Standards Administration	20, VI
Federal Acquisition Regulation	48, 29
Federal Contract Compliance Programs, Office of	41, 60

Agency	CFR Title, Subtitle or Chapter
National Security Council and Office of Science and Technology Policy	47, II
National Technical Information Service	15, XI
National Telecommunications and Information Administration	15, XXIII; 47, III, IV, V
National Transportation Safety Board	49, VIII
Natural Resources Conservation Service	7, VI
Natural Resource Revenue, Office of	30, XII
Navajo and Hopi Indian Relocation, Office of	25, IV
Navy, Department of	32, VI
Federal Acquisition Regulation	48, 52
Neighborhood Reinvestment Corporation	24, XXV
Northeast Interstate Low-Level Radioactive Waste Commission	10, XVIII
Nuclear Regulatory Commission	2, XX; 5, XLVIII; 10, I
Federal Acquisition Regulation	48, 20
Occupational Safety and Health Administration	29, XVII
Occupational Safety and Health Review Commission	29, XX
Ocean Energy Management, Bureau of	30, V
Oklahoma City National Memorial Trust	36, XV
Operations Office	7, XXVIII
Overseas Private Investment Corporation	5, XXXIII; 22, VII
Patent and Trademark Office, United States	37, I
Payment From a Non-Federal Source for Travel Expenses	41, 304
Payment of Expenses Connected With the Death of Certain Employees	41, 303
Peace Corps	2, XXXVII; 22, III
Pennsylvania Avenue Development Corporation	36, IX
Pension Benefit Guaranty Corporation	29, XL
Personnel Management, Office of	5, I, XXXV; 5, IV; 45, VIII
Human Resources Management and Labor Relations Systems, Department of Homeland Security	5, XCVII
Federal Acquisition Regulation	48, 17
Federal Employees Group Life Insurance Federal Acquisition Regulation	48, 21
Federal Employees Health Benefits Acquisition Regulation	48, 16
Pipeline and Hazardous Materials Safety Administration	49, I
Postal Regulatory Commission	5, XLVI; 39, III
Postal Service, United States	5, LX; 39, I
Postsecondary Education, Office of	34, VI
President's Commission on White House Fellowships	1, IV
Presidential Documents	3
Presidio Trust	36, X
Prisons, Bureau of	28, V
Privacy and Civil Liberties Oversight Board	6, X
Procurement and Property Management, Office of	7, XXXII
Public Contracts, Department of Labor	41, 50
Public and Indian Housing, Office of Assistant Secretary for	24, IX
Public Health Service	42, I
Railroad Retirement Board	20, II
Reclamation, Bureau of	43, I
Refugee Resettlement, Office of	45, IV
Relocation Allowances	41, 302
Research and Innovative Technology Administration	49, XI
Rural Business-Cooperative Service	7, XVIII, XLII
Rural Development Administration	7, XLII
Rural Housing Service	7, XVIII, XXXV
Rural Telephone Bank	7, XVI
Rural Utilities Service	7, XVII, XVIII, XLII
Safety and Environmental Enforcement, Bureau of	30, II
Saint Lawrence Seaway Development Corporation	33, IV
Science and Technology Policy, Office of	32, XXIV
Science and Technology Policy, Office of, and National Security Council	47, II
Secret Service	31, IV
Securities and Exchange Commission	5, XXXIV; 17, II

Agency	CFR Title, Subtitle or Chapter
Selective Service System	32, XVI
Small Business Administration	2, XXVII; 13, I
Smithsonian Institution	36, V
Social Security Administration	2, XXIII; 20, III; 48, 23
Soldiers' and Airmen's Home, United States	5, XI
Special Counsel, Office of	5, VIII
Special Education and Rehabilitative Services, Office of	34, III
State, Department of	2, VI; 22, I; 28, XI
Federal Acquisition Regulation	48, 6
Surface Mining Reclamation and Enforcement, Office of	30, VII
Surface Transportation Board	49, X
Susquehanna River Basin Commission	18, VIII
Tennessee Valley Authority	5, LXIX; 18, XIII
Trade Representative, United States, Office of	15, XX
Transportation, Department of	2, XII; 5, L
Commercial Space Transportation	14, III
Emergency Management and Assistance	44, IV
Federal Acquisition Regulation	48, 12
Federal Aviation Administration	14, I
Federal Highway Administration	23, I, II
Federal Motor Carrier Safety Administration	49, III
Federal Railroad Administration	49, II
Federal Transit Administration	49, VI
Maritime Administration	46, II
National Highway Traffic Safety Administration	23, II, III; 47, IV; 49, V
Pipeline and Hazardous Materials Safety Administration	49, I
Saint Lawrence Seaway Development Corporation	33, IV
Secretary of Transportation, Office of	14, II; 49, Subtitle A
Transportation Statistics Bureau	49, XI
Transportation, Office of	7, XXXIII
Transportation Security Administration	49, XII
Transportation Statistics Bureau	49, XI
Travel Allowances, Temporary Duty (TDY)	41, 301
Treasury, Department of the	2, X;5, XXI; 12, XV; 17, IV; 31, IX
Alcohol and Tobacco Tax and Trade Bureau	27, I
Community Development Financial Institutions Fund	12, XVIII
Comptroller of the Currency	12, I
Customs and Border Protection	19, I
Engraving and Printing, Bureau of	31, VI
Federal Acquisition Regulation	48, 10
Federal Claims Collection Standards	31, IX
Federal Law Enforcement Training Center	31, VII
Financial Crimes Enforcement Network	31, X
Fiscal Service	31, II
Foreign Assets Control, Office of	31, V
Internal Revenue Service	26, I
Investment Security, Office of	31, VIII
Monetary Offices	31, I
Secret Service	31, IV
Secretary of the Treasury, Office of	31, Subtitle A
Truman, Harry S. Scholarship Foundation	45, XVIII
United States and Canada, International Joint Commission	22, IV
United States and Mexico, International Boundary and Water Commission, United States Section	22, XI
U.S. Copyright Office	37, II
Utah Reclamation Mitigation and Conservation Commission	43, III
Veterans Affairs, Department of	2, VIII; 38, I
Federal Acquisition Regulation	48, 8
Veterans' Employment and Training Service, Office of the Assistant Secretary for	41, 61; 20, IX
Vice President of the United States, Office of	32, XXVIII
Wage and Hour Division	29, V
Water Resources Council	18, VI
Workers' Compensation Programs, Office of	20, I, VII
World Agricultural Outlook Board	7, XXXVIII

List of CFR Sections Affected

All changes in this volume of the Code of Federal Regulations (CFR) that were made by documents published in the FEDERAL REGISTER since January 1, 2014 are enumerated in the following list. Entries indicate the nature of the changes effected. Page numbers refer to FEDERAL REGISTER pages. The user should consult the entries for chapters, parts and subparts as well as sections for revisions.

For changes to this volume of the CFR prior to this listing, consult the annual edition of the monthly List of CFR Sections Affected (LSA). The LSA is available at *www.fdsys.gov*. For changes to this volume of the CFR prior to 2001, see the "List of CFR Sections Affected, 1949–1963, 1964–1972, 1973–1985, and 1986–2000" published in 11 separate volumes. The "List of CFR Sections Affected 1986–2000" is available at *www.fdsys.gov*.

2014

14 CFR

79 FR Page

Chapter II

234.13 Removed....................37945

235 Added....................37945

398 Policy statement....................60951

Chapter III

406.9 (a) revised....................61992

2015

14 CFR

80 FR Page

Chapter II

250.5 Amended; (e)(3) added....................30147

250.9 Amended....................30147

251 Added....................166

254.4 Amended....................30147

254.5 (b) amended....................30147

375.11 Revised; interim....................78648

375.38 Added; interim....................78648

383.2 (b)(3) amended....................30147

Chapter III

400.2 Revised....................31834

401.5 Amended....................30151, 31834

Regulation at 80 FR 30151 eff. date confirmed....................45051

413.7 (a) revised....................30151

Regulation at 80 FR 30151 eff. date confirmed....................45051

414.11 (a) revised....................30151

Regulation at 80 FR 30151 eff. date confirmed....................45051

2016

14 CFR

81 FR Page

Chapter II

234 Authority citation revised....................76306

234.2 Amended....................76306, 76826

234.3 Revised....................76826

234.4 (a) introductory text revised; (k) added....................76826

234.6 Revised....................76306

(b) revised....................76827

244.2 (a) amended....................76827

244.3 (a) introductory text revised....................76827

250.2b (c) revised....................76827

250.5 (c)(3) amended....................76827

250.10 Revised....................76827

252 Authority citation revised....................11427

252.1 Revised....................11427

252.2 Revised....................11427

252.3 Revised....................11427

252.4 Added....................11427

252.5 Revised....................11427

252.7 Removed....................11428

252.8 Revised....................11428

252.13 Removed....................11428

252.15 Removed....................11428

252.17 Revised....................11428

252.19 Removed....................11428

255 Removed....................76828

256 Added....................76828

257.3 Amended....................76828

257.5 Revised....................76828

259.8 (a) introductory text amended; (a)(1) revised....................76829

382 Technical correction....................38573, 43463

14 CFR—Continued

81 FR Page

Chapter II—Continued

382.27 (a) revised 33120
382.133 Revised 33120
383 Authority citation revised 52765
383.1 Revised; interim 52765
383.2 Revised; interim 52766
399.80 (h) removed 76829

Chapter III

406.9 (a) revised; interim 43469
415.35 (a) amended 59439
415.37 (a)(1) amended 59439
415.41 Amended 59439
415.55 Amended 59439
417.15 (b) amended 59439
417.107 (b)(1) through (4) revised 47026
(e)(2) amended 59439
417.121 (c) amended 59439
417.231 (a) amended 59439
417.301 Duplicate (d)(1) removed 59439
417.303 (j) amended 59439
417.305 Duplicate (c)(1) removed 59439
417 Appendices A, E and I amended 59439
420.19 (a)(1) revised 47026
420.23 (a)(2), (b)(3) and (c)(1)(ii) revised 47026
420.25 (b) revised 47027
420 Appendices C and D amended 47027
431.35 (b)(1) revised 47027
431.43 (d)(2) revised 47027
431.79 (a)(3) amended 59440
435.35 Revised 47027
440.3 Amended 55122
440.17 (b) through (f) revised 55122
440 Appendix B revised 55124
Appendix C revised 55130

2017

14 CFR

82 FR Page

Chapter II

234.6 (a) and (b) introductory text amended 14438
Revised 14605

14 CFR—Continued

82 FR Page

Chapter III

406.9 (a) revised 17101

2018

14 CFR

83 FR Page

Chapter II

Chapter II Policy statement 53991
205 Notification 18734
295 Added; eff. 2-14-19 46874
298 Authority citation revised; eff. 2-14-19 46877
298 Notification 18734
298.80 Revised; eff. 2-14-19 46877
298.90—298.92 (Subpart I) Added; eff. 2-14-19 46877
382 Policy statement 23804
383 Revised 60743

Chapter III

404 Heading revised 28534
404.1—404.9 (Subpart A) Heading removed 28534
404.1 Revised 28534
404.3 Heading, (a)(3), (b), (c), and (d) revised; (e), (f), and (g) added 28534
404.5 Revised 28534
404.7 Added 28534
404.9 Added 28534
404.11—404.19 (Subpart B) Heading removed 28534
404.11 Revised 28534
404.13 Revised 28534
404.15 Removed 28535
405 Heading revised 28535
406.9 (a) revised 60743
420.1 Revised 28535
420.23 (a)(3), (b)(4), and (c)(2) revised; (c)(3) removed 28535
420.25 (a) revised 28535
431.1 Revised 28535
435.1 Revised 28535
437.1 Revised 28535
437.65 (b) revised 28535
460.5 (d) revised 28535

○

www.ingramcontent.com/pod-product-compliance
Lightning Source LLC
LaVergne TN
LVHW052202200926
848481LV00001B/8

* 9 7 8 1 6 4 0 2 4 5 3 3 4 *